PRENTICE HALL

MAGRUDER'S AMERICAN GOVERNMENT

William A. McClenaghan Professor Emeritus, Oregon State University

PEARSON

Boston, Massachusetts   Chandler, Arizona   Glenview, Illinois   Upper Saddle River, New Jersey

Acknowledgments appear on pages 861–864, which constitute an extension of this copyright page.

ISBN 13: 978-0-13-373172-9
ISBN 10:   0-13-373172-3
Student Edition with Online Student Center 6-year access   ISBN: 0-13-373603-2
3 4 5 6 7 8 9 10   V052   15 14 13 12 11

Revised yearly by William A. McClenaghan,
Professor Emeritus, Oregon State University

Magruder's American Government, first published in 1917 and revised annually, is an enduring symbol of the author's faith in American ideals and American institutions. The life of Frank Abbott Magruder (1882–1949) was an outstanding example of Americanism at its very best. His career as a teacher, author, and tireless worker in civic and religious undertakings remains an inspiring memory to all who knew him.

Grant Wiggins, Program Consultant

Grant Wiggins is the President of Authentic Education in Hopewell, New Jersey. He earned his Ed.D. from Harvard University and his B.A. from St. John's College in Annapolis. Grant consults with schools, districts, and state education departments on a variety of reform matters; organizes conferences and workshops; and develops print materials and Web resources on curricular change. He is the co-author, with Jay McTighe, of *Understanding By Design* and *The Understanding By Design Handbook,* the award-winning and highly successful materials on curriculum published by ASCD. His work has been supported by the Pew Charitable Trusts, the Geraldine R. Dodge Foundation, and the National Science Foundation.

Over the past twenty years, Wiggins has worked on some of the most influential reform initiatives in the country, including Vermont's portfolio system and Ted Sizer's Coalition of Essential Schools. He has established statewide Consortia devoted to assessment reform for the states of North Carolina and New Jersey. Grant is the author of *Educative Assessment* and *Assessing Student Performance*, both published by Jossey-Bass. His many articles have appeared in such journals as Educational Leadership and Phi Delta Kappan.

Unit 1

Foundations of American Government

1

Essential Question What should be the goals of government?

Go online with Unit 1
Find these interactive resources at PearsonSuccessNet.com

⭐ **GOVERNMENT** ONLINE
How Government Works

- **Checks and Balances**
- **Amending the Constitution**
- **Louisiana Becomes a State**

⭐ **GOVERNMENT** ONLINE
Government on the Go

- **Political Dictionary**
- **Audio Review**
- **Downloadable Interactivities**

⭐ **GOVERNMENT** ONLINE
WebQuest

- **Explore Essential Questions online**

⭐ **GOVERNMENT** ONLINE
Government Online

- **Interactivities**
- **In the News**
- **Citizenship Activity Pack**
- **Online Self-Test**
- **Audio Tours**
- **Updates**
- **Documents**

Unit 2

Political Behavior: Government By the People
119

Essential Question In what ways should people participate in public affairs?

Go online with Unit 2
Find these interactive resources at
PearsonSuccessNet.com

GOVERNMENT ONLINE
How Government Works

- Minor Parties in History
- Five Methods of Nomination
- What Happens to a Ballot
- Grass-roots Organizing

GOVERNMENT ONLINE
Government on the Go

- Political Dictionary
- Audio Review
- Downloadable Interactivities

GOVERNMENT ONLINE
WebQuest

- Explore Essential Questions online

GOVERNMENT ONLINE
Government Online

- Interactivities
- In the News
- Citizenship Activity Pack
- Online Self-Test
- Audio Tours
- Updates
- Documents

Unit 3

The Legislative Branch

265

Essential Question What makes a successful Congress?

Go online with Unit 3
Find these interactive resources at PearsonSuccessNet.com

GOVERNMENT ONLINE
How Government Works

- **Gerrymandering: Choosing Their Voters**
- **The Impeachment Process**
- **Congressional Checks on the Presidential Treaty-Making Power**
- **How a Bill Becomes a Law**

GOVERNMENT ONLINE
Government on the Go

- **Political Dictionary**
- **Audio Review**
- **Downloadable Interactivities**

GOVERNMENT ONLINE
WebQuest

- **Explore Essential Questions online**

GOVERNMENT ONLINE
Government Online

- **Interactivities**
- **In the News**
- **Citizenship Activity Pack**
- **Online Self-Test**
- **Audio Tours**
- **Updates**
- **Documents**

Unit 4

The Executive Branch

361

Go online with Unit 4
Find these interactive resources at
PearsonSuccessNet.com

GOVERNMENT ONLINE
How Government Works

- **Presidential Succession**
- **The Race to the Presidency**
- **Confirmation Process**
- **The Executive Branch**
- **The Executive Departments**
- **Regulatory Commissions**
- **Creating the Federal Budget**
- **The State Department**
- **Civilian Control of the Military**
- **Department of Homeland Security**

GOVERNMENT ONLINE
Government on the Go

- **Political Dictionary**
- **Audio Review**
- **Downloadable Interactivities**

GOVERNMENT ONLINE
WebQuest

- **Explore Essential Questions online**

GOVERNMENT ONLINE
Government Online

- **Interactivities**
- **In the News**
- **Citizenship Activity Pack**
- **Online Self-Test**
- **Audio Tours**
- **Updates**
- **Documents**

Unit 5

The Judicial Branch 517

Essential Question What should be the role of the judicial branch?

Go online with Unit 5
Find these interactive resources at PearsonSuccessNet.com

GOVERNMENT ONLINE
How Government Works

- The Appellate Path in the Federal Courts
- How a Case Reaches the Supreme Court
- The *Lemon* Test
- Freedoms of Speech and Press
- Exceptions to the Exclusionary Rule
- Rights of the Accused

GOVERNMENT ONLINE
Government on the Go

- Political Dictionary
- Audio Review
- Downloadable Interactivities

GOVERNMENT ONLINE
WebQuest

- Explore Essential Questions online

GOVERNMENT ONLINE
Government Online

- Interactivities
- In the News
- Citizenship Activity Pack
- Online Self-Test
- Audio Tours
- Updates
- Documents

Unit 6

Comparative Political and Economic Systems

643

Essential Question How should a government meet the needs of its people?

Go online with Unit 6
Find these interactive
resources at
PearsonSuccessNet.com

⚡ **GOVERNMENT** ONLINE
How Government Works

- The Federal Reserve System

⚡ **GOVERNMENT** ONLINE
Government on the Go

- Political Dictionary
- Audio Review
- Downloadable
  Interactivities

⚡ **GOVERNMENT** ONLINE
WebQuest

- Explore Essential
  Questions online

⚡ **GOVERNMENT** ONLINE
Government Online

- Interactivities
- In the News
- Citizenship Activity
  Pack
- Online Self-Test
- Audio Tours
- Updates
- Documents

Unit 7

Participating in State and Local Government   705

Essential Question What is the right balance of local, State, and federal government?

Go online with Unit 7
Find these interactive resources at PearsonSuccessNet.com

GOVERNMENT ONLINE
How Government Works

- Amending State Constitutions
- Initiative and Referendum
- Choosing Executive Officers
- Criminal and Civil Law
- Municipalities and Townships
- Alternate Forms of City Government
- State and Local Spending
- State and Local Revenues

GOVERNMENT ONLINE
Government on the Go

- Political Dictionary
- Audio Review
- Downloadable Interactivities

GOVERNMENT ONLINE
WebQuest

- Explore Essential Questions online

GOVERNMENT ONLINE
Government Online

- Interactivities
- In the News
- Citizenship Activity Pack
- Online Self-Test
- Audio Tours
- Updates
- Documents

Learning With Essential Questions

Magruder's American Government is organized around Essential Questions. An essential question is a launching pad for exploring ideas. It doesn't have just one right answer. The answer to an essential question changes as you learn more or as circumstances change.

GOVERNMENT ONLINE
Webquest
To complete the Chapter Essential Question Webquest, visit **PearsonSuccessNet.com**

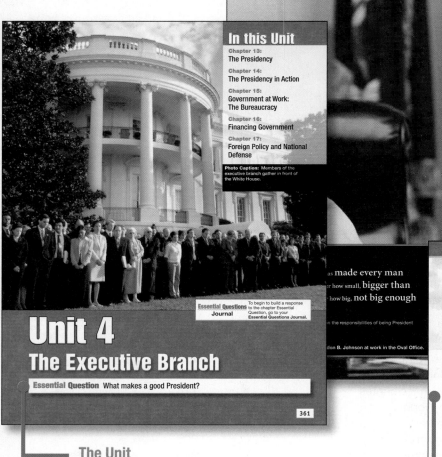

In this Unit

Chapter 13:
The Presidency

Chapter 14:
The Presidency in Action

Chapter 15:
Government at Work: The Bureaucracy

Chapter 16:
Financing Government

Chapter 17:
Foreign Policy and National Defense

Photo Caption: Members of the executive branch gather in front of the White House.

Unit 4
The Executive Branch

Essential Question What makes a good President?

361

Essential Questions Journal To begin to build a response to the chapter Essential Question, go to your Essential Questions Journal.

as made every man
r how small, **bigger than**
how big, **not big enough**

n the responsibilities of being President

don B. Johnson at work in the Oval Office.

CHAPTER 14

The Presidency in Action

Essential Question
How much power should the President have?

Section 1:
The Growth of Presidential Power

Section 2:
The Executive Powers

Section 3:
Diplomatic and Military Powers

Section 4:
Legislative and Judicial Powers

The Chapter Essential Question addresses the main idea of each chapter. Answering the Chapter Essential Question helps you answer the Unit Essential Question.

SECTION 1

The Growth of Presidential Power

Guiding Question
What factors have contributed to the growth of presidential power? Use a concept web like the one below to keep track of the main ideas on the growth of presidential power.

Reasons for the Growth of Presidential Power

Political Dictionary
• Executive Article
• imperial presidency

Objectives
1. Explain why Article II of the Constitution can be described as "an outline" of the presidential office.
2. List several reasons for the growth of presidential power.
3. Explain how the Presidents' own views have affected the power of the office.

Images Above: President George Washington; Mount Rushmore (background)

The presidency is regularly called "the most powerful office in the world," and it is. But is this what the Framers had in mind when they created the post in 1787? At Philadelphia, they purposely created a single executive with very broadly stated powers. Still, they agreed with Thomas Jefferson, who wrote in the Declaration of Independence that "a Tyrant is unfit to be the ruler of a free people." So, just as purposefully, they constructed a "checked," or limited, presidency.

Article II

Article II of the Constitution is known as the **Executive Article**, which in only a few words established the presidency. It begins this way:

FROM THE CONSTITUTION

The executive Power shall be vested in a President of the United States of America.

—Article II, Section 1

With this one sentence, the Framers laid the basis for the vast power and influence the nation's chief executive possesses today.

The Constitution also sets out other, somewhat more specific grants of presidential power. Thus, the President is given the power to command the armed forces, to make treaties, to approve or veto acts of Congress, to send and receive diplomatic representatives, and to "take Care that the Laws be faithfully executed." [1]

Still, the Constitution lays out the powers of the presidency in a very sketchy fashion. Article II reads almost as an outline. It has been called "the most loosely drawn chapter" in the nation's fundamental law. [2] It does not

[1] Most of the specific grants of presidential power are found in Article II, Sections 2 and 3. A few are elsewhere in the Constitution—for example, the veto power, in Article I, Section 7, Clause 2.
[2] Edward S. Corwin, *The President: Office and Powers.*

400 The Presidency in Action

The Unit Essential Question addresses the main idea of the unit.

The guiding questions steer you to the main ideas of each section of the chapter. Answering the section guiding questions helps you think about the Chapter Essential Question.

"Once you have learned to question and to persist in your questioning, nothing can stop you. That's why a curriculum framed around Essential Questions is so important."
—Grant Wiggins, coauthor of *Understanding by Design*

▲ Grant Wiggins talks with high school students.

Essential Questions Journal

Use your Essential Questions Journal to build answers to Essential Questions.

Also available online at PearsonSuccessNet.com

Learning Online

▶ Online Student Center

It all starts with the Online Student Center! There you can access a wide array of 21st century learning tools to help personalize learning.

Access *Magruder's American Government* Online

Go to the Online Student Center at PearsonSuccessNet.com to find your textbook.

Connect with content using Government ▶ on the Go Audio and Video

Study anywhere, anytime with downloadable audio and video files.

- Political Dictionary Audio in English
- Political Dictionary Audio in Spanish
- Audio Review in English
- Audio Review in Spanish
- Audio Tour Animations

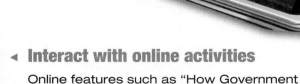

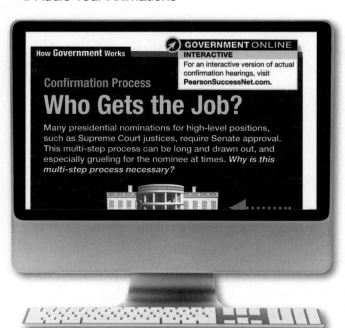

How Government Works

GOVERNMENT ONLINE
INTERACTIVE
For an interactive version of actual confirmation hearings, visit PearsonSuccessNet.com.

Confirmation Process

Who Gets the Job?

Many presidential nominations for high-level positions, such as Supreme Court justices, require Senate approval. This multi-step process can be long and drawn out, and especially grueling for the nominee at times. *Why is this multi-step process necessary?*

◀ Interact with online activities

Online features such as "How Government Works" help you visualize key concepts and information.

Research online with Webquests

Research current and relevant information using a wide range of preselected, reliable Web sites.

Monitor progress with online assessment

Online self-tests help you monitor your learning.

Study Skills

▶ Prepare To Read

Get more from your reading by answering the guiding questions and filling in note-taking graphic organizers that appear at the beginning of each section.

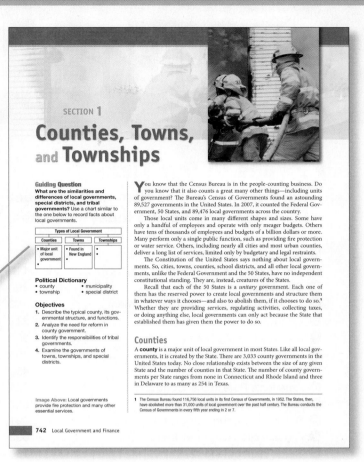

Graphic organizers help you answer the guiding question at the beginning of each section.

▶ Quick Study Guide

Review for tests with charts that organize unit and chapter Essential Questions, political dictionary terms, and the key concepts of each chapter.

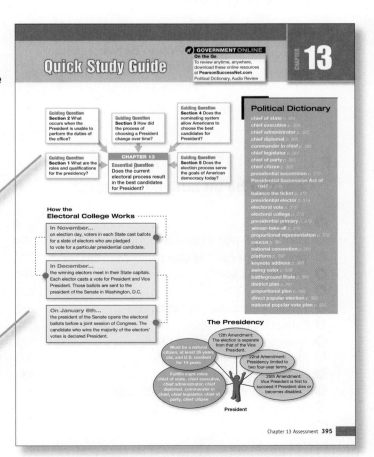

A graphic organizer helps you see how the guiding questions for each chapter help you answer the chapter's Essential Question.

Charts, diagrams, and tables summarize key information.

Special Features

▶ Issues Of Our Time

Confront key issues from new perspectives. Learn the facts behind today's debates.

GOVERNMENT ONLINE
with Online Enhancement

Many charts, graphs, diagrams, and illustrations are expanded online with interactivities, audio tours, and updates. To view these enhanced graphics, go to **PearsonSuccessNet.com** The ⟲ on these pages indicates an online enhancement.

A timeline shows the connection between today's debate and past events.

Consider the viewpoints of prominent Americans on the issues that impact our lives.

▶ Citizenship 101

Learn to be an active citizen.

Practice your citizenship skills with online activities.

Focus on the Supreme Court

▶ Landmark Decisions of the Supreme Court

Learn the complete story behind groundbreaking decisions of the U.S. Supreme Court.

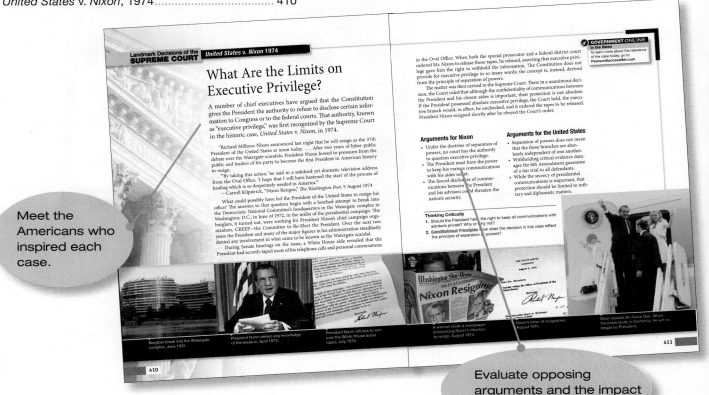

Meet the Americans who inspired each case.

Evaluate opposing arguments and the impact of the Court's decision.

▶ Supreme Court-at-a-Glance

Identify the defining facts of important Supreme Court cases.

See the Supreme Court Glossary for summaries of key cases, p. 805.

SUPREME COURT
at a glance

▶ **Case:** *Gideon v. Wainwright,* 1963

▶ **Issue:** 6th Amendment right to counsel

▶ **Decision:** Clarence Earl Gideon (below) defended himself at his trial and was found guilty. He wrote to the Supreme Court, saying that he had been unconstitutionally denied counsel. The Court agreed and ordered a new trial, holding that an attorney must be provided to those who cannot afford one.

▶ From The Constitution

Trace enduring government concepts to the words of the U.S. Constitution.

Focus on passages from the United States Constitution.

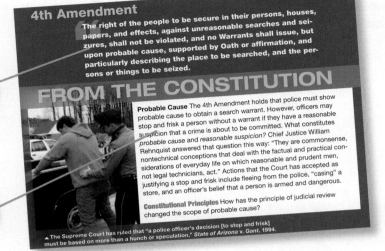

4th Amendment

The right of the people to be secure in their persons, houses, papers, and effects, against unreasonable searches and seizures, shall not be violated, and no Warrants shall issue, but upon probable cause, supported by Oath or affirmation, and particularly describing the place to be searched, and the persons or things to be seized.

FROM THE CONSTITUTION

Probable Cause The 4th Amendment holds that police must show probable cause to obtain a search warrant. However, officers may stop and frisk a person without a warrant if they have a reasonable suspicion that a crime is about to be committed. What constitutes *probable cause* and *reasonable suspicion*? Chief Justice William Rehnquist answered that question this way: "They are commonsense, nontechnical conceptions that deal with the factual and practical considerations of everyday life on which reasonable and prudent men, not legal technicians, act." Actions that the Court has accepted as justifying a stop and frisk include fleeing from the police, "casing" a store, and an officer's belief that a person is armed and dangerous.

Constitutional Principles How has the principle of judicial review changed the scope of probable cause?

▲ The Supreme Court has ruled that "a police officer's decision [to stop and frisk] must be based on more than a hunch or speculation," *State of Arizona* v. *Gant*, 1994.

Learn the significance behind key constitutional principles.

Recall the words and ideas behind today's government with excerpts from the Constitution throughout the text.

▶ How Government Works

Find out about the processes by which our government functions through detailed diagrams and infographics.

> Complex content is displayed visually to explain how our government works.

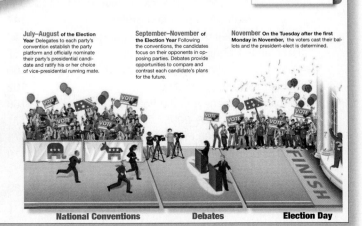

How Government Works

The Race for the Presidency

The race begins as members of the same party vie to become their party's frontrunner. As the pace intensifies, the field dwindles to a contest between two major party candidates, each striving for the ultimate victory—the presidency. *How does the race to the White House reflect the American democratic ideal?*

⚡ GOVERNMENT ONLINE
For an interactive version about the race to the presidency, visit PearsonSuccessNet.com

1–4 Years Before Election The first steps for potential candidates include broadening their visibility, testing their appeal nationwide, and developing committees to explore their viability as a candidate. If the results are favorable, the runner will officially announce his or her candidacy.

1–4 Years Before Election The cost of running for office is huge and raising funds is an ongoing effort throughout the campaign. Lack of funds often causes runners to drop out of the race.

January–June of the Election Year Primaries and caucuses help determine the party's nominee. At this stage voters choose their party's frontrunner, and many candidates concede defeat.

July–August of the Election Year Delegates to each party's convention establish the party platform and officially nominate their party's presidential candidate and ratify his or her choice of vice-presidential running mate.

September–November of the Election Year Following the conventions, the candidates focus on their opponents in opposing parties. Debates provide opportunities to compare and contrast each candidate's plans for the future.

November On the Tuesday after the first Monday in November, the voters cast their ballots and the president-elect is determined.

Start the Race | **Fundraising** | **Primaries and Caucuses** | **National Conventions** | **Debates** | **Election Day**

▶ Infographics, Charts, Graphs, and Tables

Visualize key government concepts and interpret relevant data through infographics, charts, graphs, and tables.

Charts, graphs, and diagrams help deepen your understanding of important concepts.

▶ Political Cartoons

Examine historical and modern political cartoons for insights into American government.

▶ Document-Based Assessment

Analyze enduring issues and prepare for high-stakes tests by examining documents, data, and political cartoons.

▶ Maps

Explore the intersection of government and geography.

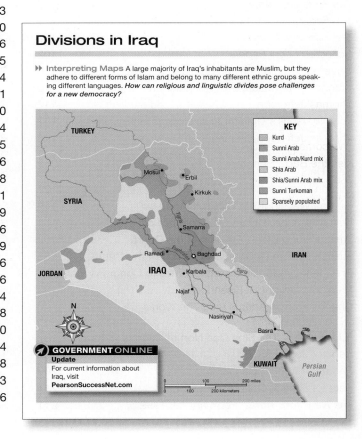

Divisions in Iraq

▸▸ Interpreting Maps A large majority of Iraq's inhabitants are Muslim, but they adhere to different forms of Islam and belong to many different ethnic groups speaking different languages. *How can religious and linguistic divides pose challenges for a new democracy?*

KEY
- Kurd
- Sunni Arab
- Sunni Arab/Kurd mix
- Shia Arab
- Shia/Sunni Arab mix
- Sunni Turkoman
- Sparsely populated

⦿ **GOVERNMENT** ONLINE
Update
For current information about Iraq, visit
PearsonSuccessNet.com

▶ Primary Sources

Gain insights as you read through the words of people who shaped American government.

Constitution Quick Study Guide

Amendments

1st Amendment: Freedom of Religion, Speech, Press, Assembly, and Petition

2nd Amendment: Right to Keep, Bear Arms

3rd Amendment: Lodging Troops in Private Homes

4th Amendment: Search, Seizures, Proper Warrants

5th Amendment: Criminal Proceedings, Due Process, Eminent Domain

6th Amendment: Criminal Proceedings

7th Amendment: Jury Trials in Civil Cases

8th Amendment: Bail; Cruel, Unusual Punishment

9th Amendment: Unenumerated Rights

10th Amendment: Powers Reserved to the States

11th Amendment: Suits Against the States

12th Amendment: Election of President and Vice President

13th Amendment: Slavery and Involuntary Servitude
- Section 1. Slavery and Involuntary Servitude Prohibited
- Section 2. Power of Congress

14th Amendment: Rights of Citizens
- Section 1. Citizenship; Privileges and Immunities; Due Process; Equal Protection
- Section 2. Apportionment of Representation
- Section 3. Disqualification of Officers
- Section 4. Public Debt
- Section 5. Powers of Congress

15th Amendment: Right to Vote—Race, Color, Servitude
- Section 1. Suffrage Not to Be Abridged
- Section 2. Power of Congress

16th Amendment: Income Tax

17th Amendment: Popular Election of Senators
- Section 1. Popular Election of Senators
- Section 2. Senate Vacancies
- Section 3. Inapplicable to Senators Previously Chosen

18th Amendment: Prohibition of Intoxicating Liquors
- Section 1. Intoxicating Liquors Prohibited
- Section 2. Concurrent Power to Enforce
- Section 3. Time Limit on Ratification

19th Amendment: Equal Suffrage—Sex
- Section 1. Suffrage Not to Be Abridged
- Section 2. Power of Congress

20th Amendment: Commencement of Terms; Sessions of Congress; Death or Disqualification of President-Elect
- Section 1. Terms of President, Vice President, members of Congress
- Section 2. Sessions of Congress
- Section 3. Death or Disqualification of President-Elect
- Section 4. Congress to Provide for Certain Successors
- Section 5. Effective Date
- Section 6. Time Limit on Ratification

21st Amendment: Repeal of 18th Amendment
- Section 1. Repeal of Prohibition
- Section 2. Transportation, Importation of Intoxicating Liquors
- Section 3. Time Limit on Ratification

22nd Amendment: Presidential Tenure
- Section 1. Restriction on Number of Terms
- Section 2. Time Limit on Ratification

23rd Amendment: Inclusion of District of Columbia in Presidential Election Systems
- Section 1. Presidential Electors for District
- Section 2. Power of Congress

24th Amendment: Right to Vote in Federal Elections—Tax Payment
- Section 1. Suffrage Not to Be Abridged
- Section 2. Power of Congress

25th Amendment: Presidential Succession; Vice Presidential Vacancy; Presidential Inability
- Section 1. Presidential Succession
- Section 2. Vice Presidential Vacancy
- Section 3. Presidential Inability

26th Amendment: Right to Vote—Age
- Section 1. Suffrage Not to Be Abridged
- Section 2. Power of Congress

27th Amendment: Congressional Pay

UNITED STATES CONSTITUTION: Constitution Quick Study Guide

The Preamble states the broad purposes the Constitution is intended to serve—to establish a government that provides for greater cooperation among the States, ensures justice and peace, provides for defense against foreign enemies, promotes the general well-being of the people, and secures liberty now and in the future. The phrase We the People emphasizes the twin concepts of popular sovereignty and of representative government.

Legislative Department

Section 1. Legislative power; Congress

Congress, the nation's lawmaking body, is bicameral in form; that is, it is composed of two houses: the Senate and the House of Representatives. The Framers of the Constitution purposely separated the lawmaking power from the power to enforce the laws (Article II, the Executive Branch) and the power to interpret them (Article III, the Judicial Branch). This system of separation of powers is supplemented by a system of checks and balances; that is, in several provisions the Constitution gives to each of the three branches various powers with which it may restrain the actions of the other two branches.

Section 2. House of Representatives

♦ **Clause 1. Election** Electors means voters. Members of the House of Representatives are elected every two years. Each State must permit the same persons to vote for United States representatives as it permits to vote for the members of the larger house of its own legislature. The 17th Amendment (1913) extends this requirement to the qualification of voters for United States senators.

♦ **Clause 2. Qualifications** A member of the House of Representatives must be at least 25 years old, an American citizen for seven years, and a resident of the State he or she represents. In addition, political custom requires that a representative also reside in the district from which he or she is elected.

♦ **Clause 3. Apportionment** The number of representatives each State is entitled to is based on its population, which is counted every 10 years in the census. Congress reapportions the seats among the States after each census. In the Reapportionment Act of 1929, Congress fixed the permanent size of the House at 435 members with each State having at least one representative. Today there is one House seat for approximately every 700,000 persons in the population.

The words "three-fifths of all other persons" referred to slaves and reflected the Three-Fifths Compromise reached by the Framers at Philadelphia in 1787; the phrase was made obsolete, was in effect repealed, by the 13th Amendment in 1865.

---

* The black lines indicate portions of the Constitution altered by subsequent amendments to the document.

♦ **Clause 4. Vacancies** The executive authority refers to the governor of a State. If a member leaves office or dies before the expiration of his or her term, the governor is to call a special election to fill the vacancy.

United States Constitution

PREAMBLE

We the People of the United States, in Order to form a more perfect Union, establish Justice, insure domestic Tranquility, provide for the common defence, promote the general Welfare, and secure the Blessings of Liberty to ourselves and our Posterity, do ordain and establish this Constitution for the United States of America.

Article I.
Section 1.

All legislative Powers herein granted shall be vested in a Congress of the United States, which shall consist of a Senate and House of Representatives.

Section 2.

♦ 1. The House of Representatives shall be composed of Members chosen every second Year by the People of the several States, and the Electors in each State shall have the Qualifications requisite for Electors of the most numerous Branch of the State Legislature.

♦ 2. No Person shall be a Representative who shall not have attained to the age of twenty-five Years, and been seven Years a Citizen of the United States, and who shall not, when elected, be an Inhabitant of that State in which he shall be chosen.

♦ 3. Representatives and direct Taxes* shall be apportioned among the several States which may be included within this Union, according to their respective Numbers, which shall be determined by adding to the whole Number of free Persons, including those bound to Service for a Term of Years and excluding Indians not taxed, three fifths of all other Persons. The actual Enumeration shall be made within three Years after the first Meeting of the Congress of the United States, and within every subsequent term of ten Years, in such Manner as they shall by Law direct. The Number of Representatives shall not exceed one for every thirty Thousand, but each State shall have at Least one Representative; and, until such enumeration shall be made, the State of New Hampshire shall be entitled to choose three, Massachusetts eight, Rhode Island and Providence Plantations one, Connecticut five, New York six, New Jersey four, Pennsylvania eight, Delaware one, Maryland six, Virginia ten, North Carolina five, South Carolina five, and Georgia three.

♦ 4. When vacancies happen in the Representation from any State, the Executive Authority thereof shall issue Writs of Election to fill such Vacancies.

◆5. The House of Representatives shall choose their Speaker and other Officers; and shall have the sole Power of Impeachment.

Section 3.

◆1. The Senate of the United States shall be composed of two Senators from each State ~~chosen by the Legislature thereof~~ for six Years; and each Senator shall have one Vote.

◆2. Immediately after they shall be assembled in Consequences of the first Election, they shall be divided, as equally as may be, into three Classes. The Seats of the Senators of the first Class shall be vacated at the Expiration of the second Year; of the second Class, at the Expiration of the fourth Year; and of the third Class, at the Expiration of the sixth Year; so that one-third may be chosen every second Year; ~~and if Vacancies happen by Resignation, or otherwise, during the Recess of the Legislature of any State, the Executive thereof may make temporary Appointments until the next Meeting of the Legislature, which shall then fill such Vacancies.~~

◆3. No Person shall be a Senator who shall not have attained to the Age of thirty Years, and been nine Years a Citizen of the United States, and who shall not, when elected, be an Inhabitant of that State for which he shall be chosen.

◆4. The Vice President of the United States shall be President of the Senate but shall have no Vote, unless they be equally divided.

◆5. The Senate shall choose their other Officers, and also a President pro tempore, in the Absence of the Vice President, or when he shall exercise the Office of President of the United States.

◆6. The Senate shall have the sole Power to try all Impeachments. When sitting for that Purpose, they shall be on Oath or Affirmation. When the President of the United States is tried, the Chief Justice shall preside: And no Person shall be convicted without the Concurrence of two thirds of the Members present.

◆7. Judgment in Cases of Impeachment shall not extend further than to removal from Office, and disqualification to hold and enjoy any Office of honor, Trust, or Profit under the United States: but the Party convicted shall nevertheless be liable and subject to Indictment, Trial, Judgment and Punishment, according to Law.

◆**Clause 5. Officers; impeachment** The House elects a Speaker, customarily chosen from the majority party in the House. Impeachment means accusation. The House has the exclusive power to impeach, or accuse, civil officers; the Senate (Article I, Section 3, Clause 6) has the exclusive power to try those impeached by the House.

Section 3. Senate

◆**Clause 1. Composition, election, term** Each State has two senators. Each serves for six years and has one vote. Originally, senators were not elected directly by the people, but by each State's legislature. The 17th Amendment, added in 1913, provides for the popular election of senators.

◆**Clause 2. Classification** The senators elected in 1788 were divided into three groups so that the Senate could become a "continuing body." One-third of the Senate's seats are up for election every two years.

The 17th Amendment provides that a Senate vacancy is to be filled at a special election called by the governor; State law may also permit the governor to appoint a successor to serve until that election is held.

◆**Clause 3. Qualifications** A senator must be at least 30 years old, a citizen for at least nine years, and must live in the State from which elected.

◆**Clause 4. Presiding officer** The Vice President presides over the Senate, but may vote only to break a tie.

◆**Clause 5. Other officers** The Senate chooses its own officers, including a president pro tempore to preside when the Vice President is not there.

◆**Clause 6. Impeachment trials** The Senate conducts the trials of those officials impeached by the House. The Vice President presides unless the President is on trial, in which case the Chief Justice of the United States does so. A conviction requires the votes of two-thirds of the senators present.

No President has ever been convicted. In 1868 the House voted eleven articles of impeachment against President Andrew Johnson, but the Senate fell one vote short of convicting him. In 1974 President Richard M. Nixon resigned the presidency in the face of almost certain impeachment by the House. The House brought two articles of impeachment against President Bill Clinton in late 1998. Neither charge was supported by even a simple majority vote in the Senate, on February 12, 1999.

◆**Clause 7. Penalty on conviction** The punishment of an official convicted in an impeachment case has always been removal from office. The Senate can also bar a convicted person from ever holding any federal office, but it is not required to do so. A convicted person can also be tried and punished in a regular court for any crime involved in the impeachment case.

Section 4. Elections and Meetings

◆**Clause 1.** **Election In 1842** Congress required that representatives be elected from districts within each State with more than one seat in the House. The districts in each State are drawn by that State's legislature. Seven States now have only one seat in the House: Alaska, Delaware, Montana, North Dakota, South Dakota, Vermont, and Wyoming. The 1842 law also directed that representatives be elected in each State on the same day: the Tuesday after the first Monday in November of every even-numbered year. In 1914 Congress also set that same date for the election of senators.

◆**Clause 2.** **Sessions Congress** must meet at least once a year. The 20th Amendment (1933) changed the opening date to January 3.

Section 5. Legislative Proceedings

◆**Clause 1.** **Admission of members; quorum** In 1969 the Supreme Court held that the House cannot exclude any member-elect who satisfies the qualifications set out in Article I, Section 2, Clause 2.

A majority in the House (218 members) or Senate (51) constitutes a quorum. In practice, both houses often proceed with less than a quorum present. However, any member may raise a point of order (demand a "quorum call"). If a roll call then reveals less than a majority of the members present, that chamber must either adjourn or the sergeant at arms must be ordered to round up absent members.

◆**Clause 2.** **Rules** Each house has adopted detailed rules to guide its proceedings. Each house may discipline members for unacceptable conduct; expulsion requires a two-thirds vote.

◆**Clause 3.** **Record** Each house must keep and publish a record of its meetings. The Congressional Record is published for every day that either house of Congress is in session, and provides a written record of all that is said and done on the floor of each house each session.

◆**Clause 4.** **Adjournment** Once in session, neither house may suspend (recess) its work for more than three days without the approval of the other house. Both houses must always meet in the same location.

Section 4.

◆1. The Times, Places and Manner of holding Elections for Senators and Representatives, shall be prescribed in each State by the Legislature thereof; but the Congress may at any time by law make or alter such Regulations, except as to the Places of choosing Senators.

◆2. The Congress shall assemble at least once in every Year, and such Meeting shall be on the first Monday in December, unless they shall by Law appoint a different Day.

Section 5.

◆1. Each House shall be the Judge of the Elections, Returns and Qualifications of its own Members, and a Majority of each shall constitute a Quorum to do Business; but a smaller Number may adjourn from day to day, and may be authorized to compel the Attendance of absent Members, in such Manner, and under such Penalties, as each House may provide.

◆2. Each House may determine the Rules of its Proceedings, punish its Members for disorderly Behavior, and, with the Concurrence of two thirds, expel a Member.

◆3. Each House shall keep a Journal of its Proceedings, and from time to time publish the same, excepting such Parts as may in their Judgment require Secrecy; and the Yeas and Nays of the Members of either House on any question shall, at the Desire of one fifth of those Present, be entered on the Journal.

◆4. Neither House, during the Session of Congress, shall, without the Consent of the other, adjourn for more than three days, nor to any other Place than that in which the two Houses shall be sitting.

Section 6.

♦1. The Senators and Representatives shall receive a Compensation for their Services, to be ascertained by Law, and paid out of the Treasury of the United States. They shall in all Cases, except Treason, Felony, and Breach of the Peace, be privileged from Arrest during their Attendance at the Session of their respective Houses, and in going to and returning from the same; and for any Speech or Debate in either House, they shall not be questioned in any other Place.

♦2. No Senator or Representative shall, during the Time for which he was elected, be appointed to any civil Office under the Authority of the United States, which shall have been created, or the Emoluments whereof shall have been increased during such time; and no Person holding any Office under the United States, shall be a Member of either House during his Continuance in Office.

Section 7.

♦1. All Bills for raising Revenue shall originate in the House of Representatives; but the Senate may propose or concur with amendments as on other Bills.

♦2. Every Bill which shall have passed the House of Representatives and the Senate, shall, before it become a law, be presented to the President of the United States: If he approve, he shall sign it, but if not he shall return it, with his Objections to that House in which it shall have originated, who shall enter the Objections at large on their Journal, and proceed to reconsider it. If after such Reconsideration two thirds of the House shall agree to pass the Bill, it shall be sent, together with the Objections, to the other House, by which it shall likewise be reconsidered, and if approved by two thirds of that House, it shall become a Law. But in all such Cases the Votes of both Houses shall be determined by Yeas and Nays, and the Names of the Persons voting for and against the Bill shall be entered on the Journal of each House respectively. If any Bill shall not be returned by the President within ten Days (Sunday excepted) after it shall have been presented to him, the Same shall be a law, in like Manner as if he had signed it, unless the Congress by their Adjournment, prevent its Return, in which Case it shall not be a Law.

♦3. Every Order, Resolution, or Vote to which the Concurrence of the Senate and House of Representatives may be necessary (except on a question of adjournment) shall be presented to the President of the United States; and before the Same shall take Effect, shall be approved by him, or, being disapproved by him, shall be repassed by two thirds of the Senate and House of Representatives, according to the Rules and Limitations prescribed in the Case of a Bill.

Section 6. Compensation, Immunities, and Disabilities of Members

♦**Clause 1. Salaries; immunities** Each house sets its members' salaries, paid by the United States; the 27th Amendment (1992) modified this pay-setting power. This provision establishes "legislative immunity." The purpose of this immunity is to allow members to speak and debate freely in Congress itself. Treason is strictly defined in Article III, Section 3. A felony is any serious crime. A breach of the peace is any indictable offense less than treason or a felony; this exemption from arrest is of little real importance today.

♦**Clause 2. Restrictions on office holding** No sitting member of either house may be appointed to an office in the executive or in the judicial branch if that position was created or its salary was increased during that member's current elected term. The second part of this clause—forbidding any person serving in either the executive or the judicial branch from also serving in Congress—reinforces the principle of separation of powers.

Section 7. Revenue Bills, President's Veto

♦**Clause 1. Revenue bills** All bills that raise money must originate in the House. However, the Senate has the power to amend any revenue bill sent to it from the lower house.

♦**Clause 2. Enactment of laws; veto** Once both houses have passed a bill, it must be sent to the President. The President may (1) sign the bill, thus making it law; (2) veto the bill, whereupon it must be returned to the house in which it originated; or (3) allow the bill to become law without signature, by not acting upon it within 10 days of its receipt from Congress, not counting Sundays. The President has a fourth option at the end of a congressional session: If he does not act on a measure within 10 days, and Congress adjourns during that period, the bill dies; the "pocket veto" has been applied to it. A presidential veto may be overridden by a two-thirds vote in each house.

♦**Clause 3. Other measures** This clause refers to joint resolutions, measures Congress often passes to deal with unusual, temporary, or ceremonial matters. A joint resolution passed by Congress and signed by the President has the force of law, just as a bill does. As a matter of custom, a joint resolution proposing an amendment to the Constitution is not submitted to the President for signature or veto. Concurrent and simple resolutions do not have the force of law and, therefore, are not submitted to the President.

Section 8. Powers of Congress

♦**Clause 1.** The 18 separate clauses in this section set out 27 of the many expressed powers the Constitution grants to Congress. In this clause Congress is given the power to levy and provide for the collection of various kinds of taxes, in order to finance the operations of the government. All federal taxes must be levied at the same rates throughout the country.

♦**Clause 2.** Congress has power to borrow money to help finance the government. Federal borrowing is most often done through the sale of bonds on which interest is paid. The Constitution does not limit the amount the government may borrow.

♦**Clause 3.** This clause, the Commerce Clause, gives Congress the power to regulate both foreign and interstate trade. Much of what Congress does, it does on the basis of its commerce power.

♦**Clause 4.** Congress has the exclusive power to determine how aliens may become citizens of the United States. Congress may also pass laws relating to bankruptcy.

♦**Clause 5.** has the power to establish and require the use of uniform gauges of time, distance, weight, volume, area, and the like.

♦**Clause 6.** Congress has the power to make it a federal crime to falsify the coins, paper money, bonds, stamps, and the like of the United States.

♦**Clause 7.** Congress has the power to provide for and regulate the transportation and delivery of mail; "post offices" are those buildings and other places where mail is deposited for dispatch; "post roads" include all routes over or upon which mail is carried.

♦**Clause 8.** Congress has the power to provide for copyrights and patents. A copyright gives an author or composer the exclusive right to control the reproduction, publication, and sale of literary, musical, or other creative work. A patent gives a person the exclusive right to control the manufacture or sale of his or her invention.

♦**Clause 9.** Congress has the power to create the lower federal courts, all of the several federal courts that function beneath the Supreme Court.

♦**Clause 10.** Congress has the power to prohibit, as a federal crime: (1) certain acts committed outside the territorial jurisdiction of the United States, and (2) the commission within the United States of any wrong against any nation with which we are at peace.

Section 8.

The Congress shall have Power

♦1. To lay and collect Taxes, Duties, Imposts and Excises to pay the Debts and provide for the common Defence and general Welfare of the United States; but all Duties, Imposts and Excises, shall be uniform throughout the United States;

♦2. To borrow Money on the credit of the United States;

♦3. To regulate Commerce with foreign Nations, and among the several States, and with the Indian Tribes;

♦4. To establish an uniform Rule of Naturalization, and uniform Laws on the subject of Bankruptcies throughout the United States;

♦5. To coin Money, regulate the Value thereof, and of foreign Coin, and fix the Standard of Weights and Measures;

♦6. To provide for the Punishment of counterfeiting the Securities and current Coin of the United States;

♦7. To establish Post Offices and post Roads;

♦8. To promote the Progress of Science and useful Arts, by securing, for limited Times to Authors and Inventors the exclusive Right to their respective Writings and Discoveries;

♦9. To constitute Tribunals inferior to the supreme Court;

♦10. To define and punish Piracies and Felonies committed on the high Seas, and Offences against the Law of nations;

11. To declare War, grant Letters of Marque and Reprisal, and make Rules concerning Captures on Land and Water;

12. To raise and support Armies; but no Appropriation of Money to that Use shall be for a longer Term than two Years;

13. To provide and maintain a Navy;

14. To make Rules for the Government and Regulation of the land and naval Forces;

15. To provide for calling forth the Militia to execute the Laws of the Union, suppress Insurrections and repel Invasions;

16. To provide for organizing, arming, and disciplining the Militia, and for governing such Part of them as may be employed in the Service of the United States, reserving to the States respectively the Appointment of the Officers, and the Authority of training the Militia according to the discipline prescribed by Congress;

17. To exercise exclusive Legislation in all Cases whatsoever, over such District (not exceeding ten Miles square) as may, by Cession of Particular States, and the Acceptance of Congress, become the Seat of the Government of the United States, and to exercise like Authority over all Places purchased by the Consent of the Legislature of the State in which the Same shall be, for the Erection of Forts, Magazines, Arsenals, Dockyards and other needful Buildings;—And

18. To make all Laws which shall be necessary and proper for carrying into Execution the foregoing Powers and all other Powers vested by this Constitution in the Government of the United States, or in any Department or Officer thereof.

Section 9.

1. The Migration or Importation of such Persons as any of the States now existing shall think proper to admit, shall not be prohibited by the Congress prior to the Year one thousand eight hundred and eight, but a Tax or duty may be imposed on such Importation, not exceeding ten dollars for each Person.

♦ **Clause 11.** Only Congress can declare war. However, the President, as commander in chief of the armed forces (Article II, Section 2, Clause 1), can make war without such a formal declaration. Letters of marque and reprisal are commissions authorizing private persons to outfit vessels (privateers) to capture and destroy enemy ships in time of war; they were forbidden in international law by the Declaration of Paris of 1856, and the United States has honored the ban since the Civil War.

♦ **Clauses 12 and 13.** Congress has the power to provide for and maintain the nation's armed forces. It established the air force as an independent element of the armed forces in 1947, an exercise of its inherent powers in foreign relations and national defense. The two-year limit on spending for the army insures civilian control of the military.

♦ **Clause 14.** Today these rules are set out in three principle statutes: the Uniform Code of Military Justice, passed by Congress in 1950, and the Military Justice Acts of 1958 and 1983.

♦ **Clauses 15 and 16.** In the National Defense Act of 1916, Congress made each State's militia (volunteer army) a part of the National Guard. Today, Congress and the States cooperate in its maintenance. Ordinarily, each State's National Guard is under the command of that State's governor; but Congress has given the President the power to call any or all of those units into federal service when necessary.

♦ **Clause 17.** In 1791 Congress accepted land grants from Maryland and Virginia and established the District of Columbia for the nation's capital. Assuming Virginia's grant would never be needed, Congress returned it in 1846. Today, the elected government of the District's 69 square miles operates under the authority of Congress. Congress also has the power to acquire other lands from the States for various federal purposes.

♦ **Clause 18.** This is the Necessary and Proper Clause, also often called the Elastic Clause. It is the constitutional basis for the many and far-reaching implied powers of the Federal Government.

Section 9. Powers Denied to Congress

♦ **Clause 1.** The phrase "such persons" referred to slaves. This provision was part of the Commerce Compromise, one of the bargains struck in the writing of the Constitution. Congress outlawed the slave trade in 1808.

◆**Clause 2.** A writ of habeas corpus, the "great writ of liberty," is a court order directing a sheriff, warden, or other public officer, or a private person, who is detaining another to "produce the body" of the one being held in order that the legality of the detention may be determined by the court.

◆**Clause 3.** A bill of attainder is a legislative act that inflicts punishment without a judicial trial. See Article I, Section 10, and Article III, Section 3, Clause 2. An ex post facto law is any criminal law that operates retroactively to the disadvantage of the accused. See Article I, Section 10.

◆**Clause 4.** A capitation tax is literally a "head tax," a tax levied on each person in the population. A direct tax is one paid directly to the government by the taxpayer—for example, an income or a property tax; an indirect tax is one paid to another private party who then pays it to the government—for example, a sales tax. This provision was modified by the 16th Amendment (1913), giving Congress the power to levy "taxes on incomes, from whatever source derived."

◆**Clause 5.** This provision was a part of the Commerce Compromise made by the Framers in 1787. Congress has the power to tax imported goods, however.

◆**Clause 6.** All ports within the United States must be treated alike by Congress as it exercises its taxing and commerce powers. Congress cannot tax goods sent by water from one State to another, nor may it give the ports of one State any legal advantage over those of another.

◆**Clause 7.** This clause gives Congress its vastly important "power of the purse," a major check on presidential power. Federal money can be spent only in those amounts and for those purposes expressly authorized by an act of Congress. All federal income and spending must be accounted for, regularly and publicly.

◆**Clause 8.** This provision, preventing the establishment of a nobility, reflects the principle that "all men are created equal." It was also intended to discourage foreign attempts to bribe or otherwise corrupt officers of the government.

Section 10. Powers Denied to the States

◆**Clause 1.** The States are not sovereign governments and so cannot make agreements or otherwise negotiate with foreign states; the power to conduct foreign relations is an exclusive power of the National Government. The power to coin money is also an exclusive power of the National Government. Several powers forbidden to the National Government are here also forbidden to the States.

◆**Clause 2.** This provision relates to foreign, not interstate, commerce. Only Congress, not the States, can tax imports; and the States are, like Congress, forbidden the power to tax exports.

◆2. The Privilege of the Writ of Habeas Corpus shall not be suspended, unless when in Cases of Rebellion or Invasion the public safety may require it.

◆3. No Bill of Attainder or ex post facto Law shall be passed.

◆4. No Capitation, ~~or other direct,~~ Tax shall be laid, unless in Proportion to the Census of Enumeration hereinbefore directed to be taken.

◆5. No Tax or Duty shall be laid on Articles exported from any State.

◆6. No Preference shall be given by any Regulation of Commerce or Revenue to the Ports of one State over those of another: nor shall Vessels bound to, or from, one State, be obliged to enter, clear or pay Duties in another.

◆7. No Money shall be drawn from the Treasury, but in Consequence of Appropriations made by Law; and a regular Statement and Account of the Receipts and Expenditures of all public Money shall be published from time to time.

◆8. No Title of Nobility shall be granted by the United States: And no Person holding any Office of Profit or Trust under them, shall, without the Consent of the Congress, accept of any present, Emolument, Office, or Title, of any kind whatever, from any King, Prince, or foreign State.

Section 10.

◆1. No State shall enter into any Treaty, Alliance, or Confederation; grant Letters of Marque and Reprisal; coin Money; emit Bills of Credit; make any Thing but gold and silver Coin a Tender in Payment of Debts; pass any Bill of Attainder, ex post facto Law, or Law impairing the Obligation of Contracts, or grant any Title of Nobility.

◆2. No State shall, without the Consent of the Congress, lay any Imposts or Duties on Imports or Exports, except what may be absolutely necessary for executing its inspection Laws; and the net Produce of all Duties and Imposts, laid by any State on Imports or Exports, shall be for the Use of the Treasury of the United States; and all such Laws shall be subject to the Revision and Control of the Congress.

♦ 3. No State shall, without the Consent of Congress, lay any Duty of Tonnage, keep Troops, or Ships of War in time of Peace, enter into any Agreement or Compact with another State, or with a foreign Power, or engage in War, unless actually invaded, or in such imminent Danger as will not admit of delay.

Article II
Section 1.

♦ 1. The executive Power shall be vested in a President of the United States of America. He shall hold his Office during the Term of four Years, and, together with the Vice President, chosen for the same Term, be elected as follows:

♦ 2. Each State shall appoint, in such Manner as the Legislature thereof may direct, a Number of Electors, equal to the whole Number of Senators and Representatives to which the State may be entitled in the Congress: but no Senator or Representative, or Person holding an Office of Trust or Profit, under the United States, shall be appointed an Elector.

♦ 3. ~~The Electors shall meet in their respective States, and vote by Ballot for two Persons, of whom one at least shall not be an Inhabitant of the same State with themselves. And they shall make a List of all the Persons voted for, and of the Number of Votes for each; which List they shall sign and certify, and transmit sealed to the Seat of the Government of the United States, directed to the President of the Senate. The President of the Senate shall, in the Presence of the Senate and House of Representatives, open all the Certificates, and the Votes shall then be counted. The Person having the greatest Number of Votes shall be the President, if such Number be a majority of the whole Number of Electors appointed; and if there be more than one who have such Majority, and have an equal Number of Votes, then, the House of Representatives shall immediately choose by Ballot one of them for President; and if no Person have a Majority, then from the five highest on the List the said House shall in like Manner choose the President. But in choosing the President, the Votes shall be taken by States, the Representatives from each State having one Vote; a quorum for this Purpose shall consist of a Member or Members from two thirds of the States, and a Majority of all the States shall be necessary to a Choice. In every Case, after the Choice of the President, the Person having the greatest Number of Votes of the Electors shall be the Vice President. But if there should remain two or more who have equal Votes, the Senate shall choose from them by Ballot the Vice President.~~

♦ **Clause 3.** A duty of tonnage is a tax laid on ships according to their cargo capacity. Each State has a constitutional right to provide for and maintain a militia; but no State may keep a standing army or navy. The several restrictions here prevent the States from assuming powers that the Constitution elsewhere grants to the National Government.

Executive Department
Section 1. President and Vice President

♦ **Clause 1. Executive power, term** This clause gives to the President the very broad "executive power," the power to enforce the laws and otherwise administer the public policies of the United States. It also sets the length of the presidential (and vice-presidential) term of office; see the 22nd Amendment (1951), which places a limit on presidential (but not vice-presidential) tenure.

♦ **Clause 2. Electoral college** This clause establishes the "electoral college," although the Constitution does not use that term. It is a body of presidential electors chosen in each State, and it selects the President and Vice President every four years. The number of electors chosen in each State equals the number of senators and representatives that State has in Congress.

♦ **Clause 3. Election of President and Vice President** This clause was replaced by the 12th Amendment in 1804.

National convention to nominate candidates for President and Vice President

Clause 4. Date Congress has set the date for the choosing of electors as the Tuesday after the first Monday in November every fourth year, and for the casting of electoral votes as the Monday after the second Wednesday in December of that year.

Clause 5. Qualifications The President must have been born a citizen of the United States, be at least 35 years old, and have been a resident of the United States for at least 14 years.

Clause 6. Vacancy This clause was modified by the 25th Amendment (1967), which provides expressly for the succession of the Vice President, for the filling of a vacancy in the Vice Presidency, and for the determination of presidential inability.

Clause 7. Compensation The President now receives a salary of $400,000 and a taxable expense account of $50,000 a year. Those amounts cannot be changed during a presidential term; thus, Congress cannot use the President's compensation as a bargaining tool to influence executive decisions. The phrase "any other emolument" means, in effect, any valuable gift; it does not mean that the President cannot be provided with such benefits of office as the White House, extensive staff assistance, and much else.

Clause 8. Oath of office The Chief Justice of the United States regularly administers this oath or affirmation, but any judicial officer may do so. Thus, Calvin Coolidge was sworn into office in 1923 by his father, a justice of the peace in Vermont.

Section 2. President's Powers and Duties

Clause 1. Military, civil powers The President, a civilian, heads the nation's armed forces, a key element in the Constitution's insistence on civilian control of the military. The President's power to "require the opinion, in writing" provides the constitutional basis for the Cabinet. The President's power to grant reprieves and pardons, the power of clemency, extends only to federal cases.

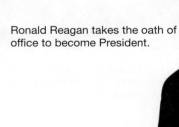

Ronald Reagan takes the oath of office to become President.

4. The Congress may determine the Time of choosing the Electors, and the Day on which they shall give their Votes; which Day shall be the same throughout the United States.

5. No Person except a natural born Citizen, or a Citizen of the United States, at the time of the Adoption of this Constitution, shall be eligible to the Office of President; neither shall any person be eligible to that Office who shall not have attained to the Age of thirty-five Years, and been fourteen Years a Resident within the United States.

6. ~~In Case of the Removal of the President from Office, or of his Death, Resignation, or Inability to discharge the Powers and Duties of the said Office, the Same shall devolve on the Vice President,~~ and the Congress may by Law provide for the Case of Removal, Death, Resignation or Inability, both of the President and Vice President, declaring what Officer shall then act as President, and such Officer shall act accordingly, until the Disability be removed, or a President shall be elected.

7. The President shall, at stated Times, receive for his Services, a Compensation, which shall neither be increased nor diminished during the Period for which he shall have been elected, and he shall not receive within that Period any other Emolument from the United States, or any of them.

8. Before he enter on the Execution of his Office, he shall take the following Oath or Affirmation:
"I do solemnly swear (or affirm) that I will faithfully execute the Office of President of the United States, and will to the best of my Ability, preserve, protect and defend the Constitution of the United States."

Section 2.

1. The President shall be Commander in Chief of the Army and Navy of the United States, and of the Militia of the several States, when called into the actual Service of the United States; he may require the Opinion, in writing, of the principal Officer in each of the executive Departments, upon any Subject relating to the Duties of their respective Offices, and he shall have Power to Grant Reprieves and Pardons for Offences against the United States, except in Cases of Impeachment.

♦ 2. He shall have Power, by and with the Advice and Consent of the Senate, to make Treaties, provided two thirds of the Senators present concur; and he shall nominate, and by and with the Advice and Consent of the Senate, shall appoint Ambassadors, other public Ministers and Consuls, Judges of the supreme Court, and all other Officers of the United States, whose Appointments are not herein otherwise provided for, and which shall be established by Law: but the Congress may by Law vest the Appointment of such inferior Officers, as they think proper, in the President alone, in the Courts of Law, or in the Heads of Departments.

♦ 3. The President shall have Power to fill up all Vacancies that may happen during the Recess of the Senate, by granting Commissions which shall expire at the End of their next Session.

Section 3.

He shall from time to time give to the Congress Information of the State of the Union, and recommend to their Con-sideration such Measures as he shall judge necessary and expedient; he may, on extraordinary Occasions, convene both Houses, or either of them, and in Case of Disagreement between them, with Respect to the Time of Adjournment, he may adjourn them to such Time as he shall think proper; he shall receive Ambassadors and other public Ministers; he shall take Care that the Laws be faithfully executed, and shall Commission all the Officers of the United States.

Section 4.

The President, Vice President and all Civil Officers of the United States, shall be removed from Office on Impeachment for and Conviction of, Treason, Bribery, or other high Crimes and Misdemeanors.

Article III
Section 1.

The judicial Power of the United States, shall be vested in one supreme Court, and in such inferior Courts as the Congress may from time to time ordain and establish. The Judges, both of the supreme and inferior Courts, shall hold their Offices during good Behaviour, and shall, at stated Times, receive for their Services, a Compensation, which shall not be diminished during their Continuance in Office.

♦ **Clause 2. Treaties, appointments** The President has the sole power to make treaties; to become effective, a treaty must be approved by a two-thirds vote in the Senate. In practice, the President can also make executive agreements with foreign governments; these pacts, which are frequently made and usually deal with routine matters, do not require Senate consent. The President appoints the principal officers of the executive branch and all federal judges; the "inferior officers" are those who hold lesser posts.

♦ **Clause 3. Recess appointments** When the Senate is not in session, appointments that require Senate consent can be made by the President on a temporary basis, as "recess appointments." Recess appointments are valid only to the end of the congressional term in which they are made.

Section 3. President's Powers and Duties

The President delivers a State of the Union Message to Congress soon after that body convenes each year. That message is delivered to the nation's lawmakers and, importantly, to the American people, as well. It is shortly followed by the proposed federal budget and an economic report; and the President may send special messages to Congress at any time. In all of these communications, Congress is urged to take those actions the Chief Executive finds to be in the national interest. The President also has the power: to call special sessions of Congress; to adjourn Congress if its two houses cannot agree for that purpose; to receive the diplomatic representatives of other governments; to insure the proper execution of all federal laws; and to empower federal officers to hold their posts and perform their duties.

Section 4. Impeachment

The Constitution outlines the impeachment process in Article I, Section 2, Clause 5 and in Section 3, Clauses 6 and 7.

Judicial Department
Section 1. Courts, Terms of Office

The judicial power conferred here is the power of federal courts to hear and decide cases, disputes between the government and individuals and between private persons (parties). The Constitution creates only the Supreme Court of the United States; it gives to Congress the power to establish other, lower federal courts (Article I, Section 8, Clause 9) and to fix the size of the Supreme Court. The words "during good behaviour" mean, in effect, for life.

Section 2. Jurisdiction

◆**Clause 1.** Cases to be heard This clause sets out the jurisdiction of the federal courts; that is, it identifies those cases that may be tried in those courts. The federal courts can hear and decide—have jurisdiction over—a case depending on either the subject matter or the parties involved in that case. The jurisdiction of the federal courts in cases involving States was substantially restricted by the 11th Amendment in 1795.

◆**Clause 2.** Supreme Court jurisdiction Original jurisdiction refers to the power of a court to hear a case in the first instance, not on appeal from a lower court. Appellate jurisdiction refers to a court's power to hear a case on appeal from a lower court, from the court in which the case was originally tried. This clause gives the Supreme Court both original and appellate jurisdiction. However, nearly all of the cases the High Court hears are brought to it on appeal from the lower federal courts and the highest State courts.

◆**Clause 3.** Jury trial in criminal cases A person accused of a federal crime is guaranteed the right to trial by jury in a federal court in the State where the crime was committed; see the 5th and 6th amendments. The right to trial by jury in serious criminal cases in the State courts is guaranteed by the 6th and 14th amendments.

Section 3. Treason

◆**Clause 1.** Definition Treason is the only crime defined in the Constitution. The Framers intended the very specific definition here to prevent the loose use of the charge of treason—for example, against persons who criticize the government. Treason can be committed only in time of war and only by a citizen or a resident alien.

◆**Clause 2.** Punishment Congress has provided that the punishment that a federal court may impose on a convicted traitor may range from a minimum of five years in prison and/or a $10,000 fine to a maximum of death; no person convicted of treason has ever been executed by the United States. No legal punishment can be imposed on the family or descendants of a convicted traitor. Congress has also made it a crime for any person (in either peace or wartime) to commit espionage or sabotage, to attempt to overthrow the government by force, or to conspire to do any of these things.

Section 2.

◆1. The judicial Power shall extend to all Cases, in Law and Equity, arising under this Constitution, the Laws of the United States, and Treaties made, or which shall be made, under their Authority;— to all Cases affecting Ambassadors, other public ministers, and Consuls;— to all Cases of Admiralty and maritime Jurisdiction;— to Controversies to which the United States shall be a Party;— to Controversies between two or more States;— ~~between a State and Citizens of another State;~~— between Citizens of different States;— between Citizens of the same State claiming Lands under Grants of different States, ~~and between a State, or the Citizens thereof, and foreign States, Citizens, or Subjects.~~

◆2. In all Cases affecting Ambassadors, other public Ministers and Consuls, and those in which a State shall be a Party, the supreme Court shall have original Jurisdiction. In all the other Cases before mentioned, the supreme Court shall have appellate Jurisdiction, both as to Law and Fact, with such Exceptions, and under such Regulations as the Congress shall make.

◆3. The trial of all Crimes, except in Cases of Impeachment, shall be by Jury; and such Trial shall be held in the State where the said Crimes shall have been committed; but when not committed within any State, the Trial shall be at such Place or Places as the Congress may by Law have directed.

Section 3.

◆1. Treason against the United States shall consist only in levying War against them, or in adhering to their Enemies, giving them Aid and Comfort. No Person shall be convicted of Treason unless on the Testimony of two Witnesses to the same overt Act, or on Confession in open Court.

◆2. The Congress shall have Power to declare the Punishment of Treason, but no Attainder of Treason shall work Corruption of Blood, or Forfeiture except during the Life of the Person attainted.

Article IV

Section 1.

Full Faith and Credit shall be given in each State to the public Acts, Records, and judicial Proceedings of every other State. And the Congress may by general Laws prescribe the Manner in which such Acts, Records and Proceedings shall be proved, and the Effect thereof.

Section 2.

♦1. The Citizens of each State shall be entitled to all Privileges and Immunities of Citizens in the several States.

♦2. A Person charged in any State with Treason, Felony, or other Crime, who shall flee from justice, and be found in another State, shall on Demand of the executive Authority of the State from which he fled, be delivered up, to be removed to the State having Jurisdiction of the Crime.

♦3. ~~No Person held to Service or Labor in one State, under the Laws thereof, escaping into another, shall, in Consequence of any Law or Regulation therein, be discharged from Service or Labor, but shall be delivered up on Claim of the Party to whom such Service or Labor may be due.~~

Section 3.

♦1. New States may be admitted by the Congress into this Union; but no new State shall be formed or erected within the Jurisdiction of any other State; nor any State be formed by the Junction of two or more States, or Parts of States, without the Consent of the Legislatures of the States concerned as well as of the Congress.

♦2. The Congress shall have Power to dispose of and make all needful Rules and Regulations respecting the Territory or other Property belonging to the United States; and nothing in this Constitution shall be so construed as to Prejudice any Claims of the United States, or of any particular State.

Section 4.

The United States shall guarantee to every State in this Union a Republican Form of Government, and shall protect each of them against Invasion; and on Application of the Legislature, or of the Executive (when the Legislature cannot be convened) against domestic Violence.

Relations Among States

Section 1. Full Faith and Credit

Each State must recognize the validity of the laws, public records, and court decisions of every other State.

Section 2. Privileges and Immunities of Citizens

♦**Clause 1.** Residents of other States In effect, this clause means that no State may discriminate against the residents of other States; that is, a State's laws cannot draw unreasonable distinctions between its own residents and those of any of the other States. See Section 1 of the 14th Amendment.

♦**Clause 2.** Extradition The process of returning a fugitive to another State is known as "interstate rendition" or, more commonly, "extradition." Usually, that process works routinely; some extradition requests are contested however—especially in cases with racial or political overtones. A governor may refuse to extradite a fugitive; but the federal courts can compel an unwilling governor to obey this constitutional command.

♦**Clause 3.** Fugitive slaves This clause was nullified by the 13th Amendment, which abolished slavery in 1865.

Section 3. New States; Territories

♦**Clause 1.** New States Only Congress can admit new States to the Union. A new State may not be created by taking territory from an existing State without the consent of that State's legislature. Congress has admitted 37 States since the original 13 formed the Union. Five States—Vermont, Kentucky, Tennessee, Maine, and West Virginia—were created from parts of existing States. Texas was an independent republic before admission. California was admitted after being ceded to the United States by Mexico. Each of the other 30 States entered the Union only after a period of time as an organized territory of the United States.

♦**Clause 2.** Territory, property Congress has the power to make laws concerning the territories, other public lands, and all other property of the United States.

Section 4. Protection Afforded to States by the Nation

The Constitution does not define "a republican form of government," but the phrase is generally understood to mean a representative government. The Federal Government must also defend each State against attacks from outside its border and, at the request of a State's legislature or its governor, aid its efforts to put down internal disorders.

Provisions for Amendment

This section provides for the methods by which formal changes can be made in the Constitution. An amendment may be proposed in one of two ways: by a two-thirds vote in each house of Congress, or by a national convention called by Congress at the request of two-thirds of the State legislatures. A proposed amendment may be ratified in one of two ways: by three-fourths of the State legislatures, or by three-fourths of the States in conventions called for that purpose. Congress has the power to determine the method by which a proposed amendment may be ratified. The amendment process cannot be used to deny any State its equal representation in the United States Senate. To this point, 27 amendments have been adopted. To date, all of the amendments except the 21st Amendment were proposed by Congress and ratified by the State legislatures. Only the 21st Amendment was ratified by the convention method.

National Debts, Supremacy of National Law, Oath

Section 1. Validity of Debts

Congress had borrowed large sums of money during the Revolution and later during the Critical Period of the 1780s. This provision, a pledge that the new government would honor those debts, did much to create confidence in that government.

Section 2. Supremacy of National Law

This section sets out the Supremacy Clause, a specific declaration of the supremacy of federal law over any and all forms of State law. No State, including its local governments, may make or enforce any law that conflicts with any provision in the Constitution, an act of Congress, a treaty, or an order, rule, or regulation properly issued by the President or his subordinates in the executive branch.

Section 3. Oaths of Office

This provision reinforces the Supremacy Clause; all public officers, at every level in the United States, owe their first allegiance to the Constitution of the United States. No religious qualification can be imposed as a condition for holding any public office.

Ratification of Constitution

The proposed Constitution was signed by George Washington and 37 of his fellow Framers on September 17, 1787. (George Read of Delaware signed for himself and also for his absent colleague, John Dickinson.)

Article V

The Congress, whenever two thirds of both Houses shall deem it necessary, shall propose Amendments to this Constitution, or, on the Application of the Legislatures of two thirds of the several States, shall call a Convention for proposing Amendments, which, in either Case, shall be valid to all Intents and Purposes, as Part of this Constitution, when ratified by the Legislatures of three fourths of the several States, or by Conventions in three fourths thereof, as the one or the other Mode of Ratification may be proposed by the Congress; Provided that no Amendment which may be made prior to the Year One thousand eight hundred and eight shall in any Manner affect the first and fourth Clauses in the Ninth section of the first Article; and that no State, without its Consent, shall be deprived of its equal Suffrage in the Senate.

Article VI

Section 1.

All Debts contracted and Engagements entered into, before the Adoption of this Constitution, shall be as valid against the United States under this Constitution, as under the Confederation.

Section 2.

This Constitution, and the Laws of the United States which shall be made in Pursuance thereof; and all Treaties made, or which shall be made, under the Authority of the United States, shall be the supreme Law of the Land; and the Judges in every State shall be bound thereby, anything in the constitution or Laws of any State to the Contrary notwithstanding.

Section 3.

The Senators and Representatives before mentioned, and the Members of the several State legislatures, and all executive and judicial Officers, both of the United States and of the several States, shall be bound by Oath or Affirmation, to support this Constitution; but no religious Test shall ever be required as a Qualification to any Office or public Trust under the United States.

Article VII

The ratification of the Conventions of nine States, shall be sufficient for the Establishment of this Constitution between the States so ratifying the same.

Nine States had to approve the Constitution before it could become effective.

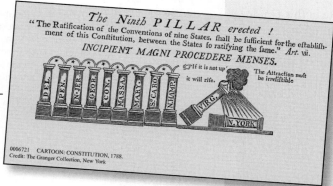

0006721 CARTOON: CONSTITUTION, 1788.
Credit: The Granger Collection, New York

Done in Convention by the Unanimous Consent of the States present the Seventeenth Day of September in the Year of our Lord one thousand seven hundred and Eighty-seven and of the Independence of the United States of America the twelfth. In witness whereof We have hereunto subscribed our Names.

Attest:
William Jackson,
Secretary
George Washington,
President and Deputy from Virginia

New Hampshire
John Langdon
Nicholas Gilman

Massachusetts
Nathaniel Gorham
Rufus King

Connecticut
William Samuel Johnson
Roger Sherman

New York
Alexander Hamilton

New Jersey
William Livingston
David Brearley
William Paterson
Jonathan Dayton

Pennsylvania
Benjamin Franklin
Thomas Mifflin
Robert Morris
George Clymer
Thomas Fitzsimons
Jared Ingersoll
James Wilson
Gouverneur Morris

Delaware
George Read
Gunning Bedford, Jr.
John Dickinson
Richard Bassett
Jacob Broom

Maryland
James McHenry
Dan of St. Thomas Jennifer
Daniel Carroll

Virginia
John Blair
James Madison, Jr.

North Carolina
William Blount
Richard Dobbs Spaight
Hugh Williamson

South Carolina
John Rutledge
Charles Cotesworth Pinckney
Charles Pinckney
Pierce Butler

Georgia
William Few
Abraham Baldwin

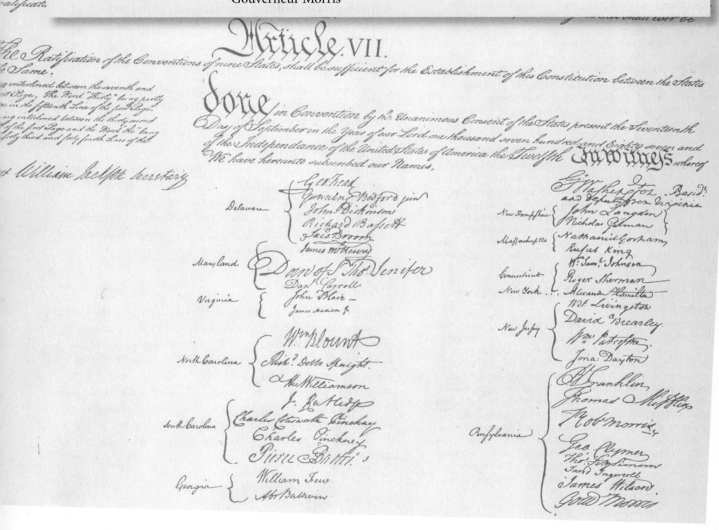

The United States Constitution

Amendments

The first 10 amendments, the Bill of Rights, were each proposed by Congress on September 25, 1789, and ratified by the necessary three-fourths of the States on December 15, 1791. These amendments were originally intended to restrict the National Government—not the States. However, the Supreme Court has several times held that most of their provisions also apply to the States, through the 14th Amendment's Due Process Clause.

1st Amendment. Freedom of Religion, Speech, Press, Assembly, and Petition

The 1st Amendment sets out five basic liberties: The guarantee of freedom of religion is both a protection of religious thought and practice and a command of separation of church and state. The guarantees of freedom of speech and press assure to all persons a right to speak, publish, and otherwise express their views. The guarantees of the rights of assembly and petition protect the right to join with others in public meetings, political parties, interest groups, and other associations to discuss public affairs and influence public policy. None of these rights is guaranteed in absolute terms, however; like all other civil rights guarantees, each of them may be exercised only with regard to the rights of all other persons.

2nd Amendment. Bearing Arms

Each State has the right to maintain a militia, an armed force for its own protection—today, the National Guard. The National Government and the States can and do regulate the private possession and use of firearms.

3rd Amendment. Quartering of Troops

This amendment was intended to prevent what had been common British practice in the colonial period; see the Declaration of Independence. This provision is of virtually no importance today.

4th Amendment. Searches and Seizures

The basic rule laid down by the 4th Amendment is this: Police officers have no general right to search for or seize evidence or seize (arrest) persons. Except in particular circumstances, they must have a proper warrant (a court order) obtained with probable cause (on reasonable grounds). This guarantee is reinforced by the exclusionary rule, developed by the Supreme Court: Evidence gained as the result of an unlawful search or seizure cannot be used at the court trial of the person from whom it was seized.

5th Amendment. Criminal Proceedings; Due Process; Eminent Domain

A person can be tried for a serious federal crime only if he or she has been indicted (charged, accused of that crime) by a grand jury. No one may be subjected to double jeopardy—that is, tried twice for the same crime. All persons are protected against self-incrimination; no person can be legally compelled to answer any question in any governmental proceeding if that answer could lead to that person's prosecution. The 5th Amendment's Due Process Clause prohibits unfair, arbitrary actions by the Federal Government; a like prohibition is set out against the States in the 14th Amendment. Government may take private property for a legitimate public purpose; but when it exercises that power of eminent domain, it must pay a fair price for the property seized.

1st Amendment

Congress shall make no law respecting an establishment of religion, or prohibiting the free exercise thereof, or abridging the freedom of speech, or of the press; or the right of the people peaceably to assemble, and to petition the Government for a redress of grievances.

2nd Amendment

A well-regulated Militia being necessary to the security of a free State, the right of the people to keep and bear Arms, shall not be infringed.

3rd Amendment.

No Soldier shall, in time of peace be quartered in any house, without the consent of the Owner, nor, in time of war, but in a manner to be prescribed by law.

4th Amendment.

The right of the people to be secure in their persons, houses, papers, and effects, against unreasonable searches and seizures, shall not be violated, and no Warrants shall issue, but upon probable cause, supported by Oath or affirmation, and particularly describing the place to be searched, and the persons or things to be seized.

5th Amendment.

No person shall be held to answer for a capital, or otherwise infamous crime, unless on a presentment or indictment of a Grand Jury, except in cases arising in the land or naval forces, or in the Militia, when in actual service in time of War, or public danger; nor shall any person be subject for the same offence to be twice put in jeopardy of life or limb; nor shall be compelled in any criminal case to be a witness against himself, nor be deprived of life, liberty, or property, without due process of law; nor shall private property be taken for public use, without just compensation.

Jury swearing in

6th Amendment

In all criminal prosecutions, the accused shall enjoy the right to a speedy and public trial, by an impartial jury of the State and district wherein the crime shall have been committed, which district shall have been previously ascertained by law, and to be informed of the nature and cause of the accusation; to be confronted with the witnesses against him; to have compulsory process for obtaining witnesses in his favor, and to have the Assistance of Counsel for his defence.

7th Amendment

In Suits at common law, where the value in controversy shall exceed twenty dollars, the right of trial by jury shall be preserved, and no fact tried by a jury, shall be otherwise re-examined in any Court of the United States, than according to the rules of the common law.

8th Amendment

Excessive bail shall not be required, nor excessive fines imposed, nor cruel and unusual punishment inflicted.

9th Amendment

The enumeration in the Constitution, of certain rights, shall not be construed to deny or disparage others retained by the people.

10th Amendment

The powers not delegated to the United States by the Constitution, nor prohibited by it to the States, are reserved to the States respectively, or to the people.

6th Amendment. Criminal Proceedings

A person accused of crime has the right to be tried in court without undue delay and by an impartial jury; see Article III, Section 2, Clause 3. The defendant must be informed of the charge upon which he or she is to be tried, has the right to cross-examine hostile witnesses, and has the right to require the testimony of favorable witnesses. The defendant also has the right to be represented by an attorney at every stage in the criminal process.

7th Amendment. Civil Trials

This amendment applies only to civil cases heard in federal courts. A civil case does not involve criminal matters; it is a dispute between private parties or between the government and a private party. The right to trial by jury is guaranteed in any civil case in a federal court if the amount of money involved in that case exceeds $20 (most cases today involve a much larger sum); that right may be waived (relinquished, put aside) if both parties agree to a bench trial (a trial by a judge, without a jury).

8th Amendment. Punishment for Crimes

Bail is the sum of money that a person accused of crime may be required to post (deposit with the court) as a guarantee that he or she will appear in court at the proper time. The amount of bail required and/or a fine imposed as punishment must bear a reasonable relationship to the seriousness of the crime involved in the case. The prohibition of cruel and unusual punishment forbids any punishment judged to be too harsh, too severe for the crime for which it is imposed.

9th Amendment. Unenumerated Rights

The fact that the Constitution sets out many civil rights guarantees, expressly provides for many protections against government, does not mean that there are not other rights also held by the people.

10th Amendment. Powers Reserved to the States

This amendment identifies the area of power that may be exercised by the States. All of those powers the Constitution does not grant to the National Government, and at the same time does not forbid to the States, belong to each of the States, or to the people of each State.

11th Amendment. Suits Against States

Proposed by Congress March 4, 1794; ratified February 7, 1795, but official announcement of the ratification was delayed until January 8, 1798. This amendment repealed part of Article III, Section 2, Clause 1. No State may be sued in a federal court by a resident of another State or of a foreign country; the Supreme Court has long held that this provision also means that a State cannot be sued in a federal court by a foreign country or, more importantly, even by one of its own residents.

12th Amendment. Election of President and Vice President

Proposed by Congress December 9, 1803; ratified June 15, 1804. This amendment replaced Article II, Section 1, Clause 3. Originally, each elector cast two ballots, each for a different person for President. The person with the largest number of electoral votes, provided that number was a majority of the electors, was to become President; the person with the second highest number was to become Vice President. This arrangement produced an electoral vote tie between Thomas Jefferson and Aaron Burr in 1800; the House finally chose Jefferson as President in 1801. The 12th Amendment separated the balloting for President and Vice President; each elector now casts one ballot for someone as President and a second ballot for another person as Vice President. Note that the 20th Amendment changed the date set here (March 4) to January 20, and that the 23rd Amendment (1961) provides for electors from the District of Columbia. This amendment also provides that the Vice President must meet the same qualifications as those set out for the President in Article II, Section 1, Clause 5.

Vice President Joseph R. Biden, President Barack Obama

13th Amendment. Slavery and Involuntary Servitude

Proposed by Congress January 31, 1865; ratified December 6, 1865. This amendment forbids slavery in the United States and in any area under its control. It also forbids other forms of forced labor, except punishments for crime; but some forms of compulsory service are not prohibited—for example, service on juries or in the armed forces. Section 2 gives to Congress the power to carry out the provisions of Section 1 of this amendment.

11th Amendment

The Judicial power of the United States shall not be construed to extend to any suit in law or equity, commenced or prosecuted against one of the United States by Citizens of another State, or by Citizens or Subjects of any Foreign State.

12th Amendment

The Electors shall meet in their respective States and vote by ballot for President and Vice President, one of whom, at least, shall not be an inhabitant of the same State with themselves; they shall name in their ballots the person voted for as President, and in distinct ballots the person voted for as Vice President, and they shall make distinct lists of all persons voted for as President, and of all persons voted for as Vice President, and of the number of votes for each, which lists they shall sign and certify, and transmit sealed to the seat of the government of the United States, directed to the President of the Senate;— The President of the Senate shall, in the presence of the Senate and the House of Representatives, open all the certificates and the votes shall then be counted;— the person having the greatest Number of votes for President shall be the President, if such number be a majority of the whole number of Electors appointed; and if no person have such a majority, then, from the persons having the highest numbers not exceeding three on the list of those voted for as President, the House of Representatives shall choose immediately, by ballot, the President. But in choosing the President, the votes shall be taken by States, the representation from each State having one vote; a quorum for this purpose shall consist of a member or members from two thirds of the States, and a majority of all the States shall be necessary to a choice. And if the House of Representatives shall not choose a President whenever the right of choice shall devolve upon them, before the fourth day of March next following, then the Vice President shall act as President, as in case of death or other constitutional disability of the President. The person having the greatest number of votes as Vice President, shall be the Vice President, if such number be a majority of the whole number of Electors appointed, and if no person have a majority, then from the two highest numbers on the list, the Senate shall choose the Vice President; a quorum for the purpose shall consist of two thirds of the whole number of Senators, a majority of the whole number shall be necessary to a choice. But no person constitutionally ineligible to the office of President shall be eligible to that of Vice-President of the United States.

13th Amendment

Section 1. Neither slavery nor involuntary servitude, except as a punishment for crime whereof the party shall have been duly convicted, shall exist within the United States, or any place subject to their jurisdiction.

Section 2. Congress shall have power to enforce this article by appropriate legislation.

14th Amendment

Section 1. All persons born or naturalized in the United States and subject to the jurisdiction thereof, are citizens of the United States and of the State wherein they reside. No State shall make or enforce any law which shall abridge the privileges or immunities of citizens of the United States; nor shall any State deprive any person of life, liberty, or property, without due process of law; nor deny to any person within its jurisdiction the equal protection of the laws.

Section 2. Representatives shall be apportioned among the several States according to their respective numbers, counting the whole number of persons in each State, excluding Indians not taxed. But when the right to vote at any election for the choice of electors for President and Vice President of the United States, Representatives in Congress, the Executive and Judicial officers of a State, or the members of the Legislature thereof, is denied to any of the male inhabitants of such State, being twenty-one years of age and citizens of the United States, or in any way abridged, except for participation in rebellion, or other crime, the basis of representation therein shall be reduced in the proportion which the number of such male citizens shall bear to the whole number of male citizens twenty-one years of age in such State.

Section 3. No person shall be a Senator or Representative in Congress, or elector of President and Vice President, or hold any office, civil or military, under the United States, or under any State, who, having previously taken an oath, as a member of Congress, or as an officer of the United States, or as a member of any State legislature, or as an executive or judicial officer of any State, to support the Constitution of the United States, shall have engaged in insurrection or rebellion against the same, or given aid or comfort to the enemies thereof. But Congress may, by a vote of two thirds of each House, remove such disability.

Section 4. The validity of the public debt of the United States, authorized by law, including debts incurred for payment of pensions and bounties for services in suppressing insurrection or rebellion, shall not be questioned. But neither the United States nor any State shall assume or pay any debt or obligation incurred in aid of insurrection or rebellion against the United States, or any claim for the loss or emancipation of any slave; but all such debts, obligations and claims shall be held illegal and void.

Section 5. The Congress shall have power to enforce, by appropriate legislation, the provisions of this article.

14th Amendment. Rights of Citizens

Proposed by Congress June 13, 1866; ratified July 9, 1868. Section 1 defines citizenship. It provides for the acquisition of United States citizenship by birth or by naturalization. Citizenship at birth is determined according to the principle of jus soli—"the law of the soil," where born; naturalization is the legal process by which one acquires a new citizenship at some time after birth. Under certain circumstances, citizenship can also be gained at birth abroad, according to the principle of jus sanguinis—"the law of the blood," to whom born. This section also contains two major civil rights provisions: the Due Process Clause forbids a State (and its local governments) to act in any unfair or arbitrary way; the Equal Protection Clause forbids a State (and its local governments) to discriminate against, draw unreasonable distinctions between, persons.

Most of the rights set out against the National Government in the first eight amendments have been extended against the States (and their local governments) through Supreme Court decisions involving the 14th Amendment's Due Process Clause.

The first sentence here replaced Article I, Section 2, Clause 3, the Three-Fifths Compromise provision. Essentially, all persons in the United States are counted in each decennial census, the basis for the distribution of House seats. The balance of this section has never been enforced and is generally thought to be obsolete.

This section limited the President's power to pardon those persons who had led the Confederacy during the Civil War. Congress finally removed this disability in 1898.

Section 4 also dealt with matters directly related to the Civil War. It reaffirmed the public debt of the United States; but it invalidated, prohibited payment of, any debt contracted by the Confederate States and also prohibited any compensation of former slave owners.

15th Amendment. Right to Vote—Race, Color, Servitude

Proposed by Congress February 26, 1869; ratified February 3, 1870. The phrase "previous condition of servitude" refers to slavery. Note that this amendment does not guarantee the right to vote to African Americans, or to anyone else. Instead, it forbids the States from discriminating against any person on the grounds of his "race, color, or previous condition of servitude" in the setting of suffrage qualifications.

16th Amendment. Income Tax

Proposed by Congress July 12, 1909; ratified February 3, 1913. This amendment modified two provisions in Article I, Section 2, Clause 3, and Section 9, Clause 4. It gives to Congress the power to levy an income tax, a direct tax, without regard to the populations of any of the States.

17th Amendment. Popular Election of Senators

Proposed by Congress May 13, 1912; ratified April 8, 1913. This amendment repealed those portions of Article I, Section 3, Clauses 1 and 2 relating to the election of senators. Senators are now elected by the voters in each State. If a vacancy occurs, the governor of the State involved must call an election to fill the seat; the governor may appoint a senator to serve until the next election, if the State's legislature has authorized that step.

18th Amendment. Prohibition of Intoxicating Liquors

Proposed by Congress December 18, 1917; ratified January 16, 1919. This amendment outlawed the making, selling, transporting, importing, or exporting of alcoholic beverages in the United States. It was repealed in its entirety by the 21st Amendment in 1933.

19th Amendment. Equal Suffrage—Sex

Proposed by Congress June 4, 1919; ratified August 18, 1920. No person can be denied the right to vote in any election in the United States on account of his or her sex.

15th Amendment

Section 1. The right of citizens of the United States to vote shall not be denied or abridged by the United States or by any State on account of race, color, or previous condition of servitude.

Section 2. The Congress shall have power to enforce this article by appropriate legislation.

16th Amendment

The Congress shall have power to lay and collect taxes on incomes, from whatever source derived, without apportionment among the several States, and without regard to any census or enumeration.

17th Amendment

The Senate of the United States shall be composed of two Senators from each State, elected by the people thereof, for six years; and each Senator shall have one vote. The electors in each State shall have the qualifications requisite for electors of the most numerous branch of the State legislatures.

When vacancies happen in the representation of any State in the Senate, the executive authority of such State shall issue writs of election to fill such vacancies: Provided, That the legislature of any State may empower the executive thereof to make temporary appointments until the people fill the vacancies by election as the legislature may direct.

This amendment shall not be so construed as to affect the election or term of any Senator chosen before it becomes valid as part of the Constitution

18th Amendment.

Section 1. After one year from the ratification of this article the manufacture, sale, or transportation of intoxicating liquors within, the importation thereof into, or the exportation thereof from the United States and all territory subject to the jurisdiction thereof for beverage purposes is hereby prohibited.

Section 2. The Congress and the several States shall have concurrent power to enforce this article by appropriate legislation.

Section 3. This article shall be inoperative unless it shall have been ratified as an amendment to the Constitution by the legislatures of the several States, as provided in the Constitution, within seven years of the date of the submission hereof to the States by Congress.

19th Amendment

The right of citizens of the United States to vote shall not be denied or abridged by the United States or by any State on account of sex.

Congress shall have power to enforce this article by appropriate legislation.

20th Amendment

Section 1. The terms of the President and Vice President shall end at noon on the 20th day of January, and the terms of Senators and Representatives at noon on the 3d day of January, of the years in which such terms would have ended if this article had not been ratified; and the terms of their successors shall then begin.

Section 2. The Congress shall assemble at least once in every year, and such meeting shall begin at noon on the 3d day of January, unless they shall by law appoint a different day.

Section 3. If, at the time fixed for the beginning of the term of the President, the President elect shall have died, the Vice President elect shall become President. If a President shall not have been chosen before the time fixed for the beginning of his term, or if the President-elect shall have failed to qualify, then the Vice President elect shall act as President until a President shall have qualified; and the Congress may by law provide for the case wherein neither a President elect nor a Vice President elect shall have qualified, declaring who shall then act as President, or the manner in which one who is to act shall be selected, and such person shall act accordingly until a President or Vice President shall have qualified.

Section 4. The Congress may by law provide for the case of the death of any of the persons from whom the House of Representatives may choose a President whenever the right of choice shall have devolved upon them, and for the case of the death of any of the persons from whom the Senate may choose a Vice President whenever the right of choice shall have devolved upon them.

Section 5. Sections 1 and 2 shall take effect on the 15th day of October following the ratification of this article.

Section 6. This article shall be inoperative unless it shall have been ratified as an amendment to the Constitution by the legislatures of three fourths of the several States within seven years from the date of its submission.

21st Amendment

Section 1. The eighteenth article of amendment to the Constitution of the United States is hereby repealed.

Section 2. The transportation or importation into any State, Territory, or possession of the United States for delivery or use therein of intoxicating liquors, in violation of the laws thereof, is hereby prohibited.

Section 3. This article shall be inoperative unless it shall have been ratified as an amendment to the Constitution by conventions in the several States, as provided in the Constitution, within seven years from the date of the submission hereof to the States by the Congress.

20th Amendment. Commencement of Terms; Sessions of Congress; Death or Disqualification of President-Elect

Proposed by Congress March 2, 1932; ratified January 23, 1933. The provisions of Sections 1 and 2 relating to Congress modified Article I, Section 4, Clause 2, and those provisions relating to the President, the 12th Amendment. The date on which the President and Vice President now take office was moved from March 4 to January 20. Similarly, the members of Congress now begin their terms on January 3. The 20th Amendment is sometimes called the "Lame Duck Amendment" because it shortened the period of time a member of Congress who was defeated for reelection (a "lame duck") remains in office.

This section deals with certain possibilities that were not covered by the presidential selection provisions of either Article II or the 12th Amendment. To this point, none of these situations has occurred. Note that there is neither a President-elect nor a Vice President-elect until the electoral votes have been counted by Congress, or, if the electoral college cannot decide the matter, the House has chosen a President or the Senate has chosen a Vice President.

Congress has not in fact ever passed such a law. See Section 2 of the 25th Amendment, regarding a vacancy in the vice presidency; that provision could some day have an impact here.

Section 5 set the date on which this amendment came into force.

Section 6 placed a time limit on the ratification process; note that a similar provision was written into the 18th, 21st, and 22nd amendments.

21st Amendment. Repeal of 18th Amendment

Proposed by Congress February 20, 1933; ratified December 5, 1933. This amendment repealed all of the 18th Amendment. Section 2 modifies the scope of the Federal Government's commerce power set out in Article I, Section 8, Clause 3; it gives to each State the power to regulate the transportation or importation and the distribution or use of intoxicating liquors in ways that would be unconstitutional in the case of any other commodity. The 21st Amendment is the only amendment Congress has thus far submitted to the States for ratification by conventions.

22nd Amendment. Presidential Tenure

Proposed by Congress March 21, 1947; ratified February 27, 1951. This amendment modified Article II, Section I, Clause 1. It stipulates that no President may serve more than two elected terms. But a President who has succeeded to the office beyond the midpoint in a term to which another President was originally elected may serve for more than eight years. In any case, however, a President may not serve more than 10 years. Prior to Franklin Roosevelt, who was elected to four terms, no President had served more than two full terms in office.

BETTER A THIRD TERMER THAN A THIRD RATER

Political button supporting FDR's third term.

23rd Amendment. Presidential Electors for the District of Columbia

Proposed by Congress June 16, 1960; ratified March 29, 1961. This amendment modified Article II, Section I, Clause 2 and the 12th Amendment. It included the voters of the District of Columbia in the presidential electorate; and provides that the District is to have the same number of electors as the least populous State—three electors—but no more than that number.

24th Amendment. Right to Vote in Federal Elections—Tax Payment

Proposed by Congress August 27, 1962; ratified January 23, 1964. This amendment outlawed the payment of any tax as a condition for taking part in the nomination or election of any federal officeholder.

25th Amendment. Presidential Succession, Vice Presidential Vacancy, Presidential Inability

Proposed by Congress July 6, 1965; ratified February 10, 1967. Section 1 revised the imprecise provision on presidential succession in Article II, Section 1, Clause 6. It affirmed the precedent set by Vice President John Tyler, who became President on the death of William Henry Harrison in 1841. Section 2 provides for the filling of a vacancy in the office of Vice President. The office had been vacant on 16 occasions and remained unfilled for the rest of each term involved. When Spiro Agnew resigned the office in 1973, President Nixon selected Gerald Ford per this provision; and, when President Nixon resigned in 1974, Gerald Ford became President and chose Nelson Rockefeller as Vice President.

22nd Amendment

Section 1. No person shall be elected to the office of the President more than twice, and no person who has held the office of President, or acted as President, for more than two years of a term to which some other person was elected President shall be elected to the office of the President more than once. But this Article shall not apply to any person holding the office of President, when this Article was proposed by the Congress, and shall not prevent any person who may be holding the office of President, or acting as President, during the term within which this Article becomes operative from holding the office of President or acting as President during the remainder of such term.

Section 2. This article shall be inoperative unless it shall have been ratified as an amendment to the Constitution by the legislatures of three fourths of the several states within seven years from the date of its submission to the States by the Congress.

23rd Amendment.

Section 1. The District constituting the seat of Government of the United States shall appoint in such manner as the Congress may direct:

A number of electors of President and Vice President equal to the whole number of Senators and Representatives in Congress to which the District would be entitled if it were a State, but in no event more than the least populous State; they shall be in addition to those appointed by the States, they shall be considered, for the purposes of the election of President and Vice President, to be electors appointed by a State; and they shall meet in the District and perform such duties as provided by the twelfth article of amendment.

24th Amendment.

Section 1. The right of citizens of the United States to vote in any primary or other election for President or Vice President, for electors for President or Vice President, or for Senator or Representative in Congress, shall not be denied or abridged by the United States or any State by reason of failure to pay any poll tax or other tax.

Section 2. The Congress shall have power to enforce this article by appropriate legislation.

25th Amendment.

Section 1. In case of the removal of the President from office or of his death or resignation, the Vice President shall become President.

Section 2. Whenever there is a vacancy in the office of the Vice President, the President shall nominate a Vice President who shall take office upon confirmation by a majority vote of both Houses of Congress.

Section 3. Whenever the President transmits to the President pro tempore of the Senate and the Speaker of the House of Representatives his written declaration that he is unable to discharge the powers and duties of his office, and until he transmits to them a written declaration to the contrary, such powers and duties shall be discharged by the Vice President as Acting President.

Section 4. Whenever the Vice President and a majority of either the principal officers of the executive departments or of such other body as Congress may by law provide, transmit to the President pro tempore of the Senate and the Speaker of the House of Representatives their written declaration that the President is unable to discharge the powers and duties of his office, the Vice President shall immediately assume the powers and duties of the office as Acting President.

Thereafter, when the President transmits to the President pro tempore of the Senate and the Speaker of the House of Representatives his written declaration that no inability exists, he shall resume the powers and duties of his office unless the Vice President and a majority of either the principal officers of the executive department or of such other body as Congress may by law provide, transmit within four days to the President pro tempore of the Senate and the Speaker of the House of Representatives their written declaration that the President is unable to discharge the powers and duties of his office. Thereupon Congress shall decide the issue, assembling within forty-eight hours for that purpose if not in session. If the Congress, within twenty-one days after receipt of the latter written declaration, or, if Congress is not in session, within twenty-one days after Congress is required to assemble, determines by two-thirds vote of both Houses that the President is unable to discharge the powers and duties of his office, the Vice President shall continue to discharge the same as Acting President; otherwise, the President shall resume the powers and duties of his office.

26th Amendment.

Section 1. The right of citizens of the United States, who are eighteen years of age or older, to vote shall not be denied or abridged by the United States or by any State on account of age.

Section 2. The Congress shall have the power to enforce this article by appropriate legislation.

27th Amendment.

No law varying the compensation for the services of the Senators and Representatives, shall take effect, until an election of Representatives shall have intervened.

This section created a procedure for determining if a President is so incapacitated that he cannot perform the powers and duties of his office.

Section 4 deals with the circumstance in which a President will not be able to determine the fact of incapacity. To this point, Congress has not established the "such other body" referred to here. This section contains the only typographical error in the Constitution; in its second paragraph, the word "department" should in fact read "departments."

26th Amendment. Right to Vote—Age
Proposed by Congress March 23, 1971; ratified July 1, 1971. This amendment provides that the minimum age for voting in any election in the United States cannot be more than 18 years. (A State may set a minimum voting age of less than 18, however.)

27th Amendment. Congressional Pay
Proposed by Congress September 25, 1789; ratified May 7, 1992. This amendment modified Article I, Section 6, Clause 1. It limits Congress's power to fix the salaries of its members—by delaying the effectiveness of any increase in that pay until after the next regular congressional election.

Skills Handbook

The following pages provide you with the skills you need to learn and demonstrate your knowledge of American government.

Writing

Writing is one of the most powerful communication tools you will use for the rest of your life. Beyond the ability of the written word to inspire, inform, and entertain, research also shows that writing about what you read actually helps you learn new information and form new ideas. A systematic approach to writing—including prewriting, drafting, revising, and proofreading—can help you write better, whether you are writing an essay or a research paper.

Narrative Essay

Narrative writing tells a story, often about a personal experience. In a government or civics course, this story, for example, might be a narrative essay that recounts how participation in a campaign or a summer job working for a government agency affected you, your friends, or your family.

❶ Prewriting

Choose a topic. The focus of your essay should be an experience of significance to you. Use these suggestions as a guide.
- Look at photos that show you with friends or family. Perhaps you attended a political rally or worked on a community event for a cause or charity you cared about.
- Scan the news in print or through electronic media. Consider how current events, court decisions, or election results have affected you or people you know. Brainstorm with family or friends. How did you react or respond to these events? Jot down ideas like the ones below.

Connections to Government and Politics This Year
- participated in a mock legislative assembly
- watched televised debates between candidates at election time
- attended a climate change rally and circulated a petition for stricter controls on greenhouse emissions

Consider audience and purpose. As you write, think about who your reader will be.
- Keep the knowledge and experience level of your audience in mind. Make sure you provide any necessary background information.
- Think about the purpose of the essay. Is your goal to entertain or inform? If your goal is to inform, you might share insights, describe lessons learned, or convey how the experience changed you.

Gather details. Collect the facts and details you need to tell your story.
- Research and include any background information about the experience that readers might need to know to understand how it affected you.
- List details about your own perceptions of the experience.

② Drafting

Organize information. Narratives are usually told in chronological order. Identify the climax of the decisive moment in your story. Then logically organize your work into a beginning, middle, and end.

Write an opening sentence. Open strongly with an engaging sentence that will catch your reader's attention.

Use sensory details. Use sights, sounds, or smells to make the story vivid for readers. Describe people's actions and gestures. Pinpoint and describe locations.

Write a conclusion. Sum up the significance of the experience.

A strong opening engages the reader.	→Practicing my speech in front of my bedroom mirror wasn't so bad. Now, however, I was saying these same words out loud in a crowded high school auditorium filled with seniors who would rather be somewhere else.
Sensory details make the experience more vivid for the reader.	→My heart pounded wildly. My first thought was "What am I doing here?" As I began to talk, some of those bored expressions began to change. Others, however, whispered to their neighbors or stared off into space. Couldn't they see that climate change might someday have a dramatic effect on their lives? I learned that day that knowing how you feel about an issue is
Insight or significance tells the reader what this event means to you.	→easy. Convincing others to take that issue seriously is a much tougher challenge. My political education was just beginning.

③ Revising

Add dialogue or description. Dialogue (a person's thoughts or feelings in his or her own words) can make a narrative more convincing. Look for places in the story where the emotions are especially intense. In the model, this might be when the speaker first faces the bored audience.

First Draft	Revision
Despite the many times I had practiced my speech in front of a mirror, I was still nervous. My heart was beating fast as I looked out at the auditorium.	Practicing my speech in front of my bedroom mirror wasn't so bad. Now, however, I was saying these same words in a crowded high school auditorium filled with seniors who would rather be somewhere else. My heart pounded wildly.

Revise word choice. Replace general words with more specific, colorful ones. Choose vivid action verbs, precise adjectives, and specific nouns to convey your meaning. In the example above, notice how much more effective the revised version is at conveying the experience.

Read your draft aloud. Listen for grammatical errors and statements that are unclear. Revise your sentences as necessary.

④ Publishing and Presenting

Highlight text you want to emphasize, and then read your essay aloud to the class. Invite and respond to questions.

Expository Writing

Expository writing explains ideas or information in detail. The strategies on these pages examine several expository writing styles.

① Prewriting

Choose a topic. In a government course, the focus of your writing might be explaining the process of a bill becoming law, comparing and contrasting the positions of political candidates, identifying a problem and proposing a solution, or examining the causes and effects behind policy changes. The following suggestions are a guide.

- For writing about a process, consider the question *how*. For example, you might ask, "How does a bill become a law?" Then you would identify the steps or procedures involved.

Question: How does a bill become a law?
Answer: A proposed law is introduced in the House or Senate, then sent to the appropriate committee to be studied. If the committee votes to pass the bill, it is debated by the full House or Senate. After debate, members vote on the bill. If passed, it is sent to the other house and goes through the same process. If it passes that house, it is sent to the President for his approval or veto.

- With a partner, visit the Web site of two candidates for office. Choose three issues that both candidates address and note each candidate's viewpoint on the issues you've chosen.

- With a small group, write problems related to each of these challenges on slips of paper: global warming, universal healthcare, and energy alternatives. Have each person take a slip of paper and brainstorm possible solutions to each problem with the group.

- Write down questions to ask a school board member about policy or other changes they are considering. Ask why these changes are being considered. Understanding why is the basis of a cause-and-effect essay.

Consider audience and purpose. Consider how much your readers know about the process, comparison, problem, or event you will address. Adjust your writing to your audience's knowledge or provide explanations of unfamiliar ideas.

Research the topic. Use library and Internet resources and interviews with local officials or experts if possible. Also consider your personal experience. You might know about a local community problem from firsthand experience.

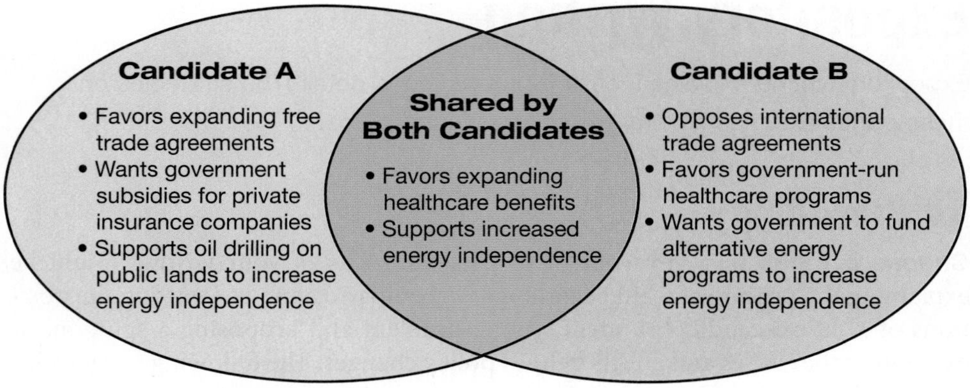

Candidate A
- Favors expanding free trade agreements
- Wants government subsidies for private insurance companies
- Supports oil drilling on public lands to increase energy independence

Shared by Both Candidates
- Favors expanding healthcare benefits
- Supports increased energy independence

Candidate B
- Opposes international trade agreements
- Favors government-run healthcare programs
- Wants government to fund alternative energy programs to increase energy independence

Create a graphic organizer. For cause-and-effect or problem-solution essays, use a two-column chart. Process writing can be a bulleted list of steps. A Venn diagram can help you compare and contrast.

Fine-tune your ideas. For a problem-solution essay, choose a solution and narrow its scope to ensure that it is achievable in cost, effort, and timing. If your solution has been tried by others, describe successes or failures and how your approach will differ. Keep in mind that problem-solution and process writing often involve cause-effect relationships. Look for causes and effects as you organize your material.

② Drafting

Match structure to purpose. Typically, problem-solution essays benefit from block organization, which presents the entire problem and then proposes a solution. Put process and cause-and-effect essays in sequential order. Organize compare/contrast essays by subject or by point.

By subject: Discuss the issues and viewpoints of Candidate A, and then compare and contrast them with those of Candidate B.
By point: Introduce each issue, such as healthcare or trade agreements. Relate views of both candidates on the issue, comparing or contrasting them in your discussion. Then, move on to the next issue.

Give background. To discuss a policy, program, or process, orient the reader to context. Ensure readers know why a law was passed or what the court case was about. Choose the important facts, but don't overwhelm the reader with details.

Elaborate for interest and emphasis. Give details about each point in your essay. To clarify a cause-and-effect relationship, add facts that explain the link between the reason for a decision or action and its consequences. In a problem-solution essay, readers are more likely to support proposed solutions if essays clearly show how these solutions will solve the problem. Sum up in a brief conclusion.

One of the most serious problems Americans face today is the rising cost of healthcare. For several decades, the cost of healthcare has risen much faster than personal wages. At the same time, the number of Americans without health insurance continues to rise. In 2006, 14.8 percent of Americans were uninsured. To further complicate the problem, the retirement of the baby boom generation is just beginning. Experts predict that in the decade ahead these changes will greatly increase the demand for healthcare.

Healthcare policy analysts offer several strategies for reducing costs. First, allow the government to negotiate with drug companies for lower prescription prices, and allow cheaper drugs to be brought in from other countries. Second, pay doctors and other providers lower fees similar to those paid to providers in other industrialized nations. Finally, make consumers pay more of their own healthcare costs so that they will weigh the necessity of treatments. Many experts see consumers' reliance on high-cost specialists rather than primary care doctors as a key cost factor. A carefully implemented plan to put these ideas into action will give more Americans access to quality healthcare.

Identify the topic to orient readers.

Point out causes of the problem.

List possible solutions.

Conclude by summarizing the goal of the solution.

❸ Revising

Remember purpose. Your essay should answer the question or thesis with which you began. In a problem-solution essay, your purpose is to convince readers to support your solution. Try to anticipate opposing arguments and respond to them.

Review organization. Number your main points. Reorganize these points until they flow in a logical order.

Add transition words. Make cause-and-effect relationships clear with such words as *because* and *so*. To compare and contrast, use linking words, such as *similarly* or *in contrast*. Use words such as *first* and *next* to show steps in a process.

First Draft	Revision
The Federal Drug Administration monitors small clinical trials. These trials show the drug to be safe, and FDA officials conduct larger trials.	First, the Federal Drug Administration monitors small clinical trials. Next, if the results of these trials show the drug to be safe and effective enough for further study, FDA officials conduct larger trials.

Add details. For a process essay, be sure to include all steps; don't assume readers will make connections. When writing about cause and effect, stress the way one event leads to the next. Add more background if necessary for clarity.

Revise. Vary sentence length. Scan for vague words, such as *good,* and replace them with specific words. Use technical terms sparingly and define them.

Peer review. Ask a classmate to review your draft. Revise areas of confusion.

❹ Publishing and Presenting

Create a government manual. Contribute your explanation of a government process to a class manual of Government How-Tos.

Research Writing

A research paper presents information about a particular topic from several different sources. The author must then tie this information together with a single unifying idea and present it to the reader.

1 Prewriting

Choose a topic. Often, a teacher will assign your research topic. If not, you may have flexibility in choosing your focus, or you may have the opportunity to completely define your topic. The following suggestions are a guide.

- Using an online or electronic library catalog, search for topics that interest you. When a title looks promising, find the book on the shelves. Because libraries group research materials by subject, you should find other books on similar subjects that may help you decide on your final topic.

- Review your class notes. Jot down topics that you found interesting. For example, you might find a starting point for research into students' legal rights in schools from a Supreme Court case that you studied in class.

- Brainstorm topics with a group. List interesting current events issues such as the economy, healthcare, the environment, and privacy. Within each category, take turns adding subtopics. The chart below looks at different topics related to the Internet, politics, and government.

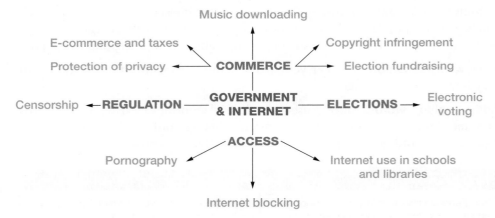

Music downloading

E-commerce and taxes

Copyright infringement

Protection of privacy — **COMMERCE** — Election fundraising

Censorship ← **REGULATION** — **GOVERNMENT & INTERNET** — **ELECTIONS** → Electronic voting

ACCESS

Pornography

Internet use in schools and libraries

Internet blocking

Analyze the audience. Your research and your paper should be strongly influenced by the audience. How much will readers already know about this topic and how much will you have to teach them?

Gather details. Collect the facts and details you need to write your paper. Use a variety of resources, including nonfiction books or journal articles, newspapers, newsmagazines, and government publications. Search the Internet for reliable information and opinions on your topic, starting with online encyclopedias and news organizations. Look for interviews with experts on your topic.

Organize evidence and ideas. Create notecards or a computer file on your topic to record information and to help you organize your thoughts. Start by writing down a possible thesis statement. Then begin reading and taking notes. Write a heading at the top of each notecard and add subtopics below. List your information sources on a separate card, giving each a number. Use that number to identify the source for each subtopic on your cards. In the examples below, the number *3* is used to identify the information source. Use the same number for additional topic cards derived from the same source.

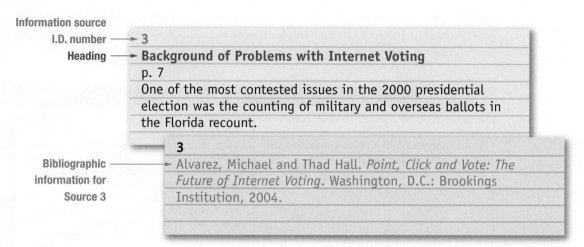

Information source I.D. number → **3**

Heading → **Background of Problems with Internet Voting**

p. 7
One of the most contested issues in the 2000 presidential election was the counting of military and overseas ballots in the Florida recount.

3

Bibliographic information for Source 3 → Alvarez, Michael and Thad Hall. *Point, Click and Vote: The Future of Internet Voting*. Washington, D.C.: Brookings Institution, 2004.

❷ Drafting

Fine-tune your thesis. Review your notes to find relationships between ideas. Shape a thesis that is supported by the majority of your information, then check that it is specific enough to address thoroughly in the time and space allotted. You can fine-tune your thesis further as you draft or even when you revise.

Organize the information to fit your purpose. Consider your reason for exploring this topic, and identify the structure that will best help you reach this goal. Decide whether you want to present arguments that will compare and contrast aspects of a topic, persuade readers to support your position on an issue or policy, or argue for a particular solution to a problem. Then organize appropriately. For example, if your goal is to persuade readers that electronic voting should be allowed in national elections, begin by stating arguments in favor of your position. Follow by presenting opposing views with your counterarguments or rebuttals to those points.

Make an outline. Create an outline in which you identify each topic and subtopic in a single phrase. Turn these phrases into sentences and then into the topic and supporting sentences of your draft paragraphs. Write an introduction, at least three body paragraphs, and a conclusion. Support all of your statements with the facts and details you gathered.

An outline helps you organize your information.

Each body paragraph examines a part of the main topic.

Internet Voting

Outline

I. Introduction

II. What Are the Benefits of Internet Voting?
   A. Appeal to young voters and increased voter turnout
   B. Ease and convenience of voting

III. What Are the Risks of Internet Voting?
   A. Inequality of access (Counterargument: Computers in schools and libraries expand access)
   B. Potential for voter fraud and tampering (Counterargument: Technological improvements make Internet voting more secure)

IV. Conclusion: Benefits Outweigh Risks

❸ Revising

Add detail. Mark points in your essay where more details would strengthen your statements. In the following example, notice the added details in the revised version. When adding facts, be sure they are accurate.

First Draft	Revision
Internet voting can increase voter participation by making it easier to cast a ballot. Even people who don't own computers can vote in schools and libraries.	Internet voting can increase voter participation by making the process more convenient, especially for citizens with disabilities and Americans living abroad. Critics argue that online voting unfairly favors wealthier Americans who are more likely to own computers. In many places, however, voters who do not own computers will be able to cast their ballots at Internet terminals in public schools and libraries.

Make the connection for readers. Help readers find their way through your ideas. First, check that your body paragraphs and the information within them flow in a logical sequence. If they do not, revise to correct this. Then add transition words to link ideas and paragraphs.

Give credit. Check that you have used your own words or given proper credit to other sources. For quoted text, add parenthetical notes that include the author's last name and the relevant page number from the source. For example, you could cite the notecard on page 57 as (Alvarez and Hall, p. 7). The surest way to avoid plagiarism is to take notes in your own words, and then write from your notes, not from the original source.

❹ Publishing and Presenting

Share your research. Gather a group of classmates and present your research projects. If time allows, create visual materials to accompany your presentations. After you share your papers, hold a question-and-answer session.

Persuasive Essay

Persuasive writing supports an opinion and often takes the form of a position paper, editorial, blog, or Op-Ed piece. Persuasive essays in government often argue for or against government policies, candidates, or political issues.

1 Prewriting

Choose a topic. Choose a topic that provokes discussion and has at least two sides. Use these suggestions as a guide.

- Talk with classmates in a round-table discussion about issues you have studied recently. Outline pro and con positions on these issues.
- Scan the table of contents or flip through the pages of your textbook. Focus on issues that interest you.
- Look at blogs, editorials, or Op-Ed pieces online or in current newspapers. Develop a position on an issue of importance today.

Narrow your topic. Choose a subsection of the topic to cover if the subject is complex. Write for five minutes on the general topic. Circle the most important idea. Then write for five minutes on that idea. Continue looping until the topic is manageable.

Consider your audience. Choose arguments that will appeal to your audience and that are likely to persuade readers to agree with your views.

Gather evidence. Collect evidence that will help you support your position convincingly.

Identify pros and cons. Use a graphic organizer like the one below to list points on both sides of the issue.

Position: State and local governments should provide funds to build a new soccer stadium.	
Pro ◄——————————————————————————————► **Con**	
• Create new jobs, both temporary construction jobs and permanent service jobs • Attract customers to local businesses • Increase tax revenue • Increase sense of community and civic pride	• Costly to build and maintain • Money spent on this project will result in less money for schools, public transit, and other pressing needs. • Increase in traffic and use of public facilities will require improved infrastructure and more cost.

2 Drafting

State your thesis. Clearly state your position, as in this example:

> Local and State government officials should provide funding for the construction of a new soccer stadium because of the economic and social benefits it will bring to the city and the region.

Write your introduction Use your introduction to provide context. Tell your readers when and why the issue arose, and identify the key decision makers involved.

Acknowledge the opposition. State, and then refute, opposing arguments.

Use facts and details. Include quotations, statistics, or comparisons to build your case. Include personal experiences or reactions to the topic, such as the opinions of officials who were interviewed.

Write a conclusion. Return to your thesis and close with a strong, compelling argument or a brief summary of the three strongest arguments.

Background orients readers. →	A plan to build a world-class soccer stadium has been proposed at both the State and local levels. Is this a good idea for our city? I believe that
Thesis identifies your main argument. →	it is. Local and State government officials should provide funding for construction of a new soccer stadium because of the economic and social benefits it will bring to the city and the region. Those who oppose the
Acknowledging opposing argument and then refuting it solidifies your position. →	stadium project focus mainly on its costs to the public. The new stadium will bring many benefits that don't show up on a balance sheet—entertainment, excitement, and most importantly, a sense of enhanced community pride. Studies show that cities with professional sports teams
Supporting argument clarifies your thesis and sums up your position. →	attract more tourists. Equally important, residents get a positive message about their community every time they turn on their TVs and see the local team on the new playing field.

③ Revising

Add information. Extra details can generate interest in your topic. For example, add a quotation from a news article supporting your argument.

Review arguments. Make sure your arguments are logical and clear. Avoid faulty logic such as circular reasoning (arguing a point by merely restating it differently). Evidence is the best way to support your points. Notice how much more effectively the revised version supports the argument in the following example.

First Draft	Revision
Building a new stadium will bring money to the city, which will help residents.	A 2008 study commissioned by the city manager estimated that stadium construction would create 1,700 construction jobs and provide $2 million in tax revenues. The study also concluded that spending at local hotels, restaurants, and shops by visiting soccer teams and fans would bring in an additional $1.1 million per year.

Use transition words to guide readers. To show contrast, use *although,* or *despite.* To point out a reason, use *because,* or *if.* To signal a conclusion, use *so,* or *then.*

④ Publishing and Presenting

Persuasive speech. Many persuasive essays are delivered orally. Prepare your essay as a speech, highlighting words for emphasis, and adding cues for changes in tone, volume, or speed.

Writing for Assessment

Assessment writing allows fewer choices than other writing and usually imposes a time limit. In government and political science courses, you will be required to write both short-answer and extended responses.

① Prewriting

Choose a topic. Short-answer questions seldom offer a choice of topics. For extended response, however, you may have a choice of more than one question.

- Analyze what each question is asking. Identify key words such as those listed.

Key Words	What You Need in an Answer
• Explain	• Give a clear, complete account.
• Compare/Contrast	• Show how two or more things are alike and different.
• Define	• Give examples to explain meaning.
• Argue, Convince, Support, Persuade	• Take a position on an issue and present strong reasons to support your opinion.
• Summarize	• Provide the most important elements.
• Evaluate/Judge	• Assign a value or explain an opinion.

Notice in the examples below that the key words are underlined.

> **Short-Answer Question:** <u>Explain</u> why the ability to communicate is an important aspect of presidential leadership.
>
> **Extended-Response Question:** What <u>leadership qualities</u> have the nation's most outstanding Presidents displayed? Give examples to <u>support your choices</u>.

- After choosing a question, try to plot the answer quickly in your mind. If you cannot do so easily, choose another question.

Measure your time. Divide your time: one-quarter on prewriting, half on drafting, one-quarter on revising. For short-answer questions, decide how much of the overall test time you can spend on each question.

Organize your response. For extended-response questions, divide your topic into subtopics that fit the type of question. Jot down facts and details for each. For a question on presidential leadership, consider the following.

Leadership Qualities of Outstanding Presidents
• ability to communicate and build consensus on major policies (1)
• ability to gain the trust and respect of the American public (2)
• vision or clear idea of where to lead the nation (3)
• openness to new ideas; flexibility in changing conditions (4)
Example of President Exhibiting Specific Leadership Qualities
• Franklin Roosevelt: ability to communicate, gain trust, try new ideas (New Deal)

② Drafting

Choose an appropriate organization. For short-answer responses, write one to three complete sentences. Extended responses require a more elaborate structure. For an extended response on presidential leadership, describe the leadership qualities of each President, and give examples. For problem-solution questions, describe the problem, and propose a solution. For compare/contrast questions, present similarities first, then differences.

Open and close strongly. Start by using the question's language to state your position. This helps you focus and shows that you understand the question. Conclude by restating your position. For short answers, include language from the question in your response.

Support your ideas. Each paragraph should support your main idea.

> The opening restates the question and presents the main idea. → By itself, no single quality makes an exceptional leader. In the careers of the nation's most outstanding Presidents, many of their qualities built upon and complemented one another. Franklin Roosevelt was a highly
>
> The writer uses information from the graphic organizer to build an argument. → effective communicator and flexible leader. (1) Despite his privileged upbringing, his skills as a communicator enabled him to convey his compassion for the poor and earned him the trust and respect of the American people. He used his communication skills to convince the people in his administration to work together. Roosevelt showed
>
> The writer supports the second subtopic. → flexibility in responding to the difficult economic and social challenges of the Depression (2) by his advocacy of the many experimental programs and policies of his New Deal initiative. President Roosevelt provides an
>
> The conclusion recaps the main idea and uses the question's language. → excellent example of several key qualities of an exceptional leader.

③ Revising

Examine word choice. Replace general words with specific words. Add transitions where they improve clarity. Read the following examples. The revised version shows the relative importance of the writer's supporting evidence.

First Draft	Revision
No single quality makes a good leader. Qualities build upon and complement one another. Franklin Delano Roosevelt was a highly effective communicator because he won the trust and support of the American people. He convinced people to work together.	<u>By itself</u> no single quality makes an exceptional leader. <u>In the careers of the nation's most outstanding Presidents,</u> many qualities built upon and complemented one another. <u>For example,</u> Franklin Delano Roosevelt was a highly effective communicator, <u>who</u> won the trust and support of the American people; <u>in addition,</u> the President convinced the people in his administration to work together.

Check organization. Make sure your introduction includes a main idea and briefly defines each subtopic. Review each paragraph for a single main idea. Check that your conclusion summarizes the information you have presented.

④ Publishing and Presenting

Edit and proofread. Check spelling, grammar, and mechanics. Make sure that tenses match, subjects agree with verbs, and all sentences include a subject and verb. Confirm that you have responded to all the questions you were asked.

Writing Rubric

Use this chart, or rubric, to evaluate your writing.

Criteria	Exceeds standard	Meets standard	Approaches standard	Does not meet standard
Thesis	Sharp, well-developed thesis with clear connection to topic	Sharp and mostly developed thesis with clear connection to topic	Somewhat clear thesis with limited connection to topic	No thesis, or unclear thesis, with little connection to topic
Introduction	Clear, direct focus; highly interesting and engaging; provides excellent context for discussing topic	Focused and interesting, provides context for discussing topic	Somewhat focused and interesting, provides some limited context for discussing topic	Too broad, provides little context for discussing topic; uses throwaway phrases like "throughout history"
Organization	Recognizable beginning, middle, and ending; logically organized with a variety of transitions	Clear beginning, middle, and ending; generally logical organization with some transition words used	Beginning, middle, and ending unclear; connections between ideas weak and few transition words used	No beginning, middle, or ending; no connections between ideas and no transition words used
Supporting evidence and facts	Substantial facts and evidence	Sufficient facts and evidence	Uneven use of facts and evidence	Insufficient facts and evidence
Analysis	Effective, logical, sophisticated analysis supported by facts and evidence; demonstrates keen insight into and understanding of topic	Effective, logical analysis supported by facts and evidence; demonstrates clear understanding of topic	General analysis only, and/or somewhat illogical or inconsistent; facts and evidence somewhat enhance analysis; demonstrates basic understanding of topic	Limited analysis and/or illogical; uses descriptive and storytelling format rather than analysis; demonstrates limited understanding of topic
Conclusion	Ties together main ideas to arrive at a logical and insightful conclusion that shows deep understanding of the topic	Ties together main ideas to arrive at a logical and insightful conclusion	Demonstrates some understanding of the topic and/or relies heavily on summary	Demonstrates general and shallow understanding of the topic or is summary only
Mechanics	Extremely few or no grammatical, spelling, punctuation, or other mechanical errors	A few grammatical and spelling errors, which do not distract from the overall quality of the paper	Some errors in spelling, grammar, punctuation, word choice, and capitalization; includes repetition, fragments, conversational prose	Many grammatical, spelling, punctuation, and other errors, which detract from the quality of the paper

21st Century Skills **WRITING**

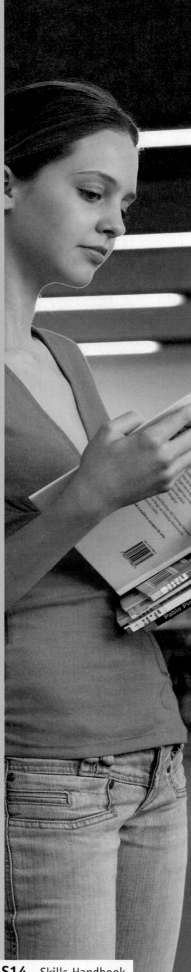

Critical Thinking

Analyze Sources

A primary source is a firsthand account of an event. Examples include letters and photographs. A secondary source is an account based on primary sources. Follow these steps to analyze primary and secondary sources.

1 Identify the document. Identify the source of the document. Determine when, where, and why it was written. Is the document a primary or secondary source?

2 Find the main idea. After identifying the main idea, identify details or sections of text that support the main idea.

3 Evaluate the source for point of view and bias. Primary sources often have a strong point of view or bias. It is important to analyze primary sources critically.

> For three weeks in September 1957, . . . Little Rock became the focus of a showdown over integration as Gov. Orval Faubus blocked nine black students from enrolling at all-white Central. Although the U.S. Supreme Court had declared segregated classrooms unconstitutional in 1954 . . . Faubus said he feared violence if the races mixed in a public school. The showdown soon became a test for President Dwight D. Eisenhower, who has been derided by some historians as being silent on civil rights. . . .
> David A. Nichols, author of *A Matter of Justice: Eisenhower and the Beginning of the Civil Rights Revolution*, argues that the showdown . . . showed the 34th president's true feelings about desegregation. "I think the intervention in Little Rock revealed who Eisenhower really was on this issue," . . .
>
> —*USA Today*, September 22, 2007

> Newport, Rhode Island,
> September 27, 1957
>
> The Honorable Richard B. Russell [Georgia]
> United States Senate
> Washington, D.C.
>
> Few times in my life have I felt as saddened as when the obligations of my office required me to order the use of force [federal troops] within a state to carry out the decisions of a Federal Court. My conviction is that had the police powers of the State of Arkansas been utilized not to frustrate the orders of the Court but to support them, the ensuing violence and open disrespect for the law would never have occurred . . . . When a State, by seeking to frustrate the orders of a Federal Court, encourages mobs of extremists to flout the orders of a Federal Court, and when a State refuses to utilize its police powers to protect against mobs persons who are peaceably exercising their right under the Constitution . . . the oath of office of the President requires that he take action . . . . "

Practice and Apply the Skill

Use the sources above to answer the following questions.

1. What makes the letter a primary source and the article a secondary source?

2. Based on the letter, what is Eisenhower's reason for sending federal troops?

3. What point does the article make about Eisenhower's role in the Little Rock crisis? How is this point supported by the letter?

Compare Viewpoints

Many factors shape a person's viewpoint, including values, age, prejudices, gender, and past experiences. Comparing viewpoints will help you understand issues and form your own opinions. Use the following steps to learn about comparing viewpoints. Then analyze the speeches below and answer the questions.

① Identify the authors. Determine when and where each person was speaking. Identify the intended audience for each speech and its purpose.

② Determine the author's frame of reference. Consider how each speaker's attitudes; beliefs; values; social, economic, or political concerns and affiliations; as well as past experiences, might affect his or her viewpoint.

③ Determine the author's bias. Bias may be revealed in the use of emotionally charged words, faulty logic, or exaggerated claims. In written or spoken materials, be sure to identify which statements are facts and which are opinions.

④ Compare and contrast. Determine how the viewpoints are similar and different. Consider factors that might have contributed to differing positions.

Passage A

It is time to check and reverse the growth of government which shows signs of having grown beyond the consent of the governed. It is my intention to curb the size and influence of the Federal establishment . . . . Now . . . it is not my intention to do away with government. It is, rather, to make it…stand by our side, not ride on our back…. It is no coincidence that our present troubles . . . are proportionate to the intervention and intrusion into our lives that result from unnecessary and excessive growth of government.

—Ronald Reagan, First Inaugural Address, January 20, 1981

Passage B

My view is to . . . recognize that [the federal government] has a role in our lives and a partnership role to play. We have made the Government smaller. . . . We have . . . been working . . . to reduce the burden of unnecessary regulation. But we believe Government has important work to do, to expand opportunity, to give people the tools they need to make the most of their own lives, to enhance our security. That's why we support adding 100,000 police . . . more affordable college loans . . . the minimum wage legislation now before Congress. . . .

—Bill Clinton, Press Conference, March 4, 1995

Practice and Apply the Skill

Use the excerpts above to answer the following questions.

1. Who are the speakers, where did they speak, and who was the intended audience?

2. What issue are both Presidents addressing? How do Reagan and Clinton's viewpoints differ?

3. How do you think each President's political background influenced his viewpoint?

4. How does Reagan's statement that government should "not ride on our back" reflect a bias, if any, on this issue?

Analyze Cause and Effect

Recognizing a cause-effect relationship means examining how one event or action brings about others. Government decision makers face a complex web of choices and often need to understand relationships among events to set or improve policy. Use the following steps to learn how to understand the relationships between causes and effects. Then read the passage below and answer the questions.

1 Identify the central event. Determine what event is the most important and decide if it is a cause or effect.

2 Look for signal words and phrases. Words and phrases such as *because, due to,* and *on account of* signal causes. Words and phrases such as *so, thus, therefore,* and *as a result* signal effects.

3 Decide if an event has more than one cause or effect. Most events have multiple causes and many have more than one effect.

4 Identify events that are both causes and effects. Events can form a chain of causes and effects. For example, a decrease in taxes might result in a decrease in State funding for new highway construction, which in turn might cause increased traffic delays.

Fewer Youths Jump Behind the Wheel at 16
by Mary Chapman and Micheline Maynard, *The New York Times*, February 25, 2008

For generations, driver's licenses have been tickets to freedom for America's 16-year-olds, prompting many to line up at motor vehicle offices the day they were eligible to apply.

No longer. In the last decade, the proportion of 16-year-olds nationwide who hold driver's licenses has dropped from nearly half to less than one-third, according to . . . the Federal Highway Administration.

Reasons vary, including tighter state laws governing when teenagers can drive, higher insurance costs and a shift . . . . to expensive private driving academies. . . .

[E]xperts also add parents . . . willing to chauffeur their children to activities, and pastimes like surfing the Web that keep them indoors . . . .

The way students learn has undergone a major change, too. Twenty-five years ago most teenagers took driver's education in their local schools. But the number of school systems offering the program has plummeted to about 20 percent today, from 90 percent in the 1980s, said Allen Robinson, of American Driver and Traffic Safety Education Association. . . .

"High schools are out of the business because of the cost," said Henning Mortensen, owner of Bond Driving School in Sacramento. Commercial driving academies have stepped in to fill the gap. . . .

Driving schools charge higher rates. . . .

Graduated driver-licensing laws, which delay awarding a full license until a teenager spends time . . . driving under certain conditions, are also keeping down the number of 16-year-olds on the road, said Frederik R. Mottola . . . of the National Institute for Driver Behavior. . . .

Practice and Apply the Skill

Use the article above to answer the following questions.

1. What is the issue discussed in this article?

2. According to the article, what are the causes of the decline in 16-year-old drivers?

3. What two causes are cited in paragraph four?

Problem Solving

Every year elected officials at all levels of government face problems. Whether they are dealing with traffic congestion, airport safety, or hurricane relief, the ability to solve problems is a valuable skill. Use the following steps to learn more about problem solving. Then read the passage below and answer the questions.

❶ Identify the problem. Begin by clearly identifying the problem. Write a statement or question that summarizes the problem you are trying to solve.

❷ Gather information and identify options. Collect information and data, considering both the causes of the problem and strategies for addressing it. Most problems have multiple solutions. Identify as many options as possible.

❸ Consider advantages and disadvantages of each option. Analyze each option by predicting benefits, drawbacks, and possible outcomes.

❹ Choose, implement, and evaluate a solution. Pick the option with the most benefits and fewest drawbacks. Once the chosen option has been implemented, evaluate the outcome to decide if the strategy worked.

> "Like most large cities in America today, Minneapolis continues to face violent crime. . .
>
> We have met the challenge of crime with a multi-faceted plan of attack. . . The most. . . powerful tool in our crime fighting strategy has been increasing the visibility and presence of police officers on the street. We are growing our police force by over 100 officers. . .
>
> To a larger more diverse, more visible police force, we added groundbreaking public safety technology. . . The addition of dozens of safety cameras and dramatically increased police patrol has made our downtown one of the safest in America. The safety cameras. . . have helped provide essential evidence to arrest and successfully charge criminals. . . .
>
> The technology we are implementing increases prosecutions by providing needed court evidence, but we also invested in better prosecution with more funding for community prosecutors. . . . The number of our most chronic criminals. . . who were convicted has increased from 81 convictions in 2005 to 129 convictions in 2006—a 60% increase in one year. . . .
>
> Working. . . with our juvenile crime unit, we are identifying young offenders early and getting them into programs that offer a productive alternative to gangs. . . .
>
> We have also focused. . . efforts to get illegal guns off the street. . . . The results. . . are beginning to be seen. After a surge of crime during the summer of 2005 and first half of 2006, violent crime began trending down in the later months of 2006. As we end the first quarter of 2007, for the first time in years, violent crime is falling, down 22 percent city-wide. . . . "
>
> —Minneapolis Mayor R.T. Rybak,
> State of the City Address,
> March 19, 2007

Practice and Apply the Skill

Use the passage above to answer the following questions.

1. What problem is the mayor concerned about, and what is his problem-solving goal?

2. What options does the mayor identify for solving this problem?

3. What are the advantages and drawbacks of the safety camera option?

4. How did the mayor assess the effectiveness of efforts to prosecute criminals?

5. What kinds of information can the mayor use to evaluate his solutions?

Decision Making

Decision making plays a key role in the political process in every branch of government. Although the types of decisions Presidents, cabinet heads, governors, and city councilors make differ, they all involve the steps below.

1 Identify the problem and gather information. Define and clarify what needs to be decided. Consider the goal or the intended outcome. Decide what information is needed to make an informed decision. Apply existing knowledge and research about the subject. Consider strategies others have used to address the issue.

2 List and review possible options. A decision requires choosing among two or more alternatives. List all possible options.

3 Identify possible consequences and make a decision. Consider the possible outcomes and predict the consequences of each option. Then review all options and choose those with the fewest drawbacks and greatest number of benefits. Read about one school's tardiness problem and possible solutions.

The Problem
A large portion of the student body has been tardy more than usual this semester.
- The city has cancelled bus service past the school due to budget cuts. The school is located on a low-use bus route, and student discount passes did not generate enough revenue to keep the bus route going.
- Since many parents now drive their children to school, traffic has increased, causing school buses and parents to be late.
- Many students are unable to walk because they live too far away from the school.
- Students are missing the first five to twenty minutes of their first-period class, when attendance is taken.
- Students are either marked as tardy, or absent if they come in excessively late.

Potential Solutions
- Require all students to take school buses.
- Circulate a petition, demanding the city reinstate its bus service.
- Work with city councilors to establish a reasonable fare, or a reduced schedule that will allow city buses to run during school hours.
- Create a car-pooling program for students who live close to one another.
- Establish first period as a study hall, and take attendance at the end of the period in order to allow students time to arrive at school.

Practice and Apply the Skill

Use the list above to answer the following questions.

1. What is the major concern for the school?

2. What is the advantage of requiring all students to take the bus to school?

3. What are the disadvantages of turning first period into a study hall?

4. What do you think is the best solution to the problem? Why?

Draw Inferences and Conclusions

Drawing inferences means reading between the lines—that is, forming conclusions based on information that is not stated directly, but only suggested. Use the following steps to learn how to draw inferences and arrive at conclusions. Then read the passage below and answer the questions.

1 Summarize information. Confirm your understanding of the text by identifying the main idea. To find information that is suggested but unstated in a passage, you have to understand the stated content of the passage.

2 Study the facts. Determine what facts and information the text provides.

3 Apply other facts or prior knowledge. Consider what you know about the topic. Use this prior knowledge to evaluate the information. A combination of what you already know and what you learn from reading the passage can help you draw inferences.

4 Summarize the information to form a conclusion. Combine the inferences you made to form a conclusion about the topic.

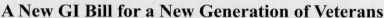

A New GI Bill for a New Generation of Veterans
Editorial, *The Sacramento Bee*, 2008

. . . [W]e must accept our duty to care for those who have borne the battle. . . .

That's why the GI Bill of Rights, which President Franklin D. Roosevelt signed in June 1944, was so important. That law gave returning soldiers benefits to compensate for opportunities they lost while they served in the military. It eased their transition to civilian life.

Before World War II, less than 10 percent of Americans went to college and home ownership was unreachable for most. The GI Bill spurred a college education and home ownership boom. It has been rightly called the "Magic Carpet to the Middle Class."

The nation should have a similar package ready when those who have served tours in Afghanistan and Iraq move . . . to civilian life. . . .

To that end, Sen. Jim Webb, D-Va., introduced a 21st century GI Bill of Rights (S. 22). Most soldiers in the current war enlisted right after high school, so 90 percent do not have a college degree. As Webb notes, current law is designed only for peacetime service. (It requires a $1,200 fee to enroll, provides no money for books and housing and covers only half the cost of the average public college education). . . .

The cost [of the new bill]: $2 billion a year. That's less than one week of the Iraq war. . . .

Many veterans say they're frustrated . . . a new GI Bill still hasn't [passed]. They should be. The two houses of Congress need to get their act together and get this done, . . .

Practice and Apply the Skill

Use the editorial above to answer the following questions.

1. What is the main idea in this editorial?

2. Why was Roosevelt's GI Bill called "The Magic Carpet to the Middle Class"?

3. What does the author of this editorial imply when he says that the new GI bill will cost less than one week of the Iraq war?

4. What conclusion can you draw about the planned effects of the new GI bill, should it pass?

Note Taking and Active Listening

Note taking and active listening are two skills that can increase your ability to remember and understand a speech or lecture. Use the following steps to learn more about note taking and active listening. Then read the excerpted speech below and answer the questions.

1 Identify the topic and main ideas. The title of the text often gives clues to its content. Once you identify the topic, it is easier to identify main ideas. Many speakers start their speeches by listing the key points they will develop. At the conclusion of the talk, they often restate their main ideas and then summarize their conclusions.

2 Take notes selectively. Do not write down every word you hear. Instead, jot down important terms and summarize key points and details that support these points.

3 Practice active listening. Active listening is a key component of the communication process. Like all communication, it requires engaged participation. Look at and listen to the speaker. Think about what you hear and see.

4 Listen for transitions, repetition, and emphasis. Listen for words or phrases that indicate key points or transition from one point to the next. Be alert for repetition. Statements that are repeated or said with emphasis are important points. Pay attention for phrases, gestures, or expressions that suggest strong opinions.

Speech On Stewardship of the Earth by James E. Hansen, NASA chief climate scientist, 2007

. . . Global warming differs from previous pollution problems in two fundamental ways. With water pollution or common air pollution, smog, the problems occur immediately. . . . If we . . . stop emitting them, the problem goes away. However, global warming is caused by greenhouse gases that have a lifetime of hundreds of years. . . .

The second major difference . . . is that the climate system responds slowly to the gases that we add to the air. . . .The Earth has warmed one and one-half degrees Fahrenheit so far. . . . Moreover, there are surely more gases in the pipeline, because of power plants . . . and vehicles. . . . One and one-half degrees! Who cares about that? . . . Well, we had better all care about it, because we have already brought the planet close to some tipping points. . . .

Let me mention three major consequences of global warming, if we go down the business-as-usual path. . . . First, there is the extermination of species. . . . [A] given mean temperature line is moving poleward, . . . about 35 miles per decade. That rate will accelerate under business-as-usual. Many species cannot migrate that fast. Besides, there is no place colder for polar species to go. . . . Second, there is potential instability of the ice sheets. If additional global warming exceeds two degrees Fahrenheit, the West Antarctic ice sheet and part of Greenland surely will become unstable, causing eventual sea level rise of several meters. . . . Third, there will be a noticeable increase in climate extremes. . . . Heavy rains and floods will increase, but so will . . . droughts and forest fires. . . .

Practice and Apply the Skill

Use the excerpt above to answer the following questions.

1. What is the topic of this speech?

2. What three main points would you list as consequences of global warming?

3. What statements in this speech suggest greater emphasis or strong emotion?

Give a Multimedia Presentation

Government officials are often asked to make presentations. You too will be asked to give presentations in school and at work. One key to an effective presentation is to combine text, video, audio, and graphics. Use these steps for an effective presentation.

1 Define your topic. When choosing a topic, consider the time allotted for the presentation and the complexity of the subject. Multimedia presentations lend themselves to topics that have several subtopics. However, a topic that is too broad is hard to cover adequately in a limited amount of time. Consider how to narrow the topic.

2 Determine what types of media are available for the presentation. Do you have a computer and the software to create a podcast, PowerPoint presentation, or slide show? Do you have access to video, film, or audio clips of speeches or historic events?

3 Make a storyboard. Create a storyboard by brainstorming ideas for covering your topic in various media. Then make a detailed outline of the information you will present. Identify the medium that will work best for each part of the presentation. Plan the transitions between each part of the presentation.

4 Practice your presentation. A trial run gives presenters a chance to time each segment, identify technical problems, and make sure all participants know their roles.

Below is a storyboard for a presentation on reducing traffic congestion.

1 (2 mins)

Gridlock: Traffic cam of city at rush hour
Introduce issue by explaining how traffic congestion affects everyone in the audience.
• Wastes time
• Wastes gas
• Increases energy dependence

2 (3 mins)

Graphs
• Rise in peak period travel times
• Costs of congestion
• Smog and poor air quality

1996 2000 2004 2008

3 (4 mins)

Video clip of transportation expert or newscaster talking about possible solutions to traffic problems

4 (4 mins)

Solutions
• More emphasis on public transportation: buses, light rail, metro
• Construction of Park and Ride lots
• Incentives by local businesses to encourage employees to carpool
• Fast passes

5 (4 mins)

Solutions
• Toll roads
• HOV lanes
• Better signal control
• Businesses encourage employees to commute at different times through flextime

6 (5 mins)

Summarize possible solutions in sections 4 and 5
What we recommend

Practice and Apply the Skill

Use the storyboards above to answer the following questions.

1. What media will be used in the presentation?

2. How did the presenters narrow or focus the presentation of their topic?

3. How did the presenters stay within the time limit of the presentation?

Analyze Political Cartoons

Political cartoons express the cartoonist's opinion on a recent issue or current event. Often the cartoon's purpose is to influence public opinion about political leaders, government policies, or economic and political issues. To achieve this goal, cartoonists use humor and exaggeration. When analyzing a political cartoon, be sure to examine all words, images, and labels to help you fully understand the cartoon's intent. Use the following steps to analyze a political cartoon.

1 **Identify the symbols in the cartoon.** Analyze the cartoon to determine what each image or symbol represents. Read the title and any labels or captions.

2 **Analyze the meaning of the cartoon.** Consider how the cartoonist uses the images and symbols in the cartoon to express his or her opinion.

3 **Draw conclusions about the cartoon's intent.** Determine the main idea, message, or point of view expressed in the cartoon.

Medicare Cuts

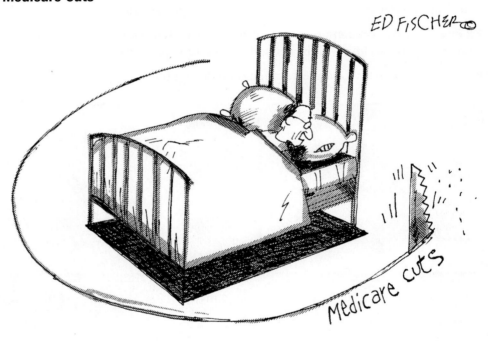

Practice and Apply the Skill

Use the cartoon above to answer the following questions.

1. Who does the figure in the bed represent?

2. What symbol represents cuts to the senior insurance program, Medicare?

3. According to the cartoon, what will be the result of Medicare cuts?

4. What is the main idea of this cartoon?

Innovate and Think Creatively

An innovation is a new idea that improves on an existing product or process. Use the steps below to learn how to think innovatively and creatively. Then read the passage below and answer the questions.

1 Identify what it is that needs improving. Describe a specific problem to be solved. Are there faster, better, or more efficient ways of getting a job or task done? Consider the intended outcome.

2 Brainstorm solutions. Generate as many ideas as possible. Be open to all ideas. If you are working in a group, don't criticize the ideas of others and don't hesitate to suggest ideas that might seem strange or impractical. Innovation often results from a chain of related ideas leading to an unexpected insight.

3 Understand how to achieve the innovation. Think about the skills, tools, or methods needed to realize the goal. Identify such factors as ease of use, resources, costs, and time. Get input from likely users. Involve people who are knowledgeable about the process, and work to build their support. Establish benchmarks for success and compare the results of the innovation with the original process.

Homeless Project's Army of Citizens Calls Year Success
by Kevin Fagan, *San Francisco Chronicle*, 10/19/05

Barry Cowart stood in front of the Bill Graham Civic Auditorium, staring at the 200 homeless people in a line . . . .

"Last April, that was me in that line," he said. "I'd been sleeping in the Greyhound bus station for months, and then I came here to this *thing* they do every month. That day, they got me into a residential hotel room . . . .

The "thing" he referred to is Project Homeless Connect, San Francisco Mayor Gavin Newsom's monthly gathering of volunteers to help his city's street people . . . .

On Oct. 13, 2004, the mayor kicked off his concept . . . with a handful of participants and street counselors . . . . By the end of the day, they had placed 24 into shelter and housing . . .

Since that first foray, Project Homeless Connect became a veritable citizen army that assembles between 1,000 and 2,000 community and government volunteers from all over the nation at the auditorium every other month to help more than 1,000 homeless people get into shelter, permanent housing, counseling and health care. While the homeless are being hooked up to those services, they get . . . food, clothing, blankets, and even kibble for their dogs or cats . . . .

. . . [R]epresentatives of cities from New York and Chicago to Los Angeles . . . have come to check out the past few gatherings . . . .

"It's daunting . . . to even consider doing something this big," said Kathleen Gardipee, a representative of Portland, Ore., who came to help prepare her city for its own Connect . . . . "But this is amazing . . . ."

Over the past year . . . the Connect efforts have helped 6,822 homeless people, putting 646 into shelter or housing, 1,583 into medical or mental health care, and the rest into legal counseling, food programs or other services. A total 11,382 individual volunteers pitched in.

Practice and Apply the Skill

Use the newspaper article to answer the following questions.

1. What problem did Mayor Newsom want to solve through the creation of PHC?

2. What was innovative about the mayor's solution?

3. Why do you think many cities are interested in San Francisco's innovation?

4. How did the mayor's office measure the effectiveness of this program?

Digital Age Literacy

The Internet is a valuable research tool that provides links to millions of sources of information created by government agencies, schools, businesses, and individuals all over the world. E-mail, wikis, and blogs all provide ways for Internet users to share information and express opinions. Follow the steps below to learn how you can use e-mail, wikis, and blogs effectively.

Writing an E-mail

1 **Identify the purpose of the email.** Clearly indicate the topic in the subject line. A busy recipient is more likely to open the e-mail promptly if the subject is stated.

2 **Focus on why you are writing.** Include the subject of your e-mail in the first sentence. State why you are writing and what you expect to receive in terms of information or action from the recipient. Try to limit messages to three or four key points and keep paragraphs short.

3 **Respect your reader.** If you are responding to or following up on an e-mail query or request that is more than a few days old, remind the recipient of why you are writing. It is often helpful to leave the original e-mail in your response for reference. Identify yourself clearly if the recipient is someone you don't know. If you are uncertain about whether your language and tone should be formal or informal, examine the e-mail received and take your cues from it.

4 **Proofread e-mails before sending.** Once you have composed your e-mail, use a spell checker or other tool to check grammar, punctuation, and spelling. Remember that e-mail is not private. Think carefully about sending messages that you would not want shared with others. Below is an example of an e-mail sent from one student to another.

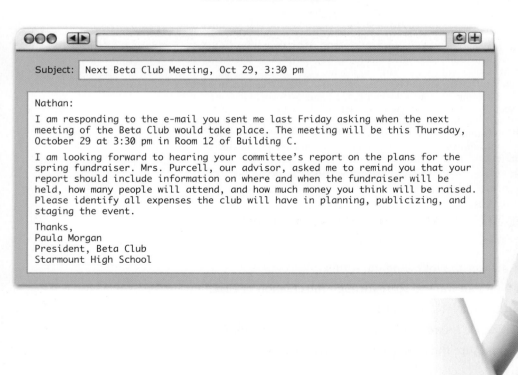

Subject: Next Beta Club Meeting, Oct 29, 3:30 pm

Nathan:

I am responding to the e-mail you sent me last Friday asking when the next meeting of the Beta Club would take place. The meeting will be this Thursday, October 29 at 3:30 pm in Room 12 of Building C.

I am looking forward to hearing your committee's report on the plans for the spring fundraiser. Mrs. Purcell, our advisor, asked me to remind you that your report should include information on where and when the fundraiser will be held, how many people will attend, and how much money you think will be raised. Please identify all expenses the club will have in planning, publicizing, and staging the event.

Thanks,
Paula Morgan
President, Beta Club
Starmount High School

Understanding and Evaluating Wikis

A wiki is a Web site that allows users to make, edit, and link Web pages to create an online document. As communal Web sites, many wikis are used for collaborative writing and research activities. Each entry includes a list of changes made by successive writers or editors. While many Internet users are enthusiastic about wikis, critics question their reliability and fear that users will accept information without verifying its accuracy.

Follow the steps below to learn about evaluating wikis.

1 Identify the sources of the information on the Web site. Scan the entry to find out who provided the information. Consider whether the writer has expertise or special knowledge of this topic that would make his or her opinion authoritative, or whether the author is not credible at all, making the information unreliable.

2 Determine when the article was written. Look for a date indicating when the article was written or last updated. Does the entry reflect changing events or provide current information on this topic?

3 Verify information by looking at other sources. Compare the information on the wiki with information from official sources such as government Web sites, Web sites sponsored by respected organizations, or traditional encyclopedias. Do further research if your sources disagree.

Reading and Assessing Blogs

Blogs are online journals. The word *blog* is short for *weblog*. Most blogs are short posts expressing an author's opinions. Blog writers, or bloggers, typically focus on a particular subject. Blogs can be found on every topic from politics to fashion. Blogs usually include the writer's previous posts as well as links to posts on other blogs, Web sites, and news articles. Some also include photos and video or audio files. Most blogs are interactive, providing a space for readers to comment.

1 Identify the writer. Look for the author's name and his or her professional affiliation, if any, as well as any biographical information.

2 Assess sources. Evaluate the credibility and accuracy of recommended sources.

3 Identify the writer's bias. Consider the arguments and evidence the writer presents. Are positions stated in rational language and presented in a balanced way that acknowledges other points of view, or is the language clearly one-sided? Do the posts contain frequent misspellings and grammatical errors? Scan reader comments to determine whether the blog allows opposing points of view.

Practice and Apply the Skill

Use the information above to answer these questions.

1. How might the language in a business e-mail differ from the language in an e-mail sent to friends?

2. How are wikis useful for projects that require input from multiple participants?

3. How does a blog differ from an editorial in a newspaper?

Analyze Graphic Data

A graph is a useful way to visually present large amounts of data. Every day, government policymakers, economists, and statisticians use different kinds of graphs to present and summarize data. Line graphs describe changes over time. Bar graphs show the relationships between two or more sets of data, and suggest trends. Circle graphs show how individual parts relate to a whole. Use the steps below to analyze graphic data.

❶ Identify the type of information presented. Before you can interpret the information in a graph, you must identify what is being shown. Note the title, all labels, and the key, if there is one. On a bar or line graph, use the graph title, the axis labels, and the key to interpret the data. On a circle graph, examine labels of all segments of the graphs. Identify the source of the data for the graph.

❷ Read the data. Before studying overall patterns, look at specific elements on the graph. On line graphs and bar graphs, determine what the numbers on the x-axis (horizontal) and the y-axis (vertical) represent. Then determine the relationship between the numbers.

❸ Interpret the graph and draw conclusions. Study the data in the graph to draw conclusions. Look for patterns or trends, such as changes over time or comparisons of different groups.

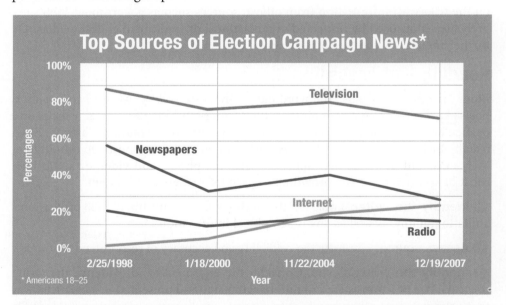

Practice and Apply the Skill

Use the graph above to answer the questions below.

1. (a) What is the subject of the graph? (b) What is the time frame? (c) What do the numbers on the x-axis and y-axis represent?

2. What does the graph indicate about the relationship between Internet use and newspaper readership among 18- to 25-year-olds?

3. Based on the graph, what prediction can you make about the use of Internet and television as sources in the future?

Analyze Maps

Maps bring information to life in a way that words alone cannot. Election maps, for example, can be valuable tools for identifying and understanding voting patterns. Political analysts often study voting patterns from previous elections to make predictions about winners and losers on election night. Use the steps below to analyze an election map.

2006 Missouri Senate Race Election Results by County

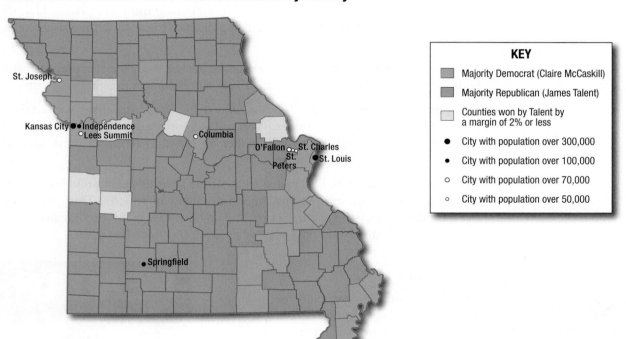

1 **Identify the purpose of the map.** Study the title to identify the purpose of the map and to make sure that you understand what information is shown.

2 **Determine the scope of the analysis.** For a national election map, analysis might focus on voting by State or region. Analysis of map of a State's election data might focus on voter turnout by county or by precinct. Here, it is by county.

3 **Use the key.** Analyze and apply the information in the map key to determine what data is shown. In an election map, you might look for color patterns. These might include areas of the State where voter turnout was strong for one political party or the other.

Practice and Apply the Skill

Use the Missouri county election map above to answer the following questions.

1. What does the map's title tell you?

2. What does each color on the map represent?

3. What voting pattern can you find in the counties with the State's largest cities?

4. How was McCaskill able to win the election despite winning only the city of St. Louis and 25 of Missouri's 114 counties?

Analyze Images

During elections, images of candidates and the issues they support fill television screens, newspapers, and Web sites. They seek to inform, persuade, and influence the viewer's opinion on a particular candidate or issue. It is important to be able to analyze an image, especially in advertising, for bias, emotional appeals, or inaccurate statements. Use the steps below to practice analyzing images.

1 Identify the content. When viewing an advertisement, look closely at the images and text and determine which information is most important. Identify themes or issues that the advertisement highlights. Notice how the images reinforce the overall message.

2 Note emotions. In analyzing the images of people, study facial expressions and body positions. Consider the emotions these expressions or positions suggest.

3 Consider context. Determine the context in which the image was created. Evaluate the accuracy of any information and supporting facts presented. Read all captions and credits. When possible, gather information about who produced or paid for the image or advertisement.

4 Identify the purpose. Determine whether the advertisement provides primarily factual information or opinions about a candidate or an issue. Does it emphasize a candidate's positive features or present an issue in a positive or balanced way, or is it intended to show an opponent or decision in a negative light?

Image A

This advertisement, paid for by a national organization that represents large private nursing home chains, refers to a Congressperson who voted in favor of a bill that might have reduced Medicare funding.

Image B

This poster is from Ronald Reagan's 1980 presidential campaign.

Practice and Apply the Skill

Use the political ads above to answer the following questions.

1. (a) What issue does Image A focus on? (b) What is the purpose of Image A?

2. Why do you think the producers of Image A chose this image?

3. In what ways could Image A be considered a negative, or attack, ad?

4. (a) Does Image B make the candidate seem presidential? How? (b) What is the impact of the phrase at the bottom of the poster?

5. How does the purpose of Image B differ from the purpose of Image A?

Analyze Timelines

A timeline allows readers to analyze a sequence of historical events in chronological order and to find relationships, such as causes and effects, among those events. Use the steps below to analyze a timeline.

1 Identify the topic and time period. Read the timeline's title. Then determine the span of time represented by the entire timeline.

2 Determine how the timeline is divided. Most timelines are divided into equal segments, or increments, of time—years, decades, or centuries.

3 Read each entry. Read each caption carefully. Where possible, connect each one to the events before and after it. Note the date when each event occurred.

4 Look for relationships. Decide if any of the events fall into a common category. Identify any recurring events. Look for events that might be causes and/or effects of other events.

Voting Rights in the United States, 1964–2009

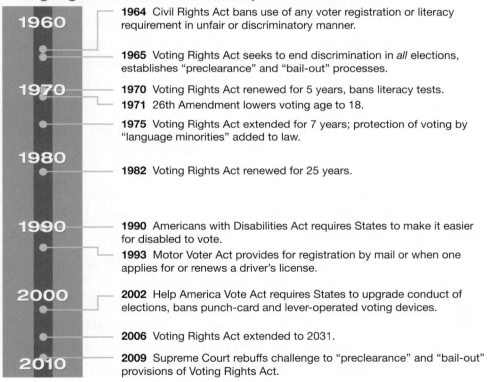

1964 Civil Rights Act bans use of any voter registration or literacy requirement in unfair or discriminatory manner.

1965 Voting Rights Act seeks to end discrimination in *all* elections, establishes "preclearance" and "bail-out" processes.

1970 Voting Rights Act renewed for 5 years, bans literacy tests.

1971 26th Amendment lowers voting age to 18.

1975 Voting Rights Act extended for 7 years; protection of voting by "language minorities" added to law.

1982 Voting Rights Act renewed for 25 years.

1990 Americans with Disabilities Act requires States to make it easier for disabled to vote.

1993 Motor Voter Act provides for registration by mail or when one applies for or renews a driver's license.

2002 Help America Vote Act requires States to upgrade conduct of elections, bans punch-card and lever-operated voting devices.

2006 Voting Rights Act extended to 2031.

2009 Supreme Court rebuffs challenge to "preclearance" and "bail-out" provisions of Voting Rights Act.

Practice and Apply the Skill

Use the timeline above to answer the following questions.

1. What span of time does the timeline cover?
2. How many years is each segment of the timeline?
3. What was the impact of the Americans with Disabilities Act on voting rights?
4. What event recurs on the timeline?
5. What was the longest interval between renewals of the Voting Rights Act?

Perspectives

PREFACE

This is a book about government—and, more particularly, about government in the United States. Over the course of its 25 chapters, you will consider the ways in which government in this country is organized, the ways in which it is controlled by the people, the many things that it does, and the various ways that it does them.

The American system of government is extraordinarily dynamic. Change—growth, adaptation, innovation—is the basic element of its character. While it is true that our government's fundamental principles and its basic structure have remained constant over time, many of its other characteristics have changed. They continue to do so—from year to year and, frequently, from one day to the next, and sometimes remarkably.

To underscore the critical importance of this fact of continuing change, dwell for a moment on the phrase "the American system of government." You will come across it again and again, for it is an apt description of government in the United States. As you will soon discover, that system is a very complex one.

It is complex because it is made up of many different parts, performing many different functions. It is a system because its many different parts are interrelated. The whole cannot be understood without a knowledge of its several interacting parts; and those parts cannot be understood without a knowledge of the whole. Given all of this, the vital effects of ongoing change in the system are obvious.

Every effort has been made to see that this book is as accurate, as up-to-date, as readable, and as interesting and usable as possible. The wealth of factual information it contains has been drawn from the most current and reliable of sources. This is not a book about current events, however. It does contain much data and draws many examples from the contemporary scene. But they are purposefully woven into the context of its primary objective: the description, analysis, and explanation of the American system of government.

— William A. McClenaghan

Photo: U.S. Capitol dome

Essential Questions Journal To begin to build a response to the unit Essential Question, go to your **Essential Questions Journal.**

Unit 1 Foundations of American Government

Essential Question What should be the goals of government?

Principles of Government

Essential Question
Is government necessary?

Section 1:
Government and the State

Section 2:
Forms of Government

Section 3:
Basic Concepts of Democracy

> In framing **a government** which is to be administered **by men over men,** the great **difficulty** lies in **this:** You must first enable the government to **control the governed;** and in the next place oblige it to **control itself.**
>
> —*The Federalist* No. 51

Photo: The Statue of Liberty is an enduring symbol of American democracy.

GOVERNMENT ONLINE
On the Go

To study anywhere, anytime, download these online resources at PearsonSuccessNet.com
• Political Dictionary
• Audio Review
• Downloadable Interactivities

SECTION 1

Government and the State

What is government and what is its purpose? Use an outline like the one below to take notes on the definition and purposes of government.

A. Definition of Government
  a. _____
  b. _____
B. Characteristics of a State
  a. _____
  b. _____
C. Purposes of Government
  a. _____
  b. _____

Political Dictionary

- government
- public policies
- legislative power
- executive power
- judicial power
- constitution
- dictatorship
- democracy
- state
- sovereign

Objectives

1. Define government and the basic powers every government holds.
2. Describe the four defining characteristics of a state.
3. Identify four theories that attempt to explain the origin of the state.
4. Understand the purpose of government in the United States and other countries.

Image Above: Flags representing several countries fly outside of the European Parliament in Strasbourg, France.

This is a book about government—and, more particularly, about government in the United States. Why should you read it? Why should you study government? These are legitimate questions, and they can be answered in several different ways—as you will see throughout the pages of this book. But, for now, consider this response: you should know as much as you possibly can about government because government affects you in an uncountable number of very important ways. It does so today, it did so yesterday, and it will do so every day for the rest of your life.

Think of the point in this light: What would your life be like *without* government? Who would protect you, and all of the rest of us, against terrorist attacks and against other threats from abroad? Who would provide for education, guard the public's health, and protect the environment? Who would pave the streets, regulate traffic, punish criminals, and respond to fires and other human-made and natural disasters? Who would protect civil rights and care for the elderly, the poor, and those who cannot care for themselves? Who would protect consumers and property owners?

Government does all of these things, of course—and much more. In short, if government did not exist, we would have to invent it.

What Is Government?

Government is the institution through which a society makes and enforces its public policies. Government is made up of those people who exercise its powers, all those who have authority and control over people.

The **public policies** of a government are, in short, all of those things a government decides to do. Public policies cover matters ranging from taxation, defense, education, crime, and healthcare to transportation, the environment, civil rights, and working conditions. Indeed, the list of public policy issues handled by government is nearly endless.

Governments must have power in order to make and carry out public policies. Power is the ability to command or prevent action, the ability to achieve a desired end.

Every government has and exercises three basic kinds of power: (1) **legislative power**—the power to make laws and to frame public policies; (2) **executive power**—the power to execute, enforce, and administer laws; and (3) **judicial power**—the power to interpret laws, to determine their meaning, and to settle disputes that arise within the society. These powers of government are often outlined in a country's constitution. A **constitution** is the body of <u>fundamental</u> laws setting out the principles, structures, and processes of a government.

The ultimate responsibility for the exercise of these powers may be held by a single person or by a small group, as in a **dictatorship.** In this form of government, those who rule cannot be held responsible to the will of the people. When the responsibility for the exercise of these powers rests with a majority of the people, that form of government is known as a democracy. In a **democracy,** supreme authority rests with the people.

Government is among the oldest of all human inventions. Its origins are lost in the mists of time. But, clearly, government first appeared when human beings realized that they could not survive without some way to regulate their own actions, as well as those of their neighbors.

The earliest known evidences of government date from ancient Egypt and the sixth century B.C. More than 2,300 years ago, the Greek philosopher Aristotle observed that "man is by nature a political animal."[1] When he wrote those words, Aristotle was only recording a fact that, even then, had been obvious for thousands of years.

What did Aristotle mean by "political"? That is to say, what is "politics"? Although people often equate the two, politics and government are very different things. Politics is a process, while government is an institution.

More specifically, politics is the process by which a society decides how power and resources will be distributed within that society. Politics enables a society to decide who will <u>reap</u> the benefits, and who will pay the costs, of its public policies.

The word *politics* is sometimes used in a way that suggests that it is somehow immoral or something to be avoided. But, again, politics is the means by which government is conducted. It is neither "good" nor "bad," but it is necessary. Indeed, it is impossible to conceive of government without politics.

The State

Over the course of human history, the state has emerged as the dominant political unit throughout the world. The **state** can be

<u>reap</u>
v. to gain, receive, take in

<u>fundamental</u>
adj. basic, essential, primary

The Three Basic Powers of Government

In the United States, the three basic powers of government are held in three separate branches. *Why do you think the Framers of the Constitution separated these powers?*

The President is the Head of State, and executes the laws.

Executive

Congress creates the laws and frames public policy.

Legislative

The Supreme Court interprets the laws and determines their constitutionality.

Judicial

---

1 In most of the world's written political record, the words *man* and *men* have been widely used to refer to all of humankind. This text follows that form when presenting excerpts from historical writings or documents and in references to them.

Four Characteristics of a State

What do you need to make a state?

Every state in the world has the following four characteristics. Each characteristic may vary widely from state to state. *Which of these characteristics is represented by the map in the background?*

Population

Large or small, every state must be inhabited—that is, have a population.

Territory

Every state must have land, with known and recognized borders.

Sovereignty

The state has absolute power within its territory. It can decide its own foreign and domestic policies.

Government

Government is the mechanism through which a state makes and enforces its policies.

---

populous
adj. relating to the number of people in a given region

defined as a body of people, living in a defined territory, organized politically (that is, with a government), and with the power to make and enforce law without the consent of any higher authority.

There are more than 200 states in the world today. They vary greatly in size, military power, natural resources, and economic importance. Still, each of them possesses all four of the characteristics of a state. That is, each of them has population, territory, sovereignty, and government.

Note that the word *state* describes a legal entity. In popular usage, a state is often called a "nation" or a "country." In a strict sense, however, the word *nation* is an ethnic term, referring to races or other large groups of people. The word *country* is a geographic term, referring to a particular place, region, or area of land.

Population Clearly, a state must have people—a population. The size of that population, however, has nothing directly to do with the existence of a state. One of the world's smallest states, in population terms, is San Marino. Bound on all sides by Italy, it has only some 30,000 people. The People's Republic of China is the world's most

populous state, with more than 1.3 billion people—just about one fifth of all of the world's population. The more than 300 million people who live in the United States make it the world's third most populous state, after China and India.

The people who make up a state may or may not be homogeneous. The adjective *homogeneous* describes members of a group who share customs, a common language, and ethnic background. Today, the population of the United States includes people from a wide variety of backgrounds. Still, most Americans think of themselves as exactly that: Americans.

Territory Just as a state cannot exist without people, so it must have land—territory—with known and recognized boundaries. The states in today's world vary as widely in terms of territory as they do in population. Here, too, San Marino ranks among the world's smallest states. It covers less than 24 square miles, and so is smaller than thousands of cities and towns in the United States. The United States also recognizes the state of Vatican City, which is completely surrounded by the city of Rome. It has a permanent population of less than 900 and an area of only 109 acres.

Russia, the world's largest state, stretches across some 6.6 million square miles. The total area of the United States is slightly less than 3.8 million square miles.

Sovereignty Every state is **sovereign**—that is, it has supreme and absolute power within its own territory and can decide its own foreign and domestic policies. It is neither subordinate nor responsible to any other authority. Sovereignty is the one characteristic that distinguishes the state from all other, lesser political units in the world.

Thus, as a sovereign state, the United States can determine its form of government, frame its own economic system, and shape its own foreign policies. The States within the United States are not sovereign and so are not states in the international, legal sense. Each State is subordinate to the Constitution of the United States.²

Government Every state is politically organized. That is, every state has a government. Recall, a government is the institution through which society makes and enforces its public policies. A government is the agency through which the state exerts its will and works to accomplish its goals. Government includes the machinery and the <u>personnel</u> by which the state is ruled.

---

2 In this book, *state* printed with a small *s* denotes a state in the family of nations, such as the United States, Great Britain, and Mexico. *State* printed with a capital *S* refers to a State in the American union.

Government is necessary to avoid what the English philosopher Thomas Hobbes (1588–1679) called "the war of every man against every man." Without government, said Hobbes, there would be "continual fear and danger of violent death and the life of man [would be] solitary, poor, nasty, brutish, and short." The world has seen a number of examples over recent years of what happens when a government disappears: In Lebanon, Bosnia, Somalia, and many other places, life became "nasty, brutish, and short."

Origin of the State

For centuries, historians, philosophers, and others have pondered the question of the origin of the state. What set of circumstances first brought it into being?

Over time, many different answers have been offered, but history provides no conclusive evidence to support any of them. However, four theories have emerged as the most widely accepted explanations for the origin of the state.

The Force Theory Many scholars have long believed that the state was born of force. They hold that one person or a small group claimed control over an area and forced all within it to submit to that person's or group's rule. When that rule was established, all the basic elements of the state—population, territory, sovereignty, and government—were present.

✔ **Checkpoint**
What is the definition of *sovereignty?*

personnel
n. people who work for an organization

China (left) and Barbados (below) are on opposite ends of the population scale. Both, however, are sovereign states.

Origins of the State

There are four theories as to how the state came to be. Each theory brings together the four characteristics of the state in different ways. *Which of the theories best describes the origin of the United States? Why?*

GOVERNMENT ONLINE

Audio Tour
To listen to a guided audio tour of theories about how the state formed, visit **PearsonSuccessNet.com**

Force Theory

An individual or group claimed control over a **territory** and forced the **population** to submit. In this way, the state became **sovereign,** and those in control formed a **government.**

Evolutionary Theory

A **population** formed out of primitive families. The heads of these families became the **government.** When these families settled in one **territory** and claimed it as their own, they became a **sovereign** state.

Divine Right Theory

God created the state, making it **sovereign.** The **government** is made up of those chosen by God to rule a certain **territory.** The people **(population)** must obey their ruler.

Social Contract Theory

A **population** in a given place **(territory)** gave up as much power to a **government** as needed to promote the well-being of all. In doing so, they created a **sovereign** state.

The Evolutionary Theory Others claim that the state developed naturally out of the early family. They hold that the primitive family, of which one person was the head and thus the "government," was the first stage in political development. Over countless centuries, the original family became a network of related families, a clan. In time, the clan became a tribe. When the tribe first turned to agriculture and gave up its nomadic, wandering ways, tying itself to the land, the state was born.

The Divine Right Theory The theory of **divine right** was widely accepted in much of the Western world from the fifteenth through the eighteenth centuries. It held that God created the state and that God had given those of royal birth a "divine right" to rule. The people were bound to obey their ruler as they would God; opposition to "the divine right of kings" was both treason and a mortal sin.

During the seventeenth century, philosophers began to question this theory. Much of the thought upon which present-day democracies rests began as a challenge to the theory of divine right.

The notion of divine right was not unique to European history. The rulers of many ancient civilizations, including the Chinese, Egyptian, Aztec, and Mayan civilizations, were held to be gods or to have been chosen by the gods. The Japanese emperor, the *mikado,* governed by divine right until 1945.

The Social Contract Theory In terms of the American political system, the most significant of the theories of the origin of the state is that of the "social contract." Philosophers such as Thomas Hobbes, James Harrington (1611–1677), and John Locke (1632–1704) in England and Jean Jacques Rousseau (1712–1778) in France developed this theory in the seventeenth and eighteenth centuries.

Hobbes wrote that in earliest history humans lived in unbridled freedom, that is in a "state of nature," in which no government existed and no person was subject to any superior power. That which people could take by force belonged to them. However, all people were similarly free in that state of nature. No authority existed to protect one person from the aggressive actions of another. Thus, individuals were only as secure as their own physical strength and intelligence could make them.

Human beings overcame their unpleasant condition, says the social contract theory, by agreeing with one another to create a state. By contract, people within a given area agreed to give up to the state as much power as was needed to promote the safety and well-being of all. In the contract (that is, through a constitution), the members of the state created a government to exercise the powers they had voluntarily given to the state.

In short, the social contract theory argues that the state arose out of a voluntary act of free people. It holds that the state exists only to serve the will of the people, that they are the sole source of political power, and that they are free to give or to withhold that power as they choose from the government. The theory may seem somewhat far-fetched today. The great concepts that this theory promoted, however—popular sovereignty, limited government, and individual rights— were immensely important to the shaping of the American governmental system.

The Declaration of Independence (see pages 43–47) justified its revolution through the social contract theory, arguing that King George III and his ministers had violated the contract. Thomas Jefferson called the document "pure Locke."

▸▸ **Interpreting Cartoons** This cartoon pokes fun at organized government. *Which types of government might restrict people from "having it as good as this"? Why?*

The Purpose of Government

What does government do? You can find a very meaningful answer to that question in the Constitution of the United States. The American system of government was created to serve the purposes set out there.

❝ FROM THE CONSTITUTION

We the People of the United States, in Order to form a more perfect Union, establish Justice, insure domestic Tranquility, provide for the common defence, promote the general Welfare, and secure the Blessings of Liberty to ourselves and our Posterity, do ordain and establish this Constitution for the United States of America.

—Preamble to the Constitution

Form a More Perfect Union The United States, which had just won its independence from Great Britain, faced an altogether uncertain future in the postwar 1780s. In 1781, the Articles of Confederation, the nation's first constitution, created "a firm league of friendship" among the 13 States. That league soon proved to be neither very firm nor very friendly. The government created by the Articles was powerless to overcome the intense rivalries and jealousies among the States that marked the times.

The Constitution of today was written in 1787. The original States adopted it in order to link themselves, and the American people, more closely together. That Constitution was built in the belief that in union there is strength.

✔ **Checkpoint**
What is the Social Contract Theory?

Reproduced by permission of Johnny Hart and Field Enterprises

A Coast Guard cutter stands guard in New York Harbor. *Against what kinds of threats does the Coast Guard defend the nation?*

can only imagine what it would be like to live in a state of anarchy—without government, law, or order. In fact, people do live that way in some parts of the world today. For years now, Somalia, located on the eastern tip of Africa, has not had a permanent functioning government; rival warlords control different parts of the country.

In *The Federalist* No. 51, James Madison observed: "If men were angels, no government would be necessary." Madison, who was perhaps the most thoughtful of the Framers of the Constitution, knew that most human beings fall far short of that standard.

Provide for the Common Defense Defending the nation against foreign enemies has always been one of government's major responsibilities. You can see its importance in the fact that defense is mentioned far more often in the Constitution than any of the other functions of government.

The nation's defense and its foreign policies are but two sides of the same coin: the security of the United States. To provide this security, the nation maintains an army, navy, air force, and coast guard. Departments such as the Department of Homeland Security keep watch for threats to the country and its people.

The United States has become the world's most powerful nation, but the world remains a dangerous place. This country must maintain its vigilance and its armed strength. Just a glance at today's newspapers or at one of this evening's television news programs will furnish <u>abundant</u> proof of that fact.

Establish Justice To provide justice, said Thomas Jefferson, is "the most sacred of the duties of government." No purpose, no goal of public policy, can be of greater importance in a democracy.

But what is justice? The term is difficult to define, for justice is a concept—an idea, an invention of the human mind. Like other concepts, such as truth, liberty, and fairness, justice means what people want it to mean.

As the concept of justice has developed over time in American thought and practice, it has come to mean this: The law, in both its content and its <u>administration,</u> must be reasonable, fair, and impartial. Those standards of justice have not always been met in this country. We have not attained our professed goal of "equal justice for all." However, this must be said: The history of this country can be told largely in terms of our continuing attempts to reach that goal.

"Injustice anywhere," said Martin Luther King, Jr., "is a threat to justice everywhere." You will encounter this idea again and again in this book.

Insure Domestic Tranquility Order is essential to the well-being of any society, and keeping the peace at home has always been a prime function of government. Most people

Promote the General Welfare Few people realize the extent to which government acts as the servant of its citizens, yet you can see examples everywhere. Public schools are one illustration of government's work to promote the general welfare. So, too, are its efforts to protect the quality of the air you breathe, the water you drink, and the food you eat. The list of tasks government performs for your benefit goes on and on.

Some governmental functions that are common in other countries—operating steel mills, airlines, and coal mines, for example— are not carried out by government in this country. In general, the services that government provides in the United States are those

administration
n. a performance of duties

abundant
adj. available in large quantity, plentiful

that benefit all or most people. Many of them are the services that are not very likely to be provided by the voluntary acts of private individuals or groups.

Secure the Blessings of Liberty This nation was founded by those who loved liberty and prized it above all earthly possessions. They believed with Thomas Jefferson that "the God who gave us life gave us liberty at the same time." They subscribed to Benjamin Franklin's <u>maxim</u>: "They that can give up essential liberty to obtain a little temporary safety deserve neither liberty nor safety."

The American dedication to freedom for the individual recognizes that liberty cannot be absolute. It is, instead, a relative matter. No one can be free to do whatever he or she pleases, for that behavior would interfere with the freedoms of others. As Clarence Darrow, the great defense lawyer, once said: "You can only be free if I am free."

Both the Federal Constitution and the State constitutions set out many guarantees of rights and liberties for the individual in this country. That does not mean that those guarantees are so firmly established that they exist forever, however. To preserve and protect them, each generation must learn and understand them anew, and be willing to stand up for them when necessary.

For many people, the inspiration to protect our rights and liberties arises from deep

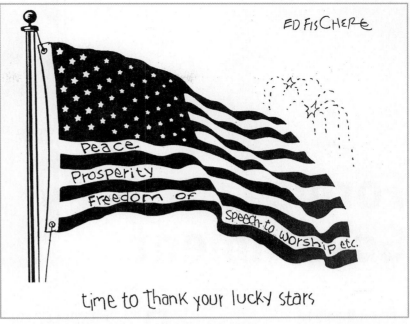

▸▸ **Analyzing Political Cartoons** In this cartoon, some of the liberties secured by the Constitution are written on the flag. **What is the phrase "thank your lucky stars" referring to?**

feelings of patriotism. Patriotism is the love of one's country; the passion that drives one to serve one's country, either by defending it from invasion or by protecting its rights and maintaining its laws and institutions. Patriotism is the defining characteristic of a good citizen, the noblest passion that animates a man or a woman in the character of a citizen. As a good citizen, you, too, must agree with Thomas Jefferson: "Eternal vigilance is the price of liberty."

maxim
n. a general truth or rule of conduct

Essential Questions
Journal
To continue to build a response to the chapter Essential Question, go to your **Essential Questions Journal.**

SECTION 1 ASSESSMENT

1. **Guiding Question** Use your completed outline to answer this question: What is government and what is its purpose?

Key Terms and Comprehension

2. What is the difference between a **state** and a nation?

3. **(a)** How is government conducted under a **dictatorship? (b)** How does a dictatorship differ from a **democracy?**

4. How does a **constitution** help to make it possible for a government to carry out its **public policies?**

Critical Thinking

5. **Summarize (a)** Summarize the four leading theories of the origin of the state. **(b)** Which two best describe the origin of dictatorships?

6. **Draw Inferences (a)** What is meant by "standards of justice have not always been met"? **(b)** What are some examples of efforts made to reach the goal of justice for all?

Quick Write

Expository Writing: Ask Questions When explaining a topic, you want to answer *Who, What, When, Where, Why,* and *How.* Develop these questions to explain the origins of either dictatorship or democracy. For example, if you choose dictatorship, you may ask these questions: *Who are some well-known dictators? When did dictatorships first develop?* You will answer these questions as you research the topic.

Forms of Government

Guiding Question

What are some forms of government in the world today?
Use a table like the one below to take notes on the different kinds of government in the world today.

Forms of Government	
Democracy	**Dictatorship**
•	•
•	•
•	•
•	•

Political Dictionary

- autocracy
- oligarchy
- unitary government
- federal government
- division of powers
- confederation
- presidential government
- parliamentary government

Objectives

1. Classify governments according to three sets of characteristics.
2. Define systems of government based on who can participate.
3. Identify different ways that power can be distributed, geographically, within a state.
4. Describe a government by the distribution of power between the executive branch and legislative branch.

Image Above: Members of the House of Lords in the British Parliament wear traditional robes and wigs.

Does the form a government takes, the way in which it is structured, have any importance? Political scientists, historians, and other social commentators have long argued that question. The English poet Alexander Pope weighed in with this couplet in 1733:

PRIMARY SOURCE

For Forms of Government let fools contest; Whate'er is best adminster'd is best. . . ."

—Essay on Man

Was Pope right? Does it matter what form a government takes? Pope thought not. You can form your own opinion as you read this section.

Classifying Governments

No two governments are, or ever have been, exactly alike, for governments are the products of human needs and experiences. All governments can be classified according to one or more of their basic features, however. Over time, political scientists have developed many bases upon which to classify (and so to describe, compare, and analyze) governments.

Three of those classifications are especially important and useful. These are classifications according to (1) who can participate in the governing process, (2) the geographic distribution of governmental power within the state, and (3) the relationship between the legislative (lawmaking) and the executive (law-executing) branches of the government.[3]

Who Can Participate

To many people, the most meaningful of these classifications is the one that depends on the number of persons who can take part in the governing process.

---

3 Note that these classifications are not mutually exclusive. For example, the government of the United States is federal in form, and it is also presidential and democratic.

Here there are two basic forms to consider: democracies and dictatorships.

Democracy In a democracy, supreme political authority rests with the people. The people hold the sovereign power, and government is conducted only by and with the consent of the people.[4]

Abraham Lincoln gave immortality to this definition of democracy in his Gettysburg Address in 1863: "government of the people, by the people, for the people." Nowhere is there a better, more <u>concise</u> statement of the American understanding of democracy.

A democracy can be either direct or indirect in form. A direct democracy, also called a pure democracy, exists where the will of the people is translated into public policy (law) directly by the people themselves, in mass meetings. Clearly, direct democracy can work only in small communities, where the citizenry can meet in a central place, and where the problems of government are few and relatively simple.

Direct democracy does not exist at the national level anywhere in the world today. However, the New England town meeting, which you will read about in Chapter 25, and the *Landsgemeinde* in a few of the smaller Swiss <u>cantons</u> is an excellent example of direct democracy in action.[5]

Americans are more familiar with the indirect form of democracy—that is, with representative democracy. In a representative democracy, a small group of persons, chosen by the people to act as their representatives, expresses the popular will. These agents of the people are responsible for carrying out the day-to-day conduct of government—the making and executing of laws and so on. They are held accountable to the people for that conduct, especially at periodic elections.

At these elections, the people have an opportunity to express their approval or disapproval of their representatives by casting ballots for or against them. To put it another way, representative democracy is government by popular consent—government with the consent of the governed.

Some people insist that the United States is more properly called a republic rather than a democracy. They hold that in a republic the sovereign power is held by those eligible to vote, while the political power is exercised by representatives chosen by and held responsible to those citizens. For them, democracy can be defined only in terms of direct democracy.

✔ **Checkpoint**
How does a direct democracy differ from an indirect democracy?

concise
adj. brief; to the point

canton
n. a local governmental unit in Switzerland

Direct
Democracy

- Also called pure democracy
- Occurs when the will of the people translates directly into public policy
- Works only on a small, local level

Image: Town meeting

Direct and Indirect Democracy
Who governs?

Democratic government derives its power from the people. The picture above shows citizens of a small town voting. Below, a representative casts her vote. The board behind her records the votes of each representative. *Why might direct democracy be more appropriate for a smaller population? Why might indirect democracy be better for a larger population?*

Indirect
Democracy

- Also called representative democracy
- A group of persons chosen by the people express the will of the people.
- Widely used on a national, State, and local level

Image: A legislator votes.

---

4 The word *democracy* is derived from the Greek words *demos* meaning "the people" and *kratia* meaning "rule" or "authority." The Greek word *demokratia* means "rule by the people."

5 The *Landsgemeinde*, like the original New England town meeting, is an assembly open to all local citizens qualified to vote. In a more limited sense, lawmaking by initiative petition is also an example of direct democracy; see Chapter 24.

regimes
n. particular governments

prestige
n. a reputation based on achievement

elite
n. a select group, a privileged class

Many Americans use the terms *democracy, republic, representative democracy,* and *republican form of government* interchangeably, although they are not the same. Whatever the terms used, remember that in a democracy the people are sovereign. They are the only source for any and all of government's power. In other words, the people rule.

Dictatorship A dictatorship exists where those who rule cannot be held responsible to the will of the people. The government is not accountable for its policies, nor for how they are carried out. Dictatorship is probably the oldest, and it is certainly the most common, form of government known to history.[6]

Dictatorships are sometimes identified as either autocracies or oligarchies. An **autocracy** is a government in which a single person holds unlimited political power. An **oligarchy** is a government in which the power to rule is held by a small, usually self-appointed elite.

All dictatorships are authoritarian; those in power hold absolute and unchallengeable authority over the people. Modern dictatorships have tended to be totalitarian, as well. That is, they exercise complete power over nearly every aspect of human affairs. Their power embraces all matters of human concern.

The leading examples of dictatorship in the modern era have been those in Fascist Italy (from 1922 to 1943), in Nazi Germany (from 1933 to 1945), in the Soviet Union (from 1917 until the late 1980s), and one that still exists in the People's Republic of China (where the present regime came to power in 1949).

Although they do exist, one-person dictatorships are not at all common today. A few close approaches to such a regime can now be found in Libya, which has been dominated by Muammar al-Qaddafi since 1969, and in some other Arab and African states.

Most present-day dictatorships are not nearly so absolutely controlled by a single person or by a small group as may appear to be the case. Outward appearances may hide the fact that several groups—the army, religious leaders, industrialists, and others—compete for power in the political system.

Dictatorships often present the outward appearance of control by the people. The people often vote in popular elections; but the vote is closely controlled, and ballots usually contain the candidates of but one political party. An elected legislative body often exists, but only to rubber-stamp the policies of the dictatorship.

Typically, dictatorial regimes are militaristic in character. They usually gain power by force. The military holds many of the major posts in the government. After crushing all effective opposition at home, these regimes may turn to foreign aggression to enhance the country's military power, political control, and prestige.

Geographic Distribution of Power

In every system of government, the power to govern is located in one or more places geographically. From this standpoint, three basic forms of government exist: unitary, federal, and confederate.

Unitary Government A **unitary government** is often described as a centralized government. All powers held by the government belong to a single, central agency. The central (national) government creates local units of government for its own convenience. Those local governments have only those powers that the central government chooses to give them.

Most governments in the world are unitary in form. Great Britain is a classic illustration. A single central organization, the Parliament, holds all of the government's power. Local governments do exist—but solely to relieve Parliament of burdens it could perform only with much difficulty and inconvenience. Though unlikely, Parliament could do away with all local government in Britain at any time.

Be careful not to confuse the unitary form of government with a dictatorship. In the unitary form, all of the powers held by the government are concentrated in the central government.

---

6 The word *dictatorship* comes from the Latin *dictare,* meaning "to dictate, issue orders," "to give authoritative commands." *Dictator* was the ancient Roman republic's title for the leader who was given extraordinary powers in times of crisis. Julius Caesar (100–44 B.C.) was the last of the Roman dictators.

Democracies and Dictatorships

Every country has a different approach to government. Below are four examples: two democracies and two dictatorships. In each image, the people are expressing their will. *How are the people's methods and the governments' reactions different in each image?*

Democracy

Dictatorship

United States	United Kingdom	Popular Name	China	Myanmar (Burma)
United States of America (photo above left)	United Kingdom of Great Britain and Northern Ireland	**Official Name**	People's Republic of China	Union of Myanmar (photo above right)
Constitution-based federal republic	Constitutional monarchy	**Form of Government**	Communist state	Military junta (a faction that rules after a coup)
President Barack Obama	Queen Elizabeth II	**Chief of State**	President Hu Jintao	Sr. General Than Shwe
President Barack Obama	Prime Minister Gordon Brown	**Head of Government**	Premier Wen Jiabao	Lt. General Thein Sein
The Constitution was ratified by the States in 1787–88, establishing the Federal Government.	Power has gradually shifted from the monarchy to the Parliament over the last 800 years.	**Origins of Current Government**	In 1949, Mao Zedong established the People's Republic of China as a socialist autocracy.	The military has ruled since 1962, despite defeat in free elections in 1990.
The President and members of Congress are chosen by the people.	The monarchy is hereditary; the prime minister is the head of the leading party in Parliament, which is elected by the people.	**Elections**	The president is chosen by the National People's Congress. The president nominates the premier, who is confirmed by the Congress, which is chosen by regional congresses.	There are no elections. The junta has banned the legislature and taken over judicial power.

Distribution of Power

Power can be distributed between central (national) and local governments in three different ways. *Which diagram best describes the distribution of power in the United States?*

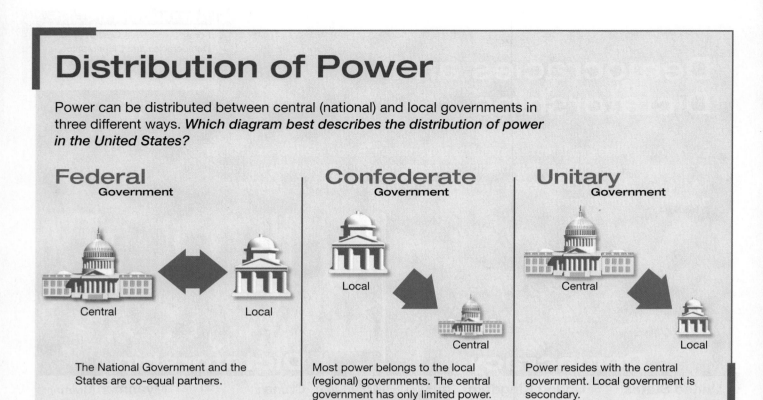

Federal
Government

Central   Local

The National Government and the States are co-equal partners.

Confederate
Government

Local

Central

Most power belongs to the local (regional) governments. The central government has only limited power.

Unitary
Government

Central

Local

Power resides with the central government. Local government is secondary.

That government might not have all power, however. In Great Britain, for example, the powers held by the government are limited. British government is unitary and, at the same time, democratic.

Federal Government A **federal government** is one in which the powers of government are divided between a central government and several local governments. An authority superior to both the central and local governments makes this **division of powers** on a geographic basis; and that division cannot be changed by either the local or national level acting alone. Both levels of government act directly on the people through their own sets of laws, officials, and agencies.

In the United States, for example, the National Government has certain powers and the 50 States have others. This division of powers is set out in the Constitution of the United States. The Constitution stands above both levels of government; and it cannot be changed unless the people, acting through both the National Government and the States, agree to the change.

Australia, Canada, Mexico, Switzerland, Germany, India, and some 20 other states also have federal forms of government today. In the United States, the phrase "the Federal Government" is often used to identify the National Government, the government headquartered in Washington, D.C. Note, however, that each of the 50 State governments in this country is unitary, not federal, in form.

Confederate Government A **confederation** is an alliance of independent states. A central organization, the confederate government has the power to handle only those matters that the member states have assigned to it. Typically, confederate governments have had limited powers and only in such fields as defense and foreign affairs.

Most often, confederate governments have not had the power to make laws that apply directly to individuals, at least not without some further action by the member states. A confederate structure of government makes it possible for the several states to cooperate in matters of common concern and, at the same time, retain their separate identities.

Confederations have been rare in the modern world. The European Union (EU) is the closest approach to one today. The EU, formed by 12 countries in 1993, has established free trade among its now 27 member-nations, launched a common currency, and seeks to coordinate its members' foreign and defense policies.

In our own history, the United States under the Articles of Confederation (1781–1789) and the Confederate States of America (1861–1865) also provide examples of this form of government.

Legislative and Executive Branches

Political scientists also classify governments based on the relationship between their legislative and executive agencies. This grouping yields two basic forms of government: presidential and parliamentary.

Presidential Government
A **presidential government** features a separation of powers between the executive and the legislative branches of the government. The two branches are independent of one another and <u>coequal.</u> The chief executive (the president) is chosen by the people, independently of the legislature. He or she holds office for a fixed term, and has a number of significant powers that are not subject to the direct control of the legislative branch.

The details of this separation of the powers of these two branches are almost always spelled out in a written constitution—as they are in the United States. Each of the branches is regularly given several powers with which it can block actions of the other branch.

✔ **Checkpoint**
How is the executive branch related to the legislative branch in a presidential government?

coequal
adj. equal with one another, of the same rank

Choosing a Chief Executive

In a presidential democracy, the people choose their representatives as well as their President. In a parliamentary democracy, the representatives (members of parliament) choose the prime minister. *Which method seems best for choosing a chief executive? Why?*

Voters elect the legislature and the chief executive.

Legislative Branch

Chief Executive

Executive Branch
The two branches are independent and coequal.

Presidential

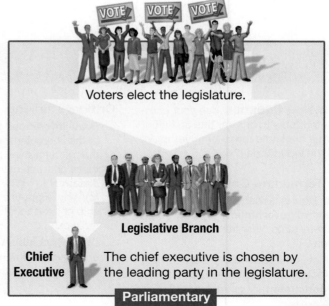

Voters elect the legislature.

Legislative Branch

Chief Executive
The chief executive is chosen by the leading party in the legislature.

Parliamentary

▲ Members of the South African parliament are sworn into office.

The United States is the world's leading example of presidential government. In fact, the United States invented the form. Nearly all of the other presidential systems in the world today are also found in the Western Hemisphere.

Parliamentary Government In a **parliamentary government,** the executive branch is made up of the prime minister or premier, and that official's cabinet. The prime minister and cabinet are themselves members of the legislative branch, the parliament. The prime minister is the leader of the majority party or of a like-minded group of parties (a coalition) in parliament and is chosen by that body. With parliament's approval, the prime minister selects the members of the cabinet from among the members of parliament. The executive is thus chosen by the legislature, is a part of it, and is subject to its direct control.

The prime minister and the cabinet (often called "the government") remain in office only as long as their policies and administration have the support of a majority in parliament. If the parliament defeats the prime minister and cabinet on an important matter, the government may receive a "vote of no confidence," and the prime minister and his cabinet must resign from office. Then a new government must be formed. Either parliament chooses a new prime minister or, as often happens, all the seats in parliament go before the voters in a general election.

A majority of the governmental systems in the world today are parliamentary, not presidential, in form—and they are by a wide margin. Parliamentary government avoids one of the major problems of the presidential form: prolonged conflict and sometimes deadlock between the executive and legislative branches. However, the protections against arbitrary government found in the checks and balances of presidential government are not a part of the parliamentary system.

Essential Questions Journal — To continue to build a response to the chapter Essential Question, go to your **Essential Questions Journal.**

SECTION **2** ASSESSMENT

1. **Guiding Question** Use your completed table to answer this question: What are some forms of government in the world today?

Key Terms and Comprehension

2. **(a)** How is power distributed in a **federal government? (b)** How does a federal state differ from a confederate state?

3. What is the relationship between the executive and legislative branches in a **parliamentary government?**

Critical Thinking

4. **Draw Inferences (a)** What are some of the characteristics of democracy that dictatorships adopt? **(b)** Are these characteristics of a true dictatorship? Why or why not? **(c)** Why might the rulers of a dictatorship choose to take on these characteristics?

5. **Draw Conclusions** Explain how a unitary government might be either democratic or dictatorial in form.

Quick Write

Expository Writing: Research Your Topic Use several sources to find the answers to the questions you posed in Section 1. The answers will help you gather details you will need to fully explain either a democracy or a dictatorship. Then put all of your facts and details in chronological order to help the reader follow the growth of democracy or dictatorship.

Volunteering

In one of his State of the Union addresses, President George W. Bush called on Americans to volunteer. He also announced the creation of USA Freedom Corps, an organization that links Americans to thousands of volunteer opportunities. USA Freedom Corps has helped many volunteer organizations—including Learn and Serve America, which supports student volunteers—gain recognition and support for their causes.

A substantial number of students volunteer their time and skills every year. According to the Department of Labor, about one in five citizens between the ages of 16 and 24 has volunteered in recent years.

While volunteering is not required of U.S. citizens, it is an important responsibility that many students fulfill in their spare time. More recently, the number of volunteers between 16 and 24 years old has fallen. Many essential programs suffer when the number of people willing to give time and money declines.

All citizens of the United States benefit from services provided by the government. Citizens can attend public schools, receive mail, and enjoy national parks. However, sometimes the government lacks funding or manpower to provide these services to their greatest extent.

Volunteers provide services that the government may not have the time or the resources to offer. A student may tutor a younger student after school. A volunteer group might maintain hiking trails in a national park.

In addition, volunteers fulfill services that the government is not required to provide. These include visiting the elderly or providing community theater. Volunteers are particularly necessary in times of war. The United Service Organizations (USO) support troops overseas with comforts such as entertainment, packages from home, and phone cards to call the United States.

1. **Make a List** To volunteer, make a list of activities that interest you and talents that you possess. Many people find it rewarding to share their talents and interests with others. For example, if you like to play soccer, you may be able to coach for a children's team.

2. **Seek Out Opportunities** Look for volunteer opportunities that are connected to your interests and strengths. Ask your teacher or use the Internet to find organizations that fit your criteria.

3. **Make Contact** Write an e-mail to or call the contact person for your chosen organization. Some organizations require a resume, references, or a list of past experiences. Make sure you have these on hand.

▸▸ What do you think?

1. How does volunteering benefit all citizens? Why is volunteering an important civic responsibility?

2. The United States has seen a drop in the number of volunteers in the last few years. How could teenagers be persuaded to volunteer? Brainstorm two ways to get people interested in volunteering.

3. **You Try It** Locate some volunteer opportunities in your community. Make a list of the ones that interest you, and how you would get involved. Is it easy or difficult to get involved in these organizations? What are the steps that you must take? Are these causes ones to which you would give some of your time?

⌖ GOVERNMENT ONLINE
Citizenship Activity Pack
For an activity to help you explore volunteering, go to **PearsonSuccessNet.com**

SECTION 3

Basic Concepts of Democracy

What are the basic concepts of democracy? Use a concept web like the one below to take notes on the basic concepts of democracy.

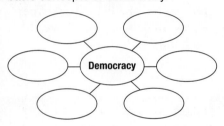

Democracy

Political Dictionary
- majority rule
- compromise
- citizen
- free enterprise system

Objectives
1. Understand the foundations of democracy.
2. Analyze the connections between democracy and the free enterprise system.

Image Above: Children gather to celebrate Flag Day in New York City.

What do you make of this assessment of democracy by British statesman James Bryce: "No government demands so much from the citizen as Democracy, and none gives so much back"? What does democratic government demand from you? What does it give you in return?

Foundations

Democracy is not <u>inevitable.</u> It does not exist in the United States simply because Americans regard it as the best of all possible political systems. Rather, democracy exists in this country because the American people believe in its basic concepts. It will continue to exist only for as long as we, the people, continue to subscribe to and practice those concepts.

Sir Winston Churchill (1874–1965) once put the argument for democracy this way: "No one pretends that democracy is perfect or all-wise. Indeed, it has been said that democracy is the worst form of government except all those other forms that have been tried from time to time."

The American concept of democracy—what we believe democracy means—rests on these basic notions:

1. Recognition of the fundamental worth and dignity of every person;

2. Respect for the equality of all persons;

3. Faith in majority rule and an insistence upon minority rights;

4. Acceptance of the necessity of compromise; and

5. Insistence upon the widest possible degree of individual freedom;

Of course, these concepts can be worded in other ways. No matter what the wording, however, they form the very minimum with which anyone who professes to believe in democracy must agree.

Worth of the Individual Democracy is firmly based upon a belief in the fundamental importance of the individual. Each individual, no matter what his or her station in life, is a separate and distinct being.

This concept of the dignity and worth of the individual is of overriding importance in democratic thought. At various times, of course, the welfare of one or a few individuals is <u>subordinated</u> to the interests of the many in a democracy. People can be forced to do certain things whether they want to or not. Examples range from paying taxes to registering for the draft to stopping at a stop sign.

When a democratic society forces people to pay a tax or obey traffic signals, it is serving the interests of the many. However, it is not simply serving the interests of the many who as a mass of people happen to outnumber the few. Rather, it is serving the many who, as individuals, together make up that society.

The distinction we are trying to make here between *an* individual and *all* individuals may be difficult to grasp. It is, however, critically important to a real understanding of the meaning of democracy.

Equality of All Persons Hand in hand with the belief in the worth of the individual, democracy stresses the equality of all individuals. It holds, with Jefferson, that "all men are created equal."

Certainly, democracy does not imply an equality of condition for all persons. Thus, it does not claim that all are born with the same mental or physical abilities. Nor does it hold that all persons have a right to an equal share of worldly goods.

Rather, the democratic concept of equality means that every person is entitled to (1) equality of opportunity and (2) equality before the law. That is, the democratic concept of equality holds that no person should be held back for any such <u>arbitrary</u> reasons as those based on race, color, religion, or gender. It states that each person must be free to develop himself or herself as fully as he or she wishes to, and that each person should be treated as the equal of all other persons under the law.

We have come a great distance toward the goal of equality for all in this country. It is clear, however, that we are still a considerable distance from a genuine, universally recognized and respected equality for all of America's people.

Majority Rule, Minority Rights In a democracy, the will of the people and not the dictate of the ruling few determines public policy. But what is the popular will, and how is it determined? Some device must exist by which these crucial questions can be answered. The only satisfactory device democracy knows is that of **majority rule.** Democracy holds that a majority will be right more often than it will be wrong, and that the majority will also be right more often than any one person or small group will.

✔ **Checkpoint**
To what are citizens entitled under the democratic concept of equality?

subordinate
v. of lesser rank

arbitrary
adj. based on unsupported opinion, random choice

inevitable
adj. unavoidable, sure to happen

In *Brown* v. *Board of Education,* (1954) the Supreme Court ruled that segregation denied African Americans equality guaranteed by the Constitution and the democratic system. Arkansas fought the integration of its schools. Elizabeth Eckford (inset) was one of nine African Americans who enrolled at Central High School in Little Rock in 1957. Below, seven of the students known as the Little Rock Nine sit with Thurgood Marshall, who argued the case.

Democracy can be described as an experiment or a trial-and-error process designed to find satisfactory ways to order human relations. Democracy does not dictate that the majority will always arrive at the best decisions on public matters. In fact, the democratic process is not meant to come up with "right" or "best" answers. Rather, the democratic process is a search for *satisfactory* solutions to public problems.

Of course, in a democracy the majority's decisions will usually be more, rather than less, satisfactory. Democracy does admit the possibility of mistakes; there is the possibility that "wrong" or less satisfactory answers will sometimes be found. Democracy also recognizes that seldom is any solution to a public problem so satisfactory that it cannot be improved upon, and that circumstances can change over time. So, the process of experimentation, of seeking answers to public questions, is a never-ending one.

Certainly, a democracy cannot work without the principle of majority rule. Unchecked, however, a majority could destroy its opposition and, in the process, destroy democracy itself. Thus, democracy requires majority rule restrained by minority rights. The majority must always recognize the right of any minority to become, if it can by fair and lawful means, the majority. The majority must always be willing to listen to a minority's argument, to hear its objections, to bear its criticisms, and to welcome its suggestions.

Necessity of Compromise In a democracy, public decision making must be largely a matter of give-and-take among the various competing interests. It is a matter of compromise in order to find the position most acceptable to the largest number. **Compromise** is the process of blending and adjusting competing views and interests.

Compromise is an essential part of the democratic concept for two major reasons. First, remember that democracy puts the individual first and, at the same time, insists that each individual is the equal of all others. In a democratic society made up of many individuals and groups with many different opinions and interests, how can the people make public decisions except by compromise?

Second, few public questions have only two sides. Most can be answered in several ways. Take the apparently simple question of how a city should pay for the paving of a public street. Should it charge those who own property along the street? Or should the costs be paid from the city's general treasury? Or should the city and the adjacent property owners share the costs? What about those who will use the street but do not live in the city? Should they have to pay a toll?

Remember, compromise is a process, a way of achieving majority agreement. It is never an end in itself. Not all compromises are good, and not all are necessary.

Individual Freedom It should be clear by this point that democracy can thrive only in an atmosphere of individual freedom. However, democracy does not and cannot insist on complete freedom for the individual. Absolute freedom can exist only in a state of anarchy—the total absence of government. Anarchy can only lead, inevitably and quickly, to rule by the strong and ruthless.

Democracy does require that each individual must be as free to do as he or she pleases as far as the freedom of all will allow. Justice Oliver Wendell Holmes once had this to say about the relative nature of each individual's rights: "The right to swing my fist ends where the other man's nose begins."

▸▸ **Analyzing Cartoons** *Who do the chefs represent in this cartoon?*

Drawing the line between the rights of one individual and those of another is not easy. Still, the drawing of that line is a continuous and vitally important function of democratic government. As John F. Kennedy put it: "The rights of every man are diminished when the rights of one man are threatened."

Striking the proper balance between freedom for the individual and the rights of society as a whole is similarly difficult—and vital. Abraham Lincoln described democracy's problem in these words:

PRIMARY SOURCES

Must a government, of necessity, be too *strong* for the liberties of its own people, or too *weak* to maintain its own existence?

—Message to Congress, July 4, 1861

Human beings desire both liberty and authority. Democratic government must work constantly to strike the proper balance between the two. The authority of government must be <u>adequate</u> to the needs of society. At the same time, that authority must never be allowed to become so great that it restricts the individual beyond what is absolutely necessary.

Duties and Responsibilities of Citizenship

Over the centuries, any number of statesmen, philosophers, and others have told us that citizenship carries with it both duties and responsibilities. Theodore Roosevelt put that point this way in 1902: "The first requisite of a good citizen in our republic is that he should be able and willing to pull his weight."

In a democratic society, the *duties* of "a good citizen" all revolve around his or her commitment to obey the law—a point long accepted in this country. In his Farewell Address in 1796, George Washington put that obligation this way: "the very idea of the power and right of the People to establish Government presupposes the duty of every individual to obey the established Government."

The several *responsibilities* of "a good citizen" in a free society all come down to this: an abiding respect for each of the core beliefs on which democracy is based in this country. A **citizen** is one who holds both rights and responsibilities in a state. Look again at page 20 and then ask yourself this question: Do I understand and am I committed to honoring the basic concepts of American democracy?

Democracy and the Free Enterprise System

The American commitment to freedom for the individual is deep-rooted, and it is as evident in the nation's economic system as it is in the political system. The American economic system is often called the **free enterprise system.** It is an economic system characterized by the private ownership of capital goods; investments made by private decision, not by government directive; and success or failure determined by competition in the marketplace. The free enterprise system is based on four fundamental factors: private ownership, individual <u>initiative,</u> profit, and competition.

✔ **Checkpoint**
Name two duties of every U.S. citizen.

<u>adequate</u>
adj. enough to meet the needs of a situation

<u>initiative</u>
n. enterprise, resourcefulness

Duties and Responsibilities of Citizenship

Duties	Responsibilities
• Serving on a **jury**	• **Voting**
• Serving as a **witness** when called	• **Volunteering**
• Attending **school**	• **Participating** in civic life
• Paying **taxes**	• **Understanding** the workings of our government
• Registering for the **draft** (men only)	
• **Obeying** local, State, and national **laws**	
• Respecting the **rights of others**	

▶▶ Analyzing Charts Many duties and responsibilities come with being a citizen. *Why might obeying the law be a duty rather than a responsibility?*

antitrust laws
n. laws that regulate business practices in order to promote competition

zoning ordinances
n. laws that regulate the uses of property in certain areas

How the System Works The free enterprise system is often called capitalism. It is also known as the private enterprise system and as a market-based system. It does not rely on government to decide what items are to be produced, how much of any particular item should be produced, or how much any item is to sell for. Rather, those decisions are made in the marketplace. Millions of producers and consumers obey the unwritten law of supply and demand: When supplies of goods and services become plentiful, prices will tend to drop; when, on the other hand, supplies become scarce, prices will very likely rise.

Democracy and the free enterprise system are not the same thing. One is a political system, and the other is an economic system. However, both are firmly based on the concept of individual freedom. America's experience with both systems clearly suggests that the two reinforce one another in practice.

Government and the Free Enterprise System The basis of the American economic system is the free market. However, government does play a role in the American economy, and it always has. Government's participation in the economy serves a two-fold purpose: to protect the public and to preserve private enterprise.

Government's participation in the economy can be seen at every level in this country: national, State, and local. Here are but a few

examples: Economic activities are regulated by government through <u>antitrust laws,</u> pure food and drug laws, antipollution standards, and city and county <u>zoning ordinances</u> and building codes.

The nation's economic life is promoted in a great number of public ways. The government grants money for transportation systems and the growing of particular food crops, builds roads and operates public schools, provides services such as the postal system and weather reports, and much more.

Thus, some activities that might be carried out privately are in fact conducted by government. Public education, local fire departments, and city bus systems are long-standing examples of the point.

How much should government participate, regulate, promote, police, and serve? Many heated debates in American politics center on that question, and we are often reminded of Abraham Lincoln's advice:

PRIMARY SOURCES

The legitimate object of government, is to do for a community of people, whatever they need to have done, but can not do, *at all,* or can not, *so well do,* for themselves—in their separate, and individual capacities.

—Abraham Lincoln

Essential Questions Journal To continue to build a response to the chapter Essential Question, go to your **Essential Questions Journal.**

SECTION 3 ASSESSMENT

1. **Guiding Question** Use your completed concept web to answer this question: What are the basic concepts of democracy?

Key Terms and Comprehension

2. **(a)** In what two ways does democracy require the equality of all persons? **(b)** What kind of equality is *not* guaranteed by democracy?

3. Why is **compromise** so important in a democracy?

4. What does it mean to be a good **citizen?**

Critical Thinking

5. **Predict Consequences (a)** What must a good citizen do in order to help preserve democracy? **(b)** What might be the consequences if citizens were not required to pay taxes? To serve on a jury?

6. **Draw Conclusions** How might the government react to a downturn in the economy?

Quick Write

Quick Write Expository Writing: Create an Outline Using the notes from the research you conducted in Section 2, create an outline to help you further organize your information. The outline should follow the chronological order you established.

Quick Study Guide

GOVERNMENT ONLINE
On the Go
To review anytime, anywhere, download these online resources at **PearsonSuccessNet.com**
Political Dictionary, Audio Review

Guiding Question
Section 2 What are some forms of government in the world today?

Guiding Question
Section 1 What is government and what is its purpose?

CHAPTER 1
Essential Question
Is government necessary?

Guiding Question
Section 3 What are the basic concepts of democracy?

Political Dictionary

government *p. 4*
public policies *p. 4*
legislative power *p. 5*
executive power *p. 5*
judicial power *p. 5*
constitution *p. 5*
dictatorship *p. 5*
democracy *p. 5*
state *p. 5*
sovereign *p. 7*
autocracy *p. 14*
oligarchy *p. 14*
unitary government *p. 14*
federal government *p. 16*
division of powers *p. 16*
confederation *p. 16*
presidential government *p. 17*
parliamentary government *p. 18*
majority rule *p. 21*
compromise *p. 22*
citizen *p. 23*
free enterprise system *p. 23*

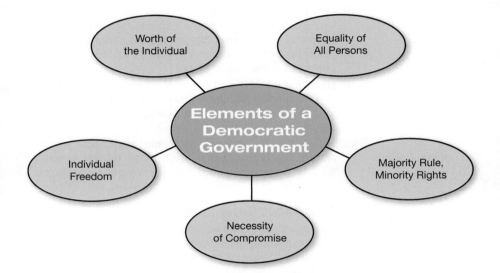

Worth of the Individual

Equality of All Persons

Elements of a Democratic Government

Individual Freedom

Majority Rule, Minority Rights

Necessity of Compromise

Origin of the State

Force Theory	Evolutionary Theory	Divine Right Theory	Social Contract Theory
One person or a small group took control of a population by force.	The state developed naturally out of the early family.	God created the state and gave those of royal birth the "divine right" to rule.	People agreed to give up as much freedom as needed to create a state that provided safety and well-being for all (Hobbes).

Chapter Assessment

 **GOVERNMENT** ONLINE
Self-Test
To test your understanding of key terms and main ideas, visit **PearsonSuccessNet.com**

Comprehension and Critical Thinking

Section 1

1. What are the three basic powers exercised by government?
2. **(a)** What four characteristics does every state possess? **(b)** How does the force theory account for those four characteristics? **(c)** Which of those theories best explains the rise of democratic states? Why?
3. **(a)** What are the six purposes of government established by the Constitution? **(b)** Cite three ways in which the Federal Government promotes the general welfare that are not listed in the text.
4. **Analyze Political Cartoons (a)** What form of government does the king represent? **(b)** What is the king implying when he says that he doesn't get to vote either? **(c)** Is this a misleading statement? Why or why not?

"So what? — I don't get to vote *either,* you know!"

Section 2

5. **(a)** Explain the fundamental ideas of democracy. **(b)** How is a republic different from a democracy? **(c)** Why do some people hold that the United States is more properly called a republic rather than a democracy?
6. **(a)** What is the difference between an autocracy and an oligarchy? **(b)** According to the text, which of these types of dictatorship are you more likely to find today?
7. **(a)** How is power distributed in a presidential government? **(b)** How is power distributed in a parliamentary government? **(c)** Which system seems to give the most power to the legislative branch?

Section 3

8. **(a)** When looking at majority rule versus minority rights, why would some people argue that the United States is not a true democracy? **(b)** How are the rights of the individual protected in a true democracy? **(c)** How are they protected in the United States?
9. **(a)** How might the application of purely democratic ideas to a functioning government cause a problem for a large federal state? **(b)** How might it cause a problem for minority groups within that state?
10. Explain how the following duties and responsibilities of citizenship contribute to the good of all: **(a)** paying taxes, **(b)** voting, and **(c)** volunteering. **(d)** Which do you think is most important? Why?

Writing About Government

11. Use your Quick Write activities to write an expository piece explaining democracy or dictatorship. Use your outline as a basis for your expository piece. See pp. S3–S5 in the Skills Handbook.

Apply What You've Learned

12. **Essential Question Activity** You are the leaders of a group of formerly independent states now coming together to form a new country. The new country will be large in area, with a large population. Choose a form of government (federal, confederate, or unitary) that you think would best suit this situation.

    (a) Work out the details of your new government based on information from the chapter. Answer the following questions: Will the country run under a free enterprise system? Will it be a direct or representative democracy? What major functions will the government be required to perform?

    (b) Write an organizational plan for your government and present it to the class. Allow time for questions. Revise your plan according to issues your classmates point out.

13. **Essential Question Assessment** Use the work from the activity and the content of this chapter to help you write a paragraph that answers the Essential Question: **Is government necessary?** Then, as a class, discuss your responses. Discuss why or why not government is necessary.

Essential Questions
Journal
To respond to the chapter Essential Question, go to your **Essential Questions Journal.**

Document-Based Assessment

The Roots of Democracy

Its invention is usually attributed to ancient Greece, but democracy existed well before the Greeks coined the term around 2,500 years ago. However, the Greek philosophers wrote extensively on the subject. Some supported it, while others—like Plato—did not.

Document 1

Thus it is manifest that the best political community is formed by citizens of the middle class, and that those states are likely to be well-administered in which the middle class is large, and stronger if possible than both the other classes, or at any rate than either singly; for the addition of the middle class turns the scale, and prevents either of the extremes from being dominant. Great then is the good fortune of a state in which the citizens have a moderate and sufficient property; for where some possess much, and the others nothing, there may arise an extreme democracy, or a pure oligarchy; or a tyranny may grow out of either extreme— either out of the most rampant democracy, or out of an oligarchy; but it is not so likely to arise out of the middle constitutions and those akin to them. . . . The mean condition of states is clearly best, for no other is free from faction; and where the middle class is large, there are least likely to be factions and dissensions [disagreements].

—Discussion on the mean condition from Aristotle's *Politics*, Part XI

Document 2

How grandly does [democracy] trample all these fine notions of ours under her feet, never giving a thought to the pursuits which make a statesman, and promoting to honor any one who professes to be the people's friend. . . .

And when they [democratic principles] have emptied and swept clean the soul of him [the individual] who is now in their power and who is being initiated by them in great mysteries, the next thing is to bring back to their house insolence [ill-mannered behavior] and anarchy [lawlessness, chaos] and waste and impudence [disrespect] in bright array having garlands on their heads, and a great company with them, hymning their praises and calling them by sweet names; insolence they term breeding, and anarchy liberty, and waste magnificence, and impudence courage.

—Discussion about democracy from Plato's *Republic*, Book 8

Use your knowledge of the concepts of democracy, other forms of government, and Documents 1 and 2 to answer Questions 1–3.

1. According to Aristotle, what is the best condition for political stability?
   A. extreme democracy
   B. moderate democracy
   C. pure oligarchy
   D. tyranny

2. Based on the excerpt from Plato's *Republic,* what is Plato's attitude toward democracy? Cite two supporting details from the passage.

3. **Pull It Together** How might Aristotle address Plato's concerns? Write a paragraph from Aristotle's point of view.

GOVERNMENT ONLINE

Documents
To find more primary sources on democracy, visit
PearsonSuccessNet.com

Origins of American Government

Essential Question
How does the Constitution reflect the times in which it was written?

"**Why** stand we here idle?… Is **life** so dear or **peace** so sweet as to be purchased at the price of **chains** and **slavery?** Forbid it, Almighty God! I know not what course others may take, but as for me, **give me liberty or give me death!**

—Patrick Henry, Speech at the Virginia Convention, March 1775

Painting: The colonists meet the British army at Lexington, Massachusetts.

GOVERNMENT ONLINE
On the Go

To study anywhere, anytime, download these online resources at PearsonSuccessNet.com
• Political Dictionary
• Audio Review
• Downloadable Interactivities

SECTION 1

Our Political Beginnings

Guiding Question

What ideas and traditions influenced government in the English colonies? Use a concept web like the one below to take notes on the ideas that shaped American colonists' concepts of government.

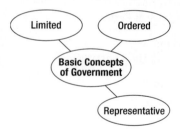

Political Dictionary

- limited government
- representative government
- Magna Carta
- due process
- Petition of Right
- English Bill of Rights
- charter
- bicameral
- proprietary
- unicameral

Objectives

1. Identify the three concepts of government that influenced the American colonies.
2. Explain the significance of three landmark English documents.
3. Describe the three types of colonies that the English established in the American colonies.

Image Above: King John signs the Magna Carta, limiting his own power.

The American system of government did not suddenly spring into being with the signing of the Declaration of Independence in 1776. Nor was it created by the Framers of the Constitution in 1787.

The beginnings of what was to become the United States can be found in the mid-sixteenth century when explorers, traders, and settlers first made their way to North America. The French, Dutch, Spanish, Swedes, and others came to explore and settle what would become this nation—and to dominate those Native Americans who were here for centuries before the arrival of the first Europeans. It was the English, however, who came in the largest numbers. And it was the English who soon controlled the 13 colonies that stretched for some 1,300 miles along the Atlantic seaboard.

Basic Concepts of Government

The earliest English settlers brought with them knowledge of a political system—of established laws, customs, practices, and institutions—that had been developing in England for centuries.

Some aspects of that governing system had come to England from other times and places. Thus, the concept of the rule of law that influenced English political ideas has roots in the early civilizations of Africa and Asia.[1] More directly, the ancient Romans occupied much of England from A.D. 43 to 410. They left behind a legacy of law, religion, and custom. From that rich political history, the English colonists brought to North America three basic notions that were to loom large in the shaping of government in the United States.

Ordered Government The English colonists saw the need for an orderly regulation of their relationships with one another—that is, a need for government. They created local governments, based on those they had known in England.

---

[1] For example, King Hammurabi of Babylonia developed a system of laws known as Hammurabi's Code around 1750 B.C. Its 282 legal rules covered real estate, trade, and business transactions, as well as criminal law. The code distinguished between major and minor offenses, established the state as the authority to enforce the law, and tried to guarantee social justice. Because of the Babylonians' close contact with the Hebrews, many of their laws became part of Hebrew law and thus later a part of the Old Testament of the Bible—for example, "An eye for an eye." The English were quite familiar with and devoutly attracted to this Biblical concept of the rule of law.

Many of the offices and units of government they established are with us yet today: the offices of sheriff and justice of the peace, the grand jury, counties, and several others.

Limited Government The colonists also brought with them the idea that government is restricted in what it may do, and every individual has certain rights that government cannot take away. This concept is called **limited government,** and it was deeply rooted in English belief and practice by the time the first English ships set sail for America. It had been planted in England centuries earlier, and had been developing there for nearly 400 years before Jamestown was settled in 1607.

Representative Government The early English settlers also carried another important concept across the Atlantic: **representative government.** This idea that government should serve the will of the people had also been developing in England for several centuries. With it had come a growing insistence that the people should have a voice in deciding what government should and should not do. As with the concept of limited government, the idea of "government of, by, and for the people" flourished in America.

Landmark English Documents

These basic notions of ordered government, limited government, and representative government can be traced to several <u>landmark</u> documents in English history.

The Magna Carta A group of determined barons forced King John to sign the **Magna Carta**—the Great Charter—at Runnymede in 1215. Weary of John's military campaigns and heavy taxes, the barons who prompted the Magna Carta were seeking protection against heavy-handed and <u>arbitrary</u> acts by the king.

The Magna Carta included guarantees of such fundamental rights as trial by jury and **due process** of law (protection against the arbitrary taking of life, liberty, or property). Those protections against the absolute power of the king were originally intended for the

privileged classes only. Over time, however, they became the rights of all English people and were incorporated into other documents. The Magna Carta established the critical idea that the monarchy's power was not absolute.

The Petition of Right The Magna Carta was respected by some monarchs and ignored by others for 400 years. Over that period, England's Parliament slowly grew in influence. In 1628, when Charles I asked Parliament for more money in taxes, Parliament refused until he agreed to sign the **Petition of Right.**

The Petition of Right limited the king's power in several ways. Most importantly, it demanded that the king no longer imprison or otherwise punish any person but by the lawful judgment of his peers or by the law of the land. The document also insisted that the king may not impose martial law, or military rule, in times of peace, or require homeowners to shelter the king's troops without their consent. The Petition declared that no man should be

" PRIMARY SOURCE
compelled to make or yield any gift, loan, benevolence, tax, or such like charge, without common consent by act of parliament.

—Petition of Right

The Petition challenged the idea of the divine right of kings, declaring that even a monarch must obey the law of the land.

The English Bill of Rights In 1689, after years of revolt and turmoil, Parliament offered the crown to William and Mary of Orange. The events surrounding their ascent to the throne are known as the Glorious Revolution. To prevent abuse of power by William and Mary and all future monarchs, Parliament, in 1689, drew up a list of provisions to which William and Mary had to agree.

This document, the **English Bill of Rights,** prohibited a standing army in peacetime, except with the consent of Parliament,

✔ **Checkpoint**
What is representative government?

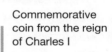

Commemorative coin from the reign of Charles I

landmark
adj. historical, pivotal, highly significant

arbitrary
adj. not restrained or limited in the exercise of power

Foundations of American Rights

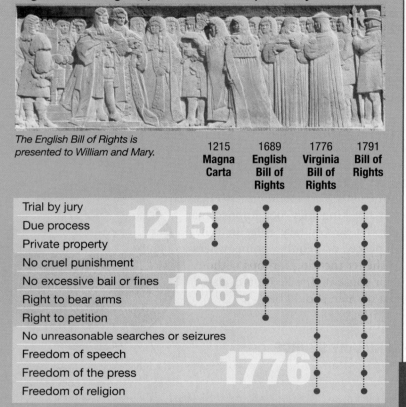

GOVERNMENT ONLINE
Audio Tour
Listen to a guided audio tour of the rights in these documents at PearsonSuccessNet.com

The rights established in these landmark documents were revolutionary in their day and influenced government in many countries. *How might the right to petition, first granted in the English Bill of Rights, prevent abuse of power by a monarch?*

The English Bill of Rights is presented to William and Mary.

	1215 Magna Carta	1689 English Bill of Rights	1776 Virginia Bill of Rights	1791 Bill of Rights
Trial by jury	●	●	●	●
Due process	●			●
Private property	●			
No cruel punishment		●	●	●
No excessive bail or fines		●	●	●
Right to bear arms		●		●
Right to petition		●	●	●
No unreasonable searches or seizures			●	●
Freedom of speech			●	●
Freedom of the press			●	●
Freedom of religion			●	●

✔ **Checkpoint**
What were the limitations set by the English Bill of Rights?

venture
n. an undertaking involving risk

levy
v. to impose, to collect by legal authority

and required that all parliamentary elections be free. In addition, the document declared

" **PRIMARY SOURCE**

that the pretended power of suspending the laws, or the execution of laws, by regal authority, without consent of Parliament is illegal . . .

that **levying** money for or to the use of the Crown . . . without grant of Parliament . . . is illegal . . .

that it is the right of the subjects to petition the king . . . and that prosecutions for such petitioning are illegal . . .

—**English Bill of Rights**

The English Bill of Rights also included such guarantees as the right to a fair trial, as well as freedom from excessive bail and from cruel and unusual punishment.

Our nation has built upon, changed, and added to those ideas and institutions that settlers brought here from England. Still, much in American government and politics today bears the stamp of those early English ideas. Surely, this is not so strange when you recall that the colonial period of American history lasted for some 170 years and that the United States has existed as an independent nation for only a slightly longer period.

The Thirteen Colonies

England's colonies in North America have been described as "13 schools of government." The colonies were the settings in which Americans first began to learn the difficult art of government.[2]

The 13 colonies were established, separately, over a span of some 125 years. During that long period, outlying trading posts and isolated farm settlements developed into organized communities. The first colony, Virginia, was founded with the first permanent English settlement in North America at Jamestown in 1607.[3] Georgia was the last to be formed, with the settlement of Savannah in 1733.

Each of the colonies was born out of a particular set of circumstances. Virginia was originally organized as a commercial <u>venture</u>. Its first colonists were employees of the Virginia Company of London (also called the London Company), a private trading corporation. Massachusetts was first settled by

---

2 The English and other Europeans brought their own notions of government, but that is not to say that they introduced the idea of government to the Americas. Several Native American societies had developed systems of government. Some Native American political organizations were very complex. For example, five Native American tribes in what is now New York State—the Seneca, Cayuga, Oneida, Onondaga, and Mohawk—formed a confederation known as the Iroquois League. The League was originally created to end conflicts among the tribes. It proved so successful as a form of government that it lasted for some 200 years.

3 St. Augustine, Florida, is the oldest continuously populated European settlement in what is now the United States. St. Augustine was founded by Pedro Menéndez de Aviles in 1565 to establish Spanish authority in the region.

people who came to North America in search of greater personal and religious freedom. King George granted Georgia to 21 trustees, who governed the colony.

But the differences among the colonies are of little importance. Of much greater significance is the fact that all of them were shaped by their English origins. The many similarities among all 13 colonies far outweighed their differences.

Each colony was established on the basis of a **charter,** a written grant of authority from the king. This grant gave colonists or companies a grant of land and some governing rights, while the Crown retained a certain amount of power over a colony. Over time, these instruments of government led to the development of three different types of colonies: royal, proprietary, and charter.

Royal Colonies The royal colonies were subject to the direct control of the Crown. On the eve of the American Revolution in 1775, there were eight: New Hampshire, Massachusetts, New York, New Jersey, Virginia, North Carolina, South Carolina, and Georgia.

The Virginia colony did not enjoy the quick success its sponsors had promised. In addition, the colony's government was evolving into one of popular rule. The king disapproved of the local government's methods, as well as their attempt to grow tobacco. So, in 1624, the king revoked the London Company's charter, and Virginia became the first of the royal colonies. Later, as the charters of other colonies were canceled or withdrawn for a variety of reasons, they became royal colonies.

A pattern of government gradually emerged for each of the royal colonies. The king named a governor to serve as the colony's chief executive. A council, also named by the king, served as an advisory body to the royal governor. Later, the governor's council became both the upper house of the colonial legislature and the colony's

highest court. The lower house of a **bicameral** (two-house) legislature was elected by those property owners qualified to vote.[4] It owed much of its influence to the fact that it shared with the governor and his council the power of the purse—the power to tax and spend. The governor, advised by the council, appointed judges for the colony's courts.

The laws passed by the legislature had to be approved by the governor and the Crown. Royal governors often ruled with a stern hand, following instructions from London. Much of the resentment that finally flared into revolution was fanned by their actions.

The Proprietary Colonies By 1775, there were three **proprietary** colonies: Maryland,

---

4 The Virginia legislature held its first meeting in Jamestown on July 30, 1619, and was the first representative body to meet in the North American English colonies. It was made up of burgesses—that is, representatives—elected from each settlement (each borough) in the colony. Virginia called the lower house of its colonial legislature the House of Burgesses; South Carolina, the House of Commons; Massachusetts, the House of Representatives.

The Thirteen Colonies, 1775

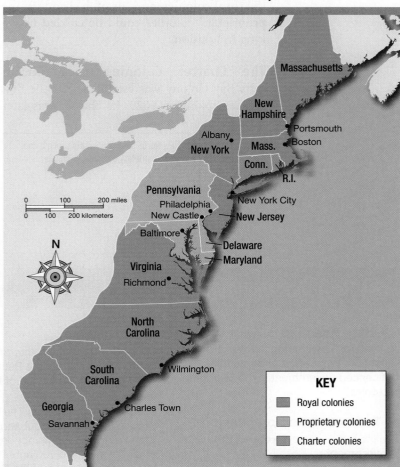

▶▶ Analyzing Maps Despite the differing government systems within the colonies, they were all influenced by their English roots. *How many royal colonies were left at this time? How were royal colonies and charter colonies different?*

haven
n. a place of safety

Pennsylvania, and Delaware. These colonies were organized by a proprietor, a person to whom the king had made a grant of land. By charter, that land could be settled and governed much as the proprietor chose. In 1632, the king granted Maryland to Lord Baltimore, which was intended as a <u>haven</u> for Catholics. In 1681, Pennsylvania was granted to William Penn. In 1682, Penn also acquired Delaware. [5]

The governments of these three colonies were much like those in the royal colonies. The governor, however, was appointed by the proprietor. In Maryland and Delaware, the legislatures were bicameral. In Pennsylvania, the legislature was a **unicameral** body. It consisted of only one house. The Frame of Government, a constitution that William Penn drew up for that colony in 1682, was, for its time, exceedingly democratic. As in the royal colonies, appeals of decisions in the proprietary colonies could be carried to the king in London.

The Charter Colonies The Massachusetts Bay Colony was established as the first charter colony in 1629. Its charter was later

revoked, and Massachusetts became a royal colony in 1691.

Connecticut and Rhode Island were charter colonies founded by religious dissidents from Massachusetts. Connecticut was founded in 1633, and granted a charter in 1662. Rhode Island was founded in 1636, and granted a charter in 1663. Both colonies were largely self-governing.

The governors of Connecticut and Rhode Island were elected each year by the white, male property owners in each colony. Although the king's approval was required before the governor could take office, it was not often asked. Laws made by their bicameral legislatures were not subject to the governor's veto, nor was the Crown's approval needed. Judges in the charter colonies were appointed by the legislature, but appeals could be taken from the colonial courts to the king.

The Connecticut and Rhode Island charters were so liberal for their time that, after independence, they were kept with only minor changes as State constitutions until 1818 and 1843, respectively. In fact, many historians say that if Britain had allowed the other colonies the same freedoms and self-government found in the charter colonies, the Revolution might never have occurred.

---

[5] New York, New Jersey, North Carolina, South Carolina, and Georgia also began as proprietary colonies. Each later became a royal colony.

Essential Questions Journal To continue to build a response to the chapter Essential Question, go to your **Essential Questions Journal.**

SECTION 1 ASSESSMENT

1. **Guiding Question** Use your completed flowchart to answer this question: What ideas and traditions influenced government in the English colonies?

Key Terms and Comprehension

2. Define the concept of **representative government.**

3. Explain why the barons forced King John to sign the **Magna Carta.**

4. **(a)** What is a **bicameral** legislature? **(b)** How was the lower house of the legislature chosen in the royal colonies?

Critical Thinking

5. **Make Comparisons** What principles do the Magna Carta, the Petition of Right, and the English Bill of Rights have in common?

6. **Predict Consequences** The English Crown gave Connecticut and Rhode Island many freedoms not enjoyed by other colonies. Do you agree with the historians who say that the Revolution may have never happened if all colonies enjoyed the same freedoms? Why or why not?

Quick Write

Narrative Writing: Choose a Colony Choose one of the 13 colonies and write questions about its founding, its original government, and how it changed throughout the Revolutionary period. You will later research answers for these questions and write a narrative nonfiction piece. For example, if you choose Connecticut, you might ask: What was Connecticut's reaction to the English government's treatment of the colonies?

ISSUES OF OUR TIME

Adopting a Constitution

▶▶ Track the Issue

The need for a constitution has been debated in different nations and international groups like the European Union (E.U.). Most have adopted constitutions, while a few have not.

1788

The Constitution is ratified after nearly a year of heated debate.

1861

The Confederate States of America ratifies a constitution that closely resembles the Constitution of the United States.

1949

The Federal Republic of Germany adopts a constitution based on the principles of the American Constitution and the British government.

2005

Voters in France and the Netherlands reject the E.U. constitution; a new charter has been proposed.

October 2005

The Iraqi people vote to approve their new constitution during U.S. occupation.

The Iraqi Governing Council held their signing ceremony on March 8, 2004. ▼

▶▶ Perspectives

On July 13, 2003, twenty-five individuals representing the many religious and ethnic groups in Iraq met to write a new constitution. Called the Iraqi Governing Council, its goal was to create a federal and democratic government for its diverse population, much like our Constitutional Convention of 1787. After more than two years of debate, a constitution was written and ratified, but not without opposition. Many people, including members of the Sunni Arab community in Kirkuk, feared a federal system would divide the nation rather than unite it.

"The constitution will not be complete or legitimate unless those who did not participate in the previous elections or those who are not represented in the National Assembly are involved in it. Among these are the Sunni Arabs. If they do not take part in writing the constitution, the constitution will not be at all legitimate. It will be a lame constitution which will be met with objection and rejection by a large sector of the Iraqi society."
—**Sheik Khalaf Salih al-Ulayyan, head of National Dialogue Council**

"Kirkuk's Arabs refuse any constitution that would divide the country by different names, which is at odds with Islam and with the Arabic nation of Iraq."
—**Sheik Abdul Rahman Mished, leader of Kirkuk's Arab Assembly**

▶▶ Connect to Your World

1. **Understand (a)** Why does Sheik Abdul Rahman Mished oppose a federal system? **(b)** Do you agree or disagree with him?
2. **Compare and Contrast (a)** What were the arguments for and against the ratification of the American Constitution? **(b)** What similarities exist between the arguments of the Anti-Federalists and those of the Sunni Arabs?

GOVERNMENT ONLINE
In the News
For updates about the Iraqi constitution, visit
PearsonSuccessNet.com

35

SECTION 2

The Coming of Independence

Guiding Question

What events and ideas led to American independence? Use a flowchart like the one below to record major events that led to American independence.

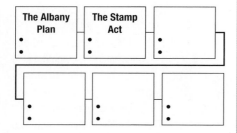

The Albany Plan	The Stamp Act	
•	•	•
•	•	•

•	•	•
•	•	•

Political Dictionary
• confederation
• Albany Plan of Union
• delegate
• popular sovereignty

Objectives

1. Explain how Britain's colonial policies contributed to the growth of self-government in the colonies.
2. Identify the major steps that led to growing feelings of colonial unity.
3. Compare the First and the Second Continental Congresses.
4. Analyze the ideas in the Declaration of Independence.
5. Summarize the common features of the first State constitutions.

Image Above: Benjamin Franklin was a leading member of the Second Continental Congress.

"**W**e must all hang together, or assuredly we shall all hang separately." Benjamin Franklin is said to have spoken these words on July 4, 1776, as he and the other members of the Second Continental Congress approved the Declaration of Independence. Those who heard him may have chuckled. But they also may have felt a shiver, for Franklin's humor carried a deadly serious message.

In this section, you will follow the events that led to the momentous decision to break with Great Britain.[7] You will also consider the new State governments that were established with the coming of independence.

Britain's Colonial Policies

The 13 colonies were separately controlled under the king, largely through the Privy Council and the Board of Trade in London. Parliament took little part in the management of the colonies. Although it did become increasingly interested in matters of trade, it often left administrative matters to the Crown.[8]

Over the century and a half that followed the first settlement at Jamestown, the colonies developed within that framework of royal control. In theory, they were governed from London. But London was more than 3,000 miles away, and it took nearly two months to sail that distance. The colonists became used to a large measure of self-government.

Each colonial legislature began to assume broad lawmaking powers. Many found the power of the purse to be very effective. They often bent a royal governor to their will by not voting the money for his salary until he came to terms with them. As one member of New Jersey's assembly put it: "Let us keep the dogges poore, and we'll make them do as we please."

By the mid-1700s, the relationship between Britain and the colonies had become, in fact if not in form, federal. This meant that the central government

---

7 England became Great Britain by the Act of Union with Scotland in 1707.
8 Much of British political history can be told in terms of the centuries-long struggle for supremacy between the monarch and Parliament. That conflict was largely settled by England's Glorious Revolution of 1688, but it did continue through the American colonial period and into the nineteenth century. However, Parliament paid little attention to the American colonies until very late in the colonial period.

in London was responsible for colonial defense and for foreign affairs. It also provided a uniform system of money and credit and a common market for colonial trade. Beyond that, the colonies were allowed a fairly wide amount of self-rule. Little was taken from them in direct taxes to pay for the central government. The few regulations set by Parliament, mostly about trade, were largely ignored.

This was soon to change. Shortly after George III came to the throne in 1760, Britain began to deal more firmly with its colonies. Restrictive trading acts were expanded and enforced. New taxes were imposed, mostly to support British troops in North America.

Many colonists took strong exception to those policies. They objected to taxes imposed on them from afar. That arrangement, they claimed, was "taxation without representation." They saw little need for the costly presence of British troops on North American soil, since the French had been defeated and their power broken in the French and Indian War (1754–1763). Yet, the colonists still considered themselves British subjects loyal to the Crown.

The king's ministers were poorly informed and stubborn. They pushed ahead with their policies, despite the resentments they stirred in America. Within a few years, the colonists faced a fateful choice: submit or revolt.

Growing Colonial Unity

A decision to revolt was not one to be taken lightly—or alone. The colonies would need to learn to work together if they wanted to succeed. Indeed, long before the 1770s, several attempts had been made to promote cooperation among the colonies.

Early Attempts In 1643, the Massachusetts Bay, Plymouth, New Haven, and Connecticut settlements formed the New England Confederation, a "league of friendship" for defense against Native American tribes. A **confederation** is a joining of several groups for a common purpose. As the danger passed and frictions among the settlements grew, the confederation lost importance and finally dissolved in 1684.

In 1696, William Penn offered an elaborate plan for intercolonial cooperation, largely in trade, defense, and criminal matters. It received little attention and was very quickly forgotten.

The Albany Plan In 1754, the British Board of Trade called a meeting of seven of the northern colonies at Albany. The main purpose of the meeting was to discuss the problems of colonial trade and the danger of attacks by the French and their Native American allies. Here, Benjamin Franklin offered what came to be known as the **Albany Plan of Union.**

In his plan, Franklin proposed the creation of an annual congress of **delegates** (representatives) from each of the 13 colonies. That body would have the power to raise military and naval forces, make war and peace with the Native Americans, regulate trade with them, tax, and collect customs <u>duties</u>.

✔ **Checkpoint**
How did Britain's dealings with the colonies change? When did they change?

<u>duty</u>
n. a tax on imports

▶▶ **Analyzing Political Cartoons** (1) A colonial cartoonist mocks British Lord William on stilts fishing for popularity in the Atlantic after the Stamp Act disaster. (2) A British cartoon depicts the colonists, forcing tea down the throat of a tarred-and-feathered tax collector. Both Britain and the colonies had their own opinions about the taxes. *How does the British cartoon depict the colonists? How does this differ from the colonial cartoon?*

The Road to Independence

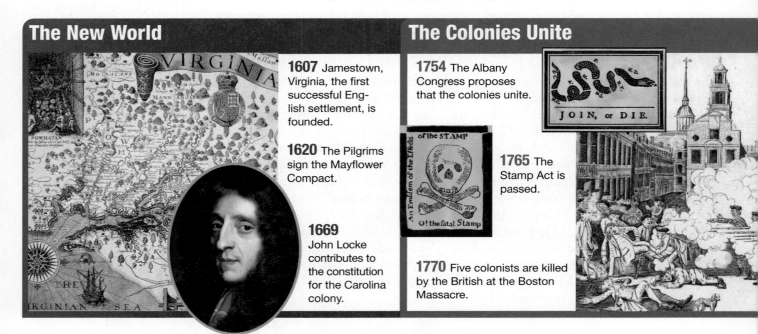

The New World

1607 Jamestown, Virginia, the first successful English settlement, is founded.

1620 The Pilgrims sign the Mayflower Compact.

1669 John Locke contributes to the constitution for the Carolina colony.

The Colonies Unite

1754 The Albany Congress proposes that the colonies unite.

1765 The Stamp Act is passed.

1770 Five colonists are killed by the British at the Boston Massacre.

▶▶ **Interpreting Timelines** English colonists brought with them the ideas of the Enlightenment and limited government. In time, these ideas began to shape the ideals of American government and the actions of the colonists. *How did early events contribute to the signing of the Declaration of Independence?*

repeal
v. to cancel

boycott
n. a refusal to buy or sell certain goods

Franklin's plan was ahead of its time. It was agreed to by the representatives attending the Albany meeting, but it was turned down by the colonies and by the Crown.

The Stamp Act Congress Britain's harsh tax and trade policies fanned resentment in the colonies. Parliament had passed a number of new laws, among them the Stamp Act of 1765. That law required the use of tax stamps on all legal documents, on certain business agreements, and on newspapers.

The new taxes were widely denounced, in part because the rates were perceived as severe, but largely because they amounted to "taxation without representation." In October of 1765, nine colonies—all except Georgia, New Hampshire, North Carolina, and Virginia—sent delegates to a meeting in New York, the Stamp Act Congress. There, they prepared a strong protest, called the Declaration of Rights and Grievances, against the new British policies and sent it to the king. The Stamp Act Congress marked the first

time a significant number of the colonies had joined to oppose the British government.

Parliament <u>repealed</u> the Stamp Act, but frictions still mounted. New laws were passed and new policies made to tie the colonies more closely to London. Colonists showed their resentment and anger by completely evading the laws. Mob violence erupted at several ports, and many colonists supported a <u>boycott</u> of English goods. On March 5, 1770, British troops in Boston fired on a jeering crowd, killing five, in what came to be known as the Boston Massacre.

Organized resistance was carried on through Committees of Correspondence, which had grown out of a group formed by political leader Samuel Adams in Boston in 1772. Those committees soon spread throughout the colonies, providing a network for cooperation and the exchange of information among the patriots.

Protests multiplied. The Boston Tea Party took place on December 16, 1773. A group of men, disguised as Native Americans, boarded

War Begins

Independence

1773 The Tea Act is passed. Colonists respond with the Boston Tea Party.

1775 The battles of Lexington and Concord spark the Revolution.

1776 The Declaration of Independence is signed.

three tea ships in Boston Harbor. They broke open the chests and dumped the ship's cargo into the sea to protest British control of the tea trade.

First Continental Congress

In the spring of 1774, Parliament passed yet another set of laws, this time to punish the colonists for the troubles in Boston and elsewhere. These new laws, denounced in America as the Intolerable Acts, prompted widespread calls for a meeting of the colonies.

Delegates from every colony except Georgia met in Philadelphia on September 5, 1774. Many of the <u>ablest</u> men of the day were there: Samuel Adams and John Adams of Massachusetts; Roger Sherman of Connecticut; Stephen Hopkins of Rhode Island; John Dickinson and Joseph Galloway of Pennsylvania; John Jay and Philip Livingston of New York; George Washington, Richard Henry Lee, and Patrick Henry of Virginia; and John Rutledge of South Carolina.

For nearly two months, the members of that First Continental Congress discussed the worsening situation and debated plans for action. They sent a Declaration of Rights,

protesting Britain's colonial policies, to King George III. The delegates urged the colonies to refuse all trade with England until the hated taxes and trade regulations were repealed. The delegates also called for the creation of local committees to enforce that boycott.

The meeting adjourned on October 26, 1774, with a call for a second congress to be convened the following May. Over the next several months, all 13 colonial legislatures gave their support to the actions of the First Continental Congress.

Second Continental Congress

During the fall and winter of 1774–1775, the British government continued to refuse to compromise, let alone reverse, its colonial policies. It reacted to the Declaration of Rights as it had to other expressions of colonial discontent—with even stricter and more repressive measures.

The Second Continental Congress met in Philadelphia on May 10, 1775. By then, the Revolution had begun. The "shot heard 'round the world" had been fired. The battles of Lexington and Concord had been fought three weeks earlier, on April 19.

✔ **Checkpoint**
What did the First Continental Congress accomplish?

ablest
adj. the most talented, capable, competent, skillful

The Delegates Each of the 13 colonies sent representatives to the Congress. Most of those who had attended the First Continental Congress were again present. Most notable among the newcomers were Benjamin Franklin of Pennsylvania and John Hancock of Massachusetts.

Hancock was chosen president of the Congress.[9] Almost at once, a continental army was created, and George Washington was appointed its commander-in-chief. Thomas Jefferson then took Washington's place in the Virginia delegation.

Our First National Government The Second Continental Congress became, by force of circumstance, the nation's first national government. However, it rested on no constitutional base. It was condemned by the British as an unlawful assembly and a den of traitors. But it was supported by the force of public opinion and practical necessity.

The Second Continental Congress served as the first government of the United States for five fateful years, from the formal adoption of the Declaration of Independence in July 1776 until the Articles of Confederation went into effect on March 1, 1781. During that time, the Second Continental Congress fought a war, raised armies and a navy, borrowed funds, bought supplies, created a money system, made treaties with foreign powers, and did other things that any government would have had to do in those circumstances.

The unicameral Congress exercised both legislative and executive powers. In legislative matters, each colony—later, State—had one vote. Executive functions were handled by committees of delegates.

The Declaration of Independence

Slightly more than a year after the Revolution began, Richard Henry Lee of Virginia proposed to the Congress:

---

9 Peyton Randolph, who had also served as president of the First Continental Congress, was originally chosen to the office. He resigned on May 24, however, because the Virginia House of Burgesses, of which he was the speaker, had been called into session. Hancock was then elected to succeed him.

PRIMARY SOURCE

" Resolved, That these United Colonies are, and of right ought to be, free and independent States, that they are absolved from all allegiance to the British Crown, and that all political connection between them and the State of Great Britain is, and ought to be, totally dissolved.

—Resolution of June 7, 1776

Congress named a committee of five—Benjamin Franklin, John Adams, Roger Sherman, Robert Livingston, and Thomas Jefferson—to prepare a proclamation of independence. Their momentous product, the Declaration of Independence, was very largely the work of Jefferson.

On July 2, the final break came. The delegates agreed to Lee's resolution—but only after spirited debate, for many of the delegates had serious doubts about the wisdom of a complete separation from England. Two days later, on July 4, 1776, they adopted the Declaration of Independence, proclaiming the existence of the new nation.

At its heart, the Declaration proclaims:

PRIMARY SOURCE

" We hold these truths to be self-evident, that all men are created equal, that they are endowed by their Creator with certain unalienable Rights, that among these are Life, Liberty and the pursuit of Happiness. That to secure these rights, Governments are instituted among Men, deriving their just powers from the consent of the governed; That whenever any Form of Government becomes destructive of these ends it is the Right of the People to alter or to abolish it, and to institute new Government, laying its foundations on such principles and organizing its powers in such form, as to them shall seem most likely to effect their Safety and Happiness.

—The Unanimous Declaration of the Thirteen United States of America

The members of the Second Continental Congress signed the Declaration of Independence on July 4, 1776. *By signing this document, what were these men risking? Why were they willing to sign it?*

> "And for the support of this Declaration, with a firm reliance on the protection of Divine Providence, we mutually pledge to each other, our lives, our Fortunes, and our sacred Honor.
> — Declaration of Independence

No political system had ever been founded on the notion that the people should rule instead of being ruled, nor on the idea that every person is important as an individual, "created equal," and endowed with "certain unalienable rights." The Declaration was also groundbreaking because it was founded on the concept of "the consent of the governed," not divine right or tradition as the basis for the exercise of power.

With the adoption of the Declaration, the United States was born. The 13 colonies became free and independent States.

The First State Constitutions

In January 1776, New Hampshire adopted a constitution to replace its royal charter. Less than three months later, South Carolina followed suit. Then, on May 10, nearly two months before the adoption of the Declaration of Independence, the Congress urged each of the colonies to adopt "such governments as shall, in the opinion of the representatives of the people, best conduce to the happiness and safety of their constituents."

Drafting State Constitutions In 1776 and 1777, most of the States adopted written

constitutions—bodies of fundamental laws setting out the principles, structures, and processes of their governments. Assemblies or conventions were commonly used to draft and then adopt these new documents.

Massachusetts set a lasting example in the constitution-making process. There, a popularly elected convention submitted its work to the voters for ratification. The Massachusetts constitution of 1780 is the oldest of the present-day State constitutions, and the oldest written constitution in force in the world today.[10]

Common Features The first State constitutions differed, sometimes widely, in their details. Yet they were on the whole more alike than not. The most common features were the principles of **popular sovereignty** (a government that exists only with the consent of the governed), limited government, civil rights and liberties, separation of powers, and checks and balances.

Popular Sovereignty. Everywhere, the people were recognized as the only source of

---

[10] From independence until that constitution became effective in 1780, Massachusetts relied on its colonial charter, in force prior to 1691, as its fundamental law.

Common Features of State Constitutions

▶ **Popular Sovereignty**　　▶ **Separation of Powers**
▶ **Limited Government**　　　▶ **Checks and Balances**
▶ **Civil Rights and Liberties**

Once the seat of Massachusetts government, the Old State House in Boston has endured just as the State constitution has. Shown here: the Old State House as seen in 1870 and present day.

✓ **Checkpoint**
How did the State constitutions separate governmental power?

unalienable
adj. cannot be surrendered or transferred, sacred

governmental authority. In the new United States, government could be conducted only with the consent of the governed.

Limited Government. The new State governments could exercise only those powers granted to them by the people through the constitution. The powers that were given were hedged with many restrictions.

Civil Rights and Liberties. In every State, it was made clear that the sovereign people held certain rights that government must at all times respect. Seven of the new documents began with a bill of rights, setting out the "unalienable rights" held by the people.

Separation of Powers, Checks and Balances. The powers granted to the new State governments were divided among three distinct branches: executive, legislative, and judicial. Each branch was given powers with which to check, or restrain the actions of, the other branches of the government.

Beyond those basics, the new State constitutions were rather brief documents. They were, for the most part, declarations of principle and statements of limitation on governmental power. Memories of the royal governors were fresh, and State governors were given little real power. Most of the authority that was granted to government was placed in the legislature. Elective terms of office were made purposely short, seldom more than one or two years. The right to vote was limited to those adult white males who could meet rigid qualifications, including property ownership.

We shall come back to the State constitutions later, in Chapter 24. For now, note this very important point: The earliest of those documents were, within a very few years, to have a marked impact on the drafting of the Constitution of the United States.

Essential Questions Journal To continue to build a response to the chapter Essential Question, go to your **Essential Questions Journal.**

SECTION 2 ASSESSMENT

1. **Guiding Question** Use your completed concept web to answer this question: What events and ideas led to American independence?

Key Terms and Comprehension

2. **(a)** What is a **confederation?**
   (b) What was the purpose of the New England Confederation?
3. In your own words, explain what "taxation without representation" means.

Critical Thinking

4. **Summarize** What major events led to the calling of the First Continental Congress?
5. **Make Comparisons (a)** Compare the goals of the First and Second Continental Congresses.
   (b) What challenges did each meeting face?

Quick Write

Narrative Writing: Research Your Colony Using the questions you drafted in Section 1, conduct preliminary research to find the answers. Add any additional questions that you may have after reading Section 2. Browse the Internet or other sources and take notes on what you find. Use the information to begin a story about your colony's involvement in the shaping of the American government.

Thomas Jefferson was the primary author of the Declaration of Independence. *What principles from the three British documents did he incorporate in the Declaration?*

The Declaration of Independence

The Declaration of Independence is composed of four parts: a Preamble, a Declaration of Natural Rights, a List of Grievances, and a Resolution of Independence.

IN CONGRESS, JULY 4, 1776

The Unanimous Declaration of the Thirteen United States of America

► **Preamble:** The Preamble explains why the Declaration was written.

► **Declaration of Natural Rights:** This paragraph lists the basic rights to which all people are entitled. It describes those rights as being unalienable. They cannot be taken away. The government gets its power from the people. When the government usurps (takes) power from the people and does not protect their rights, the people have the right and responsibility to throw off that government and to create a new one.

► **List of Grievances:** This section lists the colonists' 27 complaints against the British Crown. In essence, King George III had chosen to rule as a tyrant rather than govern with the people's well-being in mind.

► The people refuse to give up their right to representation—a right the colonists considered vital.

► The king had dissolved representative houses and refused to allow the election of new legislators. Without legislators, the colonists were without protection from foreign invasion or convulsions (riots) from within.

► **When in the Course of human events** it becomes necessary for one people to dissolve the political bands which have connected them with another, and to assume among the powers of the earth, the separate and equal station to which the Laws of nature and of nature's God entitle them, a decent respect to the opinions of mankind requires that they should declare the causes which impel them to the separation.

► We hold these truths to be self-evident, that all men are created equal, that they are endowed by their Creator with certain unalienable Rights, that among these are Life, Liberty and the Pursuit of Happiness. That to secure these rights, Governments are instituted among Men, deriving their just powers from the consent of the governed; That whenever any Form of Government becomes destructive of these ends it is the Right of the People to alter or to abolish it, and to institute new Government, laying its foundation on such principles and organizing its powers in such form, as to them shall seem most likely to effect their Safety and Happiness. Prudence, indeed, will dictate that Governments long established should not be changed for light and transient causes; and accordingly all experience hath shown, that mankind are more disposed to suffer, while evils are sufferable, than to right themselves by abolishing the forms to which they are accustomed. But when a long train of abuses and usurpations, pursuing invariably the same Object evinces a design to reduce them under absolute Despotism, it is their right, it is their duty, to throw off such Government, and to provide new Guards for their future security.

► Such has been the patient sufferance of these Colonies; and such is now the necessity which constrains them to alter their former Systems of Government. The history of the present King of Great Britain is a history of repeated injuries and usurpations, all having in direct object the establishment of an absolute Tyranny over these States. To prove this, let Facts be submitted to a candid world.

He has refused his Assent to Laws, the most wholesome and necessary for the public good.

He has forbidden his Governors to pass Laws of immediate and pressing importance, unless suspended in their operation till his Assent should be obtained; and when so suspended, he has utterly neglected to attend to them.

He has refused to pass other Laws for the accommodation of large districts of people, unless those people would relinquish the right of Representation in the Legislature, a right inestimable to them and formidable to tyrants only.

He has called together legislative bodies at places unusual, uncomfortable, and distant from the depository of their Public Records, for the sole purpose of fatiguing them into compliance with his measures.

► He has dissolved Representative Houses repeatedly, for opposing with manly firmness his invasions on the rights of the people.

He has refused for a long time, after such dissolutions, to cause others to be elected; whereby the Legislative powers, incapable of Annihilation, have returned to the People at large for their exercise; the State remaining in the mean time exposed to all the dangers of invasions from without, and convulsions within.

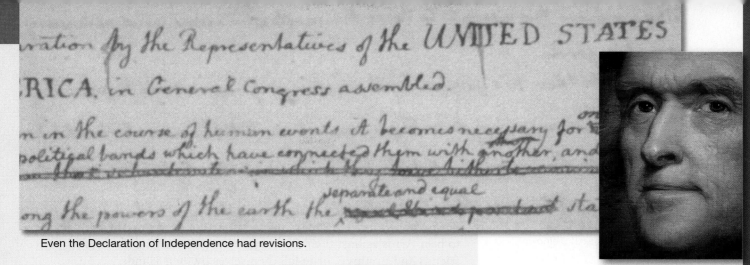

Even the Declaration of Independence had revisions.

Thomas Jefferson

▶ He has endeavored to prevent the population of these States; for that purpose obstructing the Laws for Naturalization of Foreigners; refusing to pass others to encourage their migration hither, and raising the conditions of new Appropriations of Lands.

He has obstructed the Administration of Justice, by refusing his Assent to Laws for establishing Judiciary powers.

▶ He has made Judges dependent on his Will alone for the tenure of their offices, and the amount and payment of their salaries.

He has erected a multitude of New Offices, and sent hither swarms of Officers to harass our people and eat out their substance.

He has kept among us in time of peace, Standing Armies, without the Consent of our legislatures.

He has affected to render the Military independent of, and superior to, the Civil Power.

He has combined with others to subject us to a jurisdiction foreign to our constitutions, and unacknowledged by our laws; giving his Assent to their Acts of pretended Legislation:

▶ For quartering large bodies of armed troops among us;

For protecting them, by a mock Trial, from punishment for any Murders which they should commit on the Inhabitants of these States;

For cutting off our Trade with all parts of the world;

For imposing Taxes on us without our Consent;

For depriving us, in many cases, of the benefits of Trial by Jury;

For transporting us beyond Seas to be tried for pretended offenses;

▶ For abolishing the free System of English Laws in a neighboring Province, establishing therein an Arbitrary government, and enlarging its Boundaries so as to render it at once an example and fit instrument for introducing the same absolute rule into these Colonies;

For taking away our Charters, abolishing our most valuable Laws, and altering fundamentally the Forms of our Governments;

For suspending our own Legislatures, and declaring themselves invested with Power to legislate for us in all cases whatsoever.

▶ The king had tried to slow population growth by preventing individuals from other countries from becoming citizens of the colonies.

▶ This grievance was later addressed in Article III, Section 1 of the Constitution, which states that federal judges shall hold office "during good Behaviour."

▶ The king forced colonists to lodge British soldiers in their homes. The Bill of Rights addressed this in the 3rd Amendment, which states that no soldier can be lodged in "any house" without the consent of the owner.

▶ Here, the Declaration refers to Canada. The colonists feared that they, too, would fall under absolute rule. Britain extended the border of Quebec to the Ohio Valley, cutting it off to colonial settlers.

He has abdicated Government here, by declaring us out of his Protection, and waging War against us.

He has plundered our seas, ravaged our Coasts, burned our towns, and destroyed the lives of our people.

He is at this time transporting large Armies of foreign mercenaries to complete the works of death, desolation and tyranny, already begun with circumstances of Cruelty and perfidy scarcely paralleled in the most barbarous ages, and totally unworthy the Head of a civilized nation.

▶ The king had forced captive sailors to fight against their own people, or die.

He has constrained our fellow Citizens taken Captive on the high Seas to bear Arms against their Country, to become the executioners of their friends and Brethren, or to fall themselves by their Hands.

He has excited domestic insurrections amongst us, and has endeavored to bring on the inhabitants of our frontiers the merciless Indian Savages whose known rule of warfare, is an undistinguished destruction of all ages, sexes, and conditions.

▶ The colonists tried repeatedly to petition the king to correct his wrongs. However, their protests were met by harsh laws. Therefore, he does not deserve to rule the colonies.

In every stage of these Oppressions We have Petitioned for Redress in the most humble terms. Our repeated Petitions have been answered only by repeated injury. A Prince, whose character is thus marked by every act which may define a Tyrant, is unfit to be the ruler of a free People.

▶ The colonists still felt a common identity with citizens of Britain. However, their fellow British subjects ignored their appeals for help.

Nor have We been wanting in attentions to our British brethren. We have warned them from time to time of attempts by their legislature to extend an unwarrantable jurisdiction over us. We have reminded them of the circumstances of our emigration and settlement here. We have appealed to their native justice and magnanimity, and we have conjured them by the ties of our common kindred to disavow these usurpations, which, would inevitably interrupt our connections and correspondence. They too have been deaf to the voice of justice and of consanguinity. We must, therefore, acquiesce in the necessity, which denounces our Separation, and hold them, as we hold the rest of mankind, Enemies in War, in Peace Friends.

▶ **The Resolution of Independence:** The colonies declare themselves free and independent States, by authority of the people of the States and of God. Therefore, the States have the power to declare war, make peace, create alliances and trade with foreign powers, and do all other acts afforded to independent States.

We, therefore, the Representatives of the United States of America, in General Congress, Assembled, appealing to the Supreme Judge of the world for the rectitude of our intentions, do, in the Name, and by the Authority of the good People of these Colonies, solemnly publish and declare, That these United Colonies are, and of right ought to be Free and Independent States; that they are Absolved from all Allegiance to the British Crown, and that all political connection between them and the State of Great Britain, is and ought to be totally dissolved, and that as Free and Independent States, they have full Power to levy War, conclude Peace, contract Alliances, establish Commerce, and to do all other Acts and Things which Independent States may of right do. And for the support of this Declaration, with a firm reliance on the protection of Divine Providence, we mutually pledge to each other our Lives, our Fortunes, and our sacred Honor.

New Hampshire:
Josiah Bartlett
William Whipple
Mathew Thornton

Massachusetts Bay:
John Hancock
Samuel Adams
John Adams
Robert Treat Paine
Elbridge Gerry

Rhode Island:
Stephan Hopkins
William Ellery

Connecticut:
Roger Sherman
Samuel Huntington
William Williams
Oliver Wolcott

New York:
William Floyd
Philip Livingston
Francis Lewis
Lewis Morris

New Jersey:
Richard Stockton
John Witherspoon
Francis Hopkinson
John Hart
Abraham Clark

Delaware:
Caesar Rodney
George Read
Thomas M'Kean

Maryland:
Samuel Chase
William Paca
Thomas Stone
Charles Carroll
of Carrollton

Virginia:
George Wythe
Richard Henry Lee
Thomas Jefferson
Benjamin Harrison
Thomas Nelson, Jr.
Francis Lightfoot Lee
Carter Braxton

Pennsylvania:
Robert Morris
Benjamin Rush
Benjamin Franklin
John Morton
George Clymer
James Smith
George Taylor
James Wilson
George Ross

North Carolina:
William Hooper
Joseph Hewes
John Penn

South Carolina:
Edward Rutledge
Thomas Heyward, Jr.
Thomas Lynch, Jr.
Arthur Middleton

Georgia:
Button Gwinnett
Lyman Hall
George Walton

As president of the Second Continental Congress, John Hancock was the first to sign the Declaration of Independence, approving it with his now-famous signature.

Reviewing the Declaration

Vocabulary
Choose ten unfamiliar words in the Declaration. Look them up in the dictionary. Then, on a piece of paper, copy the sentence in the Declaration in which each unfamiliar word is used. After the sentence, write the definition of the unfamiliar word.

Comprehension
1. Name the three "unalienable rights" listed in the Declaration.
2. From what source do governments derive their "just powers"?
3. According to the Declaration, what powers belong to the United States as "Free and Independent States"?

Critical Thinking
4. **Recognize Cause and Effect** Why do you think the colonists were unhappy with the fact that their judges' tenure and salaries were dependent on the king?
5. **Identifying Assumptions** Do you think that the words "all men are created equal" were intended to apply to all those who lived in the colonies? Which groups were most likely not included?
6. **Drawing Conclusions** What evidence is there that the colonists had already and unsuccessfully voiced their concerns to the king?

SECTION 3

The Critical Period

Guiding Question

What weaknesses in the Articles of Confederation made a lasting government impossible? Use an outline like the one below to take notes on the reasons why the Articles of Confederation failed.

I. The Articles of Confederation
  A. Weaknesses
    1. _____
    2. _____
  B. Effects of the Weaknesses
    1. _____
    2. _____

Political Dictionary

• Articles of Confederation
• ratification

Objectives

1. Describe the structure of the government set up under the Articles of Confederation.
2. Explain why the weaknesses of the Articles led to a critical period for the country in the 1780s.
3. Describe how a growing need for a stronger national government led to plans for a Constitutional Convention.

Image Above: Daniel Shays' rebellion made the need for a stronger government clear.

The First and Second Continental Congresses rested on no legal base. They were called in haste to meet an emergency, and they were intended to be temporary. Something more regular and permanent was clearly needed. In this section, you will look at the first attempt to establish a lasting government for the new nation.

The Articles of Confederation

Richard Henry Lee's resolution that led to the Declaration of Independence also called on the Second Continental Congress to propose "a plan of confederation" to the States. Off and on, for 17 months, Congress debated the problem of uniting the former colonies. Finally, on November 15, 1777, the **Articles of Confederation** were approved.

The Articles of Confederation established "a firm league of friendship" among the States. Each State kept "its sovereignty, freedom, and independence, and every Power, <u>Jurisdiction</u>, and right . . . not . . . expressly delegated to the United States, in Congress assembled." The States came together "for their common defense, the security of their Liberties, and their mutual and general welfare. . . ." In effect, the Articles created a structure that more closely resembled an alliance of independent states than a government "of the people."

The Articles did not go into effect immediately, however. The **ratification** (formal approval) of each of the 13 States was needed first. Eleven States approved the document within a year. Delaware added its approval in February 1779. Maryland did not ratify until March 1, 1781. The Second Continental Congress declared the Articles effective on that date.

Governmental Structure The government set up by the Articles was quite simple. A Congress was the sole body created. It was unicameral, made up of delegates chosen yearly by the States in whatever way their legislatures might direct. Each State had only one vote in the Congress, no matter its population or wealth.

The Articles established no executive or judicial branch. These functions were to be handled by committees of the Congress. Each year the Congress would choose one of its members as its president. That person would be its presiding officer, but not the president of the United States. Civil officers such as postmasters were to be appointed by the Congress.

Powers of Congress Several important powers were given to the Congress. It could make war and peace, send and receive ambassadors, make treaties, borrow money, set up a money system, establish post offices, build a navy, raise an army by asking the States for troops, fix uniform standards of weights and measures, and settle disputes among the States.

State Obligations By agreeing to the Articles, the States pledged to obey the Articles and acts of the Congress. They promised to provide the funds and troops requested by Congress; treat citizens of other States fairly and equally within their own borders; and give full faith and credit to the public acts, records, and judicial proceedings of every other State. In addition, the States agreed to surrender fugitives from justice to one another, submit their disputes to Congress for settlement, and allow open travel and trade among the States.

Beyond those few obligations, the States retained those powers not explicitly given to the Congress. They, not the Congress, were primarily responsible for protecting life and property, and for promoting "the safety and happiness of the people."

Weaknesses The powers of the Congress appear, at first glance, to have been considerable. Several important powers were missing, however. Their omission, together with other weaknesses, soon proved the Articles inadequate for the needs of the time.

The Congress did not have the power to tax. It could raise money only by borrowing and by asking the States for funds. Borrowing was, at best, a poor source. The Second Continental Congress had borrowed heavily to support the Revolution, and many of those debts had not been paid. And, while the Articles remained in force, not one State came close to meeting the financial requests made by the Congress.

Nor did the Congress have the power to regulate trade between the States. This lack of a central mechanism to regulate the young

✔ **Checkpoint**
What powers did Congress hold under the Articles of Confederation?

jurisdiction
n. legal authority

presiding officer
n. the chair of a meeting

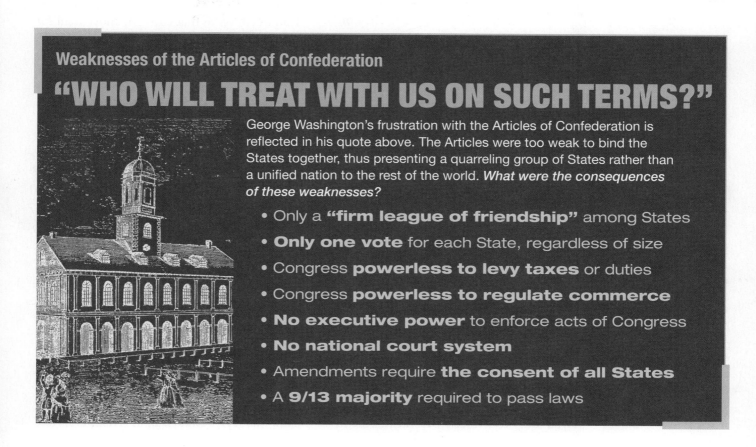

Weaknesses of the Articles of Confederation

"WHO WILL TREAT WITH US ON SUCH TERMS?"

George Washington's frustration with the Articles of Confederation is reflected in his quote above. The Articles were too weak to bind the States together, thus presenting a quarreling group of States rather than a unified nation to the rest of the world. *What were the consequences of these weaknesses?*

- Only a **"firm league of friendship"** among States
- **Only one vote** for each State, regardless of size
- Congress **powerless to levy taxes** or duties
- Congress **powerless to regulate commerce**
- **No executive power** to enforce acts of Congress
- **No national court system**
- Amendments require **the consent of all States**
- A **9/13 majority** required to pass laws

nation's growing commerce was one of the major factors that soon led to the adoption of the Constitution.

The Congress was further limited by a lack of power to make the States obey the Articles of Confederation or the laws it made. Congress could exercise the powers it did have only with the consent of 9 of the 13 State delegations. Finally, the Articles themselves could be changed only with the consent of all 13 of the State legislatures.

arsenal
n. a store of arms or military equipment

The Critical Period, the 1780s

The long Revolutionary War finally ended on October 19, 1781. America's victory was confirmed by the signing of the Treaty of Paris in 1783. Peace, however, brought the new nation's economic and political weaknesses into sharp focus. Problems, made even more difficult by the weaknesses of the Articles, soon surfaced.

With a central government unable to act, the States bickered among themselves. They grew increasingly jealous and suspicious of one another. They often refused to support the new central government, financially and in almost every other way. Several of them made agreements with foreign governments without the approval of the Congress, even though that was forbidden by the Articles. Most organized their own military forces. George Washington complained, "…we are one nation today and 13 tomorrow. Who will treat with us on such terms?"

The States taxed one another's goods and even banned some trade. They printed their own money, often with little backing. Economic chaos spread throughout the colonies as prices soared and sound credit vanished. Debts, public and private, went unpaid. Violence broke out in a number of places.

The most spectacular of these events played out in western Massachusetts in a

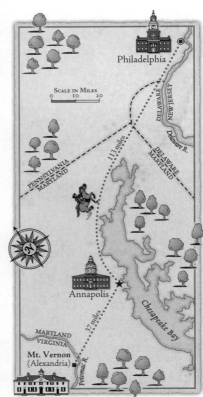

Delegates met first at Alexandria. They met again at Annapolis. The First and Second Continental Congresses met at Philadelphia.

series of incidents that came to be known as Shays' Rebellion. As economic conditions worsened there, property holders, many of them small farmers, began to lose their land and possessions for lack of payment on taxes and other debts. In the fall of 1786, Daniel Shays, who had served as an officer in the War for Independence, led an armed uprising that forced several State judges to close their courts. Early the next year, Shays mounted an unsuccessful attack on the federal <u>arsenal</u> at Springfield. State forces finally moved to quiet the rebellion and Shays fled to Vermont. In response to the violence, the Massachusetts legislature eventually passed laws to ease the burden of debtors.

A Need for Stronger Government

The Articles had created a government unable to deal with the nation's troubles. Inevitably, demand grew for a stronger, more effective national government. Those who were most threatened by economic and political instability—large property owners, merchants, traders, and other creditors—soon took the lead in efforts to that end. The movement for change began to take concrete form in 1785.

Mount Vernon Maryland and Virginia, plagued by bitter trade disputes, took the first step in the movement for change. Ignoring the Congress, the two States agreed to a conference to resolve conflicts over commerce and navigation on the Potomac River and Chesapeake Bay. Representatives from the two States met at Alexandria, Virginia, in March 1785. At George Washington's invitation, they moved their sessions to his home at nearby Mount Vernon.

Their negotiations proved so successful that on January 21, 1786, the Virginia General Assembly called for "a joint meeting of [all of] the States to consider and recommend a federal plan for regulating commerce."

Annapolis That joint meeting opened at Annapolis, Maryland, on September 11, 1786. Turnout was poor, with representatives from only five of the 13 States attending: New York, New Jersey, Pennsylvania, Delaware, and

Virginia. Although New Hampshire, Massachusetts, Rhode Island, and North Carolina had appointed delegates, none attended the Annapolis meeting. Disappointed but still hopeful, Alexander Hamilton, a delegate from New York, and Virginia's James Madison persuaded the gathering to call for yet another meeting of the States.

By mid-February of 1787, seven of the States had named delegates to the Philadelphia meeting: Delaware, Georgia, New Hampshire, New Jersey, North Carolina, Pennsylvania, and Virginia. On February 21, the Congress, which had been hesitating, also called upon the States to send delegates to Philadelphia

Primary Source

❝ . . . for the sole and express purpose of revising the Articles of Confederation and reporting to Congress and the several legislatures such alterations and provisions therein as shall when agreed to in Congress and confirmed by the States render the [Articles] adequate to the exigencies of Government and the preservation of the Union.

—The United States in Congress Assembled, February 21, 1787

That Philadelphia meeting became the Constitutional Convention. What began as an assembly to revise the existing Articles

❝ . . . at Philadelphia on the second Monday in May next, to take into consideration the situation of the United States, to devise such further provisions as shall appear to them necessary to render the constitution of the Federal Government adequate to the exigencies of the Union.
— Call of the Annapolis Convention

Independence Hall served as the meeting place for both the Second Continental Congress and the Constitutional Convention. *What significance might this building have had for the Constitutional Convention?*

of Confederation soon evolved into a meeting dedicated to a different purpose—the creation of an entirely new kind of government for the United States of America. This government would derive its power from a constitution.

Essential Questions Journal To continue to build a response to the chapter Essential Question, go to your **Essential Questions Journal.**

SECTION 3 ASSESSMENT

1. **Guiding Question** Use your completed outline to answer this question: What weaknesses in the Articles of Confederation made a lasting government impossible?

Key Terms and Comprehension

2. What was the goal of the **Articles of Confederation?**

3. **(a)** Under the Articles of Confederation, was Congress unicameral or bicameral? **(b)** How were representatives chosen to serve in Congress?

Critical Thinking

4. **Synthesize Information** When the States ratified the Articles, they agreed to obey the Articles and all acts of Congress. **(a)** Did the States honor their agreement? **(b)** How do you know?

5. **Identify Point of View** Washington was referring to foreign affairs when he complained, "We are one nation today and 13 tomorrow. Who will treat with us on such terms?" **(a)** What did Washington fear would happen? **(b)** Do you agree with his point of view? Why or why not?

Quick Write

Narrative Writing: Details and Anecdotes When writing narrative nonfiction, it is important to have details and anecdotes to keep your reader's interest. Choose some important dates or events that you wish to highlight. Research them further to find personal accounts or interesting examples from that time.

SECTION 4

Creating the
Constitution

Guiding Question

What compromises enabled the Framers to create the Constitution? Use a flowchart like the one below to record details about the Framers' compromises.

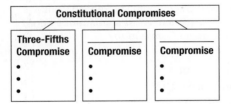

Constitutional Compromises

Three-Fifths Compromise	Compromise	Compromise
•	•	•
•	•	•
•	•	•

Political Dictionary

- Framers
- Virginia Plan
- New Jersey Plan
- Connecticut Compromise
- Three-Fifths Compromise
- Commerce and Slave Trade Compromise

Objectives

1. Identify the Framers of the Constitution and discuss how they organized the Philadelphia Convention.
2. Compare and contrast the Virginia Plan and the New Jersey Plan.
3. Summarize the convention's major compromises and the effects of those decisions.
4. Describe the delegates' reactions to the Constitution.

Image Above: George Washington was president of the Constitutional Convention.

Picture the scene. It is hot—sweltering, in fact. Yet all of the windows of the State House are closed and shuttered to discourage eavesdroppers. Outside, soldiers keep curious onlookers and others at a distance. Inside, the atmosphere is frequently tense as 50 or so men exchange sometimes heated views. Indeed, some who are there become so upset that they threaten to leave the hall, and a few actually do so.

This was often the scene at the Philadelphia meeting, which finally began on May 25, 1787.[11] Over the long summer months, until mid-September, the Framers of what was to become the Constitution worked to build a new government that could meet the needs of the nation. In this section, you will consider that meeting and its outcome.

The Framers

Twelve of the 13 States, all but Rhode Island, sent delegates to Philadelphia.[12] In total, 74 delegates were chosen by the legislatures in those 12 states. For a number of reasons, however, only 55 of them actually attended the convention.

Of that 55, this much can be said: Never, before or since, has so remarkable a group been brought together in this country. Thomas Jefferson, who was not among them, later called the delegates "an assembly of demi-gods."

The delegates who attended the Philadelphia Convention, known as the **Framers** of the Constitution, included many outstanding individuals. These were men of wide knowledge and public experience. Many of them had fought in the Revolution; 46 had been members of the Continental Congress or the Congress of the Confederation, or both. Eight had served in constitutional conventions in their own States, and seven had been State governors. Eight had signed the Declaration of Independence. Thirty-four of the delegates had attended college in a day when there were but a few colleges in the land. Two were to become

---

11 Not enough States were represented on the date Congress had set, May 14, to begin the meeting. The delegates who were present met and adjourned each day until the 25th, when a quorum (a majority) of the States was on hand.

12 The Rhode Island legislature was controlled by the soft-money forces, mostly debtors and small farmers, who were helped by inflation and so were against a stronger central government. The New Hampshire delegation, delayed mostly by lack of funds, did not reach Philadelphia until late July.

Presidents of the United States, and one a Vice President. Nineteen later served in the Senate and thirteen in the House of Representatives.

Is it any wonder that the product of such a gathering was described by the English statesman William E. Gladstone, nearly a century later, as "the most wonderful work ever struck off at a given time by the brain and purpose of man"?

Remarkably, the average age of the delegates was only 42, and most of the leaders were in their 30s—James Madison was 36, Gouverneur Morris 35, Edmund Randolph 34, and Alexander Hamilton, 30. At 81, Benjamin Franklin was the oldest. His health was failing, however, and he was not able to attend many of the meetings. George Washington, at 55, was one of the few older members who played a key role at the Convention. Jonathan Dayton of New Jersey was, at 26, the youngest delegate.

By and large, the Framers of the Constitution were of a new generation in American politics. Several of the leaders of the Revolutionary period were not in Philadelphia. Patrick Henry said he "smelt a rat" and refused to attend. Samuel Adams, John Hancock, and Richard Henry Lee were not selected as delegates by their States. Thomas Paine was in Paris. So was Thomas Jefferson, as American minister to France. John Adams was the <u>envoy</u> to England and Holland at the time.

Organization and Procedure

The Framers met in the State House (now Independence Hall), probably in the same room in which the Declaration of Independence had been signed 11 years earlier.

They organized immediately on May 25, unanimously electing George Washington president of the convention. Then, and at the second session on Monday, May 28, they adopted several rules of procedure. A majority of the States would be needed to conduct

✔ **Checkpoint**
What were some of the Framers' accomplishments?

envoy
n. a representative, especially in diplomatic affairs

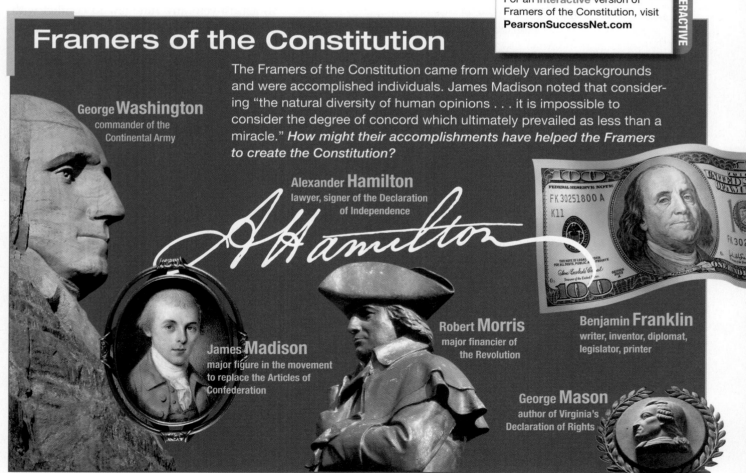

Framers of the Constitution

The Framers of the Constitution came from widely varied backgrounds and were accomplished individuals. James Madison noted that considering "the natural diversity of human opinions . . . it is impossible to consider the degree of concord which ultimately prevailed as less than a miracle." *How might their accomplishments have helped the Framers to create the Constitution?*

George **Washington**
commander of the Continental Army

Alexander **Hamilton**
lawyer, signer of the Declaration of Independence

James **Madison**
major figure in the movement to replace the Articles of Confederation

Robert **Morris**
major financier of the Revolution

Benjamin **Franklin**
writer, inventor, diplomat, legislator, printer

George **Mason**
author of Virginia's Declaration of Rights

business. Each State delegation was to have one vote on all matters, and a majority of the votes cast would carry any proposal.

The Framers met on 92 of the 116 days from May 25 through their final meeting on September 17. They did most of their work on the floor of the convention. They handled some matters in committees, but the full body ultimately settled all questions.[13]

A Momentous Decision Remember, Congress had called the Philadelphia Convention "for the sole and express purpose" of recommending revisions to the Articles of Confederation. However, almost at once the delegates agreed that they were meeting to create an entirely new government for the United States. On May 30 they adopted this proposal:

PRIMARY SOURCE

Resolved, . . . that a national Government ought to be established consisting of a supreme Legislative, Executive and Judiciary.

—Edmund Randolph, Delegate from Virginia

With this momentous decision, the Framers redefined the purpose of the convention. From that point on, they set about writing a new constitution, intended to replace the Articles of Confederation. (However, much that would go into this new constitution would come directly from the Articles of Confederation.) Their debates were spirited, even bitter. At times the convention seemed near collapse. Once they had passed Randolph's resolution, however, the resolve of most of the delegates never wavered.

Proposals

Once the Framers resolved to replace the Articles of Confederation, two major plans were offered for the new government, the Virginia Plan and the New Jersey Plan.

---

[13] Twenty-nine delegates from seven States were present on the first day. The full number of 55 was not reached until August 6, when John Francis Mercer of Maryland arrived. In the meantime, some delegates had departed, and others were absent from time to time. Some 40 members attended most of the daily sessions of the convention.

Virginia Plan No State had more to do with the calling of the convention than Virginia. It was not surprising, then, that its delegates should offer the first plan for a new constitution. On May 29, the **Virginia Plan,** largely the work of Madison, was presented by Randolph.

The Virginia Plan called for a new government with three separate branches: legislative, executive, and judicial. The legislature—Congress—would be bicameral. Representation in each house was to be based either on each State's population or on the amount of money it gave for the support of the central government. The members of the lower house, the House of Representatives, were to be popularly elected in each State. Those of the upper house, the Senate, were to be chosen by the House from lists of persons nominated by the State legislatures.

Congress was to be given all of the powers it held under the Articles. In addition, it would have the power "to legislate in all cases to which the separate States are incompetent" to act, to veto any State law in conflict with national law, and to use force if necessary to make a State obey national law.

Under the proposed Virginia Plan, Congress would choose a "National Executive" and a "National Judiciary." Together, these two branches would form a "Council of revision." They could veto acts passed by Congress, but a veto could be overridden by the two houses. The executive would have "a general authority to execute the National laws." The judiciary would "consist of one or more supreme tribunals [courts], and of inferior tribunals."

The Virginia Plan also provided that all State officers should take an oath to support the Union, and that each State be guaranteed a republican form of government. Under the plan, Congress would have the exclusive power to admit new States to the Union.

The Virginia Plan, then, would create a new constitution by thoroughly revising the Articles. Its goal was the creation of a truly national government with greatly expanded powers and, importantly, the power to enforce its decisions.

The Virginia Plan set the agenda for much of the convention's work. But some delegates—especially those from New York and the smaller States of Delaware, Maryland, and New Jersey—found it too radical.[14] Soon they developed their counterproposals. On June 15, William Paterson of New Jersey presented the position of the small States.

The New Jersey Plan Paterson and his colleagues offered several amendments to the Articles, but not nearly so thorough a revision as that proposed by the Virginia Plan. The **New Jersey Plan** retained the unicameral Congress of the Confederation, with each of the States equally represented. In addition to those powers Congress already had, the plan would add closely limited powers to tax and to regulate trade between the States.

The New Jersey Plan also called for a "federal executive" of more than one person. This plural executive would be chosen by Congress and could be removed by it at the request of a majority of the States' governors. The "federal judiciary" would be composed of a single "supreme Tribunal," appointed by the executive.

Among their several differences, the major point of disagreement between the two plans centered on this question: How should the States be represented in Congress? Would it be on the basis of their populations or financial contributions, as in the Virginia Plan? Or would it be on the basis of State equality, as in the Articles and the New Jersey Plan?

For weeks the delegates returned to this conflict, debating the matter again and again. The lines were sharply drawn. Several delegates on both sides of the issue threatened to withdraw. Finally, the dispute was settled by one of the key compromises the Framers were to make as they built the Constitution.

Compromises

The disagreement over representation in Congress was critical. The larger States expected to dominate the new government. The smaller States feared that they would not be able to protect their interests. Tempers flared on both sides. The debate became so

---

14 The Virginia Plan's major support came from the three most populous States: Virginia, Pennsylvania, and Massachusetts. New York was then only the fifth most populous State.

The Enlightenment and American Government

The 17th and 18th centuries are known as the Enlightenment; a period where thinkers based their philosophies on reason. This movement greatly influenced the leaders of the new American government. Read these quotes from four Enlightenment thinkers.

In what ways do they parallel the principles of American Government?

"The end of law is not to abolish or restrain, but to preserve and enlarge freedom. For in all the states of created beings capable of law, where there is no law, there is no freedom. —*The Second Treatise of Government*, 1690

john Locke

"The people, in whom the supreme power resides, ought to have the management of everything within their reach: that which exceeds their abilities must be conducted by their ministers. But they cannot be said to have their ministers [agents], without the power of nominating them: . . . therefore . . . the people should choose their ministers. —*The Spirit of Laws*, 1748

baron de Montesquieu

"If we enquire wherein lies precisely the greatest good of all, which ought to be the goal of every system of law, we shall find that it comes down to two main objects, *freedom* and *equality*: freedom because any individual dependence means that much strength drawn from the body of the state, and equality because freedom cannot survive without it. —*The Social Contract*, 1762

jean jacques Rousseau

"The absolute rights of man . . . are usually summed up in one general appellation [name] . . . of acting as one thinks fit, without any restraint or control, unless by the law of nature: being a right inherent in us by birth, and one of the gifts of God to man at his creation, when he endued [provided] him with the faculty of free-will. —*Commentaries on the Laws of England*, 1765–1769

william Blackstone

Slavery in the United States, 1790

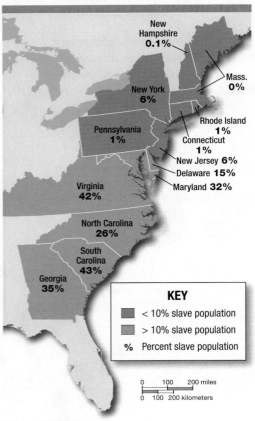

New Hampshire 0.1%
Mass. 0%
New York 6%
Rhode Island 1%
Connecticut 1%
Pennsylvania 1%
New Jersey 6%
Delaware 15%
Maryland 32%
Virginia 42%
North Carolina 26%
South Carolina 43%
Georgia 35%

KEY
■ < 10% slave population
■ > 10% slave population
% Percent slave population

0   100   200 miles
0   100   200 kilometers

▶▶ **Analyzing Maps** The southern States had a larger slave population than did the northern States at the time of the Constitutional Convention. *How might this have affected their stance on the Three-Fifths and Commerce and Slave Trade compromises?*

✔ **Checkpoint**
What was the Connecticut Compromise?

intense that Benjamin Franklin was moved to suggest that "henceforth prayers imploring the assistance of Heaven . . . be held in this Assembly every morning before we proceed to business."

Connecticut Compromise

The conflict was settled by a compromise suggested by the Connecticut delegation. In the **Connecticut Compromise,** it was agreed that Congress should be composed of two houses. In the smaller Senate, the States would be represented equally. In the House, the representation of each State would be based upon its population.

By combining basic features of the plans, the convention's most serious dispute was resolved. The agreement satisfied the smaller States in particular, allowing them to support the creation of a strong central government.

The Connecticut Compromise was so pivotal to the writing of the Constitution that it has often been called the Great Compromise.

Three-Fifths Compromise

Once it had been agreed to base the seats in the House on each State's population, this question arose: Should slaves be counted in figuring the populations of the States?

Again debate was fierce. Most delegates from the southern States argued that slaves should be counted. Most of the northerners took the opposing view. All could see the contradictions between slavery and the sentiments expressed in the Declaration of Independence, but slavery was legal in every State except

Massachusetts. The slave population was concentrated in the southern States, however, as you can see from the map on this page.

Finally, the Framers agreed to the **Three-Fifths Compromise.** It provided that all "free persons" should be counted, and so, too, should "three fifths of all other persons" (Article I, Section 2, Clause 3). For "all other persons," read "slaves." For the three fifths won by the southerners, the northerners exacted a price. That formula was also to be used in fixing the amount of money to be raised in each State by any direct tax levied by Congress. In short, the southerners could count their slaves, but they would have to pay for them.

This odd compromise disappeared from the Constitution with the adoption of the 13th Amendment, abolishing slavery, in 1865. For nearly 150 years, there have been no "all other persons" in this country.

Commerce and Slave Trade Compromise

The Framers generally agreed that Congress must have the power to regulate foreign and interstate trade. To many southerners, that power carried a real danger, however. They worried that Congress, likely to be controlled by northern commercial interests, would act against the interests of the agricultural South.

They were particularly fearful that Congress would try to pay for the new government out of export duties, and southern tobacco was the major American export of the time. They also feared that Congress would interfere with the slave trade.

Before they would agree to the commerce power, the southerners insisted on certain protections. So, according to the **Commerce and Slave Trade Compromise,** Congress was forbidden the power to tax the export of goods from any State. It was also forbidden the power to act on the slave trade for a period of at least 20 years. It could not interfere with "the migration or importation of such persons as any State now existing shall think proper to admit," except for a small head tax, at least until the year 1808.[15]

---

15 Article I, Section 9, Clause 1. Congress promptly banned the importation of slaves in 1808, and, in 1820, it declared the slave trade to be piracy. The smuggling of the enslaved into this country continued until the outbreak of the Civil War, however.

The Connecticut Compromise

"All legislative Powers herein granted shall be vested in a Congress of the United States, which shall consist of a Senate and House of Representatives." —Article 1, Section 1

FROM THE CONSTITUTION

The Great Compromise The Connecticut delegates Roger Sherman, Oliver Ellsworth, and William Samuel Johnson presented their compromise to the Philadelphia Convention as a means to end the deadlock between supporters of the rival New Jersey and Virginia Plans. The compromise incorporated parts of each plan in order to resolve the dispute over representation.

Constitutional Principles
In what ways did each plan propose to limit the powers of the legislative and executive branches?

▲ Seated at the table are William Samuel Johnson (left) and Roger Sherman at the signing of the Constitution.

A "Bundle of Compromises" The convention spent much of its time, said Franklin, "sawing boards to make them fit." The Constitution drafted at Philadelphia has often been called a "bundle of compromises." Those descriptions are <u>apt</u>, if they are properly understood.

There were differences of opinion among the delegates, certainly. After all, the delegates came from 12 different States widely separated in geographic and economic terms, and the delegates often reflected the particular interests of their own States. Bringing those interests together did require compromise. Indeed, final decisions on issues such as the selection of the President, the treaty-making process, the structure of the national court system, and the amendment process were all reached as a result of compromise.

But by no means did all, or even most, of what shaped the document come from compromises. The Framers were agreed on many of the basic issues they faced. Thus, nearly all the delegates were convinced that a new national government, a federal government, had to be created, and that it had to have the powers necessary to deal with the nation's grave social and economic problems. The Framers were also dedicated to the concepts of popular sovereignty and limited government. None questioned for a moment the wisdom of representative government. The principles of separation of powers and of checks and balances were accepted almost as a matter of course.

Many disputes did occur, and the compromises by which they were resolved came only after hours, days, and even weeks of heated debate. The point here, however, is that the differences were not over the most fundamental of questions. They involved, instead, such vital but lesser points as these: the details of the structure of Congress, the method by which the President was to be chosen, and the practical limits that should be put on the several powers to be given to the new central government.

For several weeks, through the hot Philadelphia summer, the delegates took up resolution after resolution. On September 8, a committee was named "to revise the stile of and arrange the articles which had been agreed to" by the

apt
adj. appropriate, correct, fit

convention. That committee, the Committee of Stile and Arrangement, put the Constitution into its final form. Finally, on September 17, the convention approved its work and 39 names were placed on the finished document.[16] Because not all of the delegates were willing to sign the Constitution, its final paragraph was very carefully worded to give the impression of unanimity: "Done in Convention by the Unanimous Consent of the States present. . . ."

Perhaps none of the Framers was completely satisfied with their work. Nevertheless, wise old Benjamin Franklin put into words what many of them must have thought on that final day:

"Sir, I agree with this Constitution with all its faults, if they are such; because I think a general Government necessary for us . . . I doubt . . . whether any other Convention we can obtain, may be able to make a better Constitution. For when you assemble a number of men to have the advantage of their joint wisdom, you inevitably assemble with those men, all their prejudices, their passions, their errors of opinion, their local interests, and their selfish views. From such an assembly can a perfect production be expected? It therefore astonishes me, Sir, to find this system approaching so near to perfection as it does . . . "

—*Notes* of Debates in the Federal Convention of 1787, James Madison

On Franklin's motion, the Constitution was signed. Madison tells us that

PRIMARY SOURCE

. . . Doctor Franklin, looking towards the President's chair, at the back of which a rising sun happened to be painted, observed to a few members near him, that painters had found it difficult to distinguish in their art a rising sun from a setting sun. 'I have,' said he, 'often and often in the course of the Session . . . looked at that behind the President without being able to tell whether it was rising or setting: But now at length I have the happiness to know that it is a rising and not a setting Sun.'

—*Notes* of Debates in the Federal Convention of 1787, James Madison

---

16 Three of the 41 delegates present on that last day refused to sign the proposed Constitution: Edmund Randolph of Virginia, who later supported ratification and served as Attorney General and then Secretary of State under President Washington; Elbridge Gerry of Massachusetts, who later became Vice President under Madison; and George Mason of Virginia, who continued to oppose the Constitution until his death in 1792. George Read of Delaware signed both for himself and for his absent colleague John Dickinson.

Essential Questions Journal To continue to build a response to the chapter Essential Question, go to your **Essential Questions Journal.**

SECTION 4 ASSESSMENT

1. **Guiding Question** Use your completed flowchart to answer this question: What compromises enabled the Framers to create the Constitution?

Key Terms and Comprehension

2. **(a)** What was the goal of the **Framers** when they met at Independence Hall? **(b)** How did that goal change?

3. What was the purpose of keeping the discussions within the Constitutional Convention a secret?

Critical Thinking

4. **Test Conclusions** The Framers abandoned the Articles of Confederation in favor of an entirely new constitution. Do you agree with their decision? Why or why not?

5. **Identify Central Issues** Explain the differences between the Virginia Plan and the New Jersey Plan. How were these differences resolved?

Quick Write

Narrative Writing: Choose a Main Idea When writing narrative nonfiction, it is important to have a main idea. This idea will help you stay on track as you write the story of your colony. Look through your notes and write a main idea.

Ratifying the
Constitution

Guiding Question

What issues aroused the vigorous debate over the ratification of the Constitution? Use an outline like the one below to keep track of the issues debated during ratification.

I. Ratification of the Constitution
  A. Federalist Arguments
    1. _____
    2. _____
  B. Anti-Federalist Arguments
    1. _____
    2. _____

Political Dictionary

• Federalist   • Anti-Federalist

Objectives

1. Identify the opposing sides in the fight for ratification and describe the major arguments for and against the proposed Constitution.
2. Describe the inauguration of the new government of the United States of America.

Image Above: This poster celebrates the bicentennial of Virginia's ratification of the Constitution.

Today, the Constitution of the United States is the object of unparalleled admiration and respect, both here and abroad. But in 1787 and 1788, it was widely criticized, and in every State there were many who opposed its adoption. The battle over the ratification of the document was not easily decided.

The Fight for Ratification

Remember, the Articles of Confederation provided that changes could be made to them only if *all* of the State legislatures agreed. But the Framers had determined that the new Constitution would replace, not <u>amend</u>, the Articles. They had seen how crippling the requirement of unanimity could be. So, the new Constitution provided that

FROM THE CONSTITUTION

The ratification of the conventions of nine States shall be sufficient for the establishment of this Constitution between the States so ratifying the same.

—Article VII

The Congress of the Confederation agreed to this irregular procedure. On September 28, 1787, it sent copies of the new document to the States.

Federalists and Anti-Federalists The Constitution circulated widely and was debated vigorously. Two groups quickly emerged in each of the States: the **Federalists,** who favored ratification, and the **Anti-Federalists,** who opposed it.

The Federalists were led by many of those who attended the Philadelphia Convention. Among the most active were James Madison and Alexander Hamilton. The opposition was headed by such well-known Revolutionary War figures as Patrick Henry, Richard Henry Lee, John Hancock, and Samuel Adams.

The Federalists stressed the weaknesses of the Articles. They argued that the many difficulties facing the Republic could be overcome only by the creation of new government based on the Constitution.

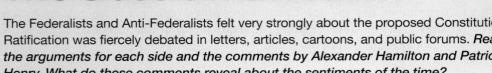
Checkpoint
What change did the
Framers make to the
ratification process?

amend
v. to change or modify

The Anti-Federalists attacked nearly every part of the document. Many objected to the ratification process. Several worried that the presidency could become a monarchy and that Congress would become too powerful. In Massachusetts, Amos Singletary, a delegate to the ratifying convention, condemned the Federalists:

"These lawyers, and men of learning, and monied men, that talk so finely and gloss over matters so smoothly, to make us poor illiterate people, swallow down the pill, expect to get into Congress themselves; they expect to . . . get all the power and all the money into their own hands, and then they will swallow up all us little folks . . . just as the whale swallowed up Jonah."[17]

—Amos Singletary

[17] S.B. Harding, "The Contest Over the Ratification of the Federal Constitution in the State of Massachusetts," 1896, as quoted in Carl Van Doren, *The Great Rehearsal*, 1948.

The lack of one major feature of the proposed Constitution drew the heaviest fire: a bill of rights. The new document did contain some protections of individual rights—for example, a provision for the writ of habeas corpus, which is a protection against arbitrary arrest. The Framers had made no provision for such basic liberties as freedom of speech, press, and religion, however—largely because those matters were covered by the existing State constitutions. They also believed that because the powers to be granted to the new government would be fragmented among three branches, no branch of the government could become powerful enough to threaten the rights of the people.

Everywhere, the Anti-Federalists bore down on the absence of a bill of rights. At Virginia's ratifying convention, Patrick Henry said of the proposed Constitution, "I look on that paper as the most fatal plan that could possibly be conceived to enslave a free

GOVERNMENT ONLINE

Audio Tour
Listen to a guided audio tour of these arguments at
PearsonSuccessNet.com

The Federalist/Anti-Federalist Argument

Two Sides of Ratification

The Federalists and Anti-Federalists felt very strongly about the proposed Constitution. Ratification was fiercely debated in letters, articles, cartoons, and public forums. *Read the arguments for each side and the comments by Alexander Hamilton and Patrick Henry. What do these comments reveal about the sentiments of the time?*

Federalist
- The Articles of Confederation are too weak.
- Only a stronger national government can overcome the difficulties the Republic faces.
- Liberties that could be included in a bill of rights are covered in the State constitutions.

Anti-Federalist
- The States would no longer have the power to print money.
- The national government would be given too much power.
- There should be a bill of rights.

The subject speaks its own importance; comprehending in its consequences nothing less than the existence of the UNION, the safety and welfare of the parts of which it is composed, the fate of an empire in many respects the most interesting in the world.
—Alexander Hamilton,
The Federalist, No. 1, 1787

The fate of this question and America may depend on this: Have they said, we the States? Have they made a proposal of a compact between States? If they had this would be a confederation...
— Patrick Henry,
Speech before the
Virginia Ratifying
Convention,
June 5, 1788

United we stand—Divided we fall

▶▶ Columns representing the States that had ratified the Constitution are placed in a row by the hand of God. **Is this a Federalist or Anti-Federalist cartoon? In which States was ratification won by only a narrow margin?**

Ratification of the Constitution

State	Date	Vote
Delaware	Dec. 7, 1787	30–0
Pennsylvania	Dec. 12, 1787	46–23
New Jersey	Dec. 18, 1787	38–0
Georgia	Jan. 2, 1788	26–0
Connecticut	Jan. 9, 1788	128–40
Massachusetts	Feb. 6, 1788	187–168
Maryland	April 28, 1788	63–11
South Carolina	May 23, 1788	149–73
New Hampshire	June 21, 1788	57–46
Virginia	June 25, 1788	89–79
New York	July 26, 1788	30–27
North Carolina*	Nov. 21, 1789	195–77
Rhode Island	May 29, 1790	34–32

* Second vote; ratification was originally defeated on August 4, 1788, by a vote of 184–84.

people." Stung by the criticism, the Federalists promised that the Constitution, once adopted, would be amended to overcome this fault.

Over the course of the struggle for ratification, an extraordinary number of essays, speeches, letters, and other commentaries were printed. Of them all, the most remarkable were a series of 85 essays that first appeared in various newspapers in New York in the fall of 1787 on into the spring of 1788. Those essays, supporting the Constitution, were written by Alexander Hamilton, James Madison, and John Jay, and they were soon published in book form as *The Federalist: A Commentary on the Constitution of the United States.* All of the essays bore the pen name "Publius" (Latin for "Public Man"), and they were reprinted throughout the 13 States. They remain an excellent commentary on the Constitution and rank among the finest of all political writings in the English language.

The Anti-Federalists' attacks were also published widely. Among the best of their works were several essays usually attributed to Robert Yates, who had been one of New York's delegates to the Philadelphia Convention; they were signed by "Brutus" and appeared in the *New York Journal* at the same time that the paper carried several of the *Federalist* essays. The Anti-Federalists' views were also presented in pamphlets and letters written by Richard Henry Lee of Virginia, who used the pen name "The Federal Farmer."

Nine States Ratify Ratification came fairly quickly in a few States and only after a bitter struggle in others. Delaware was the first to approve the Constitution, on December 7. Pennsylvania followed five days later. In Pennsylvania, however, where the legislature had been slow to call a ratifying convention, several Federalists, angered by Anti-Federalist delays, took matters into their own hands. They broke into a Philadelphia boarding house, seized two legislators hiding there, and forcibly marched them to the State house so the assembly could vote to schedule the convention.

The contest for ratification was close in several States, but the Federalists finally prevailed in all of them. On June 21, 1788, New Hampshire brought the number of ratifying States to nine.

Under Article VII, New Hampshire's ratification should have brought the Constitution into effect, but it did not. Neither Virginia nor New York had yet ratified. Without either of those key States the new government could not hope to succeed.

Virginia's Ratification Virginia's vote for ratification followed New Hampshire's by just four days. The brilliant debates in its convention were followed closely throughout the

✔️ **Checkpoint**
Why did the Framers not include a bill of rights in the original Constitution?

inauguration
n. a ceremonial induction into office

quorum
n. a majority

unanimous
adj. having the approval or consent of all

State. The Federalists were led by Madison, John Marshall, and Governor Edmund Randolph (even though he had refused to sign the Constitution at Philadelphia). Patrick Henry, leading the opposition, was joined by James Monroe, Richard Henry Lee, and George Mason (another of the nonsigners).

Although George Washington was not one of the delegates to Virginia's convention, his strong support for ratification proved vital. With Madison, he was able to get a reluctant Thomas Jefferson to support the document. Had Jefferson fought as did other Anti-Federalists, Virginia might never have ratified the Constitution.

New York, The Last Key State In New York, the ratifying convention was bitterly divided. The Anti-Federalists were led by Governor George Clinton and two of the State's three delegates to the Philadelphia convention: Robert Yates and John Lansing, who had quit Philadelphia in late July, claiming that the convention had gone beyond its authority.

New York's approval of the Constitution was absolutely necessary, for that large commercial State effectively separated New England from the rest of the nation. Its ratification of the Constitution, on July 26, brought the number of ratifying States to 11. The victory there was largely won by Alexander Hamilton.

Inauguration

On September 13, 1788, with 11 of the 13 States "under the federal roof," the Congress of the Confederation paved the way for its successor.[18] It chose New York City as the temporary capital.[19] It set the first Wednesday in January as the date on which the States would choose presidential electors. The first Wednesday in February was set as the date on which those electors would vote, and the first Wednesday in March as the date for the inauguration of the new government.

The new Congress convened on March 4, 1789. It met in Federal Hall, on Wall Street in New York City. But because it lacked a quorum, it could not count the electoral votes until April 6. Finally, on that day, it found that George Washington had been elected President by a unanimous vote. John Adams was elected Vice President by a large majority.

On April 30, after a historic trip from Mount Vernon to New York, Washington took the oath of office as the first President of the United States.

---

[18] Neither North Carolina nor Rhode Island had ratified the new Constitution before it became effective. The Constitution failed in a first convention in North Carolina and was finally approved by a second one in late November of 1789. Rhode Island did not hold a ratifying convention until May of 1790.

[19] The District of Columbia did not become the nation's capital until 1800.

| Essential Questions | To continue to build a |
| Journal | response to the chapter |

Essential Question, go to your **Essential Questions Journal.**

SECTION 5 ASSESSMENT

1. **Guiding Question** Use your completed outline to answer this question: What issues aroused the vigorous debate over the ratification of the Constitution?

Key Terms and Comprehension

2. Explain why the **Anti-Federalists** opposed the presidency.

3. Explain the importance of adding a bill of rights to the Constitution.

Critical Thinking

4. **Identify Point of View** Reread the quote by Amos Singletary in this section. According to Singletary, why did the Federalists support ratifying the Constitution?

5. **Make Inferences** Recall Virginia's role in writing the Declaration of Independence and in the Second Continental Congress. Why do you think it was important for Virginia to ratify the Constitution?

Quick Write

Narrative Writing: Create an Outline When writing a narrative nonfiction piece, it helps to have an outline of your thoughts and ideas. Create an outline using your main ideas and supporting details. Revise your outline as needed to make sure that the story progresses in an interesting and clear way.

Quick Study Guide

GOVERNMENT ONLINE
On the Go
To review anytime, anywhere, download these online resources at PearsonSuccessNet.com
Political Dictionary, Audio Review

Guiding Question
Section 2 What events and ideas led to American independence?

Guiding Question
Section 3 What weaknesses in the Articles of Confederation made a lasting government impossible?

Guiding Question
Section 4 What compromises enabled the Framers to create the Constitution?

Guiding Question
Section 1 What ideas and traditions influenced government in the English colonies?

CHAPTER 2
Essential Question
How does the Constitution reflect the times in which it was written?

Guiding Question
Section 5 What issues aroused the vigorous debate over the ratification of the Constitution?

Political Dictionary

limited government *p. 31*
representative government *p. 31*
Magna Carta *p. 31*
due process *p. 31*
Petition of Right *p. 31*
English Bill of Rights *p. 31*
charter *p. 33*
bicameral *p. 33*
proprietary *p. 33*
unicameral *p. 34*
confederation *p. 37*
Albany Plan of Union *p. 37*
delegate *p. 37*
popular sovereignty *p. 41*
Articles of Confederation *p. 48*
ratification *p. 48*
Framers *p. 52*
Virginia Plan *p. 54*
New Jersey Plan *p. 55*
Connecticut Compromise *p. 56*
Three-Fifths Compromise *p. 56*
Commerce and Slave Trade Compromise *p. 56*
Federalist *p. 59*
Anti-Federalist *p. 59*

Key Documents

Declaration of Independence: Key Facts	Constitution: Key Facts
• In 1776, the Second Continental Congress approved the Declaration of Independence.	• The New Jersey Plan: A unicameral Congress with each State equally represented
• Written by Thomas Jefferson, the Declaration proclaimed the natural rights of all citizens, and outlined how the king had violated those rights.	• The Virginia Plan: A bicameral Congress with representation based on population or the amount of money each State contributed to Congress each year
• With the approval of the Declaration, the 13 colonies became free and independent States.	• The Connecticut Compromise: A bicameral Congress with each State equally represented in the Senate and represented by population in the House
	• The Three-Fifths Compromise: Three fifths of the slave population was counted for representation in the House and for taxation.
	• The Constitution was hotly debated by Federalists and Anti-Federalists.

The Road to the Constitution

1215: Magna Carta
1628: Petition of Right
1689: English Bill of Rights

1765: Parliament passes the Stamp Act.
1774: The First Continental Congress meets.
1775: The American Revolution begins.
1776: The Declaration of Independence
1777: Articles of Confederation approved.

1787: The Framers sign the Constitution.
1789: The Constitution takes effect.

Chapter Assessment

Comprehension and Critical Thinking

Section 1

1. **(a)** Name and explain the three concepts of government that the English brought with them to the colonies. **(b)** How did these ideas shape the creation of the 13 colonies?

2. Describe the limitations on the monarchy imposed by these documents: **(a)** the Magna Carta, **(b)** the Petition of Right, **(c)** the English Bill of Rights.

3. In the royal colonies, why might the colonists resent the "stern hand" of a royal governor?

Section 2

4. The Declaration of Independence states, "Governments are instituted among Men, deriving their just powers from the consent of the governed." What kind of government is this?

5. **(a)** What were the complaints of the Stamp Act Congress? **(b)** What was meant by "taxation without representation"?

6. **Analyze Political Cartoons** Look at the cartoon below. **(a)** How has the artist drawn the horse "America"? **(b)** How does this reflect British attitudes toward the American colonies?

THE HORSE AMERICA, throwing his Master.

Section 3

7. **(a)** Explain the responsibilities of Congress under the Articles of Confederation. **(b)** Which of these responsibilities were taken over by the States? **(c)** Why did this cause a problem?

Section 4

8. **(a)** Why did the Framers consider it necessary to replace the Articles of Confederation? **(b)** What obstacles did they face in creating a strong central government?

9. How did the Constitution improve upon the Articles of Confederation? Give examples from the text.

10. Look at the population density map in Section 4 and reread the paragraphs concerning the Three-Fifths Compromise. Why, in addition to moral reasons, might the northern States have wished to abolish slavery?

Section 5

11. **(a)** Why was a bill of rights not included in the original Constitution? **(b)** Why might the Anti-Federalists have wanted a bill of rights in the document?

Writing About Government

12. Use your Quick Write exercises to write a narrative non-fiction piece about a State's role in the formation of the national government. Make sure that you use your outline as the frame of your story. Include interesting details and anecdotes wherever possible. See pp. S1–S2 in the Skills Handbook.

Apply What You've Learned

13. **Essential Question Activity** Research a recently created constitution for a foreign nation or international association.
    (a) Identify the writer(s) of the constitution, and what their qualifications were.
    (b) Research the process through which the constitution was created. How did the writers decide on what to include? What did they think were the most important rights to protect?
    (c) Did the constitution go through a ratification process? How was the process conducted?

14. **Essential Question Assessment** Based on your research and this chapter, make a chart comparing the process used to create the U.S. Constitution with a more recently written constitution. This comparison will help you answer the Essential Question: **How does the Constitution reflect the times in which it was written?** Include details such as the concerns of the creators, and the process of ratification in your chart.

Essential Questions Journal To respond to the chapter Essential Question, go to your **Essential Questions Journal.**

Document-Based Assessment

The Constitution and the Revolutionary War Era

The Declaration of Independence espoused the highest principles of Enlightenment thinking. However, a significant percent of the new nation's population remained disenfranchised under their new Constitution. The text below refers to two of those groups.

Document 1

I long to hear that you have declared an independency — and by the way in the new code of Laws which I suppose it will be necessary for you to make I desire you would Remember the Ladies, and be more generous and favourable to them than your ancestors. Do not put such unlimited power into the hands of the Husbands. Remember all Men would be tyrants if they could. If perticuliar care and attention is not paid to the Ladies we are determined to foment a Rebelion, and will not hold ourselves bound by any Laws in which we have no voice, or Representation.

—**Letter from Abigail Adams to John Adams, March 31, 1776**

Document 2

Would any one believe that I am Master of Slaves, of my own purchase! I am drawn along by the general inconvenience of living here without them. I will not, I cannot justify it. However culpable my Conduct, I will so far pay my devoir to Virtue, as to own the excellence & rectitude of her Precepts, & lament my want of conforming to them.

I believe a time will come when an opportunity will be offered to abolish this lamentable Evil. Every thing we can do is to improve it, if it happens in our day; if not, let us transmit to our descendants, together with our Slaves, a pity for their unhappy Lot, & our abhorrence for Slavery. If we cannot reduce this wished for Reformation to practice, let us treat the unhappy victims with lenity. It is the furthmost advance we can make towards Justice. It is a debt we owe to the purity of our Religion, to show that it is at variance with that Law which, warrants Slavery.

—**Patrick Henry on slavery, in a letter to Robert Pleasants, January 18, 1773**

Use your knowledge of the social reality of the Revolutionary War era and the documents above to answer Questions 1–3.

1. What warning did Abigail Adams issue to her husband in Document 1?
   A. The new nation will fail if slaves are not freed.
   B. Families will fail if women are not equal partners with their husbands.
   C. Women will rise up if their rights are not answered.
   D. The War for Independence will fail if women do not join the battle.

2. How do Patrick Henry's comments reflect the differences between the ideals of the War for Independence and the reality of life in those times?

3. **Pull It Together** Does the culture of the time in which the Constitution was written excuse inequalities that the document allowed?

GOVERNMENT ONLINE
Online Documents
To find more primary sources on colonial suffrage, visit
PearsonSuccessNet.com

The Constitution

Essential Question
How has the Constitution lasted through changing times?

" These **principles** form the bright **constellation** which has gone before us and **guided our steps** through an age of **revolution** and **reformation**.

—Thomas Jefferson, 1801

▶ **Photo:** Sculptures of the Framers at the National Constitution Center in Philadelphia

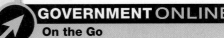

GOVERNMENT ONLINE
On the Go

To study anywhere, anytime, download these online resources at PearsonSuccessNet.com
• Political Dictionary
• Audio Review
• Downloadable Interactivities

SECTION 1

Basic Principles

Guiding Question

What are the six main principles on which the Constitution is based?
Use a concept web like the one below to take notes on the six basic principles of the Constitution.

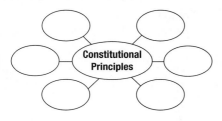

Constitutional Principles

Political Dictionary

- popular sovereignty
- limited government
- constitutionalism
- rule of law
- separation of powers
- checks and balances
- veto
- judicial review
- unconstitutional
- federalism

Objectives

1. Understand the basic outline of the Constitution.
2. Understand the six basic principles of the Constitution: popular sovereignty, limited government, separation of powers, checks and balances, judicial review, and federalism.

Image Above: Voters express their will to the government. This concept is called popular sovereignty.

The Constitution of the United States dates from the latter part of the eighteenth century. Written in 1787, it took effect in 1789. The fact that it is more than 220 years old does not mean, however, that in the twenty-first century, it is only an interesting historical artifact, best left to museums and dusty shelves. On the contrary, it remains a vitally important and vibrant document.

The Constitution is this nation's fundamental law. It is, by its own terms, "the supreme Law of the Land"—the highest form of law in the United States.

An Outline of the Constitution

The Constitution sets out the basic principles upon which government in the United States was built and operates today. The document lays out the ways in which the Federal Government is organized, how the leaders of that government are selected, and many of the procedures those leaders must follow as they perform their duties. Of utmost importance, it sets out the limits within which government must conduct itself.

The Constitution also lays out the basic rules of American politics. By doing so, it helps to determine who wins and who loses in the political arena. To really understand government and politics in this country, we must know a good deal about the Constitution and how it has been interpreted and applied thoughout our history.

Even with its 27 amendments, the Constitution is a fairly brief document. Its little more than 7,000 words can be read in half an hour. You will find the text of the Constitution at the beginning of the book. As you read it, remember that this document has successfully guided this nation through more than two centuries of tremendous growth and change. One of the Constitution's greatest strengths is that it deals largely with matters of basic principle. Unlike most other constitutions—those of the 50 States and those of other nations—the Constitution of the United States is not weighted down with detailed and cumbersome provisions.

As you read the Constitution, you will also see that it is organized in a simple and straightforward way. It begins with a short introduction, the Preamble. The balance of the original document is divided into seven numbered

68 The Constitution

sections called articles. The first three articles deal with the three branches of the National Government: Congress, the presidency, and the federal court system. These articles outline the basic organization and powers of each branch, and the methods by which the members of Congress, the President and Vice President, and federal judges are chosen. Article IV deals mostly with the place of the States in the American Union and their relationships with the National Government and with one another. Article V indicates how formal amendments may be added to the document. Article VI declares that the Constitution is the nation's supreme law; Article VII provided for the ratification of the Constitution.

The seven articles of the original document are followed by 27 amendments, printed in the order in which each provision was adopted.

The Constitution is built around six basic principles. They are popular sovereignty, limited government, separation of powers, checks and balances, judicial review, and federalism.

Popular Sovereignty

In the United States, all political power resides in the people, a concept known as **popular sovereignty.** The people are the *only* source for any and all governmental power. Government can govern only with the consent of the governed.

The principle of popular sovereignty is woven throughout the Constitution. In its opening words—the Preamble—that document declares: "We the People of the United States . . . do ordain and establish this Constitution for the United States of America."

The people have given the United States Government whatever powers it has, through the Constitution. That government exercises those powers through popularly elected leaders who are chosen by the people to represent them in the exercise of the people's power.

Limited Government

The principle of **limited government** holds that no government is all-powerful. That government may do *only* those things that the people have given it the power to do.

✔ **Checkpoint**
What is the purpose of the Preamble of the Constitution?

political arena
n. the setting in which political activity occurs

provision
n. a clause in a document or agreement

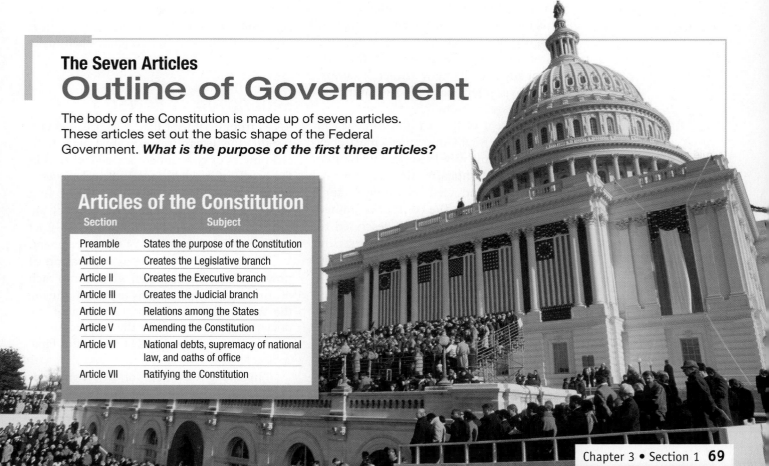

The Seven Articles
Outline of Government

The body of the Constitution is made up of seven articles. These articles set out the basic shape of the Federal Government. *What is the purpose of the first three articles?*

Articles of the Constitution

Section	Subject
Preamble	States the purpose of the Constitution
Article I	Creates the Legislative branch
Article II	Creates the Executive branch
Article III	Creates the Judicial branch
Article IV	Relations among the States
Article V	Amending the Constitution
Article VI	National debts, supremacy of national law, and oaths of office
Article VII	Ratifying the Constitution

Basic Principles of the Constitution

These cartoons illustrate the six principles of government set out in the Constitution. ***According to the cartoons, what is the role of the judicial branch? What are the roles of citizens?***

Popular Sovereignty

Limited Government

Separation of Powers

enshrined
v. set out with respect; honored

In effect, the principle of limited government is the other side of the coin of popular sovereignty. It is that principle stated the other way around: The people are the only source of any and all of government's authority; and government has only that authority the people have given to it.

The concept of limited government can be put another way: Government must obey the law. Stated this way, the principle is often called **constitutionalism**—that is, government must be conducted according to constitutional principles. The concept of limited government is also frequently described as the **rule of law,** which holds that government and its officers, in all that they do, are always subject to—never above—the law.

In large part, the Constitution is a statement of limited government. Much of it reads as prohibitions of power to government. For example, notice the Constitution's guarantees of freedom of expression. Those great guarantees—of freedom of religion, of speech, of the press, of assembly, and of petition—are

prohibition
n. a denial; a ban

vital to democratic government. They are enshrined in the 1st Amendment, which begins with the words: "Congress shall make no law. . . ."

Separation of Powers

Recall from Chapter 1 that in a parliamentary system, the legislative, executive, and judicial powers of government are all gathered in the hands of a single agency. British government is a leading example of the form. In a presidential system, these basic powers are distributed—separated—among three distinct and independent branches of the government.

This concept is known as **separation of powers.** The idea had been written into each of the State constitutions adopted during the Revolution. A classic expression of the doctrine can be found in the Massachusetts constitution written in 1780 (Part the First, Article XXX):

"In the government of this commonwealth, the legislative department shall never

Checks and Balances

Judicial Review

Federalism

exercise the executive and judicial powers, or either of them: The executive shall never exercise the legislative and judicial powers, or either of them: The judicial shall never exercise the legislative and executive powers, or either of them: to the end it may be a government of laws and not of men."

The Constitution of the United States distributes the powers of the National Government among the Congress (the legislative branch), the President (the executive branch), and the courts (the judicial branch). This separation of powers is clearly set forth in the opening words of each of the first three Articles of the Constitution.

Article I, Section 1 declares: "All legislative Powers herein granted shall be <u>vested</u> in a Congress of the United States. . . ." Thus, Congress is the lawmaking branch of the National Government.

Article II, Section 1 declares: "The executive Power shall be vested in a President of the United States of America." Thus, the President is given the law-executing, law-

enforcing, and law-administering powers of the National Government.

Article III, Section 1 declares: "The judicial Power of the United States shall be vested in one supreme Court, and in such inferior Courts as the Congress may from time to time ordain and establish." Thus, the federal courts, and most importantly the Supreme Court, interpret and apply the laws of the United States in cases brought before them.

Remember, the Framers intended to create a stronger central government for the United States. Yet they also intended to limit the powers of that government. The doctrine of separation of powers was designed to accomplish just that.

In *The Federalist,* No. 47, James Madison wrote of this arrangement: "The accumulation of all powers, legislative, executive, and judiciary, in the same hands, whether of one, a few, or many . . . may justly be pronounced the very definition of tyranny."

The earliest of the State constitutions provided for a separation of powers among the

✔ **Checkpoint**
How does the separation of powers keep government from becoming too powerful?

<u>vested</u>
v. given to, conferred upon

legislative, executive, and judicial branches of the new governments they established. This was a reflection of the mistrust and suspicion toward any government common to the people of the new United States in the late 1700s. Thus, the inclusion of the doctrine of separation of powers was both natural and inevitable in the writing of the Constitution.

Checks and Balances

The National Government is organized around three separate branches. As you have just seen, the Constitution gives to each branch its own field of governmental authority: legislative, executive, and judicial.

These three branches are not entirely separated nor completely independent of one another. Rather, they are tied together by a complex system of **checks and balances.** This means that each branch is subject to a number of constitutional checks, or restraints, by the other branches. In other words, each branch has certain powers with which it can check the operations of the other two.

Congress has the power to make laws, but the President may **veto** (reject) any act of Congress. In its turn, Congress can <u>override</u> a presidential veto by a two-thirds vote in each house. Congress can refuse to provide funds requested by the President, or the Senate may refuse to approve a treaty or an appointment made by the chief executive. The President is the commander in chief of the armed forces, but Congress provides that military force; and so on.

The system of checks and balances links the judicial branch to the legislative and the executive branches. The President has the power to name all federal judges. Each appointment, however, must be approved by a majority vote in the Senate. At the same time, the courts have the power to determine the constitutionality of acts of Congress and of presidential actions, and to strike down those they find unconstitutional.

Head-on clashes between the branches of government do not often happen. The check-and-balance system operates all the time, however, and in routine fashion. The very fact that it exists affects much of what happens in Washington, D.C.

For example, when the President picks someone to serve in some important office in the executive branch—as, say, secretary of state or director of the Office of National Intelligence—the President is quite aware that the Senate must confirm that appointment. So, the chief executive is apt to pick someone who very likely will be approved by the Senate. In a similar sense, when Congress makes a law, it does so with a careful eye on both the President's veto power and the power of the courts to review its actions.

Spectacular clashes—direct applications of the check-and-balance system—do sometimes occur, of course. The President does veto some acts of Congress. On rare occasions, Congress does override a veto. And, even more rarely, the Senate does reject a presidential appointee. Twice in our history, the House of Representatives has impeached (brought charges against) a President, seeking his removal: Andrew Johnson in 1868 and Bill Clinton in 1998. On both occasions the President was acquitted by the Senate.

But, again, these and other direct confrontations are not common. Congress, the President, and even the courts try to avoid them. The check-and-balance system makes compromise necessary—and, remember, compromise is a vital part of democratic government.

Over time, the check-and-balance system has worked quite well. It has done what the Framers intended it to do; it has prevented "an unjust combination of a majority." At the same time, the system of checks and balances has not often forestalled a close working relationship between the executive and legislative branches of the Federal Government.

Note, however, that that working relationship runs more smoothly when the President and a majority in both houses of Congress are of the same political party. When the other party controls one or both houses, <u>partisan</u> friction and conflict play a larger-than-usual part in that relationship.

Through most of our history, the President and a majority of the members of both houses of Congress have been of the same party. Over the past 50 years or so, however, the American people have become quite familiar with divided government—that is, a political

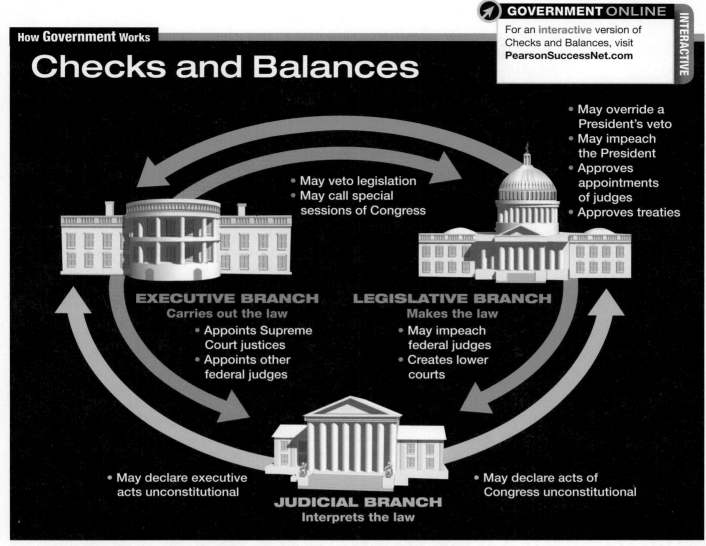

Checks and Balances

GOVERNMENT ONLINE

For an interactive version of Checks and Balances, visit **PearsonSuccessNet.com**

INTERACTIVE

- May veto legislation
- May call special sessions of Congress

- May override a President's veto
- May impeach the President
- Approves appointments of judges
- Approves treaties

EXECUTIVE BRANCH
Carries out the law
- Appoints Supreme Court justices
- Appoints other federal judges

LEGISLATIVE BRANCH
Makes the law
- May impeach federal judges
- Creates lower courts

- May declare executive acts unconstitutional

- May declare acts of Congress unconstitutional

JUDICIAL BRANCH
Interprets the law

▸▸ **Interpreting Diagrams** Under the system of checks and balances, each branch of government can check the actions of the others. ***In what ways can the power of the executive be checked by the other two branches?***

environment in which one party occupies the White House and the other controls one or both houses of Congress.

Most recently, Republican President George W. Bush faced an opposing Congress in the last two years of his eight-year presidency. In 2008, Barack Obama recaptured the White House for the Democrats, and the Democratic Party strengthened their slim majorities in both houses on Capitol Hill.

Judicial Review

One aspect of the principle of checks and balances is of such importance in the American constitutional system that it stands by itself, as one of that system's basic principles. The

power of **judicial review** may be defined as the power of a court to determine the constitutionality of a governmental action.

In part, then, judicial review is the power to declare **unconstitutional**—to declare illegal, null and void, of no force and effect—a governmental action found to violate some provision in the Constitution. The power of judicial review is held by all federal courts and by most State courts, as well.[1]

The Constitution does not provide for judicial review in so many words. Yet it seems

---

1 Generally, the power is held by all courts of record. These are courts that keep a record of their proceedings and have the power to punish for contempt. Usually, only the lowest courts in a State—justice of the peace courts—are not courts of record.

clear that the Framers intended that the federal courts, and in particular the Supreme Court, should have that power. In *The Federalist* No. 51, James Madison described the judicial power as one of the "<u>auxiliary</u> precautions" against the possible domination of one branch of the government over another.

In *The Federalist* No. 78, Alexander Hamilton wrote:

> "The interpretation of the laws is the proper and peculiar province of the courts. A constitution is, in fact, and must be regarded by the judges as a fundamental law. It therefore belongs to them to ascertain its meaning, as well as the meaning of any particular act proceeding from the legislative body. If there should happen to be an irreconcilable variance between the two, that which has the superior obligation and validity ought, of course, to be preferred; or, in other words, the Constitution ought to be preferred to the statute. . . ."

In practice, the Supreme Court established the power of judicial review in the landmark case of *Marbury* v. *Madison* in 1803. Since *Marbury,* the Supreme Court and other federal and State courts have used the power in thousands of cases. For the most part, those courts have upheld challenged governmental actions. That is, in most cases in which the power of judicial review is exercised, the actions of government are found to be constitutional.

That is not always the case, however. To date, the Supreme Court has decided some 150 cases in which it has found an act or some part of an act of Congress to be unconstitutional. It has struck down several presidential and other executive branch actions as well. The Court has also voided hundreds of actions of the States and their local governments, including some 1,200 State laws and local ordinances.

Federalism

As you know, the American governmental system is federal in form. The powers held by government are distributed on a territorial basis. The National Government holds some of those powers. Others belong to the 50 States.

auxiliary
adj. extra; supportive; supplemental

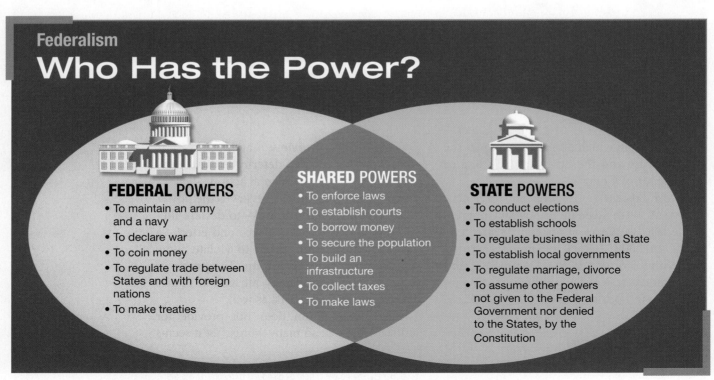

Federalism
Who Has the Power?

FEDERAL POWERS
- To maintain an army and a navy
- To declare war
- To coin money
- To regulate trade between States and with foreign nations
- To make treaties

SHARED POWERS
- To enforce laws
- To establish courts
- To borrow money
- To secure the population
- To build an infrastructure
- To collect taxes
- To make laws

STATE POWERS
- To conduct elections
- To establish schools
- To regulate business within a State
- To establish local governments
- To regulate marriage, divorce
- To assume other powers not given to the Federal Government nor denied to the States, by the Constitution

Interpreting Diagrams The Constitution divides power among the State and Federal governments. *Why does the Constitution give the power to regulate trade among the States to the Federal Government?*

The principle of **federalism**—the division of power among a central government and several regional governments—came to the Constitution out of both experience and necessity. At Philadelphia, the Framers faced a number of difficult problems, not the least of them: How to build a new, stronger, more effective National Government while preserving the existing States and the concept of local self-government.

The colonists had rebelled against the harsh rule of a powerful and distant central government. They had fought for the right to manage their own local affairs without the meddling and dictation of the king and his ministers in far-off London. Surely, the colonists would not now agree to another such government.

The Framers found their solution in federalism. In short, they constructed the federal arrangement, with its division of powers, as a compromise. It was an alternative to both the system of nearly independent States, loosely tied to one another in the weak Articles of Confederation, and to a much feared, too powerful central government.

We shall explore the federal system at length in the next chapter. For now, keep in mind that among so many other reasons, federalism is an important part of the Constitution's web of protections of individual freedom. Remember, the Framers were dedicated to the concept of limited government. They were convinced (1) that governmental power poses a threat to individual liberty, (2) that, therefore, the exercise of governmental power must be restrained, and (3) that to divide governmental power, as federalism does, is to curb it and so prevent its abuse. James Madison addressed this point in this passage from *The Federalist Papers*:

> ## PRIMARY SOURCE
>
> In the compound republic of America, the power surrendered by the people is first divided between two distinct governments, and then the portion allotted to each is subdivided among distinct and separate departments. Hence a double security arises to the rights of the people. The different governments will control each other, at the same time that each will be controlled by itself.
> —*The Federalist* No. 51

> ✓ **Checkpoint**
> Identify two powers that the States hold, but that the Federal Government does not.

Essential Questions	To continue to build a response to the chapter Essential Question, go to your **Essential Questions Journal.**
Journal	

SECTION **1** ASSESSMENT

1. **Guiding Question** Use your completed concept web to answer this question: What are the six main principles on which the Constitution is based?

Key Terms and Comprehension

2. How do the first three **articles** differ from the other four articles?

3. **(a)** Into what three branches are the powers of the Federal Government separated? **(b)** Give a brief summary of the **checks and balances** in place for each of the three branches.

4. **(a)** Explain the concept of the **rule of law. (b)** Why would this concept have been important for the Framers? **(c)** What might happen if there were no rule of law?

Critical Thinking

5. **Summarize (a)** Explain the concept of judicial review. **(b)** How was this power formally established?

6. **Express Problems Clearly** What issues might arise when the legislative and executive branches are controlled by different parties?

Quick Write

Writing for Assessment: Develop a Main Idea Some essay tests provide a list of topics from which you must choose. Try to select a topic for which you can quickly develop a main idea. For example:
(a) The relationship between the separation of powers, checks and balances, and judicial review
(b) The importance of federalism to the survival of the U.S. government
(c) The importance of separating powers between the State and Federal governments

What is judicial review?

"It is emphatically the province and duty of the Judicial Department to say what the law is."

Those words, penned by Chief Justice John Marshall, lie at the heart of the Supreme Court's decision in *Marbury* v. *Madison* in 1803—the landmark case in which the High Court established the principle of judicial review. The Constitution does not, in so many words, grant that power to the courts. Yet its exercise has long since become a major feature of the American system of constitutional government.

Marbury arose in the aftermath of the contentious elections of 1800, in which Thomas Jefferson and his Democratic-Republicans captured both the presidency and control of Congress. The Federalists, stung by defeat, tried to pack the federal courts with loyal party members. The outgoing Congress created dozens of new judgeships, and President John Adams promptly filled those posts with tried-and-true Federalists.

William Marbury had been named a justice of the peace for the District of Columbia, and the Senate had confirmed that appointment. President Adams signed his and several other commissions of office late the night of March 3, 1801. Jefferson became President at noon the following day, and he found that Marbury's and the other commissions had not yet been delivered. Angered by the Federalists' court-packing scheme, he directed the new secretary of state, James Madison, not to deliver those documents to the "midnight justices."

Secretary of State James Madison refused to deliver William Marbury's commission of office.

Marbury asked the Supreme Court to order Madison to make delivery of Marbury's commission.

Refusing Marbury's request, Chief Justice John Marshall established the power of judicial review.

Angered in turn, Marbury went to the Supreme Court, seeking a writ of mandamus—a court order directing an officer of government to perform a lawfully required duty. Congress had authorized such suits in the Judiciary Act of 1789. A section of that law gave the Supreme Court the power to hear them in its original jurisdiction—that is, directly, not on appeal from a lower court.

Marbury's suit put Chief Justice Marshall in a most difficult position. His Court had yet to become the coequal of the President and Congress in the still quite new Federal Government. If it granted the writ, the President would almost certainly ignore the action. The Court had no power with which it could enforce its decision, and its place in the system of separation of powers would surely suffer. On the other hand, to deny the writ meant that Marbury would not receive the commission to which he was clearly entitled.

Finally, after sitting on the case for nearly two years, Marshall hit upon a shrewd—indeed, a brilliant and calculatingly farsighted—solution. Unanimously, the Court rejected Marbury's plea. It found that the section of the Judiciary Act on which Marbury depended was in conflict with a provision of the Constitution and was, therefore, invalid. Said the Court: "A law repugnant [completely unacceptable] to the Constitution is void; and the courts, as well as the other departments, are bound by that instrument."

With this ruling, the Court established its power to determine the constitutionality of governmental actions. In doing so, it had in effect upheld President Jefferson's refusal to deliver Marbury's commission. However, that short-term success pales in the light of John Marshall's triumph: the Supreme Court had acquired the power of judicial review.

GOVERNMENT ONLINE
In the News
To learn more about the relevance of the case today, go to **PearsonSuccessNet.com**

Think Critically

1. Should the Supreme Court have the power to declare an act of Congress unconstitutional? Why or why not?
2. **Constitutional Principles** Explain why the power of judicial review is an important part of the system of checks and balances.

Exercising its power of judicial review, the High Court has found several congressional and presidential actions unconstitutional. Thus, in *New York Times* v. *United States*, 1971, the Court held that the government could not bar the publication of secret documents relating to the war in Vietnam.

SECTION 2
Formal Amendment

Guiding Question

How has the Constitution been amended through the formal amendment process? Use an outline like the one below to take notes on how the Constitution can be amended.

I. Formal Amendment Process
A. First Method
  1. _____
  2. _____
B. Second Method
  1. _____
  2. _____

Political Dictionary

- amendment
- ratification
- formal amendment
- Bill of Rights

Objectives

1. Identify the four different ways by which the Constitution may be formally changed.
2. Explain how the formal amendment process illustrates the principles of federalism and popular sovereignty.
3. Understand that several amendments have been proposed, but not ratified.
4. Outline the 27 amendments that have been added to the Constitution.

Image Above: Inez Milholland fought to amend the Constitution to allow women's suffrage.

The Constitution of the United States has now been in force for more than 200 years—longer than the written constitution of any other nation in the world.[2]

When the Constitution became effective in 1789, the United States was a small agricultural nation of fewer than four million people. That population was scattered for some 1,300 miles along the eastern edge of the continent. The 13 States, joined together mostly by travel on horseback and sailing ships, struggled to stay alive in a generally hostile world.

Today, well over 300 million people live in the United States. The now 50 States stretch across the continent and beyond, and the country has many far-flung commitments. The United States is the most powerful nation on Earth, and its modern, highly industrialized and technological society has produced a standard of living that has long been the envy of many other countries.

How has the Constitution, written in 1787, endured and kept pace with that astounding change and growth? The answer lies in this highly important fact: The Constitution of today is, and at the same time is not, the document of 1787. Many of its words are the same, and much of their meaning remains the same. But some of its words have been changed, some have been eliminated, and some have been added. And, very importantly, the meanings of many of its provisions have been modified, as well.

This process of constitutional change, of modification and growth, has come about in two basic ways: (1) by formal amendment and (2) by other, informal means. In this section, you will look at the first of them: the addition of formal amendments to the Constitution.

Formal Amendment Process

The Framers knew that even the wisest of constitution makers cannot build for all time. Thus, the Constitution provides for its own **amendment**—that is, for changes in its written words.

---

2 The British constitution dates from well before the Norman Conquest of 1066, but it is not a single, written document. Rather, it is an "unwritten constitution," a collection of principles, customs, traditions, and significant parliamentary acts that guide British government and practice. Israel, which has existed only since 1948, is the only other state in the world without a written constitution.

Article V sets out two methods for the proposal and two methods for the **ratification** of amendments. So, there are four possible methods of **formal amendment**—changes or additions that become part of the written language of the Constitution itself. The diagram below sets out these two methods of proposal and two methods of ratification.

First, an amendment may be proposed by a two-thirds vote in each house of Congress and ratified by three fourths of the State legislatures. Today, at least 38 State legislatures must approve an amendment to make it a part of the Constitution. Of the Constitution's 27 amendments, 26 were adopted in this manner.

Second, an amendment may be proposed by Congress and ratified by <u>conventions</u>, called for that purpose, in three fourths of the States. Only the 21st Amendment (1933) was adopted in this way.

When Congress proposes an amendment, it chooses the method of ratification.

State conventions were used to ratify the 21st Amendment, largely because the lawmakers felt that the conventions' popularly elected delegates would be more likely to reflect public opinion on the question of the repeal of nationwide prohibition than would State legislators.

Third, an amendment may be proposed by a national convention, called by Congress at the request of two thirds of the State legislatures—today, 34. As you can see in the diagram, it must then be ratified by three fourths of the State legislatures. To this point, Congress has not called such a convention.[3]

---

3   The calling of a convention was a near thing twice over the past 40 years or so. Between 1963 and 1969, 33 State legislatures, one short of the necessary two thirds, sought an amendment to erase the Supreme Court's "one-person, one-vote" decisions; see Chapter 24. Also, between 1975 and 1983, 32 States asked for a convention to propose an amendment that would require that the federal budget be balanced each year, except in time of war or other national emergency.

convention
n. a meeting to deal with matters of common concern

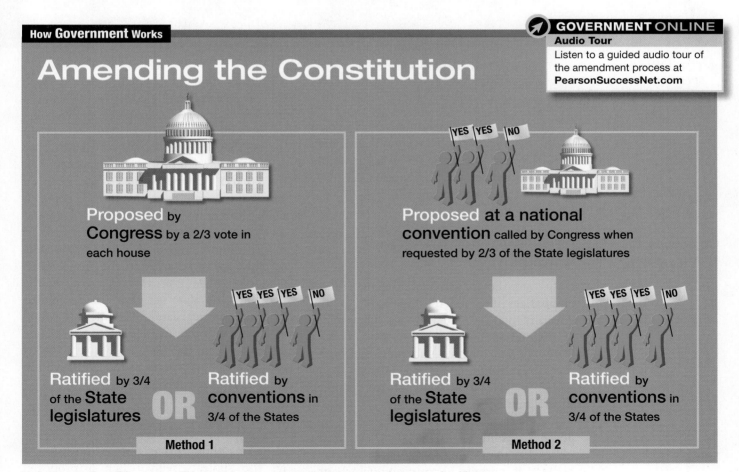

How **Government** Works

Amending the Constitution

Proposed by Congress by a 2/3 vote in each house

YES YES NO

Proposed at a national convention called by Congress when requested by 2/3 of the State legislatures

Ratified by 3/4 of the **State legislatures**

OR

YES YES YES NO

Ratified by **conventions** in 3/4 of the States

Method 1

Ratified by 3/4 of the **State legislatures**

OR

YES YES YES NO

Ratified by **conventions** in 3/4 of the States

Method 2

▶▶ **Interpreting Diagrams** There are two ways to propose an amendment, each with two means of ratification. *Which method has been used to ratify most amendments?*

The 27 Amendments

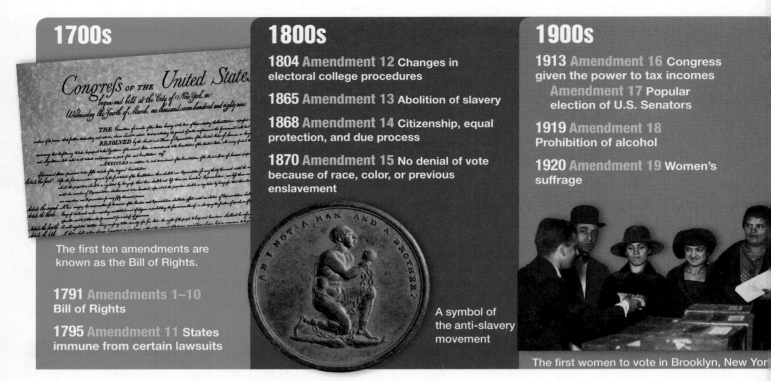

1700s

The first ten amendments are known as the Bill of Rights.

1791 Amendments 1–10 Bill of Rights

1795 Amendment 11 States immune from certain lawsuits

1800s

1804 Amendment 12 Changes in electoral college procedures

1865 Amendment 13 Abolition of slavery

1868 Amendment 14 Citizenship, equal protection, and due process

1870 Amendment 15 No denial of vote because of race, color, or previous enslavement

A symbol of the anti-slavery movement

1900s

1913 Amendment 16 Congress given the power to tax incomes
Amendment 17 Popular election of U.S. Senators

1919 Amendment 18 Prohibition of alcohol

1920 Amendment 19 Women's suffrage

The first women to vote in Brooklyn, New Yor

▶▶ **The Amendments** Only 27 amendments have been added to the Constitution thus far. *Why do you think the Constitution has been amended so infrequently since 1789?*

And fourth, an amendment may be proposed by a national convention and then ratified by conventions in three fourths of the States. Remember, the Constitution itself was adopted in much this same way.

Federalism and Popular Sovereignty

Note that the formal amendment process emphasizes the federal character of the governmental system. Proposal takes place at the national level and ratification is a State-by-State matter. Also note that when the Constitution is amended, that action represents the expression of the people's sovereign will.

Some criticize the practice of sending proposed amendments to the State legislatures rather than to ratifying conventions, especially because it permits a constitutional change without a clear-cut expression by the people.

The critics point out that State legislators, who do the ratifying, are elected to office for a mix of reasons, including party membership, name familiarity, and their stands on certain issues. They are almost never chosen because of their stand on a proposed amendment. On the other hand, the delegates to a ratifying convention would be chosen by the people on the basis of only one factor: a yes-or-no stand on the proposed amendment.

The Supreme Court has held that a State cannot require an amendment proposed by Congress to be approved by a vote of the people of the State before it can be ratified by that State's legislature. It made that ruling in *Hawke* v. *Smith,* in 1920. However, a State legislature can call for an advisory vote by the people before it acts, as the Court held in *Kimble* v. *Swackhamer,* in 1978.

Proposed Amendments

The Constitution places only one restriction on the subjects with which a proposed amendment may deal. Article V declares

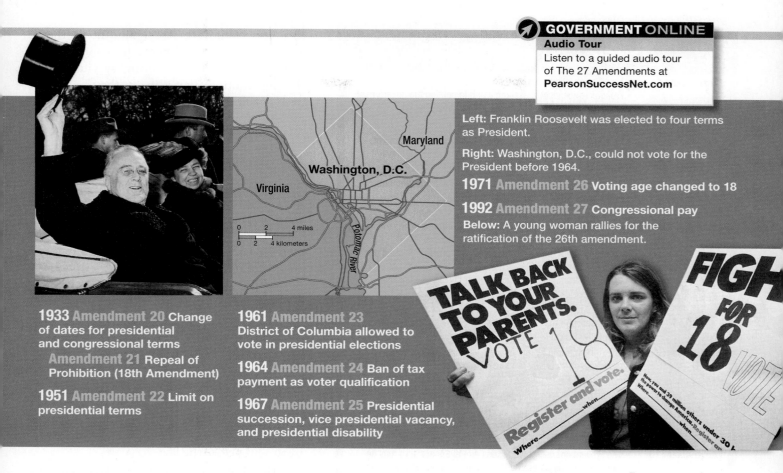

Left: Franklin Roosevelt was elected to four terms as President.

Right: Washington, D.C., could not vote for the President before 1964.

1971 Amendment 26 Voting age changed to 18

1992 Amendment 27 Congressional pay

Below: A young woman rallies for the ratification of the 26th amendment.

Maryland

Washington, D.C.

Virginia

Potomac River

0   2   4 miles
0   2   4 kilometers

1933 Amendment 20 Change of dates for presidential and congressional terms
Amendment 21 Repeal of Prohibition (18th Amendment)

1951 Amendment 22 Limit on presidential terms

1961 Amendment 23 District of Columbia allowed to vote in presidential elections

1964 Amendment 24 Ban of tax payment as voter qualification

1967 Amendment 25 Presidential succession, vice presidential vacancy, and presidential disability

TALK BACK TO YOUR PARENTS. VOTE 18
Register and vote.
Where _____ when _____

FIGHT FOR 18 VOTE

---

that "no State, without its Consent, shall be deprived of its equal Suffrage in the Senate."

When both houses of Congress pass a resolution proposing an amendment, Congress does not send it to the President to be signed or vetoed, though the Constitution would seem to require it[4]—because when Congress proposes an amendment, it is not making law (not legislating). Although the chief executive has no formal role in the amendment process, his or her political influence can affect the success or failure of any attempt to amend the Constitution, of course.

If a State rejects a proposed amendment, it is not forever bound by that action. It may later reconsider and ratify the proposal. Most constitutional scholars agree that the reverse is not true, however. Once a State has approved an amendment, that action cannot be undone; and no governor's veto power

extends to the ratification of a proposed amendment.

Some 15,000 joint resolutions calling for amendments to the Constitution have been proposed in Congress since 1789. Only 33 of them have been sent on to the States. Of those, only 27 have been finally ratified. One of the unratified amendments had been offered by Congress in 1789—along with 10 other proposals that became the Bill of Rights in 1791, and another that became the 27th Amendment in 1992.

The unratified amendment of 1789 dealt with the distribution of seats in the House of Representatives. A second, proposed in 1810, would have voided the citizenship of anyone accepting any foreign title or other honor. Another, in 1861, would have prohibited forever any amendment relating to slavery. A fourth, in 1924, was intended to give Congress the power to regulate child labor. A fifth one, proclaiming the equal rights of women (ERA), was proposed in 1972; it fell three States short of ratification and died in 1982. An amendment to give the District of

✔ **Checkpoint**
How does the formal amendment process reflect the concept of federalism?

---

4 See Article I, Section 7, Clause 3. This practice of not submitting proposed amendments to the President is an example of the many changes in the Constitution that have been made by means other than formal amendment, a matter addressed in the next section.

The First Ten Amendments

Amendment 1	• Freedom of religion, speech, and the press • Freedom to peaceably assemble and to petition the government
Amendment 2	• The right to maintain a militia • The right to bear arms
Amendment 3	• Protection from having to quarter (house) soldiers in time of peace without the consent of the owner, nor in time of war except as provided by law
Amendment 4	• Protection against arbitrary searches and seizures without proper warrant or probable cause
Amendment 5	• Protection from prosecution without an indictment • Protection from being tried for the same crime twice • Protection from having to testify against oneself • Protection from the loss of life, liberty, or property without due process of law • Protection from loss of property without just compensation
Amendment 6	• The right to a speedy trial by an impartial jury • The right to be informed of the charges, to cross-examine witnesses, and to present favorable witnesses • The right to an attorney
Amendment 7	• The right to a trial by jury in any civil case where the amount of money involved is $20 or more
Amendment 8	• Protection from excessive bail or fines • Protection from cruel and unusual punishment
Amendment 9	• The fact that the Constitution spells out a number of civil rights does not mean that there are not other, unwritten, rights held by the people.
Amendment 10	• The powers not delegated to the Federal Government may be exercised by the States, as long as they are not prohibited by the Constitution.

▶▶ The first ten amendments protect many fundamental rights held by the people. *Why is it important to spell out these rights?*

✔ **Checkpoint**
What is the purpose of the Bill of Rights?

Columbia seats in Congress was proposed in 1978; it died in 1985.

When Congress proposed the 18th Amendment in 1917, it set a seven-year deadline for its ratification. The Supreme Court held that Congress can place "a reasonable time limit" on the ratification process, in a case from California, *Dillon* v. *Gloss,* in 1921. Congress has set a similar limit on the ratification period for each of the amendments (except the 19th) that it has proposed since then. It also granted a three-year extension of the deadline for the Equal Rights Amendment in 1979.

The 27 Amendments

The Constitution's 27 amendments are summarized on pages 80 and 81, and in the table above. As you review them, note

this important fact: As significant as they are, those 27 amendments have not been responsible for the extraordinary vitality of the Constitution. That is to say, they have not been a major part of the process by which the Constitution has kept pace with more than two centuries of change.

The Bill of Rights The first ten amendments were added to the Constitution less than three years after it became effective. They were proposed by the first session of the First Congress in 1789 and were ratified by the States in late 1791. Each of these amendments arose out of the controversy surrounding the ratification of the Constitution itself. Many people, including Thomas Jefferson, had agreed to support the Constitution only if a listing of the basic rights held by the people were added to it, immediately.

Collectively, the first ten amendments are known as the **Bill of Rights.** They set out the great constitutional guarantees of freedom of belief and expression, of freedom and security of the person, and of fair and equal treatment before the law.

The first ten amendments were added to the Constitution so quickly that, for all intents and purposes, they might just as well be regarded as a part of the original Constitution. In point of fact, they were not. We shall look at the 1st through the 9th amendments at some length in Chapters 19 and 20. The 10th Amendment does not deal with civil rights, as such. Rather, it spells out the concept of reserved powers held by the States in the federal system.

The Later Amendments Each of the other amendments that have been added to the Constitution over the past 200 years also grew out of some particular, and often interesting, set of circumstances. For example, the 11th Amendment declares that no State may be sued in the federal courts by a citizen of another State or by a citizen of any foreign state. It was proposed by Congress in 1794 and ratified in 1795, after the State of Georgia had lost a case in the United States Supreme Court. The case (*Chisholm* v. *Georgia,* decided by the Court in 1793) arose out of a dispute over the ownership of some land in Georgia.

It had been brought to the brand new federal court system by a man who lived in South Carolina.

The 12th Amendment was added in 1804 after the electoral college had failed to produce a winner in the presidential election of 1800. Thomas Jefferson became the third President of the United States in 1801, but only after a long, bitter fight in the House of Representatives.

The 13th Amendment, added in 1865, provides another example. It abolished slavery in the United States and was a direct result of the Civil War. The 14th Amendment, with its definition of citizenship (in 1868), and the 15th Amendment on the right to vote (in 1870) also resulted from that conflict.

The 18th Amendment, establishing a nationwide prohibition of alcohol, was ratified in 1919. Known as "the noble experiment," it lasted fewer than 14 years. The 18th Amendment was repealed by the 21st in 1933.

The 22nd Amendment (1951), limiting the number of terms in which a President may serve to two, was proposed in 1947, soon after the Republican Party had gained control of Congress for the first time in 16 years. Over that period, Franklin D. Roosevelt, a Democrat, had won the presidency four times.

The 26th Amendment was added in 1971. It lowered the voting age to 18 in all elections in the United States. Many who

HE'S GOT A WARRANT!

offthemark.com

▶▶ **Analyzing Political Cartoons** This cartoon illustrates the 4th Amendment. *What is this cartoon conveying about that amendment?*

backed the amendment began to work for its passage during World War II, creating the slogan "Old enough to fight, old enough to vote." Its ratification was spurred by the war in Vietnam.

The most recent amendment, the 27th, was written by James Madison and was among the first to be offered by Congress, in 1789. It forbids members of Congress from raising their own pay during that term. It finally became a part of the Constitution in 1992, when the 38th State, Michigan, ratified it.

Essential Questions Journal To continue to build a response to the chapter Essential Question, go to your **Essential Questions Journal.**

SECTION 2 ASSESSMENT

1. **Guiding Question** Use your completed outline to answer this question: How has the Constitution been amended through the formal amendment process?

Key Terms and Comprehension

2. **(a)** Which method of **formal amendment** has been used only once? **(b)** For which **amendment** was it used?

3. Explain how the **ratification** process is an example of popular sovereignty.

Critical Thinking

4. **Predict Consequences (a)** Why was the Bill of Rights added to the Constitution? **(b)** What rights do these amendments protect? **(c)** How might news reports differ if freedom of speech and the press were not part of the Constitution?

5. **Identify Central Issues** Some people have criticized the ratification of amendments by State legislatures instead of by popularly elected delegates. **(a)** Why has this process been criticized? **(b)** Do you agree? Why or why not?

Quick Write

Writing for Assessment: Gather Details Reread the topic you chose in the previous section. What is this question asking for? For example, when you see the word *effect* in a question, you know you are looking for a cause-and-effect relationship. Gather details from the reading that specifically answer the question. Leave out unnecessary details.

Identifying Political Roots and Attitudes

What is your position on these questions:
- **Should all Americans be covered by healthcare insurance?**
- **Should the Federal Government do more to protect the environment?**
- **Has outsourcing jobs to other countries harmed the nation's economy?**

Your position on these issues probably reflects a number of factors, especially your background and personal experiences. Family, friends, and teachers, as well as their party affiliations, may also influence you. The part of the country in which you live may be at the root of your political attitudes, as well.

Political attitudes evolve from a variety of sources. People settle in different parts of the country. They belong to different ethnic and cultural groups. Career paths and education also have a major impact.

These political attitudes affect the way a citizen votes. They also affect the way senators and representatives vote, and how Presidents choose the issues they support or oppose. Use these steps to determine where your classmates stand on one of the above issues.

1. **Choose a Question** Look at the questions above. Do you have opinions about these issues? Where do you think your opinions came from? Have you read articles about these issues? Have you heard others talking about them?

2. **Choose One Question** Choose one of these questions and look at opinion polls from various sources to see how people across the country feel about the issue. Do you notice trends? For example, how do people in the city feel about the environment and how do people from rural areas feel about it? What is the opinion of each of the political parties?

3. **Create and Ask Polling Questions** Now, create your own polling questions on the issue. Ask fellow students their opinion on the subject. Make sure your questions are neutral in nature.

Ask them how much they have read or heard about the matter, as well as how they think of themselves politically. Are they conservative? Liberal? With which party do they most often identify? How did they come to identify with this party?

Collect your information to present to the class. Then, review what you've learned. Where do your political roots originate? Has your opinion on this issue changed? Understanding your own political roots and attitudes can help you judge where you stand on an issue, and how you would make the best choice when voting.

▸▸ What do you think?

1. What personal experiences and individuals have influenced your political attitudes?

2. What has had the greatest effect on your political attitudes: the place where you live, your family's party affiliation, or your cultural background? Explain your answer.

3. **You Try It** Write five interview questions about political roots and attitudes. Answer each question yourself. Then interview a friend or family member about their views.

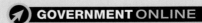

GOVERNMENT ONLINE
Citizenship Activity Pack
For an activity on political roots and attitudes, go to
PearsonSuccessNet.com

SECTION 3

Change by Other Means

Guiding Question

How have the day-to-day workings of government affected how we interpret the Constitution? Use a cause-and-effect chart like the one below to take notes on the workings of government.

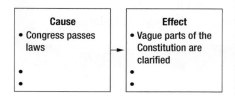

Cause	Effect
• Congress passes laws	• Vague parts of the Constitution are clarified
•	•
•	•

Political Dictionary

- executive agreement
- treaty
- electoral college
- Cabinet
- senatorial courtesy

Objectives

1. Identify how basic legislation has added to our understanding of the Constitution over time.
2. Describe the ways in which the executive and judicial branches have interpreted the Constitution.
3. Analyze the role of party practices and custom in interpreting the Constitution.

Image Above: Delegates, like the one above, play an important role in shaping the U.S. government.

Surely, the Framers would be surprised to learn that only 17 amendments have been added to their handiwork since the adoption of the Bill of Rights more than two centuries ago. That so few formal changes have been made is, in part, a tribute to the wisdom of the Framers. But it is also due, in no small part, to the fact that many of the Constitution's provisions are cast in almost outline-like form; they are brief and seldom very detailed or specific. In short, their skeletal nature virtually guarantees interpretation.

So, to understand the Constitution, you must grasp this key point: There is much in that document—in fact, a great deal—that cannot be seen with the naked eye.

To put this essential point another way: Over time, many interpretations have been made in the Constitution that have not involved any changes in its written words. This vital process of constitutional change by means other than formal amendment has taken place—and continues to occur—in five key ways: through (1) the passage of basic legislation by Congress; (2) actions taken by the President; (3) key decisions of the Supreme Court; (4) the activities of political parties; and (5) custom and usage.

Basic Legislation

Congress has been a major agent of constitutional change in two important ways. First, it has passed a number of laws to clarify several of the Constitution's brief provisions. That is, Congress has added flesh to the bones of those sections of the Constitution that the Framers left purposely skeletal—provisions they left for Congress to detail as circumstances required.

Take the structure of the federal court system as an example. In Article III, Section 1, the Constitution provides for "one supreme Court, and . . . such inferior Courts as the Congress may from time to time <u>ordain</u> and establish." Beginning with the Judiciary Act of 1789, all of the federal courts, except the Supreme Court, have been created by acts of Congress. Or, similarly, Article II creates only the offices of President and Vice President. The many departments, agencies, and offices in the now huge executive branch have been created by acts of Congress.

The State of the Union

"The President shall from time to time give to Congress information of the State of the Union and recommend to their Consideration such measures as he shall judge necessary and expedient.

—Article II, Section 3

FROM THE CONSTITUTION

Creating a Custom While an address to Congress is required by the Constitution, the method of address is left to each President. Both George Washington and then John Adams delivered their speeches to joint sessions of Congress. But Thomas Jefferson submitted a written document in 1801 and set a precedent that lasted for more than a century. In 1913 Woodrow Wilson revived the practice of appearing before Congress, and every President since then has followed his lead. Calvin Coolidge's 1923 speech was the first broadcast by radio and Harry Truman's 1947 address was the first to be televised.

Constitutional Principles How does the State of the Union address reflect the system of checks and balances?

▲ President Harry Truman delivers the first televised State of the Union.

✔ **Checkpoint**
Name the two methods by which Congress has shaped the government.

succession
n. the process by which one follows in order (succeeds) to an office

ordain
v. to order, direct, decree

As an additional example, the Constitution deals with the matter of presidential <u>succession</u>, but only up to a point. The 25th Amendment says that if the presidency becomes vacant, the Vice President automatically succeeds to the office. Who becomes President if both the presidency and the vice presidency are vacant? Thus, the Constitution leaves the answer to that question to Congress.

Second, Congress has added to the Constitution by the way in which it has used many of its powers. The Constitution gives to Congress the expressed power to regulate foreign and interstate commerce.[5] But what is "foreign commerce" and "interstate commerce"? What, exactly, does Congress have the power to regulate? The Constitution does not say. Congress has done much to

define those words, however, by exercising its commerce power with the passage of literally thousands of laws. As it has done so, Congress has, in a very real sense, expanded the Constitution.

Executive Action

The manner in which various Presidents, especially the more vigorous ones, have used their powers has also contributed to the growth of the Constitution. For example, the document says that only Congress can declare war.[6] But the Constitution also makes the President the commander in chief of the nation's armed forces.[7] Acting under that authority, several Presidents have made war without a declaration of war by

---

5 See Article I, Section 8, Clause 3.

6 See Article I, Section 8, Clause 11.
7 See Article II, Section 2, Clause 1.

Congress. In fact, Presidents have used the armed forces abroad in combat without such a declaration on several hundred occasions in our history.

Take the use of executive agreements in the conduct of foreign affairs as another example. An **executive agreement** is a pact made by the President directly with the head of a foreign state. A **treaty,** on the other hand, is a formal agreement between two or more sovereign states. The principal difference between agreements and treaties is that executive agreements need not be approved by the Senate. They are as legally binding as treaties, however. Recent Presidents have often used them in our dealings with other countries, instead of the much more cumbersome treaty-making process outlined in Article II, Section 2 of the Constitution.

Additionally, most Presidents have insisted that the phrase "executive Power" in Section 1 of Article II includes much more than the particular presidential powers set out in that article. Thus, Thomas Jefferson engineered the Louisiana Purchase in 1803, doubling the size of the United States—even though the Constitution does not say that the President has the power to acquire territory.

Court Decisions

The nation's courts, most <u>tellingly</u> the United States Supreme Court, interpret and apply the Constitution in many of the cases they hear. You have already encountered several of these instances of constitutional interpretation by the Court, most notably in *Marbury* v. *Madison,* 1803.

Recall that the Court established the power of judicial review—which is not specifically mentioned in the Constitution. You will find many more instances throughout the pages of this book—for the Supreme Court is, as Woodrow Wilson once put it, "a constitutional convention in continuous session."

Party Practices

The nation's political parties have been a major agent of constitutional change over the course of our political history, despite the fact that the Constitution makes no mention

of them. In fact, most of the Framers were opposed to political parties. In his Farewell Address in 1796, George Washington warned the people against what he called "the baneful effects of the spirit of party." He and many others feared the divisive effect of party politics on government. Yet, even as he spoke, parties were developing. They have had a major place in the shaping of government and its processes ever since. Illustrations of that point are almost endless.

Neither the Constitution nor any law provides for the nomination of candidates for the presidency. From the 1830s on, however, the major parties have held national conventions to do just that. The parties have converted the **electoral college,** the body that makes the formal selection of the nation's President, from what the Framers intended into a "rubber stamp" for each State's popular vote in presidential elections. Both houses of Congress are organized and conduct much of their business on the basis of party. The President makes appointments to office with an eye to party politics. In short, government in the United States is in many ways government through party.

Custom and Usage

Unwritten customs may be as strong as written law, and many of them have developed in our governmental system. Again, there are many examples. By custom, not because the Constitution says so, the heads of the 15 executive departments make up the **Cabinet,** an advisory body to the President.

On each of the eight occasions when a President died in office, the Vice President succeeded to that office—most recently Lyndon Johnson, following John Kennedy's assassination in 1963. Yet, the written words of the Constitution did not provide for this practice until the adoption of the 25th Amendment in 1967. Until then, the Constitution said only that the powers and duties of the presidency—but *not* the office itself—"shall devolve on" (be transferred to) the Vice President.[8]

---

8 Read carefully Article II, Section 1, Clause 6, and then read Section 1 of the 25th Amendment.

✔ **Checkpoint**
How have political parties changed the way we interpret the Constitution?

<u>**tellingly**</u>
adv. striking, with marked effect

▲ The President and three Cabinet secretaries (from left): Eric Shinseki (Veterans Affairs), Shaun Donovan (Education), and Ken Salazar (Interior).

✔ **Checkpoint**
Which two customs did the 22nd and 25th amendments establish as law?

It is a long-established custom that the Senate will approve only those presidential appointees, such as a federal judge or a United States marshal, who are acceptable to the senator or senators of the President's party from the State involved. This practice is known as **senatorial courtesy,** and it amounts to an unwritten rule that is closely followed in the Senate. Notice that its practical effect is to shift a portion of the appointing power from the President, where the formal wording of the Constitution puts it, to certain members of the Senate.

Both the strength and the importance of unwritten customs can be seen in the reaction to the rare circumstances in which one of them has not been observed. For nearly 150 years, the "no-third-term tradition" was a closely followed rule in presidential politics. The tradition began in 1796, when George Washington refused to seek a third term as President, and several later Presidents followed that lead. In 1940, and again in 1944, however, Franklin Roosevelt broke the no-third-term custom. He sought and won a third and then, four years later, a fourth term in the White House. As a direct result, the 22nd Amendment was added to the Constitution in 1951, limiting the President to two terms. What had been an unwritten custom, an informal rule, became part of the written Constitution itself.

Essential Questions Journal To continue to build a response to the chapter Essential Question, go to your **Essential Questions Journal.**

SECTION **3** ASSESSMENT

1. **Guiding Question** Use your completed cause-and-effect chart to answer this question: How have the day-to-day workings of government affected how we interpret the Constitution?

Key Terms and Comprehension

2. **(a)** Did the Framers lay out the provisions of the Constitution in a general or specific manner? **(b)** In what way has the Framers' plan eased change throughout the last two centuries?

3. In what two ways has Congress "added flesh to the bones" of the Constitution? Give an example of each.

Critical Thinking

4. **Predict Consequences** Several Presidents have deployed troops to various conflicts without asking Congress for a declaration of war. What might be the consequences of setting aside this check **(a)** on the executive branch? **(b)** on Congress? **(c)** How might it change the interpretation of the Constitution?

5. **Draw Conclusions (a)** Name two examples of customs that have endured despite their absence in the Constitution. **(b)** How important is custom in the workings of the Federal Government? Why?

Quick Write

Writing for Assessment: Outline and Answer Once you have gathered the details you need for the topic you selected in Section 1, write an outline to organize the information. Remember, you may not have much time. Make your outline brief and to the point. Use the outline as a framework to write your response.

Quick Study Guide

GOVERNMENT ONLINE
On the Go
To review anytime, anywhere, download these online resources at **PearsonSuccessNet.com**
Political Dictionary, Audio Review

Guiding Question
Section 2 How has the Constitution been amended through the formal amendment process?

Guiding Question
Section 1 What are the six main principles on which the Constitution is based?

CHAPTER 3
Essential Question
How has the Constitution lasted through changing times?

Guiding Question
Section 3 How have the day-to-day workings of government affected how we interpret the Constitution?

Political Dictionary

popular sovereignty *p. 69*
limited government *p. 69*
constitutionalism *p. 70*
rule of law *p. 70*
separation of powers *p. 70*
checks and balances *p. 72*
veto *p. 72*
judicial review *p. 73*
unconstitutional *p. 73*
federalism *p. 75*
amendment *p. 78*
ratification *p. 79*
formal amendment *p. 79*
Bill of Rights *p. 82*
executive agreement *p. 87*
treaty *p. 87*
electoral college *p. 87*
Cabinet *p. 87*
senatorial courtesy *p. 88*

The Six Basic Principles

Popular Sovereignty	The people give the government its power.
Limited Government	Government has only those powers that the people give it.
Separation of Powers	The powers of government are split among the judicial, legislative, and executive branches.
Checks and Balances	Each branch has the power to check the other two branches.
Judicial Review	The courts have the power to determine if government actions violate the Constitution.
Federalism	The powers of government are divided between the Federal Government and the States.

The Formal Amendment Process

By Congress
- **Proposal** by a 2/3 vote in each house of Congress
- **Ratification** by 3/4 of State legislatures or by conventions in 3/4 of the States

By a National Convention
- **Proposal** by a national convention called by Congress
- **Ratification** by 3/4 of State legislatures or by conventions in 3/4 of the States

Chapter Assessment

GOVERNMENT ONLINE
Self-Test
To test your understanding of key terms and main ideas, visit **PearsonSuccessNet.com**

Comprehension and Critical Thinking

Section 1

1. **(a)** What checks exist between the legislative and executive branches? **(b)** How do these checks represent the intentions of the Framers?

2. Reread the excerpt from the Massachusetts Constitution in Section 1. **(a)** What restrictions does it put on the three branches of the State government? **(b)** What is meant by "a government of laws and not of men"?

3. **(a)** Why were the Framers so careful to limit the powers of the Federal Government? **(b)** Which branch of the Federal Government seems to have the least amount of checks against its power? **(c)** How might the power of this branch be further limited?

4. **Analyze Political Cartoons (a)** Which checks on government does this cartoon suggest? **(b)** How does it reflect "a government of laws and not of men"?

"How come everything / like is always unconstitutional?"

Section 2

5. **(a)** Of the four methods of formal amendment, which has been used the most to amend the Constitution? **(b)** How does this method preserve the intention of the Framers to create a federal government?

6. In most cases, amendments have been added as the result of a specific issue. What issue gave rise to **(a)** the 13th, 14th, and 15th amendments? **(b)** the 22nd Amendment?

7. **(a)** When an amendment is proposed, why is it not sent to the President to sign or veto? **(b)** Do you agree with this practice? Why or why not?

8. How does the process of constitutional amendment reflect the goals of the Framers?

Section 3

9. **(a)** How have party practices changed the way we interpret the Constitution? **(b)** How did the Framers—in particular, George Washington—feel about political parties? **(c)** Do you agree with Washington's assessment of political parties? Why or why not?

10. **(a)** List two ways in which custom has influenced government. **(b)** How important is custom to our government?

Writing About Government

11. Use your Quick Write exercises to write a brief essay answering the question you chose. Make sure that you use your outline as the frame for your essay. Try to make your point in three or four paragraphs, with an introduction, a body, and a conclusion. See pp. S11–S12 in the Skills Handbook.

Apply What You've Learned

12. **Essential Question Activity** Propose your own amendment to the Constitution.

    (a) Research a current government issue, something that you feel should be made a permanent part of the Constitution.

    (b) Create an outline of arguments for and against your proposed addition to the Constitution.

    (c) Create a plan detailing which method you would use to get your amendment proposed and ratified.

    (d) Bring your amendment before the class and explain why it should be passed.

13. **Essential Question Assessment** Based on your work from the activity and the content you have learned in this chapter, hold a group discussion to help you answer the Essential Question: **How has the Constitution lasted through changing times?** Take notes on your ideas from the discussion.

Essential Questions Journal To respond to the chapter Essential Question, go to your **Essential Questions Journal.**

Document-Based Assessment

Amendments for a Growing City

In 1790, Congress chose a site along the Potomac River for the nation's capital. The map illustrates the plan for the new city. This site would belong to no State. It would be under the authority of Congress. The image reflects the city's small population at its beginnings. In 1950, Washington, D.C., was home to over 800,000 residents, who could not vote for their President. Document 1 shows the amendment that changed that situation.

Document 1

Section 1. The District constituting the seat of Government of the United States shall appoint in such manner as the Congress may direct:

A number of electors of President and Vice President equal to the whole number of Senators and Representatives in Congress to which the District would be entitled if it were a State, but in no event more than the least populous State; they shall be in addition to those appointed by the States, they shall be considered, for the purposes of the election of President and Vice President, to be electors appointed by a State; and they shall meet in the District and perform such duties as provided by the twelfth article of Amendment.

Section 2. Congress shall have the power to enforce this article by appropriate legislation.

—23rd Amendment

Document 2

—Washington, D.C., circa 1790

Use your knowledge of the Constitution, the amendment process, and Documents 1 and 2 to answer Questions 1–3.

1. What was the purpose of the 23rd Amendment to the Constitution?
   - **A.** to include voters of Washington, D.C., in all elections
   - **B.** to include voters of Washington, D.C., in presidential elections
   - **C.** to include members of Congress, living in Washington, D.C., in presidential elections
   - **D.** to include members of Congress, living in Washington, D.C., in all elections

2. Why did the Constitution not address the issue of voters in the national capital?

3. **Pull It Together** How does the example of Washington, D.C., help to explain why the Constitution has endured through changing times?

GOVERNMENT ONLINE
Online Documents
To find more primary sources on Washington, D.C., visit
PearsonSuccessNet.com

Federalism

Essential Question
Is the federal system the best way to govern the United States?

> Let the **thirteen states**, bound together in a **strict** and **indissoluble Union**, concur in erecting **one great American system**

—Alexander Hamilton, *The Federalist* No. 11

GOVERNMENT ONLINE
On the Go

To study anywhere, anytime, download these online resources at PearsonSuccessNet.com
• Political Dictionary
• Audio Review
• Downloadable Interactivities

▶ **Photo:** President Obama discusses the economy with Virginia Governor Tim Kaine at John Tyler Community College.

SECTION 1

Federalism: Powers Divided

How is power divided between the Federal Government and the States? Use a Venn diagram like the one below to take notes on the powers of the Federal and State Governments.

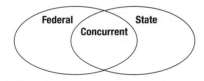

Political Dictionary

- federalism
- division of powers
- delegated powers
- expressed powers
- implied powers
- inherent powers
- reserved powers
- exclusive powers
- concurrent powers
- Supremacy Clause

Objectives

1. Define federalism and explain why the Framers chose this system.
2. Identify powers delegated to and denied to the National Government, and powers reserved for and denied to the States.
3. Explain the difference between exclusive and concurrent powers.
4. Examine the Constitution as "the supreme Law of the Land."

Image Above: Members of the New York National Guard

You know that federal law requires young men to register for military service at age 18, that most employers must pay their workers at the least a minimum wage set by act of Congress, and that no person can be denied a job on the basis of his or her race or ethnicity.

You also know that State law says that you must have a driver's license in order to drive a car, that it is illegal for anyone under 21 to buy alcoholic beverages, and that only those persons who can satisfy certain requirements can buy or own firearms.

Those three examples illustrate a very complex matter: the division of the powers of government in this country between the National Government, on the one hand, and the 50 States on the other. This section will help you to better understand that sometimes complicated, but very important, arrangement.

The Framers Choose Federalism

When the Framers of the Constitution met at Philadelphia in 1787, they faced a number of difficult questions. Not the least of them: How could they possibly create a new central government that would be strong enough to meet the needs of the day and would, at the same time, preserve the already existing States?

Few of the Framers favored a strong central government based on the British model, and all of them knew that the Revolution had been fought in the name of local self-government. They also knew that the government established under the Articles of Confederation had proved too weak to deal with the new nation's many problems.

While the Framers favored a stronger national government, they also knew firsthand the importance of limiting federal powers. They were convinced that (1) governmental power inevitably poses a threat to individual liberty, (2) that therefore the exercise of governmental power must be restrained, and (3) that to divide governmental power, as federalism does, is to prevent its abuse.

Federalism Defined

Federalism is a system of government in which a written constitution divides the powers of government on a territorial basis, between a central government and several regional governments, usually called states or provinces. Each of those basic levels of government has its own substantial set of powers. Neither level, acting alone, can change the basic division of powers the constitution has created. Additionally, each level of government operates through its own agencies and acts directly through its own officials and laws.

The American system of government stands as a prime example of federalism. The basic design of that system is set out in the Constitution. The document provides for a **division of powers** between the National Government and the governments of the 50 States. That is, it assigns certain powers to the National Government and reserves others to the States. This division of powers was implied in the original Constitution and then spelled out in the 10th Amendment.

In effect, federalism produces a dual system of government. That is, it provides for two basic levels of government, each with its own field of authority, and each operating over the same people and the same territory at the same time.

In the American federal system, each of the two basic levels of government can make certain decisions and do certain things that the other level cannot. For example, only the Federal Government can regulate interstate commerce—that is, trade conducted between and among the various States. On the other hand, each of the States decides for itself whether those who commit certain crimes in that State can be put to death.

Federalism's major strength lies in this central fact: It allows local action in matters of local concern and national action in matters of wider concern. Local traditions, needs, and desires vary from one State to another, and federalism allows for differing circumstances among the States.

Illustrations of this point are nearly endless. For example, in 48 States most gas stations are self-service; in New Jersey and Oregon, the law forbids motorists to pump their own gas. Only one State—North Dakota—does not require voters to register in order to cast their ballots. Only Nebraska

Reserved Powers

> The powers not delegated to the United States by the Constitution, nor prohibited by it to the States, are reserved to the States respectively, or to the people.
>
> —10th Amendment

FROM THE CONSTITUTION

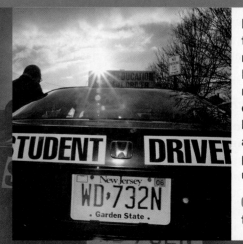

States usually require driver's license applicants to take driving lessons.

Regulating Driving Issuing driver's licenses is a power reserved to the States, and every State has its own set of rules and requirements. Most States require a written, on-road, and vision test. However, the age at which teenagers can get a license and the rules new drivers must follow vary from State to State. Thus, in California, drivers under 20 must be accompanied by someone age 25 or older between the hours of 11 P.M. and 5 A.M. In Massachusetts, a teenager cannot get a driver's license until age 16-and-a-half, at which point the new driver is given a restricted Junior Operator's License until age 18.

Constitutional Principles Under which of the six basic principles do the reserved powers fall?

enumerated
adj. specified, listed, identified

reprieve
n. postponement or delay in the execution of a sentence

has a unicameral (one-house) legislature. Oregon and Washington are the only States that have legalized physician-assisted suicide. Only five States—Alaska, Delaware, New Hampshire, Montana, and Oregon—do not impose a general sales tax.

Federalism also allows for experimentation and innovation in solving public policy problems. Indeed, the several States have long been described as so many "laboratories of government." New approaches to difficult matters may originate in one State and then be adopted in another or even be put in place at the national level.

The Welfare Reform Act passed by Congress in 1996 affords a useful illustration of the point. That landmark statute revolutionized the Federal Government's approach to providing welfare assistance to millions of Americans on the lower rungs of the nation's economic ladder—and its basic features were first suggested by welfare administrators in the States of Wisconsin, California, and Michigan.

In its most noteworthy provisions, the law abolished the Aid to Families with Dependent Children (AFDC) program, replacing it with block grants to the States. The several States now have wide discretion in the determination of eligibility for financial assistance.

While federalism allows individual States to handle State and local matters, it also provides for the strength that comes from union. National defense and foreign affairs offer useful illustrations of this point. So, too, do domestic affairs. Take, for example, a natural disaster. When a flood, drought, hurricane, or other catastrophe hits a particular State, the resources of the National Government and all of the other States can be mobilized to aid the stricken area.

Powers of the Federal Government

The National Government is a government of **delegated powers.** That is, that government has only those powers delegated (granted) to it in the Constitution. There are three distinct types of delegated powers: expressed, implied, and inherent.

The Expressed Powers The **expressed powers** are those powers delegated to the National Government in so many words—spelled out, expressly, in the Constitution. Those powers are also sometimes called the "<u>enumerated</u> powers."

You can find most of the expressed powers in Article I, Section 8. There, in 18 separate clauses, the Constitution expressly gives 27 powers to Congress. They include the power to lay and collect taxes, to coin money, to regulate foreign and interstate commerce, to raise and maintain armed forces, to declare war, to fix standards of weights and measures, to grant patents and copyrights, and to do many other things.

Several other expressed powers are set out elsewhere in the Constitution, as well. Article II, Section 2 gives several powers to the President—including the power to act as commander in chief of the armed forces, to grant <u>reprieves</u> and pardons, to make treaties, and to appoint major federal officials. Article III grants "the judicial Power of the United States" to the Supreme Court and other courts in the federal judiciary. And, finally, several expressed powers also are found in various amendments to the Constitution; thus, the 16th Amendment gives Congress the power to levy an income tax.

The Implied Powers The **implied powers** are not expressly stated in the Constitution, but they are reasonably suggested—implied—by the expressed powers. The constitutional basis for the implied powers is found in one of the expressed powers. Article I, Section 8, Clause 18 gives Congress the "necessary and proper power." The Necessary and Proper Clause says that Congress has the power

FROM THE CONSTITUTION

to make all Laws which shall be necessary and proper for carrying into Execution the foregoing Powers and all other Powers vested by this Constitution in the Government of the United States, or in any Department or Officer thereof.

—Article I, Section 8, Clause 18

Expressed Powers

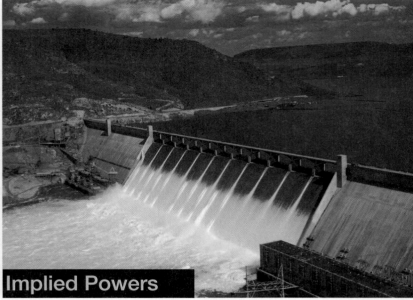

Implied Powers

Congress has the expressed power to provide for naturalization—the process by which aliens become citizens. Its implied powers allow it to do such things as create hydroelectric dams. *Where does the Constitution provide for dam-building?*

Through decades of congressional and court interpretation, the words *necessary and proper* have come to mean, in effect, "convenient and useful." Indeed, the Necessary and Proper Clause is sometimes called the Elastic Clause, because, over time, it has been stretched to cover so many different situations.

Here are but a few of the thousands of examples of the exercise of implied powers: Congress has provided for the regulation of labor-management relations, the building of hydroelectric power dams, and the building of the 42,000-mile interstate highway system. It has made federal crimes of such acts as moving stolen goods, gambling devices, and kidnapped persons across State lines. It has prohibited racial discrimination in granting all people access to such places as restaurants, theaters, hotels, and motels. Congress has taken these actions, and many more, because the power to do so is reasonably implied by just one of the expressed powers: the power to regulate interstate commerce.[1]

The Inherent Powers The **inherent powers** are those powers that belong to

the National Government because it is the national government of a sovereign state in the world community. Although the Constitution does not expressly provide for them, they are powers that, over time, all national governments have come to possess. It stands to reason that the Framers of the Constitution intended the National Government they created would also hold those several constitutional powers.

The inherent powers are few in number. The major ones include the power to regulate immigration, to <u>deport</u> aliens, to acquire territory, to grant diplomatic recognition to other states, and to protect the nation against rebellion or other attempts to overthrow the government by force or violence.

One can argue that most of the inherent powers really are implied by one or more of the expressed powers. For example, the power to regulate immigration is suggested by the expressed power to regulate foreign trade. The power to acquire territory can be drawn from the treaty-making power and the several war powers. But the doctrine of inherent powers holds that it is not necessary to go to these lengths to find these powers in the Constitution. In short, these powers exist because the United States exists.

> ✔ **Checkpoint**
> Why is the Necessary and Proper Clause sometimes referred to as the Elastic Clause?

> <u>deport</u>
> *v.* to order that one be sent to another country

---

[1] Article I, Section 8, Clause 3. The doctrine of implied powers is treated in greater detail in Chapter 11.

Powers Denied to the Federal Government

Although the Constitution delegates certain powers to the National Government, it also *denies* certain powers to that level of government in order to keep federalism intact. It does so in three distinct ways.

First, the Constitution denies some powers to the National Government in so many words—*expressly*.[2] Among them are the powers to levy duties on exports; to take private property for public use without the payment of just compensation; to prohibit freedom of religion, speech, press, or assembly; to conduct illegal searches or seizures; and to deny to any person accused of a crime a speedy and public trial or a trial by jury.

Second, several powers are denied to the National Government because of the *silence* of the Constitution. Recall that the National Government is a government of delegated powers; it has only those powers the Constitution gives to it.

Among the many powers not granted to the National Government are the powers to do such things as create a public school system for the nation, enact uniform marriage and divorce laws, and set up units of local government. The Constitution says nothing that would give the National Government the power to do any of those things, expressly, implicitly, or inherently. In short, the lack of any such provision—the silence of the Constitution—denies power to the National Government.

Third, some powers are denied to the National Government because of the federal system itself. Clearly the Constitution does not intend that the National Government should have the power to take any action that would threaten the existence of that system. For example, in the exercise of its power to tax, Congress cannot tax any of the States or any of their local units in the conduct of their various governmental functions. If it could, it would have the power to destroy—tax out of existence—one or more, or all, of the States.[3]

---

2 Most of the expressed denials of power are found in Article I, Section 9 and in the 1st through the 8th amendments.

3 But notice that when a State, or one of its local units, performs a so-called nongovernmental function—for example, maintains liquor stores, runs a bus system, or operates a farmers market—it is liable to federal taxation. We shall return to this point later, in Chapter 25.

Inherent Powers

▲ President George W. Bush meets with Chancellor Angela Merkel of Germany at the 2007 G8 Summit as part of his diplomatic role.

The States

The 50 States are the other half of the very complicated equation we call federalism. Their many-sided role in the American federal system is no less important than that of the National Government.

Powers Reserved to the States Recall, the 10th Amendment states that the States are governments of **reserved powers.** The reserved powers are those powers that the Constitution does not grant to the National Government and does not, at the same time, deny to the States.

Thus, any State can forbid persons under 18 to marry without parental consent. It can ban the sale of pornography, outlaw prostitution, and permit some forms of gambling and prohibit others. A State can require that doctors, lawyers, hairdressers, and plumbers be licensed in order to practice in the State. It can <u>confiscate</u> automobiles and other property used in connection with such <u>illicit</u> activities as drug trafficking. It can establish public schools, enact land use laws, regulate the services and restrict the profits of such public utilities as natural gas, oil, electric power, and telephone companies, and do much, much more.

In short, the sphere of powers held by each State—the scope of the reserved powers—is huge. The States can do all of those things just mentioned, because the Constitution does not give the National Government the power to do those things, and it does not deny the States the power to do them.

How broad the reserved powers really are can be understood from this fact: Most of what government does in this country today is done by the States (and their local governments), not by the National Government. The point can also be seen from this fact: The reserved powers include the vitally important police power—the power of a State to protect and promote the public health, the public morals, the public safety, and the general welfare.

The Constitution does not grant expressed powers to the States, with one notable exception. Section 2 of the 21st Amendment gives the States a virtually unlimited power to regulate the manufacture, sale, and consumption of alcoholic beverages.

Powers Denied to the States Just as the Constitution denies many powers to the National Government, so it denies many powers to the States. Some of those powers are denied to the States in so many words.[4] For example, no State can enter into any treaty, alliance, or confederation. Nor can a State print or coin money or deprive any person of life, liberty, or property without due process of law.

Some powers are denied to the States inherently—that is, by the existence of the federal system. Thus, no State (and no local government) can tax any of the agencies or functions of the National Government. Remember, too, each State has its own constitution. Those documents also deny many powers to the States.[5]

The Exclusive and the Concurrent Powers

Most of the powers that the Constitution delegates to the National Government are **exclusive powers.** That is, they can be exercised only by the National Government; they cannot be exercised by the States under any circumstances.

Some of these powers are expressly denied to the States—for example, the power to coin money, to make treaties with foreign states, and to lay duties (taxes) on imports. Some of them are not expressly denied to the States but are, nonetheless, among the exclusive powers of the Federal Government because of the nature of the particular power involved. The power to regulate interstate commerce is a leading example of this point.

---

4 Most of those expressed prohibitions of powers to the States (and so, too, to their local governments) are found in Article I, Section 10 and in the 13th, 14th, 15th, 19th, 24th, and 26th Amendments.

5 Note the many provisions in your own State's constitution that deny various powers to your State and its many local governments. As you do, note the significance of these too-little noticed words in the 10th Amendment of the Federal Constitution: "or to the people." We shall look at State constitutions later, and in more detail, in Chapter 24.

✔ **Checkpoint**
Why did the Framers reserve some powers for the States?

confiscate
v. to take or seize legally

illicit
adj. illegal, unlawful, outlawed

GOVERNMENT ONLINE

Audio Tour
Listen to a guided audio tour of
the concurrent powers at
PearsonSuccessNet.com

Concurrent Powers
Sharing Responsibility

Some powers are exercised by both levels of government, as you can see in the circle. *Why do both levels of government have the power to establish law enforcement agencies?*

- Levy and collect taxes
- Borrow money
- Establish courts
- Define crimes and set punishments
- Set environmental and health standards
- Claim private property for public use
- Establish a police force
- Protect national borders

An Idaho State trooper patrols a **STATE** highway.

FBI and volunteers look for evidence of a **FEDERAL** crime.

If the States could exercise that power, trade between and among the States would be at best chaotic and at worst impossible.[6]

Some of the powers delegated to the National Government are **concurrent powers.** That is, they are powers that both the National Government and the States possess and exercise. Those powers include the power to levy and collect taxes, to define crimes and set punishments for them, and to condemn (take) private property for public use.

The concurrent powers are held and exercised separately and simultaneously by the two basic levels of government. That is, the concurrent powers are those powers that the Constitution does not grant exclusively to the National Government and that, at the same time, does not deny to the States. The concurrent powers, in short, are those powers that make it possible for a federal system of government to function.

---

6 The States cannot regulate interstate commerce as such, but they can and do *affect* that trade. For example, in regulating highway speeds, the States regulate not only those vehicles operating within the State, but also those operating from State to State. Generally, the States can *affect* interstate commerce but they cannot impose an unreasonable burden upon it.

Although government in the United States is often discussed in terms of three levels—national, State, and local—there are, in fact, only two basic levels in the federal system: the National Government and the State governments. The more than 87,000 units of local government in the United States today are subunits of the various State governments. Local governments can provide services, regulate activities, collect taxes, and do many other things only because the State has given them the power to do so. In short, when local governments exercise their powers, they are actually exercising State powers.

Another way of putting all of this is to remind you of a point that we first made in Chapter 1. Each of the 50 States has a *unitary* form of government—an arrangement in which a central government that creates local units of government for its own convenience.

Supreme Law of the Land

As you have just seen, the division of powers in the American federal system produces a dual system of government, one in which two basic levels of government operate over the same territory and the same people at the same time. Such an arrangement is bound to result in conflicts between national and State law.

The Supremacy Clause The Framers anticipated those conflicts—and so they wrote the **Supremacy Clause** into the Constitution. That provision declares that

FROM THE CONSTITUTION

This Constitution, and the Laws of the United States which shall be made in <u>Pursuance</u> thereof; and all Treaties made, or which shall be made, under the Authority of the United States, shall be the supreme Law of the Land; and the Judges in every State shall be bound thereby, anything in the Constitution or Laws of any State to the Contrary notwithstanding.

—Article VI, Section 2

The Constitution and the laws and treaties of the United States are "the supreme Law of the Land." This means that the Constitution ranks above all other forms of law in the United States. Acts of Congress and treaties stand immediately beneath the Constitution.[7]

The Supremacy Clause has been called the "linchpin of the Constitution" because it joins the National Government and the States into a single governmental unit, a federal government. In other words, the Supremacy Clause is the provision in the Constitution that makes the complex federal system a working reality.

Our political history is studded with challenges to the concept of national supremacy. Recall that this nation fought a horrific Civil War over that very matter in the years 1861 to 1865. Those who have rejected the concept of national supremacy have insisted that the

Constitution is, at base, a compact among sovereign States, rather than one between and among "We the People of the United States." They believe that the powers that compact does give to the National Government are to be very narrowly defined and applied. Echoes of that view can still be found in contemporary American politics.

The Supreme Court and Federalism The Supreme Court is the umpire in the federal system. One of its chief duties is to apply the Constitution's Supremacy Clause to the conflicts that the dual system of government inevitably produces.

The Court was first called to settle a clash between a national and a State law in 1819. The case, *McCulloch* v. *Maryland*, involved the controversial Second Bank of the United States. The bank had been chartered by Congress in 1816. In 1818, the Maryland legislature, hoping to cripple the bank, placed a tax on all notes issued by its Baltimore branch. James McCulloch, the branch cashier, refused to pay the tax, and the Maryland courts convicted him for that refusal. (See pp. 310–311.)

The Supreme Court unanimously reversed the Maryland courts. Speaking for the Court, Chief Justice John Marshall based

✔ Checkpoint
How is a local government different from a State government?

pursuance
n. a carrying out of an execution of something

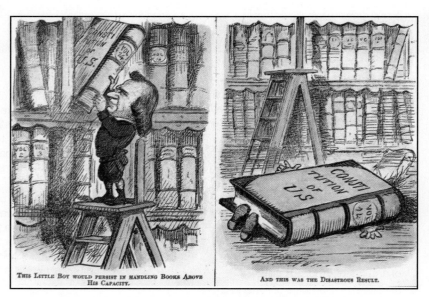

THIS LITTLE BOY WOULD PERSIST IN HANDLING BOOKS ABOVE HIS CAPACITY.

AND THIS WAS THE DISASTROUS RESULT.

▸▸ **Analyzing Cartoons** This cartoon ran in *Harper's Weekly* when Congress attempted to remove President Andrew Johnson. *How does the "disastrous result" illustrate the Supremacy Clause?*

---

7 Acts of Congress and treaties stand on equal planes with one another. Neither can conflict with any provision in the Constitution. In the rare case of conflict between the provisions of an act and those of a treaty, the one more recently adopted takes precedence as the latest expression of the sovereign people's will. The Supreme Court has regularly held to that position from the first cases it decided on the point, *The Head Money Cases,* in 1884.

the decision squarely on the Constitution's Supremacy Clause:

imperil
v. to endanger, put at risk, threaten

PRIMARY SOURCE

[If] any one proposition could command the universal assent of mankind, we might expect it would be this—that the government of the Union, though limited in its powers, is supreme within its sphere of action. . . . [T]he states have no power . . . to retard, impede, burden, or in any manner control, the operations of the constitutional laws enacted by Congress. . . . [8]

—*McCulloch* v. *Maryland,* 1819

Since the decision in this landmark case, it has been impossible to overstate the significance of the role of the Court as the umpire of the federal system. Had the Court not assumed this role, the American federal system and probably the United States itself could not have survived its early years. Justice Oliver Wendell Holmes once made that point in these words:

---

8 The case is also critically important in the development of the constitutional system because, in deciding it, the Court for the first time upheld the doctrine of implied powers. It also held that the National Government is immune from any form of State taxation, a point we shall return to in Chapter 25.

PRIMARY SOURCE

I do not think the United States would come to an end if we [the Court] lost our power to declare an Act of Congress void. I do think the Union would be **imperiled** if we could not make that declaration as to the laws of the several States.

—*Collected Legal Papers*

The Supreme Court first held a State law to be unconstitutional in a case from Georgia, *Fletcher* v. *Peck,* in 1810. The Court found that a Georgia law passed in 1794 that sold some 35 million acres of public land for 1.5 cents an acre amounted to a contract between the State and Peck and other buyers. Despite the obvious corruption involved, it found that the legislature's later (1796) repeal of the law violated the Constitution's Contract Clause (Article I, Section 10, Clause 1). That provision prohibits the States the power to pass any "Law impairing the Obligation of Contracts." Over the centuries since then, the High Court has found thousands of State laws and local ordinances unconstitutional, but it has upheld the constitutionality of thousands of others.

Essential Questions Journal To continue to build a response to the chapter Essential Question, go to your **Essential Questions Journal.**

SECTION 1 ASSESSMENT

1. **Guiding Question** Use your completed Venn diagram to answer this question: How is power divided between the Federal Government and the States?

Key Terms and Comprehension

2. **(a)** How is power divided under the concept of **federalism? (b)** What is the purpose of this **division of powers?**

3. **(a)** What are the three kinds of **delegated powers** held by the Federal Government? **(b)** Cite two examples of **inherent powers.**

4. **(a)** Cite two examples of **reserved powers** held by the States. **(b)** How does the Constitution determine which powers are to be held by the States?

Critical Thinking

5. **Draw Conclusions (a)** Why might the Framers have wanted to reserve specific powers for the States? **(b)** Why might they have wanted to deny certain powers, such as the power to make alliances or enter into treaties, to the States?

6. **Make Comparisons (a)** What purpose does government at a local level serve? **(b)** How does the source of the powers given to governments at the local level differ from the source of the delegated powers of the Federal Government?

Quick Write

Compare and Contrast: Choose and Research a Topic A compare-contrast essay holds two subjects side-by-side and looks at their differing and similar aspects. For this exercise, compare and contrast State powers with the powers of the Federal Government. Research and take notes on the various powers held by the State and Federal Governments.

The National Government and the 50 States

Guiding Question

According to the Constitution, what must the National Government guarantee to each State? Use a chart like the one below to take notes on the Federal Government's responsibilities.

Responsibilities of the Federal Government

Republican Government		
•	•	•
•	•	•
•	•	•

Political Dictionary

- enabling act
- act of admission
- grants-in-aid program
- categorical grant
- block grant
- project grant

Objectives

1. Summarize the obligations that the Constitution places on the National Government with regard to the States.
2. Explain the process for admitting new States to the Union.
3. Examine the many and growing areas of cooperative federalism.

Image Above: Residents of Hawaii celebrate their newly acquired Statehood in 1959.

Have you ever really focused on the words *United States,* and what those two words say? The United States is a union of States, the several States joined together, the States united.

The Framers of the Constitution created that union of States, and they intended to preserve it. To that end, the Constitution (1) requires the National Government to guarantee certain things to the States and (2) makes it possible for the National Government to do certain things for the States.

The Nation's Obligations

The Constitution places several obligations on the National Government for the benefit of the States. Most of them are found in Article IV.

Republican Form of Government The Constitution requires the National Government to "guarantee to every State in this Union a Republican Form of Government."[9] The Constitution does not define "Republican Form of Government," and the Supreme Court has regularly refused to do so. The term is generally understood to mean a "representative government."

The Supreme Court has held that the question of whether a State has a republican form of government is a "political question." That is, it is one to be decided by the political branches of the government—the President and Congress—and not by the courts.[10]

The only extensive use ever made of the republican-form guarantee came in the years immediately following the Civil War. Congress declared that several southern States did not have governments of a republican form, and refused to admit senators and representatives from those States until they had ratified the 13th, 14th, and 15th amendments and broadened their laws

---

9 Article IV, Section 4. The provision is sometimes called "the Guarantee Clause."

10 The leading case here is *Luther* v. *Borden* (1849). This case grew out of Dorr's Rebellion, a revolt led by Thomas W. Dorr against the State of Rhode Island in 1841–1842. Dorr and his followers had written a new constitution for the State. When they tried to enforce the new document, the governor in office under the original constitution declared martial law (temporary rule by military authorities), and called on the Federal Government for help. President John Tyler took steps to put down the revolt, and it quickly collapsed. Although the question of which of the competing governments was the legitimate one was a major issue in *Luther* v. *Borden,* the Supreme Court refused to decide the matter.

to recognize the voting and other rights of African Americans.

Invasion and Internal Disorder The
Constitution states that the National Government must also

> ### FROM THE CONSTITUTION
>
> protect each of them [the States] against Invasion; and on Application of the Legislature, or of the Executive (when the Legislature cannot be convened) against domestic Violence.
>
> —Article IV, Section 4

Today it is clear that an invasion of any one of the States would be met as an attack on the United States itself. This constitutional guarantee is therefore now of little significance.

That was not the case in the late 1780s. Then it was not at all certain that all 13 States would stand together if a foreign power attacked one of them. So, before the States agreed to give up their war-making powers, each demanded that an attack on any one of the States would be met as an attack on all of them.

The federal system assumes that each of the 50 States will keep the peace within its own borders. Thus, the primary responsibility for curbing insurrection, riot, or other internal disorder rests with the individual States. However, the Constitution does recognize that a State might not be able to control some situations. It therefore guarantees protection against internal disorder, or what the Constitution calls "domestic Violence."

The use of federal force to restore order within a State has been a rare event historically. Several instances did occur in the 1960s, however. When racial unrest exploded into violence in Detroit during the "long, hot summer" of 1967, President Lyndon Johnson ordered units of the United States Army into the city. He acted at the request of the governor of Michigan, George Romney, and only after Detroit's police and firefighters, supported by State police and National Guard units, could not control riots, arson, and looting in the city. In 1968, again at the request of the governors involved, federal troops were sent into Chicago and Baltimore to help put down the violence that erupted following the assassination of Martin Luther King, Jr. In 1992, President George H.W. Bush ordered members of the National Guard, the Army, and the Marines to Los Angeles to restore order after three days of rioting. The violence was sparked by the acquittal of four white officers charged with beating Rodney King, a black motorist, after he led them on a high-speed chase.

Normally, a President has sent troops into a State only in answer to a request from its governor or legislature. If national laws are being broken, national functions interfered with, or national property endangered, however, a President does not need to wait for such a plea.[11]

The ravages of nature—storms, floods, drought, forest fires, and the like—can be far more destructive than human violence. Here, too, acting to protect the States against "domestic Violence," the Federal Government stands ready to aid stricken areas.

Respect for Territorial Integrity The
National Government is constitutionally bound to respect the territorial integrity of each of the States. That is, the National Government must recognize the legal existence and the physical boundaries of each State.

The basic scheme of the Constitution imposes this obligation. Several of its provisions do so, as well. For example, Congress must include, in both of its houses, members chosen in each one of the States.[12] Recall, too, that Article V of the Constitution declares that no State can be deprived of its equal representation in the United States Senate without its own consent.

integrity
n. a single, undivided whole

insurrection
n. a revolt against a government

---

11 President Grover Cleveland ordered federal troops to end rioting in the Chicago rail yards during the Pullman Strike in 1894 despite the objections of Illinois Governor William Altgeld. The Supreme Court upheld his actions in *In re Debs* (1895). The Court found that rioters had threatened federal property and impeded the flow of the mail and interstate commerce. Thus, more than "domestic Violence" was involved. Since then, several Presidents have acted without a request from the State involved. Most recently, President Dwight Eisenhower did so at Little Rock, Arkansas, in 1957, and President John Kennedy did so at the University of Mississippi in 1962 and at the University of Alabama in 1963. In each of those instances, the President acted to halt the unlawful obstruction of school integration orders issued by the federal courts.
12 In the House, Article I, Section 2, Clause 1; in the Senate, Article I, Section 3, Clause 1 and the 17th Amendment.

Admitting New States

That new States would soon join the original 13 as members of the new United States was generally accepted as fact in the 1780s. To that end, the Congress of the Confederation, meeting as the Framers were drafting what was to become the Constitution, enacted the Northwest Ordinance of 1787—clearly, the most important measure passed by that body in its eight years as the government of the United States.

The ordinance anticipated the creation of new States in what was then known as the Northwest Territory—a roughly defined area lying north of the Ohio River and west of New York, Pennsylvania, and Virginia. The measure provided for the eventual Statehood of any sector in that region that acquired a population of at least 60,000 persons. It made provision for local self-government, for civil and political rights, and for the support of education. An earlier measure, the Ordinance of 1785, had created the township system for the dividing of land for the support of local schools. Its provisions were folded into the 1787 enactment.

The Northwest Ordinance was readopted by the new Congress under the Constitution in 1790, and it served as the basis for later legislation regarding the nation's territorial possessions. It established that those territories were not to be kept in a second-class

Territorial Expansion of the U.S.

GOVERNMENT ONLINE
Audio Tour
Listen to a guided audio tour of American expansion at **PearsonSuccessNet.com**

▸▸ **Analyzing Maps** Until the early 20th century, the Federal Government steadily acquired land and admitted new States (indicated by years). *From which 19th-century acquisition were the most States created?*

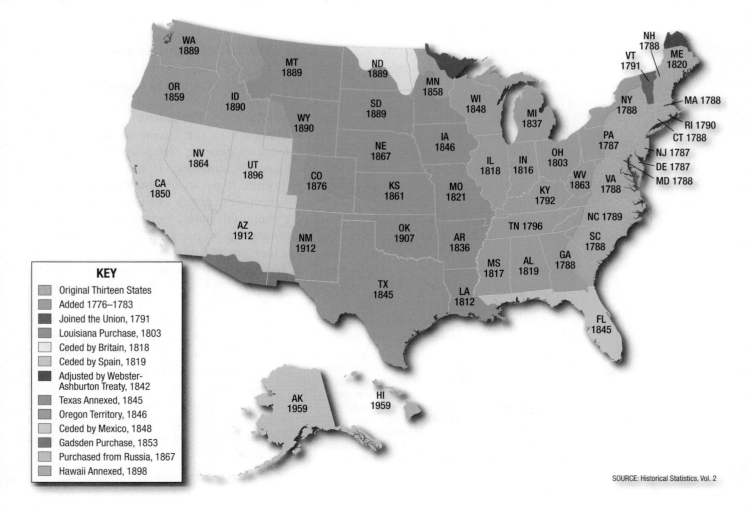

KEY
- Original Thirteen States
- Added 1776–1783
- Joined the Union, 1791
- Louisiana Purchase, 1803
- Ceded by Britain, 1818
- Ceded by Spain, 1819
- Adjusted by Webster-Ashburton Treaty, 1842
- Texas Annexed, 1845
- Oregon Territory, 1846
- Ceded by Mexico, 1848
- Gadsden Purchase, 1853
- Purchased from Russia, 1867
- Hawaii Annexed, 1898

SOURCE: Historical Statistics, Vol. 2

Louisiana Becomes a State

Louisiana was once part of a larger territory bought from France by President Thomas Jefferson in 1803. The Louisiana Purchase (right) nearly doubled the size of the country. Those who lived within the area became citizens of the United States, and the land was divided into territories. The Territory of Orleans constituted what is now Louisiana. By 1810, 77,000 people lived there, and many wished to acquire Statehood. Orleans submitted a petition for admittance to Congress in 1812, and on April 30, 1812, Louisiana became the 18th State. *Which power gave Jefferson the right to acquire territory?*

GOVERNMENT ONLINE

For an interactive version of Louisiana statehood, visit **PearsonSuccessNet.com**

status but were to be groomed for Statehood on an equal footing with the existing States.

Congress and New States Only Congress has the power to admit new States to the Union, and the Constitution places only one restriction on that power: A new State cannot be created by taking territory from one or more of the existing States without the consent of the legislature(s) of the State(s) involved.[13]

Congress has admitted 37 States since the original 13 formed the Union, as the map on page 105 shows. Four States (Kentucky, Tennessee, Maine, and West Virginia) were created from parts of already existing States. Texas and Vermont were independent republics before admission. California was admitted shortly after being ceded to the United States by Mexico.

13 Article IV, Section 3, Clause 1. Some argue that this restriction was violated with West Virginia's admission in 1863. It was formed from the 40 western counties that had broken away from Virginia over secession from the Union at the start of the Civil War. The consent required by the Constitution was given by a minority of the members of the Virginia legislature—those who represented the 40 western counties. Congress accepted their action, holding that they were the only group legally capable of acting as the Virginia legislature at the time.

Each of the other 30 States entered the Union only after a longer period of time, frequently more than 15 years, as an organized territory.

Admission Procedure The process of admission to the Union is usually simple. The area desiring Statehood first asks Congress for admission. If and when Congress chooses, it passes an **enabling act,** an act directing the people of the territory to frame a proposed State constitution. A territorial convention prepares the constitution, which is then put to a popular vote in the proposed State. If the voters approve the document, it is submitted to Congress for its consideration. If Congress still agrees to Statehood after reviewing the proposed constitution, it passes an **act of admission,** an act creating the new State. If the President signs the act, the new State enters the Union.

The two newest States, Alaska and Hawaii, shortened the usual admission process. Each adopted a proposed constitution without waiting for an enabling act, Hawaii in 1950 and Alaska in 1956. Both became States in 1959.

Conditions for Admission Before finally admitting a new State, Congress has often set certain conditions. For example, in 1896, Utah was admitted on condition that its constitution outlaw polygamy, the practice of having more than one spouse at a time. In admitting Alaska to the Union, Congress forever prohibited that State from claiming title to any lands legally held by any Native American.

Each State enters the Union on an equal footing with each of the other States. Thus, although Congress can set certain conditions like those just described, it cannot impose conditions of a political nature. For example, when Oklahoma was admitted to the Union in 1907, Congress said the State could not move its capital from Guthrie to any other place before 1913. In 1910, however, the Oklahoma legislature moved the State's capital to Oklahoma City. When that step was challenged, the Supreme Court held, in *Coyle* v. *Smith* (1911) that Congress can set conditions for a prospective State's admission, but those conditions cannot be enforced if they compromise the independence of a State to manage its own internal affairs.

Consider one more example: President William Howard Taft vetoed a resolution to admit Arizona to the Union in 1911. He did so because Arizona's proposed constitution provided that members of the State's judiciary could be recalled (removed from office) by popular vote. This provision meant, said Taft, that in deciding cases a judge would have to keep one eye on the law and the other on public opinion. In response to the President's concern, Arizona removed the recall section from the document. In 1912 Congress passed, and the President signed, another act of admission for Arizona. Almost immediately after admission, however, the new State amended its new constitution to provide for the recall of judges. That provision remains a valid part of Arizona's constitution today.

Cooperative Federalism

Remember, federalism produces a dual system of government, one in which *two* basic levels operate over the same people and the same territory at the same time. As a result of this complex arrangement, competition, tensions, and conflict are a regular and ongoing part of American federalism. In short, the American federal system is much like a tug-of-war, a continuing power struggle between the National Government and the States.

The American federal system also involves a broad area of *shared* powers. That is, in addition to the two separate spheres of power held and exercised by the two basic levels of government, there are large and growing areas of cooperation between them.

Federal Grants-in-Aid Perhaps the best-known examples of this intergovernmental cooperation are the many federal **grants-in-aid programs**—grants of federal money or other resources to the States and their cities, counties, and other local units. Many of these governments are regularly strapped for funds; these grants often help them perform a large share of their everyday functions.

The history of grants-in-aid programs goes back more than 200 years, to the period before the Constitution. In the Northwest Ordinance, the Congress under the Articles of Confederation provided for the government of the territory beyond the Ohio River and set aside sections of land for the support of public education in those future States.

On through the nineteenth century, most States received grants of federal lands for a number of purposes: schools and colleges, roads and canals, flood control work, and several others. A large number of the major State universities, for example, were founded as land-grant colleges. These schools were built with the money that came from the sale of public lands given to the States by the Morrill Act of 1862.

Congress began to make grants of federal money quite early, too. In 1808, it gave the States $200,000 to support the militia, the <u>forerunner</u> of the present-day National Guard. Cash grants did not play a large role, however, until the Depression years of the 1930s. Many of the New Deal programs aimed at bringing the nation out of its economic crisis were built around grants of money.

Since then, Congress has set up hundreds of grants-in-aid programs. In fact, more than 500 are now in operation. Dozens of programs function in a variety of areas: in education,

✓ **Checkpoint**
What must a territory do once an enabling act is passed by Congress?

forerunner
n. one that comes before, precedes

Three Types of Federal Grants
Where Does the Money Go?

Its taxing power gives Congress the implied power to make grants-in-aid to States and their local governments. *What kinds of organizations might receive a block grant?*

GOVERNMENT ONLINE

For an interactive version of the three types of federal grants, visit **PearsonSuccessNet.com**

INTERACTIVE

CATEGORICAL
Tens of billions of dollars fund interstate roads each year.

BLOCK
Congress gives millions of dollars to the States for homeland security purposes.

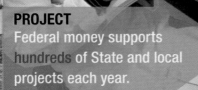

PROJECT
Federal money supports hundreds of State and local projects each year.

mass transit, highway construction, healthcare, and many others.

Grants-in-aid are based on the National Government's taxing power. The Constitution gives Congress that power in order

unwarranted
adj. without legal authority

" FROM **THE** CONSTITUTION

to pay the Debts and provide for the common Defense and general Welfare of the United States. . . .
—Article I, Section 8, Clause 1

Today, these grants total about $400 billion, and account for about a third of all State and local government spending each year.

In effect, grants-in-aid blur the division-of-powers line in the federal system. They make it possible for the Federal Government to operate in many policy areas in which it would otherwise have no constitutional authority—for example, in such fields as education, low-income housing, local law enforcement, and mental health.

Critics of grants-in-aid have long made this point. They also argue that the grants, which usually come with strings attached, often give Washington a major—and, they say, an <u>unwarranted</u>—voice in the making of public policy at the State and local levels.

Types of Federal Grants Today, Congress appropriates money for three types of grants-in-aid: categorical grants, block grants, and project grants.

Over time, most grants have been categorical. **Categorical grants** are made for some specific, closely defined purpose—for school lunches or for the construction of airports or wastewater treatment plants, for example. Categorical grants are usually made with conditions attached. These "strings" require the State to (1) use the federal monies only for the specific purpose involved; (2) make its own monetary contribution, often a matching amount but sometimes much less; (3) provide an agency to administer the grant; and (4) obey a set of guidelines tailored to the particular purpose for which the monies are given.

Block grants have come into wide use over the last several years. They are made for much more broadly defined purposes than are categorical grants—for healthcare, social services, or welfare, for example. They are also made with fewer strings attached, so State and local governments have greater freedom in deciding just how and on what to spend block grant dollars. From the 1980s on, many programs once supported by separate and fragmented categorical grants have been merged into broader block grants.

Congress also provides money for **project grants.** These are grants made to States, localities, and sometimes private agencies that apply for the grants. The Department of Health and Human Services makes many project grants—through its National Institutes of Health, for example, to support scientists engaged in research on cancer, diabetes, neurological disease, and other medical issues. Many State and local governments also apply for these grants to fund their job training and employment programs.

Other Forms of Federal Aid The National Government aids the States in several other important ways. For example, the FBI gives extensive help to State and local police. The army and the air force equip and train each State's National Guard units. The Census Bureau's data are essential to State and local school, housing, and transportation officials as they plan for the future.

Many other forms of aid are not nearly so visible. "Lulu payments," for example, are federal monies that go to local governments in those areas in which there are large federal landholdings. These direct payments are made in lieu of (to take the place of) the property taxes that those local governments cannot collect from the National Government. These payments are also known as PILTs (payment in lieu of taxes).

State Aid to the National Government
Intergovernmental cooperation is a two-way street. That is, the States and their local governments also aid the National Government in many ways.

Thus, State and local election officials conduct national elections. These elections are financed with State and local funds, and they are regulated largely by State laws. The legal process by which aliens can become citizens, called naturalization, takes place most often in State courts. The examples go on and on.

Essential Questions Journal To continue to build a response to the chapter Essential Question, go to your **Essential Questions Journal.**

SECTION 2 ASSESSMENT

1. **Guiding Question** Use your completed chart to answer this question: According to the Constitution, what must the National Government guarantee to each State?

Key Terms and Comprehension

2. **(a)** What is the purpose of an **enabling act? (b)** What does Congress do once the requirements of the enabling act are met?

3. **(a)** Why does the Federal Government make **grants-in-aid** to the States? **(b)** Why are grants-in-aid controversial?

4. **(a)** What are the three main types of grants-in-aid? **(b)** For what is the money used in each type?

Critical Thinking

5. **Draw Conclusions (a)** Why might the Framers have included standards in the Constitution that each territory must meet before it can become a State? **(b)** Why is Congress barred from including conditions concerning a State's government? **(c)** How is this restriction an example of the federalist system?

6. **Summarize (a)** What is cooperative federalism? **(b)** How does this practice help the States to fulfill their several responsibilities?

Quick Write

Compare and Contrast: Create a Venn Diagram Use a Venn diagram to organize the research you gathered in Section 1. Put examples of the States' powers on one side, examples of the Federal Government's powers on the other, and examples of concurrent powers in the middle. You will use the Venn Diagram to create your final essay.

ISSUES OF OUR TIME

The Environment and States' Rights

▶▶ Track the Issue

Over time, the Federal Government has taken many, often controversial, steps to protect the environment.

1872

Congress sets aside land in three States for Yellowstone National Park, the country's first national park.

1907

Theodore Roosevelt sets aside 16 million acres of new forest preserves with a presidential proclamation.

1948

The Clean Water Act is passed by Congress. It has been amended several times.

1963

Congress passes the Clean Air Act. It, too, has been amended several times.

2004

The Supreme Court rules that the EPA can override States on the environment, *Alaska Department of Environmental Conservation* v. *EPA.*

Bush administration
EPA Administrator
Stephen L. Johnson ▶

▶▶ Perspectives

In 2007, California Governor Arnold Schwarzenegger asked the EPA to allow his State to impose stricter emissions controls than those the EPA had put in place for all 50 States. Then-EPA Administrator Stephen Johnson denied that request and California went to court over the matter. When Lisa Jackson became the new EPA Administrator in the Obama administration, she promptly reversed the EPA's decision. Today California and other States do impose stricter controls than those put in place by the EPA.

"The authority of states to address greenhouse gas emissions from motor vehicles has been clearly and unequivocally supported—by the Supreme Court, a federal court decision in Vermont, and in December by a federal court here in California. On this issue, the U.S. EPA has failed to lead, it has failed to follow the states' lead and we are prepared to force it out of the way in order to protect the environment."

–Governor Arnold Schwarzenegger,
April 2, 2008

"I believe that Congress by passing a unified federal standard of 35 mpg [miles per gallon] delivers significant reductions that are more effective than a state-by-state approach. This applies to all 50 states, not one state, not 12 states, not 15 states. It applies to all 50 states, and that's great for the economy, for national security, and for the environment."

– EPA Administrator
Stephen L. Johnson, 2007

▶▶ Connect to Your World

1. **Predict Consequences** Why might Governor Schwarzenegger oppose federal regulations on carbon emissions?
2. **Identify Central Issues (a)** Does the Federal Government have the right to restrict what a State may or may not do within its borders? **(b)** Should States be able to set their own environmental standards?

🔘 **GOVERNMENT ONLINE**
In the News
For updates on environmental cases, visit
PearsonSuccessNet.com

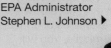

SECTION 3

Interstate Relations

Guiding Question

How do the States work together to preserve the Union? Use an outline like the one below to take notes on how the States cooperate.

I. The States Work Together
  A. Interstate Compacts
    1. _____
    2. _____
  B. _____
    1. _____
    2. _____
  C. _____

Political Dictionary

- interstate compact
- Full Faith and Credit Clause
- extradition
- Privileges and Immunities Clause

Objectives

1. Explain why States make interstate compacts.
2. Understand the purpose of the Full Faith and Credit Clause.
3. Describe the Extradition Clause and explain its purpose.
4. Explain the purpose of the Privileges and Immunities Clause.

Image Above: A person stands where the borders of Utah, Colorado, Arizona, and New Mexico meet to create "The Four Corners."

You know that rivalries, conflicts, and jealousies among the newly independent States was a principal reason for the writing and the adoption of the Constitution. The fact that the new document strengthened the hand of the National Government, especially with regard to trade among the States, reduced many of those frictions. So, too, did several of the new Constitution's provisions dealing with the States' relationships with one another.

Interstate Compacts

No State can enter into any treaty, alliance, or confederation, says the Constitution. However, the States can, with the consent of Congress, enter into **interstate compacts**—agreements among themselves and with foreign states.[14]

The States made few of these agreements for several decades—only 36 of them by 1920. The number has grown steadily since then, however. New York and New Jersey led the way in 1921 with a pact creating what is now the Port Authority of New York and New Jersey to manage the harbor facilities bordering both States. More than 200 compacts are now in force, and many involve several States. In fact, all 50 States have joined in two of them: the Compact for the Supervision of Parolees and Probationers and the Compact on Juveniles. These two compacts enable States to share important law-enforcement data.

Other agreements cover a widening range of subjects. They include pacts that coordinate the development and conservation of such resources as water, oil, wildlife, and fish; counter the effects of global climate change; and encourage the cooperative use of public universities.

Full Faith and Credit

In Article IV, Section 1, the Constitution commands that: "Full Faith and Credit shall be given in each State to the public Acts, Records, and judicial Proceedings of every other State."

---

[14] Article 1, Section 10, Clause 3: The Supreme Court has held that congressional consent is not needed for any compact that does not tend to increase the political power of a State (*Virginia* v. *Tennessee*, 1893). But it is often difficult to decide whether an interstate agreement is political or nonpolitical in nature. So, nearly all compacts are submitted to Congress as a matter of course.

✔ **Checkpoint**
Name two examples of interstate compacts. How do the States benefit from these compacts?

probate
v. to establish the validity of a will

The term *public acts* refers to the laws of a State. *Records* refers to such documents as birth certificates, marriage licenses, deeds to property, car registrations, and the like. The words *judicial proceedings* relate to the outcome of court actions: damage awards, the probating of wills, divorce decrees, and so forth.

The **Full Faith and Credit Clause** most often comes into play in court matters. Take this example: Allen sues Bill in Florida, and the Florida court awards Allen $50,000 in damages. Bill cannot escape payment of the damages by moving to Georgia, because Allen could simply ask the Georgia courts to enforce the damage award. Nor would the case have to be retried in Georgia. Instead, the Georgia courts would have to give full faith and credit to—recognize and respect the validity of—the judgment made by the Florida court.

In a similar vein, a person can prove age, place of birth, marital status, title to property, and similar facts by securing the necessary documents from the State where the record was made. The validity of these documents will be recognized in each of the 50 States.

Exceptions The Full Faith and Credit Clause is regularly observed, and it usually operates routinely between the States. There are two notable exceptions to the rule, however. First,

The Full Faith and Credit Clause ensures that all States recognize public records, such as these.

it applies only to *civil*, not *criminal*, matters. One State cannot enforce another State's criminal law. Second, full faith and credit need not be given to certain divorces granted by one State to residents of another State.

On the second exception, the key question is always this: Was the person who obtained the divorce in fact a resident of the State that granted it? If so, the divorce will be accorded full faith and credit in other States. If not, the State granting the divorce did not have the authority to do so, and another State can refuse to recognize it.

Marriage and Divorce The matter of interstate "quickie" divorces has been troublesome for decades, and especially since the Supreme Court's decision in a 1945 case, *Williams* v. *North Carolina*. In that case, a man and a woman traveled to Nevada, where each wanted to obtain a divorce so they could marry one another. They lived in Las Vegas for six weeks, the minimum period of State residence required by Nevada's divorce law. The couple were granted their divorces, were married, and returned to North Carolina the next day.

Problems arose when that State's authorities refused to recognize their Nevada divorces. North Carolina brought the couple to trial and a jury convicted each of them of the crime of bigamous cohabitation (marrying and living together while a previous marriage is still legally in effect).

On appeal, the Supreme Court upheld North Carolina's denial of full faith and credit to the Nevada divorces. It ruled that the couple had not in fact established *bona fide*—good faith, valid—residence in Nevada. Rather, the Court held that the couple had remained legal residents of North Carolina. In short, it found that Nevada lacked the authority to grant their divorces.

A divorce granted by a State court to a *bona fide* resident of that State must be given full faith and credit in all other States. To become a legal resident of a State, a person must intend to reside there permanently, or at least indefinitely. Clearly, the Williamses had not intended to do so.

The *Williams* case, and later ones like it, have cast dark clouds of doubt over the validity of thousands of other interstate divorces.

The later marriages of people involved in these divorces, and the frequently tangled estate problems produced by their deaths, suggest the confused and serious nature of the matter.

Even the legality of some marriages differs among the States. Today, most States and the Federal Government prohibit same-sex unions. However, six States do provide that such marriages can be legally performed within their borders.

In 2003, Massachusetts' Supreme Judicial Court held that that State's constitutional guarantees of equal rights to all persons in the State means that same-sex couples have exactly the same marriage rights as those enjoyed by all male-female couples in Massachusetts.

Since then, by court decision or legislative action, five other States have come to the same position. Connecticut did so in 2008, Iowa, Maine, and Vermont in 2009; and New Hampshire in 2010.

New York and Washington, D.C., are among the many jurisdictions that do not allow for the marriage of gay or lesbian couples. Both, however, do recognize the validity of such weddings performed elsewhere.

If a same-sex couple, legally married to one another in one State, moves to a State where those unions are outlawed, does the Full Faith and Credit Clause require the second State to recognize the validity of that couple's marriage? That thorny question has not yet (2010) reached the Supreme Court, but it almost certainly will—and soon.

Congress stepped into this building controversy in its early stages with the passage of the Defense of Marriage Act (DOMA) in 1996. That law declares that only those marriages that unite a man and a woman are legal in the United States. And it also provides that no State can be required to give full faith and credit to any same-sex marriage performed in any other State.

For several years now, critics of same-sex unions have urged Congress to propose a federal marriage amendment to the Constitution. That amendment would, in effect, write DOMA into the nation's fundamental law. To this point at least, those efforts have not been successful in either house.

▲ In 1958, Richard and Mildred Loving married in Washington, D.C., but were subsequently arrested in their home State of Virginia, where their interracial marriage was illegal. The Supreme Court ruled the Virginia law unconstitutional, and that all States must recognize interracial marriage.

Extradition

The Constitution makes provisions for those who flee to another State to avoid punishment for a crime.

FROM THE CONSTITUTION

A Person charged in any State with Treason, Felony, or other Crime, who shall flee from Justice, and be found in another State, shall on Demand of the executive Authority of the State from which he fled, be delivered up, to be removed to the State having Jurisdiction of the Crime.

—Article IV, Section 2, Clause 2

This clause refers to **extradition,** the legal process by which a fugitive from justice in one State can be returned to that State. Extradition is designed to prevent a person from escaping justice by fleeing a State.

The return of a fugitive from justice is usually a routine matter; governors regularly approve the extradition requests they receive from other States' chief executives. Some of those requests, however, are contested. This is especially true in cases with strong racial or political overtones, and in cases of parental kidnapping of children involved in custody disputes.

Until the 1980s, governors could, and on occasion did, refuse to return fugitives. In *Kentucky* v. *Dennison* (1861) the Supreme Court had held that the Constitution did not give the Federal Government any power with which to compel a governor to act in an extradition case. So, for more than a century,

jurisdiction
n. the authority to interpret and apply the law

fugitive
n. one who flees

the Constitution's word *shall* in the Extradition Clause had to be read as "may."

The Court overturned that ruling in 1987, however. In *Puerto Rico* v. *Branstad,* a unanimous Court held that the federal courts can indeed order an unwilling governor to extradite a fugitive.

Privileges and Immunities

The Constitution also protects citizens who move between the States.

FROM THE CONSTITUTION

The Citizens of each State shall be entitled to all Privileges and Immunities of Citizens in the several States.
—Article IV, Section 2, Clause 1[15]

This clause, known as the **Privileges and Immunities Clause,** means that no State can draw unreasonable distinctions between its own residents and those persons who happen to live in another State.

Each State must recognize the right of any American to travel in or become a resident of that State. It must also allow any citizen, no matter where he or she lives, to use its courts and make contracts; buy, own, rent, or sell property; or marry within its borders.

15 The provision is reinforced in the 14th Amendment.

However, a State cannot do such things as try to relieve its unemployment problems by requiring employers to hire in-State residents first. Thus, the Supreme Court struck down an Alaskan law requiring employers to prefer Alaskan workers to construct that State's oil and gas pipelines (*Hicklin* v. *Orbeck,* 1978). The Court overturned a California law that set the welfare benefits for newly arrived residents from States with lower welfare benefit levels at a lower level than those paid to long-term residents (*Saenz* v. *Roe,* 1999).

However, the Privileges and Immunities Clause does allow States to draw *reasonable* distinctions between its own residents and those of other States. Thus, any State can require that a person live within the State for some time before he or she can vote or hold public office. It also can require some period of residence before one can be licensed to practice law, medicine, dentistry, and so on.

In another example, the wild fish and game in a State are considered the common property of the people of that State. So, a State can require nonresidents to pay higher fees for fishing or hunting licenses than those paid by residents—who pay taxes to provide fish hatcheries, enforce game laws, and so on. By the same token, State colleges and universities regularly set higher tuition rates for out-of-State students.

Essential Questions Journal	To continue to build a response to the chapter Essential Question, go to your **Essential Questions Journal.**

SECTION 3 ASSESSMENT

1. **Guiding Question** Use the completed outline to answer this question: How do the States work together to preserve the Union?

Key Terms and Comprehension

2. **(a)** Cite two **interstate compacts.**
   (b) What purpose do these compacts serve?

3. **(a)** Cite two examples of records that a State must recognize under the **Full Faith and Credit Clause.**
   (b) What are the two exceptions to that recognition?

Critical Thinking

4. **Synthesize Information** If a person commits a felony in one State and flees to another, why might that person face extradition? Why wouldn't he or she be tried for his or her crime in the second State?

5. **Summarize (a)** How does the Privileges and Immunities Clause protect the rights of U.S. citizens? **(b)** Give three examples of rights that may be protected under this clause.

Quick Write

Compare and Contrast: Draft Your Essay Use the Venn diagram you created in Section 2 as the outline for your essay. You may want to order your outline by first describing one set of powers, followed by the second set of powers, and finally putting the concurrent powers at the end.

Quick Study Guide

GOVERNMENT ONLINE

On the Go
To review anytime, anywhere, download these online resources at **PearsonSuccessNet.com**
Political Dictionary, Audio Review

CHAPTER 4

Guiding Question
Section 2 According to the Constitution, what must the National Government guarantee to each State?

Guiding Question
Section 1 How is power divided between the Federal Government and the States?

CHAPTER 4
Essential Question
Is the federal system the best way to govern the United States?

Guiding Question
Section 3 How do the States work together to preserve the Union?

Political Dictionary

federalism p. 94
division of powers p. 95
delegated powers p. 96
expressed powers p. 96
implied powers p. 96
inherent powers p. 97
reserved powers p. 99
exclusive powers p. 99
concurrent powers p. 100
Supremacy Clause p. 101
enabling act p. 106
act of admission p. 106
grants-in-aid program p. 107
categorical grant p. 108
block grant p. 109
project grant p. 109
interstate compact p. 111
Full Faith and Credit Clause p. 112
extradition p. 113
Privileges and Immunities Clause p. 114

Republican form of government

The Nation's Obligations to the States

Protection from invasion and internal disorder

Respect for territorial integrity

Division of Power

Federal Powers	Concurrent Powers	State Powers
Coin money	Levy and collect taxes	License marriage
Control commerce with foreign nations	Borrow money	License professionals
Determine standards of weight and measure	Establish courts	Maintain public schools
Declare war	Define crimes and set punishments	License drivers
Make laws that are "necessary and proper"	Claim private property for public use	Ratify amendments to the Constitution
Regulate interstate commerce	Establish a police force	Regulate elections
Control immigration	Set environmental and health standards	Oversee intrastate commerce
Acquire territory		Set speed limits
Conduct diplomatic relations with other countries		Establish standards of health and safety
		Exercise those powers not given to the Federal Government and not restricted by the Constitution

Chapter Assessment

GOVERNMENT ONLINE
Self-Test
To test your understanding of key terms and main ideas, visit **PearsonSuccessNet.com**

Comprehension and Critical Thinking

Section 1

1. **(a)** Define federalism. **(b)** How are powers divided among the States and the National Government? **(c)** Why are certain powers left to the States rather than given to the National Government?

2. Give an example of an expressed power that the Constitution gives to **(a)** the President; **(b)** Congress; **(c)** the courts. **(d)** Under what Constitutional principle do these powers fall?

3. **(a)** What is the Elastic Clause? **(b)** What powers does this clause give to Congress? **(c)** Do you think that the Elastic Clause is broad enough to cover some of the powers that Congress has assumed? Why or why not? Cite specific examples.

4. **Analyze Political Cartoons (a)** Is the subject of this cartoon an example of reserved, exclusive, or concurrent powers? **(b)** Does the cartoonist favor or oppose State anti-pollution laws? How can you tell? **(c)** Why do you think one State may have different policies than another

"They have very strict anti-pollution laws in this state."

on the same issue? **(d)** Which level of government do you think should have the basic responsibility for regulating the quality of the environment? Why?

Section 2

5. **(a)** Name three obligations that the National Government has with regard to the States. **(b)** How do these obligations illustrate the concept of federalism?

6. **(a)** Briefly describe the process by which a new State can be admitted to the Union. **(b)** What types of conditions may not be imposed by the Federal Government on a territory as it becomes a State?

7. **(a)** Define cooperative federalism. **(b)** Name two types of federal aid given to the States. **(c)** How might federal aid be used to heighten the Federal Government's influence on State matters?

Section 3

8. **(a)** Until 1987, a governor could challenge an extradition order. Under what circumstances was this allowed? **(b)** According to *Puerto Rico* v. *Branstad,* who can order an unwilling governor to extradite a fugitive? **(c)** Do you think this infringes on States' rights? Why or why not?

9. **(a)** Under the Privileges and Immunities Clause, what reasonable distinctions can a State make between its own residents and those of other States? **(b)** What distinction may a State not draw?

Writing About Government

10. Use your Quick Write exercises to write a compare-and-contrast essay that compares State and federal powers. Refer back to your Venn diagram if you need help organizing your essay. See pp. S3–S5 in the Skills Handbook.

Apply What You've Learned

11. **Essential Question Activity** Create a federal grant proposal.

    (a) Identify some local activity (education, law enforcement, traffic control, etc.) that could be, but is not currently, supported by a federal grant.

    (b) Create a grant proposal for that activity. How large would the grant be? What strings might be attached?

    (c) Present your grant proposal to the class for its consideration.

12. **Essential Question Assessment** Based on your work from the grant proposal activity, write an Op-Ed for a local newspaper that addresses the Essential Question: **Is the federal system the best way to govern the United States?** Apply what you learned about grants and the grant process to answer this question. Make sure you back up your opinion with facts from the textbook and from your research.

Essential Questions Journal To respond to the chapter Essential Question, go to your **Essential Questions Journal.**

Document-Based Assessment

The Power Divide

Debate over the extent of the powers of the new National Government in the federal system continued beyond the ratification of the Constitution in 1789. Thomas Jefferson and John Marshall were leading participants in that debate.

Document 1

". . . to take from the states all the powers of self-government, & transfer them to a general & consolidated government, . . . is not for the peace, happiness or prosperity of these states: and that therefore this commonwealth [Kentucky] is determined, . . . to submit to undelegated & consequently unlimited powers in no man, or body of men on earth: that in cases of an abuse of the delegated powers . . . a change by the people would be the constitutional remedy; but where powers are assumed which have not been delegated a nullification of the act is the rightful remedy: that every state has a natural right, . . . to nullify . . . all assumptions of power by others within their limits . . .

—Opposition to the Alien and Sedition Act from Thomas Jefferson's draft of the "Kentucky Resolution," 1798

Document 2

"America has chosen to be, in many respects and to many purposes, a nation; and for all these purposes her government is complete; to all these objects, it is competent. The people have declared that in the exercise of all powers given for these objects, it is supreme. It can, then, in effecting these objects, legitimately control all individuals or governments within the American territory. The Constitution and laws of a State, so far as they are repugnant to the Constitution and laws of the United States, are absolutely void. These States are constituent parts of the United States. They are members of one great empire—for some purposes sovereign, for some purposes subordinate.

—John Marshall's Opinion from *Cohens* v. *Virginia,* 1821

Use your knowledge of the Constitution, the federal system, and Documents 1 and 2 to answer Questions 1–3.

1. Jefferson's resolution declares
   A. the right of the States to nullify a federal statute or federal law.
   B. the right of the States to initiate amendments to the Constitution.
   C. the absolute power of the Federal Government over the States.
   D. the authority of the Supreme Court to review State court judgments.

2. According to Marshall, what is the test of the constitutionality of State laws?

3. **Pull It Together** Which of these arguments best describes our government today? Why?

> **GOVERNMENT ONLINE**
> **Documents**
> To find more primary sources on federalism, visit
> **PearsonSuccessNet.com**

Essential Question

What should be the goals of government?

For every government, there exists a set of goals unique to the country's needs and history. For the United States government, those goals have been discussed and debated for the more than 200 years of the nation's existence.

"

ON THE GOALS OF GOVERNMENT:

A wise and frugal [thrifty] government . . . shall restrain men from injuring one another, shall leave them otherwise free to regulate their own pursuits of industry and improvement, and shall not take from the mouth of labor the bread it has earned. This is the sum of good government.

—Thomas Jefferson, First Inaugural Address, March 4, 1801

"

ON WHERE GOVERNMENT DERIVES ITS POWER:

Here, sir, the people govern; here they act by their immediate representatives.

—Alexander Hamilton, on ratifying the Constitution, June 27, 1788

"

ON WHAT MAKES A GOOD GOVERNMENT:

Good government is a trust, and the officers of the government are trustees; and both the trust and the trustees are created for the benefit of the people.

—Sen. Henry Clay,
   Speech at Ashland, Kentucky, 1829

Essential Question Warmup

Throughout this unit, you studied the origins and elements of various governments, including those of the United States. Use what you have learned and the quotations above to answer the following questions. Then, go to your **Essential Questions Journal.**

1. How might a government's goals be affected by that government's form?

2. What are some other factors that might determine a government's goals?

3. What are the goals of the U.S. government?

4. How did the Framers develop these goals?

Essential Questions
Journal

To continue to build a response to the unit Essential Question, go to your **Essential Questions Journal.**

Photo: Barack Obama greets supporters.

Essential Questions Journal To begin to build a response to the unit Essential Question, go to your **Essential Questions Journal.**

Unit 2 Political Behavior: Government By the People

Essential Question In what ways should people participate in public affairs?

Political Parties

Essential Question
Does the two-party system help or harm democracy?

"No **America** without **democracy**, no democracy without **politics**, no politics without **parties**, no parties without **compromise** and **moderation**....

—Clinton Rossiter, *Parties and Politics in America*

Photo: Republican convention delegates cheer their party's 2008 presidential and vice presidential nominees, Sen. John McCain (R., Arizona) and Gov. Sarah Palin (R., Alaska).

GOVERNMENT ONLINE
On the Go

To study anywhere, anytime, download these online resources at PearsonSuccessNet.com
• Political Dictionary
• Audio Review
• Downloadable Interactivities

SECTION 1
Parties and What They Do

Guiding Question

What are political parties, and how do they function in our two-party system? Use an outline to organize the main features of political parties, their roles, and types of party systems.

I. What Parties Do
  A. Definition
  B. Functions
II. Types of Party Systems
  A. Two Party
  B. _____
  C. _____

Political Dictionary

- political party
- political spectrum
- partisanship
- single-member districts
- plurality
- bipartisan
- consensus
- coalition

Objectives

1. Define a *political party*.
2. Describe the major functions of political parties.
3. Identify the reasons why the United States has a two-party system.
4. Understand multiparty and one-party systems and how they affect the functioning of a political system.

Image Above: National party conventions are opportunities for parties to show their support.

"**W**inning isn't everything; it's the only thing." So said legendary football coach Vince Lombardi. Lombardi was talking about teams in the National Football League. He might just as well have had the Republican and Democratic parties in mind. They, too, are in the business of competing and winning.

What Is a Party?

A **political party** is a group of persons who seek to control government through the winning of elections and the holding of public office. This definition of a political party is broad enough to cover any political party including the two major parties in American politics, the Republicans and the Democrats. Another, more specific definition can be used to describe most political parties, both here and abroad: A group of persons, joined together on the basis of certain common principles, who seek to control government in order to secure the adoption of certain public policies and programs.

This latter definition, with its emphasis on principles and policy positions, will not fit the two major parties in the United States. The Republican and Democratic parties are not primarily principle- or issue-oriented. They are, instead, election-oriented.

You can better understand the two major parties if you recognize that each of them is an organization made up of three separate but closely related elements, three separate groups of party loyalists:

1. *The party organization.* This element of the party includes its leaders, its other activists, and its many "hangers-on"—all those who give their time, money, and skills to the party. In short, these are the party "professionals," those who run the party at the national, State, and local levels.

2. *The party in government.* This component includes the party's candidates and officeholders, those thousands of persons who hold elective or appointive offices in the executive, legislative, and judicial branches at the federal, State, and local levels of government.

3. *The party in the electorate.* These are the millions of people who call themselves Republicans or Democrats, and who support the party and its candidates through thick and thin. Many of them cast their votes on the basis of the party label, without regard to candidates or issues in an election. Observers sometimes criticize this kind of voting behavior as thoughtless. Yet knowing that a candidate is a Republican or Democrat often provides useful clues about where a candidate stands on key issues.

What Parties Do

It is clear from our history, and from the histories of other peoples as well, that political parties are absolutely essential to democratic government. They are a vital link between the people and their government, between the governed and those who govern. Indeed, many observers argue that political parties are the principal means by which the will of the people is made known to government and by which government is held accountable to the people.

Parties serve the democratic ideal in another significant way: They work to blunt conflict; they are "power brokers." Political parties seek to modify the contending views of various interests and groups, encourage compromise, and so help to unify, rather than divide, the American people. They are very often successful in their attempts to soften the impact of <u>extremists</u> at both ends of the **political spectrum,** or range of political views.

Again, parties are indispensable to democratic government and, so, to American government. That fact is underscored by the several significant functions they perform.

Nominating Candidates The major function of a political party is to nominate—name—candidates for public office. That is, parties select candidates and then present them to the voters. Then the parties work to help those nominees win elections.

In a functioning democracy, there must be some way to find (choose and recruit) candidates for office. There must also be some mechanism to gather support for those candidates. Parties are the best device yet found to do these jobs.

The nominating function is almost exclusively a party function in the United States.[1] It is the one activity that most clearly sets political parties apart from all of the other groups that operate in the political process.

Informing and Activating Supporters Parties inform the people, and inspire and activate their interest and their participation in public affairs. Other groups also perform this function—in particular, the news media and interest groups.

Parties try to inform and inspire voters in several ways. Mostly, they do so by campaigning for their candidates, taking stands on current issues and criticizing opposing candidates and the positions they adopt.

Each party tries to inform the people as it thinks they should be informed—to its own advantage. It conducts its "educational" efforts through pamphlets, signs, buttons, and stickers; advertisements in newspapers and magazines and via radio, television, the Internet, and text messaging; at speeches, rallies, and conventions; and in a variety of other ways.

Remember, both parties want to win elections, and that consideration has much to do with the stands they take on most issues. Both Republicans and Democrats try to shape positions that will attract as many voters as possible—and at the same time, offend as few as possible.

✔ **Checkpoint**
What are the three elements that make up a political party?

<u>extremist</u>
n. one on the extreme right or left in politics

In 2008, the Democratic presidential contest pitted New York Senator Hillary Clinton against Illinois Senator Barack Obama, splitting loyalties in the party. ▼

---

1 The exceptions are in nonpartisan elections and in those rare instances in which an independent candidate enters a partisan contest. Nominations are covered at length in Chapter 7.

rascal
n. a mean, unprincipled, or dishonest person

The Bonding Agent Function In the business world, a bond is an agreement that protects a person or a company against loss caused by a third party. In politics, a political party acts as a "bonding agent," to ensure the good performance of its candidates and elected officeholders. In choosing its candidates, the party tries to make sure that they are men and women who are both qualified and of good character—or, at the least, that they are not unqualified for the public offices they seek.

The party also prompts its successful candidates to perform well in office. The democratic process imposes this bonding agent function on a party, whether the party really wants to perform it or not. If it fails to assume the responsibility, both the party and its candidates may suffer the consequences of that failure in future elections.

Governing In several respects, government in the United States is government by party. For example, public officeholders—those who govern—are regularly chosen on the basis of party. Congress and the State legislatures are organized on party lines, and they conduct much of their business on the basis of **partisanship**—the strong support of their party and its policy stands. Most appointments to executive offices, at both the federal and State levels, are made with an eye to party.

In yet another sense, parties provide a basis for the conduct of government. In the complicated separation of powers arrangement, the executive and legislative branches must cooperate with one another if government is to accomplish anything. It is political parties that regularly provide the channels through which these two branches are able to work together.

Political parties have played a significant role in the process of constitutional change. Consider this important example: The Constitution's cumbersome system for electing the President works principally because political parties reshaped it in its early years, and they have made it work ever since.

cumbersome
adj. unwieldy; clumsy

The Watchdog Function Parties act as watchdogs over the conduct of the public's business. This is particularly true of the party out of power. It plays this role as it criticizes the policies and behavior of the party in power. In American politics, the party in power is the party that controls the executive branch of government—the presidency at the national level or the governorship at the State level.

In effect, the party out of power attempts to convince the voters that they should "throw the rascals out," that the "outs" should become the "ins" and the "ins" the "outs." The scrutiny and criticism by the "out" party tends to make the "rascals" more careful of their public charge and more responsive to the wishes and concerns of the people. In short, the party out of power plays the important role of "the loyal opposition"—opposed to the party in power but loyal to the people and the nation.

Again, these functions performed by political parties and, particularly, the two major parties, testify to the important role they play in making democracy work in this country. You might well remember that point the next time a comedian on late-night television ridicules some candidate, party, or officeholder.

There was a time when the parties played an even larger role in the nation's affairs than they do today. For example, in what has been called "the golden age of parties," from roughly the late nineteenth to the mid-twentieth century, party organizations operated as major welfare organizations in many places in the United States. They regularly helped newly arrived immigrants and many others among the poor to obtain food, housing, and jobs. Often they did this to win the support of these people at the polls. That once important welfare function has long since been taken over by a number of government programs put in place in the twentieth century.

The Two-Party System

Two major parties, the Republicans and the Democrats, dominate American politics. That is to say, this country has a two-party system. In a typical election in the United States, only the Republican or the Democratic Party's candidates have a reasonable chance of winning public office.

It is true that in some States, and in many local communities, one of the two

How Parties
Communicate

For the better part of two centuries now, political parties have used a wide variety of strategies to communicate with voters. *How do the images shown here reflect attempts to reach potential voters?*

▲ At recent national conventions, both parties gave limited edition macaroni and cheese to press and delegates.

▲ Parties have created their own Web sites and tried to connect with voters by joining popular social networking sites.

major parties may be overwhelmingly dominant, winning election after election. And it may do so for a long time—as, for example, the Democratic Party dominated the politics of the South from the years after the Civil War into the 1960s. But, on the whole, and through most of our history, the United States has been a two-party nation.

Several factors explain why America has had and continues to have a two-party system. No one of these factors, alone, offers a wholly satisfactory explanation for the phenomenon. Taken together, however, they are quite persuasive.

The Historical Basis The two-party system in the United States is rooted in the beginnings of the nation itself. The Framers of the Constitution were opposed to political parties. As you know, the ratification of the Constitution gave rise to America's first two parties: the Federalists, led by Alexander Hamilton, and the Anti-Federalists. In short, the American party system began as a two-party system.

The Framers hoped to create a unified country; they sought to bring order out of the chaos of the Critical Period of the 1780s. To most of the Framers, parties were "factions," and therefore agents of divisiveness and disunity. George Washington reflected this view when, in his Farewell Address in 1796, he warned the new nation against "the <u>baneful</u> effects of the spirit of party."

In this light, it is hardly surprising that the Constitution made no provision for political parties. The Framers could not foresee the ways in which the governmental system they created would develop. Thus, they could not possibly know that two major parties

✔ **Checkpoint**
How did the Framers view political parties?

baneful
adj. causing distress

would emerge as prime instruments of government in the United States. Nor could they know that those two parties would tend to be moderate, to choose "middle-of-the-road" positions, and so help to unify rather than divide the nation.

The Force of Tradition Once established, human institutions are likely to become self-perpetuating. So it has been with the two-party system. The very fact that the nation began with a two-party system has been a leading reason for the retention of a two-party system in this country. Over time, it has become an increasingly important, self-reinforcing reason as well.

The point can be made this way: Most Americans accept the idea of a two-party system simply because there has always been one. This inbred support for the arrangement is a principal reason why challenges to the system—by minor parties, for example—have made so little headway. In other words, America has a two-party system because America has a two-party system.

The Electoral System Several features of the American electoral system tend to promote the existence of but two major parties. The basic shape, and many of the details, of the election process work in that direction and to discourage minor parties.

Political Spectrum

Where Do the Parties Stand?

LEFT ⬅ ➡ CENTER RIGHT

Radical	Liberal	Moderate	Conservative	Reactionary
Favors extreme change to create an altered or entirely new social system.	Believes that government must take action to change economic, political, and ideological policies thought to be unfair.	Holds beliefs that fall between liberal and conservative views, usually including some of each.	Seeks to keep in place the economic, political, and social structures of society.	Favors extreme change to restore society to an earlier, more conservative state of affairs.

Democratic Platform 2008

Labor

"Democrats are committed to an economic policy that produces good jobs with good pay and benefits. That is why we support the right to organize. We know that when unions are allowed to do their job of making sure that workers get their fair share, they pull people out of poverty and create a stronger middle class."

Healthcare

"The American people understand that good health is the foundation of individual achievement and economic prosperity. Ensuring quality, affordable health care for every single American is essential to children's education, workers' productivity, and businesses' competitiveness. We believe that covering all is absolutely necessary to making our health care system workable and affordable."

Republican Platform 2008

Labor

"We affirm both the right of individuals to voluntarily participate in labor organizations and bargain collectively and the right of States to enact Right-to-Work laws. But the nation's labor laws . . . should be modernized to make it easier for employers and employees to plan, execute, and profit together."

Healthcare

"Americans have the best doctors, the best hospitals, the most innovative medical technology, and the best facilities anywhere in the world. Our challenge and opportunity is to build around them the best health-care system. Republicans believe the key to real reform is to give control of the health-care system to patients and their health-care providers, not bureaucrats in government or business."

▶▶**Critical Thinking** *How do the platforms differ on the issues of labor and healthcare? How are they similar? How do the party platforms reflect the political spectrum?*

The prevalence of **single-member districts** is one of the most important of these features. Nearly all of the elections held in this country—from the presidential contest to those at the local levels—are single-member district elections. That is, they are contests in which only one candidate is elected to each office on the ballot. They are winner-take-all elections. The winning candidate is the one who receives a **plurality,** or the largest number of votes cast for the office. Note that a plurality need not be a majority, or more than half of all votes cast in any given election.

The single-member district pattern works to discourage minor parties. Because only one winner can come out of each contest, voters usually face only two <u>viable</u> choices: They can vote for the candidate of the party holding the office, or they can vote for the candidate of the party with the best chance of replacing the current officeholder. In short, the single-member district arrangement has led many voters to think of a vote for a minor party candidate as a "wasted vote."

Another important aspect of the electoral system works to the same end. Much of American election law is purposely written to discourage non-major-party candidates.[2] The GOP and the Democrats regularly act in a **bipartisan** way in this matter.[3] That is, the two major parties find common ground here. They work together to shape election laws in such a way that minor party or independent candidates have a much harder time winning elective office.

Every four years, the presidential contest offers a striking illustration of this situation. In 2008, Republican John McCain and Democrat Barack Obama were listed on the ballots

of all 50 States and the District of Columbia. However, none of the other serious presidential hopefuls—the non-major parties' candidates—made it to the ballot in every State.

Independent candidate Ralph Nader was on the ballots of 45 States and the District of Columbia in 2008; and the Libertarian Party's Bob Barr also made it to the ballot in 45 States. The Green Party's Cynthia McKinney was listed in 41 States and the Constitution Party's Chuck Baldwin in 38. All of the other minor party candidates fell far short of those totals, however. Indeed, most suffered their usual fate: they managed to make the ballots of only one or a few States.

The American Ideological Consensus

Americans are, on the whole, an <u>ideologically</u> homogeneous people. That is, over time, the American people have shared many of the same ideals, the same basic principles, and the same patterns of belief.

This is not to say that Americans are all alike. Clearly, this is not the case. The United States is a pluralistic society—one consisting of several distinct cultures and groups. Increasingly, the members of various ethnic, racial, religious, and other social groups compete for and share in the exercise of political power in this country. Still, there is a broad **consensus**—a general agreement among various groups—on matters of fundamental importance.

Nor is it to say that Americans have always agreed with one another in all matters. The nation has been deeply divided at times: during the Civil War and in the years of the Great Depression, for example, and over such critical issues as racial discrimination, the war in Vietnam, and abortion.

Still, note this very important point: This nation has not been regularly plagued by sharp and unbridgeable political divisions. The United States has been free of long-standing, bitter disputes based on such factors as economic class, social status, religious beliefs, or national origin.

Those conditions that could produce several strong rival parties simply do not exist in this country. In this way, the United States differs from most other democracies. In short, the realities of American society and

viable
adj. reasonable, practical, sensible

ideologically
adv. relating to or concerned with ideas

---

2 Nearly all election law in this country is State law, not federal law—a point discussed at length in the next two chapters. However, note this very important point: Almost all of the nearly 7,400 State legislators—nearly all of those persons who make State law—are either Democrats or Republicans. Only a handful of minor party members or independents now sit, or have ever sat, in State legislatures.

3 GOP is common shorthand for the Republican Party. The initials stand for Grand Old Party, a nickname acquired in the latter part of the 19th century. The nickname may owe its origins to British politics. Prime Minister William Gladstone was dubbed "the Grand Old Man," often abbreviated "GOM," by the English press in 1882. Soon after, "GOP" appeared in headlines in the *New York Tribune,* the *Boston Post,* and other American papers.

politics simply do not permit more than two major parties.

This ideological consensus has had another very important impact on American parties. It has given the nation two major parties that look very much alike. Both tend to be moderate. Both are built on compromise and regularly try to occupy "the middle of the road." Both parties seek the same prize: the votes of a majority of the electorate. To do so, they must win over essentially the same people. Inevitably, each party takes policy positions that do not differ a great deal from those of the other major party.

This is not to say that there are no significant differences between the two major parties today. There are many. For example, the Democratic Party, and those who usually vote for its candidates, are more likely to support such things as social welfare programs, government regulation of business practices, and efforts to improve the status of minorities. On the other hand, the Republican Party and its supporters are much more likely to favor the play of private market forces in the economy and to argue that the Federal Government should be less extensively involved in social welfare programs.

Multiparty Systems

Some critics argue that the American two-party system should be scrapped. They would replace it with a multiparty arrangement, a system in which several major and many lesser parties exist, seriously compete for, and actually win, public offices. Multiparty systems have long been a feature of most European democracies, and they are now found in many other democratic societies elsewhere in the world.

In the typical multiparty system, the various parties are each based on a particular interest, such as economic class, religious belief, sectional attachment, or political ideology. Those who favor such an arrangement for this country say that it would provide for a broader representation of the electorate and be more responsive to the will of the people. They claim that a multiparty system would give voters a much more meaningful choice among candidates and policy alternatives than the present two-party system does.

Multiparty systems do tend to produce a broader, more diverse representation of the electorate. That strength, however, is also a major weakness of a multiparty system. It often leads to instability in government. One party is often unable to win the support of a majority of the voters. As a result, the power to govern must be shared by a number of parties in a **coalition.** A coalition is a temporary alliance of several groups who come together to form a working majority and so

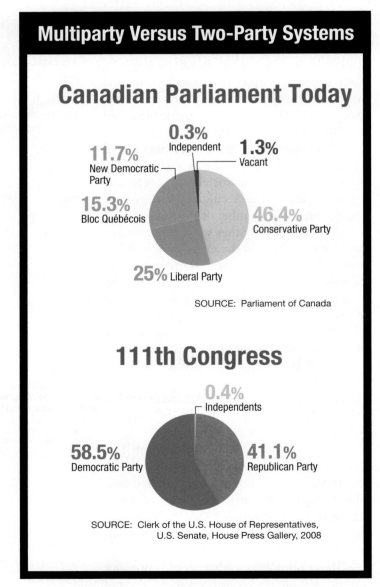

Multiparty Versus Two-Party Systems

Canadian Parliament Today

0.3% Independent
1.3% Vacant
11.7% New Democratic Party
15.3% Bloc Québécois
46.4% Conservative Party
25% Liberal Party

SOURCE: Parliament of Canada

111th Congress

0.4% Independents
58.5% Democratic Party
41.1% Republican Party

SOURCE: Clerk of the U.S. House of Representatives, U.S. Senate, House Press Gallery, 2008

▶▶ **Analyzing Charts** In Canada's multiparty system, power is shared by several parties, none with a majority. In the American system, two parties have a monopoly on power. *How are majorities built in the Canadian Parliament?*

to control a government. Several of the multiparty nations of Western Europe have experienced frequent changes in party control as coalitions shift and dissolve.

Historically, the American people have shunned a multiparty approach to politics. They have refused to give substantial support to any but the two major parties and their candidates. Two of the factors mentioned here—single-member districts and the American ideological consensus—seem to make the multiparty approach impossible in the United States.

One-Party Systems

In the typical dictatorship, only one political party, the party of the ruling clique, is allowed to exist. For all practical purposes, the resulting one-party system really amounts to a "no-party" system.

Many Americans are quite familiar with one-party systems of a quite different sort. What are often called "modified one-party systems" are found in roughly a fourth of the States today. That is, in those States one of the two major parties—either the Republicans or the Democrats—consistently wins most of the elections held there. Although in the remaining States there is more or less vigorous two-party competition at the Statewide level, there are also many locales in most of them where the political landscape is regularly dominated by a single party.

"My goodness, if I'd known how badly you wanted democracy I'd have given it to you ages ago."

▶▶ **Analyzing Political Cartoons** *What is this cartoon saying about one-party systems?*

From the 1870s into the 1960s, the Democratic Party was so dominant throughout the southern States that that quarter of the country came to be known as the Solid South. Over the past 40 years or so, however, the GOP has become the leading party in that part of the country.

Essential Questions Journal To continue to build a response to the chapter Essential Question, go to your **Essential Questions Journal.**

SECTION 1 ASSESSMENT

1. **Guiding Question** Use your completed outline to answer this question: What are political parties, and how do they function in our two-party system?

Key Terms and Comprehension

2. How do **political parties** help to unify the American people?

3. Explain the bonding agent function of political parties in your own words.

4. What is a **single-member district**?

5. How is the ideological **consensus** of the American electorate reflected in the membership of the major parties?

Critical Thinking

6. **Recognize Propaganda** Do you think political parties are a valid source of information about candidates and their views? Why or why not?

7. **Compare Points of View** Explain why a person might consider a vote for a minor-party candidate even knowing that candidate is not likely to win.

Quick Write

Persuasive Writing: Choose a Topic The first step in writing a persuasive essay is to explore a topic. Make a list of five controversial national issues from history or the present that you feel strongly about or are familiar with. Examples might include immigration, labor, intervention in international affairs, education, the environment, or healthcare.

SECTION 2

Two-Party System in American History

Guiding Question

How has the two-party system affected the history of American government? Use the table to record details about the history of the two-party system in American history.

Two-Party System in American History	
Early Parties	
1800–1860	
1860–1932	
1932–1968	
1968–Present	

Political Dictionary

- incumbent
- faction
- spoils system
- electorate
- sectionalism

Objectives

1. Understand the origins of political parties in the United States.
2. Identify and describe the three major periods of single-party domination and describe the current era of divided government.

Henry Ford, the great auto maker, once said that all history is "bunk." Mr. Ford knew a great deal about automobiles and mass production, but he did not know much about history, or its importance.

Listen, instead, to William Shakespeare: "What's past is prologue." Today is the product of yesterday. You are what you are today because of your history. The more you know about your past, the better prepared you are for today, and for tomorrow.

Much the same can be said about the two-party system in American politics. The more you know about its past, the better you will understand its workings today.

The Nation's First Parties

The beginnings of the American two-party system can be traced to the battle over the ratification of the Constitution. The conflicts of the time, centering on the proper form and role of government in the United States, were not stilled by the adoption of the Constitution. Rather, those disputes were carried over into the early years of the Republic, and they led directly to the formation of the nation's first full-blown political parties.

The Federalist Party was the first to appear. It formed around Alexander Hamilton, who served as secretary of the treasury in the new government organized by George Washington. The Federalists were, by and large, the party of "the rich and the well-born." Most of them had supported the Constitution.

Led by Hamilton, the Federalists worked to create a stronger national government. They favored vigorous executive leadership and a set of policies designed to correct the nation's economic ills. The Federalists' program appealed to financial, manufacturing, and commercial interests. To reach their goals, they urged a liberal interpretation of the Constitution.

Thomas Jefferson, the nation's first secretary of state, led the opposition to the Federalists.[4] Jefferson and his followers were more sympathetic to the

Images Above: James Madison (left) and Alexander Hamilton were founders of the nation's two earliest political parties.

---

4 As you recall, George Washington was opposed to political parties. As President, he named arch foes Hamilton and Jefferson to his new Cabinet to get them to work together—in what proved to be an unsuccessful attempt to avoid the creation of formally organized and opposing groups.

130 Political Parties

"common man" than were the Federalists. They favored a very limited role for the new government created by the Constitution. In their view, Congress should dominate that new government, and its policies should help the nation's small shopkeepers, laborers, farmers, and planters. The Jeffersonians insisted on a strict construction of the provisions of the Constitution.

Jefferson resigned from Washington's Cabinet in 1793 to concentrate on organizing his party. Originally, the new party took the name Anti-Federalist. Later it became known as the Jeffersonian Republicans or the Democratic-Republicans. Finally, by 1828, it became the Democratic Party.

These two parties first clashed in the election of 1796. John Adams, the Federalists' candidate to succeed Washington as President, defeated Jefferson by just three votes in the electoral college. Over the next four years, Jefferson and James Madison worked tirelessly to build the Democratic-Republican Party. Their efforts paid off in the election of 1800. Jefferson defeated the **incumbent,** the current officeholder, President Adams; Jefferson's party also won control of both houses of Congress. The Federalists never returned to power.

Four Major Eras

The history of the American party system since 1800 can be divided into four major periods. Through the first three of these periods, one or the other of the two major parties was dominant, regularly holding the presidency and usually both houses of Congress. The nation is now in a fourth period, much of it marked by divided government.

In the first of these periods, from 1800 to 1860, the Democrats won 13 of 15 presidential elections. They lost the office only in the contests of 1840 and 1848. In the second era, from 1860 to 1932, the Republicans won 14 of 18 elections, losing only in 1884, 1892, 1912, and 1916.

The third period, from 1932 to 1968, began with the Democrats' return to power and Franklin Roosevelt's first election to the presidency. The Democrats won seven of the nine presidential elections, losing only in

1952 and 1956. Through the fourth and current period, which began in 1968, the Republicans have won seven of eleven presidential elections. Today, the Democrats occupy the White House, however, and they also control both houses of Congress—as they have done over much of this most recent period.

The Era of the Democrats

Thomas Jefferson's election in 1800 marked the beginning of a period of Democratic domination that was to last until the Civil War. The Federalists, soundly defeated in 1800, had disappeared altogether by 1816.

For a time, through the "Era of Good Feeling," the Democratic-Republicans were unopposed in national politics. However, by the mid-1820s they had split into a number of **factions,** or competing groups. By the time of Andrew Jackson's administration (1829–1837), a potent party had arisen to challenge the Democrats, known as the National Republicans and then Whigs. The major issues of the day—conflicts over public lands, the Second Bank of the United States, high tariffs, and slavery—all had made new party alignments inevitable.

✔ **Checkpoint**
How are the politics of today different from past eras?

potent
adj. powerful, strong

alignment
n. arrangement, grouping

▸▸ **Analyzing Political Cartoons** This cartoon ridicules the fighting in Congress between Federalists and Anti-Federalists soon after John Adams, a Federalist, was elected President in 1796. *Why was the election of 1796 so significant to each party?*

The Democrats, led by Jackson, were a coalition of small farmers, debtors, frontier pioneers, and slaveholders. They drew much of their support from the South and West. The years of Jacksonian democracy produced three fundamental changes in the nation's political landscape: (1) voting rights for all white males, (2) a huge increase in the number of elected offices around the country, and (3) the spread of the **spoils system**—the practice of awarding public offices, contracts, and other governmental favors to those who supported the party in power.

The Whig Party was led by the widely popular Henry Clay and the great orator Daniel Webster. The party consisted of a loose coalition of eastern bankers, merchants and industrialists, and many owners of large southern plantations. The Whigs were opposed to the tenets of Jacksonian democracy and strongly supported a high tariff. However, the Whigs' victories were few. Although they were the other major party from the mid-1830s to the 1850s, the Whigs were able to elect only two men to the White House, both of them war heroes: William Henry Harrison in 1840 and Zachary Taylor in 1848.

By the 1850s, the growing crisis over slavery split both major parties. Left leaderless by the deaths of statesmen Clay and Webster, the Whig Party fell apart. Meanwhile, the Democratic Party split into two sharply divided camps, in the North and South. Through the decade, the nation drifted toward civil war.

Of the several groupings that arose to compete for supporters among the former Whigs and the fragmented Democrats, the Republican Party was the most successful. Founded in 1854, it drew many Whigs and antislavery Democrats to its ranks. The Republicans nominated their first presidential candidate, John C. Frémont, in 1856; and they elected their first President, Abraham Lincoln, in 1860.

With Abraham Lincoln's election, the Republican Party became the only party in the history of American politics to make the jump from third-party to major-party status. As you will see, even greater things were in store for the Republicans.

The Era of the Republicans

The Civil War signaled the beginning of the second era of one-party sway. For nearly 75 years, the Republicans were to dominate the national political scene. They were supported by business and financial interests, and by farmers, laborers, and newly freed African Americans.

The Democrats, crippled by the war, were able to survive as a national party largely because of their hold on the Solid South in the years following the end of Reconstruction in the mid-1870s. Southern resentment of the Republicans' role in the defeat of the South, coupled with fears that the Federal Government would act to advance the rights of African Americans, meant that the Democrats would monopolize southern politics for the next 100 years.

For the balance of the century, the Democratic Party struggled to rebuild its national electoral base. In all that time, they were able to place only one candidate in the White House: Grover Cleveland in 1884 and again in 1892. His two victories marked only short breaks in Republican control, however. Riding the crest of popular acceptance and unprecedented prosperity, the GOP remained the dominant party well into the twentieth century.

The election of 1896 was especially critical in the development of the two-party system. It climaxed years of protest by small business owners, farmers, and the emerging labor unions against big business, financial monopolies, and the railroads. The Republican Party nominated William McKinley and supported the gold standard. The Democratic candidate was William Jennings Bryan, a supporter of free silver, who was also endorsed by the Populist Party.

With McKinley's victory in 1896, the Republicans regained the presidency. In doing so, they drew a response from a broader range of the **electorate**—the people eligible to vote. This new strength allowed the GOP to maintain its role as the dominant party in national politics for another three decades.

The Democratic Party lost the election of 1896, but it won on another score. Bryan, its young, dynamic presidential nominee,

Party Identity: Past and Present

▸▸ **Analyzing Political Cartoons**
Cartoonist Thomas Nast has been credited with creating the party symbols in his 1874 cartoons for the magazine *Harper's Weekly*. Originally, neither party adopted his ideas. Over time, each party assumed and revised the symbols, which have since become synonymous with party identity. *What characteristics of the donkey and elephant do you think appeal to Democrats and Republicans? How have the parties modernized the symbols since the publication of Nast's cartoons?*

Democrats ▸

Republicans ▴

campaigned throughout the country as the champion of the "little man." He helped to push the nation's party politics back toward the economic arena, and away from the divisions of **sectionalism** that had plagued the nation for so many years. Sectionalism emphasizes a devotion to the interests of a particular region.

The Republicans suffered their worst setback of the era in 1912, when they renominated incumbent President William Howard Taft. Former President Theodore Roosevelt, denied the nomination of his party, left the Republicans to become the candidate of his "Bull Moose" Progressive Party. Traditional Republican support was divided between Taft and Roosevelt. As a result, the Democratic nominee, Woodrow Wilson, was able to capture the presidency although with less than fifty percent of the popular vote. Wilson also managed to keep the office four years later by a very narrow margin.

Again, however, the Democratic successes of 1912 and 1916 proved only a brief <u>interlude</u>. The GOP reasserted its control of the nation's politics by winning each of the next three presidential elections: Warren Harding of Ohio in 1920, Calvin Coolidge of Vermont in 1924, and Herbert Hoover of California in 1928.

The Return of the Democrats

The Great Depression, which began in 1929, had a massive impact on nearly all aspects of American life including the political landscape. The landmark presidential election of 1932 brought Franklin Roosevelt and the Democrats back to power at the national level. That election also marked a basic shift in the public's attitude toward the proper role of government in the nation's social and economic life.

Franklin Roosevelt and the Democrats won in 1932 with a new electoral base, built largely of southerners, small farmers, organized labor, and big-city political organizations. Roosevelt's revolutionary economic and social welfare programs further strengthened that coalition. It also brought increasing support from African Americans and other minorities to the Democrats.

The historic election of 1932 made the Democratic Party the clear majority party in American politics—a position it was to keep for the better part of the next 40 years. President Roosevelt won overwhelming reelection in 1936, an unprecedented third term in 1940, and another term in the midst of World War II, in 1944. Vice President Harry S Truman completed that fourth term, following FDR's death in April of 1945. President Truman was elected to a full term of his own in 1948

✓ **Checkpoint**
What third-party candidate had an influence on the election of 1912? Explain.

<u>interlude</u>
n. intervening time

Political Parties From 1800 to Today

Era of Democrats 1800–1860

1800 Thomas Jefferson (below) is elected President, ushering in an era of Democratic domination that lasted until the Civil War.

1828 President Andrew Jackson's (right) Democratic Party includes small farmers, debtors, frontier pioneers, and slaveholders.

1854 The Republican Party is born, attracting many former Whigs and antislavery Democrats.

Era of Republicans, 1860–1932

1860 The election of Abraham Lincoln (below) and the start of the Civil War mark the beginning of 75 years of Republican Party supremacy.

▶▶ **Analyzing Timelines** This timeline shows which parties have dominated the presidency since the election of 1800. *What issues or events had an impact on elections held before the current era?*

in a close election against GOP challenger Thomas E. Dewey of New York. The Republicans regained the White House in 1952, and kept it in 1956, with World War II hero Dwight Eisenhower. Both times, the widely popular Eisenhower defeated the Democrat Adlai Stevenson.

The GOP's return to power was brief, however. Senator John F. Kennedy recaptured the presidency for the Democrats in 1960. He did so with a razor-thin victory over the Republican Party's standard bearer, and then Vice President Richard M. Nixon.

Lee Harvey Oswald shot and killed President Kennedy in Dallas, Texas, on November 22, 1963, and so Vice President Lyndon B. Johnson became President. Mr. Johnson won a full term of his own in 1964, crushing Republican Barry Goldwater of Arizona.

Era of Divided Government

Richard Nixon made a successful return to presidential politics eight years after his narrow loss to John Kennedy in 1960. In 1968 he defeated Vice President Hubert Humphrey, the candidate of a Democratic Party torn apart by conflicts over the war in Vietnam, civil rights, and a variety of social issues. That election also had a strong third-party effort from American Independent Party candidate George Wallace. Mr. Nixon won only a slim plurality of the votes cast in that election.

President Nixon retained the White House in 1972, routing the choice of the still-divided Democrats, Senator George McGovern of South Dakota. However, the Watergate scandal forced him from office in August of 1974.

Vice President Gerald Ford then became President and served the remainder of the second Nixon term in the White House. Beset by problems in the economy, by the continuing effects of Watergate, and by his pardon of former President Nixon, Mr. Ford lost the presidency in 1976. In a very close election, the voters rejected his bid for a full term, preferring instead the Democratic Party's candidate, Jimmy Carter, the former governor of Georgia.

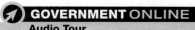

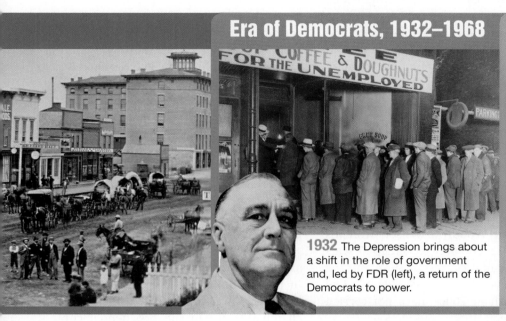

Era of Democrats, 1932–1968

1932 The Depression brings about a shift in the role of government and, led by FDR (left), a return of the Democrats to power.

Era of Divided Government, 1968–Today

1968 From this election on, neither party consistently holds the presidency, and Congress is often controlled by the opposing party.

The Republican Advantage A steadily worsening economy, political fallout from the Iranian hostage crisis, and his own inability to establish himself as an effective President spelled defeat for Jimmy Carter in 1980. Led by Ronald Reagan, the former governor of California, the Republicans scored an impressive victory over President Carter and the independent bid of former Republican Congressman John Anderson of Illinois. Mr. Reagan won a second term by a landslide in 1984; the Democratic candidate Vice President Walter Mondale could carry only his home State of Minnesota and the District of Columbia.

The GOP kept the White House with a third straight win in 1988. Their candidate, George H.W. Bush of Texas, had served as Vice President through the Reagan years and became the first sitting Vice President to win the presidency since Martin Van Buren in 1836. Mr. Bush trounced his Democratic opponent, Governor Michael Dukakis of Massachusetts.

The Reagan and Bush victories of the 1980s triggered wide-ranging efforts to alter many of the nation's foreign and domestic policies. Despite the hugely successful Persian Gulf War of 1990–1991, Mr. Bush was done in by problems that plagued the nation's economy in the 1980s into the 1990s. He was defeated in 1992 by Democrat Bill Clinton, then governor of Arkansas, who also turned back an independent challenge by Texas billionaire H. Ross Perot.

Into the Twenty-First Century Bill Clinton won a second term in 1996, handily defeating the Republican candidate, longtime senator from Kansas, Bob Dole, and, at the same time, <u>thwarting</u> a third-party bid by Mr. Perot. The Republican-controlled Congress mounted an unsuccessful attempt to impeach and remove President Clinton in the midst of his second term.

The GOP did regain the White House in the exceedingly close presidential contest of 2000. Their candidate, George W. Bush, son of the former Republican President, was then the governor of Texas. The younger Mr. Bush failed to win the popular vote contest in 2000, but he did capture a bare majority of the electoral votes and so the White House. His Democratic opponent, Vice President Al Gore, became the first presidential nominee since 1888 to win the popular vote and yet

✔ **Checkpoint**
What factors contributed to Jimmy Carter's defeat in the 1980 election?

thwart
v. to defeat, stop

prodigious
adj. of great size, power, extent

fail to win the presidency; you will read more about this in Chapter 13.

The years since Richard Nixon won the presidency in 1968 have been marked by divided government, or a situation in which one of the major parties occupies the White House and the other party holds a majority of the seats in one or both houses of Congress. Over much of the past 40 years, Republicans have lived in the White House and Democrats have controlled Capitol Hill.[5] That circumstance was reversed from 1995 to 2001, though.

Through much of our history, newly elected Presidents have regularly swept many of their party's candidates into office with them—"on their coattails." Thus, the Democrats gained 62 seats in the House of Representatives when Woodrow Wilson won his first term in 1912, and they picked up 97 seats when FDR was first elected in 1932. But the victories of several recent Presidents—like George W. Bush in 2000—have not carried the coattail effect.

The Republicans lost seats in the House and Senate in 2000 but did manage to keep a narrow hold on both chambers. The Democrats reclaimed the upper house in 2001, when a senator switched parties.

---

5 The Democrats held almost uninterrupted control of Congress from 1933 to 1995. Over those years, the Republicans controlled both houses of Congress for only two two-year periods—first, after the congressional elections of 1946, and then after those of 1952. The GOP did win control of the Senate (but not the House) in 1980; the Democrats recaptured the upper chamber in 1986.

Sparked by the prodigious campaign efforts of President Bush, the Republicans won back the Senate and padded their slim majority in the House in the off-year elections of 2002 and continued their winning ways in 2004. Mr. Bush defeated his Democratic opponent, Senator John Kerry of Massachusetts, and his party kept its narrow grip on both the House and Senate in the hard-fought congressional elections of that year.

The GOP suffered significant losses in the most recent off-year elections, however. The Democrats, riding the wave of increasing dissatisfaction with several Bush administration policies and, in particular, mounting opposition to the war in Iraq, regained control of both houses of Congress in the November 2006 elections.

The Democrat's slim margins in the House and Senate were strengthened considerably in the elections of 2008, as they took even more seats away from the Republicans in both chambers. And in the presidential contest, their candidate, Senator Barack Obama of Illinois, bested his Republican rival, Senator John McCain of Arizona. A majority of the nation's voters turned to the Democrats, hoping that a change of party would help solve the many grave problems this country faced. With their congressional and presidential victories of 2008, the Democratic Party was in a position it had not been in since 1994—when the GOP took control of Congress in the midst of Bill Clinton's first term.

Essential Questions Journal To continue to build a response to the chapter Essential Question, go to your **Essential Questions Journal.**

SECTION 2 ASSESSMENT

1. **Guiding Question** Use your completed table to answer the question: How has the two-party system affected the history of American government?

Key Terms and Comprehension

2. Briefly describe the overall pattern in the way the two major parties have competed for and held power in American history.

3. What is **sectionalism**?

4. What characterizes the present political era that began in 1968?

Critical Thinking

5. **Draw Conclusions** Do you think one-party rule or divided government comes closer to the ideal the Framers had when they envisioned a government without political parties?

6. **Synthesize Information** How do political and economic crises hinder or help candidates get elected? Use specific examples from the section to support your answer.

Quick Write

Persuasive Writing: Gather Details Using the Internet or other resources, carry out research to find out how political parties view (or viewed) one of the issues that you listed in Section 1. Take notes on your findings.

The Minor Parties

Guiding Question

What role have minor parties played in American politics? Use a flowchart to take notes on the role of minor parties in American politics.

Minor Parties			
Ideological	Single-Issue	Economic Protest	Splinter
• • •	• • •	• • •	• • •

Political Dictionary

- ideological parties
- single-issue parties
- economic protest parties
- splinter parties

Objectives

1. Identify the types of minor parties that have been active in American politics.
2. Understand why minor parties are important despite the fact that none has ever won the presidency.

Images Above: George C. Wallace, governor of Alabama, campaigned for President in 1968 as a member of the American Independent Party.

Libertarian, Reform, Socialist, Prohibition, Natural Law, Communist, American Independent, Green, Constitution—these are only some of the many parties that have fielded presidential candidates in recent years and continue to do so. You know that none of these parties or their candidates has any real chance of winning the presidency. But this is not to say that minor parties are unimportant. The bright light created by the two major parties too often blinds us to the vital role several minor parties have played in American politics.

Minor Parties in the United States

Their number and variety make minor parties difficult to describe and classify. Some have limited their efforts to a particular locale, others to a single State, and some to one region of the country. Still others have tried to woo the entire nation. Most have been short-lived, but a few have existed for decades. And, while most have lived, mothlike, around the flame of a single idea, some have had a broader, more practical base. Still, four distinct types of minor parties can be identified.

Ideological Parties The **ideological parties** are those based on a particular set of beliefs—a comprehensive view of social, economic, and political matters. Most of these minor parties have been built on some shade of Marxist thought; the Socialist, Socialist Labor, Socialist Worker, and Communist parties are leading examples of that fact.

A few ideological parties have had a quite different approach, however—especially the Libertarian Party of today, which emphasizes individualism and calls for doing away with most of government's present functions and programs. The ideological parties have seldom been able to win many votes. As a rule, however, they have been long-lived.

Single-Issue Parties The **single-issue parties** focus on a single public question. Their names have usually indicated their primary concern. Thus, the Free Soil Party opposed the spread of slavery in the 1840s and 1850s; the American Party, also called the "Know Nothings," opposed Irish-Catholic immigration in the 1850s; and the Right to Life Party opposes abortion today.

smorgasbord
n. widely varied assortment or collection

agrarian
adj. relating to the land or its cultivation

Most of the single-issue parties have faded into history. They died away as events have passed them by, as their themes have failed to attract voters, or as one or both of the major parties have taken their key issues as their own.

Economic Protest Parties The **economic protest parties** have been rooted in periods of economic discontent. Unlike the socialist parties, these groups have not had any clear-cut ideological base. Rather, they have proclaimed their disgust with the major parties and demanded better times, and have focused their anger on such real or imagined enemies as the monetary system, "Wall Street bankers," the railroads, or foreign imports.

Often, they have been sectional parties, drawing their strength from the agricultural South and West. The Greenback Party tried to take advantage of agrarian discontent from 1876 through 1884. It appealed to struggling farmers by calling for the free coinage of silver, federal regulation of the railroads, an income tax, and labor legislation. A descendant of the Greenbacks, the Populist Party of the 1890s also demanded public ownership of railroads, telephone and telegraph companies, lower tariffs, and the adoption of the initiative and referendum.

Each of these economic protest parties has disappeared as the nation has climbed out of the difficult economic period in which that party arose.

Splinter Parties Those that have split away from one of the major parties are known as **splinter parties.** Most of the more important minor parties in our politics have been splinter parties. Among the leading groups that have split away from the Republicans are Theodore Roosevelt's "Bull Moose" Progressive Party of 1912 and Robert La Follette's Progressive Party of 1924. From the Democrats have come Henry Wallace's Progressive Party and the States' Rights (Dixiecrat) Party, both of 1948, and George Wallace's American Independent Party of 1968.

Most splinter parties have formed around a strong personality—most often someone who has failed to win his or her major party's presidential nomination. These parties

have faded or collapsed when that leader has stepped aside. Thus, the Bull Moose Progressive Party passed away when Theodore Roosevelt returned to the Republican fold after the election of 1912. Similarly, the American Independent Party lost nearly all of its brief strength when Governor George Wallace rejoined the Democrats after his strong showing in the presidential race in 1968.

Like many minor parties in American politics, the Green Party, founded in 1996, is difficult to classify. The Green Party began as a classic single-issue party but, as the party has evolved, it simply will not fit into any of the categories set out here. The Green Party came to prominence in 2000, with Ralph Nader as its presidential nominee. His campaign was built around a smorgasbord of issues—environmental protection, of course, but also universal healthcare, campaign finance reform, restraints on corporate power, and much more.

The Greens refused to nominate Ralph Nader in either 2004 or 2008. In 2004, they instead chose attorney and political activist David Cobb—who built his presidential campaign around most of the positions the Greens had supported in 2000.

In 2008, the Green Party nominated Cynthia McKinney, a former Democratic congresswoman from Georgia. Among the positions supported by McKinney were an end to the war in Iraq, universal health care, and repeal of the Patriot Act.

Why Minor Parties Are Important

Even though most Americans do not support them, minor parties have still had a considerable impact on American politics and on the major parties. For example, it was a minor party, the Anti-Masons, that first used a national convention to nominate a presidential candidate in 1831. The National Republicans and then the Democrats followed suit in 1832. Ever since, national conventions have been used by both the Democrats and the Republicans to pick their presidential tickets.

Minor parties can have a telling effect in other ways. Thus, a strong third-party candidacy can play a decisive role—often a

GOVERNMENT ONLINE

For an **interactive** version of Minor Parties in History, visit **PearsonSuccessNet.com**

INTERACTIVE

Minor Parties in History

Minor parties have played important roles in our political history, sometimes forcing one or both major parties to adopt new positions on public policy matters. *Have any third-party candidates had an impact on presidential elections in recent years? Explain.*

FREE SOIL CANDIDATES FOR PRESIDENT AND VICE-PRESIDENT.

▲ The Free Soil Party is an example of a single-issue party. It campaigned against the spread of slavery into the western States and territories. Former Democratic President Martin Van Buren ran as the party's presidential candidate in 1848.

▶ Eugene Debs, pictured far right on this 1912 campaign button, led the Socialist Party, an ideological party founded in 1900.

"SOCIALISM IS THE HOPE OF THE WORLD"

DEBS-SEIDEL

TIME
The Weekly News-Magazine

▶ In 1924, Robert La Follette led the Progressive Party, a splinter party that broke away from the Republican Party.

Strong Minor Party Efforts, 1848 to Today*

Year	Party	% Popular Vote	Electoral Votes
1848	Free Soil	10.13	---
1856	Whig-American	21.55	8
1860	Constitutional Union	12.64	39
1880	Greenback	3.36	---
1888	Prohibition	2.19	---
1892	Populist	8.54	22
	Prohibition	2.19	---
1904	Socialist	2.98	---
1908	Socialist	2.82	---
1912	Progressive (Bull Moose)	27.39	88
	Socialist	5.99	---
1916	Socialist	3.17	---
1920	Socialist	3.45	---
1924	Progressive	16.61	13
1932	Socialist	2.22	---
1948	States' Rights (Dixiecrat)	2.41	39
	Progressive	2.37	---
1968	American Independent	13.53	46
1996	Reform	8.40	---
2000	Green	2.74	---

*Includes all minor parties that polled at least 2% of the popular vote. SOURCE: U.S. Census Bureau; *Historical Statistics of the United States, Colonial Times to 1970*

▶▶ **Analyzing Charts** Minor parties have sometimes had significant impact on presidential elections. *Using the data in the chart, which of these minor parties may have changed election results?*

Former President Theodore Roosevelt became the Progressive or "Bull Moose" party's nominee in 1912 after losing the Republican Party's nomination. **How might this image have been used by the Progressive Party in the 1912 election?**

✔ **Checkpoint**
How do minor parties act as critics of the major parties?

innovator
n. one who introduces a new approach

"spoiler role"—in an election. In a presidential contest, even if a minor party ticket fails to win any electoral votes, it can still pull enough support away from one of the major parties to affect the outcome of the election. Many analysts think that Ralph Nader and the Green Party did exactly that to Al Gore and the Democratic Party in 2000. The spoiler effect can occur in any national, State, or local election.

In 1912, a split in the Republican Party resulted in Theodore Roosevelt's third-party candidacy. Almost certainly, if Roosevelt had not quit the Republican Party, William Howard Taft would have fared much better, and Woodrow Wilson would not have become President.

Historically, however, minor parties have been most important in their roles of critic and innovator. Unlike the major parties, they have been ready, willing, and able to take quite clear-cut stands on controversial issues. Many of the more important issues of American politics were first brought to the public's attention by a minor party—among them, the progressive income tax, women's suffrage, and railroad and banking regulation. Oddly enough, this very important innovator role of the minor parties has also been a major source of their frustration. When their proposals have gained any real degree of popular support, one and sometimes both of the major parties have taken over those ideas. The late Norman Thomas, who was six times the Socialist Party's candidate for President, often complained that "the major parties are stealing from my platform."

Altogether, 21 minor-party and independent presidential candidates, some of them nominated by more than one party, appeared on the ballots of at least one State in 2008. The most visible minor-party presidential campaigns in the most recent election were those of the Green, Libertarian, Constitution, and Socialist parties. More than a thousand minor-party and independent candidates also sought seats in Congress and ran for various State and local offices around the country.

Essential Questions Journal To continue to build a response to the chapter Essential Question, go to your **Essential Questions Journal.**

SECTION 3 ASSESSMENT

1. **Guiding Question** Use your completed flowchart to answer the question: What role have minor parties played in American politics?

Key Terms and Comprehension

2. How do **ideological parties** differ from **single-issue parties**?

3. **(a)** Why do **splinter parties** develop? **(b)** What usually happens to these break-away parties?

4. In what ways can minor parties impact elections in this country?

Critical Thinking

5. **Identify Points of View** Why do you think a leader or group might seek to create a minor party even though their chances for winning are less than those of a major party?

6. **Express Problems Clearly** A minor party is likely to be a victim of its own success. Explain the meaning of this statement.

Quick Write

Persuasive Writing: Review Arguments Make a list of each party's most persuasive arguments on the issue you selected in Sections 1 and 2. Review your lists and decide with which party you most agree or disagree. Note any arguments from the opposing party that you find compelling.

Working on a Political Campaign

CAMPAIGNING IN FULL SWING DURING LAST DAYS OF ELECTION
"In the final days of the campaign, both camps worked furiously for success on election day. Phone banks made thousands of calls to convince undecided voters and supporters held campaign signs at every intersection. The candidates themselves rushed from appearance to appearance, all in an exhausting sprint to the finish in this hotly contested election."

Elections are a great celebration of our democratic system. Even if you cannot vote, you can still play a part in deciding who our leaders will be. While many political campaigns have paid staff, it is the volunteers who perform much of the actual work. A strong volunteer group can spell the difference between victory and defeat. Here's how:

1. **Get to Know the Candidate** One excellent way to learn about the candidates is to visit their Web sites. Candidates might have a short biography, videos, press releases, and blogs posted. If a candidate does not have a Web site, his or her campaign office can provide similar information. You might also try to see the candidate in person.

2. **Choose a Candidate** Once you are more familiar with a candidate and his or her positions, decide if that candidate's beliefs match your own. It is important to volunteer your time for a person you believe in. Be prepared to talk about his or her views convincingly.

3. **Find Out About Volunteer Opportunities** Political campaigns offer a wide range of volunteer opportunities. A candidate may be looking for people to go door-to-door to seek support. The campaign may need people to host or even just attend events. Most campaigns need people to make phone calls or send out mailings of campaign

literature. Campaigns also appreciate financial contributions.

4. **Choose a Task** Before you choose a task, be sure you are capable of fulfilling it. For example, if you do not have access to a car or a ride, avoid a task that would need transportation. If your studies are demanding, do not commit to making phone calls every night. Though you may not be able to do every job, you will be able to find some way to get involved and hopefully you will find it a rewarding experience.

▸▸ What do you think?

1. Whom should you contact to find out which candidates are running for office in your town or State?

2. How might volunteering for a campaign help you become a more informed voter?

3. **You Try It** Follow the steps above to work on a political campaign. Keep a journal about your activities during the campaign and reflect on your experience.

GOVERNMENT ONLINE
Citizenship Activity Pack
For an activity about working on a political campaign, go to
PearsonSuccessNet.com

Party Organization

Guiding Question

How are political parties organized at the federal, State, and local levels? Use a table to take notes on how political parties are organized.

Party Organization		
National	**State**	**Local**
•	•	•
•	•	•
•	•	•

Political Dictionary
• ward
• precinct

Objectives
1. Understand why the major parties have a decentralized structure.
2. Describe the national party machinery and party organization at the State and local levels.

How strong, how active, and how well organized are the Republican and Democratic parties in your community? Contact the county chairperson or another official in one or both of the major parties. They are usually not very difficult to find. For starters, try the telephone directory.

The Decentralized Nature of the Parties

The two major parties are often described as though they were highly organized, close-knit, well-disciplined groups. However, neither party is anything of the kind. They are, instead, highly decentralized, fragmented, and often plagued by factions and internal squabbling.

Neither party has a chain of command running from the national through the State to the local level. Each of the State party organizations is only loosely tied to the party's national structure. By the same token, local party organizations are often quite independent of their parent State organizations. These various party units usually cooperate with one another, of course—but that is not always the case.

The Role of the Presidency The President's party is almost always more solidly united and better organized than the other major party. The President is automatically the party's leader, and asserts that leadership with such tools as ready access to the media, personal popularity, the power to make appointments to federal office, and the ability to dispense other favors.

The other party has no one in an even faintly comparable position. Indeed, in the American party system, there is seldom any one person who can truly be called its leader. Rather, a number of personalities, frequently in competition with one another, form a loosely identifiable leadership group in the party out of power.[6]

Image Above: Howard Dean served as the Democratic Party's national chairperson in the 2008 election.

6 The party out of power does have a temporary leader for a brief time every fourth year: its presidential candidate, from nomination to election day. A defeated presidential candidate is often called the party's "titular leader"—a leader in title, by custom, but not in fact. What's more, if he or she lost by a wide margin, the defeated nominee may have little or no role to play in ongoing party affairs.

The Impact of Federalism Federalism is a major reason for the decentralized nature of the two major political parties. Remember, the basic goal of the major parties is to gain control of government by winning elective offices.

Today there are more than *half a million* elective offices in the United States. We elect more people to public office in this country than do the voters of any other country on the planet. In the American federal system, those offices are widely distributed over the national, State, and local levels. In short, because the governmental system is highly decentralized, so too are the major parties that serve it.

The Nominating Process The nominating process is also a major cause of party decentralization. Recall, from Section 1, that the nominating process has a central role in the life of political parties. You will consider the selection of candidates at some length in Chapter 7, but, for now, look at two related aspects of that process.

First, candidate selection is an intraparty process. That is, nominations are made *within* the party. Second, the nominating process can be, and often is, a <u>divisive</u> one. Where there is a fight over a nomination, that contest pits members of the same party against one another: Republicans fight Republicans; Democrats battle Democrats. In short, the prime function of the major parties—the making of nominations—is also a prime cause of their highly fragmented character.

National Party Machinery

At the national level, both major parties are composed of five basic elements. They are structured around a national convention, a national committee, a national chairperson, and two congressional campaign committees.

The National Convention The national convention, often described as the party's national voice, meets in the late summer of every presidential election year to pick the party's presidential and vice-presidential candidates. It also performs a few other functions, as you will see in Chapter 13, including the adoption of the party's rules and the writing of its platform.

Beyond that, however, the convention has little authority. It has no control over the party's selection of candidates for any other offices nor over the policy stands those nominees take. Often, a national convention does play a role in making peace among various factions in the party, helping them to accept a party platform that will appeal to a wide range of voters in the general election.

The National Committee Between conventions, the party's affairs are handled, at least in theory, by the national committee and by the national chairperson. For years, each party's national committee was composed of a committeeman and a committeewoman from each State and several of the territories. They were chosen by the State's party organization. Over the past several years, however, both parties have expanded the committee's membership.

Today, the Republican National Committee (RNC) also seats the party chairperson from each State and members from the District of Columbia, Guam, American Samoa, Puerto Rico, and the Virgin Islands.

✔ **Checkpoint**
How does the nomination process contribute to intraparty conflict?

<u>divisive</u>
adj. causing disagreement

▶▶ Analyzing Political Cartoons *How does this cartoon illustrate the decentralized nature of political parties?*

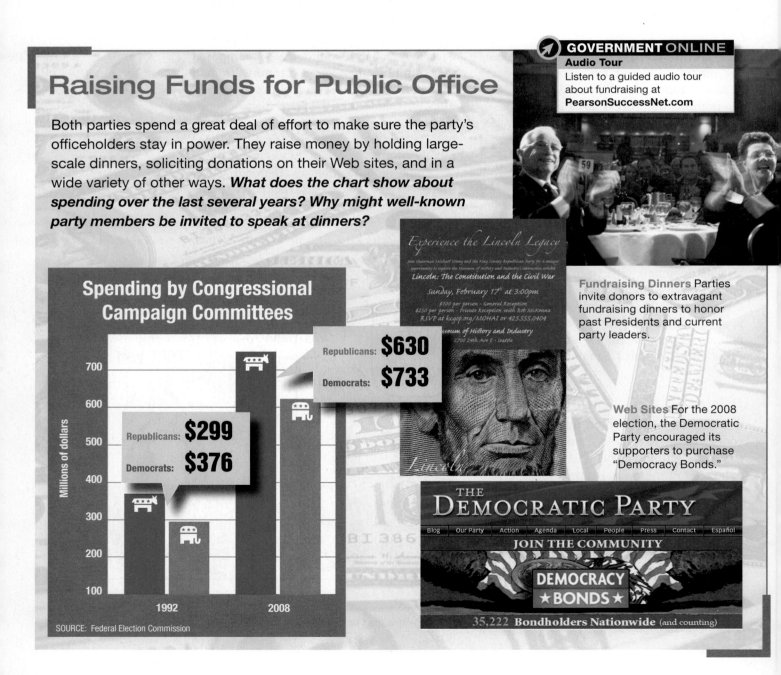
Representatives of such GOP-related groups as the National Federation of Republican Women also serve on the RNC.

The Democratic National Committee (DNC) is an even larger body. In addition to the committeeman and -woman from each State, it now includes the party's chairperson and vice-chairperson from every State and the territories. Moreover, its ranks now include a few dozen members from the party organizations of the larger States, and up to 75 at-large members chosen by the DNC itself. Several members of Congress, as well as governors, mayors, and members of the Young Democrats, also have seats on the DNC.

On paper, the national committee appears to be a powerful organization loaded with many of the party's leading figures. In fact, it does not have a great deal of clout. Most of its work centers on the staging of the party's national convention every four years.

The National Chairperson In each party, the national chairperson is the leader of the national committee. He or she is chosen to a four-year term by the national committee, at a

Raising Funds for Public Office

Both parties spend a great deal of effort to make sure the party's officeholders stay in power. They raise money by holding large-scale dinners, soliciting donations on their Web sites, and in a wide variety of other ways. *What does the chart show about spending over the last several years? Why might well-known party members be invited to speak at dinners?*

Spending by Congressional Campaign Committees

Republicans: **$630**
Democrats: **$733**

Republicans: **$299**
Democrats: **$376**

Millions of dollars

700
600
500
400
300
200
100

1992   2008

SOURCE: Federal Election Commission

Fundraising Dinners Parties invite donors to extravagant fundraising dinners to honor past Presidents and current party leaders.

Experience the Lincoln Legacy

Join Chairman Michael Young and the King County Republican Party for a unique opportunity to explore the Museum of History and Industry's interactive exhibit

Lincoln: The Constitution and the Civil War

Sunday, February 17ᵗʰ at 3:00pm

$100 per person - General Reception
$250 per person - Private Reception with Rob McKenna
RSVP at kcgop.org/MOHAI or 425.555.0404

Museum of History and Industry
2700 24th Ave E - Seattle

Web Sites For the 2008 election, the Democratic Party encouraged its supporters to purchase "Democracy Bonds."

THE
DEMOCRATIC PARTY

Blog   Our Party   Action   Agenda   Local   People   Press   Contact   Español

JOIN THE COMMUNITY

DEMOCRACY ★BONDS★

35,222 **Bondholders Nationwide** (and counting)

meeting held right after the national convention. The choice is made by the just-nominated presidential candidate and is then ratified by the national committee.

Only two women have ever held that top party post. Jean Westwood of Utah chaired the DNC from her party's 1972 convention until late 1972; and Mary Louise Smith of Iowa headed the RNC from 1974 until early 1977. Each lost her post soon after her party lost a presidential election. To this point, only two African Americans have served as major party chairmen: Ron Brown, who headed the DNC from 1989 to 1993, and Michael Steele, who now chairs the RNC.

The national chairperson directs the work of the party's headquarters and its professional staff in Washington. In presidential election years, the committee's attention is focused on the national convention and then the campaign. In between presidential elections, the chairperson and the committee work to strengthen the party and its fortunes. They do so by promoting party unity, raising money, recruiting new voters, and otherwise preparing for the next presidential season. Both parties have lately established state-of-the-art technical facilities to help their candidates and officeholders better communicate with voters. Those sophisticated facilities include such things as television studios, satellite uplinks, constantly updated Web sites, and computerized voter registration lists.

Congressional Campaign Committees

Each party also has a campaign committee in each house of Congress.[7] These committees work to reelect incumbents and to make sure that "open seats," seats given up by retiring members, remain in the party. The committees also take a hand in carefully selected campaigns to unseat incumbents in the other party, in those races where the chances for success seem to justify those efforts.

In both parties and in both houses, the members of these congressional campaign committees are chosen by their colleagues.

---

7 In the House: the National Republican Congressional Committee and the Democratic Congressional Campaign Committee; in the Senate: the National Republican Senatorial Campaign Committee and the Democratic Senatorial Campaign Committee

Local Party Organization

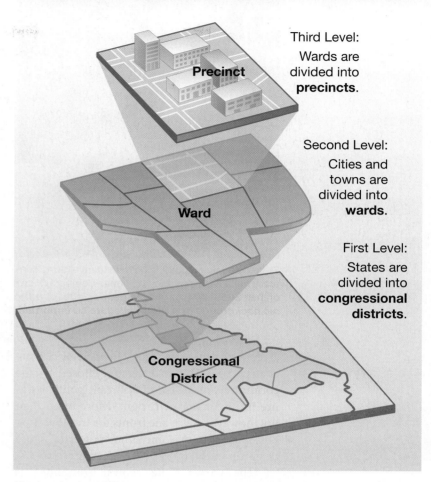

Third Level: Wards are divided into **precincts**.

Second Level: Cities and towns are divided into **wards**.

First Level: States are divided into **congressional districts**.

▶▶ **Analyzing Diagrams** Local party organization can vary from State to State, but a common example is shown here. *What kind of party jobs do you think exist at each level of organization?*

They serve for two-year terms—that is, for a term of Congress.

State and Local Party Machinery

National party organization is largely the product of custom and of rules adopted by the party's national conventions over time. At the State and local levels, on the other hand, party structure is largely determined by State law.

The State Organization In most States, party structure is decentralized, much as it is at the national level. It is usually built around

✔ **Checkpoint**
What do the national committees do between presidential elections?

State delegates attending national conventions generally must represent the population demographics of their State. **Why might the gender, age, or ethnic background of a State delegate be important?**

defy
v. resist, frustrate

Because most of these committees meet only infrequently, the chairperson has great independence in conducting the party's affairs.

Together, the chairperson and the central committee work to further the party's interests in the State. Most of the time, they attempt to do this by building an effective organization and promoting party unity, finding candidates and campaign funds, and so on. Remember, however, both major parties are highly decentralized, fragmented, and sometimes torn by struggles for power. This can really complicate the chairperson's and the committee's job.

Local Organization Local party structures vary so widely that they nearly <u>defy</u> even a brief description. Generally, they follow the electoral map of the State, with a party unit for each district in which elective offices are to be filled: congressional and legislative districts, counties, cities and towns, wards, and precincts. A **ward** is a unit into which cities are often divided for the election of city council members. A **precinct** is the smallest unit of election administration; the voters in each precinct cast their ballots at one polling place located within the precinct.

a State central committee, headed by a State chairperson. The chairperson, chosen by the committee, may be an important political figure in his or her own right. More often than not, however, he or she fronts for the governor, a U.S. senator, or some other powerful figure or group in the politics of the State.

The party's State central committee is almost everywhere composed of members who represent major geographic subdivisions, usually counties. They are chosen in primary elections, by local caucuses, or at State conventions.

In most larger cities, a party's organization is further broken down by residential blocks and sometimes even by apartment buildings. In some places, local party organizations are active year-round, but most often they are inactive except for those few hectic months before an election.

Essential Questions
Journal
To continue to build a response to the chapter Essential Question, go to your **Essential Questions Journal.**

SECTION 4 ASSESSMENT

1. **Guiding Question** Use your completed table to answer the question: How are political parties organized at the federal, State, and local levels?

Key Terms and Comprehension

2. Describe the place of the presidency in national party organization.
3. Describe the role of the congressional campaign committees for each party.
4. What is the difference between a **ward** and a **precinct**?

Critical Thinking

5. **Recognize Cause and Effect** Why is party unity harder to achieve for the party out of power than it is for the party in power?
6. **Expressing Problems Clearly** Why do you think direct primaries create more conflict within parties than the other forms of the nominating process?

Quick Write

Persuasive Writing: Decide on a Structure Using the list of arguments from Section 3, arrange them in order from most persuasive to least persuasive or vice versa. Decide whether you would be more likely to persuade a reader by starting with weaker reasons and building to the best argument or, conversely, leading with your best argument.

Quick Study Guide

GOVERNMENT ONLINE

On the Go

To review anytime, anywhere, download these online resources at **PearsonSuccessNet.com**
Political Dictionary, Audio Review

Guiding Question
Section 2 How has the two-party system affected the history of American government?

Guiding Question
Section 3 What role have minor parties played in American politics?

Guiding Question
Section 1 What are political parties, and how do they function in our two-party system?

CHAPTER 5
Essential Question
Does the two-party system help or harm democracy?

Guiding Question
Section 4 How are political parties organized at the federal, State, and local levels?

Political Dictionary

political party *p. 122*
political spectrum *p. 123*
partisanship *p. 124*
single-member district *p. 127*
plurality *p. 127*
bipartisan *p. 127*
consensus *p. 127*
coalition *p. 128*
incumbent *p. 131*
faction *p. 131*
spoils system *p. 132*
electorate *p. 132*
sectionalism *p. 133*
ideological parties *p. 137*
single-issue parties *p. 137*
economic protest parties *p. 138*
splinter parties *p. 138*
ward *p. 146*
precinct *p. 146*

Rooted in American history and political tradition

Promoted by the electoral system and single-member districts

Two-party System in American Government

Characterized by eras of one-party domination

Encouraged by American ideological consensus

Political Parties in the United States

Major Parties	Minor Parties
• Historically, one of two parties with a realistic chance to win elections	• Have difficulty winning elections in the American party system
• Currently Democratic and Republican parties	• May form based on an ideology or single issue, as a result of bad economic times, or from an existing party
• One party may dominate national elections at times.	• Though rarely successful, they influence elections and the major parties.
• Both parties agree on some important issues and disagree on others.	

Chapter Assessment

Comprehension and Critical Thinking

Section 1

1. Provide an example of a political party performing in the following roles: **(a)** nominating, **(b)** informing and activating, **(c)** serving as a bonding agent, **(d)** governing, **(e)** serving as a watchdog.

2. **(a)** What features of the electoral system support the existence of a two-party system? **(b)** Analyze one of these features and explain its role.

3. Compare and contrast two-party with multiparty systems, noting the strengths and weaknesses of each.

Section 2

4. **Analyze Political Cartoons (a)** Who is represented in the political cartoon below? **(b)** What does this cartoon imply about party loyalty? **(c)** Do you think people are loyal to a certain party?

"Yes, son, we're Republicans."

5. **(a)** Describe the circumstances that led to the development of the first two political parties in American history. **(b)** Explain, using specific examples, how political parties strengthen or weaken U.S. democracy.

6. Consider the eras of one-party domination. What factors are necessary to cause a transition from one era to another?

Section 3

7. Explain what type of minor party is likely to develop around the following: **(a)** a strong personality, **(b)** the collapse of the stock market, **(c)** a specific theory about government, **(d)** growing concern about climate change.

8. **(a)** State three reasons why a person might wish to vote for a minor party candidate in a presidential election. **(b)** How do minor parties strengthen or weaken the two-party system?

Section 4

9. **(a)** What does it mean to say that the major parties in American politics are decentralized? **(b)** Would a more centralized political party be more or less effective in winning elections? Explain your answer.

10. **(a)** Define **ward** and **precinct**. **(b)** How does party organization contribute to the strength of the two-party system?

Writing About Government

11. Use your Quick Write exercises from the chapter to write a newspaper editorial persuading others to support or oppose a political party on the issue you selected. Begin your editorial with the following prompt: I agree (or disagree) with the _____ party on the issue of _____. Cover both sides of the issue but take a clear stand on one side. See pp. S9–S10 of the Skills Handbook.

Apply What You've Learned

12. **Essential Question Activity** Interview close friends or relatives who voted in the last election. Ask them if they identify themselves as members of a political party. Consider:

    (a) If they do not identify themselves as a member of a party, ask them why not.

    (b) If they do identify themselves as a party member, ask on what issues do they most agree and/or disagree with the party.

    (c) Ask them what might make them change their party

affiliation. Then have them consider whether or not the two-party system helps or harms democracy.

13. **Essential Question Assessment** Based on your interviews and the content you have learned in this chapter, write an anonymous magazine profile about the people you interviewed that helps answer the Essential Question: **Does the two-party system help or harm democracy?**

Essential Questions Journal To respond to the chapter Essential Question, go to your **Essential Questions Journal.**

Document-Based Assessment

Political Parties

The Constitution says nothing about political parties. Yet they soon developed and quickly became a significant part of the governmental system—sometimes, a controversial part, as illustrated by the documents below.

Document 1

Let me now take a more comprehensive view, and warn you in the most solemn manner against the baneful effects of the spirit of party generally.

This spirit, unfortunately, is inseparable from our nature, having its root in the strongest passions of the human mind. It exists under different shapes in all governments, more or less stifled, controlled, or repressed; but, in those of the popular form, it is seen in its greatest rankness, and is truly their worst enemy.

The alternate domination of one faction over another, sharpened by the spirit of revenge, natural to party dissension, which in different ages and countries has perpetrated the most horrid enormities, is itself a frightful despotism . . . and sooner or later the chief of some prevailing faction, more able or more fortunate than his competitors, turns this disposition to the purposes of his own elevation, on the ruins of public liberty.

Without looking forward to an extremity of this kind (which nevertheless ought not to be entirely out of sight), the common and continual mischiefs of the spirit of party are sufficient to make it the interest and duty of a wise people to discourage and restrain it.

—George Washington, *Farewell Address,*
September 17, 1796

Document 2

Use your knowledge of political parties and Documents 1 and 2 to answer Questions 1–3.

1. Which answer best summarizes the point of Document 1?
   A. Political parties promote good government.
   B. Parties are likely to lead to the rise of a despot in the long run.
   C. Party conflict and rivalry is a necessary evil in government.
   D. Parties work best in a government that is not based on democratic principles.

2. What does Document 2 suggest about the differences between Democratic and Republican candidates for office?

3. **Pull It Together** What are the advantages and disadvantages of political parties?

GOVERNMENT ONLINE
Documents
To find more primary sources on political parties, visit
PearsonSuccessNet.com

Essential Question
Why do voters act as they do?

> "People often say that in a **democracy,** decisions are made by a majority of the **people. . . . Decisions** are made by a **majority** of those who make **themselves heard** and who **vote**—a very different thing."
>
> —Walter Judd, *Wit and Wisdom of Politics*

Photo: A college student casts her first-ever vote in a presidential election in Springfield, Missouri.

GOVERNMENT ONLINE
On the Go

To study anywhere, anytime, download these online resources at PearsonSuccessNet.com
• Political Dictionary
• Audio Review
• Downloadable Interactivities

The Right to Vote

Guiding Question

How have voting rights changed over the course of American history? Use a graphic organizer to take notes on the history of voting rights in this country.

History of Voting Rights	
Early 1800s	
1870	
1920	
1960s	
1970s	

Political Dictionary

- suffrage
- franchise
- electorate
- disenfranchised
- poll tax

Objectives

1. Summarize the history of voting rights in the United States.
2. Identify and explain constitutional restrictions on the States' power to set voting qualifications.

Image Above: A volunteer helps a voter with instructions to vote.

Soon, you will be eligible to vote—but will you exercise that right? The record suggests that while you may do so, many of your friends will not, at least not for some time. The record also suggests that some of your friends will never vote. Yet, clearly, the success of democratic government depends on popular participation and, in particular, on the regular and informed exercise of the right to vote.

The History of Voting Rights

The Framers of the Constitution purposely left the power to set suffrage qualifications to each State. **Suffrage** means the right to vote. **Franchise** is a synonym for the right to vote.[1]

Expansion of the Electorate When the Constitution went into effect in 1789, the right to vote was generally restricted to white male property owners. In fact, probably not one in fifteen adult white males could vote in elections in the various States. Benjamin Franklin often made fun of this situation. He told of a man whose only property was a jackass and noted that the man would lose the right to vote if his jackass died. "Now," asked Franklin, "in whom is the right of suffrage? In the man or the jackass?"

Today, the size of the American **electorate**—the potential voting population—is truly impressive. More than 230 million people, nearly all citizens who are at least 18 years of age, qualify to vote. That huge number is a direct result of the legal definition of suffrage. In other words, it is the result of those laws that determine who can and cannot vote. It is also the result of more than 200 years of continuing, often bitter, and sometimes violent struggle over the right to vote.

The history of American suffrage since 1789 has been marked by two long-term trends. First, the nation has experienced the gradual elimination of

---

1 Originally, the Constitution had only two suffrage provisions. Article I, Section 2, Clause 1 requires each State to allow anyone qualified to vote for members of "the most numerous Branch" of its own legislature to vote as well for members of the national House of Representatives. Article II, Section 1, Clause 2 declares that presidential electors be chosen in each State "in such Manner as the Legislature thereof may direct."

several restrictions on the right to vote. Those restrictions were based on a variety of factors, including religious belief, property ownership, tax payment, race, and gender. Second, a significant share of what was originally the States' power over the right to vote has been gradually assumed by the Federal Government.

Extending Suffrage: The Five Stages The growth of the American electorate has come in five identifiable stages. The two trends described above—growing federal control over suffrage and the elimination of voting restrictions—are woven through those stages.

1. The first stage of the struggle to extend voting rights came in the early 1800s. Religious qualifications, put in place in colonial days, quickly disappeared. No State has had a religious test for voting since 1810. Then, one by one, States began to eliminate property ownership and tax payment qualifications.

By mid-century, almost all white adult males could vote in every State.

2. The second major effort to broaden the electorate followed the Civil War. The 15th Amendment, ratified in 1870, was intended to protect any citizen from being denied the right to vote because of race or color. Still, for nearly another century, African Americans were systematically <u>barred</u> from voting, and they remained the largest group of **disenfranchised** citizens, or citizens denied the right to vote, in the nation's population.

3. The 19th Amendment prohibited the denial of the right to vote because of sex. Its ratification in 1920 completed the third expansion of suffrage. Wyoming, while still a territory, had given women the vote in 1869.[2]

---

2 Women did vote in some elections in this country before Wyoming acted in 1869, however—notably in New Jersey, where women could and did vote in all elections from 1776 to 1807.

✔ **Checkpoint**
What was the first voting qualification to disappear?

bar
v. to prevent, prohibit, ban

The Five Stages of Expanding Suffrage

Suffrage was gradually expanded over a period of nearly 200 years.
As more and more Americans gained the right to vote, how might election results have been affected?

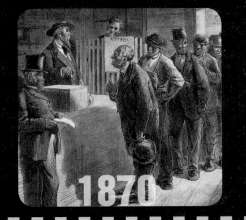

Early 1800s
Religious, property, and tax qualifications begin to disappear in every State.

1870
15th Amendment prohibits voting restrictions based on race or color.

1920
19th Amendment removes voting restrictions based on sex.

1965
The Voting Rights Act of 1965 enforces racial equality at polling places.

1971
26th Amendment sets the minimum voting age at 18.

Women's Suffrage In 1919

▸▸ **Interpreting Maps** Before the 19th Amendment was adopted across the U.S., several States and territories had given women suffrage in various capacities. This map shows the type of suffrage granted. *What observations can you make about women's suffrage in different regions?*

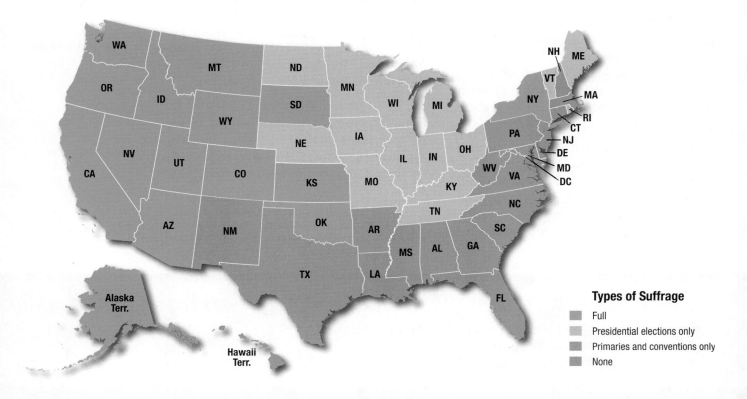

Types of Suffrage

- Full
- Presidential elections only
- Primaries and conventions only
- None

By 1920, more than half of the States had followed that lead.

4. A fourth major extension took place during the 1960s. During that time, federal legislation and court decisions focused on securing African Americans a full role in the electoral process in all States. With the passage and <u>vigorous</u> enforcement of a number of civil rights acts, especially the Voting Rights Act of 1965 and its later extensions, racial equality finally became fact in polling booths throughout the country.

The 23rd Amendment, passed in 1961, added the voters of the District of Columbia to the presidential electorate. The 24th Amendment, ratified in 1964, eliminated the poll tax (and any other tax) as a condition for voting in any federal election. A **poll tax** was a tax imposed by several States as a qualification for voting.

5. The fifth and latest expansion of the electorate came with the adoption of the 26th Amendment in 1971. It provides that no State can set the minimum age for voting at more than 18 years of age. In other words, those 18 and over were given the right to vote by this amendment.

The Power to Set Voting Qualifications

Again, the Constitution does not give the Federal Government the power to set suffrage qualifications. Rather, that matter is reserved to the States. The Constitution does,

<u>vigorous</u>
adj. strong or powerful

however, place five restrictions on the ability of the States to exercise that power:

1. Any person whom a State allows to vote for members of the "most numerous Branch" of its own legislature must also be allowed to vote for representatives and senators in Congress.[3] This restriction is of little real meaning today. With only minor exceptions, each of the States allows the same voters to vote in all elections within the State.

2. No State can deprive any person of the right to vote "on account of race, color, or previous condition of servitude" (15th Amendment).[4]

3. No State can deprive any person of the right to vote on account of sex (19th Amendment).[5]

4. No State can require payment of any tax as a condition for taking part in the nomination or election of any federal officeholder. That is, no State can levy any tax in connection with the selection of the President, the Vice President, or members of Congress (24th Amendment).

---

3 Article I, Section 2, Clause 1; the 17th Amendment extended the "most numerous Branch" provision to the election of senators.

4 The phrase "previous condition of servitude" refers to slavery. This amendment does not guarantee the right to vote to African Americans, or to anyone else. Instead, it forbids discrimination on these grounds when the States set suffrage qualifications.

5 This amendment does not guarantee the right to vote to women as such. Technically, it forbids States the power to discriminate against males or females in establishing suffrage qualifications.

5. No State can deprive any person who is at least 18 years of age of the right to vote because of age (26th Amendment).[6]

Beyond these five restrictions, remember that no State can violate any other provision in the Constitution in the setting of suffrage qualifications—or in anything else that it does. A case decided by the Supreme Court in 1975, *Hill* v. *Stone,* illustrates the point.

There, the Court struck down a section of the Texas constitution that declared that only those persons who owned taxable property could vote in city bond elections. The Court found the drawing of such a distinction for voting purposes—between those who do and those who do not own taxable property—to be an unreasonable classification prohibited by the 14th Amendment's Equal Protection Clause.

---

6 This amendment does not prevent any State from allowing persons younger than age 18 to vote. It does prohibit a State from setting a maximum age for voting, however.

✔ **Checkpoint**
What did the 26th Amendment do?

Suffragists published newspapers and pamphlets in support of their cause. *How might weekly or daily publications help in the fight for women's suffrage?*

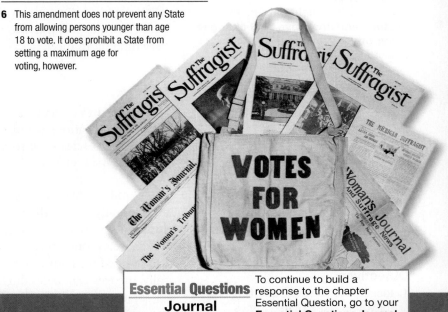

Essential Questions Journal

To continue to build a response to the chapter Essential Question, go to your **Essential Questions Journal.**

SECTION **1** ASSESSMENT

1. Guiding Question Use your completed graphic organizer to answer this question: How have voting rights changed over the course of American history?

Key Terms and Comprehension

2. Briefly summarize the history of **suffrage** qualifications in this country.

3. (a) What is a **poll tax? (b)** Which amendment eliminated it?

4. (a) What is the American **electorate? (b)** Approximately how large is it?

Critical Thinking

5. Identify Central Issues (a) What was the voting experience of African Americans after the Civil War? **(b)** What does this suggest about the legal expansion of voting rights?

6. Recognize Ideologies (a) What does the Constitution say about suffrage qualifications? **(b)** How does this reflect the Framers' ideas about the role of the Federal Government in the nation's political system?

Quick Write

Narrative Essay: Choose a Topic Choose a significant event in the history of suffrage such as the coming of women's suffrage or the abolition of the poll tax. You may want to do preliminary research online or at the library. Write a paragraph summarizing the event and its importance. Include details such as who, what, when, where, and why.

SECTION 2

Voter Qualifications

Guiding Question

What are the qualifications for voting, and how have they changed over time? Use the flowchart to record information about voter qualifications in the United States.

Voting Qualifications		
Citizenship	Residence	Age
• • •	• • •	• • •

Political Dictionary

- alien
- transient
- registration
- purge
- poll books
- literacy

Objectives

1. Identify the universal qualifications for voting in the United States.
2. Explain the other requirements that States use or have used as voting qualifications.

Image Above: Members of the armed forces stationed abroad vote by absentee ballot.

Are you qualified to vote? Probably not—at least not yet. Do you know why? In this section, you will see how the States, including yours, determine who can vote. You will also see that the various qualifications they set are not very difficult to meet.

Universal Requirements

Today, every State requires that any person who wants to vote must be able to satisfy qualifications based on three factors: (1) citizenship, (2) residence, and (3) age. The States have some leeway in shaping the details of the first two of these factors; they have almost no discretion with regard to the third one.

Citizenship **Aliens,** foreign-born residents who have not become citizens, are generally denied the right to vote in this country. Still, nothing in the Constitution says that aliens cannot vote, and any State could allow them to do so if it chose. At one time, about a fourth of the States permitted those aliens who had applied for naturalization—that is, applied for citizenship—to vote. Typically, the western States did so to help attract settlers.[7]

States may draw a distinction between native-born and naturalized citizens with regard to suffrage. The Pennsylvania constitution says that one must have become a citizen at least one month before an election in order to vote in that State.

Residence In order to vote in this country today, one must be a legal resident of the State in which he or she wishes to cast a ballot. In many States, a person must have lived in the State for at least a certain period of time before he or she can vote.

The States adopted residence requirements for two reasons: (1) to keep a political machine from bringing in enough outsiders to affect the outcome of an election (a once common practice), and (2) to allow new voters at least some time in which to become familiar with the candidates and issues in an upcoming election.

---

7 Arkansas, the last State in which aliens could vote, adopted a citizenship requirement in 1926. In a few States, local governments can permit noncitizens to vote in local contests—e.g., city council elections—and a handful do.

Residence Requirements
Where You Live Determines Where You Vote

In order to vote in elections today, voters must be citizens with established residence in their voting locations. *Why do you think some States have different residence requirements?*

Large ceremonies (at right) are often held when people are sworn in as citizens. ▶

▶ States require voters to be residents.

▶ A person can have only one residence.

▶ Some States have provided registration qualifications that require people to have lived in a place for a certain amount of time.

▶ Naturalized citizens can vote once they become citizens.

For decades, every State imposed a fairly lengthy residence requirement—typically, a year in the State, 60 or 90 days in the county, and 30 days in the local precinct or ward.[8] The requirement was longer in some southern States—for example, one year in the State, six months in the county, and three months in the precinct in Alabama, Louisiana, and South Carolina, and in Mississippi a year in the State, a year in the county, and six months in the precinct.

Residence requirements are not nearly so long today. In fact, most States now require that a voter be a legal resident but do not attach a time period to that qualification. About a third of them say that a voter must have lived in the State for at least 30 days. In a few, the period is somewhat shorter—for example, 29 days in Arizona, 20 in Minnesota, and 10 in Wisconsin.[9]

Today's much shorter requirements are a direct result of a 1970 federal law and a 1972 Supreme Court decision. In the Voting Rights Act Amendments of 1970, Congress banned any requirement of longer than 30 days for voting in presidential elections.[10] And in *Dunn* v. *Blumstein,* 1972, the Court found Tennessee's requirement—at the time, a year in the State and 90 days in the county—unconstitutional. The Court found such a lengthy requirement to be an unsupportable discrimination against new residents and so in conflict with the 14th Amendment's Equal Protection Clause. The Supreme Court said that "30 days appears to be an ample period of time." Election law and practice among the States quickly accepted that standard.

Nearly every State does prohibit **transients,** persons who plan to live in a State for only a short time, from gaining legal residence status there. Thus, a traveling sales agent, a member of the armed services, or a college student usually cannot vote in a State

✓ Checkpoint
When and why did residence requirements begin to get shorter?

8 Recall from Chapter 5, the precinct is the smallest unit of election administration. The ward is a unit into which cities are often divided for the election of members of the city council.

9 Until recently, Arizona imposed a 50-day requirement period. The Supreme Court upheld Arizona's residence law in *Marston* v. *Lewis* in 1973, but it also declared in another case that a similar law "approaches the outer constitutional limits."

10 The Supreme Court upheld this provision in the law in *Oregon* v. *Mitchell* in 1970.

infirmity
n. physical or mental weakness

fraudulent
adj. deceitful; false

eligibility
n. qualifications

where he or she has only a temporary physical presence. In several States, however, the courts have held that college students who claim the campus community as their legal residence must be allowed to vote there.

Age The 26th Amendment, added to the Constitution in 1971, declares,

FROM THE CONSTITUTION

The right of citizens of the United States, who are eighteen years of age or older, to vote shall not be denied or abridged by the United States or by any State on account of age.

—26th Amendment

Thus, no State can set the minimum age for voting in any election at more than 18. In other words, the amendment extends suffrage to citizens who are at least 18 years of age. Notice, however, that any State can set the age at less than 18, if it chooses to do so.

Until the 26th Amendment was adopted, the generally accepted age requirement for voting was 21. In fact, until 1970, only four States had put the age at less than 21. Georgia was the first State to allow 18-year-olds to vote; it did so in 1943, in the midst of World War II. Kentucky followed suit in 1955. Alaska entered the Union in 1959 with the voting age

set at 19, and Hawaii became a State later that same year with a voting age of 20.

Both Alaska and Hawaii set the age above 18 but below 21 to avoid potential problems caused by high school students voting in local school-district elections. Whatever the fears at the time, there have been no such problems in any State since the passage of the 26th Amendment.

Efforts to lower the voting age to 18 nationwide began in the 1940s, during World War II. Those efforts were capped by the adoption of the 26th Amendment in 1971, during the war in Vietnam. That amendment was ratified more quickly than any other amendment to the Constitution. This fact is testament to the emotional weight of the principal argument in its favor: "Old enough to fight, old enough to vote."

How have 18 to 20-year-olds responded to the 26th Amendment? In short, not very well. In election after election, young voters are much less likely to vote than any other age group in the electorate. In 1972, 48 percent of the 18-to-20 age group voted, but by 2000 that figure had plummeted to 28 percent. It rose again, substantially, in 2004 and topped 48 percent in 2008. But contrast that figure with the turnout of Americans 65 and older. Despite the infirmities that may accompany their age, their voting rate regularly exceeds 60 percent, and it did so again in the presidential election of 2008.

In a growing number of States, some 17-year-olds can now cast ballots in primary elections. Those States allow anyone whose 18th birthday falls after the primary but before the general election to vote in the primary election.

Several states have come very close to effectively lowering the voting age to 17 for *all* elections. In Nebraska, for example, any person who will be 18 by the Tuesday following the first Monday in November can qualify to vote in any election held during that calendar year.

Registration

One other significant qualification, registration, is nearly universal among the States today. **Registration** is a procedure of voter

The Vietnam War spurred the lowering of the voting age to 18.

identification intended to prevent <u>fraudulent</u> voting. It gives election officials a list of those persons who are qualified to vote in an election. Several States also use voter registration to identify voters in terms of their party preference and, thus, their <u>eligibility</u> to take part in closed primaries.

Requirements Forty-nine States—all except North Dakota—require that most, and usually all, voters be registered in order to cast ballots. Voter registration became a common feature of State election law in the early 1900s. Today, most States require all voters to register in order to vote in any election held within the State. A few, however, do not impose the requirement for all elections.

Maine and Wisconsin allow voters to register at any time, up to and including election day. Elsewhere, a voter must be registered by a certain date, often 20 or 30 days before an election.[11] That cutoff gives election officials time to prepare the poll books for an upcoming election.

Typically, a prospective voter must register his or her name, age, place of birth, present address, length of residence, and similar facts. The information is logged by a local official, usually a registrar of elections or the county clerk. A voter typically remains registered unless or until he or she moves, dies, is convicted of a serious crime, or is committed to a mental institution.

State law directs local election officials to review the lists of registered voters and to remove the names of those who are no longer eligible to vote. This process, known as **purging,** is usually done every two or four years. Unfortunately, the requirement is often ignored. When it is, the **poll books** (the official lists of qualified voters in each precinct) soon become clogged with the names of many people who, for one reason or another, are no longer eligible to vote.

Controversies There are some who think that the registration requirement should be abolished everywhere. They see the qualifica-

---

[11] In Idaho, Minnesota, New Hampshire, and Wyoming, a person who is qualified to vote but misses the deadline can register (and then vote) on election day.

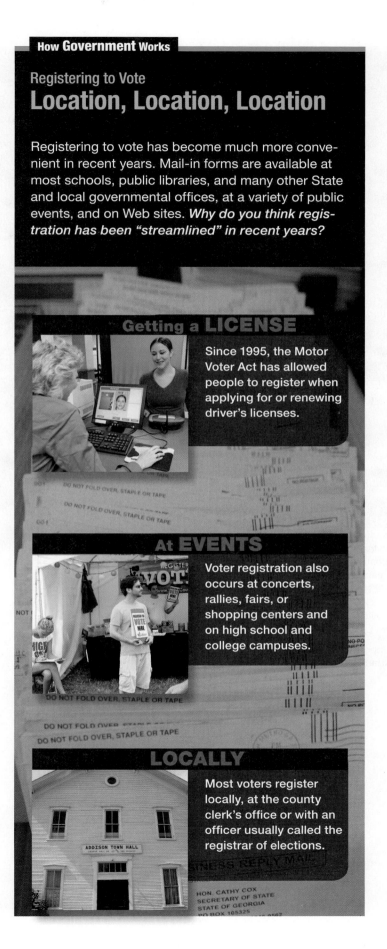

How Government Works

Registering to Vote
Location, Location, Location

Registering to vote has become much more convenient in recent years. Mail-in forms are available at most schools, public libraries, and many other State and local governmental offices, at a variety of public events, and on Web sites. *Why do you think registration has been "streamlined" in recent years?*

Getting a LICENSE

Since 1995, the Motor Voter Act has allowed people to register when applying for or renewing driver's licenses.

At EVENTS

Voter registration also occurs at concerts, rallies, fairs, or shopping centers and on high school and college campuses.

LOCALLY

Most voters register locally, at the county clerk's office or with an officer usually called the registrar of elections.

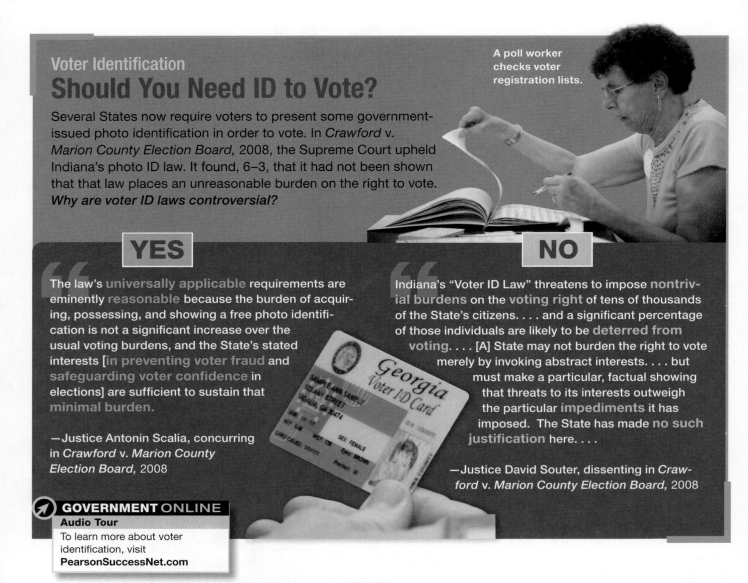

Voter Identification
Should You Need ID to Vote?

Several States now require voters to present some government-issued photo identification in order to vote. In *Crawford* v. *Marion County Election Board,* 2008, the Supreme Court upheld Indiana's photo ID law. It found, 6–3, that it had not been shown that that law places an unreasonable burden on the right to vote. **Why are voter ID laws controversial?**

A poll worker checks voter registration lists.

YES

"The law's universally applicable requirements are eminently reasonable because the burden of acquiring, possessing, and showing a free photo identification is not a significant increase over the usual voting burdens, and the State's stated interests [in preventing voter fraud and safeguarding voter confidence in elections] are sufficient to sustain that minimal burden.

—Justice Antonin Scalia, concurring in *Crawford* v. *Marion County Election Board,* 2008

NO

"Indiana's "Voter ID Law" threatens to impose nontrivial burdens on the voting right of tens of thousands of the State's citizens. . . . and a significant percentage of those individuals are likely to be deterred from voting. . . . [A] State may not burden the right to vote merely by invoking abstract interests. . . . but must make a particular, factual showing that threats to its interests outweigh the particular impediments it has imposed. The State has made no such justification here. . . .

—Justice David Souter, dissenting in *Crawford* v. *Marion County Election Board,* 2008

GOVERNMENT ONLINE
Audio Tour
To learn more about voter identification, visit
PearsonSuccessNet.com

buttress
v. to support, reinforce, strengthen

tion as a bar to voting, especially by the poor and less educated.

Those critics <u>buttress</u> their case by noting that voter turnout began to decline in the early 1900s, just after most States adopted a registration requirement. They also point to the fact that voter turnout is much higher in most European democracies than in the United States. In those countries, voter registration is not a matter of individual choice but is the law. Public officials must enter the names of all eligible citizens on registration lists. The United States is the only democratic country in which each person decides whether or not to register to vote.

Most people who have studied the problem favor keeping the registration requirement as a necessary defense against fraud. However, they also favor making the process

a more convenient one. In short, they see the problem in these terms: Where is the line between making it so easy to vote that fraud is encouraged, and making it so difficult that legitimate voting is discouraged?

Most States have eased the registration process over the last several years. In 1993, Congress passed a law that required every State (but North Dakota) to do so. That law, dubbed the "Motor Voter Act," became effective in 1995. It directs the States to (1) allow all eligible citizens to register to vote when they apply for or renew a driver's license; (2) provide for voter registration by mail; and (3) make registration forms available at the local offices of State employment, welfare, and other social service agencies. The Federal Election Commission reported that by the year 2000, approximately 8 million persons had registered to vote as a direct result of the Motor Voter Law.

The law also requires every State to mail a questionnaire to each of its registered voters every four years, so that the poll books can be purged for deaths and changes of residence. It also forbids the States to purge for any other reason, including failure to vote.

Several States now have so-called voter ID laws that require people to prove their identity when they seek to register or vote. Some government-issued photo ID—a passport or a driver's license, for example—will usually satisfy the requirement to confirm their identity at the polls.

The statutes are quite controversial. Their sponsors, usually Republican State legislators, insist that the measures are intended to prevent people from voting under false identities, also known as fraudulent voting. Fraudulent voting, they argue, weakens the value of legally-cast votes by diluting them with illegitimate votes. Critics, mostly Democrats, say that they are really designed to discourage voting by the elderly, disabled, poor, and minority groups, who are less likely to have State-issued driver's licenses or federally issued passports. They also argue that very few cases of voter fraud have been identified and prosecuted in recent years.

The Supreme Court upheld Indiana's photo ID law in *Crawford* v. *Marion County Election Board* in 2008. The Court ruled, 6–3, that the opponents of the law had not shown that it puts so unreasonable a burden on some groups of voters that it violates the 14th Amendment's Equal Protection Clause. The Court will likely hear other challenges to these laws as they are applied in future elections.

Literacy, Tax Payment

Suffrage qualifications based on two other factors—literacy and tax payment—were once fairly common among the States. They had a fairly long history but are no longer to be found anywhere.

Literacy Today, no State has a suffrage qualification based on voter **literacy**—a person's ability to read and write. At one time, the literacy requirement could be, and in many places was, used to make sure that a qualified voter had the capacity to cast an informed ballot. Some States asked potential voters to prove that they could read; others asked for the ability to both read and write. And still others required those who registered to vote to show that they could read and write and also understand some piece of printed material—often, a passage from the State or Federal Constitution.

Connecticut adopted the first literacy qualifications in 1855. Massachusetts followed in 1857. Both States were trying to limit voting by Irish Catholic immigrants. Mississippi adopted a literacy requirement in 1890, and soon after, most of the other southern States followed suit. The literary qualification in most southern States included an "understanding" clause. Often, whites were asked to "understand" some short, plainly worded constitutional provision; but African Americans had to interpret a long, complex passage to the satisfaction of local election officials.

While those qualifications had been aimed at disenfranchising African Americans, they sometimes had unintended effects. Several States soon found that they needed to adjust their voting requirements by adding so-called grandfather clauses to their constitutions. These grandfather clauses were designed to enfranchise those white males who were unintentionally disqualified by their failure to meet the literacy or taxpaying requirements.

A grandfather clause was added to the Louisiana constitution in 1898; Alabama, Georgia, Maryland, North Carolina, Oklahoma, and Virginia soon added them as well. These clauses stated that any man, or his male descendants, who had voted in the State before the adoption of the 15th Amendment (1870) could become a legal voter without regard to any literacy or taxpaying qualifications. The Supreme Court found the Oklahoma provision, the last to be adopted (in 1910), in conflict with the 15th Amendment in *Guinn* v. *United States* in 1915.

A number of States outside the South also adopted literacy qualifications, including Wyoming, California, Washington, New

✔ **Checkpoint**
What are the requirements of the "Motor Voter Law Act?"

Registration Requirements

Literacy tests (below) were used in many places to try to deny African Americans the right to vote. The questions below are reproduced from one of the many versions of those tests in use during that time. The tests were changed frequently, making it impossible to study for them. *How might these questions discourage eligible citizens from registering to vote?*

A voter fills out a registration form. ▶

Can you answer these?

1. If you have been employed by another during the last five years, state the nature of your employment and the name or names of such employer or employers and his or their addresses.

2. Give the names of the places, respectively, where you have lived during the last five years; and the name or names by which you have been known during the last five years.

3. Are you now or have you ever been affiliated with any group or organization which advocates the overthrow of the Unites States Government or the government of any State of the United States by unlawful means?

4. Name some of the duties and obligations of citizenship. Do you regard those duties and obligations as having priority over the duties and obligations you owe to any other secular organization when they are in conflict?

Source: The Honorable Rufus A. Lewis Collection at Trenholm State Technical College Archives

---

✔ **Checkpoint**
Which amendment outlawed the poll tax?

Hampshire, Arizona, New York, Oregon, and Alaska. Its unfair use finally led Congress to ban literacy qualifications in 1970. The Court agreed in *Oregon* v. *Mitchell,* 1970:

PRIMARY SOURCE

In enacting the literacy test ban . . . Congress had before it a long history of the discriminatory use of literacy tests to disfranchise voters on account of their race.

—Justice Hugo Black, Opinion of the Court

Some form of the literacy requirement was in place in 18 States when Congress finally banned its use.

Tax Payment Property ownership, proved by the payment of property taxes, was once a very common suffrage qualification. For decades, several States also demanded the payment of a special tax, called the poll tax, as a condition for voting. Those requirements and others that

called for the payment of a tax in order to vote have disappeared over the years.

The poll tax was once found throughout the South. Beginning with Florida in 1889, each of the 11 southern States adopted the poll tax as part of the effort to discourage voting by African Americans. The device proved to be of only limited effectiveness, however. That fact, and opposition to the use of the poll tax from within the South as well as elsewhere, led most of those States to abandon it. By 1966, the tax was still in use in only Alabama, Mississippi, Texas, and Virginia.[12]

The 24th Amendment, ratified in 1964, outlawed the poll tax, or any other tax, as a condition for voting in any federal election. The Supreme Court finally eliminated the poll tax in 1966 as a qualification for voting in all elections. In *Harper* v. *Virginia Board of Elections,* the Court held the Virginia poll tax to be

---

[12] By that time, the poll tax had been abolished in North Carolina (1920), Louisiana (1934), Florida (1937), Georgia (1945), South Carolina (1951), Tennessee (1953), and Arkansas (1965).

in conflict with the 14th Amendment's Equal Protection Clause. The Court could find no reasonable relationship between the act of voting on one hand and the payment of a tax on the other. Justice William O. Douglas, writing for the majority, put the point this way:

PRIMARY SOURCE

Once the franchise is granted to the electorate, lines may not be drawn which are inconsistent with the Equal Protection Clause. . . . Voter qualifications have no relation to wealth nor to paying this or any other tax. . . . Wealth, like race, creed, or color, is not germane to one's ability to participate intelligently in the electoral process.

—Justice William O. Douglas,
Opinion of the Court

▲ Several groups hold voter registration drives targeting the homeless, especially in larger cities. *Why might it be important to register the homeless in a large city?*

Persons Denied the Vote Clearly, democratic government can exist only where the right to vote is widely held. Still, every State does purposely deny the vote to certain persons. For example, few of the 50 States allow people in mental institutions, or any other persons who have been legally found to be mentally incompetent, to vote.

Most States disqualify, at least temporarily, those persons who have been convicted of serious crimes. Until fairly recently, that disqualification was almost always a permanent one. Over recent years, however, most States have made it possible for the majority of convicted felons to regain the right to vote, although those guilty of such election-related offenses as bribery and ballot-box stuffing, however, are still regularly banned. A few States also do not allow anyone dishonorably discharged from the armed forces to cast a ballot.

Essential Questions Journal To continue to build a response to the chapter Essential Question, go to your **Essential Questions Journal.**

SECTION 2 ASSESSMENT

1. **Guiding Question** Use your completed flowchart to answer the question: What are the qualifications for voting, and how have they changed over time?

Key Terms and Comprehension

2. What does the Constitution say about the voting rights of **aliens?**
3. **(a)** What is the purpose of laws requiring voter **registration? (b)** How do registration laws vary among States?
4. Why should election officials regularly **purge** voter lists?

Critical Thinking

5. **Express Problems Clearly (a)** What are the pros and cons of voter registration? **(b)** Do you think the "Motor Voter Law" has had a positive or negative impact on voting? Explain.
6. **Draw Inferences (a)** Why were literacy requirements originally added to some State's voting requirements? **(b)** How did the establishment of "grandfather clauses" call into question the motives of States that had literacy test requirements?

Quick Write

Narrative: Consider Audience and Purpose Once you have chosen an event, think about who your audience is. Will you be writing for your fellow classmates, your teacher, or someone outside of your class? Consider how much background information you need to provide to your reader. Write a brief paragraph describing your audience.

SECTION 3
Suffrage and Civil Rights

Guiding Question

How did the U.S. fulfill the promise of the 15th Amendment? Use the chart to record details of the history of voting rights for African Americans.

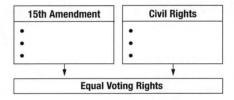

15th Amendment	Civil Rights
•	•
•	•
•	•

Equal Voting Rights

Political Dictionary

- gerrymandering
- injunction
- preclearance

Objectives

1. Describe the tactics often used to deny African Americans the right to vote despite the command of the 15th Amendment.
2. Understand the significance of the civil rights laws enacted in 1957, 1960, and 1964.
3. Analyze the provisions and effects of the Voting Rights Act of 1965.

Image Above: Dr. Martin Luther King, Jr., casts his ballot in Atlanta, Georgia, on November 3, 1964.

How important is the right to vote? For those who do not have it, that right can seem as important as life itself. Indeed, in the Deep South of the 1960s, civil rights workers suffered arrest, beatings, shocks with electric cattle prods, even death—all in the name of the right to vote. Their efforts inspired the nation and led to large-scale federal efforts to secure that right for African Americans and other minority groups in the United States.

The 15th Amendment

The effort to extend the franchise to African Americans began with the 15th Amendment, which was ratified in 1870. It declares that the right to vote cannot be denied to any citizen of the United States because of "race, color, or previous condition of servitude." The amendment was plainly intended to ensure that African American men, nearly all of them former slaves and nearly all of them living in the South, could vote.

The 15th Amendment is not self-executing, however. In other words, simply stating a general principle without providing for a means of enforcement was not enough to carry out the intention of the amendment. To make it effective, Congress had to act. Yet for nearly 90 years the Federal Government paid little attention to the voting rights of African Americans.

History During that period, African Americans were generally and systematically kept from the polls in much of the South. White supremacists employed a number of tactics to that end. Their major weapon was violence. Other tactics included more subtle threats and social pressures—for example, firing an African American man who tried to register or vote, or denying his family credit at local stores.

More formal "legal" devices were used, as well. The most effective were literacy tests. White officials regularly manipulated those tests to disenfranchise African Americans. Registration laws served the same end. As written, they applied to all potential voters. In practice, however, they were often administered to keep African Americans from qualifying to vote. Poll taxes, "white primaries," gerrymandering, and several other devices were also used.

Gerrymandering is the practice of drawing electoral district lines (the boundaries of the geographic area from which a candidate is elected to a public office) in order to limit the voting strength of a particular group or party.

The white primary arose out of the decades-long Democratic domination of politics in the South. It was almost a given that the Democratic candidate for an office would be elected. Therefore, only the Democrats ordinarily nominated candidates, generally in primaries. In several southern States, political parties were defined by law as "private associations" that could exclude whomever they chose, and the Democrats regularly refused to admit African Americans. Because only party members could vote in the party's primary, African Americans were then excluded from a critical step in the public election process.

Court Rulings

The Supreme Court outlawed the white primary in a case from Texas, *Smith* v. *Allwright,* in 1944. The Court held that nominations are an integral part of the election process. So, when a political party holds a primary, it is performing a public function and is bound by the 15th Amendment.

The Supreme Court outlawed gerrymandering used for purposes of racial discrimination in *Gomillion* v. *Lightfoot,* 1960. There, the Alabama legislature had redrawn the electoral district boundaries of Tuskegee, effectively excluding blacks from the city limits. The Court ruled that the legislature's action violated the 15th Amendment, because the irregularly shaped district clearly was created to deprive blacks of political power.

Led by these decisions, the lower federal courts struck down many practices designed to deny the vote to African Americans in the 1940s and 1950s. Still, the courts could act only when those who claimed to be victims of discrimination sued. That case-by-case method was, at best, agonizingly slow.

Early Civil Rights Legislation

Finally, largely in response to the civil rights movement led by Dr. Martin Luther King, Jr., Congress was moved to act. In the late 1950s, it began to enact civil rights laws specifically intended to implement the 15th Amendment.

Acts of 1957 and 1960

The first of the laws Congress passed to enforce the 15th Amendment was the Civil Rights Act of 1957, which created the United States Commission on Civil Rights. One of the Commission's major duties is to inquire into claims of voter discrimination. The Commission reports its findings to Congress and the President and, through the media, to the public. The 1957 law also gave the attorney general the power to seek federal court orders to prevent interference with any person's right to vote in any federal election.

The Civil Rights Act of 1960 added an additional safeguard. It provided for the appointment of federal voting referees. Those officers were to serve anywhere a federal court found voter discrimination. They were given the power to help qualified persons to register and vote in federal elections.

The Civil Rights Act of 1964

The Civil Rights Act of 1964 is much broader and more effective than either of the two earlier measures. It outlaws discrimination in several areas, especially in job-related matters. With regard to voting rights, its most important section forbids the use of any voter registration or literacy requirement in an unfair or discriminatory manner.

The 1964 law continued a pattern set in the earlier laws. It relied on judicial action to overcome racial barriers and emphasized the use of federal court orders called injunctions. An **injunction** is a court order that either <u>compels</u> or restrains the performance of some act by a private individual or public official. The violation of an injunction amounts to contempt of court, a crime punishable by fine and/or imprisonment.

Dramatic events in Selma, Alabama, soon revealed the shortcomings of this approach. Dr. King mounted a voter registration drive in that city in early 1965. He and his supporters hoped that they could focus national attention on the issue of African American voting rights—and they most certainly did.

Their registration efforts were met with insults and violence by local white <u>civilians</u>, by city and county police, and then by State troopers. Three civil rights workers were murdered, and many were beaten when they attempted a peaceful march to the State

✓ **Checkpoint**
What is gerrymandering and how was it used to keep African Americans from voting?

<u>**white supremacist**</u>
n. advocate of the superiority of the white race, racist

<u>**compel**</u>
v. to force, require

<u>**civilian**</u>
n. any person not an active member of the armed forces or having police power

African Americans and the Vote

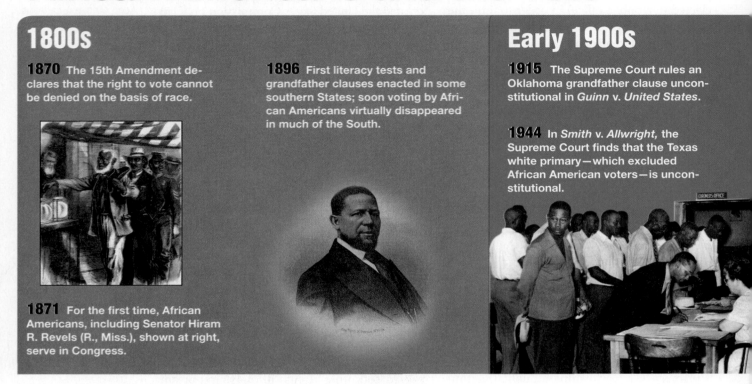

1800s

1870 The 15th Amendment declares that the right to vote cannot be denied on the basis of race.

1871 For the first time, African Americans, including Senator Hiram R. Revels (R., Miss.), shown at right, serve in Congress.

1896 First literacy tests and grandfather clauses enacted in some southern States; soon voting by African Americans virtually disappeared in much of the South.

Early 1900s

1915 The Supreme Court rules an Oklahoma grandfather clause unconstitutional in *Guinn* v. *United States.*

1944 In *Smith* v. *Allwright,* the Supreme Court finds that the Texas white primary—which excluded African American voters—is unconstitutional.

▶▶ **Analyzing Timelines** The 15th Amendment did not really become an effective part of the Constitution until the 1960s. *Why do you think it took so long for the 15th Amendment to become truly effective?*

Capitol. The nation saw much of the drama on television and was shocked. An outraged President Lyndon Johnson urged Congress to pass new and stronger legislation to ensure the voting rights of African Americans. Congress responded, and quickly.

Voting Rights Act of 1965

The Voting Rights Act of 1965 made the 15th Amendment, at long last, a truly effective part of the Constitution. Unlike its predecessors, this act applied to *all* elections held anywhere in this country—State and local, as well as federal.

Originally, the Voting Rights Act was to be in effect for a period of five years. Congress has extended its life on four occasions, in the Voting Rights Act Amendments of 1970, 1975, 1982, and, most recently, 2006. The present version of the law was made effective for 25 years; its provisions will not expire until 2031.

predecessor
n. one who goes before, forerunner

The 1965 law directed the attorney general to challenge the constitutionality of the remaining State poll-tax laws in the federal courts. That provision led directly to *Harper* v. *Virginia Board of Elections,* 1966, as you may recall from Section 2.

The law also suspended the use of any literacy test or similar device in any State or county where less than half of the electorate had been registered or had voted in the 1964 presidential election. The law authorized the attorney general to appoint voting examiners to serve in any of those States or counties. It also gave these federal officers the power to register voters and otherwise oversee the conduct of elections in those areas.

Preclearance The Voting Rights Act of 1965 imposed another restriction on those States where a majority of the electorate had not voted in 1964. The act declared that no new election laws, and no changes in existing election laws, could go into effect in any

Today

1965 The Voting Rights Act protects African Americans against various tactics intended to prevent them from voting.

1966 Edward W. Brooke III (R., Mass.) becomes the first African American elected to the Senate since the 1870s.

2008 Senator Barack Obama (D., Illinois) is the first African American elected President of the United States.

Left: Civil rights marchers approach Alabama's State Capitol during a voter registration protest march in 1965.
Right: Voter registration in New York City

of those States unless first approved—given **preclearance**—by the Department of Justice. Only those new or revised laws that do not <u>dilute</u> the voting rights of minority groups can survive the preclearance process and take effect.

The preclearance hurdle has produced a large number of court cases over the years. Those cases show that the laws most likely to <u>run afoul</u> of the preclearance requirement are those that make these kinds of changes: (1) the location of polling places; (2) the boundaries of election districts; (3) the deadlines in the election process; (4) a shift from ward or district election to at-large elections; or (5) the qualifications candidates must meet in order to run for office.

Any State or county subject to the voter-examiner and preclearance provisions can be removed from the law's coverage through a "bail-out" process. That relief can come if the State shows the United States District Court in the District of Columbia that it has not applied any voting procedures in a discriminatory way for at least 10 years.

The voter-examiner and preclearance provisions of the 1965 Voting Rights Act originally applied to six entire States: Alabama, Georgia, Louisiana, Mississippi, South Carolina, and Virginia. In addition, these provisions applied to 40 counties in North Carolina.

The Supreme Court upheld the Voting Rights Act in 1966. In *South Carolina* v. *Katzenbach*, a unanimous Court rejected the claim that the law—and, most particularly, its preclearance provisions—violated the reserved power of each State to shape its own electoral system. Instead the Court found the Voting Rights Act to be a proper exercise of the power granted to Congress in Section 2 of the 15th Amendment. That provision authorizes Congress to enact "appropriate legislation" to enforce the constitutional prohibition against racial discrimination in voting set out in Section 1 of the amendment.

✔ **Checkpoint**
What provision about literacy tests was in the Voting Rights Act of 1965?

dilute
v. to weaken, diminish, water down

run afoul
v. to come into conflict with, be at odds with

Amendments to the Act The Voting Rights Act Amendments of 1970 extended the law for another five years. The 1968 elections were taken into account in determining jurisdictions with concerns; the result was that a number of counties in six more States (Alaska, Arizona, California, Idaho, New Mexico, and Oregon) were included in the law's coverage.

That 1970 law also provided that, for five years, no State could use literacy as the basis for any voting requirement. That temporary ban as well as residence provisions outlined in the law were upheld by the Supreme Court in *Oregon* v. *Mitchell* in 1970.

In 1975, the law was extended again, this time for seven years, and the five-year ban on literacy tests was made permanent. Since 1975, no State has been able to apply *any* sort of literacy qualification to *any* aspect of the election process. The law's voter-examiner and preclearance provisions were also broadened in 1975. Since then, they have also covered any State or county where more than 5 percent of the voting-age population belongs to certain "language minorities." These groups are defined to include all persons of Spanish heritage, Native Americans, Asian Americans, and Alaskan Natives.

This addition expanded the law's coverage to all of Alaska and Texas and to several counties in 24 other States, as well. In these areas, all ballots and other official election materials must be printed both in English and in the language of the minorities involved.

The 1982 amendments extended the basic features of the act for another 25 years. In 1992, the law's language-minority provisions were revised: they now apply to any community that has a minority-language population of 10,000 or more.

Over the years, several States and a handful of counties in a few other States have been removed from the law's coverage, through the "bail-out" process. Today, eight entire States remain subject to the Voting Rights Act: Alabama, Alaska, Arizona, Georgia, Louisiana, Mississippi, South Carolina, and Texas. At least some counties in six other States are also covered by the statute: California, Florida, New York, North Carolina, South Dakota, and Virginia, as well as two townships in Michigan and ten towns in New Hampshire.

The Court still faces challenges to the Voting Rights Act, most recently in *Northwest Austin Municipal Utility District* v. *Holder* in 2009. There, a small Texas water district argued that, given the many significant changes in race relationships over the past 40 years, the 2006 extension of the law was unnecessary and is, therefore, unconstitutional.

In deciding the case, the Court sidestepped the question of the law's constitutionality. It did so by holding, 8–1, that because the water district had no history of race-based discrimination it was not subject to the law's preclearance provisions. Clearly, the future holds more challenges to the validity of the Voting Rights Act.

Essential Questions Journal To continue to build a response to the chapter Essential Question, go to your **Essential Questions Journal.**

SECTION 3 ASSESSMENT

1. **Guiding Question** Use your completed chart to answer the question: **How did the United States fulfill the promise of the 15th Amendment?**

Key Terms and Comprehension

2. How has **gerrymandering** been used to prevent the fulfillment of the 15th Amendment?

3. **(a)** What is **preclearance**? **(b)** What is the process meant to prevent?

Critical Thinking

4. **Synthesize Information** Why, for nearly a century, was the 15th Amendment largely ineffective?

5. **Make Comparisons (a)** In what key way did the Voting Rights Act of 1965 differ from earlier civil rights laws? **(b)** How have more recent legislation and court decisions helped further refine that Act?

Quick Write

Narrative: Gather Details Gather any additional details about the event you chose in Section 1 that may be important to your essay. List details in order of importance.

Casting Your Vote

Voting is one of the greatest privileges a citizen enjoys. It means that you have a role in deciding who your elected officials will be. Yet voting is a big responsibility. It takes some planning to ensure your eligibility, prepare yourself to become an informed voter, and eventually cast your vote.

Casting your vote in an election requires two different kinds of preparation. First, you must become aware of the rules and procedures concerning registering to vote and submitting your ballot where you live. Beyond that, you must consider several factors and examine the issues and candidates involved in the election in order to make an informed decision.

1. **Understand Eligibility Rules** In order to vote, you must be a United States citizen. You must be of age. This generally means being 18, though some States allow people to vote at a younger age in some circumstances. Be sure to find out what the rules are where you live. Also find out about residence require-ments. You must be a resident of the place where you plan to vote, though how you prove residency does vary.

2. **Register to Vote** You can register to vote by visiting the city or town election offices, or when you get or renew a driver's license. You may also be able to register by mail or even online. Find out what you must do in your State to register as well as how soon before the election. Pay close attention to whether or not you will need to declare a political party when registering.

3. **Educate Yourself** As the election approaches, research the candidates and issues that will appear on the ballot. Read newspaper and online news coverage. Watch televised debates. Review candidate websites to learn about views and positions. By doing these things and thinking critically about what you learn, you are closer to being an informed voter.

4. **Vote** Voting requires that you make the effort to come to the polling place on election day and cast your ballot. Find out ahead of time when the polls will be open, and make plans to take the time necessary to meet this responsibility. If you think you will not be present on election day, find out about absentee voting. If advance voting is used where you live, be sure you understand the rules and procedures for casting a ballot.

▸▸ What do you think?

1. Of the steps listed, which do you think is most important to casting a vote?

2. Why is it important to be an informed voter?

3. **You Try It** Follow the steps above and write a step-by-step description of how you would cast a ballot, using details specific to your community.

GOVERNMENT ONLINE
Citizenship Activity Pack
For an activity to help you learn more about voting, go to **PearsonSuccessNet.com**

Voter Behavior

Guiding Question

What factors influence voter behavior? Use the outline to record details about voter behavior.

Factors that Influence Voters
A. Sociological
　1. _____
　2. _____
　3. _____
B. Psychological

Political Dictionary

- off-year election
- ballot fatigue
- political efficacy
- political socialization
- gender gap
- party identification
- straight-ticket voting
- split-ticket voting
- independent

Objectives

1. Examine the problem of nonvoting in this country.
2. Identify those people who typically do not vote.
3. Examine the behavior of those who vote and those who do not.
4. Understand the sociological and psychological factors that affect voting and voter behavior.

Image Above: Reviewing a ballot on election day

"Your vote is your voice. Use it." That's the advice of Rock the Vote, an organization that encourages young voters ages 18 to 25 to participate in the election process. In the United States, and in other democratic countries, we believe all voices should be heard. That is, we believe in voting.

Most elections in this country are built around two-candidate contests. How many choices does a voter have in a two-candidate race? More than most people think. Not just two but, in fact, *five* options. He or she can (1) vote FOR Candidate A, (2) vote AGAINST Candidate A, (3) vote FOR Candidate B, (4) vote AGAINST Candidate B, or (5) decide not to vote for either candidate.

Over the next several pages, you will look at voter behavior in this country—at who votes and who does not, and at why those people who do vote cast their ballots as they do.

Nonvoting

The word *idiot* came to our language from the Greek. In ancient Athens, idiots *(idiotes)* were those citizens who did not vote or otherwise take part in public life.

Tens of millions of Americans vote in presidential and congressional elections; in State elections; and in city, county, and other public elections. Still, there are many millions of other Americans who, for one reason or another, do not vote. There are some quite valid reasons for not voting, as you will see. But this troubling fact remains: Most of the millions of Americans who could—but do not—go to the polls cannot claim any of those justifications. Indeed, they would have been called idiots in the Greece of 2500 years ago.

On election day in 2008, there were an estimated 228 million persons of voting age in the United States. Yet only some 131 million of them—only 60 percent—actually voted in the presidential election. Nearly 100 million persons who might have voted did not.

In 2008, some 121 million votes were cast in the elections held across the country to fill the 435 seats in the House of Representatives. That is, only some 53 percent of the electorate voted in those congressional contests. (Notice the even lower rates of turnout in the **off-year elections**—that is, in the congressional elections held in the even-numbered years, between presidential elections.)

Several <u>facets</u> of the nonvoter problem are not very widely known. Take, for example, this striking fact: There are millions of nonvoters *among those who vote*. Some 10 million persons who voted in the last presidential election could also have voted for a congressional candidate, but they did not choose to do so.

"Nonvoting voters" are not limited to federal elections. In fact, they are much more common in State and local elections. As a general rule, the farther down the ballot an office is, the fewer the number of votes that will be cast for it. This phenomenon is sometimes called **ballot fatigue.** The expression suggests that many voters exhaust their patience and/or their knowledge as they work their way down the ballot. More votes are generally cast for the governorship than for other Statewide offices, such as lieutenant governor or secretary of state. More voters in a county usually vote in the races for Statewide offices than vote in the contests for such county offices as sheriff, county clerk, and so on.

There are other little-recognized facets of the nonvoter problem, too. Turnout in congressional elections is consistently higher in presidential years than it is in off-year elections. That same pattern holds among the States in terms of the types of elections; more people vote in general elections than in either primary or special elections.

Why People Do Not Vote

Why so many nonvoters? Why, even in a presidential election, do as many as half of those who could vote stay away from the polls?

Clearly, the time that it takes to vote should not be a significant part of the answer. For most people, it takes more time to choose a DVD to watch than it does to go to their neighborhood polling place and cast a ballot. So we must look elsewhere for answers.

"Cannot-Voters" To begin with, look at another of those little-recognized aspects of the nonvoter problem. Several million persons who are regularly identified as nonvoters can be much more accurately described as "cannot-voters." That is, although it is true that they do not vote, the fact is that they cannot do so.

The 2008 data support the point. Included in that figure of nearly 100 million who did not vote in the last presidential election are at least 10 million who are resident aliens. Remember, they are barred from the polls in

✔ **Checkpoint**
What are "nonvoting voters"?

<u>**facet**</u>
n. side or aspect

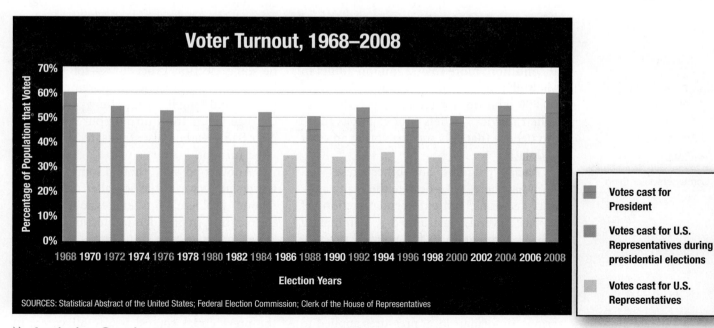

Voter Turnout, 1968–2008

SOURCES: Statistical Abstract of the United States; Federal Election Commission; Clerk of the House of Representatives

Legend:
- Votes cast for President
- Votes cast for U.S. Representatives during presidential elections
- Votes cast for U.S. Representatives

▶ Analyzing Graphs Voter turnout varies from election to election, but presidential elections always draw more voters than off-year elections. *What factor does the blue at the top of each bar represent, and what is this factor called?*

✓ **Checkpoint**
Why do people choose not to vote?

alienate
vt. to feel unfriendly or hostile to, isolated from

idolatry
n. excessive devotion to some person or thing

every State. Another 5 to 6 million citizens were so ill or otherwise physically disabled that they simply could not vote in an election. An additional 2 to 3 million persons were traveling suddenly and unexpectedly, and so could not vote.

Other groups of cannot-voters can be discovered in the nonvoting group. They include some 500,000 persons in mental health care facilities or under some other form of legal restraint because of their mental condition; more than 2 million adults in jails and prisons; and perhaps as many as 100,000 who do not (cannot) vote because of their religious beliefs—for example, those who believe that acts such as voting amount to idolatry.

Racial, religious, and other biases still play a part here, too—despite the many laws, court decisions, and enforcement actions of the past several years aimed at eliminating such discrimination in the political process. An unknown but certainly significant number of people cannot vote today because of (1) the purposeful administration of election laws to keep them from doing so, and/or (2) various "informal" local pressures applied to that same end.

Actual Nonvoters Even so, there are millions of actual nonvoters in the United States. Thus, in 2008, more than 80 million Americans who could have voted in the presidential election did not. There are any number of reasons for that behavior. As a leading example: Many who could go to the polls do not because they are convinced that it makes little real difference which candidate wins a particular election.

That fairly large group includes two quite different groups of nonvoters. On the one hand, there are many who generally approve of the way the public's business is being managed—that is, many who believe that no matter who wins an election, things will continue to go well for themselves and for the country.

On the other hand, that group also includes many people who feel alienated— that is, many who deliberately refuse to vote because they don't trust political institutions and processes. They either fear or scorn "the system." To them, elections are meaningless, choiceless exercises.

Another large group of nonvoters is composed of people who have no sense of **political efficacy.** That is, they lack any feeling of influence or effectiveness in politics. They do not believe that they or their votes can have any real impact on what government does or does not do.

Other factors can also dictate whether voters show up at the polls or not. Cumbersome election procedures—for example, inconvenient registration requirements, long ballots, and long lines at polling places—discourage voters from turning out on election day. Bad weather also tends to discourage voter turnout.

Another possible, though somewhat controversial, factor is the so-called "time-zone fallout" problem. This expression refers to the fact that, in presidential elections, polls in States in the Eastern and Central time zones close an hour or more before polls in States in the Mountain and Pacific time zones. Based on early returns from the East and Midwest, the news media often project the outcome of the presidential contest before all voters in the West have gone to the polls. Some people fear that such reports discourage western voters from casting their ballots.

Of all the reasons that may be cited, however, the chief cause for nonvoting is, purely and simply, a lack of interest. Those who are <u>indifferent</u>, who just cannot be bothered, are usually woefully uninformed. Most often, they know little or nothing about the candidates and issues in an election. There are many who argue that the democratic process is well served by the fact that most of these people do not go to the polls.

Comparing Voters and Nonvoters One useful way to get a handle on the problem of nonvoting is to contrast those persons who tend to go to the polls regularly with those who do not.

The people most likely to vote display such characteristics as higher levels of income, education, and occupational status. They are usually well integrated into community life. They tend to be long-time residents who are active in, or at least comfortable with, their surroundings. They are likely to have a strong sense of party identification, and to believe that voting is an important act. They are also likely to live in those areas where laws, customs, and competition between the parties all promote turnout.

The opposite characteristics produce a profile of those less likely to vote. Nonvoters are likely to be younger than age 35, unmarried, and unskilled. More nonvoters live in the South and in rural locales. Men are less likely to vote than women—a fact that first became apparent in the 1980s.

A few of the factors that help determine whether or not a person will vote are so important that they influence turnout even when they conflict with other factors. For example, those persons with a high sense of political efficacy are likely to vote—no matter what their income, education, age, race, and so on may be. The degree of two-party competition also has an extraordinary impact on participation. Thus, the greater the competition between candidates, the more likely people will be to go to the polls, regardless of other factors.

Despite the greater weight of some of these factors, however, note this point: It is the combined presence of several factors, not one of them alone, that tends to determine whether a person will or will not vote.

Voters and Voting Behavior

As you have read, tens of millions of potential voters do not go to the polls in this country. But many millions more do. How do those who do vote behave? What prompts many to vote most often for Republicans and many others to support the Democratic Party? Research has produced a huge amount of information about why people tend to vote as they do.

Studying Voting Behavior Most of what is known about voter behavior comes from three sources.

1. *The results of particular elections.* How individuals vote in a given election is secret in the United States. However, careful study of the returns from areas populated largely by, say, African Americans or Catholics or high-income families will indicate how those groups voted in a given election.

2. *The field of survey research.* The polling of scientifically determined cross sections of the population is the method by which public opinion is most often identified and measured. The Gallup Organization and the Pew Research Center conduct perhaps the best known of these polls today.

3. *Studies of political socialization.* **Political socialization** is the process by which people gain their political attitudes and opinions. That complex process begins in early childhood and continues through each person's life. Political socialization involves all of the experiences and relationships that lead people to see the political world, and to act in it, as they do.

Factors That Influence Voters Observers still have much to learn about voter behavior, but many sociological and psychological factors clearly influence the way people cast their ballots. Sociology is the study of groups and how people behave within groups. The sociological factors affecting voter behavior are really the many pieces of a voter's social and economic life. Those pieces are of two

✔ **Checkpoint**
What three sources are used to gather data about voter behavior?

indifferent
adj. uninterested, uncaring, not concerned

broad kinds: (1) a voter's personal characteristics—age, race, income, occupation, education, religion, and so on; and (2) a voter's group affiliations—family, co-workers, friends, and the like.

Psychology is the study of the mind and individual behavior. The psychological factors that influence voter behavior are a voter's perceptions of politics—that is, how the voter sees the parties, the candidates, and the issues in an election.

The differences between these two kinds of influences are not nearly so great as they might seem. In fact, they are closely related and they constantly interact with one another. How voters look at parties, candidates, or issues is often shaped by their own social and economic backgrounds.

Sociological Factors

Using data from past elections, you can draw a composite picture of the American voter in terms of a number of sociological factors. A word of caution here: Do not make too much of any one of these factors. Remember, each voter possesses not just one, but in fact *several* of the many characteristics involved here.

To illustrate the point: College graduates are more likely to vote Republican. So are persons over age 50. African Americans, on the other hand, are more likely to vote for Democrats. So are members of labor unions. How, then, would a 55-year-old, college-educated African American who belongs to the AFL-CIO decide to vote?

Income and Occupation Voters in lower income brackets are more likely to be Democrats. Voters with higher incomes tend to be Republicans. This pattern has held up over time, no matter whether a particular election was a cliffhanger or a blow-out. The 2008 election proved to be an exception, however. In that contest, those making under $50,000 did favor Democrat Barack Obama by an overwhelming majority. However, those with incomes of $50,000 and up were fairly evenly divided between the two candidates, and President Obama made significant inroads among those who make over $200,000, winning 52 percent of their votes.

Most often, how much one earns and what one does for a living are closely related. Professional and business people, and others with higher incomes, regularly tend to vote for Republican candidates. Manual workers, and others in lower income groups, usually vote for Democrats. Thus, with the exception of 1964 and 2008, professional and business people have voted heavily Republican in every presidential election in the modern era.

Education Studies of voter behavior reveal that there is also a close relationship between the level of a voter's education and how he or she tends to vote. College graduates vote for Republicans in higher percentages than high-school graduates; and high-school graduates vote Republican more often than those who have only gone through grade school. Again, however, the 2008 election proved an exception to this trend.

Gender, Age There are often measurable differences between the partisan choices of men and women today. This phenomenon is known as the **gender gap,** and it first appeared in the 1980s. Women generally tend to favor the Democrats by a margin of five to ten percent, and men often give the GOP a similar edge. In 2008, however, President Obama won 56 percent of all votes cast by women, while men's votes were evenly split between the candidates.

A number of studies show that men and women are most likely to vote differently when such issues as abortion, health care or other social welfare matters, or military involvements abroad are prominent in an election.

Traditionally, younger voters have been more likely to vote Democratic than Republican. Older voters are likely to find the GOP and its candidates more attractive. Thus, in every presidential election from 1960 through 1980, the Democrats won a larger percentage of the votes of the under-30 age group than of the 50-and-over age bracket.

That long-standing pattern was broken by Ronald Reagan's appeal to younger voters in 1984, and by George H.W. Bush in 1988. However, Bill Clinton restored the Democrats' claim to those voters in 1992 and 1996.

And John Kerry won the major slice of the votes of that age group—54 percent—in 2004. The 2008 election upheld this tradition of younger voters favoring the Democrats, and in a big way, with Barack Obama winning 66 percent of the under 30 vote.

Religion, Ethnic Background Historically, a majority of Protestants have most often preferred the GOP. Catholics and Jews have tended to be Democrats.[14] The 2008 elections supported this trend, with President Obama winning just 45 percent of the votes cast by all Protestants and only 34 percent of those cast by white Protestants. Fifty-four percent of all Catholic voters backed the President, and he won a huge 78 percent of the ballots cast by Jewish voters.

Moral issues, notably same-sex marriage, were unusually prominent in 2004 and 2008. Church attendance has also emerged as a major indicator of partisan

14 In 1960, John F. Kennedy became the first Roman Catholic President. His election marked a sharper split between Catholic and Protestant voters than in any other recent election.

Checkpoint
How do sociological factors affect voting?

GOVERNMENT ONLINE
Audio Tour
Listen to a guided audio tour on voting at
PearsonSuccessNet.com

Group Voting, 2008 Presidential Election

Analyzing Charts This chart reports the voting behavior of several major segments of the American electorate in the most recent presidential election. As you analyze this data, remember that every voter belongs to not just one, but all of these groups. ***How might a 45-year-old, college-educated, Hispanic woman who makes $60,000 per year vote? Explain your reasoning.***

	GROUPS (percentage of total)	REPUBLICAN	DEMOCRATIC
	All voters (100%)*	45%	53%
GENDER Women vote Democratic more often than men.	Men (46%)	48%	49%
	Women (54%)	43%	56%
RACE African Americans vote heavily Democratic.	White (74%)	55%	43%
	African American (13%)	4%	95%
	Latino/a (9%)	31%	67%
	Asian (2%)	35%	62%
AGE Older people vote more heavily Republican.	18–29 years (18%)	32%	66%
	30–44 years (29%)	46%	52%
	45–64 years (37%)	49%	50%
	65 years (16%)	53%	45%
INCOME People with higher incomes tend to vote Republican.	Less than $50,000/year (38%)	38%	60%
	$50,000 or more/year (62%)	49%	49%
EDUCATION Republican voting tends to increase with level of education.	No high school (4%)	35%	63%
	High school graduate (20%)	46%	52%
	Some college (31%)	47%	51%
	College graduate (28%)	48%	50%
	Postgraduate study (17%)	40%	58%
PARTY IDENTIFICATION Most significant predictor of how one will vote.	Democratic (39%)	10%	89%
	Republican (32%)	90%	9%
	Independent (29%)	44%	52%

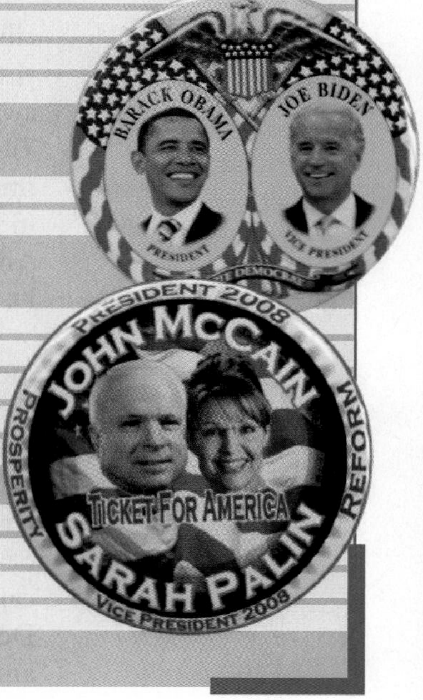

SOURCE: CNN exit poll

*Exit poll results may not match vote totals.

▶▶ Analyzing Political Cartoons *Is it really true that only those persons who vote have a right to complain? Why or why not?*

preference. Fifty-five percent of voters who go to church at least once a week marked their ballots for Mr. McCain in 2008.

For decades now, African Americans have supported the Democratic Party consistently and massively. They form the only group that has given the Democratic candidate a clear majority in every presidential election since 1952. There are now more than 40 million African Americans, and they make up the second largest minority in the country.

In the North, African Americans generally voted Republican until the 1930s, but, with the coming of the New Deal, they moved away from the party of Abraham Lincoln. The civil rights movement of the 1960s led to much greater African American participation in the politics of the South. Today, African Americans vote overwhelmingly Democratic in that region, too.

The United States is now home to more than 45 million Latinos, people with Spanish-speaking backgrounds. Latinos generally favor Democratic candidates. Note, however, that the label "Latino" conceals differences among Cuban Americans, who most often vote Republican, and Mexican Americans and Puerto Ricans, who are strongly Democratic. While the rate of turn-out among Latinos increased significantly in the

historic election of 2008, it was still comparatively low—well below 50 percent.

Geography Geography—the part of the country, State, and/or locale in which a person lives—also has a measurable impact on voter behavior. After the Civil War, the States of the old Confederacy voted so consistently Democratic that the southeast quarter of the nation became known as the Solid South. For more than a century, most Southerners, regardless of any other factor, identified with the Democratic Party.

The Solid South is now a thing of the past. Republican candidates have been increasingly successful throughout the region over the past half-century. The GOP now carries at least most of the Southern States in the presidential contest every four years, and it is now widely successful at the State and local levels across the region, too.

Those States that have most consistently supported Republican candidates over time have been Idaho, Wyoming, and Utah in the West and Kansas, Nebraska, and the Dakotas in the Midwest. The Democrats have made significant inroads in former Republican strongholds in New England, over the past two decades or so.

Voters' attitudes also vary in terms of the size of the communities in which they live. Generally, the Democrats draw strength from the big cities of the North and East and on the Pacific Coast. Many white Democrats have moved from the central cities and taken their political preferences with them, but Republican voters still dominate much of suburban America. Voters in smaller cities and rural areas are also likely to be Republicans.

Family and Other Groups To this point, you have seen the American voter sketched in terms of several broad social and economic characteristics. The picture can also be drawn on the basis of much smaller and more personal groupings, especially such primary groups as family, friends, and co-workers.

Typically, the members of a family vote in strikingly similar ways. Nine out of ten married couples share the same partisan leanings. As many as two out of every three voters follow the political attachments of their parents. Those who work together and circles of friends also tend to vote very much alike.

This like-mindedness is hardly surprising. People of similar social and economic backgrounds tend to associate with one another. In short, a person's group associations usually reinforce the opinions he or she already holds.

Psychological Factors

Although they are quite important, it would be wrong to give too much weight to the sociological factors in the voting mix. For one thing, those factors are fairly static. That is, they tend to change only gradually and over time. To understand voter behavior, you must look beyond such factors as occupation, education, ethnic background, and place of residence. You must also take into account a number of psychological factors. That is, you must look at the voters' perceptions of politics: how they see and react to the parties, the candidates, and the issues in an election.

Party Identification A majority of Americans identify themselves with one or the other of the two major parties early in life. Many never change. They support that party, election after election, with little or no regard for either the candidates or the issues involved in a particular election.

The hefty impact of **party identification**—the loyalty of people to a particular political party—is the single most significant and lasting predictor of how a person will vote. A person who is a Democrat or a Republican will, for that reason, very likely vote for all or most of that party's candidates in any given election. The practice of voting for candidates of only one party in an election is called **straight-ticket voting.**

Party identification is, therefore, a key factor in American politics. Among many other things, it means that each of the major parties can regularly count on the votes of millions of faithful supporters in every election.

Several signs suggest that, while it remains a major factor, party identification has lost some of its impact in recent years. One of those signs is the weakened condition of the parties themselves. Another is the

marked increase in **split-ticket voting**—the practice of voting for the candidates of more than one party in an election. That behavior, which began to increase in the 1960s, is fairly common today.

Another telling sign is the large number of voters who now call themselves **independents.** That term is regularly used to identify those people who have no party affiliation. It includes voters who are independent of both the Republicans and the Democrats (and of any minor party as well). "Independent" is a tricky term, however.[15] Many who claim to be independents actually vote most often for the candidates of one or the other of the major parties.

The loose nature of party membership makes it difficult to determine just what proportion of the American electorate is independent. However, the best guesses put the number of independents at somewhere between a fourth and a third of all voters today. The role that these independent voters play is especially critical in those elections

---

15 Note that the term "independent" is sometimes mistakenly used to suggest that independents form a more or less cohesive group that can be readily compared with Republicans and Democrats. In short, independents in American politics are not only independent of Republicans and Democrats; each of them is also independent of all other independents.

✔● **Checkpoint**
What is straight-ticket voting?

Family can influence party identification.

where the opposing major party candidates are more or less evenly matched.

Until fairly recently, the typical independent was less concerned, less well informed, and less active in politics than those voters who identified themselves as Republicans or Democrats. That unflattering description still fits many independents.

However, a new breed of independent voter began to appear in the 1960s and 1970s, and their ranks have grown over the years since then. Largely because of the political events and personalities of that period, these "new" independents preferred not to join either of the two major parties. Today, these independents are often young and above average in education, income, and job status.

Candidates and Issues Party identification is a long-term factor. While most voters identify with one or the other of the major parties and most often support its candidates, they do not always vote that way. One or more short-term factors can cause them to switch sides in a particular election, or at least vote a split ticket. Thus, in 2008, several exit polls indicated that about 10 percent of those voters who regularly identify themselves as Democrats actually marked their ballots for the Republican nominee, Senator John McCain. And just about that same

tumultuous
adj. chaotic, stormy, agitated

percentage of Republicans crossed over and voted for the Democratic senator from Illinois, Barack Obama, in that election.

The most important of these short-term factors are the candidates and the issues in an election. Clearly, the impression a candidate makes on the voters can have an impact on how they vote. What image does a candidate project? How do the voters see that candidate in terms of personality, character, style, appearance, past record, abilities, and so on? And how do voters see the opposing candidate?

Just as clearly, issues can also have a large impact on voter behavior. The role of issues varies, however, depending on such things as the emotional content of the issues themselves, the voters' awareness of them, and the ways in which the contending candidates present them to the electorate.

Issues have become increasingly important to voters over the past 40 years or so. The tumultuous nature of politics over the period—highlighted by the civil rights movement, the Vietnam War, the feminist movement, the Watergate scandal, economic problems, and, over recent years, such critical matters as a severe economic recession and the ongoing wars in Iraq and Afghanistan—is most likely responsible for this heightened voter concern.

Essential Questions Journal To continue to build a response to the chapter Essential Question, go to your **Essential Questions Journal.**

SECTION 4 ASSESSMENT

1. **Guiding Question** Use your completed outline to answer this question: What factors influence voter behavior?

Key Terms and Comprehension
2. What are **off-year elections**?
3. (a) How does a person's sense of **political efficacy** affect voting behavior? (b) What other factors affect how a person will vote?
4. What is the meaning and significance of the **gender gap**?

Critical Thinking
5. **Predict Consequences (a)** In some democracies, voters are required to vote. Do you think such mandatory voting would work in the United States? **(b)** Why or why not?
6. **Draw Inferences (a)** How do factors such as income and level of education impact rates of voter participation? **(b)** Why do you think this is the case?

Quick Write

Narrative: Select a Narrative Structure Using your research and the list of details, identify what the climax, or most interesting and vivid part of your story, is. Narratives are usually told in chronological order with the climax near the end. Organize the details you collected for your essay into a beginning, middle, and end.

Quick Study Guide

Guiding Question
Section 2 What are the qualifications for voting, and how have they changed over time?

Guiding Question
Section 3 How did the U.S. fulfill the promise of the 15th Amendment?

Guiding Question
Section 1 How have voting rights changed over the course of American history?

CHAPTER 6
Essential Question
Why do voters act as they do?

Guiding Question
Section 4 What factors influence voter behavior?

Political Dictionary

suffrage p. 152
franchise p. 152
electorate p. 152
disenfranchised p. 153
poll tax p. 154
alien p. 156
transient p. 157
registration p. 158
purge p. 159
poll book p. 159
literacy p. 161
gerrymandering p. 165
injunction p. 165
preclearance p. 167
off-year election p. 170
ballot fatigue p. 171
political efficacy p. 172
political socialization p. 173
gender gap p. 175
party identification p. 177
straight-ticket voting p. 177
split-ticket voting p. 177
independent p. 177

Expansion of Voting Rights in the U.S.

Original Electorate
Voting generally limited to white male property owners.

Expansion Era #1
Religious qualifications and property-ownership requirements eliminated; by the mid-1800s most white males could vote.

Expansion Era #2
After the Civil War, the 15th Amendment intended to protect any male citizen from being denied the vote because of race or color.

Expansion Era #3
The 19th Amendment, ratified in 1920, gave women the right to vote in every State.

Expansion Era #4
Court decisions and federal legislation, especially the Voting Rights Act of 1965 and its later extensions, finally made the 15th Amendment truly effective.

Expansion Era #5
In 1971, the 26th Amendment lowered the voting age to 18.

Influences on Voter Behavior

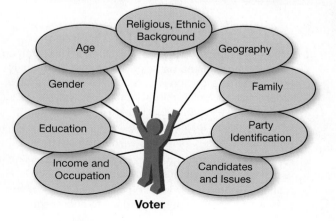

Age

Religious, Ethnic Background

Geography

Gender

Family

Education

Party Identification

Income and Occupation

Candidates and Issues

Voter

Chapter Assessment

🔀 **GOVERNMENT** ONLINE
Self-Test
To test your understanding of key terms and main ideas, visit **PearsonSuccessNet.com**

Comprehension and Critical Thinking

Section 1

1. (a) Which level of government is primarily responsible for establishing voter qualifications in the United States? **(b)** Why has the Federal Government gradually assumed a larger role in the setting of those qualifications?

2. (a) Identify the restrictions that prevented some citizens from voting in the past. **(b)** What has been the most effective and common way to overturn those restrictions? **(c)** Why do you think this is?

Section 2

3. (a) Why do States set residence requirements? **(b)** How have those requirements changed over time? **(c)** Why have those changes occurred?

4. (a) What was the primary argument made in favor of lowering the voting age to 18? **(b)** How has youth participation in elections changed since then? **(c)** Why do you think this is?

5. (a) What was the original purpose of literacy tests? **(b)** What prompted the removal of literacy requirements?

Section 3

6. (a) Why was the 15th Amendment adopted? **(b)** Why was that amendment largely ineffective for nearly a century?

7. (a) What were some of the legal means used to keep African Americans from voting? **(b)** What were some of the illegal means used? **(c)** How were the efforts to disenfranchise African Americans finally overcome?

Section 4

8. (a) What is a nonvoting voter? **(b)** What is the cause of ballot fatigue?

9. (a) What are some of the characteristics of a likely voter? **(b)** How does a closely contested race usually affect voter turnout?

10. (a) What is split-ticket voting? **(b)** What psychological factors tend to produce split-ticket voting?

11. Analyzing Political Cartoons Study the cartoon below that references a World War II monument. **(a)** What is the message of the cartoon? **(b)** Why does the cartoonist use a soldier as the voice of this cartoon?

Writing About Government

12. Use your Quick Write exercises from the chapter to write a narrative essay about an important event in the history of suffrage. You should review the paragraph you wrote

Apply What You've Learned

13. Essential Question Activity Conduct research on voter registration and participation in your community. Find out what a person who wishes to vote must do in order to cast a ballot, and what may disqualify a person from voting. Then interview friends or relatives about why they do or do not vote. Ask:

(a) What must a person who wishes to vote do?

(b) How easy or difficult is the registration process? If it is difficult, how might it be made easier?

(c) If the friends or relatives you interviewed do not vote, ask what, if anything, might be done to encourage voting.

14. Essential Question Assessment Based on your research and what you learned in this chapter, create a brochure explaining the registration process for someone who has recently moved into your community. You might also include statistics or some information about why people do or do not vote. Your brochure should help you to answer the Chapter Essential Question: **Why do voters act as they do?**

Essential Questions Journal To respond to the chapter Essential Question, go to your **Essential Questions Journal.**

Document-Based Assessment

The American Electorate

Since the nation's founding, the size of the electorate has grown remarkably. Much of that growth has involved extending the right to vote to such originally disenfranchised groups as African Americans and women. To many, efforts to expand the electorate represent the highest ideals of the American system of government, as illustrated by the documents below.

Document 1

"This was the first nation in the history of the world to be founded with a purpose. The great phrases of that purpose still sound in every American heart, North and South: "All men are created equal." "Government by consent of the governed." "Give me liberty or give me death." Well, those are not just clever words, or those are not just empty theories. In their name Americans have fought and died for two centuries, and tonight around the world they stand there as guardians of our liberty, risking their lives.

Those words are promised to every citizen that he shall share in the dignity of man. This dignity cannot be found in a man's possessions. It cannot be found in his power or in his position. It really rests on his right to be treated as a man equal in opportunity to all others. It says that he shall share in freedom. He shall choose his leaders, educate his children, provide for his family according to his ability and his merits as a human being....

Many of the issues of civil rights are very complex and most difficult. But about this there can and should be no argument: every American citizen must have an equal right to vote.

—President Lyndon Johnson
Address to Congress, March 15, 1965

Document 2

—Cartoon by Thomas Nast,
published November 22, 1869

Use your knowledge of voting rights and Documents 1 and 2 to answer Questions 1–3.

1. Which answer best summarizes the point of Document 1?

   A. Voting rights are only one of the many important civil rights guaranteed to the American people.

   B. The right to vote is one of the most basic rights possessed by the American people.

   C. Only those people who are well informed should be allowed to vote.

   D. More people will have to fight and die in order to secure voting rights.

2. What are the people celebrating in Document 2, and what does the picture suggest will result?

3. **Pull It Together** Why do you think that securing voting rights for African Americans was essential to securing equal rights as citizens of the United States?

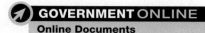

Online Documents

To find more primary sources on the electorate, visit **PearsonSuccessNet.com**

The Electoral Process

Essential Question
How fair and effective is the electoral process?

Section 1:
The Nominating Process

Section 2:
Elections

Section 3:
Money and Elections

> The **future** of this **republic** is in the hands of the **American voter.**
>
> —President Dwight D. Eisenhower

GOVERNMENT ONLINE
On the Go

To study anywhere, anytime, download these online resources at PearsonSuccessNet.com
• Political Dictionary
• Audio Review
• Downloadable Interactivities

Photo: Governor Christine Gregoire (D., Washington) greets schoolchildren.

SECTION 1

The Nominating Process

Guiding Question

What methods are used to choose candidates for public office? Use the diagram to write down information about the various methods of nominating candidates to run for office.

Political Dictionary

- nomination
- general election
- caucus
- direct primary
- closed primary
- open primary
- blanket primary
- runoff primary
- nonpartisan election

Objectives

1. Explain why the nominating process is a critical first step in the election process.
2. Describe self-announcement, the caucus, and the convention as nominating methods.
3. Discuss the direct primary as the principal nominating method used in the United States today.
4. Understand why some candidates use the petition as a nominating device.

Image Above: Minnesota's Democratic-Farmer-Labor Party nominates a candidate for governor at a State convention.

Suppose your teacher stood in front of the class and said: "Here's a $1,000 bill. Who'd like to have it?" You, and everyone else in the room, would promptly say, or at least think: "Me!" Suppose the teacher then said: "Okay, we'll hold an election. The person who wins the most votes gets the money."

What would happen? If the election were held immediately, it is likely that each member of the class would vote for himself or herself. A few might vote for a friend. Almost certainly, however, the election would end in a tie. No one would win the money.

But suppose the teacher said: "We'll hold the election tomorrow." What do you suppose would happen then? As you think about the answer to that question, you begin to get a sense of the practical importance of the nominating process—the first step in the process of electing candidates for public office.

A Critical First Step

The nominating process is the process of candidate selection. **Nomination**—the naming of those who will seek office—is a critically important step in the election process.

You have already seen two major illustrations of the significance of the nominating process. In Chapter 5, you read about the making of nominations (1) as a prime function of political parties in American politics, and (2) as a leading reason for the decentralized character of the two major parties in the United States.

The nominating process also has a very real impact on the right to vote. In the typical election in this country, voters can choose between only two candidates for each office on the ballot. They can vote for the Republican or they can vote for the Democratic candidate.[1] This is another way of saying that we have a two-party system in the United States. It is also another way to say that the nominating stage is a critically important step in the electoral process. Those who make nominations place real, very practical limits on the choices that voters can make in the general election.

---

1   Other choices are sometimes listed, of course—minor party or independent nominees. These are not often meaningful alternatives, however; most voters choose not to "waste" their votes on candidates who cannot win. Also, nonpartisan elections are an exception to this statement, of course, since candidates are not identified by party labels.

In one-party constituencies (those areas where one party regularly wins elections), the nominating process is usually the only point at which there is any real contest for public office. Once the dominant party has made its nomination, the general election is little more than a formality.

Dictatorial regimes point up the importance of the nominating process. Many of them hold **general elections**—regularly scheduled elections at which voters make the final selection of officeholders—much as democracies do. But, typically, the ballots used in those elections list only one candidate for each office—the candidate of the ruling <u>clique</u>; and those candidates regularly win with majorities approaching 100 percent.

Nominations are made in five different ways in this country. Candidates are named to the ballot by (1) self-announcement, (2) caucus, (3) convention, (4) direct primary, and (5) petition.

Self-Announcement

Self-announcement is the oldest form of the nominating process in American politics. First used in colonial times, it is still often found at the small-town and rural levels in many parts of the country.

The method is quite simple. A person who wants to run for office simply announces that fact. Modesty or local custom may dictate that someone else actually makes the candidate's announcement, but, still, the process amounts to the same thing.

Self-announcement is sometimes used by someone who failed to win a regular party nomination or by someone unhappy with the party's choice. Note that whenever a write-in candidate appears in an election, the self-announcement process has been used.

In recent history, four prominent presidential contenders have made use of the process: George Wallace, who declared himself to be the American Independent Party's nominee in 1968; and independent candidates Eugene McCarthy in 1976; John Anderson in 1980; and Ross Perot in 1992. And all of the 135 candidates who sought to replace Governor Gray Davis of California in that State's recall election in 2003—including the winner, Arnold Schwarzenegger—were self-starters.

The Caucus

As a nominating device, a **caucus** is a group of like-minded people who meet to select the candidates they will support in an upcoming election. The first caucus nominations were made during the later colonial period, probably in Boston in the 1720s. John Adams described the caucus this way in 1763:

PRIMARY SOURCE

"This day learned that the Caucus Club meets, at certain times, in the garret of Tom Dawes, the Adjutant of the Boston Regiment. He has a large house, and he has a moveable partition in his garret which he takes down, and the whole club meets in one room. There they smoke tobacco till you cannot see from one end of the garret to the other. There they drink flip, I suppose, and they choose a moderator, who puts questions to the vote regularly; and selectmen, assessors, collectors, wardens, fire-wards, and representatives, are regularly chosen before they are chosen in the town."

—Charles Francis Adams (ed.)
The Works of John Adams (1856)

✔ **Checkpoint**
What is nomination?

<u>clique</u>
n. an exclusive group

▶▶ **Analyzing Cartoons** Ross Perot launched his 1992 presidential campaign via self-announcement. *Why might self-announcement attract candidates with the personal wealth to finance their own campaigns?*

Five Methods of Nomination

Candidates for public office can reach the general election ballot in, altogether, five different ways in the United States. State law and party practice determine which of these methods can be used in a particular State. *Which method of nomination is the most democratic?*

PRIMARY

Qualified voters cast ballots in private for their preferred candidate. The person who receives the most votes is nominated.

CAUCUS

Party members and supporters debate the merits of the candidates and then vote to select a nominee.

CONVENTION

Local districts select delegates to represent them at a higher-level meeting where the nominee is chosen.

SELF-ANNOUNCEMENT

The candidate announces his or her intention to run for office, usually as an independent or a write-in candidate.

PETITION

Candidates collect a specified number of signatures from voters to qualify for the general election.

VOTE
Ada County Elections

DFL
STATE CONVENTION

GOVERNMENT ONLINE
Audio Tour
Listen to a guided audio tour of this table at
PearsonSuccessNet.com

Originally the caucus was a private meeting of a few influential figures in the community.[2] As political parties began to appear in the late 1700s, they took over the device and soon broadened the membership of the caucus considerably.

The coming of independence brought the need to nominate candidates for State offices: governor, lieutenant governor, and others above the local level. The legislative caucus—a meeting of a party's members in the State legislature—took on the job. At the national level, both the Federalists and the Democratic-Republicans in Congress were, by 1800, choosing their presidential and vice-presidential candidates through the congressional caucus.

The legislative and congressional caucuses were quite practical in their day. Transportation and communication were difficult at best. Since legislators were already gathered regularly in a central place, it made sense for them to take on the nominating responsibility. The spread of democracy, especially in the newer States on the frontier, spurred opposition to the use of caucuses, however. They were widely condemned for their closed, unrepresentative character.

Criticism of the caucus reached its peak in the early 1820s. The supporters of three of the leading contenders for the presidency in 1824—Andrew Jackson, Henry Clay, and John Quincy Adams—boycotted the Democratic-Republicans' congressional caucus that year. In fact, Jackson and his supporters made "King Caucus" a leading campaign issue. The other major contender, William H. Crawford of Georgia, became the caucus nominee at a meeting attended by fewer than one third of the Democratic-Republican Party's members in Congress.

Crawford ran a poor third in the electoral college balloting in 1824, and the reign of

2 The origin of the term *caucus* is not clear. Most authorities agree that it comes from the word *caulkers*, because the Boston Caucus Club met in a room formerly used as a meeting place by caulkers in the Boston shipyards. (Caulkers made ships watertight by filling seams or cracks in the hulls of sailing vessels with tar or oakum.) The term is also used to refer to a group whose members (often members of a legislative body) unite to promote some particular interest—for example, in Congress today, the Congressional Black Caucus.

King Caucus at the national level was ended. With its death in presidential politics, the caucus system soon withered at the State and local levels, as well.

The caucus is still used to make local nominations in some places, especially in New England. There, a caucus is open to all members of a party, and it only faintly resembles the original closed and private process.

The Convention

As the caucus method collapsed, the convention system took its place. The first national convention to nominate a presidential candidate was held by a minor party, the Anti-Masons, in Baltimore in 1831. The newly formed National Republican (soon to become Whig) Party also held a convention later that same year. The Democrats picked up the practice in 1832. All major-party presidential nominees have been chosen by conventions ever since. By the 1840s, conventions had become the principal means for making nominations at every level in American politics.

On paper, the convention process seems perfectly suited to representative government. A party's members meet in a local caucus to pick candidates for local offices and, at the same time, to select delegates to represent them at a county convention.[3]

At the county convention, the delegates nominate candidates for county offices and select delegates to the next rung on the convention ladder, usually the State convention. There, the delegates from the county conventions pick the party's nominees for governor and other Statewide offices. State conventions also send delegates to the party's national convention, where the party selects its presidential and vice-presidential candidates.

In theory, the will of the party's rank and file membership is passed up through each of its representative levels. Practice soon pointed up the weaknesses of the theory, however, as party bosses found ways to manipulate the process. By playing with the selection of delegates, usually at the local levels, they soon dominated the entire system.

As a result, the caliber of most conventions declined at all levels, especially during the late 1800s. How low some of them fell can be seen in this description of a Cook County (Chicago), Illinois, convention in 1896:

PRIMARY SOURCE

Of [723] delegates, those who had been on trial for murder numbered 17; sentenced to the penitentiary for murder or manslaughter and served sentence, 7; served terms in the penitentiary for burglary, 36; served terms in the penitentiary for picking pockets, 2; served terms in the penitentiary for arson, 1; . . . jailbirds identified by detectives, 84; keepers of gambling houses, 7; keepers of houses of ill-fame, 2; convicted of mayhem, 3; ex-prize fighters, 11; poolroom proprietors, 2; saloon keepers, 265; . . . political employees, 148; no occupation, 71; . . .

—R.M. Easley
"The Sine qua Non of Caucus Reform"
Review of Reviews (Sept. 1897)

Many people had hailed the change from caucus to convention as a major change for the better in American politics. The abuses of the new device soon dashed their hopes. By the 1870s, the convention system was itself under attack as a major source of evil in the nation's politics. By the 1910s, the direct primary had replaced the convention in most States as the principal nominating method in American politics.

Conventions still play a major role in the nominating process in some States—notably, Connecticut, Michigan, South Dakota, Utah, and Virginia. And, as you will see, no adequate substitute for the device has yet been found at the presidential level.

The Direct Primary

A **direct primary** is an *intra*party election. It is held within a party to pick that party's candidates for the general election. Wisconsin

✔ **Checkpoint**
What is the caucus and how has its popularity changed?

---

3 The meetings at which delegates to local conventions are chosen are still often called caucuses. Earlier, they were also known as primaries—that is, first meetings. The use of that name gave rise to the term *direct primary*, to distinguish that newer nominating method from the convention process.

adopted the first Statewide direct primary law in 1903; several other States soon followed its lead. Every State now makes at least some provision for its use.

In most States, State law requires that the major parties use the primary to choose their candidates for the United States Senate and House of Representatives, for the governorship and all other Statewide offices, and for most local offices as well. In a few States, however, different combinations of convention and primary are used to pick candidates for the top offices.

In Michigan, for example, the major parties choose their candidates for the U.S. Senate and House, the governorship, and the State legislature in primaries. Nominees for lieutenant governor, secretary of state, and attorney general are picked by conventions.[4]

Although the primaries are party-nominating elections, they are closely regulated by law in most States. The State usually sets the dates on which primaries are held, and it regularly conducts them, too. The State, not the parties, provides polling places and election officials, registration lists and ballots, and otherwise polices the process.

---

[4] In most States, minor parties are required to make their nominations by other, more difficult processes, usually in conventions or by petition. This is another of the several ways in which State election laws often, purposely, make life difficult for minor parties.

Caucuses are also found in the presidential selection process. They are used to select national convention delegates in a handful of States, as you will see in Chapter 13.

Two basic forms of the direct primary are in use today: (1) the closed primary and (2) the open primary. The major difference between the two lies in the answer to this question: Who can vote in a party's primary—*only* those qualified voters who are party members, or *any* qualified voter?

The Closed Primary Today, 25 States provide for the **closed primary**—a party's nominating election in which only declared party members can vote. The party's primary is closed to all but those party members.[5]

In most of the closed primary States, party membership is established by registration. When voters appear at their polling places on primary election day, their names are checked against the poll books and each voter is handed the primary ballot of the party in which he or she is registered. The voter can mark only that party's ballot; he or she can vote only in that party's primary.

In some of the closed primary States, however, a voter can change his or her party registration on election day. In those States, then, the primary is not as completely "closed" as it is elsewhere.

The Open Primary The **open primary**—also known as the crossover primary—is a party's nominating election in which *any* qualified voter can cast a ballot. Although it is the form in which the direct primary first appeared, it is now found in only 17 States.

When voters go to the polls in some open primary States, they are handed a ballot of each party holding a primary. Usually, they receive only two ballots, those of the Republican and

---

[5] The Supreme Court has held that a State's closed primary law cannot forbid a party to allow independent voters to participate in its primary if the party itself chooses to allow them to do so. In *Tashjian* v. *Republican Party of Connecticut*, 1986, the Court struck down such a State law. Note that the Court did not outlaw the closed primary in this case, nor did it hold that a political party *must* allow independents to vote in its primary. The Court found that the Connecticut law violated the 1st and 14th Amendments' guarantees of the right of association—here the right of Connecticut Republicans to associate with independents (invite independents to join them) in making GOP nominations.

Volunteers wave signs for candidates Rep. Ron Paul (R., Texas) and Gov. Mike Huckabee (R., Arkansas) during the 2008 Republican presidential primaries.

the Democratic parties. Then, in the privacy of the voting booth, each voter marks the ballot of the party in whose primary he or she chooses to vote. In other open primary States, a voter must ask for the ballot of the party in whose primary he or she wants to vote. That is, each voter must make a *public* choice of party in order to vote in the primary.

Through 2000, three States used a different version of the open primary—the **blanket primary,** sometimes called the "wide-open primary." Washington adopted the first blanket primary law in 1935. Alaska followed suit in 1970, and California did so in 1996. In a blanket primary, every voter received the same ballot—a long one that listed *every* candidate, regardless of party, for every nomination to be made at the primary. Voters could participate however they chose. They could confine themselves to one party's primary; or they could switch back and forth between the parties' primaries, voting to nominate a Democrat for one office, a Republican for another, and so on down the ballot.

The Supreme Court found California's version of the blanket primary unconstitutional in 2000, however. In *California Democratic Party* v. *Jones*, the High Court held that that process violated the 1st and 14th amendments' guarantees of the right of association. It ruled that a State cannot force a political party to associate with outsiders—that is, with members of other parties or with independents—when it picks its candidates for public office.

The Court's decision in *Jones* made the blanket primary a thing of the past. Two of the three States that used the device—Alaska and California—now provide for more traditional versions of the open primary. Washington, on the other hand, has gone a different route.

Washington now provides for the "top-two" form of the open primary. There, the names of all those who seek nomination are listed, by office, on a single primary ballot. Then the top two vote getters for each office, regardless of party, face one another in the general election. Thus, two Republicans, or two Democrats, may battle one another in November.

Louisiana uses yet another version of the open primary, under what is sometimes called its "open-election law." There, as in Washington, all candidates for nomination

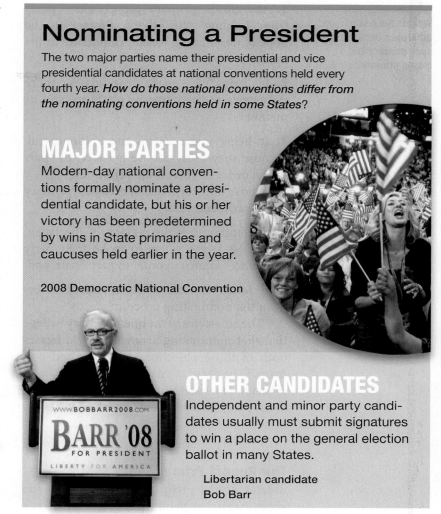

Nominating a President

The two major parties name their presidential and vice presidential candidates at national conventions held every fourth year. *How do those national conventions differ from the nominating conventions held in some States?*

MAJOR PARTIES

Modern-day national conventions formally nominate a presidential candidate, but his or her victory has been predetermined by wins in State primaries and caucuses held earlier in the year.

2008 Democratic National Convention

OTHER CANDIDATES

Independent and minor party candidates usually must submit signatures to win a place on the general election ballot in many States.

Libertarian candidate Bob Barr

are listed on a single ballot, and the top two vote getters, regardless of party, face off in the general election. But if a candidate wins a majority of the votes in the primary, he or she is declared the winner of the office involved—so, the primary becomes, in effect, the election.[6]

Closed vs. Open Primaries The merits of the two basic forms of the direct primary have been argued for decades. Those who support the closed primary rely on three major arguments. They regularly claim that:

---

6 Louisiana's "open-election" primary law applies to its State and local elections, which are held in November of the *odd*-numbered years. Since 1872, federal law has directed that congressional elections be held in November of the *even*-numbered years, and Louisiana abides by that law. It holds traditional closed primaries in the *even*-numbered years to choose candidates for seats in the U.S. House and Senate.

1. The closed primary prevents one party from "raiding" the other's primary in the hope of nominating weaker candidates in the opposition party.

2. It helps to make candidates more responsive to the party, its platform, and its members.

3. It helps make voters more thoughtful, because they must choose between the parties in order to vote in the primaries.

Those who criticize the closed primary usually contend that:

1. It compromises the secrecy of the ballot, because it forces voters to make their party preferences known in order to participate, and

2. It tends to exclude independent voters from the nominating process.[7]

The advocates of the open primary believe that that nominating arrangement addresses both of those objections to the closed primary. They say that in the typical open primary (1) voters are not forced to make their party preferences a matter of public record, and (2) independent voters are not excluded from the nominating process.

The Runoff Primary In most States, candidates need to win only a plurality of the votes cast in the primary to win their party's nomination.[8] (Remember, a *plurality* is the greatest number of votes won by any candidate, whether a *majority* or not.) In 8 States, however, an absolute majority is needed to carry a primary.[9] If no one wins a majority in a race, a **runoff primary** is held a few weeks later. In that runoff contest, the two top vote getters in the first primary face one another to determine the party's nomination,

and the winner of that vote becomes the party's nominee.

The Nonpartisan Primary In most States all or nearly all of the elected school and municipal offices are filled in **nonpartisan elections**. These are elections in which candidates are not identified by party labels. About half of all State judges are chosen on nonpartisan ballots, as well. The nomination of candidates for these offices takes place on a nonpartisan basis, too, and most often in nonpartisan primaries.

Typically, a contender who wins a clear majority in a nonpartisan primary then runs unopposed in the general election, subject only to write-in opposition. In many States, however, a candidate who wins a majority in the primary is declared elected at that point. If there is no majority winner, the names of the two top contenders are placed on the general election ballot.

The primary first appeared as a partisan nominating device. Many have long argued that it is not well suited for use in nonpartisan elections. Instead, they favor the petition method, as you will see in a moment.

The Presidential Primary The presidential primary developed as an offshoot of the direct primary. It is *not* a nominating device, however. Rather, the presidential primary is an election that is held as one part of the process by which presidential candidates are chosen.

The presidential primary is a very complex process that was in place in a large majority of States in the most recent presidential election. It is one or both of two things, depending on the State involved. It is a process in which a party's voters elect some or all of a State party organization's delegates to that party's national convention; and/or it is a preference election in which voters can choose (vote their preference) among various contenders for the grand prize, the party's presidential nomination.

Much of what happens in presidential politics in the early months of every fourth year centers on this very complicated process. (See Chapter 13 for an extended discussion of the presidential primary.)

---

7 See the discussion of *Tashjian v. Republican Party of Connecticut,* 1986, in footnote 5. The closed primary States have amended their election laws to comply with that decision.

8 In Iowa, if no candidate wins at least 35 percent of the votes in a primary, the party must then nominate its candidate for that office by convention.

9 Alabama, Arkansas, Georgia, Mississippi, Oklahoma, South Carolina, Texas—and Louisiana under its unique "open election" law. In North Carolina a runoff is held when no candidate wins 40 percent of the primary vote. In South Dakota, if no one who seeks a party's nomination for governor, U.S. senator, or U.S. representative wins at least 35 percent, the party's candidate for that office must be picked in a runoff primary two weeks later.

Forms of Primaries Among the States, 2008

GOVERNMENT ONLINE
Audio tour
Listen to a guided audio tour of this map at **PearsonSuccessNet.com**

Analyzing Maps The direct primary, whatever its form, intends to put the nominating function in the hands of a party's rank-and-file membership. *What form of the primary is used in your State?*

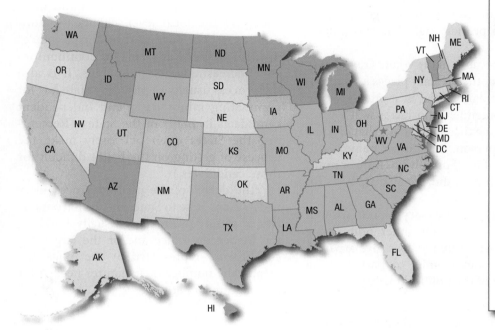

KEY

☐ **Closed Primary**
Unaffiliated Voters Excluded
Primaries are limited to voters registered with that party. Unaffiliated voters cannot vote in primaries.

☐ **Closed Primary**
Unaffiliated Voters Permitted
Primaries are limited to voters registered with that party and unaffiliated voters, who may vote in any party's primary.

☐ **Open Primary**
Private Choice
Voters may vote in any party's primary. Their choice of party remains private.

☐ **Open Primary**
Public Declaration
Voters may vote in any party's primary. Election officials record which party's ballot they choose.

☐ **Open Election**
All candidates appear on a single ballot open to all voters. If no candidate receives 50 percent, the top two vote getters proceed to a run-off.

★ **Unaffiliated voters permitted to vote in Republican race only**

Evaluation of the Primary

The direct primary, whether open or closed, is an *intra*party nominating election. It came to American politics as a reform of the boss-dominated convention system. It was intended to take the nominating function away from the party organization and put it in the hands of the party's rank-and-file membership.

The basic facts about the primary have never been very well understood by most voters, however. So, in closed primary States, many voters resent having to declare their party preference in order to vote in the primary. And, in both open and closed primary States, many are upset because they cannot express their support for candidates in more than one party. Many are also annoyed by the "bed-sheet ballots" they regularly see in primary elections—not realizing that the use of the direct primary almost automatically

means a long ballot. And some are concerned because the primary (and, in particular, its closed form) tends to exclude independents from the nominating process.

All of these factors, combined with a lack of appreciation of the important role that primaries play in the election process, result in this unfortunate and significant fact: Nearly everywhere, voter turnout in primary elections is usually less than half what it is in the general elections in November.

Primary contests can be quite costly. The fact that successful contenders must then wage—and finance—a general election campaign adds to the money problems that <u>bedevil</u> American politics. Unfortunately, the financial facts of political life in the United States mean that some well-qualified people refuse to seek public office simply because they cannot muster the funding absolutely necessary to finance a campaign.

bedevil
v. irritate, bother

The nominating process, whatever its form, can have a very divisive effect on a party. Remember, the process takes place *within* the party—so, when there is a contest for a nomination, that is where the contest occurs: Republicans fight with Republicans, Democrats do battle with Democrats. A bitter fight in the primaries can so wound and divide a party that it cannot recover in time to present a united front for the general election. Many a primary fight has cost a party an election.

Finally, because many voters are not very well informed, the primary places a premium on name familiarity. That is, it often gives an edge to a contender who has a well-known name or a name that sounds like that of some well-known person. But, notice, name familiarity in and of itself usually has little or nothing to do with a candidate's qualifications for public office.

Obviously, the primary is not without its problems, nor is any other nominating device. Still, the primary does give a party's members the opportunity to participate at the very core of the political process.

---

10 The petition device is also an important part of the recall and the initiative and referendum processes; see Chapter 24.

Petition

One other nominating method is used fairly widely at the local level in American politics today—nomination by petition. Where this process is used, candidates for public office are nominated by means of petitions signed by a certain number of qualified voters in the election district.[10]

Nomination by petition is found most widely at the local level, chiefly for nonpartisan school posts and municipal offices in medium-sized and smaller communities and, increasingly, for judgeships. It is also the process usually required by State law for nominating minor party and independent candidates in many of the States. (Remember, the States often purposely make the process of getting on the ballot difficult for those candidates.)

The details of the petition process vary widely from State to State, and even from one city or county to the next. Usually, however, the higher the office and/or the larger the constituency represented by the office, the greater the number of signatures needed for nomination by petition.

Essential Questions
Journal

To continue to build a response to the chapter Essential Question, go to your **Essential Questions Journal.**

SECTION 1 ASSESSMENT

1. Guiding Question Use your completed diagram to answer this question: What methods are used to choose candidates for public office?

Key Terms and Comprehension

2. What is the purpose of **nomination** in the electoral system?

3. In addition to primaries, what nominating methods are used in the United States?

4. What is the difference between a **closed primary** and an **open primary**?

5. How does the presidential primary differ from those primaries used in State and local nominations?

Critical Thinking

6. Express Problems Clearly Summarize the relationship between the will of the people and the power of party organizations. How has this relationship changed the way that parties nominate candidates?

7. Draw Inferences What do you think explains the usually low level of turnout in primary elections in most States?

Quick Write

Explanatory Essay: Choose a Topic Using the Internet, other media sources, and your textbook, find an example of a recent election that took place at the national level or in your State or local community. Write a brief summary of the election—who the candidates were and when the race took place.

SECTION 2
Elections

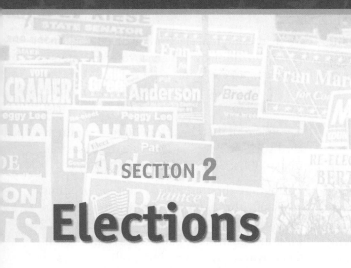

Guiding Question

How are elections conducted in the United States? Use the chart to record information about how elections are administered and conducted.

Elections		
Administration	**Ballots**	**Voting Procedures**
• • •	• • •	• • •

Political Dictionary

- ballot
- absentee voting
- coattail effect
- precinct
- polling place

Objectives

1. Analyze how the administration of elections in the United States helps make democracy work.
2. Define the role of local precincts and polling places in the election process.
3. Describe the various ways in which voters can cast their ballots.
4. Outline the role that voting devices play in the election process.

Image Above: Campaign lawn signs express support for specific candidates.

Most high school students are not old enough to vote. In some parts of the country, though, high school students can serve on local election boards. First in Hawaii and Oregon and now in several States, 16- and 17-year-olds can become full-fledged members of the panels that administer local elections.

We hold more elections in this country and we vote more often than most people realize. Indeed, Sundays and holidays are about the only days of the year on which people do not go to the polls somewhere in the United States. We also elect *far* more officeholders than most people realize—in fact, more than 500,000 of them, more than in any other country in the world.

The Administration of Elections

Democratic government cannot possibly hope to succeed unless its elections are free, honest, and accurately reported. Many people see the details of the election process as much too complicated, too legalistic, too dry and boring to worry about. Those who do really miss the vital part that those details play in making democracy work. *How* something can be done very often shapes *what* is in fact done—and that fact is as true in politics as it is in all other areas of human concern.

Extent of Federal Control Nearly all elections in the United States are held to choose the more than 500,000 persons who hold elective office in the more than 89,000 units of government at the State and local levels. It is quite understandable, then, that most election law in the United States is *State*—not federal—law.

Even so, a body of federal election law does exist. The Constitution gives Congress the power to fix "[t]he Times, Places, and Manner of holding Elections" of members of Congress.[11] Congress also has the power to set the time for choosing presidential electors, to set the date for casting the electoral votes, and to regulate other aspects of the presidential election process.[12]

---

11 Article I, Section 4, Clause 1; 17th Amendment
12 Article II, Section 1, Clause 4; 12th Amendment

Congress has set the date for holding congressional elections as the first Tuesday following the first Monday in November of every even-numbered year. It has set the same date every fourth year for the presidential election.[13] Thus, an off-year round of congressional contests was scheduled for November 2, 2010, followed by a presidential election on November 6, 2012.

Congress has required the use of secret ballots and allowed the use of voting machines and similar devices in federal elections. It has also acted to protect the right to vote, as you saw in Chapter 6. Congress has also prohibited various corrupt practices and regulates the financing of campaigns for federal office, as you will see in the pages ahead.

Congress expanded the body of federal election law with the passage of the Help America Vote Act of 2002. That law came in response to the many ballot and voter registration problems that plagued several States

in the presidential election in 2000. A **ballot**[14] is the medium by which a voter registers a choice in an election.

In its major provisions, the law requires the States to

1. replace all their lever-operated and punch-card voting devices by 2006—a deadline that, in fact, most States failed to meet;

2. upgrade their administration of elections, especially through the better training of local election officials and of those more than 2 million (mostly low-paid workers and volunteers) who work in precinct polling places on election day;

3. centralize and computerize their voter registration systems, to facilitate the identification of qualified voters on election day and so minimize fraudulent voting;

4. provide for provisional voting, so a person whose eligibility to vote has been challenged

---

13 Congress has made an exception for Alaska. Because of the possibility of severe weather in much of Alaska in early November, that State may, if it chooses, elect its congressional delegation and cast its presidential vote in October. To this point, however, Alaska has chosen to use the November date.

14 The word comes from the Italian *ballotta*, "little ball," and reflects the practice of dropping black or white balls into a box to indicate a choice. The term *blackball* also comes from that practice. The ancient Romans used paper ballots as early as 139 B.C.

GOVERNMENT ONLINE
Audio tour
Listen to a guided audio tour of this diagram at
PearsonSuccessNet.com

Counting Facility
Ballots usually are counted in a central location and stored in case a recount is required.

How **Government** Works

What Happens to a Ballot?

The several States offer voters different ways to cast their votes, in both paper formats and electronically, and on election day or earlier. *Why is it important for local officials to guard and track ballots after they are cast?*

Paper Ballot
Usually collected at polling place, taken to counting facility

Absentee Ballot
Mailed to the counting facility
OR
Brought to the polling place and combined with other ballots

Electronic Ballot
Data transported manually on disks or drives
OR
Votes transmitted electronically to counting facility

can nonetheless cast a ballot that will be counted if it is later found that he or she is, in fact, qualified to vote.

State law deals with all other matters relating to national elections—and with all of the details of State and local elections as well.

Election Day Most States hold their elections to fill State offices on the same date Congress has set for national elections: in November of every even-numbered year. The "Tuesday-after-the-first-Monday" formula prevents election day from falling on (1) Sundays (to maintain the principle of separation of church and state) and (2) the first day of the month, which is often payday and therefore peculiarly subject to campaign pressures.

Some States do fix other dates for some offices, however. Louisiana, Mississippi, New Jersey, and Virginia elect the governor, other executive officers, and State legislators in November of *odd*-numbered years. In Kentucky, the governor and other executive officers are chosen in odd-numbered years, but legislators are elected in even-numbered years. City, county, and other local election dates vary from State to State. When those elections are not held in November, they generally take place in the spring.

Early Voting Millions of Americans cast their ballots before election day. Indeed, some 32 million did so in 2008. Many of them did so by **absentee voting**—a process by which they could vote without going to their polling places on election day. Congress was responsible for the first instance of absentee voting. In the midst of the Civil War, it provided for the casting of absentee ballots by federal troops in the elections of 1864. Over the years, every State has made at least some provision for the process.

Now, almost everywhere, voters can apply for an absentee ballot some weeks before an election. They mark those ballots and return them to the local election office, usually by mail, in a sealed envelope, and before election day.

State absentee voting was originally intended to serve a relatively small group of voters, especially the ill or disabled and those who expected to be away from home on election day. Most States have broadened their laws over recent years, however—to the point where, in most of them, any qualified voter can cast an absentee ballot simply because he or she wants to vote that way.

Two thirds of the States have now formalized early voting. They allow any voters who choose to do so to cast their ballots at any time over a period of several days before an election—not as an absentee ballot but as though they were voting on election day itself. Indeed, in many places, election day is now just the final day on which votes can be cast.

The Coattail Effect The **coattail effect** occurs when a strong candidate running for an office at the top of the ballot helps attract voters to other candidates on the party's ticket. In effect, the lesser-known office seeker "rides the coattails" of the more prestigious personality—for example, a Franklin Roosevelt, a Ronald Reagan, or a Barack Obama. The coattail effect is usually most apparent in presidential elections. However, a popular candidate for senator or governor can have the same kind of pulling power in State and local elections.

A reverse coattail effect can occur, too. This happens when a candidate for some major office is less than popular with many voters—for example, Barry Goldwater as the Republican presidential nominee in 1964, and George McGovern for the Democrats in 1972. President Jimmy Carter's coattails were also of the reverse variety in 1980.

Some have long argued that all State and local elections should be held on dates other than those set for federal elections. This, they say, would help voters pay more attention to State and local candidates and issues and lessen the coattail effect a presidential candidate can have.

Precincts and Polling Places

A **precinct** is a voting district. Precincts are the smallest geographic units for the conduct of elections. State law regularly restricts their size, generally to an area with no more than 500 to 1,000 or so qualified voters. A **polling place**—the place where the voters who live in a precinct actually vote—is located somewhere in or near each precinct.

✔ **Checkpoint**
What is early voting?

A precinct election board supervises the polling place and the voting process in each precinct. Typically, the county clerk or county board of elections draws precinct lines, fixes the location of each polling place, and picks the members of the precinct boards.

The precinct board opens and closes the polls at the times set by State law. In most States, the polls are open from 7:00 or 8:00 A.M. to 7:00 or 8:00 P.M. The precinct election board must also see that the ballots and the ballot boxes or voting devices are available. It must make certain that only qualified voters cast ballots in the precinct. Often the board also counts the votes cast in the precinct and then sends the results to the proper place, usually to the county clerk or county board of elections.

Poll watchers, one from each party, are allowed at each polling place. They may challenge any person they believe is not qualified to vote, check to be sure that their own party's supporters do vote, and monitor the whole process, including the counting of the ballots.

Casting the Ballot

A ballot can take a number of different forms, ranging from a piece of paper to optical scanners and touch screens. Whatever its form, however, it is clearly an important and sensitive part of the election process.

Each State now provides for a secret ballot. That is, State law requires that ballots be cast in such manner that others cannot know how a person has voted.

Voting was a quite public process through much of the nation's earlier history, however. Paper ballots were used in some colonial elections, but voting was more commonly *viva voce*—by voice. Voters simply stated their choices, in public, to an election board. With suffrage limited to the privileged few, many people defended oral voting as the only "manly" way in which to participate. Whatever the merits of that view, the expansion of the electorate brought with it a marked increase in intimidation, vote buying, and other corruptions of the voting process.

Paper ballots were in general use by the mid-1800s. The first ones were unofficial—slips of paper that voters prepared themselves and dropped in the ballot box. Soon candidates and parties began to prepare ballots and hand them to voters to cast, sometimes paying them to do so. Those party ballots were often printed on distinctively colored paper, and anyone watching could tell for whom voters were voting.

Political machines—local party organizations capable of mobilizing or "manufacturing" large numbers of votes on behalf of candidates for political office—flourished in many places in the latter 1800s. They fought all attempts to make voting a more dependably fair and honest process. The political corruption of the post–Civil War years brought widespread demand for ballot reforms.

The Australian Ballot A new voting arrangement was devised in Australia, where it was first used in an election in Victoria in 1856. Its successes there led to its use in other countries. By 1900 nearly all of the States were using it, and it remains the basic form of the ballot in this country today.

The Australian Ballot has four essential features: It (1) is provided at public expense; (2) lists the names of all candidates in an election; (3) is given out only at the polls, one to each qualified voter; and (4) can be marked in secret.

Two basic forms of the Australian ballot, shown on p. 197, have been used in this country over the past century. Most States now use the office-group ballot; only a handful of them rely on the party-column ballot.

Sample Ballots Sample ballots, clearly marked as such, are available in most States before an election. In some States they are mailed to all voters, and they appear in most newspapers and on the Internet. They cannot be cast, but they can help voters prepare for an election.

First in Oregon (1907), and now in several States, an official voter's pamphlet is mailed to voters before every election. It lists all candidates and measures that will appear on the ballot. In Oregon, each candidate is allowed space to present his

Mechanical voting machines like the one below were outlawed by Congress in 2002.

or her qualifications and position on the issues. Supporters and opponents of ballot measures are allowed space to present their arguments as well.

Bed-sheet Ballots The ballot in a typical American election is lengthy, often and aptly called a "bed-sheet" ballot. It frequently lists so many offices, candidates, and ballot measures that even the most well-informed voters have a difficult time marking it intelligently.

The long ballot came to American politics in the era of Jacksonian Democracy in the 1830s. Many held the view at the time that the greater the number of elective offices, the more democratic the governmental system. That idea remains widely accepted today.

Generally, the longest ballots are found at the local level, especially among the nation's 3,000-odd counties. The list of elected offices is likely to include several commissioners, a clerk, a sheriff, one or more judges, a prosecutor, coroner, treasurer, assessor, surveyor, school superintendent, engineer, sanitarian, and even the proverbial dogcatcher.

Critics of the bed-sheet ballot reject the notion that the more people you elect, the more democratic the system. Instead, they say, the fewer the offices voters have to fill, the better they can know the candidates and their qualifications. Those critics often point to the factor of "ballot fatigue"—that is, to the drop-off in voting that can run as high as 20 to 30 percent at or near the bottom of the typical (lengthy) ballot.

There seems little, if any, good reason to elect such local officials as clerks, coroners, surveyors, and engineers. Their jobs do not carry basic policy-making responsibilities. Rather, they carry out policies made by others. Many believe that to shorten the ballot and promote good government, the rule should be: Elect those who make public policies; appoint those whose basic job it is to administer those policies.

Automated Voting

Well over half the votes now cast in national elections are cast on some type of voting machine—and, increasingly, on some type of electronic voting device.

Ballot Types

Also called the Massachusetts ballot, from its early use (1888) in that State, the office-group ballot is the most common form of the ballot in use in the United States today. *How does a party-column ballot encourage voters to vote along party lines?*

OFFICE-GROUP BALLOT

▶ All candidates for an office are grouped together under the title of that office. It is sometimes called the "office block" ballot because the names appear as a block. Names may be listed in random order to avoid giving any candidate an unfair advantage.

Favored by many authorities because voters consider each choice, office by office.

OFFICIAL BALLOT
FOR PRESIDENT AND VICE PRESIDENT OF THE UNITED STATES (VOTE FOR ONE ONLY)
(Republican Party)
John S. McCain, III/Sarah Palin .... ( )
(Democratic Party)
Barack Obama/Joseph Biden .... ( )
(Libertarian Party)
Bob Barr/Wayne Root .... ( )
(Green Party)
Cynthia McKinney/Rosa Clemente .... ( )
FOR UNITED STATES SENATOR (VOTE FOR ONE ONLY)
(Republican Party)
Brett Locker .... ( )
(Democratic Party)
Paula Robinson .... ( )
(Green Party)
Phoebe J. Bowne .... ( )

PARTY-COLUMN BALLOT

▶ Also known as the Indiana ballot, from its early use (1889) in that State, the party-column ballot lists all candidates under their party's name.

OFFICIAL BALLOT

OFFICE TITLE	A LIBERTARIAN	B DEMOCRAT	C REPUBLICAN	D GREEN
President and Vice President of the United States *Vote for One*	Bob BARR Wayne ROOT ☐	Barack OBAMA Joseph BIDEN ☐	John S. McCAIN III Sarah PALIN ☐	Cynthia McKINNEY Rosa CLEMENTE ☐
United States Senator *Vote for One*		Paula ROBINSON ☐	Brett LOCKER ☐	Phoebe J. BOWNE ☐

Favored by *politicians* because it encourages straight-ticket voting and the coattail effect.

Memory cards record votes cast on electronic voting machines.

Electronic Vote Counting Electronic data processing (EDP) techniques were first applied to the voting process in the 1960s. California and Oregon led the way and EDP is now a vital part of that process in most States.

For some years, the most widely used adaptations of EDP involved punch-card ballots, counted by computers. But punch-card ballots often produced problems—most frequently because voters failed to make clean punches. Their incomplete perforations left "hanging chads" that made the cards difficult or impossible for computers to read.

Punch-card ballots played a major role in the disputed presidential election vote count in Florida in 2000; and that fiasco led to the passage of the Help America Vote Act of 2002. As we noted on page 194, that law required the elimination of all punch-card voting devices (and all lever-operated voting machines, as well).

Most States have turned to two other EDP-based voting systems. One of them involves the same optical-scanning technology used to grade the standardized tests students take in school. Voters mark their ballots by filling in circles, ovals, or rectangles or by completing arrows. A computer scans the marked ballots, counting and recording the votes cast.

The other system utilizes direct response electronic voting machines (DREs). Those machines are much like ATMs or cash machines. Voters make their choices on most models by touching a screen or, on some, by pushing buttons. Their votes are recorded electronically.

DREs have proved troublesome in many places. Some models have malfunctioned and some do not provide a paper record of voters' choices. Many computer scientists insist that DREs can be easily compromised by hackers. Several States abandoned them for 2008. They turned, instead, to optical-scanning systems or went back to hand-counted paper ballots.

Vote-by-Mail Elections A number of States now conduct at least some of their elections by mail. Voters receive a ballot in the mail, mark them, and mail the ballots back to election officials. The first such election was held in Monterey County, California, in 1977; and the first large-scale use of mail-in ballots took place in San Diego in 1981.

Thomas Edison patented the first voting machine—the first mechanical device for the casting and counting of votes—in 1868, and the Myers Automatic Booth was first used in a public election in Lockport, New York, in 1892. The use of similar but much-improved devices soon spread to polling places across the country.

For the better part of a century, most voting machines were lever-operated, and quite cumbersome. Voters had to pull various levers in order to cast their ballots—one lever to open (unlock) the machine, others to indicate their choices of candidates, and yet another to close (lock) the machine and record their votes.

Those lever-operated machines did speed up the voting process; and they reduced both fraud and counting errors. The machines were quite expensive, however, and they also posed major storage and transport problems from one election to the next.

To this point, most vote-by-mail elections have been confined to the local level and to voting on city or county measures, not on candidates for local offices. But, recall, as we noted a few pages ago, vote-by-mail is an integral part of the absentee voting process, and voting by absentee ballot is becoming an increasingly common practice in many places.

In fact, one State, Oregon, now holds *all* of its elections by mail, and it has done so since 1998. That State held the first-ever all-mail primary election and then the first all-mail general election (including the presidential election) in 2000.

Voting by mail has stirred controversy, of course. Critics fear that the process threatens the secret ballot principle. They worry about fraud, especially the possibility that some voters may be subjected to undue pressures when they mark their ballots at home or any place other than a secure voting booth.

Supporters, on the other hand, say that more than ten years of voting by mail in Oregon indicates that that process can be as fraud-proof as any other method of voting. They also make this point: The mail-in process increases voter participation in elections and, at the same time, reduces the costs of conducting them.

Online Voting Online voting—casting ballots via the Internet—has attracted considerable attention and some support in recent years. Will e-voting become widespread, even commonplace, as some predict? Obviously, only time will tell.

Online voting is not an entirely new phenomenon. The first e-vote was cast in November 1997. Election officials in Harris County, Texas, allowed astronaut David Wolf to vote in Houston's city election by e-mail from the space station *Mir*.

The first public election in which some votes were cast by computer was held in 2000, in Arizona's Democratic presidential primary. The Defense Department enabled 84 members of the military stationed abroad to vote electronically in the general election that year, but chose not to repeat the program because of worries about ballot security. In 2008, Arizona became the first State to allow registered voters living abroad (both civilian and military) to vote early and online. Several thousand Arizonans did so.

A number of public officials and private companies promote online voting. They claim that it will make participation much more convenient, increase voter turnout, and reduce election costs.

Many skeptics believe that the electronic infrastructure is not ready for e-voting. Some fear digital disaster: jammed phone lines, blocked access, hackers, viruses, denial-of-service attacks, fraudulent vote counts, and violations of voter secrecy. Critics also point out that because not everyone can afford home computers, online voting could undermine the basic American principle of equality.

✔ **Checkpoint**
How successful have vote-by-mail and online voting been?

Essential Questions Journal To continue to build a response to the chapter Essential Question, go to your **Essential Questions Journal.**

SECTION 2 ASSESSMENT

1. **Guiding Question** Use your completed chart to answer the question: How are elections conducted in the United States?

Key Terms and Comprehension

2. What is the Federal Government's role in the administration of elections?
3. What is the role of the **precinct** in elections?
4. How have **ballots** changed over time?
5. What factors have complicated the move to automated voting?

Critical Thinking

6. **Predict Consequences** What might happen if people lost confidence that their ballots were being counted and recorded properly?
7. **Synthesize Information** Present an argument for or against a proposal to use only hand-counted ballots in all elections.

Quick Write

Explanatory Essay: Research the Topic Use the Internet or other resources to collect information about the election you chose in Section 1. Gather as much information as you can about the candidates and the balloting. Record your information carefully.

Campaign Finance

▶▶ Track the Issue

When regulating campaign finance, the Federal Government has tried to balance free speech rights against the potential for corruption.

1828

After winning a costly and bitter presidential race, Andrew Jackson replaces many government officials with his own campaign supporters.

1907

Congress bans corporate contributions to federal candidates.

1947

The Taft-Hartley Act blocks labor unions from donating to candidates. In response, unions donate through political action committees (PACs).

1974

Congress creates the Federal Election Commission to enforce strict new laws on campaign fundraising.

2002

The Bipartisan Campaign Reform Act is passed and signed, placing strict limits on the use of so-called soft money.

Sen. John McCain
(R., Arizona) ▶

▶▶ Perspectives

Campaigns must raise money to organize and get their message out to voters. The boom in "soft money" in the 1990s, allowing almost unlimited donations to parties by some individuals, led to successful attempts to impose new limits. These efforts, led by Sen. John McCain, sparked debate over government's proper role in regulating political activity.

"This system of unregulated soft money . . . bred public cynicism about the workings of our institutions of government. At a minimum, the actions of Congress and the executive branch were severely tainted by the specter of six-figure soft-money donations by special interests with a stake in legislation and policies pending before the Federal Government."
— *Senator John McCain*
(R., Arizona)

"I think the practical effect of [limits on soft money] would dramatically push Americans out of the political process, putting restrictions on Political Action Committees means that Americans can't band together, pool their resources, and support the candidates of their choice. . . . [Under] the First Amendment of the Constitution, people are free to express themselves and the Supreme Court has said that campaign spending is speech. . . ."
— *Senator Mitch McConnell*
(R., Kentucky)

▶▶ Connect to Your World

1. **Understand (a)** What argument against soft money does Senator McCain make? **(b)** What is Senator McConnell's argument against regulation of soft money?
2. **Draw Conclusions (a)** Why do you think the appearance of corruption alone worries people? **(b)** Do you believe government should be able to act against the appearance of corruption?

🔄 **GOVERNMENT** ONLINE
In the News
For updates about campaign finance, visit
PearsonSuccessNet.com

Money and Elections

Guiding Question

What role does money play in electoral politics? Use a flowchart to record information about the role of money in electoral politics and the efforts of government to regulate it.

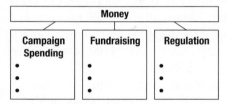

Political Dictionary

- political action committee (PAC)
- subsidy
- hard money
- soft money

Objectives

1. Explain the issues raised by campaign spending.
2. Describe the various sources of funding for campaign spending.
3. Examine federal laws that regulate campaign finance.
4. Outline the role of the Federal Election Commission in enforcing campaign finance laws.
5. Distinguish hard money from soft money.

Image Above: Senator Russ Feingold (D., Wisconsin) has led efforts to regulate campaign contributions.

Running for public office costs money—and often quite a lot of it. That fact creates some very real problems. It presents the possibility that candidates will try to buy their way into office. It also makes it possible for special interests to try to buy favors from those who hold office.

Clearly, government by the people must be protected from those dangers. But how? Parties and candidates must have money. Without it, they cannot campaign or do any of the many other things they must do to win elections.

In short, dollars are absolutely necessary campaign resources. Yet, the getting and spending of campaign funds can corrupt the entire political process.

Campaign Spending

No one really knows how much money is spent on political campaigns in the United States. Remember, there are more than 500,000 elective offices in this country—most of them at the State and particularly the local level. More or less reliable estimates of total spending in presidential election years—on all efforts to win nominations and to gain offices at all levels—can be seen in the table on the next page.

The presidential election consumes by far the largest share of campaign dollars. For 2008, total spending for all of the major and minor party presidential efforts—for primaries and caucuses, conventions, general election campaigns, for everything—reached a mind-boggling $2.5 billion.

The vast sums spent on congressional campaigns also continue to climb, election after election. That spending has doubled over the past decade. A candidate must now raise and spend at least $1 million in a typical race for a seat in the House. A Senate campaign can cost as much as twenty times that amount. All told, some $1.5 billion was spent on House and Senate contests in 2008.

Radio and television time, professional campaign managers and consultants, newspaper advertisements, pamphlets, buttons, posters and bumper stickers, office rent, polls, data processing, mass mailings, Web sites, travel—these and a host of other items make up the huge sums spent in campaigns. Television ads are far and away the largest item in most campaign budgets

Total Campaign Spending, 1964–2008

Year	Estimated spending	Voter turnout*	Spending per voter
1964	$200 million	70.6 million	$2.83
1968	$300 million	73.2 million	$4.10
1972	$425 million	77.7 million	$5.47
1976	$540 million	81.6 million	$6.62
1980	$1.2 billion	86.6 million	$13.87
1984	$1.8 billion	92.7 million	$19.42
1988	$2.7 billion	91.6 million	$29.48
1992	$3.2 billion	104.4 million	$30.65
1996	$4.0 billion	96.5 million	$41.45
2000	$5.1 billion	105.4 million	$48.39
2004	$6.0 billion	120.2 million	$49.92
2008	$7.0 billion	130.9 million	$53.48

*Presidential elections
SOURCES: Federal Election Commission; Herbert E. Alexander, *Financing Politics*

Analyzing Charts Total campaign spending has risen dramatically in recent elections. **What factors may account for this rise?**

today, even at the local level. As humorist Will Rogers put it years ago, "You have to be loaded just to get beat."

The total amount spent in particular races varies widely, of course. How much depends on several things: the office involved, the candidate and whether he or she is the incumbent or the challenger, the nature of the opposition, and much more—including, not least, the availability of campaign funds.

Sources of Funding

Parties and their candidates draw their money from two basic sources: private contributors and the public treasury.

Private and Public Sources Private givers have always been the major source of campaign funds in American politics. They come in various shapes and sizes:

1. Small contributors—those who give $5 or $10 or so, and only occasionally. Only about 10 percent of people of voting age ever make a campaign contribution, so parties and candidates must look to other places for much of their funding.

2. Wealthy individuals and families—the "fat cats," who can make large donations and find it in their best interest to do so.

3. Candidates—both incumbents and challengers, their families, and, importantly, people who hold and want to keep appointive public offices. Ross Perot holds the all-time record in this category. He spent some $65 million of his own money on his independent bid for the presidency in 1992.

4. Various nonparty groups—especially **political action committees (PACs).** Political action committees are the political arms of special-interest groups and other organizations with a stake in electoral politics.

5. Temporary organizations—groups formed for the immediate purposes of a campaign, including fundraising. Hundreds of these short-lived units spring up every two years, and at every level in American politics.

Then, too, parties and their candidates often hold fundraisers of various sorts. The most common are $100-, $500-, and $1,000-a-plate luncheons, dinners, picnics, receptions, and similar gatherings. Some of these events now reach the $100,000-or-more level in presidential campaigns. Direct mail requests, telethons, and Internet solicitations are also among the oft-used tools of those who raise campaign money.

Over recent years, the Internet has become, by far, the most productive of those tools. Often, donations spiked immediately after an important speech or primary election victory or when the candidate challenged donors to give. Web sites including Daily Kos and Act Blue identified and profiled congressional candidates for their readers to support.

Public funds—subsidies from the federal and some State treasuries—are now another prime source of campaign money. A **subsidy** is a grant of money, usually from a government. Subsidies have so far been most important at the presidential level, as you will see shortly. Several States also provide some form of public funding of parties and/or candidacies.

Why People Give Campaign donations are a form of political participation. Those who donate do so for a number of reasons. Many small donors give simply because they believe in a party or in a candidate. Many of those who give, however, want something in return. They want access to government, and hope to get it by helping their "friends" win elections. And, notice, some contributors give to both sides in a contest: Heads they win and tails they still win.

Some big donors want appointments to public office, and others want to keep the ones they have. Some long for social recognition. For them, dinner at the White House, meeting with a Cabinet official, or knowing the governor on a first-name basis may be enough. Organized labor, business, professional, and various other groups have particular policy aims. They want certain laws passed, changed, or repealed, or certain administrative actions taken.

Regulating Finance

Congress first began to regulate the use of money in federal elections in 1907. In that year, it became unlawful for any corporation or national bank to make "a money contribution in any election" to candidates for federal office. Since then, Congress has passed several laws to regulate the use of money in presidential and congressional campaigns. Today, these regulations are found in four detailed laws: the Federal Election Campaign Act (FECA) of 1971, the FECA Amendments of 1974 and of 1976, and the Bipartisan Campaign Reform Act of 2002.

The earliest federal laws were loosely drawn, not often obeyed, and almost never enforced. The 1971 law replaced them. The 1974 law was the major legislative response to the Watergate scandal of the Nixon years. The 1976 law was passed in response to a landmark Supreme Court decision, *Buckley* v. *Valeo*, in 1976. The 2002 law attempted to close the "soft-money" loophole in the 1974 and 1976 statutes; it was upheld by the High Court in *McConnell* v. *FEC* in 2003.

Congress does not have the power to regulate the use of money in State and local

✔ **Checkpoint**
Where do campaign contributions come from?

GOVERNMENT ONLINE
Audio Tour
Listen to a guided audio tour of this diagram at **PearsonSuccessNet.com**

Internet Fundraising
A Trickle Becomes a Flood

Candidates use the Internet to raise more money, faster, from many more donors than in the past. Insurgent candidates, not those favored by party leaders and traditional donors, have made the greatest leaps in Internet fundraising. *Why did outside candidates like McCain, Dean, and Obama need to find new ways to raise money?*

Obama Shatters Records

Gov. Dean Leads the Way

New Hampshire Surprise

2000 — **$1 Million**
John McCain raised $1 million via the Internet after an upset in the New Hampshire primary.

2004 — **$20 Million**
Howard Dean raised $20 million for the Democratic primaries, creating a comprehensive Internet strategy later adopted by other candidates.

2008 — **$230 Million**
Barack Obama raised some $230 million via the Internet for his primary campaign. More than 80 percent of that amount came in sums of less than $100.

elections. Every State now regulates at least some aspects of campaign finance, however—some of them do so more effectively than others.[15]

Federal Election Commission

The Federal Election Commission (FEC) administers all federal law dealing with campaign finance. Set up by Congress in 1974, the FEC is an independent agency in the executive branch. Its six members are appointed by the President, with Senate confirmation.

Federal campaign finance laws are both strongly worded and closely detailed. But they are not very well enforced. In large part this is because the FEC has been both underfunded and understaffed. That is to say, members of Congress—who, remember, raise and spend campaign money—have made it practically impossible for the FEC to do an effective job.

---

[15] State campaign finance laws are summarized in *The Book of the States,* an annual publication of the Council of State Governments.

In short, the FEC finds itself in a situation much like that of the chickens who must guard the fox house.

The laws that the FEC is supposed to enforce cover four broad areas. They (1) require the timely disclosure of campaign finance data, (2) place limits on campaign contributions, (3) place limits on campaign expenditures, and (4) provide public funding for several parts of the presidential election process.

Disclosure Requirements Congress first required the reporting of certain campaign finance information in 1910. Today, the disclosure requirements are intended to spotlight the place of money in federal campaigns. Those requirements are so detailed that most candidates for federal office must now include at least one certified public accountant in their campaign organization.

No individual or group can make a contribution in the name of another. Cash gifts of more than $100 are prohibited, as are contributions and spending from foreign sources.

GOVERNMENT ONLINE

For an interactive version of campaign spending, visit **PearsonSuccessNet.com**

INTERACTIVE

Rising Campaign Costs

Candidates are raising and spending more money than ever, and no campaign demands more than the presidential contest. John McCain and Barack Obama set new spending records in 2008, as data averaged from both campaigns for just one month indicate. *How does campaign spending reflect the importance of television?*

TRAVEL $4,100,000   TELEVISION AND RADIO ADVERTISING TIME $25,200,000   SOURCE: Federal Election Commission, September 2008

CAMPAIGN WORKER SALARIES $2,000,000   POLLING $800,000

All contributions to a candidate for federal office must be made through a single campaign committee. Only that committee can spend that candidate's campaign money. All contributions and spending must be closely accounted for by that one committee. Any contribution or loan of more than $200 must be identified by source and by date. Any spending over $200 must also be identified by the name of the person or firm to whom payment was made, by date, and by purpose.

Any contribution of more than $5,000 must be reported to the FEC no later than 48 hours after it is received. So, too, must any sum of $1,000 or more received in the last 20 days of a campaign.

Limits on Contributions Congress first began to regulate campaign contributions in 1907, when it outlawed donations by corporations and national banks. A similar ban was first applied to labor unions in 1943. Individual contributions have been regulated since 1939.

Today, no person can give more than $2,300 to any federal candidate in a primary election, and no more than $2,300 to any federal candidate's general election campaign. Also, no person can give more than $5,000 in any year to a political action committee (PAC), or $28,500 to a national party committee. The total of any person's contributions to federal candidates and committees now must be limited to no more than $108,200 in an election cycle (the two years from one general election to the next one). The FEC adjusts those figures, to account for inflation, every two years.

Those limits may seem generous; in fact, they are very tight. Before limits were imposed in 1974, many wealthy individuals gave far larger amounts. In 1972, for example, W. Clement Stone, a Chicago insurance executive, contributed more than $2 million (equal to more than $20 million in today's money) to President Richard Nixon's reelection campaign.

PAC Contributions Neither corporations nor labor unions can contribute to any candidate running for a federal office. Their political action committees, however, can and do.

Political action committees (PACs) seek to affect the making of public policy, and so they are very interested in the outcome of elections in the United States. Some 4,400 PACs are active today, and those organizations are of two distinct types:

1. Most PACs are the political arms of special interest groups—and especially of business associations, labor unions, and professional organizations. These groups are known in the law as "segregated fund committees." They can raise funds *only* from their members—from the executives, the employees, and the stockholders of a corporation, from the members of a labor union, and so on. They *cannot* seek contributions from the general public. Each of these PACs is a part of its parent organization.

BIPAC (the Business-Industry Political Action Committee) and COPE (the AFL-CIO's Committee on Political Education) are among the most active of these groups.

2. A few hundred PACs are "unconnected committees." Each of them was established as an independent entity, not as a unit in some larger organization. Many are ideologically based. These PACs can raise money from the public at large. One major example is EMILY's List, which actively recruits and funds pro-choice women as Democratic candidates. (The group takes its name from this political maxim: Early Money Is Like Yeast, it makes the dough rise.)

PACs fill their war chests with contributions from the members of the PAC's parent organization or with the dollars they raise from the public. They "bundle" the money they gather—that is, each PAC pools its many contributions into a single large fund. Then they distribute that money to those candidates who (1) are sympathetic to the PAC's policy goals, and (2) have a reasonable chance of winning their races.

No PAC can give more than $5,000 to any one federal candidate in an election, or $10,000 per election cycle (primary and general election). However, there is no overall limit on PAC giving to candidates. Each PAC can give up to $5,000 per election to each of as many candidates as it chooses. A PAC may also contribute up to $15,000 a year to a political party.

Barack Obama refused PAC contributions in 2008. Even so, those groups poured $416 million into the presidential and congressional

✓ **Checkpoint**
What does the Federal Election Commission (FEC) do?

▲ Former Massachusetts governor Mitt Romney promoted his bid for the GOP presidential nomination with a widely publicized telethon in 2008. **Why must candidates spend significant time on fundraising activities?**

campaigns that year. And they funneled untold other millions into State and local contests around the country, as well.

Limits on Expenditures Congress first began to limit federal campaign spending in 1925. Most of the limits now on the books apply only to presidential (not congressional) elections. This fact is due mostly to the Supreme Court's decision in *Buckley* v. *Valeo*, 1976.

In *Buckley*, the High Court struck down all but one of the spending limits set by the FECA Amendments of 1974. It held each of the other restrictions to be contrary to the 1st Amendment's guarantees of free expression. In effect, said the Court, in politics "money is speech."

The one limit the Court did uphold is a cap on spending by those presidential contenders who accept FEC subsidies for their preconvention and/or their general election campaigns. As you will see in a moment, those who seek the presidency can either accept or reject that public money for their campaigns. In *Buckley*, the Court said that those who take the subsidies must take a

spending limit along with them, as part of their deal with the FEC.[16]

Public Funding for Presidential Campaigns Congress first began to provide for the public funding of presidential campaigns in the Revenue Act of 1971. It broadened sections of that law in 1974 and again in 1976.

The 1971 law created the Presidential Election Campaign Fund. Every person who files a federal income tax return can "check off" (assign) three dollars of his or her tax bill (six dollars on a joint return) to the fund. The money in the fund is used every four years to subsidize preconvention campaigns (including the primary campaigns), national conventions, and presidential election campaigns. The FEC administers the various subsidies involved.

Preconvention Campaigns. Presidential primary and caucus campaigns are supported by private contributions and, if the candidate applies for them, the public money he or she receives from the FEC. To be eligible for the public funds, a contender must raise at least $100,000 in contributions from individuals (not organizations). That amount must be gathered in $5,000 lots in each of at least 20 States, with each lot built from individual donations of no more than $250. That convoluted requirement is meant to discourage frivolous candidacies.

For each presidential hopeful who passes that test and applies for the subsidy, the FEC will match the first $250 of each individual contribution to the candidate, up to a total of half of the overall limit on preconvention spending. So, in 2008, the FEC could give a contender about $21 million, because the preconvention ceiling was slightly more than $42 million. The FEC does not match contributions from PACs or from any other political organizations.

In 2008, Senator John McCain spent about $100 million to win the GOP nomination—some $7 million of it from the FEC. Senator Barack Obama, on the other hand, refused the public money. He raised and

---

[16] Until 2008, only a handful of major party aspirants refused the public money. George W. Bush, in 2000 and again in 2004, and his Democratic opponent in 2004, John Kerry, won nomination without the public money. However, both Bush and Kerry did take the FEC funds for their general election campaigns.

spent more than $230 million in private contributions in his campaign for the Democratic Party's nomination.[17]

National Conventions. If a major party applies for the money, it automatically receives a grant to help pay for its national convention. The FEC gave the Republicans and the Democrats $16.4 million each for that purpose in 2008.

Presidential Election Campaigns. Each major party nominee automatically qualifies for a public subsidy to pay for the general election campaign. For 2008, that subsidy was $84.1 million. A candidate can refuse that funding, of course, and, in that event, be free to raise however much he or she can from private sources.

Until 2008, the nominees of both major parties took the public money each time. Because they did, each (1) could spend no more than the amount of the subsidy in the general election campaign and (2) could not accept campaign funds from any other source.

For 2008, only Republican John McCain ran with the FEC money and so could spend only that $84.1 million in the fall campaign. The Republican National Committee, other party organizations, and several independent groups also backed the McCain effort, however—to the tune of some $210 million.

Barack Obama, on the other hand, became the first presidential nominee in the 32-year history of the program to reject the public money. He raised and spent more than $500 million on his successful ten-week post-convention campaign.

The fact that several contenders, in both parties, rejected the FEC money for their pre-convention campaigns and Senator Obama's abstention for the general election have led many to predict the collapse of the public funding arrangements in federal law. That development is a direct result of two major factors: (1) a continuing decline in the number of taxpayers willing to contribute to the Presidential Election Campaign Fund and, especially, (2) the continuing and accelerating rise in the costs of campaigning.

The massive effect of that second factor, soaring costs, on the whole matter of campaign finance and its regulation can be seen in this stunning fact: For 2008, just one item, television advertising, accounted for at least $300 million in presidential campaign spending.

A minor party's candidate can also qualify for the FEC funding, but none does so automatically. For a minor party nominee to be eligible, his or her party must either (1) have won at least five percent of the popular vote in the last presidential election, or (2) win at least that much of the total vote in the current election. Since 1972, only Ross Perot in 1992 and 1996 has come even close to qualifying.

In the latter case, the public money is received *after* the election and so could not possibly help the candidate win votes in that election. (Remember, many provisions in both federal and State election law are purposely drawn to discourage the efforts of minor party and independent candidacies.)

Hard Money, Soft Money

More than 40 years ago, President Lyndon Johnson described the then-current body of

✓ **Checkpoint**
How are presidential campaigns financed?

Hard Money and Soft Money

Historically, hard money was tightly regulated and more difficult to raise, while soft money could be procured easily from fewer people in larger sums. *How has regulation of hard and soft money changed since the 1990s?*

---

17 His chief opponent for the Democratic nomination, Senator Hillary Clinton, also refused FEC funds. She raised and spent nearly $200 million in her unsuccessful bid.

federal campaign finance law as "more loophole than law." Over recent years, we have come dangerously close to the point where LBJ's description can be applied to the federal election money statutes of today—particularly because of soft money.

Since the 1970s, federal law has placed limits on **hard money**—that is, those contributions that are given directly to candidates for their campaigns for Congress or the White House, are limited in amount, and must be reported. That kind of campaign money is usually more difficult to raise than **soft money**—funds given to parties or to other political organizations, in unlimited amounts, to be used for such "party-building activities" as voter registration or get-out-the-vote drives or for campaigns for or against particular public policies, for example, gun control or minimum wage hikes.

Both major parties began to raise soft money (began to exploit the soft-money loophole) in the 1980s, and they intensified their efforts in the 1990s. The Republican and Democratic National Committees and their House and Senate campaign committees gathered millions of unregulated dollars from wealthy individuals, labor unions, corporations, and other interest groups. Officially, those funds were to be used for party-building purposes; but both parties found it easy to filter them into their presidential and congressional campaigns.

The torrent of money rushing through the soft-money loophole rose from about $19 million in 1980 to some $500 million in 2000. Those huge numbers have convinced a great many people that the nation's campaign finance laws are in serious need of reform. As a step in that direction, Congress finally enacted the Bipartisan Campaign Reform Act (the BCRA) of 2002 after years of debate and delay. The measure is also known as the McCain-Feingold Law, after its chief Senate sponsors.

The BCRA was aimed principally at the soft-money problem. It bans soft-money contributions to political parties. But the law does not say that other political organizations cannot raise and spend those dollars.

Almost immediately, a number of independent groups—organizations with no formal ties to any party—sprang up to do just that. In short, creative minds in both parties quickly found ways to skirt the ban on soft money. Some $200 million poured through that loophole in 2004 and even more for the congressional elections of 2006 and the presidential campaigns in 2008.

Many of these independent organizations are known as "527s," after the section in the Internal Revenue code under which they operate as tax-free entities. In 2008, Senator Obama initially discouraged the help of 527 organizations, while his opponent, Republican Senator John McCain encouraged that help.

SECTION **3** ASSESSMENT

Essential Questions Journal
To continue to build a response to the chapter Essential Question, go to your Essential Questions Journal.

1. **Guiding Question** Use your completed chart to answer the question: What role does money play in electoral politics?

Key Terms and Comprehension

2. Why do people contribute to political campaigns?

3. What are the four ways in which the FEC attempts to regulate the role of money in campaigns?

4. What are **political action committees,** and what is their role in the political process?

5. What is the difference between **hard money** and **soft money?**

Critical Thinking

6. **Summarize** Why do the huge amounts of money required for most political campaigns concern many observers?

7. **Identify Central Issues** The Supreme Court has ruled that "Money is speech." What does this observation mean for efforts to regulate and limit donations and spending in political campaigns?

Quick Write

Explanatory Essay: Write a Thesis Statement A thesis statement sets out what, specifically, you will cover in your essay. Write a thesis statement for an explanatory essay about the election you chose in Section 1.

Quick Study Guide

GOVERNMENT ONLINE
On the Go
To review anytime, anywhere, download these online resources at **PearsonSuccessNet.com**
Political Dictionary, Audio Review

Guiding Question
Section 2 How are elections conducted in the United States?

Guiding Question
Section 1 What methods are used to choose candidates for public office?

CHAPTER 7
Essential Question
How fair and effective is the electoral process?

Guiding Question
Section 3 What role does money play in electoral politics?

Political Dictionary

- **nomination** *p. 184*
- **general election** *p. 185*
- **caucus** *p. 185*
- **direct primary** *p. 187*
- **closed primary** *p. 188*
- **open primary** *p. 188*
- **blanket primary** *p. 189*
- **runoff primary** *p. 190*
- **nonpartisan election** *p. 190*
- **ballot** *p. 194*
- **absentee voting** *p. 195*
- **coattail effect** *p. 195*
- **precinct** *p. 195*
- **polling place** *p. 195*
- **political action committee (PAC)** *p. 202*
- **subsidy** *p. 202*
- **hard money** *p. 208*
- **soft money** *p. 208*

Path to Elected Office

Nominating Candidates
- Self-announcement
- Caucus
- Conventions
- Direct Primary
  - *Closed Primary*
  - *Open Primary*
- Petition

Electing Candidates
- Elections administered by State and local goverments
- Some federal oversight
- Citizens vote by mail or at polling places
- Paper ballots and electronic voting in use

Campaign Contributions
- Individual Donors
- Political Action Committees (PACs)
- Public Financing by Government

Regulating Campaign Finance
- Contributions by individuals and groups are protected by 1st Amendment guarantee of free speech
- Direct contributions by unions and corporations to campaigns are illegal
- Federal campaigns must record donations and report regularly to Federal Election Commission

Chapter Assessment

GOVERNMENT ONLINE
Self-Test
To test your understanding of key terms and main ideas, visit
PearsonSuccessNet.com

Comprehension and Critical Thinking

Section 1

1. **(a)** What is the essential difference between the nominating and the election stages in the political process? **(b)** Explain why the two-party system makes the nominating process especially significant.

2. **(a)** What factors led to the convention replacing the caucus as a widely used nominating method? **(b)** How well did the convention method succeed in improving upon the caucus method?

3. **(a)** What is the role of political parties in primary elections? **(b)** Why do you think a political party might object to the use of a blanket primary? **(c)** Are closed primaries a fair way to nominate candidates? Explain.

Section 2

4. **(a)** Provide three examples of areas in which the Federal Government has established election law. **(b)** What are the goals of the Federal Government in regulating elections?

5. **(a)** What are some of the problems that the secret ballot is designed to prevent? **(b)** How did the Australian ballot improve the voting process?

6. **(a)** Why do you think there has been an interest in automating the voting process in recent times? **(b)** What are the possible benefits and drawbacks of voting via the Internet? **(c)** Do the advantages of voting via the Internet outweigh its drawbacks? Explain.

Section 3

7. **(a)** What factors affect how much money is spent in a political campaign? **(b)** How do campaign contributions help candidates running for office? **(c)** Does the private rather than the public financing of campaigns make elections more effective? Why or why not?

8. **(a)** The Supreme Court has held that campaign contributions are a form of political speech. Explain why you agree or disagree. **(b)** Why was this ruling significant?

9. **Analyzing Political Cartoons** The cartoon below was drawn following the 2008 Democratic presidential primaries in which Senator Obama defeated Senator Clinton. **(a)** Why is Senator Obama holding a sign reading "Unity"? **(b)** What does this cartoon say about primary rivalries?

THE TIMES·PICAYUNE © 2 0 0 8   SKELLY

cartoonistgroup.com

Writing About Government

10. Use the Quick Write exercises from this chapter to complete a 3–5 paragraph explanatory essay that describes and explains the key steps and features of the election you selected. See pages S3–S5 of the Skills Handbook.

Apply What You've Learned

11. **Essential Question Activity** Prepare an outline for each side of a debate about the topic: Money is essential to the electoral process.

    (a) Develop a compelling argument both for and against the statement.

    (b) Describe existing efforts to regulate the role of money in elections.

    (c) Identify the main sources of campaign funding and analyze the impact each source has on elections.

    (d) Analyze the potential effects of removing all money from the political process, or, alternatively, removing all regulation of money.

12. **Essential Question Assessment** After you have considered and written about both sides of the question about the role of money in government, write a brief essay explaining your own views on the role of money in the electoral process today. Your essay should help you answer the Essential Question: **How fair and effective is the electoral process?**

Essential Questions
Journal
To respond to the chapter Essential Question, go to your **Essential Questions Journal.**

Document-Based Assessment

Nominating Candidates in Our Electoral System

Nominating candidates to run for office is a function of political parties. It is also a key step in the democratic process. This dual quality of the nominating process can create tension, as the party's wishes and the voice of the people do not always agree.

Document 1

Tonight, after fifty-four hard-fought contests, our primary season has finally come to an end. Sixteen months have passed since we first stood together on the steps of the Old State Capitol in Springfield, Illinois. Thousands of miles have been traveled. Millions of voices have been heard. . . .

There are those who say that this primary has somehow left us weaker and more divided. Well I say that because of this primary, there are millions of Americans who have cast their ballot for the very first time.

—Senator Barack Obama, June 3, 2008

Document 2

President [George H.W.] Bush received a jarring political message in the New Hampshire primary today, scoring a less-than-impressive victory over Patrick J. Buchanan, the conservative commentator. . . .

The signal to Mr. Bush was unmistakable. Even though Mr. Buchanan's support represented more than 63,000 actual votes, it amounted to a roar of anger from those who voted in the Republican primary, and it showed the power of a "send a message" campaign against him in times of economic distress. . . .

Republicans loyal to Mr. Bush tried to play down the results. . . . But there was alarm in the White House. . . .

—*The New York Times,* February 19, 1992

Document 3

Senator [Warren G.] Harding's nomination was the outcome of a complex situation that did not begin to clear until last evening. After four ineffective ballots yesterday the convention had adjourned until this morning. Four additional ballots in the forenoon and early afternoon of today had developed Harding strength, but General Leonard Wood and Governor Frank O. Lowden had remained in the lead. . . .

Interesting, and even thrilling, as the open proceedings in the convention were, moves behind the scenes, of which most of the convention knew nothing, had their dramatic side. The nomination of the candidate for President was arranged in conferences in hotel rooms.

—*The New York Times,* June 12, 1920

Use your knowledge of the nominating process and Documents 1, 2, and 3 to answer Questions 1–3.

1. According to Barack Obama in Document 1, which of the following is **not** an advantage of the primary process?
   A. The candidates competed in many States across the country.
   B. Primaries divided the party and upset many voters.
   C. Primaries brought millions of new voters into the nomination process.
   D. The candidates met many voters in their travels.

2. In Document 2, why do you think the message received by President Bush was so jarring?

3. Does the nominating process described in Document 3 seem democratic? Explain your answer.

4. **Pull It Together** How do the interests of voters and the interests of party officials sometimes come into conflict during the nomination process?

GOVERNMENT ONLINE
Online Documents
To find more primary sources on the nominating process, visit **PearsonSuccessNet.com**

E CYCLISM
DE FRANCE JULY 3-25
HE TOUR DE F ANCE -- STAGE 16 TI
SON
MILITANT
EN ATTACKS AGAINST PO
ARMSTRON
HE OVERALL LEAD IN THE

Essential Question
What is the place of the media and public opinion in a democracy?

> **What** the **public knows** about **politics** and **government** is the **result** of what the **media** do, what the **politicians** do, and what use the **public** makes of the resulting **information.**
>
> —Guido H. Stempel III, *Media and Politics in America*

Photo: Onlookers watch the news in Times Square, New York City.

GOVERNMENT ONLINE
On the Go

To study anywhere, anytime, download these online resources at PearsonSuccessNet.com
• Political Dictionary
• Audio Review
• Downloadable Interactivities

The **Formation** of **Public Opinion**

Guiding Question

What is public opinion, and what factors help to shape it? Use a concept web like the one below to show the factors that influence public opinion.

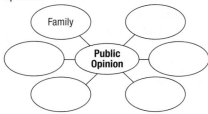

Political Dictionary
- public affairs
- public opinion
- mass media
- peer group
- opinion leader

Objectives

1. Examine the term *public opinion* and understand why it is so difficult to define.
2. Analyze how family and education help shape public opinion.
3. Describe four other factors that shape public opinion.

Image Above: Guests on *Meet the Press* discuss the 2008 presidential election.

Do you like broccoli? Blue fingernail polish? Tattoos? Hard rock music? What about sports? Old cars? You almost certainly have an opinion on each of those things. On some of them, you may hold strong opinions, and those opinions may be very important to you. Still, each of those opinions is your own view, your *private* opinion. None of them qualifies as *public* opinion.

What Is Public Opinion?

Few terms in American politics are more widely used, and less well understood, than the term *public opinion.* It appears regularly in newspapers and magazines and on blogs, and you hear it frequently on radio and television.

Quite often, the phrase is used to suggest that all or most of the American people hold the same view on some public issue, such as global warming or deficit spending. Thus, time and again, politicians say that "the people" want such and such, television commentators tell us that "the public" favors this or opposes that, and so on.

In fact, there are very few matters about which all or nearly all of "the people" think alike. "The public" holds many different and often conflicting views on nearly every public issue.

To understand what public opinion is, you must recognize this important point: Public opinion refers to a complex collection of the opinions of many different people. It is the sum of all of their views. It is *not* the single and undivided view of some mass mind.

Different Publics Many publics exist in the United States—in fact, too many to be counted. Each public is made up of all those individuals who hold the same view on some particular public issue. Each group of people with a differing point of view is a *separate* public with regard to that issue.

For example, the people who think that Congress should establish a national health insurance program belong to the public that holds that view. People who believe that the President is doing an excellent job as chief executive, or that capital punishment should be abolished, or that prayer should be permitted in public school, are members of separate publics with those particular opinions. Clearly, many people can and do belong to more than one of those publics; but almost certainly only a very few belong to all four of them.

Notice this important point: Not many issues capture the attention of all—or even nearly all—Americans. In fact, those that do are few and far between. Instead, most public issues attract the interest of *some* people (and sometimes millions of them), but those same issues are of little or no interest to many (and sometimes millions of) other people.

This point is crucial, too: In its proper sense, public opinion includes only those views that relate to public affairs. **Public affairs** include politics, public issues, and the making of public policies—those events and issues that concern the people at large. To be a *public* opinion, a view must involve something of general concern and of interest to a significant portion of the people as a whole.

Of course, the American people as a whole are interested in many things—rock groups and symphony orchestras, the New York Yankees and the Dallas Cowboys, candy bars and green vegetables, and a great deal more. Many people have opinions on each of these things, views that are sometimes loosely called "public opinion." But, again, in its proper sense, public opinion involves only those views that people hold on such things as political parties and candidates, taxes, unemployment, welfare programs, national defense, foreign policy, and so on.

Definition Clearly, public opinion is so complex that it cannot be readily defined. From what has been said about it to this point, however, **public opinion** can be described this way: those attitudes held by a significant number of people on matters of government and politics.

As we have suggested, you can better understand the term in the plural—that is, as public opinions, the opinions of different publics. Look at it this way: public opinion is made up of expressed group attitudes.

A view must be *expressed* in order to be an opinion in the public sense. Otherwise, it cannot be identified with any public. That expression need not be oral (spoken). It can take any number of other forms, as well: a protest demonstration, a film, a billboard, a vote for or against a candidate, and so on. The point is that a person's private thoughts on an issue enter the stream of public opinion only when those thoughts are expressed publicly.

Family and School

No one is born with a set of attitudes about government and politics. Instead, each of us learns our political opinions, and we do so in a lifelong "classroom" and from many different "teachers." In other words, public opinion is formed out of a very complex process. The factors involved in it are almost <u>infinite.</u>

✔ **Checkpoint**
What do public affairs include?

infinite
adj. uncountable, neverending, limitless

Top Issues for 2008 Presidential Election

Opinions about public affairs often vary widely across the voting population. In the summer before the 2008 election, voters had different opinions about which issues were most important in the presidential election. *How might the information on this chart change in the election of 2012? 2016?*

- Economy
- Iraq
- Gas prices
- Healthcare
- Terrorism
- Personal characteristics

49%
25%
18%
16%
7%
7%

49%
of voters thought **the economy** was the **most important** issue in their **vote** for President.

SOURCE: Henry J. Kaiser Family Foundation

monopoly
n. dominant or exclusive control

impressionable
adj. easily influenced, receptive

indoctrinate
v. to teach, instruct

You have already considered that point. Recall the detailed look at why people vote as they do in Chapter 6. Those pages amounted to an extensive look at how public opinion is formed. Also in that chapter, you considered the process by which each person acquires his or her political opinions—the process of *political socialization.* That complex process begins in early childhood, and it continues on through one's lifetime. It involves all of the many experiences and relationships that lead each of us to see the political world and to act in it as we do.[1]

There are many different agents of political socialization at work in the opinion-shaping process. Again, you looked at these agents in Chapter 6: age, race, income, occupation, residence, group affiliations, and many others. Here, look again at two of them, the family and school. They have so large an impact that they deserve another and slightly different discussion here.

Family Most parents do not think of themselves as agents of political socialization, nor do other members of most families. Parents and other family members do nonetheless play an important part in this process.

Children first see the political world from within the family and through the family's eyes. They begin to learn about politics much as they begin to learn about most other things in life. They learn from what their parents have to say, from the stories that their older brothers and sisters bring home from school, from watching television with the family, and so on.

Most of what smaller children learn in the family setting cannot really be described as political opinions. Clearly, toddlers are not concerned with the wisdom of spending billions of dollars on an antimissile defense system, with the causes of global warming, or the pros and cons of the monetary policies of the Federal Reserve Board.

---

1 The concept of socialization comes from the fields of sociology and psychology. There, it is used to describe all of the ways in which a society transforms individuals into members of that society. To put this another way: Socialization is the multi-sided, lifelong process in which people come to know, accept, and follow the beliefs and practices of their society. *Political socialization* is a part of that much broader process.

Young children do pick up some fundamental attitudes, however. With those attitudes, they acquire a basic slant toward such things as authority and rules of behavior, property, neighbors, people of other racial or religious backgrounds, and the like. In short, children lay some foundations on which they will later build their political opinions.

A large number of scholarly studies report what common sense also suggests. The strong influence the family has on the development of political opinions is largely a result of the near <u>monopoly</u> the family has on the child in his or her earliest, most <u>impressionable</u> years. Those studies also show that:

> "Children raised in households in which the primary caregivers are Democrats tend to become Democrats themselves, whereas children raised in homes where their caregivers are Republican tend to favor the GOP."
>
> —**Benjamin Ginsberg, Theodore Lowi, and Margaret Weir,** *We the People*

School The start of formal schooling marks the initial break in the influence of the family. For the first time, children become regularly involved in activities outside the home.

From the first day, schools teach children the values of the American political system. They work to <u>indoctrinate</u> the young, to instill in them loyalty to a particular cause or idea. In fact, preparing students to become good citizens is an important part of our educational system.

Students may salute the flag, recite the Pledge of Allegiance, and sing patriotic songs. They learn about George Washington, Abraham Lincoln, Susan B. Anthony, Martin Luther King, Jr., and other great Americans. From the early grades on, they pick up growing amounts of specific political knowledge, and they begin to form political opinions. In high school, they are often required to take a course in American government and even to read books such as this one.

School involves much more than books and classes, of course. It is a complex bundle of experiences and a place where a good deal of informal learning occurs—about the similarities and differences among individuals

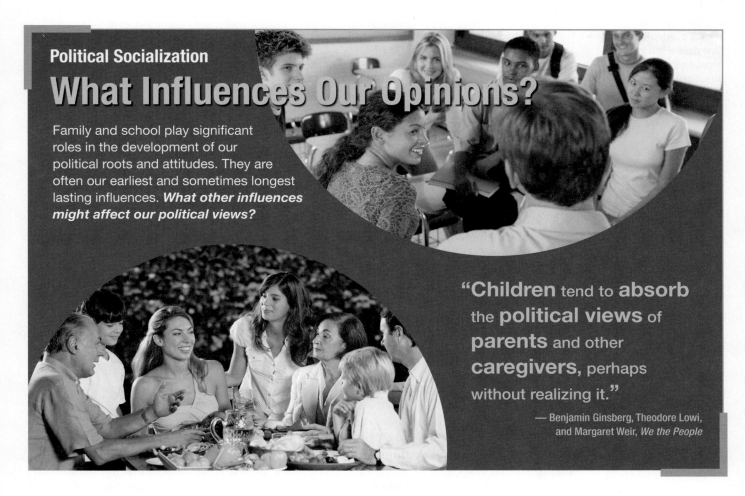

Political Socialization

What Influences Our Opinions?

Family and school play significant roles in the development of our political roots and attitudes. They are often our earliest and sometimes longest lasting influences. *What other influences might affect our political views?*

"**Children** tend to **absorb** the **political views** of **parents** and other **caregivers,** perhaps without realizing it."

— Benjamin Ginsberg, Theodore Lowi, and Margaret Weir, *We the People*

and groups, about the various ways in which decisions can be made, and about the process of compromise that must often occur in order for ideas to move forward.

Once again, the family and school are *not* the only forces at work in the process by which opinions are formed. A number of other influences are part of the mix. These two factors are singled out here to highlight their leading roles in that process.

Other Factors

No factor, by itself, shapes a person's opinion on any single issue. Some factors do play a larger role than others, however. Thus, in addition to family and school, occupation and race are usually much more significant than, say, gender or place of residence.

For example, on the question of national health insurance, the particular job a person has—how well-paying it is, whether its benefits include coverage by a private health-insurance plan, and so on—will

almost certainly have a greater impact on that person's views than his or her gender or place of residence.

On the other hand, the relative weight of each factor that influences public opinion also depends on the issue in question. If the issue involves, say, equal pay for women or the restoration of Lake Michigan, then gender or where one lives will almost certainly loom larger in the opinion-making mix.

Besides family, school, and such factors as occupation and race, four other factors have a major place in the opinion-making process. They are the mass media, peer groups, opinion leaders, and historic events.

Mass Media The **mass media** include those means of communication that reach large, widely underlinedispersed audiences (masses of people) simultaneously. No one needs to be told that the mass media, including newspapers, magazines, radio, and in particular, television and the Internet, have a huge effect on the formation of public opinion.

dispersed
adj. scattered, spread out

Take this as but one indication: There is at least one television set in more than 98 percent of the nation's 115 million households. There are two or more sets in more than 80 million homes and millions more in many other places. Most of those sets are turned on for at least eight hours a day, for a mind-boggling total of more than a *billion* hours a day. You will take a longer look at the influence of the mass media later in this chapter.

Peer Groups People with whom one regularly associates, including friends, classmates, neighbors, co-workers, and the like, make up one's **peer group.** When a child enters school, friends and classmates become important agents in shaping his or her attitudes and behavior. The influence of peer groups continues on through adulthood.

Belonging to a peer group usually reinforces what a person has already come to believe. One obvious reason for this is that most people trust the views of their friends. Another is that the members of a peer group have shared many of the same socializing experiences, and so tend to think along the same or similar lines.

To put this observation another way, contradictory or other unsettling opinions are not often heard within a peer group. Most people want to be liked by their friends and associates. As a result, they are usually reluctant to stray too far from what their peers think and how they behave.

Opinion Leaders The views expressed by **opinion leaders** also bear heavily on the formation of public opinion. An opinion leader is any person who, for any reason, has an unusually strong influence on the views of others. These opinion shapers are a distinct minority in the total population, of course, but they are found everywhere.

Many opinion leaders hold public office. Some write for newspapers or magazines, or express their opinions on radio or television or the Internet. Others are prominent in business, labor, agriculture, and civic organizations. Many are professionals—doctors, lawyers, teachers, ministers, and rabbis—and have regular contact with large numbers of people. Many others are active members of their neighborhood or church, or have leadership roles in their local communities.

Whoever they may be—the President of the United States, a network television commentator, the governor, the head of a local citizens committee, or even a local talk-show host—these opinion leaders are people to whom others listen and from whom others draw ideas and convictions. Whatever their political, economic, or social standing or outlook may be, opinion leaders play a significant role in the formation of public opinion.

Historic Events Historic events can have a major impact on the views of large numbers of people—and so have a major impact on the content and direction of public policy. Clearly, the events of September 11, 2001, and the onset of the global war on terror constitute a leading illustration of that point. American views on national security and foreign policy have undergone dramatic shifts as a result of those events.

Our history affords many other examples, as well—not the least of them the Great Depression, which began in 1929 and lasted for the better part of a decade.

The Depression was a shattering national experience. Almost overnight, need and

"WE DO WANT TO WARN YOU THAT THIS NEWS HAS YET TO BE SPUN, SO YOU MAY HAVE TO FORMULATE YOUR OWN OPINION."

▶▶ **Analyzing Cartoons** An effort to shape the public's response is known as "spin." *What is the cartoonist implying about the media here?*

poverty became massive national problems. Hunger and despair stalked the land. In 1929, some two million people were unemployed in the United States. By just four years later, that number had climbed to 13.5 million. In 1935, some 18 million men, women, and children were wholly dependent on public emergency relief programs. Some 10 million workers had no employment other than that provided by temporary public projects.

All of this changed people's view of the proper place of government in the United States. The Depression persuaded a large majority of Americans to support an expanded role for government—in particular, for the National Government—in the nation's economic and social life.

The Great Depression also prompted a majority of Americans to shift their loyalties from the Republicans to the Democrats. The Republicans had dominated the national political scene from Lincoln's election in 1860 to the onset of the Depression. That situation changed abruptly when Franklin D. Roosevelt's landslide victory in 1932 began nearly 40 years of Democratic domination.

The turbulent politics of the 1960s and early 1970s furnish another example of the way in which significant occurrences can impact and shape opinions. The American people had emerged from World War II and the prosperity of the 1950s with a largely optimistic view of the future and of the United States' place in the world. That rose-colored outlook was reflected in a generally favorable, even respectful, attitude toward government in this country.

The 1960s and early 1970s changed all that. Those years were highlighted by a number of traumatic events. Of special note were the assassinations of President John Kennedy in 1963 and of the Reverend Martin Luther King, Jr., and Senator Robert Kennedy in 1968. This period also included the civil rights movement and the Vietnam War, with all of the protests, violence, and strong emotions that accompanied both of those chapters in this nation's life. The era ended with the Watergate scandal and the near-impeachment and subsequent resignation of President Richard Nixon in 1974.

Those years of turmoil and <u>divisiveness</u> produced a dramatic decline in the American people's estimate of their government—and most especially in their evaluation of its trustworthiness.

Many Americans became Democratic voters as a result of the Great Depression.

divisiveness
n. result of disagreement, tending to divide

Essential Questions
Journal
To continue to build a response to the chapter Essential Question, go to your **Essential Questions Journal.**

SECTION **1** ASSESSMENT

1. **Guiding Question** Use your completed concept web to answer this question: What is public opinion, and what factors help to shape it?

Key Terms and Comprehension

2. What does it mean to say that there are different "publics" that help make up **public opinion?**

3. To what kinds of issues and affairs is **public opinion** limited?

4. What are the two most important early influences on many people's political socialization?

5. What are the roles of **mass media, peer groups,** and **opinion leaders** in influencing public opinion?

Critical Thinking

6. **Make Generalizations** What features of peer groups explain why they tend to reinforce rather than challenge what a person believes?

7. **Identify Central Issues** What are some of the public issues that were brought to the forefront of public opinion in the wake of the terrorist attacks of September 11, 2001?

Quick Write

Cause-and-Effect Essay: Choose a Topic Using the Internet, other sources, and your textbook, identify a public affairs issue, such as the environment or energy, about which there are strong public opinions. Write a brief summary of the issue and cite at least two of the more prominent public opinions about the topic.

SECTION 2

Measuring Public Opinion

Guiding Question

How is public opinion measured and used? Use a table like the one below to take notes on the section.

Measuring Public Opinion	
Elections	Voting results can sometimes reflect public opinion.

Political Dictionary

- mandate
- interest group
- public opinion poll
- straw vote
- universe
- sample
- random sample
- quota sample

Objectives

1. Describe the challenges involved in measuring public opinion.
2. Explain why scientific opinion polls are the best way to measure public opinion.
3. Identify the five steps in the polling process.
4. Understand the problems in evaluating polls.
5. Recognize the limits on the impact of public opinion in a democracy.

Image Above: NBC News pollster conducts an election exit poll.

How often have you heard the phrase: "According to a recent poll . . ."? Probably more than you can count, especially in the months leading up to an election. Polls are one of the most common means of gauging public opinion.

If public policy is to reflect public opinion, one needs to be able to find the answers to these questions: What are people's opinions on a particular issue? How many people share a given view on that issue? How firmly do they hold that view? In other words, there must be a way to "measure" public opinion.

Measuring Public Opinion

The general shape of public opinion on an issue can be found through a number of key indicators. They include voting; lobbying; books; pamphlets; magazine and newspaper articles; editorial comments in the press and on radio, television, and the Internet; paid advertising; letters to editors and public officials; and so on.

These and other means of expression are the devices through which the general direction of public opinion becomes known. Usually though, the means by which a view is expressed tells little—and often nothing reliable—about the size of the group that holds that opinion or how strongly it is held. In the American political system, this information is critically important. To find it, some effort must be made to measure public opinion. Elections, interest groups, the media, and personal contacts with the public all—at least to some degree—provide the means by which that measurement can be done.

Elections In a democracy, the voice of the people is supposed to express itself through the ballot box. Election results are thus very often said to be indicators of public opinion. The votes cast for the various candidates are regularly taken as evidence of the people's approval or rejection of the stands taken by those candidates and their parties. As a result, a party and its victorious candidates regularly claim to have received a mandate to carry out their campaign promises. In American politics, a **mandate** refers to the instructions or commands a constituency gives to its elected officials.[2]

---

2 The term *mandate* comes from the Latin *mandatum,* meaning "a command."

In reality, however, election results are seldom an accurate measure of public opinion. Voters make choices in elections for any of several reasons, as you have seen. Very often, those choices have little or nothing to do with the candidates' stands on public questions. Then, too, candidates often disagree with some of the planks of their party's platform. And, as you know, candidates and parties often express their positions in broad, generalized terms.

In short, much of what you have read about voting behavior, and about the nature of parties, adds up to this: Elections are, at best, only useful indicators of public opinion. To call the typical election a mandate for much of anything other than a general direction in public policy is to be on very shaky ground.

Interest Groups Private organizations whose members share certain views and objectives, and who work to shape the making and the content of public policy are called **interest groups.** These organizations are also very <u>aptly</u> known as pressure groups and special-interest groups.

Interest groups are a chief means by which public opinion is made known. They present their views (exert their pressures) through their lobbyists, by letters, telephone calls, and e-mails, in political campaigns, and by other methods. In dealing with them, however, public officials often have difficulty determining two things: How many people does an interest group really represent? How strongly do those people hold the views that an organization says they hold?

The Media Earlier, you read some impressive numbers about television that help describe the place of the media in the opinion process; you will read more of those numbers later. Here, recognize this point: The media are also a gauge for assessing public opinion.

The media are frequently said to be "mirrors" as well as "molders" of opinion. It is often claimed that the views expressed in newspaper editorials, syndicated columns, news magazines, television commentaries, and blogs are fairly good indicators of public opinion. In fact, however, the media are not very accurate mirrors of public opinion, often reflecting only the views of a vocal minority.

Personal Contacts Most public officials have frequent and wide-ranging contacts in many different forms with large numbers of people. In each of these contacts, they try to read the public's mind. Indeed, their jobs demand that they do so.

✔ **Checkpoint**
How do interest groups present their views?

<u>aptly</u>
adv. fittingly, appropriately, suitably

How **Government** Works

Using Public Opinion

Public officials seek to measure public opinion through a variety of sources, as shown below. Whether or not a public official gets reelected may depend on how he or she responds to public opinion. *For what reasons is public opinion measured?*

Media	Serve as mirrors and molders of public opinion
The People	Convey their opinions in e-mails, letters, phone calls, or public meetings
Interest Groups	Share the views of their members in hopes of influencing policy

A candidate for office shakes hands with a voter on his way into a polling place. ▶

▶▶ **Analyzing Cartoons** A pollster is a person or group who researches public opinion. ***What do you think the cartoonist is saying about pollsters here?***

mishap
n. calamity, disaster, misfortune

Members of Congress receive bags of mail and hundreds of phone calls and e-mails every day. Many of them make frequent trips "to keep in touch with the folks back home." Top administration figures are often on the road, too, selling the President's programs and gauging the people's reactions. Even the President does some of this, with speaking trips to different parts of the country.

Governors, State legislators, mayors, and other officials also have any number of contacts with the public. These officials encounter the public in their offices, in public meetings, at social gatherings, community events, and even at ball games.

Can public officials find "the voice of the people" in all of those contacts? Many can and do, and often with surprising accuracy. But some public officials cannot. They fall into an ever-present trap: They find only what they want to find, only those views that support and agree with their own.

Public Opinion Polls

Public opinion is best measured by **public opinion polls,** devices that attempt to collect information by asking people questions.[3] The more accurate polls are based on scientific polling techniques.

Straw Votes Public opinion polls have existed in this country for more than a century. Until the 1930s, however, they were far from scientific. Most earlier polling efforts were of the **straw vote** variety.[4] That is, they were polls that sought to read the public's mind simply by asking the same question of a large number of people. Straw votes are still fairly common. Many radio talk-show hosts pose questions that listeners can respond to by telephone, and television personalities regularly invite responses by e-mail.

The straw-vote technique is highly unreliable, however. It rests on the mistaken assumption that a relatively large number of responses will provide a fairly accurate picture of the public's views on a given question. The problem is this: The respondents are self-selected. Nothing in the process ensures that those who respond will represent a reasonably accurate cross section of the total population. The straw vote emphasizes the quantity rather than the quality of the sample to which its question is put.

The most famous of all straw-polling mishaps took place in 1936. A widely read periodical, the *Literary Digest,* mailed postcard ballots to more than 10 million people and received answers from more than 2 million of them. Based on that huge return, the magazine confidently predicted the outcome of the presidential election that year. It said that Governor Alfred Landon, the Republican nominee, would easily defeat incumbent Franklin Roosevelt. Instead, Roosevelt won in a landslide. He captured more than 60 percent of the popular vote and carried every State but Maine and Vermont.

The *Digest* had drawn its sample on a faulty basis: from automobile registration lists and telephone directories. The *Digest* had failed to consider that in the mid-Depression year of 1936, millions of people could not afford to own cars or have private telephones.

The *Digest* poll failed to reach most of the vast pool of the poor and unemployed,

---

3 *Poll* comes from the old Teutonic word *polle,* meaning "the top or crown of the head," the part that shows when heads are counted.

4 The odd name comes from the fact that a straw, thrown up in the air, will indicate which way the wind is blowing.

millions of blue-collar workers, and most of the ethnic minorities in the country. Those were the very segments of the population from which Roosevelt and the Democrats drew their greatest support. The magazine had predicted the winner of each of the three previous presidential elections, but its failure to do so in 1936 was so colossal that it ceased publication not long thereafter.

Scientific Polling Serious efforts to take the public's pulse on a scientific basis date from the mid-1930s. They began with the work of such early pollsters as George Gallup and Elmo Roper. The techniques that they and others have developed over the decades since then have reached a highly sophisticated level.

There are now more than 1,000 national and regional polling organizations in this country. Many of them do mostly commercial work. That is, they tap the public's preferences on everything from toothpastes and headache remedies to television shows and thousands of other things. However, at least 200 of these polling organizations also poll the political preferences of the American people.

Among the best known of the national pollsters today are the Gallup Organization (the Gallup Poll) and the Pew Research Center for People and the Press.

A number of the leading national polls are joint efforts of major news-gathering and professional polling organizations. Their polls regularly report public attitudes on matters of current interest—including, for example, the level of public support of the President and/or Congress or, in election seasons, candidates running for such major offices as governor or member of the House or Senate. Those joint ventures that can most frequently be found in print and on television and the Internet include the ABC News/*The Washington Post* poll, the CBS News/*The New York Times* poll, the NBC/*The Wall Street Journal* poll, and the CNN/*USA Today*/Gallup poll.

The Polling Process

Scientific poll-taking is an extremely complex process that can best be described in five basic steps. In their efforts to discover and report public opinion, pollsters must

✔ **Checkpoint**
What do national polls do?

The Effect of Poll Wording on Reliability

How you ask the question...

"The Federal Government should see to it that all people have adequate housing.

55.1% Agree

44.9% Disagree

"Some people feel the Federal Government should see to it that all people have adequate housing, while others feel each person should provide his or her own housing. Which comes closest to how you feel about this?

44.6% Government responsible

55.4% Government not responsible

"Some people feel each person should provide his or her own housing, while others feel the Federal Government should see to it that all people have adequate housing. Which comes closest to how you feel about this?

29.5% Government responsible

70.5% Government not responsible

...affects the answer.

SOURCE: Questions and Answers in Attitude Surveys, 1981 & 1996

▸▸ Analyzing Charts This chart demonstrates the importance of carefully wording each question in a poll. ***Which question is worded in the least biased manner? How can you tell?***

sufficient
adj. adequate, enough

deliberately
adv. on purpose, knowingly, intentionally

(1) define the universe to be surveyed; (2) construct a sample; (3) prepare valid questions; (4) select and control how the poll will be taken; and (5) analyze and report their findings to the public.

Defining the Universe The **universe** is a term that means the whole population that the poll aims to measure. It is the group whose opinions the poll will seek to discover. That universe can be all voters in Chicago, or every high school student in Texas, or all Republicans in New England, or all Democrats in Georgia, or all Catholic women over age 35 in the United States, and so on.

Constructing a Sample If the universe is very small—say, the 30 members of a high school class—the best way to discover what that entire universe thinks about some matter would be to question all of its members. Most polls involve much larger universes, however—for example, all of the people who live in a particular city or State or the United States. Clearly, each of those universes is so large that it would be impossible to interview all of its members. So pollsters construct a **sample**—a representative slice of the total universe.

Most pollsters draw random samples (often called probability samples). A **random sample** is composed of randomly selected people, and so it is one in which all the members of its universe stand an equal chance of being interviewed. Recall, the sample used for the infamous *Literary Digest* poll in 1936 was not picked at random and so did not accurately reflect the universe it sought to measure.

Most major national polls regularly use samples composed of some 1,500 or so people to represent the nation's adult population (of more than 200 million people) today. How can the views of so few people possibly represent the views of so many?

The answer to that question lies in the mathematical law of probability. Flip a coin a thousand times. The law of probability says that, given an honest coin and an honest flip, heads will come up 500 times. The results of that exercise will be the same no matter how often it is repeated.

The law of probability is regularly applied in any number of situations—by insurance companies to compute life expectancies, by food quality inspectors to grade a farmer's truckload of beans, and by many others who "play the odds," including pollsters when they draw random samples.

In short, if the sample is of sufficient size and is properly selected at random from the entire universe, the law of probability says that the result will be accurate to within a small and predictable margin of error. Mathematicians tell us that a properly drawn random sample of some 1,500 people will reflect the opinions of the nation's entire adult population and be accurate to within a margin of plus or minus (±) 3 percent.

Pollsters agree that it is impossible to construct a sample that would be an absolutely accurate reflection of a large universe. Hence, the allowance for error. A margin of error of ±3 percent means a spread of 6 percentage points, of course. To reduce the sampling error from ±3 percent to ±1 percent, the size of the sample would have to be at least 9,500 people. The time and expense to interview so huge a sample make that impractical.

Some pollsters do use a less complicated, but less reliable, sampling method. They draw quota samples. A **quota sample** is one deliberately constructed to reflect the major characteristics of a given universe.

For example, if 51.3 percent of a universe is female, 17.5 percent of it is African American, and so on, then the quota sample will be made up of 51.3 percent females, 17.5 percent African Americans, and so on. Most of the people in the sample will belong to more than one of the categories used to build the sample. That fact is a major reason why such samples are less reliable than random samples.

Asking Well-Drawn Questions The way in which the questions are phrased is critically important to the reliability of any poll. To illustrate that point, most will probably say "yes" to a question put this way: "Should local taxes be reduced?" Many will also answer "yes" if asked this question: "Should the size of the city's police force be increased to fight the rising tide of crime in our community?" Yet, expanding the police force would almost certainly require more local tax dollars.

Evaluating Polls
Questions to Ask About Polls

Poll results are often published in newspapers, magazines, or online. You should learn to analyze such results carefully. Use the following questions as a starting point. *Why is it important to read poll results critically?*

WHO?
Who is responsible for the poll?

Polls sponsored by political campaigns may aim to mislead as much as inform.

WHAT?
What is the poll's universe?

The universe is the population the poll aims to measure. This allows you to judge whether the sample is truly representative.

HOW?
How was the sample chosen?

Samples should be selected randomly. How were questions written and asked? The method of creating and asking questions can alter the results.

WHY?
Why is the poll being conducted?

Polls meant to boost a candidate's approval ratings are not reliable.

WHEN?
When was the data collected?

Opinions change quickly during elections—so knowing when the data was collected is important.

Responsible pollsters recognize the problem and construct their questions with great care. They try to avoid "loaded," emotionally charged words and terms that are difficult to understand. They also try to avoid questions that are worded in a way that tends to shape the answers that will be given to them.

Interviewing How pollsters communicate with respondents can also affect accuracy. For decades, most polls were conducted door-to-door, face-to-face. That is, the interviewer questioned the respondent in person. Today, however, most pollsters do their work by telephone, with a sample selected by *random digit dialing.* Calls are placed to randomly chosen numbers within randomly chosen area codes around the country. Telephone surveys are less labor intensive and less expensive than door-to-door polling. Still, most professional pollsters see advantages and drawbacks to each approach. But they all agree that only one technique, not a combination of the two, should be used in any given poll.

The interview itself is a very sensitive point in the process. An interviewer's tone of voice or the emphasis he or she gives to certain words can

influence a respondent's replies and so affect the validity of a poll. If the questions are not carefully worded, some of the respondent's replies may be snap judgments or emotional reactions. Others may be answers that the person being interviewed thinks "ought" to be given. Thus, polling organizations try to hire and train their interviewing staffs very carefully.

Analyzing Findings Polls, whether scientific or not, try to measure people's attitudes. To be of any real value, however, someone must analyze and report the results. Scientific polling organizations today collect huge amounts of raw data. In order to handle these data, computers and other electronic hardware have become routine parts of the process. Pollsters use these technologies to tabulate and interpret their data, draw their conclusions, and then publish their findings.

Evaluating Polls

How good are polls? On balance, the major national polls are fairly reliable. So, too, are most of the regional surveys around the country. Still, they are far from perfect. Fortunately, most responsible pollsters readily acknowledge the limits of their polls. Many of them are involved in continuing efforts to refine every aspect of the polling process.

Pollsters know that they have difficulty measuring the intensity, stability, and relevance of the opinions they report. *Intensity* is the strength of feeling with which an opinion is held. *Stability* (or fluidity) is the relative permanence or changeableness of an opinion. *Relevance* (or pertinence) is how important a particular opinion is to the person who holds it.

Polls and pollsters are sometimes said to shape the opinions they are supposed to measure. Some critics say that in an election, for example, pollsters often create a "bandwagon effect." That is, some voters, wanting to be with the winner, jump on the bandwagon of the candidate who is ahead in the polls.

In spite of these criticisms, it is clear that scientific polls are the most useful tools there are for the difficult task of measuring public opinion. Although they may not always be precisely accurate, they do offer reasonably reliable guides to public thought. Moreover, they help to focus attention on public questions and to stimulate the discussion of them.

Limits on the Impact

More than a century ago, the Englishman Lord Bryce described government in the United States as "government by public opinion." Clearly, the energy devoted to measuring public opinion in this country suggests something of its powerful role in American politics. However, Lord Bryce's observation is true only if it is understood to mean that public opinion is the major, but by no means the only, force at work to influence public policy in this country.

Most importantly, remember that our system of constitutional government is not designed to give free, unrestricted play to public opinion—and especially not to majority opinion. In particular, the doctrines of separation of powers and of checks and balances, and the constitutional guarantees of civil rights and liberties are intended to protect minority interests against the excesses of majority views and actions.

Finally, polls are not elections, nor are they substitutes for elections. It is when faced with a ballot that the voter must decide for himself or herself what is important and what is not. He or she must be able to tell the difference between opinions and concrete information, and appreciate the difference between personalities and platforms.

Democracy involves far more than a simple measuring of the various opinions people hold. At base, democracy is all about making careful choices among leaders and their positions on public issues, and among the actions that may flow from those choices.

Essential Questions Journal To continue to build a response to the chapter Essential Question, go to your **Essential Questions Journal.**

SECTION 2 ASSESSMENT

1. **Guiding Question** Use your completed table to answer the question: How is public opinion measured and used?

Key Terms and Comprehension

2. Why do victorious candidates sometimes claim a **mandate**?

3. Why is it difficult to determine much about public opinion based on the actions of **interest groups?**

4. Why are **straw votes** a generally unreliable form of measuring public opinion?

5. Identify the five steps in the polling process.

Critical Thinking

6. **Analyze Information** What are the benefits and drawbacks of releasing to the public the results of public opinion polls on upcoming elections?

7. **Recognize Ideologies** Give an example of how our system of government works to minimize the influence of public opinion on certain types of decisions.

Quick Write

Cause-and-Effect Essay: Research the Topic Use the Internet and other resources to collect information about the history of the topic you chose in Section 1. Find out when the topic first gained prominence in American social life and what events, trends, or factors have had a significant impact on public opinion about that topic.

Conducting a Poll

We live in a representative democracy in which the voters elect representatives to act on their behalf. Your school's student government may operate the same way. One way representatives can gain insight into the thoughts and feelings of their constituents—that is, understand public opinion—is to conduct a poll. A well-constructed poll can help provide solid information about what a group of people thinks. Yet putting together a good poll requires knowledge and skill.

Follow these simple steps to conduct an effective poll.

1. **Define the universe.** In polling, the universe is the group of people whose opinion you are interested in learning about. For a presidential candidate, it may be all the voters in the country. For a candidate for student council, it may be all the students in a school, and so on.

2. **Construct your sample.** In some cases, you may be able to poll every person in the universe. If that is not possible, you must identify whom you will poll—your *sample*. Your sample should be a number of people chosen randomly from the universe. The goal is to poll a group that represents the whole universe in its views and attitudes.

Note: The people who volunteer to be polled or who walk by a specific corner of your school or community are not a random sample.

3. **Prepare valid questions.** Good poll questions do not lead people to an answer or convey a strong attitude about an issue. They provide enough information to frame the question properly, but not so much that they promote one response or another. Before you conduct your poll, invite friends or colleagues to review your questions to help ensure their reliability and objectivity.

4. **Conduct interviews carefully.** Just as a pollster must prepare questions carefully, he or she must ask questions carefully. Remember, the goal is to get answers that truly reflect people's attitudes at the time. An interviewer must be careful not to seem to lead respondents to a particular answer.

5. **Interpret the results.** Polls are not perfect. If you have used a random sample, your results will contain a margin of error. When you interpret your results, remember to analyze the intensity, the stability, and the relevance of the opinions you collect.

▸▸ What do you think?

1. Why do you think that selecting your sample from volunteers or from a group that passes by a specific hallway or corner might not be a valid random sample?

2. Explain how an interviewer's behavior affects the way people respond to a poll question.

3. **You Try It** Follow the steps laid out here, and design a public opinion poll about an issue in your school or community with detailed descriptions of the universe, how you will construct your sample, and what questions you will ask.

GOVERNMENT ONLINE
Citizenship Activity Pack
For activities on conducting polls, go to
PearsonSuccessNet.com

SECTION 3

The Mass Media

Guiding Question

How has the development of different media helped inform the public about politics? Use the flowchart like the one below to take notes on the development of different media.

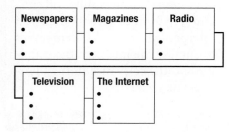

Political Dictionary
- medium
- weblog
- public agenda
- sound bite

Objectives
1. Examine the role of the mass media in providing the public with political information.
2. Explain how the mass media influence politics.
3. Understand the factors that limit the influence of the media.

Image Above: People get their news from various media outlets, such as the Internet.

How much television do you watch each day? Little or none? Two hours a day? Three hours? More? However much you watch, you no doubt know that your peers spend a great deal of time in front of the TV. Studies show that by the time the average student graduates from high school today, he or she will have spent nearly 11,000 hours in classrooms and nearly 15,000 hours watching television. On average, high school students now watch more than 20 hours of TV programming each week.

Television has an extraordinary impact on the lives of everyone in this country. So do all of the other elements of the mass media.

The Role of Mass Media

A **medium** is a means of communication; it transmits some kind of information. *Media* is the plural of medium. The *mass media* include those means of communication that can reach large, widely dispersed audiences simultaneously.

Five major elements of the mass media are especially significant in American politics today. Ranked in terms of their impact, they are television, the Internet, newspapers, radio, and magazines. Other forms of the media, including books, films, and satellite radio, play a lesser but still relevant role in the political process.

Importantly, the mass media do not function as an arm of government in the United States. They are, instead, almost entirely privately owned and operated. And, unlike political parties and interest groups, their prime goal is *not* that of influencing the course of public affairs. They are, nonetheless, an extremely potent force in American politics.

Along with entertainment, the media provide political information. They do so directly when they report the news, in a television newscast or in the news columns of a newspaper, for example. The media also provide a large amount of political information less directly—for example, in radio and television programs, magazine articles, and blogs. These venues often deal with such public topics as crime, healthcare, climate change, or some aspect of American foreign policy. Either way, people acquire most of what they know about government and politics from the various forms of media.

Television Politics and television have gone hand in hand since the technology first appeared. The first public demonstration of television occurred at the New York World's Fair in 1939. President Franklin Roosevelt opened the fair on camera, and a <u>comparative</u> handful of local viewers watched him do so on tiny five- and seven-inch screens.

World War II interrupted the development of the new medium, but it began to become generally available in the late 1940s. Television boomed in the 1950s. The first transcontinental broadcast came in 1951, when President Harry Truman, speaking in Washington, D.C., addressed the delegates attending the Japanese Peace Treaty Conference in San Francisco.

Today, television is <u>all-pervasive.</u> As you read earlier, there is at least one television set in 98 percent of the nation's 115 million households. Just a few years ago, there were more homes in this country with television sets than with indoor plumbing facilities!

Television replaced newspapers as the principal source of political information for a majority of Americans in the early 1960s. Now, television is the principal source of news for an estimated 80 percent of the population.

The more than 1,700 television stations in this country include more than 1,400 commercial outlets and some 350 public broadcasters. Three major national networks have dominated television from its infancy: the Columbia Broadcasting System (CBS), the American Broadcasting Company (ABC), and the National Broadcasting Company (NBC). Those three giants furnish most of the programming for more than 500 local stations, and that programming accounts for nearly half of all television viewing time today.

The major networks' audience share has been declining in recent years, however. The main challenges to them have come from three sources: (1) several independent broadcasting groups—for example, the Fox Network; (2) cable broadcasters, such as Turner Broadcasting, and especially its Cable News Network (CNN); and (3) the Public Broadcasting System (PBS) and its more than 350 local stations.[5]

Newspapers The first regularly published newspaper in America, the *Boston News-Letter,* appeared in 1704.[6] Other papers soon followed, in Boston and then in Philadelphia, New York, Annapolis, and elsewhere. By 1775, 37 newspapers were being published

✔ **Checkpoint**
What is the principal news source for the majority of Americans?

comparative
adj. by comparison

all-pervasive
adj. spread throughout

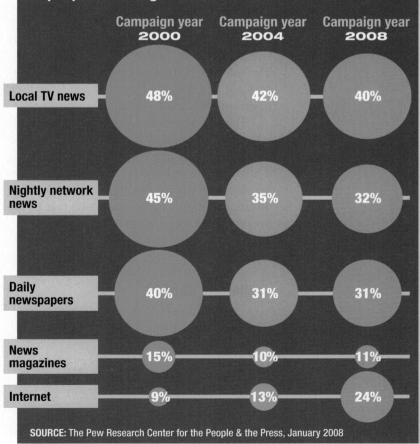

Where do we get our campaign news?

The number of Americans who use the Internet as their source for campaign news has more than doubled since 2000. *How does this compare with the number of people watching network or local television?*

	Campaign year 2000	Campaign year 2004	Campaign year 2008
Local TV news	48%	42%	40%
Nightly network news	45%	35%	32%
Daily newspapers	40%	31%	31%
News magazines	15%	10%	11%
Internet	9%	13%	24%

SOURCE: The Pew Research Center for the People & the Press, January 2008

---

5 C-SPAN, the Cable-Satellite Public Affairs Network, is sponsored by the cable industry. C-SPAN, C-SPAN2, and C-SPAN3 cover a broad range of public events—including major floor debates and committee hearings in Congress, presidential and other press conferences, and speeches by notable public figures.

6 The world's first newspaper was almost certainly the *Acta Diurna,* a daily gazette in Rome dating from 59 B.C. Another very early forerunner of today's newspapers was *Tsing Pao,* a court journal in Beijing. Press historians believe that its first issues, printed from stone blocks, were published beginning in A.D. 618; its last issue appeared in 1911.

The Power of the Press

The phrase "yellow journalism" came about in the late 1800s when competing newspaper owners William Randolph Hearst and Joseph Pulitzer used dramatic headlines and editorials instead of facts to stir up public opinion in favor of war with Spain—and to sell more papers. Historians say that "nothing better illustrates the power of the press and the misuse of that power" as well as the Spanish-American War. ***Does yellow journalism exist today?***

"You furnish the pictures . . . I'll furnish the war."

—William Randolph Hearst, 1897

in the colonies. All of them were weekly papers, and they were printed on one sheet that was usually folded to make four pages. The nation's first daily newspaper, the *Pennsylvania Evening Post and Daily Advertiser,* began publication in 1783.

Those first papers regularly carried political news. Several spurred the colonists to revolution, carrying the news of independence and the text of the Declaration of Independence to people throughout the colonies. Thomas Jefferson marked the vital role of the press in the earliest years of the nation when, in 1787, he wrote to a friend:

PRIMARY SOURCE

. . . were it left to me to decide whether we should have a government without newspapers or newspapers without a government, I should not hesitate a moment to prefer the latter.

—Thomas Jefferson, Letter to Colonel Edward Carrington, January 16, 1787

The 1st Amendment, added to the Constitution in 1791, made the same point regarding the importance of newspapers with its guarantee of the freedom of the press.

Today, more than 10,000 newspapers are published in the United States, including some 1,430 dailies, more than 7,200 weeklies, some 550 semiweeklies, and several hundred foreign-language papers. Those publications have a combined circulation of about 150 million copies per issue. About 45 percent of the nation's adult population read a newspaper every day, and they spend, on average, a half hour doing so.

The number of daily newspapers has been declining for decades, however, from more than 2,000 in 1920 to 1,745 in 1980 and to about 1,430 today. Radio and television, and more recently the Internet, have been major factors in that downward trend.

Nevertheless, newspapers are still an important source of information about government and politics. Most papers cover stories in greater depth than television does, and many try to present various points of view in their editorial sections. Those newspapers that have the most substantial reputations and national influence today include *The New York Times, The Washington Post, The Wall Street Journal,* and *USA Today.*

Most newspapers are local papers. That is, most of their readers live in or near the communities in which those papers are published. While many local papers do provide some national and international news coverage, most of them focus on events closer to home.

Advances in telecommunications and computerized operations are changing that basic fact, however. Now, each day's editions of *USA Today, The New York Times,* and *The Wall Street Journal* are generally available on the day of publication around the country.

Radio Radio as it exists today began in 1920. On November 2 of that year, station KDKA in Pittsburgh went on the air with presidential election returns. The new medium soon became immensely popular.

By the 1930s, radio had assumed much of the role in American society that television has today. It was a major entertainment medium, and millions of people planned their daily schedules around their favorite programs. The networks also provided the nation with dramatic coverage of important events, and radio exposed the American people to national and international politics as never before.

President Franklin Roosevelt was the first major public figure to use radio effectively. The late author David Halberstam described the impact of FDR's famous fireside chats:

"

PRIMARY SOURCE

He was the first great American radio voice. For most Americans of [that] generation, their first memory of politics would be of sitting by a radio and hearing that voice, strong, confident, totally at ease. . . . Most Americans in the previous 160 years had never even seen a President; now almost all of them were hearing him, in their own homes. It was literally and figuratively electrifying.

—David Halberstam, *The Powers That Be*

Many thought that the arrival of television would bring the end of radio as a major medium. Radio has survived, however, in large part because it is so conveniently available. People can hear music, news, sports, and other radio programs in a great many places where they cannot watch television—in their cars, at work, in remote areas, and in any number of other places and situations. The arrival of satellite radio has added to radio's popularity. With this new technology, digital radio signals are beamed from a communications satellite, allowing subscribers to tune into their favorite station anywhere in the country, and often with no commercial interruptions.

Radio remains a major source of news and other political information. The average person hears some 15 hours of radio each week. No one knows how many millions of radios there are in this country—in homes, offices, cars, backpacks, and a great many other places. Those radios can pick up some 14,000 stations on the AM and FM dials.

Many AM stations are affiliated with one or another of the national networks. Unlike television, however, most radio programming is local. There are also some 700 public radio stations, most of them on the FM dial. These noncommercial outlets are part of National Public Radio (NPR), which is radio's counterpart of television's PBS.

Most radio stations spend little time on public affairs today. Many do devote a few minutes every hour to "the news"—really, to a series of headlines. All-news stations are now found in most of the larger and many medium-sized communities. They are usually on the air 24 hours a day, and they do provide somewhat more extensive coverage of the day's events. A growing number of stations now serve the preferences of Latino Americans, African Americans, and other minority listeners.

Over recent years, talk radio has become an important source of political comment. The opinions and analyses offered by a number of talk show hosts can be found on hundreds of stations across the United States. Among the most prominent talk broadcasters today are conservatives Rush Limbaugh, Sean Hannity, and Bill O'Reilly, and liberals Thom Hartmann and Rachel Maddow. Their programs air nationally and attract millions of listeners every weekday.

Magazines Several magazines were published in colonial America. Benjamin Franklin began one of the very first, his *General Magazine,* in Philadelphia in 1741. On into the early 1900s, most magazines published in the United States were generally devoted to literature and the social graces. The first political magazines—among them, *Harper's Weekly* and the *Atlantic Monthly*—appeared in the mid-1800s.

The progressive reform period in the early 1900s spawned several journals of opinion, including a number that featured articles by the day's leading muckrakers.[7] For decades before radio and television, magazines constituted the only national medium.

Some 12,000 magazines are published in the United States today. Most are trade publications,

---

7 The *muckrakers* were journalists who exposed wrongdoing in politics, business, and industry. The term was coined by Theodore Roosevelt in 1906 and is derived from the raking of muck—that is, manure and other barnyard debris. The muckrakers set the pattern for what is now called investigative reporting.

---

such as *Veterinary Forum* and the *Automotive Executive,* or periodicals that target some special personal interest, such as *Golf Digest, Teen,* and *American Rifleman.* Among magazines with the highest circulation today: *AARP the Magazine, Reader's Digest,* and *National Geographic.* They each sell some 10 to 20 million or more copies per issue.

Three news magazines, *Time, Newsweek,* and *U.S. News & World Report,* rank in the top 35 periodicals in terms of circulation. They have a combined circulation of nearly 10 million copies a week, and they are important sources of political news and comment. There are a number of other magazines devoted to public affairs, most of them vehicles of opinion, including the *Nation,* the *New Republic,* the *National Review,* and the *Weekly Standard.*

The Internet The Internet is fast becoming a leading source of political news and information for the American people. Its roots can be traced to a Defense Department research project of the Cold War era. In 1969, the DoD's Advanced Research Projects Agency established a four-computer network in the

The Transformation of Mass Media

As media have changed, so too has the way that people participate. *What has been the impact of the Internet on political discussion?*

Radio spread widely in the 1920s and 1930s, giving a national voice to elected officials and gifted speakers.

The **"big three" networks,** ABC, CBS, and NBC, dominated the limited channels of early television. Nightly news programs by respected anchors, such as Walter Cronkite (right), commanded large audiences and set the agenda for the nation.

THEN... A Few Voices Imparting Information

Pentagon designed to protect military secrets from hostile actions. Two years later that grid (ARPANET) had grown to include some two dozen computers at 15 widely scattered locations across the country.

From those beginnings, the Internet has grown phenomenally, and it continues to do so. By the 1990s, it had expanded into the private sector, and by the beginning of the 21st century, it had become a mass medium. Today, more than 75 percent of the American people report that they have access to a computer at home, in the workplace, or at school, and nearly two-thirds of them say they go online on a regular basis.

Television remains the most widely used source for political news and information, but the Internet is now in second place, ahead of newspapers, radio, and magazines. One of every four people say they regularly go online to "get the news." Younger people are especially <u>inclined</u> to do so.

Other media have recognized the Internet's capabilities. Nearly all newspapers have Web sites where all or most of the stories carried in their print versions can be found. Most magazines are also available online, and most television stations maintain home pages that provide links to many other sources. With only a few exceptions, media outlets allow visitors to view their Web sites free of charge.

Much the same can be said of virtually all government agencies, interest groups, political parties, elected officials, and candidates' campaign organizations. The extraordinary range of printed, audio, and visual information available on the Internet really defies description. To the point, much of the updated factual content of this textbook has been drawn from reliable Internet sources.

The Internet has <u>spawned</u> the growth of **weblogs**—often called "blogs"—Web site postings usually devoted to some specific subject. Many are written by single authors, others are the work of several contributors, and many allow visitors to post their own comments. Those blogs devoted to government and politics typically feature links to articles and commentaries from a variety of sources. Podcasts, digital recordings that are posted and can be downloaded from the Internet, have also grown spectacularly over recent years.

✔ **Checkpoint**
What are weblogs?

spawned
v. produced, brought forth

inclined
adj. persuaded, convinced

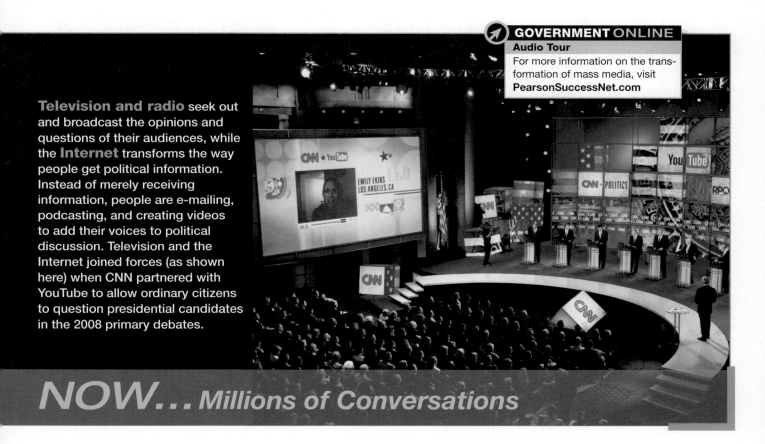

Television and radio seek out and broadcast the opinions and questions of their audiences, while the **Internet** transforms the way people get political information. Instead of merely receiving information, people are e-mailing, podcasting, and creating videos to add their voices to political discussion. Television and the Internet joined forces (as shown here) when CNN partnered with YouTube to allow ordinary citizens to question presidential candidates in the 2008 primary debates.

GOVERNMENT ONLINE
Audio Tour
For more information on the transformation of mass media, visit **PearsonSuccessNet.com**

NOW... Millions of Conversations

Media Influence

The mass media have a great impact on the issues that people focus on and how they think about the world around them. **What do these cartoons say about media influence?**

"That's not my political opinion. That's just stuff I hear on the radio."

The Media and Politics

Clearly, the media play a significant role in American politics. Just how significant that role is, and just how much influence the media have, is the subject of a long, still unsettled debate.

Whatever its weight, the media's influence can be seen in any number of situations. It is most visible in two particular areas: (1) the public agenda and (2) the field of electoral politics.

The Public Agenda The media play a very large role in shaping the **public agenda,** the societal problems that the nation's political leaders and the general public agree need government attention. As they report and comment on events, issues, policies, and personalities, the media determine to a very large extent what public matters the people will think and talk about—and, so, those matters about which public-policy makers will be most concerned.

Put another way, the media have the power to focus the public's attention on a specific issue. They do so by emphasizing some things and downplaying others. For example, they feature certain items on the front page or at the top of the newscast and bury others in the latter pages or segments of the program.

It is not correct to say that the media tell the people *what* to think; but it is clear that they tell the people what to think *about.* A look at any issue of a daily newspaper or a quick review of the content of any television or Internet news story will demonstrate that point. Remember, people rely on the media for most of the information they receive on public issues.

The mass media also have a direct impact on the nation's leaders. Some years ago, Stephen Hess, a widely respected authority on the media, identified several news organizations that form the "inner ring" of influence in Washington, D.C. He cited the three major television networks, CBS, ABC, and NBC; three newspapers, *The New York Times, The Washington Post,* and *The Wall Street Journal;* the leading news wire service, the Associated Press (AP); and the three major news weeklies, *Time, Newsweek,* and *U.S. News & World Report.* CNN, MSNBC, Fox News, Reuters, and *USA Today* have since joined that select group.

Top political figures in and out of government pay close and continuing attention to these sources. In fact, the President receives a daily digest of the news reports, analyses, and editorial comments that these and other sources broadcast and publish.

Electoral Politics You have seen several illustrations of the media's importance in electoral politics as you have read this book. Recall, for example, the fact that the media, and in particular television, have contributed to a decline in the place of political parties in American politics.

Television has made candidates far less dependent on party organizations than they once were. Before television, the major parties generally dominated the election process. They recruited most candidates who ran for office, and they ran those candidates' campaigns. The candidates depended on party organizations in order to reach the voters.

Now, both television and the Internet allow candidates to appeal directly to the people, without the help of a party organization. Candidates for office need not be experienced politicians who have worked their way up a party's political ladder over the course of several elections. It is not unusual for candidates to assemble their own campaign organizations and operate with only loose connections to their political parties.

Remember, too, that how voters see a candidate—the impressions they have of that candidate's personality, character, abilities, and so on—is one of the major factors that influence voting behavior. Candidates and professional campaign managers are quite aware of this fact. They know that the kind of "image" a candidate projects in the media can have a telling effect on the outcome of an election.

Candidates regularly try to manipulate media coverage to their advantage. Campaign strategists understand that, even with the Internet, most people learn almost everything they know about a candidate from

television. They therefore plan campaigns that emphasize television exposure. Such technical considerations as timing, location, lighting, and camera angles loom large, often at the expense of such substantive matters as the issues involved in an election or a candidate's qualifications for public office.

Good campaign managers also know that most television news programs are built out of stories that (1) take no more than a minute or two of air time, and (2) show people doing something interesting or exciting. Newscasts seldom feature "talking heads," speakers who drone on and on about some complex issue.

Instead, newscasts featuring candidates are usually short, sharply focused **sound bites**—snappy reports that can be aired in 30 or 45 seconds or so. Staged and carefully orchestrated visits to historic sites, factory gates, toxic-waste dumps, football games, and the like, have become a standard part of the electoral scene.

Limits on Media Influence

Having said all this, it is all too easy to overstate the media's role in American politics. A number of built-in factors work to limit the media's impact on the behavior of the American voting public.

For one thing, few people follow international, national, or even local political events very closely. Many studies of voting behavior show that in the typical election, only about 10 percent of those who can vote and only about 15 percent of those who do vote are well informed on the many candidates and issues involved in that election. In short, only a small part of the public actually takes in and understands much of what the media have to say about public affairs.

Moreover, most people who do pay some attention to politics are likely to be selective about it. That is, they most often watch, listen to, and read those sources that generally agree with their own viewpoints. They regularly ignore those sources with which they disagree. Thus, for example, many Democrats do not watch the televised campaign appearances or visit the Web sites of Republican candidates. Nor do many Republicans

✔ **Checkpoint**
How do candidates use media coverage to their advantage?

read newspaper stories about the campaign efforts of Democratic candidates.

Another important limit on the media's impact is the content the media carries. This is especially true of radio and television. Most television programs, for example, have little or nothing to do with public affairs, at least not directly. (A number of popular programs do relate to public affairs in an indirect way, however. Thus, many are "crime shows," and crime is certainly a matter of public concern. Many also carry a political message—for example, that the police are hard-working public servants.)

Advertisers who pay the high costs of television air time want to reach the largest possible audiences. Because most people are more interested in being entertained than in being informed about public issues, few public-affairs programs air in prime time. There are exceptions, however, including *60 Minutes, 20/20, Dateline,* and *Anderson Cooper 360.*

Radio and television mostly "skim" the news. They report only what their news editors determine to be the most important or the most interesting stories of the day. Even on widely watched evening news programs, most reports are presented in 60- to 90-second time slots. In short, the broadcast media seldom give the kind of in-depth coverage that a good newspaper can supply.

Newspapers are not as <u>hampered</u> as many other media in their ability to cover public affairs. Still, much of the content of most newspapers is nonpolitical. Like nearly all of television and radio, newspapers depend on their advertising revenues, which in turn depend on producing a product with the widest possible appeal. Newspaper readers are often more interested in the sports pages and the social, travel, advertising, and entertainment sections of a newspaper than they are in its news and editorial pages.

In-depth coverage of public affairs is available in the media to those who want it and will seek it out. There are a number of good newspapers around the country. In-depth coverage can also be found on the Internet, in several magazines, and on a number of radio and television stations, including public broadcast outlets. Remember, however, that there is nothing about democracy that guarantees an alert and informed public. Like voting and other forms of political participation, being an informed citizen requires some effort.

hampered
v. restricted, curbed, limited

SECTION **3** ASSESSMENT

Essential Questions Journal To continue to build a response to the chapter Essential Question, go to your **Essential Questions Journal.**

1. **Guiding Question** Use your completed flowchart to answer this question: How has the development of different media helped inform the public about politics?

Key Terms and Comprehension

2. Cite an example of an influential **medium** in our society.

3. What is the status of newspapers today compared to, say, 1980, and what are the likely explanations for the change that has occurred?

4. What is the media's role in shaping the **public agenda?**

5. What are **sound bites,** and what do they suggest about the limits of the media's influence?

Critical Thinking

6. **Predict Consequences** What might happen to the influence of the media if the 1st Amendment guarantee of freedom of the press were to be repealed?

7. **Recognize Cause and Effect** What are some of the effects of the fact that most television viewers want to be entertained rather than informed?

Quick Write

Cause-and-Effect Essay: Write a Thesis Statement A thesis outlines the subject of your essay. Write a thesis statement for a cause-and-effect essay on the topic you chose in Section 1. You will use your thesis to develop an organizational structure for your essay.

GOVERNMENT ONLINE

On the Go
To review anytime, anywhere,
download these online resources
at **PearsonSuccessNet.com**
Political Dictionary, Audio Review

CHAPTER **8**

Quick Study Guide

Guiding Question
Section 2 How is
public opinion
measured and used?

Guiding Question
Section 1 What is
public opinion, and
what factors help to
shape it?

CHAPTER 8
Essential Question
What is the place of the
media and public
opinion in a democracy?

Guiding Question
Section 3 How has
the development of
different media helped
inform the public about
politics?

Political Dictionary

public affairs p. 215
public opinion p. 215
mass media p. 217
peer group p. 218
opinion leader p. 218
mandate p. 220
interest group p. 221
public opinion poll p. 222
straw vote p. 222
universe p. 224
sample p. 224
random sample p. 224
quota sample p. 224
medium p. 228
weblog p. 233
public agenda p. 234
sound bite p. 235

The Mass Media's Impact on Public Opinion

Benefits	Limits
• Help shape the public agenda	• Only a small number of people follow media very closely.
• Influence electoral politics	• People tend to be selective in choosing political coverage.
• In-depth media coverage is available to those who look for it, particularly on the Internet.	• Much media content is shallow and unrelated to political affairs.
• Changing nature of the media allows for more people to actively participate in discussions.	• Media, such as radio and television, tend to carry only short reports on general news and politics.
• Publication of poll results allows media to show how public opinion is measured.	• Newspapers and television depend on advertising revenue, which can sometimes dictate coverage.

Media Influence on American Politics

Public Agenda	Electoral Politics
● Direct the public's attention to certain issues	● Allow candidates to be less dependent on political parties
● Influence public officials through editorials, analyses, and news reports	● Help candidates reach people directly through television and the Internet

Chapter Assessment

Comprehension and Critical Thinking

Section 1

1. **(a)** What constitutes a "public" in the United States? **(b)** Why is the opinion of the public about a popular movie or television program not a good example of public opinion?

2. **(a)** What are the earliest influences on a person's attitudes about public matters? **(b)** What are factors that might influence a person's public opinions after he or she leaves school?

3. **(a)** What factors do you think give an opinion leader the ability to shape public opinion? **(b)** What kinds of historic events are most likely to lead to a significant change in public opinion?

Section 2

4. **Analyze Political Cartoons (a)** What does this cartoon suggest about opinion polls? **(b)** How does the cartoon exaggerate or down, lay the import of opinion polls?

5. **(a)** Why are many interested in learning the content of public opinion? **(b)** What can you learn by examining such measures of public opinion as magazine and newspaper articles, editorials, and letters to the editor? **(c)** What is the relationship between elections and public opinion?

6. **(a)** Why are scientifically conducted polls described as the best measure of public opinion? **(b)** What features must a poll have in order to be considered an accurate measure of public opinion?

7. **(a)** What are three factors that even scientifically constructed polls have difficulty accounting for? **(b)** In addition to their occasional inaccuracy, what is another common criticism of polls? **(c)** Why do polls sometimes differ from election results?

Section 3

8. **(a)** What makes television perhaps the most effective of the different forms of media? **(b)** How has the growth of the Internet affected other media?

9. **(a)** What are the two ways the media affect politics? **(b)** How does the concept of the "sound bite" illustrate how the media affect politicians and how they work today?

10. **(a)** How does the content of most media programming limit the media's influence on public opinion? **(b)** How do the attitudes of the American people affect the influence of the media on public opinion?

Writing About Government

11. Use your Quick Write exercises from each Section Assessment to write a cause-and-effect essay about the public affairs issue you selected in Section 1. Be sure to clearly highlight the causes and effects of the issue. Note that there can be multiple causes. See pp. S3–S5 in the Skills Handbook.

Apply What You've Learned

12. **Essential Question Activity** For five days, keep a log of all the time you spend viewing or otherwise interacting with a form of mass media. In addition to keeping track of the number of hours you spend, record:

    (a) what programs you watch or listen to, and what articles you read;

    (b) whether the program discusses any public affairs topics (include entertainment programs that deal with public affairs topics); and

    (c) what you learned about public affairs.

13. **Essential Question Assessment** Based on your research and the content you have learned in this chapter, write a newspaper editorial that helps to answer the Essential Question: **What is the place of the media and public opinion in a democracy?** Your editorial should focus on your interaction with the media and how or whether it had any impact on your opinions on public affairs.

Essential Questions **Journal**	To respond to the chapter Essential Question, go to your **Essential Questions Journal.**

Document-Based Assessment

The Impact of Television on Political Events

In 1960, most people who listened to the Nixon-Kennedy debates on the radio thought the candidates performed equally well, but those who watched the debates on television, thought John Kennedy looked vibrant while Richard Nixon looked pale and listless. The power of the media to influence public opinion—and shape history—is well demonstrated throughout our history, as shown in the documents below.

Document 1

The Nixon-Kennedy debates' significance extended well beyond 1960. The use of television to transmit an image or idea instantly to millions soon made presidential campaigns more of a spectator sport—leading to campaign concepts and phrases such as 'catchy sound bites,' the 'likability' factor and mass marketing.

—Excerpt from "JFK, Nixon usher in marriage of TV, politics" by Greg Botelho from cnn.com

Document 2

Document 3

In the area of political affairs, the impact of television has been widely condemned. As the dominant form of mass communication, television is said to have contributed to a variety of maladies including reduced voter turnout, discounting of substantive issues in political campaigns, decline of the political parties, [and] automatic reelection of incumbents. . . . As the public's 'mind's eye,' television effectively sets the political agenda; the themes and issues that are repeated in television news coverage become the priorities of viewers.

—Excerpt from *Is Anyone Responsible?: How Television Frames Political Issues* by Shanto Iyengar

---

Use your knowledge of the media and Documents 1–3 to answer the following questions.

1. Which statement best summarizes Document 1?
   A. The use of television in the Nixon-Kennedy debates led to increased voter turnout.
   B. The Nixon-Kennedy debates had a huge impact on television programming.
   C. Presidential campaigns as they were known changed dramatically when television began to broadcast the debates.
   D. The phrase "catchy sound bites" came out of the debates.

2. In Document 2, what is the cartoonist's point of view regarding television news?

3. What does Document 3 suggest about the influence of television?

4. **Pull It Together** How do you think the impact of television, and the media in general, will change over time? Consider audience, users, and technology.

GOVERNMENT ONLINE
Documents
To find additional primary sources on the impact of the media, visit **PearsonSuccessNet.com**

Interest Groups

Essential Question
To what extent do interest groups advance or harm democracy?

" For all our **variety,** we are **interconnected, intersected,** and **interwoven** by organizations— arguably more so than any other modern nation.

—James Cortada and Edward Waking, *Betting on America,* 2002

Photo: UNITE HERE, a powerful interest group, marches in New York City's Labor Day parade.

GOVERNMENT ONLINE
On the Go

To study anywhere, anytime, download these online resources at PearsonSuccessNet.com
• Political Dictionary
• Audio Review
• Downloadable Interactivities

241

SECTION 1

The **Nature** of **Interest Groups**

Image Above: Members of an environmental group express their support for a "greener" city.

An **interest group** is a collection of people who share certain views on public matters and work to shape public policy to their benefit. They try to persuade public officials to respond to their positions favorably. You may not think that you belong to this sort of group, but as you read this section you will likely discover that you do. You might, in fact, belong to several of them. You will probably also realize that you will become a member of many more of these groups in the years to come—because these organizations provide one of the most effective ways in which Americans can get government to react to their needs and wants.

The Role of Interest Groups

Where do you stand on the question of gun control? What about global warming? National health insurance? Abortion? Prayer in public schools? What can you do to promote your views on these and other public questions? How can you increase the chance that your positions will carry the day?

Joining with others who share your opinions is both practical and democratic. Organization can provide the route to power, and organized efforts to further group interests are a fundamental part of the democratic process. Moreover, the right to do so is protected by the Constitution. Remember, the 1st Amendment guarantees "the right of the people peaceably to assemble, and to petition the Government for a redress of grievances."

Interest groups are sometimes called "pressure groups" and often "organized interests" or "special interests." They try to influence what government does in some specific area of special interest to them. They give themselves a variety of labels: leagues, associations, clubs, federations, unions, committees, and so on. But whatever they call themselves, every interest group seeks to influence the making and content of **public policy.** Used in this general sense, public policy includes all of the goals that a government pursues in the many areas of human affairs in which it is involved—everything from seat belts, speed limits, and zoning to flood control, old-age pensions, and the use of military force in international affairs.

Because interest groups exist to shape public policy, they can be found wherever those policies are made or can be influenced. They operate at every level of government—on Capitol Hill and elsewhere in Washington, D.C., in every one of the 50 State capitals, in thousands of city halls and county courthouses, and in many other places at the local level all across the country. In short, as diplomat and historian Lord Bryce put it somewhat indelicately more than a century ago: "Where the body is, there will the vultures be gathered."

Remember, our society is <u>pluralistic</u>. It is not dominated by any one <u>elite</u>. It is, instead, composed of several distinct cultures and groups. Increasingly, the members of various ethnic, racial, religious, and other groups compete for and share in the exercise of political power in the United States.

Parties and Interest Groups

Interest groups are made up of people who join together for some political purpose, much like political parties. Parties and interest groups overlap in a number of ways. They differ from each other in three significant ways, however: (1) with respect to the making of nominations, (2) in their primary focus, and (3) in the scope of their interests.

First, parties nominate candidates for public office; interest groups do not. Recall, the making of nominations is a prime function of political parties. If an interest group were to nominate candidates, it would, in effect, become a political party.

Interest groups do attempt to affect the outcome of primaries and other nominating contests. They do not pick candidates who then run for office under their labels, however. It may be widely known that a particular interest group supports this or that candidate, but the candidate seeks votes as a Republican or a Democrat.[1]

Second, parties are chiefly interested in winning elections and thereby controlling government. Interest groups are chiefly concerned with controlling or influencing the policies of government. Unlike parties, those groups do not face the problems involved in trying to appeal to the largest possible

number of people. In short, political parties are mostly interested in the *who*, and interest groups are mostly concerned with the *what*, of government. To put it another way, parties focus mostly on the candidate; interest groups focus mostly on policy questions.

Third, political parties are necessarily concerned with the whole range of public affairs, with everything of concern to voters. Interest groups almost always concentrate only on those issues that most directly affect the interests of their members.

In addition, interest groups are private organizations. Unlike political parties, they are not accountable to the public. Their members, not the voters, pass judgment on their performance.

Interest Groups: Good or Bad?

Do interest groups pose a threat to the well-being of the American political system? Or are they, instead, a valuable part of that system? The argument over the merit of interest groups goes back to the beginnings of the Republic.

Two Early Views Many have long viewed interest groups with suspicion and <u>foreboding</u>. They have feared that some would become so powerful that they would be able to shape public policies to their own narrow and selfish ends. James Madison gave voice to that view in 1787. In *The Federalist* No. 10, he argued that, inevitably, people join together to pursue common interests. They form "factions," Madison's term for what we now call interest groups. He warned that those factions, left unchecked, could dominate public decision making because of size, resources, and/or leadership.

✔ **Checkpoint**
Where do interest groups operate?

<u>pluralistic</u>
adj. made up of several groups with different ethnic, religious, political backgrounds

<u>elite</u>
n. select, privileged group in a society

<u>foreboding</u>
n. an expectation of trouble

▶▶ **Analyzing Political Cartoons**
AARP is a well-known interest group for people over 50; it responds to the needs of older Americans. **What is this cartoon saying about AARP and similar interest groups?**

---

1 Note that this discussion centers on the differences between interest groups and the *major* parties. There are many striking parallels between interest groups and most minor parties—for example, in terms of their scope of interest.

Madison believed that a society could eliminate factions only by eliminating the people's fundamental freedoms. He argued that "the mischiefs of factions" could best be controlled by a political system in which the powers of government, or the ability to make public policies, are fragmented. That is a major reason why, he said, the Constitution provides for a separation of powers and checks and balances, and for a federal system of government—to make it unlikely that one group can override the interests of other (competing) groups.[2]

2 You can read the full text of *The Federalist* No. 10 in the historic documents section at the end of this book.

Nearly fifty years later, Alexis de Tocqueville was deeply impressed by the vast number of organizations he found in this country. Tocqueville, a Frenchman, toured much of what was the United States in the 1830s. In his work, *Democracy in America,* he wrote that

PRIMARY SOURCE

In no country in the world has the principle of association been more successfully used, or more unsparingly applied to a multitude of different objects, than in America.

—Alexis de Tocqueville

GOVERNMENT ONLINE
Audio Tour
To learn more about early interest groups, visit
PearsonSuccessNet.com

Early Interest Groups

Interest groups have always sought a wide variety of goals. The people shown here fought for equality, labor, and economic reforms. *What tactics might these people and groups have used to accomplish their goals?*

Frederick Douglass, 1818–1895, former slave, American Anti-Slavery Society

Mary Church Terrell, 1863–1954, founder, National Association of Colored Women

Lewis Hine, 1874–1940, photographer, National Child Labor Committee

Oliver Hudson Kelly, 1826–1913, farmer, founder of current-day group, "the Grange"

"**Congress shall make no law . . . abridging . . . the right of the people** peaceably to assemble, and to **petition the Government for a redress of grievances.**
—1st Amendment

This Sioux Indian delegation traveled to Washington, D.C., in 1891 to protest the actions of the United States Cavalry troops at the battle of Wounded Knee, South Dakota, where about 300 Native Americans were killed.

And, in a similar vein, he also observed that

"Americans of all ages, all conditions, and all dispositions, constantly form associations . . . not only commercial and manufacturing . . . but . . . of a thousand other kinds—religious, moral, serious, futile, extensive or restricted, enormous or diminutive."
—Alexis de Tocqueville

Are those "associations," or interest groups, good or bad? To answer that question you must weigh, on the one hand, the functions those groups perform in American politics and, on the other, the various criticisms often leveled at them.

Their Valuable Functions *First*, among their several <u>commendable</u> functions, organized interests help to stimulate awareness of and interest in **public affairs.** Public affairs are those issues and events that concern the people at large. Interest groups raise awareness of public affairs mostly by developing and publicizing those policy positions they favor and by opposing those they see as threats to the interests of their members.

Second, interest groups represent their members on the basis of shared attitudes rather than on the basis of geography—by what their members think as opposed to where they happen to live. Public officials are elected from districts drawn on maps. But many of the issues that concern and unite people today have less to do with where they live than with, say, how they make a living. A labor union member who lives in Chicago may have much more in common with someone who does the same kind of work in Seattle than he or she does with someone who owns a business in Chicago or runs a farm in another part of Illinois.

Third, organized interests often provide useful, specialized, and detailed information to government—for example, on employment, price levels, or the sales of new and existing homes. These data are important to the making of public policy, and government officials often cannot obtain them from any other source. This flow of information works both ways: interest groups frequently get useful information from public agencies and pass it along to their members.

Fourth, interest groups are vehicles for political participation. Most people are not inclined to run for and hold public office, or even to volunteer for a campaign. For many Americans, then, interest groups are a convenient and less time-consuming way to help shape public policy. They are a means through which like-minded citizens can pool their resources and channel their energies into collective political action. One mother concerned about drunk driving cannot accomplish very much acting alone. Thousands of people united in an organization like MADD (Mothers Against Drunk Driving) certainly can and do.

Fifth, interest groups add another element to the checks-and-balances feature of the political process. Many of them keep close tabs on the work of various public agencies and officials and thus help to make sure that they perform their tasks in responsible and effective ways.

Finally, interest groups regularly compete with one another in the public arena. That competition places a very real limit on the lengths to which some groups might otherwise go as they seek to advance their own interests. For example, the automotive industry may work to weaken or postpone auto emission standards imposed under the Clean Air Act. Their efforts may be opposed—and to some extent counterbalanced—by environmental and health-related organizations.

Criticisms All of what has just been said is not meant to suggest that interest groups are above <u>reproach</u>. On the contrary, they can be, and often are, criticized on several counts.

The potentially negative side of interest groups is sometimes all too apparent. Many groups push their own special interests which, despite their claims to the contrary, are not always in the best interests of other Americans. Their critics often make several more specific charges.

First, some interest groups have an influence far out of proportion to their size, or, for that matter, to their importance or contribution to the public good. Thus, the

<u>commendable</u>
adj. admirable, praiseworthy

<u>reproach</u>
n. blame, criticism

Colleges and high schools often hold events where interest groups try to recruit new members. **Why might those places be good locations for recruiting?**

overt
adj. open, observable

dole
vt. to give or distribute

Third, many groups do not in fact represent the views of all of the people for whom they claim to speak. Very often, both in and out of politics, an organization is dominated by an active minority who conduct the group's affairs and make its policy decisions.

Finally, some groups use tactics that, if they were to become widespread, would undermine the whole political system. These practices include bribery and other heavy-handed uses of money, <u>overt</u> threats of revenge, and so on. Instances of that sort of behavior are not at all common; they are not altogether unknown, however.

The illegal behavior of a number of representatives of special interests was exposed in Washington during the Abramoff scandal. Jack Abramoff, several of his associates, and a member of Congress are now serving time in federal prison, convicted of bribery and other offenses. Abramoff and the other special interest representatives funneled hundreds of thousands of dollars into congressional campaigns, provided all-expense-paid trips to resorts and <u>doled</u> out such things as skybox tickets to professional football games, free dinners, and even jobs for some congressional spouses—all in exchange for legislative favors. Those favors included the introduction of bills written to benefit Abramoff's clients and other attempts to shape lawmaking to that same end.

contest over "who gets what, when and how" is not always a fair fight. The more highly organized and better-financed groups often have a decided advantage in that struggle.

Second, it is sometimes hard to tell just who or how many people a group really represents. Many groups have titles that suggest that they have thousands—even millions—of dedicated members. Some organizations that call themselves such things as "The American Citizens Committee for . . ." or "People United Against . . ." are, in fact, only "fronts" for a very few people with very narrow interests.

Essential Questions Journal To continue to build a response to the chapter Essential Question, go to your **Essential Questions Journal.**

SECTION 1 ASSESSMENT

1. **Guiding Question** Use your completed table to answer this question: What roles do interest groups play in our political system?

Key Terms and Comprehension

2. What are **interest groups** and how do they attempt to shape public policy?

3. How do political parties and interest groups differ from one another?

4. How do interest groups raise awareness of **public affairs?**

5. **(a)** Summarize public attitudes about interest groups. **(b)** What is their role in the American political system?

Critical Thinking

6. **Express Problems Clearly (a)** What were James Madison's concerns about "factions" in *The Federalist* No. 10? **(b)** Do you think Madison's concerns were justified? Use evidence from the text and your personal observations to support your point of view.

7. **Understand Point of View** What does it mean to say that joining interest groups is both practical and democratic?

Quick Write

Assessment Writing: Gather Details Writing for assessment often means that you have a limited time to answer an essay question. It may help to plan your response carefully using a graphic organizer. As you have read, interest groups are seen as both positive and negative. What do you think? To answer this question, gather details and list the positive and negative points of interest groups on a graphic organizer.

Types of Interest Groups

Guiding Question

What are the different types of interest groups at work in American society? Use the outline to record notes about different types of interest groups.

I. Types of Interest Groups
  A. Economic Interests
    1. _____
    2. _____
  B. Other Interest Groups
  C. Public-Interest Groups

Political Dictionary

- trade association
- labor union
- public-interest group

Objectives

1. Explain how the American tradition of joining organizations has resulted in a wide range of interest groups.
2. Describe four categories of groups based on economic interests.
3. Outline the reasons other interest groups have been created.
4. Identify the purpose of public-interest groups.

Image Above: Former American Medical Association President Dr. J. Edward Hill discusses medical liability reform at a news conference in 2006.

"**E**verything from A to Z." That expression can certainly be applied to the many interest groups in this country. They include, among thousands of others, AAA (the American Automobile Association), ACLU (the American Civil Liberties Union), Amnesty International, the Zionist Organization of America, and the Zoological Association of America. All of those thousands of organizations can be more or less readily classified and, so, usefully described as interest groups.

An American Tradition

The United States has often been called "a nation of joiners." Recall Alexis de Tocqueville's observations cited in the previous section. His comments, true when he made them, have become even more accurate over time.

No one really knows how many associations exist in the United States today. There are thousands upon thousands of them, however, and at every level in society. Each one becomes an interest group whenever it tries to influence the actions of government in order to promote its own goals.

Interest groups come in all shapes and sizes. They may have thousands or even millions of long-established members or only a handful of new or temporary members. They may be well or little known, highly structured or quite loose and informal, wealthy or with few resources. No matter what their characteristics, they are found in every field of human activity in this country.

The largest number of these groups has been founded on the basis of an economic interest, and especially on the bases of business, labor, agricultural, and professional interests. Some groups are grounded in a geographic area.

Others have been born out of a cause or an idea, such as prohibition of alcohol, environmental protection, or gun control. Many groups seek to influence some aspect of the nation's foreign policy. Still others exist to promote the welfare of certain groups of people—veterans, senior citizens, a racial minority, the homeless, women, people with disabilities, and so on.

Many people belong to a number of local, regional, or national interest groups—often without realizing they do. A car dealer, for example, may belong to the local Chamber of Commerce, a car dealers' association, the

American Legion, a local taxpayers' league, a garden club, a church, and the American Cancer Society. All of these are, to one degree or another, interest groups—including the church and the garden club, even though the car dealer may never think of these groups in that light.[3]

Many people may belong to groups that take conflicting stands on political issues. For example, the taxpayers' league may endorse a plan to eliminate plantings in traffic islands while the garden club wants to keep and even enlarge them.

Economic Interest Groups

Most interest groups are formed on the basis of economic interests. Among those groups, the most active—and certainly the most effective—are those representing business, labor, agriculture, and certain professions.

Business Groups Business has long looked to government to promote and protect its interests. Recall that it was merchants, <u>creditors</u>, and property owners who were most responsible for calling the Constitutional Convention in 1787. In the early years of the Republic, business interests fought for and won the <u>protective tariff</u>. Along with organized labor, many of them continue to work to maintain it, even now.

The United States Brewers Association, the oldest organized interest group at work in national politics today, was born in 1862 when Congress first levied a tax on beer. The association's stated purpose was to assure the brewing trade that its interests would be "vigorously <u>prosecuted</u> before the legislative and executive departments."

Hundreds of business groups now operate in Washington, D.C., in the 50 State capitals, and at the local level across the country. The two best-known business organizations are the National Association of Manufacturers (NAM) and the Chamber of Commerce of the United States.

Formed in 1895, NAM now represents some 12,000 firms. It generally speaks for "big business" in public affairs. The U.S. Chamber of Commerce, founded in 1912, is a major voice for the nation's thousands of smaller businesses. It has some 3,000 local chambers with about 3 million total members.

A major group comprising chief executive officers of the nation's largest companies, the Business Roundtable has also taken a large role in promoting and defending the business community in recent years.

Most segments of the business community also have their own interest groups, often called **trade associations.** They number in the hundreds and include the American Trucking Association, the Association of American Railroads, the National Restaurant Association, and many more. The several trade associations that represent the pharmaceutical, oil, and natural gas industries are generally regarded as the most powerful and effective interest groups today.

Despite their common goal of promoting business interests, business groups do not always present a solid front. In fact, they often disagree and sometimes fight among themselves. The trucking industry, for example, does its best to get as much federal aid as possible for highway construction. The railroads, however, are unhappy with what they see as "special favors" for their competition. At the same time, the railroads see federal taxes on gasoline, oil, tires, and other "highway users' fees" as legitimate sources of federal income. The truckers disagree, of course.

Labor Groups A **labor union** is an organization of workers who share the same type of job or who work in the same industry. Labor unions press for government policies that will benefit their members.

The strength of organized labor has <u>ebbed</u> over the past several years. Some 16 million Americans, only about 12 percent of the nation's labor force, belong to labor unions today. In the 1940s and 1950s, as many as a third of all working Americans were union members; in 1975, union

creditor
n. one to whom money is owed

protective tariff
n. import duty, imposed to give advantage to domestic industries

prosecute
vt. to follow up or pursue

ebb
vi. to weaken or lessen

---

3 Churches often take stands on such public issues as drinking, curfew ordinances, and legalized gambling, and they often try to influence public policy on those matters. Garden clubs frequently try to persuade cities to do such things as improve public parks and beautify downtown areas. Not every group to which people belong can properly be called an interest group, of course. But the point is that many groups that are not often thought to be interest groups are, in fact, just that.

The Changing State of Labor

GOVERNMENT ONLINE
Audio Tour
To learn more about labor unions, visit **PearsonSuccessNet.com**

Union membership has declined as the economy has shifted from manufacturing to services. However, the voice of unions remains strong politically with education, training, and library occupations having the highest rates of union membership. Unions have also become increasingly diverse demographically. *How might the interests of labor unions have shifted with the changing economy?*

Manufacturing
Manufacturing jobs, like at this automobile plant, employed half of all unionized workers in the 1950s.

Union Membership in 1955: 28%

Service
Two in five public sector employees, including teachers and other government employees (shown at left), belong to a union.

Union Membership Today: 12%

membership accounted for about a fourth of the labor force.

Organized labor is composed of a host of groups today. The AFL-CIO (the American Federation of Labor and Congress of Industrial Organizations) is by far the largest.[4] It is now made up of 56 separate unions, including, for example, the International Brotherhood of Electrical Workers (the IBEW) and the International Union of Automotive, Aerospace, and Agricultural Implement Workers (the UAW). All told, the AFL-CIO has 10 million dues-paying members today. Each of its member-unions is, like the AFL-CIO itself, organized on a national, State, and local basis.

The industrial sector of the nation's economy has declined over recent years. Because of this, <u>blue-collar workers</u> in such basic industries as automobiles and steel now represent a decreasing percentage of the working population. That decline has forced organized labor leaders to look elsewhere for new members. The AFL-CIO has been particularly active in efforts to unionize migrant farm workers, service workers, and, most recently, public employees.

In fact, the overall decline in union membership has been partially offset by an upswing in the unionization of government workers in recent years. Public-sector unions now have more than 7 million members, and that number is likely to continue to grow.

Quarrels over how to <u>rejuvenate</u> the labor movement led several unions to leave the AFL-CIO in 2005. Chief among them were the Service Employees International Union (the SEIU), with 2 million members, and the International Brotherhood of Teamsters (the

---

4 The AFL was formed in 1886 as a federation of craft unions. A craft union is made up of those workers who have the same craft or skill—for example, carpenters, plumbers, or electricians. The growth of mass-production industries created a large class of workers not skilled in any particular craft, however. The AFL found it difficult to organize those workers. Many of its craft unions opposed the admission of unions of unskilled workers to the AFL. In 1935, after years of bitter fighting, a group led by John L. Lewis of the United Mine Workers was expelled from the AFL. They formed the independent CIO in 1938. The rivalries between these unions eased to the point where a merger took place in 1955, creating the AFL-CIO.

✓ **Checkpoint**
Give an example of a situation in which business groups might disagree with one another.

blue-collar worker
n. one who does manual or industrial work—e.g., a miner, mechanic

rejuvenate
vt. restore, breathe new life into

IBT), with 1.4 million members, who formed a new 5-million-member group, the Change to Win Coalition.

There are also several independent unions not associated with either the AFL-CIO or Change to Win. Among the largest of them is the Communications Workers of America (the CWA), with approximately 700,000 members.

Organized labor generally speaks with one voice on such social welfare and job-related matters as Social Security, minimum wages, and unemployment. Labor does sometimes oppose labor, however. White-collar and blue-collar workers, for example, do not always share the same economic interests. Sectional interests (East-West, urban-rural, and so on) sometimes divide labor. Production and transportation interests (trucks versus railroads versus airplanes, for example) can create divisions, as well.

Agricultural Groups For much of our history, most Americans lived in rural areas on farms. The First Census, taken in 1790, set the nation's population at 3,929,214. It found that nearly all Americans then—94.9 percent of them—lived outside any city or town.

plummet
vi. fall or drop

The nation's population has increased dramatically since 1790, of course—to well over 300 million today. Over that period the farm population has <u>plummeted</u>. Less than two percent of the population live on farms today. Still, farmers' influence on the government's agricultural policies has been and is enormous. Many powerful associations serve the interests of agriculture. They include several broad-based farm groups and organizations that represent farmers who raise particular <u>commodities</u>.

commodity
n. anything bought and sold

The most prominent farm groups today are the National Grange, the American Farm Bureau Federation, and the National Farmers Union. The Grange, which was established in 1867, is now as much a social as a political organization. Most of its 300,000 farm-family members live in the Northeast and Mid-Atlantic States.

The Farm Bureau, formed in 1919, is the largest and most effective of the three major agricultural groups. It has over 5 million members today and is especially strong in the Midwest.

The National Farmers Union draws its strength from smaller and less prosperous farmers. The NFU often calls itself the champion of the dirt farmer, and it is frequently at odds with the Grange and the Farm Bureau.

Many other groups speak for the producers of specific farm products—these include the National Association of Wheat Growers, the National Cattlemen's Beef Association, the National Milk Producers Federation, and many others. Then, too, farm-related businesses such as pesticide manufacturers and farm implement dealers have their own organizations.

As with business and labor, farm groups sometimes find themselves at odds with one another. Thus, cotton, corn, soybean, and dairy associations compete as each of them tries to influence State laws regulating margarine and yogurt. California and Florida citrus growers are sometimes pitted against one another, and so on.

Professional Associations The professions are generally defined as those occupations that require extensive formal training, and, often government licensing—for example, medicine, law, and teaching. Most professional associations are not nearly as large, well-organized, well-financed, or effective as most business, labor, and farm groups.

Three professional groups are exceptions, however: the American Medical Association (AMA), the American Bar Association (ABA), and the National Education Association (NEA). Each has a very real impact on public policies, and at every level of government.

There are hundreds of less well-known professional groups. Most pharmacists join the National Association of Retail Druggists, librarians join the American Library Association, optometrists join the American Optometric Association, and so on. Still, not all professionals are members of the organizations that claim to represent them. Thus, fewer than half of all licensed medical doctors in the United States belong to the AMA.

Additional Interest Groups

Again, most organized interests are born out of economic concerns. Many others have been formed for other reasons, however, and many of these other groups have a good deal of political <u>clout</u>.

Issue-Oriented Groups Many groups exist to promote a cause or an idea. It would take several pages just to list them here, and so what follows is just a sampling of the more important ones.

The American Civil Liberties Union was born in 1920. It fights in and out of court to protect civil and political rights. Common Cause dates from 1970, calls itself "the citizen's lobby," and works for major reforms in the political process. The League of Women Voters and its many local leagues have been dedicated to stimulating participation in and greater knowledge about public affairs since 1919.

The list of groups devoted to causes goes on and on. Many, such as the National Women's Political Caucus, carry the women's rights banner. Others, including the National Wildlife Federation, the Sierra Club, and the Wilderness Society, are pledged to conservation and environmental protection.

Some groups are devoted to opposing or supporting certain causes. The National Right-to-Life Committee, Women Exploited by Abortion, and other groups oppose abortion. They are countered by the National Abortion and Reproduction Rights Action League, Planned Parenthood, and their allies. Similarly, the National Rifle Association (NRA) fights most forms of gun control; Handgun Control, Inc., works for it.

Washington's many "think tanks"—research institutions staffed by scholars and experts in a variety of fields—also qualify as interest groups. They promote their particular policy views and oppose those of others in books, newspaper articles, journals, and tele-

✔ **Checkpoint**
How do professional associations differ from business, labor, and farm groups?

<u>clout</u>
n. power, influence

Influencing International Events

Can interest groups make a difference?

Years of conflict in the Sudan between the government and rebel groups in Darfur have left hundreds of thousands dead and made refugees of millions more. Amnesty International, the Save Darfur Coalition, Human Rights Watch, and other groups provide various resources to the refugees and press the United States, other nations, and the UN to act in this critical situation. *What could these groups do to persuade governments to respond to this problem?*

Schools raise awareness and funds for Darfur.

Refugees flee their homes in Darfur.

centrist
adj. having moderate views

vision appearances. The more prominent among them include the more conservative Cato Institute and the Heritage Foundation; the more liberal Institute for Policy Studies; and the centrist American Enterprise Institute and Brookings Institution.

Organizations for Specific Groups Hundreds of interest groups seek to promote the welfare of certain segments of the population. Among the best known and most powerful are the American Legion and the Veterans of Foreign Wars, which work to advance the interests of the country's veterans. Groups like Older Americans, Inc., and AARP are very active in such areas as pensions and medical care for senior citizens.

pension
n. retirement or other benefit payment

Several organizations—notably the National Association for the Advancement of Colored People (NAACP) and the National Urban League—are concerned with public policies affecting African Americans. Other organizations, such as the Japanese American Citizens League, the Mexican American Legal Defense Fund, and the National Association of Arab Americans, support the country's many ethnic groups.

Religious Organizations Religious groups have long been involved in American politics, and many work to affect public policy in several important areas today. Many Protestants do so through the National Council of Churches, the Christian Voice, and the Christian Coalition.

The National Catholic Welfare Council speaks for the interests of Roman Catholics. The American Jewish Congress and B'nai B'rith's Anti-Defamation League promote the interests of the Jewish community.

Public-Interest Groups

The typical interest group seeks public policies that are of special benefit to its members and works against policies seen as threats. Some organizations have a broader focus and work for the "public good." That is, a **public-interest group** is an organization that works for the best interests of the overall community, rather than the narrower interests of one segment. It seeks policies that benefit all or most people, whether or not they belong to or support the organization.[5]

Public-interest groups have become quite visible over the past 30 years or so. Among the best known and most active are Common Cause, the League of Women Voters, and the several organizations that make up Ralph Nader's Public Citizen, Inc.

---

5 Nearly all interest groups claim that they work for the "public good." Thus, the National Association of Manufacturers (NAM) says that lower taxes on business will stimulate the economy and so help everyone. The AFL-CIO says the same thing about spending public dollars for public works programs. But, as a general rule, most interest groups support or oppose public policies on a much narrower basis: on what they see to be the best interests of their members.

Essential Questions Journal To continue to build a response to the chapter Essential Question, go to your **Essential Questions Journal.**

SECTION 2 ASSESSMENT

1. **Guiding Question** Use your completed outline to answer this question: What are the different types of interest groups at work in American society?

Key Terms and Comprehension

2. What factor distinguishes an interest group from other associations or organizations?

3. **Labor unions** and **trade associations** are formed on the basis of what interest?

4. What is a **public-interest group,** and how does it differ from other types of interest groups?

Critical Thinking

5. **Determine Cause and Effect**
(a) How have economic changes in the United States transformed the nature and types of labor unions in the country? (b) What are the results of those changes?

6. **Draw Conclusions** Why do you think that groups involved with economic interests are the most numerous type of interest group in the United States today?

Quick Write

Assessment Writing: Write Strong Opening and Closing Statements When writing for assessment, it is important to craft strong opening and closing statements. Using the graphic organizer you created in Section 1, begin to draft complete sentences that expand your argument. Remember: Your opening sentences should clearly state your position and your closing statement should complete your argument with a clear and logical conclusion.

ISSUES OF OUR TIME

Lobbying the Federal Government

Track the Issue

The 1st Amendment, which guarantees the right to peaceably assemble and petition the government for a redress of grievances, protects the rights of interest groups to lobby government.

1876

The House passes a temporary measure that, for the first time, requires all lobbyists to register with the clerk of the House.

1905

A series of articles entitled "The Treason of the Senate" appears in *Cosmopolitan*, alleging widespread corruption on the part of interest groups in Congress.

1946

Congress passes the Federal Regulation of Lobbying Act.

1995

Congress attempts to address shortcomings of the 1946 law with the Lobbying Disclosure Act.

2007

Congress and the President respond to a major lobbying scandal with the Honest Leadership and Open Government Act.

Rep. Rosa DeLauro (D., Conn.), left, greets a lobbyist at a conference. ▶

Perspectives

Recent scandals involving several lobbyists and some members of Congress and other public officials have raised questions about the influence of lobbyists and interest groups. Amid charges that lobbyists had improperly used gifts and travel to gain support in government, the nation again debated the benefits and drawbacks of lobbying.

Good lobbyists do their homework and help members of Congress understand the impact of legislation, the outcome of which citizens must live with every day. Good lobbyists understand the industry or organization that he or she is representing. Good lobbyists are great sources of information. Good lobbyists are factual. Good lobbyists are truthful.

——*Lobbyist and former Congressman Bill Sarpalius, 2006*

We want Congress to enact lobby reform legislation that sets new contribution and fundraising limits on lobbyists and lobbying firms; fundamentally changes the gift, travel, and employment relationships among members of Congress, lobbyists and lobbying firms; and institutes new and effective enforcement mechanisms. Congress needs an independent office or commission to oversee and enforce ethics rules and lobbying laws, receive allegations and complaints, conduct investigations and present cases to congressional ethics committees.

——*League of Women Voters, 2008*

Connect to Your World

1. **Understand (a)** How, according to Mr. Sarpalius, does lobbying contribute to the American system of government? **(b)** What are some lobbyist activities that concern the League of Women Voters?

2. **Draw Conclusions (a)** What might be a constitutional argument against increased restrictions on lobbyists? **(b)** How might the League of Women Voters defend its proposals against a 1st Amendment challenge? **(c)** Which do you think poses a greater danger: restricting lobbyists or giving them practically free reign? Why?

GOVERNMENT ONLINE

In the News

For updates about the regulation of lobbyists, visit
PearsonSuccessNet.com

SECTION 3

Interest Groups at Work

Guiding Question

In what ways do interest groups attempt to influence government and public opinion? Use the chart to record details of how interest groups work in our government and society.

How Interest Groups Work	
Direct Approach	**Indirect Approach**
• • •	• • •

Political Dictionary

- lobbying
- lobbyist
- *amicus curiae* brief
- grass-roots pressures

Objectives

1. Understand the difference between the *direct* and *indirect* approaches of interest groups.
2. Describe how lobbyists influence the legislative, executive, and judicial branches of government.
3. Examine how interest groups use grass-roots lobbying.
4. Identify how interest groups use media, propaganda, and political campaigns to influence public opinion and policy.

Image Above: Lobbyist Jack James of the AFL-CIO (right) speaks with Bennie Thompson (D., Miss.), chairman of the House committee on Homeland Security.

Interest groups exist to influence the making and the content of public policy, and they do so in a great many ways and in a great many places. They are, in effect, an excellent illustration of political scientist Harold D. Lasswell's notion that politics is all about "who gets what, when and how."

Interest groups approach government both directly and indirectly in their attempts to influence policy. Their *direct* efforts involve immediate, face-to-face contacts with policymakers. Their *indirect* efforts entail more subtle tactics—for example, mobilizing "the folks back home" to contact their members of Congress with letters, phone calls, faxes, and e-mails for or against a particular bill.

The Direct Approach

Again, the direct approach, bringing group pressures to bear directly on public policymakers, is another way of saying "lobbying." **Lobbying** is the process by which organized interests attempt to affect the decisions and actions of public officials.[6] **Lobbyists** are those people who try to persuade public officials to do those things that interest groups want them to do.

Lobbying occurs wherever public policy is made, including Washington, D.C., every State capital, and all of the county courthouses and city halls across the country. It is a big business today. Every important interest and many lesser ones—business groups, labor unions, farm organizations, the professions, churches, veterans, environmental groups, and many more—maintain lobbyists in Washington. Best estimates put the number of people who earn at least part of their living by lobbying Congress at no fewer than 30,000, and they spend more than $2 billion per year doing their jobs.

Most lobbyists are professionals. Some are freelancers, "hired guns" who will use their contacts and talents for anyone willing to pay what they charge.

---

6 The term was first used in Great Britain some 200 years ago, referring to journalists and special-interest pleaders who waited in the public lobbies of the House of Commons to talk with members of Parliament. The term *lobby-agent* was being used to identify favor-seekers at sessions of New York's legislature in Albany by the late 1820s. By the 1830s it had been shortened to *lobbyist* and was in wide use in Washington, D.C., and elsewhere. Lobbying is still frequently defined in terms of legislators and legislation. As we note, however, it has a much broader application today.

Most larger companies and labor unions have their own full-time lobbyists. Many work for the hundreds of Washington law firms and public relations agencies, concentrated along K Street, that specialize in that kind of work.

The Abramoff scandal prompted Congress to tighten the statutes regulating lobbyists' behavior in 2007. As the law now stands, all persons and organizations that seek to influence members of Congress, their staffers, or any policy-making officer in the executive branch must register with the clerk of the House and the secretary of the Senate. They are required to supply such basic information as name, address, and principal place of business, plus a general description of their activities. Every lobbyist must describe his or her ongoing work in detail and account for the income from it in quarterly reports.

Former senators and top-level executive branch officials must now wait two years, but ex-House members wait only one year, before they can become lobbyists. And, since 2007, no member of Congress can receive *any* gift from lobbyists or their clients.

Lobbying Congress The benefits of maintaining close relationships with members of Congress are fairly obvious, for Congress is the prime place for the making of public policy in the Federal Government. Some lobbying efforts target individual lawmakers and their staffs, but most are aimed at the standing committees of the House and Senate. More than a century ago, Woodrow Wilson described "Congress in its committee rooms" as "Congress at work," and that remains the case today, as you will see in Chapter 12.

Lobbyists testify before congressional committees and regularly submit prepared statements that set out their organization's views on proposed legislation. What happens in a legislative body often excites the interest of several different and competing groups. For example, if the House Committee on the Judiciary is considering a bill to regulate the sale of firearms, those companies that make guns, those that sell them, and those that produce or sell ammunition and a host of other related products all have a clear stake in the bill's contents and its fate. So, too, do law enforcement agencies, hunters, wildlife

conservationists, such groups as the National Rifle Association and the American Civil Liberties Union, and several others. Representatives of all of these groups are certain to be invited, or to ask for the opportunity, to present their views to the committee.

Lobbyists often provide useful information to Congress. To the point, John F. Kennedy, who served three terms in the House and was in his second term in the Senate when he won the presidency, observed:

PRIMARY SOURCE
Competent lobbyists can present the most persuasive arguments in support of their positions. Indeed, there is no more effective manner of learning all important arguments and facts on a controversial issue than to have the opposing lobbyists present their case.

—John F. Kennedy

Lobbyists are ready to do such things as make campaign contributions, provide information, write speeches, and even draft legislation. The contributions are welcome,

✔ **Checkpoint**
How do lobbyists try to influence Congress?

Many interest groups have offices on or near Washington, D.C.'s K Street, which has also become a nickname for the vast power and influence of lobbyists. *If you heard a candidate promise to heed "Main Street, not K Street," what would you think he or she meant?*

Checkpoint
Why do lobbyists target the executive branch?

nurture
vt. to foster, encourage, promote

the information is usually quite accurate, the speeches are forceful, and the bills are well drawn. Most lobbyists know that if they behaved otherwise (gave false or misleading information, for example) they would damage, if not destroy, their credibility and then their overall effectiveness.

Lobbyists work hard to influence committee action, floor debate, and then the final vote in a legislative body. If they fail in one house, they carry their fight to the other. If they lose there, too, they may turn to the executive branch, and perhaps to the courts, as well.

Lobbying the Executive Branch A vast amount of public policy is made by those who administer the law—that is, by the executive branch. Many of the laws that Congress enacts are written in fairly broad terms. More specific details, such as the day-to-day enforcement of the measure, are left to be worked out in the executive branch. As a practical matter, Congress cannot do such things as prescribe the design specifications for military aircraft, or dictate the advice that federal extension agents are to give to farmers, or determine which of several vaccines will be most effective in the next flu season.

Because meetings with the President and Cabinet officers are difficult to arrange, most executive-branch lobbying focuses, instead, on senior aides in the White House and on the various agencies in the President's administration. The primary job of one of those White House aides, the Director of Public Liaison, is to <u>nurture</u> good relations with major interest groups, especially those that support the President's policies.

Organized interests regularly try to influence the President's appointment of the top officials in various agencies. If an industry group is successful in such efforts, it can improve its chances for favorable treatment by, for example, the Federal Communications Commission or the Bureau of Reclamation in the Department of the Interior.

The most successful lobbyists rely on their networks of contacts as they deal with federal agencies. Ed Rollins, sometime lobbyist and major White House aide in recent Republican administrations, puts that point this way:

PRIMARY SOURCE

" I've got many friends all through the agencies and equally important, I don't have many enemies. . . . I tell my clients I can get your case moved to the top of the pile.

—Ed Rollins

GOVERNMENT ONLINE
For an **interactive** exploration of lobbying, visit
PearsonSuccessNet.com

INTERACTIVE

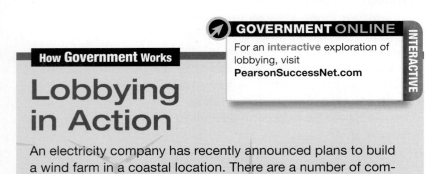

How Government Works

Lobbying in Action

An electricity company has recently announced plans to build a wind farm in a coastal location. There are a number of competing interests involved and each is taking steps to make sure their influence is felt. *What actions might these interest groups take to build public support and further their views?*

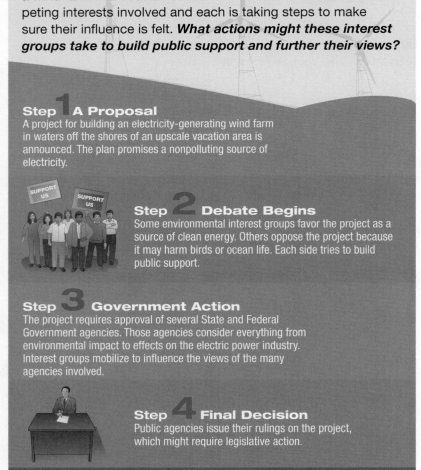

Step 1 A Proposal
A project for building an electricity-generating wind farm in waters off the shores of an upscale vacation area is announced. The plan promises a nonpolluting source of electricity.

Step 2 Debate Begins
Some environmental interest groups favor the project as a source of clean energy. Others oppose the project because it may harm birds or ocean life. Each side tries to build public support.

Step 3 Government Action
The project requires approval of several State and Federal Government agencies. Those agencies consider everything from environmental impact to effects on the electric power industry. Interest groups mobilize to influence the views of the many agencies involved.

Step 4 Final Decision
Public agencies issue their rulings on the project, which might require legislative action.

Lobbying and the Courts Organized interests have only recently recognized the fact that they can use the courts to realize their policy goals. You almost certainly know that in 1954, in *Brown* v. *Topeka Board of Education,* the United States Supreme Court held that segregation by race in public schools is unconstitutional. But do you know that *Brown* was taken to the Supreme Court by an interest group, the National Association for the Advancement of Colored People? The massive impact that that case has had made the special-interest community realize just how useful the courts can be.

Lawsuits brought by interest groups are not at all uncommon today. For some, like the American Civil Liberties Union, legal action is the primary means by which they seek to influence public policy. The ACLU regularly takes on unpopular causes—for example, those involving the free speech rights of <u>fringe groups.</u> Those causes usually have little chance of success in legislative bodies, but they may prevail in a courtroom.

An interest group may also file an ***amicus curiae*** ("friend of the court") **brief** in a case to which it is not itself a party but in which it does have a stake. An *amicus* brief consists of written arguments presented to a court in support of one side in a dispute. More than 100 different organizations submitted *amicus* briefs to the Supreme Court in 2003, arguing for or against the University of Michigan's affirmative action policies in *Gratz* v. *Bollinger* and *Grutter* v. *Bollinger.*

Organized interests often try to influence the selection of federal judges. Thus, over recent years, both pro-life and pro-choice organizations have urged Republican and Democratic administrations to make nominees' stances on abortion a major condition for appointment to the federal bench.

The Indirect Approach

Organized interests also approach government in a number of indirect ways. No matter the particular tactic used, however, the goal is exactly the same as it is when they approach public officials directly— that is, to shape policies to their liking. Not infrequently, interest groups try to mask their involvement in some indirect approach, hoping to make the effort appear to be spontaneous. Their indirect approaches include what is often called "grass-roots lobbying," the molding of public opinion, and various election-related activities.

Grass-roots Lobbying Most lobbyists know how to bring **grass-roots pressures**—pressures from members of an interest group or from the people at large, often beginning at a very basic level—to bear on public officials. Many of the groups that the lobbyists speak for can mount campaigns using letters, post-cards, phone calls, faxes, and e-mails from their supporters, often on very short notice.

Some members of Congress downplay the effectiveness of such efforts, and all of them know that groups orchestrate outpourings of letters, phone calls, e-mails, and the like. Still, every congressional office monitors those communications as a way of tracking <u>constituents'</u> opinions.

No organization uses grass-roots lobbying more effectively than AARP, a group originally known as the American Association of Retired Persons. Founded in 1958, it now has more than 39 million members and a staff of more than 1,600. Whenever legislation or some administrative action that affects retirees is pending, AARP swings into action. Members of Congress receive more letters, phone calls, and e-mails from members of AARP than they do from any other group.

The Internet has been a real <u>boon</u> to interest groups, and to cause-related organizations in particular. Nearly every organized interest has a Web site and an expanding e-mail list, as well. Blogging is used by many groups and has proved most effective in reaching people in younger age groups.

Cyberspace has been especially useful to those who want to organize a group but can do so only on a low-budget. Left-leaning MoveOn.org is a prime example of the Internet's capacity to organize. It was started by a handful of activists working out of a garage in Berkeley, California, in 1998. By 2004, they had formed an Internet network linking hundreds of thousands of citizens who could be mobilized to support liberal candidates and causes. MoveOn.org raised more than $3 million for Democratic

✔ **Checkpoint**
How does the indirect approach to lobbying differ from the direct approach?

fringe group
n. a group holding less popular, often extreme, views

constituent
n. represented by a legislator

boon
n. welcome benefit, stroke of good fortune

GOVERNMENT ONLINE
Audio Tour
To learn more about grass-roots organizing, visit
PearsonSuccessNet.com

Grass-roots Organizing
Going Digital

Advances in technology, notably the Internet, have drastically changed the way that interest groups organize on a grass-roots level. Having access to instantaneous and convenient communication tools allows smaller groups to mobilize and raise money as quickly as larger, more influential interests do. *What might be the potential drawbacks of relying on technology to organize?*

Appeals
to government officials can be made using cell phones, PDAs or other mobile technologies.

Members
organize faster and easier online, as well as being able to send important data to one another on the move.

Petitions
are a way for groups to quickly garner a large number of signatures and increase interest instantly online.

Fundraising
can be conducted more easily with credit cards and online donation forms.

Organizers
can set up Web sites based on their interests and connect with other members remotely.

congressional candidates in 2006 and even more in 2008; and it also conducted a massive get-out-the-vote effort in both elections.

Demonstrations and protest marches are another form of grass-roots lobbying. Most are efforts to show public officials that some group's cause does have broad public support. Some involve an element of political theater or an eye-catching gimmick to attract media (especially television) coverage. Thus, for example, peace groups often stage "die-ins" to protest war, and farmers might drive their tractors to Washington in "tractorcades" to dramatize their opposition to some agricultural policy.

Several groups now publish ratings of members of Congress. These rankings are based on the votes cast on measures these groups regard as crucial to their interests. Among the more prominent organizations that do so are such liberal groups as Americans for Democratic Action (ADA) and the American Civil Liberties Union (ACLU) and such conservative ones as the American Conservative Union (ACU) and the Chamber of Commerce of the United States.

Each of these groups sees to it that the mass media publicize their ratings. They also distribute them to the group's membership. Their ultimate objective is either to persuade less-than-friendly legislators to change their voting behavior or to help bring about their defeat in future elections.

Shaping Public Opinion Many organized interests spend much of their time and energy on attempts to mold public opinion. Groups that can make enough people regard them and their cause in the best possible way, and can persuade enough people to convey that feeling to public officials, have taken a major step toward achieving their policy goals.

Television screens, newspapers, and magazines are filled with costly advertisements by oil, cell phone, drug, and insurance companies, and many others—all seeking to cast the sponsor of the ad in a favorable light. Most of those ads go well beyond promoting some particular product and try also to suggest that the organizations behave as good citizens or defend family values or protect the environment, and so on.

A group's own membership can be used to shape opinions. Thus, in its decades-long opposition (since abandoned) to national health insurance proposals, the American Medical Association persuaded many doctors to put literature condemning those proposals as "socialized medicine" in their waiting rooms and to talk with patients about the issue. Using those tactics, the AMA capitalized on the tendency of most patients to respect their own physicians and regard them as experts.

Many groups use well-regarded personalities or trusted public figures to persuade people to support the group's cause. The late Charlton Heston served two terms as president of the NRA. Mr. Heston had a long record of support for the 2nd Amendment, but he was much better known from his long career as an actor. The wide recognition of his name and the moral authority associated with many of the characters he played in movies were extremely helpful to the NRA in its efforts to protect and expand the rights of Americans to keep and bear arms.

Almost certainly, though, the most effective vehicle for the molding of opinions and attitudes is the mass media. Interest groups know that people are more likely to regard their positions favorably if their activities are covered by the media as news rather than presented to the public in paid advertisements. With that in mind, interest groups produce a veritable flood of press releases, interviews, studies, and other materials, hoping to attract media coverage.

Propaganda Interest groups try to create the public attitudes they want by using propaganda.[7] Propaganda is a technique of persuasion aimed at influencing individual or group behaviors. Its goal is to create a particular belief among the audience. That belief may be completely true or false, or it may lie somewhere between those extremes. Today, people tend to think of propaganda as a form of lying and deception. As a technique,

▲ Muhammad Ali (left) and Michael J. Fox lend their names to raising money for Parkinson's disease, an illness from which both men suffer. *How might Ali's and Fox's celebrity status help their cause?*

however, propaganda is neither moral nor immoral; it is, instead, amoral.

Propaganda does not use objective logic. Rather, it begins with a conclusion. Then it brings together any evidence that will support that conclusion and disregards information that will not. Propagandists are advertisers, persuaders—and occasionally even brainwashers—who are interested in influencing others to agree with their point of view.

The development of the mass media in this country encouraged the use of propaganda, first in the field of commercial advertising, and then in politics. To be successful, propaganda must be presented in simple, interesting, and credible terms. Talented propagandists almost never attack the logic of a policy they oppose. Instead, they often attack it with name-calling. That is, they attach such labels as "communist" or "fascist." Other labels include "ultraliberal," "ultraconservative," "pie-in-the-sky," or "greedy." Or, they try to discredit a policy or person by card-stacking—that is, presenting only one side of the issue.

Policies that propagandists support receive labels that will produce favorable reactions. They use such glittering generalities as "American," "sound," "fair," and "just." Symbols are often used to elicit those positive reactions from people, too: Uncle Sam and the American flag are favorites. So, too,

---

7 The term comes from the Latin *propagare*—to propagate, to spread, to disseminate. It has been part of the American political vocabulary since the 1930s.

▶▶ **Analyzing Political Cartoons** This cartoon shows a politician kissing the hand of a political action committee member rather than a baby. ***What is this cartoonist saying about the influence of PACs on candidates for office?***

speeches—in fact, through every form of mass communication. The more controversial or less popular a group's position, the more necessary the propaganda campaign becomes.

Electioneering The most useful and the most appreciated thing that an interest group can do for a public official is to help that person win office. From the group's perspective, electing officeholders like members of Congress, State legislators, governors, and other State and local policymakers sympathetic to their interests is among the most effective things it can do. Once elected, these individuals can shape legislation and allocate money to meet the needs of the interest groups.

Groups can and do help those who run for office, and they do so in a variety of ways. Many do so through their political action committees. Recall that PACs are, as we said in Chapter 7, political arms of interest groups. They make financial contributions and hold fundraisers for candidates. They conduct voter registration and get-out-the-vote drives, supply professional campaign consultants, and provide information to be used in campaign speeches. Occasionally they even provide audiences to hear those speeches. And PACs do such other things as help staff local campaign offices, distribute campaign literature, work phone banks, and take voters to the polls on election day.

are testimonials—endorsements, or supporting statements, from such well-known personalities as television stars or professional athletes. The bandwagon approach, which urges people to follow the crowd, is another favorite technique. The plain-folks approach, in which the propagandist pretends to be one of the common people, gets heavy use, too.

Propaganda is spread through newspapers, radio, television, the Internet, movies, billboards, books, magazines, pamphlets, posters,

---

Essential Questions Journal To continue to build a response to the chapter Essential Question, go to your **Essential Questions Journal.**

SECTION 3 ASSESSMENT ★ ★ ★

1. **Guiding Question** Use your completed chart to answer this question: In what ways do interest groups attempt to influence government and public opinion?

Key Terms and Comprehension

2. How do direct and indirect approaches to lobbying differ?
3. What is a lobbyist?
4. At what levels of government does lobbying take place?
5. How do interest groups use the media and propaganda to influence the public?

Critical Thinking

6. **Predict Consequences (a)** What might happen if nothing were done to limit the role of lobbyists on the government? **(b)** Do you think government should regulate lobbyists' behavior?
7. **Draw Inferences** Why do interest groups value a positive public image?
8. **Identify Central Issues** Using celebrity spokespeople is a popular way for interest groups to gain influence. Do interest groups gain undue influence when celebrities back their causes? Explain.

Quick Write

Assessment Writing: Support and Revise Ideas As you begin to draft your complete essay, review what you have written and check to make sure that each paragraph includes a main idea. Build further upon the details gathered in Section 1 and compose a coherent, specific argument. Review word choice and write clear transitions between paragraphs.

Quick Study Guide

GOVERNMENT ONLINE

On the Go
To review anytime, anywhere, download these online resources at **PearsonSuccessNet.com**
Political Dictionary, Audio Review

Guiding Question
Section 2 What are the different types of interest groups at work in American society?

Guiding Question
Section 1 What roles do interest groups play in our political system?

CHAPTER 9
Essential Question
To what extent do interest groups advance or harm democracy?

Guiding Question
Section 3 In what ways do interest groups attempt to influence government and public opinion?

Political Dictionary

interest group *p. 242*
public policy *p. 242*
public affairs *p. 245*
trade association *p. 248*
labor union *p. 248*
public-interest group *p. 252*
lobbying *p. 254*
lobbyist *p. 254*
amicus curiae brief *p. 257*
grass-roots pressures *p. 257*

How Lobbying Works

Lobbying occurs . . .
wherever public policy is made—at the national, State, and local levels of government all across the country.

Lobbyists are . . .
the representatives of a wide variety of interest groups.

Lobbying involves . . .
writing speeches, providing information to officeholders, making campaign contributions, drafting legislation, filing court briefs, and much more.

Lobbyists use . . .
a variety of techniques to shape opinions, including grass-roots pressures, propaganda, and election-related activities.

Features of Interest Groups

Positive	Negative
• Provide ways to participate in public life	• Focus on special (narrow) interests of group
• Inform and raise interest in public matters	• Often represent small segment of population
• Promote interests important to group members	• Occasionally use unethical tactics

Chapter Assessment

Comprehension and Critical Thinking

Section 1

1. **(a)** Explain how interest groups are both practical and democratic. **(b)** Give examples of interest groups behaving in both practical and democratic ways.

2. Consider the role of interest groups in American society and in your own life. **(a)** Identify some positive impacts of these groups. **(b)** Summarize some common criticisms. **(c)** Which argument do you think is more persuasive?

3. **(a)** How do interest groups contribute to the checks-and-balances feature of the political process? **(b)** Do you think their contribution adds to the democratic process? **(c)** Why or why not?

"Well, if you feel so left out, why don't you join one of those Citizens Concerned About Something groups?"

4. **Analyze Political Cartoons (a)** What is the cartoon at left saying about interest groups? **(b)** Do you think the cartoonist sees interest groups as a positive or negative influence in society? Explain.

Section 2

5. Give an example of each of the following: **(a)** a group based on economic interests, **(b)** a group based on other special interests, and **(c)** a public interest group.

6. **(a)** What is the biggest category of interest group? **(b)** Why do you think this is? **(c)** Do you think this category is representative of the most important American interests?

7. **(a)** Why might interest groups with shared interests sometimes disagree with one another? **(b)** How might these disagreements affect their ability to influence policy?

Section 3

8. **(a)** What techniques might a lobbyist use to influence Congress? **(b)** Which of these techniques might be most effective, and why? **(c)** How do lobbyists balance ethics with effectiveness?

9. **(a)** How do lobbyists use public opinion? **(b)** How is this similar to advertising? **(c)** Would you be more or less likely to support a special interest group if it garnered positive public opinion?

10. **(a)** What involvements do lobbyists have in political campaigns? **(b)** How does this affect campaign finance?

Writing About Government

11. Use your Quick Write exercises from this chapter to complete a 3–5 paragraph essay supporting your argument concerning interest groups. See pages S11–S12 of the Skills Handbook.

Apply What You've Learned

12. **Essential Question Activity** Study the role of an interest group in your school or community and then investigate the role of a larger lobbying firm, such as those found on K Street in Washington, D.C. Then, answer the following:

    (a) What are the goals of these groups?

    (b) How does each group pursue its goals?

    (c) Do you think these groups are effective in their attempts to shape policy?

13. **Essential Question Assessment** Based on your research and what you have learned in this chapter, stage a press conference with classmates acting as reporters or as members of interest groups presenting their points of view. At a press conference, reporters are given the opportunity to ask questions, so allow time for both groups to participate. Try to answer the Essential Question: **To what extent do interest groups advance or harm democracy?**

Essential Questions
Journal
To respond to the chapter Essential Question, go to your **Essential Questions Journal.**

Document-Based Assessment

Regulating Special Interests

In 2007, Congress passed a new law limiting the reach of lobbyists. Several members were very concerned about "earmarks" (funding for specific projects in appropriations bills) and the fact that former members often become well-paid lobbyists.

Document 1

Here are some earmarks from 2008 appropriations bills:
Alaska Native Education Equity Assistance Program ($34,500,000)
AFL-CIO Working for American Institute ($1,500,000)
YMCA of Central Stark County, Ohio ($500,000)
Detroit Renaissance ($231,000)
Coastal Wind, Ohio ($100,000)
> —**Taxpayers for Common Sense,**
> **FY2008 Appropriations Bills database**

Facilities and Equipment for Hudson Alpha Institute for Biotechnology ($310,000)
> —**Office of Management and Budget**

Document 2

" This bill won't even begin to stop corruption in Washington, because the earmark favor factory will remain open and ready for business. Politicians will still be able to use these secret earmarks to direct millions of taxpayer dollars to special interests. You can hear the champagne bottles being uncorked all over K Street, because the lobbyists know it will be business as usual.
> —**Senator Jim DeMint (R., South Carolina),**
> press release from his Web site

Document 3

Document 4

" What we did today was momentous. The link between lobbyists and legislation that we have broken is something that will make a difference in the lives of the American people. . . We are free to act in the people's interest instead of the special interest.
> —**House Speaker Nancy Pelosi (D., California),**
> quoted in *USA Today,* August 1, 2007

Use your knowledge of lobbying, and Documents 1, 2, 3 and 4 to answer Questions 1–3.

1. Summarize Documents 2 and 4.
   A. Both speakers think the new law will have little effect on lobbyists.
   B. Both speakers feel it will make a big difference.
   C. Speaker 4 sees it as an important step to regulate special interests whereas Speaker 2 doesn't think the law will have any effect on corruption.
   D. Speaker 2 thinks the law will be ineffective; Speaker 4 sees it as a very positive step in the regulation of lobbying.

2. How does Document 3 illustrate the link between Congress and lobbyists?

3. How might some of the earmarks in Document 1 show the influence of special interests?

4. **Pull It Together** Do you think lobbying regulation will be effective? Why or why not?

GOVERNMENT ONLINE
Documents
To find more primary sources on lobbyists and interest groups, visit **PearsonSuccessNet.com**

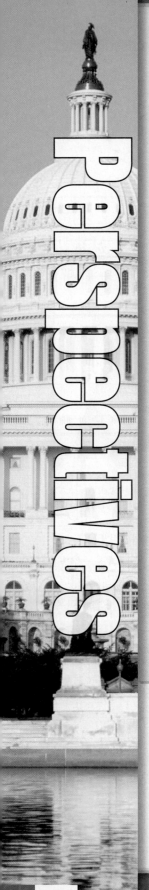

Perspectives

Essential Question

In what ways should people participate in public affairs?

Political parties, the media, voting, belonging to interest groups—Americans today have unprecedented opportunities to take part in public affairs. How and why should we do so?

"

ON THE FREE PRESS:

Freedom of expression—in particular, freedom of the press—guarantees popular participation in the decisions and actions of government, and popular participation is the essence of . . . democracy.

—Corazon Aquino, former President of the Philippines

ON A VOTER'S RESPONSIBILITIES:

"I'm undecided, but that doesn't mean I'm apathetic or uninformed."

"

ON GOVERNMENT AND THE PEOPLE:

It is not the function of our Government to keep the citizen from falling into error; it is the function of the citizen to keep the Government from falling into error.

—Justice Robert H. Jackson, *American Communications Association* v. *Douds,* 1950

Essential Question Warmup

Throughout this unit, you studied how people and government interact. Use what you have learned and the quotations and opinions above to answer the following questions. Then go to your **Essential Questions Journal.**

1. What responsibilities do the media have, if any?
2. Can citizens "keep the Government from falling into error" through voting alone?
3. Are interest groups vital to democratic government?
4. How successfully do political parties link citizens with their government?

Essential Questions Journal

To continue to build a response to the unit Essential Question, go to your **Essential Questions Journal.**

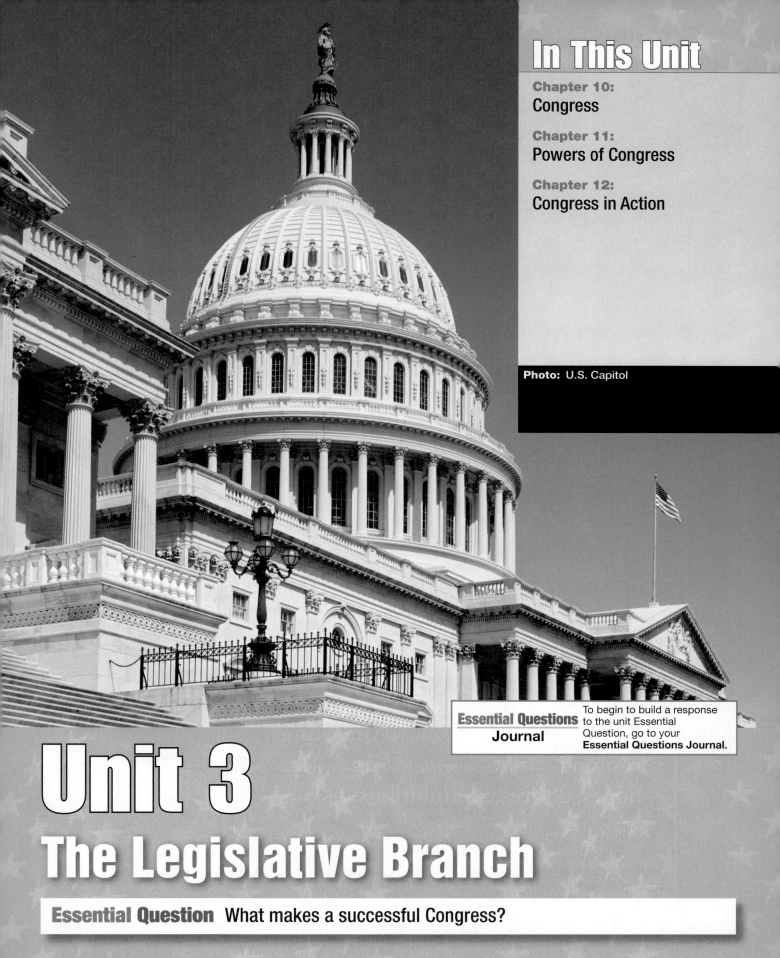

Photo: U.S. Capitol

Essential Questions Journal To begin to build a response to the unit Essential Question, go to your **Essential Questions Journal.**

Unit 3
The Legislative Branch

Essential Question What makes a successful Congress?

"

Congress—with all of its faults—is the most representative body in the land. It **reflects**—however imperfectly—the bigness and diversity of **America**. It **responds**—however imperfectly—to the expressed **hopes, desires,** and **ambitions** of the American people.

—Acceptance Remarks from The Honorable Lee H. Hamilton, U.S. Capitol Historical Society, 2005

Photo: Incoming Speaker of the House Nancy Pelosi (D., California) is congratulated as Rep. James Clyburn (D., South Carolina) looks on.

Congress

Essential Question
Whose views should members of Congress represent when voting?

Section 1:
The National Legislature

Section 2:
The House of Representatives

Section 3:
The Senate

Section 4:
The Members of Congress

GOVERNMENT ONLINE
On the Go

To study anywhere, anytime, download these online resources at PearsonSuccessNet.com
- Political Dictionary
- Audio Review
- Downloadable Interactivities

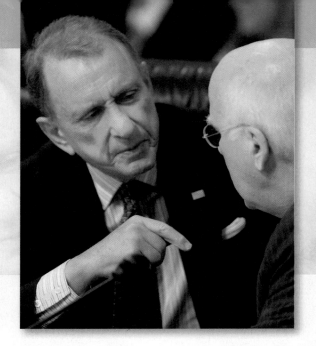

SECTION 1

The National Legislature

Guiding Question

Why does the Constitution establish a bicameral legislature?
Use a table to take notes on the reasons for a bicameral legislature.

Reason	Summary
Historical	
Practical	
Theoretical	

Political Dictionary
- bicameral
- term
- session
- convene
- adjourn
- recess
- prorogue
- special session

Objectives

1. Explain why the Constitution provides for a bicameral Congress.
2. Explain the difference between a term and a session of Congress.
3. Describe a situation in which the President may convene or end a session of Congress.

Image Above: Senators Arlen Specter (D., Penn.) and Patrick Leahy (D., Vt.)

Y ou live in a democracy, and you know that in a democracy the people rule. But what does that really mean? You are one of "the people," but you do not rule, at least not in the literal, hands-on sense. You do not make laws, collect taxes, arrest criminals, or decide court cases.

You do not do those or all of the many other things that government does because you live in a representative democracy. Here, it is the representatives of the people who do the day-to-day, hands-on work of government.

Congress stands as a prime example of that point. It is the nation's lawmaking body, the legislative branch of its National Government. It is charged with the most basic of governmental functions in a democratic society: Translating the public will into public policy in the form of law.

Yet Congress has never been very widely admired by the American people. Mark Twain amused his audiences with comments like, "Suppose you were an idiot. And suppose you were a member of Congress. But I repeat myself." Television personalities such as Jay Leno or Jon Stewart often make similar comments.

Still, despite those belittlings, Congress is immensely important in the American scheme of democratic government. James Madison called Congress "the first branch" of the National Government. Just how profoundly important he and the other Framers thought Congress to be is indicated by this fact: The very first and longest of the articles of the Constitution is devoted to it.

FROM THE CONSTITUTION

All legislative Powers herein granted shall be vested in a Congress of the United States, which shall consist of a Senate and House of Representatives.

—Article I, Section 1

A Bicameral Congress

Immediately, the Constitution establishes a **bicameral** legislature—that is, a legislature made up of two houses. It does so for historical, practical, and theoretical reasons.

Historical The British Parliament had consisted of two houses since the 1300s. The Framers and most other Americans knew the British system of bicameralism quite well. Most of the colonial assemblies and, in 1787, all but two of the new State legislatures were also bicameral. Among the original thirteen colonies, only Georgia and Pennsylvania had unicameral colonial and then State legislatures. Georgia's legislature became bicameral in 1789 and Pennsylvania's in 1790. (Only one State, Nebraska, has a unicameral legislature today.)

Practical The Framers had to create a two-chambered body to settle the conflict between the Virginia and the New Jersey Plans at Philadelphia in 1787. Recall, the most <u>populous</u> States wanted to distribute the seats in Congress in proportion to the population of each State, while the smaller States demanded an equal voice in Congress.

Bicameralism is a reflection of federalism. Each of the States is equally represented in the Senate and each is represented in line with its population in the House.

Theoretical The Framers favored a bicameral Congress in order that one house might act as a check on the other.

A leading constitutional historian recounts a conversation between Thomas Jefferson and George Washington at Mount Vernon. Jefferson, who had just returned from France, told Washington that he was opposed to a two-chambered legislature. As he made his point, he poured his coffee into his saucer, and Washington asked him why he did so. "To cool it," replied Jefferson. "Even so," said Washington, "we pour legislation into the senatorial saucer to cool it."[1]

The Framers were generally convinced that Congress would dominate the new National Government. As Madison observed,

Primary Source

In a republican government, the legislative authority necessarily <u>predominates</u>. The remedy for this inconveniency is to divide the legislature into different branches.
—The Federalist No. 51

1 Max Farrand, *The Framing of the Constitution* (1913).

Checkpoint
What practical problem did the Framers solve by creating a bicameral legislature?

populous
adj. with many people

predominates
v. holds controlling power or influence

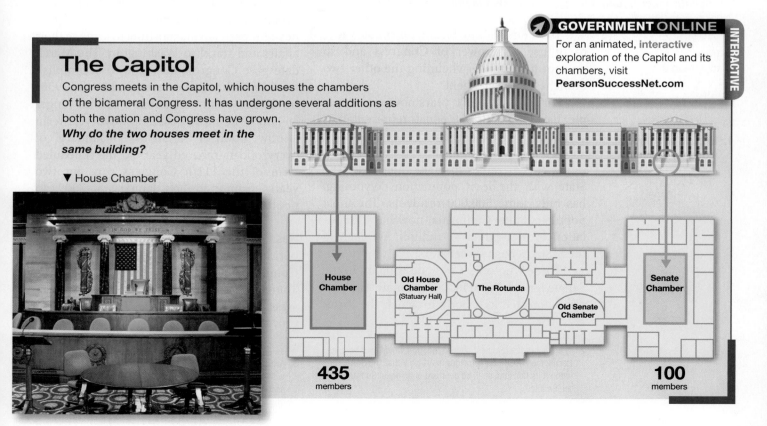

GOVERNMENT ONLINE
For an animated, interactive exploration of the Capitol and its chambers, visit **PearsonSuccessNet.com**

INTERACTIVE

The Capitol

Congress meets in the Capitol, which houses the chambers of the bicameral Congress. It has undergone several additions as both the nation and Congress have grown.
Why do the two houses meet in the same building?

▼ House Chamber

House Chamber

Old House Chamber (Statuary Hall)

The Rotunda

Old Senate Chamber

Senate Chamber

435 members

100 members

Representation in Congress

State	Population*	Senators	House Members
Wyoming	493,782	2	1
California	33,871,648	2	53

*Census of 2000 — SOURCE: U.S. Census Bureau

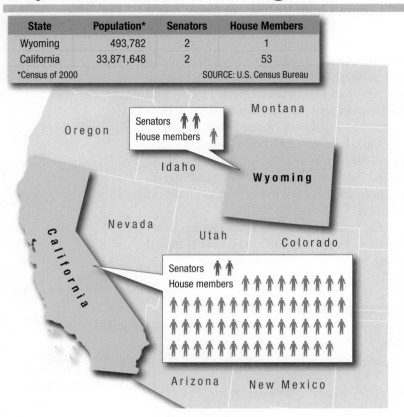

▶▶ **Interpreting Maps** California and Wyoming each elect two senators, despite a huge difference in their populations. *How does the distribution of Senate seats among the States illustrate the principle of federalism?*

diffuse
v. to spread out

The Framers saw bicameralism as a way to <u>diffuse</u> the power of Congress and so prevent it from overwhelming the other two branches of government.

For more than 200 years now, some people have argued that equal representation of the States in the Senate is undemocratic and should be eliminated.[2] They often point to the two extremes to make their case. The State with the least population, Wyoming, has only some 500,000 residents. The most populous State, California, now has a population of more than 37 million. Yet each of these States has two senators.

Those who object to State equality in the Senate ignore a vital fact. The Senate was purposely created as a body in which the States would be represented as coequal members and partners in the Union. Remember, if the Framers had been unable to agree that the States would be equally represented in the Senate, there might never have been a Constitution.

Terms and Sessions

It is said that a woman, incensed at something her senator had done, said to him, "You know, the 535 of you people in Congress meet every two years. Well, Senator, there are some of us who think that it would be much better if just two of you met every 535 years."

Whether that story is true or not, that woman's advice has never been followed. Ever since 1789, Congress has met for two-year terms.

Terms of Congress Each **term** of Congress lasts for two years, and each of those two-year terms is numbered consecutively.[3] Congress began its first term on March 4, 1789. That term ended two years later, on March 3, 1791.

The date for the start of each new term was changed by the 20th Amendment in 1933. In an earlier era, the several months from election to March 4 allowed for delays in communicating election results, and it gave newly chosen lawmakers time to arrange their affairs and travel to Washington. The March date gave Congress less time to accomplish its work each year, however, and by the 1930s travel and communications were no longer an issue. The start of each new two-year term is now "noon of the 3d day of January" of every odd-numbered year. So the scheduled term of the 111th Congress runs for two years—from noon on January 3, 2009, to noon on January 3, 2011.

Sessions A **session** of Congress is that period of time during which, each year, Congress assembles and conducts business. There are two sessions to each term of Congress—one session each year. The Constitution provides the following:

---

2 There is not the remotest chance that that would ever be done. Recall, the Constitution provides in Article V that "no State, without its Consent, shall be deprived of its equal Suffrage in the Senate."

3 Article I, Section 2, Clause 1 dictates the two-year term by providing that members of the House "shall be . . . chosen every second Year."

In fact, Congress often does "appoint a different day." The second session of each two-year term frequently **convenes** (begins) a few days or even a few weeks after the third of January.

Congress **adjourns,** or suspends until its next session, each regular session as it sees fit. Until World War II, the nation's lawmakers typically met for four or five months each year. Today, the many pressing issues facing Congress force it to remain in session through most of each year. Both houses do **recess** for several short periods during a session. That is, they temporarily suspend business.

Neither house may adjourn *sine die* (finally, ending a session) without the other's consent. The Constitution provides that

Article II, Section 3 of the Constitution does give the President the power to **prorogue** (end, discontinue) a session, but only when the two houses cannot agree on a date for adjournment. No President has ever had to use that power.

Special Sessions Only the President may call Congress into **special session**—a meeting to deal with some emergency situation.[4] Only 27 of these special joint sessions of Congress have ever been held. President Harry Truman called the most recent one in 1948, to consider anti-inflation and welfare measures in the aftermath of World War II.

Note that the President can call Congress or either of its houses into a special session. The Senate has been called alone on 46 occasions, to consider treaties or presidential appointments, but not since 1933. The House has never been called alone.

Of course, the fact that Congress now meets nearly year-round reduces the likelihood of special sessions. That fact also lessens the importance of the President's power to call one. Still, as Congress nears the end of a session, the President sometimes finds it useful to threaten a special session if the two chambers do not act on some measure high on the administration's legislative agenda.

agenda
n. list of things to be done

---

4 Article II, Section 3 says that the President "may, on extraordinary Occasions, convene both Houses, or either of them. . . ."

✔**Checkpoint**
How many sessions make up each congressional term?

Essential Questions Journal To continue to build a response to the chapter Essential Question, go to your **Essential Questions Journal.**

SECTION 1 ASSESSMENT

1. **Guiding Question** Use your completed table to answer this question: Why does the Constitution establish a bicameral legislature?

Key Terms and Comprehension

2. What is a **bicameral** legislature?
3. What is the difference between a **term** and a **session** of Congress?
4. How is a congressional **recess** different from an **adjournment**?

Critical Thinking

5. **Determine Cause and Effect** What might have happened if the Framers had created a legislature with only one house?
6. **Draw Inferences** Why is the President's power to convene and dismiss Congress very limited?
7. **Make Comparisons** The Articles of Confederation provided for a Congress that met for one-year terms. Why do you suppose the Framers created a Congress that meets for two-year terms?

Quick Write

Expository Writing: Gather Information Do research to gather information about Britain's two houses of Parliament. Include information about historical background, formal qualifications for office, salary and benefits of members, terms, and elections. Make a parallel list for the U.S. Congress. Continue to add information to your list as you read.

Writing a Letter to a Public Official

Terrorism, drunk driving, climate change, discrimination, immigration—Do you have a strong opinion about an issue that's being debated in Congress? A brief, well-written letter or e-mail is a very effective way to let your representative and senators know about it. Members of Congress pay attention to constituents who take the time to write to them.

Follow these simple steps when writing your letter:

1. **Find out who represents you in Congress.** If you don't know who your representative and senators are, look in your local newspaper, which may have a weekly record of how they voted on recent bills. You could also go to the Senate or House of Representatives Web site and type your zip code or State in the Search box. You can be sure you are using an official government Web site if the address ends in *.gov.* You can also use the blue (government) pages of your phone book to look up your members of Congress and their office addresses.

2. **Organize your thoughts.** Identify your issue clearly. Before you write, list the reasons you hold your opinion and arrange them in order of importance. Choose only the top two or three to include in your letter.

3. **Clearly state what action you want your member of Congress to take.** For example, you might say, "I am writing to urge you to vote for Senate Bill 244, the bill that will continue funding for Job Corps." If you don't know the number of a bill, identify it as closely as you can by name.

4. **Explain your reasons.** Tell your member of Congress why you think he or she should support your position. Be sure to include specific details and personal experiences that have led you to your position: "I dropped out of high school in tenth grade and couldn't get a job. My cousin learned auto mechanics in Job Corps and ended up with a really good job, so I applied. Job Corps turned my life around. I earned my GED and trained as a computer technician. This year I'm working part time and going to college. I'm writing to you to say that this is a great program. Please vote for funding to make sure it will continue to help young people who want a chance to succeed."

5. **Prepare your letter.** Make sure to address your letter correctly. Include your full name, phone number, and mailing address on the letter or in the e-mail.

▸▸ What do you think?

1. Why might an elected official want to hear about your experiences?
2. Why might it be important to limit yourself to explaining only the top two or three reasons for the position you hold?
3. **You Try It** Follow the steps above to write a letter on an issue that is important to you.

GOVERNMENT ONLINE
Citizenship Activity Pack
For an activity to help you write a letter to a public official, go to **PearsonSuccessNet.com**

SECTION 2

The **House** of **Representatives**

Guiding Question

How are the seats in the House distributed and what qualifications must members meet? Use a concept web to take notes on the House of Representatives.

Political Dictionary

- apportion
- reapportion
- off-year election
- single-member district
- at-large
- gerrymander
- incumbent

Objectives

1. Explain how House seats are distributed and describe the length of a term in the House.
2. Explain how House seats are reapportioned among the States after each census.
3. Describe a typical congressional election and congressional district.
4. Analyze the formal and informal qualifications for election to the House.

Image Above: Members of the media follow Rep. John Conyers (D., Mich.) (front right), the chairman of the House Judiciary Committee.

Every other autumn, hundreds of men and women seek election to the House of Representatives. Most of them try to attract supporters and win votes with posters, yard signs, billboards, flyers, buttons, and other eye-catching campaign materials. Nearly all make their "pitches" with radio and television spots, newspaper ads, and Web sites. In this section, you will discover the general shape of the office that all of those candidates so eagerly pursue.

Size and Terms

The exact size of the House of Representatives—today, 435 members—is not fixed by the Constitution. Rather, it is set by Congress. The Constitution provides that the total number of seats in the House of Representatives shall be **apportioned** (distributed) among the States on the basis of their respective populations.[5] Each State is guaranteed at least one seat no matter what its population. Today, seven States have only one representative apiece: Alaska, Delaware, Montana, North Dakota, South Dakota, Vermont, and Wyoming.

Voters in the District of Columbia, Guam, the Virgin Islands, and American Samoa each elect a delegate to represent them in the House, and Puerto Rico chooses a resident commissioner. Those officials are not, however, fullfledged members of the House of Representatives and do not vote on bills.

Article I, Section 2, Clause 1 of the Constitution provides that "Representatives shall be . . . chosen every second Year"—that is, they are elected for two-year terms. This rather short term means that, for House members, the next election is always just around the corner. That fact tends to make them pay close attention to "the folks back home."

There is no constitutional limit on the number of terms any member of Congress may serve. A considerable effort was made in the 1990s to persuade Congress to offer a constitutional amendment to limit congressional terms. Most versions of such an amendment would have put a three- or four-term limit on service in the House and a two-term limit for the Senate.[6]

---

5 Article I, Section 2, Clause 3.

6 The States do not have the power to limit the number of terms their members of Congress may serve, *United States* v. *Thornton*, 1995.

Reapportionment

Article I of the Constitution directs Congress to **reapportion** (redistribute) the seats in the House every ten years, after each census.[7] Until a first census could be taken, the Constitution set the size of the House at 65 seats. That many members served in the First and Second Congresses (1789–1793). The census of 1790 showed a national population of 3,929,214 persons; so in 1792 Congress increased the number of House seats by 41, to 106.

A Growing Nation As the nation's population grew over the decades, and as the number of States also increased, so did the size of the House. It went to 142 seats after the census of 1800, to 182 seats 10 years later, and so on.[8] By 1912, following the census of 1910 and the admission of Arizona and then New Mexico to the Union, the House had grown to 435 seats.

---

7 Article I, Section 2, Clause 3. A decennial census is one taken every ten years.

8 Once, following the census of 1840, the size of the House was reduced from 242 to 232 seats.

With the census of 1920, Congress found itself in a difficult political position. The House had long since grown too large for effective floor action. To reapportion without adding more seats, however, would mean that some States would have to lose seats.

Congress met the problem by doing nothing. So, despite the Constitution's command, there was no reapportionment on the basis of the 1920 census.

Reapportionment Act of 1929 Faced with the 1930 census, Congress avoided repeating its earlier lapse by passing the Reapportionment Act of 1929. That law, still on the books, sets up what is often called an "automatic reapportionment." It provides:

1. The "permanent" size of the House is 435 members. Of course, that figure is permanent only so long as Congress does not decide to change it. Congress did enlarge the House temporarily in 1959 when Alaska and then Hawaii became States. Today each of the 435 seats in the House represents an average of some 700,000 persons.

Congressional Apportionment 2003-2013

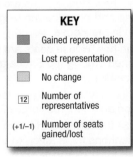

GOVERNMENT ONLINE
Audio Tour
Listen to a guided audio tour of this map at
PearsonSuccessNet.com

▸▸ **Interpreting Maps** The 435 seats in the House are reapportioned among the States every ten years. *What regions are gaining or losing population?*

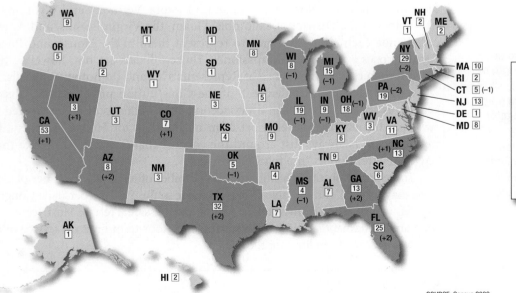

KEY

■	Gained representation
■	Lost representation
■	No change
[12]	Number of representatives
(+1/–1)	Number of seats gained/lost

SOURCE: Census 2000

2. Following each census, the Census Bureau is to determine the number of seats each State should have.

3. When the Bureau's plan is ready, the President must send it to Congress.

4. If, within 60 days of receiving it, neither house rejects the Census Bureau's plan, it becomes effective.

The plan set out in the 1929 law has worked quite well through eight reapportionments. The law leaves to Congress its constitutional responsibility to reapportion the House, but it gives to the Census Bureau the mechanical chores and the political "heat" that go with that task.

Congressional Elections

According to the Constitution, any person whom a State allows to vote for members of "the most numerous Branch" of its own legislature is qualified to vote in congressional elections.[9] The Constitution also provides that

FROM THE CONSTITUTION

The Times, Places and Manner of holding [Congressional] Elections . . . shall be prescribed in each State by the Legislature thereof; but the Congress may at any time by Law make or alter such Regulations. . . .[10]

—Article I, Section 4, Clause 1

Date Congressional elections are held on the same day in every State. Since 1872 Congress has required that those elections be held on the Tuesday following the first Monday in November of each even-numbered year. Congress has made an exception for Alaska, which may hold its election in October. To date, however, Alaskans have chosen to use the November date.

In that same 1872 law, Congress directed that representatives be chosen by written or printed ballots. The use of voting machines was approved in 1899. Today, most votes cast in congressional elections are cast on some type of (usually electronic) voting device.

Off-Year Elections Those congressional elections that occur in nonpresidential years— that is, between presidential elections—are called **off-year elections.** The next ones will occur in 2010 and 2014.

Far more often than not, the party that holds the presidency loses seats in the off-year elections. The most recent exception occurred in 2002, in the first election to be held after the terrorist attacks on September 11, 2001. The Republicans, sparked by the campaign efforts of President Bush, regained control of the Senate and padded their slim majority in the House. The party in power suffered major losses in the 2006 off-year elections, however. The Democrats, riding a wave of popular dissatisfaction with several Bush administration policies and, in particular, mounting opposition to the war in Iraq, captured control of both houses of Congress.

Districts The 435 members of the House are chosen by the voters in 435 separate congressional districts across the country. Recall that seven States each have only one seat in the House. There are, then, 428 congressional districts within the other 43 States.

The Constitution makes no mention of congressional districts. For more than half a century, Congress allowed each State to decide whether to elect its members by a general ticket system or on a **single-member district** basis. Under the single-member district arrangement, the voters in each district elect one of the State's representatives from among a field of candidates running for a seat in the House from that district.

Most States quickly set up single-member districts. However, several States used the general ticket system. Under that arrangement, all of the State's seats were filled **at-large**—that is, elected from the State as a whole, rather than from a particular district. Every voter could vote for a candidate for each one of the State's seats in the House.

✓ **Checkpoint**
Which party typically gains seats in off-year elections?

---

9 Article I, Section 2, Clause 1.
10 The Constitution allows only one method for filling a vacancy in the House—by a special election, which may be called only by the governor of the State involved (Article I, Section 2, Clause 4).

Gerrymandering
Choosing Their Voters

Each State's congressional districts must be redrawn every ten years, to bring the districts into line with the federal census. This gives State legislatures the opportunity to redistrict the State to the advantage of the majority party. *Why do some people think gerrymandering should be outlawed?*

● **Registered Green Party voter**

● **Registered Orange Party voter**

★ **Each star represents incumbent**

PACKING Packing happens when the State legislators "pack" as many voters from the opposing party into a single district as possible. This makes the other districts "safe" for the party in power.

Result: Two districts are safe for the Orange Party.

grossly
adv. obviously

peculiar
adj. unusual, odd

At-large elections proved <u>grossly</u> unfair. A party with even a very small plurality of voters statewide could win all of a State's seats in the House. Congress finally did away with the general ticket system in 1842. Thereafter, all of the seats in the House were to be filled from single-member districts in each State. Since the seven States with the fewest residents each have only one representative in the House, these representatives are said to be elected "at-large." Although each of them does represent a single-member district, that district covers the entire State.

The 1842 law made each State legislature responsible for drawing any congressional districts within its own State. It also required that each congressional district be made up of "contiguous territory." That is, it must be one piece, not several scattered pieces. In 1872, Congress added the command that the districts within each State have "as nearly as practicable an equal number of inhabitants." In 1901, it further directed that all the districts be of "compact territory"—in other words, a comparatively small area.

These requirements of contiguity, population equality, and compactness were often disregarded by State legislatures, and Congress made no real effort to enforce them. The requirements were left out of the Reapportionment Act of 1929. In 1932, the Supreme Court held (in *Wood* v. *Broom*) that they had therefore been repealed. Over time, then, and most notably since 1929, the State legislatures have drawn many districts with very <u>peculiar</u> geographic shapes. Moreover, until fairly recently, many districts were also of widely varying populations.

CRACKING Cracking happens when the party in power splits up (spreads out) the voters who support the opposing party. This results in the minority party winning fewer seats.

Result: The Orange Party wins three districts.

KIDNAPPING Kidnapping happens when the party in power redraws the district lines to move a minority-party incumbent into a different district where she or he is less likely to win reelection.

Result: The Orange Party wins three seats. The Green Party incumbent "loses" his district.

Gerrymandering Congressional district maps in several States show one and sometimes several districts of very odd shapes. Some look like the letters S or Y, some resemble a dumbbell or a squiggly piece of spaghetti, and some defy description. Those districts have usually been **gerrymandered**. That is, they have been drawn to the advantage of the political party that controls the State's legislature.

Gerrymandering is widespread today—and not just at the congressional district level. Districts for the election of State legislators are regularly drawn for the advantage of one party. In fact, gerrymandering can be found in most places where lines are drawn for the election of public officeholders—in cities, counties, school districts, and elsewhere.

Most often gerrymandering takes one of two forms. The lines are drawn either (1) to concentrate the opposition's voters in one or a few districts, thus leaving the other districts comfortably safe for the dominant party; or (2) to spread the opposition as thinly as possible among several districts, limiting the opposition's ability to win anywhere in the region. Gerrymandering's main goal is to create as many "safe" districts as possible—districts almost certain to be won by the party in control of the line-drawing process. And the computer-driven map-making techniques of today make the practice more effective than ever in its storied past.

Gerrymandering is the principle reason why, presently, only a handful of seats in the House are actually at risk in an election. In most elections, no more than 40 members now represent districts that cannot be classified as more or less safe districts.

For decades, gerrymandering produced congressional districts that differed widely

✓ **Checkpoint**
What is gerrymandering and what are its purpose and result?

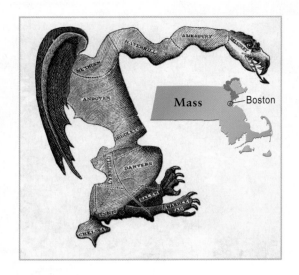

Gerrymandering takes its name from Massachusetts Governor Elbridge Gerry, who in 1812, drew the State's legislative districts to favor his party. A noted painter added a head, wings, and claws to a district map hanging over the desk of a newspaper editor. "That will do for a salamander," the artist said. "Better say Gerrymander," growled the editor. ▶

✔ **Checkpoint**
What did the Supreme Court rule in the 1964 case of *Wesberry* v. *Sanders*?

gouging
v. cheating, swindling

in the number of people they included. State legislatures were responsible for this situation, of course. A number of them regularly drew district lines on a partisan basis—with the Republicans <u>gouging</u> the Democrats in those States where the GOP controls the legislature, and the Democrats doing the same thing to the Republicans where they hold sway. In fact, that circumstance exists in several States today. Historically, most States were carved up on a rural versus urban basis as well as a partisan one—because, through much of history, the typical State legislature was dominated by the less-populated (and over-represented) rural areas of the State.[11]

Wesberry **v.** *Sanders,* **1964** The long-standing pattern of congressional districts of widely varying populations and, as a result, the long-standing fact of rural overrepresentation in the House came to an abrupt end in the mid to late 1960s. That dramatic change was the product of an historic Supreme Court decision in 1964. In a case from Georgia, *Wesberry* v. *Sanders*, the Supreme Court held that the Constitution demands that the States draw congressional districts of substantially equal populations.

---

[11] The pattern of rural overrepresentation in the State legislatures has now all but disappeared as a consequence of the Supreme Court's several "one person, one vote" decisions of the 1960s and 1970s. In the leading case, *Reynolds* v. *Sims*, 1964, the Court held that the 14th Amendment's Equal Protection Clause commands that the seats in both houses of a State's legislature must be apportioned on the basis of population equality.

The Court's "one person, one vote" decision in *Wesberry* had an immediate and extraordinary impact on the makeup of the House, on the content of public policy, and on the shape of electoral politics in general. The nation's cities and suburbs now speak with a much louder voice in Congress than they did before that decision. But notice, it remains quite possible for States to draw their congressional (or any other) district lines in accord with the "one person, one vote" rule and, at the same time, gerrymander those districts.

Gerrymandering based solely on race, however, is a violation of the 15th Amendment, *Gomillion* v. *Lightfoot*, 1960. So-called "majority-minority districts" were drawn in some States following the census in 1990 and again in 2000. Those districts were crafted to include a majority of African Americans and/or Latinos and so were likely to send African Americans and Latinos to Congress. The Supreme Court struck down those race-based districts in several cases—most notably in two cases from Texas, *Bush* v. *Vera*, 1996 and *United Latin American Citizens* v. *Perry*, 2006. However, the Court has also held this: While race cannot be the controlling factor in drawing district lines, race can be one of the mix of factors that shape that process. It did so in a case from North Carolina, *Hunt* v. *Cromartie*, in 2001.

The Court has said that under some circumstances, which it has never spelled out, excessively partisan gerrymandering might be unconstitutional. It did so for the first time in a 1986 case, *Davis* v. *Bandemer*. In 2003, Texas became the first State to redistrict between censuses, with the purpose of increasing the number of Republican-held Texas seats in the U.S. House of Representatives. In a dramatic showdown, the Republican governor called a special session. Democratic legislators fled the State, but ultimately they were unable to stop the redistricting. In a 2006 decision, a bare majority of the Court ruled that neither the Constitution nor any act of Congress prevents a State from redrawing its district lines whenever the party in control of the legislature believes that it might be to its advantage to do so, *United Latin American Citizens* v. *Perry*.

Qualifications for Office

You know that there are 435 members of the House of Representatives, and that each one of them had to win an election to get there. Each one of them also had to meet two quite different sets of qualifications to win office: the formal qualifications for membership in the House set out in the Constitution and a number of informal qualifications imposed by the realities of politics.

Formal Qualifications The Constitution says that a member of the House must (1) be at least 25 years of age, (2) have been a citizen of the United States for at least seven years, and (3) be an inhabitant of the State from which he or she is elected.[12]

Custom, not the Constitution, also requires that a representative must live in the district he or she represents. The custom is based on the belief that the legislator should be familiar with the locale he or she represents, its people, and its problems. Rarely, then, does a district choose an outsider to represent it.

The Constitution makes the House "the Judge of the Elections, Returns and Qualifications of its own Members."[13] Thus, when the right of a member-elect to be seated is challenged, the House has the power to decide the matter. Challenges are rarely successful.

The House may refuse to seat a member-elect by majority vote. It may also "punish its Members for disorderly Behavior" by majority vote, and "with the Concurrence of two thirds, expel a Member."[14]

For decades, the House viewed its power to judge the qualifications of members-elect as the power to impose additional standards. It did so several times. In 1900, it refused to seat Brigham H. Roberts of Utah because he was a polygamist—that is, he had more than one wife. In 1919 and again in 1920, the House excluded Victor L. Berger of Wisconsin, the first Socialist Party candidate

---

12 Article I, Section 2, Clause 2; see also Article I, Section 6, Clause 2.
13 Article I, Section 5, Clause 1.
14 Article I, Section 5, Clause 2.

> ✔ **Checkpoint**
> What are the formal qualifications for members of the House?

Paths to Congress

More members of Congress are lawyers by profession than any other occupation. Voters, however, have seen fit to elect representatives with widely varying backgrounds. *What qualifications do these representatives bring to their positions?*

Heath Shuler (D., North Carolina) Unlike many members of Congress, Heath Shuler had no political experience before his first election to the House in 2006. Shuler had been a quarterback in the National Football League and, later, started a real estate business. Both parties approached Shuler to run for public office. In Congress, he is a member of the Blue Dog Coalition, a group of fiscally conservative Democrats who, among other goals, are dedicated to balancing the budget.

Ileana Ros-Lehtinen (R., Florida) In 1989, Ileana Ros-Lehtinen became the first Cuban American and Hispanic woman elected to the House of Representatives. Born in Havana, her family fled to Florida when she was seven years old. She graduated from community college before earning master's and doctoral degrees in education. After founding a private elementary school, she was elected to the Florida legislature in 1982. She is the ranking member of the House Committee on Foreign Affairs and an advocate for human rights.

sedition
n. attempt to overthrow the government by force

to win a House seat. During World War I, Mr. Berger wrote several newspaper articles denouncing America's participation in that conflict. In 1919, he was convicted of <u>sedition</u> for obstructing the war effort and sentenced to twenty years in prison. The Supreme Court reversed that conviction in 1921. Mr. Berger was reelected to the House three more times and seated each time without challenge.

In *Powell* v. *McCormack,* 1969, however, the Supreme Court held that the House could not exclude a member-elect who meets the Constitution's standards of age, citizenship, and residence. The House has not excluded anyone since that decision.

Over more than 200 years, the House has expelled only five members. Three were ousted in 1861 for their "support of rebellion." Michael Myers (D., Penn.) was expelled for corruption in 1980. James Traficant (D., Ohio) was ejected after his conviction for bribery, fraud, and tax evasion in 2002. Over time, a few members have resigned to avoid almost certain expulsion. Randy "Duke" Cunningham (R., Calif.) resigned after pleading guilty in bribery charges in 2005.

The House has not often punished a member for "disorderly Behavior," but such actions are not nearly so rare as expulsions. For example, the House voted to "reprimand" Barney Frank (D., Massachusetts) in 1990 for conduct stemming from his relationship with a male prostitute. Mr. Frank has been easily reelected by the voters in his congressional district every two years since then.

Informal Qualifications The realities of politics produce a number of informal qualifications for membership in the House, beyond those requirements set out in the Constitution. Those informal yardsticks vary from time to time, sometimes from State to State, and even from one congressional district to another within the same State. Clearly, some of those factors that attract or repel voters in a heavily urbanized district differ from some of those that influence how voters see candidates in a largely rural setting.

These informal qualifications have to do with a candidate's vote-getting abilities. They include such considerations as party identification, name familiarity, gender, ethnic characteristics, and political experience. Being the **incumbent,** the person who currently holds the office, almost always helps. Regularly, well over 90 percent of those members of the House who seek reelection do so successfully.

Much more so today than in the past, a candidate's fundraising abilities also figure into the mix of informal qualifications. Like all other races, congressional campaigns have become very expensive. The average amount spent on a winning bid for the House topped the million dollar mark in 2008. Several winners, and some losers, spent a good deal more than that.

The "right" combination of these informal measurements will help a candidate win nomination and then election to the House of Representatives. The "wrong" mix will almost certainly spell defeat.

Essential Questions Journal To continue to build a response to the chapter Essential Question, go to your **Essential Questions Journal.**

SECTION 2 ASSESSMENT

1. **Guiding Question** Use your completed concept web to answer this question: How are seats in the House distributed and what qualifications must members meet?

Key Terms and Comprehension

2. How are seats in the House of Representatives **apportioned**?

3. How do elections in a **single-member district** differ from elections in States that filled their seats **at-large**?

4. Why do politicians **gerrymander** districts?

Critical Thinking

5. **Draw Inferences** How did *Wesberry* v. *Sanders* change the makeup of the House?

6. **Make Comparisons** Explain how informal qualifications for House membership might vary in rural areas versus urban areas within the same State, in different States or regions, and at different times in history.

Quick Write

Expository Writing: Compare and Contrast Using the lists you started in Section 1 about the British Parliament and the U.S. Congress, draw a Venn diagram in which you can organize features unique to the British Parliament, features unique to the U.S. Congress, and overlapping or shared features. Add to the diagram as you read Sections 3 and 4.

SECTION 3

The **Senate**

Guiding Question

How does the Senate differ from the House? Use a concept web to take notes on the Senate.

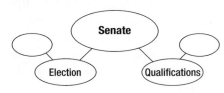

Political Dictionary

• continuous body
• constituency

Objectives

1. Compare the size of the Senate to the size of the House of Representatives.
2. Describe how senators are elected.
3. Explain how and why a senator's term differs from a representative's term.
4. Describe the qualifications for election to the Senate.

Image Above: The late Senator Edward Kennedy (D., Massachusetts) was first elected to Congress in 1962.

You should not be very surprised by these facts: Nearly a third of the present members of the Senate once served in the House of Representatives; none of the current members of the House has ever served in the Senate. Indeed, many of the men and women who now serve in the House look forward to the day when, they hope, they will sit in the Senate. As you read this section, you will come to see why the Senate is often called the "upper house."

Size, Election, and Terms

Why are there 100 members of the United States Senate? Have the members of the Senate always been elected by the voters of their States? Why do senators serve six-year terms? What qualifications must candidates for the Senate meet? Read on to find the answers to these and other questions.

Size The Constitution says that the Senate "shall be composed of two Senators from each State," and so the Senate is a much smaller body than the House of Representatives.[15] Today, however, the Senate is much larger body than the Framers imagined. The Senate had only 22 members when it held its first session in March of 1789, and 26 members by the end of the 1st Congress in 1791. Like the House, the size of the upper chamber has grown with the country. Today, 100 senators represent the 50 States.

The Framers hoped that the smaller Senate would be a more enlightened and responsible body than the House. Many of them thought that the House would be too often swayed by the immediate impact of events and by the passions of the moment, mostly because of the short term of office for members of the lower chamber. They reinforced that hope by giving senators a longer term of office and by setting the qualifications for membership in the Senate a cut above those they set for the House.

James Madison saw those provisions as "a necessary fence" against the "fickleness and passion" of the House of Representatives. Nearly a century later, Woodrow Wilson agreed with Madison:

---

15 Article I, Section 3, Clause 1 and the 17th Amendment.

Senators: Policy and Prestige

Senators are Washington celebrities—members of what is often called "the world's most exclusive club." Their names are frequently household words and their activities draw media coverage that allows them to call attention to issues they consider important. Many senators make use of the spotlight to launch campaigns for the presidency. *In what ways are senators national leaders?*

From left: Maria Cantwell (D., Washington) is known for her environmentalism; presidential campaign buttons; a bipartisan group of senators holds a press conference

"It is indispensable that besides the House of Representatives which runs on all fours with popular sentiment, we should have a body like the Senate which may refuse to run with it at all when it seems to be wrong—a body which has time and security enough to keep its head, if only now and then and but for a little while, till other people have had time to think."

—**Woodrow Wilson, Congressional Government**

Each one of the 100 members of the upper house represents an entire State. That same thing can be said of only a few members of the lower house—the seven representatives from those States with only one seat in the House. Consequently, nearly all of the members of the Senate represent a much larger and more diverse population and a much broader range of interests than do the several representatives from their State. If you look at your own State—at the size, diversity, and major characteristics of its population and at its history, geography, and economy—you will see the point.

Election Originally, the Constitution provided that the members of the Senate were to be chosen by the State legislatures. Since the ratification of the 17th Amendment in 1913, however, senators have been picked by the voters in each State at the regular November elections. Only one senator is elected from a State in any given election, except when the other seat has been vacated by death, resignation, or expulsion.[16]

Before the coming of popular election, the State legislatures often picked well-liked and qualified men to be senators. On other occasions, however, their choice was the result of <u>maneuvering</u> and infighting among the leaders of various factions in the State. These personalities all spent a great deal of energy trying to gain (and sometimes buy) enough legislators' votes to win a seat in the United States Senate. In fact, by the late 1800s, the Senate was often called the "Millionaires' Club," because so many wealthy party and business leaders sat in that chamber.

The Senate twice defeated House-passed amendments to provide for popular election. In 1912, it finally bowed to public opinion and agreed to what became the 17th Amendment the next year. The Senate was also

maneuvering
n. deal-making or strategy

---

16 The 17th Amendment gives each State a choice of methods for filling a Senate vacancy. A State may (1) fill the seat at a special election called by the governor or (2) allow the governor to appoint someone to serve until the voters fill the vacancy at such a special election or at the next regular (November) election. Most States use the appointment–special election method.

persuaded by the fact that several States had already devised ways to ensure that their legislatures would choose senators who were supported by the people of the State.

Each senator is elected from the State at-large. The 17th Amendment declares that all persons whom the State allows to vote for members of "the most numerous Branch" of its legislature are automatically qualified to vote for candidates for the U.S. Senate.

Term Senators serve for six-year terms, three times the length of those for which members of the House are chosen.[17] The Constitution puts no limit on the number of terms to which a senator may be elected. Senator Robert Byrd (D., West Virginia), who is now serving his ninth term in the upper house, holds the all-time record for service in that body. He was elected to his first term in the Senate in 1958 and was most recently reelected in 2006.

Senators' terms are staggered. Only a third of them—33 or 34 terms—expire every two years. The Senate is, then, a **continuous body.** That is, all of its seats are never up for election at the same time.

The six-year term gives senators a somewhat greater degree of job security than that enjoyed by members of the lower house. Those six years give senators some insulation from the rough-and-tumble of day-to-day politics. The six-year term also tends to make senators less subject to the pressures of public opinion and less <u>susceptible</u> to the pleas

of special interests than their colleagues in the House.

The larger size and the geographic scope of their **constituencies**—the people and interests the senators represent—are designed to have much the same effect. That is to say, senators are supposed to be less concerned with the interests of some particular small locality and more focused on the "big picture" of national concerns. Indeed, senators are much more likely to be regarded as national political leaders than are most House members.

The large size of the House generally prevents representatives from gaining as much notice and public exposure as most members of the Senate attract. Senators, and especially those who have presidential ambitions, are better able to capture national media attention. Over the past several elections, the Senate has emerged as a prime source of contenders for the presidential nomination in both parties. Senators also find it easier to establish themselves as the champions of public policies that appeal to large segments of the American people—for example, social security or national health care.

Senators are also more likely to be covered by the media in their States. And they tend to have more <u>clout</u> in their State's politics than that enjoyed by members of the House of Representatives.

Qualifications for Office

A senator must meet a higher level of qualifications for office than those the Constitution sets for a member of the House. A senator must (1) be at least 30 years of age, (2) have been a citizen of the United States for at least nine years, and (3) be an inhabitant of the State from which he or she is elected.[18]

Senators must satisfy a number of informal qualifications for office—various <u>extralegal</u> yardsticks based on such factors as party, name familiarity, gender, ethnic characteristics, and political experience. Both

Checkpoint
How were senators chosen before and after the passage of the 17th Amendment?

clout
n. power, influence

extralegal
adj. informal, not covered by law

susceptible
adj. likely to be affected by, vulnerable

---

17 Article I, Section 3, Clause 1.

18 Article I, Section 3, Clause 3. Under the inhabitant qualification, a senator need not have lived in the State for any particular period of time. Most often, of course, senators have been longtime residents of their States.

"According to our estimates, a campaign budget around six point two million is needed to successfully sing your praises."

▶▶ **Analyzing Political Cartoons** In this cartoon, a campaign manager talks to a candidate. *What clues in the cartoon tell you where this is taking place and who the characters may be?*

majority vote and "with the Concurrence of two thirds, expel a Member."[20]

Fifteen members of the Senate have been expelled by that body, one in 1797 and 14 during the Civil War. Senator William Blount of Tennessee was expelled in 1797 for conspiring to lead two Native American tribes, supported by British warships, in attacks on Spanish Florida and Louisiana. The 14 senators ousted in 1861 and 1862 were all from States of the Confederacy and had supported secession.

Over time, a few senators have resigned in the face of almost certain expulsion. In 1995, the Senate's Ethics Committee found that four-term senator Bob Packwood (R., Oregon) had been involved in several instances of blatant sexual harassment, and it urged his dismissal. Senator Packwood fought the charges for a time but resigned when it became apparent that his colleagues had had more than enough of his behavior.

The punishing of a senator for "disorderly Behavior" has also been rare. In the most recent case, in 1990, the Senate formally "denounced" Senator David Durenberger (R., Minnesota). The Ethics Committee had found him guilty on several counts of financial misconduct. The Senate called Senator Durenberger's conduct "reprehensible" and declared that he had "brought the Senate into dishonor and disrepute." Senator Durenberger chose not to seek reelection to a third term in 1994.

incumbency
n. the current holding of the office

concurrence
n. agreement

incumbency and a talent for fundraising are also major assets in Senate races.

The Senate can also judge the qualifications of its members when and if they are challenged, and it may exclude a member-elect by a majority vote.[19] The upper house has refused to seat someone on three occasions. It has not exercised that power since 1867, however. The chamber may also "punish its Members for disorderly Behavior" by

[19] Article I, Section 5, Clause 1.
[20] Article I, Section 5, Clause 2.

SECTION 3 ASSESSMENT

Essential Questions
Journal
To continue to build a response to the chapter Essential Question, go to your **Essential Questions Journal.**

1. **Guiding Question** Use your completed concept web to answer this question: How does the Senate differ from the House?

Key Terms and Comprehension

2. Why is the Senate called a **continuous body**?

3. How does a senator's **constituency** differ from that of a typical member of the House?

4. Why do most senators receive more public attention than their colleagues in the House?

Critical Thinking

5. **Determine Cause and Effect** Based on your reading, why do you think the 17th Amendment gained wide public support?

6. **Make Comparisons** How do the different terms of office for the House and Senate allow each house of Congress to make a unique contribution to national decision-making?

7. **Draw Inferences** Do the differences between the Senate and the House of Representatives ensure that the people are well represented?

Quick Write

Expository Writing: Make an Outline Using the Venn diagram you started in Section 2, make a detailed outline for an essay describing similarities and differences between the British Parliament and the U.S. Congress. Organize your points into a logical order so that, when you are ready to write your essay, your outline can serve as a guide.

SECTION 4

The Members of Congress

Guiding Question

What roles and functions do members of Congress perform?
Use a concept web to take notes on the roles and functions of members of Congress.

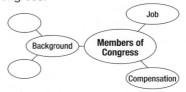

Political Dictionary

- delegate
- trustee
- partisan
- politico
- bill

- floor consideration
- oversight function
- franking privilege

Objectives

1. Describe the personal and political backgrounds of present-day members of Congress.

2. Identify the major roles played by those who serve in Congress.

3. Describe the compensation and privileges of members of Congress.

Image Above: GOP congressional leaders: Representative John Boehner (Ohio) and Senators John Kyl (Arizona) and Mitch McConnell (Kentucky)

Can you name your two senators? Your representative? Regrettably, most Americans cannot—let alone tell you much about the backgrounds, qualifications, or voting records of those who represent them in Congress.

Personal and Political Background

Whatever else they may be, the 535 members of Congress are *not* a representative cross section of the American people. Rather, the "average" member is a white male in his late 50s. The median age of the members of the House is just over 58 and about 64 for those in the Senate.

There are more women in the 111th Congress than ever—78 in the House and 17 in the Senate—and they are moving into positions of leadership. Nancy Pelosi (D., California) became the Speaker of the House in 2007, and she is now second in the line of succession to the presidency. Two standing committees in the House and two in the Senate are chaired by women today.

There are now 42 African Americans, 25 Hispanics, seven Asian Americans, and one Native American in the House. One African American, one Hispanic, one Asian American, and one Native Hawaiian sit in the Senate. The one African American in the upper chamber, Roland Burris (D., Illinois), was appointed in 2009, to fill the Senate seat of now President Barack Obama. Senator Burris is only the sixth African American ever to be a member of the upper house.

Nearly all members are married, a few are divorced, and they have, on average, two children. Only a few members say they have no religious affiliation. Just over half are Protestants, three in ten are Roman Catholics, nearly one in ten are Jewish, two are Buddhists, and two are Muslim.

Well over a third of the members of the House and over half the senators are lawyers. More than four out of five have a college degree and most, in fact, have advanced degrees.

Most senators and representatives were born in the States they represent. Only a handful were born outside the United States. Sprinkled among the members of Congress are several millionaires. A surprisingly large number of the men and women who sit in the House depend on their congressional salaries as their major source of income, however.

How Representative Is Congress?

COLLEGE DEGREES	WOMEN	AGE 60 AND OLDER	FOREIGN-BORN
27% of Americans	**51%** of Americans	**17%** of Americans	**13%** of Americans
93% of 110th Congress	**17%** of 110th Congress	**40%** of 110th Congress	**2%** of 110th Congress
In the 1st Congress, elected in 1789, only 48.4% of the members had college degrees. Today, 44% of senators and representatives have law degrees.	The first woman in Congress was Jeanette Rankin (R., Montana), a suffragist and peace activist first elected in 1916.	The 110th Congress was, on average, the oldest that has ever served. The oldest member was 83, the youngest was 31.	Foreign-born members of Congress have come from Canada, Cuba, Hungary, Japan, Mexico, the Netherlands, Pakistan, Taiwan, and many other places.

SOURCES: U.S. Census Bureau; Congressional Research Service; Biographical Directory of the United States Congress; *Politics in the First Congress, 1789–1791*

Analyzing Charts Over time, the membership of Congress has become more educated, older, and more diverse. *To what extent should the composition of Congress reflect that of the general population? Why?*

✔ **Checkpoint**
Describe the gender, ethnic, and religious diversity of members of Congress.

Most members of Congress have had considerable political experience. The average senator is serving a second term, and the typical representative has served four terms. Nearly a third of the senators once sat in the House. Several senators are former governors. A few senators have held Cabinet seats or other high posts in the executive branch of the Federal Government. The House includes a large number of former State legislators and prosecuting attorneys among its members.

Again, Congress is not an accurate cross section of the nation's population. Rather, it is made up of upper-middle-class Americans, who are, on the whole, quite able and hardworking people.

The Job

One leading commentary on American politics describes Congress and the job of a member of Congress this way:

"Congress has a split personality. On the one hand, it is a lawmaking institution and makes policy for the entire nation. In this capacity, all the members are expected to set aside their personal ambitions and perhaps even the concerns of their constituencies. Yet Congress is also a representative assembly, made up of 535 elected officials who serve as links between their constituents and the National Government. The dual roles of making laws and responding to constituents' demands forces members to balance national concerns against the specific interests of their States or districts."

—**James M. Burns, et al.,**
Government by the People

Members of both houses of Congress play five major roles. They are most importantly (1) legislators and (2) representatives of their constituents. Beyond those roles, they are also (3) committee members, (4) servants of their constituents, and (5) politicians. You will take a close look at their lawmaking function in the next two chapters. Here, we consider their representative, committee member, and servant functions.

Representatives of the People Senators and representatives are elected to represent the people. What does that really mean? The members of both houses cast hundreds of votes during each session of Congress. Many of those votes involve quite routine, relatively unimportant matters; for example, a bill to designate a week in May as National Wildflower Week. But many of those votes, including some on matters of organization and procedure, do involve questions of far-reaching importance.

Therefore, no questions about the law-making branch can be more vital than these: How do the people's representatives represent the people? On what basis do they cast their votes?

In broadest terms, each lawmaker has four voting options. He or she can vote as a delegate, a trustee, a partisan, or a politico.

Delegates see themselves as the agents of the people who elected them. They believe that they should discover what "the folks back home" think about an issue and vote that way. They are often willing to suppress their own views, ignore those of their party's leadership, and turn a deaf ear to the arguments of their colleagues and of special interests from outside their constituencies.

Trustees believe that each question they face must be decided on its merits. Conscience and judgment are their guides. They reject the notion that they must act as robots or rubber stamps. Instead, they call issues as they see them, regardless of the views held by a majority of their constituents or by any

of the other groups that seek to influence their decisions.

Partisans believe that they owe their first allegiance to their political party. They feel duty-bound to cast their votes in line with the party platform and the views of their party's leaders. Most studies of legislators' voting behavior indicate that partisanship is the leading factor influencing lawmakers' votes on most important questions.

Politicos attempt to combine the basic elements of the delegate, trustee, and partisan roles. They try to balance these often conflicting factors: their own view of what is best for their constituents and/or the nation as a whole, the political facts of life, and the <u>peculiar</u> pressures of the moment.

Committee Members In every session of Congress, proposed laws, known as **bills,** are referred to the various committees in each chamber. As committee members, senators and representatives must screen those proposals. They decide, in committee, which measures will go on to **floor consideration**—that is, be considered and acted upon by the full membership of the House or Senate.

✔ **Checkpoint**
What is the leading factor in how legislators vote?

peculiar
adj., unique, special, particular

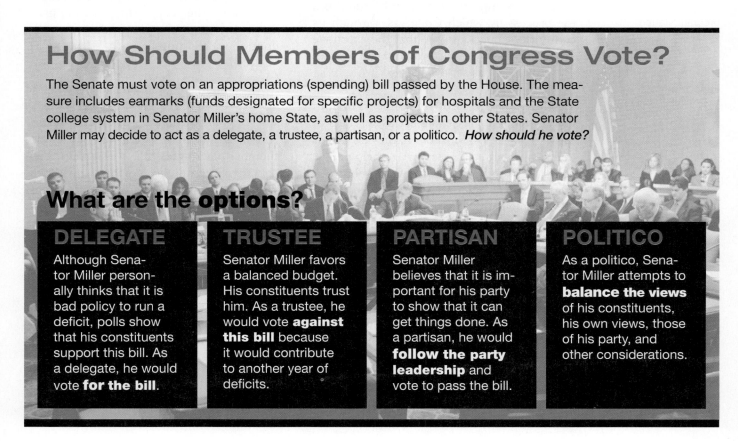

How Should Members of Congress Vote?

The Senate must vote on an appropriations (spending) bill passed by the House. The measure includes earmarks (funds designated for specific projects) for hospitals and the State college system in Senator Miller's home State, as well as projects in other States. Senator Miller may decide to act as a delegate, a trustee, a partisan, or a politico. *How should he vote?*

What are the **options?**

DELEGATE
Although Senator Miller personally thinks that it is bad policy to run a deficit, polls show that his constituents support this bill. As a delegate, he would vote **for the bill**.

TRUSTEE
Senator Miller favors a balanced budget. His constituents trust him. As a trustee, he would vote **against this bill** because it would contribute to another year of deficits.

PARTISAN
Senator Miller believes that it is important for his party to show that it can get things done. As a partisan, he would **follow the party leadership** and vote to pass the bill.

POLITICO
As a politico, Senator Miller attempts to **balance the views** of his constituents, his own views, those of his party, and other considerations.

Rep. José Serrano (D., New York), far right, takes part in the ceremonial first delivery of a program to bring discounted heating oil to his constituents. He worked with nonprofit groups and foreign officials to get the program started. **What role is Serrano fulfilling?**

appropriate
v., provide funds for a public purpose

Although Congress enacts laws and <u>appropriates</u> the money to implement them, the Constitution assigns the task of executing those laws to the executive branch. Congress must see that executive agencies carry out those laws faithfully and spend that money properly. It does so through the exercise of its critically important **oversight function,** the process by which Congress, through its committees, checks to see that the executive branch agencies are carrying out the policies that Congress has set by law.

Servants of the People Members of both the House and the Senate act as servants of their constituents. Most often, they do this as they (and their staff aides) try to help people in various dealings with the federal bureaucracy. Those interactions may involve a Social Security benefit, a passport application, a small business loan, or any one of a thousand other matters.

Some of "the folks back home" seem to think that members of Congress are sent to Washington mostly to do favors for them. Most members are swamped with constituent requests from the moment they take office. The range of these requests is almost without limit—everything from help in securing a government contract or an appointment to a military academy, to asking for a free sightseeing tour of Washington

or even a personal loan. Consider this job description offered only half-jokingly by a former representative:

"A Congressman has become an expanded messenger boy, an employment agency, getter-outer of the Navy, Army, Marines, ward heeler, wound healer, trouble shooter, law explainer, bill finder, issue translator, resolution interpreter, controversy oil pourer, gladhand extender, business promoter, convention goer, civil ills skirmisher, veterans' affairs adjuster, ex-serviceman's champion, watchdog for the underdog, sympathizer with the upper dog, namer and kisser of babies, recoverer of lost luggage, soberer of delegates, adjuster for traffic violators, voter straying into Washington and into toils of the law, binder up of broken hearts, financial wet nurse, Good Samaritan, contributor to good causes—there are so many good causes—cornerstone layer, public building and bridge dedicator, ship christener—to be sure he does get in a little flag waving—and a little constitutional hoisting and spread-eagle work, but it is getting harder every day to find time to properly study legislation—the very business we are primarily here to discharge, and that must be done above all things."

—Rep. Luther Patrick (D., Alabama)

Most members of Congress know that to deny or fail to respond to most of these requests would mean to lose votes in the next election. This is a key fact, for all of the roles a member of Congress plays—legislator, representative, committee member, constituent servant, and politician—are related, at least in part, to their efforts to win reelection.

Compensation

The Constitution says that members of Congress "shall receive a Compensation for their Services, to be ascertained by Law. . . ."[21] That is, the Constitution says that Congress fixes its own pay. The late Senator Russell Long (D., Louisiana) once characterized this provision as one that gives to members of Congress "a power that no good man would want and no bad man should have."

Salary Today, senators and representatives are paid $174,000 per year. A few members are paid somewhat more. The Speaker of the House makes $223,500 per year. The Vice President makes $227,300 per year. The Senate's president pro tem and the floor leaders in both houses receive $193,400 per year.

Nonsalary Compensation Members receive a number of "<u>fringe benefits</u>," and some are quite substantial. Thus, each member has a special tax deduction. That deduction recognizes the fact that most members of Congress must maintain two residences, one in his or her home State and one in Washington.

Generous travel allowances <u>offset</u> the cost of several round trips each year between home and Washington. Members pay relatively small amounts for life and health insurance and for outpatient care by a medical staff on Capitol Hill; they can get full medical care, at very low rates, at any military hospital. They also have a generous retirement plan, to which they contribute. The plan pays a pension based on years of service in Congress, and longtime members can retire with an income of $150,000 or more per year. The lawmakers are also covered by Social Security's retirement and Medicare programs.

Members are also provided with offices in one of the several Senate and House office buildings near the Capitol and allowances for offices in their home State or district. Each member is given funds for hiring staff and for the operating costs related to running those offices. The **franking privilege** is a well-known benefit that allows them to mail letters and other materials postage-free by substituting their facsimile signature (frank) for the postage.

Congress has also provided its members with the free printing—and through franking, the free distribution—of speeches, newsletters, and the like. Radio and television tapes can be produced at very low cost. Each member can choose among several fine restaurants and two first-rate gymnasiums. Members receive still more privileges, including such things as the

help of the excellent services of the Library of Congress and free parking in spaces reserved for them at the Capitol and also at Washington's major airports.[22]

The Politics of Pay There are only two real limits on the level of congressional pay. One is the President's veto power. The other and more potent limit is the fear of voter backlash, an angry reaction by constituents at the ballot box. That fear of election-day fallout has always made most members reluctant to vote to raise their own salaries.

Congress has often tried to skirt the politically sensitive pay question. It has done so by providing for such fringe benefits as a special tax break for those who must maintain two residences, a liberal pension plan, more office and travel funds, and other perquisites, or "perks"—items of value that are much less apparent to "the folks back home."

---

[21] Article I, Section 6, Clause 1. The 27th Amendment modified this pay-setting authority. It declares that no increase in members' pay can take effect until after the next congressional election—that is, not until after voters have had an opportunity to react to the pay raise.

[22] For decades, many members of Congress supplemented their salaries with honoraria—speaking fees and similar payments from private sources, mainly special interest groups. Critics long attacked that widespread practice as at least unseemly and, at its worst, a form of legalized bribery. The House finally prohibited its members from accepting honoraria in 1989, and the Senate did so in 1991.

☑ **Checkpoint**
Name five "fringe benefits" for members of Congress.

fringe benefits
n., compensation in addition to a base salary

offset
v., to balance, counteract, or compensate for

▶▶ **Analyzing Political Cartoons** To eliminate the need to vote for their own raises, Congress now receives an automatic annual salary increase to keep up with inflation. It is known as a "cost of living adjustment," or C.O.L.A. Critics, however, point out that they have not provided the same automatic adjustment for the minimum wage. ***What information can you learn from studying this cartoon?***

contentious
adj., controversial

The debate over congressional pay is not likely to end soon—at least not as long as the current method of establishing salaries remains in effect. All sides of the issue present reasonable arguments. Certainly, decent salaries—pay in line with the responsibilities of the job—will not automatically bring the most able men and women to Congress, or to any other public office. But certainly, decent salaries can make public service much more appealing to qualified people.

Membership Privileges Beyond the matter of their salaries and other compensation, members of Congress enjoy several privileges. The Constitution commands that senators and representatives

FROM THE CONSTITUTION

shall in all Cases, except Treason, Felony and Breach of the Peace, be privileged from Arrest during their Attendance at the Session of their respective Houses, and in going to and returning from the same. . . .
—Article I, Section 6, Clause 1

The provision dates from English and colonial practice, when the king's officers often harassed legislators on petty grounds. It has been of little importance in our national history, however.[23]

Another much more important privilege is set out in the same place in the Constitution.

The Speech or Debate Clause of Article I, Section 6, Clause 1 declares ". . . for any Speech or Debate in either House, they shall not be questioned in any other Place." The words "any other Place" refer particularly to the courts.

The privilege is intended to "throw a cloak of legislative immunity" around members of Congress. The clause protects members from suits for libel or slander arising out of their official conduct. The Court has held that the immunity applies "to things generally done in a session of the House [or Senate] by one of its members in relation to the business before it."[24] The protection includes work in committees and all other things generally done by members of Congress in relation to congressional business.

The important and necessary goal of this provision is to protect freedom of legislative debate. Clearly, members must not feel restrained in their vigorous discussion of the sometimes contentious issues of the day. However, this provision is not designed to give members unbridled freedom to attack others verbally or in writing. Thus, a member is not free to defame another person in a public speech, an article, a conversation, or otherwise.

23 The courts have held that "Breach of the Peace" covers criminal offenses. So the protection covers only arrest for civil (noncriminal) offenses while engaged in congressional business.
24 The leading case is *Kilbourn* v. *Thompson,* 1881. The holding has been affirmed many times since. In *Hutchinson* v. *Proxmire,* 1979, however, the Court held that members of Congress may be sued for libel for statements they make in news releases or in newsletters.

Essential Questions Journal To continue to build a response to the chapter Essential Question, go to your **Essential Questions Journal.**

SECTION 4 ASSESSMENT

1. **Guiding Question** Use your completed concept web to answer this question: What roles and functions do members of Congress perform?

Key Terms and Comprehension
2. What is the **oversight function**?
3. What is the difference between a **bill** and a law?
4. What are the five major roles played by members of Congress in their jobs?

Critical Thinking
5. **Draw Inferences** What does the profile of the average member of Congress tell you about the informal qualifications for the office?
6. **Make Decisions** Rank the options that members of Congress have when voting: trustee, delegate, partisan, and politico. Number one should be the option you would want your representatives and senators to use when voting. For each, explain why you would or would not favor each option.

Quick Write

Expository Writing: Write Topic Sentences Extend the outline you began in Section 3. Then write a topic sentence for each of the major headings in your outline. Topic sentences should introduce the information under that heading. If your headings are too broad to write a comprehensive topic sentence, revise the outline so that each topic sentence serves as an introduction to what follows.

Quick Study Guide

GOVERNMENT ONLINE

On the Go

To review anytime, anywhere, download these online resources at **PearsonSuccessNet.com**
Political Dictionary, Audio Review

Guiding Question
Section 2 How are the seats in the House distributed and what qualifications must members meet?

Guiding Question
Section 3 How does the Senate differ from the House?

Guiding Question
Section 1 Why does the Constitution establish a bicameral legislature?

CHAPTER 10
Essential Question
Whose views should members of Congress represent when voting?

Guiding Question
Section 4 What roles and functions do members of Congress perform?

Political Dictionary

bicameral *p. 268*
term *p. 270*
session *p. 270*
convene *p. 271*
adjourn *p. 271*
recess *p. 271*
prorogue *p. 271*
special session *p. 271*
apportion *p. 273*
reapportion *p. 274*
off-year election *p. 275*
single-member district *p. 275*
at-large *p. 275*
gerrymander *p. 277*
incumbent *p. 280*
continuous body *p. 283*
constituency *p. 283*
delegate *p. 287*
trustee *p. 287*
partisan *p. 287*
politico *p. 287*
bill *p. 287*
floor consideration *p. 287*
oversight function *p. 288*
franking privilege *p. 289*

Comparing the House and the Senate

House of Representatives	Senate
Two-year term	Six-year term
435 voting members	100 members
Smaller constituencies: Elected from districts of approximately equal populations	Larger constituencies: Elected from entire State
All elected every two years	One third elected every two years
Modest prestige, less national media attention	High prestige, more media attention

Reasons for a Bicameral Congress

Historical	Practical	Theoretical
Most colonies had bicameral legislatures. British Parliament was bicameral.	Larger States wanted representation based on population; smaller States favored equal representation.	The Framers wanted to divide the lawmaking power so that the legislative branch would not become too powerful.

Chapter Assessment

GOVERNMENT ONLINE
Self-Test
To test your understanding of key terms and main ideas, visit **PearsonSuccessNet.com**

Comprehension and Critical Thinking

Section 1

1. **(a)** Give a historical, a practical, and a theoretical reason why the Framers created a bicameral legislature. **(b)** Explain the following statement: *Bicameralism is an expression of federalism.*

2. **(a)** How is a session of Congress related to a term? **(b)** Under what circumstances may the President convene or end a session of Congress?

Section 2

3. **(a)** Describe how members of Congress are elected in a single-member district arrangement. **(b)** Explain how the terms reapportion and gerrymander are related. **(c)** In your opinion, what criteria should legislators use when drawing district lines?

Section 3

4. **(a)** How do the qualifications for membership in the Senate differ from those of the House? **(b)** How does the length of their term of office protect senators from the political pressures faced by the members of the House? **(c)** Under what circumstances might a senator's role as a national leader conflict with his or her role as a representative of a State?

5. **Analyze Political Cartoons** The 1890 cartoon to the right is a commentary on the process of State legislatures choosing senators before the passage of the 17th Amendment. **(a)** What is the candidate placing in the box? **(b)** What point is the artist making? **(c)** Compare the role of money in elections before the passage of the 17th Amendment to its role today.

Section 4

6. **(a)** List the five major roles played by members of Congress in doing their jobs. **(b)** In your opinion, what is the most important role of a member of Congress? Why?

7. **(a)** What are the advantages and disadvantages of paying our elected representatives a salary? **(b)** How much do you think that members of Congress should be paid in comparison with other professions? Explain. **(c)** How important is it for members of Congress to be well paid?

Writing About Government

8. Use the Quick Write exercises from this chapter to write an expository essay explaining similarities and differences between the British Parliament and the U.S. Congress. Before writing, make an outline and decide how to organize your essay. See pp.S3–S5 in the Skills Handbook.

Apply What You've Learned

9. **Essential Question Activity** Members of Congress are legislators for the National Government, yet they must please their constituents in order to be reelected. One way to do that is through earmarks.

    (a) Research earmarks using news stories and other current media. Summarize the controversy over earmarks. Why do some people oppose them? What effect do earmarks have on the nation?

    (b) Would the earmarks sponsored by your members of Congress make you more likely to vote for them? Would you support the earmarks if they benefited another State?

10. **Essential Question Assessment** Based on the results of your research and the content you learned in this chapter, write a paragraph answering this question: How should members of Congress balance their roles as national leaders and State or local leaders? This question will help you think about the chapter Essential Question: **Whose views should members of Congress represent when voting?**

Essential Questions Journal To respond to the chapter Essential Question, go to your **Essential Questions Journal.**

Document-Based Assessment

Members of Congress Cast Their Votes

Members of Congress must decide how to vote on any number of issues during each session. As Document 1 shows, voters would prefer that members of Congress act as delegates. However, members may feel that it is in their constituents' best interest to vote as trustees or politicos.

Document 1

When your representative in Congress votes on an issue, which should be more important?

The Representative's own principles and judgment about what is best for the country

25% AGREE

The way voters in your district feel about that issue

68% AGREE

SOURCE: The Center on Policy Attitudes, 1999

Document 2

I am now here in Congress . . . I am at liberty to vote as my conscience and judgment dictates to be right, without the yoke of any party on me . . . Look at my arms, you will find no party hand-cuff on them! . . . But you will find me . . . the people's faithful representative, and the public's most obedient, very humble servant.

—Davy Crockett, Representative from Tennessee, 1834

Document 3

There is an old story about Lyndon Johnson meeting with a group of new congressmen while he was President. One of them asked Johnson for advice on how to vote during his time in office. The President responded that he should do whatever his party leadership told him. Outside the meeting a few minutes later, a reporter asked Johnson if he'd given any advice to the new legislators. Surely, Johnson replied: "Always vote in the best interests of the American people."

That pretty well captures the realities of Washington. Out in the glare of the television lights, "the people's" interests are trotted out and given the starring role. But behind closed doors, there's a gaggle of competing interests every legislator must weigh. If the President is of your party, there's a natural desire to support him. So, too, with your party's leaders, who can advance your career and make it easier for you to help your constituents. Then there are your constituents, your campaign contributors, lobbyists . . . All of them have some claim on your loyalties.

—Lee Hamilton (D., Indiana), *"Whose Team Should a Member of Congress Be On?"* 2005

Use your knowledge of Congress and Documents 1, 2, and 3 to answer Questions 1–3.

1. Which statement does Document 1 support?
   A. Members of Congress should vote in the best interest of large corporations.
   B. Members of Congress should vote in the best interests of the nation.
   C. Members of Congress should vote in the way their constituents would choose.
   D. Members of Congress should vote for what they consider morally correct.

2. What factors would Crockett and Johnson have considered when voting on bills?

3. **Pull It Together** Based on these documents, what factors do you think are most important for members of Congress to consider when casting their votes? Why?

GOVERNMENT ONLINE
Documents
To find more primary sources on Congress, visit
PearsonSuccessNet.com

Essential Question
What should be the limits on the powers of Congress?

> Though the President is Commander in Chief, **Congress is his commander; . . .** this is **not** a Government of **kings . . .,** but a Government **of the people,** and . . . Congress **is the people.**
>
> —Rep. Thaddeus Stevens, 1867

Photo: Members of the House of Representatives are sworn in.

GOVERNMENT ONLINE
On the Go

To study anywhere, anytime, download these online resoures at PearsonSuccessNet.com
• Political Dictionary
• Audio Review
• Downloadable Interactivities

SECTION 1

The Expressed Powers

of Money and Commerce

Guiding Question

What powers over money and commerce does the Constitution give to Congress and what limits does it put on these powers? Use a table to keep track of the powers of Congress and their limits.

Money and Commerce	
Expressed Power	**Limits on Power**
•	•
•	•
•	•

Political Dictionary

- expressed powers
- implied powers
- inherent powers
- commerce power
- tax
- public debt
- deficit financing
- bankruptcy
- legal tender

Objectives

1. Describe the three types of powers delegated to Congress.
2. Analyze the importance of the commerce power.
3. Summarize key points relating to the taxing power.
4. Explain how the bankruptcy and borrowing powers work.
5. Explain why the Framers gave Congress the power to issue currency.

Image Above: Congress created the Coast Guard under its expressed power.

A typical day in either chamber of Congress might suggest that there is no limit to what Congress can do. On any given day, the House might consider bills dealing with such varying matters as the interstate highway system, an increase in the minimum wage, and grazing on public lands. Meanwhile, the Senate might be considering aid to a famine-stricken country in Africa, the President's nomination of someone to fill a vacancy on the Supreme Court, or any number of other matters.

Still, remember, there are very real limits on what Congress can do. Recall that (1) government in the United States is limited government, and (2) the American system of government is federal in form. These two fundamental facts work to shape and also to limit the powers of Congress.

The Delegated Powers

Remember, Congress has only those powers delegated (granted, given) to it by the Constitution. Large areas of power are denied to Congress in so many words in the Constitution, by the Constitution's silence on many matters, and because the Constitution creates a federal system.

There is much that Congress cannot do. It cannot create a national public school system, require people to vote or attend church, or set a minimum age for marriage or drivers' licenses. It cannot abolish jury trials, confiscate all handguns, or censor the content of newspaper columns or radio or television broadcasts. Congress cannot do these and a great many other things because the Constitution does not delegate to it any power to do so.

Still, Congress does have the power to do many things. The Constitution grants it a number of specific powers—and, recall, it delegates those powers in three different ways: (1) explicitly, in its specific wording—the **expressed powers;** (2) by reasonable deduction from the expressed powers—the **implied powers;** and (3) by creating a national government for the United States—the **inherent powers.**

The Framers very purposefully created a limited government. Given that fact, it is understandable that the existence and the scope of both the implied and the inherent powers have been the subject of dispute ever since the adoption of the Constitution. Later in the chapter, we shall examine the conflict between the strict constructionists, who interpret congressional power narrowly, and the liberal constructionists, who favor a broader interpretation.

The Expressed Powers

Most, but not all, of the expressed powers of Congress are found in Article I, Section 8 of the Constitution. There, in 18 separate clauses, 27 different powers are explicitly given to Congress.[1]

These grants of power are brief. What they do and do not allow Congress to do often cannot be discovered by merely reading the few words involved. Rather, their meaning is found in the ways in which Congress has exercised its powers since 1789, and in scores of Supreme Court cases arising out of the measures Congress has passed.

As a case in point, take the Commerce Clause, in Article I, Section 8, Clause 3. It gives Congress the power "to regulate Commerce with foreign Nations, and among the several States, and with the Indian Tribes." What do these words mean? Over the past two centuries, Congress and the Court have had to answer hundreds of questions about the scope of the Commerce Clause. Here are but a few examples: Does "commerce" include people crossing State lines or entering or leaving the country? What about business practices? Working conditions? Radio and television broadcasts? The Internet? Does Congress have the power to ban the shipment of certain goods from one State to another? To prohibit discrimination? What trade is "foreign" and what is "interstate"? And what trade is neither?

In answering these and dozens of other questions arising out of this one provision, Congress and the Court have defined—and are still defining—the meaning of the Commerce Clause. So it is with most of the other constitutional grants of power to Congress.

The commerce power and, with it, the expressed power to tax have provided much of the basis upon which Congress and the courts have built nearly all of the implied powers. Most of what the Federal Government does, day to day and year to year, it does as the result of legislation enacted by Congress in the exercise of those two powers.

The Commerce Power

Commerce, generally, is the buying and selling of goods and services. The **commerce power**—the power of Congress to regulate interstate and foreign trade—is vital to the welfare of the nation. Its few words have prompted the growth of the greatest open market in the world. The Commerce Clause proved to be more responsible for the building of a strong and *United* States out of a weak confederation than any other provision in the Constitution.

***Gibbons* v. *Ogden*, 1824** The first case involving the Commerce Clause to reach the Supreme Court, *Gibbons* v. *Ogden*, was decided in 1824. The case arose out of a clash over the regulation of steamboats by the State of New York, on the one hand, and the Federal Government, on the other. In 1807, Robert Fulton's steamboat, the *Clermont*, had made its first successful run up the Hudson River, from New York City to Albany. The State legislature then gave Fulton an exclusive, long-term grant to navigate the waters of the State by steamboat. Fulton's monopoly then gave Aaron Ogden a permit for steamboat navigation between New York City and New Jersey.

Thomas Gibbons, operating with a coasting license from the

Inherent powers are those that belong to all sovereign nations—for example, the power to control a nation's borders.

Expressed powers are those stated in the Constitution—for example, the power to regulate both foreign and interstate commerce.

Implied powers are not stated in the Constitution, but drawn from the expressed powers. Based on the expressed power to regulate commerce, Congress has set a minimum wage for hourly workers.

▶▶ This chart gives an example of each type of congressional power. *From which type of power does Congress derive most of its current authority?*

---

1 Several of the expressed powers of Congress are set out elsewhere in the Constitution. Thus, Article IV, Section 3 grants Congress the power to admit new States to the Union (Clause 1) and to manage and dispose of federal territory and other property (Clause 2). The 16th Amendment gives Congress the power to levy an income tax. The 13th, 14th, 15th, 19th, 24th, and 26th amendments grant Congress the "power to enforce" the provisions of the amendments "by appropriate legislation."

✓ **Checkpoint**
What was the Court's decision in *Gibbons* v. *Ogden?*

sweeping
adj. wide-ranging

Federal Government, began to carry passengers on a competing line. Ogden sued, and the New York courts ruled in his favor, holding that Gibbons could not sail by steam in New York waters.

Gibbons appealed that ruling to the Supreme Court. He claimed that the New York grant conflicted with the congressional power to regulate interstate commerce. The Court agreed. It rejected Ogden's argument that "commerce" should be defined narrowly, as simply "traffic" or the mere buying and selling of goods. Instead, the Court read the Commerce Clause in very broad terms:

PRIMARY SOURCE

Commerce, undoubtedly, is traffic, but it is something more; it is intercourse. It describes the commercial intercourse between nations, and parts of nations, in all its branches, and is regulated by prescribing rules for carrying on that intercourse.

—Chief Justice John Marshall

The Court's ruling was widely popular at the time because it dealt a death blow to steamboat monopolies. Freed from restrictive State regulation, many new steamboat companies came into existence. As a result, steam navigation developed rapidly. Within a few years, the railroads were similarly freed, which revolutionized transportation within the United States.

Over the decades, the Court's <u>sweeping</u> definition of commerce has brought an extension of federal authority into many areas of American life—a reach of federal power beyond anything the Framers could have imagined. As another of the many examples of the point, note this: It is on the basis of the commerce power that the Civil Rights Act of 1964 prohibits discrimination in access to or service in hotels, motels, theaters, restaurants, and in other public accommodations on grounds of race, color, religion, or national origin.[2]

---

2 The Supreme Court upheld this use of the commerce power in *Heart of Atlanta Motel* v. *United States* in 1964. The unanimous Court noted that there was "overwhelming evidence of the disruptive effect that racial discrimination has had on commercial intercourse." You will look at this case again in Chapter 21.

The Commerce Clause

The Congress shall have Power . . . To regulate Commerce with foreign Nations, and among the several States, and with the Indian Tribes.

—Article I, Section 8, Clause 3

FROM THE CONSTITUTION

Enabling Commerce The commerce power played a major role in the formation of the Union. The weak Congress created under the Articles of Confederation had no power to regulate interstate trade and little authority over foreign commerce. The 1780s were marked by intense commercial rivalries and bickering among the States. High trade barriers and spiteful State laws created chaos and confusion in much of the country. That circumstance led the Framers to write the Commerce Clause into the Constitution.

Constitutional Principles *How does the Commerce Clause reflect the principle of federalism?*

▲ Acting under its commerce power, Congress created the interstate highway system.

The Americans with Disabilities Act

Based on the commerce power, Congress passed the Americans with Disabilities Act (ADA) in 1990. It prohibits discrimination against people with disabilities in areas such as employment, public accommodation, public transportation, and access to commercial buildings. *How do these photographs illustrate problems addressed by the ADA?*

Limits on the Commerce Power The congressional power to regulate commerce is not unlimited. It, too, must be exercised in accord with all other provisions in the Constitution. Thus, for example, the Supreme Court struck down the Gun-Free School Zone Act of 1990 in *United States* v. *Lopez,* 1995. That act had made it a federal crime for anyone other than a police officer to possess a firearm in or around a school. The Court could find no useful connection between interstate commerce and guns at school. It held that Congress had in this case invaded the reserved powers of the States.

In more specific terms, the Constitution places four explicit limits on the use of the commerce power. The Constitution declares that Congress

1. cannot tax exports (Article I, Section 9, Clause 5);

2. cannot favor the ports of one State over those of any other in the regulation of trade (Article I, Section 9, Clause 6);

3. cannot require that "Vessels bound to, or from, one State, be obliged to enter, clear, or pay Duties in another" (Article I, Section 9, Clause 6); and, finally,

4. could not interfere with the slave trade, at least not until the year 1808 (Article I, Section 9, Clause 1). This last limitation, part of the curious Slave-Trade Compromise the Framers struck at Philadelphia, has been a dead letter for more than two centuries.

The Power to Tax

The Constitution gives Congress the power

FROM THE CONSTITUTION

To lay and collect Taxes, Duties, Imposts and Excises, to pay the Debts and provide for the common Defense and general Welfare of the United States. . . .

—Article I, Section 8, Clause 1

Remember, the Articles of Confederation had not given Congress the power to tax. Congress did have the power to requisition funds from the States; that is, Congress could ask (in reality, beg) each of the 13 States for money. But, through the 1780s, not a single State came even remotely close to meeting the few requests that Congress made, and a number of them paid nothing at all. The government was <u>impotent</u>, and the lack of a power to tax was a leading cause for the creation of the Constitution.

impotent
adj. powerless

The Purpose of Taxes We shall take another and longer look at the taxing power in Chapter 16. But, here, a number of important points: The Federal Government will take in some $2.1 trillion in fiscal year 2009, and almost certainly an even larger sum in 2010. Most of that money—well over 95 percent of it—will come from the various taxes levied by Congress.

"I assure you, Madam, that every penny you pay in taxes goes straight into the government's pocket."

▸▸ **Interpreting Cartoons** Congress levies taxes and created the Internal Revenue Service to collect them. This cartoon shows a taxpayer and an IRS agent. ***In what ways does this cartoon show a negative attitude toward taxes?***

✔**Checkpoint**
Name three purposes for which the government collects taxes.

A **tax** is a charge levied by government on persons or property to raise money to meet public needs. But notice, Congress does sometimes impose taxes for other purposes as well. The protective tariff is perhaps the oldest example of this point. Although it does bring in some revenue every year, its real goal is to "protect" domestic industry against foreign competition by increasing the cost of imported goods.

Taxes are also sometimes levied to protect the public health and safety. The Federal Government's regulation of narcotics is a case in point. Only those who have a proper federal license can legally manufacture, sell, or deal in those drugs—and licensing is a form of taxation.

Limits on the Taxing Power Congress does not have an unlimited power to tax. As with all other powers, the taxing power must be used in accord with all other provisions of the Constitution. Thus, Congress cannot lay a tax on church services, for example—because such a tax would violate the 1st Amendment. Nor could it lay a poll tax as a condition for voting in federal elections, for that would violate the 24th Amendment.

More specifically, the Constitution places four explicit limitations on the congressional power to tax:

1. Congress may tax only for public purposes, not for private benefit. Article I, Section 8, Clause 1 says that taxes may be levied only "to pay the Debts and provide for the common Defence and general Welfare of the United States. . . ."

2. Congress may not tax exports. Article I, Section 9, Clause 5 declares "[n]o Tax or Duty shall be laid on Articles exported from any State." Thus, customs duties (tariffs), which are taxes, can be levied only on goods brought into the country (imports), not on those sent abroad (exports).

3. Direct taxes must be apportioned among the States, according to their populations:

FROM THE CONSTITUTION

No Capitation, or other direct, Tax shall be laid, unless in Proportion to the Census of enumeration herein before directed to be taken.
—**Article I, Section 9, Clause 4**

A direct tax is one that must be paid directly to the government by the person on whom it is imposed—for example, a tax on the ownership of land or buildings, or a capitation (head or poll) tax.

An income tax is a direct tax, but it may be laid without regard to population:

FROM THE CONSTITUTION

The Congress shall have power to lay and collect taxes on incomes, from whatever source derived, without apportionment among the several States, and without regard to any census or enumeration.
—**16th Amendment**

Wealth (which translates to the ability to pay taxes) is not evenly distributed among the States. So, a direct tax levied in proportion to population would fall more heavily on the residents of some States than it would on others—and would, therefore, be grossly unfair. Consequently, Congress has not levied any direct tax—except for the income tax—outside the District of Columbia since 1861.

4. Article I, Section 8, Clause 1 provides that "all Duties, Imposts and Excises shall be uniform throughout the United States." That is, all indirect taxes levied by the Federal Government must be levied at the same rate in every part of the country. Those indirect taxes include the federal levies on gasoline, alcoholic beverages, and tobacco products.

As a general rule, an indirect tax is one first paid by one person but then passed on to another. It is indirectly paid by that second person. Take, for example, the federal tax on cigarettes. It is paid to the Treasury by the tobacco company, but is then passed on through the wholesaler and retailer to the person who finally buys the cigarettes.

The Borrowing Power

Article I, Section 8, Clause 2 gives Congress the power "[t]o borrow Money on the credit of the United States." There are no constitutional limits on the amount of money Congress may borrow, and no restriction on the purposes for borrowing.

The Treasury does the actual borrowing. Usually, it issues Treasury Notes (T-bills) for short-term borrowing and bonds for long-term purposes. Those securities are, in effect, promissory notes—IOUs—for which the government agrees to pay investors a certain sum plus interest on a certain date.

Congress has put a statutory ceiling on the public debt, however. The **public debt** is all of the money borrowed by the Federal Government over the years and not yet repaid, plus the accumulated interest on that money. That legal ceiling has never amounted to much more than a political gesture, however. Congress regularly raises the limit whenever the debt threatens to overtake it. The public debt now exceeds $12 trillion.

For decades, the Federal Government has practiced **deficit financing.** That is, it regularly spends more than it takes in each year and then borrows to make up the difference. Thus, the government has relied on deficit financing, on borrowing, to deal with the economic Depression of the 1930s, to meet

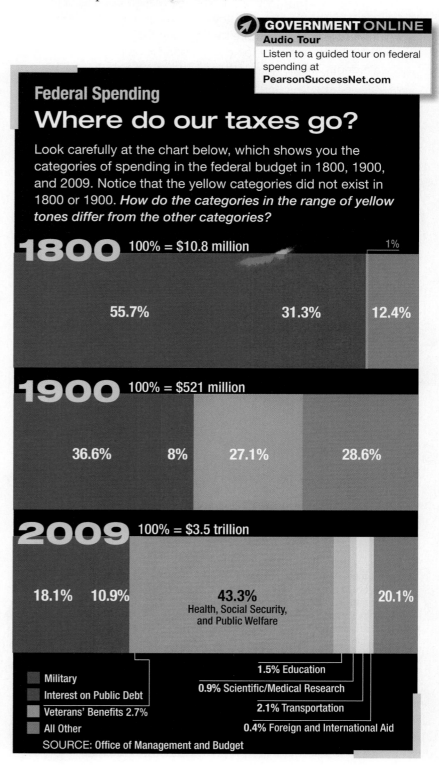

GOVERNMENT ONLINE
Audio Tour
Listen to a guided tour on federal spending at
PearsonSuccessNet.com

Federal Spending

Where do our taxes go?

Look carefully at the chart below, which shows you the categories of spending in the federal budget in 1800, 1900, and 2009. Notice that the yellow categories did not exist in 1800 or 1900. *How do the categories in the range of yellow tones differ from the other categories?*

1800 100% = $10.8 million 1%
55.7%   31.3%   12.4%

1900 100% = $521 million
36.6%   8%   27.1%   28.6%

2009 100% = $3.5 trillion
18.1%   10.9%   43.3% Health, Social Security, and Public Welfare   20.1%

Military
Interest on Public Debt
Veterans' Benefits 2.7%
All Other

1.5% Education
0.9% Scientific/Medical Research
2.1% Transportation
0.4% Foreign and International Aid

SOURCE: Office of Management and Budget

What Is Personal Bankruptcy?

GOVERNMENT ONLINE
Audio Tour
Listen to a guided audio tour about bankruptcy at **PearsonSuccessNet.com**

Regulating bankruptcy is one of the expressed powers of Congress. Declaring bankruptcy is a legal process through which people who owe more money than they can pay are relieved of part or all of their debt. It cannot be used for certain debts, including mortgages and taxes, but it can be used for medical expenses and other debts. *Why is bankruptcy a function of the Federal Government?*

Steps in Filing for Bankruptcy

1 A debtor must choose one of two kinds of bankruptcy:

The debtor gives up most of his or her property, which is then sold to pay creditors, people who are owed money.

OR

The debtor works out a payment plan with creditors, who may accept a reduced amount in exchange for total repayment over time.

▶ **Chapter 7** Liquidation Bankruptcy

▶ **Chapter 13** Individual Debt Adjustment

2 The application for bankruptcy requires detailed documentation of income, expenses, assets, liabilities, and all recent financial transactions.

Assets · Income · Liabilities · Expenses

3 When a bankruptcy application is filed, the court assumes responsibility for the debtor's finances and issues an order informing all creditors and stopping them from taking steps to collect their debts without court permission.

CREDITORS

4 With a court-appointed trustee, the debtor meets with creditors to negotiate and agree on how much each will be paid. The trustee's job is to recover as much money as possible for creditors.

5 At a hearing, a federal judge then declares the debt discharged — that is the debtor is free of debt.

---

the extraordinary costs of World War II, and to pay for wars and social programs over the decades since then.

In fact, the government's books showed a deficit in all but seven years from 1930 to 1969. And they were in the red *every* year from 1969 to 1998. As a result, the public debt climbed to more than $5.5 trillion at the beginning of fiscal year 1998.

A concerted effort by a Republican-controlled Congress and President Bill Clinton did curb the soaring debt. In fact, it produced four straight years of budget surpluses from 1998 to 2002.

Deficits are once again the order of the day, however. The Treasury has reported a deficit for every fiscal year since 2002. The shortfall topped $1.4 trillion in 2009—as you will see when we return to this whole matter of government finance in Chapter 16.

The Bankruptcy Power

Article I, Section 8, Clause 4 gives Congress the power "[t]o establish . . . uniform Laws on the subject of Bankruptcies throughout the United States." A bankrupt individual or company or other organization is one a court has found to be insolvent—that is, unable to pay debts in full. **Bankruptcy** is the legal proceeding in which the bankrupt's assets—however much or little they may be—are distributed among those to whom a debt is owed. That proceeding frees the bankrupt from legal responsibility for debts acquired before bankruptcy.

The States and the National Government have concurrent power to regulate bankruptcy. Today, however, federal bankruptcy law is so broad that it all but excludes the States. Nearly all bankruptcy cases are now heard in federal district courts.

The Currency Power

Article I, Section 8, Clause 5 gives Congress the power "[t]o coin Money [and] regulate the Value thereof." The States are expressly denied that power.[3]

---

3 Article I, Section 10, Clause 1 forbids the States the power to coin money, issue bills of credit (paper money), or make anything but gold and silver legal tender.

Until the Revolution, the English money system, built on the shilling and the pound, was in general use in the colonies. With independence, that stable currency system collapsed. The Second Continental Congress and then the Congress under the Articles issued paper money. Without sound backing, and with no taxing power behind it, however, the money was practically worthless. Each of the 13 States also issued its own currency. Adding to the confusion, people still used English coins, and Spanish money circulated freely in the southern States.

Nearly all the Framers agreed on the need for a single, national system of "hard" money. So the Constitution gave the currency power to Congress, and it all but excluded the States from that field. Currency is money in any form when it is in use as a medium of exchange. From 1789 on, among the most important of all of the many tasks performed by the Federal Government has been that of providing the nation with a uniform, stable monetary system.

From the beginning, the U.S. has issued coins in gold, silver, and other metals. Congress chartered the first Bank of the United States in 1791 and gave it the power to issue bank notes—that is, paper money. Those notes were not legal tender, however. **Legal tender** is any kind of money that a <u>creditor</u> must by law accept in payment for debts.

Congress did not create a national paper currency, and make it legal tender, until 1862. Its new national notes, known as Greenbacks, had to compete with other paper currencies already in the marketplace. Although the States could not issue paper money themselves, State governments could and did charter (license) private banks, whose notes did circulate as money. When those private bank notes interfered with the new national currency, Congress (in 1865) laid a ten percent tax on their production. The private bank notes soon disappeared. The Supreme Court upheld the 1865 law as a proper exercise of the taxing power in *Veazie Bank* v. *Fenno*, 1869.

At first, the Greenbacks could not be redeemed for gold or silver. Their worth fell to less than half their face value on the open market. Then, in 1870, the Supreme Court held their issuance to be unconstitutional. In *Hepburn* v. *Griswold* it said "to coin" meant to stamp metal and so the Constitution did not authorize the National Government to issue paper money.

The Court soon changed its mind, however, in the *Legal Tender Cases* in 1871 and again in *Juliard* v. *Greenman* in 1884. In both cases, it held the issuing of paper money as legal tender to be a proper use of the currency power. The Court also declared this a power properly implied from both the borrowing and the war powers.

✔ **Checkpoint**
How did Congress stop private bank notes from interfering with the national currency?

creditor
n. person to whom money is owed

SECTION 1 ASSESSMENT

Essential Questions	To continue to build a
Journal	response to the chapter Essential Question, go to your **Essential Questions Journal.**

1. **Guiding Question** Use your completed table to answer this question: What powers over money and commerce does the Constitution give to Congress and what limits does it put on these powers?

Key Terms and Comprehension

2. Explain the difference between the **expressed powers** and the **implied powers.**

3. What is the **commerce power** and why is it important?

Critical Thinking

4. **Make Decisions** Based on your understanding of the commerce power, explain whether Congress has the power to regulate the Internet.

5. **Draw Inferences** Why did the Framers place limits on the power of Congress to levy taxes?

6. **Express Problems Clearly** Why did the Framers explicitly grant the powers of currency, borrowing, and bankruptcy to Congress?

Quick Write

Persuasive Writing: Gather Evidence Choose one power of Congress described in this section. Then list the pros and cons of Congress exercising that power. Use your list to help you form an opinion on whether Congress has taken use of that power too far or not far enough.

SECTION 2

The Other Expressed Powers

Guiding Question

How do the expressed powers reflect the Framers' commitment to creating a strong but limited National Government? Use a table to organize information about the expressed powers of Congress.

Powers of Congress	
Foreign Policy	**Domestic Policy**
•	• Naturalization laws
•	•
•	•

Political Dictionary

- copyright
- patent
- territory
- eminent domain
- naturalization

Objectives

1. Identify the key sources of the foreign relations powers of Congress.
2. Describe the power-sharing arrangement between Congress and the President on the issues of war and national defense.
3. List other key domestic powers exercised by Congress.

Image Above: Congress has the expressed power to establish post offices and post roads.

We have just reviewed the several expressed powers that Congress has with regard to money and to foreign and interstate commerce. The Constitution gives Congress a number of other—and very important—expressed powers, and they are the focus of this section.

Congress and Foreign Policy

The Federal Government has greater powers in the field of foreign affairs than it does in any other area of public policy. The 50 States that comprise the Union are not sovereign, so they have no standing in international law. In short, the Constitution does not allow them to take part in foreign relations.[4]

The Constitution gives the President primary responsibility for the conduct of American foreign policy. As the Supreme Court stated in *United States v. Curtiss-Wright Export Corp.* in 1936, the chief executive is "the sole organ of the Federal Government in the field of international relations."

Still, the Constitution does give Congress a significant place in the field of foreign affairs. Its authority in that area arises from two sources: (1) from a number of the expressed powers, most especially the spending power, the power to regulate foreign commerce, and the war powers; and (2) from the fact that the United States is a sovereign state in the world community. As the lawmaking body of the sovereign United States, Congress has the inherent power to act on matters affecting the security of the nation—for example, the regulation of immigration and the enactment of measures to combat terrorism here and abroad. We shall return to this vitally important subject—foreign policy—in Chapter 17.

The War Powers

Six of the 27 expressed powers set out in Article I, Section 8 deal explicitly with the subject of war and national defense.[5] Remember that here, too, Congress shares power with the chief executive. The Constitution makes the

---

4 See Article I, Section 10, Clauses 1 and 3.
5 The war powers of Congress are contained in Clauses 11 through 16.

Congress shares power with the chief executive. The Constitution makes the President commander in chief of the nation's armed forces,[6] and, as such, the President dominates the field.

The congressional war powers are, however, both extensive and substantial. Only Congress can declare war. It alone has the power to raise and support armies, to provide and maintain a navy, and to make rules for the governing of the nation's military forces. Congress also has the power to provide for "calling forth the Militia" (today, the National Guard), and for the organizing, arming, and disciplining of that force. And Congress is also given the power to grant letters of marque and reprisal,[7] and to make rules concerning captures on land and water.

---

6 Article II, Section 2, Clause 1.

We shall return to the war powers in Chapter 14 and there consider, at some length, this question: Does the Constitution give the President the power to make war in the absence of a declaration of war by Congress? Many argue that it does not, but more than 200 years of American history argue otherwise. Indeed, most Presidents have used the armed forces of the United States abroad, in combat, without a congressional declaration of war.

---

7 A few of the expressed powers are of little importance today. Thus, Congress has the power to grant letters of marque and reprisal (Article I, Section 8, Clause 11), and the States are denied the power to issue them (Article I, Section 10, Clause 1). Letters of marque and reprisal are written grants of power authorizing private persons to outfit vessels to capture and destroy enemy vessels in time of war. In effect, they authorize a form of legalized piracy. Letters of marque and reprisal are forbidden in international law by the Declaration of Paris, 1856, and the United States honors the rule.

✔ **Checkpoint**
What war powers does Congress have?

The Expressed Powers of Congress
Why These Powers?

Of all the many powers the Framers could have granted to Congress, why did they choose these? In the *Federalist Papers,* James Madison answered this question by grouping the enumerated powers into the five categories below. Only Clause 9, bestowing the power to create courts inferior to the Supreme Court was not included. *Which of these powers do you think is most important? Explain.*

Security against foreign danger:
Clause 1 levy taxes, duties, and excises
Clause 2 borrow money
Clause 11 declare war
Clause 12, 13, 14 raise, regulate and provide for armies and navy
Clause 15 and 16 organize, arm, discipline, and call forth the militia to execute federal laws, suppress uprisings, and repel invasions

Regulation of the intercourse with foreign nations:
Clause 3 regulate foreign commerce
Clause 10 define and punish crimes committed on the high seas and offenses against the law of nations

Maintenance of harmony and proper intercourse among the States:
Clause 3 regulate commerce among the several States and the Indian tribes
Clause 4 establish a uniform rule of naturalization and uniform laws of bankruptcy
Clause 5 coin money, regulate the value of domestic and foreign coin, fix the standard of weights and measures
Clause 6 provide for the punishment of counterfeiting
Clause 7 establish post offices and post roads

Miscellaneous objects of general utility:
Clause 8 establish patent and copyright laws
Clause 17 legislate for the seat of the federal capital and other federal territories

Provisions for giving due efficacy to all these powers:
Clause 18 The Necessary and Proper Clause

"The powers delegated by the proposed Constitution to the federal government are few and defined. Those which are to remain in the State governments are numerous and indefinite. The former will be exercised principally on external objects, . . .
— James Madison, *The Federalist No.* 45

How does copyright law affect me?

The Internet makes sharing information easier than ever, but laws regulate what information can or cannot be shared freely. Copyright protection may be inconvenient for those who want music or other content for free, but it is important to protect the rights of writers and artists. *What determines fair use?*

Alex, Ryan, and Chris form a band. They practice their favorite popular songs and sometimes play for their friends after school. They are asked to play at a school dance. **WARNING:** Although they do not charge for their performance and they are not taking money away from the copyright holder, the band could be sued for using someone else's copyrighted work.

Ryan suggests they record an album of cover songs and distribute it for free. WARNING: The band could lose its case if sued in court for copyright infringement. If they record current songs, some people might download their version instead of buying it. That would take money from the original artist or copyright holder.

In today's world, no one can doubt that the President must have the power to respond, rapidly and effectively, to any threat to the nation's security. Still, many people have long warned of the dangers inherent in a presidential power to involve the country in undeclared wars.

Again, we shall revisit this matter in Chapter 14. But here, in the context of the war powers of Congress, we must examine the War Powers Resolution, a statute enacted by Congress in 1973.

The war-making power as it was exercised by Presidents Johnson and Nixon during the undeclared war in Vietnam (1964–1973) moved Congress to enact the War Powers Resolution. That law provides that the chief executive can commit American military forces to combat abroad only (1) if Congress has declared war or (2) when Congress has specifically authorized a military action or (3) when an attack on the United States or any of its armed forces has occurred.

If troops are ordered into combat in the third circumstance, the President is directed to report that fact to Congress within 48 hours. Any such commitment of military forces must end within 60 days, unless Congress agrees to a longer involvement. And Congress can end a commitment at any time.

The constitutionality of the War Powers Resolution remains in dispute. A determination of the question must await a situation in which Congress demands that its provisions be obeyed but the President refuses to do so.

Domestic Powers

The other expressed powers relate to domestic matters. Each of them has a direct and a considerable effect on the daily lives of the American people.

Copyrights and Patents The Constitution gives Congress the power

FROM THE CONSTITUTION

To promote the Progress of Science and useful Arts, by securing for limited Times to Authors and Inventors the exclusive Right to their respective Writings and Discoveries.

—Article I, Section 8, Clause 8

The band sells their songs over the Internet, but discover that some people are sharing the songs with friends who have not paid. **WHAT CAN THEY DO?** They can sue those who are illegally distributing and copying their compositions. If they do not take action, they could forfeit their copyright.

The band members write songs and record them. They should then copyright their compositions, registering them with the Copyright Office. **CAUTION:** The band must protect their copyrights by suing anyone who uses their songs without permission.

A rival band records one of Ryan, Chris, and Alex's songs and sells the CDs at school. **WHAT CAN THEY DO?** They can sue the other band for copyright infringement. If they can prove that they wrote the song or recorded it first, they could win and force the other band to pay damages.

Fair Use Determining an infringement of copyright depends upon whether the test of "fair use" is met. The factors considered are: **1** the purpose and character of the use, **2** the nature of the copyrighted work, **3** the amount and substantiality of the portion used, and **4** the effect of the use on the value of the copyrighted work.

In addition, the Supreme Court has held that the courts should focus on the extent that the new work is transformative—that is, does it alter the work with new expression, meaning, or message? The more transformative the new work, the less will be the significance of the other factors.

A **copyright** is the exclusive right of an author to reproduce, publish, and sell his or her creative work. That right may be assigned—transferred by contract—to another, as to a publishing firm by mutual agreement between the author and the other party.

Copyrights are registered by the Copyright Office in the Library of Congress. Under present law, they are good for the life of the author plus 70 years. They cover a wide range of creative efforts: books, magazines, newspapers, musical compositions and lyrics, dramatic works, paintings, sculptures, cartoons, maps, photographs, motion pictures, sound recordings, and much more.[8] The Office registers more than 500,000 copyrights each year.

The Copyright Office does not enforce the protections of a copyright. If the holder thinks a copyright has been violated, he or she may bring a suit for damages in the federal courts.

A **patent** grants a person the sole right to manufacture, use, or sell "any new and useful process, machine, manufacture, or composition of matter, or any new and useful improvement thereof." A patent is good for up to 20 years. The term of a patent may be extended only by a special act of Congress. The Patent and Trademark Office in the Department of Commerce administers patent laws.[9]

The Postal Powers Article I, Section 8, Clause 7 gives Congress the power "[t]o establish Post Offices and Post roads"—in effect, the power to provide for the carrying of the mail. "Post roads" are all postal routes, including rail lines, airways, and waters within the United States, during the time mail is being carried on them.

Carrying the mail is among the oldest of all governmental functions. Its origins date back at least to Egyptian practice before

✔ **Checkpoint**
Who enforces copyrights?

---

8 Not all publications can be protected by copyright. Thus, the Supreme Court has held that such "factual compilations" as telephone directories "lack the requisite originality" for copyright protection (*Feist Publications, Inc., v. Rural Telephone Service Co.,* 1991).

9 The power to protect trademarks is an implied power drawn from the commerce power. A trademark is some distinctive word, name, symbol, or device used by a manufacturer or merchant to identify his goods or services and distinguish them from those made or sold by others. A trademark need not be original, merely distinctive. The registration of a trademark carries the right to its exclusive use in interstate commerce for 10 years. The right may be renewed an unlimited number of times.

▶▶ The Constitution gives Congress the power to provide for the management of public lands and other federal property, and for a "seat of government" for the United States. *What does "Taxation without representation" on the license plate refer to?*

Today, the Postal Service functions as an independent agency in the executive branch. It serves the nation through some 37,000 post offices. The nearly 700,000 career employees of the Postal Service handle more than 200 billion pieces of mail every year.

Congress has established a number of crimes based on the postal power. It is, for example, a federal crime for anyone to obstruct the mails or to use the mails to commit any criminal act. It has also prohibited the mailing of many items, among them poisons, explosives, intoxicating liquors, some live animals, libelous or obscene matter, lottery tickets, and any articles dangerous to the mails or postal workers. Any article prohibited by a State's laws—for example, switchblade knives or firecrackers—cannot be sent into that State by mail.

The States and their local governments cannot interfere with the mails in any unreasonable way. Nor can they require licenses for Postal Service vehicles, tax the gas they use, or tax post offices or any other property of the United States Postal Service.

Territories and Other Areas In two places—in Article I, Section 8, Clause 17 and in Article IV, Section 3, Clause 2—the Constitution delegates to Congress the power to acquire, manage, and dispose of various federal areas. That power relates to the District of Columbia and to the several federal **territories,** parts of the United States that are not admitted as States and that have their own systems of government, including Puerto Rico, Guam, and the Virgin Islands. It also covers hundreds of military and naval installations, arsenals, dockyards, post offices, prisons, parks and forest preserves, and many other federal holdings.

The Federal Government may acquire property by purchase or gift. It may also do so through the exercise of the power of **eminent domain,** the inherent power to take private property for public use. Notice that the Taking Clause in the 5th Amendment restricts the Federal Government's use of the power with these words: "nor shall private property be taken for public use, without just compensation." Private property may be taken

4000 B.C. The first post office in America was established in Boston in 1639, by the General Court of the Massachusetts Bay Colony. The first successful postal system in the colonies, the Penn Post, was begun by William Penn in 1683. He established a post office in Philadelphia and provided a regular weekly service along a thirty-mile route from there to New Castle, Delaware.

The United States Postal Service traces its history back to the early colonial period. The remarkable Benjamin Franklin is generally recognized as the father of the present-day postal system. He served as Co-Deputy Postmaster of the British Colonies in North America from 1753 to 1774, when the British removed him from office because of his political activities. In 1775, he became, by unanimous choice of the Second Continental Congress, the first Postmaster General of the United States.

by eminent domain only (1) for a public use, (2) with proper notice to the owner, and (3) for a fair price. What in fact constitutes a public use, proper notice, or a fair price often becomes a matter for courts to decide.

Territory may also be acquired from a foreign state as the result of the exercise of the power of Congress to admit new States (in Article IV), the war powers, or the President's treaty-making power (in Article II). Under international law, any sovereign state may acquire unclaimed territory by discovery.

Weights and Measures
Article I, Section 8, Clause 5 gives Congress the power to "fix the Standard of Weights and Measures" throughout the United States. The power reflects the absolute need for accurate, uniform gauges of time, distance, area, weight, volume, and the like.

In 1838, Congress set the English system of pound, ounce, mile, foot, gallon, quart, and so on, as the legal standards of weights and measures in this country. In 1866, Congress also legalized the use of the metric system of gram, meter, kilometer, liter, and so on.

In 1901, Congress created the National Bureau of Standards in the Commerce Department. Now known as the National Institute of Standards and Technology, the agency keeps the original standards for the United States. It is these standards by which all other measures in the United States are tested and corrected.

Naturalization
Citizens of one country become citizens of another through a process called **naturalization.** Article I, Section 8, Clause 4 gives Congress the exclusive power "[t]o establish an uniform Rule of Naturalization." Today, the nation's population includes more than 14 million naturalized citizens.

Judicial Powers
As a part of the system of checks and balances, the Constitution gives Congress several judicial powers. Thus, it has the power to create all of the federal courts below the Supreme Court and otherwise provide for the organization and composition of the federal judiciary. The federal court system is treated at length in Chapter 18.

Congress also has the power to define federal crimes and set the punishments that may be imposed on those who violate federal law. The Constitution mentions only four. Three are found in Article I, Section 8: counterfeiting, piracies and felonies committed on the high seas, and offenses against international law. Treason is listed in Article III, Section 3. But, as you will see, Congress has used its implied powers to establish more than 100 other federal crimes.

✔ **Checkpoint**
What restrictions does the Constitution place on the exercise of eminent domain?

Essential Questions Journal To continue to build a response to the chapter Essential Question, go to your **Essential Questions Journal.**

SECTION 2 ASSESSMENT

1. **Guiding Question** Use your completed table to answer this question: How do the expressed powers reflect the Framers' commitment to creating a strong but limited National Government?

Key Terms and Comprehension
2. Explain how Congress and the President share power in foreign policy and defense.
3. How does a **copyright** differ from a **patent?**
4. What judicial powers does Congress have?

Critical Thinking
5. **Predict Consequences** How might the foreign policy of the United States be different if the Constitution had not forbidden the individual States from making treaties or alliances with foreign powers?
6. **Draw Conclusions** Some people believe that the U.S. Postal Service should be abolished because its functions could be performed more efficiently by for-profit mail companies. Do you agree? Explain.

Quick Write
Persuasive Writing: Identify Your Audience Think about who you would like to persuade to share your point of view about the power of Congress that you selected in Section 1. For example, a group of students may be interested in how Congress affects education. Make a list of the strongest evidence to persuade your audience that Congress has used that power too little or too much.

What Are the Limits on the Implied Powers of Congress?

Since the nation's founding, Americans have disagreed about the extent of the powers delegated to Congress. The Constitution had barely come into force when the meaning of the Necessary and Proper Clause was called into question.

In 1791, Congress established the Bank of the United States, despite objections from those who insisted that the Constitution did not give Congress the power to do so. Practical necessity carried the day, but the Bank's charter expired in 1811. In 1816, Congress created the Second Bank of the United States after yet another hard-fought battle over the extent of the powers of Congress.

In both instances, those who favored a stronger national government argued that a national bank was needed to stabilize the country's financial system. They also argued that its creation was clearly related to the taxing, borrowing, commerce, and currency powers. Opposing that view, those who favored a smaller national government said Congress had no authority to establish a national bank.

In 1818, the Maryland legislature placed a tax on all notes issued by any bank not chartered by Maryland law. James McCulloch, an officer of the Baltimore branch of the Second Bank, issued notes on which the tax had not been paid. The Maryland courts upheld the State's power to tax the Bank, but the United States, acting for McCulloch, appealed that decision to the Supreme Court.

Chief Justice John Marshall, quite aware of the great importance of the Court's decision in the case, declared:

Congress charters the First Bank of the United States with the support of Alexander Hamilton, 1791

Alexander Hamilton is the first Secretary of the Treasury, from 1789 to 1795.

Congress charters the Second Bank of the United States, 1816.

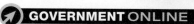
"The conflicting powers of the government of the Union … are to be discussed; and an opinion given, which may essentially influence the great operations of the government. No tribunal can approach such a question without a deep sense of its importance, and of the awful responsibility involved in its decision. But it must be decided peacefully, or remain a source of hostile legislation, perhaps of hostility of a still more serious nature; . . ."

In one of its most important decisions, the Court unanimously reversed the Maryland courts, upholding the concept of implied powers. It held that the Constitution need not expressly empower Congress to create a bank. The creation of the Second Bank of the United States, said the Court, was "necessary and proper" to the execution of the taxing, borrowing, currency, and commerce powers.

As to the question of whether Maryland had the right to tax the Bank, the Court said, "the power to tax involves the power to destroy." If States had the power to tax the Federal Government, they could destroy it. This was not, said the Court, the intention of the people when they ratified the Constitution.

Arguments for Maryland

- The Constitution gives the Federal Government no right to establish a bank.
- The power to establish banks is therefore reserved to the States.
- States are sovereign and may tax any bank within their borders.

Arguments for McCulloch and the National Bank

- The Necessary and Proper Clause gives Congress the right to do what is necessary to carry out any of its expressed powers.
- No State can lawfully tax any agency of the Federal Government.

Thinking Critically

1. What standard should be used to decide whether an act of Congress is or is not "necessary and proper"?
2. **Constitutional Principles** Did the decision in *McCulloch* v. *Maryland* strengthen or weaken the federal system?

President Andrew Jackson vetoes a bill to renew the charter of the Second Bank of the United States, 1832.

The National Banking Act creates a uniform currency for the United States, 1863.

President Woodrow Wilson signs the Federal Reserve Act, creating the Federal Reserve System, 1913.

SECTION 3
The Implied Powers

Guiding Question

How has the doctrine of implied powers increased the powers of Congress? Use a chart to record information about the implied powers.

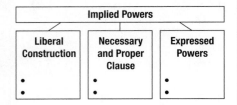

Political Dictionary

- Necessary and Proper Clause
- strict constructionist
- liberal constructionist
- consensus
- appropriate

Objectives

1. Explain how the Necessary and Proper Clause gives Congress flexibility in lawmaking.
2. Compare the strict construction and liberal construction positions on the scope of congressional power.
3. Describe the ways in which the implied powers have been applied.

Image Above: Congress established the United States Border Patrol as a major federal police agency.

What does the Constitution have to say about education? Nothing, not a word. Still, Congress provides tens of billions of dollars every year for the United States Department of Education to spend in a variety of ways throughout the country. Look around you. What indications of these federal dollars can you find in your school? If you attend a public school anywhere in the United States, that evidence should not be hard to spot.

How can this be? You know that Congress has only those powers delegated to it by the Constitution, and that document says nothing about education. The answer to that question lies in the central topic of this section: the implied powers of Congress.

The Necessary and Proper Clause

Remember, the implied powers are those powers that are not set out in so many words in the Constitution but are, rather, implied by (drawn from) those that are. The constitutional basis for the existence of the implied powers is found in one of the expressed powers. The **Necessary and Proper Clause,** the final clause in the lengthy Section 8 of Article I in the Constitution, gives to Congress the expressed power .

FROM THE CONSTITUTION

To make all Laws which shall be necessary and proper for carrying into Execution the foregoing Powers, and all other Powers vested by this Constitution in the Government of the United States, or in any Department or Officer thereof.

—Article I, Section 8, Clause 18

Much of the vitality and adaptability of the Constitution can be traced directly to this provision, and even more so to the ways in which both Congress and the Supreme Court have interpreted and applied it over the years. In effect, the Necessary and Proper Clause allows Congress to choose the means "for carrying into Execution" the many powers given to it by the Constitution.

The manner in which Congress has viewed the concept, together with the supporting decisions of the Supreme Court, have made the final clause in Article I, Section 8, truly the "Elastic Clause." It has earned that name, for it has been stretched so far and made to cover so much over the years.

Strict Versus Liberal Construction The Constitution had barely come into force when the meaning of the Elastic Clause became the subject of one of the most important disputes in American political history. The Framers of the Constitution intended to create a new and stronger National Government. The ratification of their plan was opposed by many, and that opposition was not stilled by the adoption of the Constitution. Rather, the conflict between the Federalists and the Anti-Federalists continued into the early years of the Republic. Much of that conflict centered on the powers of Congress and the meaning of the Elastic Clause. Just how broad, in fact, were those powers?

The **strict constructionists,** led by Thomas Jefferson, continued to argue the Anti-Federalist position from the ratification period. They insisted that Congress should be able to exercise (1) its expressed powers and (2) only those implied powers absolutely necessary to carry out those expressed powers. They maintained that the States should keep as much power as possible. They agreed with Jefferson that "that government is best which governs least."

Most of these Jeffersonians did acknowledge a need to protect interstate trade, and they recognized the need for a strong national defense. At the same time, they feared the consequences of a strong National Government. They believed, for instance, that the interests of the people of Connecticut were

✔ Checkpoint
What was the argument of the strict constructionists?

GOVERNMENT ONLINE
Audio Tour
Listen to a guided audio tour about these powers at
PearsonSuccessNet.com

The Implied Powers of Congress

Many of the laws Congress makes today stem from the Necessary and Proper Clause. The Framers could not have made provisions for every situation that might arise in the modern world. ***Without its implied powers, how effectively could Congress address new situations?***

The expressed power to lay and collect taxes	Implies the power to: • Punish tax evaders • Regulate (license) some commodities (such as alcohol) and outlaw the use of others (such as narcotics) • Require States to meet certain conditions to qualify for federal funding
The expressed power to borrow money	Implies the power to establish the Federal Reserve System of banks
The expressed power to create naturalization law	Implies the power to regulate and limit immigration
The expressed power to raise armies and a navy	Implies the power to draft Americans into the military
The expressed power to regulate commerce	Implies the power to: • Establish a minimum wage • Ban discrimination in workplaces and public facilities • Pass laws protecting the disabled • Regulate banking
The expressed power to establish post offices	Implies the power to: • Prohibit mail fraud and obstruction of the mails • Bar the shipping of certain items through the mail

not the same as those of South Carolinians or Marylanders or Pennsylvanians. They argued that only the States—not the far-off National Government—could protect and preserve those differing interests.

The **liberal constructionists,** led by Alexander Hamilton, had led the fight to adopt the Constitution. Now they favored a liberal interpretation of that document, a broad construction of the powers it gives to Congress. They believed that the country needed, as Hamilton put it in *The Federalist* No. 70, "an energetic Executive."

The strict constructionists were sorely troubled by that broad view of the powers of Congress. They were sure that it would all but destroy the reserved powers of the States.

Liberal Construction Prevails You know that the Supreme Court upheld the concept of implied powers in *McCulloch* v. *Maryland* in 1819. That victory for the liberal constructionists set a pattern that, in general, has been followed ever since. Over the years, the powers wielded by the National Government have grown to a point that even the most <u>ardent</u> supporters of liberal construction could not

ardent
adj. committed, passionate

have imagined. It is impossible to see how the United States could have developed as it has over the past two centuries had the Court not ruled as it did in *McCulloch.*

Several factors, working together with the liberal construction of the Constitution, have been responsible for that marked growth in national power. They have included wars, economic crises, and other national emergencies. Spectacular advances, especially in transportation and communication, have also had a real impact on the size and the scope of government. Equally important have been the demands of the people for more and still more services from government.

Congress has been led by these and other factors to view its powers in broader and broader terms. Most Presidents have regarded their powers in like fashion. The Supreme Court has generally taken a similar position in its decisions in cases involving the powers of the National Government.

Moreover, the American people have generally agreed with a broader rather than a narrow reading of the Constitution. This **consensus,** or general agreement, has prevailed even though our political history has

Congress and Education

The Constitution does not mention education. The power to act in that major area of public policy is, instead, reserved to the States. Still, Congress has been able to rely on several of its implied powers to establish programs vital to the nation's public schools. *What illustrations of that fact can you find in your school?*

The Civil Rights Act of 1964 directed the attorney general to bring court actions to eliminate race-based and other discrimination in the nation's public schools and colleges.

Civil Rights Act, 1964

Photo: Despite a federal court order to desegregate the schools, the U.S. Army had to protect African American students who enrolled at Central High School in Little Rock, Arkansas, in 1957. That situation helped to persuade Congress to pass the 1964 law.

been marked, and still is, by controversies over the proper limits of national power.

The Doctrine in Practice

The ways in which the Necessary and Proper Clause has been construed (interpreted) and applied over the last 200 years has enabled the National Government to meet the changing needs of the times. As a result, it has virtually eliminated the need for frequent amendment of the Constitution.

Instances of the exercise of the <u>doctrine</u> of implied powers are almost too numerous to count. The concept of implied powers has made it possible for the Government of the United States to meet any number of problems that could not possibly have been foreseen by the Framers. It does not stretch matters too much to say that, today, the Constitution's words "necessary and proper" really mean "convenient and useful."

Every exercise of implied powers must be based on at least one of the expressed powers. Thus, in *McCulloch* v. *Maryland* the Supreme Court found that the creation of the Bank of the United States was "necessary and proper"

to the execution of four expressed powers held by Congress: the taxing, borrowing, currency, and commerce powers.

Over the years, Congress has most often found a basis for the exercise of implied powers in (1) the commerce power, (2) its power to tax and spend, and (3) the war powers.

The Commerce Clause As you know, the Commerce Clause gives Congress the power to regulate both foreign and interstate trade. And you are aware, too, of the Supreme Court's hugely expansive reading of that provision, beginning with *Gibbons* v. *Ogden* in 1824. The word "commerce" has been held to include the production and the buying and selling of goods as well as the transportation of people and commodities. Commerce has been defined so broadly that it encompasses virtually every form of economic activity today. Congress has the authority to regulate manufacturing, wages and hours, labor-management relations, foods and drugs, air travel, and much more. It can provide for the building of interstate highways, consumer protection, the protection of the environment—the list goes on and on. In 1998,

✔ **Checkpoint**
What factors have led to the growth of national power?

<u>doctrine</u>
n. a principle or concept

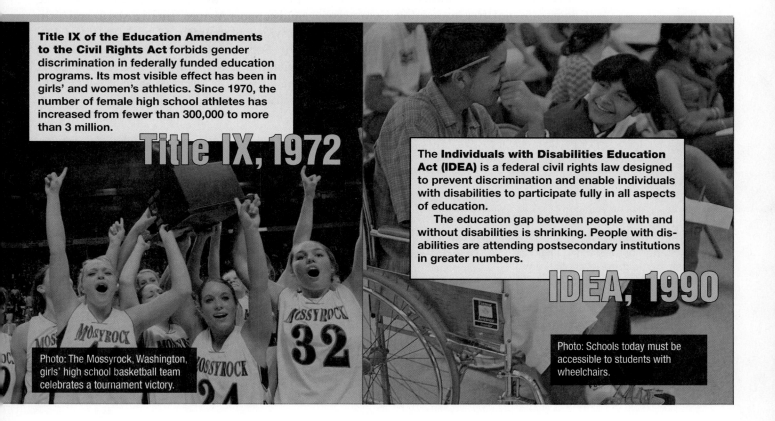

Title IX of the Education Amendments to the Civil Rights Act forbids gender discrimination in federally funded education programs. Its most visible effect has been in girls' and women's athletics. Since 1970, the number of female high school athletes has increased from fewer than 300,000 to more than 3 million.

Title IX, 1972

Photo: The Mossyrock, Washington, girls' high school basketball team celebrates a tournament victory.

The **Individuals with Disabilities Education Act (IDEA)** is a federal civil rights law designed to prevent discrimination and enable individuals with disabilities to participate fully in all aspects of education.
The education gap between people with and without disabilities is shrinking. People with disabilities are attending postsecondary institutions in greater numbers.

IDEA, 1990

Photo: Schools today must be accessible to students with wheelchairs.

"I do want a war, but I'd like to be asked nicely."

▸▸ **Interpreting Cartoons** Congress has several war powers, but the President has primary responsibility for the conduct of wars. **To which war power does this cartoon refer?**

Congress cannot pass a law based solely on the grounds that a measure will somehow promote "the general Welfare of the United States." But it can and does levy taxes and provide for the spending of money for that purpose. Thus, for example, as we said on the opening page of this section, Congress **appropriates**—assigns to a particular use—tens of billions of dollars per year to support education. And, similarly, it does so to provide for such things as farm subsidies, unemployment compensation, Social Security, Medicare, and a host of other programs.

The War Powers The several war powers reflect the fact that the National Government is responsible for the protection of this country against aggression and, when necessary, for the waging of war. As with its other expressed powers, Congress has the authority to do whatever is necessary and proper for the execution of its war power—with the exception that, in doing so, it cannot violate any other provision of the Constitution. Among many other examples of the point, Congress has the power to provide for compulsory military service—a draft—because Article I, Section 8 gives it the expressed power "[t]o raise and support Armies" (in Clause 12) and "[t]o provide and maintain a Navy" (in Clause 13). The Supreme Court originally upheld the constitutionality of a draft in a series of cases challenging the Selective Service Act of 1917 (*Selective Draft Law Cases,* 1918).

moratorium
n. temporary suspension

Congress used the Commerce Clause to impose a three-year <u>moratorium</u> on State taxation of e-commerce and other Internet activities; that freeze was extended in 2007.

Limits on the Commerce Power Still, Congress is not free to use the Commerce Clause to do whatever it chooses. The Constitution places four explicit limitations on the exercise of the commerce power. And the Supreme Court does, at least on occasion, find that the lawmaking branch has overstepped its authority under that provision.

Essential Questions Journal To continue to build a response to the chapter Essential Question, go to your **Essential Questions Journal.**

SECTION 3 ASSESSMENT

1. **Guiding Question** Use your completed chart to answer this question: How has the doctrine of implied powers increased the powers of Congress?

Key Terms and Comprehension

2. What is the **Necessary and Proper Clause** and why is it important?

3. Summarize the main disagreements between **strict constructionists** and **liberal constructionists**.

Critical Thinking

4. **Draw Inferences** How have war and economic crises increased the power of the National Government?

5. **Predict Consequences** If the strict constructionists had won the battle to limit the implied powers, how might the United States be different today?

6. **Draw Conclusions** Why is the Commerce Clause, written in 1787, still adequate to meet the needs of the nation in the 21st century?

Quick Write

Persuasive Writing: Make an Outline Write a thesis statement expressing your view and explaining the power you chose in Section 1. Explain why the Framers delegated this power to Congress and how it has been interpreted. Then use your lists from Sections 1 and 2 to make an outline of the arguments you will use to support it.

Congressional War Powers

▶▶ Track the Issue

The Constitution divides the war powers between Congress and the President. However, it remains unclear whether Congress may control the conduct of war.

1770s–1780s

Continental Congress acts as the civilian authority over the armed forces.

1860s

President Abraham Lincoln clashes with Congress over the conduct of the Civil War, the appointment of generals, and the freeing of slaves.

1898

Congress approves the use of force to secure Cuban independence, but prohibits its annexation.

1969

The War Powers Resolution limits the President's ability to send troops abroad without Congressional approval.

2001

President George W. Bush requests military authority to combat terrorism; Congress approves force only against those involved in the 9/11 attacks.

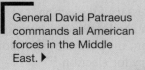

General David Patraeus commands all American forces in the Middle East. ▶

▶▶ Perspectives

Several years into the Iraq war, the 2006 mid-term elections produced Democratic majorities in both the House and Senate. The Democrats, including President Barack Obama, elected in 2008, have pledged to end that increasingly unpopular war. The Bush administration had fought the efforts of Congress to assert control over the conflict.

"[Congressional war] powers. . . . are a clear and direct statement that Congress has authority to declare, to define, and ultimately to end a war. . . . By prohibiting funds . . . , Congress can force the President to bring our forces out of Iraq. . . . Since the President is adamant about pursuing his failed policies in Iraq, Congress has the duty to stand up and use its power to stop him."

—*Senator Russell D. Feingold (D., Wisconsin), 2007*

"Congress does, of course, play a critical role in . . . the conduct of a war. That role is defined and limited by the Constitution. After all, the military answers to one commander-in-chief in the White House, not 535 commanders-in-chief on Capitol Hill. Congress does have the purse strings. . . . We expect the House and Senate to meet the needs of our military and the generals leading the troops in battle on time and in full measure."

—*Vice President Richard B. Cheney, 2007*

▶▶ Connect to Your World

1. **Understand (a)** What reason did Senator Feingold give for his argument that Congress should end the war in Iraq? **(b)** How did Vice President Cheney describe the role of Congress?
2. **Compare and Contrast (a)** How are the two views of congressional war powers alike and how do they differ? **(b)** Whose view do you agree with? Why?

🔘 **GOVERNMENT** ONLINE

In the News

For updates about congressional war powers, visit **PearsonSuccessNet.com**

The **Nonlegislative Powers**

What nonlegislative powers does the Constitution delegate to Congress? Use a concept web to record the congressional powers described in this section.

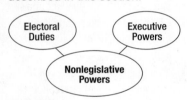

Political Dictionary

- successor
- impeach
- acquit
- perjury
- censure
- subpoena

Objectives

1. Describe the role of Congress in amending the Constitution and its electoral duties.
2. Describe the power of Congress to impeach, and summarize presidential impeachment cases.
3. Identify the executive powers of Congress.
4. Describe the investigatory powers of Congress.

Image Above: Bill Gates testifies at a congressional hearing on technological innovation.

Congress is a legislative body; its primary function is to make law. But the Constitution does give it some other chores—several nonlegislative duties—to perform as well.

Constitutional Amendments

Article V says that Congress may propose amendments to the Constitution by a two-thirds vote in each house. All 33 of the amendments thus far added to the document have been proposed by Congress. Article V also provides that Congress may call a national convention of delegates from each of the States to propose an amendment—but only if requested to do so by at least two thirds (34) of the State legislatures. No such convention has ever been called.

In recent years, several State legislatures have petitioned Congress for amendments—among them measures that would require Congress to balance the federal budget each year, prohibit flag burning, permit prayer in public schools, outlaw abortions, impose term limits on members of Congress, and prohibit same-sex marriages.

Electoral Duties

The Constitution gives certain electoral duties to Congress. But they are to be exercised only in very unusual circumstances.

The House may be called on to elect a President. The 12th Amendment says that if no one receives a majority of the electoral votes for President, the House, voting by States, is to decide the issue. It must choose from among the three highest contenders in the electoral college balloting. Each State has but one vote to cast, and a majority of the States is necessary for election.

The Senate must choose a Vice President if no candidate wins a majority of the electoral votes for that office. In that situation, the vote is by individual senators, with a majority of the full Senate necessary for election.[10]

---

10 Notice that the 12th Amendment makes it possible for the President to be of one party and the Vice President another. On the matter of presidential and vice-presidential selection, see Chapter 13.

The House has had to choose a President twice: Thomas Jefferson in 1801 and John Quincy Adams in 1825. The Senate has had to pick a Vice President only once: Richard M. Johnson in 1837.

Remember that the 25th Amendment provides for the filling of a vacancy in the vice presidency. When one occurs, the President nominates a **successor**—a replacement, someone to fill the vacancy, subject to a majority vote in both houses of Congress. That process has also been used twice: Gerald Ford was confirmed as Vice President in 1973 and Nelson Rockefeller in 1974.

Impeachment

The Constitution provides that the President, Vice President, and all civil officers of the United States may "be removed from Office on Impeachment for, and Conviction of, Treason, Bribery, or other high Crimes and Misdemeanors."[11] A close reading of those words suggests that the Framers expected that only serious criminal offenses, not political disagreements, would lead to impeachment. Politics has, nevertheless, been at the root of most impeachment controversies.

The House has the sole power to **impeach**—to accuse, bring charges. The Senate has the sole power to try—to judge, to sit as a court—in impeachment cases.[12]

Impeachment requires only a majority vote in the House; conviction requires a two-thirds vote in the Senate. The Chief Justice presides over the Senate when a President is to be tried. The penalty for conviction is removal from office. The Senate may also prohibit a convicted person from ever holding federal office again; and he or she can be tried in the regular courts for any crime involved

in the events that led to the impeachment. To date, there have been 17 impeachments and seven convictions; all seven persons removed by the Senate were federal judges.[13]

Two Presidents have been impeached by the House: Andrew Johnson in 1868 and Bill Clinton in 1998. The Senate voted to **acquit** both men—that is, it found them not guilty.

Andrew Johnson The unsuccessful attempt to remove Andrew Johnson grew out of the turmoil that followed the Civil War. Mr. Johnson had become the nation's 17th President when Abraham Lincoln was assassinated in April of 1865, and he soon became

✔ • **Checkpoint**
What is the penalty if a President is impeached and convicted?

How Government Works

Electoral Duties of Congress
Who Wins?

Presidents regularly come from the two major parties. No law says that only two people may run in the general election, but the Constitution does say that the winner must receive a majority of the electoral college votes, now 270. *What would happen if a minor party candidate won enough electoral votes to prevent any candidate winning a majority?*

STEP 1:
No candidate receives a majority of the **electoral college votes.**

246 **25** **267**

STEP 2:
Each State's **House** delegation must decide which of the top three candidates to support. Each State has **one vote** in the contest. Failure to agree means the loss of that State's vote.

STEP 3:
A candidate who wins a **majority** (26) of the votes of the States' delegations **wins the presidency.** If no candidate wins a majority of the States' votes, another vote must be taken.

Winner!

---

[11] Article II, Section 4. Military officers are not considered "civil officers," nor are members of Congress.

[12] Article I, Section 2, Clause 5; Section 3, Clause 6.

[13] Seven other federal judges were impeached by the House but later acquitted by the Senate. Two federal judges impeached by the House resigned before the Senate could act in their cases. One of the seven judges removed from office was later elected to Congress. The only other federal officer ever impeached was William W. Bellknap, President Grant's Secretary of War. Bellknap had been accused of accepting bribes and, although he had resigned from office, was impeached by the House in 1876. He was then tried by the Senate and found not guilty.

enmeshed
v. entangled; caught up in

conciliatory
adj. producing agreement

enmeshed in a series of disputes with the Radical Republicans who controlled both houses of Congress. Many of those disagreements centered around the treatment of the defeated Southern States in the immediate post-war period.

President Johnson sought to carry out the conciliatory Reconstruction policies favored by Abraham Lincoln—policies that Mr. Lincoln had summarized in these memorable words in his Second Inaugural Address on March 4, 1865: "With malice toward none, with charity for all. . . ." The Radical Republicans supported a much harsher approach to Reconstruction.

Matters came to a head when Congress passed the Tenure of Office Act, over the President's veto, in 1867. President Johnson's violation of that law triggered his impeachment by a House bent on political revenge. The Senate fell just one vote short of removing him from office.

Bill Clinton Bill Clinton was impeached by the House in 1998. In proceedings steeped in partisanship, the House voted two articles of impeachment against him on December 19. Both articles arose out of the President's admitted "inappropriate relationship" with a White House intern. The first article charged the President with **perjury**—that is, lying under oath. The second article accused him of obstruction of justice because he had withheld information about his affair with the intern.

Members of the House who supported the articles of impeachment contended that the acts of lying under oath and of withholding evidence were within the meaning of the Constitution's phrase "other high Crimes and Misdemeanors." Therefore, they argued, the President's immediate removal from office was justified.

Their opponents argued that the facts involved in the case did not justify either charge. They insisted that, while the President's conduct was deplorable and should be condemned, that conduct did not rise to the level of an impeachable offense. Many of them pressed, instead, for a resolution to **censure** the President—that is, for a formal condemnation of his behavior.

The Senate received the articles of impeachment when the new Congress convened in 1999, and it began to sit in judgment of the President on January 7.

Richard Nixon A few officeholders have resigned in the face of almost certain impeachment—most notably, Richard Nixon, who resigned the presidency in mid-1974. President Nixon's second term in office was cut short by the Watergate scandal.

The term *Watergate* comes from a June 1972 attempt by Republican operatives to break into the Democratic Party's national headquarters in the Watergate office complex in Washington, D.C. The investigation of that incident, by the *Washington Post* and then by other media, led to official investigations by the Department of Justice and by the Senate's Select Committee on Presidential Campaign Activities, popularly known as the Senate Watergate Committee.

The probes unearthed a long list of illegal acts, including bribery, perjury, income tax fraud, and illegal campaign contributions.

Gerald Ford became President by Congressional confirmation, without election to the presidency or vice-presidency. He acquired each post upon the resignation of others.

GOVERNMENT ONLINE
Audio Tour
Listen to a guided audio tour about impeachment at
PearsonSuccessNet.com

The Impeachment Process

President Clinton's Impeachment

This chronology details the complex impeachment process and shows how the process worked in the impeachment of President Bill Clinton. *What measures did the Framers build into the impeachment process to ensure its fairness? Why do you think the attempt to remove Clinton failed?*

1998

The House Judiciary Committee considers charges against the accused and votes on whether to send articles of impeachment to the full House. A simple majority vote is needed to start the process. ▼

December 11–12, 1998 After three months of hearings, the House Judiciary Committee approves four articles.

Acting much like a grand jury, the House considers the charge(s) brought by the Judiciary Committee. It can subpoena witnesses and evidence. It hears and debates arguments. ▼

December 18–19, 1998 The House holds 13 hours of bitter, partisan debate, in which more than 200 House members speak. Democrats briefly walk out to protest Republican leaders' refusal to consider the lesser punishment of censure.

Newspapers weighed in on the proceedings.

The House votes on each article. If any article is approved by a majority vote, the official is impeached, which is similar to being indicted. The House sends the article(s) of impeachment to the Senate. ▼

December 19, 1998 The House votes to impeach Mr. Clinton on two counts. The votes are 228-206 on the count of perjury and 221-212 on obstruction of justice. Voting is mostly along party lines.

1999

The Senate tries the case. If the President is to be tried, the Chief Justice of the United States presides. Selected members of the House act as managers (prosecutors). ▼

January 7, 1999 Chief Justice William Rehnquist opens a televised trial. Representative Henry Hyde of Illinois leads a team of 13 House managers. White House Counsel Charles Ruff leads the defense.

Republican leaders held a press conference.

Senators hear testimony and evidence. House prosecutors and lawyers for both sides present their cases. Additional witnesses may be called. Senators may also vote to curb testimony. ▼

January 7–February 11, 1999 With public distaste for impeachment growing, the Senate limits testimony to three witnesses, the intern among them. Closing arguments follow. For three days, the Senate deliberates in secret (despite Democrats' objections).

Protesters rallied outside the Capitol.

The Senate debates the articles, publicly or privately. It need not render a verdict. It could, for example, vote to drop the case and instead censure the official. A two-thirds vote is required for conviction. ▼

February 12, 1999 In a televised session, the Senate acquits the President on both charges, falling well short of the two-thirds vote needed for conviction. There are 55 Republicans and 45 Democrats in the Senate. On the perjury count, 45 Democrats and 10 Republicans vote not guilty. On the obstruction charge, 5 Republicans break with their party to vote with all of the Democrats against conviction.

Top: Congress reviewed tapes of Clinton's testimony.
Bottom: House Democrats walked out to protest the impeachment resolution.

How Government Works

Congressional Checks on the Presidential Treaty-Making Power
Congressional Influence

The Senate approves high-level appointments by the President, including the secretary of state, as well as ambassadors to foreign nations, who often play a role in the treaty-making process. Senator Charles Schumer, right, introduces Hilary Rodham Clinton during her confirmation hearing for secretary of state.

The President consults with Congress during the negotiation of treaties. Above, Senate Foreign Relations Committee member Senator Richard Lugar talks to reporters after meeting with President George W. Bush about a nuclear arms reduction treaty with Russia.

They also revealed the use of the Federal Bureau of Investigation, the Internal Revenue Service, and other government agencies for personal and partisan purposes.

The House Judiciary Committee voted three articles of impeachment against President Nixon in late July 1974. He was charged with obstruction of justice, abuse of power, and failure to respond to the Judiciary Committee's **subpoenas.** A committee's subpoena is a legal order directing one to appear before that body and/or to produce certain evidence. Mr. Nixon had ignored the committee's subpoena of several tape recordings of Watergate-related conversations in the Oval Office.

It was quite apparent that the full House would impeach the President and that the Senate would convict him. Those facts prompted Mr. Nixon to resign the presidency on August 9, 1974.

Beyond doubt, the Watergate scandal involved the most extensive and the most serious violations of public trust in the nation's history. Among its other consequences, several Cabinet officers, presidential assistants, and others were convicted of various felonies and misdemeanors—and many of them served jail time.

Executive Powers

The Constitution gives two executive powers to the Senate. One of those powers has to do with appointments to office, and the other with treaties made by the President.[14]

Appointments All major appointments made by the President must be confirmed by the Senate by majority vote. Each of the President's nominations is referred to the appropriate standing committee of the Senate. That committee may then hold hearings to decide whether or not to make a favorable recommendation to the full Senate for that appointment. When the committee's recommendation is brought to the floor of the Senate, it may be, but seldom is, considered in executive (secret) session.

The appointment of a Cabinet officer or of some other top member of the President's "official family" is rarely rejected by the Senate. The Senate has rejected only 12

---

14 Article II, Section 2, Clause 2

15 The first was Roger B. Taney, Andrew Jackson's choice for secretary of the treasury in 1832. Jackson later named Taney Chief Justice. The most recent rejection came in 1989, when the Senate refused President George H.W. Bush's nomination of John Tower as secretary of defense.

Presidents may need to make changes in a treaty at the behest of Congress. This ensures that there is broad consensus for any such agreement among the American people. Above, protesters oppose NAFTA outside Oklahoma's State Capitol.

Even after a treaty has been approved, Congress can abrogate (repeal) it, by passing a law that is inconsistent with its terms, or by directing the President to abrogate. Right, a lock in the Panama Canal. The Panama Canal Treaty of 1903 was replaced by a new treaty in 1979, which returned the canal to Panama.

of more than 600 Cabinet appointments.[15] More commonly, the President will withdraw a nomination if the Senate sends signals that it will reject the nominee in a confirmation vote. For example, President George W. Bush withdrew the nomination of Harriet Miers, his White House Counsel, to the Supreme Court. Bush later nominated Samuel Alito, who was confirmed by the Senate.

It is with the President's appointment of federal officers who serve in the various States (for example, U.S. attorneys and federal marshals) that the unwritten rule of "senatorial courtesy" comes into play. The Senate will turn down such a presidential appointment if it is opposed by a senator of the President's party from the State involved. The Senate's observance of this unwritten rule has a significant impact on the President's exercise of the power of appointment; in effect, this rule means that some senators virtually dictate certain presidential appointments.

Treaties The President makes treaties "by and with the Advice and Consent of the Senate, . . . provided two thirds of the Senators present <u>concur</u>."[16] For a time after the adoption of the Constitution, the President asked the advice of the Senate when a treaty

was being negotiated and prepared. Now the President most often consults the members of the Senate Foreign Relations Committee and other influential senators of both parties.

The Senate may accept or reject a treaty as it stands, or it may decide to offer amendments, reservations, or understandings to it. Treaties are sometimes considered in executive session. Because the House has a hold on the public purse strings, influential members of that body are often consulted in the treaty-making process, too.

The Power to Investigate

Congress has the power to investigate—to inquire into, or inform itself on—any matter that falls within the scope of its lawmaking authority. The authority to do so is implied by the Constitution's grant of the legislative power to Congress, in Article I, Section 1. As

---

16 Article II, Section 2, Clause 2. It is often said that the Senate "ratifies" a treaty. It does not. The Senate may give or withhold its "advice and consent" to a treaty made by the President. Once the Senate has consented to a treaty, the President ratifies it by exchanging "instruments of ratification" with other parties to the agreement. We discuss the treaty-making process at some length in Chapter 14.

✔ **Checkpoint**
What is the unwritten rule known as "senatorial courtesy"?

<u>concur</u>
v. agree

CONGRESSIONAL OVERSIGHT

▶▶ **Interpreting Cartoons** In February 2007, the House passed a nonbinding resolution opposing the President's plan to send more troops to Iraq. *What point does the cartoonist make?*

✔ **Checkpoint**
What are some of the reasons that Congress holds hearings?

we noted, both the House and Senate exercise that power through the standing committees and their subcommittees and often through special committees, as well.

Both houses may choose to conduct investigations for any one or a number of reasons. Most often, those inquiries are held to (1) gather information necessary to the framing of legislation, (2) oversee the operations of various agencies in the executive branch, (3) focus public attention on some particular matter, (4) expose the questionable activities of some public official or private

person or group, and/or (5) promote the particular interests of some members of Congress. Notice that the second of these motives, oversight, is a little-noted but quite important aspect of the constitutional system of checks and balances. Note, too, that Congress is more inclined to exercise its oversight function when one or both of its chambers is controlled by the party that does not hold the presidency, most recently in 2007 and 2008.

Over recent years, Congress has improved its ability both to inform itself and to perform its oversight responsibilities by increasing the staff resources available to the standing committees of both houses. The three little-known agencies in the legislative branch which also add to that capability are:

1. the Congressional Budget Office, which committees of both houses rely on quite heavily in taxing, spending, and other budget-related matters;

2. the Congressional Research Service, in the Library of Congress, whose several hundred staff specialists provide members with factual information on virtually any subject; and

3. the Government Accountability Office, also called Congress' watchdog because it has broad authority to monitor the work of the Federal Government and report its findings to Congress.

Essential Questions Journal To continue to build a response to the chapter Essential Question, go to your **Essential Questions Journal.**

SECTION 4 ASSESSMENT

1. **Guiding Question** Use your completed concept web to answer this question: What nonlegislative powers does the Constitution delegate to Congress?

Key Terms and Comprehension

2. If the vice presidency becomes vacant, how is a **successor** chosen?

3. Summarize the circumstances of President Richard Nixon's resignation from office.

4. Outline the process by which Congress approves or rejects presidential appointments.

5. What powers does Congress have with regard to treaties negotiated by the President?

Critical Thinking

6. **Draw Conclusions** In what two ways may Congress propose amendments to the Constitution? Do you think the Framers made amending the Constitution too difficult? Explain.

7. **Determine Cause and Effect** How do each of the nonlegislative powers of Congress illustrate the principle of checks and balances?

Quick Write

Persuasive Writing: Review and Revise Review and revise your outline from Section 3, making sure that your points are presented in a logical sequence. Use transition words, such as *although, because,* and *then* to guide readers through your ideas. Add details that will make your presentation more interesting.

Quick Study Guide

GOVERNMENT ONLINE

On the Go

To review anytime, anywhere, download these online resources at **PearsonSuccessNet.com**

Political Dictionary, Audio Review

Guiding Question
Section 2 How do the expressed powers reflect the Framers' commitment to creating a strong but limited national government?

Guiding Question
Section 3 How has the doctrine of implied powers increased the powers of Congress?

CHAPTER 11
Essential Question
What should be the limits on the powers of Congress?

Guiding Question
Section 1 What powers over money and commerce does the Constitution give to Congress and what limits does it put on these powers?

Guiding Question
Section 4 What nonlegislative powers does the Constitution delegate to Congress?

Political Dictionary

expressed powers p. 296
implied powers p. 296
inherent powers p. 296
commerce power p. 297
tax p. 300
public debt p. 301
deficit financing p. 301
bankruptcy p. 302
legal tender p. 303
copyright p. 307
patent p. 307
territory p. 308
eminent domain p. 308
naturalization p. 309
Necessary and Proper Clause p. 312
strict constructionist p. 313
liberal constructionist p. 314
consensus p. 314
appropriate p. 316
successor p. 319
impeach p. 319
acquit p. 319
perjury p. 320
censure p. 320
subpoena p. 322

Legislative Checks and Balances

On the Executive Branch	On the Judicial Branch
• Provides funding for the armed forces	• Congress creates courts inferior to the Supreme Court
• The power to declare war	• Senate must confirm appointments of federal judges
• Senate must approve treaties	
• Senate must approve appointments	

Comparing the House and the Senate

Only the House has the power to	Only the Senate has the power to
• Impeach executive and judicial officers	• Try impeachments
• Originate tax bills	• Approve or reject treaties
	• Confirm the appointment of all federal judges, Cabinet members, and other top-level officers

Chapter Assessment

Comprehension and Critical Thinking

Section 1

1. **(a)** Identify the three different types of congressional powers. **(b)** Explain how the Constitution limits the power of Congress.

2. **(a)** Describe the commerce power. **(b)** Why did the Framers grant this power to Congress? **(c)** What was the significance of the Supreme Court's decision in *Gibbons* v. *Ogden?*

3. **(a)** Why did the Framers grant Congress the power to tax? **(b)** What is the purpose of taxes? **(c)** How is the borrowing power related to the taxing power?

4. Why did Congress create a national currency?

Section 2

5. **(a)** What powers does the Constitution grant to Congress affecting war and national defense? **(b)** Why do you think the Framers gave Congress the sole power to declare war? **(c)** What tensions may arise from the division of the war powers between the Congress and the President?

6. **(a)** How do copyrights and patents "promote the Progress of Science and useful Arts"? **(b)** Why do you think the Framers granted these powers to Congress?

7. **(a)** List the expressed powers of Congress. **(b)** Are there any powers which, in your view, Congress should possess, but does not? Explain.

Section 3

8. **(a)** Describe the conflict over the meaning of the Necessary and Proper Clause. **(b)** Why is that clause also called the Elastic Clause?

9. **(a)** What is the significance of the Court's decision in *McCulloch* v. *Maryland?* **(b)** Does the concept of implied powers undercut federalism? Why or why not?

Section 4

10. **(a)** What nonlegislative powers does the Constitution grant to Congress? **(b)** How does each of those powers check or balance the executive branch?

11. **(a)** Outline the steps of the impeachment process. **(b)** Has the definition of "high crimes and misdemeanors" as impeachable offenses been stretched too far? Explain.

Writing About Government

12. **Persuasive Writing** Use your Quick Write exercises from this chapter to write a persuasive essay arguing that Congress has used its power too little or too much. Remember that your writing will be most effective if you emphasize arguments your audience will find convincing. See pp. S9—S10 in the Skills Handbook.

Apply What You've Learned

13. **Essential Question Activity** Do research to identify the major pieces of legislation that Congress enacted in a recent session. Choose two pieces of legislation that are based on the expressed powers of Congress and two pieces that are based on implied powers. Summarize each of the measures and explain which power allows Congress to be involved.

14. **Essential Question Assessment** Based on your summaries and the content of this chapter, explain in a paragraph how current congressional activity might be different if the Constitution were interpreted strictly. This will help you think about the chapter Essential Question: **What should be the limits on the powers of Congress?**

**Essential Questions
Journal**
To respond to the chapter Essential Question, go to your **Essential Questions Journal.**

Document-Based Assessment

Strict v. Liberal Construction of the Constitution

The dispute over the extent of the powers the Constitution grants to the National Government has continued to the present day. As you can see in Document 1, some make the argument that big government can be dangerous. Others see small government as insufficient to meet the needs of the people, as in Document 2.

Document 1

"[Americans] are a lot better economists than most economists care to admit. They know that a government big enough to give you everything you want is a government big enough to take from you everything you have.

—**President Gerald R. Ford,**
Remarks to a Joint Session
of Congress

Document 2

How much pruning can we do and still get apples?

Use your knowledge of the debate over the limits of federal power and these two documents to answer Questions 1–3.

1. In Document 2, what do "apples" represent?
   A. Supreme Court rulings
   B. wasteful federal programs
   C. things people want from government
   D. taxes

2. What did President Ford mean when he said that "a government big enough to give you everything you want is a government big enough to take from you everything you have"?

3. **Pull It Together** Compare the viewpoints of each document. How do you think the Federal Government should balance these points of view?

GOVERNMENT ONLINE
Documents
To find more primary sources on interpreting the Constitution, visit **PearsonSuccessNet.com**

Congress in Action

Essential Question
Can and should the lawmaking process be improved?

"Congress **in session** is Congress on **public exhibition,** whilst Congress in its **committee-rooms** is Congress **at work.**

—Woodrow Wilson, *Congressional Government: A Study in American Politics,* 1885

Photo: Members of the press take photographs at a Senate Select Committee on Intelligence session.

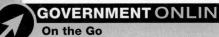

GOVERNMENT ONLINE
On the Go

To study anywhere, anytime, download these online resources at PearsonSuccessNet.com
• Political Dictionary
• Audio Review
• Downloadable Interactivities

SECTION 1

Congress Organizes

What comes to mind when you hear the word *Congress?* The Capitol? Your members of Congress? Some particular bill? Those senators and representatives you often see on the evening news? Of course, you know that the nation's lawmaking body is much more than that. It is in fact a very complex enterprise, and much larger than most people realize. Some 30,000 men and women work for the legislative branch today; and Congress appropriates some $4 billion every year to finance its own many-sided operations.[1]

Congress Convenes

Congress convenes—begins a new term—every two years, on January 3 of every odd-numbered year. Each new term follows the general elections in November.

Opening Day in the House Every other January, the 435 men and women who have been elected to the House come together at the Capitol to begin a new term. At that point, they are, in effect, just so many representatives-elect. Because all 435 of its seats are up for election every two years, the House technically has no sworn members, no rules, and no organization until its opening-day ceremonies are held.

Senator Sherrod Brown (D., Ohio) sat in the House of Representatives for seven terms before he won election to the Senate in 2006. He remembers his first opening day, in 1993, this way:

PRIMARY SOURCE

"Walking around the chamber the first day, I was awed and nervous. . . . [Q]uestions gnawed at me when I walked into that august [grand] room, when I met several members about whom I had read and whom I had seen on television. And then I thought about the President of the United States coming to address us— 'Do I deserve to be here with all these people? How did I get here? Will I measure up? How was I chosen for this privilege?'"

—Sherrod Brown, *Congress From the Inside*

The clerk of the House in the preceding term <u>presides</u> at the beginning of the first day's session.[2] The clerk calls the chamber to order and checks the roll of representatives-elect. Those members-to-be then choose a Speaker, who will be their permanent presiding officer. By custom, the Speaker is a long-standing member of the majority party, and election on the floor is only a formality. The majority party's members in the House have settled the matter beforehand.

The Speaker then takes the oath of office. By tradition, the oath is administered by the Dean of the House, the member-elect with the longest record of service in the House.[3] With that accomplished, the Speaker swears in the rest of the members, as a body. The Democrats take their seats to the right of the center aisle; the Republicans, to the left.

Next, the House elects its clerk, parliamentarian, sergeant at arms, chief administrative officer, and chaplain. None of these people are members of the House, and their elections are also a formality. The majority party has already decided the matter.

Then, the House adopts the rules that will govern its proceedings through the term. The rules of the House have been developing for over 200 years, and they are contained in a volume of about 400 pages. They are readopted, most often with little or no change, at the beginning of each term, though they are occasionally and sometimes extensively amended during a term. Thus, in 2009, the rules were amended to repeal a limit on the number of terms any member can chair any House committee. That controversial limit (of three terms, six years) had been adopted by a newly elected Republican majority at the beginning of the 104th Congress in 1995.

Finally, members of the 20 permanent committees of the House are appointed by a floor vote. With that, the House is organized.

Opening Day in the Senate The Senate is a continuous body. It has been organized without interruption since its first session in 1789. Recall that only one third of the seats are up for election every two years. Two thirds of the Senate's membership is carried over from one term to the next. As a result, the Senate does not face large organizational problems at the beginning of a term. Its first-day session is nearly always fairly short and routine, even when the elections have brought a change in the majority party. Newly elected and reelected members must be sworn in, vacancies in Senate organization and on committees must be filled, and a few other details attended to.

State of the Union Message When the Senate is notified that the House of Representatives is organized, a joint committee of the two chambers is appointed and instructed "to wait upon the President of the United States and inform him that a <u>quorum</u> of each House is assembled and that the Congress is ready to receive any communication he may be pleased to make."

Within a few weeks—in late January or early February—the President delivers the

<u>preside</u>
v. to act in the role of chairperson

<u>quorum</u>
n. a minimum number of members required to do business

Opening day in the House of Representatives, February 8, 1906

---

1 More than 15,000 of those who work in the legislative branch have jobs in the House or Senate—in members' offices, as committee staff, or in some part of the congressional administrative organization. The other 15,000 or so work in the various support agencies Congress has, over time, established within the legislative branch—including the Library of Congress, the Government Printing Office, the Congressional Budget Office, and the Government Accountability Office.

2 The clerk, a nonmember officer of the House, is picked by the majority party and usually keeps the post until that party loses control of the chamber.

3 Today, John D. Dingell (D., Michigan), who first became a member of the House on December 13, 1955.

annual State of the Union message to a joint session of Congress. The speech is a major political event and is based on this constitutional command:

> ## FROM THE CONSTITUTION
>
> **He shall from time to time give to the Congress Information of the State of the Union, and recommend to their Consideration such Measures as he shall judge necessary and expedient . . .**
>
> —Article II, Section 3

From Woodrow Wilson's first message in 1913, the President has almost always presented his annual assessment in person. Members of Congress, together with the members of the Cabinet, the justices of the Supreme Court, the foreign diplomatic corps, and other dignitaries, assemble in the House chamber to hear him.

In the address, the President reports on the state of the nation as he or she sees it, in both domestic and foreign policy terms. The message is widely covered by the news media, and it is very closely followed, both here and abroad. In fact, the chief executive's speech is as much a message to the American people, and to the world, as it is an address to Congress. In it, the President lays out the broad shape of the policies the administration expects to follow and the course the chief executive has charted for the nation. The message regularly includes a number of specific legislative recommendations, along with a plea that Congress will enact them. Its presentation is soon followed by scores of bills drawn up in the executive branch and introduced in the House and Senate by various members of the President's party.

With the conclusion of the speech, the joint session is adjourned. Each house then separately turns to the legislative business that will come before it.

The Presiding Officers

The Constitution provides for the presiding officers of each house of Congress—the Speaker of the House and the President of the Senate. Article I, Section 2, Clause 5 directs that "The House of Representatives shall choose their Speaker and other Officers. . . ." And Article I, Section 3, Clause 4 declares: "The Vice President of the United States shall be President of the Senate. . . ."

The Speaker of the House Of the two positions, the **Speaker of the House** is by far the more important and more powerful within the halls of Congress. This is particularly so because the Speaker is both the elected presiding officer of the House and the acknowledged leader of its majority party.

Although neither the Constitution nor its own rules require it, the House has always chosen the Speaker from among its own members. Today, the post is held by Nancy Pelosi (D., California). The first woman to serve as Speaker, she was originally elected to the House in 1987 and became Speaker in 2007.[4]

The Speaker is expected to preside in a fair and judicious manner, and she regularly does. The Speaker is also expected to aid the fortunes of the majority party and its legislative goals, and regularly does that, too.

Nearly all of the Speaker's powers revolve around two duties: to preside and to keep order. The Speaker chairs most sessions of the House, but often appoints another member as temporary presiding officer. No member may speak until he or she is recognized by the Speaker. The presiding officer also interprets and applies the rules, refers bills to committee, rules on points of order (questions of procedure raised by members), puts motions to a vote, and decides the outcome of most votes taken on the floor of the House. (The Speaker can be overridden by a vote of the House, but that almost never happens.) The Speaker also names the members of all select and conference committees and must sign all bills and resolutions passed by the House.

As an elected member of the House, the Speaker may debate and vote on any matter

judicious
adj. reasonable

---

4 Speaker Pelosi is the 52nd person to hold the post. The first Speaker, elected by the House in 1789, was Frederick A. C. Muhlenburg, a Federalist from Pennsylvania. Sam Rayburn (D., Texas) held the office for a record of nearly ten terms in the period from 1940 to 1961. Ms. Pelosi succeeded Dennis Hastert (R., Illinois). Only two Republicans—Newt Gingrich of Georgia (1995–1999) and Mr. Hastert (1999–2007)—have held the Speakership over the past 50 years.

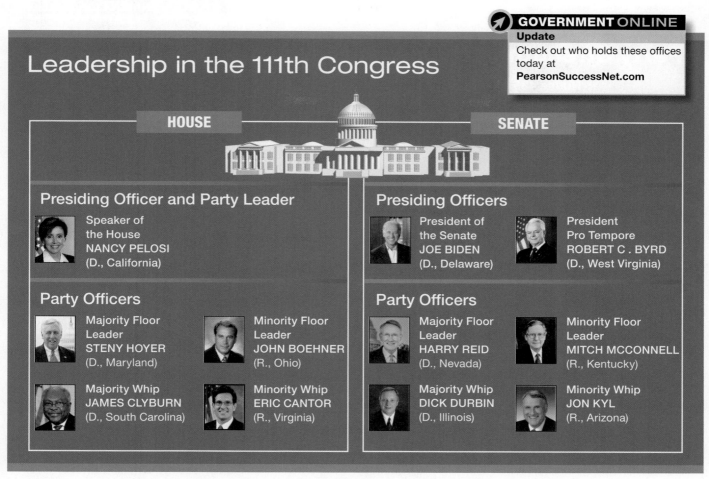

Leadership in the 111th Congress

GOVERNMENT ONLINE
Update
Check out who holds these offices today at
PearsonSuccessNet.com

HOUSE

SENATE

Presiding Officer and Party Leader

Speaker of
the House
NANCY PELOSI
(D., California)

Presiding Officers

President of
the Senate
JOE BIDEN
(D., Delaware)

President
Pro Tempore
ROBERT C. BYRD
(D., West Virginia)

Party Officers

Majority Floor
Leader
STENY HOYER
(D., Maryland)

Minority Floor
Leader
JOHN BOEHNER
(R., Ohio)

Majority Whip
JAMES CLYBURN
(D., South Carolina)

Minority Whip
ERIC CANTOR
(R., Virginia)

Party Officers

Majority Floor
Leader
HARRY REID
(D., Nevada)

Minority Floor
Leader
MITCH MCCONNELL
(R., Kentucky)

Majority Whip
DICK DURBIN
(D., Illinois)

Minority Whip
JON KYL
(R., Arizona)

▶▶ **Interpreting Charts** Party and constitutional leadership roles are very important in both houses of Congress. *How can you tell which party holds power in the House? The Senate?*

before that body. That seldom happens, but when it does, the Speaker appoints another member as the temporary presiding officer and he or she then occupies the Speaker's chair. The Speaker does not often vote, and the House rules say only that the Speaker *must* vote to break a tie. Notice then, that because a tie vote defeats a question, the Speaker occasionally votes to cause a tie and so defeat a proposal.

The Speaker of the House follows the Vice President in the line of succession to the presidency. That fact is a considerable testimony to the power and importance of both the office and the person who holds it.

The President of the Senate The Constitution makes the Vice President the **President of the Senate,** the Senate's presiding officer. This means that (1) unlike the House, the Senate does not choose its own presiding

officer and (2) unlike the Speaker of the House, the Senate's presiding officer is not in fact a member of that body. Indeed, the Vice President might not even be a member of the party that controls the Senate.

All of this adds up to the major reason why the Vice President plays a much less powerful role in the Senate than that played by the Speaker in the House. Also note this important point: the Vice President's career path, the route traveled to the post, is a much different path than the one the Speaker has followed. The Vice President has not become the Senate's presiding officer out of long service in that body. He has, instead, come to the post out of a much different process—as you will see when we take a more detailed look at the vice presidency in Chapter 13.

The president of the Senate does have the usual powers of a presiding officer: to recognize members, put questions to a vote, and so

✔ **Checkpoint**
When must the Speaker vote?

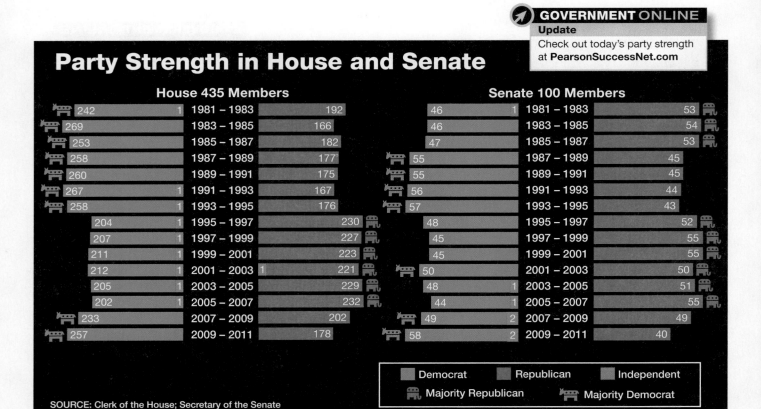

Party Strength in House and Senate

House 435 Members

Democrat	Ind	Term	Republican
242	1	1981 – 1983	192
269		1983 – 1985	166
253		1985 – 1987	182
258		1987 – 1989	177
260		1989 – 1991	175
267	1	1991 – 1993	167
258	1	1993 – 1995	176
204	1	1995 – 1997	230
207	1	1997 – 1999	227
211	1	1999 – 2001	223
212	1	2001 – 2003	1 / 221
205	1	2003 – 2005	229
202	1	2005 – 2007	232
233		2007 – 2009	202
257		2009 – 2011	178

Senate 100 Members

Democrat	Ind	Term	Republican
46	1	1981 – 1983	53
46		1983 – 1985	54
47		1985 – 1987	53
55		1987 – 1989	45
55		1989 – 1991	45
56		1991 – 1993	44
57		1993 – 1995	43
48		1995 – 1997	52
45		1997 – 1999	55
45		1999 – 2001	55
50		2001 – 2003	50
48	1	2003 – 2005	51
44	1	2005 – 2007	55
49	2	2007 – 2009	49
58	2	2009 – 2011	40

■ Democrat   ■ Republican   ■ Independent
🐘 Majority Republican   🫏 Majority Democrat

SOURCE: Clerk of the House; Secretary of the Senate

▶▶ **Analyzing Charts** This chart shows the strength of each party at the start of the past fifteen terms of Congress. Independents are placed with their caucus party. *What is the largest majority that each party has held in each house over the past 30 years?*

✔ **Checkpoint**
Who presides over the Senate if the Vice President is absent?

on. However, the Vice President cannot take the floor to speak or debate and may vote *only* to break a tie.

Any influence a Vice President may have in the Senate is largely the result of personal abilities and relationships. Several of the more recent Vice Presidents came to that office from the Senate: Harry Truman, Alben Barkley, Richard Nixon, Lyndon Johnson, Hubert Humphrey, Walter Mondale, Dan Quayle, Al Gore, and Joseph Biden. Each of them was able to build at least some power into the position out of that earlier experience.

The Senate does have another presiding officer, the **President *pro tempore*,** who serves in the Vice President's absence. The President *pro tempore,* or President *pro tem* for short, is elected by the Senate itself and is always a leading member of the majority party—usually its longest serving member. Today, the post is occupied by Senator Robert C. Byrd (D., West Virginia). Senator Byrd, who was elected to his first term in the upper house in 1958, became President *pro tempore* in 2007.

The President *pro tem* follows the Speaker of the House in the line of presidential succession. From time to time, other senators preside over the Senate, on a temporary basis; newly elected members regularly do so early in their terms.

Party Officers

Congress is a political body. This is so for two leading reasons: (1) Congress is the nation's central policy-making body, and (2) Congress is partisan. Reflecting its political character, both houses of Congress are organized along party lines.

The Party Caucus The **party caucus** is a closed meeting of the members of each party in each house. These meetings are regularly held just before Congress convenes in January and occasionally during a session. In recent years the Republicans have called their caucus in each house the party conference, and the Democrats now use this term in the Senate, too.

A caucus deals mostly with matters related to party organization, such as the selection of the party's floor leaders and questions of committee membership. It sometimes takes stands on particular bills, but neither party tries to force its members to follow its caucus decisions, nor can it.[5]

The policy committee is composed of the party's top leadership. It acts as an executive committee for the party caucus. That body is known as the policy committee in each party's structure in the Senate and in the Republicans' organization in the House. However, it is called the steering and policy committee by the Democrats in the lower chamber.

✔ **Checkpoint**
What is a party caucus?

---

5 A number of informal groupings of members of Congress meet to discuss matters of mutual interest. Some are partisan, others are bipartisan, and several use the word *caucus* in their titles. Some of these groups include, for example, the Congressional Black Caucus, the House Republican Study Committee, the Pro-Life Caucus, and the Congressional Hispanic Caucus.

Representation by State, 111th Congress

🡒 **GOVERNMENT ONLINE**
Update
Check out updated representation by State at
PearsonSuccessNet.com

The colors on these maps indicate the party composition of each State's delegation in the House and Senate. **Which States are the same color on both maps?**

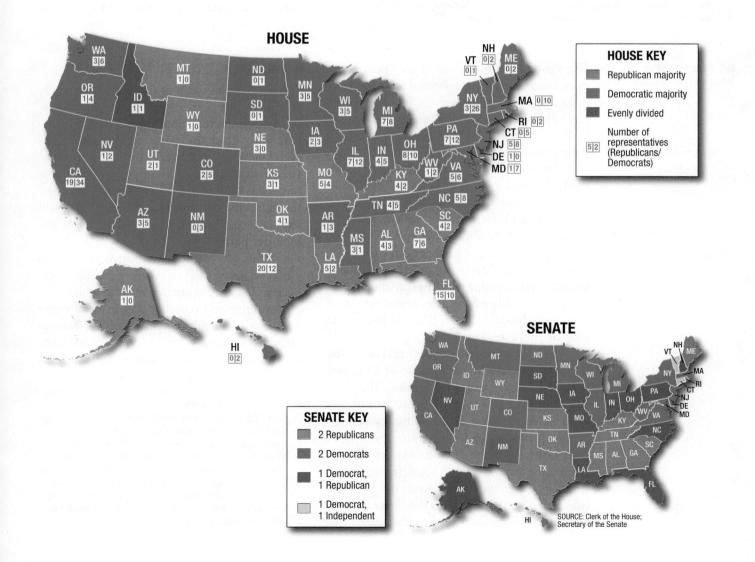

HOUSE

WA 3|6
OR 1|4
MT 1|0
ID 1|1
WY 1|0
ND 0|1
SD 0|1
MN 3|5
WI 3|5
MI 7|8
VT 0|1
NH 0|2
ME 0|2
NY 3|26
MA 0|10
RI 0|2
CT 0|5
NV 1|2
UT 2|1
CO 2|5
NE 3|0
IA 2|3
IL 7|12
IN 4|5
OH 8|10
PA 7|12
NJ 5|8
DE 1|0
MD 1|7
CA 19|34
KS 3|1
MO 5|4
KY 4|2
WV 1|2
VA 5|6
AZ 3|5
NM 0|3
OK 4|1
AR 1|3
TN 4|5
NC 5|8
SC 4|2
MS 3|1
AL 4|3
GA 7|6
TX 20|12
LA 5|2
AK 1|0
FL 15|10
HI 0|2

HOUSE KEY
Republican majority
Democratic majority
Evenly divided
5|2 Number of representatives (Republicans/ Democrats)

SENATE

SENATE KEY
2 Republicans
2 Democrats
1 Democrat, 1 Republican
1 Democrat, 1 Independent

SOURCE: Clerk of the House; Secretary of the Senate

DEFINE "TORTURE"!

HAVING to TESTIFY BEFORE THIS COMMITTEE.

SENATE HEARING

CIA

Schwadron

▶▶ **Interpreting Cartoons** Congressional committees hold hearings about a wide variety of matters. *What does the cartoon say about the feelings of those who are asked to give testimony?*

☑ **Checkpoint**
What do floor leaders do?

The Floor Leaders Next to the Speaker, the **floor leaders** in the House and Senate are the most important officers in Congress. They do not hold official positions in either chamber. Rather, they are party officers, picked for their posts by their party colleagues.

The floor leaders are legislative strategists. Assisted by paid staff, they try to carry out the decisions of their parties' caucuses and steer floor action to their parties' benefit. Each of them is also the chief spokesman for his party in his chamber. All of that calls for political skills of a high order. Senator Howard Baker (R., Tennessee), one of the Senate's most effective floor leaders, often likened his job to that of "herding cats."

The floor leader of the party that holds the majority of seats in each house of Congress is known as the **majority leader.** The floor leader of the party that holds the minority of seats in each house is the **minority leader.** The majority leader is the more powerful in each house—for the obvious reason that the majority party has more seats (more votes) than the other party has. And, the majority leader very largely controls the order of business on the floor in his or her chamber.

The two floor leaders in each house are assisted by party **whips.** The majority whip and the minority whip are, in effect, assistant floor leaders. Each of them is chosen at the party caucus, almost always at the floor leader's recommendation. A number of assistant whips serve in the House.

Whips serve as a liaison—a two-way link—between the party's leadership and its rank-and-file members.[6] The whips check with party members and tell the floor leader which members, and how many votes, can be counted on in any particular matter. The whips also see that all members of the party are present for important votes and that they vote with the party leadership. If a member must be absent for some reason, a whip sees that that member is paired with a member of the other party who will also be absent that day or who agrees not to vote on certain measures at that day's session—so one nonvote cancels out another.

Committee Chairmen

The bulk of the work of Congress, especially in the House, is really done in committee. Thus, **committee chairmen**—those members who head the standing committees in each chamber—hold very strategic posts. The chairman of each of these permanent committees is chosen from the majority party by the majority party caucus.[7] These men and women are always ranking members of the majority party.

Although committee chairmen are less powerful now than in years past, they still have a major say in such matters as which bills a committee will consider and in what order and at what length, whether public hearings are to be held, and what witnesses the committee will call. When a committee's bill has been

---

6 The term *whip* was borrowed from British politics. There, it came from the "whipper-in" in a fox hunt, the rider who is supposed to keep the hounds bunched in a pack.

7 The title *chairman* is used here because this is the form used in both houses of Congress today, both officially and informally. Only 24 women (seven in the Senate, seventeen in the House) have chaired a standing committee. Six standing committees (three in the Senate, three in the House) are chaired by women today, as you can see in the tables in Section 2, where the current chairmen of the standing committees are identified.

reported—approved for consideration—to the floor, the chairman usually manages the debate and tries to steer it to final passage.

We shall take a closer look at committees and their chairs in a moment. But, first, consider the seniority rule.

The Seniority Rule

The **seniority rule** is, in fact, an unwritten custom. It dates from the late 1800s, and is still more or less closely followed in both houses today. The seniority rule provides that the most important posts in Congress, in both the formal and the party organizations, will be held by those party members with the longest records of service. (Notice that seniority rule does not apply to the presiding officers or to the floor leaders in either chamber. As you've seen, their selection is otherwise provided for.)

The rule is applied most strictly to the choice of committee chairmen. The head of each committee is almost always the longest-serving majority party member of that committee. The rule is also followed quite closely in the selection of those members who chair the several subcommittees into which nearly all the standing committees are divided.

Criticism of the Seniority Rule

Critics of the seniority rule are many, and they do make a strong case. They insist that the seniority system ignores ability, rewards mere length of service, and works to discourage younger members. Its opponents also note that the rule means that a committee head often comes from a "safe" constituency—a State or district in which one party regularly wins the seat. With no play of fresh and conflicting forces in those places, critics claim, the chairman of a committee is often out of touch with current public opinion.

Defenders of the seniority rule argue that it ensures that a powerful and experienced member will head each committee. They also say that the rule encourages members to stay on a particular committee and so, over time, gain a wide-ranging knowledge of matters that fall within that committee's jurisdiction. In addition, they note that the rule is fairly easy to apply and that it very nearly eliminates the possibility of fights within the party.

The rule's opponents have gained some ground in recent years. Thus, the House Republican Conference (caucus) now picks several GOP members of House committees by secret ballot. House Democrats use secret ballots to choose a committee chairman whenever 20 percent of their caucus requests that procedure.

Whatever the arguments against the seniority rule, it is unlikely to be eliminated. Those members with the real power to abolish the rule are also the ones who reap the largest benefits from it.

jurisdiction
n. the range of matters under the committee's control

SECTION 1 ASSESSMENT

Essential Questions Journal To continue to build a response to the chapter Essential Question, go to your **Essential Questions Journal.**

1. **Guiding Question** Use your completed table to answer this question: How do constitutional and party officers keep Congress organized?

Key Terms and Comprehension

2. Describe opening day in the House.
3. Summarize the duties of the **floor leaders** in each house.
4. **(a)** What is the **seniority rule?** **(b)** What are the arguments for and against it?

Critical Thinking

5. **Understand Point of View (a)** Senator Howard Baker likened his job as majority leader to that of "herding cats." What does that mean? **(b)** What problems do majority leaders face?
6. **Make Comparisons** Compare and contrast the positions of Speaker of the House and President of the Senate. Which is more powerful, and why?
7. **Draw Conclusions** How important are committee chairmen in Congress? Explain.

Quick Write

Persuasive Essay: Gather Details The structure of Congress has evolved over time. As you read the chapter, take notes on the organizational structure and how it affects the lawmaking process.

SECTION 2
Committees in Congress

Guiding Question

How do committees help Congress do its work? Use a table to keep track of the purpose and characteristics of each type of congressional committee.

Standing Committee	Select Committee	Joint Committee	Conference Committee
•	• usually temporary	•	•
•		•	•
•	•	•	•
	•		

Political Dictionary

- standing committee
- subcommittee
- select committee
- joint committee
- conference committee

Objectives

1. Explain how standing committees function.
2. Describe the responsibilities and duties of the House Rules Committee.
3. Describe the role of select committees.
4. Compare the functions of joint and conference committees.

Image Above: Former Secretary of Defense Donald Rumsfeld testifying at a defense appropriations hearing

Do you know the phrase "a division of labor"? It means dividing the work to be done, assigning the several parts of the overall task to various members of the group. The House and the Senate are both so large, and their agendas are so crowded with so many different matters, that both chambers must rely on a division of labor. That is to say, much of the work that Congress does is in fact done by committees. Indeed, Representative Clem Miller (D., Calif.) once described Congress as "a collection of committees that come together in a chamber periodically to approve of one another's actions."

Standing Committees

In 1789, the House and Senate each adopted the practice of naming a special committee to consider each bill as it was introduced. By 1794, there were more than 300 committees in each chamber. Each house then began to set up permanent panels, **standing committees,** to which all similar bills can be sent. The number of these committees has varied over the years. There are 20 standing committees in the House and 16 in the Senate today. Each House committee has from 10 to as many as 75 members, and each Senate committee has from 14 to 28. Representatives are normally assigned to one or two standing committees and senators to three or four.

The pivotal role these committees play in the lawmaking process cannot be overstated. Most bills receive their most thorough consideration in these bodies. Members of both houses regularly respect the decisions and follow the recommendations they make. Thus, the fate of most bills is decided in the various standing committees, not on the floor of either house. More than a century ago, Woodrow Wilson described "Congress in its committee rooms" as "Congress at work," and that remains true today.

Some panels are more prominent and more influential than others. As you would expect, most members try to win assignments to one of these major panels. The leading committees in the House are the Rules, Ways and Means, Appropriations, Armed Services, Judiciary, Foreign Affairs, and Agriculture committees. In the Senate, senators usually compete for places on the Foreign Relations; Appropriations; Finance; Judiciary; Armed Services; and Banking, Housing, and Urban Affairs committees.

Of course, some of the other committees are particularly attractive to some members. Thus, a representative whose district lies wholly within a major city might want to sit on the House Committee on Education and the Workforce. A senator from one of the western States might angle for assignment to the Senate's Committee on Energy and Natural Resources.

Most of the standing committees review bills dealing with particular policy matters—say, public lands, taxes, or veterans' affairs. However, there are four standing committees that are not organized as subject-matter bodies: in the House, the Rules Committee, the Committee on House Administration, and the Committee on Standards of Official Conduct, and in the Senate, the Committee on Rules and Administration.

When a bill is introduced in either house, the Speaker or the President of the Senate refers the measure to the appropriate standing committee. Thus, the Speaker sends all tax measures to the House Ways and Means Committee; in the Senate, tax measures go to the Finance Committee. A bill dealing with the creation of additional federal district judgeships will be sent to the Judiciary Committee in both chambers, and so on.

Recall that the chairman of each of the standing committees is chosen according to the seniority rule. As a consequence, most committee chairmen have served in Congress for at least 12 years and some much longer. The seniority rule is also closely applied in each house when it elects the other members of each of its committees.

The members of each standing committee are formally elected by a floor vote at the beginning of each term of Congress. In fact, each party has already drawn up its own committee roster before that vote, and the floor vote merely ratifies those party choices.

The majority party always holds a majority of the seats on each standing committee.[8] The other party is well represented, however.

---

8 The only exception is the House Committee on Standards of Official Conduct, with five Democrats and five Republicans. Often called the House Ethics Committee, it investigates allegations of misconduct by House members. In the Senate, a six-member bipartisan Select Committee on Ethics plays a similar role.

A Bill in the House

In the past, bills were usually referred to one committee. Recent bills, however, have often been referred to multiple committees. Here is the path of the Food and Energy Security Act through the House in 2007. **How many subcommittees studied the bill?**

Introduced in the House

Speaker Referred Bill

• The Speaker of the House sent the bill to two committees.

▶ Committee on Agriculture

Subcommittees

• *Conservation, Credit, Energy, and Research*

• *Department Operations, Oversight, Nutrition, and Forestry*

• *General Farm Commodities and Risk Management*

• *Horticulture and Organic Agriculture*

• *Livestock, Dairy, and Poultry*

• *Specialty Crops, Rural Development and Foreign Agriculture*

▶ Committee on Foreign Affairs

• *Quickly discharged; not referred to subcommittees*

Bill Was Reported

• The bill was discharged from the Committee on Foreign Affairs and reported by the Committee on Agriculture. Then it went to the Rules Committee.

• The Rules Committee set aside one hour for general debate, plus time to consider amendments. It also instructed the House to consider the bill in the Committee of the Whole (see Section 3).

Bill Was Sent to Full House

• The bill was considered in the Committee of the Whole—that is, the full House sitting as a committee of itself.

House Standing Committee Chairs

Committee	Name, Party, State, Year Elected
Agriculture	Collin C. Peterson (D., Minn.), 1990
Appropriations	David Obey (D., Wis.), 1969
Armed Services	Ike Skelton (D., Mo.), 1976
Budget	John M. Spratt, Jr. (D., S.C.), 1982
Education and Labor	George Miller (D., Calif.), 1974
Energy and Commerce	Henry A. Waxman (D., Calif.), 1974
Financial Services	Barney Frank (D., Mass.), 1980
Foreign Affairs	Howard Berman (D., Calif.), 1982
Homeland Security	Bennie G. Thompson (D., Miss.), 1993
House Administration	Robert A. Brady (D., Penn.), 1998
Judiciary	John Conyers, Jr. (D., Mich.), 1964
Natural Resources	Nick J. Rahall II (D., W. Va.), 1976
Oversight and Government Reform	Edolphus Towns (D., N.Y.), 1982
Rules	Louise M. Slaughter (D., N.Y.), 1986
Science and Technology	Bart Gordon (D., Tenn.), 1984
Small Business	Nydia M. Velazquez (D., N.Y.), 1992
Standards of Official Conduct	Zoe Lofgren (D., Calif.), 1994
Transportation and Infrastructure	James L. Oberstar (D., Minn.), 1974
Veterans' Affairs	Bob Filner (D., Calif.), 1992
Ways and Means	Charles B. Rangel (D., N.Y.), 1970

SOURCE: *Congressional Directory* and Clerk of the House

▸▸ **Analyzing Charts** These are the House standing committees and their chairs. *What predictions can you make about the committees' jurisdiction based on their titles?*

GOVERNMENT ONLINE

Update

To check out who holds these positions today, go to **PearsonSuccessNet.com**

gauge
v. to measure; judge

Subcommittees Most standing committees are divided into **subcommittees**—divisions of standing committees which do most of the committees' work. Each subcommittee is responsible for a portion of the committee's workload. There are now some 150 subcommittees in the two houses—nearly 70 in the Senate and 99 in the House.

Take a quick look at the Senate's 19-member Judiciary Committee (currently composed of 11 Democrats and 8 Republicans). It does most of its work in its six subcommittees. Each member serves on at least two of these bodies, and their titles describe their focuses: Administrative Oversight and the Courts; Antitrust, Competition Policy and Consumer Rights; The Constitution; Crime and Drugs; Immigration, Refugees and Border Security; and Terrorism and Homeland Security.

The House Rules Committee The House Committee on Rules is the Speaker's "right arm." It controls the flow of bills to the floor and sets the conditions for their consideration there. The panel is often described as the "traffic cop" in the lower house. So many measures are introduced in the House each term that some sort of screening device is absolutely necessary.

Most bills die in the committees to which they are referred. Still, several hundred are reported out every year. So, before most of these bills can reach the floor of the House, they must also clear the Rules Committee.

Normally, a bill gets to the floor only if it has been granted a rule—been scheduled for floor consideration—by the Rules Committee. The committee decides whether and under what conditions the full House will consider a measure. As you will see, this means that the powerful 13-member Rules Committee can speed, delay, or even prevent House action on a measure. In the smaller Senate, where the process is not so closely regulated, the majority leader controls the appearance of bills on the floor.

Select Committees

At times, each house finds a need for a **select committee,** sometimes called special committees. They are panels set up for some specific purpose and, most often, for a limited time. The Speaker of the House or the President of the Senate appoints the members of these special committees, with the advice of the majority and minority leaders.

The congressional power to investigate is an essential part of the lawmaking function. Congress must decide on the need for new laws and gauge the adequacy of those already on the books. It also must exercise its vital oversight function, to ensure that federal agencies are following the laws it has already passed. At times, too, a committee may conduct an investigation of an issue—for example, the threat of domestic terrorism—in order to focus public attention on that matter. Most investigations are conducted by standing committees, or by their subcommittees.

However, select committees are sometimes formed to investigate a current issue, as the Senate's Select Committee on Indian Affairs recently did. That 15-member panel spent nearly three years investigating the behavior of a number of well-connected lobbyists who represented several Native American tribes as they sought to establish gambling casinos. The committee's extensive probe uncovered massive instances of fraud, bribery, tax evasion, and other illegal activities for which several offenders began to serve long prison sentences in 2006 and 2007. The most prominent of those <u>miscreants</u> were Washington-based lobbyist Jack Abramoff and a member of Congress, Representative Robert Ney (R., Ohio), who had been chairman of the House Committee on Administration.

At times, select committees have been spectacularly important. This happened, for example, with the Senate's Select Committee on Presidential Campaign Activities, popularly known as the Senate Watergate Committee. As the Watergate scandal began to unfold in 1973, the Senate created that committee. Chaired by Senator Sam Ervin (D., North Carolina), its job was to investigate "the extent, if any, to which illegal, improper, or unethical activities were engaged in by any persons . . . in the presidential election of 1972." Its sensational hearings riveted the nation for months. Eventually, they formed a key link in the chain of events that led to President Richard Nixon's resignation from office in mid-1974.

Another notable instance came in 1987, with the work of two panels: the Senate's Select Committee on Secret Military Assistance to Iran and the Nicaraguan Opposition, and the House Select Committee to Investigate Covert Arms Transactions with Iran. These twin committees, often referred to jointly as the Iran-Contra Committee, probed the Reagan administration's conduct of two highly secret projects abroad: the sale of arms to Iran and efforts to give military aid to the Contra rebels in Nicaragua. The operation in Iran was intended, at least in part, as an arms-for-hostages deal, and it failed. The aid to the Contras was funded in part with money from the Iranian arms sales, despite an act of Congress that expressly prohibited such aid by the United States.

Most congressional investigations are not nearly so visible, nor so historic. Their more usual shape can be seen when, for example, the House Committee on Agriculture probes the spruce budworm problem (an infestation affecting trees in the Pacific Northwest) or the Senate's Armed Services Committee looks at the Army's recruiting programs.

Joint and Conference Committees

A **joint committee** is one composed of members of both houses. Some of these are select committees set up to serve some temporary purpose. Most are permanent groups that serve on a regular basis. Because the standing committees of the two houses often duplicate one another's work, many have long urged that Congress make much greater use of the joint committee device.

Some joint committees are investigative in nature and issue periodic reports to the

✔ **Checkpoint**
What is a select committee?

miscreants
n. criminals, wrongdoers

Senate Standing Committee Chairs

Committee	Name, Party, State, Year Elected
Agriculture, Nutrition, and Forestry	Blanche Lincoln (D., Arkansas), 1998
Appropriations	Daniel Inouye (D., Hawaii), 1962
Armed Services	Carl Levin (D., Mich.), 1978
Banking, Housing, and Urban Affairs	Christopher C. Dodd (D., Conn.),1980
Budget	Kent Conrad, (D., N.D.), 1986
Commerce, Science, and Transportation	Jay Rockefeller (D., W.Va.), 1984
Energy and Natural Resources	Jeff Bingaman (D., N.M.), 1982
Environment and Public Works	Barbara Boxer (D., Calif.), 1992
Finance	Max Baucus (D., Mont.), 1978
Foreign Relations	John Kerry, Jr. (D., Mass.), 1984
Health, Education, Labor, and Pensions	Tom Harkin (D., Iowa), 1984
Homeland Security and Governmental Affairs	Joseph L. Lieberman (I., Conn.), 1988
Judiciary	Patrick T. Leahy (D., Vt.), 1974
Rules and Administration	Charles Schumer (D., N.Y.), 1998
Small Business and Entrepreneurship	Mary Landrieu (D., La.), 1996
Veterans' Affairs	Daniel K. Akaka (D., Hawaii), 1990

SOURCE: *Congressional Directory* and Secretary of the Senate

▸▸ **Analyzing Charts** This chart lists the Senate's committees and their chairs. *Why do you think the Senate has fewer committees than the House?*

GOVERNMENT ONLINE
Update
To check out who holds these positions today, go to **PearsonSuccessNet.com**

Joint Committees of Congress

- The **Joint Economic Committee** addresses matters related to the U.S. economy.
  Chair: Rep. Carolyn B. Maloney (D., N.Y.)

- The **Joint Committee on the Library** addresses matters related to the Library of Congress.
  Chair: Sen. Dianne Feinstein (D., Calif.)

- The **Joint Committee on Printing** oversees the Government Printing Office and other printing by the Federal Government.
  Chair: Rep. Robert A. Brady (D., Penn.)

- The **Joint Committee on Taxation** is involved in legislation about taxes. The chair position rotates between the chair of the House Ways and Means Committee and the Senate Finance Committee.

▶▶ **Analyzing Charts** The Joint Committees of Congress include members from both houses. *Why do you think these matters are dealt with by joint committees?*

House and Senate—for example, the Joint Committee on Taxation. It conducts in-depth studies of the federal tax system and presents its findings to the House Ways and Means Committee and the Senate's Finance Committee. Most often, those committees

perform more routine duties—for example, the Joint Committee on the Library oversees the administration of that remarkable institution, the Library of Congress.

Before a bill may be sent to the President, each house must pass it in identical form. Sometimes, the two houses pass differing versions, and the first house will not agree to the changes the other has made. When this happens, a **conference committee**—a temporary, joint body—is created to iron out the differences in the bill. Its job is to produce a compromise bill that both houses will accept—as you will see shortly.

Senator Charles Schumer (D., N.Y.) testifies during a hearing on food prices by the Senate's Committee on Agriculture, Nutrition, and Forestry. ▼

Essential Questions Journal To continue to build a response to the chapter Essential Question, go to your **Essential Questions Journal.**

SECTION 2 ASSESSMENT

1. **Guiding Question** Use your completed table to answer this question: How do committees help Congress to do its work?

Key Terms and Comprehension

2. **(a)** What are **standing committees?** **(b)** What rule determines which members of Congress will serve as chairs and which as members of each committee?

3. Describe the role of **(a) select committees, (b) joint committees,** and **(c) conference committees.**

4. Why is the power of Congress to investigate a vital part of its legislative functions?

Critical Thinking

5. **Predict Consequences** What might happen if all proposed bills were sent directly to the full House for a vote?

6. **Express Problems Clearly** What are the benefits and drawbacks of the committee and subcommittee system used by Congress?

Quick Write

Persuasive Essay: Establish a Point of View Make a graphic organizer to keep track of the pros and cons of each aspect of congressional organization. Start thinking about whether you would change any aspect of how Congress is organized to make it more efficient or effective.

SECTION 3

Making Law:
The House

Guiding Question

What steps does a successful bill follow as it moves through the House? Use a flowchart to keep track of the progress of a bill through the House.

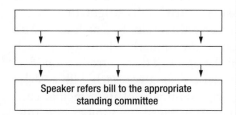

Speaker refers bill to the appropriate standing committee

Political Dictionary

- bill
- joint resolution
- concurrent resolution
- resolution
- rider
- pigeonhole
- discharge petition
- quorum
- engrossed

Objectives

1. Identify the first steps in the introduction of a bill to the House.
2. Describe what happens to a bill once it is referred to a committee.
3. Explain how House leaders schedule debate on a bill.
4. Explain what happens to a bill on the House floor, and identify the final step in the passage of a bill in the House.

Image Above: Rep. Greg Walden (R., Ore.) waves a bill during a committee work session.

These numbers may surprise you: From 6,000 to 9,000 bills and resolutions are introduced in the House and Senate during each session of Congress. Fewer than 10 percent become law. Where do all those measures come from? Why are so few of them passed? How, by what process, does Congress make law?

The First Steps

A **bill** is a proposed law presented to the House or Senate for consideration. Most bills introduced in either house do not originate with members themselves. Instead, however, many of the most important bills are born somewhere in the executive branch. Business, labor, agriculture, and other special interest groups often draft measures, as well. And some bills, or at least the ideas for them, come from private citizens who think "there ought to be a law. . . ." Many others are born in the standing committees of Congress.

According to Article I, Section 7, Clause 1 of the Constitution, "bills for raising Revenue shall originate in the House." In other words, tax bills must first be acted upon by the House. Measures dealing with any other matter may be introduced in either chamber. Only members can introduce bills in the House, and they do so by dropping them into the hopper, a box hanging on the edge of the clerk's desk. [9]

Often, before a member introduces a bill, he or she will circulate a letter informing other members about the measure and why its sponsor thinks it should become law. That is, he or she hopes to persuade several other members to become cosponsors, thereby increasing the chances that the bill will be passed. By the time many measures are introduced, in either house, a number of members are listed on them as cosponsors.

Types of Bills and Resolutions The thousands of measures—bills and resolutions—Congress considers take several forms. To begin with, there are two types of bills: public bills and private bills.

---

[9] Puerto Rico's resident commissioner and the delegates from the District of Columbia, Guam, the Virgin Islands, American Samoa, and the Northern Mariana Islands also may introduce measures in the House. Only a senator may introduce a measure in the upper house. He or she does so by addressing the chair.

The Democratic House leadership held a rally before an all-night debate on a bill that would withdraw U.S. troops from Iraq. *Why might members of Congress hold a public rally before holding a debate on a bill?*

✓ **Checkpoint**
How does an appropriations bill become a "Christmas tree"?

voluminous
adj. massive; lengthy

Public bills are measures applying to the nation as a whole—for example, a tax measure. Private bills are measures that apply to certain persons or places rather than to the entire nation. As an example, Congress once passed an act to give a sheep rancher $85,000 for his losses resulting from attacks by grizzly bears. The bears had been moved from Yellowstone National Park to other public lands on which the rancher grazed his flock.

Joint resolutions are similar to bills, and, when passed, have the force of law. They most often deal with unusual or temporary matters—for example, to appropriate money for the presidential inauguration ceremonies. Joint resolutions are used, too, to propose constitutional amendments, and they have also been used to annex territories.

Concurrent resolutions deal with matters in which the House and Senate must act jointly. However, they do not have the force of law and do not require the President's signature. Concurrent resolutions are used most often by Congress to state a position on some matter—for example, in foreign affairs.

Resolutions, often called "simple resolutions," deal with matters concerning either house alone and are taken up only by that house. They are regularly used for such matters as the adoption of a new rule of procedure or the amendment of some existing rule.

Like concurrent resolutions, a resolution does not have the force of law and is not sent to the President for approval.

A bill or resolution usually deals with a single subject, but sometimes a rider dealing with an unrelated matter is included. A **rider** is a provision not likely to pass on its own merit that is attached to an important measure certain to pass. Its sponsors hope that it will "ride" through the legislative process on the strength of the main measure.

Most riders are tacked onto appropriations measures, which provide money to pay for something. In fact, some money bills have so many riders attached that they are called "Christmas trees." The opponents of those "decorations" and the President are almost always forced to accept them if they want the bill's major provisions to become law.

Introduction and First Reading The clerk of the House numbers each bill as it is introduced. Thus, H.R. 3410 would be the 3,410th measure introduced in the House during the congressional term. Bills originating in the Senate receive the prefix S.—such as S. 210. Resolutions are similarly identified in each house in the order of their introduction.[10]

The clerk also gives each bill a short title—a brief summary of its principal contents. Having received its number and title, the bill is then entered in the House *Journal* and in the *Congressional Record* for the day.

The *Journal* contains the minutes, the official record, of the daily proceedings in the House or Senate. The *Congressional Record* is a voluminous account of the daily proceedings (speeches, debates, other comments, votes, motions, etc.) in each house. The *Record* is not quite a word-for-word account, however. Members have five days in which to make changes in each temporary edition. They often insert speeches that were in fact never made, reconstruct "debates," and revise thoughtless or inaccurate remarks.

With these actions the bill has received its first reading. All bills are printed immediately after introduction and distributed to all members of the House.

Each bill that is finally passed in either house is given three readings along the legislative route. In the House, second reading comes during floor consideration, if the measure gets that far. Third reading takes place just before the final vote on the measure. Each reading is usually by number and title only: "H.R. 3410, A bill to provide. . . ." However, the more important or controversial bills are read in full and taken up line by line, section by section, at second reading.

The three readings, an ancient parliamentary practice, are intended to ensure careful consideration of bills. Today, the readings are little more than way stations along the legislative route. They were quite important in the early history of Congress, however, when some members could not read.

After first reading, the Speaker refers the bill to the appropriate standing committee. A bill's content largely determines where it will go. The Speaker does have some discretion, however, particularly over complex measures with provisions covering a number of subjects. Which committee gets a bill can matter. For example, a controversial provision in the bill might receive a more favorable welcome in one committee than it might in another.

The Bill in Committee

The Constitution makes no mention of standing committees. These bodies do play an absolutely essential role in the lawmaking process, however—and in both houses of Congress. Indeed, their place is so pivotal that they are sometimes called "little legislatures."

The standing committees act as <u>sieves</u>. They sift through all of the many bills referred to them—rejecting most, considering and reporting only those they find to be worthy of floor consideration. In short, the fate of most bills is decided in these committees rather than on the floor of either house.

The Number of Bills That Become Laws

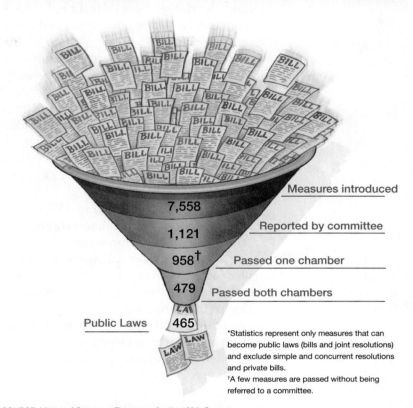

Measures introduced — 7,558
Reported by committee — 1,121
Passed one chamber — 958†
Passed both chambers — 479
Public Laws — 465

*Statistics represent only measures that can become public laws (bills and joint resolutions) and exclude simple and concurrent resolutions and private bills.
†A few measures are passed without being referred to a committee.

SOURCE: Library of Congress. Figures are for the 109th Congress.

▶▶ **Interpreting Charts** A bill must pass through many steps before it becomes law. *After which step do most bills die?*

Most of the thousands of bills introduced in each session of Congress are **pigeonholed.**[11] That is, they are buried; they die in committee. They are simply put away, never to be acted upon.

Most pigeonholed bills deserve their fate. On occasion, however, a committee buries a measure that a majority of the members of the House want to consider. When that happens, the bill can be blasted out of the committee with a discharge petition.

A **discharge petition** enables members to force a bill that has remained in committee 30 days (7 in the Rules Committee) onto the floor for consideration. Any member may file a discharge motion. If that motion is signed by a majority (218) of House members, the committee has seven days to report the bill. If it does not, any member who signed the motion may, on the second and fourth Mondays of each month, move that the bill be

✔ **Checkpoint**
What happens to the majority of bills that are introduced?

<u>sieve</u>
n. gatekeeper

---

10 Thus, H.J. Res. 12 would be the 12th joint resolution introduced in the House during the term, and similarly in the Senate, S.J. Res. 19. Concurrent resolutions are identified as H. or S. Con. Res., and simple resolutions as H. or S. Res.

11 The term comes from the old-fashioned rolltop desks with pigeonholes—slots into which papers were put and often soon forgotten. Most "by request" bills are routinely pigeonholed; they are the measures that members introduce but only because some constituent or some interest group has asked them to do so.

discharged from the committee—that is, sent to the floor. If the motion carries, the rules require the House to consider the bill at once. This maneuver is not often tried, and it seldom succeeds.

The process was most recently successful in 2002, however. What went on to become the Bipartisan Campaign Reform Act of 2002 was blasted out of the Committee on House Administration—where the House leadership had managed to bury it for several years. That measure marked the first major change in federal campaign finance law in 23 years.

The Committee at Work Once a bill reaches a committee, the chairman almost always refers it to one of several subcommittees. For an important or controversial measure, a committee, or most often one of its subcommittees, holds public hearings. Interested parties, including the representatives of interest groups, public officials, and others, are invited to testify at these information-gathering sessions. If necessary, a committee can issue a subpoena, forcing a witness to testify. [12]

Occasionally, a subcommittee will make a trip to locations affected by a measure. Thus, several members of the House Foreign Affairs Committee's Subcommittee on the Western Hemisphere may visit Rio de Janero for a first-hand look at Brazil's successful efforts to reduce that country's dependence on foreign oil.

These trips are made at public expense, and members of Congress are sometimes criticized for taking them. Some of these junkets deserve criticism. But an on-the-spot investigation often proves to be among the best ways a committee can inform itself.

Committee Actions When a subcommittee has completed its work on a bill, the measure goes to the full committee. At the chairman's direction, that body may do one of several things. It may:

1. Report the bill favorably, with a "do pass" recommendation. It is then the chairman's job to steer the bill through debate on the floor.

2. Refuse to report the bill—that is, pigeonhole it. Again, this is the fate suffered by most measures in both houses.

3. Report the bill in amended form. Many bills are changed in committee, and several bills on the same subject may be combined into a single measure.

4. Report the bill with an unfavorable recommendation. This does not often happen. Occasionally, however, a committee feels that the full House should have a chance to consider a bill or does not want to take the responsibility for killing it.

5. Report a committee bill. This is a new bill, a measure that the committee has substituted for one or several bills referred to it.

Scheduling Floor Debate

Before it goes to the floor for consideration, a bill reported by a standing committee is placed on one of several calendars in the House. A calendar is a schedule of the order in which bills will be taken up on the floor.

Calendars There are five calendars in the lower house. The *Calendar of the Committee of the Whole House on the State of the Union,* commonly known as the *Union Calendar,* is for all bills having to do with revenues, appropriations, or government property. The *House Calendar* is for all other public bills. The *Private Calendar* is for all private bills. The *Corrections Calendar,* for all bills from the Union or House Calendar taken out of order by unanimous consent of the House of Representatives. These are most often minor bills to which there is no opposition. The *Discharge Calendar* is for petitions to discharge bills from committee.

Under the rules of the House, bills are taken from each of these calendars for consideration on a regularly scheduled basis. For example, bills from the Corrections Calendar are supposed to be considered on the second and fourth Tuesdays of each month. Measures relating to the District of Columbia can be taken up on the second and fourth Mondays, and private bills on the first and third Tuesdays. On "Calendar Wednesdays," the various committee chairmen may each call

---

12 A subpoena is an order compelling one to testify and/or produce evidence. Failure to obey a subpoena may lead the House or Senate to cite the offender for contempt of Congress—a federal crime punishable by fine and/or imprisonment.

Congressional Committee Staffers

What Are Their Duties?

More than 2500 men and women serve on congressional committees. These staffers must be experts not only in the subject matter their committees cover, but in political maneuvering. Their hard work enables members of Congress to do their jobs more effectively and to keep their eyes on the bigger picture. *How might staffers contribute to the effectiveness of congressional committees?*

▶ Committee staffers deliver press copies of a Special Committee report on China's theft of U.S. nuclear weapons secrets.

▶ A committee staffer presents information about the possible impact of oil exploration on Alaska's polar bears.

up one bill from the House or Union calendars that has cleared their committees.

Rules None of these arrangements is followed too closely, however. What most often happens is even more complicated. Remember that the Rules Committee plays a critical role in the legislative process in the House. It must grant a rule before most bills can in fact reach the floor. That is, before most measures can be taken from a calendar, the Rules Committee must approve that step and set a time for its appearance on the floor.

By not granting a rule for a bill, the Rules Committee can effectively kill it. Or, when the Rules Committee does grant a rule, it may be a special rule—one setting conditions under which the members of the House will consider the measure. A special rule often sets a time limit on floor debate. It may even prohibit amendments to certain, or even to any, of the bill's provisions.

Then, too, certain bills are privileged. That is, they may be called up at almost any time, ahead of any other business before the House. The most privileged measures include major appropriations (spending) and general revenue (tax) bills, conference committee reports, and special rules granted by the Rules Committee.

On certain days, the House may suspend its rules. A motion to that effect must be approved by a two-thirds vote of the members present. When that happens, as it sometimes does, the House moves so far away from its established operating procedures that a measure can go through all the many steps necessary to enactment in a single day.

All of these—the calendars, the role of the Rules Committee, and the other complex procedures—have developed over time to help members of the House manage their heavy workload. Because of the large size of the House and the sheer number and variety of bills its members introduce, no one member could possibly know the contents, let alone the merits, of every bill on which he or she has to vote.

✔ **Checkpoint**
What power makes the Rules Committee so important?

The Bill on the Floor

If a bill finally reaches the floor, it receives its second reading in the House. Many bills the House passes are minor ones, with little or no opposition. Most of these less important measures are called from the Corrections Calendar, get their second reading by title only, and are quickly disposed of.

Nearly all of the more important measures are dealt with in a much different manner. They are considered in the Committee of the Whole, an old parliamentary device for speeding business on the floor.

The Committee of the Whole includes all the members of the House, sitting as one large committee of the House, not as the House itself. The rules of the Committee of the Whole are much less strict than the rules of the House, and floor action moves along at a faster pace. For example, a **quorum,** which is a majority of the full membership (218), must be present in order for the House to do business. Only 100 members need be present in the Committee of the Whole.

When the House resolves itself into the Committee of the Whole, the Speaker steps down because the full House of Representatives is no longer in session. Another member presides. General debate begins, and the bill receives its second reading, section by section. As each section is read, amendments may be offered. Under the five-minute rule, supporters and opponents of each amendment have just that many minutes to make their cases. Votes are taken on each section and its amendment as the reading proceeds.

When the bill has been gone through—and many run to dozens and sometimes hundreds of pages—the Committee of the Whole has completed its work. It then rises, that is, dissolves itself. Presto! The House is now back in session. The Speaker resumes the chair, and the House formally adopts the committee's work.

Debate Its large size has long since forced the House to impose severe limits on floor debate. A rule first adopted in 1842 forbids any member from holding the floor for more than one hour without unanimous consent to speak for a longer time. Since 1880, the Speaker has had the power to force any member who strays from the subject at hand to give up the floor.

The majority and minority floor leaders generally decide in advance how they will split the time to be spent on a bill. But at any time, any member may "move the previous question." That is, any member can demand a vote on the issue before the House. If that motion is adopted, debate ends. An up-or-down vote must be taken. This device is the only motion that can be used in the House to close (end) debate, but it can be a very effective one.

Voting A bill may be the subject of several votes on the floor. If amendments are offered, as they frequently are, members must vote on each of them. Then, too, a number of procedural motions may be offered, for example, one to table the bill (lay it aside), another for the previous question, and so on. The members must vote on each of these motions. These several other votes are very often a better guide to a bill's friends and foes than is the final vote itself. Sometimes, a member votes for a bill that is now certain to pass, even though he or she had supported amendments to it that, had they been adopted, would have in fact defeated the measure.

"The only solution I can see is to hold a series of long and costly hearings in order to put off finding a solution."

▶▶ **Analyzing Political Cartoons** This cartoon mocks the lawmaking process. *Is the cartoon a reference to how Congress actually works or how people think it works? Explain.*

The House uses four different methods for taking floor votes:

1. Voice votes are the most common. The Speaker calls for the "ayes" and then the "noes," the members answer in chorus, and the Speaker announces the result.

2. If any member thinks the Speaker has erred in judging a voice vote, he or she may demand a standing vote, also known as a division of the House. All in favor, and then all opposed, stand and are counted by the clerk.

3. One fifth of a quorum (44 members in the House or 20 in the Committee of the Whole) can demand a teller vote. When this happens, the Speaker names one teller from each party. The members pass between the tellers and are counted, for and against. Teller votes are rare today. The practice has been replaced by electronic voting.

4. A roll-call vote, also known as a record vote, may be demanded by one fifth of the members present.[13]

In 1973, the House installed a computerized voting system for all quorum calls and record votes to replace the roll call by the clerk. Members now vote at any of the 48 stations on the floor by inserting a personalized plastic card in a box and then pushing one of three buttons: "Yea," "Nay," or "Present." The "Present" button is most often used for a quorum call—a check to make sure that a quorum of the members is in fact present.

Otherwise, it is used when a member does not wish to vote on a question but still wants to be recorded as present.[14]

A large master board above the Speaker's chair shows instantly how each member has voted. The House rules allow the members 15 minutes to answer quorum calls or cast record votes. Voting ends when the Speaker pushes a button to lock the electronic system, producing a permanent record of the vote at the same time. Under the former roll-call process, it took the clerk up to 45 minutes to call each member's name and record his or her vote. Before 1973, roll calls took up about three months of House floor time each session.

Voting procedures are much the same in the Senate. The upper house uses voice, standing, and roll-call votes, but does not take teller votes or use an electronic voting process. Only six or seven minutes are needed for a roll-call vote in the smaller upper chamber.

Final Steps in the House Once a bill has been approved at second reading, it is **engrossed,** or printed in its final form. Then it is read a third time, by title, and a final vote is taken. Invariably, a bill is approved at third reading, and then the Speaker signs it. A page—a legislative aide—then carries it to the Senate side of the Capitol and places it on the Senate president's desk.

✔ **Checkpoint**
What are the four types of votes that the House can take?

---

13 The Constitution (Article I, Section 7, Clause 2) requires a record vote on the question of overriding a presidential veto. No record votes are taken in the Committee of the Whole.

14 A "present" vote is not allowed on some questions—for example, a vote to override a veto.

Essential Questions
Journal
To continue to build a response to the chapter Essential Question, go to your **Essential Questions Journal.**

SECTION 3 ASSESSMENT

1. **Guiding Question** Use your completed flowchart to answer this question: What steps does a successful bill follow as it moves through the House?

Key Terms and Comprehension

2. Compare and contrast a **simple resolution,** a **joint resolution,** and a **concurrent resolution.**

3. What happens to most bills in committee? Why?

Critical Thinking

4. **Make Decisions** Congressional committees are sometimes called "little legislatures." Explain this expression. Is it an accurate one? Why or why not?

5. **Draw Inferences** Why does the House use such a complicated calendar system?

Quick Write

Persuasive Essay: Make an Outline Using your graphic organizer from Section 2, choose one aspect of congressional organization that you think is very effective or one aspect that you think should be changed. Describe that point in a thesis statement and write an outline that includes at least three supporting points.

Minority Rights: The Filibuster

Track the Issue

A minority in the Senate has used strategies such as the filibuster to ensure its voice will be heard.

1790

Southern senators used the first filibuster to oppose the move of the First Congress to Philadelphia.

Early 1800s

Congress admitted new States in pairs of one slave State and one free State to ensure a balance in the Senate.

1917

The cloture rule, requiring a two-thirds vote of the Senate to end debate, arose from a filibuster against arming American merchant ships.

1960s

A newly introduced two-track option allowed the Senate to continue its work during a filibuster.

1975

The number of votes needed for cloture was reduced to three fifths.

Today

Today's Senate is often referred to as the 60-vote Senate, a reference to the number needed to invoke cloture.

Senator Robert Byrd
(D., West Virginia) ▶

Perspectives

The term *filibuster* was first used in 1851 to describe the tactic of talking a bill to death. By 2005, Democratic filibusters had prevented confirmation of a number of President Bush's judicial appointments. The Republican Majority Leader threatened to ask the Senate's presiding officer to rule judicial filibusters unconstitutional. Democrats countered by threatening to bring the Senate to a halt. A group of moderate Senate Democrats and Republicans arrived at a compromise that ended the crisis.

"[The filibuster] presents a serious challenge to…the principle so essential to our general liberty—the separation of powers….[T]he Framers concluded that the President should have the power to appoint…. But the Minority's filibuster prevents the Senate from giving "advice and consent." They deny the Senate the right to carry out its Constitutional duty….This filibuster is…a formula for tyranny by the minority."

**—Majority Leader Bill Frist
(R., Tennessee)**

"If senators are denied their right to free speech on judicial nominations, an attack on extended debate on all other matters cannot be far behind. This would mean no leverage for the minority to effect compromise, and no bargaining power for individual senators as they strive to represent the people of their states…. Let the Senate continue to be the one in which a minority can have the freedom to protect a majority from its own folly."

**—Senator Robert Byrd
(D., West Virginia)**

Connect to Your World

1. **Understand (a)** What tactic did the majority leader threaten to use to end the crisis? **(b)** Why do you think the term "nuclear option" was used to describe this tactic?
2. **Draw Inferences (a)** What does Senator Byrd say would happen if the majority used the "nuclear option"? **(b)** Do you agree or disagree with their view that this was a crisis that called for compromise?

GOVERNMENT ONLINE
In the News
For updates about minority rights visit **PearsonSuccessNet.com**

SECTION 4

Making Law:
The Senate

Guiding Question

What are the major differences in the lawmaking process in the House and the Senate? Use a Venn diagram to keep track of ways the House and Senate procedures compare.

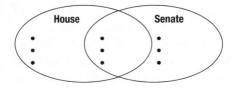

Political Dictionary

- filibuster
- cloture
- veto
- pocket veto

Objectives

1. Describe how a bill is introduced in the Senate.
2. Compare the Senate's rules for debate with those in the House.
3. Describe the role of conference committees in the legislative process.
4. Evaluate the actions the President can take after both houses have passed a bill.

Image Above: Senate pages carry copies of a bill to the Senate floor.

The House and the Senate really are two quite different places. Overall, however, the basic steps in the lawmaking process are much the same in the two chambers. Still, there are a few critical differences in their processes.

The Senate Floor

The chief differences in House and Senate procedures involve the consideration of measures on the floor. With introduction by a senator formally recognized for the purpose, a measure is given a number, read twice, and then referred to a standing committee, where it is dealt with much as are bills in the House. The Senate's proceedings are less formal and its rules less strict than those in the much larger lower house. For example, the Senate has only one calendar for all bills reported out of its committees. (Recall, there are five of these schedules in the House.) Bills are called to the Senate floor by the majority leader, usually, but not always, in consultation with the minority leader.[15]

Rules for Debate

Where debate in the House is strictly limited, it is almost unrestrained in the Senate. Indeed, most members of the Senate are intensely proud of belonging to what has often been called "the greatest deliberative body in the world."

As a general matter, a senator may speak on the floor for as long as he or she pleases. Unlike the House, the Senate has no rule that requires a member to speak only to the measure before the chamber. In short, a senator can talk about anything he or she wants to. And the Senate's rules do not allow any member to move the previous question.

Many bills, and particularly the most important pieces of legislation, come to the Senate floor under a unanimous consent agreement. The majority leader regularly negotiates these agreements with the minority leader, and they become effective only if no senator objects. Unanimous consent agreements usually limit the amount of floor time to be devoted to a particular measure

---

[15] The Senate does have one other calendar, the Executive Calendar, for treaties and appointments made by the President. The majority leader controls that schedule, too.

▶ Strom Thurmond held up the Civil Rights Act of 1957 with the longest filibuster in history.

and the number and content of amendments that may be offered to it.

The Senate does have a "two-speech rule." It provides that no senator may speak more than twice on a given question on the same legislative day. By recessing—temporarily interrupting—rather than adjourning a day's session, the Senate can prolong a "legislative day" indefinitely. Thus, the two-speech rule can successfully limit the amount of time the Senate spends on some matters.

The Senate's dedication to freedom of debate is almost unique among modern legislative bodies. That freedom is intended to encourage the fullest possible discussion of matters on the floor. But, notice, the great <u>latitude</u> it allows also gives rise to the filibuster.

The Filibuster Essentially, a **filibuster** is an attempt to "talk a bill to death." It is a stalling tactic by which a minority of senators seeks to delay or prevent Senate action on a measure. The filibusterers try to so monopolize the Senate floor and its time that the Senate must either drop the bill or change it in some manner acceptable to the minority.

Talk—and more talk—is the filibusterers' major weapon. In addition, senators may use time-killing motions, quorum calls, and other parliamentary maneuvers. Indeed, anything to delay or obstruct is grist for the minority's mill as it works to block a bill that would very likely pass if brought to a vote.

Among the many better-known filibusterers, Senator Huey Long (D., Louisiana) spoke for more than 15 hours in 1935. He stalled by reading from the Washington telephone directory and giving his colleagues his recipes for "pot-likker," corn bread, and turnip greens. Senator Strom Thurmond (R., South Carolina) set the current filibuster record. He held the floor for 24 hours and 18 minutes in an unsuccessful, one-person effort against what, despite his arguments, became the Civil Rights Act of 1957.

No later efforts have come close to matching Senator Thurmond's record. In fact, both in the past and today, nearly all filibusters are team efforts, with a number of senators taking turns on the floor, relieving one another as they monopolize the Senate's time. Well over 300 measures have been killed by filibusters. Just the *threat* of a filibuster has resulted in the Senate's failure to consider a number of bills and the amending of many others.

The Senate often tries to beat off a filibuster with lengthy, even day-and-night, sessions to wear down the participants. At times, some little-observed rules are strictly enforced. Among them are the requirements that senators stand—not sit, lean on their desks, or walk about—as they speak and that they not use "unparliamentary language" on the floor. These countermeasures seldom work.

The Cloture Rule The Senate's real check on the filibuster is its Cloture Rule, Rule XXII in the Standing Rules of the Senate. It was first adopted in 1917, after one of the most notable of all filibusters in Senate history. That filibuster, which lasted for three weeks, took place less than two months before the United States entered World War I.

German submarines had renewed their attacks on shipping in the North Atlantic, so President Wilson asked Congress to permit the arming of American merchant vessels. The bill, widely supported in the country, quickly passed the House, by a vote of 403–13. The measure died in the Senate, however, because

latitude
n. freedom of action

twelve senators filibustered it until the end of the congressional term on March 4th.

The public was outraged. President Wilson declared: "A little group of willful men, representing no opinion but their own, has rendered the great Government of the United States helpless and contemptible." The Senate passed the Cloture Rule at its next session.

Rule XXII provides for **cloture**—limiting debate. The rule is not in regular, continuing force; it can be brought into play only by a special procedure. A vote to invoke the rule must be taken two days after a petition calling for that action has been submitted by at least 16 members of the Senate. If at least 60 senators—three fifths of the full Senate—vote for the motion, the rule becomes effective. From that point, no more than another 30 hours of floor time may be spent on the measure. Then it *must* be brought to a final vote.

Of nearly 700 attempts to invoke the rule, only about a third have been successful. Many senators hesitate to vote for cloture because (1) they honor the tradition of free debate and/or (2) they worry that frequent use of cloture will undercut the value of the filibuster that they may someday want to use.

The Situation Today Filibusters have become much more common in recent years because, for more than a decade now, party control of the upper house has been a very narrow thing. In the 110th Congress (2007–2009), there were 49 Democrats and 49 Republicans in the Senate. The Democrats were able to control the chamber only because its two independent members, Joe Lieberman of Connecticut and Bernie Sanders of Vermont, chose to support them, not the Republicans, for organizational purposes.

The Democrats do have a wider margin of control in the 111th Congress: 58 seats and the two independents to the GOP's 40 seats. But the 60 votes needed to beat back a filibuster can still be hard to come by.

Over the past several years, the minority party, at times the Democrats, currently the Republicans, has made frequent use of the filibuster to block legislation backed by the majority party. And their filibusters have been regularly successful. They have because, given the Cloture Rule, the minimum

number of votes necessary to pass an important bill in the Senate today is not 51 or a simple majority of the members present and voting. It is, instead, 60, the minimum number of votes necessary to invoke cloture (end debate). It is true that filibusters can protect the minority and prevent hasty and ill-considered legislation. It is also true that they can promote gridlock, and public ridicule.

Conference Committees

As you have seen, a bill must survive any number of challenges in order to become a law. Most don't. A measure can be killed, or simply buried, in a subcommittee, in the full committee, in the House Rules Committee, or in any of the parallel committees in the Senate. The remainder must make it through votes on the floor in both houses.

Any measure that does survive the legislative process *must* have been passed by both houses in identical form. Most often, a bill approved by one house and then passed by the other is left unchanged by the second. When the House and Senate do pass different versions of the same bill, the first house usually concurs in the other's amendments, and congressional action is completed.

When one house will not accept the other's version of a bill, the measure is sent to a conference committee—a temporary joint committee of the two chambers. It seeks to produce a compromise bill acceptable to both houses.

The conferees—managers—are named by the respective presiding officers. Mostly, they are leading members of the standing committee that first handled the measure in each house.

Both chambers' rules say that a conference committee can consider only those parts of a bill on which the two houses have disagreed. In practice, however, conferees often add provisions never considered in either the House or Senate.

Once the conferees agree, their report, the compromise bill, is submitted to both houses. It must be accepted or rejected without amendment. Only rarely does either house turn down a conference committee's work. This is not surprising, for two major

✔ **Checkpoint**
What caused the Senate to pass the Cloture Rule in 1917?

How a **Bill** Becomes a Law

A bill may be introduced in either chamber. The path to the right is that of a bill that begins in the House. If a bill were to start in the Senate, steps 5, 6, and 7 would precede steps 1, 2, 3, and 4. *In what ways does the lawmaking process in the House differ from that in the Senate?*

1 H.R. 1 INTRODUCED IN HOUSE.

2 COMMITTEE ACTION
H.R. 1 referred to standing committee for study, hearings, revisions, and approval.

3 RULES COMMITTEE
The Rules Committee sets conditions for debate and amendment on the floor.

5 S. 1 INTRODUCED IN SENATE.

4 FLOOR ACTION
H.R. 1 debated, then passed or defeated. If passed, it goes to the Senate.

6 COMMITTEE ACTION
S. 1 referred to standing committee for study, hearings, revisions, and approval.

7 FLOOR ACTION
S. 1 debated, then passed or defeated.

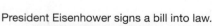

President Eisenhower signs a bill into law.

8 CONFERENCE COMMITTEE
Conference committee resolves differences between House and Senate versions of bill.

9 CONGRESSIONAL APPROVAL
House and Senate vote on final passage. Approved bill is sent to the President.

10 PRESIDENTIAL ACTION
The President signs or vetoes the bill or allows it to become law without signing. A vetoed bill returns to Congress; the veto may be (but seldom is) overridden.

A House-Senate conference committee ▲

Lawmaking Behind the Scenes

The simplified path on the facing page does not fully reveal the complexity of the lawmaking process or the subtle changes to the process over the past several decades. As partisanship has increased in Congress, the majority party leaders in both houses have taken a much more important role, and lawmakers have introduced several unofficial, informal steps to the process. *How does the majority leadership influence legislation?*

▶▶ Before a Bill Is Submitted

The Hopper in the House

Building Support Much work happens before a member of Congress submits a bill. Members may work with their own staff, experts in the field, interest groups, or the executive branch to draft the bill. They revise and edit the measure to ensure broad support and ask other members to announce their support by cosponsoring the bill. Negotiating behind the scenes is vital to the success of a proposed bill.

Getting It Right The exact wording of the bill determines its future in more ways than one. If a bill deals with matters that fall within the jurisdiction of more than one committee, the sponsors of the measure may tweak its wording to ensure that the primary responsibility for the bill will fall to the committee most likely to report it favorably.

Howard McKeon, (R., Calif.) and Roscoe G. Bartlett (R., Md.) talk during a House Armed Services Committee markup. ▼

▶▶ Committee Action

Multiple Committees The most important measures are now often referred to more than one committee. This reduces the clout of members of each committee by adding more voices to the committee debate.

Majority Rules The majority leadership in the House regularly uses the Rules Committee to advance its party's agenda. For example, the Rules Committee may restrict debate on a bill when it reaches the floor. In an emergency situation, the leadership may even bypass committees and bring a bill directly to the floor for a vote. This seldom happens, but it illustrates the increased power of party leaders over committees.

reasons: (1) the powerful membership of the typical conference committee, and (2) the fact that its report usually comes in the midst of the rush to adjournment at the end of a congressional session.

The conference committee stage is a most strategic step. A number of major legislative decisions and compromises are often made at that point. Indeed, the late Senator George Norris (R., Nebraska) once quite aptly described conference committees as "the third house of Congress."

The President Acts

The Constitution requires that bills and resolutions be sent to the President after they have passed both houses of Congress. The President has four options at this point:

1. The President may sign the bill, and it then becomes law.

2. The President may **veto**—refuse to sign—the bill. The measure must then be returned to the house in which it originated, together with the President's objections (a veto message). Although it seldom does, Congress may then pass the bill over the President's veto, by a two-thirds vote of the full membership of each house.

3. The President may allow the bill to become law without signing it—by not acting on it within 10 days, not counting Sundays, of receiving it.

4. The fourth option is a variation of the third, called the **pocket veto.** If Congress adjourns its session within 10 days of submitting a bill to the President, and the President does not act, the measure dies. (Sundays are not counted.)

Congress added another element to the President's veto power with the passage of the Line Item Veto Act of 1996. That law gave the chief executive the power to reject individual items in appropriations bills. The Supreme Court held the law unconstitutional, however, in *Clinton* v. *City of New York,* 1998.

Because Congress can seldom muster the votes necessary to override a veto, the power can play an extremely effective part in the President's dealings with Congress. The weight of power in the executive-legislative relationship is underscored by this fact: The mere threat of a veto is often enough to defeat a bill or to prompt changes in its provisions as it moves through the legislative process.

Nancy Reagan and members of Congress watch the President sign the Ronald Reagan Centennial Commission Act of 2009. ▼

Essential Questions Journal To continue to build a response to the chapter Essential Question, go to your **Essential Questions Journal.**

SECTION 4 ASSESSMENT

1. **Guiding Question** Use your completed Venn diagram to answer this question: What are the major differences in the lawmaking process in the House and the Senate?

Key Terms and Comprehension

2. **(a)** What is a **filibuster? (b)** How can it be ended?

3. What are the four options a President has when a bill reaches his desk?

Critical Thinking

4. **Draw Inferences** Consider what you have read about the filibuster. Identify two reasons why it has become a valued Senate tradition.

5. **Understand Point of View** Why might some Presidents have used the veto power frequently, while others have not used it very often?

Quick Write

Persuasive Essay: Consider Your Audience Look at your outline from Section 3. Suppose that the audience for your essay is members of Congress. Add details to your outline that will help you present your view in the most persuasive way. Begin with a clear statement of your argument. Be sure to address the various opposing points of view.

GOVERNMENT ONLINE

On the Go

To review anytime, anywhere, download these online resources at **PearsonSuccessNet.com**
Political Dictionary, Audio Review

Guiding Question
Section 2 How do committees help Congress do its work?

Guiding Question
Section 3 What steps does a successful bill follow as it moves through the House?

Guiding Question
Section 1 How do constitutional and party officers keep Congress organized?

CHAPTER 12
Essential Question
Can and should the lawmaking process be improved?

Guiding Question
Section 4 What are the major differences in the lawmaking process in the House and the Senate?

Political Dictionary

Speaker of the House p. 332
President of the Senate p. 333
President *pro tempore* p. 334
party caucus p. 334
floor leader p. 336
majority leader p. 336
minority leader p. 336
whip p. 336
committee chairman p. 336
seniority rule p. 337
standing committee p. 338
subcommittee p. 340
select committee p. 340
joint committee p. 341
conference committee p. 342
bill p. 343
joint resolution p. 344
concurrent resolution p. 344
resolution p. 344
rider p. 344
pigeonhole p. 345
discharge petition p. 345
quorum p. 348
engrossed p. 349
filibuster p. 352
cloture p. 353
veto p. 356
pocket veto p. 356

Comparing the House and the Senate

House of Representatives	Senate
• Smaller personal staffs	• Larger personal staffs
• Fewer committee assignments	• More committee assignments
• More formal, less flexible rules	• Fewer, more flexible rules
• Committee work usually more important than floor debate in shaping outcome of legislation	• Floor debate often more important than committee work in shaping outcome of legislation
• Floor debate strictly limited	• Floor debate largely unlimited, but subject to cloture vote by 60 senators to end debate

Types of Bills and Resolutions

Bill	A proposed law: a public bill applies to the entire nation; a private bill applies only to certain people or places
Joint Resolution	A proposal for some action that has the force of law when passed; usually deals with special circumstances or temporary matters
Concurrent Resolution	A statement of position on an issue, adopted by the House and Senate in identical form
Resolution	A measure dealing with some matter in one house; does not have the force of law and does not require the President's signature

Chapter Assessment

Comprehension and Critical Thinking

Section 1

1. **(a)** How often does a new term of Congress begin? **(b)** Compare opening day in the House and the Senate.
2. **(a)** How are House and Senate committee chairmen chosen? **(b)** Why are there both constitutional and party officers in Congress?

Section 2

3. **(a)** What are the standing committees in the House and Senate? **(b)** Which party holds the majority of seats on each committee? **(c)** What factors determine which committee will deal with a bill?
4. **(a)** Who determines who will serve on each congressional committee? **(b)** Why are some committee assignments more desirable than others?

Section 3

5. What type of measure would the House or Senate use if it wanted to **(a)** amend one of its rules? **(b)** express an opinion that would have the force of law on some temporary matter? **(c)** make a law affecting only one person?
6. **(a)** What are the five options a committee has when it has finished work on a bill? **(b)** Describe a situation in which a committee might decide to report a bill with an unfavorable recommendation rather than pigeonhole it. **(c)** Evaluate the usefulness of this practice.
7. Why might a member of Congress vote in favor of a bill once it is certain to pass even though he or she had supported previous attempts to scuttle it?

Section 4

FILIBUSTED.

8. **(a) Analyzing Political Cartoons** Study the cartoon above. **(a)** What point is the cartoon making? **(b)** Do you agree or disagree with its point of view?
9. **(a)** Why are conference committees rarely necessary? **(b)** Why are their recommendations usually accepted?
10. Compare and contrast the rules for debate in the House and Senate.

Writing About Government

11. Use your Quick Write exercises from this chapter to write a persuasive essay about the organization of Congress. Make sure that your thesis is stated clearly and that it is illustrated with specific examples and supported by your arguments. When you are finished, ask a friend to read the essay and give you feedback about its clarity and persuasiveness. Use this feedback to fine tune your writing. See pp. S9–S10 of the Skills Handbook.

Apply What You've Learned

12. **Essential Question Activity** Go online to find information about bills recently introduced in Congress. Find a bill that became law and another that died in committee. Make a flowchart to show the progression of each bill through Congress and explain how that process compares to the chart "How a Bill Becomes a Law" in Section 4.

13. **Essential Question Assessment** Look at your flowchart from Question 12. Using these two bills as examples, write an essay in which you evaluate the success of the current lawmaking process. This will help you answer the chapter Essential Question: **Can and should the lawmaking process be improved?**

Essential Questions Journal To respond to the chapter Essential Question, go to your **Essential Questions Journal.**

Document-Based Assessment

Divided Government

Over recent decades, the majority party in Congress has often not been the President's party. Americans disagree about this state of divided government. As Document 2 shows, independents generally favor divided government. Critics, however, point out that divided government allows each party to blame the other for government failures, as the author of Document 3 argues.

Document 1

One fallacious viewpoint too often expressed this election season is that a Democrat takeover of one or both houses of Congress would be desirable, since we then would have "divided government," with each party holding a share of power. Given the problems our nation faces today, this would be disastrous for America. . . . [T]he fundamental problems our nation faces today require a full commitment to coherent solutions, not a little of the left and a little of the right jumbled together.

—Peter Ferrara, *National Review Online,*
November 1, 2006

Document 2

The voters gave the country divided government last week, [in the 2006 congressional elections] and Americans tend to believe divided government is a good thing, although the belief is not overwhelming. 42% say it's better for the country when one party controls the Presidency and the other the Congress, while 33% (and even more Republicans) favor one party government. Independents [51%] are particularly happy with divided control.

—CBS News Poll, November 14, 2006

Document 3

[D]ivided government is the main reason voters should be mistrustful of the decisions and nondecisions made in Washington. Division produces deadlock. Deadlock produces a mélange [mix] of actions and nonactions that no elected official can or will defend, and for which every elected official in each party blames the elected officials in the other.

—Lloyd Cutler, Counsel to President Carter,
Letter to *The New York Times,* September 16, 1992

Document 4

Use your knowledge of Congress and Documents 1–4 above to answer Questions 1–3.

1. Which statement does Document 2 support?
   A. Independents are most likely to support divided government.
   B. Republicans are most likely to support divided government.
   C. Democrats are most likely to support divided government.
   D. A majority of Americans support divided government.

2. What point does Document 4 make?

3. **Pull It Together** Using these documents, explain whether divided government enhances or hinders the lawmaking process.

GOVERNMENT ONLINE
Documents
To find more resources on divided government, visit
PearsonSuccessNet.com

Essential Question

What makes a successful Congress?

There are many ways to define a successful Congress. The following examples offer perspectives on different qualities.

" ON SETTING PRIORITIES:

Congress should pass laws that reflect the will of the people; that is, Congress should be responsive to popular majorities. Congress should pass laws that deal promptly and effectively with pressing national problems. . . . Only in a perfect world would what the majority wants always accord with what policy experts deem most likely to be effective. When a conflict exists, which should take priority?"

—Barbara Sinclair, *An Effective Congress and Effective Members: What Does It Take?*, 1996

ON COMPROMISE:

" ON EFFICIENCY:

. . . Congress simply isn't set up to be efficient. . . . Its job is to understand [issues] thoroughly, weigh the beliefs and interests of an astounding variety of Americans, and consider carefully how to move forward.

—Rep. Lee Hamilton (D., Indiana), 2004

Essential Question Warmup

Throughout this unit, you studied the powers and functions of Congress. Use what you have learned and the quotations and opinions above to answer the following questions. Then go to your **Essential Questions Journal.**

1. How should members of Congress balance their roles as representatives of what voters want and as trustees who promote the best interests of the nation as a whole?

2. How should members of Congress balance their roles as party members with the need to compromise?

3. What should be the role of debate in Congress?

Essential Questions Journal To continue to build a response to the unit Essential Question, go to your **Essential Questions Journal.**

Photo: Members of the executive branch gather in front of the White House.

Essential Questions Journal To begin to build a response to the unit Essential Question, go to your **Essential Questions Journal.**

Unit 4
The Executive Branch

Essential Question What makes a good President?

Essential Question
Does the current electoral process result in the best candidates for President?

> In the **scheme** of our national **government**, the **presidency** is **preeminently** the **people's** office.
>
> —President Grover Cleveland, 1900

Photo: Citizens of Chillicothe, Ohio, greet presidential candidate Barack Obama in 2008.

GOVERNMENT ONLINE
On the Go

To study anywhere, anytime, download these online resources at PearsonSuccessNet.com
• Political Dictionary
• Audio Review
• Downloadable Interactivities

The President's Job Description

Guiding Question

What are the roles and qualifications of the office of the President? Use an outline like the one below to keep track of the presidential roles and qualifications.

I. The President's Roles
   A. Chief of state
      1. _____
      2. _____
   B. _____
      1. _____
      2. _____

Political Dictionary

- chief of state
- chief executive
- chief admin-istrator
- chief diplomat
- commander in chief
- chief legislator
- chief of party
- chief citizen

Objectives

1. Describe the President's many roles.
2. Understand the formal qualifications necessary to become President.
3. Explain how the President's term of office has changed over time.
4. Describe the President's pay and benefits.

Image Above: President Ronald Reagan addresses U.S. troops in South Korea in 1983.

Do you know who the youngest person ever to be President of the United States was? The oldest? Who held the presidency for the longest time? The shortest? Can a person born abroad become President? You will find the answers to these questions, and much more, in this section, which provides a basic overview of the presidential office.

Presidential Roles

At any given time, of course, only one person is the President of the United States. The office, with all of its awesome powers and duties, belongs to that one individual. Whoever that person may be, he—and most likely someday she[1]—must fill several different roles, and all of them at the same time. The President is simultaneously (1) chief of state, (2) chief executive, (3) chief administrator, (4) chief diplomat, (5) commander in chief, (6) chief legislator, (7) chief of party, and (8) chief citizen.

1. To begin with, the President is **chief of state,** the ceremonial head of the government of the United States. He or she is, then, the symbol of all of the people of the nation—in President William Howard Taft's words, "the personal embodiment and representative of their dignity and majesty."

In many countries, the chief of state reigns but does not rule. That is certainly true of the queens of England, Denmark, and the Netherlands; the kings of Norway, Sweden, and Belgium; the emperor of Japan; and the presidents of Italy and Germany. It is just as certainly *not* true of the President of the United States. The President both reigns and rules.

2. The President is the nation's **chief executive,** vested by the Constitution with "the executive Power" of the United States. That power is immensely broad in both domestic and foreign affairs. Indeed, the American presidency is often described as "the most powerful office in the world."

But remember, the President is not all-powerful. He or she lives in an environment filled with constitutional checks and balances in which there are

---

1 To this point, all of the Presidents have been men, but nothing in the Constitution precludes the possibility of a woman in that office.

many practical limits on what he or she can and cannot do.

3. The President is also the **chief administrator,** the director of the huge executive branch of the Federal Government. He or she heads one of the largest governmental machines the world has ever known. Today, the President directs an administration that employs more than 2.7 million civilians and spends more than $3 trillion a year.

Managing the <u>sprawling</u> executive branch is only one of the President's several jobs. Harry Truman complained that he had to spend too much of his time "flattering, kissing, and kicking people to get them to do what they were supposed to do anyway."

4. Every President is also the nation's **chief diplomat,** the main architect of American foreign policy and the nation's chief spokesman to the rest of the world. "I make foreign policy," President Truman once said—and he did. Everything the President says and does is closely followed, both here and abroad.

5. In close <u>concert</u> with the President's role in foreign affairs, the Constitution also makes him or her the **commander in chief** of the nation's armed forces. The 1.4 million men and women in uniform and all of the nation's military might are subject to the President's direct and immediate control. The Constitution does give Congress some significant powers in foreign affairs and over the military, but the President has long since become dominant in both fields.

6. The President is also the nation's **chief legislator,** the principal author of its public policies. Most often, it is the President who sets the overall shape of the congressional agenda—initiating, suggesting, requesting, insisting, and demanding that Congress enact most of the major pieces of legislation that it does.

The President and Congress do sometimes clash, and the President does not always get his or her way on Capitol Hill. Still, working with Congress occupies a major part of the President's time.

These six presidential roles all come directly from the Constitution. Yet they do not complete the list. The President has still other vital roles to play.

7. The President is, automatically, the **chief of party,** the acknowledged leader of the political party that controls the executive branch—and is virtually unchallengeable in that role. As you know, parties are not mentioned in the Constitution, but they do have a vital place in the workings of the American governmental system. Much of the real power and influence of the President depends on his or her ability to play this critical role.

8. The office also automatically makes its occupant the nation's **chief citizen.** The President is expected to be "the representative of all the people." He or she is expected to take the high road and <u>champion</u> the public interest against the many different and competing private interests. "The presidency," said Franklin Roosevelt, "is not merely an administrative office. That is the least of it. It is, preeminently, a place of moral leadership."

Listing the President's several roles is a useful and convenient way to describe the President's job. But, remember, the President

✓ Checkpoint
What are the President's responsibilities as the nation's chief legislator?

<u>sprawling</u>
adj. spreading out over a large area

<u>concert</u>
n. with all in agreement, together as one

<u>champion</u>
v. to fight for, defend, or promote

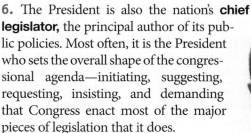

President Bill Clinton meets with Israeli and Palestinian leaders at Camp David in 2000 to conduct peace talks. ***What role is President Clinton fulfilling here?***

agonizing
adj. painful, distressing

sordid
adj. shameful

must play all of these roles simultaneously, and they are all interconnected. None of them can be performed in isolation. The manner in which a President plays any one role can have a real effect on his or her ability to play another and even all of them.

As but two illustrations of the point, take the experiences of Presidents Lyndon Johnson and Richard Nixon. Each was a strong and relatively effective President during his first years in office. But Mr. Johnson's actions as commander in chief during the <u>agonizing</u> and increasingly unpopular war in Vietnam seriously damaged his stature and effectiveness in the White House. In fact, the damage was so great that it helped persuade LBJ not to run for reelection in 1968.

The many-sided and <u>sordid</u> Watergate scandal brought President Nixon's downfall. The manner in which he filled the roles of party leader and chief citizen so destroyed Mr. Nixon's presidency that he was forced to leave office in disgrace in 1974.

Formal Qualifications

Whatever else a President must be, the Constitution says that he—and, again, likely one day she—must meet three formal qualifications for office.[2] The President must:

1. Be "a natural born Citizen . . . of the United States." Do the words "natural born" mean "native born"—that is, born in the United States? By law, a person born abroad to an American-citizen parent becomes an American citizen at birth. That law leads many to argue that it is therefore possible for a person born outside the United States to become President.[3] Some dispute that view, however. The question of what the Constitution means here cannot be answered until someone born a citizen, but born abroad, does in fact become President.

2. "[H]ave attained . . . the Age of 35 years." John F. Kennedy, at 43, was the youngest person ever elected to the office. Theodore Roosevelt reached the White House by succession at age 42. Only seven other chief executives took the oath of office before age 50: James K. Polk in 1845, Franklin Pierce in 1853, Ulysses S. Grant in 1869, James Garfield in 1881, Grover Cleveland in 1885, Bill Clinton in 1993, and Barack Obama in 2009.

Ronald Reagan, who was 69 when he was first elected in 1980, was the oldest candidate ever to win the office; and, when he left office in 1989 at age 77, he was the oldest person ever to hold the presidency. Most chief executives have been in their 50s when they gained the White House.

3. "[H]ave . . . been fourteen years a Resident within the United States." Given the elections of Herbert Hoover (in 1928) and Dwight Eisenhower (in 1952), we know that here the Constitution means any 14 years in a person's life. Both Mr. Hoover and General Eisenhower spent several years outside the country before winning the White House.

While these formal qualifications do have some importance, they are really not very difficult to meet. Indeed, well over 100 million Americans do so today. There are several other *informal* and important qualifications for the presidency, as you will see in Section 4.

The Presidential Term

The Framers considered a number of different limits on the length of the presidential term. Most of their debate centered on a four-year term, with the President eligible for reelection, versus a single six-year or seven-year term without being eligibile for reelection. They finally settled on a four-year term.[4] They agreed, as Alexander Hamilton wrote in *The Federalist* No. 71, that four years was a long enough period for a President to have gained experience, demonstrated his abilities, and established stable policies.

Until 1951, the Constitution placed no limit on the number of terms a President might serve. Several Presidents, beginning

---

2 Article II, Section 1, Clause 5.

3 Martin Van Buren, who was born December 5, 1782, was the first President actually born in the United States. His seven predecessors (and his immediate successor) were each born in the colonies, before the Revolution—that is, before there was a United States. But notice, the Constitution anticipated that circumstance with these words: "or a Citizen of the United States, at the time of the Adoption of this Constitution."

---

4 Article II, Section 1, Clause 1.

Term Limits

> "No person shall be elected to the office of the President more than twice, and no person who has held the office of President, or acted as President, for more than two years of a term to which some other person was elected President shall be elected to the office of the President more than once.
>
> —22nd Amendment

FROM THE CONSTITUTION

NO FOURTH TERM EITHER

BETTER A THIRD TERMER THAN A THIRD RATER

Shattering Precedent George Washington's refusal to seek another term as President in 1796 soon gave rise to the "no-third-term tradition" in presidential politics. That unwritten rule was followed for nearly 150 years. In 1940, however, in an election in which the third-term question was a major issue, Franklin D. Roosevelt won another term in the White House; and, four years later, in the midst of World War II, FDR won a fourth term. In 1947, Congress proposed what in 1951 became the 22nd Amendment. It says that no President may serve more than two elected terms or, at the most, ten years in office.

Constitutional Principles How does the 22nd Amendment reflect the principles of popular sovereignty, limited government, and checks and balances?

Franklin D. Roosevelt campaigning for his third term in 1940

with George Washington, refused to seek more than two terms, however. Soon, the "no-third-term tradition" became an unwritten rule.

Franklin D. Roosevelt broke the tradition by seeking and winning a third term in 1940, and then a fourth in 1944. To prevent this from recurring, the 22nd Amendment made the unwritten custom limiting presidential terms a part of the written Constitution.

Each President may now serve a maximum of two full terms—eight years—in office. A President who succeeds to the office after the midpoint in a term could possibly serve for more than eight years. In that case, the President may finish out the predecessor's term and then seek two full terms of his or her own. However, no President may serve more than ten years in the office.

Many people, including Presidents Truman, Eisenhower, and Reagan, have called for the repeal of the 22nd Amendment. They insist that the two-term rule is undemocratic because it places an <u>arbitrary</u> limit on the people's right to decide who should be President. Critics also say that it undercuts the authority of a two-term President, especially in the latter part of a second term. Supporters of the amendment defend it as a reasonable safeguard against "executive tyranny."

Several Presidents have urged a single six-year term. They and others have argued that a single, nonrenewable term would free a President from the pressures of a campaign for a second term—and so would allow the chief executive to focus on the pressing demands of the office.

arbitrary
adj. high-handed, unreasonable

▲ *Air Force One* and a fleet of automobiles are some of the benefits that come with the presidency. **Why is it necessary for these services to be made available to the President?**

Pay and Benefits

Congress determines the President's annual salary, which can neither be increased nor decreased during a presidential term. The President's pay was first set at $25,000 a year, in 1789.[5] It is now $400,000 a year. Congress set that figure in 1999, and it became effective on January 20, 2001.

Congress has also provided the President with a $50,000-a-year expense allowance. That money may be spent however the President chooses. This allowance is, in effect, a part of his or her pay, and it is taxed as part of his or her income.

The Constitution forbids the President "any other emolument [payment for work] from the United States, or any of them." This provision does not prevent the President from being provided with a great many extras, however.

They include the White House, a magnificent 132-room mansion set on an 18.3-acre estate in the heart of the nation's capital; a sizable suite of offices and a large staff to assist him; a fleet of automobiles; the lavishly fitted Air Force One and several other planes and helicopters; Camp David, the resort hideaway in the Catoctin Mountains in Maryland; the finest medical, dental, and other healthcare available; generous travel and entertainment funds; and many other fringe benefits.

---

5 Article II, Section 1, Clause 7. At Philadelphia, Benjamin Franklin argued that, as money and power might corrupt a man, the President ought to receive nothing beyond his expenses; his suggestion was not put to a vote at the Convention.

Essential Questions Journal To continue to build a response to the chapter Essential Question, go to your **Essential Questions Journal.**

SECTION 1 ASSESSMENT

1. **Guiding Question** Use your completed outline to answer this question: What are the roles and qualifications of the office of the President?

Key Terms and Comprehension

2. (a) How does the President function as **chief of state?** (b) In what manner might this role be performed simultaneously with those of **chief diplomat** and **chief citizen?**

3. (a) Which two presidential roles do not come from the Constitution? (b) How did they come about?

4. What is the purpose of the 22nd Amendment?

Critical Thinking

5. **Draw Conclusions** Why do you think the Framers chose to provide formal qualifications for the office of the President?

6. **Demonstrate Reasoned Judgment** Do you think the pay and benefits with which the President is compensated are adequate and appropriate for the job? Why or why not?

Quick Write

Research Writing: Explore a Topic Choose three Presidents from this section and write a list of questions about each one for which you will research to find the answers. Focus on their personal backgrounds and political experience prior to their election. For example, you might ask: What partisan political experience did President Dwight Eisenhower have before his election?

Evaluating Leadership

"Tuesday's election for the State Assembly seat in Gloucester County is going to be a close one. Recent polls show that Jane Arbino is leading among voters who say that coalition-building is a key factor in their choice, but that voters who favor fiscal responsibility are much more likely to vote for her opponent, Keith James."

What qualities do you consider important when you choose whom to vote for in an election? Many different factors can make someone the right candidate for you, and your factors might not be the ones that matter to someone else. It is important to decide what you consider essential before you cast your ballot.

1. Decide what factors are most important to you. Before you begin evaluating leadership abilities, you should determine which qualities you care about the most. Do you want a leader with a proven track record? Past actions can be a good indicator of what someone will do in the future. It can be important for a leader to have demonstrated his or her ability to get things done. You may wish to evaluate a candidate based on aspects of his or her personality or character. Does the candidate have the ability to motivate or inspire others? Does this person share your beliefs and values?

2. Match the skills to the job. Your evaluation of a candidate may depend on what leadership position is being filled. Your town mayor may need different leadership qualities than, say, the town clerk, and the qualities of a good senator might differ from those of a good Board of Education member. For some positions, it is important for a leader to have a strong vision and the ability to unite conflicting groups. For others, you might be looking for someone who can stand his or her ground in the face of opposition. A candidate might be a good choice for one position but not another, so you should make sure to think about the specific requirements of the job when you evaluate leadership abilities.

3. Compare their qualifications. Once you have determined the factors that are important to you and have evaluated the skills necessary for the position, you will need to compare each candidate against those factors. Who meets most of your requirements? Does your list of requirements reduce your options to one candidate? If not, you will need to compare the several choices against each other to determine who you think is the best choice for the position.

▸▸ What do you think?

1. What do you think is the most important leadership quality for a United States senator? What about for a high school principal?

2. Do you think it's a good idea for a leader to admit when he or she has made a mistake?

3. **You Try It** Make a list of the criteria that you think make someone a good leader. Choose someone in a leadership position, such as a member of Congress or the President. Evaluate that person using the leadership criteria that you selected.

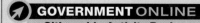

GOVERNMENT ONLINE
Citizenship Activity Pack
For activities on evaluating leadership, go to
PearsonSuccessNet.com

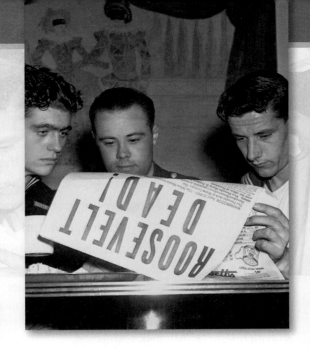

SECTION 2

Presidential **Succession** and the **Vice Presidency**

Guiding Question

What occurs when the President is unable to perform the duties of the office? Use a chart like the one below to keep track of the main ideas about presidential succession.

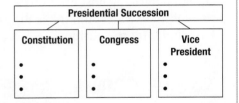

Political Dictionary
- presidential succession
- Presidential Succession Act of 1947
- balance the ticket

Objectives
1. Explain how the Constitution provides for presidential succession.
2. Understand the constitutional provisions relating to presidential disability.
3. Describe the role of the Vice President.

Image Above: Service men read of President Franklin Roosevelt's death in a newspaper, April 12, 1945.

Consider these facts. To this point, forty-seven people have served as Vice President. Fourteen of them have reached the Oval Office—most recently, George H.W. Bush in 1989. Indeed, five of the last twelve Presidents were once Vice President.

The Constitution and Succession

Presidential succession is the scheme by which a presidential vacancy is filled. If a President dies, resigns, or is removed from office by impeachment, the Vice President succeeds to the office.

Originally, the Constitution did not provide for the succession of a Vice President. Rather, it declared that "the powers and duties" of the office—not the office itself—were to "devolve on [transfer to] the Vice President."[6]

In practice the Vice President did succeed to the office when it became vacant. Vice President John Tyler was the first to do so. He set the precedent in 1841 when he succeeded President William Henry Harrison, who died of pneumonia just one month after taking office. What had been practice became a part of the written Constitution with the adoption of the 25th Amendment in 1967, which states, "In case of the removal of the President from office or of his death or resignation, the Vice President shall become President."

Congress fixes the order of succession following the Vice President.[7] The present law on the matter is the **Presidential Succession Act of 1947.** By its terms, the Speaker of the House and then the President pro tempore of the Senate are next in line. They are followed, in turn, by the secretary of state and then by each of the other 14 heads of the Cabinet departments, in order of each position's precedence—that is, the order in which their offices were created by Congress.[8]

---

6   Read carefully Article II, Section 1, Clause 6.
7   Article II, Section 1, Clause 6. On removal of the President by impeachment, see Chapter 11.
8   A Cabinet member is to serve only until a Speaker or a president pro tem is available and qualified. Notice that the 25th Amendment also provides for the filling of any vacancy in the vice presidency. In effect, that provision makes the Presidential Succession Act a law with little real significance—except in the highly unlikely event of simultaneous vacancies in the presidency and vice presidency.

Presidential Disability

Until the 25th Amendment was adopted in 1967, there were serious gaps in the arrangement for presidential succession. Neither the Constitution nor Congress had made any provision for deciding when a President was so disabled that he could not perform the duties of the office. Nor was there anything to indicate by whom such a decision was to be made.

For nearly 180 years, then, the nation played with fate. President Eisenhower suffered three serious but temporary illnesses while in office: a heart attack in 1955, ileitis in 1956, and a mild stroke in 1957. Two other Presidents were disabled for much longer periods. James Garfield lingered for 80 days before he died from an assassin's bullet in 1881. Woodrow Wilson suffered a paralytic stroke in September of 1919 and was an invalid for the rest of his second term. In fact, he was so ill that he could not meet with his Cabinet for seven months after his stroke. And, in 1981, Ronald Reagan was gravely wounded in an assassination attempt.

Sections 3 and 4 of the 25th Amendment fill the disability gap, and in detail. The Vice President is to become Acting President if (1) the President informs Congress, in writing, "that he is unable to discharge the powers and duties of his office," or (2) the Vice President and a majority of the members of the Cabinet inform Congress, in writing, that the President is so incapacitated.[9]

The President may resume the powers and duties of the office by informing Congress by "written declaration" that no inability exists. However, the Vice President and a majority of the Cabinet may challenge the President on this score. If they do, Congress has 21 days in which to decide the matter.

Thus far, the disability provisions of the 25th Amendment have come into play on three occasions: In 1985, Ronald Reagan transferred the powers of the presidency to Vice President George H.W. Bush for nearly

✔ **Checkpoint**
How did the 25th Amendment fill the gaps in the Presidential Succession Act of 1947?

---

[9] The 25th Amendment gives this authority to the Vice President and the Cabinet or to "such other body as Congress may by law provide." To this point, no "such other body" has been created.

How Government Works

Who Is Next in Line?

The Vice President is first in line to succeed to the presidency should the office become vacant. A vacancy has occurred nine times. In each case, the Vice President did succeed to the office. *When did the practice of vice presidential succession actually become part of the written Constitution?*

Lyndon B. Johnson became President when John F. Kennedy was assassinated on November 22, 1963.

The Line of Succession

1. Vice President
2. Speaker of the House
3. President pro tempore of the Senate
4. Secretary of State
5. Secretary of the Treasury
6. Secretary of Defense
7. Attorney General
8. Secretary of the Interior
9. Secretary of Agriculture
10. Secretary of Commerce
11. Secretary of Labor
12. Secretary of Health and Human Services
13. Secretary of Housing and Urban Development
14. Secretary of Transportation
15. Secretary of Energy
16. Secretary of Education
17. Secretary of Veterans Affairs
18. Secretary of Homeland Security

GOVERNMENT ONLINE
Update
Check out who holds these offices today at
PearsonSuccessNet.com

✓ Checkpoint
What are the formal duties of the Vice President?

contrive
v. to create or bring about

eight hours, while surgeons removed a tumor from Mr. Reagan's large intestine. In 2002, and again in 2007, George W. Bush conveyed his powers to Vice President Dick Cheney for some two hours, while Mr. Bush was anesthetized during a routine medical procedure.

The Vice Presidency

"I am Vice President. In this I am nothing, but I may be everything." So said John Adams, the nation's first Vice President. Those words could have been repeated, very appropriately, by each of the 47 Vice Presidents who have followed him in that office.

Importance of the Office The Constitution pays little attention to the office of the Vice President. It assigns the position only two formal duties: (1) to preside over the Senate[10] and (2) to help decide the question of presidential disability.[11] Beyond those duties, the Constitution makes the Vice President, in effect, a "President-in-waiting."

Throughout much of the nation's history, in fact, the vice presidency was treated as an

ideological
adj. having to do with the beliefs or ideas of a person or group

10 Article I, Section 3, Clause 4; see Chapter 12.
11 25th Amendment, Sections 3 and 4.

office of little real consequence and, often, as the butt of jokes. Indeed, many Vice Presidents themselves had a hand in this undermining of the office. John Adams described his post as "the most insignificant office that ever the invention of man contrived or his imagination conceived."

John Nance Garner, who served for two terms as Franklin D. Roosevelt's Vice President (1933–1941), once declared, "The vice presidency isn't worth a warm pitcher of spit." Alben Barkley, who served during Harry Truman's second term, often told the story of a woman who had two sons. One of them, Barkley said, went away to sea and the other one became Vice President, "and neither of them was ever heard from again."[12]

Despite these and a great many other unkind comments, the office is clearly an important one. Its occupant is literally "only a heartbeat away" from the presidency. Remember, eight Presidents have died in office, and one was forced to resign.

Much of the blame for the low status of the vice presidency can be laid on the two major parties and the way they choose their candidates for the office. Traditionally, each national convention names the handpicked choice of its just-nominated presidential candidate. Usually, the newly minted presidential candidate picks someone who will **"balance the ticket."** That is, the nominee chooses a running mate who can strengthen his or her chance of being elected by virtue of certain ideological, geographic, racial, ethnic, gender, or other characteristics. In short, fate—presidential succession—does not very often have a high priority in the vice presidential candidate selection process.

The Vice President Today Although the vice presidency is still at times the target of late-night television humor, recent Presidents have made much greater use of their Vice Presidents than did any of their predecessors. In effect, the office has been reinvented.

"Dad, who runs the country if anything happens to the Vice-President?"

▶▶ **Analyzing Political Cartoons** Today, there is some criticism regarding the growth of the power of the Vice President. **How does this cartoon illustrate this attitude?**

12 Indeed, one Vice President, William Rufus King, never actually served in the office. A five-term senator from Alabama, he was elected with President Franklin Pierce in 1852. Shortly after the election, he became ill and went to Cuba hoping the climate would aid his health. His condition worsened, however, and he could not return to Washington for the inauguration. Although sworn in while in Cuba, he died upon his return to the United States.

Indeed, Dick Cheney (2001–2009) is widely seen as the most influential occupant of the office in the nation's history.

Barack Obama chose Joe Biden of Delaware as his running mate in 2008, in no small part on the basis of his long record of public service. Vice President Biden's 36 years in the Senate were capped by his chairmanship of the Senate's Foreign Relations Committee—a qualification that seems particularly fitting in today's crisis-filled world.

Still, even with the elevation of the office in recent years, no President has been willing to make his Vice President a true "Assistant President." The major reason: Of all the President's official family, only the Vice President is not subject to the ultimate discipline of removal from office by the President. No matter what the circumstances, the President cannot fire the Vice President.

Vice-Presidential Vacancy

The vice presidency has been vacant 18 times thus far: nine times by succession to the presidency, twice by resignation, and seven times by death.[13] Yet not until 1967 and the 25th Amendment did the Constitution deal with the matter. The amendment provides, in part:

---

13 John C. Calhoun resigned to become a senator from South Carolina in 1832. Spiro T. Agnew resigned in 1973, after a conviction for income tax evasion. The seven who died in office were George Clinton (1812), Elbridge Gerry (1814), William R. King (1853), Henry Wilson (1875), Thomas A. Hendricks (1885), Garret A. Hobart (1899), and James S. Sherman (1912).

" FROM THE CONSTITUTION

Whenever there is a vacancy in the office of the Vice President, the President shall nominate a Vice President who shall take office upon confirmation by a majority vote of both Houses of Congress.

—25th Amendment, Section 2

This provision was first implemented in 1973. In that year, President Richard Nixon selected and Congress confirmed Gerald R. Ford to succeed Spiro Agnew as Vice President. It came into play again in 1974 when, following Mr. Nixon's resignation, President Ford named and Congress approved Nelson Rockefeller for the post.

Vice President Joe Biden addresses the press.

Essential Questions Journal	To continue to build a response to the chapter Essential Question, go to your **Essential Questions Journal.**

SECTION 2 ASSESSMENT

1. **Guiding Question** Use your completed chart to answer this question: What occurs when the President is unable to perform the duties of the office?

Key Terms and Comprehension

2. **(a)** How does the Constitution address **presidential succession? (b)** In what way did the **Presidential Succession Act of 1947** deal with this matter?

3. What duties does the Constitution assign to the Vice President?

Critical Thinking

4. **Demonstrate Reasoned Judgment** Do you think an attempt to "balance the ticket" is an acceptable method of selecting a Vice President? Why or why not?

5. **Synthesize Information** How has the office of the Vice President changed in recent years?

Quick Write

Research Writing: Narrow a Topic Using the questions you drafted in the Section 1 Quick Write, conduct preliminary research to find the answers to your questions. Browse the Internet or other sources and take notes on what you find. Then use this information to determine which President you are most interested in researching further.

SECTION 3

Presidential Selection:
The Framers' Plan

Guiding Question

How did the process of choosing a President change over time? Use a flowchart like the one below to keep track of the main ideas about selecting a President.

> 1787: The Framers of the Constitution resolve to select the President by a system of electors.

Political Dictionary

- presidential elector
- electoral vote
- electoral college

Objectives

1. Explain the Framers' original provisions for choosing the President.
2. Understand how the rise of political parties changed the process of choosing a President as set out in the Constitution.

Images Above: 1800 Presidential candidates Aaron Burr (left) and Thomas Jefferson

In formal terms, the President is chosen according to the provisions of the Constitution.[14] In practice, however, the President is elected through an altogether extraordinary process—one that is not very well understood by most Americans. It is a combination of constitutional provisions, State and federal laws, and a number of practices born of the nation's political parties. To make sense of this very complex system, you must first understand what the Framers had in mind when they designed the presidential election process.

Original Provisions

The Framers gave more time to the method for choosing the President than to any other matter. It was, said James Wilson of Pennsylvania, "the most difficult of all on which we have had to decide." The difficulty arose largely because most of the Framers were against selecting the President by either of the obvious ways: by Congress or by a direct vote of the people.

Early in the Convention, most of the delegates did favor selection by Congress. Later, nearly all of them came to believe that congressional selection would, as Alexander Hamilton said, put the President "too much under the legislative thumb." Only a few of the Framers favored choosing the President by popular vote. Nearly all agreed that that process would lead to "tumult and disorder." Most delegates felt, too, that the people, scattered over so wide an area, could not possibly know enough about the available candidates to make wise, informed choices. George Mason of Virginia spoke for most at the convention: "The extent of the Country renders it impossible that the people can have the requisite capacity to judge of the respective pretensions of the Candidates."

After weeks of debate, the Framers finally agreed on a plan first put forward by Hamilton. Under it, the President and Vice President were to be chosen by a special body of **presidential electors.** These electors would be chosen in each State in a manner the State legislature directed, and each State would have as many electors as it has senators and representatives in Congress.

---

14 The Constitution deals with the process of presidential selection in several places: Article II, Section 1, Clauses 2, 3, and 4; and the 12th, 20th, and 23rd amendments.

Once selected, these electors would each cast two **electoral votes,** each for a different candidate. The candidate with the most votes would become President. The person with the second-most votes would become Vice President.

The Framers intended the electors to be "the most enlightened and respectable citizens" from each State. They were to act as "free agents" in choosing the people best qualified to fill the nation's two highest offices.

The Rise of Parties

The **electoral college,** then, is the group of people (electors) chosen from each State and the District of Columbia to formally select the President and Vice President. The original version of the electoral college worked as the Framers intended only as long as George Washington was willing to seek and hold the presidency. He did so twice, and was unanimously elected President, in 1789 and in 1792.

<u>Flaws</u> began to appear in the system in 1796, however, with the rise of political parties. John Adams, the Federalist candidate, was elected to the presidency. Thomas Jefferson, an arch-rival and Democratic-Republican, lost to Adams by just three votes in the electoral balloting. Jefferson then became Adams's Vice President.

The Election of 1800 The system broke down altogether in the election of 1800. By then there were two well-defined parties: the Federalists, led by Adams and Hamilton, and the Democratic-Republicans, headed by Jefferson. Each of these parties nominated presidential and vice-presidential candidates. They also nominated candidates to serve as presidential electors in the several States. Those elector-candidates were picked with the clear understanding that, if elected, they would vote for their party's presidential and vice-presidential nominees.

Each of the 73 Democratic-Republicans who won posts as electors voted for his party's nominees: Thomas Jefferson and Aaron Burr. In doing so, they produced a tie for the presidency. Remember that the Constitution

<u>flaw</u>
n. a defect, shortcoming, or weakness

The Electoral College

Crisis Causes Change

The Framers saw the electoral college as an appropriate way to select the President and Vice President. They did not foresee the development of political parties, however, and the parties' participation in the election of 1800 caused a serious breakdown in the Framers' presidential selection process. *What did the Framers hope to accomplish by designing the electoral college system as they did?*

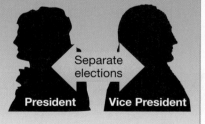

The 12th Amendment

Separate elections

President   Vice President

1787
The Framers' Original Plan

- Each elector casts two electoral votes, each for a different person for President.
- The person receiving a majority of the electoral votes becomes President.
- The person with the second highest number of electoral votes becomes Vice President.

1800
The Crisis

In accord with the Framers' original plan, in 1800 the electors cast their two votes for two different persons. Each of the 73 Democratic-Republican electors voted for that party's two nominees, producing a tie. In the end, it took 36 separate votes in the House of Representatives to finally select the President and, by default, the Vice President.

1804
Changes to the Original Plan

- The 12th Amendment to the Constitution separates the presidential and vice-presidential elections.
- Each presidential elector now casts one vote for President and one vote for Vice President.

The Election of 1800

Differing attitudes on the role of the government and the interpretation of the Constitution gave rise to political parties in the United States. ***How do the map and chart below illustrate these political divisions?***

Election of 1800

Federalist 47%
Democratic-Republican 53%

Candidate and Party	Electoral Votes
Thomas Jefferson Democratic-Republican	73
Aaron Burr Democratic-Republican	73
John Adams Federalist	65
Charles C. Pinckney Federalist	64
John Jay Federalist	1

SOURCE: National Archives and Records Administration

gave each elector two votes, each to be cast for a different person, but each to be cast for someone as President. Popular opinion clearly favored Jefferson. Still, the House of Representatives had to take 36 separate ballots before it finally settled on Mr. Jefferson as the third President of the United States.

The spectacular election of 1800 marked the introduction of three new elements into the process of selecting a President: (1) party nominations for the presidency and vice presidency, (2) nominations of candidates for presidential electors in the States who pledged to vote for their party's presidential ticket, and (3) automatic casting of the electoral votes in line with those pledges.

The 12th Amendment The election of 1800 produced another notable result: the 12th Amendment. This amendment was added to the Constitution in 1804 to make certain there would never be another such fiasco. The amendment is lengthy, but it made only one major change in the electoral college system. It separated the presidential and vice-presidential elections: "The Electors . . . shall name in their ballots the person voted for as President, and in distinct ballots the person voted for as Vice-President. . . ."[15]

With the appearance of parties, the election of 1800, and the 12th Amendment, the constitutional framework had been laid for the presidential selection system as it exists today. That system is, indeed, a far cry from what was agreed to in 1787, as you will see in the sections ahead.

---

15 Not only does the amendment mean there cannot be a repeat of the circumstances that produced a tie in 1800, it also almost certainly guarantees that the President and Vice President will be of the same party.

Essential Questions Journal To continue to build a response to the chapter Essential Question, go to your **Essential Questions Journal.**

SECTION 3 ASSESSMENT

1. **Guiding Question** Use your completed flowchart to answer this question: How did the process of choosing a President change over time?

Key Terms and Comprehension

2. How were **presidential electors** to be selected in the Framers' plan?

3. **(a)** Who makes up the **electoral college? (b)** What does it do?

4. What change did the 12th Amendment make in the presidential selection process?

Critical Thinking

5. **Recognize Bias** The Framers believed that the presidential electors would be "the most enlightened and respectable citizens" in each State. How does this statement reflect the voting population of the time?

6. **Determining Relevance** How did party allegiances complicate the election of 1800?

Quick Write

Research Writing: Gather Details When writing a research report, you should include facts, examples, descriptions, and other information to help explain your findings. Use the library and reliable Internet sources to do more in-depth research on the President you selected in Section 2. Record information on notecards to help you organize your thoughts.

Presidential Nominations

Guiding Question

Does the nominating system allow Americans to choose the best candidates for President? Use a chart like the one below to keep track of the main ideas about the nomination process.

Presidential Nominee		
Personal Characteristics • •	**Primaries and Caucuses** • •	**National Conventions** • •

Political Dictionary

- presidential primary
- winner-take-all
- proportional representation
- caucus
- national convention
- platform
- keynote address

Objectives

1. Describe the role of conventions in the presidential nominating process.
2. Evaluate the importance of presidential primaries.
3. Understand the caucus-convention process.
4. Outline the events that take place during a national convention.
5. Examine the characteristics that determine who is nominated as a presidential candidate.

Image Above: Delegates cheer on a speaker at the 2008 Democratic National Convention.

The Constitution makes no provision for the nomination of candidates for the presidency. Rather, the Framers designed a system in which presidential electors would select the "wisest and best man" to be President. But the rise of political parties and the election of 1800 altered that system drastically. In this section, you will examine what emerged from that historic revision of the Framers' plan: the modern-day presidential nominating process.

National Conventions

Recall, the congressional caucus was the first method the parties developed to pick their presidential candidates. The closed, unrepresentative character of that arrangement led to its downfall in the mid-1820s. For the election of 1832, both major parties turned to the national convention as their presidential nominating device, and it has continued to serve them ever since.

Convention Arrangements Not only does the Constitution say nothing about presidential nominations, but there is, as well, almost no federal or State statutory law on the matter. The convention process has been built over the years almost entirely by the two major parties.

In both parties, the national committee makes the arrangements for the party's convention. The committee picks the place and also sets the date for that meeting. Several of the nation's larger cities regularly bid for the honor (and the financial boost to local business) of hosting the quadrennial gatherings. For their 2008 meeting, the Democrats picked Denver, and the GOP opted for Minneapolis–St. Paul.

Apportioning Delegates With the date and the location set, the national committee issues its "call" for the convention. That formal announcement names the time and place. It also tells the party's State organizations how many delegates the States may send to the national gathering.

By tradition, both parties give each State party a certain number of delegates based on that State's electoral vote. Over the past several conventions, both parties have developed complicated formulas that also award bonus delegates to those States that have supported the party's candidates in recent elections.

For 2008, the GOP's formula produced a convention of 2,380 delegates. The Democrats' more complicated plan called for 4,233 delegates. Given those large numbers, it should be fairly clear that neither party's national convention can be called "a deliberative body," an assembly able to give each of its decisions thoughtful consideration.

Selecting Delegates There are really *three* campaigns for the presidency every four years. One is the final contest between the Republican candidate and the Democratic candidate in the fall, leading up to the election in November. The other two occur earlier and are quite different affairs. They take place *within* each of the major parties: the struggles for Republican and, separately, for Democratic convention delegates.

State laws and/or party rules fix the procedures for picking delegates in each State. That system is a reflection of federalism, and it has produced a jigsaw puzzle of presidential primaries, conventions, and caucuses among the 50 States.

To a large extent, the Republican Party leaves the matter of delegate selection to its State organizations and to State law. The Democratic Party, on the other hand, has adopted several national rules to govern the process. Most of those rules reflect the Democratic Party's attempts to broaden participation in the delegate selection process, especially by the young, African Americans, other minorities, and women.

Presidential Primaries

More than three fourths of all the delegates to both parties' conventions come from States that hold presidential primaries. Many of those primaries are major media events. Serious contenders in both the Democratic and Republican parties must make the best possible showing in at least most of them.

Depending on the State, a **presidential primary** is an election in which a party's voters (1) choose some or all of a State party organization's delegates to their party's national convention, and/or (2) express a preference among various contenders for their party's presidential nomination.[16]

History of the Presidential Primary The presidential primary first appeared in the early 1900s as part of the reform movement aimed at the party boss–dominated convention system. Wisconsin passed the first presidential primary law in 1905, providing for the popular election of national convention delegates. Several States soon followed that lead, and Oregon added the preference feature in 1910. By 1916 half the States had adopted presidential primary laws.

For a time, the primary system fell into disfavor so that by 1968, primaries were found in only 16 States and the District of Columbia. Efforts to reform the national convention process, especially in the Democratic Party, reversed that downward trend in the 1970s, however. Some form of the presidential primary can now be found in most States. For 2008, the device was in place in 40 States, and in the District of Columbia and Puerto Rico, as well.[17]

Primaries Today Recall, a presidential primary is either or both of two things: a delegate-selection process and/or a candidate preference election. Once that much has been said, however, the system becomes very hard to describe, except on a State-by-State basis.

The difficulty comes largely from two sources: (1) the fact that in each State the details of the delegate-selection process are set by State law—and those details vary from State to State, and (2) the ongoing reform efforts in the Democratic Party.

Ever since 1968, when the Democratic Party was shattered by disputes over Vietnam and civil rights policies, the Democratic National Committee has written and rewritten

---

16 Both parties allot delegates to the District of Columbia, Puerto Rico, the Virgin Islands, Guam, and American Samoa; the Democrats also provide for delegates who represent Democrats Abroad. The Democratic convention also includes a large number of "superdelegates"—mostly party officers and Democrats who hold major elective offices, and other party activists. More than 750 superdelegates were seated at the 2008 Democratic convention.

17 In a few States—South Carolina, for example—only one party held a primary. Presidential primaries were not held in ten States in 2008: Alaska, Colorado, Hawaii, Iowa, Kansas, Maine, Nebraska, Nevada, North Dakota, and Wyoming. In some States, the law permits but does not require a major party to hold a primary. In South Carolina the presidential primary is a product of party rules, not State law.

the party's rules in an effort to promote greater grass-roots participation in the Democratic primaries. Most States treat the two major parties alike in their election laws; so, as States have responded to the Democratic Party's reform efforts, the Republicans have had to revise some of their procedures, as well.

Even a matter that seems as simple as the date for the primary illustrates the <u>crazy-quilt</u> pattern of State laws. New Hampshire holds the first of the presidential primaries every four years, and it has done so since 1920. The State guards its first-in-the-nation title with a law that provides that its primary is to be held at least a week before the date any other State picks for its contest.

Most States have come to prefer an early date, so the primary schedule has become heavily "front-loaded" in recent elections. In 2008, the scramble for an earlier date meant that 16 States held their primaries on the same day—"Super Tuesday," February 5— and three fourths of the contests had been held by mid-March.

Name recognition and money have always been important factors in the primary process, and front-loading has multiplied their importance. Until lately, a candidate who was not very well-known nationally could hope to build a following from primary to primary over several weeks—as, for example, Bill Clinton did in 1992. The front-loaded process leaves little or no time for that strategy now. Contenders have to mount (and pay for) campaigns in a number of widely separated States that hold their primaries early and, often, on the same day or within a few days of one another.

Proportional Representation For decades, most presidential primaries were both delegate-selection and preference exercises. Several were also **winner-take-all** contests: The candidate who won the preference vote automatically won the support of all of the delegates chosen at that primary.

Winner-take-all primaries have now all but disappeared, however. The Democratic Party's rules actually prohibit them. Instead, the Democrats now have a complex **proportional representation** rule. Any candidate who seeks the party's presidential nomination who wins

at least 15 percent of the votes cast in a primary gets the number of that State's Democratic convention delegates that corresponds to his or her share of that primary vote. Take, for example, a State that has 40 convention delegates. If a candidate wins 45 percent of the primary vote, he or she automatically gains the support of at least 18 of the delegates.

Most States had to change their primary laws to account for the Democrats' proportional representation rule. So in many States, Republican delegates are also chosen on a proportional representation basis. Still, a few States do permit winner-take-all primaries, and the Republicans hold them where they can—in California, for example.

The proportional representation rule had another major impact on the shape of presidential primaries. It led several States—among them Oregon and Wisconsin, the States that had pioneered the presidential primary—to give up the popular selection of delegates. More than half of the presidential primary States now hold only a preference primary. The delegates themselves are actually chosen

✔ **Checkpoint**
How do State laws affect the presidential primary system?

<u>crazy-quilt</u>
adj. made up of a mixture of things, hodgepodge

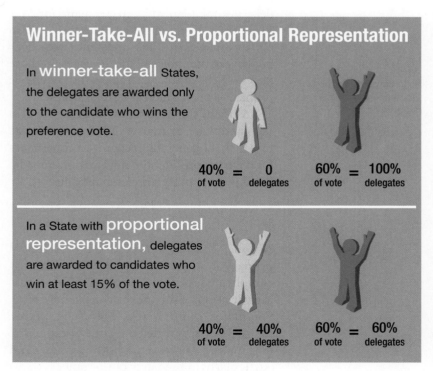

Winner-Take-All vs. Proportional Representation

In **winner-take-all** States, the delegates are awarded only to the candidate who wins the preference vote.

40% of vote = 0 delegates   60% of vote = 100% delegates

In a State with **proportional representation**, delegates are awarded to candidates who win at least 15% of the vote.

40% of vote = 40% delegates   60% of vote = 60% delegates

▶▶ Analyzing Charts As political parties' rules have changed, so has the manner in which primaries have been conducted. *Why do you think candidates who receive less than 15% of the vote are not assigned delegates?*

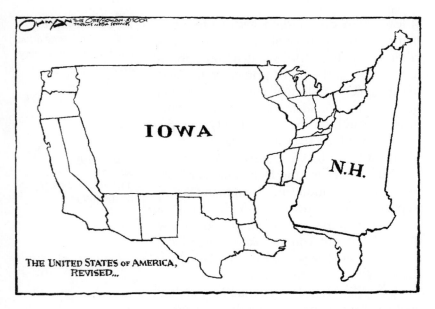

THE UNITED STATES OF AMERICA, REVISED...

▶▶ **Analyzing Political Cartoons** The first delegate-selection event in a presidential election by caucus is held in Iowa, followed afterward by the first scheduled primary in New Hampshire. ***How does this cartoon illustrate the emphasis placed on the elections held in these two States?***

✔ **Checkpoint**
Why are the primaries considered vital to the nomination process?

vie
v. to compete with someone to achieve something

later, at party conventions. In most of these States, the delegates must be picked in line with the results of the preference primary—for example, for the Republicans in 2008, so many delegates for John McCain, so many for Mitt Romney, so many for Mike Huckabee, and so on. In a few States, the preference vote does not govern the choice of the delegates. In those States—Nebraska, for example—the preference primary is often called a "beauty contest."

Most of the preference contests are also "all-candidate" primaries. These are contests in which all generally recognized contenders for a party's presidential nomination must be listed on that party's preference ballot.

Primary Appraisal

No one who has surveyed the presidential primary system needs to be told that it is complicated, or that it is filled with confusing variations. Still, these primaries are vital. For half a century now, they have played *the* major part in deciding the presidential nominating contests in both parties—and particularly in the party out of power.

Evaluation of the Primary Presidential primaries tend to democratize the delegate-selection process. And, importantly, they force would-be nominees to test their candidacies in actual political combat. For the party out of power, especially, the primaries are often "knock-down, drag-out" affairs. Without the unifying force of the President as party leader, several top personalities and factions in the party vie with one another, vigorously, for the presidential nomination. Here, a key function of the presidential primary can be seen: the screening out of the lesser possibilities to the point where only one or a few contenders for the nomination remain in the contest.

Such hard-fought contests do occur, but are not common, in the party in power. This tends to be true either because the President (1) is himself seeking reelection, or (2) has given his backing to someone he favors for the nomination. In either case the President regularly gets his way.

A sitting President is seldom challenged for his renomination, but that situation does sometimes happen. Thus, for example, Ronald Reagan made a stiff run at President Gerald Ford in the Republican Party in 1976, and Senator Edward Kennedy gave President Carter a real fight in 1980.

Reform Proposals The fact that so many States now hold presidential primaries places large demands on contenders in terms of time, effort, money, scheduling, and, not least, fatigue. The lengthy primary season tests the public's endurance, as well.

Some think that each of the major parties should hold a single, nationwide primary, and have both parties choose their presidential candidates in those contests. National conventions would be done away with—except perhaps to pick their vice-presidential nominees and/or write party platforms.

Most often, however, critics of the present arrangement favor one version or another of a regional primary plan. A series of primaries would be held at two- or three-week intervals across the country.

The prospects for reform are uncertain at best. Major changes would require joint action by Congress, the several States, and both major parties. Neither major party has ever expressed any interest in abandoning its national convention. Both parties see the conventions as a device to promote compromise and, out of it, party unity.

Caucuses

In those States that do not hold presidential primaries, delegates to the national conventions are selected in a system of local caucuses and district and/or State conventions. A **caucus** is a closed meeting of members of a political party who gather to select delegates to the national convention. The process works basically as it is described here, but the details differ from State to State.

A party's voters meet in local caucuses, most often at the precinct level. There they often express a preference among the contenders for the party's presidential nomination and select delegates to a local or district convention, where delegates to a State convention are elected. At the State level, and sometimes in the district conventions as well, delegates to the national convention are chosen.

The caucus-convention process dates back to the 1840s and is the oldest method for choosing national convention delegates. Its use has declined significantly over the years, however. In 2008, less than a fourth of all delegates to either party's national convention came from States that still use this method of delegate choice.

The Iowa caucuses generally get the most attention, largely because they are now the first delegate-selection event held in every presidential election season. Iowa schedules the start of its caucus process early, and has purposely done so ever since 1972. In 2008 the event took place on January 3, five days before New Hampshire held its first-in-the-nation presidential primary.

The national conventions are organized so that the energy and fervor heighten in intensity with each passing day. *Why do you think the conventions are designed to stir the emotions of party members?*

Securing the Nomination

Once all the primaries and caucuses have been held and all of the delegates have been chosen, another event <u>looms</u> large. The two major parties hold their **national conventions,** the <u>quadrennial</u> meetings at which the delegates select their presidential and vice-presidential candidates.

For over a century, those gatherings were highly dramatic, often chaotic, and even stormy affairs at which, after days of heated bargaining, the party would finally nominate its presidential and vice-presidential candidates. Both parties' meetings have become much tamer in recent years—largely because there is now little doubt about who will win the party's grand prize. Regularly, the leading contender has won enough delegates in the primaries and caucuses to lock up the nomination long before the convention meets.

Each party's convention remains a major event, nonetheless. The conventions have three major goals: (1) naming the party's presidential and vice-presidential candidates,

The Race for the Presidency

The race begins as presidential contenders vie to become their party's nominee. As the pace intensifies, the field narrows to a contest between two contenders for the ultimate prize—the presidency. *How does the contest for the White House reflect the American democratic ideal?*

1-4 Years Before Election The first steps for potential candidates include broadening their visibility, testing their appeal nationwide, and developing committees to explore their viability as a candidate. If the results are encouraging, the contender will officially announce his or her candidacy.

1-4 Years Before Election The costs of running for office are huge and raising funds is an ongoing effort throughout the campaign. Lack of funds often causes contenders to drop out of the race.

January–June of the Election **Year** Primaries and caucuses help determine the party's nominee. At this stage voters choose their party's frontrunner, and many candidates concede defeat.

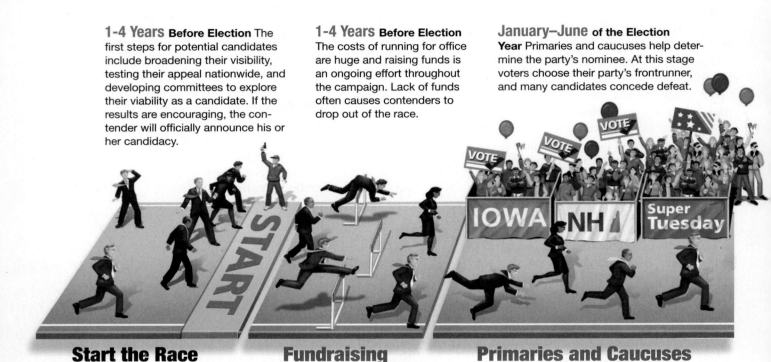

Start the Race **Fundraising** **Primaries and Caucuses**

(2) bringing the various factions and the leading personalities in the party together in one place for a common purpose, and (3) adopting the party's **platform**—its formal statement of basic principles, stands on major policy matters, and objectives for the campaign and beyond.

Both parties hope that their convention will do a number of other things, as well. They want the meeting to promote party unity, capture the interest and attention of the country at large, and generate support for the party's ticket in the upcoming campaign.

The First Days Each party's convention now meets in one or two sessions per day over three or four days. Each of those sessions is tightly scheduled and closely scripted. In short, they are now made for television.

The first day is dedicated to welcoming the delegates and organizing the convention, and to dozens of short speeches by an array of party figures. The second day sees a continuing parade of speakers but is highlighted by two major events: the adoption of the party's platform and the delivery of the keynote address.

The platform comes to the convention floor as a report by the committee on platform and resolutions. In fact, it has been drawn up by the party's leadership beforehand.

Platform-writing is a fine art. Recall, the platform is a statement of party principles and stands on policy matters. But it is also an important campaign document aimed at appealing to as many people and as many groups as possible. So both parties tend to produce somewhat generalized comments on some of the hard questions facing the nation at

GOVERNMENT ONLINE

For an interactive exploration of the steps involved in the race to the presidency, visit **PearsonSuccessNet.com**

INTERACTIVE

August–September of the Election Year Delegates to each party's convention adopt the party platform, nominate their party's presidential candidate, and ratify his or her choice of a vice-presidential running mate.

September–November of the Election Year Following the conventions, each candidate focuses on his or her opponent. Debates provide opportunities to compare and contrast each candidate's qualifications and plans for the future.

November on the Tuesday after the first Monday in November, the voters cast their ballots and the president-elect is determined.

National Conventions   **Debates**   **Election Day**

the time. Platforms are regularly criticized for blandness. Still, the platforms are important. They do set out a number of hard-and-fast stands in many policy areas. They also reflect the compromising nature of American politics and of the two major parties.

The **keynote address** is usually a <u>barnburner</u>, delivered by one of the party's most accomplished orators. The address, like nearly all the speeches the delegates hear, follows a predictable pattern. It glorifies the party, its history, its leaders, and its programs, blisters the other party, and predicts a resounding victory for the party and its candidates in November.

The Last Two Days The convention turns to its chief task on the third day: the nomination of the party's candidates for President and Vice President. The delegates turn first to the vice-presidential choice. Historically, that task often involved some suspense and a good deal of bargaining among party factions. Nowadays, however, the soon-to-be-nominated presidential candidate sometimes announces his or her choice of a running mate before the convention meets—and the delegates ratify that choice with little or no dissent.

The vice-presidential candidate then delivers his or her acceptance speech—another effort to fire up the party faithful and appeal to as many other voters as possible.

The third day's session <u>culminates</u> with the selection of the party's presidential candidate. The names of several contenders may be offered, especially in the party out of power. Once the nominating (and several seconding) speeches are made, the delegates vote. The convention secretary calls the States in

barnburner
n. an event that is very exciting or intense

culminate
v. to reach the highest point, climax

Presidential candidate Bill Clinton plays the saxophone in 1992 on the Arsenio Hall show, and candidate John McCain appeared with Jay Leno in 2008. **How do talk shows help candidates reach new audiences?**

alphabetical order, and the chair of each State delegation announces how that delegation's votes are cast. Each complete roll call is known as a ballot, and the balloting continues until one of the contenders wins a majority of the delegates' votes.

Most often, the first ballot produces a winner. Over the 28 conventions held by each party since 1900, the Republicans have made a first ballot choice 24 times and the Democrats 23 times. Indeed, the GOP has not had to take a second ballot since 1948, and the Democrats since 1952.[18]

With its candidates named, the convention comes to the final major item on its agenda: the presidential candidate's acceptance speech. That speech caps the convention and launches the party's general election campaign.

Who Is Nominated?

If an incumbent President wants another term, and the 22nd Amendment is not in play, the convention's choice is easily made. The sitting President is virtually certain to gain the nomination, and usually with no real opposition from within the party. The

President's advantages are immense: the majesty and publicity of the office and close control of the party's machinery.[19]

When the President is not in the field, up to a dozen or more contenders may surface in the preconvention period. At most, two or three of them may survive to contest the prize at the national convention.

Political Experience Who will win the nomination? The historical record suggests that this will be the usual answer: The contender who is the most electable. Both parties want to pick candidates who can win, those with the broadest possible appeal, within the party and in the electorate.

Most presidential candidates come to their nominations with substantial, well-known records in public office. Thus, in 2008, the Republicans picked John McCain, who had spent 26 years in Congress. But, notice, his Democratic opponent did not have nearly so lengthy a record. Barack Obama had served only four years in the Senate. However long the record, it is usually free of controversies that could have antagonized key elements in the party and the voting public.

Almost always, the major party candidates have served in elective offices, where they have demonstrated vote-getting abilities. Only rarely does a candidate step from the private world or from the military directly into a presidential candidacy—although Wendell Willkie did in 1940, and Dwight Eisenhower in 1952, both in the Republican Party.

Historically, the governorships of the larger States have produced the largest number of presidential candidacies. Of the 36 men nominated by the two major parties from 1908 to 2008, fifteen were either serving or had once served as a governor.

It is true that neither party picked a governor in 2008; but, notice, several governors

18 A convention can become deadlocked. In that case, a "dark horse"—that is, someone who did not seem a likely choice before the convention—may finally emerge as the nominee. The most spectacular deadlock in convention history occurred at the Democratic convention in New York in 1924. That convention took 103 ballots before John W. Davis of West Virginia won the nomination.

19 In fact, only four sitting Presidents have ever been denied nomination: John Tyler (1844), Millard Fillmore (1852), Franklin Pierce (1856), and Chester Arthur (1884).

were among the also-rans that year. The major party tickets were also notable in this respect in 2008: For the first time, both major parties selected sitting members of the United States Senate as their <u>standard bearers</u>.

Other Characteristics Most of the leading contenders for the nomination have been Protestants. The most notable exceptions to that statement, all Democrats and all Catholics, are Alfred E. Smith (1928), John F. Kennedy (1960), and John Kerry (2004).

Most nominees have also come from the larger States. So hopefuls from such pivotal States as New York, Ohio, Illinois, Texas, and California tend to have an advantage.

Television and now the Internet have reshaped this consideration, however. Thus, the Republicans nominated Bob Dole of Kansas in 1996 and John McCain of Arizona in 2008. And the Democrats selected Jimmy Carter of Georgia in 1976 and Bill Clinton of Arkansas in 1992.

Nominees usually have a pleasant and healthy appearance, seem to be happily married, and have an attractive (and exploitable) family. Only five have ever been divorced.

A well-developed speaking ability has always been a plus in American politics. The ability to project well over television, pioneered by John F. Kennedy in 1960, has long since become a must, as well.

Shattering Barriers Until 2008, neither major party had ever seriously considered a woman or nominated a member of any minority group as its presidential candidate. The Democrats broke with tradition in the most recent election, however.

Senator Hillary Clinton of New York came remarkably close to being the Democratic Party's presidential candidate in 2008. It is generally thought that the longstanding barrier to a woman at the top of a major party's national ticket has now been shattered.

The Democratic Party's presidential candidate in 2008, Barack Obama, was the child of a white mother from Kansas and a black father from Kenya. His historic election in 2008 shattered the racial barrier for the nation's highest office.

The Republicans also defied the historical record in 2008. Over time, most major party presidential candidates have been in their 50s or early 60s, with only a few in their 40s, when nominated. But none has ever been as old as John McCain, who turned 72 only a few weeks before he became the GOP's candidate in 2008. Indeed, the age spread between the two major party candidates was greater than it had been in any presidential election.

✔ **Checkpoint**
What characteristics of the presidential nominees have influenced the voting public?

<u>standard bearer</u>
v. a leader of a movement or party

SECTION 4 ASSESSMENT

Essential Questions
Journal

To continue to build a response to the chapter Essential Question, go to your **Essential Questions Journal.**

1. **Guiding Question** Use your completed chart to answer this question: Does the nominating system allow Americans to choose the best candidates for President?

Key Terms and Comprehension

2. **(a)** What is the purpose of a **presidential primary** and a **caucus? (b)** How do these processes differ?

3. **(a)** Where is the first primary held? **(b)** Why do you think there is such a great desire for a State to hold its primary as early as possible?

4. What are the three main goals of the **national conventions?**

Critical Thinking

5. **Draw Conclusions** Do you think the proportional representation rule allows for a more democratic election? Why or why not?

6. **Demonstrate Reasoned Judgment (a)** What characteristics are common to people who have been nominated to run for President by a major party? **(b)** What other characteristics would you like to see in a presidential candidate? **(c)** Explain how these characteristics would help a President perform the job more effectively.

Quick Write

Research Writing: Write a Thesis Statement As in other types of essays and reports, the backbone for a research report is the thesis, or main idea. Review your notes to find relationships between ideas. Focusing on his qualifications and administration, write a thesis statement that is supported by the majority of the information that you have found on the President you chose.

The **Presidential Election**

Guiding Question

Does the election process serve the goals of American democracy today? Use a table like the one below to keep track of the main ideas about the election process.

Electoral College	
Defects	**Significance**
• Winner-take-all system	•
•	•
•	•

Political Dictionary

- swing voter
- battleground State
- district plan
- proportional plan
- direct popular election
- national popular vote plan

Objectives

1. Describe the features of the presidential campaign.
2. Explain how the electoral college provides for the election of the President.
3. Identify the major flaws in the electoral college system.
4. Outline the advantages and disadvantages of proposed reforms of the electoral college.

Image Above: Young volunteers encourage voter participation.

As you know, the Constitution calls for a presidential election to be held every four years. The first one was held in 1789, and, like clockwork, 55 of those contests have followed along, right on schedule. That remarkable fact is unmatched in the history of any other nation in the world. Even during a civil war, two world wars, several economic depressions, and various other crises, the Constitution's command has been met.

The Presidential Campaign

The presidential campaign is an all-out effort to win the votes of the American people. For decades, that slugfest began soon after the two parties' conventions had adjourned. But, over recent decades, it has been quite apparent some weeks, or even a month or more, before the conventions who the delegates would nominate. So the campaigns have in fact begun at some point before the candidates were formally nominated.

The campaign itself is organized chaos, and it dominates the national news scene up to election day. The candidates' campaign organizations work to show their standard bearers in the best possible light and, with negative jabs, to undercut the claims of the opposition. The voters are bombarded with radio and television interviews, speeches and advertisements, direct mail, Internet messages, "whistle-stop" tours, press conferences and press releases, rallies and party dinners, stickers and buttons, pamphlets, balloons, and billboards. The candidates pose for hundreds of photographs and shake thousands of hands as each of them tries to convince the voters that he (and, one day, she) is the best bet for the country.

Both campaigns focus much of their efforts on **swing voters**—the roughly one third of the electorate who have not made up their minds at the start of the campaign and are open to persuasion by either side. Campaign strategy is also driven by the electoral college, as you will see in a moment. The would-be Presidents target the **battleground States**—those States in which the outcome is "too close to call" and either candidate could win. Both campaigns tend to concentrate their organizational efforts, campaign funds, and candidate appearances in those States.

A series of presidential debates now highlights the campaign. An incumbent President, or a candidate ahead in the polls, may not really want to debate, but both major party contenders now regularly agree to do so. [20]

The first presidential debates, in 1960, featured then-Vice President Richard Nixon and his Democratic opponent, Senator John F. Kennedy. Their four televised debates, which were really little more than joint appearances, generated a great deal of interest, and many analysts credit John Kennedy's strong performance in them as one of the keys to his very narrow victory in the election that year.

The next set of debates came in 1976, between President Gerald Ford and his Democratic opponent, Jimmy Carter; with another involving their vice-presidential running mates, Bob Dole and Walter Mondale. That general pattern has been followed in every campaign since then. Thus, in 2008, there were three debates between John McCain and Barack Obama and one that pitted Sarah Palin against Joe Biden.

The most recent presidential debates—still more joint appearances than real debates—included one on foreign policy, a second with a "town hall" format, and a third on domestic and economic policy. Whether or not, and how much, the candidates' performances in these debates affected their ratings is still being discussed. In all, an average of 57 million people watched each debate. Surprisingly, more viewers tuned in to watch the single vice-presidential debate between Democratic senator Joe Biden and Governor Sarah Palin of Alaska than watched any of the Obama-McCain debates.

The presidential campaign finally comes to an end on election day. Millions of voters go to the polls in all 50 States and the District of Columbia. But the President, whoever that is to be, is not formally elected until the presidential electors' votes are cast and counted, several weeks later.

The Election

You have arrived at one of the least understood points in the American political process. As the people vote in the presidential election, they do not cast a vote directly for one of the contenders for the office of the President. They vote, instead, for presidential electors.

Recall, the Constitution provides for the election of the President by the electoral college, in which each State has as many electors as it has members of Congress. The Framers expected the electors to use their own judgment in selecting a President. Today the electors, once chosen, are, in fact, just "rubber stamps." They are expected to vote automatically for their party's candidates for President and Vice President. In short, the electors go through the form set out in the Constitution in order to meet the letter of the Constitution, but their behavior is far from the original intent of that document.

Choosing Electors The electors are chosen by popular vote in every State on the same day everywhere: the Tuesday after the first Monday in November every fourth year.[21] So the 2012 presidential election is set for November 6, 2012. In every State except Maine and Nebraska, the electors are chosen at large.[22] That is, they are chosen on

✔ **Checkpoint**
What role does the popular vote play in a presidential election?

[20] The debates are now sponsored by an independent, nonpartisan body created by Congress, the Commission on Presidential Debates. The participants must be party-nominated candidates who are (1) supported by at least 15 percent of the respondents in five national polls and (2) listed on the ballot of States which, taken together, will cast at least a majority (270) of the electoral votes in the upcoming election. In effect, the Commission's rules exclude minor party and independent candidates from the debates.

[21] The Constitution (Article II, Section 1, Clause 2) says that the electors are to be chosen in each State "in such Manner as the Legislature thereof may direct." In several States the legislatures themselves chose the electors in the first several elections. By 1832, however, every State except South Carolina had provided for popular election. The electors were picked by the legislature in South Carolina through 1860. Since then, all presidential electors have been chosen by popular vote in every State, with two exceptions. The State legislatures chose the electors in Florida in 1868 and in Colorado in 1876.

[22] Maine (beginning in 1972) and Nebraska (1992) use the "district plan." In those States, two electors are chosen from the State at large and the others are picked in each of the State's congressional districts. The district plan was used by several States in the first few presidential elections, but every State except South Carolina had provided for the choice of the electors from the State at large by 1832. Since then, the district plan has been used only by Michigan in 1892 and by Maine and Nebraska. In 2008, Barack Obama won one electoral vote from Nebraska's 2nd congressional district.

slate
n. a list of candidates in an election

a winner-take-all basis. The presidential candidate—technically, the <u>slate</u> of elector-candidates nominated by his party—who receives the largest number of popular votes in a State regularly wins all of that State's electoral votes.

Today, the names of the individual elector-candidates appear on the ballot in only a handful of States. In most States, only the names of the presidential and vice-presidential candidates are listed. They stand as "shorthand" for the elector slates.

Counting the Electoral Votes The Constitution provides that the date Congress sets for the electors to meet "shall be the same throughout the United States."[23] The 12th

Amendment provides that "the Electors shall meet in their respective States." The electors thus meet at their State capital on the date set by Congress, now the Monday after the second Wednesday in December. There they each cast their electoral votes, one for President and one for Vice President. The electors' ballots, signed and sealed, are sent by registered mail to the President of the Senate in Washington.

Who has won a majority of the electoral votes, and who then will be the next President of the United States, is usually known by midnight of election day, more than a month before the electors cast their ballots. But the *formal* election of the President and Vice President finally takes place in early January.[24]

---

[23] Article II, Section 1, Clause 4.

[24] Usually on January 6th. Congress can choose another day in early January, however—and it did so when it moved the date to January 8 for 2009.

Electoral Votes by State

A cartogram is a thematic map that shows a relationship between two factors, distorted to convey the data. The large map below shows the electoral vote strength of each State. Note that several small, populous States have more electoral votes than many larger, rural States. ***What do these maps suggest about the electoral vote strength of the Northeast?***

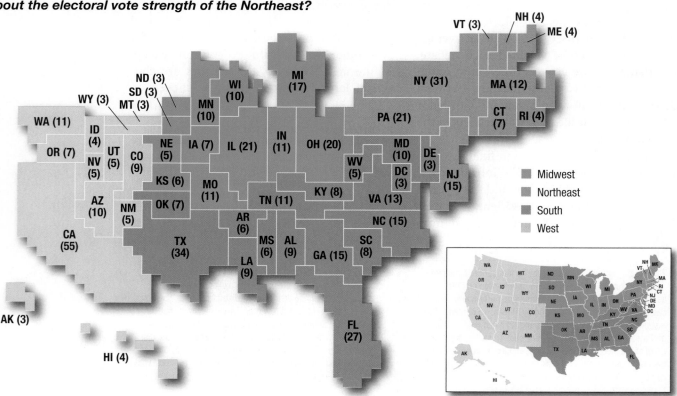

■ Midwest
■ Northeast
■ South
■ West

On that date, the president of the Senate opens the electoral votes from each State and counts them before a joint session of Congress. The candidate who receives a majority of the electors' votes for President is declared elected, as is the candidate with a majority of the votes for Vice President.

If no candidate has won a majority—at least 270 of the 538 electoral votes today—the election is thrown into the House of Representatives. This happened in 1800 and again in 1824. The House chooses a President from among the top three candidates voted for by the electoral college. Each State delegation has one vote, and it takes a majority of 26 to elect. If the House fails to choose a President by January 20, the 20th Amendment provides that the newly elected Vice President shall act as President until a choice is made.

The 20th Amendment also says that "the Congress may by law provide for the case wherein neither a President elect nor a Vice President elect shall have qualified" by Inauguration Day. Congress has done so, in the Presidential Succession Act of 1947. The Speaker of the House would "act as President . . . until a President or Vice President shall have qualified."

If no person receives a majority of the electoral votes for Vice President, the Senate decides between the top two candidates. It takes a majority of the whole Senate to elect. The Senate has chosen a Vice President only once: Richard M. Johnson in 1837.

Flaws in the Electoral College

The electoral college system is plagued by three major defects: (1) the winner of the popular vote is not guaranteed the presidency; (2) electors are not required to vote in <u>accord</u> with the popular vote; and (3) any election might have to be decided in the House of Representatives.

The First Major Defect There is the ever-present threat that the winner of the popular vote will not win the presidency. This continuing danger is largely the result of two factors. The most important is the winner-take-all

feature of the electoral college system. That is, the winning candidate customarily receives all of a State's electoral votes. Thus, in 2008, Barack Obama won just 51.5 percent of the popular vote in Ohio. Still, he won all of that State's 20 electoral votes—despite the fact that nearly 2.7 million Ohioans voted for his Republican opponent, John McCain.

The other major culprit here is the way the electoral votes are distributed among the States. Remember, two of the electors in each State are allotted because of a State's two Senate seats, regardless of population. So the distribution of electoral votes among the States does not match the facts of population and voter distribution.

Take an extreme case to illustrate this point: California, the country's most populous State, has 55 electoral votes, one for each 615,848 persons in the State, based on its 2000 population of 33,871,648 residents. Wyoming has three electoral votes, one for each 164,594 persons, based on its 2000 population of 493,782 residents.

The popular vote winner has, in fact, failed to win the presidency four times: in 1824, 1876, 1888, and most recently 2000.[25] In that latest instance, the Democratic candidate, Vice President Al Gore, won 50,999,897 popular votes—543,895 more votes than his Republican opponent, the then-governor of Texas, George W. Bush. However, Mr. Bush received 271 electoral votes—one more than the bare majority in the electoral college, and so he became the nation's 43rd President.

Florida's 25 electoral votes proved to be decisive in the 2000 election. The popular vote results in several Florida counties were challenged immediately after the polls closed there. The next five weeks were filled with partisan infighting, several recounts, and a number of court disputes.

---

[25] The election of 1876, pitting Republican Rutherford B. Hayes against Democrat Samuel J. Tilden, is often called the "Stolen Election." Two conflicting sets of electoral votes were received from Florida (4 votes), Louisiana (8 votes), and South Carolina (7 votes), and the validity of one vote from Oregon was disputed. Congress created an Electoral Commission to decide the matter. It was composed of five senators, five representatives, and five Supreme Court justices. The Commissioners, eight Republicans and seven Democrats, voted on strict party lines, so all 20 disputed votes were awarded to Hayes, who won the presidency with 185 electoral votes to Tilden's 184.

✔ **Checkpoint**
What three flaws affect the electoral college system?

<u>accord</u>
n. agreement

SUPREME COURT
at a glance

▶ **Case:** *Bush* v. *Gore,* (2000)
▶ **Constitutional Principle:**
Equal protection
▶ **Decision:** Candidate
Al Gore requested hand
recounts of votes in 4 of
Florida's 67 counties following the 2000 presidential
election. The Court ruled
that recounts must treat all
of a State's voters equally
and halted the recount.

The United States Supreme Court finally brought an end to the bitter contest on December 12. It ruled, in *Bush* v. *Gore,* that the differing ways in which various counties were recounting votes violated the 14th Amendment's Equal Protection Clause. The Court's 5–4 decision ended those recounts. It also preserved Mr. Bush's 537-vote lead in the Statewide count, and so gave him Florida's 25 electoral votes. The High Court's split decision in *Bush* v. *Gore* remains highly controversial.

To this point, 15 Presidents have won the White House with less than a majority of the popular votes cast in their elections. The most recent of these "minority Presidents" were Bill Clinton in both 1992 and 1996, and George W. Bush in 2000.

By now, you see the point: The winner-take-all factor produces an electoral vote that is, at best, only a distorted reflection of the popular vote.

The Second Major Defect Nothing in the Constitution, nor in any federal statute, requires the electors to vote for the candidate favored by the popular vote in their States. Several States do have such laws, but they are of doubtful constitutionality, and none has ever been enforced.

To this point, however, electors have "broken their pledges," refused to vote for their party's presidential nominee, on only eleven occasions—most recently in 2004. That year, one Minnesota elector, a Democrat, did not cast his ballot for his party's presidential candidate, John Kerry.

He voted, instead, for the Democrats' vice-presidential choice, John Edwards. In fact, he voted for Senator Edwards twice—once for President and then, again, on his other ballot, for Vice President.

In no case has the vote of a "faithless elector" had a bearing on the outcome of a presidential election. But the potential is most certainly there.

The Third Major Defect In any presidential election, it is possible that the contest will be decided in the House. This has happened only twice, and not since 1824. In several other elections, however—most recently, 1968—a strong third-party bid has threatened to make it impossible for either major party candidate to win a majority in the electoral college, and so throw the election into the House of Representatives.

Three serious objections can be raised regarding election by the House. First, the voting in such cases is by States, not by individual members. A State with a small population, such as Alaska, Wyoming, or Vermont, would have as much weight as the most populous State. Second, if the representatives from a State were so divided that no candidate was favored by a majority, that State would lose its vote. Third, the Constitution requires a majority of the States for election in the House—today, 26 States. If a strong third-party candidate were involved, there is a real possibility that the House could not make a decision by Inauguration Day.

In such a case, Section 3 of the 20th Amendment states that "the Vice President elect shall act as President until a President shall have qualified." If no Vice President elect is available, the Presidential Succession Act would come into play. Note that it is even mathematically possible for the minority party in the House to have control of a

Far Left: An election official uses a magnifying glass to decipher whether a "chad" was punched through on a Florida ballot in 2000. **Middle and Right:** Voters take to the streets to express their views on the contested 2000 election.

majority of the individual State delegations. That party could then elect its candidate, even though he or she may have run second or even third in both the popular and the electoral vote contests.

Proposed Reforms

The several shortcomings of the electoral college have long been recognized. To that point, Thomas Jefferson once called its original version "the most dangerous blot" on the Constitution. Amendments to revise or eliminate the electoral college have been introduced in every term of Congress since 1789. Most of the proposals fall under four headings: the district plan, the proportional plan, direct popular election, and the national popular vote plan. Over recent years, most advocates of change have supported proposals for the direct election of the President.

District and Proportional Plans Under the **district plan,** each State would choose its electors much as it chooses its members of Congress. That is, two electors would be chosen from the State at large, and they would be required to cast their electoral votes in

GOVERNMENT ONLINE
Audio Tour
Listen to a tour of this map at
PearsonSuccessNet.com

The 2008 Presidential Election
McCain vs Obama

Although John McCain won more than 45 percent of the popular vote in the 2008 election, the Republican received only 32 percent of the electoral votes. *How do these results illustrate the significance of the winner-take-all factor in State contests?*

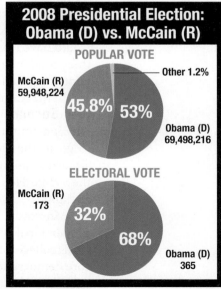

2008 Presidential Election: Obama (D) vs. McCain (R)

POPULAR VOTE
McCain (R) 59,948,224 — 45.8%
Other 1.2%
53% Obama (D) 69,498,216

ELECTORAL VOTE
McCain (R) 173 — 32%
68% Obama (D) 365

■ Barack Obama (D)
■ John McCain (R)
* One of five electoral votes to Obama

SOURCE: Federal Election Commission

✔ **Checkpoint**

How do these reform plans change the relationship between the electoral vote and the popular vote?

line with the popular vote Statewide. The State's other electors would be elected, separately, in each of that State's congressional districts. The votes of these electors would be cast in accord with the popular vote in their districts. Remember, two States—Maine and Nebraska—now choose their electors on a district plan basis.

Under the **proportional plan,** each presidential candidate would receive a share of each State's electoral vote equal to his or her share of that State's popular vote. So a candidate who won 62 percent of the votes cast in a State with 20 electors would receive 12.4 of that State's electoral votes.

In their basic forms, neither the district nor the proportional plan would require a constitutional amendment to become effective. Remember, the Constitution leaves the manner of selecting the electors up to the State legislatures. Any of them could decide to allocate the State's electoral votes by districts or on a proportional basis.

The Constitution would have to be amended to accomplish direct popular election, however. If the goal of reform is to ensure that the winner of the national popular vote would in fact win the presidency, only direct election would guarantee that result. Neither the district nor the proportional plan would do so.

If the district plan had been in place in 1960, Richard Nixon, not John F. Kennedy, would have won the presidency. And in 1976 the presidential election would almost certainly have had to be decided by the House.

If the Constitution had provided for a proportional plan in 1960, the Kennedy-Nixon election would very likely have had to go to the House. And, the House would almost certainly have had to decide who won the White House in 1968, 1976, 1992, 1996, and 2000.

Moreover, neither a district plan nor a proportional plan would overcome the electoral college arrangement that violates the core democratic value of equality. The district <u>scheme</u> prevents the weighing of all votes equally. It does, in major part, because, recall, every State has two electoral votes because it has two seats in the Senate, no matter what its population.

scheme
n. a plan or system in which things are put together

The proportional plan does do a better job of weighing popular votes equally. Still, because each of the smaller States is overrepresented by its two Senate-based electors, that arrangement would make it possible for the loser of the popular vote to win the White House in the electoral vote. And, again, the proportional plan would often throw the election into the House.

Direct Popular Election Proposals for **direct popular election** would not reform but, instead, abolish the electoral college system. The voters in all 50 States and the District of Columbia would be given the power to actually choose the President and the Vice President. Each vote, cast anywhere in the country, would count equally in the national result. The winner would, therefore, always be the choice of a majority or plurality of the nation's voters.

A majority of the American people have consistently supported direct popular election for several decades now. The fact that the loser of the popular vote nevertheless won the presidency in 2000 has given added weight to the case for direct election.

Several obstacles stand in the way of that plan, however. Not the least of them is the constitutional amendment process itself. Recall, the smaller States are heavily overrepresented in the electoral college. They would lose that advantage with direct election. It is altogether likely that enough senators, or representatives, from smaller States would oppose a direct election amendment to kill it. [26]

Some argue that direct election would weaken the federal system because the States, as States, would lose their role in the choice of a President. Others believe that direct election would put too great a load on the election process. They believe this because every vote, no matter where it was cast, would count in the national result. And so candidates would have to campaign strenuously everywhere. The impact that would have on campaign

---

[26] The House did approve a direct election amendment by the required two-thirds majority in 1969; a Senate filibuster killed the measure in 1970. A similar proposal was defeated in a Senate floor vote in 1979.

The Electoral College Today

▶▶ **Analyzing Political Cartoons** Defenders of the electoral college say that it identifies the President-elect both quickly and certainly. Critics insist that the system can and has given the presidency to candidates who did not win the popular vote. **What is this cartoon's objection to the electoral college?**

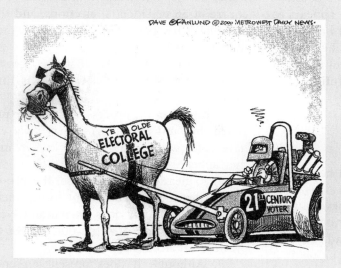

DAVE GRANLUND ©2000 METROWEST DAILY NEWS·

With 20 electoral college votes at stake, hotly contested Ohio was a major battleground State in the 2008 election.

time, effort, and finances would be huge and, opponents argue, probably unmanageable.

Some claim that, inevitably, direct election would spur various forms of voter fraud. That, they predict, would lead to lengthy, bitter, and highly explosive post-election challenges.

In several States, a Statewide election often hinges on the behavior of some particular group in the electorate. The overall result in the State depends in large part on how that group of voters cast their ballots or, often more importantly, on how heavily they do or do not turn out to vote. As but one of many examples of the point, the African American vote in Cook County (Chicago) is regularly decisive in a presidential election in Illinois. With direct election, those key groups would not have the critical power they now enjoy, and so many of them oppose direct election of the President.

Given all of this, there seems little chance that the electoral college will be abolished and direct election put in its place any time in the near future.

The National Popular Vote Plan A quite different approach to electoral college reform has recently surfaced: the **national popular vote plan**—in effect, a proposal to bring about the direct popular election of the President—and to do so without making any change in the words of the Constitution.

This new plan looks to the State legislatures to take the lead in electoral college reform. It calls upon each State's lawmaking body to (1) amend State election laws to provide that all of a State's electoral votes are to be awarded to the presidential candidate who wins the national popular vote and (2) enter into an interstate compact, the Agreement Among the States to Elect the President by National Popular Vote. That compact, and with it each State's election law changes, would come into force only if and when the compact has been agreed to by enough States to account for a majority (at least 270) of the 538 electoral votes.

The national popular vote plan is the only proposal to reform the electoral college that attracts any significant amount of public attention today. By early 2009, it had been approved by four States—Hawaii, Illinois, Maryland, and New Jersey—and is under serious consideration in several others.

This innovative plan is sponsored by a number of prominent Republicans, Democrats, and independents. It has attracted the support of several nonpartisan groups and major newspapers around the country. It has, in large part because 1) it appears to satisfy the major objections that have been raised to the electoral college as it currently operates, and 2) it does so without the need for an amendment to the Constitution.

Defending the Electoral College

Although their case is not often heard, the present electoral college system does have its defenders. They react to the several proposed reforms by raising the various objections to them you have just read. Beyond that, most of these supporters argue that critics regularly exaggerate the "dangers" they see in the present system. Thus, they note that only two presidential elections have ever gone to the House of Representatives and that none has gone there in more than 180 years.

Those who support the present electoral college system do grant the point that the candidate who loses the popular vote has in fact won the presidency four times—and as recently as 2000. But, they note, that circumstance has happened only four times over the course of 56 presidential elections, and they add that it has happened only once in more than a century.

Supporters also say that the present arrangement, whatever its warts, has three major strengths:

1. It is a known process. Each of the proposed, but untried, reforms may very well have defects that could not be known until they appeared in practice.

2. In nearly every instance, the present system identifies the President-to-be quickly and certainly. Rarely does the nation have to wait very long to know the outcome of the presidential election.

3. Although it does present an enormous obstacle to minor party candidates, the present arrangement does help promote the nation's two-party system.

Essential Questions Journal To continue to build a response to the chapter Essential Question, go to your **Essential Questions Journal.**

SECTION 5 ASSESSMENT

1. **Guiding Question** Use your table to answer this question: Does the election process serve the goals of American democracy today?

Key Terms and Comprehension

2. Why do presidential campaigns focus heavily on **swing voters** and **battleground States?**

3. **(a)** How are the members of the electoral college chosen? **(b)** What role do they play in the presidential selection process?

4. What are the four options suggested as alternatives to the electoral college?

Critical Thinking

5. **Demonstrate Reasoned Judgment (a)** Which of the alternatives to the electoral college system do you think is the most democratic? **(b)** Considering its several defects, do you think that the existing system should be reformed?

6. **Express Problems Clearly** In four presidential elections, most recently in 2000, the candidate who lost the popular vote none the less became President. **(a)** How is this outcome possible? **(b)** Do you believe that fact to be a persuasive argument for electoral college reform? Why or why not?

Quick Write

Research Writing: Make an Outline To help you structure a research report on the President you selected in Section 2, create an outline in which you identify each topic and subtopic in a single phrase. When you are ready to write your research report on how that President's professional and political experience influenced his administration, you can use the outline as a guide.

Quick Study Guide

GOVERNMENT ONLINE

On the Go
To review anytime, anywhere, download these online resources at **PearsonSuccessNet.com**
Political Dictionary, Audio Review

Guiding Question
Section 2 What occurs when the President is unable to perform the duties of the office?

Guiding Question
Section 3 How did the process of choosing a President change over time?

Guiding Question
Section 4 Does the nominating system allow Americans to choose the best candidates for President?

Guiding Question
Section 1 What are the roles and qualifications for the presidency?

CHAPTER 13
Essential Question
Does the current electoral process result in the best candidates for President?

Guiding Question
Section 5 Does the election process serve the goals of American democracy today?

Political Dictionary

chief of state *p. 364*
chief executive *p. 364*
chief administrator *p. 365*
chief diplomat *p. 365*
commander in chief *p. 365*
chief legislator *p. 365*
chief of party *p. 365*
chief citizen *p. 365*
presidential succession *p. 370*
Presidential Succession Act of 1947 *p. 370*
balance the ticket *p. 372*
presidential elector *p. 374*
electoral vote *p. 375*
electoral college *p. 375*
presidential primary *p. 378*
winner-take-all *p. 379*
proportional representation *p. 379*
caucus *p. 381*
national convention *p. 381*
platform *p. 382*
keynote address *p. 383*
swing voter *p. 386*
battleground State *p. 386*
district plan *p. 391*
proportional plan *p. 392*
direct popular election *p. 392*
national popular vote plan *p. 393*

How the Electoral College Works

In November...
on election day, voters in each State cast ballots for a slate of electors who are pledged to vote for a particular presidential candidate.

In December...
the winning electors meet in their State capitals. Each elector casts a vote for President and a vote for Vice President. Their ballots are sent to the President of the Senate.

On January 6th...
the President of the Senate opens and counts the electoral ballots before a joint session of Congress. The winners of the electoral balloting become the President and Vice President.

The Presidency

12th Amendment: Presidential and vice presidential elections separated.

Must be a natural citizen, at least 35 years old, and U.S. resident for 14 years

22nd Amendment: Presidency limited to two four-year terms

Fulfills eight roles: chief of state, chief executive, chief administrator, chief diplomat, commander in chief, chief legislator, chief of party, chief citizen

25th Amendment: Vice President succeeds to the office if President dies or becomes disabled.

President

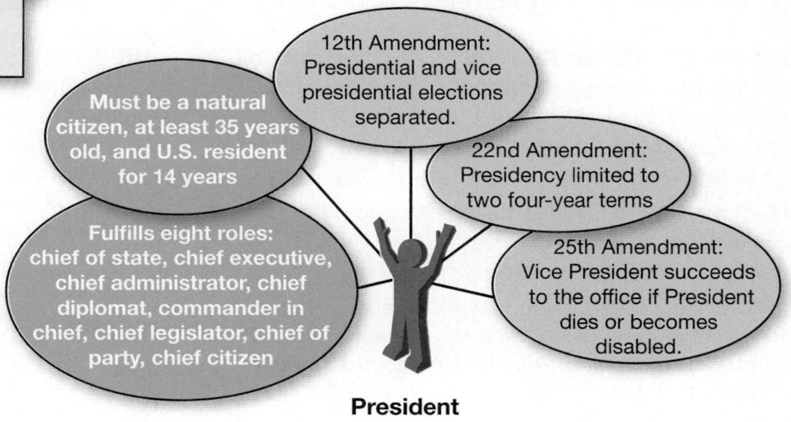

Chapter Assessment

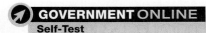

Comprehension and Critical Thinking

Section 1

1. Identify character traits that would qualify a President to best perform each of these roles: **(a)** chief executive, **(b)** chief diplomat, **(c)** commander in chief, **(d)** chief citizen.

2. Some critics of the 22nd Amendment claim it is undemocratic. **(a)** What does the 22nd Amendment do? **(b)** Does it put an unreasonable burden on the ability of voters to pick the most qualified person for the presidency?

3. **(a)** What are the formal qualifications for the presidency? **(b)** Do you think these qualifications are too mild or too restrictive? Explain your reasoning.

Section 2

4. **(a)** What are the provisions of the Presidential Succession Act of 1947 and of the 25th Amendment? **(b)** Do they provide for the best replacement for a President? **(c)** Suggest an alternative approach and identify one advantage and one disadvantage of your alternative.

5. **(a)** What are the duties of the Vice President? **(b)** Why have the responsibilities and traits of a successful Vice President changed over time?

Section 3

6. **(a)** What were the original provisions for the electoral college? **(b)** How did the election of 1800 change the voting process? **(c)** Did that election represent a failure of the Framers' vision for the electoral college? Explain.

Section 4

7. **(a)** What is a presidential primary? **(b)** What occurs to the number of presidential candidates as the primaries progress? **(c)** Is a primary vote more valuable than a general election vote in selecting a President? Explain.

8. **(a)** What is the major purpose of a national convention? **(b)** How have conventions changed over time? **(c)** Do you think that national conventions are useful today?

Section 5

9. **(a)** Explain how a presidential candidate can receive the largest number of popular votes but lose the election. **(b)** Do you think the Framers would consider this situation a flaw in the electoral college system? Why or why not?

10. **Analyze Political Cartoons (a)** At what factors in selecting a presidential candidate is the cartoonist poking fun? **(b)** Do you agree or disagree with this commentary?

Writing About Government

11. Use your Quick Write exercises from this chapter to write a research paper on how the political and professional experience of your President influenced his administration. Make sure that your report supports your thesis with accurate details. See pp. S6–S7 in the Skills Handbook.

Apply What You've Learned

12. **Essential Question Activity** With a partner, conduct research on either the Republican or Democratic primary/caucus results in your State in the most recent presidential election. Research the following:

    (a) Which method of delegate selection was used?

    (b) Where in the national election schedule did your State's primary/caucus fall?

    (c) How many candidates were in the race?

    (d) What percentage of your State's population voted in the primary/caucus? In the presidential election? Did your State's electoral college vote reflect the popular vote in your State?

13. **Essential Question Assessment** Based on your research and the content of this chapter, create a chart that illustrates how your findings show the success or failure of the American presidential selection system. Then write a letter to your governor expressing how this research helps you answer the Essential Question: **Does the current electoral process result in the best candidates for President?**

Essential Questions Journal To respond to the chapter Essential Question, go to your **Essential Questions Journal.**

Document-Based Assessment

The President's Term of Office

The tradition limiting a President to two terms in office was begun by George Washington in 1796. In 1951, the 22nd Amendment formally restricted a President to two terms, following Franklin D. Roosevelt's unique four terms in office. As the documents below illustrate, the issue of term limits is still under debate.

Document 1

"Nothing appears more plausible at first sight, nor more ill-founded upon close inspection, than a scheme . . . of continuing the Chief Magistrate in office for a certain time, and then excluding him from it, either for a limited period or forever after. This exclusion . . . would be for the most part rather pernicious [destructive] than salutary [beneficial].

One ill effect . . . would be the depriving the community of the advantage of the experience gained by the Chief Magistrate in the exercise of his office. . . .

[Another] ill effect . . . would be the banishing men from stations in which, in certain emergencies of the State, their presence might be of the greatest moment to the public interest or safety.

—*The Federalist,* No. 72

Document 2

"[T]he United States ought to be able to choose for its President anybody that it wants, regardless of the number of terms he has served. . . . Now, some people have said "You let him get enough power and this will lead toward a one-party government." That, I don't believe. I have got the utmost faith in the long-term common sense of the American people.

—Dwight D. Eisenhower, 1956

Document 3

The Oldest Mistake in the World

Use your knowledge of the presidential term limits and Documents 1–3 to answer Questions 1–3.

1. What is the main point of Document 1?
   A. Excluding candidates from reelection is democratic.
   B. Term limits deprive the voters of qualified leaders.
   C. Presidential term limits ensure that no individual can control the country in the manner of a monarch.
   D. The benefits of term limits outweigh its drawbacks.

2. What basic anxiety about leadership in a democratic system does Document 3 exploit? Explain.

3. **Pull It Together** Do you approve or disapprove of presidential term limits? Write a three-paragraph essay explaining your point of view.

GOVERNMENT ONLINE
Documents
To find more primary sources on presidential term limits, visit
PearsonSuccessNet.com

The Presidency in Action

Essential Question
How much power should the President have?

> " The presidency has **made every man** who occupied it, no matter how small, **bigger than he was**; and no matter how big, **not big enough for its demands.**
>
> —President Lyndon Johnson on the responsibilities of being President

Photo: A careworn President Lyndon B. Johnson at work in the Oval Office.

GOVERNMENT ONLINE
On the Go

To study anywhere, anytime, download these online resources at PearsonSuccessNet.com
• Political Dictionary
• Audio Review
• Downloadable Interactivities

The **Growth** of Presidential Power

Guiding Question

What factors have contributed to the growth of presidential power? Use a concept web like the one below to keep track of the main ideas on the growth of presidential power.

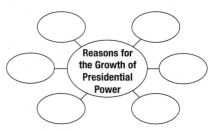

Reasons for the Growth of Presidential Power

Political Dictionary

• Executive Article
• imperial presidency

Objectives

1. Explain why Article II of the Constitution can be described as "an outline" of the presidential office.
2. List several reasons for the growth of presidential power.
3. Explain how various Presidents' views have shaped the powers of the office.

Images Above: President George Washington, with the sculptures on Mount Rushmore in the background

The presidency is regularly called "the most powerful office in the world," and it is. But is this what the Framers had in mind when they created the post in 1787? At Philadelphia, they purposely created a single executive with very broadly stated powers. Still, they agreed with Thomas Jefferson, who wrote in the Declaration of Independence that "a Tyrant is unfit to be the ruler of a free people." So, just as purposefully, they constructed a "checked," a limited presidency.

Article II

Article II of the Constitution is known as the **Executive Article,** which in only a few words established the presidency. It begins this way:

FROM THE CONSTITUTION

The executive Power shall be vested in a President of the United States of America.

—Article II, Section 1

With this one sentence, the Framers laid the basis for the vast power and influence the nation's chief executive possesses today.

The Constitution also sets out other, somewhat more specific grants of presidential power. Thus, the President is given the power to command the armed forces, to make treaties, to approve or veto acts of Congress and call special sessions of that body, to send and receive diplomatic representatives, and to "take Care that the Laws be faithfully executed." [1]

Still, the Constitution lays out the powers of the presidency in a very sketchy fashion. Article II reads almost as an outline. It has been called "the most loosely drawn chapter" in the nation's fundamental law. [2] It does not

---

[1] Most of the specific grants of presidential power are found in Article II, Sections 2 and 3. A few are elsewhere in the Constitution—for example, the veto power, in Article I, Section 7, Clause 2.

[2] Edward S. Corwin, *The President: Office and Powers.*

define "the executive Power," and the other grants of presidential power are <u>couched</u> in similarly broad terms.

Much of our political history can be told in terms of the struggle over the meaning of the constitutional phrase "executive Power"—that is, over the extent of presidential power. That struggle has pitted those who have argued for a weaker presidency, subordinate to Congress, against those who have pressed for a stronger, independent, co-equal chief executive.

That never-ending contest began at the Philadelphia Convention in 1787. There, several of the Framers agreed with Roger Sherman of Connecticut, who, according to James Madison,

Primary Source

considered the Executive Magistracy as nothing more than an institution for carrying the will of the legislature into effect, that the person or persons [occupying the presidency] ought to be appointed by and accountable to the Legislature only, which was the depository of the supreme will of the Society.

—James Madison, *Notes of Debates in the Federal Convention of 1787*

As you know, those delegates who argued for a stronger executive carried the day. The Framers established a single executive, chosen independently of Congress and with its own distinct field of powers.

The Growth of Power

The Constitution's formal grants of power to the President have not been changed since 1789. Yet presidential power has grown remarkably over the past 200 years.

Reasons for the Expansion That extraordinary expansion has come, in no small part, because of the *unity* of the presidency. The office, and its powers, are held by one person. The President is the single, commanding chief executive. In contrast, Congress is composed of two houses, and both must agree before Congress can do anything. Moreover, one of those two houses is made up of 100 separately elected members, and the other of 435.

Several other factors have also been at work here. Not least among them have been the Presidents themselves, and especially the stronger ones—Abraham Lincoln and the two Roosevelts, for example.

The nation's increasingly complex economic and social life has also had a telling effect on presidential power. As the United States has become more industrialized and technologically advanced, the people have demanded that the Federal Government take a larger and still larger role in transportation, communications, health, welfare, employment, education, civil rights, and a host of other fields. And they have looked especially to the President for leadership in those matters.

Clearly, the need for immediate and decisive action in times of crisis, and most notably in times of war, has also had a major impact here. The ability of the President—the single, commanding chief executive—to act in those situations has done much to strengthen "the executive Power."

Congress has also been involved, as it has passed the thousands of laws that have been a key part of the historic growth of the Federal Government. Congress has neither the time nor the specialized knowledge to provide much more than basic outlines of public policy. Out of necessity, it has delegated substantial authority to the executive branch to carry out the laws it has enacted.

A number of other factors have also fed the growth of executive power. Among them have been the ways several Presidents have played their roles as chief legislator, party leader, and chief citizen. Another is the huge amount of staff support a President has, both in the White House and throughout the executive branch of the Federal Government. Still another lies in the unique position from which the President can attract and hold the public's attention, and so build support for policies and actions. Every President, from Franklin Roosevelt's day to this, has purposely used the mass media—forms of communication, especially radio, television, and the Internet—to that end.

✔ **Checkpoint**
What two views of the presidency were debated by the Framers?

<u>couch</u>
v. to express using a particular style

The Means of Gaining Power

▸▸ **Analyzing Political Cartoons** The question of how much power a President should have has been hotly debated since 1787. Gradually, Presidents have increased their authority, and hence their power, both quietly and forcibly. The way in which several Presidents have exercised power has often reignited the debate over the "executive Power." *In these cartoons, how and from whom is the President gaining power?*

✔ **Checkpoint**
What limits the growth of presidential power?

imperil
v. to put in danger

seizure
n. taking by force

Limits to the Growth of Power Even with this increase of authority, no President can become all-powerful. The Constitution, which grants much power to the President, also provides for a number of restraints on the exercise of that power. Here are just two illustrations of that crucial point.

In 1952, at the height of the Korean War, a labor dispute threatened to shut down the nation's steel industry and <u>imperil</u> the war effort. To avert a strike, President Harry Truman, acting as commander in chief, ordered the Secretary of Commerce to seize and operate several steel mills. But, the Supreme Court found that here the President had overstepped his constitutional authority. It held that only Congress, acting under its commerce power, could authorize the <u>seizure</u> of private property in time of war, and it had not done so, *Youngstown Sheet & Tube Co.* v. *Sawyer*, 1952.

In June 2006, the High Court struck down President George W. Bush's plan to use military tribunals to prosecute "enemy combatants," persons captured in the war

against terrorism, held at Guantanamo Bay. The President, citing his powers as commander in chief, had ordered the formation of those tribunals. However, the Court held that the Constitution gives Congress, not the President, the power to provide for the creation of such court-like bodies.

In addition, the Court found that several features of the President's plan violated several provisions in an act of Congress (the Uniform Code of Military Justice, enacted in 1950) and a treaty of the United States (the Geneva Conventions of 1949, dealing with the treatment of prisoners of war), *Hamdan* v. *Rumsfeld*, 2006.

The Presidential View

What the presidency is at any given time depends, in large part, on how the President in office at the time sees the office and exercises its several powers. Presidents have generally taken one of two contrasting views.

The stronger, more effective chief executives have seen the office in a broad light—a view that Theodore Roosevelt called "the stewardship theory":

"My view was that every executive officer . . . was a steward of the people bound actively and affirmatively to do all that he could for the people. . . . I declined to adopt the view that what was imperatively necessary for the Nation could not be done by the President unless he could find some specific authorization to do it."

—**Theodore Roosevelt,**
Theodore Roosevelt: An Autobiography,
1913

Ironically, the most strongly worded presidential statement of the opposing view came from Roosevelt's handpicked successor in the office, William Howard Taft. Looking back on his years in the White House, Mr. Taft had this to say:

"[T]he President can exercise no power which cannot be fairly and reasonably traced to some specific grant of power or justly implied and included within such express grant. . . . Such specific grant must be either in the Federal Constitution or in an act of Congress passed in pursuance thereof. There is no undefined residuum [remnant] of power which he can exercise because it seems to him to be in the public interest."

—**William Howard Taft,**
Our Chief Magistrate and His Powers,
1916

In more recent times, critics of what they see as a too-powerful President have condemned what has been called the "**imperial presidency.**" The term paints a picture of the chief executive as a strong-willed emperor, taking various actions without consulting Congress or seeking its approval—sometimes acting in secrecy to evade or even deceive Congress. Critics of the imperial presidency worry that Presidents have become isolated policymakers who are unaccountable to the American people and their elected representatives in Congress.

Theodore Roosevelt (left) and William Howard Taft held opposing views on the presidency. *Which view has most often prevailed?* ▼

Essential Questions Journal To continue to build a response to the chapter Essential Question, go to your **Essential Questions Journal.**

SECTION 1 ASSESSMENT

1. **Guiding Question** Use your completed concept web to answer: What factors have contributed to the growth of presidential power?

Key Terms and Comprehension

2. How has the **Executive Article** fueled debate on presidential power?

3. How can the President use the mass media as a tool for the expansion of executive power?

4. How have the legislative and judicial branches influenced the growth of the power of the President?

Critical Thinking

5. **Draw Conclusions** Why do you think some people are concerned that the presidency has become too powerful?

6. **Compare Points of View** Compare and contrast the comments by Presidents Roosevelt and Taft on this page. **(a)** Which view do you favor? Why? **(b)** Whose view do you think most modern-day Presidents have favored? Explain.

Quick Write

Persuasive Writing: Take a Position The scope of presidential power has been debated for over 200 years. How do you feel about the extent of the power of the presidency? Write a thesis statement that expresses your point of view. Make sure that your thesis states your position and specifies the conclusion you intend to persuade your audience to support.

Expanding Presidential Powers

▶▶ Track the Issue

Article II of the Constitution provides only a framework for the duties and powers of the presidency. Most Presidents have tried to extend their powers in order to perform their jobs more effectively.

1787

The Constitution designs a strong National Government with an independent presidency.

1930s

President Franklin D. Roosevelt expands the executive branch to overcome the effects of the Great Depression.

1950s

President Dwight Eisenhower claims executive privilege to shield conversations from the courts and Congress.

1970s

The term "imperial presidency," in which the President ignores or misleads Congress, is used to describe the Nixon administration.

2000s

President Bush claims that the President has a practically absolute power to defend the United States.

President George W. Bush confers with Secretary of Homeland Security, Michael Chertoff in 2005. ▶

▶▶ Perspectives

Following the 9/11 terrorist attacks, President George W. Bush, acting in secret, directed the National Security Agency (NSA) to monitor communications between people in the United States and suspected terrorists. Under current law, the NSA must obtain a warrant from a federal court in order to conduct spying activities within the United States. The President defended his actions as necessary to protect the American people from harm.

"What we're trying to do is learn of communications, back and forth, from within the United States to overseas with members of al Qaeda. . . . [W]e also believe the President has the inherent authority under the Constitution, as Commander-in-Chief, to engage in this kind of activity . . . . The operators out at NSA tell me that we don't have the speed and the agility that we need, in all circumstances, to deal with this new kind of enemy."

—*Attorney General Alberto Gonzales, 2005*

"The Government appears to argue here that. . .[the President] has been granted the inherent power to violate not only the laws of the Congress but the First and Fourth Amendments of the Constitution, itself. . . . The Office of the Chief Executive has itself been created, with its powers, by the Constitution. There are. . . no powers not created by the Constitution. So all 'inherent powers' must derive from that Constitution."

—*Federal District Court Judge Anna Diggs Taylor, 2006*

▶▶ Connect to Your World

1. **Understand (a)** How did President Bush expand the power of the presidency? **(b)** How did this affect the system of checks and balances?
2. **Compare and Contrast (a)** On what constitutional basis did the attorney general support the President's order? **(b)** On what constitutional basis did Judge Diggs Taylor reject the President's order? **(c)** Which of the positions do you think most appropriate? Why?

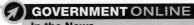

GOVERNMENT ONLINE

In the News

For updates about the expansion of presidential powers, visit **PearsonSuccessNet.com**

SECTION 2

The Executive Powers

Guiding Question

What are the executive powers and how were they established? Use a flowchart like the one below to keep track of the supporting details of the President's executive powers.

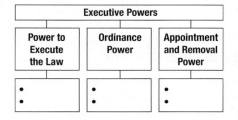

Executive Powers		
Power to Execute the Law	Ordinance Power	Appointment and Removal Power
• •	• •	• •

Political Dictionary

• executive order
• ordinance power
• executive privilege

Objectives

1. Identify the sources of the President's power to execute federal law.
2. Define the ordinance power.
3. Explain how the appointment power works and describe the limits on the removal power.
4. Examine the power of executive privilege.

Image above: President Ronald Reagan takes the oath of office in 1985.

Thomas Jefferson wrote this to a friend in 1789: "The execution of the laws is more important than the making of them." Whether Jefferson was right about that or not, in this section you will see that the President's power to execute the law endows the chief executive with extraordinary authority.

Executing the Law

As chief executive, the President executes (enforces, administers, carries out) the provisions of federal law. The power to do so rests on two brief constitutional provisions. The first of them is the oath of office sworn by the President on the day he or she takes office:

FROM THE CONSTITUTION

I do solemnly swear (or affirm) that I will faithfully execute the Office of President of the United States, and will to the best of my Ability, preserve, protect and defend the Constitution of the United States.

—Article II, Section 1, Clause 8

The other provision is the Constitution's command that "he shall take Care that the Laws be faithfully executed."[3]

The President's power to execute the law covers all federal laws. In fact, the Constitution requires the President to execute *all* federal laws no matter what the chief executive's own views of any of them may be. Their number, and the many subjects they cover, nearly boggle the mind. Social security, gun control, affirmative action, immigration, minimum wages, terrorism, environmental protection, taxes—these only begin the list. There are scores of others.

The President—and, importantly, the President's subordinates—have much to say about the meaning of laws, as do Congress and the courts. In executing and enforcing law, the executive branch also interprets it.

---

3 Article II, Section 3; this provision gives the President what is often called the "take care power."

President Bill Clinton, with Vice President Al Gore, signs the executive order establishing Utah's Grand Staircase-Escalante National Monument. **Why do you think an executive order was used for this purpose?**

discretion
n. the freedom to act according to one's judgment

To look at the point more closely: Many laws that Congress enacts are written in fairly broad terms. Congress sets out the basic policies and standards to be followed. The specific details—much of the fine print necessary to the actual, day-to-day administration of the law—are usually left to be worked out by the executive branch.

For example, immigration laws require that all immigrants seeking permanent admission to this country must be able to "read and understand some dialect or language." But what does this broadly worded requirement mean in day-to-day practice? How well must an alien be able to "read and understand"? The law does not say. Rather, the details come from within the executive branch—from the U.S. Citizenship and Immigration Services in the Department of Homeland Security.

The Ordinance Power

The job of administering and applying most federal law is the day-to-day work of all of the many departments, commissions, and other agencies of the Federal Government. All of the some 2.7 million civilian men and women who staff those agencies are subject to the President's control and direction.

The chief executive has the power to issue **executive orders,** which are directives, rules, or regulations that have the effect of law. The power to issue these orders, the **ordinance power,** arises from two sources: the Constitution and acts of Congress.

The Constitution does not mention the ordinance power in so many words, but that power is clearly intended. In granting certain powers to the President, the Constitution obviously anticipates their use. In order to exercise those powers, the chief executive must have the power to issue the necessary orders, and, as well, the power to implement them.[4]

The number, the scope, and the complexity of the problems that face the government of the United States have grown over the course of more than two centuries. As a result, Congress has found it necessary to delegate more and yet more <u>discretion</u> to the President and to top-level subordinates in the executive branch to spell out the policies and programs it has approved.

The Appointment Power

A President cannot hope to succeed without loyal subordinates who support the policies of the President's administration. To that end, the Constitution says that the President

" FROM THE CONSTITUTION

by and with the Advice and Consent of the Senate . . . shall appoint Ambassadors, other public Ministers and Consuls, Judges of the supreme Court, and all other Officers of the United States, whose Appointments are not herein otherwise provided for . . . but the Congress may by Law vest the Appointment of such inferior Officers, as they think proper, in the President alone, in the Courts of Law, or in the Heads of Departments.

—Article II, Section 2, Clause 2

Those "Officers of the United States whose Appointments are . . . otherwise provided for" are the Vice President, members of Congress, and presidential electors.

---

4 All executive orders are published in the *Federal Register,* which appears five times per week. At least once per year, all orders currently in force are published in the *Code of Federal Regulations.* Both of these publications are issued by the National Archives and Records Administration.

Acting alone, the President names only some 3,000 of the 2.7 million civilians who work for the Federal Government. The vast majority of the rest of the federal work force is hired under the civil service laws.

Appointees The President names most of the top-ranking officers of the Federal Government. Among them are (1) ambassadors and other diplomats; (2) Cabinet members and their top aides; (3) the heads of independent agencies; (4) all federal judges, U.S. marshals, and attorneys; and (5) all officers in the armed forces. When the President makes one of these appointments, the nomination is sent to the Senate. There, the support of a majority of the senators present and voting is needed for confirmation.

The unwritten rule of senatorial courtesy plays an important part in this process. That rule applies to the choice of those federal officers who serve within a State—a federal district judge or a federal marshal, for example. The rule holds that the Senate will approve only those federal appointees acceptable to the senator or senators of the President's party from the State involved. The practical effect of this custom is to place a meaningful part of the President's appointing power in the hands of particular senators.

Recess Appointments The Constitution does allow the President to make "recess appointments," that is, appointments "to fill up all Vacancies that may happen during the Recess of the Senate."[5] Any such appointment automatically expires at the end of the congressional term in which it is made.

Recess appointments have often been a matter of contention—in particular, because they make it possible for the President to bypass the Senate confirmation process. So, as a rule, Presidents have not usually given these appointments to highly controversial personalities or to someone whom the Senate has previously rejected. Over time, Presidents

---

5 Article II, Section 2, Clause 3. Over time, the words "may happen" have come to mean "may happen to exist" and "the Recess of the Senate" has come to include both the period between regular sessions of Congress and the several short recesses during a session.

GOVERNMENT ONLINE

For an **interactive** exploration of the confirmation process, visit **PearsonSuccessNet.com**

How Government Works

Confirmation Process

Who Gets the Job?

Many presidential nominations for high-level positions, such as Supreme Court justices, require Senate approval. This multi-step process can be long and drawn out, and especially grueling for the nominee at times. *Why is this multi-step process necessary?*

President Nominates

- White House staff conducts search for candidate.
- Key experts provide White House with information and guidance.
- President selects nominee and submits choice to Senate.

Senate Committee Examines

- Nominee testifies before appropriate Senate committee.
- Majority vote required before nominee is recommended to Senate.

Senate Debates

- Full Senate considers the nomination.
- Senators debate the nominee's qualifications.
- If Senate strongly opposes, President may withdraw nomination or nominee may bow out.
- Floor vote is taken.

Nominee Confirmed

- A simple majority Senate vote approves nominee.

Nominee Rejected*

- Nominee does not get a simple majority and is rejected.

* Process begins again.

▶ **Analyzing Political Cartoons** Presidential appointees are sometimes criticized for parroting the views of the President without expressing their own opinions. *How might this actually benefit the President?*

✔ **Checkpoint**
What are the two sides of the removal power debate?

have made very few recess appointments. The number tends to increase when the President's party does not control the Senate.

The Removal Power

The power to remove is the other side of the appointment coin, and is as important to presidential success as is the power to appoint. Yet, except for mention of the little-used impeachment process, the Constitution says nothing about how, by whom, or why an appointed officer may be dismissed.[6]

The Historical Debate The matter was hotly debated in the first session of Congress, in 1789. Several members argued that, if an appointment required Senate approval, Senate consent should also be required for removal. They insisted that this restriction on presidential authority was essential to congressional supervision (oversight) of the executive branch. But others argued that the President could not "take Care that the Laws be faithfully executed" without a free hand to dismiss those who were incompetent or otherwise unsuited to office.

depose
v. to remove from a position of power

---

6 In Article I, Section 2, Clause 5 and Section 3, Clauses 6 and 7, and Article II, Section 4.

The latter view prevailed. The First Congress gave the President the power to remove any officer he appointed, except federal judges. Over the years since then, Congress has sometimes tried, with little success, to restrict the President's freedom to dismiss.

One notable instance occurred in 1867. Locked with Andrew Johnson in the fight over Reconstruction, Congress passed the Tenure of Office Act. That law's plain purpose was to prevent President Johnson from removing several top officers in his administration, in particular the secretary of war, Edwin M. Stanton. The law provided that any person holding an office by presidential appointment with Senate consent should remain in that office until a successor had been confirmed by the Senate.

The President vetoed the bill, charging that it was an unconstitutional invasion of executive authority. The veto was overridden, but Mr. Johnson ignored Congress and fired Stanton anyway. The veto and Stanton's removal sparked the move for Johnson's impeachment. Ultimately, the President was acquitted, and the law was ignored in practice. It was finally repealed in 1887.

Removal and the Court The question of the President's removal power did not reach the Supreme Court until *Myers* v. *United States*, 1926. In 1876, Congress had passed a law requiring Senate consent before the President could dismiss any first-class, second-class, or third-class postmaster.

In 1920, without consulting the Senate, President Woodrow Wilson removed Frank Myers as the postmaster at Portland, Oregon. The **deposed** postmaster then sued for the salary for the rest of his four-year term. He based his claim on the point that he had been removed in violation of the 1876 law.

The Court, led by a former President, Chief Justice Taft, found the law unconstitutional. It held that the removal power was an essential part of executive power, clearly necessary to the faithful execution of the laws.

The Supreme Court did place some limits on the President's removal power in 1935, in *Humphrey's Executor* v. *United States*. President Herbert Hoover had appointed William Humphrey to a seven-year term on the

Federal Trade Commission (FTC) in 1931. When Franklin D. Roosevelt took office in 1933, he found Commissioner Humphrey to be in sharp disagreement with many of his policies. He asked the commissioner to resign, saying that his administration would be better served with someone else on the FTC. When Mr. Humphrey refused, President Roosevelt removed him. Humphrey soon died, but his heirs filed a suit for back salary.

The Supreme Court upheld the heirs' claim. It based its decision on the act creating the FTC. That law provides that a member of the commission may be removed only for "inefficiency, neglect of duty, or <u>malfeasance</u> in office."

The Court further held that Congress does have the power to set the conditions under which a member of the FTC and other such agencies might be removed by the President. It did so because those agencies, the independent regulatory commissions, are not purely executive agencies (see Chapter 15).

As a general rule, the President may remove those whom the President appoints. Occasionally, a presidential appointee does have to be fired. Most often, however, what was in fact a dismissal is called a "resignation."

Executive Privilege

At times, the nation's chief executives have insisted that the Constitution gives to the President the inherent power to refuse to disclose certain information to Congress or to the federal courts. That is, they have claimed the power of **executive privilege.** Most often, a claim of executive privilege has been made with regard to conversations and other communications between the President and his or her closest advisors.

The chief executive must, of necessity, rely on the information and advice he or she receives from key staff and their ability to speak with utmost <u>candor,</u> which depends on the confidential nature of their relationship with the President. These officials must be sure that what they say will become known publicly only if and when the President chooses to disclose that information.

Congress has never recognized executive privilege. It has often tried to compel executive officials to testify at congressional committee hearings, and Presidents have frequently resisted those efforts, citing executive privilege.

The federal courts have been reluctant to become involved in this dispute between the executive and legislative branches. However, the Supreme Court has recognized both the existence of and the need for executive privilege in a historic case, *United States* v. *Nixon*, in 1974. There, a unanimous Court said that although the President might legitimately claim executive privilege in matters involving national security, that privilege cannot be used to prevent evidence from being heard in a criminal proceeding. This decision was a key factor in Mr. Nixon's resignation.

✔ **Checkpoint**
What is the Court's stand on executive privilege?

candor
n. the quality of being open and honest in speaking

malfeasance
n. wrong or illegal conduct by a public official

Essential Questions Journal To continue to build a response to the chapter Essential Question, go to your **Essential Questions Journal.**

SECTION 2 ASSESSMENT

1. **Guiding Question** Use your completed flowchart to answer this question: What are the executive powers and how were they established?

Key Terms and Comprehension

2. How can the executive branch influence the meaning of a particular law?

3. What is the **ordinance power** and from what sources does it arise?

4. **(a)** What officers does the President appoint? **(b)** What is the Senate's role in the appointment process?

5. What is **executive privilege** and why is it controversial?

Critical Thinking

6. **Identify Central Issues** Why is the President's power of appointment so important to the success of his or her administration?

7. **Demonstrate Reasoned Judgment** Consider this statement: The unwritten rule of senatorial courtesy contradicts the principle of separation of powers. Do you agree or disagree?

Quick Write

Persuasive Writing: Generate Arguments An effective way to persuade an audience is to address both sides of the issue. Using your thesis statement from Section 1, create a chart to record facts about the debate on presidential power. In one column, record the facts that support your position, and, in the second column, note arguments that could be used against your position.

What Are the Limits on Executive Privilege?

A number of chief executives have argued that the Constitution gives the President the authority to refuse to disclose certain information to Congress or to the federal courts. That authority, known as "executive privilege," was first recognized by the Supreme Court in the historic case, *United States* v. *Nixon*, in 1974.

"Richard Milhous Nixon announced last night that he will resign as the 37th President of the United States at noon today. . . . After two years of bitter public debate over the Watergate scandals, President Nixon bowed to pressures from the public and leaders of his party to become the first President in American history to resign.

"'By taking this action,' he said in a subdued yet dramatic television address from the Oval Office, 'I hope that I will have hastened the start of the process of healing which is so desperately needed in America.'"

—Carroll Kilpatrick, "Nixon Resigns," *The Washington Post*, 9 August 1974

What could possibly have led the President of the United States to resign his office? The answers to that question begin with a botched attempt to break into the Democratic National Committee's headquarters in the Watergate complex in Washington, D.C., in June of 1972, in the midst of the presidential campaign. The burglars, it turned out, were working for President Nixon's chief campaign organization, CREEP—the Committee to Re-Elect the President. Over the next two years the President and many of the major figures in his administration steadfastly denied any involvement in what came to be known as the Watergate scandal.

During Senate hearings on the issue, a White House aide revealed that the President had secretly taped most of his telephone calls and personal conversations

Burglars break into the Watergate complex, June 1972.

President Nixon denies any knowledge of the break-in, April 1973.

President Nixon refuses to turn over the White House audio tapes, July 1973.

in the Oval Office. When both the special prosecutor and a federal district court ordered Mr. Nixon to release those tapes, he refused, asserting that executive privilege gave him the right to withhold the information. The Constitution does not provide for executive privilege in so many words; the concept is, instead, derived from the principle of separation of powers.

The matter was then carried to the Supreme Court. There in a unanimous decision, the Court ruled that although the confidentiality of communications between the President and his closest aides is important, their protection is not absolute. If the President possessed absolute executive privilege, the Court held, the executive branch would, in effect, be unchecked, and it ordered the tapes to be released. President Nixon resigned shortly after he obeyed the Court's order.

Arguments for Nixon

- Under the doctrine of separation of powers, no court has the authority to question executive privilege.
- The President must have the power to keep his various communications with his aides secret.
- The forced disclosure of communications between the President and his advisors could threaten the nation's security.

Arguments for the United States

- Separation of powers does not mean that the three branches are absolutely independent of one another.
- Withholding critical evidence damages the 6th Amendment guarantee of a fair trial to all defendants.
- While the secrecy of presidential communications is important, that protection should be limited to military and diplomatic matters.

Thinking Critically

1. Should the President have the right to keep all communications with advisors private? Why or why not?
2. **Constitutional Principles** How does the decision in this case reflect the principle of separation of powers?

A woman reads a newspaper announcing Nixon's intention to resign, August 1974.

Nixon's letter of resignation, August 1974.

Nixon boards *Air Force One*. When the plane lands in California, he will no longer be President.

SECTION 3
Diplomatic and Military Powers

Guiding Question

What tools are available to the President to implement foreign policy? Use a concept web to keep track of the main ideas and supporting details on foreign policy tools.

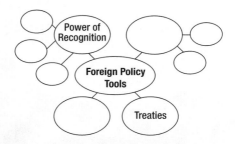

Political Dictionary
- treaty
- executive agreement
- recognition
- *persona non grata*

Objectives

1. Explain how treaties are made and approved.
2. Explain why and how executive agreements are made.
3. Summarize how the power of recognition is used.
4. Describe the President's powers as commander in chief.

Images Above: President Jimmy Carter and Chinese leader Deng Xiaoping

John F. Kennedy described the pressures of the presidency this way:

Primary Source

When I ran for the presidency . . . I knew the country faced serious challenges, but I could not realize—nor could any man who does not bear the burdens of this office—how heavy and constant would be those burdens.

—John F. Kennedy, radio broadcast (1961)

When President Kennedy made that comment, he had in mind the subject of this section: the President's awesome responsibilities as chief diplomat and as commander in chief.

Chief Diplomat

The Constitution does not say, in so many words, that the President is the nation's chief diplomat. Rather, Presidents have come to dominate the field of foreign affairs through the use of the powers of the office. In major part, they were able to do so because the Constitution makes the President the commander in chief of the nation's armed forces—and several centuries of relationships between sovereign states tells us that military force is the ultimate language of diplomacy.

The Power to Make Treaties A **treaty** is a formal agreement between two or more sovereign states. The President, usually acting through the secretary of state, negotiates these international agreements. The Senate must give its approval by a two-thirds vote of the members present before a treaty made by the President can become effective. Recall, the Constitution, in Article VI, makes treaties a part of "the supreme Law of the Land."

Contrary to popular belief, the Senate does not ratify treaties. The Constitution requires the Senate's "Advice and Consent" to a treaty made by the President. Once the Senate has given its consent, the President ratifies a treaty by the exchange of formal notifications with the other party or parties to the agreement.

Treaties have the same legal standing as acts of Congress, and their provisions are enforceable in the courts. Congress may abrogate (repeal) a treaty by passing a law contrary to its provisions, and an existing law may be repealed by the terms of a treaty. When the provisions of a treaty and an act of Congress conflict, the courts consider the latest enacted to be the law (*The Head Money Cases*, 1884). The terms of a treaty cannot conflict with any provision in the Constitution (*Missouri* v. *Holland*, 1920); but the Supreme Court has never found a treaty provision to be unconstitutional.

Treaties and the Senate The Framers considered the Senate—with, originally, only 26 members—a suitable council to advise the President in foreign affairs. Secrecy was thought to be necessary and was seen as an impossibility in a body as large as the House.

The two-thirds rule for treaty approval creates the possibility that a relatively small Senate minority can kill an international agreement. For example, in 1920, the Senate rejected the Treaty of Versailles, the general peace agreement negotiated by Woodrow Wilson to end World War I. The treaty included provisions for the League of Nations. Forty-nine senators voted for the pact and 35 against, but the vote was 7 short of the necessary two thirds. More than once, a President has been forced to bow to the views of a few senators in order to get a treaty approved, even when this has meant making concessions opposed by the majority.

At times, a President has had to turn to roundabout methods in order to achieve his goals. When a Senate minority defeated a treaty to annex Texas, President John Tyler was able to bring about annexation in 1845 by encouraging passage of a joint resolution—a move that required only a majority vote in each house. In 1898, President William McKinley used the same tactic to annex Hawaii, again after a treaty his administration had negotiated failed in the Senate.

Executive Agreements Recent Presidents have relied more heavily on executive agreements than on formal treaties in their dealings with foreign governments, especially in routine matters. An **executive agreement** is a pact between the President and the head of a foreign state, or their subordinates. Unlike treaties, these agreements do not have to be approved by the Senate.

These pacts have the same standing as treaties in the relationships between sovereign states, but they do not <u>supersede</u> federal law or the laws of any State. However, they are otherwise binding on the United States.

Most executive agreements flow out of legislation already passed by Congress or out of treaties to which the Senate has agreed. However, the President can make these agreements without any congressional action. Treaties, once made, become a permanent part of American law. Executive agreements do not. When a change of administrations occurs, only those the new President agrees to remain in force.

A few executive agreements have been extraordinary, most notably, the destroyers-for-bases deal of 1940. Under its terms, the United States gave Great Britain 50 "over-age" U.S. destroyers, naval vessels that the British needed to combat German submarine attacks in the North Atlantic. In return, the United

✔ **Checkpoint**
How do executive agreements differ from treaties?

supersede
v. to take the place of something previously in use

Secretary of State Madeleine Albright with Israeli Prime Minister Ehud Barak during Middle East peace discussions in 1999. *Why does the President rely on the secretary of state to perform diplomatic duties?*

413

Expanding Executive Power

By dividing the military powers, the Framers created an enduring tension between Congress and the President as they battle over their war power authority. However, in times of national emergency, when our safety and national interests are threatened, there is a marked shift of power to the President. *Why might Congress yield to a President's decisions regarding military actions?*

1950 Korea

President Truman orders the use of military force to defend South Korea against communist North Korea. He claims that United Nations resolutions give him the legal authority for his actions.

Congress is not consulted by the President, but makes no attempt to block his "police action."

1964 Vietnam

President Johnson, citing a report of a North Vietnamese attack on an American destroyer, asks Congress to give him the authority to do whatever he considers necessary to deal with the threat.

Congress gives the President that authority by enacting the Gulf of Tonkin Resolution.

States received 99-year leases to a string of air and naval bases extending from Newfoundland to the Caribbean.

The Power of Recognition When the President receives the diplomatic representatives of another sovereign state, the President exercises the power of **recognition.** That is, the President, acting for the United States, acknowledges the legal existence of that country and its government. The President's action indicates that the United States accepts that country as an equal member of the family of nations. Sovereign states generally recognize one another through the exchange of diplomatic representatives.[7]

Recognition does not mean that one government approves of the character or conduct of another. The United States recognizes several governments about which it has serious misgivings. Among the most notable examples today is the People's Republic of China. The facts of life in world politics make relations with these governments necessary.

Recognition is often used as a weapon in foreign relations, too. President Theodore Roosevelt's quick recognition of Panama in

1903 is a classic example of the use of the power as a diplomatic weapon. He recognized the new state less than three days after the Panamanians had begun a revolt against Colombia, of which Panama had been a part. Roosevelt's action guaranteed their success. Similarly, President Harry Truman's dramatic recognition of Israel, within minutes of its creation in 1948, helped that new state to survive among its hostile Arab neighbors.

The President may show American displeasure with the conduct of another country by asking for the recall of that nation's ambassador or other diplomatic representatives in this country. The official recalled is declared to be **persona non grata,** an unwelcome person. The same point can be made by the recalling of an American diplomat from a post in another country. The withdrawal of recognition is the sharpest diplomatic <u>rebuke</u> one government may give to another and has often been a step on the way to war.

Commander in Chief

The Constitution makes the chief executive the commander in chief of the nation's armed forces, although Congress does have extensive war powers.[8] However, the President

rebuke
n. an expression of sharp disapproval

---

7 Recognition may be accomplished by other means, such as proposing to negotiate a treaty, since in international law only sovereign states can make such agreements.

8 Article II, Section 2, Clause 1; see also Chapter 17.

1990 Kuwait

President George H.W. Bush, in reaction to Iraq's invasion of Kuwait, creates a coalition and negotiates a United Nations resolution to use "all necessary force" to stop Iraqi aggression. **Congress** passes a resolution authorizing the use of force against Iraq a month later.

2002 Iraq

President George W. Bush plans preemptive combat operations against Iraq in reaction to reports of the stockpiling of weapons of mass destruction. **Congress** passes the Iraq Resolution authorizing the President to use military force, which he exercises in 2003.

GOVERNMENT ONLINE
Audio Tour
Listen to a guided audio tour of Expanding Executive Power at **PearsonSuccessNet.com**

dominates the field of military policy. In fact, the President's powers as commander in chief are almost without limit.

Consider this illustration of the point: In 1907, Theodore Roosevelt sent the Great White Fleet around the world. He did so partly as a training exercise for the Navy, but mostly to impress other nations with America's naval might. Several members of Congress objected to the cost and threatened to block funds for the President's project. To this, Roosevelt is said to have replied, "Very well, the existing appropriation will carry the Navy halfway around the world and if Congress chooses to leave it on the other side, all right." Congress was forced to give in.

Presidents delegate much of their command authority to military subordinates. They are not required to do so, however. George Washington actually took command of federal troops and led them into Pennsylvania during the Whiskey Rebellion of 1794. Abraham Lincoln often visited the Army of the Potomac and instructed his generals in the field during the Civil War.

Most Presidents have not become so directly involved in military operations. Still, the President has the final authority over and responsibility for all military matters, and the most critical decisions are <u>invariably</u> made by the commander in chief.

Making Undeclared War Does the Constitution give the President the power to make war without a declaration of war by Congress? Although many argue that it does not, 200 years of American history argue otherwise. Presidents have often used the armed forces abroad, in combat, without a declaration of war.[9] In fact, most Presidents have done so, and on several hundred occasions.

John Adams was the first to do so, in 1798. At his command, the Navy fought and won a number of battles with French warships harassing American merchantmen in the Atlantic and the Caribbean. There have been a great many other foreign adventures since then. The long military conflicts in Korea, Vietnam, and now in Afghanistan and Iraq stand as the most extensive of these "undeclared wars."

Congressional Resolutions Congress has not declared war since World War II. On eight occasions since then, however, it has enacted joint resolutions to authorize the President to meet certain international crises with military force.

---

9 Congress has declared war 11 times. It did so against Great Britain in 1812; Mexico in 1848; Spain in 1898; Germany and Austria-Hungary in 1917; Japan, Germany, and Italy in 1941 and Bulgaria, Hungary, and Romania in 1942.

✔**Checkpoint**
How might a President exercise the role of commander in chief?

<u>invariably</u>
adv. always, without exception

President Dwight Eisenhower sought the first of these measures in 1955, to block the designs the People's Republic of China had (and still has) on Taiwan. That show of American resolve, and the presence of American warships, defused the situation.

Most recently, in 2002, Congress agreed that President George W. Bush should take whatever measures were "necessary and appropriate" to eliminate the threat posed by Saddam Hussein and his Iraqi dictatorship. In March 2003, an international coalition, led by the United States, launched Operation Iraqi Freedom—a military campaign that ousted Saddam Hussein and his government from power. Some 140,000 American troops remain in Iraq today, engaged in the difficult and often dangerous tasks of stabilizing and rebuilding that country. President Obama has declared that "our combat mission in Iraq will end by August 31, 2010" and that "all U.S. troops [will leave] Iraq by the end of 2011."

Other Uses of Military Power Since the end of World War II, there have been many other critical situations in which Presidents have deployed the nation's armed forces—without a congressional resolution to support the action. Certainly, the Korean War stands as the foremost illustration of that fact. Among the other more notable instances: the attack on Grenada, ordered by President Ronald Reagan in 1983, to frustrate a military coup in that Caribbean island nation; the invasion of Panama, at the command of President George H.W. Bush in 1989, to oust the dictatorship of General Manuel Noriega and protect American interests there; and the dispatch of American forces to the Balkans by President Bill Clinton (to Bosnia in 1995 and to Kosovo in 1999) as part of NATO's response to a vicious civil war and the horrific "ethnic cleansing" campaign conducted by the forces of Serbian President Slobodan Milosevic.

War Powers Resolution The war-making power as it was exercised by Presidents Johnson and Nixon during the undeclared war in Vietnam moved Congress to enact (over President Nixon's veto) the War Powers Resolution of 1973. That statute provides that the President can commit American military forces to combat only (1) if Congress has declared war, (2) if Congress has authorized that action, or (3) when an attack on the nation or its armed forces has occurred.

If troops are ordered into combat in the third circumstance, the President must report it to Congress within 48 hours. Any such commitment of American forces must end within 60 days, unless Congress agrees to a longer involvement. At any time, Congress can end a commitment by the passage of a concurrent resolution (which is not subject to veto). The constitutionality of the War Powers Resolution remains in dispute.

SECTION 3 ASSESSMENT

Essential Questions Journal To continue to build a response to the chapter Essential Question, go to your **Essential Questions Journal.**

1. **Guiding Question** Use your completed concept web to answer this question: What tools are available to the President to implement foreign policy?

Key Terms and Comprehension

2. Describe the treaty-making process.
3. What is the difference between a **treaty** and an **executive agreement**?
4. What is the power of **recognition** and how can the President use it as a diplomatic tool?

5. Why did Congress enact the War Powers Resolution?

Critical Thinking

6. **Synthesize Information** Why can the military powers of the President be described as almost without limit?
7. **Demonstrate Reasoned Judgment** Do you think the War Powers Resolution is constitutional? Why or why not?

Quick Write

Persuasive Writing: Sequence Your Arguments Do you want to give the audience your strongest statement first or save it until the end? In order to sequence your arguments appropriately, you will need to determine the strength of each. Using your chart from Section 2, rank the arguments that support your thesis from strongest to weakest. Then, make an outline that shows where your arguments will appear in your essay.

SECTION 4

Legislative and Judicial Powers

Guiding Question

How can the President check the actions of the legislative and judicial branches? Use a flowchart like the one below to keep track of the checks the President has on the other branches.

Presidential Powers	
Checks on the Legislative Branch	**Checks on the Judicial Branch**
• • •	• • •

Political Dictionary

- pocket veto
- line-item veto
- reprieve
- pardon
- clemency
- commutation
- amnesty

Objectives

1. Explain the President's legislative powers and how they are an important part of the system of checks and balances.
2. Describe the President's major judicial powers.

Image Above: President Barack Obama discusses the financial bailout plan.

In *The Federalist* No. 51, James Madison analyzes the Constitution's elaborate system of checks and balances. Its "constant aim," he says, "is to divide and arrange the several [branches] in such a manner as that each may be a check on the other." And he adds, "the great security against a gradual concentration of the several powers in the same department consists in giving to those who administer each department the necessary constitutional means and personal motives to resist encroachments of the others. . . . "

The Constitution gives the President certain legislative and judicial powers. They are, in Madison's phrase, "the constitutional means" that make it possible for the President to check the actions of Congress or the federal courts.

Legislative Powers

The President's legislative powers, exercised in combination with a skillful playing of the roles of chief of party and chief citizen, have made the President, in effect, the nation's chief legislator. It is the President who initiates, suggests, and demands that Congress enact much of the major legislation that it produces. However, a President whose party controls both houses on Capitol Hill may have an easier time of it than one who faces a hostile Congress.

Recommending Legislation The Constitution says that the President

FROM THE CONSTITUTION

shall from time to time give to the Congress Information of the State of the Union, and recommend to their Consideration such Measures as he shall judge necessary and expedient. . . .

—Article II, Section 3

This provision gives the President what is often called the message power.

The chief executive regularly sends three major messages to Capitol Hill each year. The first is the State of the Union message, a speech almost always delivered in person to a joint session of Congress. The President's budget message and then the annual Economic Report soon follow. The President often sends the lawmakers a number of other messages on a wide range of topics.

The Veto Power

The Constitution says that "Every Bill" and "Every Order, Resolution, or Vote to which the Concurrence of the Senate and House of Representatives may be necessary (except on a question of Adjournment) shall be presented to the President."[10] Remember, the Constitution presents the President with four options once a measure has been approved by Congress.

First, he may sign the bill, making it law, which is what usually happens. Or he can veto the bill, and the measure must then be returned to Congress.[11] Congress can then override that veto, by a two-thirds vote in each of its two chambers, but it seldom does.

As a third option, the President may allow a bill to become law by not acting on it, neither signing nor vetoing it, within ten days (excluding Sundays). This rarely happens.

The fourth option, the **pocket veto,** can be used only at the end of a congressional session. If Congress adjourns within ten days (not counting Sundays) of sending a bill to the White House and the chief executive does not act on it, the measure dies.

The veto power is an exceedingly valuable tool in the President's dealings with the legislative branch. Even the mere *threat* of a veto can defeat a bill or, at the least, prompt changes in its provisions as it moves through the legislative mill. When the chief executive makes such a threat, congressional leaders must do the math: Can they find enough votes in both houses to overcome a presidential veto?

George Washington rejected only two measures in his eight years in the presidency, and for nearly seven decades his successors also used their veto pens infrequently. But from Andrew Johnson in the 1860s onward, most chief executives have been much more willing to reject measures.

---

10 Article I, Section 7, Clauses 2 and 3. Recall that, despite these words, joint resolutions proposing constitutional amendments and concurrent resolutions, which do not have the force of law, are not sent to the President.

11 *Veto,* from the Latin meaning "I forbid."

Signing Statements

From James Monroe in the 1820s to today, various Presidents have issued "signing statements" as they approved some measures. On occasion, those statements were used to point out constitutional or other problems the President saw in a newly enacted law. More often, the statements have been used to do such things as to direct the manner in which a new law is to be enforced.

President George W. Bush issued signing statements far more often than any of his predecessors, using them to question the constitutionality of more than 1,200 provisions in various measures he signed. In doing so, he claimed a power, on one hand, to refuse to enforce those provisions or, on the other, to interpret them "in a manner consistent with" his view of "the constitutional authority of the President." His critics claim that Mr. Bush, in effect, used these statements as a substitute for the veto power, deciding which new laws he would execute and how those laws would be interpreted and applied.

President Obama has rejected his predecessor's view of signing statements. He has said that he intends to use them sparingly, and in much the same way as earlier chief executives have used them.

The Line-Item Veto

If the President decides to veto a bill, he must reject the *entire* measure. He cannot veto only a portion of it.

Since Ulysses S. Grant's day, most Presidents have favored expanding the veto power to include a **line-item veto.** That is, they have sought the power to cancel out some provisions in a measure while approving others. Most often, those who have proposed this device would restrict its application to specific dollar amounts (line items) in spending bills enacted by Congress. Many supporters argue that the line-item veto would be a potent weapon against wasteful and unnecessary federal spending.

Opponents of the line-item veto have long argued that the move would bring a massive and dangerous shift of power from the legislative branch to the executive branch. To this point, efforts to persuade Congress to propose a line-item veto amendment to the Constitution have failed.

The Power of the Veto

When the President and the majority of Congress are of the same party, vetoes tend to be rare. They tend to be more frequent during periods of divided government. *Do you think the veto gives the President too much authority?*

GOVERNMENT ONLINE

For an interactive exploration and guided audio tour of presidential vetoes, visit **PearsonSuccessNet.com**

INTERACTIVE

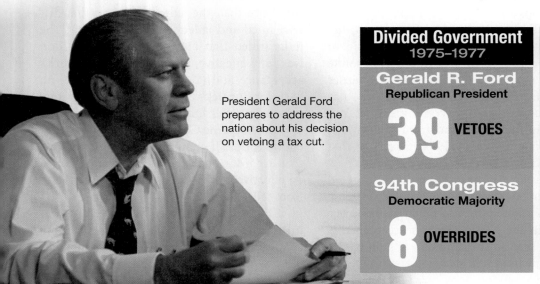

President Gerald Ford prepares to address the nation about his decision on vetoing a tax cut.

Divided Government 1975–1977	United Government 2005–2007
Gerald R. Ford Republican President	**George W. Bush** Republican President
39 VETOES	**1** VETO
94th Congress Democratic Majority	**109th Congress** Republican Majority
8 OVERRIDES	**0** OVERRIDES

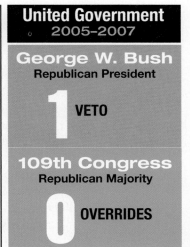

In 1996, Congress did pass a Line-Item Veto Act. The Supreme Court struck it down, however, holding that Congress lacked the power to give the President a line-item veto, *Clinton* v. *New York City*, 1998. If the chief executive is to have that authority, said the Court, it can come only as the result of an amendment to the Constitution.

Other Legislative Powers According to Article II, Section 3 of the Constitution, only the President can call Congress into special session. The fact that Congress is now in session through most of each year practically eliminates the likelihood of special sessions and also lessens the importance of the President's power to call one. Still, as Congress nears the end of a regular session, Presidents have sometimes found it useful to threaten a special session if lawmakers do not act on some particular measure. President Harry Truman called the most recent special session in 1948, in an effort to force Congress to consider anti-inflation and welfare measures in the post–World War II period.

The same constitutional provision also gives the chief executive the power to prorogue (adjourn) Congress in the event the two houses cannot agree on a date for their adjournment. That has never happened.

Judicial Powers

The Constitution gives the President the power to

> **FROM THE CONSTITUTION**
>
> . . . Grant Reprieves and Pardons for Offenses against the United States, except in Cases of Impeachment.
> —Article II, Section 2, Clause 1

A **reprieve** is the postponement of the execution of a sentence. A **pardon** is legal forgiveness of a crime.

The President's power to grant reprieves and pardons is <u>absolute</u>, except in cases of impeachment, where they may never be granted. These powers of **clemency** (mercy

✔ **Checkpoint**
How does a line-item veto differ from a regular veto?

absolute
adj. final, not subject to appeal

or leniency) may be used only in cases involving *federal* offenses.

Presidential pardons are usually granted after a person has been convicted in court. Yet the President may pardon a federal offender before that person is tried, or even before that person has been formally charged.

Pardons in advance of a trial or charge are rare. The most noteworthy pardon, by far, was granted in 1974. In that year, President Gerald Ford gave "a full, free and absolute pardon unto Richard Nixon for all offenses against the United States which he . . . has committed or may have committed or taken part in during the period from January 20, 1969, through August 9, 1974." Of course, that pardon referred to the Watergate scandal.

To be effective, a pardon must be accepted by the person to whom it is granted. When a pardon is granted prior to a charge or conviction, as in the Nixon case, its acceptance is regularly seen as an admission of guilt by the person to whom it is given.

Nearly all pardons are accepted, of course, and usually gratefully. A few have been rejected, however. One of the most dramatic refusals led to a Supreme Court case, *Burdick* v. *United States,* 1915. George Burdick, a New York newspaper editor, had refused to testify before a federal grand jury regarding the sources for certain news stories his paper had printed. Those stories reported fraud in the collection of customs duties. He invoked the 5th Amendment, claiming that his testimony could incriminate him.

President Woodrow Wilson then granted Burdick "a full and unconditional pardon for all offenses against the United States" that he might have committed in obtaining material for the news stories.

Interestingly, Burdick refused to accept the pardon, and he continued to refuse to testify. With that, the federal judge in that district fined and jailed him for contempt. The judge ruled that (1) the President's pardon was fully effective, with or without Burdick's acceptance and (2) there was, therefore, no basis for Burdick's continued claim of protection against self-incrimination.

The Supreme Court overturned the lower court's action. It unanimously upheld the rule that a pardon must be accepted in order to be effective, and it ordered Burdick's release from jail.

The pardoning power includes the power to grant conditional pardons, provided the conditions are reasonable. It also includes the power of **commutation,** or the power to reduce a fine or the length of a sentence imposed by a court.

The pardoning power also includes the power of **amnesty,** which is in effect a blanket pardon offered to a group of law violators. Thus, in 1893, President Benjamin Harrison issued a proclamation of amnesty forgiving all Mormons who had violated the antipolygamy (multiple marriage) laws in the federal territories. In 1977, President Jimmy Carter granted amnesty to Vietnam War draft evaders.

Essential Questions Journal	To continue to build a response to the chapter Essential Question, go to your **Essential Questions Journal.**

SECTION **4** ASSESSMENT

1. **Guiding Question** Use your completed flowchart to answer this question: How can the President check the actions of the legislative and judicial branches?

Key Terms and Comprehension

2. What is the purpose of issuing signing statements?

3. What is the **line-item veto** and why is it controversial?

4. Explain how these presidential judicial powers differ: **reprieve, pardon, clemency, commutation, amnesty.**

Critical Thinking

5. **Determine Relevance** How do the President's legislative and judicial powers serve the principle of checks and balances?

6. **Identify Central Issues** Why do you think the threat of a veto is an important presidential tool?

Quick Write

Persuasive Writing: Use Facts and Details To help build your case in your persuasive essay, you should have facts, statistics, quotations, and other details that support your thesis. Select the top three arguments you ranked in Section 3 and locate at least two specific details that you can use to support each of your arguments.

Quick Study Guide

GOVERNMENT ONLINE

On the Go
To review anytime, anywhere, download these online resources at **PearsonSuccessNet.com**
Political Dictionary, Audio Review

Guiding Question
Section 2 What are the executive powers and how were they established?

Guiding Question
Section 3 What tools are available to the President to implement foreign policy?

Guiding Question
Section 1 What factors have contributed to the growth of presidential power?

CHAPTER 14
Essential Question
How much power should the President have?

Guiding Question
Section 4 How can the President check the actions of the legislative and judicial branches?

Political Dictionary

Executive Article *p. 400*
imperial presidency *p. 403*
executive order *p. 406*
ordinance power *p. 406*
executive privilege *p. 409*
treaty *p. 412*
executive agreement *p. 413*
recognition *p. 414*
persona non grata *p. 414*
pocket veto *p. 418*
line-item veto *p. 418*
reprieve *p. 419*
pardon *p. 419*
clemency *p. 419*
commutation *p. 420*
amnesty *p. 420*

Diplomatic and Military Powers
- Make treaties and executive agreements
- Recognize other sovereign states
- Act as commander in chief of the armed forces

Legislative Powers
- Recommend legislation
- Veto legislation
- Call Congress into special session

Executive Powers
- Execute the law
- Direct the administration
- Appoint key officials
- Remove officials

Judicial Powers
- Grant reprieves
- Grant pardons
- Commute sentences
- Grant amnesty

The Powers of the President

Chapter Assessment

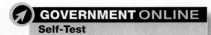
GOVERNMENT ONLINE
Self-Test
To test your understanding of key terms and main ideas, visit
PearsonSuccessNet.com

Comprehension and Critical Thinking

Section 1

1. **(a)** What were the two views of the presidency held by the Framers? **(b)** Which view did they finally choose? **(c)** Do you think the Framers' decision predetermined the nature of presidential power? Why?

2. **(a)** What factors have led to the growth of presidential power? **(b)** In what way have the people contributed to that growth? **(c)** How might this increased power affect the way voters view the qualifications of a President?

3. **Analyze Political Cartoons** How does this cartoon illustrate the presidential power controversy?

SEPARATION OF POWERS

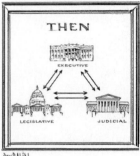

THEN

NOW

REXBABIN THE SACRAMENTO BEE

Section 2

4. **(a)** From what two sources in the Constitution does the President get the power to execute the law? **(b)** How can a President alter the substance of a law? **(c)** Do you think Congress gives the executive branch too much authority to interpret laws?

5. **(a)** What is an executive order and how is it related to the ordinance power? **(b)** How do we know that the Framers intended the President to have the ordinance power?

6. **(a)** What positions are filled by presidential appointment? **(b)** What positions are not? **(c)** Why do you think the Framers made this distinction?

Section 3

7. **(a)** What methods are available to the President to make agreements with foreign states? **(b)** Is it necessary to check the President's power to make international agreements?

8. **(a)** How does the President usually exercise the power of recognition? **(b)** How can the power be used as a weapon? **(c)** Why do you think it is important to other countries that they are recognized by the United States?

9. **(a)** What tools are available to the President as commander in chief? **(b)** How have they been limited?

Section 4

10. **(a)** What are the President's legislative powers? **(b)** What are the President's judicial powers? **(c)** How do these powers illustrate the principle of checks and balances?

11. **(a)** What is the difference between a veto and a line-item veto? **(b)** How would a line-item veto increase the President's legislative powers?

12. Why do you think the President's judicial powers are included in the Constitution?

Writing About Government

13. Use your Quick Write exercises from this chapter to write a persuasive essay regarding the debate on the extent of presidential powers. Make sure to state your position clearly in the introduction and support it with detailed arguments. See pp. S9–S10 in the Skills Handbook.

Apply What You've Learned

14. **Essential Question Activity** Take a survey of at least 10 voters (Democratic, Republican, and Independent) in your community. Ask:

   (a) Over the past decade do you think the President has overstepped his authority? If so, when?

   (b) Over the past decade do you think the President needed more authority? If so, when?

   (c) Over your lifetime, do you think the power of the President has changed? How?

15. **Essential Question Assessment** Use the results of your survey and the content of this chapter to write a paragraph that helps answer the Essential Question:

How much power should a President have? Then, as a group, work with your classmates to create a chart that consolidates the results of each survey. Using the completed chart and your prepared paragraph, discuss the Essential Question as a class and reflect on the variety of answers that arise in response to the query. Following the discussion, if you find your opinion has changed, revise your paragraph accordingly.

Essential Questions Journal	To respond to the chapter Essential Question, go to your **Essential Questions Journal**.

Document-Based Assessment

Presidential Signing Statements

Although the practice has been around since the mid 1800s, the use of presidential signing statements has recently become quite controversial. As these documents show, the already existing tensions between the executive and legislative branches have become more intense as they quarrel over the proper use of these statements.

Document 1

We are at a pivotal moment in our Nation's history, where Americans are faced with a President who makes sweeping claims for almost unchecked Executive power. One of the most troubling aspects of such claims is the President's unprecedented use of signing statements. Historically, these statements have served as public announcements containing comments from the President on the enactment of laws. But [the George W. Bush] Administration has taken what was otherwise a press release and transformed it into a proclamation stating which parts of the law the President will follow and which parts he will simply ignore. . . .

Under our constitutional system of government, when Congress passes a bill and the President signs it into law, that should be the end of the story. It is the law of the land unless and until repealed by Congress or invalidated by the courts. For this reason, there are grave and inherent dangers to the extensive and unprecedented use of signing statements.

When the President uses signing statements to unilaterally rewrite the laws enacted by the people's representatives in Congress, he creates doubt about what the rule of law means in our Nation.

—Senator Patrick Leahy (D., Vermont), 2006

Document 2

Presidential signing statements are . . . an essential part of the constitutional dialogue between the branches that has been a part of the etiquette of government since the early days of the Republic. . . . Many constitutional signing statements are an attempt to preserve the enduring balance between co-equal branches, but this preservation does not mean that the President will not enforce the provision as enacted. . . .

[S]igning statements do not diminish congressional power, because Congress has no power to enact unconstitutional laws. . . . [Also,] the statements do not augment presidential power. Where Congress, perhaps inadvertently, exceeds its own power in violation of the Constitution, the President is bound to defer to the Constitution. The President cannot adopt the provisions he prefers and ignore those he does not; he must execute the law as the Constitution requires. . . .

These statements are an established part of the President's responsibility to "take Care that the Laws be faithfully executed." Members of Congress and the President will occasionally disagree on a constitutional question. This disagreement does not relieve the President of the obligation to interpret and uphold the Constitution, but instead supports the candid public announcement of the President's views.

—Michelle E. Boardman, Deputy Assistant Attorney General, 2006

Use your knowledge of the controversy surrounding signing statements and Documents 1 and 2 to answer Questions 1–3.

1. How does each commentator cite the Constitution to his or her benefit?
   A. Both speakers claim signing statements are unconstitutional.
   B. Each speaker believes the Constitution supports signing statements.
   C. Each speaker uses it to defend his or her stance on the issue.
   D. Both take the Constitution out of context.

2. Why do you think a President would choose to approve a law with signing statements attached rather than vetoing the measure?

3. **Pull It Together** Do you think the use of signing statements follows the Framers' intention in Article II of the Constitution?

GOVERNMENT ONLINE
Documents
To find more primary sources on signing statements, visit
PearsonSuccessNet.com

Government at Work: The Bureaucracy

Essential Question
Is the bureaucracy essential to good government?

> **Bureaucracy is not an obstacle to democracy but an inevitable complement to it.**
>
> —Joseph A. Schumpeter, 1942

Photo: More than half of all income tax returns are filed electronically today; still, the IRS must deal with millions of pages of paperwork.

GOVERNMENT ONLINE
On the Go

To study anywhere, anytime, download these online resources at PearsonSuccessNet.com
• Political Dictionary
• Audio Review
• Downloadable Interactivities

425

The **Federal Bureaucracy**

Guiding Question

What is the structure and purpose of the federal bureaucracy? Use a chart like the one below to keep track of the main ideas about the federal bureaucracy.

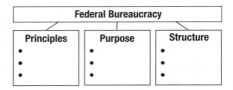

Political Dictionary

- bureaucracy
- bureaucrat
- administration
- staff agency
- line agency

Objectives

1. Define a bureaucracy.
2. Identify the major elements of the federal bureaucracy.
3. Explain how groups within the federal bureaucracy are named.
4. Describe the difference between a staff agency and a line agency.

Image Above: A Customs and Border Protection officer screens a passenger entering the United States.

The Federal Government is an immense organization. Its employees deliver the mail, regulate business practices, collect taxes, defend the nation, administer Social Security programs, manage the national forests, explore outer space, and do dozens of other things every day. Indeed, you cannot live through a single day without somehow encountering the federal bureaucracy.

What Is a Bureaucracy?

A **bureaucracy** is a large, complex administrative structure that handles the everyday business of an organization.[1] To many Americans, the word *bureaucracy* suggests such things as waste, red tape, and delay. While that image is not altogether unfounded, it is quite lopsided. Basically, bureaucracy is an efficient and an effective way to organize people (bureaucrats) to do work.

Bureaucracies are found wherever there are large organizations, in both the public and the private sectors of this country. Thus, the United States Air Force, McDonald's, the Social Security Administration, MTV, your city government, Yahoo!, the Boy Scouts of America, and the Roman Catholic Church are all bureaucracies. Even your school is a bureaucracy.

Three Features of a Bureaucracy By definition, a bureaucracy is a system of organization built on three principles: hierarchical authority, job specialization, and formalized rules.

Hierarchical authority. The word *hierarchical* describes any organization structured as a pyramid, with a chain of command running from the top of the pyramid on down to its base. The few officials and units at the top of the structure have authority over those officials and units at the larger middle level, who in turn direct the activities of the many at the bottom level.

Job specialization. Each **bureaucrat,** each person who works for the organization, has certain defined duties and responsibilities. There is, then, a precise division of labor within the organization.

---

1 The term *bureaucracy* is a combination of the French word *bureau,* which originally referred to the desk of a government official and later to the place where an official works, and the suffix *-cracy,* signifying a type of social structure.

Formalized rules. The bureaucracy does its work according to a number of established regulations and procedures. Those rules are set out in written form and so can be known by all who are involved in that work.

The Benefits of a Bureaucracy Those three features—hierarchical authority, job specialization, and formalized rules—make bureaucracy the most effective way for people to work together on large and complex tasks, whether public or private.

The hierarchy can speed action by reducing conflicts over who has the power and the appropriate authority to make decisions. The higher a person's rank in the organization, the greater the decision-making power he or she has.

Job specialization promotes efficiency because each person in the organization is required to focus on one particular job. Each worker thus gains a set of specialized skills and knowledge.

Formalized rules mean that workers can act with some speed and precision because decisions are based on a set of known standards, not on someone's likes, dislikes, or <u>inclinations.</u> Those rules also enable work to continue with little interruption even as some workers leave an organization and new workers are hired to replace them.

Recognize this very important point about public bureaucracies: their bureaucrats hold appointive offices. Bureaucrats are *unelected* makers and implementers of public policy. This is not to say that bureaucracies are undemocratic. However, in a democracy much depends on how effectively the bureaucracy is controlled by those whom the people do elect—the President and Congress. Listen to James Madison on the point:

PRIMARY SOURCE

In framing a government which is to be administered by men over men, the great difficulty lies in this: you must first enable the government to control the governed; and in the next place oblige it to control itself.
—*The Federalist* No. 51

▶▶ **Analyzing Political Cartoons** Although a bureaucracy may be the most effective governmental structure, the number of employees and time devoted to bureaucratic procedures are often criticized as a messy way to run the government. *How does this cartoon illustrate this point?*

The Federal Bureaucracy

The federal bureaucracy is all of the agencies, people, and procedures through which the Federal Government operates. It is the means by which the government makes and administers public policy—the sum of all of its decisions and actions. Nearly all of that huge bureaucracy is located in the executive branch. Not all of it, however, because both Congress and the federal court system are bureaucracies as well.

The Constitution makes the President the chief administrator of the Federal Government. Article II, Section 3 declares that "he shall take Care that the Laws be faithfully executed." But the Constitution makes only the barest mention of the administrative machinery through which the President is to exercise that power.

Article II does suggest executive departments by giving to the President the power to "require the Opinion, in writing, of the principal Officer in each of the executive Departments."[2]

Article II anticipates two departments in particular, one for military and one for

✔ **Checkpoint**
What are the benefits of the bureaucratic structure?

inclination
n. a tendency, preference, attitude

---

2 Article II, Section 2, Clause 1. There is also a reference to "Heads of Departments" in Clause 2, and to "any Department or Officer" of the government in Article I, Section 8, Clause 18.

foreign affairs. It does so by making the President the "Commander in Chief of the Army and Navy," and by giving the chief executive both the power to make treaties and to appoint "Ambassadors, other public Ministers, and Consuls."[3]

Beyond those references, the Constitution is silent on the organization of the executive branch. The Framers certainly intended that administrative agencies be created, however. They understood that no matter how wise the President and Congress, their decisions still had to be carried out in order to be effective. Without an **administration**—the government's many administrators and agencies—even the best policies would amount to just so many words and phrases. The President and Congress need millions of men and women to put policies into action in Washington, D.C., and in offices all around the country and the world.

The chief organizational feature of the federal bureaucracy is its division into areas of specialization. As you can see on the next page, the executive branch is composed of three broad groups of agencies: (1) the Executive Office of the President, (2) the 15 Cabinet departments, and (3) a large number of independent agencies.[4]

The Name Game

The titles given to the many units that make up the executive branch vary a great deal. The name *department* is reserved for agencies of Cabinet rank. Beyond the title of *department*, however, there is little <u>standardized</u> use of titles among the agencies.

The most commonly used titles for units in the executive branch include *agency, administration, commission, corporation, authority, bureau, service, office, branch,* and *division.*

The term *agency* is often used to refer to any governmental body. It is sometimes used to identify a major unit headed by

a single administrator of near-cabinet status, such as the Environmental Protection Agency. But so, too, is the title *administration;* for example, the National Aeronautics and Space Administration and the General Services Administration.

The name *commission* is usually given to agencies charged with the regulation of business activities, such as the Federal Communications Commission and the Securities and Exchange Commission. Top-ranking officers called commissioners head these units. The same title, however, is given to some investigative, advisory, and reporting bodies, including the U.S. Commission on Civil Rights and the Federal Election Commission.

Either *corporation* or *authority* is the title most often given to those agencies that conduct businesslike activities. Corporations and authorities are regularly headed by a board and a manager—as is the case with the Federal Deposit Insurance Corporation, the Commodity Credit Corporation, and the Tennessee Valley Authority.

Within each major agency, the same confusing lack of <u>uniformity</u> in the use of names is common. *Bureau* is the name often given to the major elements in a department, but *service, administration, office, branch,* and *division* are often used for the same purpose. For example, the major units within the Department of Justice include the Federal Bureau of Investigation, the United States Marshals Service, the Drug Enforcement Administration, the Office of the Pardon Attorney, the Criminal Division, and the National Drug Intelligence Center.

Many federal agencies are often referred to by their initials. The EPA, IRS, FBI, CIA, FCC, NASA, and TVA are but a few of the dozens of familiar examples we hear and read about every day.[5] A few are also known by nicknames. For example, the Government National Mortgage Association is often called "Ginnie Mae," and the National Railroad Passenger Corporation is better known to us as Amtrak.

uniformity
n. sameness, regularity

standardize
v. to set up according to a rule or model

---

3 Article II, Section 2, Clauses 1 and 2.

4 The chart is adapted from the current edition of the *United States Government Manual,* published each year by the Office of the Federal Register in the National Archives and Records Administration. The Manual includes a brief description of every agency in each of the three branches of the Federal Government. More than 580 of its now nearly 700 pages are devoted to the executive branch.

---

5 The use of acronyms can sometimes cause problems. When the old Bureau of the Budget was reorganized in 1970, it was also renamed. It is now the Office of Management and Budget (OMB). However, it was for a time slated to be known as the Bureau of Management and Budget (BOMB).

The Executive Branch

GOVERNMENT ONLINE

For an **interactive** exploration of several agencies in the executive branch, visit **PearsonSuccessNet.com**

INTERACTIVE

The executive branch of the Federal Government is composed of a large number of agencies, all of them created by act of Congress to execute the laws of the United States. Nearly 80 percent of all of the men and women who work for those agencies in fact work some place other than Washington, D.C. *Why do you think the executive branch makes up the majority of the federal bureaucracy?*

EXECUTIVE OFFICE
of the President

The Executive Office of the President is an umbrella agency composed of several sub-agencies staffed by the President's closest advisors and assistants.

- White House Office
- Office of the Vice President
- Council of Economic Advisers
- Council on Environmental Quality
- National Security Council
- Office of Administration
- Office of Management and Budget
- Office of National Drug Control Policy
- Office of Policy Development
- Office of Science and Technology Policy
- Office of the United States Trade Representative

EXECUTIVE
Departments

Often called the Cabinet departments, the executive departments and their subunits carry out much of the work of the Federal Government.

- Department of State
- Department of the Treasury
- Department of Defense
- Department of Justice
- Department of the Interior
- Department of Agriculture
- Department of Commerce
- Department of Labor
- Department of Health and Human Services
- Department of Housing and Urban Development
- Department of Transportation
- Department of Energy
- Department of Education
- Department of Veterans Affairs
- Department of Homeland Security

INDEPENDENT
Agencies*

These agencies are not attached to any of the Cabinet departments and exercise a wide range of responsibilities.

- Amtrak
- Central Intelligence Agency
- Consumer Product Safety Commission
- Environmental Protection Agency
- Equal Employment Opportunity Commission
- Farm Credit Administration
- Federal Communications Commission
- Federal Deposit Insurance Corporation
- Federal Election Commission
- Federal Reserve System
- Federal Trade Commission
- National Aeronautics and Space Administration
- National Endowment for the Arts
- National Labor Relations Board
- National Science Foundation
- National Transportation Safety Board
- Nuclear Regulatory Commission
- Office of Government Ethics
- Office of Personnel Management
- Peace Corps
- Securities and Exchange Commission
- Small Business Administration
- Social Security Administration
- Tennessee Valley Authority
- United States Postal Service

*The agencies listed are just a sampling of the more than 150 independent agencies.

✓ **Checkpoint**
How do staff agencies
differ from line agencies?

Staff and Line Agencies

The units that make up any administrative organization can be classified as either staff or line agencies. The Federal Government units are also described as such.

Staff agencies serve in a support capacity. They aid the chief executive and other administrators by offering advice and assistance in the management of the organization. **Line agencies,** on the other hand, actually perform the tasks for which the organization exists.

Congress and the President give the line agencies goals to meet, and the staff agencies help the line agencies meet these goals as effectively as possible through advising, budgeting, purchasing, management, and planning. The general public is much more aware of the work of line agencies than it is of that of most of the staff units. It is for a rather obvious reason: it is the line agencies that carry out public policies and, in doing so, deal directly with the public.

distinction
n. a difference between
two or more things

Two illustrations of the <u>distinction</u> here can be found in the several agencies that make up the Executive Office of the President and, in contrast, the Environmental Protection Agency. The agencies that make up the Executive Office of the President (the White House Office, the National Security Council, the Office of Management and Budget, and others, as you will see in the next section) each exist as staff support to the President. Their primary mission is to assist the President in the exercise of the executive power and in the overall management of the executive branch. They are not operating agencies. That is, they do not actually administer public programs.

The Environmental Protection Agency (EPA), on the other hand, has an altogether different mission. It is responsible for the day-to-day enforcement of the many antipollution laws Congress has enacted over the years. The EPA operates "on the line," where the action is.

This difference between staff agencies and line agencies can help you find your way through the complex federal bureaucracy. The distinction between the two can be oversimplified, however. For example, most line agencies do have staff units to aid them in their line operations. Thus, the Environmental Protection Agency's Office of Civil Rights is a staff unit. Its job is to ensure that the agency's personnel practices do not violate the Federal Government's antidiscrimination policies.

Essential Questions
Journal
To continue to build a response to the chapter Essential Question, go to your **Essential Questions Journal.**

SECTION **1** ASSESSMENT

1. **Guiding Question** Use your completed chart to answer this question: What is the structure and purpose of the federal bureaucracy?

Key Terms and Comprehension

2. Describe the three defining features of a **bureaucracy.**

3. List some of the more common names given to the various agencies in the executive branch.

4. What is the difference between a **staff agency** and a **line agency?**

Critical Thinking

5. **Analyze Information** Explain how the defining features of a bureaucracy both help and hurt the effectiveness and efficiency of the Federal Government.

6. **Categorize** Think of a bureaucracy that you encounter or work with on a regular basis, and identify each of the three major features of bureaucracies in that organization.

7. **Express Problems Clearly** The bureaucrats who carry out government policy are appointed, not elected. Does this mean that bureaucracies are, therefore, undemocratic? Why or why not?

Quick Write

Research Writing: Ask Questions
The numerous agencies that make up the federal bureaucracy administer public policy in a variety of fields. Think about subjects that you are interested in, for example, the economy, environment, defense, farming, transportation, or communication. Select the topic that interests you most. Then, write three questions that you would like to answer about the subject you selected as it relates to the Federal Government.

SECTION 2

Executive Office
of the President

Guiding Question

What agencies and advisors are part of the Executive Office of the President and what are their functions? Use a table like the one below to keep track of those units and their functions within the Executive Office of the President.

Executive Office of the President	
Agency	**Function**
•	•
•	•
•	•

Political Dictionary

- Executive Office of the President
- federal budget
- fiscal year
- domestic affairs

Objectives

1. Describe the Executive Office of the President.
2. Explain the duties of the White House Office, the National Security Council, and the Office of Management and Budget.
3. Identify the other agencies that make up the Executive Office of the President.

Image Above: President Barack Obama meets with his chief of staff Rahm Emanuel.

Thomas Jefferson performed his presidential duties with the help of two aides, one a messenger and the other his secretary. Like other early Presidents, he paid their salaries out of his own pocket. Indeed, Congress did not provide any money for presidential staff until 1857, when it gave President James Buchanan $2,500 for one clerk.

President Jefferson presided over an executive branch that employed, altogether, only some 2,100 people. The situation is remarkably different today. Approximately 2.7 million men and women work in the Obama administration. Two institutions—the Executive Office of the President and the President's Cabinet—are at the center of today's huge executive branch.

The Executive Office of the President

Every officer, every employee, and every agency in the executive branch of the Federal Government is legally subordinate to the President. They all exist to help the President—the chief executive—in the exercise of the executive power.

The President's right arm, however, is the **Executive Office of the President** (the EOP). The Executive Office of the President is, in fact, an umbrella agency, a complex organization of several separate agencies staffed by some 900 of the President's closest advisors and assistants.

President Franklin Roosevelt persuaded Congress to establish the Executive Office of the President in 1939. It has been reorganized in every administration since then, including the Obama Administration.

The White House Office

The nerve center of the Executive Office of the President—in fact, the nerve center of the entire executive branch of the Federal Government—is the White House Office. It houses much of the President's key personal and political staff.

The two wings on either side of the White House hold the offices of most of the President's staff. These employees occupy much of the crowded West Wing, which the public seldom sees and where the legendary Oval Office and the Cabinet Room are located.

✔ **Checkpoint**
What is the role of the
White House Office
staff?

inner circle
n. those most
influential, closest to
the center of power

The chief of staff to the President directs all of the operations of the White House Office and is among the most influential presidential aides. The counselor to the President and a number of senior advisors are also key members of the President's <u>inner circle.</u>

Several top officials work in the White House Office. A number of assistants and deputy assistants to the President aid the chief executive in such vital areas as foreign policy, defense, homeland security, the economy, political affairs, congressional relations, speech writing, and contacts with the news media and the public.

The staff of the White House Office also includes such major presidential aides as the press secretary, the appointments and scheduling assistant, and the President's physician. The first lady's very visible place in public life today is reflected by the fact that one of the assistants to the President serves as her chief of staff and one of the several deputy assistants is her press secretary.

Some 500 men and women now serve in the White House Office. The titles of some of the subunits they work for indicate the scope of their responsibilities: the Office of Energy and Climate Change Policy, the Homeland Security Council, the Office of Cabinet Affairs, and the Office of Public Liaison and Intergovernmental Affairs.

National Security Council

Most of the President's major steps in foreign affairs are taken in close consultation with the National Security Council (NSC). It meets at the President's call, often on short notice, to advise him in all domestic, foreign, and military matters that relate to the nation's security.

The President chairs the Council. Its other members include the Vice President and the secretaries of state, treasury, and defense. The Director of National Intelligence and the chairman of the Joint Chiefs of Staff regularly attend its meetings.

The NSC has a small staff of foreign and military policy experts. They work under the direction of the President's assistant for national security affairs, who is often called the President's national security advisor. The government's several intelligence agencies do much of their often super-secret work at the direction of the National Security Council.

The National Security Council is a staff agency. That is, its job is to advise the

The West Wing

The White House is a vast structure that includes two office buildings and the President's residence. The East and West wings extend from the residence and host key presidential aides and advisors. The President's closest advisors are located in the West Wing only steps away from the Oval Office. *Why is it important that these advisors be so close at hand?*

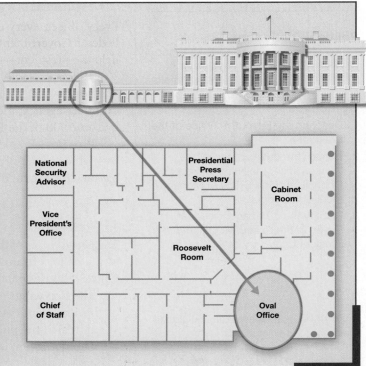

National Security Advisor

Vice President's Office

Chief of Staff

Presidential Press Secretary

Cabinet Room

Roosevelt Room

Oval Office

President in all matters affecting the nation's security. However, during the Reagan administration in the 1980s, the NSC's staff actually conducted a number of secret operations, including the sale of arms to Iran. The disclosure of the NSC's role in this sale led to the Iran-Contra scandal of the mid-1980s.

Office of Management and Budget

The Office of Management and Budget (OMB) is the largest and, after the White House Office, the most influential unit in the Executive Office. The OMB is headed by a director who is appointed by the President and confirmed by the Senate. The OMB's major task is the preparation of the federal budget, which the President must submit to Congress every year.

The **federal budget** is a very detailed estimate of receipts and expenditures, an anticipation of federal income and outgo, during the next fiscal year. A **fiscal year** is the 12-month period used by government and business for record keeping, budgeting, and other financial management purposes. The Federal Government's fiscal year runs from October 1 through September 30.

The budget is more than just a financial document. It is a plan—a carefully drawn, closely detailed work plan for the conduct of government. It is an annual statement of the public policies of the United States, expressed in dollar terms.

The creation of each fiscal year's budget is a lengthy process that begins more than a year before the start of the fiscal year for which it is intended. Each federal agency prepares detailed estimates of its spending needs for that 12-month period. The OMB reviews those proposals and gives agency officials the opportunity to defend their dollar requests. Following that agency-by-agency review, the revised (and usually lowered) spending estimates are fitted into the President's overall program before it is sent to Congress. The OMB then monitors the spending of the funds Congress appropriates.

Beyond its budget chores, the OMB is a sort of presidential "handy-man" agency. It

Federal Budget

How is the President's budget created?

The Office of Management and Budget must consider a variety of factors before it creates the President's final budget proposals. Detailed analyses of those elements help the OMB determine the appropriate level of funding for each agency. *Which of these factors might be the most difficult to quantify?*

What can the Government spend?
The OMB must estimate how much income, principally from taxes, the government will receive in an upcoming fiscal year. Much of that sum must be spent for purposes and at levels previously set by Congress (mandatory spending).

What do the People want?
The people expect the Federal Government to maintain existing programs. Only about 20 percent of all federal spending can be directed to expanding these programs and/or the creation of new ones (discretionary spending).

What does the President want?
Some spending has a higher priority in the give-and-take of the budget-making process than others—in particular, spending for those programs which are, for whatever reason, important to the President.

makes continuing studies of the organization and management of the executive branch and keeps the President up to date on the work of all its agencies. The OMB checks and clears agency stands on all legislative matters to make certain they agree with the President's policy positions. It also helps prepare the hundreds of executive orders the President must issue each year and the veto messages the chief executive occasionally sends to Congress.

Other EOP Agencies

The EOP's umbrella covers several other—and quite important—agencies. Each of those agencies provides essential staff help to the chief executive.

✔ **Checkpoint**
What are the duties of the Office of Management and Budget?

Office of National Drug Control Policy

The Office of National Drug Control Policy was established in 1988. It is headed by a director who is appointed by the President, with Senate approval. The Office prepares an annual national drug control strategy, which the President sends on to Congress. The director also coordinates the ongoing efforts of the more than 50 federal agencies that participate in the continuing war on drugs.

Council of Economic Advisers

Three of the country's leading economists, chosen by the President with Senate consent, make up the Council of Economic Advisers. The Council is the chief executive's major source of information and advice on the state of the nation's economy. It also helps the President prepare the annual Economic Report to Congress, which goes to Capitol Hill in late January or early February each year.

Other EOP Units

A number of other agencies in the Executive Office house key presidential aides. These men and women make it possible for the President to meet the many-sided responsibilities of the presidency.

The Domestic Policy Council advises the chief executive on all matters relating to the nation's **domestic affairs**—that is, all matters not directly connected to the realm of foreign affairs.

The Council on Environmental Quality aids the President in environmental policy and in writing the annual "state of the environment" report to Congress. It sees that federal agencies comply with presidential policy and the nation's environmental laws. The council's three members are appointed by the President, with the Senate's consent.

The Office of the Vice President houses the now more than fifty men and women who help the Vice President perform the duties of that office. The marked growth in the size of that staff in recent years illustrates the increase in the importance and political clout of the vice presidency.

The Office of United States Trade Representative advises the chief executive in all matters of foreign trade. The trade representative, appointed by the President and confirmed by the Senate, carries the rank of ambassador and represents the President in foreign trade negotiations.

The Office of Science and Technology Policy is the President's major advisor in all scientific, engineering, and other technological matters. Its director is drawn from the nation's scientific community.

The Office of Administration is the general housekeeping agency for all the other units in the Executive Office. It provides them with the many support services they must have in order to do their jobs.

| Essential Questions Journal | To continue to build a response to the chapter Essential Question, go to your **Essential Questions Journal.** |

SECTION 2 ASSESSMENT

1. **Guiding Question** Use your completed table to answer this question: What agencies and advisors are part of the Executive Office of the President and what are their functions?

Key Terms and Comprehension

2. Which agency in the **Executive Office of the President** has the largest impact on foreign affairs?

3. Describe the major duties of the **Office of Management and Budget.**

4. How can the **federal budget** be used to advance the President's policy agenda?

Critical Thinking

5. **Summarize** How does the White House Office help the President fulfill the role of chief administrator?

6. **Demonstrate Reasoned Judgment** Do you think that the number of agencies within the Executive Office of the President is too large, too small, or just right? Explain your answer.

7. **Draw Conclusions** Which particular agency in the executive branch do you think best illustrates the concept of checks and balances?

Quick Write

Research Writing: Gather Details When writing a research report, you should include facts, examples, and other information to help support your findings. Make a list of details related to the research topic you selected in the Quick Write of Section 1. Make sure to indicate how your topic is specific to a government agency, how the agency is organized, and what its responsibilities are.

SECTION 3

The Cabinet Departments

Guiding Question

What is the Cabinet and what does it do? Use a concept web like the one below to keep track of the supporting details about the Cabinet.

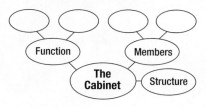

Political Dictionary

- executive department
- civilian
- secretary
- attorney general

Objectives

1. Describe the origin and work of the executive departments.
2. Explain how the members of the Cabinet are chosen.
3. Identify the role of the Cabinet in the President's decisions.

Image Above: The Bush Administration's Secretary of Agriculture Charles Kuperus (left) meets with a farmer in New Jersey.

In *The Federalist* No. 76, Alexander Hamilton declared that "the true test of a good government is its aptitude and tendency to produce a good administration." Given that comment, it seems strange that Hamilton and the other Framers of the Constitution spent so little time on the organization of the executive branch of the government they were creating. Instead, the machinery of federal administration has been built over time to meet the changing needs of the country.

Executive Departments

Much of the work of the Federal Government is done by the 15 **executive departments.** Often called the Cabinet departments, they employ nearly two-thirds of the Federal Government's **civilian,** or nonmilitary, workforce. They are the traditional units of federal administration, and each of them is built around some broad field of activity.

The First Congress created three of these departments in 1789: the Departments of State, Treasury, and War. As the size and the workload of the Federal Government grew, Congress added new departments (see chart on the following pages). Some of the newer ones took over various duties originally assigned to older departments, and gradually assumed new functions, as well. Over time, Congress has also created and later combined or abolished some departments.

Chief Officers and Staff Each department is headed by a **secretary,** except for the Department of Justice, whose work is directed by the **attorney general.** As you will see, these department heads serve in the President's Cabinet. Their duties as the chief officers of their specific department take up most of their time, however.

Each department head is the primary link between presidential policy and his or her own department. Just as importantly, each of them also strives to promote and protect his or her department with the White House, with Congress and its committees, with the rest of the federal bureaucracy, and with the media and the public.

The Executive Departments

Each of the now 15 executive departments was created by Congress. Their respective areas of responsibility generally reflect the conditions of the period and the major issues facing the nation when each of them was established. *What new department(s) do you think might be created in the 21st century?*

Industrial Era

Congress creates two new departments to address issues arising from industrialization and a growing economy.

Commerce 1903
- Founded as the Department of Commerce and Labor; separated in 1913
- Promotes international trade, economic growth, and technological development
- Grants patents and registers trademarks
- Conducts census

Federalist Era

At its first session following the adoption of the Constitution, Congress established four key departments in the executive branch.

State 1789
- Advises the President on foreign policy
- Negotiates agreements with foreign countries
- Represents the United States abroad and in international organizations

Defense 1789
- Founded as the National Military Establishment; renamed in 1949
- Provides military forces to deter war and protect the nation's security

Treasury 1789
- Produces coins and bills
- Borrows money and manages public debt
- Collects taxes

Justice 1789
- Founded as the Office of the Attorney General; renamed in 1870
- Prosecutes those accused of violating federal law
- Provides legal advice to the President
- Represents the United States in court
- Operates federal prisons

Expansion Era

As the United States expands to the west, two new departments are established to manage those lands and their use.

Interior 1849
- Manages public lands, wildlife refuges, and national parks
- Operates hydroelectric power plants
- Helps Native Americans manage their affairs

Agriculture 1889
- Assists farmers and ranchers
- Administers food stamp and school lunch programs
- Inspects food and ensures quality standards
- Manages national forests

Labor 1913
- Enforces federal laws on minimum wages, maximum hours, and safe working conditions
- Administers unemployment insurance and workers' compensation programs

---

multidimensional
adj. having several parts

An under secretary or deputy secretary and several assistant secretaries aid the secretary in his or her <u>multidimensional</u> role. These officials are also named by the President and confirmed by the Senate. Staff support for the secretary comes from assistants and aides with a wide range of titles in such areas as personnel, planning, legal advice, budgeting, and public relations.

Subunits Each department is made up of a number of subunits, both staff and line. Each of these subunits, or agencies, is usually further divided into smaller working units. Thus, the Criminal Division in the Department of Justice is composed of a number of sections, including, for example, the Counterterrorism Section and the Narcotics and Dangerous Drugs Section. Approximately 80 percent of the men and women who head the bureaus, divisions, and other major units within each of the executive departments are career people, not political appointees.

Many of the agencies in executive departments are structured geographically. Much of their work is done through regional and/or district offices, which, in turn, direct the activities of the agency's employees in the field. In fact, nearly 90 percent of all of the men and women who work as civilian employees of the Federal Government are stationed outside the nation's capital.

Postwar Era

Following World War II, the Cabinet expands to match the Federal Government's larger role in the nation's economy, social services, and education.

Health and Human Services **1953**
- Founded as the Department of Health, Education, and Welfare; separated and renamed in 1979
- Funds healthcare research programs
- Conducts programs to prevent and control disease
- Enforces pure foods and drug laws
- Administers Medicare and Medicaid

Housing and Urban Development **1965**
- Operates home-financing and public housing programs
- Enforces fair housing laws

Transportation **1967**
- Administers programs to promote and regulate highways, mass transit, railroads, waterways, air travel, and oil and gas pipelines
- Works with State and local levels on land, energy, resource, and technology programs

Energy **1977**
- Promotes production of renewable energy, fossil fuels, and nuclear energy
- Transmits and sells hydroelectric power
- Conducts nuclear weapons research and production

Education **1979**
- Administers federal aid to schools
- Ensures equal access to education
- Conducts educational research

Veterans Affairs **1989**
- Administers benefits, pensions, and medical programs for veterans of the armed forces
- Oversees military cemeteries

21st Century

The 9/11 attacks bring a new focus on national security and the newest executive department is established.

Homeland Security **2002**
- Ensures border and transportation security
- Develops emergency preparedness and response programs
- Safeguards national infrastructure and information systems

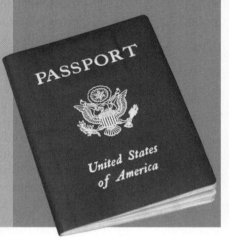

Take the Veterans Health Administration, part of the Department of Veterans Affairs, to illustrate the point. That administration does nearly all of its work providing medical care to eligible military veterans at some 150 medical centers, more than 800 outpatient clinics, and a large number of other facilities throughout the country.

The Executive Departments Today Today, the executive departments vary a great deal in terms of visibility, size, and importance. The Department of State is the oldest and the most prestigious department; but it is also among the smallest, with only some 25,000 employees. The Department of Defense is the largest, with nearly 700,000 civilian workers, and another 1.4 million men and women in the military services.

The Department of Health and Human Services has the largest budget; it accounts for just about a fourth of all federal spending each year. In contrast, the Department of Commerce has the smallest budget and contributes to less than one percent of all federal expenditures.

The Department of Homeland Security became the newest of the executive departments when Congress created it in 2002. The 15 departments, the dates they were established, and their principal functions are profiled in the chart above.

practical
adj. learned through practice or action

The Cabinet

The Cabinet is an informal advisory body brought together by the President to serve his needs. The Constitution makes no mention of this group of advisors, nor did Congress create it.[6] Instead, the Cabinet is the product of custom and usage.

At its first session in 1789, Congress established four top-level executive posts: secretary of state, secretary of the treasury, secretary of war, and attorney general. By his second term, President George Washington was regularly seeking the advice of the four outstanding people he had named to those offices: Thomas Jefferson (State), Alexander Hamilton (Treasury), Henry Knox (War), and Edmund Randolph (attorney general). So the Cabinet was born, and it has grown over time.

By tradition, the heads of the now 15 executive departments form the Cabinet. Each of the last several Presidents has regularly added a number of other top officials to the group, including the director of the Office of Management and Budget and the President's chief domestic policy advisor. The Vice President is a regular participant, and several other major figures usually attend Cabinet meetings—today, in particular, the counselor to the President, the White House chief of staff, the United States trade representative, the director of the Office of National Drug Control Policy, and the administrator of the Environmental Protection Agency.

Choosing Cabinet Members The President appoints the head of each of the 15 executive departments. Each of these appointments is subject to confirmation by the Senate, but rejections have been exceedingly rare. Of the more than 600 appointments made since 1789, only 12 have been rejected. The most recent rejection occurred in 1989, when the Senate refused to confirm President George H.W. Bush's selection of John Tower as secretary of defense.

---

6 The closest approach to it is in Article II, Section 2, Clause 1, where the President is given the power to "require the Opinion, in writing, of the principal Officer in each of the executive Departments, upon any Subject relating to the duties of their respective Offices." The Cabinet was first mentioned in an act of Congress in 1907, well over a century after its birth.

Many factors influence the President's Cabinet choices. Party is almost always important. Republican Presidents do not often pick Democrats, and vice versa. One or more of a new President's appointees invariably come from among those who played a major role in the recent presidential campaign.

Of course, professional qualifications and practical experience are also taken into account in the selection of Cabinet secretaries. Geography also plays a part. Each President tries to give some regional balance to the Cabinet. Thus, the secretary of the interior regularly comes from the West, where most of that department's wide-ranging work is carried out. The secretary of agriculture usually comes from one of the farm States in the Midwest and the secretary of housing and urban development often comes from one of the nation's major metropolitan centers.

Interest groups care about Cabinet appointments, and they influence some choices. The secretary of the treasury regularly comes out of the financial world, the secretary of commerce from the ranks of business, the secretary of education from among professional educators, the attorney general from the legal community, and so on.

Other considerations also guide the President's choices. Gender and race, management abilities and experience, and other personal characteristics—these and a host of other factors play a part in the process.

Today, a President makes Cabinet choices with an eye to racial, ethnic, and gender balance. But this has not always been the case. Thirty-one Presidents had named more than 300 Cabinet officers before Franklin Roosevelt appointed the first woman to that body: Frances T. ("Ma") Perkins, who served as secretary of labor from 1933 to 1945. In 1966, the first African American, Robert C. Weaver, was selected by Lyndon Johnson to head the Department of Housing and Urban Development. Ronald Reagan named the first Hispanic Cabinet officer, Lauro F. Cavazos, as secretary of education in 1988.

Barack Obama's Cabinet is quite diverse. It includes four women: Hillary Clinton as secretary of state, Janet Napolitano (Homeland Security), Hilda Solis (Labor), and Kathleen Sebelius (Health and Human Services).

Attorney General Eric Holder is the first African American to hold his post.

Two Hispanics sit in the Cabinet: Labor Secretary Solis and Kenneth Salazar, who heads the Interior Department. They are joined by three Asian Americans: Steven Chu (Energy), Gary Locke (Commerce), and Eric Shinseki (Veterans Affairs). The other six Cabinet officers are white males: Shaun Donovan (Housing and Urban Development), Arne Duncan (Education), Robert Gates (Defense), Timothy Geithner (Treasury), Ray LaHood (Transportation), and Tom Vilsack (Agriculture).

Four Obama Cabinet members served in Congress, two in the Senate and two in the House, and four were governors. Energy Secretary Chu is a Nobel Prize winner, in physics in 1997; and Veterans Affairs Secretary Shinseki is a retired four-star general and former Army Chief of Staff.

Defense Secretary Gates, a registered Independent, is a holdover from the Bush Cabinet; and Transportation Secretary LaHood is a former seven-term Republican member of the House of Representatives.

The Cabinet's Role Cabinet members have two major responsibilities. Individually, each is the administrative head of one of the executive departments. Collectively, they are advisors to the President.

Once a central <u>cog</u> in presidential government, the overall importance of the Cabinet has declined in recent years. Through much of our history, the Cabinet was a principal source of presidential advice. It met frequently, sometimes as often as twice a week, to offer counsel to the chief executive, and its influence could be seen in virtually all areas of public policy.

The growth of other presidential resources—particularly the vast amount of staff assistance centered in the Executive Office of the President—has <u>eclipsed</u> the Cabinet's role, however. Indeed, during his presidency, John Kennedy said that he could see no need to discuss, say, Defense Department matters with his secretaries of labor and agriculture, and he found Cabinet meetings to be "a waste of time."

Still, Presidents do continue to call Cabinet meetings, though certainly not nearly

✔ **Checkpoint**
What factors are considered when appointing executive department heads?

<u>cog</u>
n. part, element of an organization

<u>eclipse</u>
v. overshadow, surpass, outshine

President Barack Obama's Cabinet is remarkably different from that of the first such body, George Washington's Cabinet in 1789. **Why has the structure of the Cabinet changed over time?**

▲ President Franklin Roosevelt meets with Raymond Moley, a member of his "Brain Trust," in 1933. **Why might a President rely on the advice of people outside of the Cabinet?**

who was for it, declared: "Seven nays, one aye: the ayes have it."

William Howard Taft put the role of the President's Cabinet in its proper light nearly a century ago:

PRIMARY SOURCE

The Constitution . . . contains no suggestion of a meeting of all the department heads, in consultation over general governmental matters. The Cabinet is a mere creation of the President's will. . . . It exists only by custom. If the President desired to dispense with it, he could do so.

—William Howard Taft, *Our Chief Magistrate and His Powers*

as frequently as was once the case. More often than not, those sessions are held to do such things as show the administration's unified support for some particular presidential policy, rather than to thrash out the details of that matter. Cabinet members still do offer their advice—which need not be taken, of course—to the chief executive. President Abraham Lincoln once laid a proposition he favored before his seven-member Cabinet. Each member opposed it, whereupon Lincoln,

No President has ever suggested eliminating the Cabinet. However, several Presidents have leaned on other, unofficial advisory groups and sometimes depended upon them more heavily than on the Cabinet. Andrew Jackson began the practice when he became President in 1829. Several of his close friends often met with him in the kitchen at the White House and, inevitably, came to be known as the Kitchen Cabinet. Franklin Roosevelt's Brain Trust of the 1930s and Harry Truman's Cronies in the late 1940s were in the same mold.

Essential Questions Journal To continue to build a response to the chapter Essential Question, go to your **Essential Questions Journal.**

SECTION 3 ASSESSMENT

1. **Guiding Question** Use your completed concept web to answer this question: What is the Cabinet and what does it do?

Key Terms and Comprehension

2. How were the **executive departments** created?

3. (a) How are the executive department **secretaries** and **attorney general** selected? (b) What personal and professional factors are considered in the selection process?

4. How have various Presidents differed in their reliance on the Cabinet?

Critical Thinking

5. **Make Comparisons** Compare the Cabinet of today with the first Cabinet under President Washington. (a) How are the two alike? (b) How do they differ? (c) Why do you think the size of the Cabinet has grown since Washington's day?

6. **Synthesize Information** Why do you think it is important that the President select the heads of the executive departments?

Quick Write

Research Writing: Narrow Your Topic The Federal Government's involvement in the subject you selected in this chapter's Quick Writes can vary greatly. Create a concept web to help you narrow your topic to a more manageable focus. Write your subject in the middle circle, then identify subtopics in circles that link to the main subject. Include the details you have found in your research and generate specific ideas until you find a topic that is narrow enough to cover in a research paper.

SECTION 4

Independent Agencies

Guiding Question

What are the roles and structures of the independent agencies? Use a table like the one below to keep track of the distinctions among the three categories of independent agencies.

Federal Independent Agencies		
Executive	Regulatory	Corporation
•	•	•
•	•	•
•	•	•

Political Dictionary

- independent agency
- independent executive agency
- civil service
- patronage
- spoils system
- draft
- independent regulatory commission
- government corporation

Objectives

1. Explain why Congress has created the independent agencies.
2. Identify the characteristics of independent executive agencies.
3. Describe the history and formation of NASA, the OPM, and the Selective Service System.
4. Explain the structure and function of the independent regulatory commissions and government corporations.

Image Above: A Postal Service employee sorts through the day's mail.

Until the 1880s, nearly all that the Federal Government did was done through its Cabinet departments. Since then, however, Congress has created a large number of additional agencies—the **independent agencies**—located outside the departments. Today, they number more than 100. Some of the more important ones are included in the chart on page 447.

Several independent agencies administer programs similar to those of the Cabinet departments. The work of the National Aeronautics and Space Administration (NASA), for example, is similar to that of a number of agencies in the Department of Defense. NASA's responsibilities are also not very far removed from those of the Department of Transportation.

Neither the size of an independent agency's budget nor the number of its employees provides a good way to distinguish these agencies from the executive departments. Thus the Social Security Administration (SSA) is the largest of the independent agencies today. Only one Cabinet department, Health and Human Services, has a larger budget. The SSA now employs some 65,000 people—more than work for several Cabinet departments.

Why Independent Agencies?

The reasons these agencies exist outside of the Cabinet departments are nearly as many as the agencies themselves. A few major reasons stand out, however. Some have been set up outside the regular departmental structure simply because they do not fit well within any of the departments. The General Services Administration (GSA) is a leading example of the point.

The GSA is the Federal Government's major housekeeping agency. Its main chores include the construction and operation of public buildings, purchase and distribution of supplies and equipment, management of real property, and a host of similar services to most other federal agencies.

Congress has given some agencies, such as the Social Security Administration, the Federal Election Commission, and the U. S. Commission on Civil Rights, an independent status to protect them from the influence of both partisan and pressure politics. But, notice, this point can be turned on its head: Congress has located some of these agencies outside any of the Cabinet departments

✔️ **Checkpoint**
Why are some federal agencies considered independent agencies?

limelight
n. the focus of attention

catchall
n. all-inclusive, covering a wide range of possibilities

because that is exactly where certain special interest groups want them.

Some agencies were born as independents largely by accident. In short, no thought was given to the problems of administrative confusion when they were created. Finally, some agencies are independent because of the peculiar and sensitive nature of their functions. This is especially true of the independent regulatory commissions.

The label *independent agency* is really a catchall. Most of these agencies are independent only in the sense that they are not located within any of the 15 Cabinet departments. But they are not independent of the President and the executive branch. A handful of them are independent in a much more concrete way, however. For most purposes, they do lie outside the executive branch and are largely free of presidential control.

Perhaps the best way to understand all of these many independent agencies is to divide them into three main groups: (1) the independent executive agencies, (2) the independent regulatory commissions, and (3) the government corporations.

The Independent Executive Agencies

The **independent executive agencies** include most of the non-Cabinet agencies. Some are huge, with thousands of employees, multimillion-dollar or even multibillion-dollar budgets, and extremely important public tasks to perform.

The GSA, NASA, and the Environmental Protection Agency (EPA) are, for example, three of the largest of the independent executive agencies. They are organized much like the Cabinet departments: they are headed by a single administrator with subunits operating on a regional basis, and so on. The most important difference between these independent executive agencies and the 15 executive departments is simply in the fact that they do not have Cabinet status.

Some of these bureaucracies are not administrative or policy giants. But they do important work and they do sometimes attract public notice. The U. S. Commission on Civil Rights, the Peace Corps, the Small Business Administration, and the National Transportation Safety Board fall into that category.

Most independent executive agencies operate far from the limelight. They have few employees, comparatively small budgets, and rarely attract any attention. The American Battle Monuments Commission, the Citizens' Stamp Advisory Committee, and the National Indian Gaming Commission are typical of the dozens of these seldom seen or heard public bodies.

Neither the scope nor the importance of the many tasks performed by a number of these independent bureaucracies can be overstated. To make the point, take a quick look at three specific examples.

NASA The National Aeronautics and Space Administration (NASA) was created by Congress in 1958 to handle this nation's space programs. Today, the scope of those programs is truly astounding. NASA's work ranges from basic scientific research focusing on the origin, evolution, and structure of the universe, to ongoing explorations of outer space.

The military importance of NASA's work can hardly be exaggerated. Still, Congress has directed the space agency to bend its efforts "to peaceful purposes for the benefit of all humankind," as well. Its wide-ranging research and development efforts have opened new frontiers in a great many areas: in astronomy, physics, and the environmental sciences; in communication, medicine, and weather forecasting; and many more. Many scientific advances, pioneered by NASA, have been put to productive use in the civilian realm.

In the 1980s, NASA developed the space shuttle program wherein ships were reused for regular space flights in an effort to conduct research more efficiently. This and other NASA programs were so successful that its space flight and other extraterrestrial projects became routine and attracted little public notice. However, NASA's space activities were put on hold for several years following the shocking and tragic explosions of the shuttle *Challenger* in 1986 and then the shuttle *Columbia* in 2003.

Today, the shuttle delivers personnel and supplies to the international space station.

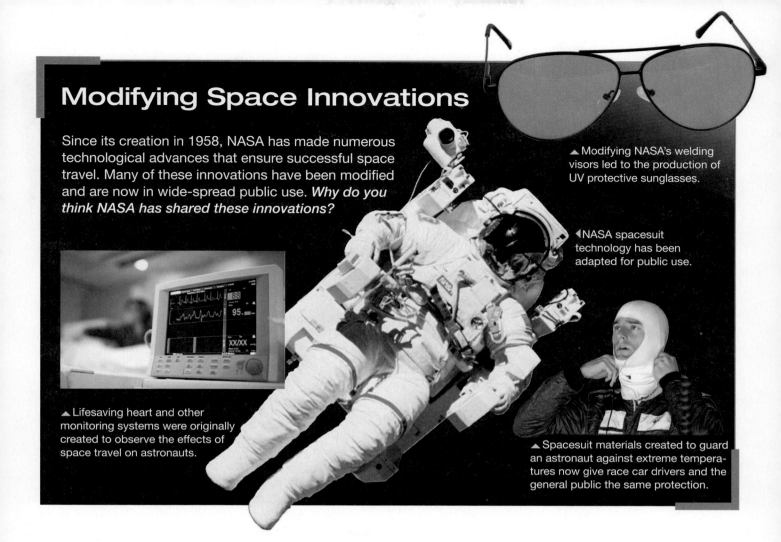

Modifying Space Innovations

Since its creation in 1958, NASA has made numerous technological advances that ensure successful space travel. Many of these innovations have been modified and are now in wide-spread public use. *Why do you think NASA has shared these innovations?*

▲ Modifying NASA's welding visors led to the production of UV protective sunglasses.

◀ NASA spacesuit technology has been adapted for public use.

▲ Lifesaving heart and other monitoring systems were originally created to observe the effects of space travel on astronauts.

▲ Spacesuit materials created to guard an astronaut against extreme temperatures now give race car drivers and the general public the same protection.

This permanently occupied station now tops NASA's to-do list. Rotating three-member international crews have lived aboard the outpost since late 2000. By 2020, in addition to the completion of this advanced research laboratory in space, NASA plans to have more robotic missions exploring Mars and other planets in the solar system and eventually return to the moon as well.

The Office of Personnel Management (OPM) The Federal Government is the nation's largest employer. Nearly 2.7 million civilians now work for Uncle Sam (and, recall, another 1.4 million men and women serve in the military today). While many people tend to stereotype all civilian employees as "faceless paper-pushers," they are, in fact, a quite diverse lot. Their ranks include computer programmers, forest rangers, electricians, chemists, physicists, FBI agents, security guards, engineers, librarians, truck drivers, botanists,

and men and women in literally hundreds of other occupations.

Most of the civilians who work for the Federal Government are members of the **civil service.** That is, they are career employees who were hired, and who are paid and promoted, in accord with acts of Congress administered by an independent agency, the Office of Personnel Management.

The History of the Civil Service For most of the first century following the adoption of the Constitution, federal employees were hired according to the **patronage** system—the practice of dispensing jobs, contracts, and other favors of government to political supporters and friends. That practice is often known, too, as the **spoils system.** The phrase comes from a comment on the floor of the Senate in 1832. Senator William Learned Marcy of New York, defending President Andrew Jackson's appointment of an

✔ **Checkpoint**
Who makes up the civil service?

stereotype
v. to regard or classify some persons or things in an oversimplified way

Careers in the Civil Service

Contrary to what many think, the civil service has a great variety of career opportunities in a wide range of fields. *With such variety in its workforce, why is working for the civil service often negatively stereotyped as paper-pushing?*

The National Zoo's chief veterinarian treats a baby panda. ▶

▲ A Department of Water Resources surveyor measures the mountain snow pack in California.

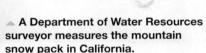

▲ A diver from the National Oceanic and Atmospheric Administration marks a marine sanctuary.

✔ Checkpoint

Why was there a push to reform the civil service in the 1800s?

ambassador, declared: "To the victor belongs the spoils of the enemy."

Every change of administration brought a new round of patronage-based rewards and punishments. Inefficiency, even corruption, became the order of the day. Huge profits were made on public contracts, at the people's expense. Political power became centered in officeholders and others who owed their livelihoods to the party in power. Able people, in and out of government, pressed for reform, but little came of their efforts.

Unfortunately, it was a tragedy that at last brought about fundamental changes in the hiring and other staffing practices of the Federal Government. In 1881, President James Garfield was fatally shot by a disappointed office-seeker, Charles J. Guiteau. Garfield had rejected the mentally unstable Guiteau's request that he be appointed to a high diplomatic post. The nation was horrified and outraged. Congress, pushed hard by Garfield's successor, Chester Arthur, passed the Pendleton Act—the Civil Service Act of 1883.

The Pendleton Act laid the foundation for the present federal civil service system. Its main purpose was to make merit—the quality of one's work—the basis for hiring, promotion, and other personnel actions in the federal workforce.

The law set up two categories of employment in the executive branch: the classified and the unclassified services. All hiring for positions in the classified service was to be based on merit. That quality was to be measured by "practical" examinations given by an independent agency, the Civil Service Commission (since 1978, the OPM).

The Pendleton Act placed only about 10 percent of the Federal Government's then 130,000 employees in the classified service; it did give the President the power to extend that coverage, however. Theodore Roosevelt championed the merit system, and by the end of his term in 1909 the classified umbrella covered two thirds of the federal workforce. Today, nearly 90 percent of all of the men and women who work for executive branch agencies are covered by the merit system.[7]

The Civil Service Today The first goal of civil service reform—the elimination of the spoils system—was largely achieved in the early years of the last century. Gradually, a new purpose emerged: recruiting and keeping the

---

7 This number does not take into account employees of the United States Postal Service and a few other federal agencies. The Postal Service is the largest agency not covered by the civil service system. It is the only federal agency in which employment policies are set by collective bargaining and labor union contracts.

best available people in the federal workforce. On the whole, efforts to reach that newer goal have succeeded. Today, most federal employees are hired through a competitive process. They are paid and promoted on the basis of written evaluations by their superiors. They are generally protected from disciplinary actions or dismissal for partisan reasons.

Still, the federal civil service is not perfect. Critics often claim that not enough attention is paid to merit in the merit system. Another independent agency, the Merit Systems Protection Board, actually enforces the merit principle in the federal bureaucracy. The Board is bipartisan—that is, its five members, appointed by the President and Senate, must include members of both major political parties. It hears appeals from those federal workers who have complaints about personnel actions—for example, denials of pay increases, demotions, or firings.

The Selective Service System Through most of our history, the nation's armed forces have depended on voluntary enlistments to fill their ranks. From 1940 to 1973, however, the **draft**—also called conscription, or compulsory military service—was a major source of military manpower.

Conscription has a long history in this country. Several colonies and later nine States required all able-bodied males to serve in their militia. However, in the 1790s, Congress rejected proposals for national compulsory military service.

Both the North and the South did use limited conscription programs during the Civil War. It was not until 1917, however, that a national draft was first used in this country, even in wartime. More than 2.8 million of the 4.7 million men who served in World War I were drafted under the terms of the Selective Service Act of 1917.

The nation's first peacetime draft came with the Selective Training and Service Act of 1940, as World War II raged in Europe but before the United States entered the war. Eventually, more than 10 million of the 16.3 million Americans in uniform during World War II entered the service under that law.

The World War II draft ended in 1947. The crises of the postwar period, however,

quickly moved Congress to revive the draft, which was reestablished by the Selective Service Act of 1948. From 1948 through 1973, nearly 5 million young men were drafted.

Mounting criticisms of compulsory military service, fed by opposition to our Vietnam policy, led many Americans to call for an end to the draft in the late 1960s. By 1972, fewer than 30,000 men were being drafted per year, and selective service was suspended in 1973. Nevertheless, the draft law is still on the books, and is administered by an independent agency, the Selective Service System.

The draft law places a military obligation on all males in the United States between the ages of 18 and 26. During the years in which the draft operated, it was largely conducted through hundreds of local selective service boards. All young men had to register for service at age 18. The local boards then selected those who were to enter the armed forces.

In 1980, President Jimmy Carter reactivated the registration requirement, and his executive order is still in force. All young males are required to sign up soon after they reach their 18th birthday. However, the President's power to order the actual <u>induction</u> of men into the armed forces expired on June 30, 1973. If the draft is ever to be reactivated, Congress must first renew that presidential authority. **8**

Independent Regulatory Commissions

The **independent regulatory commissions** stand out among the independent agencies because they are largely beyond the reach of presidential direction and control. There are eleven of these agencies today, each created to regulate—monitor, police—important aspects of the nation's economy. Their vital statistics appear in the table on page 447.

Structured for Independence The independent regulatory commissions' large measure of independence from the White House comes mainly from the way in which Congress has structured them. Each is headed by a board

induction
n. the process of installing somebody into military service

---

8 The Supreme Court upheld the constitutionality of the draft in the *Selective Draft Law Cases* in 1918. The Court also found its all-male features constitutional in *Rostker* v. *Goldberg* in 1981.

stagger
v. to arrange something so that it does not occur at the same time

or commission made up of five to seven members appointed by the President with Senate consent; and those officials have terms of such length that it is unlikely a President will gain control over any of these agencies through the appointment process, at least not in a single presidential term.

Several other features of these boards and commissions put them beyond the reach of presidential control. No more than a bare majority of the members of each board or commission may belong to the same political party. Thus, several of those officers must belong to the party out of power.

Moreover, the appointed terms of the members are <u>staggered</u> so that the term of only one member on each board or commission expires in any one year. In addition, the officers of five of these agencies can be removed by the President only for those causes Congress has specified.[9]

As with the other independent agencies, the regulatory commissions are executive bodies. That is, Congress has given them the power to administer the programs for which they were created. However, unlike other independent agencies, the regulatory commissions are also quasi-legislative and quasi-judicial bodies.[10] That is, Congress has also given these agencies certain legislative-like and judicial-like powers.

These agencies exercise their quasi-legislative powers when they make rules and regulations. Those rules and regulations have the force of law. They implement and spell out the details of the laws that Congress has directed these regulatory bodies to enforce.

To illustrate the point: Congress has said that those who want to borrow money by issuing stocks, bonds, or other securities must provide a "full and fair disclosure" of all pertinent information to prospective investors. The Securities and Exchange Commission (SEC) makes that requirement effective and indicates how those who offer securities are to meet it by issuing rules and regulations.

The regulatory commissions exercise their quasi-judicial powers when they decide disputes in those fields in which Congress has given them policing authority. For example, if an investor in Iowa thinks a local stockbroker has cheated him, he may file a complaint with the SEC's regional office in Chicago. SEC agents will investigate and report their findings, and the agency will judge the merits of the complaint much as a court would do. Decisions made by the SEC, and by the other independent regulatory bodies, can be appealed to the United States courts of appeals.

In a sense, Congress has created these agencies to act in its place. Congress could hold hearings and set interest rates, license radio and TV stations and nuclear reactors, check on business practices, and do the many other things it has directed the regulatory commissions to do. These activities are complex and time-consuming, however, and they demand constant and expert attention. If Congress were to do all of this work, it would have no time for its other and important legislative work.

Note that these regulatory bodies possess all three of the basic governmental powers: executive, legislative, and judicial. They are, then, exceptions to the principle of separation of powers. Technically, they should not be grouped with the other independent agencies. Instead, they should, somehow, be located somewhere between the executive and legislative branches, and between the executive and judicial branches, as well.

Rethinking Regulation Several authorities, and most recent Presidents, have urged that at least some of the administrative functions of the independent regulatory bodies be given to executive department agencies. Critics have raised other serious questions about these regulatory commissions and many think that they should be either abolished or, at the least, redesigned.

The most troubling questions are these: Have some of the regulatory commissions been unduly influenced by the special interests they are expected to regulate? Are all of the many and detailed rules created by these agencies really needed? Do some of those regulations have the effect of stifling

---

9 Recall the Supreme Court's holding in *Humphrey's Executor v. United States,* 1935. Congress has provided that the members of six of these bodies (the SEC, FCC, EEOC, CPSC, NRC, and CFTC) can be removed at the President's discretion.

10 The prefix *quasi-* is from the Latin, meaning "in a certain sense, resembling, seemingly."

GOVERNMENT ONLINE
Audio Tour
Listen to a guided tour about the regulatory commissions at
PearsonSuccessNet.com

Regulatory Commissions

The focus of the independent regulatory commissions is to ensure the stability of the nation's economy. Eleven federal agencies have been established to set and enforce standards on financial markets, employment, business practices, and public safety. *Should the government regulate these industries?*

Protecting
Financial Security

Federal Reserve System (The FED) est. 1913 Formulates and administers the nation's credit and monetary policy by regulating the money supply, influencing the availability of credit, and supervising banking system practices.

The Fed regulates the amount of money in circulation.

Securities and Exchange Commission (SEC) 1934 Regulates securities and other financial markets, investment companies, and brokers to ensure fair and honest transactions.

Commodity Futures Trading Commission 1974 Protects investors from fraud and improper practices related to the sale of commodity futures. Its regulations encourage sound markets and competition as well as ensure market integrity.

Equality in the workplace is enforced by the EEOC.

Ensuring
Workplace Equality

National Labor Relations Board (NLRB) 1935 Administers federal laws on labor-management and is responsible for the prevention or remedy of unfair labor practices by employers and unions.

Equal Employment Opportunity Commission (EEOC) 1964 Enforces laws prohibiting discrimination based on race, color, religion, sex, national origin, disability, or age in employment.

Securing
Business Integrity

Federal Trade Commission (FTC) 1914 Ensures consumer welfare and protects competition by regulating pricing, preventing monopolies and false advertising, stopping fraud, and protecting consumers from unfair business practices.

Federal Communications Commission (FCC) 1934 Regulates interstate and foreign communications by radio, television, wire, satellite, and cable while ensuring reasonable rates.

Federal Maritime Commission 1936 Regulates the foreign and domestic ocean-borne commerce by monitoring shipping companies, tariffs, and services to ensure compliance and fairness.

Federal Energy Regulatory Commission 1977 Regulates the transport and sale of electricity, natural gas, and oil by pipeline, licenses hydroelectric power projects, and oversees environmental issues related to energy resources.

Guarding
Public Safety

The NRC regulates the means used to store nuclear waste.

Consumer Product Safety Commission 1972 Regulates consumer products in order to protect the public from risks of injury from those products by requiring corrective action to items already on the market, establishing labeling standards, and advising the public of product recalls.

Nuclear Regulatory Commission (NRC) 1974 Licenses, regulates the use of nuclear energy to protect public health, safety, and the environment; sets rules and standards for nuclear reactors, facilities, and waste materials.

Workplace disputes are settled by the NLRB.

▶▶ **Analyzing Political Cartoons** Red tape is a term often used to describe a perceived excess of bureaucratic rules, complicated procedures, and unnecessary paperwork. *How does the use of this term convey the cartoonist's attitude toward government regulations?*

✔ **Checkpoint**
Who is ultimately responsible for regulatory agency reform?

legitimate competition in the free enterprise system? Do some of them add unreasonably to the costs of doing business and therefore to the prices that consumers must pay?

Congress sets the basic policies of the regulatory agencies, and so it has a major responsibility to answer these questions. It has responded to some questions in recent years, particularly by deregulating much of the nation's transportation industry. Airlines, bus companies, truckers, and railroads have greater freedom to operate today than they did only a few years ago. The same trend can be seen in the field of communications, notably with regard to cable television.

Two major regulatory bodies have actually disappeared in recent years. The Civil Aeronautics Board was created in 1938 to oversee commercial air traffic in the United States. For decades it assigned the routes to be flown and the rates charged by airlines and other commercial air carriers, until it was abolished by Congress in 1985.

The Interstate Commerce Commission was the very first of the regulatory commissions to be established by Congress, in 1887. For a century it issued licenses and regulated the rates and routes and most other aspects of commercial transportation by rail, highway, and water. It, too, was abolished by Congress, in 1996.

Government Corporations

A number of independent agencies are **government corporations.** They, too, are located within the vast executive branch and are subject to the presidential direction and control. Unlike the other independent agencies, however, they were set up by Congress to carry out certain businesslike activities.

Congress established the first government corporation when it chartered the Bank of the United States in 1791. However, government corporations were little used until World War I and then the Great Depression. In both periods Congress set up dozens of corporations to carry out emergency programs. Several still exist—among them, the Federal Deposit Insurance Corporation (FDIC), which insures bank deposits, and the Export-Import Bank of the United States (Eximbank), which makes loans to help the export and sale of American goods abroad.

There are now more than 50 of these corporations. They do such things as deliver the mail (the U.S. Postal Service); provide intercity rail passenger service (the National Railroad Passenger Corporation, Amtrak); protect pension benefits (the Pension Benefit Guaranty Corporation); and generate, sell, and distribute electric power (the Tennessee Valley Authority). [11]

Government v. Private Corporations The typical government corporation is set up much like a corporation in the private sector. It is run by a board of directors, with a general manager who directs the corporation's operations according to the policies laid

---

[11] State and local governments maintain their own government corporations, most often called authorities, to operate airports, turnpikes, seaports, power plants, liquor stores, and housing developments, and to conduct many other corporate activities. The Port Authority of New York and New Jersey is one of the best known.

down by the board. Most government corporations produce income that is plowed back into the business.

There are several differences between government and private corporations, however. Congress decides the purpose for which the public agencies exist and the functions they perform. Their officers are public officers; in fact, all who work for these corporations are public employees. The President selects most of the top officers of government corporations with Senate approval.

In addition, these public agencies are financed by public funds appropriated by Congress, not by private investors. The Federal Government, representing the American people, owns the stock.

The advantage most often claimed for these agencies is their flexibility. It is said that the government corporation, freed from the controls of regular departmental organization, can carry on its activities with the incentive, efficiency, and ability to experiment that make many private concerns successful. Whether that claim is valid or not is open to question. At the very least, it raises this complex issue: Is a public corporation's need for flexibility compatible with the basic democratic requirement that all public agencies be held responsible and accountable to the people?

Degrees of Independence The degree of independence and flexibility government corporations have varies considerably. In fact, some corporations are not independent at all. They are attached to an executive department.

The Commodity Credit Corporation (CCC), for example, is the government's major crop-loan and farm-subsidy agency. It is located within the Department of Agriculture, and the secretary of agriculture chairs its seven-member board. The CCC carries out most of its functions through a line agency in the Department of Agriculture—the Farm Service Agency—which is also subject to the direct control of the secretary.

Some corporations do have considerable independence, however. The Tennessee Valley Authority (TVA) is a case in point. It operates under a statute that gives it considerable discretion over its own programs. Although its budget is subject to review by the OMB, the President, and Congress, the TVA has a large say in the uses of the income its several operations produce.[12]

---

12 Congress established the TVA in the Tennessee Valley Authority Act of 1933. Its operations include electric power, flood control, reforestation, soil conservation, agricultural research, recreational facilities, and the promotion of industrial growth. The TVA's power program is self-supporting. Much of its other activities are supported by Congress.

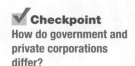

✔ **Checkpoint**
How do government and private corporations differ?

SECTION 4 ASSESSMENT

Essential Questions
Journal
To continue to build a response to the chapter Essential Question, go to your **Essential Questions Journal.**

1. **Guiding Question** Use your completed table to answer this question: What are the roles and structures of the independent agencies?

Key Terms and Comprehension

2. Why has Congress created **independent agencies?**

3. What was the **spoils system** and what replaced it?

4. How do **independent regulatory commissions** differ from the many other independent agencies?

5. **(a)** How are **government corporations** similar to private corporations? **(b)** How are they different?

Critical Thinking

6. **Identify Central Issues** Why do you think Congress purposefully structured a few independent agencies so that they are largely beyond the control of the President?

7. **Draw Conclusions** Why do you think special interest groups become involved in the structure and function of independent agencies?

Quick Write

Research Writing: Develop a Thesis A thesis statement summarizes the main idea of your research paper. Use the research you gathered and the activities you have completed for this chapter's Quick Writes and look for an idea that can be supported by the information you found. Determine how the details are related and decide on the idea that best summarizes your research. Then, write a sentence that sums up the main idea on which you will focus your paper.

The Size of Government

▶▶ Track the Issue

The Constitution makes no provisions for federal involvement in education, but in the last few decades, the Federal Government has taken an increasingly larger role in funding and supervising local schools.

1787

Thomas Jefferson argues that a democratic state must educate its citizens in order to survive.

1865

Congress establishes the Freedmen's Bureau that builds over 1,000 schools for newly freed black Americans.

1958

In response to the Soviet Union's successful launch of the Sputnik satellite, the National Defense Education Act funds math and science education in local public schools.

1979

Congress creates the Department of Education to oversee federal funding of educational programs.

2002

The No Child Left Behind Act gives the Federal Government unprecedented influence over local schools.

President George W. Bush promotes his education reforms. ▼

▶▶ Perspectives

The issue of federal involvement in schools is closely related to the larger question of the size and purpose of the Federal Government. People who favor a government with a more limited scope often point to agencies like the Department of Education as an example of unnecessary "big government" policies. However, others believe that the Federal Government has an important role to play in education.

"Our goal is nothing less than a renaissance in American education, begun by returning its control to parents, teachers, [and] local school boards. . . . The federal government has no constitutional authority to be involved in school curricula. . . . That is why we will abolish the Department of Education [and] end federal meddling in our schools. . . . We further urge that federal attempts to impose outcome- or performance-based education on local schools be ended."

—*1996 Republican Party platform*

"The quality of our public schools directly affects us all. . . . Yet too many children in America are segregated by low expectations, illiteracy, and self-doubt. . . . The federal government is partly at fault for tolerating these abysmal results. The federal government currently does not do enough to reward success and sanction failure in our educational system. [These reforms] address a general vision for . . . linking federal dollars to specific performance goals to ensure improved results."

—*President George W. Bush on the No Child Left Behind Act 2002*

▶▶ Connect to Your World

1. **Understand (a)** What role did the Republican Party suggest the Federal Government should play in education? **(b)** What issues did President Bush think governmental involvement could solve?
2. **Compare and Contrast (a)** Why did the 1996 Republican Party platform seek to limit federal involvement? **(b)** Why did President Bush suggest that it get more involved? **(c)** With which position do you agree? Why?

GOVERNMENT ONLINE

In the News

For updates about education and the Federal Government visit **PearsonSuccessNet.com**

Quick Study Guide

GOVERNMENT ONLINE
On the Go
To review anytime, anywhere, download these online resources at **PearsonSuccessNet.com**
Political Dictionary, Audio Review

CHAPTER **15**

Guiding Question
Section 2 What agencies and advisors are part of the Executive Office of the President and what are their functions?

Guiding Question
Section 3 What is the Cabinet and what does it do?

Guiding Question
Section 1 What is the structure and purpose of the federal bureaucracy?

CHAPTER 15
Essential Question
Is the bureaucracy essential to good government?

Guiding Question
Section 4 What are the roles and structures of the independent agencies?

Political Dictionary

bureaucracy *p. 426*
bureaucrat *p. 426*
administration *p.428*
staff agency *p. 430*
line agency *p. 430*
Executive Office of the President *p. 431*
federal budget *p. 433*
fiscal year *p. 433*
domestic affairs *p. 434*
executive departments *p. 435*
civilian *p. 435*
secretary *p. 435*
attorney general *p. 435*
independent agency *p. 441*
independent executive agency *p. 442*
civil service *p. 443*
patronage *p. 443*
spoils system *p. 443*
draft *p. 445*
independent regulatory commission *p. 445*
government corporation *p. 448*

Staff Agencies
- Serve in support capacity
- Offer advice and management assistance

- Form the federal administrative organizations
- Work together to meet goals

Line Agencies
- Perform specific tasks
- Meet goals set by Congress and the President
- Administer public policy

Executive Branch

Executive Office of the President	Executive Departments	Independent Agencies
White House Office comprises the President's key personal and political staff.	Traditional units of the federal administration	Located outside the executive departments
National Security Council advises on matters relating to national security.	Built around broad fields of authority	Created by Congress to perform specific functions
OMB prepares federal budget and assists in executive branch management.	Headed by a department secretary, serving as link between presidential policy and department	Nature and purpose vary from agency to agency.
Other units provide advice on issues ranging from the economy to domestic affairs.	Structured geographically, with much work done through regional offices	

Chapter Assessment

GOVERNMENT ONLINE
Self-Test
To test your understanding of key terms and main ideas, visit
PearsonSuccessNet.com

Comprehension and Critical Thinking

Section 1

1. Do you think the bureaucratic organization of the Federal Government makes it more effective or less effective?

2. **Analyze Political Cartoons (a)** What does this cartoon imply about bureaucracy? **(b)** Do you think it is an accurate portrayal? Why or why not?

Section 2

3. **(a)** Why is the Executive Office sometimes called the President's "right arm"? **(b)** Which activity of the Executive Office do you think has the most impact on the lives of the American people?

4. **(a)** Which unit of the EOP is responsible for preparing the federal budget? **(b)** What responsibility does that agency have once Congress has appropriated funds to the executive branch?

5. **(a)** What is the major responsibility of the National Security Council? **(b)** How does the constitutional system of checks and balances apply to the NSC?

Section 3

6. **(a)** What are the executive departments? **(b)** What is the process for selecting their high-ranking officers? **(c)** Do you think the department heads should be career bureaucrats? Why or why not?

7. **(a)** How are executive departments connected to the Cabinet? **(b)** Considering its relationship with the President, do you think the Cabinet can exercise too much influence on public policy?

Section 4

8. **(a)** What are the three types of independent agencies? **(b)** What is the basic role of each type? **(c)** Which type do you think affects your life the most?

9. **(a)** What is the purpose of the civil service? **(b)** How has the service changed since the enactment of the Pendleton Act in 1883?

10. **(a)** What is the function of the regulatory commissions? **(b)** Do you think laws regulating specific industries affect our personal and economic freedom? Why or why not?

Writing About Government

11. Use your Quick Write exercises from this chapter to write a research paper on how the government is involved in the administration of the topic you selected. Make sure your thesis statement is clear and supported with well-researched details, and that your conclusion reviews the key points of your thesis. See pp. S6–S7 in the Skills Handbook.

Apply What You've Learned

12. **Essential Question Activity** Look through the government pages of a local telephone book or online to locate the federal agencies in your area. Select one that interests you and conduct an interview of a civil servant who works for that agency. Ask:

    (a) In which Cabinet department is your agency located? Is it one of the larger agencies of that department?

    (b) What are your agency's key responsibilities?

    (c) How and by whom are the agency's decisions made?

    (d) Do you think the organizational structure of your agency is efficient? Could it be improved? If so, how?

13. **Essential Question Assessment** Based on your interview and this chapter's content, make a graphic organizer that illustrates the hierarchy of the agency you selected. Then, write a short essay on how this chart helps answer the Essential Question: **Is the bureaucracy essential to good government?**

Essential Questions Journal To respond to the chapter Essential Question, go to your **Essential Questions Journal.**

Document-Based Assessment

Protecting the Environment

Ecologist Rachel Carson's groundbreaking study, *Silent Spring,* was one of the earliest and most persuasive warnings of the urgent need to protect the environment, both here and abroad. As these documents show, the federal government and the public have since then become more actively involved in addressing the issue.

Document 1

Since 2001, our nation has funded nearly $10 billion in developing energy sources that are cleaner, cheaper and more reliable. [The] EPA has played a substantial role in this effort. . . . But we're not doing it alone.

Today, instead of having only 17-thousand EPA employees working to protect the environment, we now have over 300 million Americans as environmental partners. Americans from all sectors of society—communities, businesses and individuals—have begun to embrace the fact that environmental responsibility is everyone's responsibility.

—Stephen Johnson, EPA Administrator, 2007

Document 2

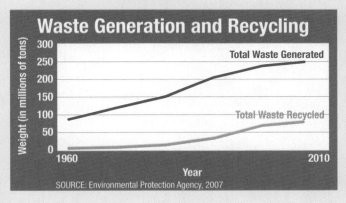

Waste Generation and Recycling

Weight (in millions of tons)

Total Waste Generated

Total Waste Recycled

Year

SOURCE: Environmental Protection Agency, 2007

Document 3

The most alarming of all man's assaults upon the environment is the contamination of air, earth, rivers, and sea with dangerous and even lethal materials. This pollution is for the most part irrecoverable. . . . In this now universal contamination of the environment, chemicals are the sinister and little-recognized partners . . . in changing the very nature of the world. . . . Many [of them] are used in man's war against nature.

These sprays, dusts, and aerosols are now applied almost universally to farms, gardens, forests, and homes—nonselective chemicals that have the power to kill every insect, the "good" and the "bad," to still the song of birds and the leaping of fish in the streams. . . .

[W]e have allowed these chemicals to be used with little or no advance investigation of their effect on soil, water, wildlife, and man himself. Future generations are unlikely to condone our lack of prudent concern for the integrity of the natural world that supports all life.

—Rachel Carson, *Silent Spring,* 1962

Use your knowledge of the independent agencies and Documents 1–3 to answer Questions 1–3.

1. What is the main point of Document 3?
   A. Chemicals are the cause of all our environmental problems.
   B. People need to take responsibility for protecting the environment.
   C. Government must regulate the chemical industry.
   D. Insecticides are good for the environment.

2. How do Documents 1 and 2 illustrate the growing emphasis on environmental concerns?

3. **Pull It Together** Should the Federal Government become more heavily involved in efforts to protect the environment? Why or why not?

GOVERNMENT ONLINE
Documents
To find more primary sources on the environment, visit
PearsonSuccessNet.com

"
The constitutional **purpose** of a **budget** is to make government **responsive** to **public opinion** and **responsible** for its **acts**.

—President William Howard Taft, message to Congress, 1909

Photo: A U.S. Mint engraver works on a plaster image of President John Adams for the current presidential dollar coin series.

Financing Government

Essential Question
How should the federal budget reflect Americans' priorities?

Section 1:
Taxes and Other Revenue

Section 2:
Borrowing and the Public Debt

Section 3:
Spending and the Budget

Section 4:
Fiscal and Monetary Policy

GOVERNMENT ONLINE
On the Go

To study anywhere, anytime,
download these online resources
at PearsonSuccessNet.com
• Political Dictionary
• Audio Review
• Downloadable Interactivities

Taxes and Other Revenue

Guiding Question

How is the Federal Government financed? Use a chart like the one below to keep track of the main ideas about financing government.

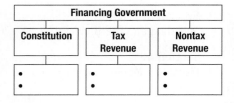

Financing Government		
Constitution	Tax Revenue	Nontax Revenue
• •	• •	• •

Political Dictionary

- fiscal policy
- progressive tax
- payroll tax
- regressive tax
- excise tax
- estate tax
- gift tax
- customs duty
- interest

Objectives

1. Explain how the Constitution gives Congress the power to tax and at the same time places limits on that power.
2. Identify the most significant federal taxes collected today.
3. Describe the nontax sources of federal revenue.

Image Above: Taxpayers filing their federal income tax forms.

This chapter is mostly about fiscal policy—a subject that has a tendency to make most people's eyes glaze over.[1] It is, nonetheless, a matter of very considerable importance to everyone in the United States.

A government's **fiscal policy** consists of the various means it uses to raise and spend money and thereby influence the nation's economy. No one needs to be told that the rate at which government takes in money and the level at which it spends that income have a very substantial impact on economic conditions. In simplest terms, it comes to this: A cut in taxes means more money in the hands of consumers, and their increased spending power means more jobs. An increase in taxes takes money away from consumers and so tends to slow the economy and reduce inflation.

In this section, we turn to taxes. Later, we shall look at borrowing—another source of governmental income, how the government spends what it takes in, and, finally, how the government's fiscal policy affects the economy.

The Power to Tax

No one really likes taxes—except, perhaps, late-night television personalities who often find fodder for their monologues in that subject. They are far from the first to joke about taxes, however. More than two centuries ago, Benjamin Franklin famously said that "in this world nothing can be said to be certain, except death and taxes."

The Constitution underscores the central importance of the power to tax by listing it first among all of the many powers granted to Congress. The Constitution gives to Congress the power

FROM THE CONSTITUTION

To lay and collect Taxes, Duties, Imposts and Excises, to pay the Debts and provide for the common Defence and general Welfare of the United States. . . .
—**Article I, Section 8, Clause 1**

---

1 The word *fiscal* comes from the Latin word *fiscus*, meaning originally a reed basket and later a purse or treasury. In ancient Rome, the *fiscus* was the public treasury, the emperor's purse.

First and foremost, Congress exercises the taxing power in order to raise the money needed to operate the Federal Government. However, Congress does sometimes exercise that power for purposes other than the raising of revenue. Usually, that other purpose is to regulate, even discourage, some activity that the government believes to be harmful to the general public.

Thus, much of the Federal Government's regulation of narcotics and other dangerous drugs is based on the taxing power. Federal law provides that only those who hold a valid license can legally manufacture, sell, or otherwise deal in those drugs—and licensing is a form of taxation. The government also regulates a number of other things by licensing—including, for example, the sale and purchasing of certain firearms, prospecting on public lands, and the hunting of migratory birds.

In 1912, Congress used its taxing power to destroy a part of the domestic match industry. It did so by <u>levying</u> a tax of two cents a hundred on matches made with white or yellow phosphorus. Those highly poisonous substances were harmful to workers who produced the matches. Matches made from other substances commonly sold for a penny a hundred at the time. So, as a result, the two-cent tax drove phosphorus matches from the market.

The Supreme Court first upheld the use of the taxing power for nonrevenue purposes in *Veazie Bank* v. *Fenno*, 1869. In 1861, Congress had created a national paper money system to provide a single, sound currency for the country. Private bank notes, which also circulated as money, soon interfered with the government's new "greenbacks." So, in 1865, Congress imposed a 10 percent tax on the issuing of those private notes—and they soon disappeared.

Constitutional Limitations The power to tax is not unlimited. As with all of its other powers, Congress must exercise the taxing power in accord with every provision in the Constitution. Thus, for example, Congress cannot levy a tax on church services—clearly, such a tax would violate the 1st Amendment. In more specific terms, the Constitution puts four expressed limits—and one very significant implied limit—on the power to tax.

First, it declares that Congress is given the power to tax in order to "pay the Debts and provide for the common Defence and general Welfare of the United States." That is, taxes can be levied *only* for public purposes, not for the benefit of some private interest.

The second expressed limit is the prohibition of export taxes. Article I, Section 9, Clause 5 declares that "No Tax or Duty shall be laid on Articles exported from any State." Thus, customs duties (tariffs) can be applied only to imports—goods brought into the United States. They may not be applied to exports, goods sent out of the country. Recall, this restriction was a part of the Commerce Compromise made by the Framers at Philadelphia in 1787.

While Congress cannot tax exports, it can and does *prohibit* the export of certain items. It does so under its expressed power to regulate foreign commerce, usually for reasons of national security. For example, Congress has banned the export of computer software that allows people to <u>encrypt</u> files in a code no government can crack.

✔ **Checkpoint**
How does the Constitution limit the power to tax?

levy
v. to charge, impose

encrypt
v. to encode, especially to prevent unauthorized access

"GIBBS, I SUBTRACTED YOUR FEDERAL, STATE AND SOCIAL SECURITY TAXES AND MEDICAL FROM YOUR PAYCHECK, AND YOU OWE THE FIRM $50."

▶▶ **Analyzing Political Cartoons** Taxes fund the programs and services the public expects from the government. Yet, some criticize the financial burden placed on taxpayers to provide government funding. *How does this cartoon illustrate this issue?*

✓ **Checkpoint**
How does a direct tax differ from an indirect tax?

Third, direct taxes must be equally apportioned—that is, evenly distributed, among the States. The Constitution originally provided that

FROM THE CONSTITUTION

No Capitation, or other direct, Tax shall be laid, unless in Proportion to the Census or Enumeration herein before directed to be taken.
—Article I, Section 9, Clause 4

This restriction was a part of the Three-Fifths Compromise the Framers made at the Philadelphia Convention. In effect, delegates from the northern States insisted that if slaves were to be counted in the populations of the southern States, those States would have to pay for them.

Recall that a direct tax is one that must be <u>borne</u> by the person upon whom it is levied. Examples include a tax on land or buildings, which must be paid by the owner of the property; or a capitation tax—a head or poll tax—laid on each person. Other taxes are indirect taxes, levies that may be shifted to another for payment—as, for example, the federal tax on liquor. That tax, placed initially on the distiller, is ultimately paid by the person who buys the liquor.

The direct tax restriction means, in effect, that any direct tax that Congress levies must be apportioned among the States according to their populations. Thus, a direct tax that raised $1 billion would have to produce just about $120 million in California and close to $10 million in Mississippi, because California has about 12 percent of the nation's population and Mississippi nearly 1 percent.

Wealth is not evenly distributed among the States, of course. So, a direct tax laid in proportion to population would be <u>grossly</u> unfair; the tax would fall more heavily on the residents of some States than it would on others. As a result, Congress has not imposed a direct tax—except for the income tax—outside the District of Columbia since 1861.

An income tax is a direct tax, but it may be laid without regard to population:

FROM THE CONSTITUTION

The Congress shall have power to lay and collect taxes on incomes, from whatever source derived, without apportionment among the several States, and without regard to any census or enumeration.
—16th Amendment

Congress first levied an income tax in 1861, to help finance the Civil War. That tax, which expired in 1872, was later upheld by the Supreme Court in *Springer* v. *United States*, 1881. A unanimous Court found that that income tax was an indirect rather than a direct tax.

However, a later income tax law, enacted in 1894, was declared unconstitutional in *Pollock* v. *Farmers' Loan and Trust Co.*, 1895. There, the Court held that the 1894 law imposed a direct tax that Congress should have apportioned among the several States. The impossibility of taxing incomes fairly in accord with any plan of apportionment led to the adoption of the 16th Amendment, in 1913.

The fourth and final limit, in Article I, Section 8, Clause 1, declares that "all Duties, Imposts and Excises shall be uniform throughout the United States." That is, all of the indirect taxes levied by the Federal Government must be set at the same rate in all parts of the country.

The Implied Limitation The Federal Government cannot tax the States or any of their local governments in the exercise of their governmental functions. That is, federal taxes cannot be imposed on those governments when they are performing such tasks as providing public education, furnishing healthcare, providing police protection, or building streets and highways.

Recall, the Supreme Court laid down that rule in *McCulloch* v. *Maryland* in 1819, when it declared that "the power to tax involves the power to destroy." If the Federal Government could tax the governmental activities of the States or their local units, it could conceivably tax them out of existence and so destroy the federal system.

The Federal Government can and does tax those State and local activities that are of a nongovernmental character, however. For

borne
v. carried as a burden

grossly
adv. very badly, glaringly

example, in 1893, South Carolina created a State monopoly to sell liquor, and it claimed that each of its liquor stores was exempt from the federal saloon license tax. But in *South Carolina* v. *United States*, 1905, the Supreme Court held that the State was liable for the tax, because the sale of liquor is not a necessary or usual governmental activity. Today, most State and many local governments are engaged in a variety of businesslike enterprises.

Current Federal Taxes

Oliver Wendell Holmes once described taxes as "what we pay for civilized society." Society does not appear to be much more civilized today than it was when Justice Holmes made that observation in 1927. However, "what we pay" has certainly gone up. In 1927, the Federal Government's tax collections altogether came to less than $3.4 billion. Compare that figure with the figures in the chart on this page.

Income Tax You will recall that the income tax was authorized by the 16th Amendment, in 1913. It is the largest source of federal revenue today. It first became the major source in 1917 and 1918. And, except for a few years in the midst of the Depression of the 1930s, it has remained so.

Several features of the income tax fit its dominant role. It is a flexible tax, because its rates can be adjusted to produce whatever amount of money Congress thinks is necessary. The income tax is also easily adapted to the principle of ability to pay. It is a **progressive tax**—that is, the higher one's income, the higher the tax rate. The tax is levied on the earnings of both individuals and corporations.

Individual Income Tax The tax on individuals' incomes regularly produces the largest amount of federal revenue. For fiscal year 2010, the individual income tax was expected to provide just over $1 trillion.

The tax is levied on each person's taxable income—that is, one's total income in the previous year less certain exemptions and deductions. On returns filed in 2010, covering income received in 2009, most taxpayers had a personal exemption of $3,650, and another

How **Government** Works

Taxes At-a-Glance

The Federal Government acquires most of its revenue through taxes. The OMB reported that the government received just over $2.1 trillion in tax revenue in fiscal year 2009. *Who bears the greatest burden in providing funding for the Federal Government?*

Individual Income Tax
A tax levied on each person's total income during the previous year, less exemptions and deductions.

43% of tax revenue **$904** billion

Payroll Taxes
A tax applied to a percentage of a person's salary, matched by the employer, to fund specific social insurance programs conducted by the government.

42% of tax revenue **$892** billion

Corporation Income Tax
A tax levied on all the earnings of a business, less its operating costs and authorized deductions.

7.1% of tax revenue **$149** billion

Excise Taxes
A tax placed on the manufacture, sale, or use of goods and/or for services rendered.

3.1% of tax revenue **$65** billion

Estate/Gift Taxes
Taxes applied to the estate of a recently deceased person and to sizeable monetary gifts between living individuals.

1.4% of tax revenue **$26** billion

Customs Duties
Taxes levied on goods imported into the United States from other countries.

1.1% of tax revenue **$23** billion

SOURCE: Office of Management and Budget

of the same amount for each dependent. The personal exemption is adjusted to account for inflation each year. Deductions are allowed for a number of things, including the cost of some medical care, most State and local taxes (except sales taxes), interest paid on home mortgages, and charitable contributions.

By April 15 of any given year, everyone who earned taxable income in the preceding calendar year must file a tax return—a declaration of that income and of the exemptions and deductions he or she claims. The returns are filed, by mail or online, with the Internal Revenue Service. The IRS now receives more than 180 million returns each year; more than 70 million of them are e-filed.

At President George W. Bush's urging, Congress passed major tax-cut legislation in 2001, 2002, and again in 2003. As a result, all taxable income earned in 2009 was taxed (in 2010) at one of six rates (brackets). Those rates range from 10 percent in the lowest bracket on up to 35 percent on the highest incomes. Thus, in the lowest bracket in 2010, a single person paid 10 percent of his or her taxable income up to $8,350. In the highest bracket, married couples sent 35 percent of their taxable income above $372,950 to the IRS.

Most people who pay income taxes do so through withholding, a pay-as-you-go plan. Employers are required to withhold a certain amount from each employee's paycheck and send that money to the IRS. When the employee files a tax return, he or she receives a refund if the employer withheld more money than the employee owed in taxes, or must pay an additional amount if too little was withheld. Those who earn income from sources not subject to withholding (for example, rent or royalties) must estimate the tax they will owe and make quarterly payments on that amount through the year.

Corporation Income Tax Each corporation must pay a tax on its net income—that is, on all of its earnings above the costs of doing business. The corporate tax is the most complicated of all federal taxes because of the many deductions allowed. Nonprofit organizations such as churches and charitable foundations are not subject to the corporation income tax.

For 2010, the corporate tax rates ran from 15 percent on the first $50,000 of taxable earnings up to a top rate of 35 percent on taxable incomes of more than $15 million.

Social Insurance Taxes The Federal Government collects huge sums to finance three major social welfare programs: (1) the Old-Age, Survivors, and Disability Insurance (OASDI) program—the basic Social Security program, established by the Social Security Act of 1935; (2) Medicare—healthcare for the elderly, added to the Social Security program in 1965; and (3) the unemployment compensation program—benefits paid to jobless workers, a program also established by the Social Security Act in 1935.

OASDI and Medicare are supported by taxes imposed on nearly all employers and their employees, and on self-employed persons. These levies are often called **payroll taxes** because the amounts owed by employees are withheld from their paychecks. For 2010, employees paid an OASDI tax of 6.2 percent on the first $106,800 of their salary or wages for the year, and their employers had to match that amount. The self-employed were taxed at 12.4 percent on the first $106,800 of their income.

For Medicare, employees pay a 1.45 percent tax on their total annual income. Employers must match the amounts withheld from their employees' paychecks. The self-employed pay the full 2.9 percent Medicare tax on their annual incomes.

The unemployment insurance program is a joint federal–State operation that makes payments to workers who lose their jobs for reasons beyond their control. The program now covers most workers in this country. Each State and the District of Columbia, Puerto Rico, and the Virgin Islands have their own unemployment compensation laws. The amount of a worker's weekly benefits, and how many weeks these benefits last, are determined by State law.

The unemployment compensation program is financed by both federal and State taxes. The federal tax is 6.2 percent of the first $7,000 an employer pays to each employee in a year. Each employer is given a credit of up to 5.4 percent against that tax for unemployment

Progressive Taxes

A progressive tax is structured so that the higher a taxpayer's income is, the greater percentage he or she must pay in taxes. The federal income tax is progressive and, in principle, works like the simplified, hypothetical example shown below. *What percentage of total income would be paid on salaries of $30,000 and $95,000?*

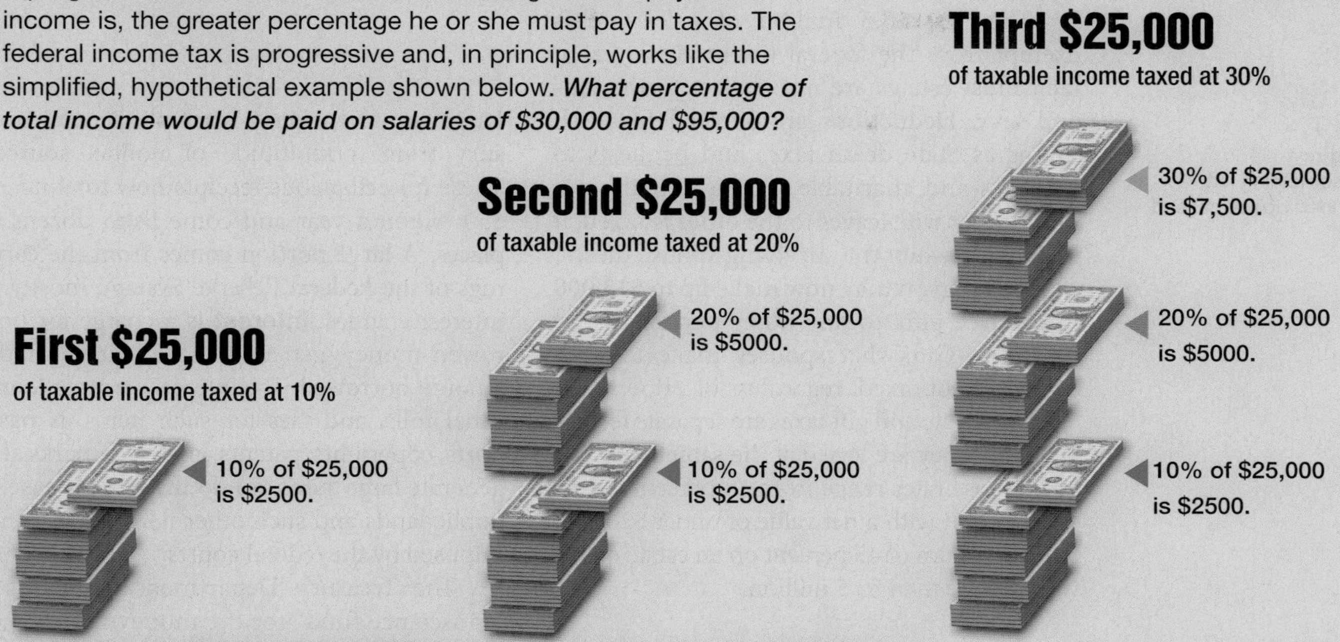

Third $25,000
of taxable income taxed at 30%

◄ 30% of $25,000 is $7,500.

◄ 20% of $25,000 is $5000.

◄ 10% of $25,000 is $2500.

Second $25,000
of taxable income taxed at 20%

◄ 20% of $25,000 is $5000.

◄ 10% of $25,000 is $2500.

First $25,000
of taxable income taxed at 10%

◄ 10% of $25,000 is $2500.

Total tax = $2,500
10% of Income

Total tax = $7,500
15% of Income

Total tax = $15,000
20% of Income

taxes that the employer pays to the State. So, the federal tax usually amounts to 0.8 percent on taxable wages.

Notice that these social insurance taxes for OASDI, Medicare, and unemployment compensation are not progressive taxes. They are, instead, **regressive taxes**—taxes levied at a fixed rate, without regard to the level of a taxpayer's income or his or her ability to pay them. In fact, the regressive OASDI and Medicare taxes now take more money out of the paychecks of many low- and middle-income workers than does the progressive federal income tax.

The IRS collects these social insurance taxes. The money is then credited to trust accounts maintained by the Treasury, and Congress appropriates funds for the social insurance programs as they are needed.

Excise Taxes An **excise tax** is a tax laid on the manufacture, sale, or consumption of goods and/or the performance of services. The Federal Government has imposed

and collected excise taxes since Congress acquired its taxing power in 1789.

Today, federal excise taxes are imposed on a long list of items, including gasoline, oil, tires, tobacco, alcohol, firearms, telephone services, airline tickets, and more. Many excise taxes are called "hidden taxes" because they are collected from producers who then figure them into the price that the retail customer finally pays. Some are called "luxury taxes" because they are imposed on goods not usually considered necessities. And some excise taxes are known as "sin taxes," particularly those laid on tobacco, alcohol, and gambling.

Estate and Gift Taxes An **estate tax** is a levy imposed on the assets (the estate) of someone who dies.[2] A **gift tax** is one imposed on a gift from one living person to another. Congress first provided for the estate

---

2 An inheritance tax is another form of the so-called death tax. It is not levied on the entire net estate but, instead, on the portion inherited by each heir. Most States impose inheritance, not estate, taxes; most States also levy gift taxes.

bequest
n. something left, handed down, passed on

dutied
adj. subjected to a tax by the government

tax in 1916. It added the gift tax in 1932 to plug a loophole in the estate tax that allowed people to avoid the estate tax by giving away money or other property before death.

The first $3.5 million of an estate is exempt from the federal tax in 2010. So, in fact, most estates are not subject to the federal levy. Deductions are allowed for such things as State death taxes and bequests to religious and charitable groups. Anything a husband or wife leaves to the other is taxed, if at all, only when the surviving spouse dies.

Any person may now make up to $13,000 in tax-free gifts to any other person in any one year. Gifts that spouses make to each other are not taxed, regardless of value.

The estate and gift taxes are separate federal taxes, but they are levied at the same rates. For 2010, those rates range from 18 percent, on an estate or gift with a net value of under $20,000, to a maximum of 45 percent on an estate or gift worth more than $3.5 million.

Customs Duties Customs duties are taxes laid on goods brought into the United States from abroad. Customs duties are also known as tariffs, import duties, or imposts. Congress decides which imports will be dutied and at what rates. Most imports are dutied; but some are not—for example, Bibles, coffee, bananas, and up to $800 of a tourist's purchases abroad. Once the major source of income for the Federal Government, custom duties now only produce just over 1 percent of government revenue taken in each year.

Nontax Revenues

Large sums of money reach the federal treasury from a multitude of nontax sources. These miscellaneous receipts now total nearly $50 billion a year and come from dozens of places. A large portion comes from the earnings of the Federal Reserve System, mostly in interest charges. **Interest** is a charge for borrowed money, generally a percentage of the amount borrowed. The interest on other loans, canal tolls, and fees for such items as passports, copyrights, patents, and trademarks also generate large sums. So do the sale or lease of public lands and such other items as the fines imposed by the federal courts.

The Treasury Department maintains a "conscience fund" for the money that people send in to ease their minds over their past taxpaying mistakes. Another little-known source of nontax money is *seigniorage*—the profit the United States Mint makes on the production of coins. The U.S. Postal Service sells more than $100 million in mint-condition stamps to collectors each year, and collectors spend untold millions more at local post offices.

Essential Questions Journal To continue to build a response to the chapter Essential Question, go to your **Essential Questions Journal.**

SECTION 1 ASSESSMENT

1. **Guiding Question** Use your completed chart to answer this question: How is the Federal Government financed?

Key Terms and Comprehension

2. What is the difference between a **progressive tax** and a **regressive tax?**

3. **Payroll taxes** support which three major social welfare programs?

4. **(a)** What are the four constitutional limitations on the power to tax? **(b)** What is the one implied limitation on that power?

Critical Thinking

5. **Demonstrate Reasoned Judgment** Which do you think is more fair, a direct or an indirect tax? Explain.

6. **Draw Conclusions** Do you think it is appropriate for the Federal Government to use taxes for regulatory purposes? Why or why not?

7. **Identify Central Issues** Why do you think the Federal Government requires employers to withhold money from each paycheck instead of allowing taxpayers to pay their taxes in one annual payment?

Quick Write

Cause-and-Effect Writing: Ask Questions To determine what our national priorities are today or once were, one must reflect on the conditions of the time. Select an administration in office between 1952 and today. Write five questions that you think will help you determine what might have influenced the Federal Government in its allocation of funds for that period. Think about subjects such as the economy, national security, and the environment.

Borrowing and the Public Debt

Guiding Question

What effect does borrowing have on the federal budget and the nation's economy? Use a concept web like the one below to keep track of the main ideas about the government's influence on the economy.

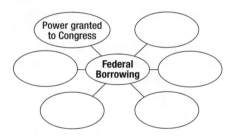

Power granted to Congress

Federal Borrowing

Political Dictionary

- deficit
- surplus
- demand-side economics
- supply-side economics
- public debt

Objectives

1. Describe federal borrowing.
2. Explain how the Federal Government's actions can affect the economy.
3. Analyze the causes and effects of the public debt.

Image Above: Work Projects Administration (WPA) workers built sidewalks during the Great Depression.

In *Hamlet*, Shakespeare wrote, "Neither a borrower nor a lender be." That advice may make good sense in many situations. However, it most certainly has *not* been followed by the government of the United States, which has been both a borrower and a lender for more than 200 years now.

Borrowing

The Constitution gives Congress the power "[t]o borrow Money on the credit of the United States" in Article I, Section 8, Clause 2. Congress first exercised that power in 1790, and it has done so hundreds of times since then. For the better part of 150 years, the power to borrow was seen as a way for the government to (1) meet the costs of crisis situations, most notably wars, and/or (2) pay for large-scale projects that could not be financed out of current income—for example, the construction of the Panama Canal in the early 1900s.

Beginning with the Depression years of the 1930s, the Federal Government has borrowed, regularly and heavily, for yet another purpose: to finance budget deficits. In nearly every one of the last 80 years, it has spent more than it has collected from taxpayers. That is, the government has run up a **deficit** (the shortfall between income and outgo) in each of those years—and it has borrowed to make up the difference.

Indeed, the government's financial books did not show a **surplus,** more income than outgo, in any fiscal year from 1970 to 1998.[3] For fiscal year 2010, which extends from October 1, 2009 to September 30, 2010, the government expects to spend some $3.7 trillion—and it will take in some $1.5 trillion less than that stupendous sum. It will have to borrow to cover that shortfall.

The Depression and Deficit Spending

The collapse of the stock market in October 1929 triggered the Great Depression of the 1930s. To meet that catastrophe, deficit financing became a constant element of federal fiscal policy.

A few statistics begin to suggest the depths of that economic calamity, and the miseries that accompanied it. Two million Americans were unemployed in

---

3 From 1930 to 2009, the Federal Government ended only 13 fiscal years "in the black"—that is, with a budget surplus: fiscal years 1930, 1947, 1948, 1949, 1951, 1956, 1957, 1960, 1969, 1998, 1999, 2000, and 2001.

1929. By 1933, that number had climbed to 13.5 million. One fifth of the nation's labor force was out of work—and millions more were working for, literally, pennies a day. By 1935, 18 million people, including children and the aged, were completely dependent on emergency public relief programs. Between 1929 and 1932, more than 5,000 banks—one of every five in the country—had failed, and their customers' deposits had vanished. By 1932, net farm income had plunged to 33 percent of its level in 1929.

Few States had made any provision for such a crisis, and those that had were overwhelmed. So, too, were churches and other private charities. Poverty and need had become national problems overnight.

stimulate
v. encourage, spur, whip up

In the elections of 1932, the voters overwhelmingly rejected the tentative efforts of President Herbert Hoover and a Republican-controlled Congress to solve the nation's economic woes. Mr. Hoover and his advisors were committed to the traditional view of the place of government in the economy. They held that government had only a very limited power to deal with what they believed was a private economic crisis. Government, they thought, should ensure a stable money supply; beyond that, the success or failure of businesses was a matter best left to the workings of the free market.

The voters turned, instead, to the Democrats. Franklin D. Roosevelt won the presidency in a landslide and his party captured huge majorities in both houses of Congress.

Keynesian Economics Almost immediately, the President and Congress launched the New Deal—a series of government spending and jobs programs designed to <u>stimulate</u> the economy and put Americans back to work. That response to the Depression was built largely on the theories advanced by British economist John Maynard Keynes. In particular, it was based on the Keynesian view that government should influence the economy by large increases in public spending in times of high unemployment.[4]

Keynesians argue that even if government must borrow to support that increased spending, the higher employment that results will soon produce higher tax revenues. This element of Keynesian economics is sometimes called **demand-side economics.**

Keynesian economic thinking continues to influence federal fiscal policy. However, President Ronald Reagan (1981–1989) and more recently George W. Bush (2001–2009) insisted that lower taxes, not greater spending, provide the best route to a stronger economy. This view, which is sometimes called **supply-side economics** or "Reaganomics," is based on the assumption that tax cuts increase the supply of money in private hands and so stimulate the economy.

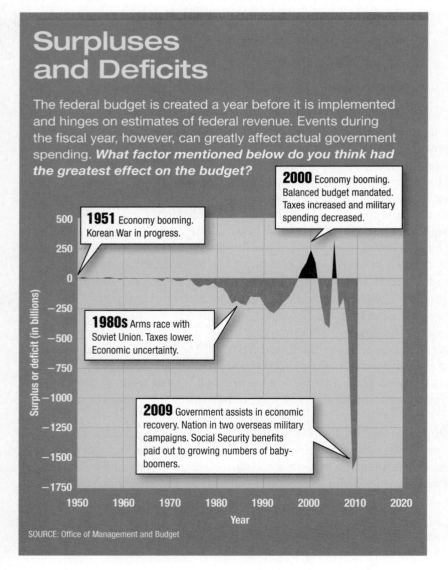

Surpluses and Deficits

The federal budget is created a year before it is implemented and hinges on estimates of federal revenue. Events during the fiscal year, however, can greatly affect actual government spending. *What factor mentioned below do you think had the greatest effect on the budget?*

1951 Economy booming. Korean War in progress.

2000 Economy booming. Balanced budget mandated. Taxes increased and military spending decreased.

1980s Arms race with Soviet Union. Taxes lower. Economic uncertainty.

2009 Government assists in economic recovery. Nation in two overseas military campaigns. Social Security benefits paid out to growing numbers of baby-boomers.

SOURCE: Office of Management and Budget

Surplus or deficit (in billions) — 500, 250, 0, −250, −500, −750, −1000, −1250, −1500, −1750

Year — 1950, 1960, 1970, 1980, 1990, 2000, 2010, 2020

4   John Maynard Keynes' (1883–1946) economic theories were most fully developed in his work *The General Theory of Employment, Interest, and Money,* published in 1936.

The Public Debt

Congress has the power to "borrow Money on the credit of the United States," and it has exercised that power ever since 1789. The public debt produced by that borrowing now exceeds $12 trillion. ***To whom does the Federal Government owe the most today?***

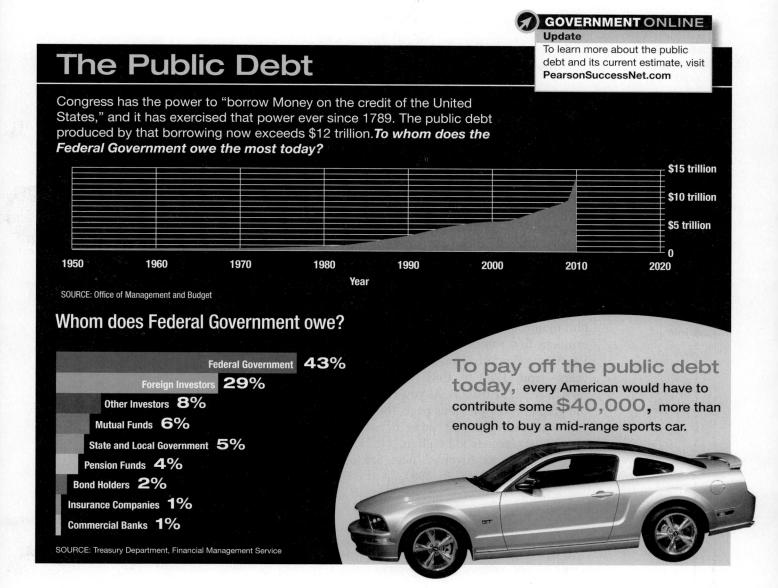

SOURCE: Office of Management and Budget

Whom does Federal Government owe?

Federal Government	**43%**
Foreign Investors	**29%**
Other Investors	**8%**
Mutual Funds	**6%**
State and Local Government	**5%**
Pension Funds	**4%**
Bond Holders	**2%**
Insurance Companies	**1%**
Commercial Banks	**1%**

SOURCE: Treasury Department, Financial Management Service

To pay off the public debt today, every American would have to contribute some **$40,000,** more than enough to buy a mid-range sports car.

A steep downturn in the nation's economy that began in 2007 and continued into 2009 led President Bush and then President Obama to persuade Congress to enact a series of "economic stimulus" plans—pump-priming measures that could very well have been written by John Maynard Keynes himself. Those laws were variously designed to inject more than $1.5 *trillion* into the nation's ailing economy in order to (1) shore up the loan-making capacities of the nation's banks and other financial institutions, (2) overcome a marked decline in consumer spending, and (3) combat a rising tide of unemployment.

How Borrowing Occurs Congress must authorize all federal borrowing. The actual borrowing is done by the Treasury Department, which issues various kinds of securities

to investors. These investors are principally individuals and banks, investment companies, and other financial institutions. The securities usually take the form of Treasury notes or bills, often referred to as T-bills, for short-term borrowing, and bonds for long-term purposes. They are, in effect, IOUs—promissory notes in which the government agrees to repay a certain sum, plus interest, on a certain date.

The Federal Government is regularly able to borrow money at lower rates of interest than the rates charged to private borrowers. This is true largely because investors can find no safer securities than those issued by the United States. If this country could not pay its debts, no one else would be able to do so, either. Federal securities are also attractive because the interest they earn cannot

✔ **Checkpoint**
How does the federal government borrow money?

accrue
v. to increase in amount
or value over time

ceiling
n. upper limit

be taxed by any of the States or their local
governments.

The Public Debt

Borrowing produces a debt, of course. The
public debt is the result of the Federal Government's borrowing over time. More precisely, the **public debt** is the total outstanding
indebtedness of the Federal Government. It
includes all of the money the government
has borrowed and not yet repaid, plus the
accrued interest on that borrowing.[5]

The Federal Government has built up a
huge debt over the years. Indeed, in the years
since the first federal budget was formulated
in 1789, the government has recorded a surplus in only 19 years. Recall, the Federal Government first went into debt during George
Washington's administration. Still, it took 192
years—from 1789 to 1981—for the public
debt to reach $1 trillion. As you can see from
the graph on the previous page, the debt has
exploded over the past three decades and
now (2010) exceeds $12 trillion.

The amounts involved here are absolutely mind-boggling. In 1981, as the debt
approached $1 trillion, President Reagan said

that he found "such a figure—a trillion dollars—incomprehensible." He then drew this
verbal picture: "[I]f you had a stack of $1,000
bills in your hand only four inches high, you'd
be a millionaire. A trillion dollars would be
a stack 67 miles high." Mr. Reagan's stack
would have to be more than 700 miles high
to equal the national debt today!

There is no constitutional limit on the
amount that may be borrowed, and so there
is no constitutional limit on the public debt.
Congress has put a statutory ceiling on the
debt, but simply raises that ceiling whenever
fiscal realities seem to call for it.

The debt has always been controversial,
and its rapid rise in recent years has fueled
the fire. The annual interest on the debt is the
amount that must be paid each year to those
from whom the government has borrowed.
That interest came to some $253 billion in
fiscal year 2008. Given the vast amounts now
being spent to combat the current economic
difficulties, that figure will be considerably
higher for each of the next several fiscal years.

Most of those who are concerned about
the size of the debt are worried about its
impact on future generations of Americans.
They say that years of shortsightedness and
failure to operate government on a pay-as-
you-go basis has produced monumental debt
and interest obligations that will have to be
met by tomorrow's taxpayers.

5 The Treasury Department's Bureau of the Public Debt acts as the
Federal Government's borrowing agent. It issues Treasury bills,
notes, and bonds and manages the U.S. Savings Bond Program.

**Essential Questions
Journal** To continue to build a
response to the chapter
Essential Question, go to your
Essential Questions Journal.

SECTION **2** ASSESSMENT

1. **Guiding Question** Use your completed concept web to answer this
   question: What effect does borrowing
   have on the federal budget and the
   nation's economy?

Key Terms and Comprehension

2. What is the difference between an annual **deficit** and the **public debt?**

3. **(a)** How does the Federal Government borrow money? **(b)** Why can it
   do so at a lower interest rate than can
   private borrowers?

4. How could the Federal Government
   create a budget **surplus?**

Critical Thinking

5. **Demonstrate Reasoned
   Judgment** Do you think deficit
   financing is an acceptable method
   to fund the Federal Government?
   Explain why or why not.

6. **Analyze Information** Why do you
   think that for many years Congress
   and the President have chosen to
   borrow money rather than balance the
   federal budget?

7. **Draw Conclusions** What do you think
   are the long-term consequences of
   ongoing deficit spending?

Quick Write

**Cause-and-Effect Writing: Gather
Details** Using magazines, newspapers, and that fiscal year's federal budget, conduct research on
the presidential administration you
selected for the Section 1 Quick
Write. Did any of the questions you
developed reflect the conditions
and priorities of the time? How did
the Federal Government respond to
those priorities? Record the results of
your research relating to each of your
questions in your notebook.

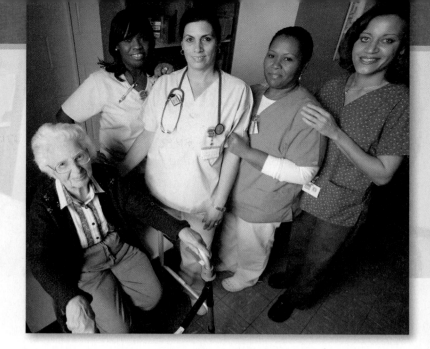

SECTION 3

Spending and the Budget

Guiding Question

How is federal spending determined? Use a concept web like the one below to keep track of how the federal budget is determined.

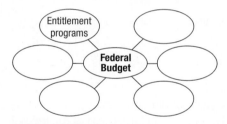

Political Dictionary

- entitlement
- controllable spending
- uncontrollable spending
- continuing resolution

Objectives

1. Identify the key elements of federal spending.
2. Define controllable and uncontrollable spending.
3. Explain how the President and Congress work together to create the federal budget.

Image Above: An elderly patient receives medical care financed by Medicare.

The Federal Government will spend more than $3.7 trillion in fiscal year 2010. If you were to place 3.7 trillion $1 bills end to end, they would stretch out some 280 million miles, which is more than the distance from Earth to the sun and back again. In this section, you will see how the Federal Government spends that vast amount of money, and how it plans for that spending through the budget process.

Federal Spending

For more than half of our national history—from independence in 1776 to the mid-1930s—the government's income and spending were so comparatively small that they had little real impact on the nation's economy. That situation changed, dramatically, with the coming of the Great Depression of the 1930s and then World War II in the early 1940s.

Today, the Federal Government takes hundreds of billions of dollars from some segments of the national economy. It then pumps those many billions back into other segments of the economy—all with huge effects on the economy as a whole, of course.

Spending Priorities Look at the right-hand side graph on the next page. As you can see, the Department of Health and Human Services now spends more money than any other federal agency—over $700 billion a year, in fact. Most of this department's spending goes for Medicare, Medicaid, and other entitlement programs.

Entitlements are benefits that federal law says *must* be paid to all those who meet the eligibility requirements—for examples, being above a certain age or below a certain income level. OASDI (the Old Age, Survivors, and Disability Insurance program)—often called "Social Security"—is the largest entitlement program today, and, recall, is funded by the social insurance taxes withheld from the paychecks of American workers. Other major examples include Medicare, Medicaid, food stamps, unemployment insurance, and veterans' pensions and benefits. The government guarantees assistance for all who qualify for those benefits. In effect, the law says that the people who receive those benefits are entitled (that is, have a right) to them.

Federal Spending Comparison

The manner in which the Federal Government spends its revenue hinges on the events of the time as well as the priorities of the American public. *What trends in federal spending can you determine from these pie charts?*

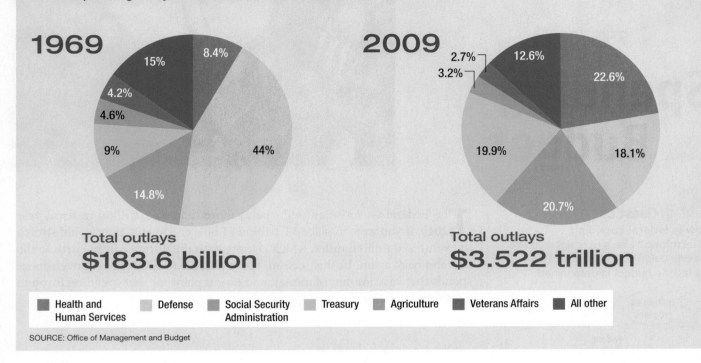

1969

8.4%
15%
4.2%
4.6%
9%
14.8%
44%

Total outlays
$183.6 billion

2009

2.7%
3.2%
12.6%
22.6%
18.1%
20.7%
19.9%

Total outlays
$3.522 trillion

■ Health and Human Services   ■ Defense   ■ Social Security Administration   ■ Treasury   ■ Agriculture   ■ Veterans Affairs   ■ All other

SOURCE: Office of Management and Budget

---

stoke
v. strengthen, stir up

OASDI is administered by an independent agency, the Social Security Administration (SSA). The department's outlays on OASDI—$727.5 billion in 2009—make SSA the third-largest government spender.

Outlays for national defense now account for a much larger share of the budget than they have over the past decade. The Department of Defense (DoD) spent more than $636 billion in 2009. It will likely spend even more in 2010, and the department's spending will continue to grow as the war on global terrorism wears on.

The defense-spending percentage in the graph is somewhat misleading, however. It does not include the defense-related expenditures of several other federal agencies, notably the nuclear weapons development work of the Department of Energy and many of the functions of the Department of Homeland Security.

Interest on the public debt is now the fourth-largest category of federal spending.

Stoked by years of deficit financing, it has consumed a larger and still larger part of the federal budget over the last several years. In the graph above, interest on the debt is included in the Treasury Department's spending. For fiscal year 2009, the net interest on the debt came to more than $383 billion.

Controllable and Uncontrollable Spending

What the Federal Government spends can be described in terms of **controllable spending** and **uncontrollable spending**. Most specific items in the federal budget are controllable. That is, Congress and the President can decide each year just how much will be spent on many of the things that the Federal Government does—for example, on national parks, highway projects, aid to education, military hardware, civil service pay, and so on. Economists often use the term "discretionary spending" to describe spending on those budget items about which Congress and the President can make choices.

Much federal spending is uncontrollable, however. It is because "mandatory spending" was built into many public programs when Congress created them. That level of spending cannot be changed unless Congress changes the law(s) that set the funding for those programs.

Take the interest on the public debt as a leading example of uncontrollable spending. That interest amounts to a fixed charge; once the Federal Government borrows the money, the interest on that loan must be paid when it comes due—and at the rate the government promised to pay.

Social Security benefits, food stamps, and most other entitlements are also largely uncontrollable. Once Congress has set the standards of eligibility for those programs, it really has no control over just how many people will meet those standards. Thus, Congress does not—really cannot—determine how many people covered by Social Security will become eligible for retirement benefits each year.

Those expenditures are not completely uncontrollable, however. Congress could redefine eligibility standards, or it could reduce the amount of money each beneficiary is to receive. But clearly those actions would be politically difficult.

In general, the percentage of federal spending that is uncontrollable has grown in recent years, while the percentage of controllable spending has decreased. In fact, the Office of Management and Budget estimates that over 60 percent of all federal spending today falls into the uncontrollable category. These trends cause concern to those officials who are responsible for maintaining control of the budget.

The Federal Budget

The Constitution gives to Congress the fabled "power of the purse"—the very significant power to control the financing of the Federal Government and all of its operations:

FROM THE CONSTITUTION

No Money shall be drawn from the Treasury, but in Consequence of Appropriations made by Law. . . .

—Article I, Section 9, Clause 7

Congress—and only Congress—has the power to provide the enormous sums that the government consumes each year. In short, it is Congress that decides *how much* the government can spend and, just as important, for exactly *what* it can spend that money.

Still, despite the fact that Congress holds the power of the purse, it is the President who initiates the process by which the Federal Government spends its money. The chief executive does so by submitting (proposing) a budget to Congress soon after that body begins each of its yearly sessions.[6]

Remember, the federal budget is a hugely important document. It is, of course, a financial statement—a lengthy and detailed estimate of federal income and proposed outgo for the upcoming fiscal year. But it is also much more than that, and much more than a dry listing of so many dollars from this and so many dollars for that. The budget is a major political statement, a declaration of the public policies of the United States. Put another way, the federal budget is the President's work plan for the conduct of the government and the execution of its public policies.

The annual budget-making process is a joint effort of the President and both houses of Congress. The President prepares the budget and submits it to Congress. Congress then reacts to the President's budget proposals, over a period of several months. It usually enacts most of those proposals, many of them in some altered form, in a number of appropriations measures.

The President and the Budget The process of building the budget is a lengthy one. In fact, it begins at least eighteen months before the start of the fiscal year for which the budget is intended. First, each federal agency prepares detailed estimates of its spending needs for that twelve-month period. Each agency then submits its spending plans to the President's budget-making agency, the Office of Management and Budget (OMB). (See Chapter 15, Section 2.)

✔ **Checkpoint**
Why is the budget both a financial and a political statement?

---

6 The word *budget* comes from the French *bougette,* meaning a small pouch or bag with its contents. In the eighteenth century, the budget was the bag in which the British chancellor of the exchequer (the treasurer) carried financial documents.

GOVERNMENT ONLINE

For an **interactive** exploration to learn more about the budget creation process, visit **PearsonSuccessNet.com**

INTERACTIVE

Creating the Federal Budget

Individually and then as one body, the House and Senate spend eight months or so determining the final allocation of federal funds. *Why are both the legislative and executive branches involved in this process?*

1 Presenting the Budget

On the first Monday in February, the President proposes a budget outlining the administration's policy and funding priorities and estimating spending, income, and borrowing for the coming fiscal year.

- President submits budget request to Congress.

2 Creating a Budget Resolution

Using the President's budget as a guide, the House and Senate work individually and then together to determine the size of the budget, estimate revenue, and set discretionary spending levels.

- House and Senate Budget Committees conduct hearings on a Budget Resolution.

- House and Senate debate and vote on their respective committee's Budget Resolution.

- Conference committee works to blend both chambers' resolutions into one final resolution.

- Each house votes on final version of the Budget Resolution.

3 Setting Appropriations

Guided by the Budget Resolution, the House and Senate work individually and then in conference to divide monies among federal agencies. Appropriations measures set out the budgets of the federal agencies in detail and provide the legal authority to spend their funds.

- House and Senate Appropriations Committees each develop 13 separate massive spending bills.

- Conference committee settles on one bill for each of the 13 appropriations measures.

- Each house votes on final version of each appropriations bill.

4 Approving the Final Budget

As each appropriations bill is approved by Congress, it is presented to the President to veto or sign into law.

- President signs or vetoes the appropriations bills. If a bill is not approved by October 1st, Congress must pass a continuing resolution for unfunded agencies to ensure their continued operation.

The OMB reviews all of the many agency proposals, often in budget hearings at which agency officials must defend their dollar requests. Following the OMB's review, revised and usually lowered spending plans for all of the agencies in the executive branch are fitted into the President's overall program. They become a part of the budget document—a part of the political statement—the President sends to Capitol Hill.[7]

Congress and the Budget Remember, Congress depends upon and works through its standing committees. The President's budget proposals, therefore, are referred to the Budget Committee in each chamber. There, in both the House and Senate committees, those money requests are studied and dissected with the help of the Congressional Budget Office (CBO).

The CBO is a staff agency created by Congress in 1974. It provides both houses of Congress and their committees with basic budget and economic data and analyses. The information that the CBO supplies is independent of the information provided by the OMB, which, recall, is the President's budget agency.

The President's budget is also sent to both the House and the Senate Appropriations Committees.[8] Their subcommittees hold extensive hearings in which they examine agency requests, quiz agency officials, and take testimony from a wide range of interested parties. Lobbyists for many of the interest groups discussed earlier (in Chapter 9) are actively involved in those hearings. They testify, bring grass-roots pressures to bear on committee members, and otherwise work to promote the interests of the organizations they represent. (And campaign contributions from these groups often find their way to members of those subcommittees—in particular, to their chairmen and ranking members.)

The two Appropriations Committees shape measures that later are reported to the

---

7 Congress enacts a separate budget to cover its own expenses. The federal courts' spending requests are prepared by the Administrative Office of the United States Courts and sent directly to Congress.

8 All tax proposals included in the President's budget are referred to the House Ways and Means Committee and, separately, to the Senate's Finance Committee.

floor of each house. Those measures are the bills that actually appropriate the funds on which the government will operate.

The two Budget Committees propose a concurrent resolution on the budget to their respective chambers. That measure, which must be passed by both houses by May 15, sets overall targets for federal receipts and spending in the upcoming fiscal year. The estimates are intended to guide the committees in both houses as they continue to work on the budget.

The two Budget Committees propose a second budget resolution in early September. Congress must pass that resolution by September 15, just two weeks before the beginning of the next fiscal year. That second budget resolution sets <u>binding</u> expenditure limits for all federal agencies in that upcoming year. No appropriations measure can provide for any spending that exceeds those limits.

Congress passes thirteen major appropriations bills each year. Recall, each of these measures must go to the White House for the President's action. Every year, Congress hopes to pass all thirteen of the appropriations measures by October 1—that is, by the beginning of the Federal Government's fiscal year.

It seldom does so, however. Congress must then pass emergency spending legislation to

Singer and songwriter John Legend testifies before a House Appropriations hearing on funding for the arts. *Why do you think the congressional appropriation hearings are open to the public?*

avoid a shutdown of those agencies for which appropriations have not yet been signed into law. That legislation takes the form of a **continuing resolution.** When signed by the President, the measure allows the affected agencies to continue to function on the basis of the previous year's appropriations. Should Congress and the President fail to act, many agencies of the Federal Government would have to suspend their operations.

binding
adj. creating a legal obligation to do something

Essential Questions
Journal

To continue to build a response to the chapter Essential Question, go to your **Essential Questions Journal.**

SECTION **3** ASSESSMENT

1. **Guiding Question** Use your completed concept web to answer this question: How is federal spending determined?

Key Terms and Comprehension
2. **(a)** What are **entitlement** programs? **(b)** List three examples of those government programs.
3. Why is **controllable spending** sometimes referred to as "discretionary spending?"
4. What is the purpose of a **continuing resolution?**
5. Describe the basic steps involved in creating the federal budget.

Critical Thinking
6. **Identify Central Issues (a)** What programs do you think are considered high priorities by most Americans? **(b)** How are these priorities taken into account during the creation of the federal budget?
7. **Predict Consequences (a)** What might occur if the OMB accepted all agency funding requests without holding budget hearings? **(b)** What would be the advantages and disadvantages if this were to occur?

Quick Write

Cause-and-Effect Writing: Identify Causes and Effects Using your research for the Section 2 Quick Write, create a graphic organizer to help you determine how government spending priorities were affected by the needs of the nation at the time and identify possible explanations for the government's actions. Were programs created? Were taxes affected? Did the actions remedy the problem? Keep in mind that there can be multiple causes and effects.

Analyzing Television News Programs

"Welcome to the Channel Four Evening News. Tonight's top story is the slashing of the interest rate by the Fed for the second time in as many weeks to address the nation's economic downturn. But first, some early speculation about the Academy Awards. . . ."

Television news programs are one of the major ways that most Americans keep up with local, national, and world events. These news programs are a valuable resource for people who want to stay aware of current events, but they also have the potential to influence public opinion.

Whenever you watch a television news program, you should think critically about how the information is presented to you.

1. **Think about the choice of stories.** There are more news events in any given day than a single news program can hope to cover. The producers of news shows have to choose which stories to report, and how long to spend on each story. By keeping track of which stories are covered, and for how long, you can get a sense of the priorities of the television news program.

2. **Pay attention to headlines and pictures.** Television news programs often use pictures and headline graphics to shape viewer reactions. For each news story, look closely at the headline graphics. Which words are the biggest? Are there any visual elements that are used just for entertainment or shock value?

3. **Compare with news coverage on other stations.** It can sometimes be very interesting to watch multiple television news programs on the same day, to see how they handle the news differently. Are they covering the same stories? Do they describe those stories the same way? Does one program include information about the news story that another program leaves out?

4. **Look for signs of bias.** You will often hear people talk about a "liberal bias" or a "conservative bias" in certain television news programs. Whatever their intentions may be, all news programs have to make choices in terms of what stories to report and how to report them, and sometimes these choices might be informed by political opinions.

▶▶ What do you think?

1. What does it mean when one television news program spends more time on a story than does another news program?

2. Other than time constraints, why would a television news program choose to leave information out of a particular story?

3. **You Try It** Watch the coverage of one local and one national television news station and compare their coverage of the same day's news. Then, write a brief summary of your investigation and indicate which of the two you think is the more useful and informative news broadcast.

GOVERNMENT ONLINE
Citizenship Activity Pack
For activities on analyzing television news programs, go to
PearsonSuccessNet.com

SECTION 4

Fiscal and Monetary Policy

Guiding Question

How does the Federal Government achieve its economic goals?
Use a table like the one below to keep track of the methods used by the government to meet its broad economic goals.

Types of Economic Policy		
Goal	Fiscal Policy	Monetary Policy
• Full employment	•	•
•	•	•

Political Dictionary

- gross domestic product
- inflation
- deflation
- recession
- fiscal policy
- monetary policy
- open market operations
- reserve requirement
- discount rate

Objectives

1. Describe the overall goals of the Federal Government's actions in the economy.
2. Explain the features and purposes of fiscal policy.
3. Explain the features and purposes of monetary policy.

"**I**t's the economy, stupid." That slogan has become a watchword in electoral politics. It first appeared during the presidential campaign of 1992, on a sign that hung on the wall of political advisor James Carville's office in Bill Clinton's campaign headquarters. Mr. Clinton, the Democratic Party's nominee, faced a daunting challenge in that election: How could he possibly convince the voters that he, not incumbent George H.W. Bush, should sit in the White House?

Mr. Bush, the 41st President of the United States, brought a substantial record to the contest—a record highlighted by the end, at long last, of the cold war and a stunning victory in the Persian Gulf War. Mr. Clinton, and Carville and Paul Begala, his chief campaign advisors, were convinced that the key to success in November lay in the domestic, not the foreign policy realm. The nation's economy was in shambles and, to their minds, the incumbent President was vulnerable on that score, and events proved them right.

The successful management of the economy is vital not only to a President's political survival. It has a very direct and immediate effect on the well-being of every man, woman, and child in this country. In this section, we explore the Federal Government's key economic goals and the principal mechanisms with which it attempts to achieve those ends.

Overall Economic Goals

The American economy is enormously complex. The nation's **gross domestic product** (GDP)—the total value of all final goods and services produced in the country each year—now exceeds $14 trillion. Over recent decades, the American people have come to expect that the government will actively and effectively control the behavior of this gigantic beast. The fortunes of presidencies, of members of Congress, and of political parties rise and fall in no small part on the basis of the economy's performance. In response to popular demand, the Federal Government seeks to achieve three main goals in the economic realm: full employment, price stability, and economic growth.

Full employment, as you might guess, means that there are enough jobs available to employ all those who are able and willing to work. The Bureau of Labor Statistics, in the Department of Labor, compiles employment and unemployment data. Its reports are a major indicator of the nation's economic health.

Price stability refers to the absence of significant ups and downs in the prices of goods and services. A general increase in prices throughout the economy is called **inflation.** A general decrease in prices is known as **deflation.** The Consumer Price Index (the CPI), also reported by the Bureau of Labor Statistics, tracks trends in the prices of consumer goods.

Both inflation and deflation have harmful effects on the economy. Higher prices due to inflation rob consumers of purchasing power because their dollars buy less than they once did. Deflation makes it difficult for people and businesses to borrow money because the assets they use to borrow against decline in value. Deflation also hurts farmers and other producers, who receive less for their products. This makes it difficult for them to pay off their loans, which in turns hurts banks and investors.

A growing economy is one in which the GDP constantly increases. That growth helps produce a higher standard of living. When there is an absence of growth and the economy shrinks, a **recession** occurs.

dampen
v. to deaden or check

tamp
v. to push down, press

President George W. Bush signs the 2008 Economic Stimulus Act. Refund checks are sent shortly thereafter. *What economic policy do these images reflect?*

Fiscal Policy

Fiscal policy is a major tool with which the Federal Government seeks to achieve its broad economic goals. Fiscal policy consists of the government's powers to tax and spend to influence the economy.

Earlier in this chapter, you read about the generating of revenue and the making of spending decisions through the federal budget process. In addition to deciding how to raise and how to spend money, policymakers must consider what effects their taxing and spending decisions will have on the overall economy. Federal spending represents about 20 percent of the nation's GDP. How money is collected and spent can have a real effect throughout the economy—on employment, on prices, and on growth.

As a general matter, an increase in government spending means heightened economic activity; spending cuts tend to dampen that activity. Tax increases take money out of people's pockets and can slow economic growth. Tax cuts can boost economic activity.

For the better part of 150 years, the Federal Government did not make vigorous use of fiscal policy. Federal income and outgo represented just a bare fraction of GDP. As recently as 1930, that fraction amounted to just over 3 percent of GDP. The Federal Government simply stood by as ups and downs rippled through the economy. Those ups and downs were seen by most economists as an inevitable and even a healthy feature of a free enterprise system.

The Great Depression of the 1930s was a particularly severe downturn. Recall that, in the midst of that crisis, British economist John Maynard Keynes advocated an increase in governmental spending and a decrease in taxes to help end the economic misery. Over time, Keynes's ideas have gained wide acceptance. Now, during a downturn, policymakers usually seek to expand the economy with greater spending and/or lower taxes. This is precisely what happened in 2008 and 2009. Recall, Congress, pressed by President Bush and then by President Obama, enacted a number of economic stimulus measures.

Fiscal policy can also be used to slow inflation. In theory, cuts in government spending and/or tax increases can tamp down inflation across the entire economy.

▶▶ **Analyzing Political Cartoons** Influencing the economy can be an extremely delicate matter. A small action can result in an unexpected outcome requiring a change in policy that may lead to unexpected results. *How does this cartoon illustrate the complexity of monetary policy?*

Fiscal policy does have its limits. For one thing, it takes time for policy changes—for example, an increase or reduction in spending—to have a measurable effect on the economy. Timing the delivery of hikes or cuts is a very tricky matter. So policymakers often resort to other means to influence economic activity.

Monetary Policy

Monetary policy is the most significant of those other means by which the Federal Government can influence the nation's economy. **Monetary policy** involves the money supply (the amount of currency in circulation) and the availability of credit in the economy.

The Federal Reserve Board (the Fed) was created in 1913. It is responsible for the execution of the government's monetary policy. Its seven members are appointed by the President and Senate to serve overlapping 14-year terms. The Board directs the work of the Federal Reserve System as an independent agency created by Congress. It was established to function as the nation's central bank.

Congress intended the Fed to impose some order on a <u>patchwork</u> banking system that had become increasingly <u>prone</u> to panics.[9] Panics occur when depositors lose confidence in banks and rush to recover their funds. If enough customers do so, a bank can be overrun and driven out of business. A panic can spread to infect other banks and, conceivably, an entire banking system. The Fed was designed to avert such a calamity. It serves as a source of emergency funding to prevent panics.

Again, the key function of the Fed is to frame monetary policy. By taking steps to increase the money supply, it can provide a short-term boost to the economy, leading to economic growth and an increase in employment. The Fed can produce the opposite

patchwork
n. something made up of many different parts

prone
adj. likely, subject or liable to

---

9 *Panic* comes from the Latin *panicus,* meaning "terrified"; also from, Pan, the Greek god of nature, thought to inspire fear.

effect by decreasing the supply of money and consequently slowing inflationary pressures.

The Fed can alter the money supply through three major mechanisms. Its tools for that purpose are open market operations, reserve requirements, and the discount rate.

Open Market Operations When the Fed seeks to alter the money supply, it does not simply send out trucks that carry bundles of cash to or from member banks. Its operations are far more sophisticated. It operates through what are called **open market operations**—a process that involves the buying or selling of government securities, such as bonds, from and to the nation's banks. By buying these government securities back from the banks, the Fed provides money to banks, which can then make loans to individuals and to businesses. If its aim is to decrease the money supply, the Fed sells government bonds through its open market operations. As it receives money from the banks that buy those securities, money is removed from circulation. Subsequently, the banks have less money to loan or invest, and so business activity slows.

Reserve Requirements The Fed can also influence or alter the amount of money in circulation by changing the reserve requirements

that all banks and similar financial institutions must meet. The **reserve requirement** is the amount of money that the Federal Reserve Board determines banks must keep "in reserve" in their vaults or on deposit with one of the 12 Federal Reserve Banks. Those funds cannot be used to make loans or for any other purpose. They remain, instead, out of circulation, available for use in the event of sudden, unexpected demand.

If the Fed sees a need to lower the money supply, on the other hand, it can require that banks increase the amount they have in reserve. Or the reserve requirement can be relaxed by the Fed to increase the amount of money in circulation.

Discount Rate The third mechanism available to the Fed involves the discount rate. The **discount rate** is the rate of interest a bank must pay when it borrows money from a Federal Reserve Bank. Interest, recall, is the cost borrowers incur and must repay in order to borrow money. If the Fed raises the discount rate, banks find it more difficult to obtain money. Banks must then charge higher interest rates to their customers; borrowing decreases and less money flows into the economy. Cutting the discount rate has the opposite effect.

Essential Questions Journal To continue to build a response to the chapter Essential Question, go to your **Essential Questions Journal.**

SECTION 4 ASSESSMENT

1. **Guiding Question** Use your completed table to answer this question: How does the Federal Government achieve its economic goals?

Key Terms and Comprehension

2. What is the **gross domestic product?**
3. What is the difference between **inflation** and **deflation?**
4. How can the use of **fiscal policy** and **monetary policy** influence the overall national economy?

Critical Thinking

5. **Identify Central Issues (a)** What are the three main economic goals the government aims to achieve? **(b)** Why do you think these goals are critical to a healthy economy?

6. **Drawing Conclusions** Should the Federal Government have the authority to take actions that can alter the nation's economy? Why or why not?

7. **Predict Consequences** Why might policymakers hesitate to use fiscal policy to influence the nation's economy?

Quick Write

Cause-and-Effect Writing: Create an Outline Review your notes and graphic organizer from Section 3 to clarify the cause-and-effect relationships between the issues and the data you found. What issues seemed to be important to Americans at the time? Did the federal budget and government actions reflect those concerns? Create an outline of the relationships with supporting data to help you determine how best to present the information—chronologically or by order of importance—to your audience.

Quick Study Guide

GOVERNMENT ONLINE
On the Go
To review anytime, anywhere, download these online resources at **PearsonSuccessNet.com**
Political Dictionary, Audio Review

Guiding Question
Section 2 What effect does borrowing have on the federal budget and the nation's economy?

Guiding Question
Section 3 How is federal spending determined?

Guiding Question
Section 1 How is the Federal Government financed?

CHAPTER 16
Essential Question
How should the federal budget reflect Americans' priorities?

Guiding Question
Section 4 How does the Federal Government achieve its economic goals?

Political Dictionary

fiscal policy p. 456
progressive tax p. 459
payroll tax p. 460
regressive tax p. 461
excise tax p. 461
estate tax p. 461
gift tax p. 461
customs duty p. 462
interest p. 462
deficit p. 463
surplus p. 463
demand-side economics p. 464
supply-side economics p. 464
public debt p. 466
entitlement p. 467
controllable spending p. 468
uncontrollable spending p. 468
continuing resolution p. 471
gross domestic product p. 473
inflation p. 474
deflation p. 474
recession p. 474
fiscal policy p. 474
monetary policy p. 475
open market operations p. 476
reserve requirement p. 476
discount rate p. 476

Sources of Government Revenue

Income tax	Progressive tax on the income of both individuals and corporations
Social insurance tax	Regressive tax withheld from employee paychecks to support social programs
Excise tax	Regressive tax on the manufacture, sale, or consumption of goods and/or on services rendered
Estate tax	Tax on the assets of someone who dies
Gift tax	Tax on a gift of money or property
Custom duty	Tax on goods imported into this country
Interest	Monies paid on charges to governmental loans
Licenses and fees	Monies paid for licenses, passports, patents, fines, etc.
Seigniorage	Income gained from production of coins and paper money
Borrowing	Monies gained through the sale of bonds

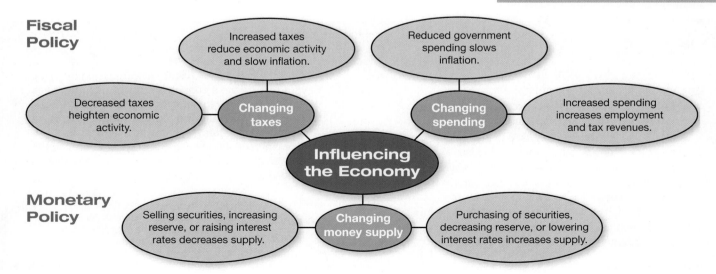

Fiscal Policy

Increased taxes reduce economic activity and slow inflation.

Reduced government spending slows inflation.

Decreased taxes heighten economic activity.

Changing taxes

Changing spending

Increased spending increases employment and tax revenues.

Influencing the Economy

Monetary Policy

Selling securities, increasing reserve, or raising interest rates decreases supply.

Changing money supply

Purchasing of securities, decreasing reserve, or lowering interest rates increases supply.

Chapter Assessment

Comprehension and Critical Thinking

Section 1

1. **(a)** What are the four limits on the power to tax as set out in the Constitution? **(b)** Why do you think these limitations were included by the Framers?

2. **(a)** What are the different types of taxes? **(b)** Which federal tax raises the most revenue? **(c)** Which tax are you most likely to pay on a regular basis? Why?

3. Do you think the current federal taxation system is equitable? Why or why not?

Section 2

4. **(a)** How does the government borrow money? **(b)** Who benefits from this borrowing system? **(c)** Who, if anyone, is disadvantaged by government borrowing?

5. **(a)** What is the public debt? **(b)** Do you think the concern about the size of the public debt is justified? Why or why not?

Section 3

6. **(a)** What is the difference between controllable and uncontrollable spending? **(b)** How would you classify entitlement programs? **(c)** Why do you think Congress structured the financing of these programs in this manner?

7. **(a)** What is the President's role in the budget-making process? **(b)** What is Congress's? **(c)** Is this process a joint effort between the President and Congress? Explain.

8. **(a)** Should the Constitution be amended to require a balanced budget each year? **(b)** What might be the results of such an amendment?

Section 4

9. **(a)** What are the principal economic goals of the Federal Government? **(b)** What methods are used by the government to meet these goals? **(c)** Should the government be involved in the economy? Why or why not?

10. **(a)** What agency is responsible for implementing monetary policy? **(b)** What tools are available to this agency to influence the nation's economy? **(c)** Which of these tools do you think might produce the quickest results? Why do you think so?

11. **Analyzing Political Cartoons (a)** Who do the characters in this cartoon represent? **(b)** What comment is being made through the doctor's diagnosis?

Writing About Government

12. Use your Quick Write exercises from this chapter to write a cause-and-effect essay on the relationship between the actions of the government and the nation's priorities. Make sure that your thesis statement is clearly stated, your ideas are well-organized and your argument is supported. See pp. S3–S5 in the Skills Handbook.

Apply What You've Learned

13. **Essential Question Activity** Take a poll of 10 to 15 individuals in your community. Ask:

    (a) What issues are priorities for Americans today? Which one is the most important to you?

    (b) Within the last six months, has the Federal Government taken any action to address that issue? If so, what?

    (c) Which federal programs or services do you think could be cut back or abolished to help deal with the issue? Would you be willing to pay additional taxes to cover the cost? If not, how should the government pay for it?

    (d) Do you think the Federal Government is responsive to the priorities of Americans? Why or why not?

14. **Essential Question Assessment** Using the results of your poll, create a chart illustrating the top priorities of Americans today to help you answer the Essential Question: **How should the federal budget reflect Americans' priorities?** Then, write a letter to your congressperson expressing the issues that are the top concerns and suggesting methods the government could use to address the issues.

Essential Questions Journal To respond to the chapter Essential Question, go to your **Essential Questions Journal.**

Document-Based Assessment

Addressing the Rising Cost of Healthcare

The costs of entitlement programs and the constraints they place on the federal budget have been debated at great length. Most Americans agree that these programs are critical to the public's well-being, however. As the documents below illustrate, keeping these programs going without undermining others is proving to be a very difficult fiscal challenge.

Document 1

In the United States a large and growing portion of both federal and state expenditures is for subsidized health insurance. In 1975, federal spending on Medicare and Medicaid was about 6 percent of total non-interest federal spending. Today, that share is about 23 percent. Because of rising costs of health care and the aging of the population, the CBO projects that, without reform, Medicare and Medicaid will be about 35 percent of non-interest federal spending in 2025. This trend implies increasingly difficult tradeoffs for legislators and taxpayers, as higher government spending on health care spending will . . . require reductions in other government programs, higher taxes, or larger budget deficits.

—Ben S. Bernanke, Chairman, Federal Reserve, 2008

Document 2

If the major entitlement programs grow as forecast, our children will be forced to choose between massive tax increases, near-elimination of all government programs outside of entitlements (including defense and essential services), or some combination. . . . Because of these rising entitlement obligations, ensuring long-term fiscal stability requires much more than addressing current spending and deficits, important as that is. Also necessary is finding a means of controlling the costs of the major entitlement programs, without compromising their essential functions.

—Katherine Baicker, Council of Economic Advisors, 2005

Document 3

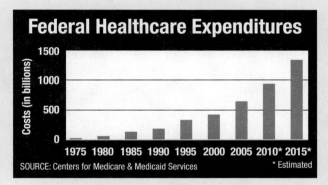

Federal Healthcare Expenditures

SOURCE: Centers for Medicare & Medicaid Services
* Estimated

Use your knowledge of financing government and the documents above to answer Questions 1–3.

1. What is the main point of Document 3?
   - **A.** Controllable expenditures are becoming uncontrollable.
   - **B.** Entitlement programs are too costly.
   - **C.** Revenue from healthcare has increased.
   - **D.** Subsidized healthcare costs have risen considerably over time.

2. What concerns are discussed in both Document 1 and Document 2?

3. **Pull It Together** Considering the expense of the entitlement program, do you think that the Federal Government should continue to provide subsidized healthcare? Why or why not?

GOVERNMENT ONLINE

Documents

To find more primary sources on the cost of healthcare, visit **PearsonSuccessNet.com**

Foreign Policy and National Defense

Essential Question
How should the United States interact with other countries?

Section 1:
Foreign Affairs and Diplomacy

Section 2:
National Security

Section 3:
American Foreign Policy Overview

Section 4:
Foreign Aid and Alliances

GOVERNMENT ONLINE
On the Go

To study anywhere, anytime, download these online resources at PearsonSuccessNet.com
• Political Dictionary
• Audio Review
• Downloadable Interactivities

" …**peace** is the **highest aspiration** of the **American people**. We **will negotiate** for it, **sacrifice** for it; we will **not surrender for it,** now or **ever.**

—Ronald Reagan, Inaugural Address, January 20, 1981

Photo: President Reagan escorts British Prime Minister Margaret Thatcher as she reviews the honor guard at the White House.

SECTION 1

Foreign Affairs and Diplomacy

Guiding Question

How is foreign policy made and conducted? Use a chart like the one below to keep track of the main themes in the conduct of American foreign policy.

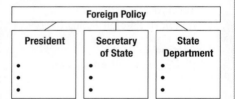

Foreign Policy		
President	**Secretary of State**	**State Department**
•	•	•
•	•	•
•	•	•

Political Dictionary

- domestic affairs
- foreign affairs
- isolationism
- foreign policy
- right of legation
- ambassador
- diplomatic immunity
- passport
- visa

Objectives

1. Explain the difference between isolationism and internationalism.
2. Define foreign policy.
3. Understand that a nation's foreign policy is composed of its many foreign policies.
4. Describe the functions, components, and organization of the Department of State.

Image Above: Secretary of State John Foster Dulles meets with General Chiang Kai-Shek.

In *The Federalist* No. 72, Alexander Hamilton noted that the "actual conduct" of America's foreign affairs would be in the hands of "the assistants or deputies of the chief magistrate," the President. Today, most of the President's "assistants or deputies" in the field of foreign affairs are located within the Department of State.

Foreign affairs have been of prime importance from the nation's very beginnings, more than a dozen years before Hamilton penned his comment in *The Federalist*. Indeed, it is important to remember that the United States would have been hard pressed to win its independence without the aid of a foreign ally, France.

Isolationism to Internationalism

With the coming of independence, and then for more than 150 years, the American people were chiefly concerned with **domestic affairs**—with events at home. **Foreign affairs,** the nation's relationships with other nations, were of little or no concern to them. Through that period, America's foreign relations were very largely shaped by a policy of **isolationism**—a purposeful refusal to become generally involved in the affairs of the rest of the world.

The period from the 1940s onward, however, has been marked by a profound change in the place of the United States in world affairs. The coming of World War II finally convinced the American people that neither they nor anyone else can live in isolation—that, in many ways, and whether we like it or not, the world of today is indeed "one world." The well-being of everyone in this country—in fact, the very survival of the United States—is affected by much that happens elsewhere on the globe. If nothing else, the realities of ultra-rapid travel and instantaneous communications make it clear that we now live in a "global village."

Wars and other political upheavals abroad have an impact on the United States and on the daily lives of the American people. Five times over the past century, the United States fought major wars abroad; and in several other instances, the nation has committed its armed forces to lesser, but significant, foreign conflicts. Terrorists in Europe, Asia, and at home; racial strife in southern Africa; conflicts in the Middle East; and other events in many around the globe have threatened the security of the United States.

Economic conditions elsewhere also have a direct and often immediate effect on and in this country. The American economy has become part of a truly global economy, linked by international banking, multinational corporations, and worldwide investments that transcend national boundaries.

Clearly, today's world cannot be described as "one world" in all respects, however. The planet remains, in many ways, a very <u>fractured</u> and dangerous place. Acts of terrorism, various civil wars, the threat of "rogue states"—these dangers, and more, make the point abundantly clear. In the interconnected yet divided world of today, only those policies that protect and promote the security of all nations can assure the security and well-being of the United States.

Foreign Policy Defined

Every nation's **foreign policy** is actually many different policies on many different topics. It is made up of all of the stands and actions that a nation takes in every aspect of its relationships with other countries—diplomatic, military, commercial, and all others. To put the point another way, a nation's foreign policy includes everything that that nation's government says and everything that it does in world affairs.

Thus, American foreign policy consists of all of the Federal Government's official statements and all of its actions as it conducts this nation's foreign relations. It involves treaties and alliances, international trade, the defense budget, foreign economic and military aid, the United Nations, nuclear weapons testing, and disarmament negotiations. It also includes the American position on oil imports, grain exports, human rights, immigration, climate change, space exploration, fishing rights, cultural exchange programs, economic <u>sanctions,</u> computer technology exports, and a great many other matters.

Some aspects of foreign policy remain largely unchanged over time. For example, an insistence on freedom of the seas has been a basic part of American policy from the nation's beginnings. Other policies are more flexible. Two decades ago, resisting the ambitions of the Soviet Union was a basic part of American foreign policy. Since the fall of the Soviet Union, the United States and Russia have built close, if not always friendly, political, military, and economic ties; the United States has also developed close relations with other former Soviet republics.

The President is both the nation's chief diplomat and the commander in chief of its armed forces. Constitutionally and by tradition, the President bears the major responsibility for both making and conducting foreign policy. The President depends on a number of officials and agencies—Hamilton's "assistants or deputies"—to meet the immense responsibilities that come with this dual role. Here we will examine the President's diplomatic support. In the next section, we will look at the defense and military departments.

The State Department

The State Department, headed by the secretary of state, is the President's right arm in foreign affairs. The President names the secretary of state, subject to confirmation by the Senate. It is to the secretary of state and to the Department of State that the President

✔ **Checkpoint**
What is foreign policy?

<u>fractured</u>
adj. divided, split

<u>sanction</u>
n. penalty imposed for some hostile act(s)

▸▸ **Analyzing Political Cartoons** In an effort to bring peace to the region, several Presidents have brokered talks between Palestinian and Israeli leaders. *According to this cartoon, why have these diplomatic efforts not been wholly successful?*

Implementing Foreign Policy

The State Department aims to achieve four major goals as it carries out America's foreign polices. It employs the methods outlined below. *How might achieving one of these goals relate to achieving the others?*

Protecting America

- Maintaining and strengthening diplomatic ties with other nations
- Managing domestic and international travel and trade policies
- Promoting global stability

Secretary of State Colin Powell arrives in Lebanon in 2002 to help ease the Arab-Israeli conflict.

Advancing Democracy

- Supporting newly established democracies
- Promoting fair voting practices and just legal systems
- Monitoring human rights issues globally

An Afghan voter reviews the ballot in an election in her country.

Promoting American Values

- Using government-supported and other media to provide information on American values to other peoples
- Supporting cultural exchange programs

A Voice of America radio journalist provides news and information on human rights to refugees in Burundi.

Supporting Diplomatic Officials

- Sending diplomats abroad to implement American foreign policy
- Protecting American diplomats and others abroad

Following terrorist threats, the U.S. embassy in Indonesia increased security with the support of local police.

looks for advice and assistance in both the formulation and the conduct of the nation's foreign policy.

The Secretary of State The secretary of state ranks first among the members of the President's Cabinet. That ranking speaks to the importance of the office, and also to the fact that the State Department was the first of the now 15 executive departments that Congress created.

A Department of Foreign Affairs had first been created in 1781 under the Articles of Confederation. Congress re-created it in 1789 as the first major unit in the executive branch under the Constitution. Later that year, its name was changed to the Department of State.

President George Washington appointed Thomas Jefferson as the nation's first secretary of state, in 1789. Bill Clinton appointed the first woman to hold the post, Madeleine Albright, in 1997. Colin Powell, who served as secretary of state in George W. Bush's first term (2001 to 2005) became the first African American to occupy the office; and his successor, Condoleezza Rice, who is both a woman and an African American, served from 2005 to 2009. Today, the post is held by another major personality—former first lady and former senator from New York, Hillary Rodham Clinton.

Today, the duties of the secretary relate almost entirely to foreign affairs. That is, they center on the making and conduct of policy and on the management of the department, its many overseas posts, and its workforce of more than 20,000 men and women.[1]

Some Presidents—most famously, Woodrow Wilson and Franklin Roosevelt—have tended to ignore their secretaries of state and have handled many foreign policy matters personally and quite often directly. Others, notably Richard Nixon, Gerald Ford, and both Bushes, have chosen instead to rely on their national security advisors (whose formal title in the Executive Office of the President is, recall, Assistant to the President for National Security Affairs). Some chief executives—in particular, the earlier ones—have chosen to delegate a large share of the responsibility for matters of foreign policy to the secretary.

Organization and Components The State Department is organized along both geographic and functional lines. Some of its agencies, such as the Bureau of African Affairs and the Bureau of Near Eastern Affairs, deal with matters involving particular regions of the world.

Other agencies have broader missions—for example, the Bureau of International Narcotics and Law Enforcement Affairs, sometimes called "Drugs 'n' Thugs." Most bureaus are headed by an assistant secretary and include several offices. Thus, both the Office of Passport Services and the Office of Visa Services are found in the Bureau of Consular Affairs.

The new U.S. Embassy in Beijing opened in 2008. Its design reflects the high-security needs of today. *Why does the United States maintain relationships with many countries with which we have significant disagreements?*

Overseas Representatives

Some 12,000 men and women now represent the United States as members of the Foreign Service, many of them serving abroad. Under international law, every nation has the **right of legation**—the right to send and receive diplomatic representatives. International law consists of those rules and principles that guide sovereign states in their dealings with one another and in their treatment of foreign nationals (private persons and groups). Its sources include treaties, decisions of international courts, and custom. Treaties are the most important source today. The right of legation is an ancient practice. Its history can be traced back to the Egyptian civilization of 6,000 years ago.

The Second Continental Congress named this nation's first foreign service officer in 1778. That year, it chose Benjamin Franklin to be America's minister to France. He served in that capacity for nearly eight years.

Ambassadors An **ambassador** is the official representative of a sovereign state in the conduct of its foreign affairs.[2] For some five

✓ Checkpoint
How are ambassadors selected?

---

1 The secretary does have some domestic responsibilities. Thus, when Richard Nixon resigned the presidency on August 9, 1974, his formal, legal announcement of that fact had to be submitted to Secretary of State Henry Kissinger. Over the years, the secretary and the department have had (and been relieved of) a fairly wide range of domestic functions—including publishing the nation's laws, issuing patents, and supervising the decennial census.

2 See Chapter 14, Section 3. An ambassador's official title is Ambassador Extraordinary and Plenipotentiary. When the office is vacant or the ambassador is absent, the post is usually filled by the next-ranking Foreign Service officer in the embassy. That officer, temporarily in charge of embassy affairs, is known as the chargé d'affaires.

Diplomatic Immunity
The Iran Hostage Crisis

An **American hostage** is paraded in front of the media by Iranian militants in 1979.

Although an embassy serves a specific diplomatic function, it is also a symbol of the nation it represents. Occasionally, tensions between nations can cause citizens of one country to protest or even attack another country's embassy to express their anger at that country.

In 1979, Iranian students occupied the U.S. embassy in the capital, Tehran, and held embassy staff hostage for 444 days. The Iran Hostage Crisis was an unusual and unprecedented assault against both a nation and international diplomatic law. *Why does the United States send diplomats to posts where political conditions are unstable?*

For the first time, **yellow ribbons** were tied to trees to symbolize public support for the hostages.

accredit
v. to appoint as an official representative of his or her country

centuries now, most of the formal contacts between sovereign nations—that is, most of their diplomatic relationships—have been conducted through their duly appointed ambassadors.

In this country, ambassadors are appointed by the President, with Senate consent, and they serve at his pleasure. Today, the United States is represented by an ambassador stationed at the capital of each sovereign state this nation recognizes. Thus, American embassies are now located in more than 180 countries around the world.

The United States now maintains over 260 diplomatic and consular offices abroad as well. There, Foreign Service officers promote American interests in a multitude of ways—for example, encouraging trade, gathering intelligence data, advising persons who seek to enter this country, and aiding American citizens who are abroad and in need of legal advice or other help.

Some ambassadorships are much desired political plums, and whenever a new President moves into the White House, he typically makes many new appointments. Too often, Presidents have appointed people to ambassadorships and other major diplomatic posts as a reward for those individuals' support—financial and otherwise—of the President's election to office. However, in many cases these ranks are filled with career diplomats in the Foreign Service.

President Harry Truman named the first African American, Edward R. Dudley, as an ambassador to Liberia, in 1949. Later that same year President Truman also appointed the first woman, Eugenie Anderson, as ambassador to Denmark.

Special Diplomats Those persons whom the President names to certain other top diplomatic posts also carry the rank of ambassador. Examples include the United States representative to the UN and the American member of the North Atlantic Treaty Council. The President also often assigns the personal rank of ambassador to those diplomats who take on special assignments abroad—for example, representing the United States at an international conference on arms limitations or Arab-Israeli relations.

Diplomatic Immunity In international law, every sovereign state is supreme within its own boundaries. All persons or things found within that state's territory are subject to its jurisdiction.

As a major exception to that rule, ambassadors are regularly granted **diplomatic immunity**—they are not subject to the laws of the state to which they are accredited. They cannot be arrested, sued, or taxed. Their official residences (embassies) cannot be entered or searched without their consent, and all official communications and other properties are protected. All other embassy personnel and their families receive this same immunity.

Diplomatic immunity is essential to the ability of every nation to conduct its foreign relations. The practice assumes that diplomats will not abuse their privileged status. If a host government finds a diplomat's conduct unacceptable, that official may be declared *persona non grata* and expelled from the country. The mistreatment of diplomats is considered a major breach of international law.

Diplomatic immunity is a generally accepted practice. There are exceptions, however. The most serious breach in modern times occurred in Iran in late 1979. Militant followers of the Ayatollah Khomeini seized the American embassy in Tehran on November 4 of that year; 66 Americans were taken hostage and 52 were held for 444 days. The Iranians finally released the hostages moments after Ronald Reagan became President on January 20, 1981.

Passports A **passport** is a legal document issued by a state that identifies a person as a citizen of that state. It grants that person a right of protection while traveling abroad and the right to return to the homeland. Passports entitle their holders to the privileges accorded to them by international custom and treaties. Few countries will admit persons who do not hold valid passports.

Travel Documents

Some years ago, a valid passport was all one needed to travel abroad and enter most other countries. Today, most countries also require a visa. ***Why do you think this is now the case?***

Passports

- Issued by a government and identifies the bearer as a citizen or national of the issuing country
- Entitles the bearer to consular protection abroad and to return to his or her country of citizenship
- Valid for 10 years
- Three types: diplomatic, official, tourist

Visas

- Issued by the country the individual requests permission to enter
- Permits the traveler to remain in a country for a specified period of time, but does not guarantee entry
- Valid only for the time period stated
- Of many types, including: transit, tourist, business, and student

The State Department's Office of Passport Services now issues more than ten million passports to Americans each year. Do not confuse passports with visas. A **visa** is a permit to enter another state and must be obtained from the country one wishes to enter. Trips to most foreign countries require visas today. Most visas to enter this country are issued at American consulates abroad.

Essential Questions Journal To continue to build a response to the chapter Essential Question, go to your **Essential Questions Journal.**

SECTION 1 ASSESSMENT

1. **Guiding Question** Use your completed chart to answer this question: How is foreign policy made and conducted?

Key Terms and Comprehension

2. Why did the United States abandon a policy of **isolationism** and move to one of internationalism?

3. **(a)** What is **foreign policy? (b)** List three examples of topics covered by American foreign policy.

4. Why is it most often advisable that an **ambassador** come from the ranks of career diplomats?

Critical Thinking

5. **Demonstrate Reasoned Judgment** Do you think it would be possible for the United States to return to a policy of isolationism? Why or why not?

6. **Draw Conclusions** Why do you think it is necessary that an American representative be assigned to work and live in each state the United States recognizes?

7. **Draw Inferences** Why is diplomatic immunity considered essential to relationships between and among nations?

Quick Write

Expository Writing: Define a Problem In order to write a problem-and-solution essay, you need to define the problem you intend to solve. Think about the types of issues the world struggles with today—economic instability, environmental destruction, famine, political unrest, and so on. What issue do you think is most important? Write a brief description of the problem you select.

National Security

Guiding Question

How does the Federal Government safeguard this nation's security?
Use a table like the one below to keep track of the methods used to safeguard the nation.

Protecting National Security	
Secretary of Defense	•
	•
	•
	•

Political Dictionary

- espionage
- terrorism

Objectives

1. Summarize the functions, components, and organization of the Department of Defense and the military departments.
2. Explain how the Director of National Intelligence and the Department of Homeland Security contribute to the nation's security.

Image Above: Two members of the Joint Service Color Guard present the colors at a military ceremony.

How many federal agencies, in addition to the Department of State, are involved with the nation's foreign affairs? Dozens of them. Thus, the FBI combats terrorism and espionage here and abroad. The Public Health Service works with the United Nations and foreign governments to conquer diseases and meet other health problems in many parts of the world. The United States Agency for International Development (USAID) provides economic help to foreign countries. The Office of the United States Trade Representative promotes this country's interests in international trade.

A recitation of this sort could go on and on. But, as you will see, this section deals with those agencies most directly involved in the areas of foreign and defense policy.

The Defense Department

Congress established what is today called the Department of Defense (DoD) in the National Security Act of 1947. It is the present-day successor to two historic Cabinet-level agencies: the War Department, created by Congress in 1789, and the Navy Department, created in 1798.

Congress created the Defense Department in order to unify the nation's armed forces. It wished to bring the then-separate army (including the air force) and the navy under the control of a single Cabinet department. Today, there are nearly 1.4 million men and women on active duty in the military, over one million in the National Guard and Reserves, and some 650,000 civilians employed by the Defense Department.

Civil Control of the Military The authors of the Constitution understood the importance of the nation's defense. They emphasized that fact clearly in the Preamble, and they underscored it in the body of the Constitution by mentioning defense more frequently than any other governmental function.

The Framers also recognized the dangers inherent in military power and the potential of its abuse. They knew that its very existence can pose a threat to free government. And, therefore, the Constitution is studded with provisions to make sure that the military is always subject to the control of the nation's civilian authorities.

Thus, the Constitution makes the elected President the commander in chief of the armed forces. To the same end, it gives broad military powers to Congress—that is, to the elected representatives of the people.[3]

---

3 Recall that the Constitution makes defense a national function and practically excludes the States from that field. Each State does have a militia, which it may use to keep the peace within its own borders. Today, the organized portion of the militia is the National Guard. Congress has the power (Article I, Section 8, Clauses 15 and 16) to "provide for calling forth the Militia" and to provide for organizing, arming, and disciplining it. Congress first delegated to the President the power to call the militia into federal service in 1795, and the commander in chief has had that authority ever since. Today, the governor of each State is the commander in chief of that State's units of the Army and the Air National Guard, except when the President orders those units into federal service.

The principle of civilian control has always been a major factor in the making of defense policy and in the creation and staffing of the various agencies responsible for the execution of that policy. The importance of civilian control is clearly illustrated by this fact: The National Security Act of 1947 provides that the secretary of defense cannot have served on active duty in any of the armed forces for at least 10 years before being named to that post.

The Secretary of Defense The Department of Defense is headed by the secretary of defense, whose appointment by the President is subject to confirmation by the Senate. The secretary, who serves at the President's

✓ **Checkpoint**
Who are the nation's civilian authorities?

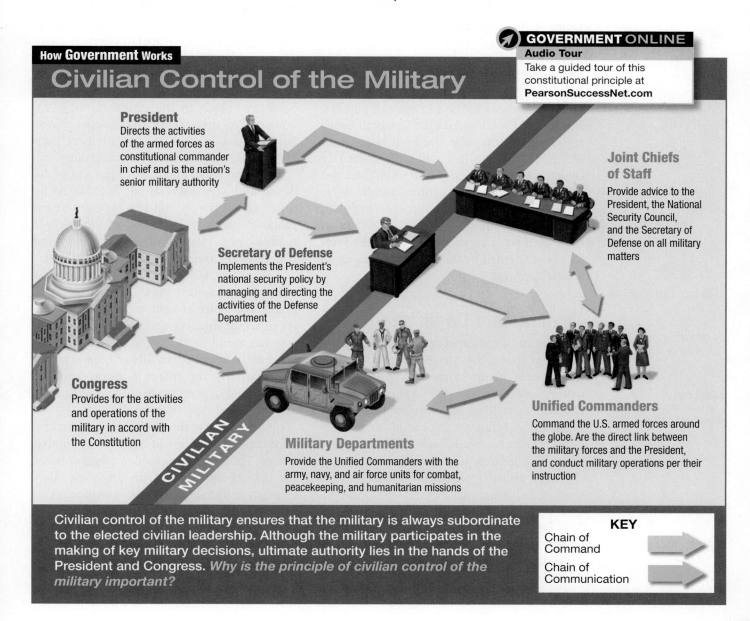

How Government Works

Civilian Control of the Military

GOVERNMENT ONLINE
Audio Tour
Take a guided tour of this constitutional principle at **PearsonSuccessNet.com**

President
Directs the activities of the armed forces as constitutional commander in chief and is the nation's senior military authority

Secretary of Defense
Implements the President's national security policy by managing and directing the activities of the Defense Department

Congress
Provides for the activities and operations of the military in accord with the Constitution

Military Departments
Provide the Unified Commanders with the army, navy, and air force units for combat, peacekeeping, and humanitarian missions

Joint Chiefs of Staff
Provide advice to the President, the National Security Council, and the Secretary of Defense on all military matters

Unified Commanders
Command the U.S. armed forces around the globe. Are the direct link between the military forces and the President, and conduct military operations per their instruction

CIVILIAN / MILITARY

Civilian control of the military ensures that the military is always subordinate to the elected civilian leadership. Although the military participates in the making of key military decisions, ultimate authority lies in the hands of the President and Congress. *Why is the principle of civilian control of the military important?*

KEY
Chain of Command
Chain of Communication

✔ **Checkpoint**
Who advises the
President on military
matters?

pleasure, is charged with two major responsibilities. He is simultaneously (1) the President's chief aide and advisor in making and carrying out defense policy, and (2) the operating head of the Defense Department.

The secretary's huge domain is often called the Pentagon—because of its massive five-sided headquarters building in Virginia, across the Potomac River from the Capitol. Its operations regularly take a large slice of the federal budget every year for more than 70 years—and nearly a fourth of all federal spending today. The global war on terrorism has forced vast increases in expenditures for the military. The Department of Defense spent nearly $300 billion in fiscal year 2001, the year of the September 11 attacks. The Department of Defense will almost certainly spend well over twice that amount in fiscal year 2010.

Chief Military Aides The six members of the Joint Chiefs of Staff serve as the principal military advisors to the secretary of defense, and to the President and the National Security Council. This collective body is made up of the chairman of the Joint Chiefs, the vice chairman, the army chief of staff, the chief of naval operations, the commandant of the Marine Corps, and the air force chief of staff. The highest ranking uniformed officers in the armed services, the members of the Joint Chiefs are named by the President, subject to Senate approval.

The Military Departments

The three military departments—the Departments of the Army, the Navy, and the Air Force—are major units and sub-Cabinet departments within the Department of Defense. A civilian secretary, named by the President and directly responsible to the secretary of defense, leads each military department. The nation's armed forces—the army, the navy, and the air force—operate within that unified structure.

The Department of the Army The army is the largest of the armed services, and the oldest. The American Continental Army, now the United States Army, was established by the Second Continental Congress on June 14, 1775—more than a year before the Declaration of Independence.

The army is essentially a ground-based force, and it is responsible for military operations on land. It must be ready (1) to defeat any attack on the United States itself, and (2) to take swift and forceful action to protect American interests in any other part of the world. To these ends, it must organize, train, and equip its active duty forces—the Regular Army, the Army National Guard, and the Army Reserve. Over 350,000 Army National Guard soldiers and reservists have been called to service since September 11, 2001, many of them for the wars in Afghanistan and Iraq. All of the army's active duty forces are under the direct command of the army's highest ranking officer, the army chief of staff.

The Regular Army is the nation's standing army, the heart of its land forces. There are now more than 550,000 soldiers on active duty—officers and enlisted personnel, professional soldiers, and volunteers. The army has been downsized in the post–cold war era, however. At the time of the collapse of the Soviet Union in 1991, there were more than 700,000 men and women on active duty.

Women make up about 15 percent of the Army and now serve in all Regular Army units, except the Special Forces. Over recent years, women's roles have come to include many combat-related duties in the army and in each of the other armed services, as well.

The army trains and equips its combat units to fight enemy forces. The infantry takes, holds, and defends land areas. The artillery supports the infantry, seeks to destroy enemy concentrations with its heavier guns, and gives anti-aircraft cover. The armored cavalry also supports the infantry, using armored vehicles and helicopters to <u>spearhead</u> assaults and oppose enemy counteroffensives.

Other units of the army provide the many services and supplies in support of combat troops. Those soldiers could not fight without the help of members of the engineer, quartermaster, signal, ordnance, transportation, military police, and medical corps.

The Department of the Navy The United States Navy was first formed as the Continental Navy—a fledgling naval force created by

spearhead
v. to lead a military force; to take the lead in

The Armed Forces Overseas

Major Military Deployments

Protecting the nation's security does not end at the nation's borders. In fact, nearly one fourth of the armed forces of the United States is now stationed abroad. Today, the top five areas to which the men and women of the American military are deployed are in East Asia, Southwest Asia, and Europe. *Why is it necessary to post the armed forces overseas in order to protect national security?*

	Total	Army	Navy	Marine Corps	Air Force
East Asia					
Japan	34,554	2,585	4,036	15,243	12,690
South Korea*	24,655	16,507	242	112	7,794
Europe					
Germany	54,043	38,633	254	300	14,856
Southwest Asia					
Afghanistan	41,300	29,100	1,700	3,300	7,200
Iraq	174,200	111,200	19,300	22,600	21,100

SOURCE: Department of Defense, Personnel and Procurement Statistics, March 2009
*2008 data

A soldier attends a farewell event prior to his deployment to Iraq.

the Second Continental Congress on October 13, 1775. Ever since, its major responsibility has been sea warfare.

The chief of naval operations is the navy's highest ranking officer and is responsible for its preparations and readiness for war and for its use in combat. Similar to the army, the navy's ranks also have been thinned in the post–cold war period. Today, some 330,000 officers and enlisted personnel serve in the navy, with women making up about 15 percent of the force.

The Second Continental Congress established the United States Marine Corps (USMC) on November 10, 1775. Today, it operates as a separate armed service within the Navy Department, but it is not under the control of the chief of naval operations. Its commandant answers directly to the secretary of the navy.

The marines are a combat-ready land force for the navy. They have two major combat missions: (1) to seize or defend land bases from which the ships of the fleet and the air power of the navy and marines can operate, and (2) to carry out other land operations essential to a naval <u>campaign.</u> Today, some 200,000 men and women serve in the USMC. The proportion of women in the marines is lower than it is in the other service branches—about 6 percent.

The Department of the Air Force The air force is the youngest of the military services. Congress established the United States Air Force (USAF) and made it a separate branch of the armed forces in the National Security Act of 1947. However, its history dates back to 1907, when the army assigned an officer and two enlisted men to a new unit called the Aeronautical Division of the Army Signal Corps. Those three men were ordered to take "charge of all matters pertaining to military ballooning, air machines and all kindred subjects."

Today, the USAF is the nation's first line of defense. It has primary responsibility for military air and aerospace operations. In time

✔ **Checkpoint**
What are the main responsibilities of each of the military departments?

campaign
n. a series of military actions taken toward a specific goal

shroud
v. to hide from view

of war, its major duties are to defend the United States; attack and defeat enemy air, ground, and sea forces; strike military and other war-related targets in enemy territory; and provide transport and combat support for land and naval operations.

Reduced by 150,000 since 1991, the air force now has about 340,000 officers and enlisted personnel, about 20 percent of whom are women. All who serve in the USAF are under the direct command of the chief of staff of the air force.

The Director of National Intelligence

The Director of National Intelligence (DNI) heads the Office of the Director of National Intelligence, established in 2005. The Office was born out of the pre-9/11 failure of the government's several intelligence agencies to collect and share information that might have warned of al Qaeda's coming attacks.

The President, with Senate approval, appoints the DNI, who is now the President's chief advisor in all matters relating to intelligence. The DNI supervises the operations of the 16 separate agencies that make up the federal intelligence community and directs the work of the National Counterterrorism Center (NCTC). The NCTC's hundreds of specialists receive and evaluate all information gathered by the intelligence community and relay it to all those who have "the need to know." As the first DNI, John Negroponte, put it: "Our job is to integrate foreign, military, and domestic intelligence in defense of the homeland and of United States interests abroad."

Some of the agencies controlled by the DNI are fairly well known, among them the FBI, the DEA, and the CIA. Indeed, for more than half a century, one of them, the Central Intelligence Agency, was—as its title suggests—the government's principal, its central, intelligence gathering organization. The CIA remains a major "cloak and dagger" agency, but the DNI now holds its once leading role in the intelligence community.

Some of the agencies in the intelligence community are little known, however, including the National Geospatial Agency,

ideological
adj. having to do with the ideas or beliefs of a group

the Defense Intelligence Agency, and the world's largest spy organization, the National Security Agency. Much of their work involves **espionage**—spying—and is shrouded in deepest secrecy. Even Congress has generally shied away from more than a passing check on their activities, and their operating funds are disguised at several places in the federal budget each year.

Nearly all Americans agree that the work of the several agencies that comprise the intelligence community is absolutely essential to the security of the United States. At the same time, however, it is essential that both the policymaking leaders in the government and the American people clearly recognize the potential dangers of a complex of government agencies whose operations are conducted in utmost secrecy.

Department of Homeland Security

The Department of Homeland Security (DHS) is charged with the awesome and complex task of protecting the United States against terrorism. **Terrorism** is the use of violence to intimidate a government or a society, usually for political or ideological reasons.

Congress created the department in 2002, and it became operational in 2003. It is responsible for the coordination and the direction of all antiterrorist activities of all of the public agencies that operate in the field of domestic security—including thousands of police departments, fire departments, emergency medical and search and rescue units, and other disaster response agencies across the country.

The Homeland Security Act of 2002 gives the department major operating responsibilities in five specific areas:

- border and transportation security
- infrastructure protection
- emergency preparedness and response
- chemical, biological, radiological, and nuclear defense
- information analysis (intelligence)

The department was built mostly of agencies transferred to it from other Cabinet departments. Those agencies include

Department of Homeland Security

Safeguarding the Nation's Security

GOVERNMENT ONLINE
Audio Tour
To learn more about the Department of Homeland Security, visit
PearsonSuccessNet.com

The attacks of September 11, 2001 illustrated the vulnerability of this nation and its people. Since those tragic events, the Department of Homeland Security was created and charged with the large and complicated task of protecting the security of this vast country. Achieving this goal requires the coordinated effort of the department's several agencies, State and local governments, and the American people. *Why do you think coordinating the efforts of all levels of government is necessary in the safeguarding of the nation's security?*

San Francisco's Golden Gate Bridge

Prevention

To detect and deter threats to the United States, the department

- Secures the nation's borders against terrorists, means of terrorism, illegal drugs, and other illegal activity
- Develops technology to detect and prevent the illegal possession and use of chemical, biological, radiological and nuclear materials
- Coordinates the collection and sharing of information
- Strengthens the security of the Nation's transportation system
- Enforces the nation's immigration laws

U.S. Border Patrol agent examines a pedestrian barrier in New Mexico.

Protection

To safeguard the nation's infrastructure, economy, and citizens from acts of terrorism, or other emergencies, the department

- Implements a plan to protect both the nation's physical infrastructure and cyber infrastructure
- Combats financial and electronic crimes and identity theft
- Protects the President and other key government officials
- Works with other agencies to protect governmental activities
- Administers a unified preparedness strategy affecting all levels of government and the private sector

Secret Service agents ensure the President's safety.

Response

To lead, manage, and coordinate the national response to acts of terrorism or other emergencies, the department

- Maintains catastrophic all-hazard plans focusing on the nation's most vulnerable communities
- Promotes response readiness through integrated planning to meet such crises as health and medical emergencies or acts of terrorism
- Provides emergency housing following major disasters
- Partners with other agencies and the private sector to assist mariners in distress and to protect property

A U.S. Coast Guard officer searches for survivors of Hurricane Katrina.

The State of Alaska and DHS jointly protect this 800-mile pipeline that carries crude oil to a seaport. *Why is the integrity of the Alaska pipeline important to national security?*

foment
v. to stir up, provoke

the Secret Service and the newly entitled U.S. Immigration and Customs Enforcement (ICE), from the Treasury Department; the Coast Guard and the Transportation Security Administration, from the Transportation Department; the renamed U.S. Citizenship and Immigration Services, from the Justice Department; and the independent Federal Emergency Management Agency (FEMA).

The threat of bioterrorism—the use of such biological agents as smallpox or anthrax as weapons—dramatizes the immensity of the problems facing the Department of Homeland Security. So, too, do these facts: There are nearly 600,000 bridges, 170,000 water systems, and more than 5,000 power plants (104 of them nuclear) in the United States. There are also 220,000 miles of rail lines, 1.5 million miles of natural gas pipelines, 25,000 miles of inland waterways, and 1,000 harbor channels. Additionally, there are some 470 skyscrapers (each over 500 feet high), nearly 19,000 airports (including some 300 major facilities), thousands of stadiums and other large gathering places, and nearly 20,000 miles of international border.

Add to those fundamental facts such critical matters as the nation's food and water supply, its healthcare system, and its communications networks, and this point becomes clear: This country cannot be protected—completely and absolutely—against terrorist acts. Terrorism thrives on unpredictability and uses it as a weapon to <u>foment</u> fear and anxiety.

It seems quite apparent that the best that can be hoped for in current circumstances is that (1) most—nearly all—terrorist attacks will be thwarted or their impacts will at least be minimized; and (2) those responsible for the attacks will be rooted out and brought to justice.

Essential Questions Journal To continue to build a response to the chapter Essential Question, go to your **Essential Questions Journal.**

SECTION 2 ASSESSMENT

1. **Guiding Question** Use your completed table to answer this question: How does the Federal Government safeguard this nation's security?

Key Terms and Comprehension

2. Who are the key advisors to the President on issues of defense?

3. Describe the main duties of each military department.

4. Why might **espionage** be considered an important tool in protecting national security?

5. What is **terrorism**?

Critical Thinking

6. **Identify Central Issues (a)** Why do you think the Framers thought civilian control of the military to be so important? **(b)** Do you think it remains a matter of valid concern today?

7. **Analyze Information (a)** What are the five areas of responsibility tasked to the Department of Homeland Security? **(b)** How might the supervision of those areas help prevent terrorist attacks in the United States?

Quick Write

Expository Writing: Brainstorm Possible Solutions Recognizing that a problem exists may be quite simple, but coming up with a solution is often a difficult task. Using the description you wrote in Section 1, brainstorm ideas for possible solutions to the problem you selected. Then, organize your list to rank the solutions from most effective to least effective.

SECTION 3

American Foreign Policy Overview

Guiding Question

How has American foreign policy changed over time? Use a timeline to keep track of the major changes in American foreign policy.

Policy of isolationism begins

1789

Political Dictionary

- collective security
- deterrence
- cold war
- containment
- détente

Objectives

1. Summarize American foreign policy from independence through World War I.
2. Show how the two World Wars affected America's traditional policy of isolationism.
3. Explain the principles of collective security and deterrence and their use during the cold war.
4. Describe American foreign policy since the end of the cold war.
5. Understand why the world remains a dangerous place.

Image Above: American diplomat Ben Franklin is received at the French court in Versailles in 1778.

The basic purpose of American foreign policy has always been to protect the security and well-being of the United States—and so it is today. It would be impossible to present a full-blown, detailed history of America's foreign relations in these pages, of course. But we can review its major themes and highlights here.

Why should you know as much as you can about the history of the United States? Because history is not "bunk," as automaker Henry Ford once described it. Let Robert Kelly, a leading historian, tell you what history really is: "History is our social memory. Our memories tell us who we are, where we belong, what has worked and what has not worked, and where we seem to be going."[4]

Foreign Policy Through World War I

From its beginnings, and for 150 years, American foreign policy was very largely built on a policy of isolationism. Throughout that period, the United States refused to become generally and permanently involved in the affairs of the rest of the world.

Isolationism arose in the earliest years of this nation's history. In his Farewell Address in 1796, George Washington declared that "our true policy" was "to steer clear of permanent alliances with any portion of the foreign world." Our "detached and distant situation," Washington said, made it desirable for us to have "as little political connection as possible" with other nations.

At the time, and for decades to come, isolationism seemed a wise policy to most Americans. The United States was a new and relatively weak nation with a great many problems, a huge continent to explore and settle, and two oceans to separate it from the rest of the world.

The policy of isolationism did not demand a *complete* separation from the rest of the world, however. From the first, the United States developed ties abroad by exchanging diplomatic representatives with other nations, making treaties with many of them, and building an extensive foreign commerce. In fact, isolationism was, over time, more a statement of our desire for

4 *The Shaping of the American Past,* 2nd ed.

doctrine
n. a rule or principle that forms the basis of a policy or belief

noninvolvement outside the Western Hemisphere than a description of United States policy within our own hemisphere.

The Monroe Doctrine James Monroe gave the policy of isolationism a clearer shape in 1823. In a historic message to Congress, he proclaimed what has been known ever since as the Monroe Doctrine.

A wave of revolutions had swept Latin America, destroying the old Spanish and Portuguese empires there. The United States viewed the prospect that other European powers would now help Spain and Portugal to take back their lost possessions as a threat to this country's security and a challenge to its economic interests.

In his message, President Monroe restated America's intentions to stay out of European affairs. He also warned the nations of Europe to stay out of the affairs of both North and South America. He declared that the United States would look on

> **Primary Source**
>
> **any attempt on their part to extend their system to any portion of this hemisphere as dangerous to our peace and safety.**
>
> —**Speech by President James Monroe to Congress, December 2, 1823**

At first, most Latin Americans took little notice of this <u>doctrine.</u> They knew that it was really the Royal Navy and British interest in Latin American trade that protected them from European domination. But in 1867, the Monroe Doctrine got its first real test. While Americans were immersed in the Civil War, France invaded Mexico. The French leader, Napoleon III, installed Archduke Maximilian of Austria as Mexico's puppet emperor. In 1867, the United States backed the Mexicans in forcing the French to withdraw, and the Maximilian regime fell.

Later, as the United States became more powerful, many Latin Americans came to view the Monroe Doctrine as a selfish policy designed to protect the political and economic interests of the United States, not the independence of other nations in the Western Hemisphere.

A World Power Following its victory in the Revolutionary War, the United States began to expand across the continent almost at once. The Louisiana Purchase in 1803 doubled the nation's size in a single stroke and the Florida Purchase Treaty in 1819 completed its expansion to the south.

Through the second quarter of the nineteenth century, the United States pursued what most Americans believed was this nation's "Manifest Destiny": the mission to

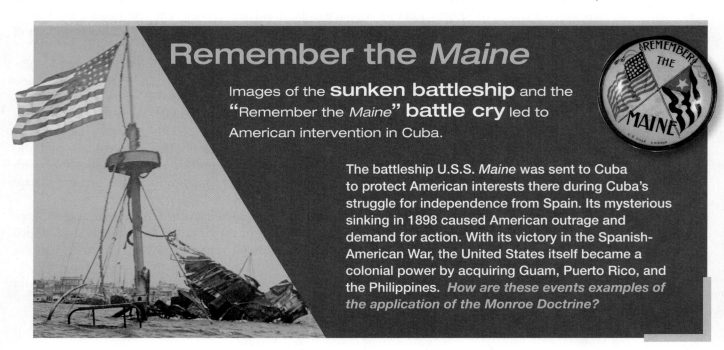

Remember the *Maine*

Images of the **sunken battleship** and the "Remember the *Maine*" **battle cry** led to American intervention in Cuba.

The battleship U.S.S. *Maine* was sent to Cuba to protect American interests there during Cuba's struggle for independence from Spain. Its mysterious sinking in 1898 caused American outrage and demand for action. With its victory in the Spanish-American War, the United States itself became a colonial power by acquiring Guam, Puerto Rico, and the Philippines. *How are these events examples of the application of the Monroe Doctrine?*

expand its boundaries across the continent to the Pacific Ocean. By 1900, the nation had not only accomplished that task, it had spread its influence beyond the continental boundaries to become both a colonial and a world power. The nation's interests now extended to Alaska, to the tip of Latin America, and across the Pacific to the Philippines.

The Good Neighbor Policy The threat of European intervention in the Western Hemisphere that troubled President Monroe declined in the second half of the nineteenth century. That threat was replaced by problems within the hemisphere. Political instability, revolutions, unpaid foreign debts, and injuries to citizens and property of other countries <u>plagued</u> Central and South America.

Under what came to be known as the Roosevelt Corollary to the Monroe Doctrine, the United States began to police Latin America in the early 1900s. Several times, the marines were used to <u>quell</u> revolutions and other unrest in Nicaragua, Haiti, Cuba, and elsewhere in Latin America.

In 1903, Panama revolted and became independent of Colombia, with America's blessing. In the same year, the United States gained the right to build a canal across the Isthmus of Panama. In 1917, the United States purchased the Virgin Islands from Denmark to help guard the canal. Many in Latin America resented these and other steps. They complained of "the Colossus of the North," of "Yankee imperialism," and of "dollar diplomacy"—and many still do.

This country's Latin American policies took a dramatic turn in the 1930s. Theodore Roosevelt's Corollary was replaced by Franklin Roosevelt's Good Neighbor Policy, a conscious attempt to win friends to the south by reducing this nation's political and military interventions in the region.

Today, the central provision of the Monroe Doctrine—the warning against foreign encroachments in the Western Hemisphere—is set out in the Inter-American Treaty of Reciprocal Assistance (the Rio Pact) of 1947. Still, the United States is, without question, the dominant power in the Western Hemisphere, and the Monroe Doctrine remains a vital part of American foreign policy.

THE WORLD CONSTABLE.

▶▶ **Analyzing Political Cartoons** To prevent European intervention in Latin America, President Theodore Roosevelt proclaimed that the United States should be the only policeman of the western hemisphere. *According to this cartoon, what is involved in implementing this policy?*

The Open Door in China Historically, American foreign-policy interests have centered on Europe and Latin America. But America has also been involved in Asia since the mid-1800s. Forty-five years before the United States acquired territory in the Pacific, the U.S. Navy's Commodore Matthew Perry had opened Japan to American trade.

By the late nineteenth century, however, America's thriving trade in Asia was being seriously threatened. The British, French, Germans, and Japanese were each ready to take slices of the Chinese coast as their own exclusive trading preserves. In 1899, Secretary of State John Hay announced this country's insistence on an Open Door policy in China. That doctrine promoted equal trade access for all nations, and demanded that China's independence and sovereignty over its own territory be preserved.

The other major powers came to accept the American position, however reluctantly. Relations between the United States and Japan worsened from that point on, up to the climax at Pearl Harbor in 1941. Over the same period, the United States built increasingly strong ties with China; but those ties were cut when communists won control of the Chinese mainland in 1949. For nearly 30 years, the United States and the People's

✔ **Checkpoint**
How did the Good Neighbor policy differ from Roosevelt's Corollary?

plague
v. to cause continuing trouble, distress

quell
v. to put down

✔ **Checkpoint**
How did World
War II change the for-
eign policy position
of the United States?

scourge
n. something that
causes great trouble or
suffering

Republic of China refused diplomatic recognition of one another.

World At War

Germany's submarine campaign against American shipping in the North Atlantic forced the United States out of its isolationist cocoon in 1917. America entered World War I "to make the world safe for democracy." However, with the defeat of Germany and the Central Powers, America pulled back from the involvements brought on by the war. The United States refused to join the League of Nations, and many Americans strongly believed that problems in Europe and the rest of the world were no concern of ours.

America's historic commitment to isolationism was finally ended by World War II. The United States became directly involved in the war when the Japanese attacked the American naval base at Pearl Harbor in Hawaii on December 7, 1941. From that point on—along with the British, the Russians, the Chinese, and our other Allies—the United States waged an all-out effort to defeat the Axis Powers (Germany, Italy, and Japan).

Under the direction and leadership of President Franklin Roosevelt, the United States became the "arsenal of democracy." American resources and industrial capacity supplied most of the armaments and other materials we and our Allies needed to win World War II. Within a very short time, the United States was transformed into the mightiest military power in the world—and it has remained so ever since.

Two New Principles

The coming of World War II brought a historic shift from a position of isolationism to one of internationalism. This nation's foreign policy has been cast in that newer direction for more than 60 years now. Even so, the overall objective of that policy remains what it has always been: the protection of the security and well-being of the United States.

Collective Security Following World War II, the United States and most of the rest of a war-weary world looked to the principle of **collective security** to keep international peace and order. America hoped to forge a world community in which at least most nations would agree to act together against any nation that threatened the peace.

To that end, this country took the lead in creating the United Nations in 1945. The organization's charter declares that the UN was formed to promote international cooperation and so "to save succeeding generations from the scourge of war . . . and to maintain international peace and security."

It soon became clear, however, that the UN would not shape the future of the world. Rather, international security would depend largely on the nature of the relations between the two superpowers, the United States and the Soviet Union. Those relations, never very close, quickly deteriorated—and for the next 40 years, American foreign policy was built around that fact.

With the breakup of the Soviet Union, the United States became the only superpower in today's world. Still, collective security remains a cornerstone of American policy. The United States has supported the United Nations and other efforts to further international cooperation. This country has also taken another path to collective security: the building of a network of regional security alliances.

Deterrence The principle of deterrence has also been a part of American foreign policy since World War II. Basically, **deterrence** is the strategy of maintaining military might at so great a level that that very strength will deter—discourage, prevent—an attack on this country by any hostile power.

President Harry Truman initiated deterrence as U.S.–Soviet relations worsened after World War II. Every President since President Truman's day has reaffirmed the strategy, and deterrence was a key factor in the collapse of the Soviet Union.

Resisting Soviet Aggression

One cannot hope to understand either recent or current American foreign policy without a knowledge of the long years of the cold war. The **cold war** was a period of more than 40 years during which relations between the two superpowers were at least tense and, more often than not, distinctly hostile. It was, for the most part, not a "hot war" of military action, but rather a time of threats, <u>posturing</u>, and military buildup.

At the Yalta Conference in early 1945, Soviet Premier Josef Stalin had agreed with President Franklin Roosevelt and British Prime Minister Winston Churchill to promote the establishment of "democratic governments" by "free elections" in the liberated countries of Eastern Europe. Instead, the Soviets imposed dictatorial regimes on those countries. The Soviets also looked to exploit postwar chaos in other nations, as well. In 1946, Churchill declared that "an iron curtain" had descended across the continent.

The Truman Doctrine The United States began to <u>counter</u> the aggressive actions of the Soviet Union in the early months of 1947. Both Greece and Turkey were in danger of falling under Soviet control. At President Harry Truman's urgent request, Congress approved a massive program of economic and military aid, and both countries remained free. In his message to Congress, the President declared that it was now

> **Primary Source**
> the policy of the United States to support free peoples who are resisting attempted subjugation by armed minorities or by outside pressures.
> —Speech by President Harry S Truman to Congress, March 12, 1947

The Truman Doctrine soon became part of a broader American plan for dealing with

☑ **Checkpoint**
What policy developed to deter the spread of communism?

posture
v. to adopt a pose, usually intended to deceive

counter
v. to oppose, contradict

GOVERNMENT ONLINE
For an **interactive** exploration of this map and to find out more about these conflicts visit
PearsonSuccessNet.com

Cold War Conflicts, 1947–1991

The ideological differences and competition for power between the two superpowers became the source of political tension worldwide. Many nations chose to side with one or the other of the superpowers. Several became battlefields and others political flashpoints where Soviet aggression and the American desire to contain communism clashed. *What do most of these locations have in common?*

KEY
☐ United States and allies
☐ Soviet Union and allies
☐ Other communist states
✳ Cold War hot spots (with dates)

SOVIET UNION

✳ Berlin (1948–1949, 1961)
Czechoslovakia (1968) ✳ ✳ Hungary (1956)
UNITED STATES
ATLANTIC OCEAN
✳ Turkey (1947)
Greece (1947) ✳
✳ Afghanistan (1979–1989)
Korea (1950–1953) ✳
Laos (1960–1962) ✳
Taiwan (1954–1955, 1958) ✳
PACIFIC OCEAN
Cuba (1962) ✳
✳ Dominican Republic (1965)
Guatemala (1954) ✳ ✳ Nicaragua (1979)
✳ Vietnam (1946–1954, 1959–1975)
Malaya (1948–1960) ✳
Angola (1974–1990) ✳
INDIAN OCEAN
Namibia (1975–1991) ✳
Chile (1973) ✳

Grateful citizens of Berlin wave to an American plane delivering badly needed supplies during the Berlin airlift. *How did the Berlin airlift symbolize America's commitment to the Truman Doctrine?*

armistice
n. an agreement to stop fighting for a time, a cease-fire

The war lasted for more than three years. It pitted the United Nations Command, largely made up of American and South Korean forces, against Soviet-trained and Soviet-equipped North Korean and communist Chinese troops. Cease-fire negotiations began in July 1951, but fighting continued until an <u>armistice</u> was signed on July 27, 1953.

The long and bitter Korean conflict did not end in a clear-cut UN victory. Still, the invasion was turned back, and the Republic of Korea remained standing. For the first time in history, armed forces of several nations fought under an international flag against aggression. There is no telling how far the tide of that aggression might have been carried had the United States not come to the aid of South Korea.

The War in Vietnam In the years following World War II, a nationalist movement arose in French Indochina—today, Vietnam. Vietnamese nationalists were seeking independence from their French colonial rulers. Made up mostly of communist forces led by Ho Chi Minh, the nationalists fought and defeated the French in a lengthy conflict. Under truce agreements signed in 1954, the country was divided into two zones. The communist-dominated North Vietnam, with its capital in Hanoi, and an anticommunist South Vietnam, with its capital in Saigon.

Almost at once, communist guerrillas (the Viet Cong), supported by the North Vietnamese, began a civil war in South Vietnam. Because President Dwight Eisenhower and other foreign policy experts believed that South Vietnam was critical to the security of all of Southeast Asia, the Eisenhower administration responded with economic and then military aid to Saigon. President John Kennedy increased that aid, and President Lyndon Johnson committed the United States to full-scale war in early 1965.

In 1969, President Richard Nixon began what he called the "Vietnamization" of the war. Over the next four years, the United States gradually pulled troops out of combat. Finally, the two sides reached a cease-fire agreement in early 1973, and the United States withdrew its last units.

the Soviet Union. From mid-1947 through the 1980s, the United States followed the policy of **containment.** That policy was rooted in the belief that if communism could be kept within its existing boundaries, it would collapse under the weight of its own internal weaknesses.

The United States and the Soviet Union confronted one another often during the cold war years. Two of those confrontations were of major, near-war proportions. The first, the Berlin blockade, occurred in 1948–1949, when the Soviets tried to force the United States and its allies to abandon the German city of Berlin to Soviet domination. The other major incident, the Cuban missile crisis, arose in 1962. The United States threatened war over the placement of Soviet nuclear missiles on the island of Cuba. In both cases, the Soviets backed down in the face of determined American resistance.

Not all cold war conflicts ended peacefully, however. During the postwar period, the United States fought two hot wars against communist forces in Asia.

The Korean War The Korean War began on June 25, 1950. Communist North Korea (the People's Democratic Republic of Korea) attacked South Korea (the UN-sponsored Republic of Korea). Immediately, the UN's Security Council called on all UN members to help South Korea repel the invasion.

The ill-fated war in Vietnam cost the United States more than 58,000 American lives. As the war dragged on, millions of Americans came to oppose American involvement in Southeast Asia—and traces of the <u>divisiveness</u> of that period can still be seen in the politics of today.

American Policies Succeed

As the United States withdrew from Vietnam, the Nixon administration embarked on a policy of **détente.** The term is French, meaning "a relaxation of tensions." In this case, the policy of détente included a purposeful attempt to improve relations with the Soviet Union and, separately, with China.

Improving Relations President Richard Nixon flew to Beijing in 1972 to begin a new era in American-Chinese relations. His visit paved the way for further contacts and, finally, for formal diplomatic ties between the United States and the People's Republic of China. Less than three months later, Mr. Nixon journeyed to Moscow. There, he and Soviet Premier Leonid Brezhnev signed the first Strategic Arms Limitations Talks agreement, SALT I—a five-year pact in which both sides agreed to a measure of control over their nuclear weapons.

Relations with mainland China have improved in fits and starts since the 1970s. Efforts at détente with the Soviets, however, proved less successful. Moscow continued to apply its expansionist pressures and provided economic and military aid to revolutionary movements around the world.

In 1979, an effort by the Soviet Union to impose a communist regime in Afghanistan was met by unexpectedly stiff resistance of armed groups of Afghans and their supporters around the region. The United States, acting largely in secret through the CIA, provided support to some of the groups resisting communist expansion. This type of war by proxy between the United States and the Soviet Union became common during the cold war. After the aggression against Afghanistan, the Carter and then the Reagan administrations placed a renewed emphasis on the containment of Soviet power.

The Cold War Ends Relations between the United States and the USSR improved remarkably after Mikhail Gorbachev came to power in Moscow in 1985. He and President Reagan met in a series of summit conferences that helped pave the way to the end of the cold war. Those meetings, focused on arms limitations, eased long-standing tensions.

Certainly, Mikhail Gorbachev deserves much credit for the fundamental change in the Soviets' approach to world affairs. But, just as certainly, that historic change was prompted by deepening political and economic chaos in Eastern Europe and within the Soviet Union itself—by conditions that ultimately brought the collapse of the Soviet Union in late 1991.

The fact that the cold war is now a matter of history should also been seen in this light:

✔ **Checkpoint**
What led to the end of the cold war?

divisiveness
n. disagreement, hostility, split

1972 President Nixon's meetings with Chinese diplomats begin the process of improving relations between the United States and China.

2000 President Clinton removes one of the last hurdles in American-Chinese relations by approving a law permitting freer trade between the two nations.

The American policies of deterrence and containment, first put in place in 1947, finally realized their goals. As President Reagan put it, the Soviet Union was left "on the ash heap of history."

Today's Dangerous World

The sudden collapse of the Soviet Union and, with it, the end of the cold war, did not mean that the world had suddenly become a peaceful place. Far from it. The planet is still plagued by conflicts and it remains a very dangerous place. Osama bin Laden, al Qaeda and other terrorist groups, and the global war against them certainly testify to that daunting fact.

Then, too, there is the worrisome fact that Iran, Iraq's neighbor in the Middle East, appears bent upon becoming a nuclear power. North Korea's nuclear aspirations may also threaten worldwide security. And there are a number of seemingly endless quarrels elsewhere in today's world—not the least of them are protracted civil wars in Africa, and repeated clashes between India and Pakistan, both nuclear powers.

In our own neighborhood, the rise of Venezuela's president Hugo Chávez raises concerns. A vocal critic of American policy, Chávez has managed to win wide support in the region. Many consider him the prime source of much anti-American feeling in Latin America today.

The Middle East The Middle East is both oil rich and conflict ridden. America's foreign policy interests in the Middle East have, for decades, been torn in two quite opposite directions: by its long-standing support of Israel and by the critical importance of Arab oil.

The United Nations created Israel as an independent state on May 14, 1948, and the United States recognized the new Jewish state within a matter of minutes. The day after it was established, Israel was invaded by Egypt, Jordan, Syria, Lebanon, and Iraq. The Israelis won that first Arab-Israeli war, decisively. Over the years since then, Israel has successfully defended itself in wars with various Arab states and against numerous terrorist attacks.

The United States has been Israel's closest friend for more than 60 years now. At the same time, however, this country has attempted to strengthen its ties with most of the Arab states in that volatile region.

With the active involvement of President Carter, Israel and Egypt negotiated a groundbreaking peace agreement, which became effective in 1979. That agreement, the Camp David Accords, led to the end of more than 30 years of hostilities between those two countries. Israel and Jordan signed a similar pact in 1994.

Israel and the Palestine Liberation Organization (PLO) took a huge, but so far unfulfilled, step toward peace in 1993. In the Oslo Accords, the PLO at last recognized Israel's right to exist. Israel recognized the PLO as the legitimate agent of the Palestinian people, and it also agreed to limited Palestinian self-rule under an autonomous Palestinian Authority.

The promise of the Oslo Accords remains to be realized. Both the United States and the UN have tried to bring the two parties together in a continuing dialogue. But recurring Palestinian terrorist attacks and Israeli military response continue.

Afghanistan The Soviet Union's invasion of Afghanistan in 1979 introduced an era of war

U.S. Special Forces and Afghan National Army personnel travel from town to town working together to bring stability to Afghanistan. *Which American foreign policy does this effort illustrate?*

502

and devastation to that Central Asian country. Although the Soviets left Afghanistan in defeat in 1989, fighting in the country continued. The groups that had defeated the Soviets now competed for power. Among the factions to emerge from this civil war was an Islamic fundamentalist movement, the Taliban. By the late 1990s, the Taliban had gained control over most of Afghanistan.

In 2001, following the terrorist attacks of September 11, the United States moved to topple the Taliban regime, which had sheltered Osama bin Laden and the al Qaeda terrorists who had carried out the attack. Initially, the war was a marked success. After a few short weeks of fighting, the Taliban took flight. The United States and its allies helped orchestrate the creation of a popularly elected government. Eventually the United States removed many of its troops, and a NATO force took the lead in providing security for the fledgling Afghan government.

Over recent years, the Taliban has reemerged as an increasingly effective foe in much of Afghanistan. In 2009 into 2010, the United States began to rebuild its military presence in that country.

Iraq The situation in Iraq has been particularly troubling for the United States. At the end of the first Gulf War in 1991, Iraq's president, Saddam Hussein, agreed to destroy his country's stock of chemical and biological weapons and to abandon his efforts to acquire a nuclear capability. He also agreed to allow UN inspectors to monitor his regime's compliance with those commitments.

Convinced that Hussein had not honored those promises and that Iraq had secretly amassed large stores of weapons, President George W. Bush sought to hold Iraq to account in 2002. Efforts to persuade the UN Security Council to support that move proved unsuccessful. But, at his urging, both houses of Congress did adopt a joint resolution authorizing the President to take those actions "necessary and appropriate" to eliminate Iraq's "continuing threat to the national security of the United States and to international peace."

In March 2003, the United States and Great Britain, supported by a number of smaller nations, launched the second Gulf War. Iraq was conquered and Saddam Hussein's regime toppled in less than six weeks.

The ongoing efforts to stabilize and rebuild Iraq, and to establish a democratic government there, have proved more than difficult. For a time, much of the country faced violence bordering on civil war, and the Iraqi government, led by Prime Minister Nouri al-Maliki, was hard put to contain it. The situation appears much improved today, and, as we noted on page 416, President Obama has declared that "our combat mission in Iraq will end by August 31, 2010."

Essential Questions Journal To continue to build a response to the chapter Essential Question, go to your Essential Questions Journal.

SECTION **3** ASSESSMENT

1. **Guiding Question** Use your completed timeline to answer this question: How has American foreign policy changed over time?

Key Terms and Comprehension

2. What is the principal aim of American foreign policy?

3. How did the creation of the United Nations reflect the principle of **collective security**?

4. **(a)** What is the policy of **deterrence**? **(b)** Is it in force today?

5. Why was **containment** a major American policy during the **cold war**?

Critical Thinking

6. **Recognize Ideologies** In 1947, President Truman said, "The free peoples of the world look to us for support in maintaining their freedoms. If we falter in our leadership, we may endanger the peace of the world, and we shall surely endanger the welfare of this nation." **(a)** Was that belief valid in 1947? **(b)** Do you think that belief remains valid in the world today? Why or why not?

Quick Write

Expository Writing: Gather Evidence Using your list of solutions from Section 2, select the one you believe is best suited to resolving the issue. Then, conduct research to find evidence that supports your proposed solution. Keep in mind which organizations you may need to carry out your solution and how your solution may affect the region concerned.

America's Role in the World

Track the Issue

United States foreign policy deals not just with military conflicts, but with humanitarian and economic matters as well.

1796

George Washington, in his Farewell Address, cautions the nation against any significant involvement in foreign affairs.

1899

With the "Open Door" policy, the United States insists that China be free to establish economic relationships with many nations.

1933

President Franklin D. Roosevelt's "Good Neighbor" policy cultivated diplomatic involvement in Latin America.

1948

Through the Marshall Plan, the United States takes an active role in the economic rebuilding of Western Europe.

2001

The United States finances humanitarian missions to many famine- and disaster-struck regions of the world.

The head of USAID with the first delivery of aid to cyclone-struck Myanmar in 2008 ▼

Perspectives

For the most part, the main goal of American economic and humanitarian foreign aid programs is to better serve our foreign policy interests and ensure this nation's security. However, some critics believe we expend too much money and human resources on international aid and place our domestic concerns at risk.

"In today's world, America's security is linked to the capacity of foreign states to govern justly and effectively. . . . We have begun an effort to relieve the poorest countries of the crushing burden of debt and we have doubled our overseas development assistance. . . . America's taxpayers must know that we are using their hard-earned dollars efficiently and effectively to improve our own security, but also to improve people's lives around the world."

—*Secretary of State Condoleezza Rice, 2006*

"[N]o country has ever done as much for another. . .as the United States has done for Iraq. We have spent hundreds of billions rebuilding their infrastructure, providing police protection,. . .giving free medical care. . . . [T]here needs to be some limit to our generosity. . . . We need to start putting our own people first. If we do not, we are soon not going to be able to pay all the Social Security and. . .other things we have promised our own people. . . ."

—*Rep. John J. Duncan, Jr. (R., Tenn.), 2007*

Connect to Your World

1. **Understand (a)** What is the intended goal of the economic development agenda described by Secretary Rice? **(b)** What is Congressman Duncan's main concern?
2. **Compare and Contrast (a)** How does Secretary Rice justify the costs of foreign aid? **(b)** How does Congressman Duncan justify cutting foreign aid? **(c)** Which argument do you find more convincing? Explain your answer.

GOVERNMENT ONLINE
In the News
For updates about American foreign aid, visit
PearsonSuccessNet.com

SECTION 4

Foreign Aid and Alliances

Guiding Question

In what ways does the United States cooperate with other nations? Use a chart like the one below to keep track of the methods used in international cooperation.

Methods of American International Cooperation		
Foreign Aid	**Security Alliances**	**United Nations**
•	•	•
•	•	•
•	•	•

Political Dictionary

- foreign aid
- regional security alliance
- NATO
- United Nations
- Security Council

Objectives

1. Identify two types of foreign aid and describe the foreign aid policy of the United States.
2. Describe the major security alliances developed by the United States.
3. Examine the role and structure of the United Nations and the problems it addresses.

Image Above: Marshall Plan funding helps in the rebuilding of West Berlin after World War II.

Do you know this ancient saying: "Those who help others help themselves"? You will see that that maxim underlies two basic elements of present-day American foreign policy: foreign aid and regional security alliances.

Foreign Aid

Foreign aid—the economic and military aid given to other countries—has been a basic feature of American foreign policy for more than sixty years. It began with the Lend-Lease program of the early 1940s, through which the United States gave nearly $50 billion in food, munitions, and other supplies to its allies in World War II. Since then, this country has sent more than $500 billion in aid to more than 100 countries around the world.

Foreign aid became an important part of the containment policy beginning with American aid to Greece and Turkey in 1947. The United States also helped its European allies rebuild after the devastation of World War II. Under the Marshall Plan, named for its author, Secretary of State George C. Marshall, the United States poured some $13 billion into 16 nations in Western Europe between 1948 and 1952.

Foreign aid has taken several different directions over the years. Immediately after World War II, American aid was primarily economic. Since that time, however, military assistance has assumed a larger role in aid policy. Until the mid-1950s, Europe received the lion's share of American help. Since then, the largest amounts have gone to nations in Asia, the Middle East, and Latin America.

Most aid, which makes up less than 1 percent of the federal budget, has been sent to those nations regarded as the most critical to the realization of this country's foreign policy objectives. In recent years, Israel, Egypt, the Philippines, and various Latin American countries have been the major recipients of American help, both economic and military.

Most foreign aid money must be used to buy American goods and services. So, most of the billions spent for that aid amounts to a substantial subsidy to both business and labor in this country. The independent United States Agency for International Development (USAID) administers most of the economic aid programs, in close cooperation with the Departments of State and Agriculture. Most military aid is channeled through the Defense Department.

The Expansion of NATO

GOVERNMENT ONLINE
Audio Tour
To find out more about the members of NATO, visit
PearsonSuccessNet.com

▶▶ **Analyzing Maps** Membership in the North Atlantic Treaty Organization has extended beyond western Europe with the addition of several nations that were once part of the Soviet-dominated Eastern Bloc. *Do you think an invitation to join will ever be extended to Russia?*

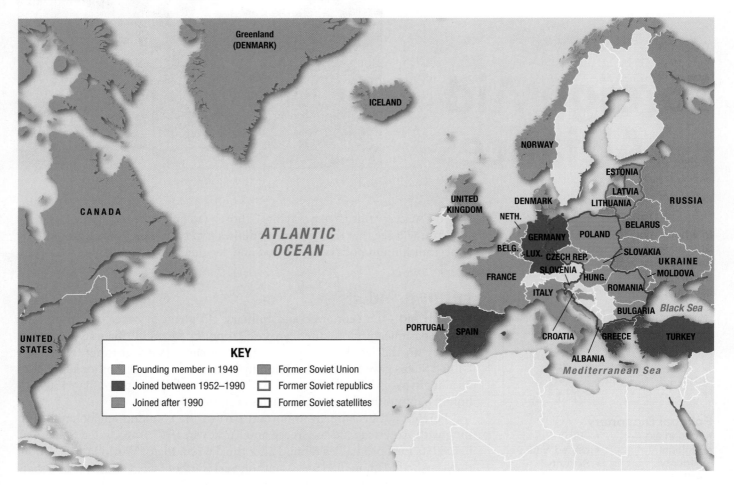

KEY

- Founding member in 1949
- Joined between 1952–1990
- Joined after 1990
- Former Soviet Union
- Former Soviet republics
- Former Soviet satellites

Security Alliances

Since World War II, the United States has constructed a network of **regional security alliances** built on mutual defense treaties. In each of those agreements, the United States and the other countries involved have agreed to take collective action to meet aggression in a particular part of the world.

NATO The North Atlantic Treaty, signed in 1949, established **NATO,** the North Atlantic Treaty Organization. The alliance was formed initially to promote the collective defense of Western Europe, particularly against the threat of Soviet aggression. NATO was originally composed of the United States and 11 other countries (see map above).

With the collapse of the Soviet Union, NATO's mutual security blanket was extended to cover much of Eastern Europe. Though it has grown in size, the alliance remains dedicated to the basic goal of protecting the freedom and security of its members through political and military action. Each of the now 28 member countries has agreed that "an armed attack against one or more of them in Europe or in North America shall be considered an attack against them all."

What has changed with NATO since its founding? Clearly, the threat of Soviet (if not Russian) aggression has lessened, yet the basic function of the alliance is the same. NATO was formed for defensive purposes and—if defense includes military intervention in conflicts that may <u>destabilize</u> Europe, and with it, the prevention of humanitarian disasters—defense remains its basic charge.

Increasingly, however, NATO is focused on what it calls "crisis management and peacekeeping." Its involvement in the Balkans provides a leading illustration of this role. First in Bosnia in 1995 and then in Kosovo in 1999, NATO air and ground forces, drawn mostly from the United States, Great Britain, and Canada, brought an end to years of vicious civil war in what was once Yugoslavia. Those military interventions also put an end to the horrific campaigns of "ethnic cleansing," directed by Serbia's President Slobodan Milosevic. NATO troops continue to maintain a fragile peace in the Balkans today.

In mid-2003, NATO took command of the International Security Assistance Force (ISAF) in Afghanistan. The United Nations established this multinational peacekeeping force in late 2001 in the wake of the American-led war that <u>ousted</u> Afghanistan's Taliban regime.

Today, ISAF is composed of over 40,000 combat and support troops drawn from 37 nations. The ISAF includes almost half of the American troops in the country. The American units now operating under NATO command battle stubborn Taliban resistance in eastern Afghanistan, in remote areas near the Pakistani border. The ISAF has assumed the leading role in rebuilding war-shattered Afghanistan. There has been disagreement within NATO, however, about how many troops member nations will commit to military operations in the country. This conflict has flared as the Taliban has shown surprising <u>resilience</u>.

Since 2005, NATO has also played a small peacekeeping role in Darfur. This conflict-plagued region of the African nation of Sudan has been the scene of what observers have described as a campaign of <u>genocide</u>, with government-backed militia targeting rival ethnic groups. NATO forces have helped train and transport troops taking part in a multinational peacekeeping mission to end the bloodshed in Darfur.

Other Alliances The Inter-American Treaty of Reciprocal Assistance, the Rio Pact, was signed in 1947. It pledges the United States, Canada, and now 32 Latin American countries to treat any "armed attack . . . against an American state . . . as an attack against all the American states." The treaty is built on the Monroe Doctrine and commits those nations to the peaceful settlement of their disputes. Cuba is not a party to the agreement.

Beyond NATO and the Rio Pact, the United States is party to several other regional alliances. Thus, the ANZUS Pact of 1951 unites Australia, New Zealand, and the United States to ensure their collective security in the Pacific region.

The Japanese Pact also dates from 1951. After six years of American military occupation, the allies of World War II (with the exception of the Soviet Union) signed a peace treaty with Japan. At the same time, the United States and Japan signed a mutual defense treaty. In return for American protection, Japan permits the United States to maintain land, sea, and air forces in and around its territory.

The Philippines Pact was ratified in 1951 as well. It, too, is a mutual defense agreement. The pact remains in force, but disagreements over its redrafting prompted the withdrawal of all American military forces from the Philippines in 1992. The Korean Pact, signed in 1953, pledges the United States to come to the aid of South Korea should it be attacked again.

The Taiwan Pact was in effect between the United States and Nationalist China from 1954 to 1980. When the United States and the People's Republic of China established full diplomatic relations in 1979, the United States withdrew its recognition of the Nationalist Chinese government, and the Taiwan pact became obsolete.

The United Nations

You know that a fundamental change occurred in American foreign policy during and immediately after World War II. That dramatic shift from isolationism to internationalism, is strikingly illustrated by this country's participation in the United Nations. Remember, the United States refused to join the League of Nations

✔ **Checkpoint**
How has NATO's purpose changed?

destabilize
v. to make something unstable, undermine, upset

oust
v. drive out, remove by force

resilience
n. ability to resume its original condition, bounce back

genocide
n. the deliberate extermination of a people or nation

The UN by the Numbers

Data can provide a great deal of insight into the nature of an organization. *What does the information below tell you about the UN?*

Membership

192 Member countries today

15 Security Council members

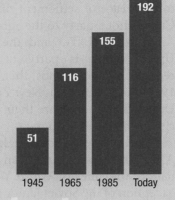

1945	1965	1985	Today
51	116	155	192

Operating Budget

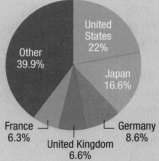

United States 22%
Japan 16.6%
Germany 8.6%
United Kingdom 6.6%
France 6.3%
Other 39.9%

$4.17 billion
Current 2-year operating budget (2008–2009)

22%
Operating budget share contributed by the United States

UN Peacekeeping

$7.1 billion
Current budget for UN peacekeeping operations

15
Peacekeeping operations in progress

91,000
UN troops deployed in peacekeeping missions around the world

SOURCE: The United Nations

after World War I. With the end of World War II, however, the American people realized that America was a world power with worldwide interests and responsibilities.

The **United Nations** (UN) came into being at the United Nations Conference on International Organization, which met in San Francisco from April 25 to June 26, 1945. There, the representatives of 50 nations—the victorious allies of World War II—drafted the United Nations Charter.[5] The charter is a treaty among all of the UN's member-states, and it serves as the body's constitution.

The United States became the first nation to ratify the UN Charter. The Senate approved it by an overwhelming vote, 89–2, on July 24, 1945. The other states that had taken part in the San Francisco Conference then ratified the charter in quick order, and it went into force on October 24, 1945. The UN held the first session of its General Assembly in London on January 10, 1946.

Charter and Organization The UN's charter is a lengthy document. It opens with an eloquent preamble which reads in part:

Primary Source

We, the peoples of the United Nations

Determined to save succeeding generations from the scourge of war, which twice in our lifetime has brought untold sorrow to mankind, and . . .

To practice tolerance and live together in peace with one another as good neighbors, and

To unite our strength to maintain international peace and security . . .

Have resolved to combine our efforts to accomplish these aims.

—Charter of the United Nations

The body of the document begins in Article I with a statement of the organization's purposes: the maintenance of international peace

---

5 Fifty nations attended the San Francisco conference. Poland did not attend, but it did sign the charter on October 15, 1945, and is considered an original member of the UN.

and security, the development of friendly relations between and among all nations, and the promotion of justice and cooperation in the solution of international problems.

The UN has 192 members today. Membership is open to those "peace-loving states" that accept the obligations of the charter and are, in the UN's judgment, able and willing to carry out those obligations. New members may be admitted by a two-thirds vote of the General Assembly, upon recommendation by the Security Council.

The charter sets forth the complicated structure of the UN. It is built around six principal <u>organs</u>: the General Assembly, the Security Council, the Economic and Social Council, the Trusteeship Council, the International Court of Justice, and the Secretariat.

The General Assembly

The UN's General Assembly has been called "the town meeting of the world." Each of the UN's members has a seat and a vote in the Assembly. It meets once a year, and sessions take place at the UN's permanent headquarters in New York City. The secretary-general may call special sessions, at the request of either the Security Council or a majority of the UN's members.

The Assembly may take up and debate any matter within the scope of the charter, and it may make whatever recommendation it chooses to the Security Council, the other UN organs, and any member-state.[6] The recommendations it makes to UN members are not legally binding on them, but these recommendations do carry some considerable weight, for they have been approved by a significant number of the governments of the world.

The Assembly elects the 10 nonpermanent members of the Security Council, the 54 members of the Economic and Social Council, and the elective members of the Trusteeship Council. In conjunction with the Security Council, it also selects the secretary-general and the 15 judges of the International Court of Justice. The Assembly shares with the Security Council the power to admit, suspend, or expel members. But the Assembly alone may propose amendments to the charter.

---

6 Except those matters currently under consideration by the Security Council.

The Security Council

The UN's **Security Council** is made up of 15 members. Five—the United States, Britain, France, Russia (originally the Soviet Union's seat), and China—are permanent members. The General Assembly chooses the 10 nonpermanent members for two-year terms; they cannot be immediately reelected. The council meets in continuous session.

The Security Council bears the UN's major responsibility for maintaining international peace. It may take up any matter involving a threat to or a breach of that peace, and it can adopt measures ranging from calling on the parties to settle their differences peacefully to placing economic and/or military sanctions on an offending nation. The only time the Security Council has undertaken a military operation against an aggressor came in Korea in 1950. It has, however, provided peacekeeping forces in several world trouble spots, with varying degrees of success.

On procedural questions—routine matters—decisions of the Security Council can be made by the affirmative vote of any nine members. On the more important matters—substantive questions—at least nine affirmative votes are also needed. However, a negative vote by any one of the permanent members is enough to kill any substantive resolution. Because of that *veto power*, the Security Council is effective only when and if the permanent members are willing to cooperate with one another.

The veto does not come into play in a situation in which one or more of the permanent members <u>abstains.</u> When, on June 25, 1950, the Security Council called on all UN members to aid South Korea in repelling the North Korean invasion, the Soviet delegate was boycotting sessions of the Security Council and so was not present to veto that action.

Economic and Social Council

The Economic and Social Council (ECOSOC) is made up of 54 members elected by the General Assembly to three-year terms. It is responsible to the Assembly for carrying out the UN's many economic, cultural, educational, health, and related activities. It coordinates the work of the UN's specialized agencies—a number of independent international

✔ **Checkpoint**
Which members of the Security Council have the veto power?

organ
n. a unit of organization that performs a specific function

abstain
v. to choose not to participate

bodies that have a working relationship with the world organization. There are several of these independent international bodies, including the World Health Organization (WHO), the International Monetary Fund (IMF), the World Bank Group, and the Food and Agriculture Organization (FAO). (See the feature below.)

Trusteeship Council The United Nations Charter requires each member to promote the well-being of the peoples of all "non-self-governing territories" as a "sacred trust." To that end, and for several decades, the Trusteeship Council monitored the way in which various UN members met that responsibility in their administration of (originally) eleven Trust

GOVERNMENT ONLINE
Audio Tour
To learn more about these specialized agencies, visit **PearsonSuccessNet.com**

The UN Economic and Social Council
The Specialized Agencies

The UN was established to eliminate "the scourge of war." To that end, the Economic and Social Council coordinates the work of 15 specialized agencies—international organizations that seek to promote economic and/or social programs in many parts of the world. *How do these agencies reflect the goals of the United Nations?*

The 15 Agencies

1 **FAO** Food and Agriculture Organization
2 **ICAO** International Civil Aviation Organization
3 **IFAD** International Fund for Agricultural Development
4 **ILO** International Labour Organization
5 **IMO** International Maritime Organization
6 **IMF** International Monetary Fund
7 **ITU** International Telecommunications Union
8 **UNESCO** United Nations Educational, Scientific, and Cultural Organization
9 **UNIDO** United Nations Industrial Development Organization
10 **UPU** Universal Postal Union
11 World Bank Group
12 **WHO** World Health Organization
13 **WIPO** World Intellectual Property Organization
14 **WMO** World Meteorological Organization
15 **WTO** World Tourism Organization

8 UNESCO
United Nations Educational, Scientific, and Cultural Organization

Promotes education for all, cultural development, protection of the worldwide cooperation in the sciences, and freedom of the press and communication.

Left: Peru's Machu Picchu, a UNESCO World Heritage site

1 FAO
Food and Agriculture Organization

Works to improve agricultural productivity and food quality, and to better the living standards of rural populations.

Below: An FAO expert teaches new farming techniques.

6 IMF
International Monetary Fund

Promotes international monetary cooperation and financial stability and provides a forum for advice and assistance on financial issues.

Below: The IMF assesses exchange rates.

12 WHO
World Health Organization

Coordinates programs aimed at solving health problems and the attainment by all people of the highest possible level of health.

Below: A WHO volunteer immunizes children against measles.

Territories. Those entities included (1) several colonies that had been mandates under the League of Nations in the years between World War I and World War II, (2) colonial possessions taken from enemy nations in World War II, and (3) some colonial areas voluntarily placed under the UN's trusteeship system by UN members. By 1994, however, the last of those Trust Territories had achieved self-governing status and so, today, the Trusteeship Council exists in name only.

International Court of Justice

The International Court of Justice (ICJ), also known as the World Court, is the UN's judicial arm. All members of the UN are automatically parties to the ICJ Statute. Under certain conditions, the services of the court are also available to nonmember states. A UN member may agree to accept the court's <u>jurisdiction</u> over cases in which it may be involved either unconditionally or with certain reservations (exceptions that may not conflict with the ICJ Statute).

The ICJ is made up of 15 judges selected for nine-year terms by the General Assembly and the Security Council. It sits in permanent session at the Peace Palace in The Hague, the Netherlands, and handles cases brought to it voluntarily by both members and nonmembers of the UN. The ICJ also advises the other UN bodies on legal questions arising out of their activities. If any party to a dispute fails to obey a judgment of the court, the other party may take that matter to the Security Council.

The Secretariat

The civil service branch of the UN is the Secretariat. It is headed by the secretary-general, who is elected to a five-year term by the General Assembly on the recommendation of the Security Council.

The secretary-general heads a staff of some 40,000 men and women who conduct the day-to-day work of the UN in New York and elsewhere around the globe. Beyond administrative chores, the Charter gives this vital power to the secretary-general: to bring before the Security Council any matter that he or she believes poses a serious threat to international peace and security.

The secretary-general prepares the UN's two-year budget, which must be approved by the General Assembly. For 2008–2009, the operating budget came to $4.17 billion. The Assembly apportions the UN's expenses for each two-year period among its member-states.

Early on, the secretary-general was seen as little more than the UN's chief clerk. The post amounts to much more than that, however, because the eight men who have thus far held it transformed the office into a major channel for the negotiated settlement of international disputes.[7]

The Work of the UN

The purpose of the United Nations can be summed up this way: to make the world a better place. To that end, the UN is involved in a wide variety of activities.

Peacekeeping is a primary function of the United Nations. More than 100,000 military and civilian personnel provided by some 120 member countries are currently engaged in 15 UN global peacekeeping operations.

The UN's specialized agencies spend some several billion dollars a year for economic and social programs to help the world's poorest nations. Those monies are beyond that loaned by the World Bank, the International Monetary Fund, and the other UN agencies that further development in poorer countries.

Health is the major concern of several UN agencies. A joint program of UNICEF and WHO has immunized 80 percent of the world's children against six killer diseases, and it is estimated that this program saves the lives of more than 2 million children a year. Smallpox, which plagued the world for centuries, has now been all but eliminated by a WHO-led campaign. Today, that organization coordinates a massive global effort to control the spread of AIDS.

The health of the environment is also a significant concern of the world organization. United Nations environmental conventions have helped reduce acid rain, lessened marine pollution, and phased out the production of

✔ ● **Checkpoint**
What is the secretary-general's role in the UN organization?

jurisdiction
n. authority of a court to hear and decide a dispute

---

7 The eight secretaries-general: Trigve Lie (Norway, 1946–1953), Dag Hammarskjold (Sweden, 1953–1961), U Thant (Burma, 1962–1972), Kurt Waldheim (Austria, 1972–1982), Javier Perez de Cuellar (Peru, 1982–1992), Boutros Boutros-Ghali (Egypt, 1992–1997), Kofi Annan (Ghana, 1997–2006), and Ban Ki-moon (South Korea, 2007–).

gases that destroy the ozone layer. The UN also helped establish the Intergovernmental Panel on Climate Change. That body was created to examine the large volume of information about climate change generated by the scientific community and to help provide government decision-makers with accurate, balanced analysis of this data.

Human rights have long been a leading priority for the United Nations. In 1948, the UN drafted the Universal Declaration of Human Rights, and it has sponsored more than 80 treaties that help protect specific rights. Various United Nations agencies work to aid and protect refugees and displaced persons, and the international organization raises more than $1 billion a year for assistance to victims of war and natural disasters.

The UN also works closely with nongovernmental organizations, NGOs, around the world. As the name suggests, NGOs are independent of governments, and the list of issues and topics that they exist to address is nearly endless. On issues ranging from public health to the environment to the status of women, these groups perform valuable work around the world. The United Nations actively seeks to partner with those organizations as a means of achieving its goals. A prime example is the International Committee of the Red Cross, a humanitarian NGO with which the UN works to assist victims of disasters ranging from military conflicts to those inflicted by Mother Nature.

The UN and the U.S.

The United States has a long and close relationship with the UN. It was President Franklin Roosevelt who, with Britain's Winston Churchill, first proposed the formation of the UN. The United States occupies a permanent place on the Security Council. Though the United States is one of 192 members of the UN, it funds some 22 percent of the UN budget. (Each member's contribution is roughly equal in proportion to its share of the world's gross domestic product.)

The relationship with the UN is complex, however. The United States has at times been critical of the UN. In fact, the United States has even withheld payment of funds to the institution. Also, the United States has not always agreed with some formal policy positions taken by the UN. In 2003, for example, the Bush administration was frustrated in its efforts to win UN support for military action against Iraq. Yet, the United States often works closely with the UN on a variety of issues to further policies that are important to both, including environmental and humanitarian causes. For example, the UN is now closely involved with American efforts to bring peace and stability to Iraq.

Essential Questions Journal To continue to build a response to the chapter Essential Question, go to your **Essential Questions Journal.**

SECTION 4 ASSESSMENT

1. **Guiding Question** Use your completed table to answer this question: In what ways does the United States cooperate with other nations?

Key Terms and Comprehension

2. (a) What is **foreign aid?** (b) Cite two examples of that policy.
3. (a) What is **NATO?** (b) How has it changed over the years?
4. Summarize the organization and function of the UN **Security Council.**

Critical Thinking

5. **Identify Central Issues** Why do you think the U.S. has formed regional security alliances around the globe?
6. **Demonstrate Reasoned Judgment** Do you think the United Nations General Assembly deserves to be called "the town meeting of the world"? Why or why not?
7. **Make Comparisons (a)** Compare the basic foreign policy of the United States early on to that of today. **(b)** How do this nation's alliances illustrate this change?

Quick Write

Expository Writing: Write a Thesis Statement A thesis statement can summarize the focus of your problem-solution essay. To help you determine your thesis statement, use the problem you identified in Section 1, the solution you selected, and its supporting research to determine how best to summarize your findings. Then, write a sentence that clearly states the purpose and goal of your essay.

Quick Study Guide

GOVERNMENT ONLINE
On the Go
To review anytime, anywhere, download these online resources at **PearsonSuccessNet.com**
Political Dictionary, Audio Review

CHAPTER **17**

Guiding Question
Section 2 How does the Federal Government safeguard this nation's security?

Guiding Question
Section 3 How has American foreign policy changed over time?

Guiding Question
Section 1 How is foreign policy made and conducted?

CHAPTER 17
Essential Question
How should the United States interact with other countries?

Guiding Question
Section 4 In what ways does the United States cooperate with other nations?

Political Dictionary

domestic affairs *p. 482*
foreign affairs *p. 482*
isolationism *p.482*
foreign policy *p. 483*
right of legation *p. 485*
ambassador *p. 485*
diplomatic immunity *p. 486*
passport *p. 487*
visa *p. 487*
espionage *p. 492*
terrorism *p. 492*
collective security *p. 498*
deterrence *p. 498*
cold war *p. 498*
containment *p. 500*
détente *p. 501*
foreign aid *p. 505*
regional security alliance *p. 506*
NATO *p. 506*
United Nations *p. 508*
Security Council *p. 509*

Key American Foreign Policies

Monroe Doctrine	Isolates the U.S. from international affairs unless North or South America is threatened.
Roosevelt Corollary	Extends the Monroe Doctrine by giving the U.S. the authority to intervene in the affairs of Latin America.
Good Neighbor Policy	Reduces American political and military interference in Latin America.
Deterrence	Maintains that superior military strength will deter hostile powers from attacking the nation.
Truman Doctrine	Affirms that the U.S. will oppose any aggressor's attempt to control another nation and its people.
Containment	Prevents the spread of communism by assisting threatened nations.
Détente	Reduces tensions between the United States and both the Soviet Union and China.
Collective Security	Brings nations together to resist any nation that threatens the peace.

U.S. Foreign Policy Positions

Isolationism
- American foreign policy until World War II
- Purposeful detachment from world affairs
- Domestic affairs are primary focus
- Allows for some ties with foreign nations
- Extended by the Monroe Doctrine to include regions of North and South America

Internationalism
- American foreign policy since World War II
- Economic and political involvement in international affairs
- Focuses on collective security
- Acknowledges impact of global events on the United States
- Embodied in the Truman Doctrine

Chapter Assessment

Comprehension and Critical Thinking

Section 1

1. **(a)** What is the difference between isolationism and internationalism? **(b)** When and why did the United States stop pursuing a largely isolationist foreign policy? **(c)** What are the advantages and disadvantages of an internationalist foreign policy?

2. **(a)** What is the major responsibility of an ambassador? **(b)** How are ambassadors appointed, and what qualifications do they usually have? **(c)** How does the work of an ambassador help advance American foreign policy?

Section 2

3. **(a)** What does "civilian control of the military" mean? **(b)** How is civilian control of the military guaranteed in the United States? **(c)** What are the dangers of a military not under civilian control?

4. **(a)** Which executive branch agencies are primarily responsible for protecting the United States from terrorist attacks? **(b)** Why is it so difficult to protect this nation completely against terrorist attacks?

Section 3

5. **(a)** What is the policy of deterrence? **(b)** How effective has it been as a tool in American foreign policy? **(c)** Do you think it is still an effective policy in today's world? Why or why not?

6. **(a)** What is the basic goal of American foreign policy? **(b)** How does the history of American foreign policy illustrate that goal? **(c)** What do you think should be the overall goal of American foreign policy?

7. **Analyze Political Cartoons**
   (a) What is the cartoonist suggesting in this cartoon?
   (b) Is it an accurate portrayal?
   (c) Should the United States armed forces be more or less involved in the affairs of other nations? Explain.

Section 4

8. **(a)** Cite three regional alliances and the countries associated with them.
   (b) What effect do you think a pact between the United States and countries in the Middle East would have on world affairs today?

9. **(a)** What is the main purpose of the United Nations?
   (b) What are the six main bodies of the UN and how do they support that purpose? **(c)** Do you think the United Nations should be a means of advancing American international policy? Why or why not?

Writing About Government

10. Use your Quick Write exercises from this chapter to write a problem-and-solution essay on a current international issue. Make sure you clearly define the problem, explain your solution, and provide supporting details illustrating how your solution could succeed. See pp. S3–S5 in the Writing Handbook.

Apply What You've Learned

11. **Essential Question Activity** Select a country to which the United States has provided humanitarian, military, or economic aid within the last 20 years. Conduct research and use the following questions to help you create a cause-and-effect chart:

    (a) What event led to U.S. involvement? For how long did the United States provide support?

    (b) Was American support military or humanitarian in nature? Did its purpose change over time?

    (c) Were other organizations involved? If so, which ones?

    (d) What were the results of American aid?

12. **Essential Question Assessment** Use the results of your research and the content of this chapter to write an editorial piece that helps express your opinion on the Essential Question: **How should the United States interact with other countries?** Remember that an Op-Ed is a form of persuasive essay. Your opinion should be well thought out and include accurate details that support the view you want to express.

Essential Questions
Journal
To respond to the chapter Essential Question, go to your **Essential Questions Journal.**

Document-Based Assessment

Deterrence and Foreign Policy

The destructive force of a nuclear weapon is horrifying, not only in its actual detonation but in the mere possibility of its use. As illustrated by the following documents, having and stockpiling weapons with such destructive capabilities became the American foreign policy of deterrence that continues to this day.

Document 1

The Japanese began the war from the air at Pearl Harbor. They have been repaid many fold. And the end is not yet. With this bomb we have now added a new and revolutionary increase in destruction to supplement the growing power of our armed forces. In their present form these bombs are now in production and even more powerful forms are in development. . . .

We are now prepared to obliterate more rapidly and completely every productive enterprise the Japanese have above ground in any city. We shall destroy their docks, their factories, and their communications. Let there be no mistake; we shall completely destroy Japan's power to make war.

**President Harry Truman,
on the bombing of Hiroshima, 1945**

Document 2

Our reluctance for conflict should not be misjudged as a failure of will. When action is required to preserve our national security, we will act. We will maintain sufficient strength to prevail if need be, knowing that if we do so we have the best chance of never having to use that strength.

**—President Ronald Reagan,
first Inaugural Address, 1981**

Document 3

The effort to develop ballistic missile defenses is part of a broader effort to move beyond the Cold War and establish a new deterrence framework for the 21st century. . . .

We no longer worry about a massive Soviet first strike. We worry about terrorist states and terrorist networks that might not be deterred by our nuclear forces. To deal with such adversaries we need a new approach to deterrence. This approach combines deep reductions in offensive nuclear forces with new, advanced conventional capabilities and defenses to protect free people from nuclear blackmail or attack. . . .

As we reduce our nuclear arsenal, we're investing in advanced conventional capabilities. . . . We're investing in the next generation of missile defenses—because these systems do more than defend our citizens, they also strengthen deterrence.

. . .[W]ith missile defenses in place, the calculus of deterrence changes in our favor. If [a] terrorist regime does not have confidence their missile attack would be successful, it is less likely to engage in acts of aggression in the first place.

**—President George W. Bush,
Global War on Terror speech, 2007**

Use your knowledge of American foreign policy and Documents 1–3 to answer Questions 1–3.

1. What is the main point of both Documents 2 and 3?
   - **A.** Deterrence is not enough to deter aggression.
   - **B.** The United States should reduce military spending.
   - **C.** New methods of deterrence are necessary.
   - **D.** Military strength will ensure national security.

2. How might President Truman's comments in Document 1 have helped deter other nations from attacking the United States?

3. **Put It Together** Do you think that nuclear weapons and weapon stockpiling have helped the United States achieve its foreign policy objectives? Why or why not?

GOVERNMENT ONLINE
Documents
To find more primary sources on deterrence, visit
PearsonSuccessNet.com

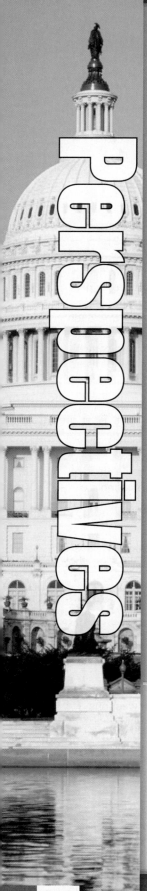

Essential Question
What makes a good President?

The more familiar you are with each of the now 44 presidencies, the better equipped you will be to identify the several factors that define a good President.

"ON THE QUALITIES OF A GREAT PRESIDENT:

. . . [R]esearch indicate[s] that great presidents, besides being stubborn and disagreeable, are more extraverted, open to experience, assertive, achievement striving, excitement seeking and more open to fantasy, aesthetics, feelings, actions, ideas and values. Historically great presidents were low on straightforwardness, vulnerability and order.

—American Psychological Association, August 2000

ON HISTORY'S JUDGMENT OF THE PRESIDENT:

RELIABLE, BASIC, SAW US THROUGH SOME ROUGH TIMES. I GUESS WE TOOK THE OLD GUY FOR GRANTED,,,

DEERING ARKANSAS DEMOCRAT-GAZETTE ©2006 CREATORS SYNDICATE, INC.

In a pun on the names of cars and Presidents, Gerald Ford joked during his presidency that he was "a Ford, not a Lincoln."

"ON THE OPPORTUNITY TO BECOME A GREAT PRESIDENT:

All our great presidents were leaders of thought at times when certain ideas in the life of the nation had to be clarified.

—Franklin D. Roosevelt, 1932

Essential Question Warmup

Throughout this unit, you studied the office and the job of the President. Use what you have learned and the opinions expressed above to answer the following questions. Then go to your **Essential Questions Journal.**

1. How do voters evaluate candidates?

2. Why does history often judge a President somewhat differently from how he was judged while in office?

3. Should a President strive to be popular or, instead, strive to be effective?

4. Can a President be great if conditions present no real opportunity to show greatness?

Essential Questions Journal

To continue to build a response to the unit Essential Question, go to your **Essential Questions Journal.**

Photo: Entrance to the Supreme Court

Essential Questions Journal To begin to build a response to the unit Essential Question, go to your **Essential Questions Journal.**

Unit 5
The Judicial Branch

Essential Question What should be the role of the judicial branch?

The Federal Court System

Essential Question
Does the structure of the federal court system allow it to administer justice effectively?

Section 1:
The National Judiciary

Section 2:
The Inferior Courts

Section 3:
The Supreme Court

Section 4:
The Special Courts

" It is **emphatically** the province and **the duty** of the judicial department to **say what the law is**....If two **laws conflict** with each other, the **courts must decide** on the operation of each.

—Chief Justice John Marshall, *Marbury* v. *Madison,* 1803

Photo: Attorney Frank Dunham holds a news conference in front of the U.S. Supreme Court building.

GOVERNMENT ONLINE
On the Go

To study anywhere, anytime, download these online resources at PearsonSuccessNet.com
• Political Dictionary
• Audio Review
• Downloadable Interactivities

The **National Judiciary**

Guiding Question

What are the structure and function of the national judiciary? Use a table like the one below to take notes on the section.

The National Judiciary	
Structure	Types of Jurisdiction
• Dual court system •	• Exclusive jurisdiction •

Political Dictionary

- inferior courts
- jurisdiction
- concurrent jurisdiction
- plaintiff
- defendant
- original jurisdiction
- appellate jurisdiction
- judicial restraint
- precedent
- judicial activism

Objectives

1. Explain why the Constitution created a national judiciary, and describe its structure.
2. Identify the criteria that determine whether a case is within the jurisdiction of a federal court, and compare the types of jurisdiction.
3. Outline the process for appointing federal judges, and list their terms of office.
4. Understand the impact of judicial philosophy.
5. Examine the roles of court officers.

Image Above: Judge Maryanne Trump Barry, U.S. Court of Appeals, Third Circuit

Joe steals a sports car in Chicago. Two days later, he is stopped for speeding in Atlanta. Where, now, will he be tried for car theft? In Illinois, where he stole the car? In Georgia, where he was caught? Joe may be on the verge of learning something about the federal court system—and about the Dyer Act of 1925, which makes it a federal crime to transport a stolen vehicle across a State line.

Creation of a National Judiciary

During the years the Articles of Confederation were in force (1781–1789), there were no national courts and no national judiciary. The laws of the United States were interpreted and applied as each State saw fit, and sometimes not at all. Disputes between States and between persons who lived in different States were decided, if at all, by the courts in one of the States involved.[1] Often, decisions by the courts in one State were ignored by courts in the other States.

Alexander Hamilton spoke to the point in *The Federalist* No. 22. He described "the want of a judiciary power" as a "circumstance which crowns the defects of the Confederation." Arguing the need for a national court system, he added, "Laws are a dead letter without courts to expound and define their true meaning and operation." The Framers created a national judiciary for the United States in a single sentence in the Constitution:

" FROM THE CONSTITUTION

The judicial Power of the United States shall be vested in one supreme Court, and in such inferior Courts as the Congress may from time to time ordain and establish.

—Article III, Section 1

Congress also is given the expressed power "to constitute Tribunals inferior to the supreme Court"—that is, create the rest of the federal court system—in Article I, Section 8, Clause 9.

---

1 The Articles of Confederation did provide (in Article IX) a very complicated procedure for the settlement of such disputes, but it was rarely used.

A Dual Court System Keep in mind this important point: There are *two* separate court systems in the United States.[2] On one hand, the national judiciary spans the country with its more than 100 courts. On the other hand, each of the 50 States has its own system of courts. Their numbers run well into the thousands, and most of the cases that are heard in court today are heard in those State, not the federal, courts.

Two Kinds of Federal Courts The Constitution establishes the Supreme Court and leaves to Congress the creation of the **inferior courts**—the lower federal courts, those beneath the Supreme Court. Over the years, Congress has created two distinct types of federal courts: (1) the constitutional courts,

and (2) the special courts. See the diagram "Types of Federal Courts" below.

The constitutional courts are those federal courts that Congress has formed under Article III to exercise "the judicial Power of the United States." Together with the Supreme Court, they now include the courts of appeals, the district courts, and the U.S. Court of International Trade. The constitutional courts are also called the regular courts and, sometimes, Article III courts.

The special courts do not exercise the broad "judicial Power of the United States." Rather, they have been created by Congress to hear cases arising out of some of the expressed powers given to Congress in Article I, Section 8. The special courts hear a much narrower range of cases than those that may come before the constitutional courts.

These special courts are also called the legislative courts and, sometimes, Article I courts. Today, they include the U.S. Court of Appeals for the Armed Forces, the U.S. Court of Appeals for Veterans Claims, the U.S. Court of Federal Claims, the U.S. Tax

---

2 Federalism does not require two court systems. Article III provides that Congress "may" establish lower federal courts. At its first session in 1789, Congress decided to construct a complete set of federal courts to parallel those of the States. In most of the world's other federal systems, the principal courts are those of the states or provinces; typically, the only significant federal court is a national court of last resort, often called the supreme court.

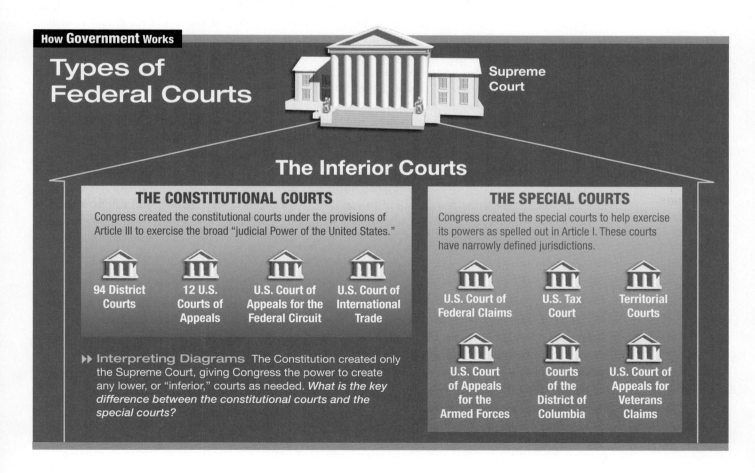

How Government Works

Types of Federal Courts

Supreme Court

The Inferior Courts

THE CONSTITUTIONAL COURTS

Congress created the constitutional courts under the provisions of Article III to exercise the broad "judicial Power of the United States."

94 District Courts

12 U.S. Courts of Appeals

U.S. Court of Appeals for the Federal Circuit

U.S. Court of International Trade

▶▶ **Interpreting Diagrams** The Constitution created only the Supreme Court, giving Congress the power to create any lower, or "inferior," courts as needed. *What is the key difference between the constitutional courts and the special courts?*

THE SPECIAL COURTS

Congress created the special courts to help exercise its powers as spelled out in Article I. These courts have narrowly defined jurisdictions.

U.S. Court of Federal Claims

U.S. Tax Court

Territorial Courts

U.S. Court of Appeals for the Armed Forces

Courts of the District of Columbia

U.S. Court of Appeals for Veterans Claims

Court, the various territorial courts, and the courts of the District of Columbia. You will look at the unique features of these tribunals later in this chapter.

Federal Court Jurisdiction

The constitutional courts hear most of the cases tried in the federal courts. That is to say, those courts have jurisdiction over most federal cases. **Jurisdiction** is defined as the authority of a court to hear (to *try* and to *decide*) a case. The term means, literally, the power "to say the law."

The Constitution gives federal courts jurisdiction over only certain cases. Recall, most cases heard in court in the United States are heard in State, not federal, courts. Article III, Section 2 provides that the federal courts may hear cases either because of (1) the *subject matter* or (2) the *parties* involved in those cases.

Subject Matter In terms of subject matter, the federal courts may hear a case if it involves a "federal question"—that is, the interpretation and application of a provision in the Constitution or in any federal statute or treaty—or a question of admiralty or maritime law. Admiralty law relates to matters that arise on the high seas or the navigable waters of the United States, such as a collision at sea or a crime committed aboard a ship. Maritime law relates to matters that arise on land but are directly related to the water, such as a contract to deliver ship supplies at dockside.

The Framers purposefully gave the federal courts exclusive jurisdiction in all admiralty and maritime cases in order to ensure national supremacy in the regulation of all waterborne commerce.

Parties A case falls within the jurisdiction of the federal courts if one of the parties involved in the case is (1) the United States or one of its officers or agencies; (2) an ambassador, consul, or other official representative of a foreign government; (3) one of the 50 States suing another State, a resident of another State, or a foreign government or one of its subjects; (4) a citizen of one State suing a citizen of another State; (5) an American citizen suing a foreign government or one of its subjects; or

(6) a citizen of a State suing another citizen of that same State where both claim title to land under grants from different States.

These criteria for determining which cases can be heard in the federal courts may seem quite complicated, and they are. But the matter is also a reflection of federalism and, so, of the dual system of courts in this country. To put the whole point of the jurisdiction of the federal courts the other way around: Those cases that are not heard by the federal courts fall within the jurisdiction of the State courts.

Types of Jurisdiction

Still more must be said on this quite complex matter of federal court jurisdiction. The federal courts exercise both *exclusive* and *concurrent* jurisdiction and, also, original and appellate jurisdiction.

Exclusive and Concurrent Jurisdiction Most of the cases that can be heard in the federal courts fall within their exclusive jurisdiction. That is, they can be tried *only* in the federal courts. Thus, a case involving an ambassador or some other official of a foreign government cannot be heard in a State court; it *must* be tried in a federal court. The trial of a person charged with a federal crime, or a suit involving the infringement of a patent or a copyright, or one involving any other matter arising out of an act of Congress is also within the exclusive (sole) jurisdiction of the federal courts.

Some cases may be tried in either a federal *or* a State court. Then, the federal and State courts have **concurrent jurisdiction,** meaning they share the power to hear these cases. Disputes involving citizens of different States are fairly common examples of this type of case. Such cases are known in the law as cases in diverse citizenship.[3]

Congress has provided that a federal district court may hear a case of diverse citizenship only when the amount of money

---

3 Congress first gave the federal courts concurrent jurisdiction in these cases in 1789, out of a perceived need for a neutral forum to settle disputes between residents of different States. Early on, it was feared that State courts (and their juries) might be prejudiced against "foreigners," people from other States. There seems little likelihood of such bias today.

Types of Jurisdiction

Which Court?

Two separate court systems, federal and State, hear and decide cases in the United States. Their jurisdictions and examples of types of cases that would be heard in each are shown in this Venn diagram. *How does the structure of this illustrated diagram explain the types of jurisdiction?*

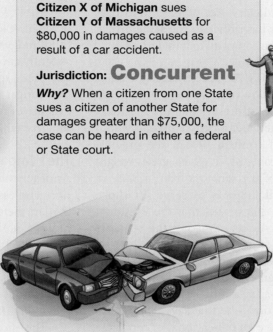

Scenario:
Citizen X of Michigan sues **Citizen Y of Massachusetts** for $80,000 in damages caused as a result of a car accident.

Jurisdiction: Concurrent

Why? When a citizen from one State sues a citizen of another State for damages greater than $75,000, the case can be heard in either a federal or State court.

Scenario:
Citizen M robs a bank in California.

Jurisdiction: Federal

Why? Bank robbery violates a federal law, regardless of the State in which the crime is committed.

Scenario:
Citizen Z of Ohio has her car repaired at AJ's, the local repair shop. Her car breaks down on her way home. She sues the repair shop for breach of contract.

Jurisdiction: State

Why? A purely local matter. Nothing in the facts of the case support federal court jurisdiction.

---

involved in that case is at least $75,000. In such a case, the **plaintiff**—the person who files the suit—may bring the case in the proper State or federal court, as he or she chooses. If the plaintiff brings the case in a State court, the **defendant**—the person against whom the complaint is made—can have the trial moved, under certain circumstances, to the federal district court.

Original and Appellate Jurisdiction A court in which a case is first heard is said to have **original jurisdiction** over that case. That court, the trial court, is often described as "the court of first instance." A court that hears a case on appeal from a lower court exercises **appellate jurisdiction** over that case.

Appellate courts do not retry cases. Rather, they determine whether a trial court

has acted in accord with applicable law. The higher court—the appellate court—may uphold, overrule, or in some way modify the decision appealed from the lower court.[4]

In the federal judiciary, the district courts have only original jurisdiction, and the courts of appeals have only appellate jurisdiction. The Supreme Court exercises both original and (most often) appellate jurisdiction.

Federal Judges

The manner in which federal judges are chosen, the terms for which they serve, and even the salaries they are paid are vital parts of the Constitution's design of an independent

---

4 Appellate comes from the Latin word *appellare,* meaning "to speak to, to call upon, to appeal to."

jurist
n. an expert in the law, especially a judge or legal scholar

premise
n. reason that forms the basis of an argument or conclusion

judicial branch. The Constitution declares that the President

> ## FROM THE CONSTITUTION
>
> **shall nominate, and by and with the Advice and Consent of the Senate, shall appoint . . . Judges of the supreme Court . . .**
>
> —Article II, Section 2, Clause 2

First, in the Judiciary Act of 1789, and ever since, Congress has provided the same procedure for the selection of all federal judges.

Selection of Judges The Senate has a major part in the selection of every federal judge. In effect, the Constitution says that the President can name to the federal bench anyone whom the Senate will confirm. Recall the practice of senatorial courtesy. It gives great weight to the wishes of the senators from a State in which a federal judge is to serve. In short, that unwritten rule means that the President almost always selects someone the senators from that State recommend.

The Court sets no age, residence, or citizenship requirements for federal judges. Nor does it require that a judge have legal training. It is tradition alone that says that federal judges must have an educational or a professional background in the law.

The President's closest legal and political aides, especially the Attorney General, take the lead in selecting federal judges. Influential senators—especially those from the nominee's home State and members of the Judiciary Committee, the President's allies and supporters in the legal profession, and various other important personalities in the President's political party also play a major role in selecting judges. Several interest groups are also quite active in the process.

Today, an increasing number of those persons who are appointed to the federal bench have had prior judicial experience. Most federal judges are drawn from the ranks of leading attorneys, legal scholars and law school professors, former members of Congress, and State court judges. Elective office (in particular, a seat in the U.S. Senate) was once a well-traveled path to the Supreme

Court; now, most justices reach the High Court from the courts of appeals.

To this point (2010), only three of the now 111 Supreme Court justices have been women: Sandra Day O'Connor (appointed in 1981), Ruth Bader Ginsburg (1993), and Sonia Sotomayor (2009). Justice Sotomayor is also the Court's first Hispanic member. Only two African Americans have thus far become justices: Thurgood Marshall (appointed in 1967) and Clarence Thomas (1991).

From George Washington's day, Presidents have looked to their own political party to fill judgeships. Republican Presidents consistently choose Republicans; Democrats usually pick Democrats. Every President knows that judges may serve for decades. So chief executives regularly look for jurists who tend to agree with their own views.

The Impact of Judicial Philosophy

Another major impact on the judicial selection process is judicial philosophy—in particular, the concepts of judicial restraint and judicial activism. All federal judges make decisions in which they must interpret and apply provisions in the Constitution and acts of Congress. That is, they often decide questions of public policy—and, in doing so, they inevitably *shape* public policy.

The proponents of **judicial restraint** believe that judges should decide cases on the basis of (1) the original intent of the Framers or those who enacted the statute(s) involved in a case, and (2) **precedent**—a judicial decision that serves as a guide for settling later cases of a similar nature. They say that the courts should defer to policy judgments made in the legislative and executive branches of the government and, in so doing, honor the basic premise of self-government: the right of the majority to determine public policy. In short, they argue that elected legislators, not appointed judges, should make law.

Those who support **judicial activism** take a much broader view of judicial power. They argue that provisions in the Constitution and in statute law should be interpreted and applied in the light of ongoing changes in conditions and values—especially in cases involving civil rights and social welfare issues. They, too, insist on the fundamental importance of majority rule and the value of precedents, but they believe that the courts should not be overly <u>deferential</u> to existing legal principles or to the judgments of elected officials.

Terms and Pay of Judges Article III, Section 1 of the Constitution reads, in part: "The Judges, both of the supreme and inferior Courts, shall hold their Offices during good Behaviour. . . . " This means that the judges of the constitutional courts are appointed for life; they serve until they resign, retire, or die in office. The Framers provided for what amounts to life tenure for these judges quite purposefully, to ensure the independence of the federal judiciary.

The very next words of the Constitution are directed to that same purpose. Article III, Section 1 continues: "and [they] shall, at stated Times, receive for their Services, a Compensation, which shall not be diminished during their Continuance in Office."

Federal judges may be removed from office only through the impeachment process. In 180

years, only 13 have ever been impeached. Of that number, seven were convicted and removed by the Senate, including three in the recent past.[5]

Those judges who sit in the special courts are not appointed for life. They are named, instead, to terms of 8 to 15 years—and may be, but seldom are, reappointed. In the District of Columbia, Superior Court judges are chosen for four-year terms; those who sit on the district's Court of Appeals are chosen for a period of eight years.

Congress sets the salaries of federal judges and has provided a generous retirement for

---

5 The judges removed from office were John Pickering of the district court in New Hampshire, for judicial misconduct and drunkenness (1804); West H. Humphreys of the district court in Tennessee, for disloyalty (1862); Robert W. Archbald of the old Commerce Court, for improper relations with litigants (1913); Halsted L. Ritter of the district court in Florida, on several counts of judicial misconduct (1936); Harry E. Claiborne of the district court in Nevada, for filing false income tax returns (1986); Alcee Hastings of the district court in Florida, on charges of bribery and false testimony (1989); and Walter Nixon of the district court in Mississippi, for perjury (1989). Four other federal judges were impeached by the House but acquitted by the Senate. Two district court judges, impeached by the House, resigned and so avoided a Senate trial.

✔ **Checkpoint**
How do the terms of office differ for judges of the constitutional courts and the special courts?

deferential
adj. respectful

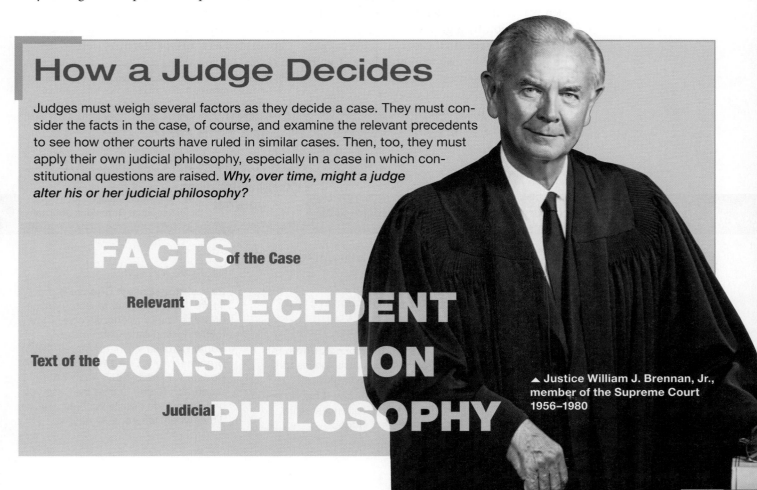

How a Judge Decides

Judges must weigh several factors as they decide a case. They must consider the facts in the case, of course, and examine the relevant precedents to see how other courts have ruled in similar cases. Then, too, they must apply their own judicial philosophy, especially in a case in which constitutional questions are raised. *Why, over time, might a judge alter his or her judicial philosophy?*

FACTS of the Case

Relevant **PRECEDENT**

Text of the **CONSTITUTION**

Judicial **PHILOSOPHY**

▲ Justice William J. Brennan, Jr., member of the Supreme Court 1956–1980

them. They may retire at age 70, and if they have served for at least 10 years, receive full salary for the rest of their lives. Or, they may retire at full salary at age 65, after at least 15 years of service. The Chief Justice may call any retired judge back to temporary duty in a lower federal court at any time.

Court Officers

Today, federal judges have little involvement in the day-to-day administrative operations of the courts over which they preside. Their primary mission is to hear and decide cases. A clerk, several deputy clerks, bailiffs, court reporters and stenographers, probation officers, and others provide support services.

The judges of each of the 94 district courts appoint one or more United States magistrates, of which there are now more than 400. They are appointed to eight-year terms and handle a number of legal matters once dealt with by the judges themselves. They issue warrants of arrest, and often hear evidence to decide whether or not a person who has been arrested on a federal charge should be held for action by a grand jury. They also set bail in federal criminal cases, and even have the power to try those who are charged with certain minor offenses.

Each federal judicial district also has at least one bankruptcy judge. These judges handle bankruptcy cases under the direction of the district court to which they are assigned.[6] There are now some 300 bankruptcy judges, all of them appointed to 14-year terms by the judges of each federal court of appeals.

The President and the Senate appoint a United States Attorney for each federal judicial district. The U.S. Attorneys and their many deputies are the government's prosecutors. They work closely with the FBI and other law enforcement agencies, and they bring to trial those persons charged with federal crimes. They also represent the United States in all civil actions brought by or against the Federal Government in their districts.

The President and Senate also select a United States marshal to serve each of the district courts. These marshals, and their several deputy U.S. marshals, perform duties much like those of a county sheriff. They make arrests in federal criminal cases, hold accused persons in custody, secure jurors, serve legal papers, keep order in courtrooms, and execute court orders and decisions. They also respond to such emergency situations as riots, mob violence, and other civil disturbances, as well as terrorist incidents. All United States Attorneys and marshals are appointed to four-year terms.

---

6 Recall that bankruptcy is a legal proceeding in which a debtor's assets are distributed among those to whom the bankrupt person, business, or other organization owes money. Although some bankruptcy cases are heard in State courts, nearly all of them fall within the jurisdiction of the federal district courts.

Essential Questions Journal To continue to build a response to the chapter Essential Question, go to your **Essential Questions Journal.**

SECTION 1 ASSESSMENT

1. **Guiding Question** Use your completed graphic organizer to answer this question: What are the structure and function of the national judiciary?

Key Terms and Comprehension

2. **(a)** What is the difference between **original jurisdiction** and **appellate jurisdiction? (b)** What kind of jurisdiction does the Supreme Court have?

3. **(a)** What is a **precedent? (b)** Write a sentence using the word **precedent**

to illustrate why it is important in the judicial system.

4. Under what circumstances do federal courts have **jurisdiction** in a case?

Critical Thinking

5. **Demonstrate Reasoned Judgment** What role should judicial philosophy play in the selection of judges?

6. **Predict Consequences** What do you think are the consequences of life tenure for federal judges?

Quick Write

Explanatory Essay: Choose a Topic Do preliminary research online or at the library to choose one of the following Supreme Court cases: *South Carolina* v. *United States*, 1905; *Brandenburg* v. *Ohio*, 1969; or *City of Boerne* v. *Flores*, 1997. Then write a paragraph to summarize the case you chose. Include details such as who, what, when, where, and why.

Judicial Restraint vs. Activism

Track the Issue

The Court's power of judicial review has long been an important part of the governing process in this country. But from *Marbury* on, this question has been the subject of intense debate: What is the appropriate role for the Supreme Court? Throughout its history, it has exercised both judicial restraint and judicial activism.

1819

In *McCulloch* v. *Maryland,* the Court exercised judicial activism, expanding constitutional provisions without citing precedent.

1849

The Court's decision in *Luther* v. *Borden* is one of the earliest cases of judicial restraint.

1954

The decision in *Brown* v. *Board of Education* provides a major example of judicial activism.

1969–1986

The Burger Court exercised a combination of judicial restraint and activism.

2005

Newly appointed Chief Justice John Roberts promises judicial restraint.

Chief Justice John Roberts ▶

Perspectives

There are two camps in the debate over judicial decision making. One side supports judicial restraint; its proponents believe that judges should consistently follow the letter of the law and apply precedent. The other supports judicial activism; its proponents think that judges should indeed consider precedent, but that they should also be willing to go further and play an active, creative role in the shaping of public policies.

"In our democratic system, responsibility for policy making properly rests with those branches that are responsible . . . to the people. It was . . . because the Framers intended the judiciary to be insulated from popular political pressures that the Constitution accords judges tenure during good behavior. . . . To the extent the term "judicial activism" is used to describe unjustified intrusions by the judiciary into the realm of policy making, the criticism is well-founded. . . . It is not part of the judicial function to make the law . . . or to execute the law."

—*John Roberts at his Senate confirmation hearing*

"We are under a Constitution, but the Constitution is what the judges say it is, and the judiciary is the safeguard of our liberty and of our property under the Constitution."

—*Charles Evan Hughes, Chief Justice of the United States 1930–1941*

Connect to Your World

1. **Understand (a)** What reasons does Justice Roberts cite for supporting judicial restraint? **(b)** How does Justice Hughes support his argument for judicial activism?
2. **Synthesize Information** To which of these competing positions—judicial restraint or judicial activism—do you think a judge should subscribe?

GOVERNMENT ONLINE
In the News
To find out more about judicial decision making, visit
PearsonSuccessNet.com

The Inferior Courts

Guiding Question

What are the structure and jurisdiction of the inferior courts?
Use a table like the one below to take notes on the structure and jurisdiction of the inferior courts.

The Inferior Courts	
Structure	**Jurisdiction**
•	•
•	•
•	•

Political Dictionary

• criminal case   • docket
• civil case   • record

Objectives

1. Describe the structure and jurisdiction of the federal district courts.
2. Describe the structure and jurisdiction of the federal courts of appeals.
3. Describe the structure and jurisdiction of the two other constitutional courts.

Image Above: An attorney for Napster, Inc., the online music firm, outside the 9th Circuit Court of Appeals

You know that the particular meaning of a word often depends on the context—the setting—in which it is used. Thus, *pitch* can be either a baseball term or a musical term; it can also refer to setting up a tent, or to a high-pressure sales talk.

The word *inferior* also has various meanings. Here, it describes the lower federal courts, those courts created by act of Congress, to function beneath the Supreme Court. The inferior courts handle nearly all of the cases tried in the federal courts.

The District Courts

The United States district courts are the federal trial courts. Their 667 judges handle more than 300,000 cases per year, about 80 percent of the federal caseload. The district courts were created by Congress in the Judiciary Act of 1789. There are now 94 of them.

Federal Judicial Districts The 50 States are divided into 89 federal judicial districts, and there are also federal district courts for Washington, D.C., Puerto Rico, the Virgin Islands, Guam, and the Northern Mariana Islands. Each State forms at least one judicial district. Some are divided into two or more districts, however—usually because of the larger amount of judicial business there. At least two judges are assigned to each district, but many districts have several. Thus, New York is divided into four judicial districts; one of them, the United States Judicial District for Southern New York, now has 44 judges.

Cases tried in the district courts are most often heard by a single judge. However, certain cases may be heard by a three-judge panel. Chiefly, these are cases that involve congressional districting or State legislative apportionment questions, those arising under the Civil Rights Act of 1964 or the Voting Rights Acts of 1965, 1970, 1975, and 1982, and certain antitrust actions.

Two little-known multi-judge panels play a key role in ongoing efforts to combat terrorism in this country and abroad. Both are shrouded in secrecy. One is the Foreign Intelligence Surveillance Court, created by Congress in 1978. It is often called the "FISA court" and is composed of 11 federal district court judges, who are appointed to seven-year terms by the Chief Justice of the United States. The court, which meets in secret, has the power to issue secret search warrants—court orders that allow the FBI and other federal law enforcement agencies to conduct covert surveillance of persons suspected of being spies or members of terrorist organizations.

The other is the Alien Terrorist Removal Court, created by Congress in 1996. It is made up of five district court judges, appointed by the Chief Justice to five-year terms. This court has the power to decide whether those persons identified as "alien terrorists" by the Attorney General of the United States should be expelled from this country.

District Court Jurisdiction The district courts have original jurisdiction over more than 80 percent of the cases that are heard in the federal court system. The only federal cases that do not begin in the district courts are those few that fall within the original jurisdiction of the Supreme Court and those cases heard by the Court of International Trade or by one of the special courts. Thus, the district courts are the principal trial courts, the "courts of first instance," in the federal judiciary.

District court judges hear a wide range of both criminal cases and civil cases. In the federal courts, a **criminal case** is one in which a defendant is tried for committing some action that Congress has declared by law to be a federal crime. A federal **civil case** involves some noncriminal matter—say, a dispute over the terms of a contract or a suit in which the plaintiff seeks damages (money) for some harm done by the defendant.

The United States is always a party to a federal criminal case, as the prosecutor. Most civil cases are disputes between private parties, but here, too, the United States may be a <u>litigant</u>, as either the plaintiff or the defendant.

✔ **Checkpoint**
What is the principal role of the federal district courts?

<u>litigant</u>
n. party to a case, either plaintiff or defendant

Federal Court Circuits and Districts

GOVERNMENT ONLINE
Audio Tour
Listen to a guided audio tour of the map at
PearsonSuccessNet.com

▸▸ **Interpreting Maps** Each State comprises at least one United States judicial district. The nation is divided into 13 judicial circuits, including the Court of Appeals for the District of Columbia and the Court of Appeals for the Federal Circuit, as shown on the map. ***Which States are in the Fifth Circuit?***

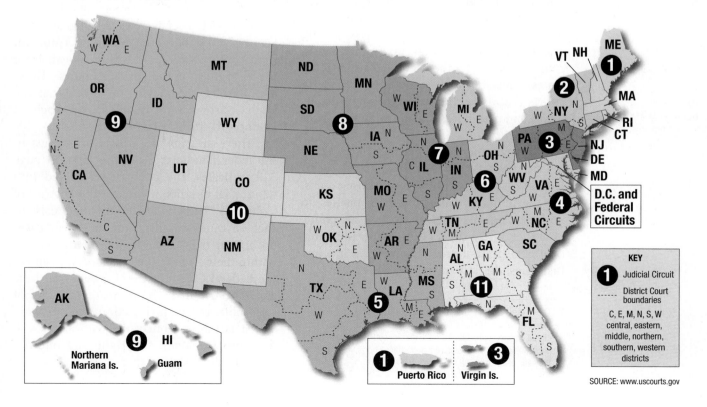

KEY

❶ Judicial Circuit

---- District Court boundaries

C, E, M, N, S, W central, eastern, middle, northern, southern, western districts

SOURCE: www.uscourts.gov

The Appellate Path in the Federal Courts

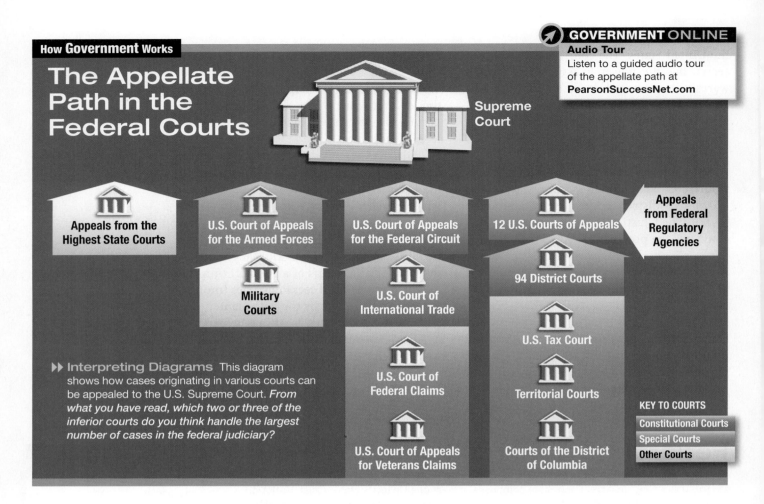

Supreme Court

Appeals from the Highest State Courts

U.S. Court of Appeals for the Armed Forces

U.S. Court of Appeals for the Federal Circuit

12 U.S. Courts of Appeals

Appeals from Federal Regulatory Agencies

Military Courts

U.S. Court of International Trade

94 District Courts

U.S. Court of Federal Claims

U.S. Tax Court

Territorial Courts

U.S. Court of Appeals for Veterans Claims

Courts of the District of Columbia

KEY TO COURTS
Constitutional Courts
Special Courts
Other Courts

▶▶ **Interpreting Diagrams** This diagram shows how cases originating in various courts can be appealed to the U.S. Supreme Court. *From what you have read, which two or three of the inferior courts do you think handle the largest number of cases in the federal judiciary?*

indict
v. accuse, bring charges against

The district courts try criminal cases ranging from bank robbery, kidnapping, and mail fraud to counterfeiting, terrorism, and tax evasion. They hear civil cases arising under bankruptcy, postal, tax, public lands, civil rights, and other laws of the United States. These trial courts are the only federal courts that use grand juries to <u>indict</u> defendants, and petit juries to determine their guilt or innocence.

Most of the decisions made in the 94 federal district courts are final. That is, most federal cases not only begin in those courts, but they end there as well. Losing parties do not often appeal a decision to a higher court. However, a few cases are taken to the court of appeals in that judicial circuit or, in a few instances, directly to the Supreme Court.

---

7 These tribunals were originally called the circuit courts of appeals. Before 1891, each Supreme Court justice "rode circuit," hearing appeals from the district courts within that geographic area. Congress renamed these courts in 1948, but they still are often called the "circuit courts."

The Courts of Appeals

The courts of appeals were created by Congress in 1891. They were established as "gatekeepers" to relieve the Supreme Court of much of the burden of hearing appeals from the decisions of the district courts. Those appeals had become so numerous that the High Court was more than three years behind its **docket**—its list of cases to be heard.

There are now 13 courts of appeals in the federal judiciary.[7] As the map on page 529 indicates, the country is divided into 12 judicial circuits, including the District of Columbia. There is one court of appeals for each of those circuits, and they hear cases on appeal from the various district courts within their circuit. The Court of Appeals for the Federal Circuit is the thirteenth of these appellate tribunals. It sits in the District of Columbia, but its jurisdiction is nationwide and it is mostly concerned with appeals of decisions in patent, copyright, and international trade cases.

Appellate Court Judges Each of these courts is composed of from 6 to 28 judges (179 in all). In addition, a justice of the Supreme Court is assigned to each. For example, the United States Court of Appeals for the Eleventh Circuit covers Alabama, Florida, and Georgia. The court is composed of 12 circuit judges and Associate Justice Clarence Thomas of the Supreme Court. The judges hold their sessions in a number of major cities within the circuit.

Each court of appeals usually sits in three-judge panels. Occasionally, however, and especially for an important case, a court will sit *en banc*—that is, with all of the judges in that circuit participating.

Appellate Court Jurisdiction The 13 courts of appeals have only appellate jurisdiction. For the 12 circuit-based courts, most cases come to them from the district courts within their circuit, but some are appealed from the Tax Court and some from the territorial courts. Recall, they are also empowered to hear appeals from the decisions of several federal regulatory agencies—for example, the Federal Trade Commission and the National Labor Relations Board.

Unlike the 12 circuit-based courts, the jurisdiction of the thirteenth, the Court of Appeals for the Federal Circuit, is nationwide in scope. Congress created it in 1982, with the special purpose of centralizing and speeding up the handling of appeals in certain types of federal civil cases.

The Court of Appeals for the Federal Circuit hears appeals from the decisions rendered in several different courts. Many of its cases come from the other constitutional court, the Court of International Trade, and still others come from two of the special courts: the Court of Federal Claims and the Court of Appeals for Veterans Claims. It also hears the appeals taken in any patent, copyright, or trademark case decided in any of the 94 federal district courts.

Again, these 13 tribunals are appellate courts. They do not conduct trials or accept new evidence in the cases they hear. Instead, they review the **record,** the transcript of proceedings made in the trial court, and they ponder the oral and written arguments (the briefs) submitted by attorneys representing parties to a case. The fact that less than one percent of their decisions are appealed to the Supreme Court underscores the importance of the place these tribunals occupy.

Court of International Trade

Congress has established one other Article III court, the Court of International Trade. Often called the Trade Court, this body was originally created in 1890, and was restructured as a constitutional court in 1980.

The Trade Court now has nine judges, including its chief judge, appointed by the President and the Senate. Like the 94 district courts, it is a federal trial court, a court of first instance. It tries all civil (but not criminal) cases that arise out of the nation's customs and other trade-related laws. Its judges sit in panels of three and often hold jury trials in such major ports as New Orleans, San Francisco, Boston, and New York.

✔ **Checkpoint**
Which inferior court hears appeals related to patents and copyrights?

Essential Questions Journal To continue to build a response to the chapter Essential Question, go to your **Essential Questions Journal.**

SECTION **2** ASSESSMENT

1. **Guiding Question** Use your completed graphic organizer to answer this question: What are the structure and jurisdiction of the inferior courts?

Key Terms and Comprehension

2. What is the difference between a **criminal case** and a **civil case?**

3. Why were the courts of appeals created?

Critical Thinking

4. **Draw Conclusions** Why do you think so many of the courts in the federal judiciary are appellate courts?

5. **Predict Consequences** What do you think might be the consequences if Congress were to follow the lead of several States by reducing the role of the grand jury in federal criminal cases?

Quick Write

Explanatory Essay: Research the Topic Research to gather more details on the Supreme Court case you chose in Section 1. Focus especially on the path the case took to reach the Supreme Court.

The **Supreme Court**

Guiding **Question**

What is the Supreme Court's jurisdiction, and how does the Court operate? Use an outline like the one below to take notes on the Supreme Court.

I. The Supreme Court
  A. Judicial review
    1. Established in *Marbury* v. *Madison,* 1803
    2. _____
  B. _____
    1. _____
    2. _____

Political Dictionary

- writ of certiorari
- certificate
- brief
- majority opinion
- concurring opinion
- dissenting opinion

Objectives

1. Define the concept of judicial review.
2. Outline the scope of the Supreme Court's jurisdiction.
3. Examine how cases reach the Supreme Court.
4. Summarize the way the Court operates.

Image Above: John Marshall, Chief Justice of the United States, 1801–1835

The eagle, the flag, Uncle Sam—you almost certainly recognize these symbols. They are used widely to represent the United States. You probably also know the symbol for justice: the blindfolded woman holding a balanced scale. She represents what is perhaps this nation's loftiest goal: equal justice under the law. Indeed, those words are chiseled in marble above the entrance to the Supreme Court building in Washington, D.C.

The Supreme Court of the United States is the only court specifically created by the Constitution, in Article III, Section 1. The Court is made up of the Chief Justice of the United States, whose office is also established by the Constitution,[8] and eight associate justices.[9]

The Framers quite purposely placed the Court on an equal plane with the President and Congress. As the highest court in the land, it stands as the court of last resort in all questions of federal law. That is, the Supreme Court of the United States is the final authority in any case involving any question arising under the Constitution, an act of Congress, or a treaty of the United States.

Judicial Review

Remember, most courts in this country, both federal and State, may exercise the critically important power of judicial review. They have the extraordinary power to decide the constitutionality of an act of government, whether executive, legislative, or judicial. The ultimate exercise of that power rests with the Supreme Court of the United States. That single fact makes the Supreme Court the final authority on the meaning of the Constitution.

The Constitution does not, in so many words, provide for the power of judicial review. Nevertheless, there is little doubt that the Framers intended that the federal courts—and, in particular, the Supreme Court—should have this power.[10]

---

8 Article I, Section 3, Clause 6.
9 Congress sets the number of associate justices and thus the size of the Supreme Court. The Judiciary Act of 1789 created a Court of six justices, including the Chief Justice. The Court was reduced to five members in 1801 but increased to seven in 1807, to nine in 1837, and to 10 in 1863. It was reduced to seven in 1866 and increased to its present size of nine in 1869.
10 See Article III, Section 2, setting out the Court's jurisdiction, and Article VI, Section 2, the Supremacy Clause.

Marbury v. *Madison* The Court first asserted its power of judicial review in *Marbury* v. *Madison* in 1803.[11] (See the Landmark Decisions of the Supreme Court feature, Chapter 3.) Recall that the case arose in the aftermath of the stormy elections of 1800. Thomas Jefferson had won the presidency and control of both houses of Congress. The outgoing Federalists, stung by their defeat, then tried to pack the judiciary with loyal party members. Congress created several new federal judgeships in the early weeks of 1801, and President John Adams quickly filled those posts with Federalists.

William Marbury had been appointed a justice of the peace for the District of Columbia. The Senate had promptly confirmed his appointment, and late on the night of March 3, 1801, President Adams signed the commissions of office for Marbury and a number of other new judges. The next day, Jefferson became President and discovered that Marbury's commission and several others had not been delivered.

Angered by the Federalists' attempted court-packing scheme, President Jefferson instructed James Madison, the new secretary of state, not to deliver those commissions. William Marbury then went to the Supreme Court, seeking a writ of mandamus to force delivery.[12] Marbury based his suit on the Judiciary Act of 1789, in which Congress had created the federal court system. That law gave the Supreme Court the right to hear such suits in its original jurisdiction (not on appeal from a lower court).

In a unanimous opinion written by Chief Justice John Marshall, the Court refused Marbury's request. It did so because it found the section of the Judiciary Act on which Marbury had based his case to be in conflict with Article III in the Constitution and, therefore, void.

The Effects of *Marbury* With the Court's decision, Chief Justice Marshall claimed for the Supreme Court the right to declare acts

✔ **Checkpoint**
What is the significance of the case *Marbury* v. *Madison*?

aftermath
n. result or consequence

---

11 It is often mistakenly said that the Court first exercised the power in this case, but in fact the Court did so at least as early as *Hylton* v. *United States* in 1796. In that case it upheld the constitutionality of a tax Congress had laid on carriages. It found that the tax was not a direct tax and so was not one that had to be apportioned among the States in accord with Article I, Section 2, Clause 3 of the Constitution.

12 A writ of mandamus is a court order compelling an officer of government to perform an act that the officer has a clear legal duty to perform.

Packing the Court

The Judiciary Act of 1789 created a Supreme Court of six justices, including the Chief Justice. The Court's size has fluctuated over time, reaching its present size of nine in 1869. In 1937, President Franklin D. Roosevelt asked Congress to increase the size of the Court, proposing that one additional justice be added for each sitting justice over age 70, to a maximum of 15 members. FDR claimed that his plan would make the Court a more efficient body. In reality, however, the proposal—which became known as "the Court-packing scheme"—was born out of the fact that the then-current Court had found several key pieces of New Deal legislation to be unconstitutional. Despite FDR's popularity, his plan was widely opposed, and it was roundly defeated in Congress, thereby protecting the separation of powers. *Why must a President be closely interested in the composition of the Supreme Court?*

of Congress unconstitutional, and so laid the foundation for the judicial branch's key role in the development of the American system of government.

The dramatic and often far-reaching effects of the Supreme Court's exercise of the power of judicial review tends to overshadow much of its other work. Each year, it hears dozens of cases in which questions of constitutionality are not raised, but in which federal law is interpreted and applied. Thus, many of the more important statutes that Congress has passed have been brought to the Supreme Court time and again for decisions. So, too, have many of the lesser ones. In interpreting those laws and applying them to specific situations, the Court has had a real impact on both their meaning and their effect.

Supreme Court Jurisdiction

The Supreme Court has both original and appellate jurisdiction. Most of its cases, however, come on appeal—from the lower federal courts and from the highest State courts. Article III, Section 2 of the Constitution spells out two classes of cases that may be heard by the High Court in its original jurisdiction: (1) those to which a State is a party, and (2) those affecting ambassadors, other public ministers, and consuls.

Congress cannot enlarge on this constitutional grant of original jurisdiction. Recall, that is precisely what the Supreme Court held in *Marbury*. If Congress could do so, it would in effect be amending the Constitution. Congress can <u>implement</u> the constitutional provision, however, and it has done so. It has provided that the Supreme Court shall have original and exclusive jurisdiction over (1) all controversies involving two or more States, and (2) all cases brought against ambassadors or other public ministers, but not consuls.

The Court may choose to take original jurisdiction over any other case covered by the broad wording in Article III, Section 2 of the Constitution. Almost without exception, however, those cases are tried in the lower courts. The Supreme Court hears only a very small number of cases in its original jurisdiction—in fact, no more than a case or two each term.

<u>implement</u>
v. to carry out, put into effect

How Cases Reach the Court

More than 8,000 cases are now appealed to the Supreme Court each term. Of these, the Court accepts only a few hundred for decision. In most cases, petitions for review are denied, usually because most of the justices agree with the decision of the lower court or believe that the case involves no significant point of law.

In short, the High Court is in the somewhat enviable position of being able to set its own agenda. It decides what it wants to decide. The Court selects those cases that it does hear according to "the rule of four": At least four of its nine justices must agree that a case should be put on the Court's docket.

More than half the cases decided by the Court are disposed of in brief orders. For example, an order may remand (return) a case to a lower court for reconsideration in light of some other recent and related case decided by the High Court. All told, the Court decides, after hearing arguments and with full opinions, fewer than 100 cases per term.

Most cases reach the Supreme Court by **writ of certiorari** (from the Latin, meaning "to be made more certain"). This writ is an order by the Court directing a lower court to send up the record in a given case for its review. Either party to a case can petition the Court to issue a writ. But, again, "cert" is granted in only a very limited number of instances—typically, only when a petition raises some important constitutional question or a serious problem in the interpretation of a statute.

When certiorari is denied, the decision of the lower court stands in that particular case. Note, however, that the denial of cert is not a decision on the merits of a case. All a denial means is that, for whatever reason, four or more justices could not agree that the Supreme Court should accept that particular case for review.

A few cases do reach the Court in yet another way: by **certificate.** This process is used when a lower court is not clear about the procedure or the rule of law that should apply in a case. The lower court asks the Supreme Court to certify the answer to a specific question in the matter.

Most cases that reach the Court do so from the highest State courts and the federal courts of appeals. A very few do come from the federal district courts and an even smaller number from the Court of Appeals for the Armed Forces.

How the Court Operates

The Supreme Court sits from the first Monday in October to sometime the following June or July. Each term is identified by the year in which it began. Thus, the 2010 term runs from October 4, 2010, into the early summer of 2011.

Oral Arguments Once the Supreme Court accepts a case, it sets a date on which that matter will be heard. As a rule, the justices consider cases in two-week cycles from October to early May. They hear oral arguments in several cases for two weeks; then recess for two weeks to consider those cases and handle other Court business.

On those days on which the Court hears arguments, it convenes at 10:00 A.M. on Mondays, Tuesdays, Wednesdays, and sometimes Thursdays. At those public sessions, the lawyers, representing the parties of those cases the Court has accepted, make their oral arguments. Their presentations are almost always limited to 30 minutes.

The justices usually listen to an attorney's arguments and sometimes interrupt them with pointed questions. After 25 minutes, a white light flashes at the lectern from which an attorney addresses the Court. Five minutes later, a red light signals the end of the presentation and it must stop, even if the lawyer is in mid-sentence.

Briefs Each party files detailed written statements—**briefs**—with the Court before they present their oral arguments. These detailed statements spell out the party's legal position and are built largely on relevant facts and the citation of precedents. Briefs often run to hundreds of pages.

The Court may also receive *amicus curiae* (friend of the court) briefs. These are briefs filed by persons or groups who are not actual parties to a case but who nonetheless have a substantial interest in its outcome. Thus, for

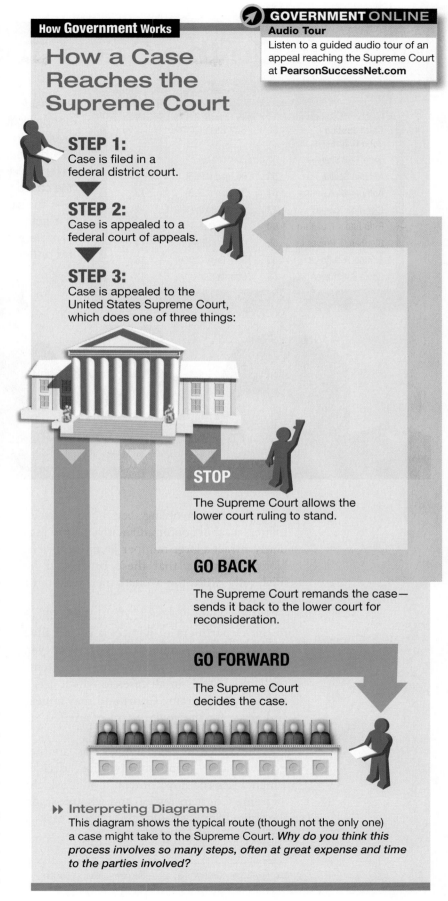

GOVERNMENT ONLINE

Audio Tour

Listen to a guided audio tour of an appeal reaching the Supreme Court at **PearsonSuccessNet.com**

How **Government** Works

How a Case Reaches the Supreme Court

STEP 1:
Case is filed in a federal district court.

STEP 2:
Case is appealed to a federal court of appeals.

STEP 3:
Case is appealed to the United States Supreme Court, which does one of three things:

STOP
The Supreme Court allows the lower court ruling to stand.

GO BACK
The Supreme Court remands the case—sends it back to the lower court for reconsideration.

GO FORWARD
The Supreme Court decides the case.

▶▶ **Interpreting Diagrams**
This diagram shows the typical route (though not the only one) a case might take to the Supreme Court. *Why do you think this process involves so many steps, often at great expense and time to the parties involved?*

Who Is On the Court Today?

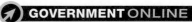

GOVERNMENT ONLINE

Update
For online updates and additional information on the Court, go to **PearsonSuccessNet.com**

Justice	Age When Appointed	Appointed by (Year)	Previous Years as a Judge
Chief Justice John G. Roberts, Jr.	50	G.W. Bush (2005)	2
John Paul Stevens	55	Ford (1975)	5
Antonin Scalia	50	Reagan (1986)	4
Anthony M. Kennedy	51	Reagan (1988)	13
Clarence Thomas	43	G.H.W. Bush (1991)	2
Ruth Bader Ginsburg	60	Clinton (1993)	13
Stephen G. Breyer	55	Clinton (1994)	14
Samuel A. Alito, Jr.	55	G.W. Bush (2006)	16
Sonia Sotomayor	55	Obama (2009)	17

A President seeks to appoint justices who share his or her political stance, but justices' views may change over time in unpredictable ways. Today's Supreme Court has a conservative majority and is often divided in its decisions, likely due to the controversial nature of the cases that it hears. The Court has recently made 5–4 decisions on topics such as public school affirmative action programs and capital punishment for juvenile offenders. *What might lead a justice to change his or her basic position in some area of the law?*

Front row: Anthony Kennedy, John Paul Stevens, Chief Justice John Roberts, Antonin Scalia, Clarence Thomas, Back row: Samuel Alito, Ruth Bader Ginsburg, Stephen Breyer, Sonia Sotomayor

example, cases involving such highly charged matters as abortion or affirmative action regularly attract a large number of *amicus* briefs. Notice, however, that these briefs can be filed only with the Court's permission or at its request.

The solicitor general, a principal officer in the Department of Justice, is often called the Federal Government's chief trial lawyer. He—and, certainly, one day she—represents the United States in all cases to which it is a party in the Supreme Court and may appear and argue for the government in any federal or State court.[13]

The solicitor general also has another extraordinary responsibility. He decides which cases the government should ask the Supreme Court to review and what position the United States should take in those cases it brings before the High Court.

---

[13] The Attorney General may argue the government's position before the Supreme Court but rarely does so.

The Court in Conference On most Fridays through a term, the justices meet in conference. There, in closest secrecy, they consider the cases in which they have heard oral arguments; and there, too, they decide which new cases they will accept for decision.

Only the Chief Justice, who presides, and the eight other members of the Court are present at the conference. The Chief Justice leads the discussion of each case to be considered—stating the facts, summarizing the questions of law involved, and usually indicating how he thinks the Court should dispose of that case. Then each of the associate justices, in order of seniority, present their views and conclusions. A majority must decide which party wins or loses a case and whether a lower court's decision in that matter is to be affirmed or reversed.

About a third of the Court's decisions are unanimous, but most find the Court divided. The High Court is sometimes criticized for its split decisions. However, most of the cases it hears pose difficult and complicated questions, and many present questions on which lower courts have disagreed. In short, most of the Court's cases excite controversy; the easy cases seldom get that far.

The Court's Opinions Once a case has been considered and decided in conference, the Court announces its decision in the matter and, with it, issues one or more written opinions. The decision indicates which party has won the dispute and by what margin among the justices. Where the decision is unanimous, the Chief Justice most often writes the Court's opinion. If there has been a split decision, the Chief Justice may write the majority opinion, or he may assign that task to another justice in the majority. When the Chief Justice is in the minority, the senior justice in the majority makes that assignment.

The **majority opinion,** officially called "the Opinion of the Court," sets out the facts in a case, identifies the issues it presents, and details the reasons that <u>underpin</u> the majority's decision.[14]

The Court's opinions are exceedingly valuable. Its majority opinions stand as precedents. The lower courts, both federal and State, are expected to follow precedent—that is, decide cases of like nature in a manner consistent with previous rulings.[15]

One or more of the justices on the majority side may write a **concurring opinion,** usually to make some point not made or not emphasized in the majority opinion. In effect, a justice who writes a concurring opinion agrees with (concurs in) the majority decision as to the winner of a case but offers different reasons for reaching that conclusion.

One or more **dissenting opinions** may be written by those justices who do not agree with the Court's majority decision. Those dissents do not become precedent. They are, instead, expressions of opposition to the majority's views in a case. Chief Justice Charles Evans Hughes once described dissenting opinions as "an appeal to the brooding spirit of the law, to the intelligence of a future day." On rare occasions, the High Court does reverse itself. The minority opinion of today could become the Court's majority position on some distant tomorrow.

---

14 Most majority opinions, and many concurring and dissenting opinions, run to dozens of pages. Some Supreme Court decisions are issued with very brief, unsigned opinions. These *per curiam* (for the court) opinions seldom run more than a paragraph or two and usually dispose of relatively uncomplicated cases. All of the High Court's opinions in every case are published online and in the *United States Reports,* the official printed record of its decisions.

15 The doctrine of precedent is often identified as *stare decisis*— Latin for "let the decision stand," or adhere to decided cases.

✔ **Checkpoint**
What happens once a case has been decided?

underpin
v. to support or strengthen

Essential Questions Journal To continue to build a response to the chapter Essential Question, go to your **Essential Questions Journal.**

SECTION 3 ASSESSMENT

1. **Guiding Question** Use your completed graphic organizer to answer this question: What is the Supreme Court's jurisdiction, and how does the Court operate?

Key Terms and Comprehension

2. **(a)** What does a **writ of certiorari** have in common with a **certificate? (b)** How do the two differ?

3. What is **majority opinion** and why is it important?

4. Explain briefly how most cases reach the Supreme Court.

Critical Thinking

5. **Summarize** Why was the Court's decision in *Marbury* v. *Madison* one of the most important cases ever decided by the Supreme Court?

6. **Determine Cause and Effect** How does the power of judicial review place the judicial branch on an equal plane with the other branches of the Federal Government?

Quick Write

Explanatory Essay: Create a Flowchart Using your research from Section 2, create a flowchart to show the path the case took to reach the Supreme Court. Be sure to use arrows or lines so that the sequence is clear.

SECTION 4

The Special Courts

Guiding Question

What are the special courts, and what are the jurisdictions of each?
Use a concept web to take notes on the special courts.

Court of Appeals for the Armed Forces

Special Courts

Political Dictionary
• court-martial
• civilian tribunal
• redress

Objectives

1. Contrast the jurisdiction of the Court of Appeals for the Armed Forces and the Court of Appeals for Veterans Claims.
2. Explain how a citizen may sue the United States government in the Court of Federal Claims.
3. Examine the roles of the territorial courts and those of the District of Columbia courts.
4. Explain what types of cases are brought to the Tax Court.

Image Above: U.S. Army attorney before a court-martial

Recall, the national court system is made up of two quite distinct types of federal courts. They are (1) the constitutional courts, sometimes called the regular or Article III courts, discussed over the last several pages, and (2) the special courts, also known as the legislative or Article I courts.

Each of the special courts was established by Congress acting under the authority delegated to it in Article I, Section 8 of the Constitution—not under the power given to it in Article III to create courts to exercise the broad "judicial Power of the United States." That is to say, each of these courts has a very narrow jurisdiction; each hears only those cases that fall into a very limited class. And the special courts differ from the constitutional courts in one other important regard. Although their judges are all appointed by the President and Senate, they serve for a fixed term—not for life "during good Behaviour."

Military and Veterans Claims Courts

Beginning in 1789, Congress has created a system of military courts for each branch of the nation's armed forces, as an exercise of its expressed power to "make Rules for the Government and Regulation of the land and naval Forces."[16] These military courts—**courts-martial**—serve the special disciplinary needs of the armed forces and are *not* a part of the federal court system. Their judges, prosecutors, defense attorneys, court reporters, and other personnel are all members of the military; most of them are officers. They conduct trials of those members of the military who are accused of violating military law. Today, the proceedings in a court-martial are fairly similar to the trials held in civilian courts across the country. There are some important differences, however. For example, at a court-martial, only two thirds of the panel (the jury in the case) must agree on a guilty verdict, in contrast to the unanimous verdict usually required in cases tried in the civilian courts.

---

[16] Article I, Section 8, Clause 14. This provision allows Congress to provide for the regulation of the conduct of members of the armed forces under a separate, noncivil legal code. The present-day system of military justice has developed over more than 230 years. Today, the Uniform Code of Military Justice, enacted by Congress in 1950, and the Military Justice Acts of 1968 and 1983 are the principal statutes that set out the nation's military law.

The Court of Appeals for the Armed Forces In 1950, Congress created the Court of Military Appeals, now titled the Court of Appeals for the Armed Forces, to review the more serious court-martial convictions of military personnel. This appellate court is a **civilian tribunal,** a part of the judicial branch, entirely separate from the military establishment. Appeals from the court's decisions can be taken to the Supreme Court. It is, then, the court of last resort in most cases that involve offenses against military law.

The Court of Appeals for Veterans Claims Acting under its power (Article I, Section 8, Clause 9) to "constitute Tribunals inferior to the supreme Court," Congress created the Court of Veterans Appeals in 1988 and changed its name in 1999 to the Court of Appeals for Veterans Claims.

This court has the power to hear appeals from the decisions of an administrative agency, the Board of Veterans' Appeals in the Department of Veterans Affairs (VA). Thus, this court hears cases in which individuals claim that the VA has denied or otherwise mishandled <u>valid</u> claims for veterans' benefits. Appeals from the decisions of the Court of Appeals for Veterans Claims can be taken to the Court of Appeals for the Federal Circuit.

Military Commissions In 2001, President Bush issued a controversial executive order creating several military commissions. These court-like bodies were set up, outside the regular courts-martial system, to try "unlawful enemy combatants"—suspected terrorists captured by American forces in Iraq and Afghanistan. Some 770 of those captives were held over a seven-year period in a military prison at the American naval base at Guantanamo Bay, Cuba.

Recall that in 2006, the Supreme Court found that those military commissions had been improperly established, *Hamdan* v. *Rumsfeld;* see page 402. The Court held that a chief executive could create such tribunals but only if authorized to do so by an act of Congress. Congress responded with the Military Commissions Act of 2006, but the commissions accomplished very little over the next three years.

President Obama suspended the military commissions and ordered the closure of the Guantanamo Bay facility by early 2010. Congressional resistance soon surfaced and the daunting problem of the fate of some 200 detainees still held there remains.

Other Special Courts

The other special courts also have very narrow jurisdictions. They include the Court of Federal Claims, the territorial courts, the District of Columbia courts, and the U.S. Tax Court.

The Court of Federal Claims The United States government cannot be sued by anyone, in any court, for any reason, without its consent.[17] The government may be taken to court

---

17 The government is shielded from suit by the doctrine of sovereign immunity. The doctrine comes from an ancient principle of English public law: "The King can do no wrong." The rule is not intended to protect public officials from charges of wrongdoing; rather it is intended to prevent government from being hamstrung in its own courts. Congress has long since agreed to a long list of legitimate court actions against the government.

valid
adj. legitimate, well-grounded

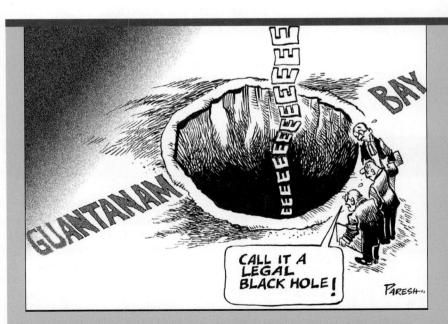

▶▶ **Analyzing Political Cartoons** Military tribunals have been established at various times in America's past—during the Mexican-American War, the Civil War, and World War II. *How do the bystanders in this cartoon view the military commissions at Guantanamo Bay?*

only in cases in which Congress has declared the United States to be open to suit. Originally, any person with a money claim against the United States could secure **redress**—satisfaction of a claim, payment—only by an act of Congress. In 1855, however, Congress set up the Court of Claims to hear such pleas.[18] That body was renamed the United States Court of Federal Claims in 1992.

The Court of Federal Claims holds trials throughout the country, hearing claims for damages against the Federal Government. Those claims it upholds cannot in fact be paid until Congress appropriates the money, which it does almost as a matter of standard procedure. Appeals from the court's decisions may be carried to the Court of Appeals for the Federal Circuit.

Occasionally, those who lose in the Claims Court still manage to win some compensation. Some years ago, a Puget Sound mink rancher lost a case in which he claimed that low-flying Navy planes had frightened his animals and caused several of the females to become sterile. He asked $100 per mink. He lost, but then his congressman introduced a private bill that eventually paid him $10 for each animal.

The Territorial Courts Acting under its power (Article IV, Section 3, Clause 2) to "make all needful Rules and Regulations

---

[18] Congress acted under its expressed power to pay the debts of the United States, Article I, Section 8, Clause 1.

respecting the Territory . . . belonging to the United States," Congress has created courts for the nation's territories. These courts sit in the Virgin Islands, Guam, and the Northern Mariana Islands. They function much like the local courts in the 50 States.

The District of Columbia Courts Acting under its power to "exercise exclusive Legislation in all Cases whatsoever, over such District . . . as may . . . become the Seat of the Government of the United States" (Article I, Section 8, Clause 17), Congress has set up a judicial system for the nation's capital. Both the federal district court and the federal Court of Appeals for the District of Columbia hear cases as constitutional courts. Congress has also established two local courts, much like the courts in the States: a superior court, which is the general trial court, and a court of appeals.

The United States Tax Court Acting under its power to tax (Article I, Section 8, Clause 1), Congress created the United States Tax Court in 1969 as "an independent judicial body" in the legislative branch. It is not, in fact, a part of the federal court system. The Tax Court hears civil but not criminal cases involving disputes over the application of the tax laws. Most of its cases, then, are generated by the Internal Revenue Service and other Treasury Department agencies. Its decisions may be appealed to the federal courts of appeals.

SECTION 4 ASSESSMENT

Essential Questions Journal To continue to build a response to the chapter Essential Question, go to your **Essential Questions Journal.**

1. **Guiding Question** Use your completed graphic organizer to answer this question: What are the special courts and what are the jurisdictions of each?

Key Terms and Comprehension

2. What is the difference between **civilian tribunals** and **courts-martial?**

3. What does it mean to seek **redress** in a court?

4. How do the special courts differ from the constitutional courts?

Critical Thinking

5. **Synthesize Information** When, if ever, do you think the establishment of a military commission is justified?

6. **Determine Relevance** Why do you think Congress has created the several special courts, rather than simply providing that all federal cases are to be tried in the regular courts?

Quick Write

Explanatory Essay: Write a Thesis Statement A thesis states specifically what you will cover in your essay. Write a thesis statement for an explanatory essay on your chosen case's path to the Supreme Court. You will use your thesis as a guide to develop an organizational plan for your essay.

Quick Study Guide

GOVERNMENT ONLINE

On the Go
To review anytime, anywhere, download these online resources at **PearsonSuccessNet.com**
Political Dictionary, Audio Review

CHAPTER **18**

Guiding Question
Section 2 What are the structure and jurisdiction of the inferior courts?

Guiding Question
Section 3 What is the Supreme Court's jurisdiction, and how does the Court operate?

Guiding Question
Section 1 What are the structure and function of the national judiciary?

CHAPTER 18

Essential Question
Does the structure of the federal court system allow it to administer justice effectively?

Guiding Question
Section 4 What are the special courts, and what are the jurisdictions of each?

Political Dictionary

inferior courts *p. 521*
jurisdiction *p. 522*
concurrent jurisdiction *p. 522*
plaintiff *p. 523*
defendant *p. 523*
original jurisdiction *p. 523*
appellate jurisdiction *p. 523*
judicial restraint *p. 524*
precedent *p. 524*
judicial activism *p. 524*
criminal case *p. 529*
civil case *p. 529*
docket *p. 530*
record *p. 531*
writ of certiorari *p. 534*
certificate *p. 534*
brief *p. 535*
majority opinion *p. 537*
concurring opinion *p. 537*
dissenting opinion *p. 537*
court-martial *p. 538*
civilian tribunal *p. 539*
redress *p. 540*

The Federal Courts

U.S. Supreme Court

Inferior Courts

Constitutional Courts	**Special Courts**
• District Courts	• U.S. Court of Appeals for the Armed Forces
• U.S. Courts of Appeals	• U.S. Court of Appeals for Veterans Claims
• U.S. Court of Appeals for the Federal Circuit	• U.S. Court of Federal Claims
• U.S. Court of International Trade	• Territorial Courts
	• Courts of the District of Columbia
	• U.S. Tax Court

How Cases Reach the Court

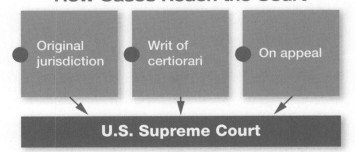

Original jurisdiction

Writ of certiorari

On appeal

U.S. Supreme Court

Chapter Assessment

Comprehension and Critical Thinking

Section 1

1. **(a)** Why did the Framers see a need for a national court system? **(b)** Why did the Framers believe that an independent judiciary was so important?

2. **(a)** What are the two general principles that determine whether the federal courts have jurisdiction over a case? **(b)** Do you think these principles are broad enough? Why or why not?

3. **(a)** Outline the process by which most federal judges are nominated and approved. **(b)** Why did the Framers create a system of judicial selection that requires the cooperation of the President and the Senate?

Section 2

4. **Analyze Political Cartoons (a)** What is happening in this scene? **(b)** What point is the cartoonist making?

Section 3

5. **(a)** What kinds of cases do the district courts hear? **(b)** Why can it be said that the federal district courts are the principal trial courts in the national judiciary?

6. **(a)** What is the principal role of the courts of appeals? **(b)** Why were they a necessary creation?

Section 3

7. **(a)** What is judicial review? **(b)** Is the power of judicial review consistent with the basic principles of democracy? Why or why not?

8. **(a)** What is the jurisdiction of the Supreme Court? **(b)** For what reasons do you think the "easy" cases do not reach the Supreme Court?

9. **(a)** What is a concurring opinion? What is a dissenting opinion? **(b)** Why do Supreme Court justices often write concurring and/or dissenting opinions in a case?

Section 4

10. **(a)** What are the special courts? Cite two examples and the jurisdiction of each. **(b)** What does it mean to say these courts have a very narrow jurisdiction?

11. **(a)** What is the function of a civilian tribunal? **(b)** Why do you think Congress established a civilian tribunal to hear the appeals of serious courts-martial convictions?

Writing About Government

12. Use your Quick Write exercises from this chapter to write an explanatory essay about the path your chosen case took to reach the Supreme Court. Be sure to write an introduction that has a strong and clear purpose, a body that identifies the steps in the process and shows how each step relates to the overall process, and a conclusion that synthesizes the information. See pp. S3–S5 in the Skills Handbook.

Apply What You've Learned

13. **Essential Question** **Activity** Interview a federal judge or lawyer who has experience with federal cases. Ask:

    (a) What do you think is the purpose of the law?

    (b) What is the role of the courts in our system of government?

    (c) What do you think are the advantages of trying a case in federal court, as compared to a State or local court? The disadvantages?

14. **Essential Question** **Assessment** Based on the interview you conducted and the content you have learned in this chapter, write an op-ed that helps to answer the Essential Question: **Does the structure of the federal court system allow it to administer justice effectively?** An op-ed is an opinion piece that you could submit to your local newspaper for publication. Op-eds present an informed view and should be engaging. Include facts and statistics to support your opinion.

Essential Questions Journal To respond to the chapter Essential Question, go to your **Essential Questions Journal.**

Document-Based Assessment

Term Limits for Federal Judges

Over recent years, many have questioned the wisdom of the provision of life tenure for federal judges, as illustrated in Document 1 below. The debate has often focused on the Supreme Court. Article III, Section 1 of the Constitution gives Supreme Court justices lifetime appointments. A Framer's viewpoint is set out in Document 2. Any change in the tenure of Supreme Court justices would require a constitutional amendment. Although both supporters and opponents of such an amendment agree that one is unlikely any time soon, the issue has led to lively debate.

Document 1

[L]ifetime tenure should be abolished. . . . [A]s the judiciary has become almost as polarized [divided] along partisan lines as the elective branches, Presidents have been seeking out younger and younger judge-ship appointees at every level of the judiciary, hoping to influence the courts long after they [the Presidents] leave the White House.

The insularity [isolation] produced by lifetime tenure, combined with youthful appointment and long service, often means that senior judges represent the views and outlooks of past generations better than the current day.

Therefore, a nonrenewable term of fifteen years is an attractive innovation. . . . This is a long time to serve— nearly four current presidential terms. . . . At the same time, it is short enough to prevent justices from becoming too detached and generationally removed from the American mainstream.

—Larry J. Sabato, *A More Perfect Constitution*

Document 2

The standard of good behavior for the continuance in office of the judicial magistracy [judges], is certainly one of the most valuable of the modern improvements in the practice of government. In a monarchy it is an excellent barrier to the despotism of the prince; in a republic it is a no less excellent barrier to the encroachments and oppressions of the representative body. And it is the best expedi-ent which can be devised in any government, to secure a steady, upright, and impartial administration of the laws.

—Alexander Hamilton, *The Federalist* No. 78

Use your knowledge of the terms of Supreme Court justices and Documents 1 and 2 to answer Questions 1–3.

1. What concern does the author of Document 1 have about life tenure for judges?
   A. Justices who are appointed to the Court at a young age lack the knowledge and experience of older justices.
   B. Justices should be required to retire from the Court at a specified age.
   C. Justices who serve long terms on the Court can become out of touch with the challenges of society today.
   D. Justices who have life tenure do not under-stand the concerns of young people.

2. What reasons does the author of Document 2 give for his opinion about lifetime tenure for justices?

3. **Pull It Together** Would you support or oppose term limits for Supreme Court justices? Why or why not?

GOVERNMENT ONLINE
Documents
To find more primary sources on judges' term limits, visit
PearsonSuccessNet.com

Civil Liberties: First Amendment Freedoms

Essential Question
How can the judiciary balance individual rights with the common good?

Section 1:
The Unalienable Rights

Section 2:
Freedom of Religion

Section 3:
Freedom of Speech and Press

Section 4:
Freedom of Assembly and Petition

> All through the years we have had to **fight for civil liberty,** and we know that there are times when the **light** grows rather dim, and every time that happens **democracy** is in danger.
>
> —Eleanor Roosevelt, 1940

Photo: Peaceful protest is a 1st Amendment right.

GOVERNMENT ONLINE
On the Go

To study anywhere, anytime, download these online resources at PearsonSuccessNet.com
- Political Dictionary
- Audio Review
- Downloadable Interactivities

SECTION 1

The Unalienable Rights

Guiding Question

How does the Constitution protect the rights of individuals against government? Use a concept web to identify three parts of the Constitution that protect individual rights.

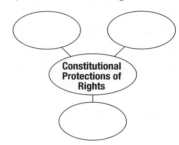

Constitutional Protections of Rights

Political Dictionary

- Bill of Rights
- civil liberties
- civil rights
- alien
- Due Process Clause
- process of incorporation

Objectives

1. Explain how Americans' commitment to freedom led to the creation of the Bill of Rights.
2. Understand that the rights guaranteed by limited government are not absolute.
3. Show how federalism affects individual rights.
4. Describe how the 9th Amendment helps protect individual rights.

Image Above: James Madison, author of the Bill of Rights

Have you ever heard of Walter Barnette? How about Toyosaburo Korematsu? Dollree Mapp? Clarence Earl Gideon? Walter Barnette was a Jehovah's Witness in West Virginia who told his children not to salute the American flag or to recite the Pledge of Allegiance in school. Toyosaburo Korematsu was an American citizen interned by the Federal Government during World War II. Dollree Mapp was jailed for keeping "lewd and lascivious books" in her boarding house in Ohio. Clarence Earl Gideon went to prison for breaking into a poolroom in Florida. You will encounter these names again as you read this chapter and the next one. Each of these people played an important part in building and protecting the rights of all Americans.

A Commitment to Freedom

A commitment to personal freedom is deeply rooted in America's colonial past. For centuries, the people of England waged a continuing struggle for individual rights, and the early colonists brought a dedication to that cause with them to America.

Their commitment to freedom took root here, and it flourished. The Revolutionary War was fought to preserve and expand those very rights: the rights of the individual against government. In proclaiming the independence of the new United States, the founders of this country declared:

PRIMARY SOURCE

We hold these truths to be self-evident, that all men are created equal, that they are endowed by their Creator with certain unalienable Rights, that among these are Life, Liberty and the pursuit of Happiness. That to secure these rights, Governments are instituted among Men. . . .

—Declaration of Independence

The Framers of the Constitution repeated the justification for the existence of government in the Preamble to the Constitution. That document, they said, was written to "secure the Blessings of Liberty to ourselves and our Posterity."

The Constitution, as it was written in Philadelphia, contained a number of important guarantees. The most notable of these can be found in Article I, Sections 9 and 10, and in Article III. Unlike many of the first State constitutions, however, the new National Constitution did not include a general listing of the rights of the people.

That omission raised an outcry. The objections were so strong that several States ratified the Constitution only with the understanding that a listing of rights would soon be added. The first session of the new Congress proposed a series of amendments. Ten of them, known as the **Bill of Rights,** were ratified by the States and became a part of the Constitution on December 15, 1791. Later amendments, especially the 13th and the 14th, have added to the Constitution's guarantees of personal freedom.

The Constitution guarantees both rights and liberties to the American people. The distinction between civil rights and civil liberties is murky at best. Legal scholars often disagree on the matter, and the two terms often are used interchangeably.

Think of the distinction this way: In general, **civil liberties** are protections *against government*. They are guarantees of the safety of persons, opinions, and property from arbitrary acts of government. Thus, freedom of religion, freedom of speech and press, and the guarantees of fair trial are prime examples of civil liberties.

In contrast, **civil rights** are often associated with *positive acts of government* that seek to make constitutional guarantees a reality for all people. Viewed from this perspective, laws against discrimination on the basis of race, sex, religious belief, or national origin set out in the Civil Rights Act of 1964 are leading examples of civil rights.

Limited Government

Remember, government in the United States is limited. The Constitution is filled with examples of this fact. Chief among them are its many guarantees of personal freedom. Each of those guarantees is either an outright prohibition or a restriction on the power of government to do something.

All governments have and use authority over individuals. The all-important difference between a democratic government and a dictatorial one lies in the extent of that authority. In a dictatorial <u>regime</u>, the government's powers are practically unlimited. The government regularly suppresses dissent, often harshly. In the United States, however, governmental authority is strictly limited. As Justice Robert H. Jackson once put the point:

" PRIMARY SOURCE

If there is any fixed star in our constitutional constellation, it is that no official, high or petty, can prescribe what shall be <u>orthodox</u> in politics, nationalism, religion, or any other matters of opinion or force citizens to confess by word or act their faith therein.

—*West Virginia Board of Education* v. *Barnette,* 1943

Rights Are Relative, Not Absolute The Constitution guarantees many rights to everyone in the United States. Still, no one has the right to do anything he or she pleases. Rather, all persons have the right to do as they please as long as they do not infringe on the rights of others. That is, each person's rights are *relative* to the rights of every other person.

To illustrate the point: Everyone in the United States has a right of free speech, but no one enjoys absolute freedom of speech. A person can be punished for

✔ **Checkpoint**
How does the Bill of Rights limit government in the United States?

regime
n. a government

orthodox
adj. standard, recognized, accepted

arbitrary
adj. random

No one has a right to play loud music if doing so infringes on the rights of others.
▼

✓ **Checkpoint**
Cite an example that
illustrates the point that
rights are relative.

vulgarity
n. an offensive or
indecent act or
expression

stringent
adj. strict, rigid, narrow

using obscene language, or for using words in a way that causes someone to commit a crime—to riot or to desert from the military, for example. The Supreme Court dealt with this point most recently in *Federal Communications Commission* v. *Fox Television Stations,* 2009. There, 5–4, it upheld the FCC's controversial policy of punishing broadcasters for even the one-time use of gross <u>vulgarities</u> on the air.

In this oft-quoted line, Justice Oliver Wendell Holmes put the relative nature of each person's rights in this way:

> ❝
> **PRIMARY SOURCE**
> The most <u>stringent</u> protection of free speech would not protect a man in falsely shouting fire in a theatre and causing a panic.
> —*Schenck* v. *United States,* 1919

When Rights Conflict On occasion, different guarantees of rights come into conflict with one another. For example, cases involving freedom of the press versus the right to a fair trial are not at all uncommon.

In one famous case, Dr. Samuel Sheppard of Cleveland, Ohio, had been convicted of murdering his wife. His lengthy trial was widely covered in the national media. On appeal, Sheppard claimed that the highly sensational coverage had denied him a fair trial. The Supreme Court agreed. In *Sheppard* v. *Maxwell,* 1966, the Court rejected the free press argument, overturned Sheppard's conviction, and ordered a new trial.

To Whom Are Rights Guaranteed? Most constitutional rights are extended to all persons. The Supreme Court has often held that "persons" includes **aliens,** people who are not citizens of the country in which they live. Not *all* rights are given to aliens, however. The right to travel freely throughout the country is guaranteed to all citizens, for example, but travel by aliens can be restricted.[1]

After the bombing of Pearl Harbor by Japan in 1941, all persons of Japanese descent living on the Pacific Coast were evacuated— forcibly moved—inland. Many suffered economic and other hardships. In 1944, the Supreme Court reluctantly upheld the forced evacuation as a reasonable wartime emergency measure.[2] Still, the relocation was strongly criticized over the years. In 1988, the Federal Government admitted that the wartime relocation had been both unnecessary and unjust. Congress voted to pay $20,000 to each living internee. It also declared, "the Congress apologizes on behalf of the nation."

The current war on terrorism has created a political climate similar to that of the early days of World War II. Did the mistreatment of Japanese Americans then provide a lesson for today? Will the rights of Muslims and others of Middle Eastern descent be respected by government as it fights terrorism here and abroad?

Federalism and Individual Rights

Federalism is a complicated governmental arrangement. It produces any number of problems—including a very complex pattern of guarantees of individual rights in the United States.

The Bill of Rights Remember, the first ten amendments to the Constitution were originally intended as restrictions on the new National Government, not on the already existing States. And that remains the fact of the matter today.[3]

To illustrate this important point: The 5th Amendment says that no person can be charged with "a capital, or otherwise infamous crime" except by a grand jury. As a part of the Bill of Rights, this provision applies

---

1 See the two Privileges and Immunities clauses, in Article IV, Section 2, and the 14th Amendment. The guarantee does not extend to citizens under some form of legal restraint—for example, in jail or out on bail awaiting trial.

2 *Korematsu* v. *United States,* 1944. However, on the same day the Court held, in *Ex parte Endo,* that once the loyalty of any citizen internee had been established, no restriction could be placed on that person's freedom to travel that was not legally imposed on all other citizens.

3 The Supreme Court first held that the provisions of the Bill of Rights restrict only the National Government in *Barron* v. *Baltimore,* 1833. This was the first case in which the point was raised. The Supreme Court has followed that holding (precedent) ever since.

GOVERNMENT ONLINE

Audio Tour
Listen to a guided audio tour
of these rights at
PearsonSuccessNet.com

The 14th Amendment's Due Process Clause
Incorporation of Rights

- Provisions of the **Bill of Rights INCORPORATED**
  into the 14th Amendment's Due Process Clause

1st AMENDMENT
- Freedom of speech
- Freedom of press
- Freedom of assembly, petition
- Free Exercise Clause
- Establishment Clause

4th AMENDMENT
- No unreasonable searches, seizures

5th AMENDMENT
- No self-incrimination
- No double jeopardy

6th AMENDMENT
- Right to counsel
- Right to confront and obtain witnesses
- Speedy trial
- Trial by jury in criminal cases

8th AMENDMENT
- No cruel, unusual punishments

- Provisions of the **Bill of Rights NOT INCORPORATED**
  into the 14th Amendment's Due Process Clause

2nd AMENDMENT
- Right to keep, bear arms

3rd AMENDMENT
- No quartering of troops

5th AMENDMENT
- Grand jury

7th AMENDMENT
- Trial by jury in civil cases

▶▶ **Interpreting Charts** This chart shows which rights the Supreme Court has "nationalized" by incorporating them into the meaning of the Due Process Clause in the 14th Amendment. *Why do you think that some, but not all, rights have been incorporated into the 14th Amendment's Due Process Clause?*

only to the National Government. The States may use the grand jury to bring accusations of serious crime—or, if they prefer, they can use some other process to do so. The grand jury is a part of the criminal justice system in all but two States and the District of Columbia, however. For additional information, see the coverage of the grand jury in the next chapter and also in Chapter 24.

The Modifying Effect of the 14th Amendment Again, the provisions of the Bill of Rights apply against the National Government, not against the States. This does *not* mean, however, that the States can deny basic rights to the people.

In part, the States cannot do so because each of their own constitutions contains a bill of rights. In addition, they cannot deny these basic rights because of the 14th Amendment's **Due Process Clause.** It says:

FROM THE CONSTITUTION

No State shall . . . deprive any person of life, liberty, or property, without due process of law. . . .
—14th Amendment, Section 1

The Supreme Court has often said that the 14th Amendment's Due Process Clause means that no State can deny to any person any right that is "basic or essential to the American concept of ordered liberty."

But what specific rights are "basic or essential"? The Supreme Court has answered that question in a long series of cases in which it has held that most (but not all) of the protections in the Bill of Rights are also covered by the 14th Amendment's Due Process Clause, and so apply against the States. In deciding those cases, the Court has engaged in what has come to be called the **process of incorporation.** It has incorporated—merged, combined—most of the guarantees in the Bill of Rights into the 14th Amendment's Due Process Clause.

The Court began that historic incorporation in *Gitlow* v. *New York*, 1925. The landmark case involved Benjamin Gitlow, a Communist, who had been convicted of criminal anarchy in the State courts. He had made several speeches and published a pamphlet calling for the violent overthrow of government in this country.

On appeal, the Court upheld Gitlow's conviction and the State law under which he had been tried. In deciding the case, however, the Court made this crucial point: Freedom of speech and press, which the 1st Amendment says cannot be denied by the National Government, are also "among the fundamental personal rights and liberties protected by the Due Process Clause of the 14th Amendment from impairment by the States."

Soon after *Gitlow*, the Court held each of the 1st Amendment's guarantees to be covered by the 14th Amendment. It struck down State laws involving speech (*Fiske* v. *Kansas*, 1927; *Stromberg* v. *California*, 1931), the press (*Near* v. *Minnesota*, 1931), assembly and petition (*DeJonge* v. *Oregon*, 1937), and religion (*Cantwell* v. *Connecticut*, 1940). In each of those cases, the Court declared a State law unconstitutional as a violation of the 14th Amendment's Due Process Clause.

In the 1960s, the Court extended the scope of the 14th Amendment's Due Process Clause even further. The key guarantees are listed in the chart on the previous page. You will look at each of the guarantees involved—the 1st Amendment rights in this chapter and the others in Chapter 20.

The 9th Amendment

The Constitution does *not* contain a complete catalog of all the rights held by Americans. The little-noted 9th Amendment says that there are, in fact, some guarantees beyond those set out in the Constitution:

FROM THE CONSTITUTION

The enumeration in the Constitution, of certain rights, shall not be construed to deny or disparage others retained by the people.

—9th Amendment

Over the years, the Supreme Court has found a number of other rights "retained by the people." They include, most notably, the guarantee that an accused person will not be tried on the basis of evidence unlawfully gained, and the right of a woman to choose to have an abortion without undue interference by government.

Essential Questions Journal To continue to build a response to the chapter Essential Question, go to your **Essential Questions Journal.**

SECTION 1 ASSESSMENT

1. **Guiding Question** Use your completed graphic organizer to answer this question: How does the Constitution protect the rights of individuals against government?

Key Terms and Comprehension

2. What is the **Bill of Rights,** and why did its omission from the original Constitution raise such an outcry?

3. Compare and contrast **civil liberties** and **civil rights.**

4. **(a)** What is the **process of incorporation? (b)** What guarantees in the Bill of Rights are covered by the 14th Amendment's **Due Process Clause?**

Critical Thinking

5. **Draw Inferences (a)** Why are individual rights not absolute? **(b)** Cite two examples of the fact that rights may come into conflict with one another.

6. **Predict Consequences** How do you think this country might be different today if the Supreme Court had not applied the process of incorporation to the 14th Amendment?

Quick Write

Persuasive Essay: Choose a Topic To write a persuasive essay, one that convinces others to accept your views, you should select a topic that you feel strongly about. Read through this section and identify a topic on which you might write such an essay—for example, proper limits on freedom of speech.

SECTION 2

Freedom of Religion

Guiding Question

How does the 1st Amendment protect the freedom of religion?
Use a chart like the one below to take notes on five Supreme Court cases that protect the freedom of religion.

Freedom of Religion	
Case	**Ruling**
• *Pierce* v. *Society of Sisters*, 1925	•
•	•
•	•

Political Dictionary

• Establishment Clause
• Free Exercise Clause
• parochial

Objectives

1. Examine why religious liberty is protected in the Bill of Rights.
2. Describe the limits imposed by the Establishment Clause of the 1st Amendment.
3. Summarize the Supreme Court rulings on religion and education as well as other Establishment Clause cases.
4. Explain how the Supreme Court has interpreted and limited the Free Exercise Clause.

Image Above: Americans are free to practice religion as they please.

I n the early 1830s, a Frenchman, Alexis de Tocqueville, came to America to observe life in the young country. He is said to have later written in his classic, *Democracy in America,* that he had searched for the greatness of America in many places: in its large harbors and deep rivers, in its fertile fields and boundless forests, in its rich mines and vast world commerce, in its public schools and institutions of higher learning, and in its democratic legislature and matchless Constitution. Yet it was not until he went into the churches that Tocqueville said he came to understand the genius and the power of this country.

Religious Liberty

The 1st Amendment sets out *two* guarantees of religious freedom. It prohibits (1) "an establishment of religion" (in the **Establishment Clause**), and (2) any arbitrary interference by government with "the free exercise thereof" (in the **Free Exercise Clause**). And, recall, both protections are extended against the States by the Due Process Clause in the 14th Amendment.[4]

These constitutional guarantees were born out of decades of colonial opposition to established churches—to official government-sponsored churches in the colonies. The Virginia Statute for Religious Freedom, adopted in 1786, was the immediate basis for the 1st Amendment. Drafted by Thomas Jefferson, that law provided for absolute religious freedom in Virginia. It declared that that State could not require that any person profess any set of religious beliefs nor support any religious institution.

Separation of Church and State

The Establishment Clause sets up, in Thomas Jefferson's words, "a wall of separation between church and state." That wall is not infinitely high, however, and it is not impenetrable. Church and government are constitutionally separated in this country, but they are neither enemies nor even strangers to one another.

---

4 Also, Article VI, Section 3 provides that "no religious Test shall ever be required as a Qualification to any Office or public Trust under the United States." In *Torcaso* v. *Watkins,* 1961, the Supreme Court held that the 14th Amendment puts the same restriction on the States.

✔️ **Checkpoint**
According to the Supreme Court, how does state-sponsored support of prayer in schools violate the 1st Amendment?

sect
n. a religious group

Government has done much to encourage churches and religion in the United States. Nearly all property of and contributions to religious <u>sects</u> are free from federal, State, and local taxation. Chaplains serve with each branch of the armed forces. Most public officials take an oath of office in the name of God. Sessions of Congress, most State legislatures, and many city councils open with prayer. The nation's anthem and its coins and currency make reference to God.

The limits imposed by the Establishment Clause remain a matter of continuing and often heated controversy. The Supreme Court did not hear its first Establishment Clause case until 1947. A few earlier cases did involve government and religion, but none of them involved a direct consideration of the "wall of separation."

The most important of those earlier cases was *Pierce* v. *Society of Sisters,* 1925. There, the Court held an Oregon compulsory school attendance law unconstitutional. That law required parents to send their children to *public* schools. It was purposely intended to eliminate private and especially **parochial** (church-related) schools.

In striking down the law, the Court did not address the Establishment Clause question. Instead, it found the law to be an unreasonable interference with the liberty of parents to direct the upbringing of their children—and so in conflict with the Due Process Clause of the 14th Amendment.

Religion and Education

The Court's first direct ruling on the Establishment Clause came in *Everson* v. *Board of Education,* a 1947 case often called the New Jersey School Bus Case. The Court upheld a State law that provided for the public, tax-supported busing of students attending any school in the State, including parochial ones.

Critics had attacked the law as a support of religion. They maintained that it relieved parochial schools of the need to pay for busing and so freed their money for other, including religious, purposes. The Court disagreed; it found the law to be a safety measure intended to benefit children, no matter what schools they might attend. Since that

decision, the largest number of the Court's Establishment Clause cases have involved, in one way or another, religion and education.

Released Time "Released time" programs allow public schools to release students during school hours to attend religious classes. In *McCollum* v. *Board of Education,* 1948, the Court struck down the released time program then in place in Champaign, Illinois, because the program used public facilities for religious purposes.

Yet in *Zorach* v. *Clauson,* 1952, the Court upheld New York City's released time program. It did so because that program required religious classes to be held in private places off school grounds.

Prayers and the Bible The Court has now decided seven major cases involving prayer and the reading of the Bible in public schools. In *Engel* v. *Vitale,* 1962, the Court outlawed the use, even on a voluntary basis, of a prayer written by the New York State Board of Regents. The prayer read: "Almighty God, we acknowledge our dependence upon Thee, and we beg Thy blessings upon us, our parents, our teachers, and our country."

In striking down the prayer, the Supreme Court held that:

❝

PRIMARY SOURCE

[T]he constitutional prohibition against laws respecting an establishment of religion must at least mean that, in this country, it is no part of the business of government to compose official prayers for any group of the American people to recite as part of a religious program carried on by government.

—Justice Hugo L. Black

The High Court extended that holding in two 1963 cases. In *Abington School District* v. *Schempp,* it struck down a Pennsylvania law requiring that each school day begin with readings from the Bible and a recitation of the Lord's Prayer. In *Murray* v. *Curlett,* the Court erased a similar rule in Baltimore. In both cases, the Court found violations of

Ruling on Religion The Court has held that public schools cannot sponsor religious exercises. It has not ruled, however, that individuals cannot pray when and as they choose in schools or in any other place. Nor has it held that students cannot study the Bible in a literary or historical context in school. The Court's rulings have nevertheless been widely criticized. Many critics have proposed that the Constitution be amended to allow voluntary group prayer in public schools. Despite the Court's decisions, both organized prayer and Bible readings are found in many public school classrooms today.

Constitutional Principles How does the separation of church and state reflect the principle of limited government?

▲ Public schools cannot sponsor prayer at school-related events.

"the command of the 1st Amendment that the government maintain strict neutrality, neither aiding nor opposing religion."

Since then, the Supreme Court has found the following to be unconstitutional:

• a Kentucky law that ordered the posting of the Ten Commandments in all public school classrooms, *Stone* v. *Graham,* 1980;

• Alabama's "moment of silence" law, *Wallace* v. *Jaffree,* 1985, which provided for a one-minute period for "meditation or voluntary prayer" at the start of each school day;

• the offering of prayer as part of a public school graduation ceremony, in a Rhode Island case, *Lee* v. *Weisman,* 1992;

• a Texas school district's policy that permitted student-led prayer at high school football games, *Santa Fe Independent School District* v. *Doe,* 2000.

Student Religious Groups The Equal Access Act of 1984 declares that any public high school that receives federal funds (nearly all do) must allow student religious groups to meet in the school on the same terms that it sets for other student organizations. The Supreme Court found that the law does not violate the Establishment Clause in a Nebraska case, *Westside Community Schools* v. *Mergens,* 1990. There, several students had tried to form a Christian club at the high school. The students had to fight the school board in the federal courts in order to win their point.

The High Court has since gone much further than it did in *Mergens*—in a case from New York, *Good News Club* v. *Milford Central School,* 2001. There, a school board had refused to allow a group of grade-school students to meet after school to sing, pray, memorize scriptures, and hear Bible lessons. The school board based its action on the Establishment Clause. The Court, however, held that the board had violated Good News Club members' 1st and 14th amendment rights to free speech.

Evolution In *Epperson* v. *Arkansas*, 1968, the Court struck down a State law forbidding the teaching of the scientific theory of evolution. It held that the Constitution

> **PRIMARY SOURCE**
> forbids alike the preference of a religious doctrine or the prohibition of theory which is deemed antagonistic to a particular dogma. . . . 'The State has no legitimate interest in protecting any or all religions from views distasteful to them.'
>
> —Justice Abe Fortas

The Court found a similar law to be unconstitutional in 1987. In *Edwards* v. *Aguillard*, it voided a 1981 Louisiana law that provided that whenever teachers taught the theory of evolution, they also had to offer instruction in "creation science."

Aid to Parochial Schools Most recent Establishment Clause cases have centered on this highly controversial question: What forms of State aid to parochial schools are constitutional? Several States give help to private schools, including schools run by church organizations, for transportation, textbooks, standardized testing, and much else.

Those who support this aid argue that parochial schools enroll many students who would otherwise have to be educated at public expense. They also point out that parents have a legal right to send their children to those schools—as, recall, the Court held in *Pierce* v. *Society of Sisters*, 1925.

To give that right real meaning, they say, the State should give some aid to parochial schools in order to relieve parents of some of the double burden they carry because they must pay taxes to support the public schools their children do not attend. Advocates also insist that schools run by religious organizations pose no real church-state problems because they devote most of their time to <u>secular</u> subjects rather than to <u>sectarian</u> ones.

Several States give aid to parochial schools for such things as student transportation.

secular
adj. nonreligious

sectarian
adj. religious

Opponents of aid to parochial schools argue that parents who send their children to parochial schools should accept the financial consequences of that choice. Many of these critics also insist that it is impossible to draw clear lines between secular and sectarian courses in parochial schools. They say that religious beliefs are bound to have an effect on the teaching of nonreligious subjects.

The *Lemon* Test The Court applies a three-pronged standard, the *Lemon* test, to decide whether a State law amounts to an "establishment" of religion. That standard states: (1) a law must have a secular, not religious, purpose; (2) it must neither advance nor inhibit religion; and (3) it must not foster an "excessive entanglement" of government and religion.

The test stems from *Lemon* v. *Kurtzman*, 1971. There, the Supreme Court held that the Establishment Clause is designed to prevent three main evils: "sponsorship, financial support, and active involvement of the sovereign in religious activity." It struck down a Pennsylvania law that provided for reimbursements (money payments) to private schools to cover their costs for teachers' salaries, textbooks, and other teaching materials in nonreligious courses.

The Court held that the State's program was of direct benefit to parochial schools, and so to the churches sponsoring them. It also found that the Pennsylvania program required such close State supervision that it produced an excessive entanglement of government with religion.

More often than not, the Court has ruled unconstitutional those laws that provide some form of public aid to church-related schools. Thus, it ruled in an Ohio case that public funds can not be used to pay for such things as field trips for parochial school students, *Wolman* v. *Walter*, 1977. Nor can tax monies be used to pay any part of the salaries of parochial school teachers, even those who teach only secular courses, *Grand Rapids School District* v. *Ball*, 1985. In this Michigan case, the Supreme Court noted that while the contents of, say, a textbook used in a course might be checked easily, the way a teacher handles that course cannot. And the Court invalidated a New York law that created a small school

GOVERNMENT ONLINE
Audio Tour
Listen to an audio tour of the Lemon test at
PearsonSuccessNet.com

The *Lemon* Test

The courts determine whether State aid to parochial schools is constitutional by applying the *Lemon* test. **How does the *Lemon* test support the Court's rulings in Wolman *v.* Walter and Mueller *v.* Allen?**

1. Secular purpose

2. Neutral toward religion

3. No "excessive" entanglement

Constitutional

district to benefit handicapped school children in a tight-knit community of Hasidic Jews, *Board of Education of Kiryas Joel* v. *Grumet,* 1994.

Some State laws have passed the *Lemon* test, however. The Court has held that New York can pay church-related schools what it costs them to administer the State's standardized tests, *Committee for Public Education and Religious Liberty* v. *Regan,* 1980. In a 1993 case from Arizona, *Zobrest* v. *Catalina Foothills School District,* it said that the use of public money to provide an interpreter for a deaf student in a Catholic high school does not violate the Establishment Clause. The Constitution, said the Court, does not place an *absolute* barrier to the placing of a public employee in a religious school.

In 1973, the Court struck down a New York law that reimbursed parents for the tuition they paid to religious schools, *Committee for Public Education* and *Religious Liberty* v. *Nyquist.* But in *Mueller* v. *Allen,* 1983, it upheld a Minnesota tax law that really accomplishes the same end.

The Minnesota law gives parents a State income tax deduction for the costs of tuition, textbooks, and transportation. Most public school parents pay little or nothing for those items, so the law is of particular benefit to parents with children in private, mostly parochial, schools. The Court found that the law meets the *Lemon* test, and it relied on this point: The tax deduction is available to all parents with children in school.

The High Court went much further in *Zelman* v. *Simmons-Harris* in 2002. There, it upheld Ohio's experimental "school choice" plan. Under that plan, parents in Cleveland can receive vouchers (grants for tuition payments) from the State and use them to send their children to private schools. Nearly all families who take the vouchers send their children to parochial schools. The Court found, 5–4, that the Ohio program is not intended to promote religion but, rather, to help children from low-income families.

Other Establishment Cases

Most church-state controversies have involved public education. Some Establishment Clause cases have arisen in other policy areas, however.

Seasonal Displays Many public organizations sponsor celebrations of the holiday season with street decorations, programs in public schools, and the like. Can these publicly sponsored observances properly include expressions of religious belief?

In *Lynch* v. *Donnelly,* 1984, the Court held that the city of Pawtucket, Rhode Island, could include the Christian nativity scene in its holiday display, which also featured non-religious objects such as Santa's sleigh and reindeer. That ruling, however, left open this question: What about a public display made up *only* of a religious symbol?

The Court faced that question in 1989. In *County of Allegheny* v. *ACLU,* it held that the

✔ **Checkpoint**
Why did the Supreme Court rule in favor of a law that gave an income tax deduction for parochial tuition?

Establishment Clause Cases
How Did the Court Rule?

Seasonal Displays

A Christmas tree sparkles in front of the California State Capitol. The Court has ruled that "government may celebrate Christmas in some manner and form, but not in a way that endorses Christian doctrine."

Chaplains

A chaplain offers the opening prayer in both houses of Congress and most State legislatures (shown here). The Court has ruled that this practice, unlike organized prayers in public schools, is constitutionally permissible.

✓ **Checkpoint**

How do each of the situations described here and in the photos above exemplify the Establishment Clause?

county's seasonal display "endorsed Christian doctrine," and so violated the 1st and 14th amendments. The county courthouse had a large display celebrating the birth of Jesus and a banner proclaiming "Glory to God in the Highest."

At the same time, the Court upheld another holiday display in *Pittsburgh* v. *ACLU*. The city's display consisted of a Christmas tree, an 18-foot menorah, and a sign declaring the city's dedication to freedom.

Chaplains

Daily sessions of both houses of Congress and most of the State legislatures begin with prayer. In Congress, and in many States, chaplains paid with public funds offer the opening prayer.

The Supreme Court has ruled that this practice, unlike prayers in the public schools, is constitutionally permissible. The ruling was made in a case involving Nebraska's one-house legislature, *Marsh* v. *Chambers,* 1983.

The Court rested its distinction between school prayers and legislative prayers on two points. First, prayers have been offered in the nation's legislative bodies "from colonial times through the founding of the Republic and ever since." Second, legislators, unlike

schoolchildren, are not "susceptible to 'religious indoctrination,' or peer pressure."

The Ten Commandments

Public displays of the Ten Commandments have ignited controversy in several places in recent years. The High Court decided its first case on the matter, *Stone* v. *Graham*, in 1980. It ruled on two other similar cases in 2005.

In *Van Orden* v. *Perry*, the Court held that the Ten Commandments monument located on the grounds of the Texas State Capitol in Austin does not violate the 1st and 14th amendments. The Court found that the monument (1) was erected in 1961 as part of a private group's campaign against juvenile delinquency, (2) is set among 37 other historical and cultural markers, and (3) had gone unchallenged for some 40 years. In short, the Court found the monument's overall message to be secular rather than religious and therefore acceptable.

In *McCreary County* v. *ACLU of Kentucky*, a differently divided 5–4 majority ruled that the display of the Ten Commandments in Kentucky county courthouses was unacceptable. They were, said the Court, an impermissible <u>endorsement</u> of religion by government.

endorsement
n. approval or backing of

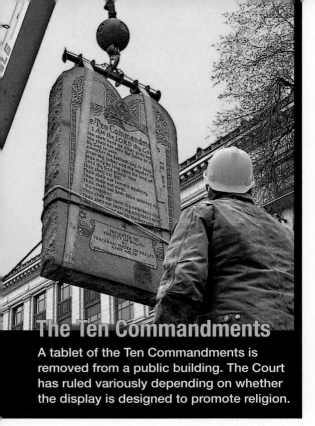

The Ten Commandments

A tablet of the Ten Commandments is removed from a public building. The Court has ruled variously depending on whether the display is designed to promote religion.

Framed copies of the Commandments were first posted in county courthouses in 1999. Nonreligious documents, including the Bill of Rights, were added to the displays some years later, but only after the original displays' content had been challenged. The Supreme Court found that the original displays had a clear religious purpose. The later additions were merely "a sham," an attempt to mask that unconstitutional religious purpose.

The Free Exercise Clause

The second part of the constitutional guarantee of religious freedom is set out in the 1st Amendment's Free Exercise Clause, which guarantees to each person the right to believe whatever he or she chooses to believe in matters of religion. No law and no other action by any government in this country can violate that absolute constitutional right. It is protected by both the 1st and the 14th amendments.

No person has an absolute right to act as he or she chooses, however. The Free Exercise Clause does *not* give anyone the right to violate criminal laws, offend public morals, or threaten community safety.

The Supreme Court laid down the basic shape of the Free Exercise Clause in the first case it heard on the issue, *Reynolds* v. *United States,* 1879. Reynolds, a Mormon, had two wives. That practice, polygamy, was allowed by his church but prohibited by federal law in any territory of the United States.

Reynolds was convicted under the law. On appeal, he argued that the law violated his right to the free exercise of his religious beliefs. The Supreme Court disagreed. It held that the 1st Amendment does not forbid Congress the power to punish those actions that are "violations of social duties or subversive of good order."

Limits on Free Exercise Over the years, the Court has approved many regulations of human conduct in the face of free exercise challenges. For example, it has upheld laws that require the vaccination of schoolchildren, *Jacobson* v. *Massachusetts,* 1905; laws that forbid the use of poisonous snakes in religious rites, *Bunn* v. *North Carolina,* 1949; and laws that require certain businesses to be closed on Sundays ("blue laws"), *McGowan* v. *Maryland,* 1961.

A State can require religious groups to have a permit to hold a parade on public streets, *Cox* v. *New Hampshire,* 1941; and organizations that enlist children to sell religious literature must obey child labor laws, *Prince* v. *Massachusetts,* 1944. The Federal Government can draft those who have religious objections to military service, *Welsh* v. *United States,* 1970.

The Court has also held that the Air Force can deny an Orthodox Jew the right to wear his yarmulke (skull cap) while on active duty, *Goldman* v. *Weinberger,* 1986. The U.S. Forest Service can allow private companies to build roads and cut timber in national forests that Native Americans have traditionally used for religious purposes, *Lyng* v. *Northwest Indian Cemetery Protective Association,* 1988.

Free Exercise Upheld Over time, however, the Court has found many actions by governments to be incompatible with the free exercise guarantee. The Court did so for the first time in one of the landmark Due Process cases cited earlier in this chapter,

✔ **Checkpoint**
What acts are not protected by the Free Exercise Clause?

✔ **Checkpoint**

How did the decision in *Barnette* differ from the decision in *Gobitis*?

Cantwell v. *Connecticut,* 1940. There, the Court struck down a law requiring a person to obtain a license before soliciting money for a religious cause. The Court reaffirmed that holding in an Ohio case, *Watchtower Bible and Tract Society* v. *Village of Stratton,* 2002.

The Supreme Court has decided a number of other cases in a similar way. Thus, Amish children cannot be forced to attend school beyond the 8th grade, because that sect's centuries-old "self-sufficient agrarian lifestyle is essential to their religious faith and is threatened by the exposure of their children to modern educational influences," *Wisconsin* v. *Yoder,* 1972. On the other hand, the Amish, who provide support for their own elderly or disabled people, must pay Social Security taxes, as all other employers do, *United States* v. *Lee,* 1982.

The Court has often held that "only those beliefs rooted in religion are protected by the Free Exercise Clause," *Sherbert* v. *Verner,* ~~1963~~. To what beliefs are "rooted in religion"? Clearly, religions that seem strange to most Americans are as entitled to constitutional protection as are the more traditional ones. For example, in *Lukumi Babalu Aye* v. *City of Hialeah,* 1993, the High Court struck down a Florida city's ordinance that outlawed animal sacrifices as part of any church services.

The Jehovah's Witnesses have carried several important religious freedom cases to the High Court. Perhaps the stormiest controversy resulting from these cases arose out of the Witnesses' refusal to salute the flag because they see such conduct as a violation of the Bible's commandment against idolatry. In *Minersville School District* v. *Gobitis,* 1940, the Court upheld a Pennsylvania school board regulation requiring students to salute the flag each morning. Walter Gobitis instructed his children not to do so, and the school expelled them. He went to court, basing his case on the constitutional guarantee.

Gobitis finally lost in the Supreme Court, which declared that the board's rule was not an infringement of religious liberty. Rather, it found the rule a lawful attempt to promote patriotism and national unity.

Three years later, in the midst of World War II, the Court reversed that decision. In *West Virginia Board of Education* v. *Barnette,* 1943, it held a compulsory flag-salute law unconstitutional. Justice Robert H. Jackson's words below are from the Court's powerful opinion in that case.

" PRIMARY SOURCE

To believe that patriotism will not flourish if patriotic ceremonies are voluntary and spontaneous, instead of a compulsory [forcibly required] routine, is to make an unflattering estimate of the appeal of our institutions to free minds.

—Justice Robert H. Jackson

SECTION **2** ASSESSMENT

Essential Questions Journal To continue to build a response to the chapter Essential Question, go to your **Essential Questions Journal.**

1. **Guiding Question** Use your completed graphic organizer to answer this question: How does the 1st Amendment protect the freedom of religion?

Key Terms and Comprehension

2. **(a)** What is the **Establishment Clause? (b)** How does it provide for a separation of church and state?

3. **(a)** What does the *Lemon* test evaluate? **(b)** How did the test originate?

4. What does the 1st Amendment's **Free Exercise Clause** guarantee?

Critical Thinking

5. **Draw Inferences** Why do you think the doctrine of separation between church and state is a continuing issue?

6. **Identify Central Issues** Some critics feel that Supreme Court decisions such as *Engel* v. *Vitale* and *Murray* v. *Curlett* limit people's free exercise of religion. Do you agree or disagree?

Quick Write

Persuasive Essay: Gather Evidence Based on the topic you chose in Section 1, gather evidence to support your position. In addition, gather information on the other side of the issue. Make a Pro and Con chart to list arguments on both sides.

SECTION 3

Freedom of Speech and Press

Guiding Question

What are the limits on the guarantees of free speech and free press? Use a table like the one below to take notes on how freedom of expression is limited in the various types of speech and media.

Type of Expression	Limitation
Seditious speech	

Political Dictionary

- libel
- slander
- sedition
- seditious speech
- prior restraint
- injunction
- shield law
- symbolic speech
- picketing

Objectives

1. Explain the importance of the two basic purposes served by the guarantees of free expression.
2. Summarize how the Supreme Court has limited seditious speech and obscenity.
3. Examine the issues of prior restraint and press confidentiality, and describe the limits the Court has placed on the media.
4. Define symbolic and commercial speech; describe the limits on their exercise.

Image Above: Network television news anchor Katie Couric

Think about this children's verse: "Sticks and stones may break my bones, but names will never hurt me." This rhyme says, in effect, that acts and words are separate things, and that acts can harm but words cannot.

Is that really true? Certainly not. You know that words can and do have consequences, sometimes powerful consequences. Words, spoken or written, can make you happy, sad, bored, informed, or entertained. They can also expose you to danger, deny you a job, or lead to other serious events.

Free Expression

The guarantees of free speech and press in the 1st and 14th amendments serve two fundamentally important purposes: (1) to guarantee to *each* person a right of free expression, in the spoken and the written word, and by all other means of communication; and (2) to guarantee to *all* persons a wide-ranging discussion of public affairs. That is, the 1st and 14th amendments give people the right to have their say *and* the right to hear what others have to say.

The American system of government depends on the ability of the people to make sound, reasoned judgments on matters of public concern. The people can best make such judgments when they know all the facts and can hear all the available interpretations of those facts.

Keep two other points in mind: First, the guarantees of free speech and press are intended to protect the expression of unpopular views. The opinions of the majority need little or no constitutional protection. These guarantees ensure, as Justice Holmes put it, "freedom for the thought that we hate," (dissenting opinion, *Schwimmer* v. *United States,* 1929). Second, some forms of expression are not protected by the Constitution. No person has an unbridled right of free speech or free press. Reasonable restrictions can be placed on those rights. Think about Justice Holmes's comment about restricting the right to falsely shout "Fire!" in a crowded theater. Or consider this restriction: No person has the right to libel or slander another. **Libel** is the false and malicious use of printed words; **slander** is the false and malicious use of spoken words.[5]

---

5 Both libel and slander involve the use of words maliciously—with vicious purpose; to injure a person's character or reputation; or to expose that person to public contempt, ridicule, or hatred.

This World War II poster warned of the dangers of careless talk and espionage. *What was the Espionage Act?* ▶

If you tell where he's going... He may never get there!

run afoul of
adv. to come into conflict with, become entangled with

insubordination
n. rebellion or disobedience

scurrilous
adj. insulting or scandalous

Truth is generally an adequate defense against a claim of libel or slander. The law does not shield public officials nearly as completely as it protects private persons, however. In *New York Times* v. *Sullivan,* 1964, the Supreme Court held that public officials cannot recover damages for a published criticism, even if it is exaggerated or false, "unless that statement was made with actual malice—that is, knowledge that it was false or with a reckless disregard of whether it was false or not."

Several later decisions have extended that ruling to cover "public figures" and even private persons who simply happen to become involved in some newsworthy event.

Similarly, the law prohibits the use of obscene words, the printing and distributing of obscene materials, and false advertising. It also condemns the use of words to prompt others to commit a crime—for example, to riot or to attempt to overthrow the government by force.

Seditious Speech

Sedition is the crime of attempting to overthrow the government by force or to disrupt its lawful activities by violent acts.[6] **Seditious speech** is the advocating, or

urging, of such conduct. It is not protected by the 1st Amendment.

The Alien and Sedition Acts Congress first acted to curb opposition to government in the Alien and Sedition Acts of 1798. Those acts gave the President the power to deport undesirable aliens and made "any false, scandalous, and malicious" criticism of the government a crime. The laws were meant to stifle the opponents of President John Adams.

The Alien and Sedition Acts were undoubtedly unconstitutional, but that point was never tested in the courts. Some 25 persons were arrested for violating them; of those, 10 were convicted. The Alien and Sedition Acts expired before Thomas Jefferson became President in 1801, and he soon pardoned those who had run afoul of them.

Sedition Act of 1917 Congress passed another sedition law during World War I, as part of the Espionage Act of 1917. That law made it a crime to encourage disloyalty, interfere with the draft, obstruct recruiting, incite insubordination in the armed forces, or hinder the sale of government bonds. The act also made it a crime to "willfully utter, print, write, or publish any disloyal, profane, scurrilous, or abusive language about the form of government of the United States."

More than 1,000 persons were convicted for violating the Espionage Act. The constitutionality of the law was upheld several times, most importantly in *Schenck* v. *United States,* 1919. Charles Schenck, an officer of the Socialist Party, had been found guilty of obstructing the war effort. He had sent fiery leaflets to some 15,000 draftees, urging them to resist the call to military service.

The Supreme Court upheld Schenck's conviction. The case is particularly noteworthy because the Court's opinion, written by Justice Oliver Wendell Holmes, established the "clear and present danger" rule:

---

6 Espionage, sabotage, and treason are often confused with sedition. Espionage is spying for a foreign power. Sabotage involves an act of destruction intended to hinder a nation's war or defense effort. Treason can be committed only in times of war and can consist only of levying war against the United States or giving aid and comfort to its enemies.

The question in every case is whether the words used are used in such circumstances and are of such nature as to create a clear and present danger that they will bring about the substantive evils that Congress has a right to prevent.

—Justice Oliver Wendell Holmes

In short, the rule says that words can be outlawed. Those who utter them can be punished if there is an immediate danger that criminal acts will follow.

The Smith Act of 1940 Congress passed the Smith Act in 1940, just over a year before the United States entered World War II. That law is still on the books. It makes it a crime for anyone to advocate the violent overthrow of the government of the United States, to distribute any material that teaches or advises violent overthrow, or to knowingly belong to any group with such an aim.

The Court upheld the Smith Act in *Dennis* v. *United States,* 1951. There, 11 Communist Party leaders had been convicted of advocating the overthrow of the Federal Government. On appeal, the Communist leaders argued that the Smith Act violated the 1st Amendment. They also claimed that no actions of theirs constituted a clear and present danger to this country. The Court disagreed.

Later, however, the Supreme Court modified the *Dennis* ruling in several cases. In *Yates* v. *United States,* 1957, for example, the Court overturned the Smith Act convictions of several Communist Party leaders. It held that merely to urge someone to *believe* something, in contrast to urging that person to *do* something, cannot be made illegal. In *Yates* and other Smith Act cases, the Court upheld the constitutionality of the law, but interpreted its provisions so that enforcing the Smith Act became practically impossible.

Obscenity

Both federal and State laws have made the <u>dissemination</u> of obscene material illegal, and the courts have generally agreed that obscenity is not protected by the 1st and 14th amendments. But what, exactly, is *obscenity?* Lawmakers and judges have wrestled with that question for decades. The Supreme Court's Justice Potter Stewart once famously said that, although he could not define the term, "I know it when I see it," *Jacobellis* v. *Ohio,* 1964.

A large part of the problem in defining *obscenity* lies in the fact that moral standards vary from time to time, place to place, and person to person. To illustrate that point: Much of what appears on television today would, in fact, have been banned as obscenity only a few decades ago.

In 1872, Congress passed the first in a series of laws that prevent the mailing of obscene matter. The current postal law, upheld in *Roth* v. *United States,* 1957, excludes "obscene, lewd, lascivious, or filthy" material from the mail. The Court found the law a proper exercise of the postal power (Article I, Section 8, Clause 7) and so not prohibited by the 1st Amendment. *Roth* marked the Court's first attempt to define obscenity.

Today, the leading case is *Miller* v. *California,* 1973. There the Court laid down a three-part test to define obscenity. A book, film, recording, or other piece of material is legally obscene if (1) "the average person applying contemporary [local] community standards" finds that the work, taken as a whole, "appeals to the prurient interest"—that is, tends to excite lust; (2) "the work depicts or describes, in a patently offensive way," a form of sexual conduct specifically dealt with in an anti-obscenity law; and (3) "the work, taken as a whole, lacks serious literary, artistic, political, or scientific value."

In recent years, the Court has heard only a handful of cases involving questions of obscenity. As you will see shortly, those cases have all involved the Internet.

Prior Restraint

The Constitution allows government to punish some <u>utterances</u> after they are made—for example, in cases involving libel or slander, or obscenity. With almost no exceptions, however, government cannot curb ideas *before* they are expressed. That is, except in

✔ **Checkpoint**
What are the provisions of the Smith Act?

<u>utterance</u>
n. remark, statement
<u>dissemination</u>
n. distribution

▶ **Case:** *Near* v. *Minnesota,* 1931

▶ **Constitutional Principle:** Limited Government

▶ **Decision:** Local public officials relied on a State law to prevent a newspaper from printing scandalous information about them. The Supreme Court struck down the State law. The Court ruled that freedom of the press does not allow such prior restraint on publications.

Articles in the *Saturday Press* in the late 1920s prompted a landmark decision in *Near* v. *Minnesota, 1931.* **What is the significance of the ruling in this case?**

the most extreme situations, government cannot place any **prior restraint** on written or spoken expression.

The concept of prior restraint is basic to the meaning of the 1st and 14th amendment protections of freedom of expression. *Near* v. *Minnesota,* 1931, is a leading case in point. There, the Supreme Court struck down a State law that allowed local public officials to prevent the publication of any "malicious, scandalous, and defamatory" periodical. Acting under that law, a local court had issued an order forbidding the publication of the *Saturday Press.* That Minneapolis newspaper had published a series of articles charging public corruption and attacking local officials as "grafters" and "Jewish gangsters."

The Court held that the guarantee of a free press does not allow a prior restraint on publication—*except* in such extreme situations as wartime, or when a publication is obscene or incites its readers to acts of violence. Even "miscreant purveyors of scandal" and anti-Semitism are entitled to constitutional protection, said the Court.

The Constitution does not forbid any and all forms of prior censorship, but "any prior restraint on expression comes to this Court with a 'heavy presumption' against its constitutional validity," *Nebraska Press Association* v. *Stuart,* 1976.[7] The Court has used that general rule several times—for example, in the famous Pentagon Papers Case, *New York Times* v. *United States,* 1971.

In that case, several newspapers had obtained copies of a set of classified documents, widely known as the Pentagon Papers. Officially titled *History of U.S. Decision-Making Process on Viet Nam Policy,* those documents had been stolen from the Defense Department and then leaked to the press.

The Nixon administration sought an **injunction** (a court order) to bar their publication, arguing that national security was at stake and the documents (government property) had been stolen. The newspaper argued the "public right to know," and it insisted that the 1st Amendment protected its right to publish the papers. The Court found that the government had not shown that printing the documents would endanger the nation's security. The government, in effect, had not overcome the "heavy presumption" against prior censorship.

The few prior restraints the Supreme Court has approved include:

• regulations prohibiting the distribution of political literature on military bases without the approval of military authorities, *Greer* v. *Spock,* 1976;

• a Central Intelligence Agency (CIA) rule that agents must never publish anything about the agency without the CIA's express permission, *Snepp* v. *United States,* 1980;

• a federal prison rule that allows officials to prevent an inmate from receiving publications considered "detrimental to the security, good order, or discipline" of the prison, *Thornburgh* v. *Abbott,* 1989.

---

7 There, a State judge had ordered the media not to report certain details of a murder trial. The Court found the judge's gag order to be unconstitutional.

The Court has also said that public school officials have a broad power to censor school newspapers, plays, and other "school-sponsored expressive activities." It did so in a case from Missouri, *Hazelwood School District* v. *Kuhlmeier*, 1988. There, the principal of a St. Louis high school had prohibited the publication of a series of articles written by student reporters for their school's paper. Those articles explored the impact that various events, among them pregnancy and parents' divorces, can have on teenagers. Three students sued, but they finally lost their case when the High Court held that school administrators can exercise "editorial control over the style and content of student speech in school-sponsored expressive activities so long as their actions are reasonably related to legitimate <u>pedagogical</u> concerns."

The Media

The 1st Amendment stands as a monument to the central importance of the media in a free society. That raises this question: To what extent can the media—whether print, radio, television, or the Internet—be regulated by government?

Confidentiality Can news reporters be forced to testify before a grand jury in court or before a legislative committee? Can those government bodies require journalists to name their sources and reveal other confidential information? Many reporters and news organizations insist that they must have the right to refuse to testify in order to protect their sources. They argue that without this right they cannot assure confidentiality, and therefore many sources will not reveal important, sensitive information.

Both State and federal courts have generally rejected the news media argument. In recent years, several reporters have refused to obey court orders directing them to give information, and they have gone to jail, thus testifying to the importance of these issues.

In the leading case, *Branzburg* v. *Hayes*, 1972, the Supreme Court held that reporters, "like other citizens, [must] respond to relevant questions put to them in the course of a valid grand jury investigation or criminal

trial." If the media are to receive any special exemptions, said the Court, they must come from Congress and the State legislatures.

To date, Congress has not acted on the Court's suggestion, but some 30 States have passed so-called **shield laws.** These laws give reporters some protection against having to disclose their sources or reveal other confidential information in legal proceedings in those States.

Motion Pictures The Supreme Court took its first look at motion pictures early in the history of the movie industry. In 1915, in *Mutual Film Corporation* v. *Ohio*, the Court upheld a State law that barred the showing of any film that was not of a "moral, educational, or amusing and harmless character." The Court declared that "the exhibition of moving pictures is a business, pure and simple," and "not . . . part of the press of the country." With that decision, nearly every State and thousands of communities set up movie review (really movie censorship) programs.

The Court reversed itself in 1952, however. In *Burstyn* v. *Wilson*, a New York censorship case, it found that "liberty of expression by means of motion pictures is guaranteed by the 1st and 14th amendments." Still, the Court has never held that the Constitution grants the film industry the same level of protection against prior restraint that it gives to newspapers. In fact, it has upheld a requirement that films be submitted to official censors so long as those censors are required to act reasonably and their decisions are subject to speedy court review, *Freedman* v. *Maryland*, 1965.

Very few of the once-common movie review boards still exist. Most people now rely on the film industry's own rating system and on the comments of movie critics to guide their viewing choices.

Radio and Television Both radio and television broadcasting are subject to extensive federal regulation. Most of this regulation is based on the often-amended Federal Communications Act of 1934, which is administered by the Federal Communications Commission (FCC). As the Supreme Court noted in

✔ **Checkpoint**
How has the Supreme Court ruled on student speech?

pedagogical
adj. educational, academic, instructional

Freedoms of Speech and Press

Rules of the Road

The 1st Amendment stands as a monument to the central importance of free speech and the media in a free society. Various forms of speech are regulated by government, however. ***Why are radio stations and network television subjected to wide-ranging federal regulation?***

The Supreme Court has ruled that school administrators can exercise "editorial control over the style and content of student speech in school-sponsored expressive activities. . . ."

The Federal Communications Act, administered by the FCC, bans the use of indecent language on the radio and on network television, and may deny violators a renewal of their operating licenses.

The Children's Internet Protection Act (CIPA) requires public libraries that receive federal money to use filters to block their computers' access to pornographic sites on the Internet.

FCC v. *Pacifica Foundation,* 1978: "Of all forms of communication, broadcasting has the most limited 1st Amendment protection."

The Court has several times upheld this wide-ranging federal regulation as a proper exercise of the commerce power. Unlike newspapers and other print media, radio and television use the public's property—the public airwaves—to distribute their materials. They have no right to use the limited broadcast frequencies without the public's permission in the form of a proper license, said the Court in *National Broadcasting Co.* v. *United States,* 1943.

The Court has regularly rejected the argument that the 1st Amendment prohibits such regulations. Instead, it has said that regulation of this industry implements the constitutional guarantee. In *Red Lion Broadcasting Co.* v. *FCC,* 1969, the Court held that there is no "unabridgeable 1st Amendment right to broadcast comparable to the right of every

individual to speak, write, or publish." However, "this is not to say that the 1st Amendment is irrelevant to public broadcasting. . . . It is the right of the viewers and the listeners, not the right of the broadcasters . . ."

The Federal Communications Act forbids prior censorship—and so the FCC cannot censor the content of programs before they are broadcast. However, the law does permit the FCC to ban the use of indecent language, and the Court has held that it can take violations of that ban into account when a station applies for the renewal of its operating license, *FCC* v. *Pacifica Foundation,* 1978.

In several recent decisions, the Supreme Court has given cable television somewhat broader 1st Amendment freedoms than those enjoyed by traditional network television. *United States* v. *Playboy Entertainment Group,* 2000, is fairly typical. There, the Court struck down an attempt by Congress to force many cable systems to limit sexually explicit

GOVERNMENT ONLINE

For an **interactive** exploration of the methods of regulating free speech, visit **PearsonSuccessNet.com**

INTERACTIVE

Except in the most extreme situations, government cannot place any prior restraint on the content of newspapers and other print media.

channels to confine their programs to late night hours. The Court agreed that shielding children from such programming is a worthy goal; nevertheless, it found the 1996 law to be a violation of the 1st Amendment.

The Internet The Internet has generated only a handful of Supreme Court cases— and each of them has involved attempts by Congress to regulate access to pornographic matter on the World Wide Web. Congress first attempted to protect minors from that material in the Communications Decency Act of 1996. That law made it a crime to "knowingly" transmit any "obscene or indecent" speech or image that is "patently offensive as measured by contemporary community standards" to any person under the age of 18.

The Court promptly declared that law unconstitutional in *Reno* v. *American Civil Liberties Union,* 1997. A majority of the justices found that the words "indecent" and

"patently offensive" were too vague and that the overall effect of that law was to deny to adults materials that are protected by the 1st Amendment. "Regardless of the strength of the government's interest in protecting children," said the Court, "the level of discourse reaching a mailbox cannot be limited to that which would be suitable for a sandbox."

The Supreme Court did uphold an act of Congress dealing with pornography, the Internet, and public libraries in *United States* v. *American Library Association,* 2003. There, a majority could find no constitutional fault in the Children's Internet Protection Act (CIPA) of 2002. That law provides that those public libraries that receive federal money—nearly all of them do—must use filters to block their computers' access to pornographic sites on the Internet.

Symbolic Speech

People also communicate ideas by their conduct, by the way they do a particular thing. Thus, a person can "say" something with a facial expression or a shrug of the shoulders, or by carrying a sign or wearing an armband. This expression by conduct is known as **symbolic speech.**

Clearly, not all conduct amounts to symbolic speech. If it did, murder or robbery or any other crime could be excused on grounds that the person who committed the act meant to say something by doing so.

Just as clearly, however, some conduct does express opinion. Take picketing in a labor dispute as an example. **Picketing** involves the patrolling of a business site by workers who are on strike. By their conduct, picketers attempt to inform the public of the controversy and to persuade others not to deal with the firm involved. Picketing is, then, a form of expression. If peaceful, it is protected by the 1st and 14th amendments.

The leading case on the point is *Thornhill* v. *Alabama,* 1940. There, the Court struck down a State law that made it a crime to loiter about or to picket a place of business in order to influence others not to trade or work there. Picketing that is "set in a background of violence," however, can be prevented. Even peaceful picketing can be restricted if it is

✔ **Checkpoint**
What is symbolic speech?

conducted for an illegal purpose—for example, forcing someone to do something that is itself illegal.

Other Symbolic Speech Cases The Court has been sympathetic to the symbolic speech argument, but it has not given blanket 1st Amendment protection to that means of expression. Note these cases:

United States v. *O'Brien,* 1968, involved four young men who had burned their draft cards to protest the war in Vietnam. A court convicted them of violating a federal law that makes that act a crime. O'Brien appealed, arguing that the 1st Amendment protects "all modes of communication of ideas by conduct." The Supreme Court disagreed, saying: "We cannot accept the view that an apparently limitless variety of conduct can be labeled 'speech' whenever the person engaging in the conduct intends thereby to express an idea."

The Court also held that acts of dissent by conduct can be punished if: (1) the object of the protest is within the constitutional powers of the government; (2) whatever restriction is placed on expression is no greater than necessary in the circumstances; and (3) the government's real interest in the matter is not to squelch dissent.

Using that three-part test, the Court has sometimes denied claims of symbolic speech. Thus, in *Virginia* v. *Black,* 2003, it upheld a State law that prohibits the burning of a cross

as an act of intimidation, a threat that can make a person fear for his safety. The Court also made this point: Those who burn crosses at rallies or parades as acts of political expression (acts not aimed at a particular person) cannot be prosecuted under the law.

Tinker v. *Des Moines School District,* 1969, on the other hand, is one of several cases in which the Court has come down on the side of symbolic speech. In *Tinker,* several students who had worn black armbands to school to dramatize their opposition to the war in Vietnam had been suspended by the district.

The Court found that school officials had overstepped their authority and violated the students' right to free expression. Said the Court: "It can hardly be argued that either students or teachers shed their constitutional rights to freedom of speech or expression at the schoolhouse gate."[8]

The Court recognized campaign donations as protected speech in *Buckley* v. *Valeo,* 1976. See Chapter 7 to learn more.

Flag Burning A sharply divided Court has twice held that burning the American flag as an act of political protest is expressive conduct protected by the 1st and 14th amendments. In *Texas* v. *Johnson,* 1989, a 5–4 majority ruled that State authorities had violated a protester's rights by prosecuting him under a law that forbids the "desecration of a venerated object." Johnson had set fire to an American flag during an anti-Reagan demonstration at the Republican National Convention in Dallas in 1984. Said the Court:

PRIMARY SOURCE

If there is a bedrock principle underlying the 1st Amendment, it is that the government may not prohibit the expression of an idea simply because society finds the

squelch
v. to silence or smother

The Supreme Court ruled in favor of John and Mary Beth Tinker (shown here), emphasizing that students' 1st Amendment rights could not be abridged just because students are on school property. ▼

---

8 Do not read too much into this, for the Court noted that it "has repeatedly emphasized the need for affirming the comprehensive authority of the States and of school officials, consistent with fundamental constitutional safeguards, to prescribe and control conduct in the schools." The fact that in *Tinker* the students' conduct did not cause a substantial disruption of normal school activities was an important factor in the Court's decision.

idea itself offensive. . . . We do not consecrate the flag by punishing its desecration, for in doing so we dilute the freedom that this cherished emblem represents.

—Justice William J. Brennan, Jr.

The Supreme Court's decision in *Johnson* set off a firestorm of criticism around the country and prompted Congress to pass the Flag Protection Act of 1989. It, too, was struck down by the Court, 5–4, in *United States* v. *Eichman*, 1990. The Court based its decision on the same grounds as those set out a year earlier in *Johnson*. Since *Johnson* and *Eichman*, Congress has rejected several attempts to propose a constitutional amendment to outlaw flag burning.

Commercial Speech

Commercial speech is speech for business purposes; the term refers most often to advertising. Until the mid-1970s, it was thought that the 1st and 14th amendments did not protect such speech. In *Bigelow* v. *Virginia*, 1975, however, the Court held unconstitutional a State law that prohibited the newspaper advertising of abortion services. The following year, in *Virginia State Board of Pharmacy* v. *Virginia Citizens Consumer Council*, it struck down another Virginia law forbidding the advertisement of prescription drug prices.

Not all commercial speech is protected, however. Government can and does prohibit false and misleading advertisements, and the advertising of illegal goods or services.

In fact, government can even forbid advertising that is neither false nor misleading. In 1970, Congress banned cigarette ads on radio and television. In 1986, it extended the ban to include chewing tobacco and snuff.

In most of its commercial speech cases, the Court has struck down arbitrary restrictions on advertising. In *44 Liquormart, Inc.* v. *Rhode Island*, 1996, the Court voided a State law that prohibited ads in which liquor prices were listed. In *Greater New Orleans Broadcasting Association* v. *United States*, 1999, it struck down a federal law that prohibited casino advertising on radio or television.

More recently, the Court dealt with limits on smokeless tobacco and cigar advertising. Massachusetts had barred outdoor ads for these <u>commodities</u> within 1,000 feet of any school or playground. The Court held that the limit was a violation of the 1st and 14th amendments' guarantee of free speech, *P. Lorillard Co.* v. *Reilly*, 2001.

✔ **Checkpoint**
Why, according to Justice Brennan, is flag burning protected by the 1st and 14th amendments?

<u>commodity</u>
n. article that can be bought or sold

Essential Questions Journal To continue to build a response to the chapter Essential Question, go to your **Essential Questions Journal.**

SECTION **3** ASSESSMENT

1. **Guiding Question** Use your completed graphic organizer to answer this question: What are the limits on the guarantees of free speech and free press?

Key Terms and Comprehension

2. **(a)** What is **libel? (b)** What is **slander?** How do the two differ?

3. Why does the government restrict **seditious speech?**

4. **(a)** What are **shield laws? (b)** Why have some States passed these laws?

Critical Thinking

5. **Draw Inferences** What do you think are the advantages and disadvantages of a free press?

6. **Identify Central Issues** The Constitution makes a particular effort to protect the expression of unpopular views. **(a)** Why is this important? **(b)** Do you think even racist or sexist expressions should be protected? Why or why not?

Quick Write

Persuasive Essay: Develop a Thesis Based on the topic you chose in Section 1 and the evidence you gathered in Section 2, identify your argument in a thesis statement, which expresses the main idea of your persuasive essay. All information that follows should support or elaborate on this statement.

Participating in Public Debate

Dear Student,

Our State Department of Education has instituted new requirements for the current school year. Effective immediately, the school year will be lengthened from 180 days to 200 days, and each school day will be extended one additional hour. The DOE feels strongly that this decision is necessary in order to remain competitive in the global economy. Statistics show that schools in China and India are in session 225–250 days a year. Students in those countries are well on their way to outperforming American students.

Thank you for your cooperation,

George Carruthers, Principal

Your right to participate in public debate is central to the founding principles of our country. If you received a letter from your school like the one above, you would probably have strong feelings about it. One way to express your views is by participating in public debate. You might speak at a city council or town hall meeting, or address your local school board. Use these opportunities to voice your opinions by following these steps:

1. **Choose an issue of concern to you, and then find out whom to contact.** Your opinion counts most when you express it to those people who have some authority or influence in the matter. That could be city council members, a private lobbying group, a school board, or a media outlet.

2. **Organize your arguments.** Decide on the best way to get your ideas across. Create an outline or a list of talking points to organize your thoughts. Think of supporting details for each point, and then identify the most important points, which you will emphasize to influence your particular audience. You might want to make

these points the first few lines of your speech. Most important, rehearse what you will say.

3. **Present your ideas.** Speak in a loud, clear voice when you present your ideas. Keep your speech lively and exciting, and be precise with the words you use. If you conduct yourself with civility and respect to win the hearts and minds of other citizens, you will persuade them to take up your cause.

▶▶ What do you think?

1. Whom might you contact to express your views in the situation presented here?

2. What short-term and long-term goals might you seek through participating in public debate?

3. **You Try It** Follow the steps above to develop a strategy for airing your views about the issue presented here. Prepare a one-minute oral argument on the issue and present it to your peers.

⊘ GOVERNMENT ONLINE
Citizenship Activity Pack
For activities on participating in public debate, go to
PearsonSuccessNet.com

Freedom of Assembly and Petition

Guiding Question

How has the Supreme Court ruled on assembly and petition cases?
Use a table like the one below to take notes on important Supreme Court cases involving freedom of assembly.

Case	Issue	Ruling

Political Dictionary

- assemble
- petition
- civil disobedience
- content neutral
- right of association

Objectives

1. Explain the Constitution's guarantees of assembly and petition.
2. Summarize how government can limit the time, place, and manner of assembly.
3. Compare and contrast the freedom-of-assembly issues that arise on public versus private property.
4. Explore how the Supreme Court has interpreted freedom of association.

Image Above: The 1st Amendment protects the people's right to assemble and protest peaceably.

A noisy street demonstration by gay rights activists or neo-Nazis; a candlelight vigil by opponents of the death penalty; pro-life supporters picketing an abortion clinic; pro-choice supporters on the steps of the State capitol . . . these are all everyday examples of freedom of assembly and petition.

The Constitution's Guarantees

The 1st Amendment guarantees "the right of the people peaceably to assemble, and to petition the Government for a redress of grievances." The 14th Amendment's Due Process Clause also protects those rights of assembly and petition against actions by the States or their local governments, *DeJonge* v. *Oregon,* 1937.

The Constitution protects the right of the people to **assemble**—to gather with one another—to express their views. It protects their right to organize to influence public policy, whether in political parties, interest groups, or other organizations. It also protects the people's right to **petition**—to bring their views to the attention of public officials by such varied means as written petitions, letters, or advertisements; lobbying; and parades or marches.

Notice, however, that the 1st and 14th amendments protect the rights of *peaceable* assembly and petition. The Constitution does not give to anyone the right to incite others to violence, block a public street, close a school, or otherwise endanger life, property, or public safety.

Note this important point as well: A significant part of the history of this country can be told in terms of **civil disobedience.** That is to say that much of our history has been built out of incidents in which people have purposely violated the law—nonviolently, but nonetheless deliberately, as a means of expressing their opposition to some particular law or public policy.

Do the 1st and 14th amendment guarantees of freedom of assembly and petition include a right of civil disobedience? That thorny question cannot be answered absolutely or without qualification because of the very nature of civil disobedience: those acts are expressions of opinion on some public matter.

Still, courts have consistently held that, as a general rule, civil disobedience is not a constitutionally protected right. Those who choose to take part

✓ **Checkpoint**
How has the Supreme Court limited the time, place, and manner of assembly?

inherent
adj. natural to or basic

in such activities are often aware of that fact, and they are usually willing to accept the consequences of their conduct.

Time-Place-Manner Rules

Government can make and enforce reasonable rules covering the time, place, and manner of assemblies. Thus, in *Grayned* v. *City of Rockford,* 1972, the Court upheld a city ordinance that prohibits making a noise or any other diversion near a school if that action has a disruptive effect on school activities. It has also upheld a State law that forbids parades near a courthouse when they are intended to influence court proceedings, *Cox* v. *Louisiana,* 1965.

Rules for keeping the public peace must be more than just reasonable, however. They must also be precisely drawn and fairly administered. In *Coates* v. *Cincinnati,* 1971, the Court struck down a city ordinance that made it a crime for "three or more persons to assemble" on a sidewalk or street corner "and there conduct themselves in a manner annoying to persons passing by, or occupants of adjacent buildings." The Court found the wording of the ordinance much too vague and therefore unconstitutional.

Government's rules must be **content neutral.** That is, although government can regulate assemblies on the basis of time, place, and manner, it cannot regulate gatherings on the basis of what might be said there. Thus, in *Forsyth County* v. *Nationalist Movement,* 1992, the Court threw out a Georgia county's ordinance that levied a fee of up to $1,000 for public demonstrations.

The law was contested by a white supremacist group seeking to protest the creation of a holiday to honor Martin Luther King, Jr. The Court found the ordinance not to be content neutral, particularly because county officials had unlimited power to set the exact fee to be paid by any group.

Public Property

Over the past several years, most of the Court's freedom of assembly cases have involved organized demonstrations. Demonstrations are, of course, assemblies.

Most demonstrations take place in public places—on streets and sidewalks, in parks or public buildings, and so on. This is the case because it is the *public* the demonstrators want to reach.

Demonstrations almost always involve some degree of conflict. Most often, they are held to protest something, and so there is an <u>inherent</u> clash of ideas. Many times there is also a conflict with the normal use of streets or other public facilities. It is hardly surprising, then, that the tension can sometimes rise to a serious level.

Given all this, the Supreme Court has often upheld laws that require advance notice and permits for demonstrations in public places. In an early leading case, *Cox* v. *New Hampshire,* 1941, it unanimously approved a State law that required a license to hold a parade or procession on a public street.

Right-to-demonstrate cases raise many difficult questions. How and to what extent can government regulate demonstrators? Does the Constitution require that police officers allow an unpopular group to continue to demonstrate even when its activities have excited others to violence? When, in the name of public peace and safety, can police order demonstrators to disband?

Gregory **v.** *Chicago* A leading and illustrative case is *Gregory* v. *Chicago,* 1969. While under police protection, comedian Dick Gregory and others marched while singing, chanting, and carrying placards, from city hall to the mayor's home some five miles away. Marching in the streets around the mayor's house, they demanded the firing of the city's school superintendent and an end to de facto segregation in the city's schools.

A crowd of several hundred people, including many residents of the all-white neighborhood, quickly gathered. Soon, the bystanders began throwing insults and threats, as well as rocks, eggs, and other objects. The police tried to keep order, but after about an hour, they decided that serious violence was about to break out. At that point, they ordered the demonstrators to leave the area. When Gregory and others failed to do so, the police arrested them and charged them with disorderly conduct.

PUBLIC PROPERTY

The Constitution protects peaceful demonstrations. In some situations, however, police efforts to prevent a rally from becoming a violent event have in fact been attempts to prevent speech. The line between crowd control and thought control can be very thin, indeed.

PRIVATE PROPERTY

The 1st and 14th Amendments do not give people a right to trespass on private property. However, a State's supreme court can interpret that State's constitution to permit a reasonable exercise of the right of petition on private property. *Why has the Court ruled differently on public and private property demonstrations?*

The convictions of the demonstrators were unanimously overturned by the Court. It noted that the marchers had exercised their constitutional rights of assembly and petition. The bystanders, not the demonstrators, had caused the disorder. As long as the demonstrators acted peacefully, they could not be punished for disorderly conduct.

Recent Cases Over recent years, many of the most controversial demonstrations have been those held by anti-abortion groups. For the most part, their efforts have been aimed at discouraging women from seeking the services of abortion clinics, and those efforts have generated many lawsuits.

There have been two particularly notable cases to date. In the first one, *Madsen* v. *Women's Health Services, Inc.,* 1994, the Supreme Court upheld a Florida judge's order directing protesters not to block access to an abortion clinic. The judge's order had drawn a 36-foot buffer zone around the clinic. The

High Court found that to be a reasonable limit on the demonstrators' activities.

The other major case is *Hill* v. *Colorado,* 2000. There, the Court upheld, 5–4, a State law that limits "sidewalk counseling" at clinics where abortions are performed. That statute creates an eight-foot buffer zone around anyone who wants to enter. No one may make an "unwanted approach" to talk, hand out a leaflet, or wave a sign.

The Court found that the Colorado law does not deal with the content of abortion protestors' speech. It is aimed, instead, at *where, when,* and *how* their message is delivered.

Private Property

What about demonstrations on private property—at shopping centers, for example? The Court has said that the 1st and 14th Amendment rights of assembly and petition do not give people a right to trespass on private property, even to express political views.

Privately owned shopping centers are not "places of public assembly." Thus, no one has a constitutional right to do such things as hand out political leaflets or ask people to sign petitions in those places.

These comments are based on the leading case here, *Lloyd Corporation* v. *Tanner*, 1972. However, since that case the Court has held this: A State supreme court may interpret the provisions of that State's constitution in such a way as to require the owners of shopping centers to allow the reasonable exercise of the right of petition on their private property.

Freedom of Association

The guarantees of freedom of assembly and petition include a **right of association**—the right to join with others to promote political, economic, and social causes. That right is not set out in so many words in the Constitution. However, in *National Association for the Advancement of Colored People* v. *Alabama*, 1958, the Supreme Court said, "it is beyond debate that freedom to engage in association for the advancement of beliefs and ideas is an inseparable aspect" of the Constitution's guarantees of free expression.

The case just cited is one of the early right-to-associate cases. There, a State law required the Alabama branch of the NAACP to disclose the names of all its members in that State. When the organization refused a court's order to do so, it was found in contempt of court and fined $100,000.

The Supreme Court overturned the contempt conviction. It said that it could find no legitimate reason why the State should have the NAACP's membership list.

A person cannot be fired from a job because of political associations—for example, membership in a political party, *Brown* v. *Socialist Workers '74 Campaign Committee*, 1982. And a person cannot be required to disclose his or her political associations to be licensed to practice law, *Gibson* v. *Florida*, 1966.

There is no absolute right of association, however. In *Boy Scouts of America* v. *Dale*, 2000, the Supreme Court held that the Boy Scouts have a constitutional right to exclude gays from their organization. The Court noted that opposition to homosexuality is a part of the Boy Scout organization's "expressive association"—that is, what they stand for.

The decision overturned a ruling by the New Jersey Supreme Court. That court had applied the State's anti-discrimination law against the Scouts. It ordered a New Jersey troop to readmit James Dale, an Eagle Scout, whom the troop had dismissed when it learned he was gay. The Court ruled that a State cannot force an organization to accept members when that action would contradict what the organization professes to believe.

Essential Questions Journal — To continue to build a response to the chapter Essential Question, go to your **Essential Questions Journal.**

SECTION 4 ASSESSMENT

1. **Guiding Question** Use your completed graphic organizer to answer this question: How has the Supreme Court ruled on assembly and petition cases?

Key Terms and Comprehension

2. What do the guarantees of freedom of assembly and petition intend to protect?

3. **(a)** What is **civil disobedience? (b)** Is it constitutionally protected? Why or why not?

4. How does the **right of association** extend the right of assembly?

Critical Thinking

5. **Draw Conclusions (a)** Why are the freedom to assemble peacefully and the freedom of association important to a democratic society? **(b)** What might happen if people were denied these rights?

6. **Demonstrate Reasoned Judgment** Why do you think the government can regulate assemblies based on time, place, and manner, but not on the basis of what might be said there?

Quick Write

Persuasive Essay: Provide Elaboration In a persuasive essay, you can build a strong case for your position by stating facts, providing statistics, and including details. Conduct research to find this information on the topic you chose in Section 1. Take notes on index cards to help you organize your persuasive essay.

Quick Study Guide

GOVERNMENT ONLINE
On the Go
To review anytime, anywhere, download these online resources at **PearsonSuccessNet.com**
Political Dictionary, Audio Review

Guiding Question
Section 2 How does the 1st Amendment protect the freedom of religion?

Guiding Question
Section 3 What are the limits on the guarantees of free speech and free press?

Guiding Question
Section 1 How does the Constitution protect the rights of individuals against government?

CHAPTER 19
Essential Question
How can the judiciary balance individual rights with the common good?

Guiding Question
Section 4 How has the Supreme Court ruled on assembly and petition cases?

Political Dictionary

Bill of Rights *p. 547*
civil liberties *p. 547*
civil rights *p. 547*
alien *p. 548*
Due Process Clause *p. 549*
process of incorporation *p. 549*
Establishment Clause *p. 551*
Free Exercise Clause *p. 551*
parochial *p. 552*
libel *p. 559*
slander *p. 559*
sedition *p. 560*
seditious speech *p. 560*
prior restraint *p. 562*
injunction *p. 562*
shield law *p. 563*
symbolic speech *p. 565*
picketing *p. 565*
assemble *p. 569*
petition *p. 569*
civil disobedience *p. 569*
content neutral *p. 570*
right of association *p. 572*

Decisions Relating to the Due Process Clause

The 14th Amendment's Due Process Clause says that no State can deny to any person any right that is essential to ordered liberty.

Gitlow v. *New York*, 1925: The guarantees of free speech and press are included within the meaning of the 14th Amendment's Due Process Clause.

Fiske v. *Kansas*, 1927: Struck down a State law that denied freedom of speech.

Near v. *Minnesota*, 1931: Struck down a State law that denied freedom of the press.

DeJonge v. *Oregon*, 1937: Struck down a State law that denied freedom of assembly and petition.

Cantwell v. *Connecticut*, 1940: Struck down a State law that denied the free exercise of religion.

First Amendment Freedoms

1st Amendment: "Congress shall make no law respecting an establishment of religion, or prohibiting the free exercise thereof; or abridging the freedom of speech, or of the press; or the right of the people peaceably to assemble, and to petition the Government for a redress of grievances."

Freedom of Religion	Freedom of Speech and Press	Freedom of Assembly and Petition
• Creates a separation of church and state (Establishment Clause) • Protects people's right to believe what they choose in matters of religion (Free Exercise Clause)	• Guarantee the right to speak, write, and otherwise communicate most ideas • Ensure the people's right to hear the ideas of others	• Protect people's right to assemble peaceably to express their views • Ensure people's right to bring their views to public attention

Chapter Assessment

Comprehension and Critical Thinking

Section 1

1. **(a)** For what unalienable rights was the American Revolution fought? **(b)** How did the Framers of the Constitution guarantee those rights?

2. **(a)** What general limitation is placed on individual rights? **(b)** What example does *Schenck* v. *United States* cite to explain this limitation? **(c)** To which conflicting rights did *Sheppard* v. *Maxwell* apply?

3. **(a)** How does federalism complicate guarantees of individual rights? **(b)** How does the 14th Amendment address this complication? **(c)** On what basis did the Supreme Court strike down many State laws after the *Gitlow* case?

4. **(a)** What does the 9th Amendment provide? **(b)** Why do you think it was included in the Bill of Rights?

Section 2

5. List five examples of the ways in which government encourages religion in the United States.

6. **(a)** Cite two arguments for allowing State aid to parochial schools. **(b)** Cite two arguments against this practice.

7. **(a)** Why has the Court allowed legislative prayers but not organized school prayers? **(b)** Do you agree with the Court's rationale? Why or why not?

8. Identify three ways in which government may properly restrict the exercise of religious belief.

Section 3

9. What two basic purposes do the guarantees of free expression serve?

10. **(a)** What does the "clear and present danger" rule say? **(b)** What case established the rule? **(c)** How is the Smith Act of 1940 consistent with that rule?

11. **(a)** What is prior restraint? **(b)** In what situations does the Supreme Court allow prior restraint?

Section 4

12. What are the time, place, and manner limits that government can put on freedom of assembly?

13. What limits on public demonstrations has the Court upheld?

14. **Analyze Political Cartoons** How do you think the Supreme Court might rule in a case like the one shown in the cartoon below: for the boys (freedom of association) or for the girl (anti-discrimination)? Explain your answer.

Writing About Government

15. Use your Quick Write exercises to write a persuasive essay supporting a civil liberties issue. Write an introduction with at least two sides, a body that provides evidence to support your position and refutes the opposing position, and a conclusion that strengthens your argument. See pp. S9–S10 in the Skills Handbook.

Apply What You've Learned

16. **Essential Question Activity** Not all assembly is protected by the 1st and 14th Amendments. Suppose you are helping to organize a demonstration for a political cause. Write three to five questions you should ask to determine if the Supreme Court would consider your demonstration to be constitutionally protected.

17. **Essential Question Assessment** Based on the questions you wrote and the content of this chapter, create a brochure for participants that helps to answer the Essential Question: **How can the judiciary balance individual rights with the common good?** Consider the freedoms of speech, press, and assembly and petition. Include examples from the chapter that show how individual rights are balanced by the courts to ensure relative guarantees for the public (the common good).

Essential Questions Journal To respond to the chapter Essential Question, go to your **Essential Questions Journal.**

Document-Based Assessment

Freedom of Speech and Assembly

Citizens burn the American flag in a protest and the Ku Klux Klan parades along Main Street. Both these controversial actions are protected by the 1st and 14th Amendments. Some Americans believe such actions should not be protected. From America's earliest days, public and judicial opinion have been divided over the extent of free speech and assembly, as shown in the documents below.

Document 1

"We have nothing to fear from the demoralizing reasonings of some, if others are left free to demonstrate their errors and especially when the law stands ready to punish the first criminal act produced by the false reasonings; these are safer corrections than the conscience of the judge.

—Thomas Jefferson, July 3, 1801

Document 2

Document 3

"[F]reedom of speech which is secured by the Constitution does not confer an absolute right to speak, without responsibility, whatever one may choose, . . . a State in the exercise of its police power may punish those who abuse this freedom by . . . tending to incite to crime, disturb the public peace, or endanger the foundations of organized government. . . .

—Whitney v. California, 1927

Document 4

"[T]he constitutional guarantees of free speech and free press do not permit a State to forbid or proscribe advocacy of the use of force or of law violation except where such advocacy is directed to inciting or producing imminent lawless action and is likely to incite or produce such action. . . . [T]he mere abstract teaching . . . of the moral propriety or even moral necessity for a resort to force and violence is not the same as preparing a group for violent action and steeling it to such action. . . .

—Brandenburg v. Ohio, 1969

Use your knowledge of 1st Amendment freedoms and Documents 1–4 to answer these questions.

1. According to Document 1, which of these should be punished?
    - **A.** violent ideas
    - **B.** "demoralizing reasonings"
    - **C.** criminal acts produced by violent ideas
    - **D.** speech whose purpose is to incite fear

2. What comment does the cartoon make about some of the Court's 1st Amendment decisions?

3. According to Document 3, when may a State exercise its police power in order to limit freedom of speech and assembly?

4. According to Document 4 (a case that overturned *Whitney*), when may speech and assembly be properly limited?

5. **Pull It Together** Which documents support tightening limits on speech and assembly? With which documents do you agree? Why?

⊘ GOVERNMENT ONLINE

Documents

To find additional primary sources on 1st Amendment freedoms, visit **PearsonSuccessNet.com**

Essential Question
To what extent has the judiciary protected the rights of privacy, security, and personal freedom?

My **belief** has always been . . . that **wherever** in this land any individual's **constitutional rights** are being **unjustly denied,** it is the **obligation** of the federal government—at point of bayonet if necessary— **to restore** that individual's constitutional **rights.**

—Ronald Reagan

Photo: Statue of Lady Justice

GOVERNMENT ONLINE
On the Go

To study anywhere, anytime, download these online resources at PearsonSuccessNet.com
• Political Dictionary
• Audio Review
• Downloadable Interactivities

SECTION 1

Due Process
of Law

Guiding Question

Why is the concept of due process important to a free society? Use a chart like the one below to take notes on due process.

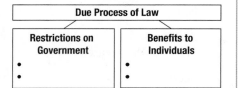

Due Process of Law	
Restrictions on Government	**Benefits to Individuals**
•	•
•	•

Political Dictionary

- due process
- procedural due process
- substantive due process
- police power
- search warrant

Objectives

1. Explain the meaning of due process of law as set out in the 5th and 14th amendments.
2. Define police power and understand its relationship to civil rights.
3. Describe the right of privacy and its origins in constitutional law.

Image Above: Evidence in a criminal case is tested in a laboratory.

Did you know that DNA evidence has led to the reversal of more than 200 wrongful convictions in recent years? That the use of evidence drawn from the scientific study of body tissues has proved that all those persons were convicted, and served time in prison, for crimes they did *not* commit? Did you know that there is a strong likelihood that an untold number of innocent persons remain in prison today? As you will soon see, this point alone illustrates the importance of due process of law.

What Due Process Means

The Constitution contains two due process clauses. The 5th Amendment declares that the Federal Government cannot deprive any person of "life, liberty, or property, without due process of law." The 14th Amendment places that same restriction on every one of the States—and, very importantly, on their local governments, as well. A thorough grasp of the meaning of these provisions is absolutely essential to an understanding of the American concept of civil rights and liberties.

It is impossible to define the two due process guarantees in exact and complete terms. The Supreme Court has consistently and purposely refused to do so. Instead, it has relied on finding the meaning of due process on a case-by-case basis. The Court first described that approach in *Davidson* v. *New Orleans,* 1878, as the "gradual process of inclusion and exclusion, as the cases presented for decision shall require."

Fundamentally, however, the Constitution's guarantee of **due process** means this: In whatever it does, government must act fairly and in accord with established rules. It may not act unfairly, arbitrarily, or unreasonably.

The concept of due process began and developed in English and then in American law as a procedural concept. That is, it first developed as a requirement that government act fairly, use fair procedures to enforce law.

Fair procedures are of little value, however, if they are used to administer unfair laws. The Supreme Court recognized this fact toward the end of the nineteenth century. It began to hold that due process requires that both the ways in which government acts *and* the laws under which it acts must be fair.

Thus, the Court added the idea of substantive due process to the original notion of procedural due process.

In short, **procedural due process** has to do with the *how* (the procedures, the methods) of governmental action. **Substantive due process** involves the *what* (the substance, the policies) of governmental action.

Examples of Due Process Any number of cases may be used to illustrate these two elements of due process. Take a classic case, *Rochin* v. *California,* 1952, to exemplify procedural due process.

Rochin was a suspected narcotics dealer. Acting on a tip, three Los Angeles County deputy sheriffs went to his rooming house. They forced their way into Rochin's room, found him sitting on a bed, and spotted two capsules on a nightstand. When one of the deputies asked, "Whose stuff is this?" Rochin popped the capsules into his mouth. Although all three officers jumped him, Rochin managed to swallow the pills.

The deputies took Rochin to a hospital, where his stomach was pumped. The capsules were recovered and found to contain morphine. The State then prosecuted and convicted Rochin for violating the State's narcotics laws.

The Supreme Court unanimously held that the deputies had violated the 14th Amendment's guarantee of procedural due process. Said the Court:

PRIMARY SOURCE

This is conduct that shocks the conscience. Illegally breaking into the privacy of the petitioner, the struggle to open his mouth and remove what was there, the forcible extraction of his stomach's contents—this course of proceeding by agents of government to obtain evidence is bound to offend even hardened sensibilities. They are methods too close to the rack and the screw. . . .

—Justice Felix Frankfurter

The case *Pierce* v. *Society of Sisters,* 1925, illustrates substantive due process. In 1922, Oregon's voters had adopted a new compulsory school-attendance law that required all persons between the ages of 8 and 16 to attend *public* schools. The law was purposely written to destroy private, especially parochial, schools in the State.

A Roman Catholic order challenged the law's constitutionality, and the Supreme Court held that its provisions violated the 14th Amendment's Due Process Clause. The Court did not find that the State had enforced the law unfairly. Rather, it held that the law itself, in its contents, "unreasonably interferes with the liberty of parents to direct

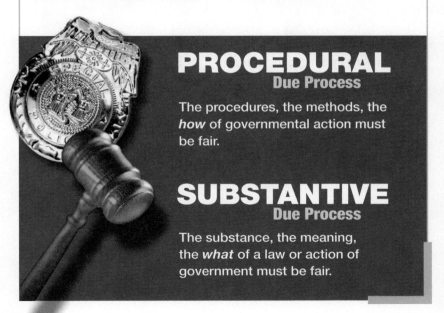

Due Process

This basic limit is placed on the Federal Government in the **5th Amendment,** and on State and local governments in the **14th Amendment:**

Government cannot deprive any person of life, liberty, or property without due process of law.

Both the **procedures** and the **laws** of government must be in accord with due process. *Why are procedural and substantive due process both necessary?*

PROCEDURAL
Due Process

The procedures, the methods, the *how* of governmental action must be fair.

SUBSTANTIVE
Due Process

The substance, the meaning, the *what* of a law or action of government must be fair.

the upbringing and education of children under their control.

The 14th Amendment and the Bill of Rights Recall these crucial points from Chapter 19: The provisions of the Bill of Rights apply against the National Government *only*. However, the Supreme Court has held that the 14th Amendment's Due Process Clause includes within its meaning most of the protections set out in the Bill of Rights.

In a long series of decisions dating from 1925, the Court extended the protections of the Bill of Rights against the States through the 14th Amendment's Due Process Clause. The chart on page 549 lists those amendments that have been incorporated—and with them the four provisions in the Bill of Rights that have not been incorporated.

The key 1st Amendment cases were discussed in Chapter 19. Those involving the 4th through the 8th amendments are treated in Sections 2, 3, and 4 of this chapter.

compulsory
adj. forced, obligatory

"What's so great about due process? Due process got me ten years."

▶ **Interpreting Political Cartoons** *Is it possible that the prisoner's complaint is justified? Explain your answer.*

The Police Power

In the federal system, the reserved powers of the States include the broad and important **police power.** The police power is the authority of each State to act to protect and promote the public health, safety, morals, and general welfare. In other words, it is the power of each State to safeguard the well-being of its people.

The Police Power and Civil Liberties The use of the police power often produces conflicts with civil liberty protections. When it does, courts must strike a balance between the needs of society, on the one hand, and of individual freedoms on the other. Any number of cases can be used to illustrate the conflict between police power and individual rights. Take as an example a matter often involved in drunk-driving cases.

Every State's laws allow the use of one or more tests to determine whether a person arrested and charged with drunk driving was in fact drunk at the time of the incident. Some of those tests are simple: walking a straight line or touching the tip of one's nose, for example. Some are more sophisticated, however, notably the breathalyzer test and the drawing of a blood sample.

Does the requirement that a person submit to such a test violate his or her rights under the 14th Amendment? Does the test involve an unconstitutional search for and seizure of evidence? Does it amount to forcing a person to testify against himself or herself (unconstitutional <u>compulsory</u> self-incrimination)? Or is that requirement a proper exercise of the police power?

Time after time, State and federal courts have come down on the side of the police power. They have supported the right of society to protect itself against drunk drivers and rejected the individual rights argument.

The leading case is *Schmerber* v. *California*, 1966. There, the Court found no objection to a situation in which a police officer had directed a doctor to draw blood from a drunk-driving suspect. The Court emphasized these points: The blood sample was drawn in accord with accepted medical practice. The officer had reasonable grounds to believe that the suspect was drunk. Further, had the officer taken time to secure a **search warrant**—a court order authorizing a search—whatever evidence was present could have disappeared from the suspect's system.

Protecting the Public Legislators and judges have often found the public's health, safety, morals, and/or welfare to be of overriding importance. For example:

1. To promote health, States can limit the sale of alcoholic beverages and tobacco, make laws to combat pollution, and require the vaccination of schoolchildren.

2. To promote safety, States can regulate the carrying of concealed weapons, require the use of seat belts, and punish drunk drivers.

3. To promote morals, States can regulate gambling and outlaw the sale of obscene materials and the practice of prostitution.

4. To promote the general welfare, States can enact compulsory education laws, provide help to the medically needy, and limit the profits of public utilities.

Clearly, governments cannot use the police power in an unreasonable or unfair way, however. In short, they cannot violate the 14th Amendment's Due Process Clause.

The Right of Privacy

The constitutional guarantees of due process create a right of privacy—"the right to be free, except in very limited circumstances, from unwanted governmental intrusions into one's privacy," *Stanley* v. *Georgia,* 1969.[1] It is, in short, "the right to be let alone."[2]

The Constitution makes no specific mention of the right of privacy, but the Supreme Court declared its existence in *Griswold* v. *Connecticut,* 1965. That case centered on a State law that outlawed birth-control counseling and prohibited the use of all birth-control devices. The Court held the law to be a violation of the 14th Amendment's Due Process Clause—and noted that the State had no business policing the marital bedroom.

Roe **v.** *Wade* The most controversial applications of the right of privacy have come in cases that raise this question: To what extent can a State limit a woman's right to an abortion? The leading case is *Roe* v. *Wade,* 1973. There, the Supreme Court struck down a Texas law that made abortion a crime except when necessary to save the life of the mother.

In *Roe,* the Court held that the 14th Amendment's right of privacy "encompass[es] a woman's decision whether or not to terminate her pregnancy." More specifically, the Court ruled that:

1. In the first trimester of pregnancy (about three months), a State must recognize a woman's right to an abortion; it cannot interfere with medical judgments in that matter during that period.

2. In the second trimester, a State, acting in the interest of women who undergo abortions, can make reasonable regulations about how, when, and where abortions can be performed but cannot prohibit the procedure.

3. In the final trimester, a State, acting to protect the unborn child, can choose to prohibit all abortions except those necessary to preserve the life or health of the mother.

Challenges to *Roe* In several later cases, the Court rejected a number of challenges to its basic holding in *Roe.* As the composition of the Court has changed, however, so has the Court's position on abortion. That shift can be seen in the Court's decisions in recent cases on the matter.

In *Webster* v. *Reproductive Health Services,* 1989, the Court upheld two key parts of a Missouri law. Those provisions prohibit abortions, except those that preserve the

Promoting safety is one of the States' police powers. *In what ways do States promote morality?*

---

[1] *Stanley* involved the possession of obscene materials in one's own home. In the most recent right to privacy case, the Court struck down a Texas law that made sexual relations between consenting gay adults a crime, *Lawrence* v. *Texas,* 2003.

[2] Justice Louis D. Brandeis, dissenting in *Olmstead* v. *United States,* 1928.

mother's life or health, (1) in any publicly operated hospital or clinic in that State, and (2) when the mother is 20 or more weeks pregnant and tests show that the fetus is viable (capable of sustaining life outside the mother's body).

Two cases in 1990 addressed the issue of minors and abortion. In those cases, the Court said that a State may require a minor (1) to inform at least one parent before she can obtain an abortion, *Ohio* v. *Akron Center for Reproductive Health*, and (2) to tell both parents of her plans, except in cases where a judge gives permission for an abortion without parental knowledge, *Hodgson* v. *Minnesota*.

The Court's most important decision on the issue since *Roe* v. *Wade* came in *Planned Parenthood of Southeastern Pennsylvania* v. *Casey* in 1992. There, the Court announced this rule: A State may place reasonable limits on a woman's right to have an abortion, but these restrictions cannot impose an "undue burden" on her choice of that procedure.

In *Casey*, the Court applied that new standard to Pennsylvania's Abortion Control Act. It upheld several sections of the law, finding that they did not place "a substantial obstacle in the path of a woman seeking an abortion of a non-viable fetus." Those provisions, it said, do not impose an "undue burden" on a woman's choice.

The Supreme Court did strike down another key part of the Pennsylvania law in *Casey*, however. That provision required that a married woman tell her husband of her plan to have an abortion. That requirement, said the Court, did indeed amount to an "undue burden."

Recent Cases The High Court has decided only two abortion cases since 1992. Its 5–4 vote in the most recent one effectively overturned its 5–4 decision in the earlier case. Together, the two cases underscore the impact that changes in the composition of the Court can have on the outcome of cases that come before it.

In *Gonzales* v. *Carhart*, 2007, the justices applied *Casey's* "undue burden" rule to an act of Congress, the Partial Birth Abortion Ban Act of 2003, and found it constitutional. That statute prohibits a particular method of abortion, a medical procedure that opponents of abortion call "partial birth abortion." In fact, that operation had been performed in very few instances.

In the earlier case, *Stenberg* v. *Carhart*, 2000, the Court had applied *Casey* to strike down a Nebraska law that also banned partial birth abortions, and in language very nearly identical to that used by Congress when it passed the federal law in 2003.

SECTION 1 ASSESSMENT

Essential Questions **Journal**	To continue to build a response to the chapter Essential Question, go to your **Essential Questions Journal**.

1. **Guiding Question** Use your completed graphic organizer to answer this question: Why is the concept of due process important to a free society?

Key Terms and Comprehension

2. **(a)** What does the phrase **due process** of law mean? **(b)** Why has the Supreme Court purposefully not defined due process exactly?

3. How do **procedural due process** and **substantive due process** differ?

4. **(a)** What is the **police power** reserved to the States? **(b)** What is the relationship between the police power and due process of law?

Critical Thinking

5. **Draw Conclusions** Considering the constitutional right of privacy, is it proper for a State to use its police power to protect and promote morals among its citizens? Explain your answer.

6. **Demonstrate Reasoned Judgment** The right of privacy is not found in the Constitution. **(a)** How did Justice Brandeis define the right of privacy? **(b)** Do you think a constitutional amendment is needed to guarantee an individual's right to privacy? Why or why not?

Quick Write

Research Essay: Choose a Topic Scan the chapter for two or three Supreme Court cases. Research the cases online, and write a summary paragraph of each case that includes the facts and issues. Select the case that most interests you.

SECTION 2

Freedom and Security of the Person

Guiding Question

How does the Constitution protect the freedom and security of the person? Use a concept web to take notes on the section.

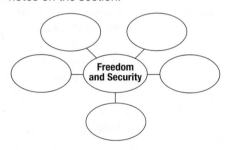

Political Dictionary

- involuntary servitude
- discrimination
- writs of assistance
- probable cause
- exclusionary rule

Objectives

1. Outline Supreme Court decisions regarding slavery and involuntary servitude.
2. Explain the intent and application of the 2nd Amendment's protection of the right to keep and bear arms.
3. Summarize the constitutional provisions designed to guarantee security of home and person.

Image Above: Police must have probable cause when they stop a vehicle.

The Constitution of the United States is, in very large part, a statement of limited government. Many of the restrictions it puts on governmental power are intended to protect the right of every American to be free. That is, those restrictions guard the right of individuals to be free from physical restraints, to be secure in their persons, and to be secure in their homes.

Slavery and Involuntary Servitude

The 13th Amendment was added to the Constitution in 1865, ending over 200 years of slavery in America. Section 1 of the amendment declares: "Neither slavery nor involuntary servitude, . . . shall exist within the United States, or any place subject to their jurisdiction." Importantly, Section 2 of this amendment gives Congress the expressed power "to enforce this article by appropriate legislation."

Until 1865, each State could decide for itself whether to allow slavery. With the 13th Amendment, that power was denied to them, and to the National Government, as well.

The 13th Amendment: Section 1 As a widespread practice, slavery disappeared in the United States more than 140 years ago. There are still occasional cases of it, however. Most often, those cases have involved **involuntary servitude**—that is, forced labor. An 1867 federal law, the Anti-Peonage Act, makes it a crime to force someone to work for another in order to fulfill a contract or satisfy a debt. Several times, the Supreme Court has struck down State laws making it a crime for any person to fail to work after having received money or other benefits by promising to do so.

The 13th Amendment does not forbid all forms of involuntary servitude, however. Thus, in 1918, the Supreme Court drew a distinction between "involuntary servitude" and "duty" in upholding the constitutionality of the selective service system (the draft).[3] Nor does imprisonment for crime violate the amendment; and those who are convicted of crime can be forced to work. Finally, note this important point: Unlike any other provision in the Constitution,

---

3 *Selective Draft Law Cases,* 1918.

the prohibitions in the 13th Amendment cover the conduct of private individuals as well as the behavior of government.

The 13th Amendment: Section 2 Shortly after the Civil War, Congress passed several civil rights laws based on the 13th Amendment. The Supreme Court, however, sharply narrowed the scope of federal authority in several cases, especially the *Civil Rights Cases,* 1883. In effect, the Court held that racial **discrimination** (prejudice, unfairness) against African Americans by *private individuals* was allowed. Private discrimination, ruled the Court, did not place the "badge of slavery" on African Americans nor keep them in servitude.

As a result, Congress soon repealed most of the civil rights laws based on the 13th Amendment. The enforcement of the few laws that remained was at best unimpressive. For years, it was generally thought that Congress did not have the power, under either the 13th or 14th Amendment, to act against those who practiced race-based discrimination.

Nearly a century later, however, in *Jones* v. *Mayer,* 1968, the Supreme Court breathed new life into the 13th Amendment. The case centered on one of the post-Civil War acts Congress had not repealed. Passed in 1866, that almost-forgotten law provided in part that:

The 13th Amendment abolished slavery in 1865. *What types of involuntary servitude are permitted today?*

Jones, an African American, had sued because Mayer had refused to sell him a home, solely because of his race. Mayer contended that the 1866 law was unconstitutional, since it sought to prohibit private racial discrimination.

The Supreme Court upheld the 1866 law, declaring that the 13th Amendment abolished slavery and also gave Congress the power to abolish "the badges and incidents of slavery." Said the Court:

PRIMARY SOURCE

At the very least, the freedom that Congress is empowered to secure under the 13th Amendment includes the freedom to buy whatever a white man can buy, the right to live wherever a white man can live.

—Justice Potter Stewart

The Court affirmed that decision in several later cases. Thus, in *Runyon* v. *McCrary,* 1976, two private schools had refused to admit two African American students. By doing so, the schools had refused to enter into a contract of admission—a contract they had advertised to the general public. The Court found that the schools had violated another provision of the 1866 law, providing that: "[All] citizens of the United States, . . . of every race and color, . . . shall have the same right, . . . to make and enforce contracts . . . as is enjoyed by white citizens. . . ."

The Court has also ruled that the Civil Rights Act of 1866 protects all "identifiable classes of persons who are subjected to intentional discrimination solely because of their ancestry or ethnic characteristics"—for example Jews, *Shaare Tefila Congregation* v. *Cobb,* 1987, and Arabs, *St. Francis College* v. *Al-Khazraji,* 1987.

More recently, the Court has backed off a bit. In *Patterson* v. *McLean Credit Union,* 1989, it declared that although the 1866 law does prohibit racial discrimination in a contract of employment, any on-the-job discrimination should be handled in accord with the Civil Rights Act of 1964. (See Chapter 21.) Nevertheless, the Court has several times held that the 13th Amendment gives Congress significant power to attack "the badges and incidents of slavery," from whatever source they may come.

Right to Keep and Bear Arms

The 2nd Amendment was added to the Constitution to protect the concept of the citizen-soldier. It reads:

FROM THE CONSTITUTION

A well regulated Militia, being necessary to the security of a free State, the right of the people to keep and bear Arms, shall not be infringed.

What, exactly, do these words mean? Do they protect *only* the right of each State to keep a militia, especially against <u>encroachments</u> by the Federal Government? Or, does the 2nd Amendment do that *and also* give to individuals a right to keep and bear arms—just as, say, the 1st Amendment protects free speech?

For decades, the Supreme Court refused to accept the latter interpretation. In its one really important 2nd Amendment ruling, in *United States* v. *Miller,* 1939, the Court rejected the individual right argument. It upheld a section of the National Firearms Act of 1934 that made it a crime to ship sawed-off shotguns or submachine guns across State lines unless the shipper had a federal license to do so. The Court said that it could find no valid link between the shotgun involved in the case and "the preservation . . . of a well-regulated militia."

In 2008, however, the holding in *Miller* was effectively overturned, 5–4, in *District of Columbia* v. *Heller.* There, the Court found the District's very strict gun control ordinance unconstitutional. It ruled, for the first time in more than 200 years, that the 2nd Amendment forbids "the absolute prohibition of handguns held and used for self-defense in the home."

The Court did say, however, that *Heller* does not overrule "long-standing prohibitions on the possession of firearms by felons or the mentally ill, or laws forbidding the carrying of firearms in sensitive places such as schools and government buildings, or laws imposing

conditions and qualifications on the commercial sale of arms."

Clearly, over the next several years both federal and State courts will handle any number of cases challenging the many State and federal laws that now limit the right to keep and bear arms. Remember, the Supreme Court has never found that the 14th Amendment's Due Process Clause covers the 2nd Amendment—a fact that will surely affect those cases.

Security of Home and Person

The 3rd and 4th amendments say that government cannot violate the home or person of anyone in this country without just cause.

The 3rd Amendment This amendment forbids the quartering (housing) of soldiers in private homes in peacetime without the owner's consent and not in wartime except "in a manner to be prescribed by law." The guarantee was added to prevent what had been British practice in colonial days.[4] The 3rd Amendment has had little importance since 1791 and has never been the subject of a Supreme Court case.

The 4th Amendment The 4th Amendment also grew out of colonial practice. It was designed to prevent the use of **writs of assistance**—blanket search warrants with which British customs officials had invaded private homes to search for smuggled goods.

Each State constitution contains a similar provision. The guarantee also applies to the States through the 14th Amendment's Due Process Clause. Unlike the 3rd Amendment,

This statue, called *The Minuteman,* honors the colonial militia. *Why was the 2nd Amendment added to the Constitution?*

encroachment
n. intrusion, invasion

---

4 Recall that among the king's many "repeated injuries and usurpations [seizures]" set out in the Declaration of Independence was that of "quartering large bodies of troops among us." See page 45.

Probable Cause The 4th Amendment holds that police must show probable cause to obtain a search warrant. However, officers may stop and frisk a person without a warrant if they have a reasonable suspicion that a crime is about to be committed. What constitutes *probable cause* and *reasonable suspicion?* Chief Justice William Rehnquist answered that question this way: "They are commonsense, nontechnical conceptions that deal with the factual and practical considerations of everyday life on which reasonable and prudent men, not legal technicians, act." Actions that the Court has accepted as justifying a stop and frisk include fleeing from the police, "casing" a store, and an officer's belief that a person is armed and dangerous.

Constitutional Principles Is probable cause an indispensable part of the guarantee against unreasonable searches and seizures?

▲ The Supreme Court has ruled that "a police officer's decision [to stop and frisk] must be based on more than a hunch or speculation," *Arizona* v. *Gant*, 1994.

the 4th Amendment has proved a highly important guarantee. See the text of the 4th Amendment above.

Probable Cause The basic rule laid down by the 4th Amendment is this: Police officers have no general right to search for evidence or to seize either evidence or persons. Except in special circumstances, they must have a proper warrant (a court order). That warrant must be obtained with **probable cause**—that is, a reasonable suspicion of crime.

Florida v. *J.L.,* 2000, illustrates the rule. There, Miami police received a tip that a teenager was carrying a concealed weapon. Two officers went to the bus stop where the tipster said the young man could be found. The police located him, searched him, pulled a gun from his pocket, and arrested him.

The Court held that the police acted illegally because they did not have a proper warrant. All they had was an anonymous tip,

unsupported by any other evidence. Their conduct amounted to just the sort of thing the 4th Amendment was intended to prevent.

Police do not always need a warrant, however—for example, when evidence is "in plain view." Thus, the Court upheld a search and seizure involving two men who were bagging cocaine. A policeman spotted them through an open window, entered the apartment, seized the cocaine, and arrested them. The Court upheld their conviction, rejecting a claim to 4th Amendment protection, *Minnesota* v. *Carter,* 1999.

Many 4th Amendment cases are complicated. In *Lidster* v. *Illinois,* 2004, for example, the Court upheld the use of so-called "informational roadblocks." In 1997, police had set up barriers on a busy highway near Chicago, hoping to find witnesses to a recent hit-and-run accident. When Robert Lidster was stopped, an officer smelled alcohol on him. Lidster failed several sobriety tests and was arrested on a drunk-driving charge. Lidster's attorney filed a motion to quash (set aside) that arrest. The lawyer argued that Lidster was forced to stop by officers who, before they stopped him, had no valid reason (no probable cause) to believe that he had committed any crime.

Lidster lost that argument. The Court upheld both his conviction and the use of informational roadblocks. Lidster had simply run afoul of the long arm of coincidence.

Arrests An arrest is the seizure of a person. When officers make a lawful arrest, they do not need a warrant to search "the area from within which [the suspect] might gain possession of a weapon or destructible evidence."[5] In fact, most arrests take place without a warrant. Police can arrest a person in a public place without one, provided they have probable cause to believe that person has committed or is about to commit a crime.[6]

Illinois v. *Wardlow,* 2000, illustrates this point. There, four police cars were patrolling a high-crime area in Chicago. When Wardlow spotted them, he ran. An officer chased him down an alley, caught him, and found that Wardlow was carrying a loaded pistol. The Court held, 5–4, that Wardlow's behavior—his flight—gave the police "common sense" grounds on which to believe that he was involved in some criminal activity. (Note, however, that the Court did not hold that police have a blanket power to stop anyone who flees at the sight of a police officer.)

When, exactly, does the 4th Amendment protection come into play? The Court has several times held that this point is reached "only when the officer, by means of physical force or show of authority, has in some way restrained the liberty of a citizen," *Terry* v. *Ohio,* 1968.

Automobiles The Court has long had difficulty applying the 4th Amendment to automobiles. It has several times held that an officer needs no warrant to search an automobile, a boat, an airplane, or some other vehicle, when there is probable cause to believe that it is involved in illegal activities—because such a "movable scene of crime" could disappear while a warrant was being sought.

Carroll v. *United States,* 1925, is an early leading case on the point. There, the Court emphasized that "where the securing of a warrant is reasonably practicable, it must be used, . . . In cases where seizure is impossible except without a warrant, the seizing officer acts unlawfully and at his peril unless he can show the court probable cause."

The Court overturned a long string of automobile search cases in 1991. Before then, it had several times held that a warrant was usually needed to search a glove compartment, a paper bag, luggage, or other "closed containers" in an automobile. But, in *California* v. *Acevedo,* 1991, the Court set out what it called "one clear-cut rule to govern automobile searches." Whenever police lawfully stop a car, they do not need a warrant to search anything in that vehicle that they have reason to believe holds evidence of a crime. "Anything" includes a passenger's belongings, *Wyoming* v. *Houghton,* 1999.

Police, upon making a routine traffic stop, do not need to secure a warrant in order to use a trained dog to sniff around (search) the outside of a car for narcotics, *Illinois* v. *Caballes,* 2005. When officers make a traffic stop, the Constitution protects passengers as well as drivers against an illegal search or seizure, *Brendlin* v. *California,* 2007. And when police stop a car and arrest the driver, they may search inside the car only if they have reason to believe that the car contains evidence of the crime for which that arrest was made, *Arizona* v. *Gant,* 2009.

The Exclusionary Rule

The heart of the guarantee against unreasonable searches and seizures lies in this question: If an unlawful search or seizure does occur, can that "tainted evidence" be used in court? If it can be used, the 4th Amendment offers no real protection to a person accused of crime.

✔ **Checkpoint**
What rule regarding automobile searches was established in *California* v. *Acevedo?*

tainted
adj. spoiled, tarnished, flawed

---

5 This rule was first laid down in *Chimel* v. *California,* 1969. Chimel was arrested, in his home, on a burglary charge and police searched for evidence of his stealing.

6 A person arrested without a warrant must be brought promptly before a judge for a probable cause hearing. In *County of Riverside* v. *McLaughlin,* 1991, the Court held that "promptly" means within 48 hours.

To meet that problem, the Supreme Court has adopted, and is still refining, the **exclusionary rule.** Essentially, the rule is this: Evidence gained as the result of an illegal act by police cannot be used at the trial of the person from whom it was seized.

The rule was first laid down in *Weeks* v. *United States*, 1914. In that narcotics case, the Court held that evidence obtained illegally by federal officers could not be used in the federal courts. For decades, however, the Court left questions of the use of such evidence in State courts for each State to decide for itself.

Mapp* v. *Ohio The exclusionary rule was finally extended to the States in *Mapp* v. *Ohio*, 1961. There, the Court held that the 14th Amendment forbids unreasonable searches and seizures by State and local officers just as the 4th Amendment bars such actions by federal officers. It also held that the fruits of an unlawful search or seizure cannot be used in the State courts, just as they cannot be used in the federal courts.

In *Mapp*, Cleveland police had entered Dollree Mapp's home, forcibly and without a warrant. They claimed to be searching for both a fugitive in a bombing case and evidence of gambling. Their lengthy search found nothing on either count. But they did turn up some "dirty books." Mapp was then convicted of the possession of obscene materials and sentenced to jail. The Court overturned that conviction, holding that the evidence against her had been found illegally and so could not be used at her trial.

Cases Narrowing the Rule The exclusionary rule has always been controversial. It was intended to put teeth into the 4th Amendment, and it has. It says to police: As you enforce the law, obey the law. The rule seeks to prevent, or at least deter, police misconduct.

Critics of the rule say that it means that some persons who are clearly guilty nonetheless go free. Why, they ask, should criminals be able to "beat the rap" on "a technicality"?

The Court has narrowed the scope of the rule most notably in the four cases in the feature on the next page.

Drug Testing Programs Federal drug-testing programs involve searches of persons, so are covered by the 4th Amendment. To date, however, the Court has held that those programs can be conducted without warrants or even any indication of drug use by those who must take the tests. It did so in two 1989 cases. One involved the mandatory testing of those drug enforcement officers of the U.S. Customs Service (now Immigration and Customs Enforcement) who carry firearms, *National Treasury Employees Union* v. *Von Raab.* The other had to do with the testing of railroad workers after a train accident, *Skinner* v. *Railway Labor Executives' Association.* In effect, the Court said in both cases that the violations of privacy involved were outweighed by a legitimate governmental interest—for example, in *Skinner,* discovering the cause of a train accident.

The Court has also upheld two local school districts' drug-testing programs, both covered by the 14th Amendment's Due Process Clause. It sustained an Oregon school district's program that requires all students who take part in school sports to agree to be tested for drug use, *Vernonia School District* v. *Acton,* 1995. That ruling was extended in a case from Oklahoma, *Board of Education of Independent School District No. 92 of Pottawatomie County* v. *Earls,* 2002. There, the Court upheld the random testing of students who want to participate in *any* competitive extracurricular activity. In both of these cases, the Court said that "a warrant and finding of probable cause are unnecessary in the public school context because [they] would unduly interfere with . . . swift and informal disciplinary procedures."

The Patriot Act The USA Patriot Act, commonly called the Patriot Act, is officially the Uniting and Strengthening America by Providing Appropriate Tools Required to Intercept and Obstruct Terrorism Act of 2001. It was passed by Congress and signed by President George W. Bush just six weeks after the terrorist attacks of 9/11. That 342-page statute

SUPREME COURT
at a glance

▶ **Case:** *Mapp* v. *Ohio,* 1961
▶ **Issue:** States' use of illegally obtained evidence
▶ **Decision:** After a warrantless search of Dollree Mapp's house, police officers turned up "lewd and lascivious material" and used it as evidence to convict Mapp. The Supreme Court struck down Mapp's conviction, holding that evidence seized illegally could not be used in either federal or State courts.

Exceptions to the Exclusionary Rule

In recent decades, the Supreme Court has narrowed the scope of the exclusionary rule by allowing evidence to be admissible in situations that it previously had not. *What is the purpose of that rule?*

◀ Evidence bag

Inevitable Discovery

Tainted evidence can be used in court if it "inevitably would have been discovered by lawful means." In *Nix* v. *Williams*, 1984, the defendant claimed the evidence against him had been found only after his confession was illegally obtained. **The Court ruled that the evidence ultimately would have been found without the defendant's statement.**

Knock-and-Announce Violation

The centuries-old "knock-and-announce" rule requires that police announce their presence before serving a warrant. The rule is intended to give residents a chance to open the door, not hide evidence. **The Court found that the rule is meant to protect persons and property from violence when police arrive,** *Hudson* v. *Michigan,* 2006.

Good Faith

In *United States* v. *Leon,* 1984, agents thought they were using a proper warrant. Their warrant was later shown to be faulty, but the Court upheld their actions nonetheless: **"When an officer acting with objective good faith has obtained a search warrant . . . and acted within its scope . . . there is nothing to deter."**

Honest Mistakes

The Court allowed the use of evidence seized in the mistaken search of an apartment, *Maryland* v. *Garrison,* 1987. Officers had a warrant to search for drugs in an apartment on the third floor of a building. Not realizing that there were two apartments, they entered and found drugs in the wrong apartment—the one for which they did not have a warrant.

Evidence is admissible

---

was renewed, after some contentious debate and with some modifications, in 2006.

The law provides for greatly increased governmental powers to combat domestic and international terrorist activities. Its major provisions focus on three broad areas: surveillance and investigation, immigration, and the financing of terrorist groups. Several provisions raise significant civil liberties issues that, over time, will be tested in the courts.

Of particular 4th Amendment concern are the act's provisions that allow the secret "sneak-and-peek searches." Under the statute, federal agents, acting with a warrant, may enter a person's home or office when no one is present and conduct a search—making notes, taking photos, and so on. The agents need not notify the person who is the subject of the search for weeks or even months—and so they are able to continue their investigation without that person's knowledge.

Wiretapping Electronic eavesdropping, such as wiretapping, videotaping, and other more sophisticated means of "bugging," is now quite widely used in the United States. These various techniques of discovery present difficult search and seizure questions that the authors of the 4th Amendment could not possibly have foreseen.

The 4th Amendment has always applied to "searches" that involve a physical intrusion—for example, a police officer entering a building or reaching inside a car. The amendment has also always applied to "seizures" that produce some tangible object—for example, a gun or a packet of methamphetamines found inside a car. Listening in on a conversation electronically, from afar, is a quite different matter.

In fact, in its first eavesdropping case, *Olmstead* v. *United States,* 1928, the Court held that the wiretapping there did not constitute a "search." The case arose when federal agents tapped a Seattle bootlegger's telephone calls. Their bugs produced evidence that led to Olmstead's conviction under the National Prohibition Act. The Court upheld that conviction. It found that, although the agents had not secured a warrant, there had been no "actual physical invasion" of Olmstead's home or office, and so no violation of the 4th Amendment because the phone lines had been tapped *outside* those places.

Olmstead stood for nearly forty years. It was finally overruled in what remains the leading case today, *Katz* v. *United States,* 1967. Katz had been convicted of transmitting gambling information across State lines. He had used a public phone booth in Los Angeles to call his contacts in Boston and Miami. Much of the evidence against him had come from an electronic tap placed on the roof—outside—of the phone booth.

The Court ruled that the bugging evidence could not be used against Katz. Despite the fact that he was in a public, glass-enclosed phone booth, he was entitled to make a *private* call, from a place where he had "a reasonable expectation of privacy." Said the Court: The 4th Amendment protects "persons, not just places." It noted, however, that the requirements of the amendment can be satisfied in such situations if police obtain a proper warrant before they install a listening device.

Congress responded to the Court's decision in *Katz* in a provision in the Omnibus Crime Control and Safe Street Act of 1968. There, Congress prohibited any wiretapping for domestic purposes except that authorized by a warrant issued by a federal judge.

Soon after September 11, President George W. Bush directed the National Security Agency (NSA), acting in secret and without court-approved warrants, to monitor the international telephone calls and e-mails of Americans with suspected ties to terrorists. The public did not become aware of that monitoring program until late 2005, and its disclosure brought a storm of protest. Many insist that this NSA activity is illegal. However, the Bush administration defended it as an appropriate exercise of the President's power as commander in chief.

| **Essential Questions** **Journal** | To continue to build a response to the chapter Essential Question, go to your **Essential Questions Journal.** |

SECTION **2** ASSESSMENT

1. **Guiding Question** Use your completed graphic organizer to answer this question: How does the Constitution protect the freedom and security of the person?

Key Terms and Comprehension

2. **(a)** What does the 13th Amendment guarantee? **(b)** How did the *Civil Rights Cases,* 1883, undermine those guarantees?

3. **(a)** How does the 4th Amendment limit government? **(b)** When does the 4th Amendment come into play during an arrest?

Critical Thinking

4. **Express Problems Clearly (a)** What does the exclusionary rule exclude? **(b)** Does the exclusionary rule serve the interests of justice? Answer this question first as the defendant in a criminal trial, and then as an arresting police officer.

5. **Identify Central Issues (a)** Why did the Court overturn the conviction in *Katz* v. *United States?* **(b)** Do you agree with the Court's decision? Why or why not?

Quick Write

Research Essay: Organize Your Notes Research to find additional information on the case you selected in Section 1, taking notes as you read. Then organize your notes under main headings. Scan the material for subtopics. Subtopics may include *What is this case about? How did it change an existing law? Why it is important to individual rights today?* Under your subtopics, write related details.

ISSUES OF OUR TIME

Balancing Security and Liberty

▶▶ **Track the Issue**

As international relations expanded in the 20th century, so too did government surveillance.

1908

The Bureau of Investigation (BOI) is formed and becomes the Federal Bureau of Investigation (FBI) in 1935.

1947

The National Security Act establishes the Central Intelligence Agency (CIA) to coordinate intelligence affecting national security.

1978

The Foreign Intelligence Surveillance Act (FISA) is passed. The FISA Court must issue warrants to authorize secret surveillance of suspected terrorists in the U.S.

2001

The Patriot Act is passed. The National Security Agency (NSA) secretly monitors international calls and e-mails of Americans with suspected ties to terrorists without court-approved warrants.

2008

The Protect America Act revises FISA warrant requirements, granting immunity to telecommunications companies that eavesdropped on Americans without warrants.

Justice Sandra Day O'Connor ▶

▶▶ **Perspectives**

Soon after September 11, President Bush directed the National Security Agency to begin the secret, warrantless monitoring of all international telephone and e-mail communications by persons within the United States. The legality of that surveillance program, which was ended in 2006, remains unsettled. To what lengths should the government be permitted to go in its efforts to combat terrorist activities?

"It is during our most challenging . . . moments that our Nation's commitment to due process is most severely tested . . . . We have . . . made clear that a state of war is not a blank check for the President when it comes to the rights of the Nation's citizens. Whatever power the . . . Constitution envisions for the Executive in its exchanges with other nations or with enemy organizations in times of conflict, it most assuredly envisions a role for all three branches when individual liberties are at stake. . . ."
—*Justice Sandra Day O'Connor, 2004*

"FISA requires the intelligence community to make a finding of probable cause. . . .[which] was never intended to be expanded to protect the rights of foreign terrorists overseas. Showing probable cause often takes time, is sometimes impossible, and makes intelligence officers spend valuable time convincing lawyers that this standard is met, rather than doing their most important task—hunting down terrorists and other foreign threats."
—*Dana Perino,*
Press Secretary, 2008

▶▶ **Connect to Your World**

1. **Understand (a)** What rights does Justice O'Connor concede to the executive branch during wartime? **(b)** How does the executive branch justify surveillance without a warrant?
2. **Draw Conclusions** Which argument do you find to be the most convincing? Why?

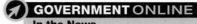

GOVERNMENT ONLINE
In the News
To find out more about balancing security and liberty, visit
PearsonSuccessNet.com

591

Rights of the Accused

Guiding Question

What protections does the Constitution set out for persons accused of crimes? Use a table to take notes on the section.

Rights of the Accused	
5th Amendment	**6th Amendment**
•	•
•	•
•	•

Political Dictionary

- writ of habeas corpus
- bill of attainder
- ex post facto law
- grand jury
- indictment
- presentment
- information
- double jeopardy
- bench trial
- Miranda rule

Objectives

1. Define writ of habeas corpus, bills of attainder, and ex post facto laws.
2. Outline how the right to a grand jury and the guarantee against double jeopardy help safeguard the rights of the accused.
3. Describe issues that arise from guarantees of speedy and public trials.
4. Determine what constitutes a fair trial by jury.
5. Examine the right to an adequate defense and the guarantee against self-incrimination.

Image Above: A suspect must be brought before a court and informed of the charges against him.

Think about this statement: "It is better that ten guilty persons go free than that one innocent person be punished." That maxim expresses one of the bedrock principles of the American legal system.

Of course, society must punish criminals in order to preserve itself. However, the law intends that any person who is suspected or accused of a crime must be presumed innocent until proven guilty by fair and lawful means.

Habeas Corpus

The **writ of habeas corpus,** sometimes called the writ of liberty, is intended to prevent unjust arrests and imprisonments.[7] It is a court order directed to an officer holding a prisoner. It commands that the prisoner be brought before the court and that the officer show cause—explain, with good reason—why the prisoner should not be released.

The right to seek a writ of habeas corpus is protected against the National Government in Article I, Section 9 of the Constitution. That right is guaranteed against the States in each of their own constitutions.

The Constitution says that the right to the writ cannot be suspended, "unless when in Cases of Rebellion or Invasion the public Safety may require it." President Abraham Lincoln suspended the writ in 1861 during the Civil War. His order covered various parts of the country, including several areas in which war was not then being waged. Chief Justice Roger B. Taney, sitting as a circuit judge, held Lincoln's action unconstitutional, *Ex parte Merryman*, 1861.

Taney ruled that the Constitution gives the power to suspend the writ to Congress alone. Congress then passed the Habeas Corpus Act of 1863. It gave the President the power to suspend the writ when and where, in his judgment, that action was necessary. In *Ex parte Milligan*, 1866, the Supreme Court ruled that neither Congress nor the President can suspend the writ in those locales where there is no actual fighting nor the likelihood of combat.

The right to the writ has been suspended only once since the Civil War and the Reconstruction Period that followed it. The territorial governor of Hawaii

---

7 The phrase *habeas corpus* comes from the Latin, meaning "you should have the body," and those are the opening words of the writ.

did so following the Japanese attack on Pearl Harbor in December 1941. The Supreme Court later ruled that the governor did not have the power to take that action, *Duncan* v. *Kahanamoku,* 1946.

In 2008, the Supreme Court held, for the first time, that foreign prisoners being held as enemy combatants at the U.S. naval base at Guantanamo Bay, Cuba, have a constitutional right to challenge their detention—that is, a right to seek writs of habeas corpus—in the federal courts, *Boumediene* v. *Bush* and *Al Odah* v. *United States.* The Bush administration had vigorously opposed that 5–4 ruling, but the Obama administration generally supports it. See page 539.

Bills of Attainder

A **bill of attainder** is a legislative act that provides for the punishment of a person without a court trial. The Constitution prohibits Congress from passing any such measure in Article I, Section 9, and it places the same prohibition on the States in Section 10.

The Framers wrote the ban on bills of attainder into the Constitution because Parliament and several of the colonial legislatures had passed many such bills. They have been quite rare in our national history, however.

The denial of the power to pass bills of attainder is both a protection of individual freedom and one of the Constitution's several provisions for separation of powers. In effect, the ban says to members of Congress and to the States' lawmakers: Be legislators, not judges. A legislative body can pass laws that define crime and set the penalties for violations of them. But it cannot pass a law that declares a person or identifiable group of persons guilty of a crime and provides for his or their punishment.

United States v. *Lovett,* 1946, is one of the few attainder cases ever decided by the Supreme Court. That case involved a provision in a law appropriating funds for the army that declared that none of the monies could be used to pay the salaries of three named persons. Several members of the House thought that those three were "subversive," and they urged the President to discharge them. The Court found that provision to be a bill of attainder.

In another similar case, *United States* v. *Brown,* 1965, the Court overturned a provision in the Landrum-Griffin Act of 1959. That provision made it a federal crime for a member of the Communist Party to serve as an officer of a labor union.

Ex Post Facto Laws

The Constitution, in Article I, Sections 9 and 10, prohibits Congress and the States from enacting ex post facto laws. An **ex post facto law** is a law applied to an act committed before the passage of that law. The phrase *ex post facto* is from the Latin, meaning "after the fact." An ex post facto law (1) is a criminal law—one defining a crime and/or providing for its punishment; (2) applies to an act committed before its passage; and (3) works to the disadvantage of the accused.

For example, a law making it a crime to sell marijuana cannot be applied to a sale that occurred before that law was passed. Or, a law that changes the penalty for murder from life in prison to death cannot be used to sentence a person who committed a murder before the punishment was made more severe.

Retroactive civil laws are *not* forbidden. Thus, a law raising income tax rates could be passed in November and applied to income earned through the whole year.

After the Japanese bombed Pearl Harbor, the governor of Hawaii suspended the writ of habeas corpus. *Who has the power to suspend the writ?*

Rights of the Accused

Steps of Justice

Any person accused of a crime is presumed to be innocent until proven guilty. *What protections does the Constitution extend to those accused of crime?*

Arrest

- Officers must have a warrant or act on probable cause.
- No unreasonable search or seizure.
- Accused may request writ of habeas corpus to challenge detention.

Interrogation

- Accused must be informed of the right to counsel and the right to remain silent.
- No third degree methods or coerced confession.

Grand Jury Proceeding

- Grand jury weighs evidence provided by prosecutor.
- Accused may be charged by indictment or presentment.
- Bail, if required, cannot be excessive.

Grand Jury

The 5th Amendment to the Constitution declares that

> ### FROM THE CONSTITUTION
>
> **No person shall be held to answer for a capital, or otherwise infamous crime, unless on a presentment or indictment of a Grand Jury. . . .**

The **grand jury** is the formal device by which a person can be accused of a serious crime—that is, any offense for which the punishment is death or imprisonment.[8] In federal cases, the grand jury is a body of from 16 to 23 persons drawn from the area of the district court that it serves. The

---

8 The 5th Amendment declares that the guarantee of grand jury does not extend to "cases arising in the land or naval forces." The conduct of members of the armed forces is regulated under a code of military law enacted by Congress, now the Uniform Code of Military Justice.

votes of at least 12 of the grand jurors are needed to return an indictment or to make a presentment.

An **indictment** is a formal complaint that the prosecutor lays before a grand jury. It charges the accused with one or more crimes. If the grand jury finds that there is enough evidence to justify a trial, it returns a "true bill of indictment." The accused person is then held for prosecution. If the grand jury does not make such a finding, the charge is dropped and the accused is set free.

A **presentment** is a formal accusation brought by the grand jury on its own motion, rather than that of the prosecutor. It is rarely used in federal courts.

A grand jury's proceedings are not a trial. Since unfair harm could come if they were public, its sessions are secret. They are also one-sided—in the law, an *ex parte* judicial proceeding. That is, only the prosecution, not the defense, is present.

Trial

- Public trial by an impartial jury within 100 days of arrest.
- Accused may request a change of venue.
- Assistance of counsel guaranteed.
- No self-incrimination.
- Favorable witnesses may be subpoenaed, opposing witnesses confronted.
- Jury's verdict to convict must be unanimous.
- No double jeopardy.

Punishment
(if found guilty)

- No excessive fine.
- No cruel and unusual punishment.

Appeals

- Either side may appeal a verdict against it.

GOVERNMENT ONLINE
Audio Tour
To learn more about the rights of the accused, visit
PearsonSuccessNet.com

The right to grand jury is intended as a protection against overzealous prosecutors. Critics say that it is too time-consuming, too expensive, and too likely to follow the dictates of the prosecutor.

The 5th Amendment's grand jury provision is the only part of the Bill of Rights relating to criminal prosecution that the Supreme Court has not brought within the coverage of the 14th Amendment's Due Process Clause. In the majority of States today, most criminal charges are not brought by grand jury indictment. They are brought, instead, by an **information,** an affidavit in which the prosecutor swears that there is enough evidence to justify a trial. (See Chapter 24.)

Double Jeopardy

The 5th Amendment's guarantee against double jeopardy is the first of several protections in the Bill of Rights especially intended to ensure fair trials in the federal courts.[9] Fair trials are guaranteed in State courts by each State's constitution and, also, recall, by the 14th Amendment's Due Process Clause.

The 5th Amendment says in part that no person can be "twice put in jeopardy of life or limb." Today, this prohibition against **double jeopardy** means that once a person has been tried for a crime, he or she cannot be tried again for that same crime. The Constitution's ban of double jeopardy applies against the States through the 14th Amendment's Due Process Clause, *Benton* v. *Maryland,* 1969.

A person can violate both a federal *and* a State law in single act, however—for example, by selling narcotics. That person can then be tried for the federal crime in a federal court and for the State crime in a State court. Thus, a single act can also result in several criminal charges. A person who breaks into a

---

9 See the 4th, 5th, 6th, 7th, and 8th amendments and Article III, Section 2, Clause 3.

store, steals liquor, and sells it can be tried for illegal entry, theft, and selling liquor without a license.

In a trial in which a jury cannot agree on a verdict (a hung jury), there is no jeopardy. It is as though no trial had been held. Nor is double jeopardy involved when a case is appealed to a higher court.[10]

Several States allow the continued confinement of violent sex predators after they have completed a prison term. The Court has twice held that that confinement is not punishment—and so does not involve double jeopardy. Rather, the practice is intended to protect the public from harm, *Kansas* v. *Hendrick*, 1987, and *Seling* v. *Young*, 2001.

Speedy and Public Trial

The 6th Amendment commands that:

> ### FROM THE CONSTITUTION
>
> **In all criminal prosecutions, the accused shall enjoy the right to a speedy and public trial, . . .**

Speedy Trial The guarantee of a speedy trial is meant to ensure that the government will try a person accused of crime within a reasonable time and without undue delay. But how long a delay is too long? The Supreme Court has recognized that each case must be judged on its own merits.

In a leading case, *Barker* v. *Wingo*, 1972, the Court listed four criteria for determining if a delay has violated the constitutional protection. They are (1) the length of the delay, (2) the reasons for it, (3) whether the delay has in fact harmed the defendant, and (4) whether the defendant had asked for a prompt trial.

The Speedy Trial Act of 1974 says that the time between a person's arrest and the beginning of his or her federal criminal trial cannot be more than 100 days. The law does allow for some exceptions, however—for

example, when the defendant must undergo extensive mental tests, or when the defendant or a key witness is ill.

The 6th Amendment guarantees a prompt trial in *federal* cases. The Supreme Court first applied this right against the States as part of the 14th Amendment's Due Process Clause in *Klopfer* v. *North Carolina*, 1967.

Public Trial The 6th Amendment says that a trial must also be public. The right to be tried in public is also part of the 14th Amendment's guarantee of procedural due process, *In re Oliver*, 1948.

A trial must not be too speedy or too public, however. The Supreme Court threw out an Arkansas murder conviction in 1923 on just those grounds. The trial had taken only 45 minutes, and it had been held in a courtroom packed by a threatening mob.

Within reason, a judge can limit both the number and the kinds of spectators who may be present at a trial. Those who seek to disrupt a courtroom can be barred from it. A judge can order a courtroom cleared when the expected testimony may be embarrassing to a witness or to someone else who is not a party to the case.

Many questions about how public a trial should be involve the media—especially newspapers and television. The guarantees of fair trial and free press often collide in the courts. On the one hand, a courtroom is a public place where the media have a right to be present. On the other hand, media coverage can jeopardize a defendant's right to a fair trial. The Supreme Court has often held that the right to a public trial belongs to the defendant, not to the media.

What about televised trials? Television cameras are barred from all federal courtrooms. Yet most States do allow some form of in-court television reporting. Can televising a criminal trial violate a defendant's rights?

In an early major case, *Estes* v. *Texas*, 1965, the Supreme Court reversed the conviction of an oil man charged with swindling investors and others out of millions of dollars. The Court found that the media coverage of his trial had been so "circus-like" and disruptive that Estes had been denied his right to a fair trial.

---

10 The Organized Crime Control Act of 1970 allows federal prosecutors to appeal sentences they believe to be too lenient. The Supreme Court has held that such appeals do not violate the double jeopardy guarantee, *United States* v. *Di Francesco*, 1980.

Sixteen years later, the Court held in *Chandler* v. *Florida,* 1981, that nothing in the Constitution prevents a State from allowing the televising of a criminal trial. At least, televising is not prohibited as long as steps are taken to avoid too much publicity and to protect the defendant's rights.

Trial by Jury

The 6th Amendment also says that a person accused of a federal crime must be tried "by an impartial jury." This guarantee reinforces an earlier one set out in the Constitution, Article III, Section 2. The right to trial by jury is also binding on the States, but only in cases involving "serious" crimes, *Duncan* v. *Louisiana* (1968).[11] The trial jury is often called the petit jury. *Petit* is the French word for "small."

The 6th Amendment adds that the members of a federal court jury must be drawn from "the State and district wherein the crime shall have been committed, which district shall have been previously ascertained by law." This stipulation gives the defendant any benefit there might be in having a jury familiar with the people and problems of the area.

A defendant may ask to be tried in another place—seek a "change of venue"—on grounds that the people of the locality are so prejudiced in the case that an impartial jury cannot be drawn. The judge must decide whether a change of venue is justified.

A defendant may also <u>waive</u> the right to a jury trial. However, he or she can do so only if the judge is satisfied that the defendant fully understands what that action means. In fact, a judge can order a jury trial even when a defendant does not want one. If a defendant waives the right, a **bench trial** is held, which means that a judge alone hears the case. (Of course, a defendant can plead guilty and so avoid any trial.)

In federal practice, the jury that hears a criminal case must have 12 members. However, some federal civil cases are tried before juries of as few as six members. Several States now provide for smaller juries, often of six members, in both criminal and civil cases.

In the federal courts, the jury that hears a criminal case can convict the accused only by a unanimous vote. Most States follow the same rule.[12]

In a long series of cases, dating from *Strauder* v. *West Virginia,* 1880, the Supreme Court has held that a jury must be "drawn from a fair cross section of the community." A person is denied the right to an impartial jury if he or she is tried by a jury from which members of any groups "playing major roles in the community" have been excluded, *Taylor* v. *Louisiana,* 1975. In short, no person can be kept off a jury on such grounds as race, color, religion, national origin, or gender.

Adequate Defense

Every person accused of a crime has the right to the best possible defense that circumstances will allow. In *Gideon* v. *Wainwright,* 1963, the Court held that an attorney must be furnished to a defendant who cannot afford one. In many places, a judge assigns a lawyer from the local community,

✔ **Checkpoint**
What are the advantages of having a local jury? Of having a change in venue?

waive
v. to give up or forgo

SUPREME COURT
at a glance

▸ **Case:** *Gideon v. Wainwright,* 1963

▸ **Issue:** 6th Amendment right to counsel

▸ **Decision:** Clarence Earl Gideon (below) defended himself at his trial and was found guilty. He wrote to the Supreme Court, saying that he had been unconstitutionally denied counsel. The Court agreed and ordered a new trial, holding that an attorney must be provided to those who cannot afford one.

---

11 In *Baldwin* v. *New York,* 1970, the Court defined serious crimes as those for which imprisonment for more than six months is possible.

12 The 14th Amendment does not say that there cannot be juries of fewer than 12 persons, *Williams* v. *Florida,* 1970, but it does not allow juries of fewer than six members, *Ballew* v. *Georgia,* 1978. Nor does it prevent a State from providing for a conviction on a less than unanimous jury vote, *Apodaca* v. *Oregon,* 1972. But if a jury has only six members, it may convict only by a unanimous vote, *Burch* v. *Louisiana,* 1979.

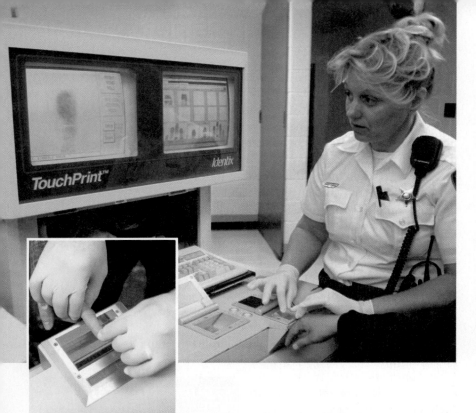

▲ The guarantee against self-incrimination does not prevent the fingerprinting of a suspect. **What does "taking the Fifth" mean?**

subpoena
v. to legally summon, order to appear

or a private legal aid association provides counsel.

The 6th Amendment says that a defendant has the right (1) "to be informed of the nature and cause of the accusation," (2) "to be confronted with the witnesses against him" and question them in open court, (3) "to have compulsory process for obtaining witnesses in his favor" (that is, favorable witnesses can be <u>subpoenaed,</u> and (4) "to have the Assistance of Counsel for his defense."

These key safeguards apply in the federal courts. Still, if a State fails to honor any of them, the accused can appeal a conviction arguing that the 14th Amendment's Due Process Clause has been violated. The Supreme Court protected the right to counsel in *Gideon* v. *Wainwright,* 1963; the right of confrontation in *Pointer* v. *Texas,* 1965; and the right to call witnesses in *Washington* v. *Texas,* 1967.

These guarantees are intended to prevent the cards from being stacked in favor of the prosecution. One of the leading right-to-counsel cases, *Escobedo* v. *Illinois,* 1964, illustrates this point.

Chicago police picked up Danny Escobedo for questioning in the death of his brother-in-law. On the way to the police station, and then while he was being questioned there, he asked several times to see his lawyer. The police denied those requests.

They did so even though his lawyer was in the police station and was trying to see him, and the police knew the lawyer was there. Through a long night of questioning, Escobedo made several damaging statements. Prosecutors later used those statements in court as a major part of the evidence that led to his murder conviction.

The Supreme Court ordered Escobedo freed from prison four years later. It held that he had been improperly denied his 14th Amendment right to counsel.

Self-Incrimination

The guarantee against self-incrimination is among the several protections set out in the 5th Amendment. That provision declares that no person can be "compelled in any criminal case to be a witness against himself." This protection must be honored in both the federal and State courts, *Malloy* v. *Hogan,* 1964.

In a criminal case, the burden of proof is always on the prosecution. The defendant does not have to prove his or her innocence. The ban on self-incrimination prevents the prosecution from shifting the burden of proof to the defendant.

Applying the Guarantee The language of the 5th Amendment suggests that the guarantee against self-incrimination applies only to criminal cases. In fact, it covers any governmental proceeding in which a person is legally compelled to answer any question that could lead to a criminal charge. Thus, a person may claim the right ("take the Fifth") in a variety of situations: in a divorce proceeding (which is a civil matter), before a legislative committee, at a school board's disciplinary hearing, and so on.

The courts, not the individuals who claim it, decide when the right can be properly invoked. If the plea of self-incrimination is pushed too far, a person can be held in contempt of court.

The guarantee against self-incrimination is a personal right.[13] One can claim it only

---

13 With this major exception: A husband cannot be forced to testify against his wife, or a wife against her husband, *Trammel* v. *United States,* 1980. One can testify against the other voluntarily, however.

for oneself. It cannot be invoked in someone else's behalf; a person can be forced to "rat" on another.

The privilege does not protect a person from being fingerprinted or photographed or required to submit a handwriting sample or appear in a police lineup. And, recall, it does not mean that a person does not have to submit to a blood test in a drunk-driving situation, *Schmerber* v. *California,* 1966.

A person cannot, however, be forced to confess to a crime under duress—that is, as a result of torture or other physical or psychological pressure. In *Ashcraft* v. *Tennessee,* 1944, for example, the Supreme Court threw out the conviction of a man accused of hiring another person to murder his wife. The confession on which his conviction rested had been secured only after some 36 hours of continuous, threatening interrogation. The questioning was conducted by officers who worked in shifts because, they said, they became so tired that they had to rest.

Miranda **v.** *Arizona* In a truly historic decision, the Court refined the Escobedo holding in *Miranda* v. *Arizona,* 1966. (See the Landmark Decisions of the Supreme Court feature on the next two pages.) In this case, a mentally challenged man, Ernesto Miranda, had been convicted of kidnapping and rape. Ten days after the crime, the victim picked Miranda out of a police lineup. After two hours of questioning, during which the police did not tell him of his rights, Miranda confessed.

The Supreme Court struck down Miranda's conviction. More importantly, it said that it would no longer uphold convictions in cases in which suspects had not been told of their constitutional rights before police questioning. It thus laid down the **Miranda rule**—the requirement that police must read a suspect his or her rights before any questioning occurs.

The Supreme Court is still refining the rule on a case-by-case basis. Most often the rule is closely followed. But there are exceptions. Thus, the Court has held that an undercover police officer posing as a prisoner does not have to tell a cell mate of his Miranda rights before prompting him to talk about a murder, *Illinois* v. *Perkins,* 1990.

The Miranda rule has always been controversial. Critics say that it "puts criminals back on the streets." Others applaud the rule, arguing that criminal law enforcement is most effective when it relies on independently secured evidence, rather than on confessions gained by questionable tactics from defendants who do not have the help of a lawyer.

✔ **Checkpoint**
What does the Miranda rule require of police officers?

Essential Questions Journal To continue to build a response to the chapter Essential Question, go to your **Essential Questions Journal.**

SECTION **3** ASSESSMENT

1. **Guiding Question** Use your completed graphic organizer to answer this question: What protections does the Constitution set out for persons accused of crimes?

Key Terms and Comprehension

2. **(a)** What does a **writ of habeas corpus** require? **(b)** When has the writ been suspended?

3. What are the three characteristics of an **ex post facto law?**

4. **(a)** Who bears the burden of proof in criminal cases? **(b)** What constitutional guarantee enforces this?

5. What rights to fair trial are guaranteed by the 6th Amendment?

Critical Thinking

6. **Express Problems Clearly (a)** What rights may come into conflict when a trial is televised? **(b)** Should television cameras be allowed in the courtroom? Why or why not?

7. **Identify Arguments** Why has the Miranda rule been both criticized and applauded?

Quick Write

Research Essay: Paraphrasing As you take notes on the case you selected in Section 1, paraphrase the source information by restating it in your own words. If you use the author's words, use quotation marks. You should cite your source even if you do not include direct quotes from them.

What Are the Rights of the Accused?

- You have the right to remain silent.
- Anything you say can and will be used against you in a court of law.
- You have the right to an attorney.
- If you cannot afford an attorney, one will be appointed for you.

These words have been made famous by countless television dramas over the past forty years. They stem from the 5th and 6th amendments: "nor shall [any person] be compelled in any criminal case to be a witness against himself," and "[the accused] shall have the Assistance of Counsel for his defence." Often called the Miranda rights, they must be spoken to suspects before police interrogation.

In 1963, Ernesto Miranda was arrested at his home in Phoenix, Arizona. Accused of kidnapping and rape, he was questioned at the police station by two police officers. After two hours of interrogation, he signed a written confession. That confession was used at his trial, where Miranda was found guilty and sentenced to 20 to 30 years in prison. Miranda's attorney appealed to the Supreme Court of Arizona, claiming that Miranda had not been informed of his right to remain silent or to have an attorney present during the interrogation. The Arizona Court upheld the conviction, however, noting that Miranda had not requested an attorney. The case was then appealed to the United States Supreme Court.

In a 5–4 decision, the Supreme Court overturned Miranda's conviction. Chief Justice Earl Warren wrote the majority opinion, which centered on what happens when a suspect is taken into custody: "Today, then, there can be no doubt that the 5th Amendment privilege is available outside of criminal court proceedings and

The Supreme Court overturned the conviction of Miranda (right). He was retried without his confession but with witnesses and other evidence. Found guilty, he served 11 years.

Justice Harlan, dissenting, wrote: "The social costs of crime are too great to call the new rules anything but a hazardous experimentation."

serves to protect persons in all settings in which their freedom of action is curtailed in any significant way from being compelled to incriminate themselves. We have concluded that without proper safeguards the process of in-custody interrogation of persons suspected or accused of crime contains inherently compelling pressures which work to undermine the individual's will to resist and to compel him to speak where he would not otherwise do so freely. In order to combat these pressures and to permit a full opportunity to exercise the privilege against self-incrimination, the accused must be adequately and effectively apprised of his rights and the exercise of those rights must be fully honored."

Arguments for Miranda

- Miranda was poor and uneducated. He did not know of his 5th Amendment right to remain silent nor his 6th Amendment right to counsel.
- Arizona ignored both the *Escobedo* rule (evidence obtained from an illegally obtained confession is inadmissible in court) and the *Gideon* rule (all felony defendants have the right to an attorney).
- Miranda's confession was illegally obtained and should be thrown out.
- Miranda's conviction was faulty, and he deserves a new trial.

Arguments for Arizona

- Miranda was no stranger to police procedures. He negotiated with police officers with intelligence and understanding.
- Miranda signed his confession of guilt willingly.
- The prosecution was proper, his conviction was based on Arizona law, and his imprisonment was just.
- The Arizona Supreme Court upheld his conviction and the rejection of its decision would cripple the work of police.

Thinking Critically

1. Is it essential that a person be given the right to counsel during police interrogation as well as during trial? Why or why not?
2. **Constitutional Principles** How does this case reflect the principle of limited government?

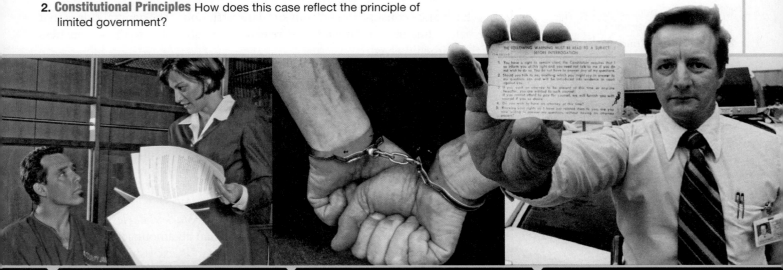

In *Miranda,* the Court said: "With a lawyer present the likelihood that the police will practice coercion is reduced."

The Miranda rights must be read to a suspect as soon as possible after he or she has been restrained.

The Miranda rule has "become part of our national culture," *Dickerson* v. *United States,* 2000.

SECTION 4
Punishment

Guiding Question

How does the Constitution set limits on punishments for crime?
Use a table like the one below to take notes on the section.

Punishment
8th Amendment Limits
•
•

Political Dictionary

- bail
- preventive detention
- capital punishment
- treason

Objectives

1. Explain the purpose of bail and preventive detention.
2. Describe the Court's interpretation of cruel and unusual punishment.
3. Outline the history of the Court's decisions on capital punishment.
4. Define the crime of treason.

Image Above: A lawyer reviews her client's paperwork before a bail hearing.

A gain, think about this proposition: "It is better that ten guilty persons go free than that one innocent person be punished." How do you react to that comment now, after reading about the rights of persons accused of crime? Consider those persons who are found guilty, those who do not go free but are instead punished. How should they be treated? The Constitution gives its most specific answers to that question in the 8th Amendment.

Bail and Preventive Detention

The 8th Amendment says, in part:

FROM THE CONSTITUTION

Excessive bail shall not be required, nor excessive fines imposed, . . .

Each State constitution sets out similar restrictions. The general rule is that the bail or fine in a case must bear a reasonable relationship to the seriousness of the crime involved.

Bail The sum of money that the accused may be required to post (deposit with the court) as a guarantee that he or she will appear in court at the proper time is called **bail**. The use of bail is justified on two bases: First, that a person should not be jailed until his or her guilt has been established; and second, that a defendant is better able to prepare for trial outside of a jail.

Note that the Constitution does not say that all persons accused of a crime are automatically entitled to bail. Rather, it guarantees that, where bail is set, the amount will not be excessive.

The leading case on bail in the federal courts is *Stack* v. *Boyle,* 1951. There, the Court ruled that "bail set at a figure higher than an amount reasonably calculated" to assure a defendant's appearance at a trial "is 'excessive' under the 8th Amendment." In *Stack,* 12 persons had been accused of violating the Smith Act of 1940, which, recall, made it a federal crime for any person to advocate the violent overthrow of government in the United States. (See Chapter 19, Section 3.)

A defendant can appeal the denial of release on bail or the amount of bail. Bail is usually set in accordance with the severity of the crime charged and with the reputation and financial resources of the accused. People with little or no income often have trouble raising bail. Therefore, the federal and most State courts release many defendants "on their own recognizance"—that is, on their honor. Failure to appear for trial, "jumping bail," is itself a punishable crime.

Preventive Detention In 1984, Congress provided for the **preventive detention** of some people accused of federal crimes. A federal judge can order that the accused be held, without bail, when there is good reason to believe that he or she will commit another serious crime before trial.

Critics of the law claim that preventive detention amounts to punishment before trial. They say it undercuts the presumption of innocence to which all defendants are entitled.

The Supreme Court upheld the 1984 law, 6–3, in *United States* v. *Salerno,* 1987. The majority rejected the argument that preventive detention is punishment. Rather, it found the practice a <u>legitimate</u> response to a "pressing societal problem." The Court held that, "There is no doubt that preventing danger to the community is a legitimate regulatory goal." All of the States have adopted preventive detention laws.

Cruel and Unusual Punishment

The 8th Amendment also forbids "cruel and unusual punishment." The 14th Amendment extends that prohibition against the States, *Robinson* v. *California,* 1962.

The Supreme Court decided its first cruel and unusual case in 1879 in *Wilkerson* v. *Utah.* There, a territorial court had sentenced a convicted murderer to death by a firing squad. The Court held that this punishment was not forbidden by the Constitution. The kinds of penalties the Constitution intended to prevent, said the Court, were such barbaric tortures as burning at the stake, crucifixion,

drawing and quartering, "and all others in the same line of unnecessary cruelty." The Court took the same position a few years later when, for the first time, it upheld the electrocution of a convicted murderer in a case from New York, *In re Kemmler,* 1890.

Since then, the Court has heard only a handful of cruel and unusual cases, except for those relating to capital punishment. More often than not, it has rejected the cruel and unusual punishment argument.[14] *Louisiana* v. *Resweber,* 1947, is fairly typical. There, the Court found that it was not unconstitutional to subject a convicted murderer to a second electrocution after the chair had failed to work properly on the first occasion. And in *Rhodes* v. *Chapman,* 1980, it held that putting two inmates in a cell that had been designed to hold only one did not violate the constitutional command.

The Court also denied the cruel and unusual claim in its most recent 8th Amendment case not involving the death penalty,

---

[14] The prohibition of cruel and unusual punishments is limited to criminal matters. It does not forbid paddling or similar punishments in the public schools, *Ingraham* v. *Wright,* 1977.

legitimate
adj. valid, sound, lawful

"OVERCROWDED—I'll say it's OVERCROWDED!"

▶▶ **Analyzing Political Cartoons** The 8th Amendment forbids cruel and unusual punishment. ***What point is the cartoonist making here?***

✔ **Checkpoint**

What was the significance of the Court's ruling in *Furman* v. *Georgia*?

capriciously
adv. unpredictably; erratically, without reason

Lockyer v. *Andrade,* 2003. That case centered on California's "three strikes" law. That statute provides that any person convicted of a third crime must be sentenced to at least 25 years in prison. Leandro Andrade had received 50 years for stealing $153.54 worth of children's videos from two K-Mart stores. The K-Mart thefts were treated as separate offenses and he had an earlier burglary conviction on his record, as well.

The Court has held some punishments to be cruel and unusual, but only a very few. It did so for the first time in *Weems* v. *United States* in 1910. There, the Court overturned the conviction of a Coast Guard official who had been found guilty of falsifying government pay records. He had been sentenced to 15 years at hard labor, constantly chained at wrist and ankle. In *Robinson* v. *California,* 1962, the Court ruled that a State law that defined narcotics addiction as a crime to be punished, rather than an illness to be treated, violated the 8th and 14th amendments.[15]

Capital Punishment

Laws providing for **capital punishment**—the death penalty—date back to at least the 18th century B.C. and the Code of Hammurabi, which set death as the penalty for more than 25 different offenses.[16] The punishment has been a part of American law since the colonial period, and both the Federal Government and 35 States provide for it today.

Over time, the Supreme Court was reluctant to face this highly charged question: Is capital punishment cruel and unusual and therefore prohibited by the 8th Amendment?

State Laws Struck Down The Court did meet the issue, finally, and more or less directly, in *Furman* v. *Georgia,* 1972. There, it struck down all of the then-existing State laws providing for the death penalty—but not because that punishment is cruel and unusual.

Rather, the Court voided those laws because they gave too much discretion to judges or juries in deciding whether to impose the ultimate penalty. The Court found that of all the people convicted of capital crimes, only "a random few," most of them African American or poor, or both, were "capriciously selected" for execution.

Immediately, most States and Congress began to write new capital punishment laws. Those new statutes took one of two forms. Several States made a death sentence mandatory for certain crimes—for example, the killing of a police officer or a murder committed during a rape, kidnapping, or arson. Others provided, instead, for a two-stage process in capital cases: first, a trial to settle the question of guilt or innocence; then, for those convicted, a second proceeding to decide if the circumstances involved in the crime justify a sentence of death.

In considering scores of challenges to these new laws, the Supreme Court found mandatory death penalty statutes unconstitutional. In *Woodson* v. *North Carolina,* 1976, it ruled that those statutes were "unduly harsh and rigidly unworkable." They were, said the Court, simply attempts to "paper over" the decision in *Furman.*

Two-Stage Approach Upheld The two-stage approach was found to be constitutional in *Gregg* v. *Georgia,* 1976. There, the Court held for the first time that the "punishment of death does not invariably violate the Constitution." It declared that well-drawn two-stage laws could practically eliminate "the risk that it [the death penalty] would be inflicted in an arbitrary or capricious manner."

Later Cases Opponents of the death penalty continue to appeal capital cases to the Supreme Court, but to no real avail. Most of their cases have centered on the application, not the constitutionality, of the punishment. The more important of those several cases have resulted in these rulings: The death penalty can be imposed only for "crimes resulting in the death of the victim," *Coker* v. *Georgia,* 1977. That penalty cannot be imposed on those who are mentally challenged, *Atkins* v. *Virginia,* 2002, or on those who were

---

15 But, notice, that does not mean that buying, selling, or possessing narcotics cannot be made a crime. Laws that criminalize such conduct are designed to punish persons for their behavior, not for being ill.

16 The phrase "capital punishment" comes from the Latin *caput,* meaning "head"; in many cultures, the historically preferred method for execution was beheading (decapitation).

Capital Punishment Debate

Capital punishment has a lengthy history, and so does the controversy surrounding it. The punishment has been a part of American law since the colonial period, and 35 States provide for it today. More than 1,100 persons have been executed in this country since the Supreme Court reinstated capital punishment in 1976. Fewer than three in every 100 death sentences imposed are ever carried out, however. Thirty-seven persons were executed in nine States in 2008. Some 3,300 persons sit on death row in American prisons today. *Do you think the maximum penalty for murder should be death or, instead, life without the possibility of parole? Explain.*

47%
prefer **death penalty**

Public Opinion

48%
prefer **life without parole**

SOURCE: Gallup poll, 2006

> Although some of the studies suggest that the death penalty may not function as a significantly greater deterrent than lesser penalties, there is no convincing empirical evidence either supporting or refuting this view. We may nevertheless assume safely that there are murderers, such as those who act in passion, for whom the threat of death has little or no deterrent effect. But for many others, the death penalty undoubtedly is a significant deterrent.
>
> —*Justice Potter Stewart,* Gregg v. Georgia, *1976*

> One area of law more than any other besmirches the constitutional vision of human dignity. . . . The barbaric death penalty violates our Constitution. Even the most vile murderer does not release the state from its obligation to respect dignity, for the state does not honor the victim by emulating his murderer. Capital punishment's fatal flaw is that it treats people as objects to be toyed with and discarded. . . . One day the Court will outlaw the death penalty. Permanently.
>
> —*William J. Brennan, former U.S. Supreme Court Justice, 1996*

under the age of 18 when their crimes were committed, *Roper* v. *Simmons, 2005.*

The question of whether the ultimate penalty is to be imposed must be decided by the jury that convicted the defendant, not the judge who presided at the trial, *Ring* v. *Arizona, 2002.*

And, most recently, these holdings: A delusional person who cannot understand why he has been sentenced to death cannot be executed, *Panetti* v. *Quarterman, 2007.* Execution by lethal injection, the method most widely used today, does not violate the 8th Amendment, *Baze* v. *Rees, 2008.* The sum of the Court's many decisions over the past thirty years or so comes down to

this: The death penalty, fairly applied, is constitutional.

Continuing Controversy Even so, capital punishment remains controversial. Public opinion polls do show that there is support for it. However, many of those supporters express misgivings about the fairness with which it is applied.

Clearly, the application of the death penalty must be closely monitored to protect the innocent and prevent wrongful convictions. The Death Penalty Information Center reports that over the past 30 years, some 125 persons who had been sentenced to death have been <u>exonerated</u> and released from prison.

exonerate
v. to declare innocent, absolve, free of blame

As retired Supreme Court Justice Sandra Day O'Connor has observed: "If statistics are any indication, the system may well be allowing some innocent defendants to be executed."

That fact has also prompted many who support capital punishment to insist that the remedies for whatever problems there may be in the administration of the penalty should not be found in its abolition. They should be found, instead, in the continuing improvement of the processes by which the ultimate penalty is imposed.

Treason

Treason against the United States is the only crime defined in the Constitution. The Framers provided a specific definition of the crime because they knew that the charge of treason has long been a favorite weapon in the hands of tyrants.

Treason, says Article III, Section 3, can consist of only two things: either (1) levying war against the United States or (2) "adhering to their Enemies, giving them Aid and Comfort." And the Constitution adds that no person can be convicted of the crime of treason "unless on the Testimony of two Witnesses to the same overt Act, or on Confession in open Court."

The law of treason covers all citizens of the United States, at home or abroad, and all permanent resident aliens. Congress has set death as the maximum sentence for someone convicted of the federal crime but no person has ever, in fact, been executed for that offense. Indeed, the death penalty was not imposed in a federal treason case until as recently as 1942. Then, four German-born American citizens were sentenced to be hanged for aiding a group of Nazi saboteurs who had been landed on the East Coast by a German submarine. But those sentences were never carried out.[17]

Treason can only be committed in wartime. But Congress has made it a crime, during times of either peace or war, to commit either espionage or sabotage, to attempt to overthrow the government by force, or to conspire to do any of these things.

Most State constitutions also condemn treason. The fabled abolitionist John Brown was hanged as a traitor by Virginia after his raid on Harpers Ferry in 1859. He is believed to be the only person ever executed for treason against a State.

---

[17] The sentence of one of the traitors was commuted to life in prison; he was later denaturalized and then deported. The other three appealed their convictions and won new trials. One of them was again convicted of treason but this time sentenced to life in prison; the other two pleaded guilty to lesser charges and received five-year prison terms.

> **Essential Questions Journal** To continue to build a response to the chapter Essential Question, go to your **Essential Questions Journal.**

SECTION 4 ASSESSMENT

1. **Guiding Question** Use your completed graphic organizer to answer this question: How does the Constitution set limits on punishments for crime?

Key Terms and Comprehension

2. **(a)** Define **bail. (b)** What is its purpose? **(c)** When is the use of bail justified?

3. What penalties has the Supreme Court considered cruel and unusual?

4. **(a)** When did the Supreme Court first hear a **capital punishment** case? What was the ruling in that case? **(b)** What is the two-stage process?

5. **(a)** Define **treason. (b)** Why does the Constitution contain a specific definition of treason?

Critical Thinking

6. **Identify Point of View** Why do some oppose preventive detention? **(b)** Why has the Supreme Court upheld it? **(c)** With which point of view do you agree? Why?

7. **Demonstrate Reasoned Judgment (a)** In capital cases, who cannot be sentenced to death? **(b)** Do you agree with the Court's ruling that mandatory death sentences are unconstitutional? Why or why not?

Quick Write

Research Essay: Opening Statement Write an opening statement, or hook, for an essay on the case you selected in Section 1. A hook should grab readers' interest. Various types of hooks motivate further reading. These include (1) a statement that hints at what is to come; (2) a fascinating description of an exciting event or action; or (3) a question that will be answered later in the essay. Your hook should connect smoothly to the introduction and the body of your essay.

Quick Study Guide

GOVERNMENT ONLINE

On the Go
To review anytime, anywhere, download these online resources at **PearsonSuccessNet.com**
Political Dictionary, Audio Review

CHAPTER **20**

Guiding Question
Section 2 How does the Constitution protect the freedom and security of the person?

Guiding Question
Section 3 What protections does the Constitution set out for persons accused of crimes?

Guiding Question
Section 1 Why is the concept of due process important to a free society?

CHAPTER 20

Essential Question
To what extent has the judiciary protected the rights of privacy, security, and personal freedom?

Guiding Question
Section 4 How does the Constitution set limits on punishments for crime?

Political Dictionary

due process p. 578
procedural due process p. 578
substantive due process p. 578
police power p. 580
search warrant p. 581
involuntary servitude p. 583
discrimination p. 584
writs of assistance p. 585
probable cause p. 586
exclusionary rule p. 588
writ of habeas corpus p. 592
bill of attainder p. 593
ex post facto law p. 593
grand jury p. 594
indictment p. 594
presentment p. 594
information p. 595
double jeopardy p. 595
bench trial p. 597
Miranda Rule p. 599
bail p. 602
preventive detention p. 603
capital punishment p. 604
treason p. 606

Protections of Freedom and Security

13th Amendment:
"Neither slavery nor involuntary servitude, . . . shall exist within the United States, or any place subject to their jurisdiction."

2nd Amendment:
"A well regulated Militia, being necessary to the security of a free State, the right of the people to keep and bear Arms, shall not be infringed."

4th Amendment:
"The right of the people to be secure in their persons, houses, papers, and effects, against unreasonable searches and seizures, shall not be violated, and no Warrants shall issue, but upon probable cause, supported by Oath or affirmation, and particularly describing the place to be searched, and the persons or things to be seized."

14th Amendment's Due Process Clause:
"No State shall . . . deprive any person of life, liberty, or property, without due process of law . . . "

Limits on Punishment

8th Amendment

"Excessive bail shall not be required, nor excessive fines imposed. . . ."

Forbids "cruel and unusual punishment"

Chapter Assessment

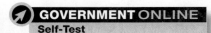 **GOVERNMENT** ONLINE
Self-Test
To test your understanding of key terms and main ideas, visit **PearsonSuccessNet.com**

Comprehension and Critical Thinking

Section 1

1. **(a)** Why are there two due process clauses in the Constitution? **(b)** In *Rochin* v. *California,* what particular actions by the deputies constituted violations of due process?

2. **(a)** Which level of government has the police power in the federal system? **(b)** Provide at least four examples of the ways in which exercises of the police power affect you.

3. **(a)** In what area has the right to privacy been most controversial? **(b)** Should the right to privacy be applied to the Census Bureau, credit card companies, and Internet sites as they collect personal information? Why or why not?

Section 2

4. **Analyze Political Cartoons (a)** Which amendment is involved in the events described in this cartoon? **(b)** What is the basic rule laid down by that amendment?

"Yes, the search was totally by-the-book. I recall covering my eyes and counting to 100 before I began looking."

5. **(a)** How did the Court apply the 13th Amendment in the late 1800s? **(b)** How did its ruling in *Jones* v. *Mayer,* 1968 revise the meaning of the 13th Amendment?

6. **(a)** Can police search a vehicle during a routine traffic stop? **(b)** Can they search both the driver and passengers? **(c)** Cite two cases to support your answers.

7. What arguments can be made for and against the exclusionary rule?

Section 3

8. **(a)** What is a bill of attainder? **(b)** How does the ban on bills of attainder protect individual freedoms?

9. **(a)** Describe five characteristics of a grand jury and four characteristics of a petit jury. **(b)** On which type of jury would you prefer to serve? Why?

10. **(a)** What is the Miranda rule? **(b)** From which two amendments is the rule drawn?

Section 4

11. **(a)** What are the constitutional guarantees regarding bail? **(b)** How is the amount of bail set? **(c)** What happens if a defendant cannot raise bail?

12. **(a)** What was the significance of *Furman* v. *Georgia?* **(b)** How does the Supreme Court view capital punishment today?

Writing About Government

13. Use your Quick Write exercises from each Section Assessment to write a research essay about the case you selected in Section 1. Use an informative writing style that describes what happened, when and where it happened, why it happened, and who was involved. Present the facts in an objective way without displaying emotion or injecting your opinion in the essay. See pp. S6–S8 in the Skills Handbook.

Apply What You've Learned

14. **Essential Question Activity** Scan the newspaper for articles concerning any guarantees of the rights of the accused shown in the illustration in Section 3 of this chapter. Prepare a brief report describing the article and the right(s) in question. Indicate how you think the issue or case should be resolved and why.

15. **Essential Question Assessment** Based on the brief report you wrote and the content of this chapter, create a poster that helps to answer the Essential Question: **To what extent has the judiciary protected the rights of privacy, security, and personal**

freedom? Your poster should list the rights of privacy, security, and/or personal freedom related to your everyday life—that is, in your home, automobile, on your computer and/or phone. On a separate piece of paper, write a paragraph that outlines the extent to which each of these freedoms is protected.

Essential Questions Journal To respond to the chapter Essential Question, go to your **Essential Questions Journal.**

Document-Based Assessment

The Patriot Act

The Patriot Act was enacted "to deter and punish terrorist acts in the United States and around the world, to enhance law enforcement investigatory tools, and for other purposes." Debate centers around whether it provides a balance between national security and the Constitution's guarantees of individual freedom, as shown in the documents below.

Document 1

The law allows our intelligence and law enforcement officials to continue to share information. It allows them to continue to use tools against terrorists that they . . . use against drug dealers and other criminals. It will improve our nation's security while we safeguard the civil liberties of our people. The legislation strengthens the Justice Department so it can better detect and disrupt terrorist threats.

—President George W. Bush, March 2006

Document 2

Just 45 days after the September 11 attacks, with virtually no debate, Congress passed the USA PATRIOT Act. There are significant flaws in the Patriot Act, flaws that threaten your fundamental freedoms by giving the government the power to access your medical records, tax records, information about the books you buy or borrow without probable cause, and the power to break into your home and conduct secret searches without telling you for weeks, months, or indefinitely.

—American Civil Liberties Union, 2003

Document 3

Delayed notification search warrants are a long-existing, crime-fighting tool upheld by courts nationwide for decades in organized crime, drug cases and child pornography. The Patriot Act simply codified the authority law enforcement had already had for decades. This tool is a vital aspect of our strategy of prevention-detecting and incapacitating terrorists before they are able to strike.

—U.S. Department of Justice, 2003

Document 4

'I need to get a bigger bat.'

Use your knowledge of the Patriot Act and Documents 1–4 to answer the following questions.

1. Document 1 implies that the overriding goal of the Patriot Act is to
   A. strengthen the Justice Department.
   B. allow law enforcement and intelligence officials to share information.
   C. safeguard civil liberties.
   D. improve the nation's security.

2. According to Document 2, what does the Patriot Act give government the power to do?

3. How does Document 3 justify the use of delayed notification search warrants?

4. What is the cartoonist saying about the Patriot Act in Document 4?

5. **Pull It Together** How do these documents illustrate the difficulty of striking a proper balance between national security and individual rights?

GOVERNMENT ONLINE
Documents
To find additional primary sources on the Patriot Act, visit
PearsonSuccessNet.com

Civil Rights: Equal Justice Under Law

Essential Question
Why are there ongoing struggles for civil rights?

Section 1:
Diversity and Discrimination

Section 2:
Equality Before the Law

Section 3:
Federal Civil Rights Laws

Section 4:
American Citizenship

" Our **Constitution** is **color-blind,** and neither knows nor tolerates classes among citizens. In respect of civil rights, all citizens are **equal before the law.** The **humblest** is the peer of the most **powerful.**

—Justice John Marshall Harlan, dissenting in *Plessy* v. *Ferguson*, 1896

Photo: March on Washington, August 28, 1963

GOVERNMENT ONLINE
On the Go

To study anywhere, anytime, download these online resources at PearsonSuccessNet.com
• Political Dictionary
• Audio Review
• Downloadable Interactivities

SECTION 1

Diversity and Discrimination

Guiding Question

How have various minority groups in American society been discriminated against? Use a table like the one below to take notes on the section.

African Americans	Native Americans	Hispanic Americans	Asian Americans
•	•	•	•
•	•	•	•
•	•	•	•

Political Dictionary

- heterogeneous
- immigrant
- reservation
- refugee
- assimilation

Objectives

1. Understand what it means to live in a heterogeneous society.
2. Summarize the history of race-based discrimination in the United States.
3. Examine discrimination against women in the past and present.

Image Above: The United States takes pride in its diversity.

Have you read George Orwell's classic, *Animal Farm?* Even if you have not, you may have heard its most oft-quoted line: "All animals are created equal, but some animals are more equal than others." You might keep Orwell's comment in mind as you read this chapter.

A Heterogeneous Society

The term **heterogeneous** is a compound of two Greek words: *hetero,* meaning "other or different," and *genos,* meaning "race, family, or kind." Something that is heterogeneous is composed of dissimilar parts, made up of elements that are unrelated to or unlike one another—in short, something composed of a mix of ingredients. "We the People of the United States" are a heterogeneous lot, and we are becoming more so, year to year.

The population of the United States is predominantly white. It is today and, as you can see in the circle graph on page 614, it has been historically. The first census in 1790 reported that there were 3,929,214 people living in this country. More than four out of five were white. African Americans made up the remaining 19 percent of the population counted in that census. As the nation's population grew over the decades, so, too, did the proportion of the American people who were white—until recently.

Today, the ethnic composition of the population is strikingly different from what it was only a generation ago. **Immigrants**—those aliens legally admitted as permanent residents—have arrived in near-record numbers every year since the mid-1960s. Over that period, the nation's African American, Hispanic American, and Asian American populations have grown at rates several times that of the white population. Indeed, the minority population now exceeds the white population in four States: California, Hawaii, New Mexico, and Texas.

A look at gender balance in the population reveals that females are more numerous than males. This has been the case for more than half a century.

As a result of these changes in the American population, the United States is more heterogeneous today than ever before. That fact is certain to have a profound effect on the American social, political, and economic landscape on through the twenty-first century.

Race-Based Discrimination

White Americans have been historically reluctant to yield to nonwhite Americans a full and equal place in the social, economic, and political life of this nation. Over time, the principal targets of that ethnic prejudice have been African Americans, Native Americans, Asian Americans, and Hispanic Americans. The white-male-dominated power structure has also been slow to recognize the claims of women to an equal place in American society.

African Americans Much of what you will read in these pages focuses on discrimination against African Americans. There are three principal reasons for this focus. First, African Americans have been the victims of consistent and deliberate unjust treatment for a longer time than any other minority group of Americans.[1] The ancestors of most African Americans came to this country in chains. Over a period of some two hundred years, tens of thousands of Africans were kidnapped, crammed aboard sailing ships, brought to America, and then sold in slave markets. As slaves, they were the legal property of other human beings. They could be bought and sold and forced to do their owners' bidding, however harsh the circumstances.

It took a civil war to end more than two centuries of slavery in this country. The 13th Amendment finally abolished slavery in 1865. Still, the Civil War and the ratification of that amendment did not end widespread racial discrimination in the United States.

Second, African Americans constitute a huge minority group in the United States. They number well over 40 million today, over 13 percent of all of the American people.

Finally, most of the gains the nation has made in translating the Constitution's guarantees of equality into a reality for all persons have come out of efforts made by and on behalf of African Americans. Recall that, for example, the struggles of Martin Luther King, Jr., and others resulted in the Civil Rights Act of 1964 and then the Voting Rights Act of 1965. See Chapter 6, Section 3.

America is now an inescapably multiracial society. Still, unlike whites, African Americans live with the consequences of America's history of racial discrimination every day of their lives. Of course, this is not to say that other groups of Americans have not also suffered the effects of discrimination. Clearly, many have.

Native Americans White settlers first began to arrive in America in relatively large numbers in the mid-1600s. At the time, some one million Native Americans were living in territory that was to become the United States.[2] By 1900, however, their number had fallen to less than 250,000.

Diseases brought by white settlers decimated those first Americans. So, too, did the succession of military campaigns that accompanied the westward expansion of the United States. To quote one leading commentator:

"'The only good Indian is a dead Indian' is not simply a hackneyed expression from cowboy movies. It was part of the strategy of westward expansion, as settlers and U.S. troops mercilessly drove the eastern Indians from their ancestral lands to the Great Plains and then took those lands too."

—Thomas E. Patterson,
The American Democracy

Today, about 3 million Native Americans live in this country. More than a third of them live on or near **reservations,** which are public lands set aside by government for use by Native American tribes.

2 An estimated 8 to 10 million Native Americans lived in all of North and South America in the mid-1600s.

1 Slavery first came to what was to become the United States in 1619; in August of that year, 20 Africans were sold to white settlers at Jamestown in colonial Virginia.

✔ **Checkpoint**
What was the impact of the 13th Amendment on racial discrimination?

Native Americans comprise a large number of ethnic groups and distinct tribes, representing a diversity of nations and lifestyles. ▼

Diversity in the United States

The Census Bureau divides the American population into groups, measuring race and Hispanic origin separately. The separate categories acknowledge the fact that persons of Hispanic origin may be of any race.

Population by Race and Hispanic Origin

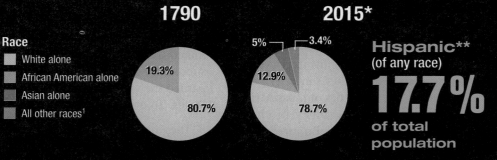

1790

2015*

Race
- White alone
- African American alone
- Asian alone
- All other races[1]

1790: 19.3%, 80.7%

2015*: 5%, 3.4%, 12.9%, 78.7%

Hispanic*
(of any race)

17.7%
of total population

Like African Americans, Native Americans have been the victims of overwhelming discrimination. The consequences of that bias have been appalling, and they remain evident today. Poverty, joblessness, and alcoholism plague many reservations. The Indian Education Act of 1972 attempted to remedy the cycle of continual poverty by providing financial assistance to local educational agencies for Native American children and adult programs. Still, the life expectancy of Native Americans living on reservations today is ten years less than the national average, and the Native American infant mortality rate is one and a half times that of white Americans.

Hispanic Americans Hispanic Americans are those in this country who have a Spanish-speaking background; many prefer to be called *Latinos*. Hispanics may be of any race. According to the Bilateral Commission on the Future of United States–Mexican Relations, Hispanic Americans "are among the world's most complex groupings of human beings. [The largest number] are white, millions . . . are mestizo,

nearly half a million in the United States are black or mulatto."[3]

Today, the number of Hispanic Americans approaches 50 million and they constitute the largest minority group in this country, having surpassed African Americans sometime around the year 2000. They are also the nation's fastest-growing population group. Hispanic Americans can generally be divided into four main subgroups:

1. *Mexican Americans* More than half of all Hispanics in the U.S., at least 29 million persons, were either born in Mexico or trace their ancestry there. Those born in this country of Mexican parents are often called *Chicanos*.

Most of the Mexican American population lives in the States of California, Arizona, New Mexico, and Texas, but that population is spreading throughout much of the country. A majority of the residents of such large cities as El Paso and San Antonio in Texas are

---

3 A *mestizo* is a person of both Spanish or Portuguese and Native American ancestry. A *mulatto* is a person of African and white ancestry.

Population Increase, 2010–2020*

Although the population of the United States remains predominantly white, minority populations are growing at a faster rate than the majority population. *What is the rate of growth for Asian Americans? What are the benefits of diversity in a community?*

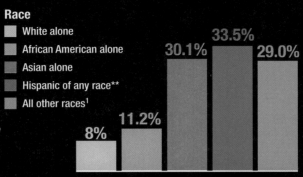

Race
- White alone
- African American alone
- Asian alone
- Hispanic of any race**
- All other races[1]

8%   11.2%   30.1%   33.5%   29.0%

Hispanic (of any race)

33.5% population increase

*Projected; **The Census Bureau added the classification of "Hispanic of any race" to better reflect the growing diversity of the nation's population.
[1]Includes American Indian and Alaska Native alone, Native Hawaiian and Other Pacific Islander alone, and Two or More Races. SOURCE: Census Bureau

Hispanic today, and such smaller border cities as Laredo and Brownsville in Texas are now over 90 percent Latino.

2. *Puerto Ricans* Another large group of Hispanics has come to the mainland from the island of Puerto Rico. The population of the United States now includes about four million Puerto Ricans. Most of them have settled in New York and New Jersey, and in other parts of the Northeast.

3. *Cuban Americans* The Hispanic population also includes some 1.5 million Cuban Americans. They are mostly people who fled the Castro dictatorship in Cuba, and their descendants. A majority of them have settled in Miami and elsewhere in South Florida.

4. *Central and South Americans* The fourth major subgroup of Hispanic Americans came here from Central and South America, many as refugees. A **refugee** is one who seeks protection (refuge) from war, persecution, or some other danger. More than three million persons have emigrated to the United States from Central and South American countries

over the past 30 years or so; they have arrived in the largest numbers from Nicaragua, El Salvador, Guatemala, Colombia, and Chile. Many have also come from the Dominican Republic, an island nation in the Caribbean.

Asian Americans The story of white America's mistreatment of Asians is a lengthy one, too. Asians have faced discrimination from the first day they arrived. As with all immigrant groups, assimilation into the white-dominated population has been difficult. **Assimilation** is the process by which people of one culture merge into and become part of another.

Chinese laborers were the first Asians to come to the United States in large numbers. They were brought here in the 1850s to 1860s as contract laborers to work in the mines and to build railroads in the West. Many white Americans, both native-born and immigrants, resented the competition of what they called "coolie labor." Their resentments were frequently expressed in acts of violence toward Asians.

Congress brought Chinese immigration to a near halt with the Chinese Exclusion

✔**Checkpoint**
What is a refugee?

Gender Discrimination

Disparity in Pay

Studies show that women earn less than 80 cents for every dollar earned by men. *What do the cartoon and graph say about equality in the workplace?*

'Another day, another eighty cents.'

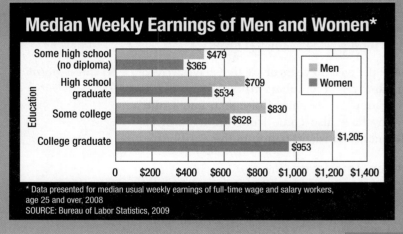

Median Weekly Earnings of Men and Women*

* Data presented for median usual weekly earnings of full-time wage and salary workers, age 25 and over, 2008
SOURCE: Bureau of Labor Statistics, 2009

virulent
adj. bitterly antagonistic, spiteful

Act of 1882. Because of this and other governmental actions, only a very small number of Chinese, Japanese, and other Asians were permitted to enter the United States for more than 80 years.

Early in World War II, the Federal Government ordered the evacuation of all persons of Japanese descent from the Pacific Coast. Some 120,000 people, two thirds of them native-born American citizens, were forcibly removed to inland "war relocation camps." Years later, the government conceded that this action had been both unnecessary and unjust.

Congress made dramatic changes in American immigration policies in 1965. Since then, some ten million Asian immigrants have come to this country, mostly from the Philippines, China, Korea, Vietnam, and India. The term "Asian American" encompasses an ever more diverse population. Asian Americans represent a tremendous variety of languages, religions, and cultures, and many recent immigrants from Asia have little in common with one another.

Today, the Asian American population exceeds 15 million. Asian Americans now live in every part of the United States. They constitute some 40 percent of the population in Hawaii and more than 10 percent of the population in California. New York City boasts the largest Chinese community outside Asia.

Discrimination Against Women

Unlike the several ethnic groups described thus far, women are not a minority in the United States. They are, in fact, a majority group. Still, traditionally in American law and public policy, women have not enjoyed the same rights as men. Their status was even lower, in many instances, than men who were themselves the target of <u>virulent</u> discrimination. Women have been treated as less than equal in a great many matters—including, for example, property rights, education, and employment opportunities.

Organized efforts to improve the place of women in American society date from July 19, 1848. On that day, a convention on women's rights met in Seneca Falls, New York, and adopted a set of resolutions that deliberately echoed the words of the Declaration of Independence. It began:

PRIMARY SOURCE

When, in the course of human events, it becomes necessary for one portion of the family of man to assume among the people of the earth a position different from that which they have hitherto occupied, . . . We hold these truths to be self-evident: that all men and women are created equal . . .

—**Declaration of Sentiments, 1848**

Those who fought and finally won the long struggle for women's suffrage believed that, with the vote, women would soon achieve other basic rights. That assumption proved to be false. Although more than 51 percent of the population is now female, women have held only a minor fraction of the nation's top public offices since 1789.

Even today, women hold less than 20 percent of the 535 seats in Congress and a little less than 25 percent of the 7,382 seats in the 50 State legislatures. Only six of the 50 State governors today are female. Women are also hugely underrepresented at the upper levels of corporate management and other power groups in the private sector. Fewer than 20 percent of the nation's doctors, lawyers, and college professors are women.

It is illegal to pay women less than men for the same work. The Equal Pay Act of 1963 requires employers to pay men and women the same wages if they perform the same jobs in the same establishment under the same working conditions. The Civil Rights Act of 1964 also prohibits job discrimination based on sex. Yet, more than 45 years after Congress passed those laws, working women earn, on the average, less than 80 cents for every dollar earned by working men. See the cartoon and graph on page 616.

Women earn less than men for a number of reasons—including the fact that the male workforce is, overall, better educated and has more job experience than the female workforce. (Note that these factors themselves can often be traced to discrimination.) In addition, some blame the so-called "Mommy track," in which women put their careers on hold to have children or work reduced hours to juggle child-care responsibilities. Others claim that a "glass ceiling" of discrimination in the corporate world and elsewhere, invisible but impenetrable, prevents women from rising to their full potential.

Certainly it is true that until quite recently women were limited to a fairly narrow range of jobs. In many cases, women were encouraged not to work outside the home once they were married. Even now, many jobs held by women are in low-paying clerical and service occupations. The Bureau of Labor Statistics reports that 97 percent of all secretaries today are women; so too are 95 percent of all child-care workers, 92 percent of all registered nurses, 92 percent of all bookkeepers and auditing clerks, 92 percent of all hairdressers and cosmetologists, and 89 percent of all dieticians and nutritionists.

Efforts on behalf of equal rights for women have gained significant ground in recent years. But, recall, that significant ground has not included an Equal Rights Amendment to the Constitution.

✔ **Checkpoint**
What was the significance of the Declaration of Sentiments?

Essential Questions Journal To continue to build a response to the chapter Essential Question, go to your **Essential Questions Journal.**

SECTION 1 ASSESSMENT

1. **Guiding Question** Use your completed graphic organizer to answer this question: How have various minority groups in American society been discriminated against?

Key Terms and Comprehension

2. Who are **immigrants**?

3. What event and which amendment outlawed slavery in this country?

4. How are **refugees** similar to and different from other **immigrants**?

5. **(a)** Identify and describe two laws intended to improve women's wages. **(b)** Summarize three reasons why women still earn less than men.

Critical Thinking

6. **Predict Consequences (a)** What is assimilation? **(b)** What could be the consequences of assimilation on a minority group?

7. **Express Problems Clearly (a)** What problems have Native Americans faced? **(b)** Does the Federal Government have a responsibility to remedy that situation? Why or why not?

Quick Write

Problem-Solution Essay: Identify a Problem Scan the chapter for a challenge that immigrants, minority Americans, or women face. Write a summary paragraph or two that includes a statement of the problem or challenge and an explanation of why and for whom it is a problem. Look at society as a whole as you consider the matter.

SECTION 2

Equality Before the Law

Guiding Question

How has the interpretation of the guarantee of equal rights changed over time? Use a flowchart like the one below to take notes on the section.

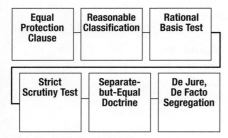

Equal Protection Clause	Reasonable Classification	Rational Basis Test
Strict Scrutiny Test	Separate-but-Equal Doctrine	De Jure, De Facto Segregation

Political Dictionary

- rational basis test
- strict scrutiny test
- segregation
- Jim Crow
- separate-but-equal doctrine
- integration
- de jure
- de facto

Objectives

1. Explain the importance of the Equal Protection Clause.
2. Describe the history of segregation in America.
3. Examine how classification by gender relates to discrimination.

Image Above: The statue *Freedom*, atop the nation's Capitol

The huge bronze statue of *Freedom* has stood atop the nation's Capitol in Washington, D.C., for about 150 years now. That bold figure is meant to symbolize the basic ideas upon which the United States exists—the concepts of individual liberty, of self-government, and of equal rights for all.

The irony is that records recently unearthed by the Architect of the Capitol show that at least 400 slaves worked on the construction of the Capitol from 1792 to its opening in 1800. And that those slaves cast the huge sculpture of *Freedom,* and even hoisted it atop the new building. Those old documents also record payments to several local slave owners—for example, "To Joseph Forest, for the hire of the Negro Charles." The owners were paid $5 a month for each slave who worked on the project.

Equal Protection Clause

The equality of all persons, proclaimed so boldly in the Declaration of Independence, is not set out in so many words in the Constitution. Still, that concept pervades the document.

The closest approach to a literal statement of equality is found in the 14th Amendment's Equal Protection Clause. It declares that "No State shall . . . deny to any person within its jurisdiction the equal protection of the laws."

Those words, added to the Constitution in 1868, were originally meant to benefit newly freed slaves. Over time, they have come to mean that the States (and their local governments) cannot draw unreasonable distinctions between any classes of persons. The Supreme Court has often held that the 5th Amendment's Due Process Clause puts the same restriction on the Federal Government.

Reasonable Classification Government must have the power to classify, to draw distinctions between persons and groups. Otherwise, it could not possibly regulate human behavior. That is to say, government must be able to *discriminate*—and it does. For example, those who rob banks fall into a special class, and they receive special treatment by government. Clearly, that sort of discrimination is reasonable.

Government may not discriminate *unreasonably,* however. Every State taxes the sale of cigarettes, and so taxes smokers but not non-smokers. No State can tax only blonde smokers, however, or only male smokers.

Over time, the Supreme Court has rejected many equal protection challenges to a wide variety of actions by government. More often than not, however, the Supreme Court has found that what those governments have done is, in fact, constitutional.

The Rational Basis Test The Supreme Court most often decides equal protection cases by applying a standard known as the **rational basis test.** This test asks: Does the classification in question bear a reasonable relationship to the achievement of some proper governmental purpose?

A California case, *Michael M.* v. *Superior Court,* 1981, illustrates that test. California law says that a man who has sexual relations with a girl under 18 to whom he is not married can be prosecuted for statutory rape. However, the girl cannot be charged with that crime, even if she is a willing partner. The Court found the law to bear a reasonable relationship to a proper public policy goal: preventing teenage pregnancies.

The Strict Scrutiny Test The Court imposes a higher standard in some equal protection cases, however. This is especially true when a case deals with (1) such "fundamental rights" as the right to vote, the right to travel between the States, or 1st Amendment rights; or (2) such "suspect classifications" as those based on race, sex, or national origin.

In these instances, the Court has said that a law must meet a higher standard than the rational basis test: the **strict scrutiny test.** A State must be able to show that some "compelling governmental interest" justifies the distinctions it has drawn between classes of people. Thus, in an alimony case, *Orr* v. *Orr,* 1979, an Alabama law that made women but not men eligible for alimony was held unconstitutional, as a denial of equal protection—because the law's distinction between men and women did not serve any compelling governmental interest.

Segregation by Race

Beginning in the late 1800s, nearly half the States—including some outside the South—passed racial segregation laws. Used in this context, **segregation** refers to the separation of one group from another on the basis of race. Most of those statutes were **Jim Crow** laws—laws aimed at African Americans in particular. Some were also drawn to affect Mexican Americans, Asian Americans, and Native Americans. They regularly required segregation by race in the use of both public and private facilities: schools, parks and playgrounds, hotels and restaurants, streetcars and railroads, public drinking fountains, restrooms, and cemeteries. Many also prohibited interracial marriages.

The Separate-but-Equal Doctrine The Supreme Court provided a constitutional basis for Jim Crow laws by creating the **separate-but-equal doctrine** in 1896. In *Plessy* v. *Ferguson,* the Court upheld a Louisiana law that required segregation in railroad coaches. It ruled that the law did not violate the Equal Protection Clause because the *separate* seating provided for African Americans was *equal* to the seating provided for whites.

✔ **Checkpoint**
What were Jim Crow laws?

SUPREME COURT
at a glance

▶ **Case:** *Plessy* v. *Ferguson,* 1896
▶ **Issues:** equal protection, constitutionality of segregation
▶ **Decision:** A Louisiana law stated that railway companies had to "provide equal but separate accommodations for the white and colored races." Homer Plessy, who was one-eighth African American, was arrested for refusing to move from a white coach. On appeal, the Supreme Court upheld the law, stating that segregation was constitutional as long as "facilities were equal."

Checkpoint

What was the result of the *Brown* v. *Board of Education* ruling?

The doctrine was soon extended to other fields. And it stood, largely unchallenged, for nearly 60 years.

Early Challenges The Supreme Court first began to chip away at the separate-but-equal doctrine in *Missouri ex rel. Gaines* v. *Canada* in 1938. Lloyd Gaines, an African American, was denied admission to the law school at the all-white University of Missouri. Gaines was fully qualified for admission—except for his race. The State did not have a separate law school for African Americans. However, it did offer to pay his tuition at a public law school in any of the four neighboring States, which did not discriminate by race. Gaines, however, insisted on a legal education in his home State.

The Court held that the separate-but-equal doctrine left Missouri with two choices: admit Gaines to the State's one law school or establish a separate-but-equal school for him. The State gave in. Gaines was admitted to the university's law school.

Over the next several years, the Court began to insist on equality of separate facilities. Thus, in 1950 the Court decided two major cases in line with its holding in Gaines: *Sweatt* v. *Painter* and *McLaurin* v. *Oklahoma*. Both cases involved African American university students for whom a State had provided separate educational facilities. The Court found that, in both instances, those separate facilities were, in fact, far from equal. Still, in neither of these cases did the Court reexamine the validity of the separate-but-equal doctrine.

Brown v. Board of Education Finally, in 1954, the Court reversed *Plessy* v. *Ferguson*. In *Brown* v. *Board of Education of Topeka*, it struck down the laws of four States requiring or allowing separate public schools for white and African American students.[4]

Unanimously, the Court held segregation by race in public education to be invalid:

---

4 Kansas, Delaware, South Carolina, and Virginia. On the same day, the High Court also struck down racially segregated public schools in the District of Columbia as a violation of the 5th Amendment, *Bolling* v. *Sharpe*, 1954.

PRIMARY SOURCE

Does segregation of children in public schools solely on the basis of race, even though the physical facilities and other 'tangible' factors may be equal, deprive the children of the minority group of equal educational opportunities? We believe that it does.

. . . To separate them from others of similar age and qualifications solely because of their race generates a feeling of inferiority as to their status in the community that may affect their hearts and minds in a way unlikely ever to be undone. . . . Separate educational facilities are inherently unequal.

—Chief Justice Earl Warren

In 1955 the Court directed the States to make "a prompt and reasonable start" to end segregation and to accomplish that goal "with all deliberate speed."

A "reasonable start" was made in Baltimore, Louisville, St. Louis, and elsewhere. In most of the Deep South, however, "massive resistance" soon developed. State legislatures passed laws, and school boards worked to block **integration**—the process of desegregation, of bringing a previously segregated group into the mainstream of society. Most of those efforts were clearly unconstitutional, but challenging them in court proved both costly and slow.

The pace of desegregation quickened after Congress passed the Civil Rights Act of 1964. That act forbids the use of federal funds to aid any State or local activity in which racial segregation is practiced. The statute also directed the Justice Department to file suits to spur desegregation efforts.

The Supreme Court hastened the process in 1969. In a case from Mississippi, *Alexander* v. *Holmes County Board of Education*, it ruled that, after 15 years, the time for "all deliberate speed" had ended. Said a unanimous Court: "[C]ontinued operation of segregated schools under a standard of allowing 'all deliberate speed' . . . is no longer constitutionally permissible."

De Jure Segregation

When the Supreme Court held separate-but-equal facilities to be constitutional in *Plessy* in 1896, the States had the law on their side. Jim Crow laws, named for a character in minstrel shows, limited voting rights and required separate facilities for African Americans. Similar laws legalized Mexican American segregation in Texas and throughout the Southwest. *What federal law quickened the pace of desegregation?*

WE SERVE WHITE'S only NO SPANISH or MEXICANS

PARAMOUNT THEATRE COLORED ENTRANCE Enjoy Good Shows in Comfort

WHITE ONLY

OPEN 7. A.M. CLOSE 11:30 PM

Separate but equal

De Jure, De Facto Segregation By the fall of 1970, school systems characterized by **de jure** segregation—segregation authorized by law—had been abolished. That is not to say that desegregation had been fully accomplished, however—far from it.[5]

Many recent integration controversies have arisen in places where the schools have never been segregated by law. They have occurred, instead, in communities in which de facto segregation has long been present, and continues. **De facto** segregation is segregation that exists in fact, even if no law requires it. Housing patterns have most often been its major cause. The concentration of African Americans in certain sections of cities inevitably led to local school systems in which the student bodies of some schools are largely African American. That condition is quite apparent in many northern as well as southern communities today.

Efforts to desegregate those school systems have taken several forms over recent decades. Thus, for example, school district lines have been redrawn and the busing of students out of racially segregated neighborhoods has been tried. Those efforts have brought strong protests in many places and violence in some of them.

The Court first <u>sanctioned</u> busing in a North Carolina case, *Swann* v. *Charlotte-Mecklenburg Board of Education,* 1971. There it held that: "Desegregation plans cannot be limited to the walk-in school." Busing has been used since then to increase the racial mix in many school districts across the country—in some by court order, in others voluntarily.

In recent years, a growing number of school systems have turned to <u>socioeconomic</u> status—

sanction
v. to authorize or permit

socioeconomic
adj. social and economic

---

5 Some States, several school districts, and many parents and private groups sought to avoid integrated schools through established or, often, newly created private schools. On this point, see the Court's holding in *Runyon* v. *McCrary,* 1976, page 584.

Checkpoint

Where does the Constitution specifically reference gender?

in particular, to income rather than race—in assigning students to schools within the district. That is, they have tried to promote schools with economically diverse student bodies. The results appear to be promising, both in terms of maintaining integrated schools and in improving the performance of disadvantaged students.

Segregation in Other Fields

Public schools have not been fully integrated. But legally enforced racial segregation in all other areas of life has been eliminated. In the process, many State and local laws have either been repealed or they have been struck down by the courts.

The Supreme Court took a leading role in that process—holding in a number of cases that segregation by race is unconstitutional in other areas as well. Thus, it has held that the 14th Amendment's Equal Protection Clause forbids segregation in public swimming pools and all other public recreational facilities, *Baltimore* v. *Dawson,* 1955; local transportation, *Gayle* v. *Browder,* 1956; and State prisons and local jails, *Lee* v. *Washington,* 1968.[6] The High Court struck down all State miscegenation laws (statutes forbidding interracial marriages) in *Loving* v. *Virginia,* 1967.

Classification by Gender

The Constitution speaks of the civil rights of "the people," "persons," and "citizens." Nowhere does it make its guarantees only to "men" or separately to "women." Its only reference to gender is in the 19th Amendment, which forbids denial of the right to vote "on account of sex." Gender has long been used as a basis of classification in the law, however. That practice reflected society's long-held view of the "proper" role of women. Most often, laws that treated men and women differently were intended to protect "the weaker sex." Over the years, the Court read that view into the 14th Amendment.

---

6   *Gayle* v. *Browder* stemmed from the lengthy bus boycott in Montgomery, Alabama—the event that first brought Dr. Martin Luther King, Jr., to national attention.

▲ In response to *United States* v. *Virginia,* 1996, women now attend the Virginia Military Institute.

First Tests In the first case to challenge sex discrimination, *Bradwell* v. *Illinois,* 1873, the Court upheld a State law barring women from the practice of law. In that case, Justice Joseph P. Bradley wrote that:

PRIMARY SOURCE

The civil law, as well as nature herself, has always recognized a wide difference in the respective spheres and destinies of man and woman. Man is, or should be, woman's protector and defender. The natural and proper timidity and delicacy which belongs to the female sex evidently unfits it for many of the occupations of civil life.

—Concurring Opinion

Even as late as 1961, in *Hoyt* v. *Florida,* the Court could find no constitutional fault with a law that required men to serve on juries, but gave women the choice of serving or not.

Circumstances Today Matters are far different today. The Court now takes a very close look at cases involving claims of sex discrimination. It first did so in *Reed* v. *Reed,* 1971; there, it struck down an Idaho law that gave fathers preference over mothers in the administration of their children's estates.

Since then, the Supreme Court has found a number of sex-based distinctions to be unconstitutional. In *Taylor* v. *Louisiana,* 1975, it held that the 14th Amendment's Equal Protection Clause forbids the States to exclude women from jury service. Among other examples of that line of cases, it struck down an Oklahoma law that prohibited the sale of beer to males under 21 and to females under 18, *Craig* v. *Boren,* 1976. And the Court found the practice of refusing to admit women to the rigorous citizen-soldier program offered by a public institution, the Virginia Military Institute, to be constitutionally unacceptable, *United States* v. *Virginia,* 1996.

The Court's changed attitude in cases involving sex-based discrimination was put this way in the majority opinion in *Frontiero* v. *Richardson* in 1973:[7]

---

7 In this case, the Court for the first time struck down a federal law providing for sex-based discrimination, as a violation of the 5th Amendment's Due Process Clause. That law gave various housing, medical, and other allowances to a serviceman for his wife and other dependents, but it made those same allowances available to a servicewoman only if her husband was dependent on her for more than half of his support.

PRIMARY SOURCE

> There can be no doubt that our Nation has had a long and unfortunate history of sex discrimination. Traditionally, such discrimination was rationalized by an attitude of 'romantic paternalism' which, in practical effect, put women, not on a pedestal, but in a cage.
>
> —Justice William J. Brennan, Jr.

Not all sex-based distinctions are unconstitutional, however. The Court has upheld a Florida law that gives an extra property tax exemption to widows, but not to widowers, *Kahn* v. *Shevin,* 1974; an Alabama law forbidding women to serve as prison guards in all-male penitentiaries, *Dothard* v. *Rawlinson,* 1977; and the federal selective service law that requires only men to register for the draft and excludes women from any future draft, *Rostker* v. *Goldberg,* 1981.

In effect, these cases say this: Classification by gender is not in and of itself unconstitutional. However, laws that treat men and women differently will be overturned by the courts unless (1) they are intended to serve an "important governmental objective" and (2) they are "substantially related" to achieving that goal.

✔ **Checkpoint**
What does the Court say today about gender-based discrimination?

Essential Questions Journal To continue to build a response to the chapter Essential Question, go to your **Essential Questions Journal.**

SECTION 2 ASSESSMENT

1. **Guiding Question** Use your completed graphic organizer to answer this question: How has the interpretation of the guarantee of equal rights changed over time?

Key Terms and Comprehension

2. **(a)** What does the 14th Amendment's Equal Protection Clause say? **(b)** To whom was it originally directed?

3. **(a)** What two tests does the High Court use when deciding equal protection cases? **(b)** How do the tests differ? **(c)** Summarize two cases that illustrate those tests.

4. **(a)** What is **integration? (b)** Which Supreme Court case led to public school integration?

5. **(a)** What is the difference between **de jure** and **de facto** segregation?

(b) What actions have school systems taken, voluntarily or otherwise, to end de facto segregation?

Critical Thinking

6. **Draw Conclusions (a)** Why do you think the Supreme Court was vague about the time frame in which to end segregation ("with all deliberate speed")? **(b)** How did the Civil Rights Act of 1964 speed up the process of integration?

7. **Recognize Bias (a)** What do you suppose Justice Bradley meant by separate "spheres and destinies of man and woman"? **(b)** Which gender-based distinctions are considered constitutional today? **(c)** Do you agree or disagree with those distinctions?

Quick Write

Problem-Solution Essay: Consider Solutions Use the problem you identified in Section 1 and research possible solutions to that problem. What solutions have been tried successfully? Unsuccessfully? Construct a chart to evaluate the pros and cons of each solution.

Is Segregation in Schools Constitutional?

The Supreme Court ruled unanimously that it was not. Third-grader Linda Brown who lived in Topeka, Kansas, had to walk a mile through a dangerous railroad yard and then take a bus to get to school. There was another school much closer to her home, but school officials would not allow her to attend that school because it was reserved for white students only. Separate elementary schools for whites and nonwhites were maintained by Topeka's Board of Education.

Oliver Brown, Linda's father, turned to the local chapter of the National Association for the Advancement of Colored People (NAACP) for help. The Topeka chapter of the NAACP believed it had the "right plaintiff at the right time," and used Brown's complaint, along with those of 13 other African American parents in Topeka, to take the case for school desegregation to the United States District Court for the District of Kansas. In the early 1950s, segregation of the races was legal, and in some States, required. Kansas gave local school districts a choice of integrating their schools. Like many States at the time, however, it chose segregation with the condition that the minority schools were to be equal to the white schools. The District Court felt "compelled" to rule in favor of the Board of Education, citing *Plessy* v. *Ferguson,* which allowed separate but equal facilities. The NAACP appealed the case to the Supreme Court, where it was combined with three other cases calling for school desegregation in Delaware, South Carolina, and Virginia.

In a unanimous 9–0 decision, the Supreme Court overturned the "separate but equal" doctrine. Chief Justice Earl Warren delivered the opinion of the Court: "we

Before *Brown,* schools designated for African Americans were separate but definitely not equal in such terms as buildings, library resources, and teachers' salaries.

Linda Brown was the subject of the landmark case. The case was a class action suit, but Oliver Brown was deliberately named plaintiff because he was male.

GOVERNMENT ONLINE
In the News
To learn more about the relevance
of the case today, go to
PearsonSuccessNet.com

cannot turn the clock back to 1868 when the [14th] Amendment was adopted, or even to 1896 when *Plessy* v. *Ferguson* was written. We must consider public education in the light of its full development and its present place in American life throughout the Nation. Only in this way can it be determined if segregation in public schools deprives these plaintiffs of the equal protection of the laws. . . .

We come then to the question presented: Does segregation of children in public schools solely on the basis of race, even though the physical facilities and other 'tangible' factors may be equal, deprive the children of the minority group of equal educational opportunities? We believe that it does. . . . To separate them from others of similar age and qualifications solely because of their race generates a feeling of inferiority as to their status in the community that may affect their hearts and minds in a way unlikely ever to be undone. . . . We conclude that in the field of public education the doctrine of 'separate but equal' has no place. Separate educational facilities are inherently unequal."

Arguments for Brown

- Segregating African American students from white students makes them feel inferior.
- A sense of inferiority affects a child's motivation to learn.
- Segregation results in the fundamentally unequal education of minority students.

Arguments for Board of Education of Topeka

- Minority schools in Topeka are equal in every way to, and sometimes have better programs than, schools for whites.
- There is no conclusive evidence that segregation by race affects the education of children.
- Segregated schools prepare black children for the segregated society they will face in adulthood.

Thinking Critically

1. On what basis did the District Court reach its decision? On what basis did the Supreme Court reach its decision?
2. **Constitutional Principles** How does this case reflect the principle of equal protection?

Thurgood Marshall, the lead attorney who argued for desegregation, would become the first African American Supreme Court justice in 1967.

People waited in long lines outside the Supreme Court building, hoping for the opportunity to hear the Court deliver its opinion in this landmark case.

As a result of the *Brown* ruling, classrooms across the country were required to desegregate.

Federal Civil Rights Laws

Guiding Question

What is the history of civil rights legislation from Reconstruction to today? Use a timeline like the one below to take notes on the section.

| 1964 | 1968 | 1972 | 1978 |

Political Dictionary

- affirmative action
- quota
- reverse discrimination

Objectives

1. Outline the history of civil rights legislation from the Reconstruction period on to today.
2. Explore the issues surrounding affirmative action.

Image Above: Dr. Martin Luther King, Jr., acknowledges the crowd at his "I Have a Dream" speech, August 28, 1963.

Those who, for one reason or another, oppose the enactment of civil rights legislation often rely on this observation: "You can't legislate morality." That is, racism, sexism, and other forms of discrimination will not be eliminated by simply passing a law.

The Reverend Dr. Martin Luther King, Jr., responded to that contention this way: "Judicial decrees," he said, "may not change the heart, but they can restrain the heartless." Clearly, Congress has agreed with Dr. King—as it has enacted a number of civil rights laws over the past 40 years or so.

Civil Rights: Reconstruction to Today

From the 1870s to the late 1950s, Congress did not pass a single piece of meaningful civil rights legislation. Several factors contributed to that fact. Among the major ones: Through that period, the nation's predominantly white population was generally unaware of or little concerned with the plight of African Americans, Native Americans, or other nonwhites in this country. And southern white Democrats, bolstered by such devices as the seniority system and the filibuster, held many of the most strategic posts in Congress.

That historic logjam was finally broken in 1957, largely as a result of the pressures brought to bear by the civil rights movement led by Dr. King (see Chapter 6, Section 3). Beginning in that year, Congress passed a number of civil rights laws—notably, the Civil Rights Acts of 1957, 1960, 1964, and 1968; the Voting Rights Acts of 1965, 1970, 1975, 1982, and 2006; and Title IX in the Education Amendments of 1972.[8]

The Civil Rights Act of 1964 The 1964 law is the most far-reaching of those statutes. It was passed after the longest debate in Senate history (83 days), and only after the Senate invoked cloture (limited debate) to kill a filibuster.

---

8 The 1957 and 1960 laws set up modest safeguards for the right to vote. You considered the voting rights provision in those statutes in Chapter 6, Section 3. The 1957 law created the U.S. Commission on Civil Rights. The commission is an independent eight-member executive branch agency that is supposed to monitor the enforcement of the various civil rights laws, investigate cases of alleged discrimination, and report its findings to the President, Congress, and the public.

Beyond its voting rights provisions, the 1964 law outlaws discrimination in a number of areas. With its several later amendments, the law's major sections now:

• provide that no person may be denied access to or refused service in various "public accommodations"—hotels, motels, restaurants, theaters, and the like—because of race, color, religion, national origin, or physical disability (Title II).[9]

• prohibit discrimination against any person on grounds of race, color, religion, national origin, sex, or physical disability in any program that receives any federal funding (Title VI).

• forbid both employers and labor unions to discriminate against any person on grounds of race, color, religion, sex, physical disability, or age in job-related matters (Title VII).[10]

The Civil Rights Act of 1968 The Civil Rights Act of 1968 is often called the Open Housing Act. With minor exceptions, it forbids anyone to refuse to sell or rent a dwelling to any person on grounds of race, color, religion, national origin, sex, or disability. It also forbids refusal to sell or rent to a family with children.

At first, the burden of enforcing the law fell on those persons who claimed to be victims of housing discrimination; they could seek damages from alleged offenders. Congress finally strengthened the law in 1988, to allow the Justice Department to bring criminal charges against those who violate its terms. Still, housing remains among the most segregated areas of American life today.

Title IX In Title IX of the Education Amendments of 1972, Congress added a key gender-based guarantee to the provisions of the Civil Rights Act of 1964. Title IX forbids discrimination on the basis of gender "in any education program or activity receiving Federal financial assistance." The statute intends to ensure that women receive equal treatment in all aspects of education. Its provisions apply to all schools, public and private, that receive federal funds, and nearly all of them do.

Since its passage, Title IX has had its most telling effect on school athletics programs, especially at the college level, by requiring roughly equal funding and opportunities for women and men. The law has been in effect for nearly four decades now; still, it continues to generate controversy.

Affirmative Action

These civil rights statutes all come down to this: Discriminatory practices based on such factors as race, color, national origin, sex, or disability are illegal. But what about the effects of *past* discrimination? Consider an African American who, for no reason of his or her own making, did not get a decent education and so today cannot get a decent job. Of what real help to that person are all of those laws that make illegal today what was done years ago?

So far, the Federal Government's chief answer to this troubling question has been a policy of **affirmative action.** That approach requires that most employers take positive steps (affirmative action) to remedy the effects of past discriminations. The policy applies to all agencies of the Federal Government, States and their local governments, and private employers who sell goods or services to any agency of the Federal

✔ **Checkpoint**
What is the Civil Rights Act of 1968?

These words would have been added to the Constitution if three additional States had ratified the Equal Rights Amendment (ERA). *Why do you think the ERA was not ratified?*

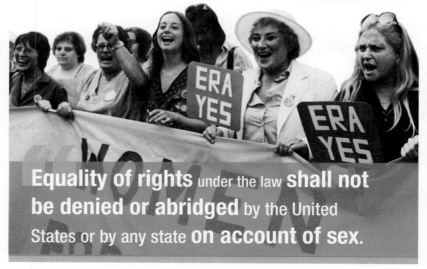

Equality of rights under the law **shall not be denied or abridged** by the United States or by any state **on account of sex.**

---

9 Congress based this section of the law on its commerce power. See Chapter 11, Section 1. Title II covers those places in which lodgings are offered to transient guests and those where a significant portion of the items sold have moved in interstate commerce. The Supreme Court upheld Title II and the use of the Commerce Clause as a basis for civil rights legislation in *Heart of Atlanta Motel, Inc.* v. *United States,* 1964.

10 The five-member Equal Employment Opportunity Commission (EEOC), an independent executive branch agency, enforces Title VII.

Equal Rights and Affirmative Action

1800s

1868 States ratify the 14th Amendment, which includes the Equal Protection Clause.

1896 The Supreme Court decision in *Plessy* v. *Ferguson* establishes the separate-but-equal doctrine.

1900s

1954 In *Brown* v. *Board of Education,* the Court overrules *Plessy,* holding that separate-but-equal public schools are unconstitutional.

1964 Civil Rights Act of 1964 overturns all Jim Crow laws.

Martin Luther King, Jr. leads a march in Washington, D.C. to promote equal rights in 1963.▶

▶▶ **Analyzing Timelines** Affirmative action programs arose in the 1960s to help rectify the harm suffered by minorities as a result of discrimination. *How did the two Michigan cases in 2003 leave the legal status of affirmative action unsettled?*

Government. The Federal Government began to demand the adoption of affirmative action programs in 1965.

To illustrate the policy, take the case of a company that does business with the Federal Government. It must adopt an affirmative action plan designed to make its workforce reflect the general makeup of the population in its locale. The plan must include steps to correct or prevent inequalities in such matters as pay, promotions, and fringe benefits.

For many employers this has meant that they must hire and/or promote more workers with minority backgrounds and more females. The share of a group necessary to satisfy a particular affirmative action requirement—say, the number of females in a company's workforce or the number of African Americans in a school's student body—is often called a **quota.**

Reverse Discrimination? Affirmative action policies remain highly controversial today. This is principally because those policies necessarily involve race-based and/or gender-based classifications.

Critics argue that affirmative action programs amount to **reverse discrimination,** or discrimination against the majority group. Affirmative action demands that preference be given to females and/or nonwhites solely on the basis of sex or race. Critics say that the Constitution requires that all public policies be "color blind."

The opponents of affirmative action have attacked the policy at the State and local levels in several places in recent years. Most often, they have relied primarily on the reverse discrimination argument as they have done so.

In 1996, California's voters gave overwhelming approval to a measure that eliminated nearly all affirmative action programs conducted by public agencies in that State. Since then, the voters in Washington (in 1998) and in Michigan (in 2004) have adopted measures nearly identical to California's.

The Bakke Case The Supreme Court decided its first major affirmative action case, *Regents of the University of California* v. *Bakke,* in 1978. Allan Bakke, a white male, had been denied admission to the university's medical school at Davis. The school had set aside 16 of the 100 seats in each year's entering class for nonwhite students. He sued the university, charging it with reverse discrimination and,

▲ Title IX increased opportunities for women to participate in sports.

1972 Title IX of the Education Amendments forbids gender discrimination in all federally funded educational programs.

1978 In *Regents of the University of California* v. *Bakke,* the Court rules that affirmative action is acceptable, but strict quotas are not.

1990 Americans with Disabilities Act prohibits discrimination on the basis of disability.

1995 In *Adarand Constructors* v. *Pena,* the Court finds that affirmative action programs will be upheld only if shown to serve some "compelling government interest."

2000s

2003 The Court finds that a State university may take race into account in admitting students, *Grutter* v. *Bollinger,* but it may not blindly give extra weight to race in that process, *Gratz* v. *Bollinger.*

2007 In *Parents Involved* v. *Seattle School District* and *Meredith* v. *Jefferson County Board of Education,* the Court overturns school integration policies that it holds, 5–4, rely too heavily on race.

so, a violation of the Equal Protection Clause. By a 5–4 majority, the Court held that Bakke had been denied equal protection and should be admitted to the medical school.

A differently composed 5–4 majority made the more far-reaching ruling in the case, however. Although the Constitution does not allow race to be used as the *only* factor in the making of affirmative action decisions, that majority of the justices held that both the Constitution and the 1964 Civil Rights Act do allow its use as one among several factors in such situations.

Later Cases The Court has decided several affirmative action cases since *Bakke.* In some of them it has upheld quotas, especially in such industries as construction, where longstanding discrimination was involved.

Note, however, that the High Court has also held that quotas can be used in only the most extreme situations. Thus, the Court held in *Richmond* v. *Croson,* 1989, that the city of Richmond, Virginia, had not shown that its minority set-aside policy was justified by a record of past discrimination by the city.

Johnson v. *Transportation Agency of Santa Clara County,* 1987, marked the first time the Court decided a case of preferential treatment on the basis of sex. The justices held that neither the Equal Protection Clause nor Title VII forbids the promotion of a woman rather than a man, even when he scored higher on a qualifying interview.

The current Supreme Court's conservative bent can be seen in its most recent affirmative action decisions. Thus, the Court's decision in *Adarand Constructors* v. *Pena,* 1995, marked a major departure from its previous rulings in such cases. Until *Adarand,* the Court had regularly upheld affirmative action laws, regulations, and programs as "<u>benign</u>" instances of "race-conscious policymaking." By this, the Court meant that it considered them to be mild but necessary restraints on behavior.

Adarand arose when a white-owned Colorado company, Adarand Constructors, Inc., challenged an affirmative action policy of the Federal Highway Administration (FHWA). Under that policy, the FHWA gave bonuses to highway contractors if 10 percent or more of their construction work was subcontracted to "socially and economically disadvantaged" businesses, including those that were owned by racial minorities.

The Court held that henceforth all affirmative action cases will be reviewed under strict scrutiny—that is, affirmative action programs will be upheld only if they can be shown to serve some "compelling governmental interest." (See page 619.)

benign
adj. harmless, mild, gentle

The Michigan Cases Two cases, *Gratz* v. *Bollinger* and *Grutter* v. *Bollinger,* both involving the admissions policies of the University of Michigan, were combined for decision by the Supreme Court in 2003. The resolution of those two cases marked the High Court's most important statement on affirmative action since its decision in *Bakke* in 1978.

Jennifer Gratz applied for admission to the University as a freshman in 1997, and Barbara Grutter sought to enter the University's law school that same year. Both women are white, and both were rejected in favor of minority applicants with lower grade point averages and lower entry test scores. Both women sued the university and its chief admissions officer, Lee Bollinger, seeking to prevent the University from using race as a factor in admissions.

The Supreme Court held, 6–3, that Gratz's rejection was the result of a race-based quota policy prohibited by the 14th Amendment's Equal Protection Clause. Grutter's rejection was upheld 5–4, however, because the law school employed a much more flexible process in making its admissions decisions.

A majority of the Court found—definitely and unambiguously—that the State of Michigan (and all States) has a compelling interest in the diversity of the student bodies of its public educational institutions. That compelling interest justifies the narrowly tailored use of race as one factor in the student admissions policies of those institutions. However, Justice Sandra Day O'Connor, writing for the majority, predicted that affirmative action would not be necessary in the future. She wrote, "We expect that 25 years from now, the use of racial preferences will no longer be necessary to further the interest approved today."

The Seattle and Louisville Cases The High Court's most recent affirmative action decision came in two cases that were combined for decision in 2007. One of those cases arose in Seattle, Washington (*Parents Involved* v. *Seattle School District*), and the other in Louisville, Kentucky (*Meredith* v. *Jefferson County Board of Education*).

Both cases centered on this question: In light of the Supreme Court's decision in *Grutter,* to what extent can public school officials now use race as a factor in assigning students to particular schools in a district as they seek to maintain racially integrated student bodies in that district?

The Court split 5–4 in the two cases. The majority found that the student assignment policies in both Seattle and Louisville relied too heavily on race and so ran afoul of the 14th Amendment's Equal Protection Clause. Indeed, four of the five justices in the majority favored the *total elimination* of race as a factor in school admission decisions.

Essential Questions Journal To continue to build a response to the chapter Essential Question, go to your **Essential Questions Journal.**

SECTION 3 ASSESSMENT

1. **Guiding Question** Use your completed timeline to answer this question: What is the history of civil rights legislation from Reconstruction to today?

Key Terms and Comprehension

2. Cite the three major provisions of the Civil Rights Act of 1964.

3. **(a)** What does the policy of **affirmative action** require? **(b)** Who must abide by the policy?

4. Under what circumstances has the Supreme Court upheld the use of **quotas?**

Critical Thinking

5. **Demonstrate Reasoned Judgment (a)** What does Title IX provide? **(b)** In what situation has it been most controversial? **(c)** Do you agree with the law? Why or why not?

6. **Synthesize Information** Some nations, such as France, require *gender parity* in government; that is, a certain number of candidates or elected leaders must be women. **(a)** How is this similar to a quota system? **(b)** Do you think the United States should adopt that system? Why or why not?

Quick Write

Problem-Solution Essay: Select the Best Solution Decide which one of the solutions you researched in Section 2 would solve the problem you identified in Section 1. Using supporting facts and details, make a list that evaluates the solution's effectiveness in achieving both short-term gains and long-term goals.

Writing a Letter to the Editor

Editor:

Regarding the article on additional budget cuts to public education ("Governor Proposes Slashing School Funding," May 9), I believe that every penny spent is a necessary investment in the future of this community. As a junior at Westfield High School, I know that these cuts would place students' futures in greater jeopardy. Last year, 15 percent of the teaching staff and 10 percent of all elective courses were eliminated due to severe reductions in funding. These cuts ultimately impacted the quality of our education, and that is a sacrifice this town should not be willing to make again.

—Thomas Grey, St. Clairsville

The Constitution guarantees all people the right to express their views. Writing a letter to the editor of your local newspaper is your chance to share your opinion about important issues that affect you and your community. Follow these steps to write an effective letter:

1. **Briefly summarize the issue.** A good letter to the editor should be brief and to the point. Begin your letter by clearly identifying the issue. If you are responding to an article published in the paper, mention the article by title and publication date in the first sentence. State your opinion up-front.

2. **Explain your position.** You should explain why you feel the way you do about the issue. Support your explanation with at least one or two specific examples. If you feel particularly passionate about the issue, let your emotions come through in your letter but remember to be civil. Never resort to name-calling or vulgar language. If you do, few people will take your letter seriously.

3. **Make a suggestion.** The main point of your letter might be to express your opinion, but you could also include suggestions for future actions. If you are writing about a problem in your community, explain what you think can be done to fix it.

4. **Identify yourself.** Sign your letter with your real name, and provide contact information. Most editors will not print anonymous letters, and they must be able to verify your identity. You can also mention any experiences you have had that are relevant to the issue.

▸▸ What do you think?

1. When writing a letter to the editor, why do you think you should be brief and to the point?

2. Why would adding suggestions for action make your letter more effective?

3. **You Try It** Choose an issue that interests you and write a letter to the editor of your local newspaper.

GOVERNMENT ONLINE
Citizenship Activity Pack
For activities on writing a letter to the editor, go to
PearsonSuccessNet.com

SECTION 4

American Citizenship

Guiding Question

How can American citizenship be attained and how has immigration policy changed over the years?
Use an outline like the one below to take notes on the section.

I. Citizenship
A. By Birth
  1. _____
  2. _____
B. _____
C. _____
II. Immigration

Political Dictionary

- citizen
- jus soli
- jus sanguinis
- naturalization
- alien
- expatriation
- denaturalization
- deportation

Objectives

1. Describe how people become American citizens by birth and by naturalization.
2. Explain how an American can lose his or her citizenship.
3. Illustrate how the United States is a nation of immigrants.
4. Compare and contrast the status of undocumented aliens and legal immigrants.

Image Above: New citizens take the oath during a naturalization ceremony in Miami, Florida.

Citizenship is the badge of membership in a political society.[11] Today, every state in the world has rules by which citizenship is determined. And much can be learned about the basic nature of a government by examining those rules. Who are and who may become citizens? Who are excluded from citizenship, and why?

The Constitution and Citizenship

An American **citizen** is one who owes allegiance to the United States and is entitled to both its protection and the privileges of its laws. As it was originally written, the Constitution referred to both "citizens of the United States" and "citizens of the States." Neither of those phrases was defined, however. Throughout much of our earlier history, it was generally agreed that national citizenship followed that of the States. That is, a person who was a citizen of, say, Maryland, was also thought to be a citizen of the United States.

Actually, the question was of little importance before the 1860s. Much of the population was the product of recent immigration, and little distinction was made between citizens and those who were not. The Civil War and the adoption of the 13th Amendment in 1865 raised the need for a constitutional definition, however.[12] The 14th Amendment met that need in 1868:

FROM THE CONSTITUTION

All persons born or naturalized in the United States and subject to the jurisdiction thereof, are citizens of the United States and of the State wherein they reside.

—14th Amendment, Section 1

---

11 The concept of citizenship—of the free inhabitants of a city—was developed by the ancient Greeks and Romans. It replaced the earlier concept of kinship—of the blood relationships of the family and the tribe—as the basis for community.

12 In the Dred Scott case (*Scott* v. *Sandford)* in 1857, the Supreme Court had ruled that neither the States nor the National Government had the power to confer citizenship on African Americans—slave or free. The dispute over that matter was one of the several causes of the Civil War.

Thus, the Constitution declares that a person may become an American citizen in either of two ways: by birth or by naturalization. The feature on page 634 summarizes the means by which American citizenship can be acquired.

Citizenship by Birth

More than 260 million Americans—nearly 90 percent—are citizens simply because they were born in this country. Another several million are also citizens by birth, although they were born outside the United States.

Two basic rules determine citizenship at birth: jus soli and jus sanguinis. According to **jus soli**—the law of the soil—citizenship is determined by place of birth, by *where* one is born.

Notice that the 14th Amendment awards American citizenship according to the location of one's birth: "All persons born . . . in the United States . . ." Congress has defined the United States to include, for purposes of citizenship, the 50 States, the District of Columbia, Puerto Rico, Guam, the Virgin Islands, and the Northern Mariana Islands, and all American embassies and all public vessels of the United States, wherever they might be.[13] Just how broad the 14th Amendment's statement of jus soli is can be seen from a leading case on citizenship, *United States* v. *Wong Kim Ark,* 1898.

Wong Kim Ark was born in San Francisco in 1873 to parents who were citizens of China. He made a brief trip to China in 1895. Upon Wong Kim Ark's return, he was refused entry to the United States by immigration officials at San Francisco. They insisted that the 14th Amendment should not be read so literally as to mean that he had become an American citizen at birth. They declared that he was an alien and so was denied entry by the Chinese Exclusion Act of 1882. The Supreme Court held, however, that under the clear wording of the 14th Amendment, he was indeed a native-born citizen of this country and so not subject to the terms of the Chinese Exclusion Act.

A very small number of persons who are born *physically* in the United States do not in fact become citizens at birth. They are those few who are born not "subject to the jurisdiction of the United States"—for example, children born to foreign diplomatic officials.

According to **jus sanguinis,** the law of the blood, citizenship at birth may also be determined by parentage, to *whom* one is born. Thus, it is altogether possible for one to become a citizen at birth even when that birth occurs outside the United States. A child born abroad can become a citizen at birth under circumstances set out in the feature on page 634. The 14th Amendment does not provide for jus sanguinis. However, Congress first recognized the doctrine in 1790 and its constitutionality has never been challenged.

Citizenship by Naturalization

Naturalization is the legal process by which a person can become a citizen of another country at some time after birth. Congress has the exclusive power to provide for naturalization.[14] No State may do so.

Individual Naturalization Naturalization is most often an individual process, conducted by a court. Generally, any person eligible to

✔ **Checkpoint**
What does the 14th Amendment say about citizenship?

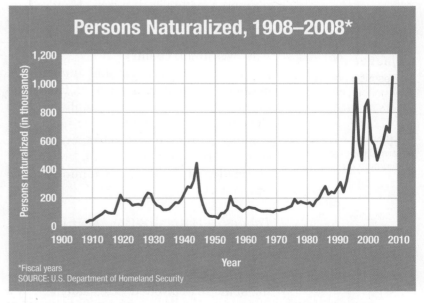

Persons Naturalized, 1908–2008*

*Fiscal years
SOURCE: U.S. Department of Homeland Security

▸▸ Analyzing Graphs *In what year were the greatest number of persons naturalized? The fewest?*

---

13 Until 1924, Native Americans born to tribal members on reservations did not become citizens at birth. They were, instead, wards (persons under legal guardianship) of the government. In that year, Congress finally did grant citizenship to all Native Americans who did not already possess it.

14 Article I, Section 8, Clause 4.

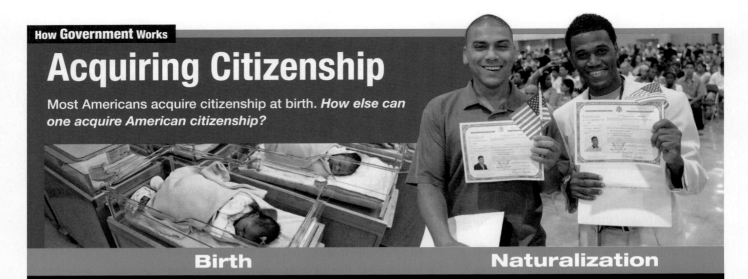

Acquiring Citizenship

Most Americans acquire citizenship at birth. *How else can one acquire American citizenship?*

Birth

Jus Soli: Law of Soil

- A child becomes an American citizen if born in the United States, Puerto Rico, Guam, Virgin Islands, Northern Mariana Islands, any U.S. embassy, or aboard a U.S. public vessel anywhere in the world.

Jus Sanguinis: Law of Blood

A child born to an American citizen on foreign soil becomes a citizen if:

- both parents are American citizens, and at least one has lived in the United States or an American territory at some time.
- one parent is an American citizen who has lived in the U.S. for at least 5 years, 2 of them after age 14, and the child has lived in the U.S. continuously for at least 5 years between the ages of 14 and 28.

Naturalization

Individually

- Naturalization of both parents (one parent if divorced or the other is deceased) automatically naturalizes children under age 16 who reside in the U.S. Adopted children born abroad are automatically naturalized if under age 18 when adoption becomes final.

Collectively

- Collective naturalization—when entire groups are naturalized—usually occurs by treaty or by act or joint resolution of Congress.

---

enter the United States as an immigrant may become a naturalized citizen. Hundreds of thousands of aliens are now naturalized each year. An **alien** is a citizen of a foreign state who lives in this country.

The U.S. Citizenship and Immigration Services in the Department of Homeland Security investigates each applicant, and then reports its findings to the judge with whom a <u>petition</u> for naturalization has been filed. If the judge is satisfied, an oath or affirmation of citizenship is administered in open court.

Collective Naturalization At various times, entire groups have been naturalized *en masse.* This has most often happened when the United States has acquired new territory. Those living in the areas involved were naturalized by a treaty or by an act or a joint resolution passed by Congress.

<u>petition</u>
n. formal request, application

The largest single instance of collective naturalization came with the ratification of the 14th Amendment, however. The most recent instance occurred in 1977, when Congress gave citizenship to the more than 16,000 native-born residents of the Northern Mariana Islands.

Loss of Citizenship

Although it rarely happens, every American citizen, whether native-born or naturalized, has the right to renounce—voluntarily abandon—his or her citizenship. **Expatriation** is the legal process by which a loss of citizenship occurs.

The Supreme Court has several times held that the Constitution prohibits automatic expatriation. That is, Congress cannot take away a person's citizenship for something he or she has done. Thus, actions such as committing a crime, voting in a foreign election, or serving in the armed forces of another country are not grounds for automatic expatriation.[15]

Naturalized citizens can lose their citizenship involuntarily. However, this process—**denaturalization**—can occur only by court order and only after it has been shown that the person became an American citizen by fraud or deception.

A person can neither gain nor lose American citizenship by marriage. The only significant effect that marriage has is to shorten the time required for the naturalization of an alien who marries an American citizen.

A Nation of Immigrants

We are a nation of immigrants. Except for Native Americans—and even they may be the descendants of earlier immigrants—all of us have come here from abroad or are descended from those who did.

Regulation of Immigration Congress has the exclusive power to regulate the crossing of this nation's borders, both inward (immigration) and outward (emigration). It alone has the power to decide who may be admitted to the country and under what conditions. In an early leading case on the point, the Court ruled that the power of the United States to "exclude aliens from its territory is . . . not open to controversy," *Chae Chan Ping* v. *United States*, 1889. The States have no power in the field, *The Passenger Cases*, 1849.

There were only some 2.5 million people in the United States when independence was declared in 1776. Since then, the population has grown more than a hundredfold, to well over 300 million today. That extraordinary population growth has come from two sources: births and immigration. Some 70 million immigrants have come here since 1820, the year when such figures were first recorded.

Congress made no serious attempt to regulate immigration for more than a century after

independence. As long as land was plentiful and expanding industry demanded more and still more workers, immigration was actively encouraged.

By 1890, however, the open frontier was a thing of the past, and labor was no longer in short supply. Then, too, the major source of immigration had shifted. Until the 1880s, most immigrants had come from the countries of northern and western Europe. The "new immigration" from the 1880s onward came mostly from southern and eastern Europe. All these factors combined to bring major changes in the traditional policy of encouraging immigration. Ultimately, the policy was reversed.

Congress placed the first major restrictions on immigration with the passage of the Chinese Exclusion Act in 1882. At the same time, it barred the entry of convicts, "lunatics," paupers, and others likely to become public charges. Over the next several years, a long list of "undesirables" was added to the law. Thus, contract laborers were excluded in 1885, immoral persons and anarchists in 1903, and illiterates in 1917. By 1920, more than 30 groups were denied admission on the basis of personal traits.

The tide of newcomers continued to mount, however. In the 10 years from 1905 through 1914, an average of more than a million persons, most of them from southern and eastern Europe, came to this country each year.

Quotas Congress responded to pressure for tighter regulation by adding quantitative limits (numerical ceilings) to the qualitative restrictions (personal characteristics) already in place. The Immigration Acts of 1921 and 1924 and the National Origins Act of 1929 assigned each country in Europe a quota—a limit on the number of immigrants who could enter the United States from that country each year. Altogether, only 150,000 quota immigrants could be admitted in any one year.

The quotas were purposely drawn to favor northern and western Europe. The quota system was not applied to the Western Hemisphere, but immigration from Asia, Africa, and elsewhere was generally prohibited.

✔ **Checkpoint**
When and why did Congress attempt to regulate immigration?

---

15 A person convicted of a federal or a State crime may lose some of the privileges of citizenship, however, either temporarily or permanently—for example, the right to travel freely or to vote or hold public office.

Immigrants in the U.S.

▶▶ **Analyzing Maps** The Immigration Act of 1990 allows 675,000 immigrants to enter the U.S. each year. The percentage of foreign-born people living in each State in 2008 ranged from less than 2 percent to more than 25 percent. *Which States have the largest immigrant populations?*

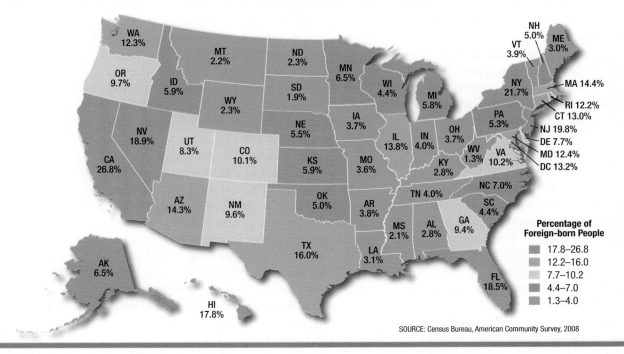

Percentage of Foreign-born People	
	17.8–26.8
	12.2–16.0
	7.7–10.2
	4.4–7.0
	1.3–4.0

SOURCE: Census Bureau, American Community Survey, 2008

✔ **Checkpoint**
What happened to the country-based quota system?

In 1952, Congress passed yet another basic law, the Immigration and Nationality Act. That statute modified the quota system, extending it to include every country outside the Western Hemisphere.

Congress finally eliminated the country-based quota system in the Immigration Act of 1965. That law allowed as many as 270,000 immigrants to enter the United States each year, without regard to race, nationality, or country of origin. The 1965 law gave special preference to immediate relatives of American citizens or of aliens legally residing in this country.

Present Immigration Policies Today, the Immigration Act of 1990 governs the admission of aliens to the United States. Like its predecessors, it was adopted only after years of intense debate, and many of its provisions are the subject of continuing controversy.

The 1990 law provided for a substantial increase in the number of immigrants who may enter the United States each year. The annual ceiling is now set at 675,000. It also continues the family-preference policy first put in place in 1965; at least one third of those persons admitted under its terms must be the close relatives of either American citizens or resident aliens. Those immigrants who have occupational talents which are in short supply in the United States (notably, highly skilled researchers, engineers, and scientists) also receive special preference.

Only those aliens who can qualify for citizenship can be admitted as immigrants. The law's list of "excludable aliens"—those barred because of some personal characteristic—is extensive. Among those excluded are: criminals (including suspected terrorists), persons with communicable diseases, drug abusers and addicts, illiterates, and mentally disturbed persons who might pose a threat to the safety of others.

Some 20 million persons—nonimmigrants—come here each year for temporary stays. They are mostly tourists, students, and people traveling for business reasons.

Deportation Most of the civil rights set out in the Constitution are guaranteed to "persons," which covers aliens as well as citizens. In one important respect, however, the status of aliens is altogether unlike that of citizens: Aliens may be subject to **deportation,** a legal process by which aliens are legally required to leave the country.

The Supreme Court has long held that the United States has the same almost-unlimited power to deport aliens as it has to exclude them. In an early major case, the Court ruled that deportation is an inherent power, arising out of the sovereignty of the United States, and that deportation is not criminal punishment, and so does not require a criminal trial, *Fong Yue Ting* v. *United States,* 1893.

An alien may be deported on any one of several grounds. The most common is illegal entry. Thousands of aliens who enter with false papers, sneak in by ship or plane, or slip across the border at night are caught each year and deported. Many of them are repeat offenders who will soon make yet another attempt to cross the border.

Conviction of any serious crime, federal or State, usually leads to a deportation order. In recent years, several thousand aliens have been expelled on the basis of their criminal records, especially narcotics violators. The war on terrorism has also quickened the pace of deportations. Because deportation is a civil, not a criminal, matter, several constitutional safeguards do not apply—for example, bail and ex post facto laws.

Undocumented Aliens

No one knows just how many undocumented aliens reside in the United States today. Best estimates put their total at about 12 million.

The number of undocumented aliens is increasing by at least half a million per year. Most of them enter the country by slipping across the Mexican or Canadian borders, usually at night. Some come with forged papers. Many others are aliens who entered legally, as nonimmigrants, but then overstayed their legal welcomes.

Well over half of all aliens who are here illegally have come from Mexico; most of the others come from other Latin American countries and from Asia. A majority of the Mexicans stay here only some four to six months a year, working on farms or in other seasonal jobs, and then return home. Most others hope to remain here permanently.

A Troublesome Situation Once here, many of these aliens find it easy to become "invisible," especially in larger cities, and law-enforcement agencies find it very difficult to locate them. Even so, immigration officials have apprehended more than a million undocumented aliens in each of the last several years. Nearly all are sent home. Most go voluntarily, but some leave only as the result of formal deportation proceedings.

The presence of so many undocumented persons has caused a number of nagging problems. Those problems have grown worse over the past several years and, until recently, not much had been done to solve them.

Consider this: Ever since 1987, it has been illegal for an employer to hire an undocumented alien to perform work anywhere in the United States. Even so, some four million persons who now hold jobs in this country came here illegally. Some employers still hire aliens who are often willing to work for substandard wages and in substandard conditions.

No one knows just how many undocumented aliens have taken jobs on farms or become day laborers. Or how many have become janitors or dishwashers, or seamstresses in sweatshops, or have found other <u>menial</u> work. However many they are, their presence has multiplied the burdens of already strained public school systems and welfare services of an increasing number of States, most notably California, Arizona, Texas, and Florida.

Current Law The problems posed by undocumented aliens trouble and divide many different interests in American politics—chief among them labor, farm, business, religious, ethnic, and civil rights organizations. After wrestling with the matter for years,

✔ **Checkpoint**
For what reasons may a person be deported?

menial
adj. unskilled, humble, lowly

Congress was finally able to pass the Immigration Reform and Control Act of 1986. Then, it enacted the Illegal Immigration Reform and Immigrant Responsibility Act of 1996.

The 1986 law did two major things. First, it established a one-year amnesty program under which many undocumented aliens could become legal residents. More than two million aliens used the process to legalize their status. Second, that law made it a crime to hire any person who is in this country illegally. Any employer who knowingly hires an undocumented alien can be fined from $250 to as much as $10,000. Repeat offenders can be jailed for up to six months.

The 1996 law made it easier to deport illegal aliens by streamlining the deportation process. It also toughened the penalties for smuggling aliens into this country, prevented undocumented aliens from claiming Social Security or public housing benefits, and allowed State welfare agencies to check the legal status of any alien who applies for any welfare benefit. The statute also doubled the size of the Border Patrol—which is, today, the largest of the several federal law enforcement agencies.

Congress has not been able to enact any meaningful immigration reform legislation for more than a decade now, however. The principal reason for the impasse is a continuing dispute over how best to approach the matter.

Many in and out of Congress insist that securing the nation's borders—stemming the flow of illegal entries—should be the nation's first concern. That thorny matter should be addressed, they say, before anything is done to meet the problems posed by the undocumented aliens already in this country. Many others argue that the need to confront these problems should not be put off to another day. In particular, many of them want to make it possible for large numbers of undocumented aliens to become legal residents and, eventually, citizens of the United States.

▶▶ Analyzing Political Cartoons *What does the cartoonist say about Congress and the immigration issue?*

SECTION 4 ASSESSMENT

Essential Questions Journal To continue to build a response to the chapter Essential Question, go to your **Essential Questions Journal.**

1. **Guiding Question** Use your completed outline to answer this question: How can American citizenship be attained and how has immigration policy changed over the years?

Key Terms and Comprehension

2. **(a)** In what two ways may a person become a U.S. **citizen? (b)** What is the difference between **jus soli** and **jus sanguinis?**

3. **(a)** What is **naturalization? (b)** About how many **aliens** are naturalized in this country each year?

Critical Thinking

4. **Demonstrate Reasoned Judgment (a)** Should U.S. citizenship be considered a right or a privilege? **(b)** Do you think citizens by birth should meet the same requirements as those set for naturalized citizens? Why or why not? **(c)** What actions, if any, do you think should result in an individual's involuntary expatriation?

5. **Identify Alternatives (a)** What did the Illegal Immigration Reform and Immigrant Responsibility Act of 1996 provide? **(b)** Do you think these provisions have been successful? Why or why not? **(c)** What changes, if any, do you think should be made to the law?

Quick Write

Problem-Solution Essay: Implement the Solution Write a specific proposal or action plan to implement the solution you selected in Section 3. Identify the steps needed to solve the problem, and then write an outline of your solution.

Quick Study Guide

GOVERNMENT ONLINE

On the Go

To review anytime, anywhere, download these online resources at **PearsonSuccessNet.com**

Political Dictionary, Audio Review

CHAPTER **21**

Political Dictionary

heterogeneous *p. 612*
immigrant *p. 612*
reservation *p. 613*
refugee *p. 615*
assimilation *p. 615*
rational basis test *p. 619*
strict scrutiny test *p. 619*
segregation *p. 619*
Jim Crow *p. 619*
separate-but-equal doctrine *p. 619*
integration *p. 620*
de jure *p. 621*
de facto *p. 621*
affirmative action *p. 627*
quota *p. 628*
reverse discrimination *p. 628*
citizen *p. 632*
jus soli *p. 633*
jus sanguinis *p. 633*
naturalization *p. 633*
alien *p. 634*
expatriation *p. 634*
denaturalization *p. 635*
deportation *p. 637*

Guiding Question
Section 2 How has the interpretation of the guarantee of equal rights changed over time?

Guiding Question
Section 3 What is the history of civil rights legislation from Reconstruction to today?

Guiding Question
Section 1 How have various minority groups in American society been discriminated against?

CHAPTER 21
Essential Question
Why are there ongoing struggles for civil rights?

Guiding Question
Section 4 How can American citizenship be attained and how has immigration policy changed over the years?

Segregation in American Society

Late 1800s: Nearly half the States pass segregation (Jim Crow) laws.

1896: The Supreme Court establishes the separate-but-equal doctrine in *Plessy* v. *Ferguson*.

1954: The Supreme Court rules in *Brown* v. *Board of Education* that the separate-but-equal doctrine is unconstitutional.

1955: Public schools begin to desegregate.

1960s: Major civil rights legislation is passed, including the Civil Rights Act of 1964.

Affirmative Action

Causes		Effects
• Discriminatory practices based on such factors as race, color, national origin, or gender	Affirmative Action Policies and Legislation	• More companies hire women and minorities
• Difficult for the underprivileged to obtain a quality education		• Reverse discrimination
• Difficult for minorities to find fair opportunities in the workforce		• Controversy and many court cases over the constitutionality and/or proper administration of affirmative action

Chapter Assessment

GOVERNMENT ONLINE
Self-Test
To test your understanding of key terms and main ideas, visit **PearsonSuccessNet.com**

Comprehension and Critical Thinking

Section 1

1. **(a)** What does it mean to say that the population of the United States is heterogeneous? **(b)** How does the ethnic balance in the United States today differ from that of colonial times? **(c)** Which ethnic groups are experiencing the most rapid population growth?

2. **(a)** How did the Indian Education Act of 1972 attempt to reduce poverty on and near reservations? **(b)** Do you think that laws can fix the damage done to Native Americans? Why or why not?

3. **(a)** When and why did Asians first come to the United States? **(b)** How did Asian immigration change after 1882? After 1965?

4. **Analyze Political Cartoons** Study the cartoon below. **(a)** What does "glass ceiling" mean? **(b)** What form of discrimination is targeted by this cartoon? **(c)** How does the cartoon reverse the usual situation?

I'M TELLIN' YA... THERE'S A GLASS CEILING IN THIS BUSINESS! HAVE YOU EVER HEARD OF A **KING** BEE? NO! IT'S A REAL PROBLEM IN OUR CULTURE!

Section 2

5. Cite an example of what you consider to be reasonable government discrimination.

6. **(a)** What was the intent of Jim Crow laws? **(b)** What landmark Supreme Court case upheld Jim Crow laws, and on what basis? **(c)** Do you think facilities can be "separate but equal"? Why or why not?

7. **(a)** Cite two cases in which the Supreme Court found sex-based distinctions to be unconstitutional. **(b)** Do you think the parameters that the Supreme Court uses when ruling on laws regarding the treatment of men and women are fair? Explain.

Section 3

8. **(a)** What do the Civil Rights Acts of 1964 and 1968 prohibit? **(b)** How was enforcement of the 1968 act given added strength?

9. **(a)** What was the first major affirmative action case ruled on by the Supreme Court? **(b)** How did the Supreme Court rule in the case? **(c)** What arguments do critics use when they claim that affirmative action is unconstitutional?

Section 4

10. **(a)** How does the 14th Amendment define citizenship? **(b)** In what circumstances may a child born abroad become an American citizen at birth?

11. **(a)** Why was immigration restricted in the 1880s and again in the 1920s? **(b)** Outline present immigration policy. **(c)** Who is excluded from entering the United States today?

Writing About Government

12. Use your Quick Write exercises from each Section Assessment to write a problem-solution essay about the topic you selected in Section 1. Begin with an interesting detail that grabs readers' attention, then explain the problem. Describe the pros and cons of two solutions, using supporting facts and details to outline the steps of what you consider to be the best proposal. Proofread and revise your rough draft into final manuscript. See pp. S3–S5 in the Skills Handbook.

Apply What You've Learned

13. **Essential Question Activity** Research major civil rights leaders in the United States, looking particularly for information on their ideals, struggles, and successes. Jot down notes as you work.

14. **Essential Question Assessment** Based on your research and the content you have learned in this chapter, create a timeline that helps to answer the Essential

Question: **Why are there ongoing struggles for civil rights?** Your timeline should include civil rights legislation and court cases, as well as quotes from famous civil rights leaders.

Essential Questions
Journal

To respond to the chapter Essential Question, go to your **Essential Questions Journal.**

Document-Based Assessment

Liberty, Equality, and Justice

"All men are created equal" were empty words for African Americans who faced de jure segregation in the South and de facto segregation in the North. These documents show that Dr. Martin Luther King, Jr., who emerged as the leader of the civil rights movement, inspired Americans to revive the civil rights struggle.

Document 1

Section 1 That all men are by nature equally free and independent and have certain inherent rights, of which, when they enter into a state of society, they cannot, by any compact, deprive or divest their posterity; namely, the enjoyment of life and liberty, with the means of acquiring and possessing property, and pursuing and obtaining happiness and safety.

—Virginia Declaration of Rights, 1776

Document 2

I say to you today, my friends, so even though we face the difficulties of today and tomorrow, I still have a dream. It is a dream deeply rooted in the American dream.

I have a dream that one day this nation will rise up and live out the true meaning of its creed: 'We hold these truths to be self-evident: that all men are created equal.'

I have a dream that one day on the red hills of Georgia the sons of former slaves and the sons of former slave owners will be able to sit down together at the table of brotherhood. . . .

I have a dream that my four little children will one day live in a nation where they will not be judged by the color of their skin but by the content of their character.

—Martin Luther King, Jr., "I Have a Dream," August 28, 1963

Document 3

Document 4

Injustice anywhere is a threat to justice everywhere. We are caught in an inescapable network of mutuality, tied in a single garment of destiny. Whatever affects one directly, affects all indirectly. Never again can we afford to live with the narrow, provincial 'outside agitator' idea. Anyone who lives inside the United States can never be considered an outsider anywhere within its bounds.

—Martin Luther King, Jr., "Letter From Birmingham Jail," April 16, 1963

Use your knowledge of civil rights and Documents 1–4 to answer the following questions.

1. Which statement best summarizes Document 4?
   A. Never stop fighting for your rights.
   B. We are all afflicted by injustice.
   C. Search your heart for the truth.
   D. All Americans should enjoy happiness and safety.

2. According to Document 1, what are the inherent rights of the American people?

3. From which founding document does King quote in Document 2?

4. What method of protest is illustrated in Document 3?

5. **Pull It Together** What is the common thread that is woven through these documents? Explain.

🢂 GOVERNMENT ONLINE

Documents

To find additional primary sources about civil rights, visit **PearsonSuccessNet.com**

Essential Question

What should be the role of the judicial branch?

Whether the role of the judicial branch should be to make law, apply law, or explain the law has been debated throughout history. The following examples each offer a perspective on the answer.

ON JUDICIAL ACTIVISM:

We want courts to settle the question of whether someone has exceeded the limits set by the law. And we want judges to be free of essential dependence upon the wielders of power so that they can do what they are supposed to do without being intimidated.

—Joseph Tussman, *Judicial Activism and the Rule of Law—Toward a Theory of Selective Intervention*

ON THE IMPLICATIONS OF LAWS WITHOUT COURTS:

Laws are dead letters without courts to expound and define their true meaning and operation.

—Alexander Hamilton, *The Federalist* No. 78

ON HOW JUSTICES RULE:

Essential Question Warmup

Throughout this unit, you studied the judicial branch. Use what you have learned and the quotations and opinions above to answer the following questions. Then go to your **Essential Questions Journal.**

1. What did Hamilton think should be the role of the judicial branch?

2. Are all laws completely constitutional or unconstitutional?

3. Should the role of the judicial branch change to adapt to changing times? Explain.

4. Should judges allow their personal views to guide their decisions? Why or why not?

Essential Questions Journal

To continue to build a response to the unit Essential Question, go to your **Essential Questions Journal.**

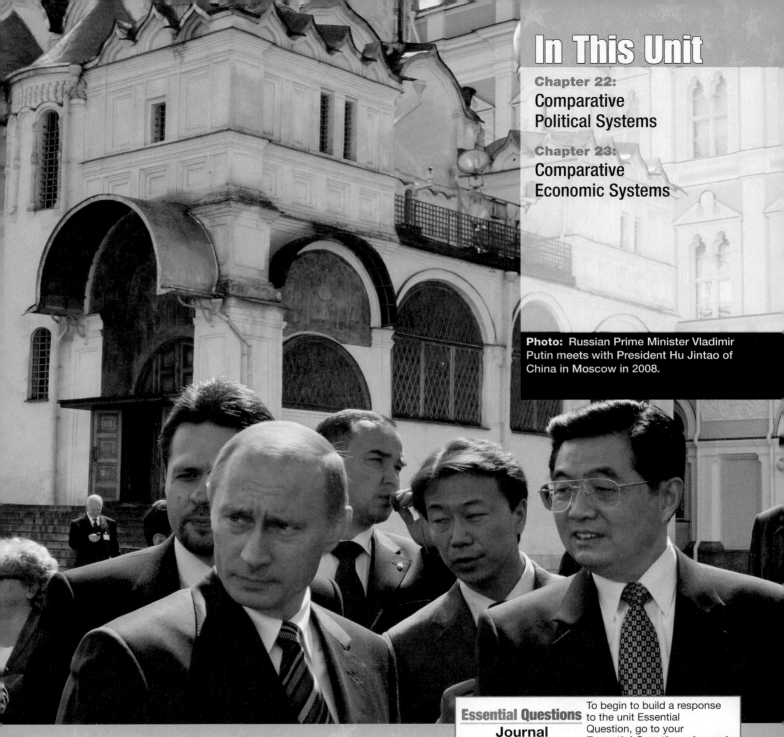

Photo: Russian Prime Minister Vladimir Putin meets with President Hu Jintao of China in Moscow in 2008.

Essential Questions Journal To begin to build a response to the unit Essential Question, go to your **Essential Questions Journal.**

Unit 6 Comparative Political and Economic Systems

Essential Question How should a government meet the needs of its people?

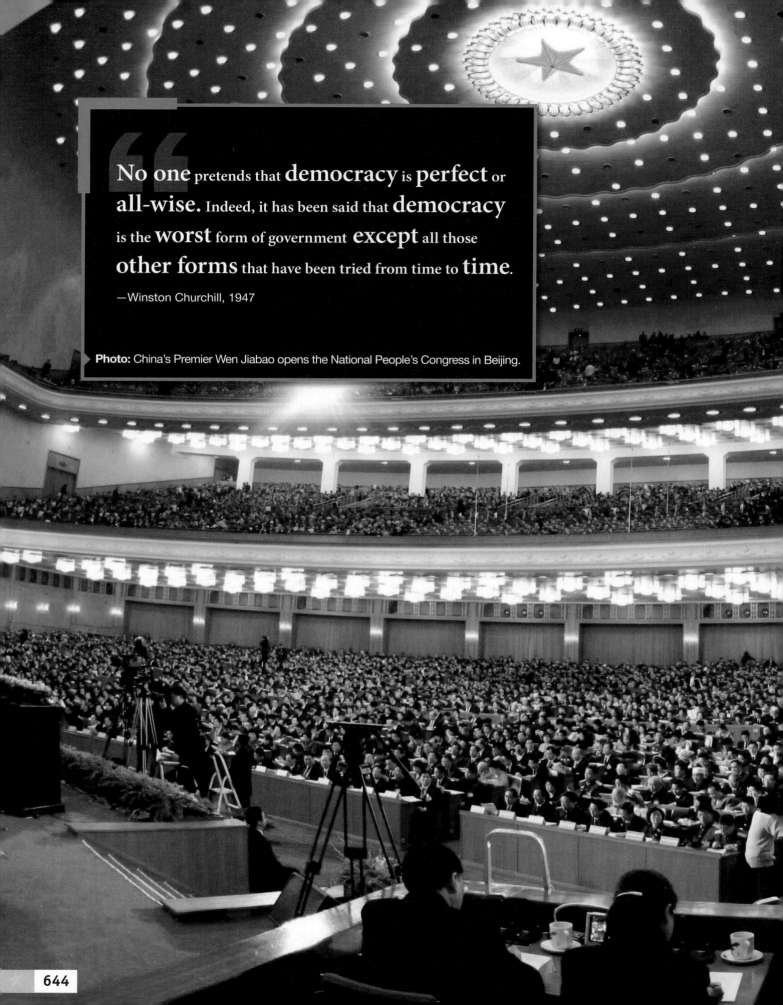

"**No one** pretends that **democracy** is **perfect** or **all-wise.** Indeed, it has been said that **democracy** is the **worst** form of government **except** all those **other forms** that have been tried from time to **time**.

—Winston Churchill, 1947

Photo: China's Premier Wen Jiabao opens the National People's Congress in Beijing.

Essential Question
How should you measure different governments?

Section 1:
Origins of the Modern State

Section 2:
Ideas and Revolutions

Section 3:
Transitions to Democracy

Section 4:
Case Studies in Democracy

GOVERNMENT ONLINE
On the Go

To study anywhere, anytime,
download these online resources
at PearsonSuccessNet.com
• Political Dictionary
• Audio Review
• Downloadable Interactivities

Origins of the Modern State

Guiding Question

On what early political ideas and traditions was modern government founded? Use an outline to take notes on the roots of modern American democracy.

I. Ancient Foundations
  A. Athens: The First Democracy
     1. _____
     2. _____
  B. _____
     1. _____
     2. _____

Political Dictionary

- patricians
- plebeians
- feudalism
- sovereignty
- legitimacy
- divine right of kings
- colonialism
- mercantilism

Objectives

1. Identify the ancient foundations of the state in Athens, in Rome, and in the feudal system.
2. Analyze the rise of sovereign states.
3. Explain how governments can achieve legitimacy.
4. Understand why European nations turned to colonialism.

Image Above: The *agora*, a large public space, was the ancient home of Athenian democracy.

As you know, government is among the oldest of all human inventions. It emerged long before the dawn of recorded history, when human beings first realized that they could not survive without it—that is, without some means by which they could regulate their own and their neighbors' behavior. The earliest evidences of government date back some 3,000 years, but clearly the institution is much older than that.

An uncountable number of governments of various forms have appeared, and disappeared, through the centuries in Europe, Asia, Africa, and the Americas. Those that survived for any length of time were those that could adapt to major changes in their environments.

The roots of democratic government in today's world—including government in the United States—lie deep in human history. They reach back most particularly to ancient Greece and Rome and also to later beliefs and practices that emerged elsewhere in Europe.

Ancient Foundations

Those who built a governmental system for the newly independent United States in the late 1700s were, on the whole, well educated. They were quite familiar with the political institutions of their day and, importantly, those of ancient Greece and Rome, as well.

Athens: The First Democracy Greek civilization began to develop some 700 to 800 years before the birth of Christ, and it reached its peak in the fourth century B.C. The Greece of that time was a loose collection of many small, independent, and somewhat isolated city-states[1]—a pattern dictated by the geography of the region, where every island, valley, and plain is cut off from its neighbors by the sea or by mountain ranges.

The concept of democracy was born in those city-states, most notably in Athens. Like the other city-states, Athens began as a monarchy. By the sixth century B.C., however, the Athenians had overthrown monarchical rule, and

---

1 Originally, the city-state (*polis*) was a defensible location to which those who lived in a particular locale could retreat when attacked. Over time, towns grew up around those defensible places.

they soon replaced it with what they called *demokratia*—literally, "rule by the people."

Athenian democracy was, at base, direct democracy. Its central feature was an Assembly (the *Ecclesia*) composed of male citizens at least 18 years of age.[2] The Assembly met 40 times a year to debate public matters and make law. Decisions in the Assembly were made by majority vote.

The Assembly's agenda was set by a Council of Five Hundred (the *boule*). That body was composed of 500 citizens who were chosen randomly, served one-month terms, and did the routine day-to-day work of government. Courts (*dikastria*) were staffed by judges who were at least 30 years of age. They, too, were chosen randomly, served one-year terms, and settled both public and private disputes.

Athens reached the peak of its glory in art, literature, and philosophy in the fifth century B.C., but it had been severely weakened by the long Peloponnesian War (431–404 B.C.) and later conquest by the Macedonians. What remained of Athenian democracy was <u>extinguished</u> by the Romans who overran Greece in 146 B.C.

In Latin, SPQR stands for "the Senate and the people of Rome," the source of all government authority in the Roman Republic. ***How well did the Senate represent the people of Rome?***

extinguish
v. end, destroy

The Roman Republic At about the time that glimmers of democracy first appeared in Greece, they began to emerge as well in Rome on the Italian peninsula. Rome was founded in 753 B.C. and, like Athens, was originally a city-state ruled by a monarchy. Monarchical rule was overthrown in 509 B.C. and was soon replaced by a rude form of popular government. The Romans referred to their new system as *res publica*, a republic.[3] The Roman Republic was to last for some 400 years, until it became the Roman Empire at the end of the first century B.C. Over that period, Rome, involved in almost continuous military conflict, expanded its domain to include most of the lands surrounding the Mediterranean Sea and nearly all of Western Europe.

The Republic was far from democratic in the modern sense. It did introduce the concept of representation, however. Much of the political history of the republican period revolved around an often violent struggle between two social classes: the **patricians,** mostly rich upper-class, landowning aristocrats; and the **plebeians,** the common folk. The Romans did hold elections to choose some public officials, but women, slaves, and the foreign-born could not participate.

Government was centered in the Senate, composed of some 300 members, and two consuls chosen by the Senate. Senators were elected by the citizenry. The patricians dominated that body, but, over time, an increasing number of plebeians were elected to the Senate and to a number of lesser assemblies. The consuls were, effectively, the heads of state. They commanded the army and conducted foreign affairs. The consuls also presided over the Senate and enforced its decrees. Interestingly, each consul had the power to veto the other's decisions. In times of crisis, the Senate could appoint a

---

2 Neither political rights nor citizenship were granted to women, slaves, or males born to noncitizens. In all, only some 30,000 of Athens' estimated 250,000 inhabitants were citizens in the fourth century B.C.

3 From the Latin *res,* meaning "thing" or "matter," and *publicus* or *publica,* meaning "the public"—thus, "the public's thing," a thing belonging to the public

epochal event
n. beginning of an era marked by notable happenings

dictator to serve in place of the consuls and exercise absolute power, but for no longer than six months.[4]

Feudalism The decline and fall of the Roman Empire in the fifth century A.D. marked the beginning of the Middle Ages— the period from that epochal event on to the 16th century. It also marked the collapse of centralized authority and organized government over vast stretches of the western world. For more than a thousand years, that world would know little or nothing of government in the modern sense of the term.

The feudal system was born in response to that chaos and disorder. It developed in fits and starts and came to hold sway over much of Europe from the ninth through the twelfth centuries. **Feudalism** was a loosely organized system in which powerful lords divided their lands among other, lesser lords. Those with land and power agreed to protect others in exchange for their loyalty, their military service, and a share of the crops they produced. The basic economic units in the feudal system were the lords' manors. Each manor contained all of a lord's land holdings, which often included a town or village, as well.

The primary relationship in the feudal chain was that between a lord and his vassals, lesser lords who pledged their loyalty to the ranking lord—who was, in some places, a monarch. The lord ruled and the vassals served him, watching over the lands in their section of the manor.

The lord did perform some functions of the state in the modern world. He provided protection for his vassals and administered a rough form of justice. In return, the vassals supported the lord's decisions and served under his military command when necessary. The lord-vassal relationship was but one part of a large complex of relationships. Often, a vassal was himself a lord to other, less powerful vassals, and a lord was sometimes a vassal under an even more powerful lord.

Serfs, the bulk of the population, lived at the bottom of the chain of feudal relationships. They were peasants, bound to the land

catalyst
n. something that prompts, brings about, change

---

[4] The word *dictator* comes from the Latin *dictare,* meaning "to say or pronounce."

they farmed. The serfs gave a share of what they grew to their vassals in return for protection in times of war. They led harsh lives. None could leave the land without the lord's permission, and their children inherited their ties and responsibilities to the lord. Most died young, never having journeyed more than a few miles from the lord's manor.

The Roman Catholic Church As the Roman Empire had spread across Western Europe, so had Roman Catholicism. The Church survived the collapse of imperial rule and now, in concert with feudalism, it provided some measure of government-like order to life in the Europe of the Middle Ages.

The Roman Catholic Church, now nearly 2,000 years old, traces its origins to the birth of Christianity and to the death of Jesus in Jerusalem, in the Roman province of Judea, in A.D. 33. Catholicism managed to overcome three centuries of often violent persecution by a succession of hostile emperors. In A.D. 380, the Roman Catholic Church became the official church of the Roman Empire.

As most of Europe was converted to Christianity—that is, as most Europeans became Catholics—the Roman Catholic Church became increasingly powerful. By the late Middle Ages, the pope and his bishops ruled vast land holdings, and they frequently vied with monarchs and lords for political as well as religious influence over people's lives.

Rise of the Sovereign State

Feudalism was, at best, a loose, makeshift basis for government. As cracks emerged in the system—between Catholics and Protestants and the feudal manor and the marketplace—the need for a more structured arrangement became apparent. The outlines of the modern, sovereign nation-state began to emerge.

The Commercial Revolution By the end of the Middle Ages, a commercial revolution began to change the ways in which people lived and did business. A horrific plague, the Black Plague of the 1340s, was a major catalyst of that revolution. In all, it killed a third of Western Europe's population. The

Roots of the Sovereign State

The defining elements of sovereign states developed over time and in different lands. *What characteristics define the United States as a sovereign state?*

GOVERNMENT ONLINE
Audio Tour
Listen to a guided audio tour on sovereignty at
PearsonSuccessNet.com

Ancient Athens

The Athenians introduced direct democracy. Citizens debated public questions and decided them by majority vote. Courts administered justice.

Roman Republic

The Roman Republic gave decision-making power to an elite Senate and consuls who could check each other and, in theory, represented the people. The laws of Rome were written for all to see.

Feudalism

In the Feudal Era, Europe's first parliaments emerged and began to limit the powers of kings. England provided for trial by a jury of one's peers.

17th century

Sovereignty emerged in the 17th century, with states with fixed borders, a national identity, and a centralized government with broad authority.

ET SAPIENTEAR: AD PRE ALIVM   CONRA·AN

Above: The Norman Invasion of 1066 brought feudalism to England.

Plague itself did not destroy the feudal system. Rather its far-reaching effects undercut that system.

After the plague, the manors still depended on the same amount of work, but from the smaller number of serfs who had survived. Serfs and free peasants found strength in the high value of their labor and began to demand higher wages and better conditions.

Because of the vast decrease in population caused by the plague, the prices of food crops fell, and so the lords made less money from their manorial lands. Merchants and artisans became increasingly wealthy and more powerful. The economy became increasingly based on money and trade, rather than land.

The Influence of Towns As you know, feudalism relied on personal relationships and agreements in which people exchanged work and food for security and justice. Over time,

lords had to find new ways to gather money. Some lords accepted money from their vassals in place of military service. Others allowed free people to set up towns on their land for a fee under a charter. In this way, towns began to spring up across Europe. Those towns were centers of trade and freedom that tested the limits of feudalism.

The most important of these towns were found in northern Italy, northern Germany, and the Netherlands. Their income came from trade with Central Europe and Asia. The merchants in these towns had uneasy relationships with the lords. Although the merchants were free, they had to pay money to lords for protection, duties on their trade goods, and the right to use roads, rivers, and bridges. Many lords tried to extend their system of justice to the towns. They often failed, because they depended on the merchants and bankers of the towns for loans. Trade <u>guilds</u> also developed

✓ **Checkpoint**
Why did feudalism endure?

<u>guild</u>
n. association of craftsmen or merchants

in the cities and towns, and their members demanded a say in government.

The Rise of Monarchies All of these factors began to undermine the feudal system, weakening the power of the lords. At the same time, the leaders of the towns began to appreciate the benefits of supporting a central authority and they allied themselves with monarchs. The monarchs, in turn, saw the towns as a source of wealth that could free them from dependence on their vassals.

Therefore, by the late 1400s the powers of the monarchs were expanding, and feudalism was fast disappearing. In nations such as England, Spain, and France, rulers centralized power, establishing national governments with national legal systems, national identities, and, most important for the monarchs, national taxes. Warfare now was between national armies, not between powerful nobles. Monarchs, whose power was absolute or nearly so, no longer needed the lords to support them and could also ignore popular representative assemblies, if they wished, for long periods of time.

To help manage the national government, monarchs hired loyal civil servants typically born in the towns and educated at local universities. Their perspectives were

charismatic
adj. having personal appeal and attractiveness

⬆ In the 1400s, King Ferdinand and Queen Isabella united their lands in marriage into what became the Kingdom of Spain. The unification of power in Spain, France, and England led to the establishment of colonies overseas.

national, not regional. The state, in the person of the monarch, now had **sovereignty,** or the utmost authority in decision making and in maintaining order. Everyone, including the nobles, was subordinate to that authority.

Because monarchs already existed within the feudal system, they enjoyed the benefits and respect of tradition. A monarch was now recognized as the strongest individual who could best govern a state and protect the people from harm. With sovereignty, the monarch now had the right to make laws for the entire nation and all its people.

Legitimacy

The development of the sovereign state was useful in creating political organization, but claiming sovereignty alone does not establish government. All governments must have legitimacy to rule.

Rulers have strong reasons to seek consent for their rule. This consent is known as **legitimacy,** the belief of the people that a government has the right to make public policy. A legitimate government is one that is accepted by its people and other governments as the sovereign authority of a nation. Leaders may use force to keep power. However, force is difficult to maintain over time.

Governments may gain legitimacy in several ways. One is by tradition. In this case, people accept a certain form of government because their society has long been governed in that way, and people expect their institutions and traditions to be carried on into the future. One type of traditional legitimacy is known as the **divine right of kings.** For hundreds of years, European monarchs based their right to rule on this belief that God had granted them that authority. To disobey a monarch was to deny the natural order of society and to commit a sin against God. In theory, monarchs who ruled by divine right did not have to answer to parliaments or to the people, only to God. The divine right of kings drew its claim to legitimacy from Europe's deep-rooted Christian values.

Another way for a government, and in particular one leader, to win legitimacy is through the power of personality. A <u>charismatic</u> person with strong leadership skills can often win popular support. The people agree to allow this person to rule them.

The final and most durable form of legitimacy is created when a government binds itself to the rule of law. The law must be seen as fair and effective for people to trust their government. Constitutional government in the United States is an excellent example of this form of legitimacy.

Colonialism

Beginning in the late 1400s and early 1500s, several European monarchies embarked on a policy of **colonialism**—the control of one nation over lands abroad. European settlers, laws, and religious beliefs spread around the world as rival nations competed for colonial possessions.

Colonial trade and its wealth brought newfound power to merchants, and monarchs adopted mercantilism to control and profit from that situation. **Mercantilism** is an economic and political theory emphasizing money as the chief source of wealth to increase the absolute power of the monarchy and the nation. The policy stressed the accumulation of precious metals, like gold and silver. It also called for the establishment of colonies and a merchant marine and the development of industry and mining to attain a favorable balance of trade with other countries. Mercantilist policies brought the monarchy and the state deep into the economy. Monarchs taxed imports heavily to protect locally produced goods. Foreigners were required to buy licenses from the state in order to trade with local merchants. Monarchs sought to fill their treasuries and enhance their own and their nations' power.

Mercantilism expanded when European explorers reached the Western Hemisphere. Their explorations there opened new opportunities for trade and farming, but only monarchs had the wealth and power to establish and control new colonies.

The high cost of exploration allowed monarchs to control overseas commerce by setting up companies to <u>monopolize</u> trade with the new regions. The company system allowed monarchs to tap new sources of wealth from distant gold and silver mines and from far-flung trade.

European colonization brought about new developments in modern government. Britain's colonial efforts led to the American Revolution and the creation of the United States and its constitutional government. The experiences of other countries originally colonized by Spain, France, Portugal, and even Great Britain, however, differed in several ways from the American experience.

Checkpoint
Why is legitimacy important?

<u>monopolize</u>
v. prevent others from sharing; control, dominate

Essential Questions Journal — To continue to build a response to the chapter Essential Question, go to your **Essential Questions Journal.**

SECTION 1 ASSESSMENT

1. **Guiding Question** Use your completed outline to answer this question: On what early political ideas and traditions was modern government founded?

Key Terms and Comprehension

2. How did the Athenian *ecclesia* differ from the Roman Senate?

3. What were the main elements of **feudalism**?

4. How did the power of **monarchs** change over time?

Critical Thinking

5. **Understanding Cause and Effect** How did the rise of towns and the commercial revolution contribute to the decline of the feudal system?

6. **Drawing Inferences** Why is it necessary that governments gain legitimacy?

Quick Write

Expository Writing: Select a Topic The goal of a compare-and-contrast essay is to analyze similarities and differences between two topics. Select two systems of government or examples of nations that developed into democracies to compare and contrast in your essay. As you read, use a Venn diagram to record similarities and differences between your two selections.

Using the Internet as a News Source

Suppose your teacher gave you the following assignment in Government class: Write a report on this week's visit of Japan's prime minister to the United States. Include major locations where the prime minister spoke and the results of any meetings with the President.

When researching current events, such as the visit of a foreign leader to the United States, Internet news sources are extremely helpful—provided you are careful about evaluating the sources which you use. Major television networks, newspapers, and magazines all have Web sites, and they are usually trustworthy. Examples include CNN, the BBC, National Public Radio, *The Wall Street Journal, The New York Times,* and so on. Government Web sites are also excellent sources.

To use the Internet as a news source, follow these steps:

1. **Determine your search term(s).** To search most effectively on the Internet, you need to determine a specific term or topic. Searching for a broad subject can yield too many responses that do not address your questions. For example, "Japan prime minister" will yield thousands of results in a search engine which would take a lot of time to sift through. In this case, you might use the prime minister's name and "U.S. visit."

2. **Use a search engine to find information on your topic or to locate specific news sources.** Type in the search term for your topic or the name of a specific news organization, such as *Newsweek,* if you already have one in mind. You can also simply type "news" into a search engine, but it will take you much longer to locate specific information on your topic. News sources that are local to the event may provide unique information and coverage.

3. **Be sure that your sources have a reputation for accurate news coverage.** Some news organizations have better reputations for accuracy and objective reporting than others, but findings from all sources should be confirmed with at least a second source. If you are unsure of a source's reliability, compare its information with similar information from a source you know to be trustworthy.

▶▶ What do you think?

1. Why is it important to determine your topic or search terms before you begin an Internet search?

2. How can you determine the reliability of a news source?

3. **You Try It** Choose a topic in the news related to the government or politics of one of the nations covered in this chapter. Determine your search terms, and then type them into a search engine. Follow the results that you think are good news sources. Take notes about the types of information you find on your topic at each of at least three Web sites you think are trustworthy—reports, editorials, photographs, video, and so on.

🔍 GOVERNMENT ONLINE
Citizenship Activity Pack

For an activity to help you use the Internet for research, go to **PearsonSuccessNet.com**

SECTION 2

Ideas and Revolutions

Guiding Question

How have some nations expanded popular sovereignty? Use a flowchart similar to the one below to record information about how different nations have expanded popular sovereignty.

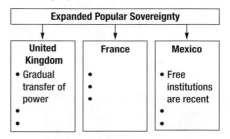

Political Dictionary

- *encomienda*
- guerrilla warfare
- fascism
- communism

Objectives

1. Understand how Enlightenment ideas helped influence the expansion of popular sovereignty.
2. Analyze the role of popular sovereignty in England, France, and around the world.
3. Describe events in Latin America, Asia, and Africa that expanded popular sovereignty.
4. Examine how fascism and communism distort the concept of popular sovereignty.

Image Above: Simón Bolivar led many South American nations to independence from Spain.

In the previous section, you traced the development of governments in Europe from ancient Greece and Rome to the rise of the sovereign state and absolute monarchy. In addition, you discovered how sovereign states gain legitimacy. In this section, you will see how legitimacy leads to stable government. You will also discover how governments without legitimacy can fall to revolutions and tyranny.

The Enlightenment

By the beginning of the eighteenth century, scientific discoveries and new thinking had led to an intellectual movement based on reason and known as the Enlightenment. Some of the most important ideas about modern government, economics, and society were developed at the time, when people began to discuss the rights of individuals to control their own fates and to have a say in their governments.

Early in the movement, English political theorist John Locke (1632–1704) put forth the notion of the natural rights of all human beings, including the rights to life, liberty, and property—ideas that later formed the basis for the Declaration of Independence. He built on the view of fellow Englishman Thomas Hobbes (1588–1679): that the people and their rulers are parties to a social contract that defines the rights and powers of each. Economists, including Adam Smith (1723–1790) and David Ricardo (1772–1823), criticized economic policies that helped monarchs grow wealthier while most of their subjects became steadily poorer and less free.

In France, the philosopher François-Marie Arouet (1694–1778), known as Voltaire, advocated reason, freedom of religion, the importance of scientific observation, and the idea of human progress. The ideas of the Baron de Montesquieu (1689–1755) were crucial to political theory during the Enlightenment. His theories about the separation of powers in government, so that different branches may check and balance each other, were integral to what was to become the Constitution of the United States.

As reason and secular thinking began to supersede religious belief, monarchs lost some of their divine legitimacy, and their God-given sovereignty came into question. More and more people began to feel that even monarchs governed only because the people granted them the power to do so. If a monarch abused his or her power, he or she broke the social contract with the people and no longer deserved to rule. In this way, popular sovereignty became increasingly important, even in a monarchy. Recall that popular sovereignty is the idea that governments can exist only with the consent of the governed.

Popular sovereignty would eventually form the basis for the many republics and democracies in the world today. Since the eighteenth century, almost every government has had to address issues of popular sovereignty in one way or another.

Two Roads to Popular Sovereignty

Two leading monarchies in Western Europe, Britain and France, took very different paths to popular sovereignty. In Britain, popular sovereignty was achieved gradually. As one of the first modern countries where the people began to have a say in their government, Britain blended popular sovereignty with deep-seated cultural traditions. Meanwhile, France took a revolutionary route to popular sovereignty and rejected many longstanding traditions.

Democracy in Britain Great Britain, now the United Kingdom, is today a constitutional monarchy. Yet that nation functions as a democracy much like the United States. Britons elect a government that is responsible to them and which draws its legitimacy from their votes and support. Great Britain was not always democratic, however. How did a country once ruled by powerful monarchs become a vibrant democracy?

The UK's history is marked by the gradual transfer of sovereignty from the monarchy to the people. The Magna Carta in 1215 was the first move toward a constitutional monarchy. In the 1640s, the English people went to war against their monarch, King Charles I. He was tried, found guilty, and executed as a tyrant and traitor in 1649. The Petition of Right of 1628 and the Bill of Rights of 1689 took more authority from the monarch and gave it to Parliament, which represented the people. Parliament controlled "the power of

Two Revolutions

Monarchies in Britain and France adapted to popular sovereignty—one nation peacefully, the other violently. Each country's transition began with a revolutionary moment that determined the shape of future events. *What were the effects of each form of revolution?*

The French Revolution

1789–1794 The French revolutionary government violently overthrew King Louis XVI, the nobility, and the Church, creating a new republic with new institutions that did not last very long.

Britain's Glorious Revolution

1688 Parliament invited William and Mary (above) to peacefully replace King James II on condition that they recognize the authority of Parliament and the rights of individuals.

the purse," the right to tax people to fund the government. Through this lever, this representative body gained more and more power over the monarchy.

The conception of exactly who "the people" are has also evolved in the UK as it has in the United States. Well into the nineteenth century, only male property owners could vote, and only those who belonged to officially recognized Protestant churches could hold public office. At times, some of the largest cities in Great Britain had no representation in Parliament at all.

Far-sighted members of Parliament recognized the need for change. In the 1800s, Parliament passed several laws to expand the right to vote. A law passed in 1829 allowed Roman Catholics to hold public office. Landmark parliamentary acts in 1832, 1867, and 1885 reduced and then removed property restrictions. Women gained the right to vote in 1918. By adapting its government to embrace popular sovereignty, Great Britain protected many of its institutions, including the monarchy, Parliament, the legal system, and the Church of England. These institutions have changed to meet the needs of a modern economy and diverse society, but they preserve a link to Britain's past.

Revolution in France France took a very different route toward popular sovereignty. While the British monarchy compromised with nobles and Parliament gained power, the French monarchy expanded and centralized its authority. Royal power reached its peak under Louis XIV (1643–1715), who famously and accurately proclaimed, "L'état, c'est moi." ("I am the state.") He was the epitome of the absolute monarch. The continuing concentration of power in the monarchy set the stage for a violent reaction led by those who adopted the concept of popular sovereignty based on reason and the natural rights of the governed.

The French Revolution of 1789 would see the end, temporarily, of the French monarchy, followed by a period of confusion and fear known as The Terror. This period was soon followed by the rise of the empire of Napoleon and war with the rest of Europe. Historic institutions like the monarchy, nobility, church, and law were destroyed and

replaced by new ones. France has undergone a number of revolutions and changes in government since the Revolution of 1789. Today, it is a representative, constitutional democracy, much like the United States, with no monarch.

Does the experience of Britain or France serve as a better model for those countries currently seeking to increase popular sovereignty? The British example was accomplished more slowly and with less bloodshed, but it took hundreds of years before all adult Britons had the right to vote. On the other hand, the instability of a revolution, as in the French model, can lead to chaos and abuse of power. In 1959, for example, many cheered when Fidel Castro overthrew the corrupt dictatorship of Fulgencio Batista in Cuba. However, the destruction of Cuba's old political system created a vacuum that Castro then filled with his own absolute authority, and Cuba is today as far from a democracy as it has ever been.

Political events in Europe significantly influenced the course of political development in Latin America, Asia, and Africa. However, the colonies in those regions would have very different experiences from those of the European states or of the 13 British colonies that became the United States.

Latin America

Spain, which controlled large portions of North and South America and the Caribbean into the 1800s, established a different system of government in its colonies than did other nations. To control the Indian population and force its subjects to labor in mining and agriculture, the Spanish crown instituted a system called the **encomienda.** Under this system, the monarch granted control of Indians living in a specific area to a settler. The grant did not include ownership of any land, but the settler could demand tribute and work from the Indians he controlled. In return, the settler was supposed to protect the Indians and see that they were instructed in the Catholic faith.

The *encomienda* system basically failed. Settlers took over Indian lands and worked the people to death in virtual slavery. The

✔ **Checkpoint**
How did democracy in the UK differ from democracy in France?

epitome
n. perfect representation, model

Latin American Independence

▶▶ **Interpreting Maps** Most countries in the Western Hemisphere won their independence from Spain or Portugal, which practiced a different form of colonial rule than had Britain in North America. *How did Spanish colonial rule continue to influence governments in Latin America after independence?*

British North America (Br.)

UNITED STATES 1776

TEXAS 1836

MEXICO 1821

ATLANTIC OCEAN

Bahamas (Br.)

Cuba (Sp.)

HAITI 1804

DOMINICAN REPUBLIC 1844

Puerto Rico (Sp.)

British Honduras

Jamaica (Br.)

GUATEMALA 1838
EL SALVADOR 1838
HONDURAS 1838
NICARAGUA 1838
COSTA RICA 1838

Mosquito Coast (Br.)

VENEZUELA 1830

British Guiana

Dutch Guiana

French Guiana

COLOMBIA 1819

ECUADOR 1822

PACIFIC OCEAN

PERU 1824

BRAZIL 1822

BOLIVIA 1825

PARAGUAY 1811

CHILE 1818

ARGENTINA 1816

URUGUAY 1828

KEY

- ▓ former British colony
- ▓ former French colony
- ▓ former Portuguese colony
- ░ former Spanish colony
- ▨ British colony
- ▨ Dutch colony
- ▨ French colony
- ▨ Spanish colony

Dates shown are dates of independence

🔘 **GOVERNMENT** ONLINE
Audio Tour
Listen to a guided audio tour of this map at
PearsonSuccessNet.com

encomienda system was eventually replaced by *haciendas,* large estates to which workers were tied, like serfs. These extensive landholdings would emerge as nearly self-sufficient centers of political and economic power throughout much of Latin America.

When Spain was conquered by Emperor Napoleon of France in the early 1800s, Latin America began to move toward independence. Many colonial elites rejected Napoleon's choice for the Spanish throne, his brother Joseph I, and remained loyal to the deposed Ferdinand VII. Other colonials, most notably Simón Bolivar, were inspired by the same Enlightenment ideas that gave rise to the American and French revolutions. They sought to create a new political order in Latin America, based on popular sovereignty.

Independence When Ferdinand VII regained the Spanish crown in 1814, he agreed to grant greater power to parliament and place some restrictions on the Church. His conservative supporters in the colonies felt betrayed. Thus, in Mexico, Agustín de Iturbide engineered that country's independence in 1821 and had himself crowned its emperor. Iturbide soon would be forced to give up his throne, and Mexico, like many of the new states of Latin America, would fall into periods of civil war throughout the nineteenth century. Most of Latin America similarly won independence from Spain (and Brazil from Portugal) in the decades after Napoleon conquered Spain and left the country too weak to control its colonies.

Obstacles to Stability It was difficult for democracy to take root in the region, however. As in Mexico, political stability was rare in most of what was postcolonial Spanish America.

Why were the new states of Latin America less able to maintain popular sovereignty than the colonies that became the United States? A main reason lay in that those 13 colonies were British, and Great Britain had a tradition of limited representative government, an expanding sense of popular sovereignty, and a population greatly influenced by the Enlightenment. The British colonists, therefore, had existing ideas that formed a basis for wanting and for justifying independence. Although the British monarch was very powerful, there was a belief among Britons that they had certain rights in the face of tyranny. Also, there were no all-powerful elites in the British colonies, as there were in Latin America, to struggle against independence.

In Latin America, social, political, and cultural traditions originated in Spain and Portugal—nations that at that time had not embraced ideas of popular sovereignty. Those nations were ruled by absolute monarchs, with little popular representation. The Catholic Church also had enormous influence and supported the <u>status quo</u>. There was little in the history or traditions of these colonials, for the most part, to help them foster or maintain democratic institutions.

Hacienda landowners were a powerful barrier to popular sovereignty. They did not want to give up their authority, property, and privileges, and they fought among themselves for control of the central government. Once in government, they faced new rebellions because they did little to solve the economic and social problems. This cycle of political disorder was common throughout Latin America well into the twentieth century.

Latin America's political troubles slowed its economic development, while relative political stability allowed countries such as Britain, France, Germany, and the United States to embrace the Industrial Revolution and the economic growth that followed.

The Mexican Revolution

Throughout the 1800s, Mexico's leaders <u>grappled</u>, often violently, with a number of questions. Should there be a centralized or, instead, a federal government? How much power should a single political leader have? How could Mexico remain independent from its powerful neighbor to the north and other major world powers?

President Porfirio Díaz brought the Republic of Mexico its first long period of stability and economic growth, from 1876 to 1910. His economic plan was based on using cheap labor to work the mineral wealth and large farms of Mexico, and inviting large foreign firms to invest in the exploitation of the country's natural resources. Those policies benefited few Mexicans. In time, the people revolted against Díaz's harsh rule, and so began a long period of civil war.

In 1917, the revolutionaries won and wrote a new constitution in which the government played a more active role in promoting the quality of Mexican social, economic, and cultural life. Though revolutionaries Emilio Zapata and Pancho Villa were assassinated, the new government absorbed their call for extensive reform in a state-supported political party. The National Revolutionary Party was formed in 1929, but later changed its name to the Institutional Revolutionary Party (PRI). The PRI controlled the government and politics of Mexico until 2000.

Latin America in the Modern Era

While Mexico remained stable under the control of the PRI, the period of the 1960s to 1980s proved to be violent elsewhere in Latin America. Throughout the nineteenth century and the first half of the twentieth century, most countries experienced cycles of dictatorship and military control, with wealth and land concentrated in the hands of a few. Democracy sprouted in the region during the 1950s, but continued economic decline and growing inequality fueled demands for real reforms. Many were inspired by the Cuban Revolution in 1959, which, based on communist ideology, promised to attend to the basic needs of the people. They often resorted to guerrilla warfare in an attempt to topple their governments. **Guerrilla warfare** is fighting carried out by small groups in hit-and-run raids.

The threat that communist guerrillas and others posed in the 1960s and 1970s led the national armed forces to take more active roles in several countries. Military leaders believed that Latin America's continued economic problems stemmed from the endless debate and corruption of politicians. In its view, the political class had to be curbed and the armed forces had to seize power to strengthen the economy and restore political

<u>status quo</u>
n. condition that currently exists

<u>grapple</u>
v. struggle, wrestle with

peace. Only then would Latin America prosper. Democracy could come later.

Despite these struggles, the idea of popular sovereignty—government in the name of the people—remained important. Every military leader who intervened in a crisis claimed to be working toward democracy. Nonetheless, military rule soon led to tyranny. Innocent civilians were caught up in heavy-handed efforts to defeat the guerrilla groups.

The events that unfolded in Latin America over this period received little official criticism from abroad. During the Cold War, the United States was concerned chiefly with the spread of the Soviet Union's communist influence in the Americas. The end of the Cold War brought new opportunities for democracy in Latin America.

Asia and Africa

Unlike Latin America, where most countries had won independence by 1830, some of Asia and most of Africa remained under colonial control through the mid-twentieth century. In theory, by this time, the ruling nations of Europe were preparing colonies in these regions for democracy. In practice, they governed with little respect for native cultures and did not provide the structures the colonies would need to thrive after independence.

The main goal of colonialism was always the control of distant lands to extract resources that would enrich the parent country. At the Conference of Berlin (1884–1885), major European powers carved nearly the entire continent of Africa into colonial holdings, with artificial boundaries that often divided tribal lands or forced diverse groups into a single colony. Not infrequently, a colonial power would favor one segment of the population over another to advance its own interests. These "divide and rule" techniques would leave lasting legacies in many places. In Rwanda, efforts by the Belgians to pit Hutus against Tutsis created tensions that exploded in the mass killings of the 1990s, more than 30 years after independence.

Economically, each colony was directed to export a few specific resources to Europe. After independence, countries often found that reliance on one or a few cash crops or raw materials could drive their economies through cycles of prosperity and depression from year to year. Thus, a fall in the world price for coffee or oil could bring tremendous hardship to an entire country.

Another major problem facing the former colonies in Africa and Asia was that most won their independence in the 1950s and 1960s, at the height of the Cold War. Many countries, such as the former French colony Vietnam, were drawn into the Cold War when the Soviet Union and United States provided arms and money to different sides fighting for control of the newly independent countries.

Under these conditions, it is not surprising that democracy failed to take hold in many newly independent nations. Countries that combined many ethnic groups had few common traditions to build upon. Conflict and mistrust made it difficult to adopt a legal system on which everyone could agree. The only way for a government to gain legitimacy was to improve the lives of the people and bring peace quickly. Unfortunately, this left

▸▸ **Interpreting Political Cartoons** The borders of many modern African nations still follow the lines drawn by European colonizing powers at the Conference of Berlin in 1884–1885. *Why is Africa* **(Afrique** *in* **French) represented by a cake in this cartoon?**

governments vulnerable to economic crises and appealing figures who easily became dictators. Because most former colonies had underdeveloped economies, there was no large middle class to balance the interests of the vast numbers of poor and of the few elite. The military often stood as the only recognizable national institution, so it could intervene in a crisis with much popular support. However, in almost every case, the military then refused to give up power after the crisis and repressed its critics.

Fascism and Communism

The experience of dictatorship has been common throughout the world. Two of the political philosophies that created the most powerful and destructive dictatorships, particularly in Europe and Asia, are fascism and Communism. **Fascism** describes a centralized, authoritarian government with policies that glorify the state over the individual. **Communism** is principally an economic theory, and you will read more about the economics of Communist states in the next chapter. In the context of government, communism describes a state based on the idea of complete government control of the economy to serve the welfare of workers, without regard for individual liberty. Although the two political movements are quite distinct, they share some traits.

Both Communist and fascist governments go to great lengths to address the idea of popular sovereignty, though in doing

✔ **Checkpoint**
What factors affected government in newly independent countries in Asia and Africa?

⊙ **GOVERNMENT** ONLINE
Audio Tour
Listen to a guided audio tour of this diagram at **PearsonSuccessNet.com**

Fascism and Communism

Fascism and communism are totalitarian political systems in which the state has complete control over society, but they differ in some goals and economic policies. *How did fascist and Communist governments benefit from identifying and attacking an "enemy of the people"?*

Similarities

- One-party states with no free elections or fair courts
- People gathered into a mass movement against an enemy
- A strong military and militarized society
- Government-controlled media broadcasting propaganda and censored news

Nazi youth parade in Germany ▶

Differences

Adolf Hitler,
Fascist dictator
Germany, 1933–1945

Fascist state

- Nation defined on racial or ethnic terms
- Foreign powers and minorities are the enemy
- State-directed economy with private enterprise
- Some religions tolerated but controlled

Communist state

- State embodies the working class
- Global capitalism is the enemy
- State-controlled economy
- Religion discouraged or outlawed

Josef Stalin,
Communist dictator
Soviet Union, 1924–1953

so they distort that concept significantly. As radical movements, they raise some concerns also found in the French Revolution, most notably: Does revolution open the door to the abuse of power?

Fascist Governments Historic examples of fascism include Adolf Hitler's Germany, (1933–1945), Benito Mussolini's Italy (1922–1943), and Francisco Franco's Spain (1936–1975). These regimes embraced a right-wing, militaristic, ultranationalist ideology that, especially in Germany, included intense racist elements. Typically, a charismatic leader heads an all-powerful political party that incites violence against all who disagree with the party or with the ruling clique. The leader also heads a state that assumes control over social and economic policy in the supposed interests of the nation. "The people" is narrowly defined to exclude cultures and ethnic groups outside the national majority, most infamously in Nazi Germany. Democratic processes are viewed with suspicion, as they lead to debate and perceived delays that prevent the government from working to help "the people." Needless to say, fascist governments rarely helped the people as much as they had promised to do.

It is not a coincidence that these governments emerged out of the economic depressions of the 1920s and the 1930s. In such difficult times, people often look for scapegoats, and, as in Latin America in later decades, they hope for a strong military hand to restore order and prosperity. Hence, in Nazi Germany, Hitler pointed to the Jews as the source of German woes, and, in Italy, many supported Mussolini because they were pleased by the fact that he "made the trains run on time."

Communist Governments Communist states promote a left-wing ideology based on the theories of Karl Marx. Marx believed that the workers of the world would overthrow the capitalist free-market system and replace it with their own rule. Unlike fascist governments, communist regimes downplay the importance of the nation in lieu of "the people," representing farmers and workers. However, they too promote a one-party rule and a strong military.

Like fascism as it was practiced in Italy and Germany, the tremendous decision-making power given to government "in the name of the people" in a communist state regularly leads to repression and suspension of civil rights. All sovereignty lies with the government and none with the people. You will read more about communism's economic goals in Chapter 23.

Essential Questions Journal To continue to build a response to the chapter Essential Question, go to your **Essential Questions Journal.**

SECTION 2 ASSESSMENT

1. **Guiding Question** Use your completed flowchart to answer this question: How have some nations expanded popular sovereignty?

Key Terms and Comprehension

2. What major ideas relating to government developed during the Enlightenment period?

3. Why were Latin American countries unable to found stable democracies after independence?

4. How does **guerrilla warfare** often lead to the strengthening of militaristic governments?

Critical Thinking

5. **Express Problems Clearly** Why did Mexico face difficulties in creating a successful democracy following independence in 1821?

6. **Draw Inferences** Why do fascist and communist governments claim that they govern by the consent of their people?

Quick Write

Expository Writing: Research for Examples and Details When writing a compare-and-contrast essay, you should include details that support the comparisons and contrasts you drew. Use your textbook, the library, and reliable Internet sources to add details and examples to the notes you made in your Venn diagram in Section 1. Review the notes to delete details that are unimportant or do not relate to both systems.

SECTION 3

Transitions to Democracy

Guiding Question

How successfully have some nations achieved democratic government? Use a table similar to the one below to record information about modern transitions to democracy.

Russia	Iraq	Yugoslavia
• 1985—soft-liner Gorbachev becomes general secretary	• • •	• •
• •		

Political Dictionary

- hard-liners
- soft-liners
- democratization
- democratic consolidation
- genocide
- failed states

Objectives

1. Understand how regimes can change from dictatorship to democracy.
2. Describe the fall of the Soviet Union in the late 1980s and early 1990s.
3. Explain the factors necessary for democratic consolidation.
4. Analyze why some countries experience setbacks or failed transitions to democracy.

Image Above: Germans celebrate the fall of the Berlin Wall in November 1989.

When the political scientist Samuel Huntington studied the rise of democracy through history, he noticed an interesting pattern: Democratization tends to happen in waves across the world. The good news from Huntington's study is that the number of democracies rises gradually over time. However, this news is tempered by his other major conclusion—that not all those countries swept up by a democratic wave achieve a stable democracy. Some do fall back into authoritarianism.

Openings for Democracy

Democracy takes root when competing groups cede the power to control a society and agree to compromise and cooperate with one another to make government work. In the modern era, new democracies have often been born out of toppled dictatorships.

Dictatorships often find themselves on the defensive in today's world. The principle of popular sovereignty forces dictators to explain why they put limits on basic freedoms. Some dictators argue that the state must be strong enough to create a better society in the long run. Others point to foreign enemies or domestic unrest to justify their repressive acts, and some lay the blame on the lack of economic development.

Both internal and external pressures can create splits and discord within a dictatorial regime. **Hard-liners,** who fight to maintain the status quo, may do battle with **soft-liners,** who want to reform governmental policies or procedures but keep the current governmental system in place.

Interestingly, soft-liners do not always prefer democratic government. Many support reforms meant to strengthen their hold on power. Nevertheless, the splits they provoke can create opportunities for change. Influential individuals can then lead social movements to bring about real reform.

Individuals from all walks of life influence democratization. Lech Walesa, a labor organizer whose struggles led to the peaceful end of communism in Poland in mid-1989, worked in a shipyard. Vaclav Havel, an intellectual, poet, and playwright, led a march to democracy in late 1989 and became president of his country, Czechoslovakia, and, later, the Czech Republic.

✓ **Checkpoint**
What do hard-liners and
soft-liners do?

Other individuals avoid politics but still influence public opinion. Russian author Alexander Solzhenitsyn wrote *The Gulag Archipelago* to expose the network of prison camps in his country and spurred the cause of human rights in the Soviet Union.

Then, too, some individuals are able to encourage democracy from beyond the borders of their own country. Pope John Paul II, a native of Poland, inspired the people of his homeland and maintained pressure on Eastern European countries to move them toward democracy.

Fall of the Soviet Union

The collapse of the Communist regimes in Eastern Europe contributed to the fall of the world's first Communist superpower, the Soviet Union, which was the successor to the Russian empire. From the Revolution of 1917 until 1990, the Communist Party was the only political party allowed to operate in the Soviet Union.

A new stage of Soviet government began in 1985 when Mikhail Gorbachev became general secretary of the party. As a soft-liner, Gorbachev undertook a reform program that rested on the principles of *perestroika* and *glasnost*. *Perestroika* called for a wide-ranging restructuring of political and economic life. *Glasnost* was the policy of openness, under which the government increased its tolerance of dissent and of freedom of expression.

flagging
adj. lagging, losing
energy

Prime Minister Vladimir Putin (right) of Russia reversed many democratic reforms of the 1990s and effectively chose his own replacement as President, Dmitry Medvedev. **Why was Putin able to assert strong control over Russia?**

Transition to Democracy Changes occurred rapidly after Boris Yeltsin was elected president of Russia in 1991. Russia was then still a republic within the Soviet Union. Although it was not independent, Yeltsin used his position to confront Gorbachev, resigning from the Communist Party and declaring the laws of the Russian Republic sovereign over Russia's population and its territory.

In August 1991, Gorbachev and his wife were vacationing when a group of hardline Communist Party leaders placed him under house arrest. They wanted a return to the policies of the old Soviet government.

When the Russian public heard of this attempted coup, thousands of protesters took to the streets of Moscow, led by Yeltsin. After several tense days, the conspirators surrendered. The coup had failed. Extraordinary events followed. The three Baltic Soviet republics of Estonia, Latvia, and Lithuania were the first to depart from the Soviet Union. Soon, the remaining 12 left the Union as well.

As the elected leader of the dominant Soviet republic of Russia, Boris Yeltsin's power overshadowed that of Gorbachev. Recognizing reality, Gorbachev resigned on December 25, 1991. By the end of the year, the Soviet Union had ceased to exist.

Independent Russia A new constitution was approved in a national referendum in late 1993. It proclaims the Russian Federation to be "a democratic, federal legally based state with a republican form of government." It also set out a new governmental structure and contains an extensive list of individual rights and freedoms.

Boris Yeltsin kept his presidential role under the new constitution, and he was reelected in 1996. Soon thereafter, the economy began to spiral downward. Yeltsin suffered serious health problems and was accused of corruption in his inner circle.

In a surprise move, Yeltsin resigned at the end of December 1999, yielding the presidency to his prime minister, Vladimir Putin. Putin won election on his own in 2000 and again in 2004. Though Putin's reputation as a political strongman allowed him to revive the flagging economy, that same reputation drew criticism as he increasingly concentrated power in the presidency and restricted civil liberties. In 2007, Putin's United Russia Party took control of the legislature in a questionable election. Putin announced he would serve as prime minister and engineered the election of an ally, Dmitry Medvedev, to the presidency, leading some observers to wonder if dictatorship had not returned to Russia.

Democratic Consolidation

So far, you have read about the process of democratization, studying the example of the Soviet Union. **Democratization** refers to the change from dictatorship to democracy and is marked by the holding of free and fair elections. What must happen, once change occurs, to ensure that democracy takes root?

Essentials of Democracy As opposed to democratization, **democratic consolidation** is a much longer process that takes place as a country firmly establishes all those factors considered necessary for a democracy to survive. These factors include a free press, a true multiparty system, civilian control over the military, a vibrant collection of interest groups, an economic system that offers clear opportunities for advancement, and a professional civil service. Some of these elements may not be present in the early stages of transition. Many take time to become firmly established.

Most of all, democratic consolidation occurs when a society establishes a sense of common trust among its citizens. Because many transitions take place following a civil war or a dictatorship that pitted one group against another, mutual trust can be difficult to establish. However, when it is achieved, democracy stands on a solid footing.

Haiti The political history of the Caribbean nation of Haiti has been very troubled. It is the poorest country in the Western Hemisphere, and the process of democratization has been extremely difficult.

The Duvalier family, which ruled the country brutally for 29 years, fled in 1986. After four years of provisional governments, a presidential election was held, and Jean-Bertrand Aristide took office. Members of the armed forces still loyal to the Duvaliers

promptly overthrew Aristide. The international community cut off aid to Haiti and called for Aristide's return, and the military rulers finally withdrew in 1994. In 1996, Aristide handed over power to his political ally, René Préval. However, Aristide and Préval each led large blocs of supporters in Haiti's parliament and refused to work together. Both sides were accused of corruption.

When Aristide recaptured the presidency in 2000 in a rigged election, the United States and other countries threatened new sanctions if democratic procedures were not followed. Instead, Aristide, once a champion of democracy, became more of a dictator. In 2004, an

✔ **Checkpoint**
What is democratic consolidation?

GOVERNMENT ONLINE

For an **interactive** exploration on how democracies succeed, visit **PearsonSuccessNet.com**

INTERACTIVE

Democratic Consolidation

What Makes Democracy Succeed?

Several factors must be in place in order for a democratic system of government to take root and flourish. *Which of these factors do you think is most important? Explain.*

Factors	Why they matter
A **free press**	The media reports on the government's actions and regularly communicates ideas for change.
Multiple parties	Competition forces the government to listen to voters.
Civilian control of the military	Clear control prevents the military from taking power.
Economic opportunity for all	Education and hard work reward people for working within the law.
Professional **civil service**	Bureaucrats are less likely to be corrupt and keep government functioning when changes in leadership occur.
Common **trust** among citizens	Everyone shares a wish for the government to thrive and settle disputes peacefully.

Divisions in Iraq

▶▶ **Interpreting Maps** A large majority of Iraq's inhabitants are Muslim, but they adhere to different forms of Islam and belong to many different ethnic groups speaking different languages. *How can religious and linguistic divides pose challenges for an emerging democracy?*

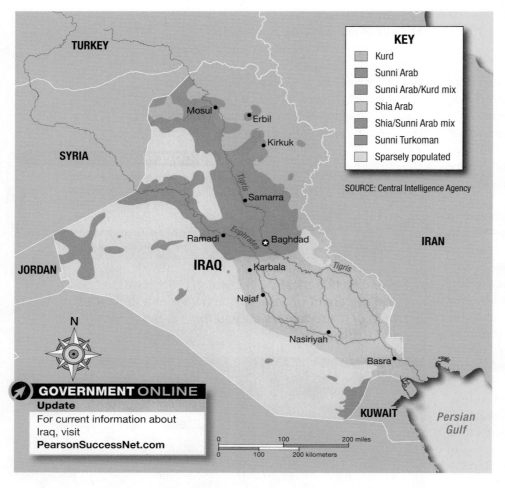

KEY
- Kurd
- Sunni Arab
- Sunni Arab/Kurd mix
- Shia Arab
- Shia/Sunni Arab mix
- Sunni Turkoman
- Sparsely populated

SOURCE: Central Intelligence Agency

GOVERNMENT ONLINE
Update
For current information about Iraq, visit
PearsonSuccessNet.com

The few instances in which one or more countries have attempted to establish democratic institutions in another country have been filled with difficulties. There have been spectacular successes, notably in Japan and Germany in the years following World War II, but what does the future hold for Iraq?

As the country has no history of free institutions upon which a democracy might be built, the effort to bring democracy to Iraq faces enormous challenges. The people of Iraq comprise many ethnic groups and religious traditions, and there are few significant unifying traditions to bring the nation's diverse Kurdish, Shia Arab, and Sunni Arab populations together as a tolerant and peaceful whole.

However, the people of Iraq have a common interest in reducing violence and restoring order in the country. Iraq has large oil reserves that could help the country to recover economically if peace returns. In 2005, Iraqis elected an interim parliament that drafted a new constitution. Iraqi voters approved the constitution, creating the basis for a new democratic government. The success of Iraqi democracy depends on the ability of the three competing groups to work together and build democratic institutions acceptable to all.

armed revolt ousted Aristide. Haiti is now ruled by a provisional government and a UN peacekeeping force. René Préval was returned to the presidency in a disputed election in 2006. Poverty and lawlessness still plague Haiti, and there are doubts that a functioning democracy can be established there any time soon.

Iraq In 2003, the United States led an invasion that toppled Saddam Hussein's brutal dictatorship in Iraq. The United States, established under the democratic principles of the Declaration of Independence and the Constitution, is committed to building a democracy amid the strife and sectarian violence there.

Setbacks and Failed Transitions

While some countries have successfully established democratic governments, and many others have begun the democratization process, a third group of countries has failed.

The costs of failure are great. Many countries today find that they must confront new problems, previously hidden by dictatorial rule, when they attempt to move toward democracy. Countries that fail to transition to democracy can pose a threat to other countries if they open safe havens for inter-national terrorist groups.

Ethnic Violence The country of Yugoslavia no longer exists. Founded in 1918, Yugoslavia included people from three major religions and many ethnic groups.

When Communist rule began to weaken in the late 1980s, regional political leaders inflamed ethnic differences for their own personal gain. By playing up old battles, they hoped to position themselves as the leaders who could correct past wrongs. The country split apart. Several prov-inces of Yugoslavia declared independence and went to war with one another for control of land that multiple ethnic groups believed was theirs by right or by history. The province of Bosnia-Herzegovina, peopled with a mix of Muslims, Serbians, and Croatians, was targeted by forces supported by neighboring Serbia and Croatia. This province saw the most intense fighting, and Bosnians suffered **genocide,** or the attempted extermination of a cultural, racial, or national group. About 200,000 civilians were killed, and many more were forced to flee the country. The conflict ended in 1995, but only after NATO intervened to stop the fighting. Instead of leading to democracy, the end of dictatorship in Yugosla-via triggered the bloody breakup of the country into at least five independent states.

Failed States Other countries remain sim-ilarly troubled. Their inability to find stability has even raised security concerns for other states. Countries such as Sudan and Afghani-stan include large regions that remain outside the control of their own governments. Soma-lia, in East Africa, does not have a function-ing government, and most of the country is ruled by warlords. These countries are known as **failed states.** In most of these areas, security is nonexistent, the economy has col-lapsed, the healthcare and school systems are in shambles, and corruption flourishes.

International terrorist groups have found refuge in these lawless lands, and have used them as bases to plan and train for acts of violence. The Soviet Union occupied Afghan-istan in the 1980s. Withdrawing in 1989, it left the country utterly devastated. Groups of Afghans who had fought against the Soviets now turned their arms against one another for control of provinces, and Afghanistan became a failed state. Other nations did not get involved in Afghanistan, and few believed anything could be done to end the fighting between warlords. The anarchy provided a haven for Osama bin Laden and his al Qaeda terrorist network to plan their attacks on the United States on September 11, 2001. In response to those attacks, a coalition of troops led by the United States moved into Afghanistan with the hope of creating a fledgling democratic government. However, large portions of the country remain outside the control of the central government.

✔ **Checkpoint**
What can happen when democracies fail?

SECTION 3 ASSESSMENT

Essential Questions Journal To continue to build a response to the chapter Essential Question, go to your **Essential Questions Journal.**

1. **Guiding Question** Use your com-pleted table to answer this question: How successfully have some nations achieved democratic government?

Key Terms and Comprehension

2. What role can **soft-liners** often play in a dictatorship?
3. What is the importance of **democratic consolidation?**

Critical Thinking

4. **Making Comparisons** Why have Iraq and Russia experienced different outcomes in their respective transitions to democracy?
5. **Drawing Inferences** How might the United States help other countries as they seek to build strong, independent democratic institutions?

Quick Write

Expository Writing: Write a The-sis Statement As in other types of essays or reports, you need to formulate a thesis statement to direct your thinking, research, and writing. Review your notes from Sections 1 and 2 to find one overarching concept that connects your categories and questions. Write a thesis statement that expresses that concept.

SECTION 4
Case Studies in Democracy

Guiding Question

What form does democratic government take in the UK and in Mexico? Use a Venn diagram to record information about the modern governments of the UK and Mexico.

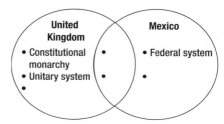

Political Dictionary
- coalition
- ministers
- shadow cabinet
- devolution

Objectives

1. Examine elements of the United Kingdom's parliamentary democracy.
2. Describe regional and local government in the United Kingdom.
3. Analyze the federal government of Mexico.

Image Above: President Felipe Calderón of Mexico

A majority of the states in the world today are representative and democratic. Each of them has developed its own set of distinctive institutions, however. The United Kingdom and Mexico present two different approaches to democratic government in today's world.

The United Kingdom: A Constitutional Monarchy

Like the United States, the United Kingdom, the UK, is a democracy. Indeed, the roots of American government are buried deep in British political and social history. Yet there are important differences between the two systems of government. Unlike government in the United States, where it is federal and presidential, government in the UK is unitary and parliamentary and rests upon an unwritten constitution.

The British constitution is not entirely unwritten. However, there is no single constitutional document, as there is in the United States. Many historic documents figure in the written portions of the UK's constitution. Especially important are the Magna Carta of 1215 and the Bill of Rights of 1689. Certain acts of Parliament also form a basic part of the British constitution.

Additionally, centuries of court decisions have created a body of law covering nearly every aspect of human conduct. Such decisions make up the common law. The truly unwritten part of the British constitution consists of the customs and practices of British politics. The written parts are called "the law of the constitution" and the unwritten parts are called "the conventions of the constitution."

In formal terms, all acts of the British government are performed in the name of the monarch. Queen Elizabeth II has been the UK's monarch since 1952. However, the prime minister and other high officials exercise the real power to govern. The monarch appoints the prime minister (traditionally the leader of the majority party in the House of Commons), but her choice is subject to the approval of that house. She has no power to dismiss the prime minister or any other government official. She has no veto power over acts of Parliament. In short, today's monarch reigns but does not rule.

British Government

Britain's storied Parliament is the core institution of government in the UK. It holds both the legislative and the executive powers of the nation—powers that in the United States are divided between separate branches of the government. It is also a bicameral body, made up of the House of Lords and the House of Commons. The latter is by far the more significant of its two chambers.

The House of Lords Historically, the House of Lords was largely composed of hereditary peers—members who inherited noble titles and, with them, seats in Parliament. Today, that largely powerless chamber's seats are held by some 700 members appointed by the Queen on the advice of the prime minister. They hold their positions mostly on the basis of their individual accomplishments in the sciences, literature, the arts, politics, or business.

The Lords have only meager law-making power: Any measure passed by the Commons but then rejected by the Lords has only to be approved a second time by the Commons in order to become law.

The House of Commons The House of Commons has 646 members today. All of them are popularly elected from single-member districts (constituencies) of roughly equal populations. There are now 529 constituencies in England, 59 in Scotland, 40 in Wales, and 19 in Northern Ireland.

The majority party in the House of Commons controls the work of that chamber. It selects the prime minister and the members of the cabinet who, together, form "the government." Its (usually) ten or so committees are generalist in nature—that is, the Speaker can refer a bill to any of those committees. All bills sent to committee must be reported to the floor, where each of them is voted up or down on a party-line basis.

The Prime Minister The prime minister, although formally appointed by the monarch, is in fact responsible to the House of Commons. When a single party holds a majority in the House of Commons, as is usually the case, that party's leader becomes prime minister. If no single party holds a majority, a coalition must be formed. A **coalition** is a temporary alliance of parties for the purpose of forming a government. Two or more parties must agree on a common choice for prime minister and on a joint slate of cabinet members.

There are no term limits on the post of prime minister. William Gladstone held the position four times from 1868 to 1894. Once a member of the Conservative Party, he broke ranks to create the Liberal Party and presided over voting reforms that expanded the electorate. Winston Churchill may be the most famous prime minister, remembered for his inspiring leadership during World War II. Margaret Thatcher, Britain's first female prime minister, led the government from 1979 to 1990 and oversaw the <u>denationalization</u> of many of Britain's coal, steel, and other basic industries. Tony Blair served as prime minister from 1997 until 2007, when he stepped down and was replaced by the current prime minister, Gordon Brown.

The Cabinet The prime minister selects the members of the cabinet, or **ministers,** from the House of Commons, although a few may sit in the House of Lords. Collectively, the prime minister and the cabinet provide

✔ **Checkpoint**
What type of government does the UK have?

denationalization
n. the transfer of a public enterprise to private owners

At the annual opening of Parliament, the British monarch reads a Speech from the Throne outlining her government's goals. The speech is written by the prime minister and cabinet. ***How does that speech symbolize the roles of the prime minister and the monarch in British government?***

United Kingdom

GOVERNMENT ONLINE
Audio Tour
LIsten to an audio guided tour about government in the UK at **PearsonSuccessNet.com**

Britain's constitutional monarchy is based on a largely unwritten constitution. The prime minister is responsible to the House of Commons and is the real head of government. *Cite examples from the text to support this statement: The British monarch reigns but does not rule.*

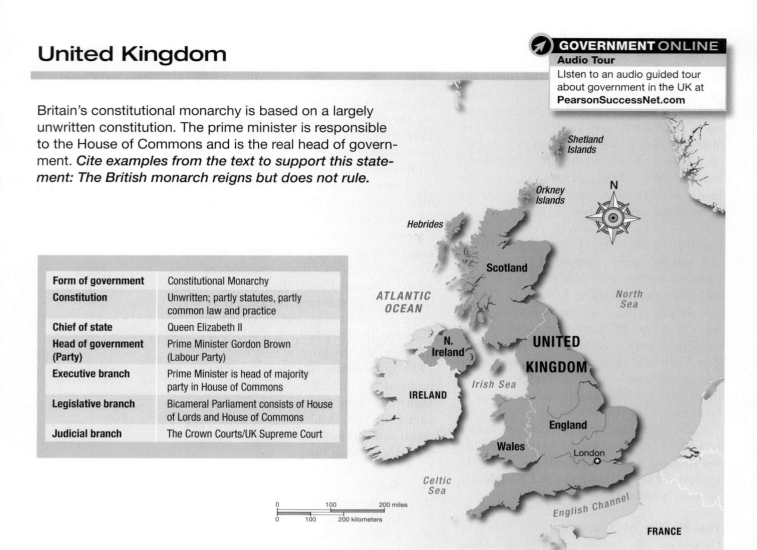

Form of government	Constitutional Monarchy
Constitution	Unwritten; partly statutes, partly common law and practice
Chief of state	Queen Elizabeth II
Head of government (Party)	Prime Minister Gordon Brown (Labour Party)
Executive branch	Prime Minister is head of majority party in House of Commons
Legislative branch	Bicameral Parliament consists of House of Lords and House of Commons
Judicial branch	The Crown Courts/UK Supreme Court

political leadership, both in making and carrying out public policy. Individually, cabinet ministers head the various executive departments, such as Defense, the Exchequer (the treasury), or Health.

The opposition parties appoint their own teams of potential cabinet members. Each opposition MP watches, or shadows, one particular member of the cabinet. If an opposition party should succeed in gaining a majority, its so-called **shadow cabinet** would then be ready to run the government.

The Courts The UK has three separate court systems—one for England and Wales, one in Northern Ireland, and one in Scotland. In England and Wales, most civil cases are tried in county courts. Serious (indictable) criminal cases are tried in the Crown Courts and less serious criminal cases in the magistrates' courts.

Judges and juries try the more serious criminal cases in the Crown Court, while judges alone hear the majority of civil disputes and less serious criminal cases. The House of Lords serves as the final court of appeal in a hierarchy of appellate courts. The court system in Northern Ireland is similar to the system in England and Wales, but the Scottish system is simpler, with fewer hierarchical layers.

Courts in the UK decide cases on the basis of (1) the common law—that is, law that has been established by judicial precedent, and (2) acts of Parliament. In the most serious cases, appeals may now be taken to a new court of last resort, the Supreme Court of the UK. That 11-judge tribunal, created by Parliament, began to hear cases in 2009. Recall, none of the courts in the UK, including the new Supreme Court, possess the power of judicial review.

The Election Process

In marked contrast to the practice in the United States, the UK does not have a fixed date for the holding of elections. Instead, the law requires only that a general election—an election in which all the seats in the Commons are at stake—be held at least once every five years. If an MP dies or resigns, a special election, called a by-election, is held in that constituency to choose a replacement.

Calling Elections Customarily, the prime minister calls an election when the political climate favors the majority party. Occasionally, an election is triggered by quite different circumstances—when the government falls because it has lost the confidence, that is, the support, of the House. This can occur if the government is defeated on a critical vote; it loses the confidence of the Commons and falls. The prime minister must then ask the monarch to dissolve Parliament (end its sessions) and call a new general election. The ability to change governments in this way means that a prime minister who becomes either ineffective or unpopular can be removed before his or her actions cause serious damage to the political system. It also means that an effective prime minister can stay in office until his or her goals are met.

Political Parties Two parties have dominated British politics in recent decades: the Conservative Party (historically known as the Tory Party or the Tories) and the Labour Party. The Conservatives have long drawn support from middle- and upper-class Britons. They tend to favor private economic initiatives over governmental involvement in the nation's economic life. The Labour Party has regularly found most of its support among working-class voters. Labour tends to favor government involvement in the economic system and a more socially equal society. Historically, the party preached doctrinaire socialism, but it moderated its views under the leadership of Prime Minister Tony Blair (1997–2007). Most recently, the Liberal Democratic Party has emerged as an alternative that blends left-wing and moderate views without the Labour Party's ties to unions.

British parties are more highly organized and centrally directed than the major parties in American politics. High levels of party loyalty and party discipline characterize the British party system. Voters regularly select candidates for the House of Commons on the basis of the candidates' party membership, not their individual qualifications.

Regional and Local Government

Recall, the United Kingdom has a unitary government. This means that there is no constitutional division of powers between the national government and regional or local governments, as in the American federal system. All power belongs to the central government. To whatever extent local governments deliver services or do anything else, they can do so only because the central government has created them, given them powers, and financed them.

Regional Government The United Kingdom is composed of four separate nations with different histories, cultures, and traditions. To provide for the distinctive governmental needs of the people of Scotland, Wales, and Northern Ireland, the United Kingdom has recently undergone a process of **devolution**—the delegation of authority from the central government back to regional governments.

✔ **Checkpoint**
How are governments formed in the UK?

▲ Scotland's Parliament flies the flags of the UK, Scotland, and the European Union.

Although the British Parliament has assigned many responsibilities to the devolved bodies, such as the Scottish Parliament that was reestablished in 1998, it has reserved for itself the exclusive power to legislate on several matters that affect the whole of the United Kingdom. These include defense, foreign policy, and macroeconomic policy. The British Parliament also continues to legislate more broadly for England, which does not have a devolved assembly.

Local Government Local government bodies have been a feature of the British political landscape for much longer than the recently established regional assemblies. Today, there are some 470 local authorities of varying types in the UK. Much as in the United States, local governments in the United Kingdom perform a broad range of functions,

entity
n. object, element

from running local schools and libraries to collecting trash and maintaining roads.

Mexico: A Federal System

Mexico has a political system similar in form to the United States. In operation, however, it is the product of a unique combination of Mexico's history and the cultural makeup of its people.

Three Branches of Government Mexico's Constitution of 1917 established a national government with three independent branches. The executive branch is headed by the president, the legislature is bicameral, and the judiciary is an independent <u>entity.</u> While this sounds much like the American political system, a major distinction can be found in the greater power of the executive branch in Mexico compared to the other branches of government.

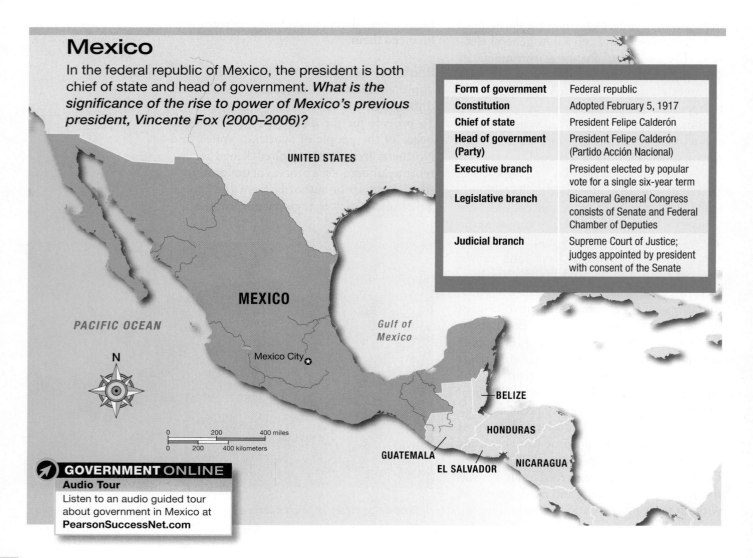

Mexico

In the federal republic of Mexico, the president is both chief of state and head of government. *What is the significance of the rise to power of Mexico's previous president, Vincente Fox (2000–2006)?*

Form of government	Federal republic
Constitution	Adopted February 5, 1917
Chief of state	President Felipe Calderón
Head of government (Party)	President Felipe Calderón (Partido Acción Nacional)
Executive branch	President elected by popular vote for a single six-year term
Legislative branch	Bicameral General Congress consists of Senate and Federal Chamber of Deputies
Judicial branch	Supreme Court of Justice; judges appointed by president with consent of the Senate

UNITED STATES

MEXICO

PACIFIC OCEAN

Gulf of Mexico

Mexico City

N

BELIZE

HONDURAS

GUATEMALA

EL SALVADOR

NICARAGUA

0   200   400 miles
0   200   400 kilometers

GOVERNMENT ONLINE
Audio Tour
Listen to an audio guided tour about government in Mexico at **PearsonSuccessNet.com**

The President The president of Mexico is popularly elected and serves one six-year term. The one-term limit is intended to prevent a popular leader from becoming a dictator by winning several reelections.

The president selects the members of the council of ministers (the cabinet) and other top civilian officers of government. He also appoints the senior officers of the armed forces and all federal judges.

In addition to the power usually held by a nation's chief executive, Mexico's president has the power to propose amendments to the constitution. Those amendments must be ratified at both the national and state levels, by a two-thirds vote in each house of Congress, and by a majority (at least 16) of the state legislatures. The president also has the power to enact laws through executive decree in some economic matters.

The Legislature The bicameral national legislature, called the General Congress, is composed of the Senate and the Chamber of Deputies. There are 64 senators—two from each of the 31 Mexican states and two from the Federal District, which includes Mexico City. Senators are elected to six-year terms. Half are elected at the time of the presidential election and half at a midterm election three years later.

The Chamber's 500 members are elected to three-year terms and cannot be reelected. Of those, 300 are directly elected from districts of more than 300,000 people. The other seats are filled from the ranks of the various political parties, based on their shares of the total vote in the national election. Thus, the Chamber is elected in a mixed system of direct and proportional representation.

The Congress meets from September 1 to December 31 each year. The combination of term limits and a short session gives the General Congress a far less significant role than that played by the Congress in the United States. Moreover, a lack of resources limits the ability of the Mexican Congress to exercise its powers. Its committees are poorly funded and understaffed, which also contributes to the dominant position of the presidency in the governmental system.

The Judicial System Mexico's independent judicial system is very similar to that of

In Mexico City, voters protested alleged election fraud after their party's candidate narrowly lost the 2006 presidential election. ***Why is election fraud a concern in Mexico?***

tribunal
n. court

the United States. However, one difference of note is that trial is by a judge alone in most criminal cases, rather than by jury. Two systems of courts—state and federal—operate within the Mexican federal system.

The federal judiciary consists of district and circuit courts that function under the Supreme Court. These <u>tribunals</u> hear all cases that arise under federal law, including those that raise constitutional issues. The 31 separate state court systems are composed of trial and appellate courts. They hear civil and criminal cases in a judicial system headed by a state Supreme Court of Justice.

Regional and Local Governments As you know, Mexico is divided into 31 states and one Federal District. The Federal District includes the capital, Mexico City, and is administered by a governor appointed by the president. Each of the 31 state constitutions provides for a governor, unicameral legislature, and state courts. Each governor is elected to a single six-year term. Legislators are elected to three-year terms. The governors appoint judges. The states have the power to legislate on local matters and to levy taxes, but most of their funding comes from the national government.

National Politics in Mexico

Mexico has a multiparty system. However, as you have read, it was dominated for decades by the PRI, which won every presidential election from 1929 until 2000. In fact, because the PRI retained its position through patronage, and opposition movements were often repressed, Mexico was not generally considered to be democratic until 2000.

The PRI The PRI's dominant position began to erode in the 1980s. The government borrowed heavily during the 1970s, expecting that oil prices would remain high. When oil prices declined sharply worldwide, the country plunged into economic chaos. Debt problems led to severe cutbacks in government programs and undermined the PRI's patronage system. Prices soared and investment capital fled the country.

The PRI made its worst showing ever in the elections of 1988. The party barely maintained control of the government, when presidential candidate Carlos Salinas de Gortari won that year. Allegations of fraud were widespread.

President Salinas pursued broad-based economic, social, and electoral reforms. He also backed the North American Free Trade Agreement (NAFTA). This agreement, about which you will learn more in the next chapter, removed trade and investment restrictions among the United States, Canada, and Mexico. In the close elections of 1994, the PRI's presidential candidate, Ernesto Zedillo, won 48.8 percent of the total vote, and the PRI retained control of the legislature.

Multiparty Democracy In the 1990s, candidates from the conservative National Action Party (PAN) and leftist Democratic Revolutionary Party (PRD) had won increasing numbers of federal, state, and local offices. Both parties took aim at the nation's highest office in 2000. Public opinion and world attention forced the PRI to guarantee a fraud-free presidential contest. When all the votes had been counted, the PAN candidate, Vicente Fox, had won with 45 percent of the vote.

Fox initially held approval ratings of over 70 percent, but those ratings later dipped below 50 percent. President Fox may have been a victim of unmet, or even unrealistic, expectations. His political rise marked a dramatic event in Mexican politics, but for many Mexicans socioeconomic conditions did not improve under his tenure. As a sign of the growing discontent, the PRI seemed to be experiencing a resurgence. Midterm elections allowed it to shore up its majority in the Senate and it almost gained a majority in the Chamber of Deputies, as well. However, PAN candidate Felipe Calderón narrowly won the presidency in the contentious 2006 election over Andrés Manuel López Obrador of the PRD. The PRI's candidate, Roberto Madrazo, came in third. PAN also gained control of both houses of Congress in that election.

Essential Questions Journal To continue to build a response to the chapter Essential Question, go to your **Essential Questions Journal.**

SECTION 4 ASSESSMENT

1. **Guiding Question** Use your completed Venn diagram to answer this question: What form does democratic government take in the United Kingdom and in Mexico?

Key Terms and Comprehension

2. Under what circumstances would a **coalition** government be formed in the United Kingdom?

3. In what major ways are the three branches of Mexican government similar to those in the United States?

4. What is the significance to Mexico of the North American Free Trade Agreement (NAFTA)?

Critical Thinking

5. **Making Comparisons** What are the major differences between **(a)** the British Parliament and the U.S. Congress? **(b)** the British prime minister and the American President?

6. **Drawing Inferences** Which form of presidential tenure do you think is preferable: the Mexican model, with one six-year term, or the American model, with a four-year term and the possibility of a second term? Explain your reasoning.

Quick Write

Expository Writing: Create an Outline To help structure your compare-and-contrast essay, create an outline in which you identify each area of comparison and contrast in a single phrase. When you are ready to write your essay, you can use the outline as a guide. Alternatively, you may create a flowchart to help you organize and order your ideas.

Quick Study Guide

GOVERNMENT ONLINE
On the Go
To review anytime, anywhere, download these online resources at **PearsonSuccessNet.com**
Political Dictionary, Audio Review

Guiding Question
Section 2 How have some nations expanded popular sovereignty?

Guiding Question
Section 3 How successfully have some nations achieved democratic government?

Guiding Question
Section 1 On what early political ideas and traditions was modern government founded?

CHAPTER 22
Essential Question
How should you measure different governments?

Guiding Question
Section 4 What form does democratic government take in the U.K. and in Mexico?

Political Dictionary

patricians p. 647
plebeians p. 647
feudalism p. 648
sovereignty p. 650
legitimacy p. 650
divine right of kings p. 650
colonialism p. 651
mercantilism p. 651
encomienda p. 655
guerrilla warfare p. 657
fascism p. 659
communism p. 659
hard-liners p. 661
soft-liners p. 661
democratization p. 663
democratic consolidation p. 663
genocide p. 665
failed states p. 665
coalition p. 667
ministers p. 667
shadow cabinet p. 668
devolution p. 670

Timeline of the Modern State

Athenian Democracy
↓
Roman Republic
↓
Feudal Era
↓
Sovereign States and Colonialism
↓
Popular Sovereignty

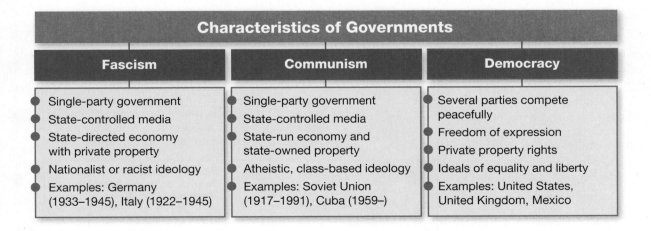

Characteristics of Governments

Fascism	Communism	Democracy
• Single-party government	• Single-party government	• Several parties compete peacefully
• State-controlled media	• State-controlled media	• Freedom of expression
• State-directed economy with private property	• State-run economy and state-owned property	• Private property rights
• Nationalist or racist ideology	• Atheistic, class-based ideology	• Ideals of equality and liberty
• Examples: Germany (1933–1945), Italy (1922–1945)	• Examples: Soviet Union (1917–1991), Cuba (1959–)	• Examples: United States, United Kingdom, Mexico

Chapter Assessment

Comprehension and Critical Thinking

Section 1

1. **(a)** What aspects of ancient Athenian democratic government exist in modern democracies? **(b)** What aspects of ancient Roman government exist in modern democracies?

2. **(a)** Why did the feudal system develop? **(b)** In what way was it a decentralized system of government? **(c)** How did feudalism meet the needs of its time?

3. **(a)** How did the rise of the sovereign state change the role of government? **(b)** How did these governments achieve legitimacy?

Section 2

4. What were the benefits and drawbacks of each method used by Britain and France to adopt popular sovereignty?

5. **(a)** Why were many Latin American countries unable to establish stable democracies after independence? **(b)** What obstacles to stability were caused by the former colonial system in Africa?

6. **(a)** What are the goals of fascist governments? **(b)** Must governments have goals to be successful? If so, what should those goals be?

Section 3

7. **(a)** Describe the difference between democratization and democratic consolidation. **(b)** How is each one important to the success of a government?

8. **Analyzing Cartoons** Study the cartoon at right. **(a)** What form of government does the hammer represent? **(b)** What is this cartoonist saying about that form of government? **(c)** From your reading and understanding of history, is this cartoon fair? Explain.

Section 4

9. **(a)** How is the United Kingdom's government similar to and different from government in the United States? **(b)** How is the United Kingdom's government similar to and different from that of Mexico?

10. **(a)** What was the role of the PRI in Mexican political life up through the 1990s? **(b)** What was the significance of the 2000 election?

Writing About Government

11. Use your Quick Write exercises from the section assessments in this chapter to write an essay that compares and contrasts the two topics you selected. Make sure that the information is accurate and that comparisons are reasoned and relevant. End your essay with a summarizing conclusion. See pp. S3–S5 in the Skills Handbook.

HUMAN RIGHTS

Apply What You've Learned

12. **Essential Question Activity** Speak with an immigrant to the United States or someone who has known an immigrant well and can answer as that person might answer. Ask:

    (a) Why did you come to the United States?

    (b) How do you view the government of your native country? What do you think worked well? How well did it meet citizens' needs? How democratic do you think it is?

    (c) How do you view the government of the United States in comparison to that of your native country?

13. **Essential Question Assessment** Based on the interview you conducted and what you have learned about democracy and American government, write a guide to the government of this country designed to help immigrants learn about its basic structure and functions in comparison with other countries. Your guide should help you answer the Essential Question: **How should you measure different governments?**

Essential Questions Journal To respond to the chapter Essential Question, go to your **Essential Questions Journal.**

Document-Based Assessment

Fascism and Communism

Communist and fascist leaders claimed to meet the needs of the people and to rule on the basis of popular sovereignty. However, communist governments, such as those in the Soviet Union and China, and fascist governments, as in Italy and Germany, became dictatorships. How did these governments use propaganda to legitimize their rule?

Document 1

" Fascism conceives of the State as an absolute, in comparison with which all individuals or groups are relative, only to be conceived of in their relation to the State. . . . The Fascist State organizes the nation, but leaves a sufficient margin of liberty to the individual; the latter is deprived of all useless and possibly harmful freedom, but retains what is essential; the deciding power in this question cannot be the individual, but the State alone. . . . Fascism is the doctrine best adapted to represent the tendencies and the aspirations of a people, like the people of Italy, who are rising again after many centuries of abasement and foreign servitude. But empire demands discipline, the coordination of all forces and a deeply felt sense of duty and sacrifice.

—Benito Mussolini, from "What Is Fascism?" 1932

Document 2

" We hold these Truths to be self-evident, that all Men are created equal, that they are endowed by their Creator with certain unalienable Rights, that among these are Life, Liberty, and the Pursuit of Happiness.

—Declaration of Independence,1776

Document 3

This Chinese Communist Party poster of 1974 calls on "workers, peasants, and soldiers" to criticize the philosopher Confucius and a discredited communist leader, Lin Biao.

工农兵是批林批孔的主力军

Use your knowledge of fascism and communism and Documents 1–3 to answer Questions 1–3.

1. In his description of fascism, Mussolini says that
   A. the people have liberty only in relation to the state.
   B. the people have absolute power over the state.
   C. the state receives its authority directly from the people.
   D. the state is democratic and has little power over the people.

2. How does Mussolini's description of freedom differ from that set out in the Declaration of Independence?

3. **Pull It Together** Italy under Mussolini and China under Mao were both authoritarian dictatorships. However, both Documents 1 and 3 make appeals to popular sovereignty. How are these appeals the same and different in each document?

GOVERNMENT ONLINE
Documents
To find more primary sources on political systems, visit
PearsonSuccessNet.com

23

Comparative Economic Systems

Essential Question
To what extent should governments participate in the economy?

Section 1:
Capitalism

Section 2:
Socialism and Communism

Section 3:
The U.S. in a Global Economy

"Freedom in **economic arrangements** is itself a component of **freedom** broadly understood.... **Economic freedom** is ... an **indispensable** means toward the **achievement** of **political freedom**.

—Milton Friedman, 1962

Photo: Traders buy and sell at the Chicago Mercantile Exchange

GOVERNMENT ONLINE
On the Go

To study anywhere, anytime, download these online resources at PearsonSuccessNet.com
• Political Dictionary
• Audio Review
• Downloadable Interactivities

Capitalism

Guiding Question

What is the role of government in the American economy? Create a chart similar to the one below to record information from the section on features of capitalism.

Features of Capitalism		

Free Enterprise	Laissez-Faire Theory	Mixed Economy
• Private ownership • Individual initiative •	• Government plays a limited role in economy •	• •

Political Dictionary

- capitalism
- factors of production
- capital
- entrepreneur
- free enterprise system

- free market
- laws of supply and demand
- monopoly
- laissez-faire theory

Objectives

1. Identify the factors of production.
2. Describe the free enterprise system and laissez-faire theory.
3. Analyze the role of government in a mixed economy.
4. Compare and contrast three types of business organizations.
5. Explain the role of profit and loss in a free enterprise system.

Image Above: Small businesses are an essential part of a free enterprise system.

You have confronted these questions several times in this book: What are the functions a government ought to undertake? What should it have the power to do? What should it not be allowed to do? Certainly these questions can be asked of just about all areas of human activity, but they are raised very significantly in the realm of economic affairs.

Questions of politics and economics are inseparable. The most important economic questions faced by a nation are also political questions. For example: Who should decide what goods will be produced? How should goods and services be distributed and exchanged within a nation? What types of income or property ought to be taxed? What social services should a government provide to its citizens?

Capitalism provides one response to all of these questions. **Capitalism** is an economic system in which individuals are free to own the means of production and maximize profits. Many aspects of capitalism will be familiar to you because the United States and most other nations in the world today have adopted this economic system.

Factors of Production

Certain resources are necessary to any nation's economy, no matter what economic system is in place. Economists call these basic resources, which are used to make all goods and services, the **factors of production.**

Land Land, which in economic terms includes all natural resources, is an important factor of production. Land has a variety of economic uses, such as agriculture, mining, and forestry. Along with farms and other property, economists categorize the water in rivers and lakes and the coal, iron, and petroleum found beneath the ground as part of the land itself.

Capital A second factor of production is **capital**—all the human-made resources that are used to produce goods and services. Physical capital (also called "capital goods") includes the buildings, machines, computers, and other materials workers need to turn land and another factor, labor, into goods and services. Note that capital is a product of the economy that is then put back into the economy.

Labor Yet another factor of production is a human resource—labor. Men and women who work in mines, factories, offices, hospitals, and other places all provide labor that is an essential part of a nation's economy. In a capitalist, or free market, economy, individuals "own" their labor and can sell it to any employer. Human capital includes the knowledge and skills that workers gain from their work experiences—an investment in themselves.

One who owns capital and puts it to productive use is called a capitalist. That term is applied to people who own large businesses or factories as well as investors and the owners of small businesses. The American economy is called capitalistic because its growth depends very largely on the energy and drive of thousands of individual capitalists, not the government.

The Role of the Entrepreneur To actually produce goods and services, someone must bring together and organize the factors of production. An **entrepreneur**—literally, an "enterpriser"—is an individual with the drive and ambition to combine land, labor, and capital resources to produce goods or offer services, and is willing to risk losses and failure. Entrepreneurs start businesses and make them grow, creating jobs and goods and services that contribute to a high standard of living.

Free Enterprise System

Capitalism is frequently referred to as a **free enterprise system,** which is an economic system characterized by private ownership of capital and by investments that are determined by private decision, not by public authorities. This system needs a **free market,** a market in which buyers and sellers are free to buy and sell as they wish. A free market is most likely to exist in a democratic nation, such as the United

✔ **Checkpoint**
Why are the factors of production important?

Factors of Production

Land, labor, and capital are the building blocks of the economy known as the factors of production. The entrepreneur brings these three factors together to create something consumers will buy. *Look up "land" and "capital" in the dictionary. How do economists' definitions differ from what you found?*

Land includes property and the resources found in nature.

Labor describes the work of individuals.

Capital includes the tools, money, and human expertise that turn labor and land into goods and services.

Entrepreneurs are risk-taking individuals who have the skill and drive to create new products or services for the market.

Goods and Services are the items people buy and the things one does for another or for the community.

✔ **Checkpoint**
What is the free enterprise system?

compensation
n. payment making up for loss

States, where security and the rule of law are protected by the government.

A free enterprise system lets consumers, entrepreneurs, and workers enjoy freedom of choice. Consumers can choose from a variety of products and services. Entrepreneurs can switch from one business to another. Workers can quit their jobs and seek new ones, and they can choose to organize labor unions as a way to bargain for better working conditions or benefits.

A capitalistic system—a free enterprise system—is based on four fundamental factors: private ownership, individual initiative, profit, and competition.

Private Ownership In a capitalistic system, private individuals and companies own most of the factors of production—the basic resources used to produce goods and services. They decide how this productive property will be used—for example, to build a business or invest in technology. What the property produces is theirs, as well. The owners of productive property are sometimes individuals, but more often they are groups of people who share ownership of a company.

In a free enterprise system, individuals own the right to their own labor. They sell that labor by taking a job, and the pay they receive represents the price paid for their work. In other economic systems, workers may have little choice as to the kinds of work they will do and little opportunity to change jobs or pay.

The protection of the rights of private ownership is also important, particularly in the United States. The 5th and 14th amendments declare that no person may be deprived "of life, liberty, or property, without due process of law." The 5th Amendment also says that "just <u>compensation</u>" must be paid to owners when private property is taken for public use.

Individual Initiative In our economy, entrepreneurs are an essential factor in the production of goods and services. Under a free enterprise system, all individuals are free to start and run their own businesses (their own enterprises). They are also free to dissolve those businesses. Importantly, the atmosphere of a free market, as well as a free society that encourages the exchange of ideas, can and often does lead to innovation and scientific and technological discoveries.

Elements of Free Enterprise

Free markets cannot succeed without these four basic elements: private ownership, individual initiative, profit, and competition. Supported by the rule of law and by the people, these factors allow for the many market transactions that define a free enterprise economy. *What is the role of the government in preserving the elements of free enterprise?*

Private ownership

UNDER NEW MANAGEMENT
NOW OPEN
COFFEE CUP CAFE

Profit

Fruity Cheerios

Individual initiative

These promote growth in the economy and often improve the quality of everyday life.

That is not necessarily true in other economic systems. In some countries, government planners decide what will be produced and how it will be made. There, centralized decision making, not individual initiative, controls the production and distribution of goods and services.

Profit Just as individuals are free to choose how they will spend or invest their capital in a free enterprise system, they are also entitled to benefit from whatever their investment or enterprise earns or gains in value. The "profit motive" is the desire to gain from business dealings. It drives entrepreneurs to create goods and services people will want to buy, and is a major reason why entrepreneurs are willing to take risks.

Competition The freedom to enter or start a new business at any time leads to competition. Competition is a situation in which a number of companies offer similar products or services. They must compete against one another for customers. In a free enterprise system, competition often helps to hold down

Competition

prices and keep quality high. This is usually the case because customers are likely to buy from the company with the best product at the lowest price. Competition promotes efficiency; the producer has the incentive (more sales) to keep costs low.

Under these competitive conditions, the **laws of supply and demand** determine the market price for goods or services. Supply is the quantity of goods or services available for sale at a range of prices. As the price increases, more of a product will be offered for sale. Demand is the desire and ability to purchase a good or service. As the price falls, more of a product will be demanded by buyers. If supply increases and demand stays the same, prices will fall. If demand decreases and supply stays the same, prices will also fall. On the other hand, if demand increases and supply stays the same, prices will rise.

Competition does not always work smoothly. Sometimes a single business becomes so successful that all its rivals go out of business. A firm that is the only source of a product or service is called a **monopoly.** Monopolies can be very powerful in the marketplace. Practically speaking, they can charge as much as they want for a product. Since there is no other supplier of that good or service, the consumer must pay the monopoly's price or do without.

In the late nineteenth century, political leaders in the United States gradually became convinced that certain monopolies were stifling competition and interfering with the free market. They were especially concerned about a type of monopoly called a trust. A trust exists when several corporations in the same line of business work together to eliminate competition from the market and regulate prices. By the latter part of the nineteenth century, trusts had gained tight-fisted control over the markets for petroleum, steel, coal, beef, sugar, and other commodities.

In response, Congress passed the Sherman Anti-Trust Act of 1890, which remains the basic law to curb monopolies today. It prohibits "every contract, combination in the form of a trust or otherwise, or conspiracy in restraint of trade or commerce among the several States, or with foreign nations."

✓ **Checkpoint**
Why is competition important?

The Anti-Trust Division in the Department of Justice watches business activities to determine whether competition within an industry is threatened. It can, for example, stop the sale or merger of a company if that move threatens competition in a particular market. On rare occasions, the Justice Department has acted to break up a monopoly to restore competition.

Laissez-Faire Theory

Early capitalist philosophers believed that, if only government did not interfere, the free enterprise system would work automatically. Adam Smith presented the classic expression of that view in his book, *The Wealth of Nations,* in 1776. Smith wrote that when all individuals are free to pursue their own private interests, an "invisible hand" works to promote the general welfare. In short, Smith introduced laissez-faire capitalism.[1]

Laissez-faire theory holds that government should play only a very limited, hands-off role in society. Governmental activity should be confined to: (1) foreign relations and national defense, (2) the maintenance of police and courts to protect private property and the health, safety, and morals of the people, and (3) those few other functions that cannot be performed by private enterprise at

a profit. The proper role of government in economic affairs should be restricted to functions intended to promote and protect the free play of competition and the operation of the laws of supply and demand.

Laissez-faire capitalism has never in fact operated in this country. The concept has had, nevertheless, and still has, a profound effect on the structure of the economic system in the United States.

A Mixed Economy

Although the American economic system is essentially private in character, government has always played a large part in it. Economists usually describe an economy in which private enterprise and governmental participation coexist as a mixed economy.

Government at every level regulates the various features of American economic life. Among its many other functions, government prohibits trusts, protects the environment, and ensures the quality of the food we eat.

Government also promotes many aspects of American economic life. It constructs roads and highways, provides such services as public health programs, the census, and weather reports, and operates Social Security and other insurance programs. It also offers many kinds of subsidies and loan programs to help entrepreneurs and businesses prosper.

Federal, State, and local governments conduct some enterprises that might well be operated privately—for example, public education, the postal system, and municipal water and power systems. It has also assumed some functions that have proved unprofitable to private enterprise—for example, many local transit systems and waste disposal and recycling projects. These sorts of public efforts are sometimes called "ash-can socialism."

Mixed economies are common in Europe and in most former communist countries. In Britain, the government provides free medical care to all. The government of the People's Republic of China owns steel mills and factories. Germany's federal government requires large companies to give workers representation on managing boards, and France once banned most companies from asking

Former Federal Reserve Chairman Alan Greenspan speaks on economics at a lecture honoring Adam Smith.

---

1 *Laissez-faire* is a French idiom meaning "to let alone."

Supply and Demand

How are prices set in a free market?

GOVERNMENT ONLINE

For an interactive exploration of supply and demand, visit **PearsonSuccessNet.com**

INTERACTIVE

In general, suppliers will produce more goods when prices are high and fewer goods when prices fall. Consumers usually seek to purchase (demand) more of a commodity at low prices and less at high prices. Where people enjoy the freedom to trade, they will find the market price that suits both sides. *What is a market signal that a price is too high?*

Price	Suppliers produce	Consumers want	What happens?
$5.00	5,000	20,000	• Not enough for sale • Empty shelves
$15.00	10,000	10,000	• Market price • Both sides happy
$30.00	20,000	5,000	• Too many t-shirts • Too few buyers

employees to work more than 35 hours per week. In each of these mixed economies, government intervention coexists with independent companies and market forces.

Types of Business Organizations

The American economy contains a number of gigantic companies with thousands of employees and factories or offices all over the world. Still, most businesses in the United States are relatively small. Over 95 percent of all businesses in this country employ fewer than 20 people. Three basic types of business organizations exist: sole proprietorships, partnerships, and corporations. Each has advantages and disadvantages.

Sole Proprietorships Businesses owned by a single individual are called sole proprietorships. Typical businesses in this category include such enterprises as hair salons, auto repair shops, and dentists' offices. About three quarters of all businesses in this country are sole proprietorships. However, because most sole proprietorships are small, they produce only a minor fraction of annual sales in the United States.

Sole proprietorships are the most flexible form of business organization. Their major advantage is that the single owner can make decisions quickly. He or she has full control of the company and can draw a salary or close the business without consulting others. A major disadvantage is that the owner is personally <u>liable</u> for the debts the business might acquire. Sole proprietorships are also limited by the owner's ability to contribute resources and manage the business.

Partnerships Businesses owned by two or more individuals, called partners, are known as partnerships. Lawyers and architects are among those professionals who often work together in partnerships.

One advantage of a partnership is that it can draw on the resources of more than one person for the capital necessary to start or expand a business. Different people bring different strengths and perspectives to a business, and a partnership can provide a

✓ **Checkpoint**
What are the three types of business organizations?

liable
adj. responsible

useful framework for entrepreneurs to use their skills to create a small business. These differences can also lead to conflict among partners, however; and partnerships may dissolve if one of the partners leaves or dies.

Corporations Corporations include both very small companies and large multinational firms. Unlike partnerships, corporations almost always have many owners, called shareholders. A share is a fraction of ownership in the corporation, and a shareholder is any person or group owning one or more shares. A corporation can continue indefinitely because a shareholder's death does not affect the legal status of the corporation. In other words, the corporation exists as its own legal entity, independent from the existence of any shareholders. The Supreme Court has often held that, under the 14th Amendment, a corporation occupies the same legal position as a person.

Corporations can draw their capital from hundreds and even thousands of investors. This characteristic enables them to finance such costly projects as artificial satellites or oil pipelines. Shareholders are responsible only for the amount of money they have invested. If the business fails, they can lose that amount, but no more. Shareholders have limited liability and are not held responsible for any debts the corporation might have.

Corporations suffer this disadvantage: The income they produce is taxed twice. First, the corporation pays a tax on its profits. Then, individual shareholders pay a tax on the dividends they receive.

Profit and Loss

What drives the capitalist economy? The best answer, most often, is profit.

To understand what profit is, you must first understand the idea of investment. An investment is a sum of money—capital—that is put into a business enterprise. For example, if you buy a van to start an express delivery business, what you pay for the van is an investment in the business.

Your profit will be the amount of money you earn from the business, after you have subtracted the costs involved in making that money—in this case, the purchase of the van and the costs of operating it, plus whatever you pay yourself. If earnings are less than the costs, the business has not made a profit; it has, instead, suffered a loss.

Taking risks and making investments are, therefore, an essential part of the capitalist system. Every year, many businesses fail because they do not produce a profit. The businesses that survive tend to be those whose owners have learned to make the most efficient use of the factors of production.

Essential Questions Journal To continue to build a response to the chapter Essential Question, go to your **Essential Questions Journal.**

SECTION 1 ASSESSMENT

1. **Guiding Question** Use your completed chart to answer this question: What is the role of government in the American economy?

Key Terms and Comprehension
2. **(a)** What is physical **capital?** **(b)** What is human capital? **(c)** How do economists define land as a **factor of production?**
3. Why are **entrepreneurs** important?
4. What is the role of government in a mixed economy?

Critical Thinking
5. **Make Comparisons** Which type of business organization would be most appropriate for: **(a)** a large bus company? **(b)** a nonchain coffee shop? Explain.
6. **Draw Conclusions** Identify two arguments that can be made for and two against government participation in a free enterprise economy.

Quick Write

Expository Writing: Select a Topic and Record Details The goal of a compare-and-contrast essay is to analyze similarities and differences between two topics. In this chapter, you will learn about different economic systems: capitalism, socialism, and communism. As you read the chapter, use a Venn diagram to record similarities and differences between two of these systems.

SECTION 2

Socialism and Communism

Guiding Question

What is the role of government under socialism and communism?
Create a table similar to the table below to record information about the role of government under socialism and communism.

Role of Government	
Socialism	**Communism**
• State owns largest industries	•
•	•
•	•

Political Dictionary

- *The Communist Manifesto*
- socialism
- communism
- welfare state
- command economy
- five-year plan
- collectivization
- privatization
- Great Leap Forward

Objectives

1. Summarize the theories of Karl Marx and their roots.
2. Identify important characteristics of socialist economies.
3. Outline the characteristics of communist economies.
4. Describe socialism and communism in action today.
5. Evaluate the effects of socialism and communism.

Image Above: Communist artwork often celebrated workers in industry and agriculture.

You know that in the United States everyone is entitled to the equal protection of the law. Political equality, of course, is not the same as economic equality. The capitalist system of the United States allows some to achieve greater financial rewards than others are able to. However, other economic systems—socialism and communism—do seek to distribute wealth more evenly across the society.

Karl Marx's Theory

Karl Marx (1818–1883), the father of modern socialism and communism, was the most significant critic of capitalism as it developed during the early stages of the Industrial Revolution. Numerous observers of working conditions in nineteenth-century factories were appalled by what they found. Those conditions led many of them to seek social and economic reforms. Marx and his colleague Friedrich Engels (1820–1895) argued for much more radical change than did most of their contemporaries.

Writings Marx and Engels first published their basic concepts in **The Communist Manifesto** in 1848. That political document condemned the miseries of the Industrial Revolution and called upon oppressed workers throughout Europe to free themselves from "capitalist enslavement." The Manifesto ended with this rallying cry:

PRIMARY SOURCE

The proletarians have nothing to lose but their chains. They have a world to win. Workingmen of all countries, unite.

—*The Communist Manifesto*

The Communist Manifesto and Marx's later multivolume work, *Das Kapital*, published in 1867, 1885, and 1894, were based on four closely related concepts: Marx's theory of history, the labor theory of value, the role of institutions, and the dictatorship of the proletariat.

commodity
n. anything bought or sold

authoritarian
adj. demanding total obedience

1. *Marx's View of History.* To Marx, all of history was a story of class struggle—of social classes competing for the control of labor and productive property. One class was the oppressor; the other, the oppressed. In the modern world, the bourgeoisie—the capitalists—oppressed the proletariat—the workers. According to Marx, the class struggle in the modern era would become so intense that, inevitably, the masses would revolt and bring down the bourgeoisie.

2. *The Labor Theory of Value.* Marx rejected the free enterprise ideas of profit and competition. In his view, the value of a commodity was set by the amount of labor put into it. A pair of shoes or a rebuilt bicycle is worth a certain amount because it takes that much labor to produce it. Marx argued that the laborer should receive that value in full.

3. *The Role of Institutions.* Marx saw the state and its government as tools by which capitalists maintained their power and privileges. Other social institutions also played a role in enforcing capitalist control over the masses. Marx described religion as "the opiate of the people"—a drug that persuades workers to tolerate their harsh lot in this life in the hope that someday they will gain what Marx called a "fictional afterlife."

4. *The Dictatorship of the Proletariat.* Marx did not believe that revolution would automatically bring about the final goal of communism—the classless society. First, he predicted a transitional phase during which an authoritarian state would represent and enforce the interests of the masses. This he called the "dictatorship of the proletariat." Once the goal of classlessness was realized, the state, he said, would "wither away."

Based on these four concepts, Marx envisioned a "free, classless society." Social classes would vanish and the people would own all property in common. Exploitation of labor and unemployment would disappear. Abundant goods would be available to all according to their needs, not necessarily how much work they contributed. Marx also expected that workers in different countries—for example, France and Germany—would share a bond far stronger than national loyalties.

Thus, he theorized that communism would also bring an end to nationalism, a major cause of European wars.

Socialists and Communists Many European workers and thinkers of the middle and late nineteenth century accepted Marx's criticisms of capitalism. His followers were deeply divided, however, by the question of how best to achieve a more equitable economy. Some argued that economic equality could be attained by peaceful, democratic means. Today, the terms **socialism** and *socialist* are usually used to identify those evolutionary ideals and the people who support them. Others argued that a fair society could come only out of a violent revolution, born out of class struggle. Over time, those who took that more strictly Marxist view came to be called communists, the advocates of **communism.**

Characteristics of Socialist Economies

Countries with a socialist government typically enact one or more of a set of public policies to achieve the basic aims of socialism. These policies include nationalization, broadening of public services, high taxation, and a command economy.

Nationalization Placing enterprises under governmental control, often by taking over privately owned industries, is called nationalization. In a socialist society, nationalization rarely includes all businesses within the country. Socialist governments usually want to control only certain segments of the economy—those having many workers, a few dominant firms, and great importance to other businesses—particularly, utilities, transportation, and steel. Many smaller companies remain in private hands. The government may also want industries that are based on new technologies to remain in private hands. It often does because individual initiative and entrepreneurship are so vital in the early phases of the development of a business.

Many socialist governments want to give each company's workers a say in deciding how a company is to be managed. Elected worker representatives now sit on the boards of directors of many major companies in both Sweden and Germany.

Public Welfare Socialists aim to guarantee the public welfare by providing for the equal distribution of such necessities and services as retirement pensions, universal healthcare, free university education, and housing. Any country that provides extensive social services at little or no direct cost to consumers is a **welfare state.**

In a welfare state, medical and dental services often are provided free or at a small charge. People who lose their jobs or who are physically unable to work receive government payments that are nearly as high as their former wages. All those who reach retirement age receive government pensions. Parents are often paid a benefit for each child until that child reaches the age of 18. Workers in several European nations receive paid maternity leave, often for both parents, and several weeks of paid vacation each year, considerably more than most American workers receive.

Taxation All governments in both capitalist and socialist states are funded by taxation. Because social welfare services are quite expensive, taxes in socialist countries tend to be relatively high. Taxes regularly take as much as 50 or 60 percent of an individual's yearly income. Socialists tend to place most of the tax burden on the upper and middle classes, in line with their aim to achieve a more equal distribution of wealth. However, gasoline and consumer goods are also subject to high taxes.

A Command Economy Economies can be divided into several categories, depending on how basic economic decisions are made. Under capitalism, key decisions are made by thousands of private individuals and companies through the give-and-take of the marketplace. Under socialism, and even more so under communism, economic decision making is more centralized. In a **command economy,** government bureaucrats plan for the development of the economy over a period of years. They set targets for production and direct investments to specific industries.

National Healthcare
What is the Cost of Free Healthcare?

The United Kingdom's National Health Service provides free healthcare to all, funded by the national government. While the ideal of national healthcare is widely popular in the UK (top), many people complain about long waits for treatment (bottom). *What might the law of supply and demand predict for a free healthcare system?*

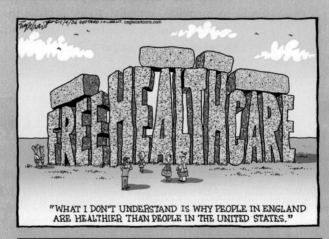

"WHAT I DON'T UNDERSTAND IS WHY PEOPLE IN ENGLAND ARE HEALTHIER THAN PEOPLE IN THE UNITED STATES."

YOUR INJURY IS IMPORTANT TO US. ALL OUR DOCTORS ARE BUSY HELPING OTHER CUSTOMERS. PLEASE WAIT, YOU ARE ADVANCING IN THE QUEUE AND YOU WILL BE SEEN AS SOON AS A DOCTOR BECOMES AVAILABLE.

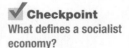

BILL PROUD

Socialism Today

Although most socialist parties in Europe have given up such traditional goals as nationalizing important industries, these parties promote socialism as it exists today. At various times in recent history, socialist parties have controlled governments and instituted socialist programs through democratic means. However, socialist parties in Britain, France, and Germany have

☑ **Checkpoint**
What defines a socialist economy?

lost power or have abandoned some of their socialist objectives that have become too expensive and unpopular to maintain.

Socialism has won a large following in developing countries in Africa and more recently in Latin America. One reason for its appeal in those nations is that large existing industries have often been owned by foreign companies. By nationalizing a foreign-owned industry and placing local people in charge, a political leader can win broad public support. He or she can also gain power by promising to provide socialist-style, "cradle-to-grave" services and to redistribute land from large land owners to the poor.

For example, after he came to power in 1999, Venezuela's President Hugo Chávez and his nationalist-socialist party, Movement for the Fifth Republic (MVR) nationalized the oil industry and used the profits to fund free education, healthcare, and low-cost housing. Chávez has also nationalized the telecommunications and electricity industries. These moves have brought support for Chávez, especially among the urban poor, and have helped him retain power, despite broad resistance to many of his socialist, or even communist, goals. Meanwhile, Venezuela's economy has experienced inflation and shortages as a result of Chávez's actions.

GOVERNMENT ONLINE

Audio Tour
Listen to a guided audio tour of Marxist Economies at **PearsonSuccessNet.com**

Marxist Economies

The writings of Karl Marx (below) inspired two competing movements to improve the lives of workers. Socialists hoped to change capitalism, while communists strove to destroy it. *How well do socialism and communism respect the rights of people as defined in a free market economy?*

SOCIALISM

Socialists came to power by promising social services and jobs for everyone while observing the rules of democracy. Many workers enjoy better pay and job protections, but young people often have trouble finding good jobs.

COMMUNISM

Revolutionaries in Russia and China overthrew governments in the name of the people and created communist dictatorships. They spread communism through war and support for foreign revolutions.

SOCIALISM	COMMUNISM
• Some central planning	• Centrally planned economy
• Most property is privately owned	• State owns all land and housing
• Only large industries are nationalized	• No privately owned businesses
• High taxes fund healthcare, child care, education	• State provides healthcare, child care, education
• Free elections	• Controlled elections
• Strong unions and worker protections	• State-controlled unions

Characteristics of Communist Economies

Socialism represents one path from Karl Marx's theories to a modern economy. Communism describes a more dramatic and frequently violent approach, one that dominated large parts of the world in the twentieth century. In practice, communism has been less successful than socialism, and has generally led to the formation of totalitarian regimes. Marx's theories did not provide a blueprint for the formation of a communist society, and communism has taken different forms in different places. However, certain common characteristics can be seen.

1. *Role of the Communist Party.* In any communist-run nation, the Communist Party holds the decision-making power in both the government and the economy. Party leaders also hold the top government positions. From top to bottom, the two institutions run parallel to one another. Inevitably, such centralized political and economic control has meant control over social, intellectual, and religious life, as well.

2. *Central Planning.* Because government makes all economic decisions, bureaucrats in a command economy must plan and supervise the production of all factories, farms, and stores in the country. Typically, a **five-year plan** plays a key role, outlining how the government wants the economy to develop. The plan sets economic goals that dictate where to emphasize growth in industry or agriculture and what and how much each individual factory and farm must produce. It also sets prices and decides how goods and services will be distributed.

3. *Collectivization.* Collective ownership—state ownership—of the means of production is a fundamental pillar of communist doctrine. The merger of small private farms into large government-owned agricultural enterprises is a major step in the creation of a communist economy. The process of **collectivization** may be voluntary in theory, but in many countries, peasant farmers were forced to give up their land. Millions died resisting collectivization in the Soviet Union.

4. *State Ownership.* Industrial enterprises, transportation, and other segments of the economy are state-owned. This aspect of the system varies greatly from country to country. In China, for example, provincial and municipal governments, not a central government ministry, own enterprises such as housing, banks, hospitals, and stores.

The Soviet Union

Marx believed that the revolution would come first in industrialized countries with large working-class populations—in particular, France, Germany, Great Britain, and then the United States. Ironically, the revolution occurred first in Russia, then an undeveloped, mainly agricultural nation, in 1917. V.I. Lenin and his followers began immediately to build a communist state in the new Soviet Union. By the time of Lenin's death in 1924, the Soviet Union had become a one-party state in control of the country's social, political, and economic institutions. Lenin's successor, Josef Stalin, tightened that control and built a totalitarian dictatorship.

The Soviet Union Under Stalin Stalin introduced centralized planning. The First Five-Year Plan (1928–1933) demanded collectivization of agriculture and a heightened production of chemicals, petroleum, and steel. Later five-year plans also emphasized heavy industry, and the Soviet Union achieved rapid, if uneven, industrialization. Unfortunately, those advances came at great cost in the form of scarce consumer goods, housing, and urban services.

The Soviet Union did provide its citizens with free education, medical care, and even summer youth camps. It was far from a classless society, however. An elite class owed its privileged status to the Communist Party. In addition, many free government services were either unavailable or of poor quality.

Transition to a Free Market By the late 1980s, under Mikhail Gorbachev's policies of *glasnost* (openness) and *perestroika* (restructuring), the Soviet Union began to dismantle the political and economic structures of communism. In 1991, the Soviet

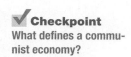

✔ Checkpoint
What defines a communist economy?

Although China still identifies itself as a communist state, private enterprise and investment have achieved remarkable growth in recent years.

The Great Leap Forward The five-year plan for 1958, the **Great Leap Forward,** was a drastic attempt to modernize China quickly. All elements of free enterprise were eliminated. Collective farms were brought together into larger units, communes. Communes grew into self-sufficient bodies run by Communist Party officials. These officials oversaw farms, industries, and government in a region, and they also managed social policy. Workers received the same rewards no matter how much they produced, so there were few incentives to work hard. The Great Leap Forward was a disastrous failure and was followed by a severe famine.

Deng Xiaoping's Reforms A new leader, Deng Xiaoping, came to power in 1977 and made great changes in the economy. Deng's program of the "Four Modernizations" was aimed at improving agriculture, industry, science and technology, and defense. He began to move China from a command economy to a market economy and opened the country to foreign investment.

Today, China's economic system is a maze of different levels of governmental bodies and economic units. Although the Communist Party remains in power and directs economic growth, the state-owned sector has shrunk. The government encourages private enterprise and investment and China has enjoyed many years of strong economic growth.

Union dissolved into 15 independent countries. The largest and most populous of them was Russia.

Many state-owned companies in Russia were privatized. **Privatization** is the process of returning nationalized enterprises to private ownership. Today, Russia is a country with some features of free enterprise but also extensive state intervention in the economy.

China

Mao Zedong, the founder of the People's Republic of China, was a Marxist. However, he believed the peasantry, not industrial workers, were the key to a successful communist revolution in agricultural China.

After Mao took control of the country in 1949, China developed its own version of a command economy. Despite its huge population, the country lacked skilled workers. The government improved technical and scientific educational opportunities and then assigned workers to jobs in the state sector. The government regulated the labor market, giving people little choice about where or for whom they worked.

Other Communist Nations

Very few communist economies exist today. Most communist nations, like China, have incorporated elements of free enterprise into their economic systems.

Cuba, led by Fidel Castro from 1959 to 2008, developed a communist economy heavily dependent on Soviet economic aid during the Cold War. As a result, the fall of the Soviet Union caused an economic crisis in Cuba. Despite modest reforms, most Cubans still live and work within the state-controlled economy.

In Southeast Asia, Vietnam and Laos are also ruled by communist parties and have centrally planned economies. However, since the late 1980s, both nations have instituted free-market reforms to open their domestic markets and promote growth and encourage investment.

Communist North Korea has achieved little growth. Its economy, army, and all civil institutions are under the total control of dictator Kim Jong-Il, and severe food shortages plague the country.

Evaluating Command Economies

Both free market and command economies have their strengths and their weaknesses. For the supporters of capitalism, it is easy to see the weaknesses in the theory and practice of socialism and communism. To the supporters of those two systems, capitalism seems filled with faults.

Critics argue that the many layers of bureaucracy in socialist countries complicate decision making and have a depressing effect on individual initiative. As a result, command economies are slow to take advantage of new technologies. In addition, many say, the smooth running of an economy is too complex to be directed by central planners. Too many unpredictable events are involved, and too many clashing interests are at stake. For all its faults, they argue, the invisible hand of the free-market economy works more efficiently than the ever-present hand of central planning.

Command economies are also criticized because they deprive people of the freedom to decide for themselves how to use their income. Since workers get to keep only a part of their earnings after taxes, they have little incentive to work harder and earn more, and no incentive to innovate or create new products. Why work hard when your basic needs will be taken care of anyway?

In response, socialists and communists say that it is fairer to supply everyone with such basic needs as medical care, housing, and education. They point to the inequalities of wealth and power that exist under capitalism. In their view, socialism makes political democracy work more smoothly by meshing it with economic democracy.

Defenders of socialism and communism also argue that these systems give workers and other ordinary citizens more control over their daily lives. Under capitalism, they say, a company's management can abruptly decide to close an unprofitable factory, even though such a decision can put thousands out of work and disrupt an entire community. This could not happen in a socialist or communist state, the argument goes. Workers and community leaders on the company's board would help decide what is best for the entire workforce and community— not just for the company's investors and shareholders.

✔ **Checkpoint**
How successful have communist economies been?

Essential Questions Journal To continue to build a response to the chapter Essential Question, go to your Essential Questions Journal.

SECTION 2 ASSESSMENT

1. **Guiding Question** Use your completed chart to answer this question: What is the role of government under socialism and communism?

Key Terms and Comprehension
2. How did Karl Marx's theories lead to **socialism** and **communism?**
3. What role does the government play in a **command economy?**
4. In your own words, describe how **communism** is intended to work.

Critical Thinking
5. **Make Comparisons** How might a capitalist, socialist, and communist government each interact with small businesses?
6. **Make Decisions** Do you think the government should have the responsibility of ensuring that every citizen has a job? Why or why not?

Quick Write

Expository Writing: Research for Examples and Details When writing a compare-and-contrast essay, you should include details that support the comparisons and contrasts you discuss. Use your textbook, the library, and reliable Internet sources to add details and examples to the notes you have made in your Venn diagram. Review the notes to delete details that are unimportant or do not relate to both systems.

Globalization and Free Trade

▶▶ Track the Issue

Until the 1940s, the United States favored protectionist policies over free trade.

Congress passes the first Tariff Act, providing the new Federal Government with its main source of revenue.

South Carolina, a rural State, threatens the unity of the country over federal tariffs protecting northern manufacturers.

Smoot-Hawley Tariff Act raises tariffs on imports to historically high levels.

The General Agreement on Tariffs and Trade (GATT) is signed, opening a new era of lower tariffs.

The North American Free Trade Agreement (NAFTA) takes effect, reducing trade barriers among the United States, Canada, and Mexico.

The World Trade Organization replaces GATT, aiming to expand global trade and resolve disputes.

President Bill Clinton promoted farm exports through NAFTA. ▶

▶▶ Perspectives

The growth of free trade has brought both benefits and challenges to Americans. While trade has expanded in some areas and the United States remains the world's largest exporter, there have also been painful job losses. What economic and social issues do government leaders need to consider in drafting free trade agreements?

Today, the global economy is enriching corporate profiteers, wealthy families and dictators, but it isn't working for working families. In the United States, we're losing high-paying, full-benefit manufacturing jobs and more and more family members are having to join the workforce to maintain living standards. Our trade deficit is eating away at economic stability and our basic industries are being hammered by . . . unfair trade practices. Around the world . . . inequality is rising, both among and within nations.

—*AFL-CIO, Campaign for Global Fairness, 2000*

With our strong institutions, deep capital markets, flexible labor markets, technological leadership, and penchant [like] for entrepreneurship and innovation, no country is better placed than the United States to benefit from increased participation in the global economy. If we resist protectionism and isolationism while working to increase the skills and adaptability of our labor force, the forces of globalization and trade will continue to make our economy stronger and our citizens more prosperous.

—*Federal Reserve Chairman Ben S. Bernanke, 2007*

▶▶ Connect to Your World

1. Understand (a) Identify five items you use each day. Where were these goods made? **(b)** How does trade affect your community in terms of jobs and the goods people buy?

2. Compare and Contrast (a) What does the AFL-CIO say are the negative effects of free trade? **(b)** Why does Bernanke think that globalization and free trade are good for the American economy? **(c)** With whom do you agree? Why?

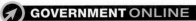

GOVERNMENT ONLINE
In the News
To find out about free trade and globalization, visit
PearsonSuccessNet.com

SECTION 3

The U.S. in a Global Economy

Guiding Question

How does the Federal Government support economic growth at home and abroad? Use an outline to take notes on the ways in which the government takes part in both the domestic and global economies.

I. The Domestic Economy
  A. Supports free enterprise
    1. _____
    2. _____
  B. _____

Political Dictionary

- globalization
- protectionism
- tariff
- import quota
- trade embargo
- NAFTA
- World Trade Organization (WTO)

Objectives

1. Describe the role of government in the domestic economy.
2. Understand the reasons why nations participate in trade.
3. Describe the role of the Federal Government in the global economy.
4. Explain the causes of globalization and its effects on the American economy.

Image Above: Traders signal an offer on the exchange floor of the Chicago Board of Trade.

Since 1789, the government of the United States has become increasingly involved in protecting, managing, and regulating this nation's economic life. With the rise of worldwide markets, free trade agreements, multinational corporations, and the use of off-shore labor—known as outsourcing—the Federal Government's participation in the economy is now more crucial than ever. Today, it has a great deal to say about how the economy operates at home and abroad. It also works to protect the economic interests of its citizens.

The Domestic Economy

For the first 120 years or so of its existence, the Federal Government played only a very limited role in the economy and in the economic well-being of the American people. However, by the early twentieth century, due to repeated economic "panics" and recessions, culminating in the Great Depression of the 1930s, the amount of governmental involvement began to change.

A vital free enterprise system fosters competition and entrepreneurship. The Federal Government tries to support this system by attempting to ensure fairness in the market place, and, with it, the health and well-being of both consumers and workers.

Recall, there are a number of independent agencies within the executive branch of the government. Many of them have an important role in the regulation of economic activities within the United States. Among the most important of them are the Federal Reserve System, the Securities and Exchange Commission (SEC), and such organizations as the Occupational Safety & Health Administration (OSHA) in the Department of Labor.

The Federal Reserve System Known as "the Fed," the Federal Reserve System is one of the most powerful tools the Federal Government uses to regulate the nation's economy. The Fed was established by Congress in 1913 to become the central banking system for the United States. It consists of a Board of Governors appointed by the President (one of whom is appointed to act as the chairperson), 12 regional banks, and many other member banks. The main purpose of the Fed is to use the tools of monetary policy to promote price stability, full employment, economic growth, and other national economic goals.

The Federal Reserve System

Twelve regional banks make up the Federal Reserve System, known as the Fed. The banks' directors and an appointed Board of Governors make important decisions that affect the national and global economy. *Why does including the regional directors improve the Fed's decisions?*

Alaska and Hawaii are part of the San Francisco District

The Fed's Responsibility: Set interest rates to encourage steady economic growth

If the Fed sets interest rates too High

- businesses will not borrow and invest
- the economy slows
- people lose jobs

If the Fed sets interest rates too Low

- too much money is borrowed
- businesses make risky investments
- prices rise quickly

KEY

⭐ Board of Governors

○ Federal Reserve Bank city

✔ **Checkpoint**
What is the Federal Reserve System?

fraudulent
adj. false, dishonest

Mainly, this means adjusting the federal funds rate—an interest rate at which banks lend money to other banks on a daily basis. The Fed does this to either contract or expand the amount of money in the economy in response to changes in inflation or unemployment. Raising interest rates makes money more expensive to borrow, and so, in theory, contracts the economy. Lowering interest rates makes money less expensive to borrow, and so tends to expand the economy. The rate adjustments that the Fed makes can affect other lending rates, foreign exchange rates, and the levels of money and credit available in the economy, as well as employment and prices. In 2008 on into 2009, the Fed took several actions to avert a panic in the financial markets. You can read more about the importance of the Fed in Chapter 16.

The Securities and Exchange Commission The Securities and Exchange Commission (SEC), is a federal regulatory agency consisting of five commissioners appointed by the President, who also selects the SEC's chairperson from among those five commissioners. Congress created the SEC in 1934 in the aftermath of the stock market crash that contributed to the Great Depression.

The commission's central task is to oversee the nation's stock markets and ensure that corporations do not engage in such abuses as insider trading, the practice of buying or selling stock based on company information not known to other investors. The SEC also ensures that publicly traded companies truthfully disclose their finances. It brings court actions against those who violate securities laws—for example, through insider trading, fraudulent accounting practices, or providing false information to investors.

The Department of Labor The Federal Government provides protections for the basic rights of workers and oversees issues of fairness and safety in the workplace. Much of this is accomplished by the Department of Labor.

To meet these aims, the Department works through its various agencies. For example, since the Occupational Safety & Health Administration (OSHA) was established in 1971, its inspectors have worked with employers and employees to decrease deaths in the workplace by 60 percent. The Employment Standards Administration (ESA) monitors fairness in contracts, benefits, and wages. The Bureau of Labor Statistics plays the important role of tracking major economic statistics, such as the unemployment rate and the consumer price index. These data are used to evaluate the health of the nation's economy.

A Global Economy

There is a growing economic <u>interdependence</u> among nations of the world. This interdependence, known as **globalization,** has been both driven and enabled by many remarkable advancements in communication and transportation technologies. Everything from the enormous increase in computing power, the Internet, communications satellites, and even the building of larger ships has increased the flow of goods, and, as well, the flow of information that connects world markets. Globalization has also developed out of the drive for increased international trade promoted by the United States in the years since the Great Depression.

The Purpose of Trade All nations engage in trade. Trade is one of the <u>hallmarks</u> of civilization, and it has been for thousands of years. However, improvements in transportation and communication technologies and the pressure to find new markets have spurred the growth of worldwide markets.

The United States produces a great many different goods, but it does not produce everything this country needs. No country does because of the unequal distribution of natural resources and other factors of production, such as skilled workers, among countries. The unequal distribution of factors of production means that one nation can more effectively specialize in producing certain goods—for example, petroleum or computer chips. That nation will then export petroleum or computer chips and use the profits to purchase, or import, goods from other nations who have an advantage in the production of, for example, food stuffs or automobiles.

Trade allows Americans to acquire the goods they want, but which this nation cannot produce as cost-effectively or efficiently as it does other goods. It is the role of the Federal Government to support trade and other economic opportunities around the world, while at the same time, protecting American producers and consumers.

American Trade Partners Today, as it has been for several decades, Canada is the United States' chief trade partner. After the North American Free Trade Agreement (NAFTA) became effective in 1994, Mexico moved up in rank to second among the United States' main trade partners. However, by the end of 2004, China had surpassed Mexico to become the United States' second leading trading partner. This remains true today.

The United States is the largest exporter of goods and services in the world. Major American exports include such goods as telecommunications, aerospace, medical, and military equipment. This country also exports soybeans, corn, fruit, automobiles, and a great many other products. Service exports are a large and quickly growing sector of world trade. The United States leads there, as well, in exporting education, information, data processing, financial services, and medical care.

The United States is also the world's number one importer of goods. About $2 trillion in imported goods and services enter the United States each year. That is nearly 20 percent of all the world's imports, and includes such consumer goods as clothing, toys, and electronics, as well as capital goods, which include computers, electronic parts, and industrial machinery. Another import category is food and beverages, including animal feed. Automobiles and auto parts constitute a fourth import category.

However, the largest category of imported goods is industrial supplies and materials, including crude oil. The United States is the largest importer of crude oil in the world,

✔ **Checkpoint**
What is the goal of globalization?

<u>interdependence</u>
n. dependence upon one another

<u>hallmark</u>
n. distinguishing feature

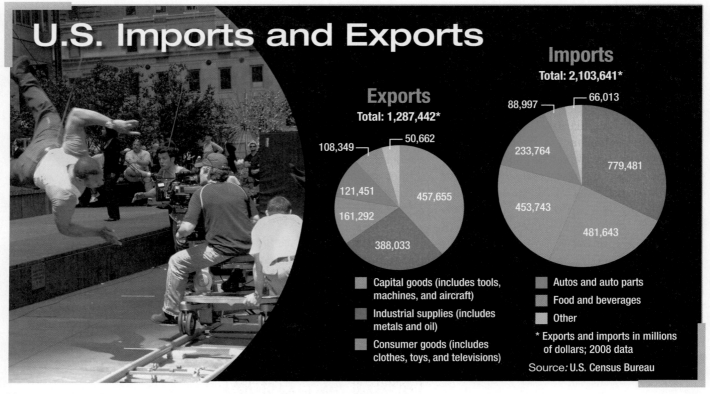

U.S. Imports and Exports

Exports
Total: 1,287,442*

- 457,655
- 388,033
- 161,292
- 121,451
- 108,349
- 50,662

■ Capital goods (includes tools, machines, and aircraft)
■ Industrial supplies (includes metals and oil)
■ Consumer goods (includes clothes, toys, and televisions)

Imports
Total: 2,103,641*

- 779,481
- 481,643
- 453,743
- 233,764
- 88,997
- 66,013

■ Autos and auto parts
■ Food and beverages
■ Other

* Exports and imports in millions of dollars; 2008 data

Source: U.S. Census Bureau

▸▸ **Analyzing Charts** The United States imports more goods and services than it exports, although film and television programs (left) are an exception to this pattern. *According to the charts, how does oil influence the trade balance of imports and exports?*

✓ **Checkpoint**
What are the main imports of the United States?

accounting for some 12 percent of all oil imports. Most of that oil comes from the countries of Canada, Saudi Arabia, Mexico, Venezuela, and Iraq.

U.S. Trade Policies

One goal of the Federal Government has often been to protect American producers and workers by keeping prices, and therefore profits, high, while minimizing competition from imports. The government must do this through such agencies as the Department of Commerce and the International Trade Commission without jeopardizing relationships with its trade partners. It has employed several tools for this tricky task.

jeopardize
v. to risk, put in danger

Economic Policy Tools Most national governments try to control imports to protect native industries from foreign competition. The goals of this practice, known as **protectionism,** include safeguarding of jobs,

protecting emerging or weakened industries, and enhancing national security. Governments often pursue these goals with trade barriers that hinder free trade and raise the prices consumers must pay for imported goods. These trade barriers are generally of three types: tariffs, import quotas, and trade embargoes.

A **tariff** is a tax on imported goods. A tariff increases the cost of an imported item, and makes American-made products more attractive to the domestic customer. The government regularly places high tariffs on goods that are produced by important American industries. For example, the tariff on steel is relatively high because Americans produce a great deal of it and the steel industry is considered vital to national security, so the government does not wish cheaper imports to put domestic steel mills out of business.

An **import quota** is a limit put on the amount of a commodity that can be imported into a country. While recently limited by international agreements, import quotas are still in place in the United States on such items as cotton, sugar, and milk. Many European nations have put a quota on American films and television shows to encourage the production of their own features and to protect national cultures.

A more significant trade barrier—and one that is more often used to apply diplomatic pressure or as a punishment rather than as an economic tool—is the trade embargo. A **trade embargo** is a ban on trade with a particular country or countries. An embargo might be placed on all goods or only specific items. It can be placed on exports or, separately, on imports. The United States has used trade embargoes largely to promote its foreign policy positions. For example, the United States has maintained a complete economic embargo on Communist Cuba since the early 1960s. Embargoes can be effective, but notice that they may also hurt the domestic economy of the nation imposing them.

NAFTA The North American Free Trade Agreement, known as **NAFTA,** became effective in 1994. NAFTA established free trade among the United States, Canada, and Mexico, and intended to eliminate, in steps, all tariffs and other barriers to trade by 2009. It created what amounts to the world's largest free trade zone.

NAFTA was approved only after a great deal of controversy and resistance, especially in the United States. Opponents of the agreement were concerned that American manufacturing operations would be moved to Mexico, where wages are lower and regulations are fewer, and lead to huge job losses. Others worried that imports without tariffs would put American businesses at a huge disadvantage. Supporters insisted that the expected increase in exports to Canada and Mexico would mean an increase in American jobs. They also argued that an improved economy would create greater prosperity and stability in Mexico, and so reduce illegal immigration from that country.

Today, nearly all <u>facets</u> of NAFTA are in place; the results seem to indicate that the pact was on the whole good for U.S. trade and investment, but not positive for all American workers. Although the long-term results are hard to distinguish from other trends, it appears that NAFTA accelerated the loss of high-paying manufacturing jobs. For example, jobs in the American textile and clothing sectors, already in decline, decreased steeply. However, many manufacturing jobs that have left the U.S. have moved to countries other than Mexico or Canada.

On the positive side, trade—in agricultural products especially—has increased dramatically with the elimination of nearly all trade barriers. Between 1993 and 2008, United States exports to Mexico rose from $41 billion to nearly $138 billion.

While NAFTA affects only trade with Canada and Mexico, it provides a model for freer trade between the United States and other countries. The United States has signed similar treaties with many other countries in Latin America and Asia involving much smaller trade flows.

International Organizations

The United States employs the tools of protectionism to support industries and workers at home. It also uses them to enlarge economic opportunities, strengthen international ties, and open new markets abroad. It often does this through membership in free trade agreements and international alliances and organizations.

Protecting the Global Economy The **World Trade Organization (WTO)** was created in 1995 to help carry out and extend the goals of a 1948 treaty, the General Agreement on Tariffs and Trade (GATT) intended to increase trade. With 151 members, the WTO provides a set of rules for international commerce, a forum for the creation of new trade agreements, and an arena in which to resolve trade issues.

The United States is also a member of, and the largest shareholder in, the World Bank. The goal of this institution is to reduce poverty and raise the standard of living around the world by making loans to poor nations to build infrastructure or reduce debt and by providing advice and training.

The International Monetary Fund (IMF) is, like the World Bank, headquartered in

<u>facet</u>
n. aspect, piece, side

tangible
adj. real, physical, touchable

Washington, D.C. It was established in 1945 to promote a healthy global economy and to prevent crises in the international monetary and financial systems. While the World Bank lends money to developing countries to build bridges, dams, and other <u>tangible</u> improvements, the IMF helps countries whose financial or banking systems are in trouble.

Another important group to which the United States belongs is the Group of 8, or "the G8," an annual meeting of the leaders of eight wealthy and industrialized nations: the United States, Canada, France, Germany, Italy, Japan, Russia, and the United Kingdom. The group has no rigid structure and leaders meet as representatives of their governments to discuss world affairs and crises.

Other Trade Alliances The European Union (EU) is the most successful of the world's free trade organizations. It is also responsible for setting policies in other areas of common concern to its members, including social issues and security. The evolution of the EU began in 1957, when six European nations established the European Common Market to coordinate economic policies and trade. Over time, most Western European nations joined the group. In 1986, they created the European Economic Community (EEC) and, in an historic step, eliminated all tariffs on trade between EU members.

In 1993, the organization went even further to blur international boundaries by forming the European Union. The EU operates much like a weak federal government, with its own parliament, its own flag, and even an anthem. Citizens of most member nations can now travel as tourists or workers across national borders freely, without a passport. In 2002, twelve of the member nations gave up their individual currencies and replaced them with the euro, which is the EU's currency. The EU is now comprised of 27 nations, including many of the former Soviet republics.

Inspired by the success of the EU, other nations have formed mostly regional trade alliances. One of the largest is the Asian-Pacific Economic Cooperation (APEC). Its 21 members include nations on the Pacific Rim, such as the United States, Japan, Canada, Chile, and China. The Southern Common Market, or MERCOSUR, is a regional trade bloc established by Brazil, Argentina, Paraguay, and Uruguay.

Top U.S. Trade Partners

The United States trades most heavily with countries in North America, East Asia, and Europe. However, we import more from each of our six largest trade partners than we export to them, leading to trade deficits. *With which country does the United States have the largest trade deficit?*

EXPORTS to U.S. and IMPORTS from U.S. in billions of dollars

	Canada	China	Mexico	Japan
EXPORTS to U.S.	335.6	337.8	215.9	139.2
IMPORTS from U.S.	261.4	71.5	151.5	66.6
TOTAL U.S. TRADE	17.6%	12%	10.8%	6.1%

SOURCE: U.S. Census, 2008 data

Impact of Trade

For the most part, a global economy seems to be a positive development. It means that more goods are available to more consumers, and that there are more markets in which producers can sell goods. Globalization and international partnerships also help developing nations to expand their economies and raise their standards of living by enabling them to sell goods to more affluent countries.

And, clearly, competition in a global market lowers the price of goods. Goods made overseas, unblocked by tariffs, are less expensive and become more affordable for Americans. Increases in jobs and higher wages, in turn, allow consumers in developing nations to buy American goods and services, and this helps to increase or at least maintain American jobs. Additionally, new, creative approaches to outsourcing may actually create new American jobs by lowering costs so that corporations are able to use the savings to grow and develop innovative products and services. Importantly, increased economic interdependence may lead to more political cooperation and so to fewer conflicts.

However, with interdependence comes risk. A crisis in another nation on which Americans depend for an important commodity can have quick, profound, and direct economic effects. Thus, in recent years, war in Iraq and instability in Nigeria—both major oil-producing nations—contributed to higher oil and gas prices in the United States.

Some people worry that international trade agreements may affect a nation's sovereignty if they have to get "permission" from partner nations to make decisions about such matters as civil rights, defense, or the environment. With <u>instantaneous</u> communications, economic downturns or market fluctuations in one part of the world now cause instability in other markets within hours.

The United States is also moving from a manufacturing economy to a service economy, in large part because American workers cannot compete with workers in other nations who are paid much less. The loss of high-paying manufacturing jobs is painful to the individuals involved, and if these workers are not retrained to begin new jobs with comparable wages, the transition will also hurt both the local and the national economy. In addition, the growth of the service sector has created many new, high-paying jobs that did not exist a decade ago, but often in different locations from where workers live.

The United States is also adversely affected by trade deficits. For example, the United States buys much more from China than China buys from the United States, and so an enormous trade deficit has developed. China has financed the deficit by lending the United States government money and by buying American assets. This means that China, along with Japan and many oil-exporting countries, owns a portion of the American economy, with implications for the economic health and future of this nation.

Tomorrow's Marketplace

As you have seen, the trend today in the world economy is toward greater interdependence among nations—

✔ Checkpoint

What is the purpose of the European Union?

instantaneous
adj. happening in an instant

GOVERNMENT ONLINE

Audio Tour
Listen to an audio guided tour on trade at
PearsonSuccessNet.com

Germany
EXPORTS to U.S. 97.6
IMPORTS from U.S. 54.7
4.5%
TOTAL U.S. TRADE

United Kingdom
EXPORTS to U.S. 58.6
IMPORTS from U.S. 53.8
3.3%
TOTAL U.S. TRADE

Selected Fast-Growing Occupations Projected increase 2006–2016

Occupation		
Home health aide +384,000	+48.7%	
Computer software engineer +226,000	+44.6%	
Personal financial advisor +72,000	+41.0%	
Medical assistant +149,000	+35.4%	

Source: The Bureau of Labor Statistics

▶▶ **Analyzing Charts** The Bureau of Labor Statistics estimates that these occupational fields will see high growth over this ten-year period. *How can education help people prepare to fill these jobs?*

increased globalization. Along with the United States, most nations are joining multiple trade alliances, such as NAFTA and the EU, to open new markets and promote free trade. Developing nations are working to diversify their economies and open their markets. The United States continues to build partnerships by establishing new trade agreements with nations such as Peru, South Korea, Singapore, and Colombia and working with China to lower the U.S. trade deficit with that nation.

The good news for Americans is that the huge increase in the demand for services worldwide means that the United States will probably continue to see an increase in service exports and retain its position as the global leader in that area. Unfortunately,

the increase in free trade and outsourcing to emerging nations means further loss of manufacturing jobs. Although economic analysts have mixed views about the overall cost in American jobs due to outsourcing, thousands or even millions of jobs could move overseas in the coming years. Federal programs such as Trade Adjustment Assistance, which retrains workers who are laid off due to outsourcing or foreign competition, will help American workers deal with this challenge.

As the economy shifts toward services, the United States will need to rely on intellectual property as much as on exported goods. Among other important challenges and issues the United States government must face in the future are the protection of American copyrights and patents against piracy and the need to foster stability in oil-producing nations and regions.

Essential Questions Journal To continue to build a response to the chapter Essential Question, go to your **Essential Questions Journal.**

SECTION 3 ASSESSMENT

1. **Guiding Question** Use your completed outline to answer this question: How does the Federal Government support economic growth at home and abroad?

Key Terms and Comprehension

2. What is the basic structure and role of the Federal Reserve System?

3. Briefly identify and define the three main **protectionist** tools available to a national government.

Critical Thinking

4. **Summarize (a)** What are the goals of **NAFTA? (b)** How has **NAFTA** affected different people in different ways?

5. **Draw Inferences** How might the U.S. benefit from participating in the World Bank, the G8, and the **WTO**?

Quick Write

Expository Writing: Create an Outline To help you structure a compare-and-contrast essay on two different economic systems, create an outline in which you identify each area of comparison and contrast in a single phrase. When you are ready to write your essay, you can use the outline as a guide. Or, you may create a flowchart to help you organize and order your ideas.

GOVERNMENT ONLINE

On the Go
To review anytime, anywhere, download these online resources at **PearsonSuccessNet.com**
Political Dictionary, Audio Review

Guiding Question
Section 2 What is the role of government under socialism and communism?

Guiding Question
Section 1 What is the role of government in the American economy?

CHAPTER 23

Essential Question
To what extent should governments partici-pate in the economy?

Guiding Question
Section 3 How does the Federal Government support economic growth at home and abroad?

Political Dictionary

capitalism p. 678
factors of production p. 678
capital p. 678
entrepreneur p. 679
free enterprise system p. 679
free market p. 679
laws of supply and demand p. 681
monopoly p. 681
laissez-faire theory p. 682
The Communist Manifesto p. 685
socialism p. 686
communism p. 686
welfare state p. 687
command economy p. 687
five-year plan p. 689
collectivization p. 689
privatization p. 690
Great Leap Forward p. 690
globalization p. 695
protectionism p. 696
tariff p. 696
import quota p. 696
trade embargo p. 697
NAFTA p. 697
World Trade Organization (WTO) p. 697

Private ownership of land, labor, and capital

Limited government participation

Free Enterprise

Free markets and prices

Competition among entrepreneurs

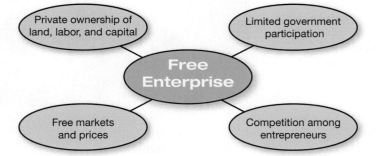

Socialism
- Some private businesses, property
- Democratic government

- State owns big industries
- Welfare state
- Planned economy

Communism
- No private property or businesses
- Dictatorship

Major Economic Institutions

U.S. Government	International Groups	Trade Agreements
Federal Reserve	World Bank	GATT and World Trade Organization
Securities and Exchange Commission	International Monetary Fund	North American Free Trade Agreement
Department of Labor	G8	
	European Union	

Chapter Assessment

Comprehension and Critical Thinking

Section 1

1. **(a)** What are the three **factors of production? (b)** What role do the factors of production play in the economy?

2. **(a)** Why is competition important in a **free market** economy? **(b)** What might happen in a market without competition? **(c)** How might government promote competition?

3. **(a)** According to **laissez-faire theory,** what are the three major concerns of government? **(b)** Do you think this amounts to too little, too much, or just about the right amount of involvement by government? Why?

Section 2

4. **(a)** Briefly explain Karl Marx's basic ideas about **capitalism. (b)** In what sense are **socialism** and **communism** a response to capitalism?

5. **(a)** What are three characteristics of socialist countries? **(b)** What are four characteristics of communist countries? **(c)** How does government participation in the economy vary in the two systems?

6. **(a)** Many people say that **socialism** and **communism** discourage individuals from taking initiatives. Is this criticism valid? Why or why not? **(b)** How does **capitalism** differ from **command economies** in the treatment of the individual?

Section 3

7. **(a)** Summarize the role of the Federal Government in the American economy. **(b)** Describe how three institutions of the Federal Government help carry out this role.

8. **Analyzing Cartoons** Study the cartoon below about a Senate candidate and tariffs on steel. **(a)** Why would steel workers and auto workers have different views on steel tariffs? **(b)** What does this indicate about the effect of tariffs on jobs? **(c)** Is this cartoon in favor of free trade, opposed to free trade, or neutral? Explain.

ARE YOU FOR STEEL TARIFFS TO HELP THE STEEL WORKERS OR AGAINST THEM TO HELP THE AUTO WORKERS?

Writing About Government

9. Use your Quick Write exercises from the section assessments in this chapter to write an essay that compares and contrasts the two topics you selected. Make sure that the information is accurate and that comparisons are reasoned and relevant. End your essay with a summarizing conclusion. See pp. S3–S5 in the Skills Handbook.

Apply What You've Learned

10. **Essential Question Activity** In small groups, meet with a business owner in your community. Ask:

    (a) How do you think the American system of government supports or encourages economic freedom?

    (b) How does a free market help your business?

    (c) In what ways do you think your life and your business would be different in a socialist or communist system?

    (d) Do you think that the Federal Government should be more or less involved in the economy, workers' rights, and social welfare?

11. **Essential Question Assessment** Based on the interview you conducted, write a political statement that expresses the views of this business owner about the relationship between economic and political freedom and the role of government in the economy. Discuss your ideas with your classmates to help you answer the Essential Question: **To what extent should governments participate in the economy?**

Essential Questions
Journal

To respond to the chapter Essential Question, go to your **Essential Questions Journal.**

Document-Based Assessment

Government and the Economy

As the United States approached its entry into World War II, President Franklin Roosevelt defined "four freedoms" government should protect, as shown in Document 1. While many question how far the government should intervene in the economy, the Federal Government often acts to influence business trends, as in Document 3.

Document 1

[W]e look forward to a world founded upon four essential human freedoms. The first is freedom of speech and expression—everywhere in the world. The second is freedom of every person to worship God in his own way—everywhere in the world. The third is freedom from want—which, translated into world terms, means economic understandings which will secure to every nation a healthy peacetime life for its inhabitants—everywhere in the world. The fourth is freedom from fear—which, translated into world terms, means a world-wide reduction of armaments to such a point and in such a thorough fashion that no nation will be in a position to commit an act of physical aggression against any neighbor—anywhere in the world.

—President Franklin D. Roosevelt, "The Four Freedoms" State of the Union Address, January 6, 1941

Document 2

I'm going to cut taxes, increase social spending and balance the budget. All you have to do is turn rocks into gold.

© Thaves. THAVES

Document 3

In 2008, President Bush sought to boost the nation's flagging economy by sending each American tax payer a payment of several hundred dollars.

This growth package must be big enough to make a difference in an economy as large and dynamic as ours . . . This growth package must be built on broad-based tax relief that will directly affect economic growth—and not the kind of spending projects that would have little immediate impact on our economy. This growth package must be temporary and take effect right away—so we can get help to our economy when it needs it most. And this growth package must not include any tax increases. . . . We're in the midst of a challenging period, and I know Americans are concerned about our economic future. But our economy has seen challenging times before—and it is resilient. In a vibrant economy, markets rise and decline. We cannot change that fundamental dynamic. As a matter of fact, eliminating risk altogether would also eliminate the innovation and productivity that drives the creation of jobs and wealth in America.

—Presidential address, January 18, 2008

Use your knowledge of government's role in the economy and Documents 1, 2, and 3 to answer Questions 1–3.

1. In his speech, Franklin Roosevelt expressed the idea that
   A. all nations should govern their people in the same way as does the United States.
   B. the most important long-term goal of all nations should be rearmament.
   C. it is the responsibility of government to ensure the welfare of all of its citizens.
   D. the global political situation is very dangerous and no one is secure.

2. How does President Bush characterize downturns in the American economy?

3. **Pull It Together** Do you think that Bush's economic growth plan fulfills the third freedom described by Roosevelt? Why or why not?

GOVERNMENT ONLINE
Go Online
To find more primary sources about the economy, visit **PearsonSuccessNet.com**

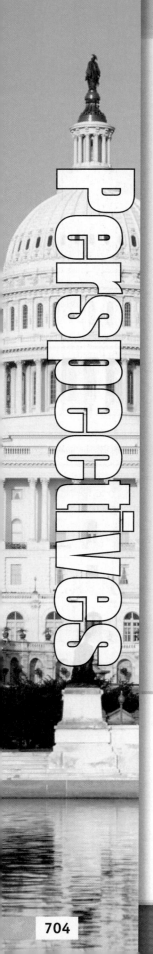

Essential Question
How should a government meet the needs of its people?

The nearly 200 sovereign states in the world today identify the needs of their people in different ways and disagree on how or to what extent government should attempt to meet those needs.

ON THE LIMITS OF GOVERNMENT:

Conservatives know that governments don't have all the answers. But if they govern with the right values, they can make a real difference.

—UK Conservative Party Manifesto, 2005

ON MEASURING THE IMPROVEMENT IN LIVES:

Prosperity Indicators, U.S.		
	1950	2008
Life Expectancy at Birth (years)	68.2	78.1 (est.)
Per Capita Gross Domestic Product (constant 2000 dollars)	$11,720*	$37,899
Population with Bachelor's Degree or higher, ages 25 and up	6.2%	29.4%
*approximate		

By most measures, Americans are healthier, better educated, and more affluent today than in the past.

ON THE RESPONSIBILITIES OF A COMMUNIST PARTY:

Without the efforts of the Chinese Communist Party . . . as the mainstay of the Chinese people, China can never achieve independence and liberation, or industrialization and the modernization of her agriculture.

—Mao Zedong, 1945

Essential Question Warmup

Throughout this unit, you studied the history and ideas behind political systems and economic systems around the world. Use what you have learned and the quotations, data, and opinions above to answer the following questions. Then go to your **Essential Questions Journal.**

1. How would you define "the needs of the people"?

2. How might other nations, and specific leaders in history, define "the needs of the people" differently?

3. Can a country led by a single party or person successfully represent a country's people?

4. How does a free market economy help meet people's needs?

Essential Questions **Journal**	To continue to build a response to the chapter Essential Question, go to your **Essential Questions Journal.**

Photo: Voters express their views at a town meeting in Hardwick, Vermont.

Essential Questions Journal To begin to build a response to the unit Essential Question, go to your **Essential Questions Journal.**

Unit 7 Participating in State and Local Government

Essential Question What is the right balance of local, State, and federal government?

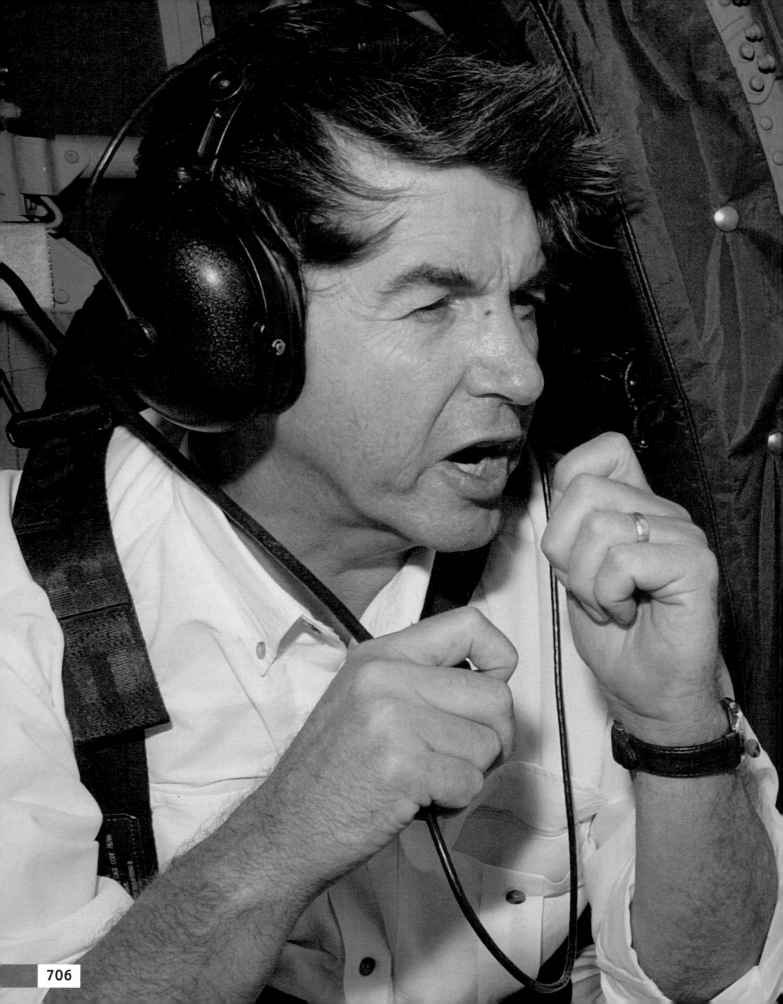

Governing the States

Essential Question
How much power should State government have?

"The Constitution, in all of its provisions, looks to an indestructible Union, composed of indestructible States.

—Chief Justice Salmon P. Chase, *Texas* v. *White*, 1869

Photo: Governor Bob Riley (R., Alabama) surveys hurricane damage.

GOVERNMENT ONLINE
On the Go

To study anywhere, anytime, download these online resources at PearsonSuccessNet.com
• Political Dictionary
• Audio Review
• Downloadable Interactivities

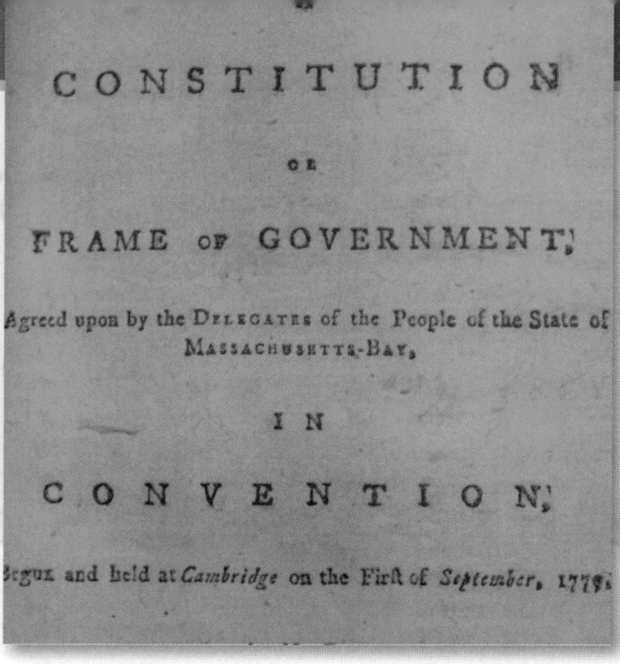

State Constitutions

CONSTITUTION
OR
FRAME OF GOVERNMENT;
Agreed upon by the DELEGATES of the People of the State of
MASSACHUSETTS-BAY,
IN
CONVENTION;
Begun and held at *Cambridge* on the First of *September*, 1779.

Guiding Question

What are the defining features of State constitutions? Use an outline to take notes on the defining qualities of State constitutions.

I. The First State Constitutions
 A. Independence
  1. _____
  2. _____
 B. _____
  1. _____
  2. _____

Political Dictionary

- popular sovereignty
- limited government
- fundamental law
- initiative
- statutory law

Objectives

1. Examine the history, content, and significance of the first State constitutions.

2. Describe the basic principles common to all State constitutions today.

3. Explain the procedures used to change State constitutions.

4. Analyze why State constitutions are in need of reform.

Image Above: Massachusetts constitution of 1780

Not very many people have ever seen a State constitution, let alone read one. Join a rather exclusive club and look at your State's document. This step should prove useful as you read this chapter.

A State constitution is that State's supreme law. It sets out the ways in which the government of the State is organized, and it distributes powers among the various branches of that government. It authorizes the exercise of power by government and, at the same time, puts limits on the exercise of power by government. Every State's constitution is superior to any and all other forms of State and local law within that State.

Recall, however: Each State's constitution is subordinate to the Constitution of the United States. No provision in any State's constitution may conflict with any form of federal law.

The First State Constitutions

Each of the 50 States has a *written* constitution. From the beginning, government in this country has been based on written constitutions.

Our experience with such documents dates from 1606, when King James I granted a charter to the Virginia Company. That act led to the settlement at Jamestown in the following year and, with it, the first government in what would become British North America. Later, each of the other English colonies was also established and governed on the basis of a written charter.

Independence When the 13 colonies became independent, each faced the problem of establishing a new government. On May 15, 1776, the Second Continental Congress, meeting in Philadelphia, advised each of the new States to adopt

"such governments as shall, in the opinion of the representatives of the people, best conduce to the happiness and safety of their constituents in particular, and America in general."

—**Second Continental Congress**

Most of the colonial charters served as models for the first State constitutions. Indeed, in Connecticut and Rhode Island, the charters seemed so well suited to the needs of the day that they were carried over into statehood as constitutions almost without change.[1]

The earliest State constitutions were adopted in a variety of ways. However, the people played no direct part in the process in any State.

Six of the revolutionary legislatures drew up new documents and proclaimed them in force in 1776. In none of those States—Maryland, New Jersey, North Carolina, Pennsylvania, South Carolina, and Virginia—was the new constitution offered to the people for their judgment.

In Delaware and New Hampshire in 1776, and in Georgia and New York in 1777, the constitutions were prepared by conventions called by the legislature. In each case, the new document had to be approved by the legislature in order to become effective, but in none was popular approval required.

In 1780, a popularly elected convention prepared a new constitution for Massachusetts. It was then ratified by a vote of the people. Thus, Massachusetts set the pattern of popular participation in the constitution-making process, a pattern generally followed among the States ever since.[2]

Assemblies representing the people drafted all of the present State constitutions; most of them became effective only after a popular vote. Only the present-day documents of Delaware (1897), Mississippi (1890), South Carolina (1895), and Vermont (1793) came into force without popular ratification.

Principles of State Constitutions

Because the first State constitutions came out of the same revolutionary <u>ferment</u>, they shared many basic features. Each proclaimed the principles of **popular sovereignty** and **limited government.** That is, in each of them the people were recognized as the sole source of authority for government, and the powers given to the new government were closely limited. Seven documents began with a lengthy bill of rights. All of them made it clear that the sovereign people held "certain unalienable rights" that government must respect.

The doctrines of separation of powers and checks and balances were also built into each of the new constitutions. In practice, however, the memory of the hated royal governors was still fresh. Thus, most of the authority that each State government had was given to the legislature. For example, only New York, Massachusetts, and South Carolina allowed the governor to veto acts of the legislature. In all the States except Georgia (until 1789) and Pennsylvania (until 1790), the legislature was bicameral.[3]

For their time, the early State constitutions were fairly democratic. Each however, contained several provisions (and some important omissions) that were quite undemocratic by today's standards. Thus, none of them provided for full religious freedom. Each one set rigid qualifications for voting and for officeholding, and all gave property owners a highly favored standing.

State Constitutions Today

The present-day State constitutions are the direct descendants of those earlier documents. Only 17 of the current State constitutions were written after 1900, and nearly all have been amended dozens of times.

Subject only to the broad limitations set out in the Federal Constitution, the people of each State can create whatever kind of "Republican Form of

✔ **Checkpoint**
Who drafted the first State constitutions?

<u>ferment</u>
n. a state of great change

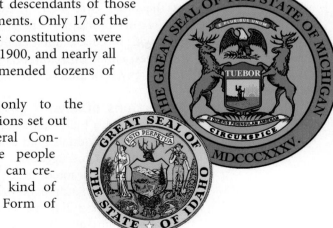

State constitutions often specify designs for State symbols, including the State seal.

---

1 Connecticut's legislature did not write a new document until 1818, and Rhode Island's waited until 1842.

2 As we noted in Chapter 2, with independence Massachusetts relied on the colonial charter in force there prior to 1691 as its first State constitution. When New Hampshire adopted its second and (present) constitution in 1784, it followed the Massachusetts model of popular convention and popular ratification.

---

3 Vermont, which became the 14th State in 1791, had a unicameral legislature until 1836. Only Nebraska has a one-house legislative body today, and it has had one since 1937.

Elements of State Constitutions

PRINCIPLES
- Popular sovereignty; power comes from the people
- Separation of powers
- Checks and balances

CIVIL RIGHTS
- Similar to U.S. Bill of Rights
- May guarantee right to education or gender equality

STRUCTURE
- Outline of State and local government
- Structure of governorship, legislature, and courts

▶▶ **Analyzing Charts** *How are the several State constitutions similar to the federal Constitution?*

☑ **Checkpoint**
When were most current State constitutions adopted?

Government" they choose. Unique provisions can be found in each of the 50 present-day State constitutions. Still, all of them are quite similar in general outline.

Basic Principles Every State's constitution is built on the principles of popular sovereignty and limited government. Each of them recognizes that government exists only with the consent of the people, and that it must operate within certain, often closely defined, bounds. In every State, the powers of government are divided among executive, legislative, and judicial branches. Each branch has powers with which it can restrain the actions of the other two. That is, each of the 50 documents proclaims separation of powers and, with it, checks and balances. Each also provides, either expressly or by implication, for the power of judicial review.

Protections of Civil Rights Each document features a bill of rights, a listing of the rights that individuals hold against the State and its officers and agencies. Most constitutions set out guarantees much like those in the first ten amendments to the national Constitution. Several of them include a number of other guarantees as well—for example, the right to self-government, to be safe from imprisonment for debt, and to organize labor unions and bargain collectively.

Governmental Structure Every State constitution deals with the structure of government at both the State and the local levels, including all three branches of State government and the organization of counties and local governments. A few follow the national pattern, providing only a broad outline. Most, however, cover the subject in considerable and often quite specific detail.

Governmental Powers and Processes Each document lists, in detail, the powers vested in the executive branch (the governor and other executive officers), the legislature, the courts, and the units of local government. The powers to tax, spend, borrow, and provide for education are very prominent. So, too, are such processes as elections, legislation, judicial procedures, and intergovernmental (State–local) relations.

Constitutional Change Constitutions are the product of human effort. None are perfect. Sooner or later, changes become necessary, or at least desirable. So, each State constitution sets out the means by which it may be revised or amended. Constitutions are **fundamental laws**—laws of such basic and lasting importance they cannot be changed as ordinary law can be. Constitutional changes are more difficult to bring about, as you shall see.

POWERS
- Lists powers held by State officials to govern and provide services
- Empowers States to tax, spend, and borrow

CHANGE
- Processes for amendment.

OTHER
- Preambles without legal force
- "Dead letter" material—provisions that no longer apply

Miscellaneous Provisions Every State constitution contains several sections of a <u>miscellaneous</u> character. Thus, most begin with a preamble, which has no legal force but does set out the purposes of those who drafted and adopted the document. Most also contain a schedule, a series of provisions for putting a new document into effect and for avoiding conflicts with its predecessor. And most include a number of "dead letter" provisions, items that have no current force or effect but nonetheless remain a part of the constitution.

Constitutional Change

Like the national Constitution, the State constitutions have been altered over time by formal amendment and by such other processes as court decisions and custom. However, those other processes have not been nearly so important at the State level as at the national level.

State constitutions are much less flexible, and much more detailed, than the national document. Constitutional change and development at the State level has come about mostly through formal amendment rather than by other means.

Two kinds of formal changes have been used: amendments, which usually deal with one or a few provisions in a constitution; and revisions, the term usually used to refer to changes of a broader scope. Revisions might include, for example, an entirely new document. Most of the formal changes made in State constitutions are made by amendment.

Procedures for Change The process of formal change involves two basic steps: proposal and then ratification. Proposals for change can be made by a constitutional convention, the legislature, or (in several States) by the voters themselves. Ratification is by popular vote in every State except Delaware.

The constitutional convention is the usual device by which new constitutions have been written and older ones revised. More than 200 such conventions have been held. In every State the legislature has the power to call a convention, and that call is generally subject to voter approval. In 14 States the question of calling a convention must be submitted to the voters at regular intervals.[4] Conventions can also propose amendments. However, because they are both costly and time-consuming, conventions are most often used for the broader purpose of revision.

Most amendments are proposed by the legislature. The process is comparatively simple in some States, while it is quite difficult in others. In Massachusetts, an amendment must

✓ **Checkpoint**
What are the six elements of State constitutions?

miscellaneous
adj. varying; not belonging to a single category

---

4 Every 20 years in Connecticut, Illinois, Maryland, Missouri, Montana, New York, Ohio, and Oklahoma; every 16 years in Michigan; every 10 years in Alaska, Iowa, New Hampshire, and Rhode Island; and every 9 years in Hawaii

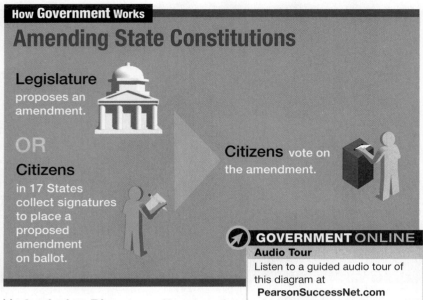

How Government Works

Amending State Constitutions

Legislature proposes an amendment.

OR

Citizens in 17 States collect signatures to place a proposed amendment on ballot.

Citizens vote on the amendment.

⊙ **GOVERNMENT** ONLINE
Audio Tour
Listen to a guided audio tour of this diagram at
PearsonSuccessNet.com

▶▶ **Analyzing Diagrams** *How does the process for amending State constitutions reflect the idea of popular sovereignty?*

✔**Checkpoint**
Describe the procedure for changing a State's constitution.

obsolete
adj. out of date

be approved by the legislature at two successive annual sessions before it goes to the voters for approval or rejection. In California, a proposal must be approved by the legislature at a single session before being sent on to the voters. Not surprisingly, more amendments are proposed (and adopted) in those States with simpler processes, such as California, than in States such as Massachusetts.

In 17 States the voters themselves can propose constitutional amendments through the **initiative,** a process in which a certain number of qualified voters sign petitions in favor of a proposal. The proposal then goes directly to the ballot, for approval or rejection by the people.

Ratification of Amendments In every State except Delaware, an amendment must be approved by vote of the people in order to become part of the constitution. The ratification process, like the proposal process, varies among the States.[5]

---

5 In Delaware, if an amendment is approved by a two-thirds vote in each house of the legislature at two successive sessions, it becomes effective. In South Carolina, final ratification, after a favorable vote by the people, depends on a majority vote in both houses of the legislature. Both the Alabama and South Carolina constitutions provide that amendments of local, as opposed to Statewide, application need be approved only by the voters in the affected locale.

Typically, the approval of a majority of those voting on an amendment adds it to the State constitution, though some States require a majority of all who vote in an election. On many occasions, in several States, amendments have been defeated though they received more *yes* votes than *no* votes. Most often, this happens because many voters fail to vote on all or at least some ballot measures.

The Need for Reform

Almost without exception, State constitutions are in urgent need of reform. The typical document is cluttered with unnecessary details, burdensome restrictions, and obsolete sections. It also carries much repetitious, even contradictory, material. Moreover, it fails to deal with many of the pressing problems that the States and their local governments currently face.

Even the newest and most recently rewritten constitutions tend to carry over a great deal of material from earlier documents and suffer from these same faults. The need for reform can be demonstrated in several ways. Looking at the documents from two standpoints, their lengths and their ages, can produce some useful insights.

The Problem of Length Length was not a problem for the first State constitutions. They were quite short, ranging from New Jersey's 1776 document (2,500 words) to the 1780 Massachusetts constitution (12,000 words). Those early constitutions were meant simply to be statements of basic principle and organization. Purposely, they left to the legislature— and to time and practice—the task of filling in the details as they became necessary.

Through the years, however, State constitutions have grown and grown. Most today are between 15,000 and 40,000 words. The shortest are those of New Hampshire (1784), with some 9,200 words, and Vermont (1793), with just over 10,200 words. At the other extreme, Alabama's 1901 constitution now runs to more than 340,000 words. A leading cause of this expansion is popular distrust of government, a historical and continuing fact of American political life. That distrust has often led to the insertion into State constitutions of detailed provisions aimed at preventing the misuse of government power.

Many restrictions on that power, which could be set out in ordinary law, have been purposely written into the State constitution, where they cannot be easily ignored or readily, and quietly, changed. Special interest groups learned long ago that public policies of particular benefit to them are much more secure in the State constitution than in a mere statute.

There has been a marked failure in every State to distinguish *fundamental law*, that which is basic and of lasting importance and should be in the constitution, from **statutory law,** that which should be enacted as ordinary law by the legislature. The line separating fundamental and statutory law may be blurry in some cases. But who can seriously argue that fundamental law includes the regulation of the length of wrestling matches, as in California's constitution, or the problem of off-street parking in the city of Baltimore, as in Maryland's document?

Two other factors have contributed to the growth of State constitutions. First, the functions performed by the States, and by most of their local governments, have multiplied over recent decades. That development has prompted many new constitutional provisions. Second, the "people" have not been stingy in the use of the initiative in those States where it is available.

The Problem of Age Most State constitutions are severely outdated. They were written for another time and are in urgent need of revision. All too often, their many amendments have aggravated the problem, adding to the clutter of the document.

The Oregon constitution provides a typical example of the situation. It was written by delegates to a territorial convention in 1857 and became effective when Oregon entered the Union in 1859. It has been amended more than 240 times; it now contains more than 55,000 words and includes *two* Articles VII and *seventeen* Articles XI!

Like most of the other State charters, the Oregon document is overloaded with statutory material. One of those Article XIs devotes nearly 2,000 words to a closely detailed treatment of veterans' farm and home loans. The document also contains a number of obsolete provisions, including one that bars any person who has ever engaged in a duel from holding any public office in the State.

Some States' charters have proved to be more stable than others. The oldest of all the constitutions are those in Massachusetts (1780), New Hampshire (1784), and Vermont (1793). Nineteen States still have the constitutions with which they entered the Union and, all told, 35 have documents that are now more than 100 years old.

A number of States have had several constitutions. Louisiana holds the record, with eleven. Georgia's current charter, its tenth, is the most recently rewritten document; it was adopted in 1982 and became effective the following year.

> ✓ **Checkpoint**
> What are the two main problems of State constitutions today?

Essential Questions Journal To continue to build a response to the chapter Essential Question, go to your **Essential Questions Journal.**

SECTION 1 ASSESSMENT

1. **Guiding Question** Use your completed outline to answer this question: What are the defining features of State constitutions?

Key Terms and Comprehension

2. Explain the concept of **popular sovereignty** as it applies to State governments.

3. **(a)** List and explain three ways changes to State constitutions may be proposed. **(b)** How are proposed changes ratified?

Critical Thinking

4. **Predict Consequences** Would early State governments have developed differently if they had not grown out of the experiences of the American Revolution?

5. **Draw Inferences** Why do you think that many State constitutions remain so lengthy and unnecessarily detailed and have so many outdated provisions?

Quick Write

Explanatory Writing: Explore a Topic Based on your prior knowledge and what you have read in this section, write at least three questions that explore the ways in which State governments affect your life. (You may also want to preview Sections 2–5 for additional questions.) For example, you might ask: Which have the most direct effect on individual citizens, State laws or federal laws?

State
Legislatures

Guiding Question

What are the defining traits and purpose of State legislatures?
Use a table similar to the one below to record the main facts about State legislatures.

Purpose/ Structure	Powers	Organization
• Purpose is to make the law	•	•
• 49 are bicameral	•	•
•	•	•

Political Dictionary
• police power
• constituent power
• referendum

Objectives
1. Describe State legislatures.
2. Explain the election, terms, and compensation of legislators.
3. Examine the powers and organization of State legislatures.
4. Describe how voters may write and pass laws through direct legislation.

Image Above: Virginia's House of Delegates

In every State, the legislature, whatever it is called, is the lawmaking branch of State government. So, its basic function goes to the very heart of democratic government: It is charged with translating the public will into the public policy of the State.

The Legislature

Several features of their lawmaking bodies vary among the 50 States. This is notably true with regard to both name and size.

Name and Structure Just over half the States call their lawmaking body, officially, the "legislature." In 19 States it is known as the "General Assembly," in two States it is called the "Legislative Assembly," and in two others the "General Court."

All but one of the 50 State legislatures are bicameral, having two chambers. The upper house is known everywhere as "the Senate." The lower house is most commonly titled "the House of Representatives," but may also be "the Assembly," "the General Assembly," or "the House of Delegates." Nebraska, the only State with a one-house legislature, calls it "the Legislature."

As with Congress, bicameralism came to the States' legislative bodies out of the colonial experience. Unicameralism is regularly cited as one of the most significant steps that could be taken to improve State legislatures. Despite its apparent successes in Nebraska, efforts to accomplish it elsewhere have been notably unsuccessful. Those who defend bicameralism usually claim that one house can and does act as a check on the other, and so prevent the passage of unwise legislation. Whether that widely held view is justified or not, it has proved a major barrier to the spread of one-chamber lawmaking bodies.

Size There may be no ideal size for a legislative body, but two basic considerations are important. First, a legislature, and each of its houses, should not be so large as to hamper the orderly conduct of the people's business. Second, it should not be so small that the many views and interests within the State cannot be adequately represented.

The upper house in most States has from 30 to 50 members, with as few as 20 senators in Alaska and as many as 67 in Minnesota. The lower house usually ranges between 100 and 150 members. However, there are only 40 seats in Alaska's lower chamber, and New Hampshire's has a whopping 400!

State Legislators

Today, there are 7,382 State legislators—5,411 representatives and 1,971 senators—among the 50 States. Nearly all of them are Republicans or Democrats; fewer than 20 belong to a minor party or are independents.

As you read these pages, keep this point in mind: To really understand your own State's lawmaking body and how it operates, and its members and the ways in which they behave, you have to know a good deal about that institution and those people that you will not find in a textbook. As one widely respected authority on State government and politics tells us,

"[Y]ou need to know about all sorts of things . . . which party is in control and by how much . . . who the governor is, and how he gets along with the legislators . . . what sorts of people those legislators are: not just what they say but how long they have been there, where they come from, what they did before they ran for office and how they got elected. . . the communities that produced them, the families that raised them and the other families they were close to; where they went to school. . . .

—**Alan Ehrenhalt, "Clueless in Boise,"** *Governing* **magazine**

Qualifications Every State's constitution sets out formal requirements of age, citizenship, and residence for legislators. Most everywhere, a representative must be at least 21 years old and senators must be at least 25. The realities of the politics of the State add informal qualifications far more difficult to meet. They have to do with a candidate's vote-getting abilities, and are based on such things as occupation, name recognition, party, race, religion, national origin, and the like.

Election Everywhere, legislators are chosen by popular vote and, almost everywhere, candidates for the legislature are nominated at party primaries. Nominees are picked by conventions in only a few States. In Nebraska, the unicameral legislature is organized on a <u>nonpartisan</u> basis. Candidates are nominated at nonpartisan primaries, and they are not identified by party in the general election.

In most States, the lawmakers are elected in November of even-numbered years. In four States, however—Mississippi, New Jersey, Virginia, and Louisiana—they are chosen in the odd-numbered years, in the hope of separating State and local issues from those in national politics.

Districts Every State's constitution requires that legislators be chosen from districts within the State, and nearly all are now elected from single-member districts. Those districts are drawn by the legislature itself in most States, and they are redrawn (reapportioned) every ten years, in line with the federal census. Gerrymandering is quite common.

Most State legislatures were long dominated by the rural, less-populated areas of the State. In *Baker* v. *Carr*, 1962, however, the United States Supreme Court held the unfair, unequal distribution of State legislative seats to be a violation of the Equal Protection Clause of the 14th Amendment. That historic

✓ **Checkpoint**
What are the qualifications for State legislators?

<u>nonpartisan</u>
adj. not belonging to or favoring any political party

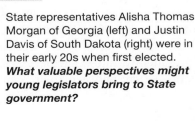

State representatives Alisha Thomas Morgan of Georgia (left) and Justin Davis of South Dakota (right) were in their early 20s when first elected. *What valuable perspectives might young legislators bring to State government?*

STUDENT DRIVER

MINIMUM WAGE

State law governs many areas of daily life, including, for example, the regulation of drivers' licenses and minimum wage rates above the federal level. *Why are these policies determined at the State level?*

✓ **Checkpoint**
How long do legislators serve?

turnover
n. rate at which people enter and leave a group

decision was soon followed by *Reynolds* v. *Sims* in 1964. There, the Court held that the Equal Protection Clause requires every State to draw its legislative districts on the basis of population equality.

Terms Legislators are elected to either two-year or four-year terms. Representatives serve two-year terms in 44 States and four-year terms in Alabama, Louisiana, Maryland, Mississippi, and North Dakota. Senators win four-year terms in 38 States (including Nebraska), and only two-year stints in the other 12.

Fifteen States now limit the number of terms any person can serve. In most, the limit is placed on service in each chamber, separately. In a few, the restriction is applied to total legislative service in either house.

The rate of <u>turnover</u> in legislative seats is fairly high, although it tends to vary from State to State and time to time. In a given year, some 20 percent of all lawmakers around the country are serving their first term in office. The major reasons for that turnover appear to be low pay, political instability, and term limits. Lawmakers tend to remain in office longer in those States that pay higher salaries and where one party regularly wins elections.

Compensation Far too often, capable men and women refuse to run for seats in the legislature because of the financial sacrifices that service usually entails. Legislative pay

varies considerably and so the situation is more trying in some States than others. California now pays lawmakers $116,208 per year, plus benefits. Oregon provides a more typical example of the compensation package. There, the total compensation per member comes to just about $30,000 per year.

Clearly, decent salaries in line with the responsibilities of the job will not automatically bring the most able men and women into State legislatures. Certainly, better salaries can make public service much more appealing to qualified people.

Sessions Little more than a generation ago, only a handful of State legislatures met in regular sessions each year, and then usually for only a few months or so. Most met only every other year. It has long since become apparent that the legislature's workload cannot be properly handled on so limited a basis.

Today, 44 State lawmaking bodies hold their regular sessions annually, and most of those sessions run for three to five months or more. Several legislatures are now in session nearly year-round.

In every State, the governor, and in three fourths of them the legislature itself, can call the body into special session. Those meetings, most common in States where legislators meet infrequently, allow lawmakers to take up urgent matters between their regularly scheduled sessions.

Powers of the Legislature

No State's constitution lists all of the powers vested in the legislature—nor could it. In each State, the legislature has all of those powers that (1) the State constitution does not grant exclusively to the executive or judicial branches or to local governments, and (2) neither the State constitution nor the United States Constitution denies to it. In effect, most of the powers held by a State are vested in its legislature.

Lawmaking Powers The fact that the legislature can enact any law that does not conflict with any provision in federal law or in the State constitution means that there can be no all-inclusive list of the legislature's powers. Its more important powers are usually set out in the State constitution, however. Those most often mentioned include the powers to tax, spend, borrow, establish courts and fix their jurisdiction, define crimes and provide for their punishment, regulate commercial activities, and maintain public schools.

Every State's legislature possesses the **police power**—the State's hugely important power to protect and promote the public health, public safety, public morals, and the general welfare. Recall, most of what government does in this country today is done by the States (and their local governments), and most of what they do is done through the exercise of the police power. In short, that extraordinarily broad authority is the power to safeguard the welfare of the people of the State, and it is the basis for much of what State legislatures do.

Nonlawmaking Powers All 50 State legislatures possess certain nonlegislative powers, in addition to those they exercise when they make a law.

In the separation of powers and checks and balances scheme, the legislature exercises some *executive* powers—for example, it has the power to approve or reject the governor's appointment of a number of officials. In some States, the legislature itself appoints various executive officers.

The legislature also has certain *judicial* powers, capped by the power of impeachment. In every State except Oregon, the legislature can remove any State officer in the executive

or judicial branch through that process. Each chamber also has the power to discipline and even expel one of its own members.

Recall that the legislature plays a significant role in both constitution-making and the constitutional amendment process. When, for example, it proposes an amendment to the State's constitution, it is not making law. It is, instead, exercising a nonlegislative power: the **constituent power.**

Organization and Lawmaking

Both the organization and the procedures of State legislatures are similar to those found in Congress. Much of what legislatures do centers around presiding officers and a committee system.

Presiding Officers Those who preside over the sessions of the States' lawmaking chambers are almost always powerful political figures, not only in the legislature itself but elsewhere in State politics.

The lower house in each of the 49 bicameral bodies elects its own presiding officer, known everywhere as the speaker. The senate chooses its own presiding officer in 27 States; in the other 23, including Nebraska, the lieutenant governor serves as president of the senate. Where the lieutenant governor does preside, the senate selects a president *pro tempore* to serve in the lieutenant governor's absence.

Except for the lieutenant governors, each of these presiding officers is chosen by a vote on the floor of his or her chamber. In fact, the majority party's caucus usually picks those who fill the leadership posts, just before the legislature begins a new term.

The chief duties of these presiding officers revolve around the conduct of the legislature's floor business. They refer bills to committee, recognize members who seek the floor, and interpret and apply the rules of their chamber to its proceedings.

Unlike the Speaker of the House in Congress, the speaker in nearly every State appoints the chair and other members of each house committee. The senate's president or president *pro tem* has that same power in just over half the States. The presiding officers

✔ **Checkpoint**
Why is the police power important?

safeguard
v. to protect or ensure

Initiative and Referendum

Voters in many States can write new laws or prevent laws from taking effect through the initiative and the referendum. *Why do you think many legislators oppose the initiative process?*

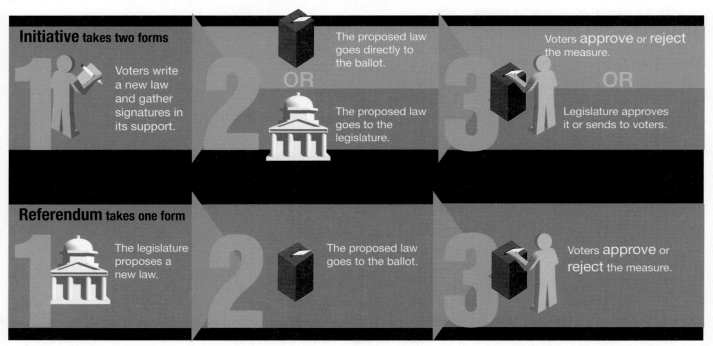

Initiative takes two forms

1 Voters write a new law and gather signatures in its support.

2 The proposed law goes directly to the ballot.

OR

The proposed law goes to the legislature.

3 Voters **approve** or **reject** the measure.

OR

Legislature approves it or sends to voters.

Referendum takes one form

1 The legislature proposes a new law.

2 The proposed law goes to the ballot.

3 Voters **approve** or **reject** the measure.

✔ **Checkpoint**
What do a legislature's presiding officers do?

sift
v. to sort or pick through carefully

regularly use this power much as they do their other powers: to reward their friends, punish their enemies, and otherwise work their influence on the legislature and its product.

Committees Several hundred or, in many larger States, several thousand measures are introduced at each session of the legislature. That flood of bills makes the committee system as practical and necessary at the State level as it is in Congress. Much of the work of the legislature is done in committee, where members sift through that pile of proposed legislation, deciding which bills will go on to floor consideration and which will fall by the wayside.

The standing committees of each house are regularly organized on a subject-matter basis—as committees on finance, education, highways, and so on. A bill referred to one of these committees may be amended or even largely rewritten there. Or, as frequently happens, it may be ignored altogether.

"Pigeonholing" occurs in the States as in Congress. In fact, in most States one of the standing committees in each house is usually the "graveyard committee." Bills are sent there to be buried. The judiciary committee, to which bills may be referred "on grounds of doubtful constitutionality," often fills this role.[6]

Sources of Bills Legally, only a member may introduce a bill in either house in any State's legislature. So, in the strictest sense, legislators themselves are the source of all measures the legislature considers. In broader terms, however, the lawmakers are the authors of only a handful of bills.

A large number of measures come from public sources, from officers and agencies in the State executive branch, and from local governments. Every State governor has a legislative program, often extensive and bold.

Many bills come from the private sector. Indeed, interest groups appear to be the

---

6 A striking illustration of a graveyard committee existed for several years in landlocked Oklahoma: the Committee on Deep Sea Navigation.

largest single source of proposed legislation. Remember, those groups and the lobbyists who represent them exist for one overriding purpose: to influence public policy to the benefit of their own particular interests. Of course, some measures do originate with private individuals—business owners, farmers, union members, and other citizens—who, for one reason or another, think, "There ought to be a law. . . ."

Direct Legislation

In several States, voters themselves can take a direct part in the lawmaking process. The main vehicles for that participation are the initiative and the referendum.

Initiative Through the initiative process, voters in 17 States can propose amendments to the State's constitution. In those States and seven others, they can also use that process to propose ordinary statutes. The initiative takes two quite different forms: the more common direct initiative and the little-used indirect initiative.

In both forms, a certain number of qualified voters (which varies from State to State) must sign petitions to <u>initiate</u> a law. Where the direct initiative is in place, a measure with sufficient signatures goes directly to the ballot, usually in the next general election. If voters approve the measure, it becomes law. If not, it dies. Where the indirect form is found,

a proposed measure goes first to the legislature for its consideration. If the lawmakers approve the measure, it becomes law. If the legislature fails to pass it, the measure then goes to the voters.

Referendum A **referendum** is a process in which the legislature refers a measure to the voters for final approval or rejection. The referendum takes three different forms: mandatory, optional, and popular.

A *mandatory referendum* occurs in those situations in which the legislature must send a measure to the voters. Recall, in every State except Delaware, a proposed constitutional amendment must be submitted to the electorate. In several States some other measures, such as those providing for the borrowing of funds, must also go to the voters.

An *optional referendum* involves a measure that the legislature has referred to the voters voluntarily. Such measures are rare. They usually involve "hot potato" issues: issues that lawmakers would prefer not to take direct responsibility for deciding themselves.

Under the *popular referendum*, a group of citizens may demand by petition that a measure passed by the legislature be referred to the voters for final action. Most attempts to use this form of the referendum fail. Most often, the opponents of a particular measure simply cannot gather the required number of signatures to force a popular vote on the target of their <u>ire</u>.

✔ **Checkpoint**
What is direct legislation?

initiate
v. to begin, launch, set in motion

ire
n. anger, outrage

Essential Questions Journal To continue to build a response to the chapter Essential Question, go to your **Essential Questions Journal.**

SECTION 2 ASSESSMENT

1. **Guiding Question** Use your completed table to answer this question: What are the defining traits and purpose of State legislatures?

Key Terms and Comprehension
2. What are the major purposes of the **police power**?
3. What three types of nonlegislative powers does a State legislature have?

Critical Thinking
4. **Demonstrate Reasoned Judgment** Do you think that State legislators should be paid a generous salary? Why or why not?
5. **Analyze Information** Would you support an amendment to your State's constitution to provide for a unicameral legislature? Why or why not?

Quick Write

Explanatory Writing: Organize Your Ideas Review your list of questions and loosely categorize them under various topics, such as "State Legislatures" or "Powers of the Executive." Select two or three categories that relate most closely to the concept of the effects of State governments on the lives of citizens. Use your textbook or other resources to take notes to answer each of the questions under your selected categories.

SECTION 3

The Governor and State Administration

Guiding Question

What are the roles and powers of a governor? Use a chart to identify the roles and responsibilities of a governor.

Roles and Responsibilities		
Executive	**Legislative**	**Judicial**
• Carry out laws	•	•
•	•	•
•	•	•

Political Dictionary

- recall
- item veto
- clemency
- pardon
- commutation
- reprieve
- parole

Objectives

1. Describe the main features of the office of governor.
2. Summarize a governor's roles, powers, duties, and the limitations of the office.
3. List and describe the other executive offices at the State level.

The governor is the principal executive officer in each of the 50 States. He or she is always a central figure in State politics and is often a well-known national personality as well. Governors today occupy an office that is the direct descendant of the earliest public office in American politics, the colonial governorship, first established in Virginia in 1607.

The Governorship

In colonial America, the actions of the royal governors inspired much of the resentment that fueled the Revolution. That attitude was carried over into the first State constitutions. Most of the powers of government were given to the legislatures; the new State governors, for the most part, had little real authority. In every State except Massachusetts and New York, the governor was chosen by the legislature, and in most of them only for a one-year term. And only in three States did the governor have a veto power.

That original separation of powers soon proved unsatisfactory. Many of the State legislatures abused their powers. Several fell prey to special interests, and the governors were unable to respond. So, as new constitutions were written, and the older ones revised, the powers of the legislatures were curbed and the powers of the governors generally increased.

Beginning with Illinois in 1917, most States have redesigned and strengthened the executive branch to make the governor the State's chief executive in more than name. Some States have gone further than others in this direction, but, overall, governors are much more powerful figures today than in decades past.

Qualifications Anyone who wants to become the governor of a State must be able to satisfy a set of formal qualifications. Typically, he or she must be an American citizen, of at least a certain age (usually 25 or 30), have lived in the State for a given period of time (most often for at least five years), and be a qualified voter.

Clearly, these formal qualifications for office are not very difficult to meet. It is the informal qualifications that have real meaning. To become a governor, a person must have those characteristics that will first attract a party's nomination, and then attract the voters in the general election. Those characteristics vary from State to State, and even from election to election within a State. Race, sex, religion, name recognition, personality, party identification, experience, ideology, the ability to use television effectively—these and several other factors are all part of the mix.

Today, most governors are attorneys in their 40s and 50s. Nearly all of them were State legislators or held another elective office in the State, such as lieutenant governor, attorney general, or mayor of a large city. California's "governator," Arnold Schwarzenegger, is a leading illustration of the fact that someone who has never held public office does sometimes win a governorship.

The first gubernatorial elections occurred in 1775 and more than 2,500 persons have now served as governors of the various States. To this point (2010), only 31 of those governors have been women.

Two women won governorships in 1924: Nellie Taylor Ross in Wyoming and Miriam "Ma" Ferguson in Texas. They were the first of several women to succeed their husbands as governors. Over the past 30 years or so, a growing number of women have won the office on their own. Six women currently hold office: Jan Brewer (R., Arizona), M. Jodi Rell (R., Connecticut), Linda Lingle (R., Hawaii), Jennifer Granholm (D., Michigan), Beverly Perdue (D., North Carolina), and Christine Gregoire (D., Washington).

Only three African Americans have ever held the office: Douglas Wilder (D., Virginia), elected in 1989; Deval Patrick (D., Massachusetts), chosen in 2006; and David Patterson (D., New York), who succeeded to the post in 2008. Governor Bobby Jindal (R., Louisiana; 2007) is a native of India.

Selection

The governor is chosen by popular vote in every State. In all but five, only a plurality is needed for election. If no candidate wins a clear majority in Arizona, Georgia, or Louisiana, the two top vote-getters meet in a runoff election. If no one wins a majority in Mississippi, the lower house of the legislature picks the new governor. In Vermont, both houses make the choice.

The major parties' gubernatorial candidates are usually picked in primaries. In a few States, however, conventions choose the nominees. Nearly half the States now provide for the joint election of the governor and the lieutenant governor. In those States, each party's candidates for those offices run as a team, and the voter casts one vote to fill both posts.

Term

The one-year gubernatorial term has long since disappeared. Governors are now chosen to four-year terms nearly everywhere. Thirty-six States limit the number of terms a chief executive may serve, most often to two terms. Those governors who seek reelection usually do so successfully.[7]

Succession

Governors are mortal. Occasionally, one of them dies in office. Many of them are also politically ambitious. Every so often, one resigns in midterm—to become a United States senator or accept an appointment to the President's Cabinet, for example.

When a vacancy does occur, it sets off a game of political musical chairs in the State. The political plans and timetables of ambition of a number of public personalities are affected by the event. No matter what causes a vacancy, every State's constitution provides for a successor. In 44 States the lieutenant governor is first in line. In Maine, New Hampshire, and West Virginia, the president of the senate succeeds. In Arizona, Oregon, and Wyoming, the office passes to the secretary of state.

Removal

The governor may be removed from office by impeachment in every State except Oregon. Only six governors have been impeached and removed since the turbulent Reconstruction years after the Civil War. The most recent to suffer that fate: Rod Blagojevich (D., Illinois) in 2009.

In 18 States, the governor may be recalled by the voters.[8] The **recall** is a petition procedure by which voters may remove an elected official from office before the completion of

✔ **Checkpoint**
What are common characteristics of governors?

gubernatorial
adj. of or relating to a governor

turbulent
adj. disorderly, stormy

plurality
n. the largest total, not necessarily a majority

---

7   The all-time record for both gubernatorial service and electoral success belongs to George Clinton of New York. He sought and won seven three-year terms as governor and held the office from 1777 to 1795 and again from 1801 to 1804. He was later Vice President of the United States, from 1805 to 1812.

8   Alaska, Arizona, California, Colorado, Georgia, Idaho, Kansas, Louisiana, Michigan, Minnesota, Montana, Nevada, New Jersey, North Dakota, Oregon, Rhode Island, Washington, Wisconsin.

▶▶ **Analyzing Political Cartoons** In 2003, California voters had to choose whether to recall the governor and, if so, which of 135 candidates should replace him. *Why did the cartoonist include a clown among the candidates?*

intangible
n. something not concrete or easily defined

his or her regular term. The process generally works this way: If a certain number of qualified voters—usually 25 percent of the number who voted in the last election held for the office—sign recall petitions, a special election must be held in which the voters decide whether to remove or instead, retain, the officeholder.

To this point, only two governors have ever been recalled: Governor Lynn J. Frazier of North Dakota, a Republican, in 1921, and Governor Gray Davis of California, a Democrat, in 2003.

Compensation In many respects, a governor's job is not unlike that of the chief executive officer of one of the nation's larger corporations. Both administer hugely complex organizations, manage the work of thousands of employees, and oversee the spending of incredible amounts of money. Governors are not paid nearly so well as the CEOs of large companies, however. The latter make tens of millions of dollars per year in salary and benefits.

fragmented
adj. split, separated into many pieces

In contrast, most governors earn little more than $100,000 per year. Salaries now range from $70,000 per year in Maine and $85,000 in Tennessee to $206,500 in California. Most States provide their chief executive with an official residence, often called a governor's mansion, and money for travel and other expenses.

To the governor's salary and other material compensations must be added the intangibles of honor and prestige that go with the office. It is this factor, and a sense of public duty, that often persuades many of our better citizens to seek the post. Several Presidents were governors before reaching the White House—most recently, Bill Clinton and George W. Bush.

A Governor's Many Roles

Much like the President, a governor plays a number of different roles. He or she is, simultaneously, an executive, an administrator, a legislator, a party leader, an opinion leader, and a ceremonial figure. What the office amounts to depends, in no small part, on how well the governor plays each—and all—of these roles. And that must depend, in turn, on his or her personality, political muscle, and overall abilities.

Many of a governor's formal powers are hedged with constitutional and other legal restrictions. Nonetheless, the powers a governor does have, together with the prestige of the office, make it quite possible for a capable, dynamic person to be a "strong" governor, one who can accomplish much for the State and for the public good.

Executive Powers

The presidency and the governorships are similar in several ways, but the comparison can be pushed too far. Remember, the Constitution of the United States makes the President *the* executive in the National Government. State constitutions, on the other hand, regularly describe the governor as the *chief* executive in the State's government. The distinction here, between *the* executive and the *chief* executive, is a critical one. The executive authority is fragmented in most States, but it is not at the national level.

In nearly every State, the executive authority is shared by a number of "executive officers"—a secretary of state, an attorney general, a treasurer, and so on. Most of these executive officers are, like the governor, popularly elected, and for that reason, very largely beyond the governor's direct control.

In short, most State constitutions so divide the executive authority that the governor can best be described as a "first among equals." Yet, whatever the realities of the distribution of power, the people look to the governor for leadership in State affairs. It is also the governor whom they hold responsible for the conduct of those affairs and for the overall condition of the State.

The governor's basic legal responsibility is regularly found in a constitutional provision that directs the chief executive to "take care that the laws be faithfully executed." Though the executive power may be divided, the governor is given a number of specific powers with which to accomplish that task.

Appointment and Removal The governor can best execute the law with subordinates of his or her own choosing. Hence, the powers of appointment and removal are, or should be, among the most important.

A leading test of any administrator is his or her ability to select loyal and able assistants. Two major factors work against the governor's effectiveness here, however. First is the existence of those other elected executives; the people choose them and the governor cannot remove them. Second, the State's constitution and statutes place restrictions on the governor's power to hire and fire. Most State constitutions require that the majority of the governor's major appointees be confirmed by the State senate.

Moreover, the legislature often sets qualifications that must be met by the governor's appointees. In a vigorous two-party State, for example, the law often requires that not more than a certain number of the members of each board or commission be from the same political party. Thus, a governor must appoint some members of the opposing party to posts.

Administering the Executive Branch The governor is the State's chief administrator. Alone and unaided, he or she could not possibly "take care that the laws be faithfully executed." The day-to-day work of enforcing the State's laws, of performing its many functions, and of delivering its many services is done by the thousands of men and women in all of the agencies that make up the executive branch. The governor must supervise that work.

Here again, the constitution and statutes of the State often limit a governor's authority. Many agencies are subject to his or her direct control, but many are not. That situation puts a <u>premium</u> on the governor's powers of persuasion and on his or her ability to operate through such informal channels as party leadership and appeals to the public.

The Budget Always remember: A government's budget is much more than a mere bookkeeping exercise. It is a political document, a statement of public policy. Its numbers, its dollar figures, reflect the struggle over "who gets what" and who doesn't.

In most States the governor prepares the budget that goes to the legislature. The lawmakers can and do make changes in the governor's financial plan. Still, the governor's recommendations carry a great deal of weight.

✔ **Checkpoint**
What are a governor's executive powers?

<u>premium</u>
n. high value

Party Control of Governorships, 2010

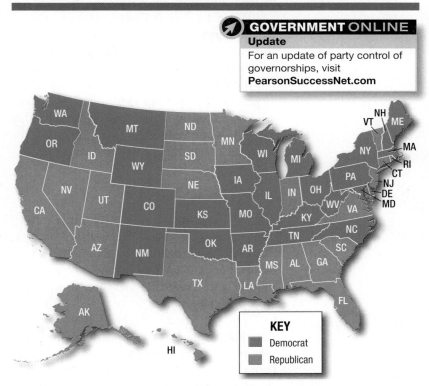

⊘ **GOVERNMENT**ONLINE
Update
For an update of party control of governorships, visit
PearsonSuccessNet.com

KEY
■ Democrat
■ Republican

▸▸ **Analyzing Maps** The two major parties compete in gubernatorial elections in every State. *Which party holds a majority of the State governorships today?*

The governor's budget-making power can be a highly effective tool with which to control State administration. Although unable to appoint or remove the head of a particular agency, for example, the governor can use the budget-making power to affect that agency's programs and have a real impact on those who work in that agency.

Military Powers Every State's constitution makes the governor the commander in chief of the State militia—in effect, of the State's units of the National Guard. The National Guard is the organized part of the State militia. In a national emergency, the National Guard may be "called up," ordered into federal service by the President.

All of the States' National Guard units were federalized in 1940 and served as part of the nation's armed forces in World War II. Many units also saw combat duty in Korea, Vietnam, and the Persian Gulf War. Today, National Guard units are on duty in such far-flung places as Bosnia, Kosovo, Afghanistan, and Iraq. Indeed, the Defense Department has relied very heavily on the Guard in the prosecution of recent wars.

When the State's Guard units are not in federal service (which is most of the time), they are commanded by the governor. On occasion, governors find it necessary to call out the Guard to deal with such emergencies as prison riots, to help fight a dangerous forest fire, to aid in relief and evacuation after a flood, to prevent looting during and after some other natural disaster, and so on.

Legislative Powers

The State's principal executive officer exercises three significant legislative powers. Those powers, together with the chief executive's personality, popularity, and political muscle, can make the governor, in fact, the State's chief legislator.

The Message Power Essentially, the message power is the power to recommend legislation. Remember, much of what lawmakers do is prompted by what the governor has urged them to do. The most effective governors push their wish lists by combining their use of the formal message power with such informal tactics as close contacts with key legislators and appeals to the public.

Special Sessions The governor in every State has the power to call the legislature into special session. As you know, that power is meant to permit the State to meet extraordinary situations. It can also be an important part of the governor's legislative arsenal. On many occasions, governors have persuaded reluctant lawmakers to pass a particular bill by threatening to call them back in a special session if they adjourn their regular meeting without having approved that measure.

The Veto Power Every governor can veto measures enacted by the legislature. The veto power—including the timely use of threats to invoke the power—can be very useful to the governor as he or she tries to influence what the legislature does or doesn't do.

In most States, the governor has only a very few days in which to sign or veto a bill—most often, five. If no action is taken within the prescribed period, the measure becomes law without his or her signature.

Only 11 States give the governor a pocket veto.[9] So, in most States, those bills a governor neither signs nor vetoes become law. Forty-four States give the governor the **item veto**—the power to eliminate one or more items from a bill without rejecting the entire measure. It is used most often on spending measures.

As in the Federal Government, the legislature may attempt to override a veto. In most States, a veto requires a two-thirds majority in both houses.

Judicial Powers

In every State the chief executive has some authority of a judicial nature. Principally, the governor has various powers of executive **clemency:** powers of mercy that may be shown to persons convicted of crime.

With the power of **pardon**, the governor may relieve someone of the legal consequences of a crime. In most States, a pardon

---

9 Alabama, Delaware, Iowa, Kansas, Massachusetts, New Mexico, New York, Ohio, Oklahoma, Vermont, Virginia

reluctant
adj. hesitant, unwilling

Choosing Executive Officers

Many jobs that are filled by presidential appointment in the Federal Government are decided by elections at the State level. *How does the direct election of executive officers empower voters in State government?*

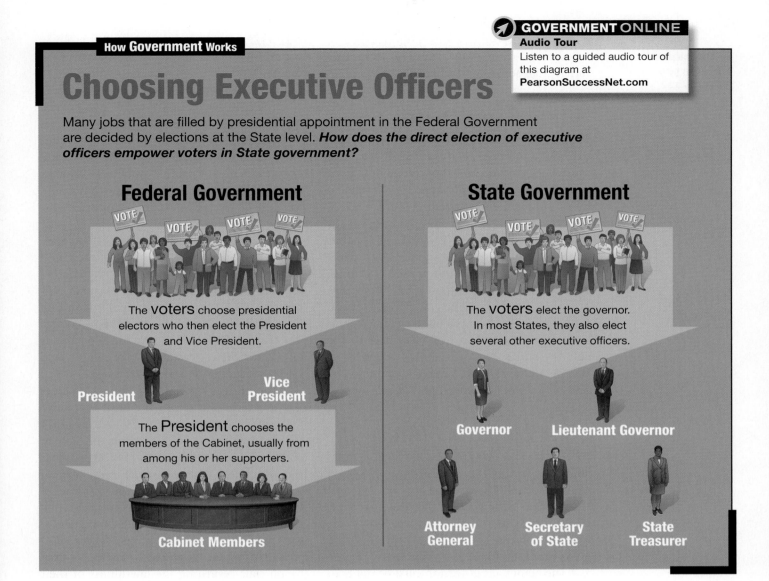

Federal Government

The **voters** choose presidential electors who then elect the President and Vice President.

President

Vice President

The **President** chooses the members of the Cabinet, usually from among his or her supporters.

Cabinet Members

State Government

The **voters** elect the governor. In most States, they also elect several other executive officers.

Governor   **Lieutenant Governor**

Attorney General   **Secretary of State**   **State Treasurer**

---

may be full or conditional, and usually it can be granted only after conviction. The power of **commutation** may be used to <u>commute</u> a sentence imposed by a court. Thus, a death sentence might be commuted to life in prison, or a sentence might be commuted to "time served," which leads to the release of a prisoner from custody.

The power to **reprieve** can be used to postpone the execution of a sentence. Reprieves are normally granted for very brief periods—for example, to allow time for an appeal or because of the late discovery of new evidence in a case. The power of **parole** permits the release of a prisoner short of the completion of a sentence.

The governor may have some or all of these powers of executive clemency. They

are often shared, however. For example, the governor may share the power to pardon with an appointed board of pardons.

Governors have not often abused their clemency powers, but in her first term (1925–1927), Governor Miriam "Ma" Ferguson of Texas pardoned 3,737 convicted felons, an average of more than five per day.[10] The pardons came so thick and fast that several Texas

commute
v. to reduce, make less severe

---

10 Governor James "Pa" Ferguson was impeached and removed by the Texas legislature in 1917. He was later pardoned by the legislature and soon announced that he would run for the governorship again. The State Supreme Court ruled the legislative pardon unconstitutional, however. All of that prompted "Ma" Ferguson to run for governor in 1924. She vented her anger over the treatment of her husband in other ways, too—for example, by refusing any and all extradition requests from other States. Mrs. Ferguson was defeated for reelection in 1926, but did win another two-year term in 1932.

newspapers ran daily "pardon columns" rather than separate news stories.

Miscellaneous Duties

In addition to the exercise of executive, legislative, and judicial powers, every chief executive must perform several other, often time-consuming duties. These duties are only hinted at by a listing of the powers of the office.

Among many other things, the governor receives official visitors and welcomes other distinguished personalities to the State, dedicates parks and public and private buildings, opens the State fair, and addresses countless organizations and public gatherings. Beyond those chores, he or she is often called upon to settle labor disputes, travel elsewhere in the country and sometimes abroad to promote the State and its trade interests, endorse any number of worthy causes, and on and on.

Other Executive Officers

In nearly every State, the governor must share control of the administration with a number of other executive officers. Most of those other officials are, like the governor, chosen by voters. The following four positions are found in most, but not all, State governments today.

The lieutenant governor must be ready to succeed to the governorship should a vacancy occur, and, in half the States, presides over the senate. The office can be a stepping-stone to the governorship by succession or by future elections. It remains, in many places, not much more than a part-time job.

The secretary of state serves as the State's chief clerk and records-keeper. He or she has charge of a great variety of public documents, records the official acts of the governor and the legislature, and usually administers the election laws.

The treasurer is the custodian of State funds, often the State's chief tax collector, and regularly the State's paymaster. Other names for this position include chief financial officer, director of finance, the commissioner of finance, and the comptroller of public accounts. The treasurer's major job is to make payments out of the State treasury to pay salaries and bills associated with State government.

The attorney general is the State's chief lawyer. He or she acts as the legal advisor to State officers and agencies as they perform their official functions, represents the State in court, and oversees the work of local prosecutors as they try cases on behalf of the State.

Much of the power of the office centers on the attorney general's formal written interpretations of constitutional and statutory law. These interpretations, called opinions, are issued to answer questions raised by officials regarding the lawfulness of their actions or proposed actions.

Essential Questions Journal To continue to build a response to the chapter Essential Question, go to your **Essential Questions Journal.**

SECTION 3 ASSESSMENT

1. **Guiding Question** Use your completed chart to answer this question: What are the roles and powers of a governor?

Key Terms and Comprehension

2. What executive powers do most governors have?

3. Briefly explain each of a governor's judicial powers: **clemency, pardon, commutation, reprieve,** and **parole.**

Critical Thinking

4. **Summarize** How has the position and power of the governor relative to the legislature evolved since the first State constitutions were written?

5. **Identify Central Issues** Should the governor of your State be able to appoint the other executive officers now chosen by voters? Why or why not?

Quick Write

Explanatory Writing: Research for Examples and Details When writing an explanatory essay, you should include examples illustrating the concepts or processes you discuss. Use your textbook, the library, or reliable Internet sources to add details and examples to the notes you have made about each of your categories. As you read each section of this chapter and learn new information, you may also want to add or replace questions.

In the Courtroom

Guiding Question

How do State and local courts apply different types of law? Use a flowchart similar to the one below to explain the significance of elements of the legal system.

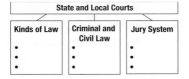

State and Local Courts		
Kinds of Law	**Criminal and Civil Law**	**Jury System**
•	•	•
•	•	•
•	•	•

Political Dictionary

- common law
- precedent
- criminal law
- felony
- misdemeanor
- civil law
- tort
- contract
- jury
- information
- bench trial

Objectives

1. Identify and define the kinds of law applied in State courts.
2. Compare and contrast criminal law and civil law.
3. Describe the types and purposes of juries and juror selection.

Image Above: Jury trial

The principal function of the State courts is to decide disputes between private parties and between private parties and government. In addition, because nearly all of these courts have the power of judicial review, they act as checks on the conduct of all other agencies of both State and local government.

Kinds of Law Applied in State Courts

The law is the code of conduct by which society is governed.[11] It is made up of several different forms, including constitutional law, statutory law, administrative law, common law, and equity.

The highest form of law in this country is *constitutional law*. It is based on the United States Constitution and the State constitutions and on judicial interpretations of those documents. *Statutory law* consists of the statutes (laws) enacted by legislative bodies, including the United States Congress, the State legislature, the people, and local governments. *Administrative law* is composed of the rules, orders, and regulations issued by federal, State, or local executive officers, acting under proper constitutional and/or statutory authority.

Common Law The common law makes up a large part of the law of each State except Louisiana.[12] **Common law** is unwritten, judge-made law that has developed over centuries from those generally accepted ideas of right and wrong that have gained judicial recognition. It covers nearly all aspects of human conduct. State courts apply common law except when it is in conflict with written law.

The common law originated in England. It grew out of the decisions made by the king's judges on the basis of local customs. It developed as judges, coming upon situations similar to those found in earlier cases, applied and reapplied the rulings from those earlier cases. Thus, little by little, the law of those cases

---

11 In its overall sense, the term *law* may be defined as the whole body of "rules and principles of conduct which the governing power in a community recognizes as those which it will enforce or sanction, and according to which it will regulate, limit, or protect the conduct of its members"; *Bouvier's Law Dictionary*, 3rd revision, Vol. II.

12 Because of an early French influence, Louisiana's legal system is largely based on French legal concepts, derived from Roman law. Nevertheless, the common law has worked its way into Louisiana law.

✔ **Checkpoint**
What forms of law
are practiced in State
courts?

compelling
adj. very good;
powerful

became *common* throughout England and, in time, throughout the English-speaking world.

American courts generally follow that same rule. A decision, once made, becomes a **precedent,** a guide to be followed in all later, similar cases, unless compelling reasons call for either an exception or its abandonment and the setting of a new precedent.

The common law is extremely important. Statutory law does override common law, but many statutes are based on the common law. A great many statutes are, in effect, common law translated into written law.

Equity This branch of the law supplements common law. It developed in England to provide equity—"fairness, justice, and right"—when remedies under the common law fell short of that goal.

The common law is mostly remedial, while equity is preventative. Thus, the common law applies to or provides a remedy for matters after they have happened; equity seeks to stop wrongs before they occur.

Suppose your neighbors plan to add a room to their house. You think that a part of the planned addition will be on your land and will destroy your rose garden. You can prevent the construction by getting an injunction, a court order prohibiting a specified action by the party named in the order.

A court is likely to grant the injunction for two reasons: (1) the immediacy of the threat to your property, and (2) the fact that the law can offer no fully satisfactory remedy once your garden has been destroyed. No money award can give back the pride or the pleasure your roses now give you.

At first, different courts administered equity and common law. In time, most States provided for the administration of both forms by the same courts, and the procedural differences between the two are disappearing.

Criminal and Civil Law

The law as it is applied by courts in this country can also be described as either criminal or civil law. **Criminal law** is that branch of the law that regulates human conduct. It identifies and defines those actions that are crimes and provides for their punishment. A crime is a public wrong considered so damaging to society at large that it has been prohibited by law. The government (State or federal) is always a party to a criminal case, as prosecutor.

Crimes are of two kinds. A **felony** is the greater offense, punishable by a heavy fine, imprisonment, or even death—for example, murder, robbery, assault, or kidnapping. A **misdemeanor** is a lesser wrong and may be punished by a lighter fine and/or a shorter jail term—for example, a traffic violation, underage drinking, or disorderly conduct.

Civil law relates to that human conduct that is not criminal in nature, to those disputes between private persons and between private persons and government that are not covered by criminal law. Civil law involves a wide range of issues, including divorce and custody disputes, torts, and contracts.

Both tort law and contract law are major and often-used branches of civil law. A **tort** is a wrongful act that involves injury to one's person, property, or reputation in a situation not covered by the terms of a contract—for example, an automobile accident, product liability, or libel. A **contract** is a legally binding agreement in which one party agrees to do something with or for another party—for example, an agreement covering the sale of property or the terms of employment.

The Jury System

A **jury** is a body of persons selected according to law to hear evidence and decide questions of fact in a court case. There are two basic types of juries in the American legal system: (1) the grand jury and (2) the petit jury.

The major function of the grand jury is to determine whether the evidence against a person charged with a crime is sufficient to justify a trial. The grand jury is used only in criminal proceedings. The petit jury is the trial jury, and it is used in both civil and criminal matters.

The Grand Jury The grand jury has from 6 to 23 persons, depending on the State. Where larger juries are used, generally at least 12 jurors must agree that an accused person is probably guilty before a formal accusation is made. Similarly, with smaller juries, an extraordinary majority is needed to indict, which means to bring the formal charge.

When a grand jury is <u>impaneled</u>, the judge instructs the jurors to find a true bill of indictment against any and all persons whom the prosecuting attorney brings to their attention and whom they think are probably guilty. The judge also instructs them to bring a presentment, an accusation, against any persons whom they, of their own knowledge, believe have violated the State's criminal laws.

The grand jury meets in secret. The prosecuting attorney presents witnesses and evidence against persons suspected of crime. The jurors may question those witnesses and may also <u>summon</u> others to testify against a suspect. After receiving the evidence and hearing witnesses, the grand jury deliberates alone and in secret. They then move to the courtroom where their report, including any indictments they may have returned, is read in their presence.

The grand jury is expensive and time-consuming. Therefore, most of the States today depend more heavily on a much simpler process of accusation: the information.

The Information An **information** is a formal charge filed by the prosecutor, without the action of a grand jury. It is used for most minor offenses and, in many States, for some serious cases. It is far less costly and time-consuming than a grand jury. Also, since grand juries most often follow the prosecutor's

✔ **Checkpoint**
What does a jury do?

<u>impaneled</u>
v. enrolled; established

<u>summon</u>
v. call

⊘ **GOVERNMENT** ONLINE
For an **interactive** exploration of criminal and civil law, visit **PearsonSuccessNet.com**
INTERACTIVE

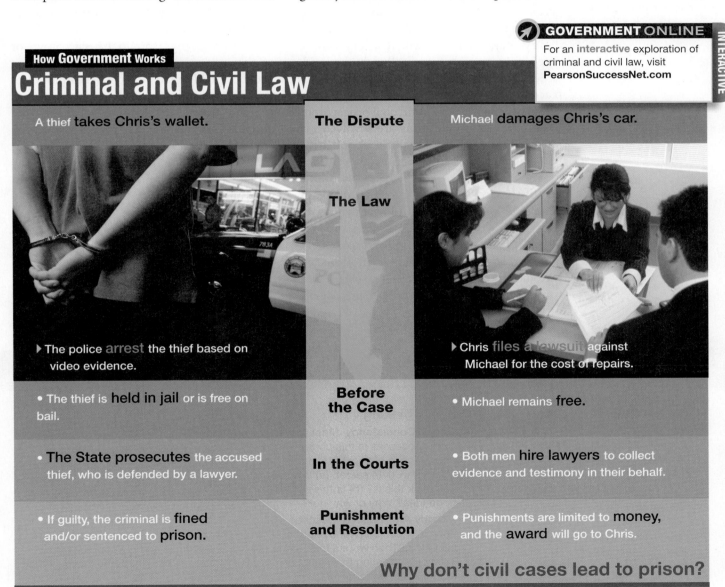

How Government Works

Criminal and Civil Law

A thief **takes** Chris's wallet.

The Dispute

The Law

▶ The police arrest the thief based on video evidence.

Before the Case

• The thief is **held in jail** or is free on bail.

In the Courts

• The State prosecutes the accused thief, who is defended by a lawyer.

Punishment and Resolution

• If guilty, the criminal is **fined** and/or sentenced to **prison.**

Michael **damages** Chris's car.

▶ Chris files a lawsuit against Michael for the cost of repairs.

• Michael remains **free.**

• Both men **hire lawyers** to collect evidence and testimony in their behalf.

• Punishments are limited to **money,** and the **award** will go to Chris.

Why don't civil cases lead to prison?

recommendations, many argue that a grand jury is really unnecessary. Others feel that the grand jury prevents prosecutors from abusing their powers.

The Petit Jury The petit jury, or trial jury, hears the evidence in a case and decides the disputed facts. In very few instances, it may also have the power to interpret and apply the law. That, however, is usually the function of the judge.

The number of trial jurors may vary. As it developed in England, the jury consisted of "12 men good and true." Although 12 is the usual total, a lesser number, often six, now fills jury boxes in several States.

In more than a third of the States, jury verdicts need not be unanimous in civil and minor criminal cases. Rather, some extraordinary majority is needed. If a jury cannot agree on a verdict (a so-called hung jury), either another trial with a new jury takes place or the matter is dropped.

Misdemeanor cases and civil proceedings in which only minor sums are involved are often heard without a jury, in a **bench trial,** by the judge alone. In several States, even the most serious crimes may be heard without a jury if the accused, fully informed of his or her rights, waives the right to trial by jury.

Selection of Jurors Jurors are picked in more or less the same way in most States. Periodically, a county official or special jury commissioners prepare a list of persons eligible for jury service, with names drawn from poll books, tax rolls, driver's license records, or other sources.[13] The sheriff serves each person with a court order to appear. After eliminating those who, for good reason, cannot serve, the judge prepares a list of those who can. Persons under 18 and over 70 years of age, illiterates, the ill, and criminals are commonly excluded. Those in occupations vital to the public interest or for whom jury service would mean real hardship are often excused, too.

As with the grand jury, the States are moving away from the use of the trial jury. Leading reasons are the greater time and cost of jury trials. The competence of the average jury and the impulses that may lead it to a <u>verdict</u> are often questioned, as well. Much criticism of the jury system is directed not so much at the system itself as at its operation.

Several things should be said in favor of the jury system, however. It has a long and honorable place in the development of Anglo-American law. Its high purpose is to promote a fair trial, by providing an impartial body to hear the charges brought against the accused. A jury tends to bring the common sense of the community to bear on the law and its application. Finally, the jury system gives citizens a chance to take part in the administration of justice, and it fosters a greater confidence in the judicial system.

---

verdict
n. decision or judgment

13 It may be the clerk of the court, the sheriff, the county governing body, or the presiding judge; in New England, it is officers of the town.

**Essential Questions
Journal**

To continue to build a response to the chapter Essential Question, go to your **Essential Questions Journal.**

SECTION 4 ASSESSMENT

1. **Guiding Question** Use your completed table to answer this question: How do State and local courts apply different types of laws?

Key Terms and Comprehension

2. Define **common law, criminal law,** and **civil law.**

3. Identify two types of **juries** and explain what they do.

Critical Thinking

4. **Check Consistency** Most government processes in this country must take place in public, but a grand jury does its work in secret. **(a)** Why do you think this is? **(b)** Is this secrecy a good idea? Why or why not?

5. **Identify Alternatives** Describe a situation in which someone might seek an injunction. Then write a brief argument in favor of granting the injunction and a brief argument against it.

Quick Write

Explanatory Writing: Write a Thesis Statement As in other types of essays or reports, you need to formulate a thesis statement to direct your thinking, research, and writing. Review your notes to find one main concept that connects your categories and questions. Write a thesis statement that expresses that concept.

Serving on a Jury

Someday, you may have the chance to participate directly in the American justice system. The right to be tried by a jury of one's peers is one of the fundamental rights afforded to citizens of a democracy, and is guaranteed by the Constitution. As a juror, you will become a major participant in the American judicial system with a duty to ensure that a fellow citizen receives justice.

How can you be selected as a potential juror? Most are chosen from voting lists, from State departments of motor vehicles, or tax rolls. How long your jury service may last can vary depending on the nature and complexity of the case involved or whether or not you are actually chosen to serve on a jury panel. Some people are excused from duty due to health issues or other hardships.

You may also be dismissed without having served at all. If you are chosen to move on to the jury selection phase, known as *voir dire*, lawyers on both sides will have questions for the potential jurors as they try to select a jury that they hope will be favorable to their case. You may be rejected.

If chosen, you and the other jurors will receive instructions prior to the beginning of the trial. These may include:

1. **Do not be influenced by bias.** Your decision in a case should not be affected by sympathies or antipathies you may have for the defendant, plaintiff, or their attorneys.

2. **Follow the law exactly as it is explained to you.** Your job as a juror is to determine whether or not someone broke the law, regardless of whether you approve of the law or not.

3. **Remember that the defendant is presumed innocent.** The government has the burden of proving a defendant guilty "beyond a reasonable doubt." If it fails to do so, the jury verdict must be "not guilty." If you feel that the government did make its case, then you must find the defendant "guilty."

4. **Keep an open mind.** Do not form or state any opinions about the case until you have heard all the evidence, the closing arguments of the lawyers, and the judge's instructions on the applicable law.

5. **During the trial, do not discuss the case.** Do not permit anyone to talk about the case with you or in your presence, except with the court's permission. Avoid media coverage of the case once the trial has begun.

▶▶ What do you think?

1. What does the concept "reasonable doubt" mean to you?

2. Why do you think jurors are instructed not to discuss a case and to avoid media coverage of it during the trial?

3. **You Try It** Create a jury simulation. Work in groups of six students to prepare a list of evidence related to a theoretical crime. After each team has completed its list, exchange lists. Following the instructions above, each team will then act as a jury to reach a verdict in another team's case. Ask each jury to discuss its verdict with the team that created the evidence.

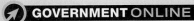

⊘ GOVERNMENT ONLINE
Citizenship Activity Pack

For activities on serving on a jury, go to
PearsonSuccessNet.com

SECTION 5

State **Courts** and Their **Judges**

Guiding Question

How are State and local courts organized and staffed? Use a table similar to the one below to record information about the types of State and local courts.

Municipal Courts	Juvenile Courts	Justice and Magistrates' Courts
•	•	•
•	•	•
•	•	•

Political Dictionary

- justice of the peace
- warrant
- preliminary hearing
- magistrate
- appellate jurisdiction

Objectives

1. Explain how State courts are organized and describe the work that each type of court does.
2. Examine and evaluate the different methods by which judges are selected among the States.

Image Above: Leah Sears, Chief Justice of the Georgia Supreme Court and first African American woman to hold that position, 2005–2009

They deal with everything from traffic tickets to murder, from disputes over nickels and dimes to settlements involving millions. They are the State and local courts and the judges who sit in them. Here, you will look at the way these courts are organized and how they conduct their business.

Organization

Each of the State constitutions creates a court system for that State. Some of the documents deal with the courts at great length, but most of them leave much of the detail of judicial organization and procedure to the legislature.

Justices of the Peace Justices of the peace—JPs—stand on the lowest rung of the State judicial ladder. They preside over what are commonly called justice courts.

JPs were once found nearly everywhere in the country. In their day, they seemed well-suited to their purpose. In justice courts, people could obtain a hearing for minor offenses quickly. JPs and their justice courts have been done away with in several States. However, they can still be found in many smaller towns and rural areas.

JPs are usually popularly elected. For the most part, they try misdemeanors—that is, cases involving such petty offenses as traffic violations, disturbing the peace, public drunkenness, and the like. JPs can almost never settle civil disputes involving more than a few hundred dollars. They do issue certain kinds of warrants, hold preliminary hearings, and often perform marriages.

A **warrant** is a court order authorizing, or making legal, some official action. Search warrants and arrest warrants are the most common of these documents. A **preliminary hearing** is generally the first step in a major criminal prosecution. There, the judge decides if the evidence is, in fact, enough to hold that person—bind that person over—for action by the grand jury or the prosecutor.

In some places, JPs are still paid out of the fines they take in. The more fines they impose, the higher their incomes. This "fee system" can lead to any number of abuses and raises serious questions about the fairness of the treatment a defendant can expect.[14]

Magistrates' Courts **Magistrates** are the city cousins of JPs. For the most part, magistrates handle those minor civil complaints and misdemeanor cases that arise in an urban setting. They preside over what often are called magistrates' courts or police courts. Magistrates, like JPs, are usually popularly elected for fairly short terms.

Municipal Courts Municipal courts were first established in Chicago in 1906. They are now found in most large cities and many smaller ones.

The jurisdiction of municipal courts is citywide. They can often hear civil cases involving several thousands of dollars as well as the usual run of misdemeanors. Many municipal courts are organized into divisions, which hear cases of a given kind—for example, civil, criminal, small claims, traffic, and probate divisions.

Consider the small claims division, often called the small claims court. Many people cannot afford the costs of suing for the collection of a small debt. A newspaper carrier, for example, can hardly afford a lawyer to collect a month's subscription from a customer. The owner of a two-family house may have the same problem with a tenant's back rent, and many merchants are forced to forget an overdue bill or sell it to a collection agency.

Small claims courts are designed for just such situations. There, a person can bring a claim for little or no cost. The proceedings are usually informal, and the judge often handles the matter without attorneys for either side.

Juvenile Courts Individuals under 18 years of age are generally not subject to the jurisdiction of the courts in which adults are tried. Minors who are arrested for some offense, or who otherwise come to the attention of the police or other authorities, may appear in juvenile courts.

The juvenile justice system is designed to address the special needs and problems of young people. This system generally emphasizes rehabilitation more than punishment. However, under some circumstances, juvenile courts do refer certain offenders to a regular criminal court for trial.

Recently, most States have responded to juvenile crime with tougher criminal laws. Often these statutes make it easier to try juveniles as adults when they are charged with serious crimes. In 46 States, juvenile court judges may assign certain cases involving juveniles to adult courts. In several States, cases that meet certain standards must be tried in adult courts.

General Trial Courts Most of the more important civil and criminal cases are heard in the States' general trial courts. Every State is divided into a number of judicial districts, or circuits, each generally covering one or more counties. For each district there is a general trial court, which may be known as a district, circuit, chancery, county, or superior court, or as a court of common pleas.

These general trial courts are courts of "first instance." That is, they exercise original jurisdiction over most of the cases they hear. Most legal actions brought under State law begin in these courts. When cases do come to them on appeal from some lower court, a new trial (a trial *de novo*) is usually held.

The cases heard in trial courts are tried before a single judge. Most often a petit jury (the trial jury) hears and decides the facts at issue in a case, and the judge interprets and applies the law involved. Criminal cases are presented for trial either by a grand jury or, most often, on motion of the prosecuting attorney.

The trial court is seldom limited as to the kinds of cases it may hear. Although this court's decision on the facts in a case is usually final, disputes over questions of law may be carried to a higher court.

✔ **Checkpoint**
What are the responsibilities of JPs, magistrates' courts, and municipal courts?

rehabilitation
n. the act of restoring, transforming one to a useful, lawful life

probate
adj. the official proving, verifying, of a will

A municipal court might handle appeals of parking tickets. ▼

---

14 Many insist that the fee system means that "JP" really stands for "judgment for the plaintiff." The practice also encourages "fee splitting"—an arrangement in which judges can increase the number of misdemeanors they hear by agreeing to share their fees with those arresting officers who bring such cases to them. The "speed trap" is probably the best known and most common result of a fee-splitting situation.

Juvenile Justice

Juvenile courts arose from decades of struggle at the State level to adapt and reform the criminal justice system. *Why do you think reformers sought separate jails and prisons for young people?*

1800s Common law preferred to have parents discipline children for most crimes. Young people accused of serious crimes were jailed with adults, and those as young as seven could be tried and sentenced in criminal courts.

1899 Cook County, Illinois, creates the first juvenile court on the principle of "the state as parent." The court protects both public safety and the needs of the juveniles accused of crimes.

1974 Congress passes the Juvenile Justice and Delinquency Prevention Act requiring that young people be jailed separately from adults and encouraging states to develop alternatives to prisons.

Today While juvenile courts still flourish, States increasingly allow juveniles accused of serious crimes to be tried and sentenced in adult courts.

Intermediate Appellate Courts Most States now have one or more intermediate appellate courts. They are courts of appeal that stand between the trial courts and the State's supreme court. These appellate courts act as "gatekeepers" to ease the burden of the State's highest court.

The appellate courts have different names among the States, but they are most often called the court of appeals.[15] Most of their work involves the review of cases decided in the trial courts. That is, these appeals courts exercise mostly **appellate jurisdiction.** Their original jurisdiction, where it exists, is limited to a few specific kinds of cases—election disputes, for example.

In exercising their appellate jurisdiction, these courts do not hold trials. Rather, they hear oral arguments from attorneys, study the briefs (written arguments) that attorneys submit, and review the record of the case in the lower court.

Ordinarily, an intermediate appellate court does not concern itself with the facts in a case. Rather, its decision turns on whether the law was correctly interpreted and applied in the court below. Its decision may be reviewed by the State's high court; its disposition of a case is usually final, however.

The State Supreme Court The State's supreme court is the highest court in its judicial system.[16] Its major function is to review the decisions of lower courts in those cases that are appealed to it.

The size of each State supreme court is fixed by that State's constitution, usually at five or seven justices. A chief justice presides over the sessions of each State's top court.

The governor appoints the justices in just over half of the States. The voters elect them elsewhere, except in two States where the legislature chooses.

The State supreme court is the court of last resort in the State's judicial system. It has the final say in all matters of State law. The United States Supreme Court *may* review some State supreme court decisions touching on federal law. But not very many State decisions actually go to the federal Supreme Court.[17] Recall

---

15 In New York, the general trial court is called the supreme court, or the county court; the intermediate appellate court is the appellate division of the supreme court; the State's highest court is known as the Court of Appeals.

16 The State's highest court is known as the Supreme Court in 45 States. But in Maine and Massachusetts it is called the Supreme Judicial Court; in Maryland and New York, the Court of Appeals; and in West Virginia, the Supreme Court of Appeals. Oklahoma and Texas have two high courts: the Supreme Court is the highest court in civil cases, and a separate Court of Criminal Appeals is the court of last resort in criminal cases.

17 Many of the cases that have reached the Supreme Court involved the 14th Amendment's Due Process and Equal Protection clauses.

that an appeal from a State's highest court will be heard in the federal Supreme Court only if (1) a "federal question"—some matter of federal law—is involved in the case and (2) the Supreme Court agrees to hear that appeal. In short, most State supreme court decisions are final.[18]

Unified Court Systems The typical State court system is organized geographically rather than by types of cases. In these map-based systems, a judge must hear cases in nearly all areas of the law. A <u>backlog</u> of cases can and often does build up in some courts while judges sit with little to do in others. Moreover, uneven interpretations and applications of the law may and sometimes do occur from one part of the State to another. To overcome these difficulties, a number of States have turned to a unified court system—one that is organized on a functional, or case-type, basis.

In a completely unified court system, there is technically only one court for the entire State. It is presided over by a chief judge or judicial council. There are a number of levels within the single court, such as supreme, intermediate appellate, and general trial sections. At each level within each section, divisions are established to hear cases in certain specialized or heavy-caseload areas of the law—criminal, juvenile, family relations, and other areas that need special attention.

In such an arrangement, a judge can be assigned to that section or division to which his or her talents and interests seem best suited. To relieve overcrowded dockets, judges may be moved from one division to another.

Selection of Judges

Clearly, the quality of any court system—indeed, the quality of justice itself—depends in large measure on the selection of competent,

well-trained judges. More than 15,000 judges now sit in the States' various trial and appellate courts. Nearly all of them came to office in one of three ways: (1) by popular election, (2) by appointment by the governor, or (3) by appointment by the legislature.

Popular election is by far the most widely used method of judicial selection. In fact, the only way to become a judge in 11 States is by popular election.[19] Midterm vacancies, caused by death or resignation, provide the only exception to that blanket rule; those vacancies are usually filled by gubernatorial appointment. Roughly half of all judicial elections are nonpartisan contests today.

Selection by the legislature is the method least often used. The lawmakers now choose all or at least most judges in only two States: South Carolina and Virginia.

Governors now select nearly a fourth of all State judges. In five States, the chief executive appoints them all. In several others, the governor has the power to appoint all or at least many judges, but under a Missouri Plan arrangement, as you will see.

How Should Judges Be Selected? Most people believe that judges should be independent, that they should "stay out of politics."

✓ **Checkpoint**
Why do some States have a unified court system?

backlog
n. a build-up of unfinished work

---

18 State law regularly gives its lower courts final jurisdiction over many types of minor cases. That is, review cannot be sought in a higher State court. In those cases, the lower court is the State's court of last resort. If any review is to be had, it can be only in the United States Supreme Court. Such reviews are extremely rare.

19 Alabama, Illinois, Kentucky, Michigan, Minnesota, Nevada, New Mexico, North Carolina, North Dakota, Pennsylvania, Wisconsin.

"My basic judicial philosophy is 'Guilty.'"

▶▶ Analyzing Political Cartoons **What does this cartoon suggest about electing judges based on their judicial philosophy?**

proponent
n. one who is actively in favor of something; a supporter

Whatever method of selection is used should be designed with that goal in mind.

Nearly all authorities agree that selection by the legislature is the most political of all the methods of choice. Few favor it. So, the question really becomes: Which is better, the popular election of judges or their appointment by the governor?

Those who favor popular election generally make the democratic argument. Because judges "say the law" (interpret and apply it), they should be chosen by and answer directly to the people. Some also argue that the separation of powers is undercut if the executive names the members of the judicial branch.

Those who favor appointment by the governor argue that the judicial function should be carried out only by those who are well qualified. The fact that a person has the support of a political party or is a good vote-getter does not mean that person has the capacity to be a good judge. Proponents of executive appointment insist that it is the best way to ensure that those persons who preside in courts will have the qualities most needed in that role: absolute honesty and integrity, fairness, and the necessary training and ability in the law.

Deciding between these two positions is difficult at best. The people have often made excellent choices, and governors have not always made wise and nonpolitical ones. Still, most authorities come down on the side of gubernatorial appointment—largely because those characteristics that make a good judge and those that make a good candidate are not too often found in the same person.

Popular election is both widely used and widely supported by citizens and party organizations. So, most moves to revise methods of judicial selection have kept at least some element of voter choice.

The Missouri Plan For most of the past century, the American Bar Association (ABA) has sponsored an approach that combines election and appointment. The method is often called "the Missouri Plan," and some form is now in place in just over half the States.

In Missouri's version of this method, the governor appoints the seven justices of the State supreme court, the 32 judges of the court of appeals, and all judges who sit in the trial courts in the most heavily populated parts of the State. The governor must make each appointment from a panel, or list, of three candidates recommended by a judicial nominating commission. The commission is made up of a sitting judge, several members of the bar, and private citizens.

Each judge named by the governor serves until the first general election after he or she has been in office for at least a year. The judge's name then appears on the ballot without opposition. The voters decide, in a retain-reject election, whether or not that judge should be kept in office. Should the voters reject a sitting judge, the process begins again.

SECTION **5** ASSESSMENT

Essential Questions
Journal
To continue to build a response to the chapter Essential Question, go to your **Essential Questions Journal.**

1. **Guiding Question** Use your completed concept web to answer this question: How are State and local courts organized and staffed?

Key Terms and Comprehension

2. **(a)** What is **appellate jurisdiction?**
   (b) Which State courts have this jurisdiction?

3. Describe the work of the general trial courts.

Critical Thinking

4. **Demonstrate Reasoned Judgment** How do you think judges should be selected? Choose one method described in this section and create a strong, well-supported argument for that method.

5. **Draw Inferences** What qualifications do you think a good judge should have? Write a help-wanted advertisement for your ideal candidate.

Quick Write

Explanatory Writing: Create an Outline To help you structure an explanatory essay on the differences in power between the national and State governments, create an outline in which you identify each topic and subtopic in a single phrase. When you are ready to write your essay, you can use the outline as a guide. Alternatively, you may create a flowchart to help you organize and order your ideas.

Quick Study Guide

GOVERNMENT ONLINE
On the Go
To review anytime, anywhere, download these online resources at **PearsonSuccessNet.com**
Political Dictionary, Audio Review

CHAPTER **24**

Guiding Question
Section 2 What are the defining traits and purpose of State legislatures?

Guiding Question
Section 3 What are the roles and powers of a governor?

Guiding Question
Section 4 How do State and local courts apply different types of law?

Guiding Question
Section 1 What are the defining features of State constitutions?

CHAPTER 24
Essential Question
How much power should State government have?

Guiding Question
Section 5 How are State and local courts organized and staffed?

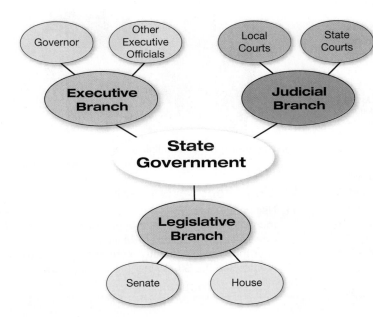

Legal Terms

Term	Purpose
Jury	To reach a just decision
Common law	To guide a judge's decisions with past examples
Equity	To stop wrongs before they occur
Criminal law	To protect the public order
Civil law	To resolve disputes between people and between people and the government

Political Dictionary

popular sovereignty p.709
limited government p. 709
fundamental law p. 710
initiative p. 712
statutory law p. 713
police power p. 717
constituent power p. 717
referendum p. 719
recall p. 721
item veto p. 724
clemency p.724
pardon p. 724
commutation p. 725
reprieve p. 725
parole p. 725
common law p. 727
precedent p. 728
criminal law p. 728
felony p. 728
misdemeanor p. 728
civil law p. 728
tort p. 728
contract p. 728
jury p. 728
information p. 729
bench trial p. 730
Justice of the Peace p. 732
warrant p. 732
preliminary hearing p. 732
magistrate p. 733
appellate jurisdiction p. 734

Chapter Assessment

GOVERNMENT ONLINE
Self-Test
To test your understanding of key terms and main ideas, visit
PearsonSuccessNet.com

Comprehension and Critical Thinking

Section 1

1. **(a)** What are the basic principles on which all State constitutions are based? **(b)** How do these basic principles reflect the origins of the first State constitutions?

2. **(a)** Explain how the process of amending a State constitution differs from amending the federal Constitution. **(b)** How might the two basic methods for changing State constitutions contribute to the need for reform?

Section 2

3. **(a)** What powers does a State legislature have? **(b)** How are those powers different from the powers of Congress?

4. **(a)** What is the difference between an initiative and a referendum? **(b)** Is the initiative process a reflection of the principle of representative government?

Section 3

5. **(a)** How does the governor's role as chief executive differ from the President's role as head of the executive branch? **(b)** Should the formal and informal qualifications for a governorship differ from those for the presidency? Why?

6. **(a)** Which of the governor's executive powers is most important? Explain. **(b)** Do the governor's judicial powers conflict with the principle of separation of powers? Why or why not?

Section 4

7. **(a)** What is common law and what are its origins? **(b)** Why do you think that it remains important to our legal system?

8. **(a)** What does the use of juries tell you about traditional American views of the proper role of citizens and government officials in the judicial process? **(b)** What does the trend away from jury trials say about trends in the American system of justice?

Section 5

9. **(a)** What are the three ways by which State and local judges are selected today? **(b)** Do you or would you approve of the Missouri Plan as a fair and effective way to select judges in your State? Why or why not?

10. **Analyzing Political Cartoons (a)** What does "streamlining the judicial process" mean? **(b)** What are the benefits to States and individuals of streamlining? **(c)** What, according to this cartoon, is a disadvantage?

"In the interest of streamlining the judicial process, we'll skip the evidence and go directly to sentencing."

Writing About Government

11. Use your Quick Write exercises from the section assessments to write an essay that explains the aspect of State government you selected. Make sure the body supports your thesis with accurate information and reasoned arguments. See pp. S3–S5 in the Skills Handbook.

Apply What You've Learned

12. **Essential Question Activity** Speak with a State legislator, legislative aide, or employee of State government. Ask:

    (a) How does State government most directly affect people's lives?

    (b) Is State government as responsible to voters as it should be?

    (c) If you could change the structure of State government, what would you do?

13. **Essential Question Assessment** Use the interview you conducted to write an editorial that helps you answer the Essential Question: **How much power should State government have?** In your editorial, propose what you think is the one most important reform that should be made to your State's government. Explain your reasoning and include information from your interview to help persuade readers of the benefits of your suggested reform.

Essential Questions Journal To respond to the chapter Essential Question, go to your **Essential Questions Journal.**

Document-Based Assessment

Direct Democracy in the States

The initiative and referendum are crucial tools of direct democracy that grew out of the Populist and Progressive reform movements of the nineteenth and early twentieth centuries as indicated in Document 1. These reforms increased control of government by the voters, but some critics wonder how effective they really are, as shown in Document 2.

Document 1

"Corruption dominates the ballot-box, the Legislatures, the Congress, and touches even. . . the bench. The people are demoralized; . . . [t]he newspapers are largely subsidized or muzzled, public opinion silenced, business [exhausted], homes covered with mortgages, labor impoverished, and the land concentrating in the hands of capitalists. . . . From the same [fertile] womb of governmental injustice we breed the two great classes—tramps and millionaires. . . . We have witnessed for more than a quarter of a century the struggles of the two great political parties for power and plunder, while grievous, wrongs have been inflicted upon the suffering people. We charge that the controlling influences dominating both these parties have permitted the existing dreadful conditions to develop without serious effort to prevent or restrain them. Neither do they now promise us any substantial reform. . . . They propose to sacrifice our homes, lives, and children on the altar of mammon; to destroy the multitude in order to secure [corrupt] funds from the millionaires. . . . RESOLVED, that we commend to the favorable consideration of the people and the reform[ist] press the legislative system known as the initiative and referendum.

—The Populist Party Platform, 1892

Document 2

Use your knowledge of the police power and Documents 1 and 2 to answer Questions 1–3.

1. Through the initiative and referendum, the Populist Party hoped to

   A. redistribute money and land to promote the economic equality of all Americans

   B. create long and confusing ballots designed to trick voters.

   C. give Americans more faith in their powerful and wealthy leaders.

   D. take power away from the wealthy and special interests and restore it to the common people.

2. What concern about ballot reforms is the cartoonist expressing in Document 2? Explain.

3. **Pull It Together** Do you think that initiatives and referenda are still effective ways for voters to influence or control government in the States? Explain.

GOVERNMENT ONLINE
Go Online head
To find more primary sources about direct democracy, visit **PearsonSuccessNet.com**

Essential Question
How local should government be?

"**Now,** we find ourselves on the brink of **great change** and we stand at **the edge of greatness**. . . . We can choose to try **new ideas,** new approaches, **new ways** of doing things.

—Philadelphia Mayor Michael Nutter

Photo: Mayor Nutter in Philadelphia's City Hall, 2008

GOVERNMENT ONLINE
On the Go

To study anywhere, anytime, download these online resources at PearsonSuccessNet.com
• Political Dictionary
• Audio Review
• Downloadable Interactivities

Counties, Towns, and Townships

Guiding Question

What are the similarities and differences of local governments, special districts, and tribal governments? Use a chart similar to the one below to record facts about local governments.

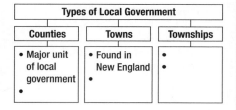

Types of Local Government		
Counties	**Towns**	**Townships**
• Major unit of local government	• Found in New England	•
•	•	•

Political Dictionary

- county
- township
- municipality
- special district

Objectives

1. Describe the typical county, its governmental structure, and functions.
2. Analyze the need for reform in county government.
3. Identify the responsibilities of tribal governments.
4. Examine the governments of towns, townships, and special districts.

You know that the Census Bureau is in the people-counting business. Do you know that it also counts a great many other things—including units of government? The Bureau's Census of Governments found an astounding 89,527 governments in the United States. In 2007, it counted the Federal Government, 50 States, and 89,476 local governments across the country.

Those local units come in many different shapes and sizes. Some have only a handful of employees and operate with only meager budgets. Others have tens of thousands of employees and budgets of a billion dollars or more. Many perform only a single public function, such as providing fire protection or water service. Others, including nearly all cities and most urban counties, deliver a long list of services, limited only by budgetary and legal restraints.

The Constitution of the United States says nothing about local governments. So, cities, towns, counties, school districts, and all other local governments, unlike the Federal Government and the 50 States, have no independent constitutional standing. They are, instead, creatures of the States.

Recall that each of the 50 States is a *unitary* government. Each one of them has the reserved power to create local governments and structure them in whatever ways it chooses—and also to abolish them, if it chooses to do so.[1] Whether they are providing services, regulating activities, collecting taxes, or doing anything else, local governments can only act because the State that established them has given them the power to do so.

Counties

A **county** is a major unit of local government in most States. Like all local governments, it is created by the State. There are 3,033 county governments in the United States today. No close relationship exists between the size of any given State and the number of counties in that State. The number of county governments per State ranges from none in Connecticut and Rhode Island and three in Delaware to as many as 254 in Texas.

---

1 The Census Bureau found 116,756 local units in its first Census of Governments, in 1952. There are, then, more than 27,000 fewer units of local government than there were a half century ago. The Bureau conducts the Census of Governments in every fifth year ending in 2 or 7.

In Louisiana, units of government known elsewhere as counties are called parishes. In Alaska, they are known as boroughs. In addition to Connecticut and Rhode Island, several other places across the country have no organized county government. About 10 percent of the nation's population lives in those areas today.

The functions of counties vary from region to region. They serve almost solely as judicial districts in some New England States. There, towns carry out most of the functions undertaken by counties elsewhere. In many mid-Atlantic and Midwestern States, counties are divided into subdivisions called **townships.** In those States, counties and townships share the functions of rural local government. In the South and the West, counties are the major governing unit in rural areas.

In terms of area, San Bernardino County in California is the largest in the continental United States; it spreads across 20,105 square miles. Kalawao County in Hawaii is the smallest; it covers just 13 square miles. Counties within each State often vary widely in area.

Counties also differ greatly in terms of population. More than 10 million people now live in Los Angeles County in California, but census-takers could find only 67 residents of Loving County, Texas, in 2000. Most counties serve populations of fewer than 50,000.

County Government Structure

The structures of county government differ, too, and often considerably. Even so, a county typically has four major elements: a governing body, a number of boards or commissions, appointed bureaucrats, and a variety of elected officials.

The Governing Body The county's governing body is frequently called the county board. It is also known as the board of commissioners, board of supervisors, police jury, assembly, legislature, and board of chosen freeholders, among other names.

The members of this governing body are almost always popularly elected. Terms of office run from two to six years, but four-year terms are the most common. Board members are usually chosen from districts within the county rather than on an at-large basis.

Generally, county boards can be grouped into two types: boards of commissioners and boards of supervisors. The board of commissioners is the smaller, more common type. It is found everywhere in the South and West, and it is also common elsewhere. A board of commissioners most often has three or five members, but some have seven or more.

The board of supervisors is typically a much larger body. It averages about 15 members but can run to 80 or more. The supervisors are elected from single-member districts in the county. Each supervisor may be an officer of his or her township, as well as a member of the countywide governing body.

The State constitution and acts of the State legislature spell out the powers held by county governing bodies. Those powers are usually both executive and legislative, despite the American tradition of separation of powers.

County governments' most important legislative powers deal with finance. Everywhere, county boards levy taxes, appropriate funds, and can <u>incur</u> limited debts. They also have a number of other legislative powers—for example, in the fields of public health and corrections.

✔ **Checkpoint**
In what ways do counties vary across the country?

incur
v. bring about, gain

The county courthouse is the center of county government, as in Sevier County, Tennessee.

County Government Structure

A typical county government is made up of a governing body, often known as a county board, and several appointed and elected officials with assigned responsibilities. *Which local government officials have the greatest impact on your daily life?*

An elected county board (above) holds broad powers over budgets and programs. Such officers as the county assessor (left) may be elected or appointed.

County Official Duties

County Board	Levies taxes and sets spending
	Administers roads, county buildings, and programs
	Appoints boards and officials
Sheriff	Runs county jail
	Provides rural police protection
	Carries out court orders
	May collect taxes
Clerk	Registers and records documents for property, birth, and death
	Runs county elections
Assessor	Sets the value of taxable property
	Collects property taxes
Treasurer	Keeps county funds
Auditor	Keeps financial records
District Attorney	Conducts criminal investigations
	Prosecutes criminal cases
School Superintendent	Administers public schools
Coroner	Investigates violent deaths
	Certifies causes of death

Most boards also carry out a number of administrative functions. They supervise the county road program and manage county property, including the courthouse, jails, hospitals, and parks. They are often responsible for the administration of welfare (cash assistance) programs and the conduct of elections. They are also responsible for the hiring of most county employees—from a few dozen or so in many rural places to several thousand in most metropolitan areas. And, importantly, they determine the pay of nearly all of the people who work for the county.

Other Elements In addition to its governing body, the typical county's government regularly includes a number of other elected officials—as you can see in the chart on this page.

Then, too, county governments usually feature several boards and commissions, whose members are also sometimes elected. Those agencies frequently include a fair board, a planning commission, a board of health, a library board, and a board of road viewers. Altogether, the nation's 3,033 counties now employ some three million men and women who do the day-to-day work of those units of local government.

Functions of Counties

Because counties are creations of the State, they are responsible for the administration of State laws. They also administer such county laws as the State's constitution and legislature allow their governing bodies to make.

Historically, nearly all counties have been institutions of rural government. Most remain rurally oriented today. Although there are some differences from State to State, the major functions of counties still reflect their rural character.

Their most common functions are to keep the peace and maintain jails and other correctional facilities; assess property for tax purposes; collect taxes and spend county funds; build and repair roads, bridges, drains, and other public works; and maintain schools. Counties record deeds, mortgages, marriage licenses, and other documents; issue licenses for such things as hunting, fishing, and marriage; administer elections; care for the poor; and work to safeguard the health of the people who live in the county.

Many counties have taken on other functions as they have become more urban. Several of these more heavily populated counties now offer many of the public services and facilities that are usually found in cities. They provide water and sewer service; have professionally trained police, fire, and medical units; and operate airports and mass transit systems. Some also enforce zoning and other land-use regulations. Many have built and now operate auditoriums, stadiums, golf courses, and other recreational facilities.

The Need for Reform

County organization is often chaotic. In the typical county, no single official can really be called the *chief* administrator. Rather, authority is divided among a number of elected boards and officials, each largely independent of the others. Too often, it is impossible to identify who is responsible for inefficiency or inaction (or worse) in the conduct of county affairs.

The large number of popularly elected officials adds to the chaos. Faced with the typical county's long ballot, voters are often hard-pressed to make informed choices. Also, many of those elected officials have no basic public policy-making responsibilities. Many people are convinced that popular election is not the best way to fill those offices.

The size and the number of counties in most States are another source of weakness. Nearly every county now in existence was laid out in the days of the horse and the stagecoach. Then, it made good sense to draw county lines so that no one lived more than a dozen miles or so from the county seat. Today, however, most counties are geographically ill-suited to the realities of the modern world.

One way in which many States have attempted to reform county government is through county home rule. That is, those 37 States allow some or all of their counties, subject to approval by the local voters, to decide the details of their own governmental structure.

Another approach to reform seeks to deal with the fragmented authority of counties. It does so by creating the position of county manager, modeled along the lines of the council-manager form of city government. Still another approach is county-city consolidation—where a major city and the county around it join into a single unit of government. San Francisco, California, and Nashville, Tennessee are leading examples.

Tribal Governments

Tribal governments exist as a distinct form of government. Unlike State, county, or community governments, however, the governments of recognized Native American nations have a unique "government-to-government" relationship with the United States. These Native American tribes are considered sovereign nations, with the right to govern their own people on their own territories unless otherwise specified by treaty or acts of Congress.

Official recognition by the Federal Government is crucial for tribal governments because it establishes their sovereignty and exempts them from State or local control. For example, some tribes have established gambling casinos on their reservations even though the territory lies within States that do not allow that type of gambling. Because the officially recognized tribes are sovereign, they are not subject to State laws and regulations. Also, recognized tribes are eligible to receive federal funds that can be used to provide local services. Today, there are some 560 federally recognized tribal governments in this country, with authority over the lives of some 1.7 million people.

Typically, a tribal government has an elected leader called a chief or chairman. Most tribes also have a council, which can vary in size from only two or three to almost 100 members. Other than these common

✔ **Checkpoint**
Why do most county governments need reform?

Native American Reservations

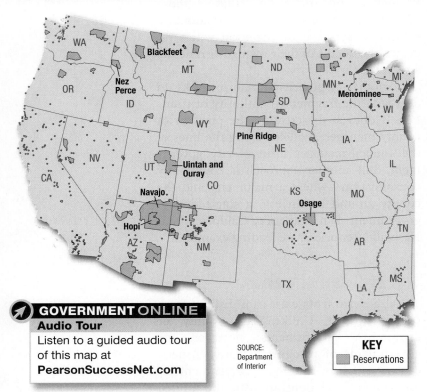

SOURCE:
Department
of Interior

KEY
Reservations

▶▶ **Analyzing Maps** Native American governments enjoy a sovereign status and a special relationship with the federal and State governments. *Why are reservations organized differently from other forms of local government?*

✔ **Checkpoint**
How do tribal governments relate to State governments?

vehicle
n. agent through which something is accomplished

constable
n. local police officer

features, tribal governments vary widely in size and structure. Some, such as the Cherokee and Navajo tribes, have a written code or constitution that provides for a State-like government with executive, legislative, and judicial branches. Others are small and loosely organized.

Like State and county governments, tribal governments use federal funds and tax revenue to provide services. These services depend on the size, history, and needs of the tribe. Many tribes have executive officers or departments that oversee policy and manage funds to provide health care, education, and welfare to tribe members. They also oversee cultural events and sites as well as distribute information about the tribe. Even smaller tribal governments provide some services, especially housing and health and education information and support.

Towns and Townships

Towns and townships exist in nearly half the States. They are little known in the South or West but are commonly found from New England to the Midwest.[2]

The New England Town In New England, the town is a major unit of local government. Except for a few major cities, each of the six States in the region is divided into towns. Each town generally includes all of the rural and the urban areas within its boundaries. The town delivers most of the services that are the responsibility of cities and counties elsewhere around the country.

The roots of the New England town reach back to the early colonial period. The Pilgrims landed at Plymouth Rock in 1620 as an organized congregation. They quickly set up a close-knit community in which their church and their government were almost one. Other Puritan congregations followed the Pilgrims' pattern.

At least in form, much of town government today is little changed from colonial times. The main feature is a town meeting, long praised as the ideal <u>vehicle</u> of direct democracy. The town meeting is an assembly open to all the town's eligible voters. It meets yearly, and sometimes more often, to levy taxes, make spending and other policy decisions, and elect officers for the next year.

Between town meetings, the board of selectmen/selectwomen chosen at the annual meeting manages the town's business. Typically, the board is a three-member body and has responsibilities for such things as roads, schools, care of the poor, and sanitation. Other officers regularly selected at the annual meeting include the town clerk, a tax assessor, a tax collector, a <u>constable</u>, road commissioners, and school board members.

The ideal of direct democracy is still alive in many smaller New England towns. It has given way, however, to the pressures

2 The term *town* is used in some States as the legal designation for smaller urban places; it is also sometimes used as another word for township. Township is also a federal public lands survey term, used to identify geographic units (often called congressional townships), each having exactly 36 square miles (36 sections).

of time, population, and the complexities of public problems in many of the larger towns. There, representative government has largely replaced it. Town officers are often elected before the yearly gathering. Many of the decisions once made by the assembled voters are now made by the selectmen and selectwomen. In recent years, several towns have gone to a town manager system for the day-to-day administration of local affairs.

Townships Townships are units of local government found principally in the Northeast and the Midwest. Nowhere do townships blanket an entire State, however.

In New York, New Jersey, and Pennsylvania, townships were formed as areas were settled and the people needed the services of local government. Consequently, the township maps of those States often resemble crazy quilts. From Ohio westward, they mostly follow the regular lines drawn in federal public land surveys. Many are perfect squares.

About half of these States provide for annual township meetings, like those held in New England towns. Otherwise, the governing body is usually a three- or five-member board, generally called the board of trustees or board of supervisors. Its members are elected for fixed terms or serve because they hold other elected township offices. Township offices often include a supervisor, a clerk, a treasurer, an assessor, a constable, a justice of the peace, and a body of road commissioners.

A **municipality** is an urban political unit within a township that usually exists as a separate governmental <u>entity</u>. As a result, township functions tend to be rural. They regularly involve such matters as roads, cemeteries, drainage, and minor law enforcement. In some States, however, the township is also the basic unit of public school administration.

Many people believe that townships have outlived their usefulness. More than half the States get along without them. Many rural townships have been abolished as a result

entity
n. unit, thing, element

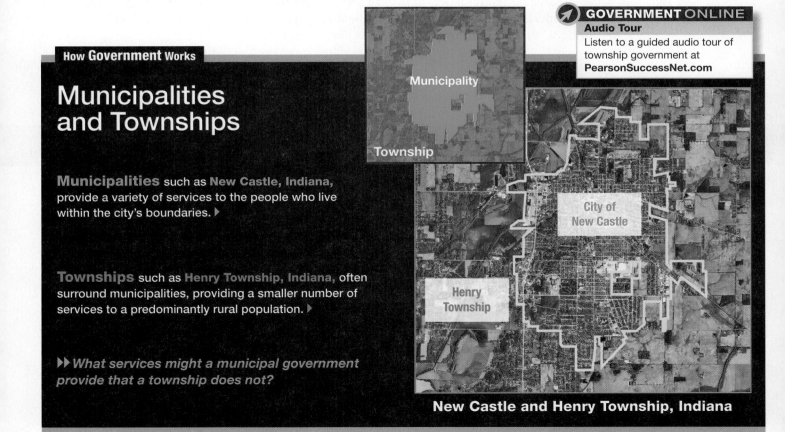

How Government Works

Municipalities and Townships

Municipalities such as New Castle, Indiana, provide a variety of services to the people who live within the city's boundaries. ▶

Townships such as Henry Township, Indiana, often surround municipalities, providing a smaller number of services to a predominantly rural population. ▶

▶▶ *What services might a municipal government provide that a township does not?*

Municipality

Township

GOVERNMENT ONLINE
Audio Tour
Listen to a guided audio tour of township government at **PearsonSuccessNet.com**

City of New Castle

Henry Township

New Castle and Henry Township, Indiana

✔**Checkpoint**
What is the purpose of a municipality?

sidestep
v. avoid, get around

of declining populations, improvements in transportation, and other factors.

Some of the more densely populated townships appear to have brighter futures than their country cousins, however. This seems especially true in the suburban areas around some larger cities. Some States, such as Pennsylvania, now allow townships to exercise many of the powers and furnish many of the services once reserved for cities.

Special Districts

There are now tens of thousands of special districts across the country. A **special district** is an independent unit created to perform one or more related governmental functions at the local level. These districts are found in mind-boggling variety and in every State. School districts—some 13,500 of them—are by far the most common example. More than 35,000 other special districts also blanket the country, and their numbers are growing.

Special districts are found most often, but not always, in rural and suburban areas. Many have been created to provide water, sewage, or electrical service; to furnish fire or police protection; and to build and maintain bridges, airports, swimming pools, libraries,

or parks. Others have been created for such purposes as soil conservation, housing, public transportation, irrigation, or reforestation. There are even, in many places, special districts for dog or mosquito control purposes.

A leading reason for the creation of special districts has been the need to provide a particular service in a wider or a smaller area than that covered by a county or a city. For example, a special district might be needed to handle pollution in the several counties through which a river flows. On the other hand, a special district might be set up to provide fire protection in some out-of-the-way locale.

In many cases, special districts have been formed because other local governments could not, or would not, provide the services desired. Others have been created to sidestep constitutional limits on the size of a city's or a county's debt; to finance a public service out of users' fees instead of general tax revenue; and to take advantage of some federal grant program.

The governing body for a special district is almost always an elected board. It has the power to lay taxes (usually on property) or charge fees, as well as the powers to spend and to carry out the function(s) for which it was created.

Essential Questions Journal To continue to build a response to the chapter Essential Question, go to your **Essential Questions Journal.**

SECTION 1 ASSESSMENT

1. **Guiding Question** Use your completed chart to answer this question: What are the similarities and differences of local governments, special districts, and tribal governments?

Key Terms and Comprehension
2. What is the main purpose of **(a)** a **township? (b)** a **special district?**
3. What factors generally make county governments inefficient?

Critical Thinking
4. **Identifying Assumptions** Consider the concept of the New England town meeting. What does this form of local government assume about the citizens of the town?
5. **Drawing Inferences** Review the functions of county and town or township government. List and describe at least three examples that show how these governing bodies affect the day-to-day lives of people in your community.

Quick Write

Writing for Assessment: Develop the Main Points When writing for assessment, carefully plot your response *before* you begin writing. Select one of the questions below. In a chart or outline, develop at least three major points that you might cover to answer that question.
(a) How do county and township governments differ from one another?
(b) What are the strengths and weaknesses of the different forms of city government?

SECTION 2

Cities and Metropolitan Areas

Guiding Question

How do city governments serve the needs of residents and other Americans? Use an outline to take notes about the ways in which city governments serve people.

I. America's Rural-Urban Shift
II. Incorporation and Charters
III. Forms of City Government
  A. Mayor-Council Form
    1._____
    2._____

Political Dictionary

- incorporation
- charter
- mayor-council government
- strong-mayor government
- weak-mayor government
- commission government
- council-manager government
- zoning
- metropolitan area

Objectives

1. Explain the process of incorporation and the function of city charters.
2. Contrast the major forms of city government.
3. Evaluate the need for city planning and list some major municipal functions.
4. Outline the challenges that face suburbs and metropolitan areas.

Image Above: City of Rochester, New York

We are fast becoming a nation of city dwellers. Where once our population was small, mostly rural, and agricultural, it is now large, mostly urban, and dominated by technology, manufacturing, and service industries. In 1790, a mere 5 percent of the population lived in the nation's few cities. Today, more than 240 million people—more than 80 percent of the population—live in the nation's cities and their surrounding suburbs.[3] For local governments, that change has had dramatic consequences.

The larger the number of people living in close contact with one another, the greater the strains on local governments. The larger the population, the greater the problems in providing water, police and fire protection, sewers, waste removal, streets and traffic regulation, public health services, schools, recreational facilities, and more. The larger the population, the more extensive—and expensive—all of this becomes.

Incorporation and Charters

Remember, each of the 50 States is a unitary government. That means that each State has complete control over all of the units of local government within its borders. All those units, including cities, were created by the State, received their powers from the State, and are subject to a variety of limitations imposed by the State.

The process by which a State establishes a city as a legal body is called **incorporation.**[4] Each State sets out in its constitution, or by statute, the conditions and the procedures under which a community may become an incorporated municipality. Typically, a State requires that a minimum number of persons live within a given area before incorporation can take place.

The fact that cities are incorporated highlights an important difference between city and county government. Cities are created largely at the request of their residents, because residents want certain public services. Counties,

---

3 Depending on local custom and State law, municipalities may be known as cities, towns, boroughs, or villages. The use and meaning of these terms vary among the States. The larger municipalities are known everywhere as cities, and the usual practice is to use that title only for those communities with significant populations.

4 The term *incorporation* comes from the Latin words *in* (into) and *corpus* (body).

✔ **Checkpoint**
How are cities established?

vest
v. granted to, bestowed upon

▶▶ **Analyzing Tables** *Why is the power to write the budget a critically important power?*

on the other hand, exist largely to serve the administrative needs of the State. Cities do act as agents of the State, of course—for example, in law enforcement and public health. But the principal reason for the existence of a city is for the convenience of those who live there.

The **charter** is a city's basic law, its constitution. Its contents may vary from city to city, but commonly the charter names the city, describes its boundaries, and declares it to be a municipal corporation. As a municipal corporation, a city has the right to sue and be sued in the courts; to have a corporate seal; to make contracts; and to acquire, own, manage, and dispose of property.

Generally, the charter sets out the other powers vested in the city and outlines its form of government. It also provides how and for what terms its officers are to be chosen, outlines their duties, and deals with finances and other matters.

Forms of City Government

Although variations can and do exist, each city has one of three basic forms of government. A city has either (1) a mayor-council, (2) a commission, or (3) a council-manager form of government.

The Mayor-Council Form The **mayor-council government** is the oldest and still the most widely used type of city government. It features an elected mayor as the chief executive and an elected council as its legislative body.

The council. The council is almost always unicameral and typically has five, seven, or nine members. Some larger cities have more. New York City has the largest council, with 51 members. Members of the council are popularly elected, almost always from districts (wards) within the city. Terms of office vary from one to six years. Four-year terms are the most common.

A move to nonpartisan city government began in the early 1900s. Its champions believed that (1) political parties were a major source of corruption in city government, and (2) partisan contests at the State and national levels have little to do with municipal problems and local issues. Today, less than one third of all cities still run their elections on a partisan basis.

The mayor. Generally, the voters elect the mayor. In some places, however, the council chooses one of its members to serve as mayor. The mayor presides at council meetings, usually may vote only to break a tie, and may recommend—and often veto—ordinances. In most cities, the council can override the veto.

Mayor-council governments are often described as either of the strong-mayor or the weak-mayor type, depending on the powers given to the mayor. This classification is useful for purposes of description. It blurs the importance of informal power in city politics, however.

In a **strong-mayor government,** the mayor heads the city's administration, usually has the veto power, can hire and fire employees, and prepares the budget. Typically, the mayor is able to exercise strong leadership in making city policy and running the city's affairs.

In a **weak-mayor government,** the mayor has much less formal power. Executive duties are shared with other elected officials—for example, a clerk, treasurer, city engineer, police chief, and even council members.

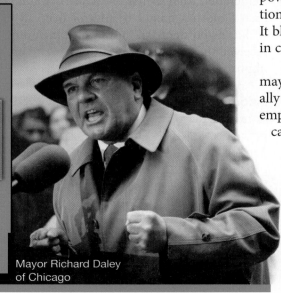

What does a mayor do?

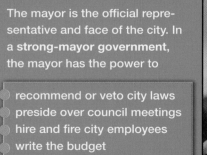

The mayor is the official representative and face of the city. In a **strong-mayor government**, the mayor has the power to

- recommend or veto city laws
- preside over council meetings
- hire and fire city employees
- write the budget

The more common **weak-mayor government** assigns most of those powers to other elected officials or the city council.

Mayor Richard Daley of Chicago

Powers of appointment, removal, and budget are shared with the council or exercised by that body alone. The mayor seldom has a veto power.

Most mayor-council cities operate under the weak-mayor rather than the strong-mayor plan. The strong-mayor form is most often found in larger cities.

The success of the mayor-council form depends in very large measure on the power, ability, and influence of the mayor. In weak-mayor cities, responsibility for action or inaction is hard to assign. The strong-mayor plan helps to solve the problems of leadership and responsibility. Still, the mayor-council form has three large defects:

1. It depends quite heavily on the capacities of the mayor.

2. An ongoing dispute between the mayor and the council can stall the workings of a city's government.

3. It is quite complicated and, so, is often little understood by the average citizen.

The Commission Form The **commission government** is simple in structure. Three to nine, but usually five, commissioners are popularly elected. Together, they form the city council, pass ordinances, and control the <u>purse strings</u>. Individually, they head the different departments of city government: police, fire, public works, finance, parks, and so on. Thus, both legislative and executive powers are centered in one body.

The commission form was born in Galveston, Texas, in 1901, after a tidal surge had devastated the city. When the existing mayor-council government proved unequal to the task, the Texas legislature gave Galveston a new charter, providing for five commissioners to make and enforce law in the stricken city. Intended to be temporary, the arrangement proved so effective that it soon spread to other communities across the country.

Depending on the city, either the voters or the commissioners themselves choose one of the commissioners to serve as the mayor. Like the other commissioners, the mayor heads one or more of the city's departments. He or she also presides at council meetings and represents the city for ceremonial purposes.

The mayor generally has no more authority than the other commissioners and rarely has a veto power.

Although many reformers supported the commission form at first, experience pointed up serious defects in the system, and its popularity fell off rapidly. Only a very few American cities have a commission form of government today.

The commission form suffers from three chief defects:

1. The lack of a single chief executive makes it difficult to assign responsibility. This can also mean that the city has no effective political leadership.

2. A built-in tendency toward "empire building" often surfaces. Each commissioner tries to draw as much of the city's money and influence as possible to his or her own department.

3. A lack of coordination <u>plagues</u> the topmost levels of policymaking and administration. Each commissioner is likely to equate the city-wide public good with the particular interests and functions of his or her department.

The Council-Manager Form The **council-manager government** is a modification of the mayor-council form. Its main features are (1) a strong council of usually five or seven members elected at-large on a nonpartisan ballot; (2) a weak mayor chosen by the voters; and (3) a manager, the city's chief administrative officer, named by the council.

The form first appeared in Ukiah, California. In 1904, that city's council appointed an "executive officer" to direct the work of city government. The first charter expressly providing for the council-manager form was granted to the city of Sumter, South Carolina, in 1912.

The council is the city's policymaking body. The manager carries out the policies the council makes. He or she is directly responsible to that body for the efficient administration of the city. The manager serves at the council's pleasure and may be dismissed at any time and for any reason.

Today, most city managers are professionally trained career administrators. As chief administrator, the manager directs the

plagues
v. disturbs, negatively affects

purse strings
n. access to financial resources

work of all city departments and has the power to hire and fire all city employees. The manager also prepares the budget for council consideration and controls the spending of the funds the council appropriates.

The council-manager plan has the backing of nearly every expert on municipal affairs, and its use has spread widely. It is now found in more than 8,000 communities, including most of those cities with populations between 25,000 and 250,000.

The council-manager plan has three major advantages over other forms of city government:

1. It is simple in form.

2. It is fairly clear who is responsible for policy, on the one hand, and for its application, on the other.

3. It relies on highly trained experts who are skilled in modern techniques of budgeting, planning, computerization, and other administrative tools.

expendable
adj. disposable, replaceable

In theory, the nonpolitical manager carries out the policies enacted by the council. Yet, in practice, sharp distinctions between policymaking and policy-application seldom exist. The manager is very often the chief source for new ideas and fresh approaches to the city's problems. On the other hand, the city council often finds it politically useful to share the responsibility for controversial decisions with the "expendable" city manager.

Some critics of the council-manager form hold that it is undemocratic because its chief executive is not popularly elected. Others say that it lacks strong political leadership. This is a particular shortcoming, they argue, in larger cities, where the population is often quite diverse and there can be many competing interests. Support for this view can be seen in the fact that only a handful of cities with more than a half a

GOVERNMENT ONLINE
Audio Tour
For a guided tour of city government, visit
PearsonSuccessNet.com

How **Government** Works

Alternate Forms of City Government

The commission (left) and council-manager (right) forms of city government provide alternatives to the traditional roles of the mayor and city council.
How does each form of government divide executive power?

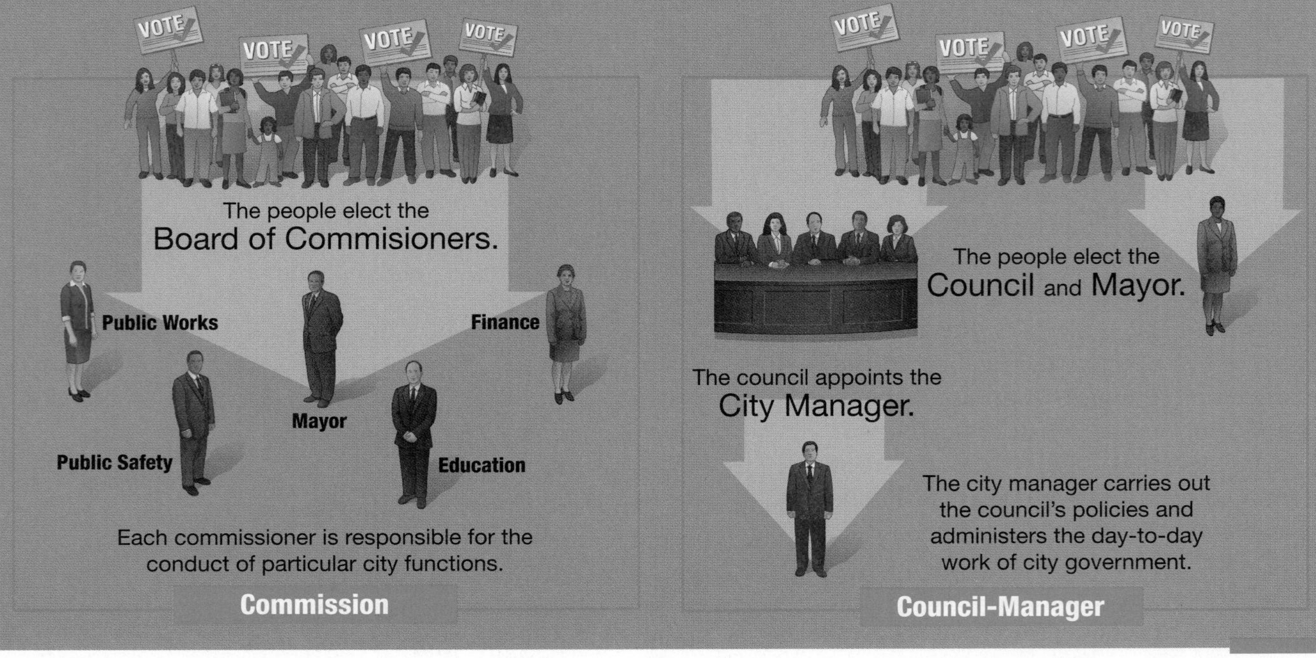

VOTE VOTE VOTE VOTE

The people elect the
Board of Commisioners.

Public Works   **Finance**

Mayor

Public Safety   **Education**

Each commissioner is responsible for the conduct of particular city functions.

Commission

VOTE VOTE VOTE VOTE

The people elect the
Council and **Mayor.**

The council appoints the
City Manager.

The city manager carries out the council's policies and administers the day-to-day work of city government.

Council-Manager

million residents have a council-manager government in place today.

City Planning

With few exceptions, most American cities developed haphazardly, without a plan, and with no eye to the future. The results of this shortsightedness can be seen in what is often called the core area or the inner city. These are the older and usually overcrowded central sections of larger cities.

Industrial plants were placed anywhere their owners chose to build them. Rail lines were run through the heart of the community. Towering buildings shut out the sunlight from the narrow streets below. Main roads were laid out too close together and sometimes too far apart. Schools, police and fire stations, and other public buildings were squeezed onto cheap land or put where the political organization could make a profit. Examples are endless.

Planning Growth Fortunately, many cities have seen the need to create order out of their random growth. Most have established some sort of planning agency. It usually consists of a planning commission, supported by a trained professional staff.

A number of factors have prompted this step. The need to correct past mistakes has often been a compelling reason, of course. Also, many cities have recognized both the advantages that can result, and the pitfalls that can be avoided, through well-planned and orderly development. Importantly, the Federal Government has spurred cities on. Most federal grant and loan programs require that cities that seek aid must first have a master plan as a guide to future growth.

City Zoning The practice of dividing a city into a number of districts, or zones, and regulating the uses to which property in each of them may be put is called **zoning.** Generally, a zoning ordinance places each parcel of land in the city into one of three spheres: residential, commercial, or industrial zones.

Each of these zones is then divided into subzones. For example, each of several residential zones may be broken down into several areas. One may be reserved for single-family residences, another may allow one-family and two-family dwellings, and a third, large apartment buildings.

Most zoning ordinances also prescribe limits on the height and area of buildings, determine how much of a lot may be occupied by a structure, and set out several other such restrictions on land use. They often have "setback" requirements, providing that structures must be placed at least a certain distance from the street and from other property lines.

Zoning still meets opposition from many who object to this interference with their right to use their property as they choose. Even so, nearly every city of any size in the United States is zoned today. The city of Houston, where zoning was turned down three times by popular vote, remains the only major exception.

Zoning ordinances must be reasonable. Remember that the 14th Amendment prohibits any State, and thus its cities, from depriving any person of life, liberty, or property without due process of law. Each of the 50 State constitutions contains a similar provision.

Clearly, zoning does deprive a person of the right to use his or her property for certain purposes. Thus, if an area is zoned for single-family dwellings only, one cannot build an apartment house or a service station on property in that zone. Zoning can also reduce the value of a particular piece of property. A choice corner lot, for example, may be much more valuable with a drive-through restaurant or gas station on the property rather than a house.[5]

While zoning may at times deprive a person of liberty or property, the key question is always this: Does it do so without due process? That is, does it do so unreasonably?

The question of reasonableness is one for the courts to decide. The Supreme Court first upheld zoning as a proper use of the police power in *Euclid* v. *Amber Realty Co.,* 1926, a case involving an ordinance enacted by the city council of Euclid, Ohio.

---

5 Nonconforming uses in existence before a zoning ordinance is passed are almost always allowed to continue. Most ordinances give the city council the right to grant exceptions, called variances, in cases where property owners might suffer undue hardships.

✔ **Checkpoint**
How do cities plan for the future?

prescribe
v. order, set down, specify

Farms, Cities, Suburbs

The United States began as a rural nation, but factories and new opportunities drew millions to cities in the 1800s and early 1900s. Today, about half of all Americans live in suburbs that bridge the gap between country and city. *How do different forms of settlement affect the responsibilities of local government?*

1790
Nearly all Americans live on farms or in small towns.

1920
For the first time, more Americans live in cities than in the countryside.

Today
Suburbs are home to half of all Americans.

SOURCE: U.S. Census

✔ **Checkpoint**
What is the purpose of zoning?

Municipal Functions

The services a city provides day in and day out are so extensive that it is almost impossible to catalog them. Most larger cities, and many smaller ones, issue annual reports on the city's condition. These are often book-length publications.

Consider just a few of the many things that most or all cities do. They provide police and fire protection. They build and maintain streets, sidewalks, bridges, street lights, parks and playgrounds, swimming pools, golf courses, libraries, hospitals, schools, correctional institutions, day-care centers, airports, public markets, parking facilities, auditoriums, and sports arenas. They furnish public health and sanitation services, including sewers and wastewater treatment, garbage collection and disposal, and disease prevention programs.

Cities operate water, gas, electrical, and transportation systems. They regulate traffic, building codes, pollution, and public utilities. Many cities also build and manage public housing projects, provide summer youth camps, build and operate docks and other harbor facilities, and maintain tourist attractions.

Metropolitan Areas

The growth of urban areas has raised many problems for city dwellers. Urban growth also affects residents of nearby suburbs.

The Suburban Boom About half of all Americans now live in suburbs. The nation's suburbs first began to grow rapidly in the years after World War II, and that growth has continued. As suburban populations have mushroomed, many of the nation's larger cities have actually lost residents.

These dramatic population shifts stemmed, in large part, from peoples' desire for more room, cheaper land, greater privacy, and less smoke, dirt, noise, and congestion. Many have also sought less crime, newer and better schools, safer streets and playing conditions, lower taxes, and higher social status. The car and the freeway turned millions of rooted city dwellers into mobile suburbanites.

Businesses followed customers to the suburbs, often clustering in shopping centers or malls instead of traditional downtowns. Many industries moved from the central city in search of cheaper land, lower taxes, and a more stable labor supply. Industries also sought an escape from city building codes, health inspectors, and other regulations.

This "suburbanitis" has added to city-dwellers' <u>woes</u>. As high-income families have moved out, they have taken their civic, financial, and social resources with them. They have left behind center cities with high percentages of older people, low-income families, and minorities. Both the need for, and the stress on, city services have multiplied.

Metropolitan Areas Suburbanites face their share of problems, too, including the need for water supplies, sewage disposal, police and fire protection, transportation, and traffic control. <u>Duplication</u> of such functions by city and suburb or by city and county can be wasteful, even dangerous. More than one fire has raged while neighboring fire departments quibbled over the responsibility for fighting it.

Attempts to meet the needs of the nation's **metropolitan areas**—cities and the areas around them—have taken several forms. Over the years, annexation has been the standard means. Outlying areas have simply been brought within a city's boundaries. Many suburbanites resist annexation, however, and many cities have been hesitant to take on the burdens involved.

Another approach has been to create special districts designed to meet the problems of heavily populated urban areas. Their boundaries frequently cut across county and city lines to include an entire metropolitan area. They often are called metropolitan districts and can serve one purpose (for example, maintaining parks) or many.

In Oregon, a regional agency known as Metro manages several activities in an area that includes Portland, the State's largest city, and 23 other municipalities. Within this region, Metro is responsible for land-use and transportation planning, solid-waste disposal programs, and the operation of the Oregon Convention Center, the Oregon Zoo, and other facilities.

Yet another approach to the challenges facing metropolitan areas is increasing the authority of counties. Among local governments around the country, counties are generally the largest in area and are most likely to include those places demanding new and increased services. In Miami-Dade County, Florida, a countywide metropolitan government took responsibility for areawide functions following a 1957 charter. Responsibilities include fire and police protection; an integrated water, sewer, and drainage system; zoning; and expressway construction. Miami and the county's other 34 municipalities continue to perform strictly local functions and services.

woe
n. problem

duplication
n. doubling

Portland's metropolitan government operates a popular regional transit system. ▼

Essential Questions Journal
To continue to build a response to the chapter Essential Question, go to your **Essential Questions Journal.**

SECTION 2 ASSESSMENT

1. **Guiding Question** Use your completed outline to answer this question: How do city governments serve the needs of residents and other Americans?

Key Terms and Comprehension

2. What are the key differences between a **strong-mayor** and a **weak-mayor government?**

3. List at least five functions of municipal government.

Critical Thinking

4. **Comparing Points of View** Zoning may be used to exclude businesses popular with young people from residential neighborhoods. **(a)** Why do you think this is so? **(b)** Is this a fair use of a local government's police power? Why or why not?

5. **Determining Cause and Effect** How have shifts in the American population led to changes in the responsibilities and organization of local government?

Quick Write

Writing for Assessment: Gather Details Reread the question you have chosen and the main points you developed in Section 1. Gather details from the text that support each of the main points to answer the question. Briefly check your final list to delete unnecessary details.

SECTION 3

Providing **Vital Services**

Guiding Question

What services do State and local governments provide? Use a concept web similar to the one below to record information about State and local government services.

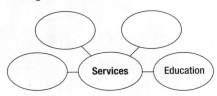

Political Dictionary
- Medicaid
- welfare
- entitlement

Objectives

1. Explain why State and local governments have a major role in providing important services.
2. Identify State and local services in the fields of education, public welfare, public safety, and highways.

Image Above: Educational spending includes computers, books, and salaries.

The 50 State governments and their tens of thousands of local governments are principally responsible for many of the public services with which most Americans are familiar. The many differences among States means that there can be variations in both the quantity and the quality of those public services, but they include, especially, those in the areas of education, public safety, welfare, streets and highways, and public health. The several States deliver services to their residents in two ways: (1) directly, through State agencies conducting State-operated programs, and (2) through the many local governments the States have created.

Education

Public education is among the oldest of all State responsibilities. Boston Latin School, in Massachusetts, is the oldest public school in continuous existence in the United States; it opened its doors in 1635. The State of New York created the first school districts in 1812. Today, public education is also among the most important of all State responsibilities. This is reflected in the fact that education is the most expensive item in every State's budget, accounting for about 30 percent of all State spending.

Funding for public education has risen sharply over recent decades, and the recent downturn in the nation's economy has almost certainly brought only a temporary dip in that trend. The amount of money spent per pupil in public schools has nearly doubled over the past 25 years.

Primary and secondary public education is largely the responsibility of local governments. Local taxes, especially property taxes, provide much of the funding for schools.

Of course, the States do provide some financial assistance to their local governments for education. The level of that aid varies, however. Some States contribute well over half the cost of primary and secondary education. Others provide only a minor fraction of the cost.

In addition, States set guidelines in order to promote quality in the schools. For example, State laws establish teacher qualifications, curricula, quality standards for educational materials, and the length of the school year.

State interest and involvement in those matters have intensified in recent years. Most States have established "curriculum frameworks" or "content standards" outlining the material that must be covered in core subjects. Every State now has an extensive Statewide testing program, fueled by the No Child Left Behind Act signed by President Bush in 2002.

At the college and university levels, the States also play a major role. States understand that, in order for businesses to succeed in the State, a ready supply of highly trained college graduates is key. Every State has a public higher education system, which may include universities, technical schools, and community colleges. Education at State universities and colleges is generally much less expensive than at private institutions. On average, <u>tuition</u> at four-year public colleges and universities is about one fourth that of private four-year schools. Nevertheless, many public institutions—for example, the University of California at Berkeley—are ranked among the world's finest schools.

Public Welfare

States take an active role in promoting the health and welfare of their residents. They pursue that goal by a variety of means.

Public Health Most States fund ambitious public health programs. States operate public hospitals and offer direct care to millions of citizens. They immunize children against dangerous childhood diseases, such as measles and mumps. With the Federal Government, they administer such programs as **Medicaid,** which provides medical care and some other health services to low-income families. Recent soaring costs in the healthcare industry have placed a great strain on many States' budgets.

Cash Assistance Another major area in which States contribute to the well-being of their citizens is cash assistance to the poor, commonly called **welfare.** States now take a leading role in this area.

✔ **Checkpoint**
What are a State's responsibilities for education?

tuition
n. fee paid for schooling

How Government Works

State and Local Spending

Public schools account for nearly three in every ten dollars spent by State and local governments. *How are the different responsibilities of State and local versus the Federal Government reflected in these categories of spending?*

GOVERNMENT ONLINE
For an **interactive** exploration of state and local expenditures, visit **PearsonSuccessNet.com**

INTERACTIVE

29%
Other

29%
Education

6%
Transportation

7%
Health care

7%
Utilities

7%
Public safety

15%
Public welfare

6% TRANSPORTATION needs drive governments to build and maintain roads, bridges, and trains. ▲

7% PUBLIC SAFETY expenditures protect people from fires and crime.

7% HEALTHCARE spending includes Medicaid for low-income Americans. ▶
SOURCE: U.S. Census

CHICAGO POLI

The Federal Government shares the cost of highway projects like Boston's Big Dig with the States and counties where they are built. **Why do local governments make most decisions about road building?**

✔ **Checkpoint**
What is the purpose of public welfare spending?

entitled
adj. eligible for, qualified to receive

recipient
n. one who receives

Between 1936 and 1996, the Federal Government provided cash assistance to needy families through the Aid to Families with Dependent Children (AFDC) program.[6] AFDC was an **entitlement** program, which means that anyone who met the eligibility requirements was <u>entitled</u> to receive benefits under the program. The Federal Government and the States shared the costs of providing AFDC benefits.

Critics of AFDC pointed to soaring costs, expanding caseloads, and the absence of time limits on benefits as serious problems with the program. Because of these issues, critics argued that the program encouraged people to depend on government assistance rather than become self-supporting.

In 1996, AFDC was replaced with a new and strikingly different program, Temporary Assistance to Needy Families (TANF). Unlike AFDC, TANF is a block grant program: The Federal Government gives States a fixed amount of money each year, regardless of whether the number of TANF <u>recipients</u> rises or falls. The States are then free to use

---

6 AFDC was authorized by Title IV of the Social Security Act of 1935. Until 1962, the program was named Aid to Dependent Children, as the 1935 act was aimed simply at needy dependent children.

the federal grant, plus the State funds they are obliged to contribute, to design and implement their own welfare programs. TANF limits recipients to a total of five years of assistance during the course of their lifetimes, and recipients must work or participate in some form of vocational training or community service.

The number of families on welfare has plunged since the mid-1990s. Many who remain on welfare must overcome a number of barriers, such as physical or mental disabilities or substance abuse, in order to obtain and hold jobs. Now that States have the primary responsibility for welfare, it is their task to find ways to help these families.

Other Efforts States do much more to promote their citizens' health and welfare. They make and enforce antipollution laws to protect the environment; they inspect factories and other workplaces to protect worker safety; they license healthcare practitioners to ensure quality care; and the list goes on and on.

Public Safety

One of the oldest law-enforcement groups, the legendary Texas Rangers, was established in 1835. Today, a variety of police forces, from the local sheriff to academy-trained State police, operate in every State to preserve law and order.

The State police are perhaps the most visible group, since they patrol the State's roads and highways. State law-enforcement forces perform other vital services, as well. They may function as the primary police force in rural communities, investigate crimes, provide centralized files for fingerprints and other information, and provide training and many other services to support local law-enforcement agencies.

Each State has its own corrections system for dealing with those convicted of State crimes. States operate prisons, penitentiaries, and other correctional facilities, including those for juvenile offenders.

Operating these disciplinary systems is a growing burden for States. Today, more than 2.5 million people are incarcerated, more than half of them in State prisons.

Two leading causes of booming prison populations are (1) increases in the number of people sentenced for violent crimes and (2) the increasing length of the average prison sentence. One result is prison overcrowding. Another result is rising State corrections spending, which has more than doubled over the past 20 years. The States now spend more than $40 billion each year to build, staff, and maintain prisons and to house prisoners.

In an effort to expand their prison capacity more affordably, many States have hired private contractors to operate some of their prisons. More than 5 percent of all State prisoners are now held in private facilities.

Highways and Other Services

Building and maintaining roads and highways is an enormous job. It regularly ranks among the most expensive of all the many items in State budgets.

Again, the Federal Government is a partner with the States in funding highways. The most impressive example is the Interstate Highway System, a network of high-speed roadways that spans the length and breadth of the continental United States. Construction of the system began with the 1956 Federal-Aid Highway Act and continues to this day.

The Interstate Highway System, now officially known as the Dwight D. Eisenhower System of Interstate and Defense Highways, is 99 percent finished. When finally complete, it will total some 45,000 miles. The Federal Government has paid roughly 90 percent of its total cost.

While the interstate system is a magnificent achievement, it constitutes only a tiny fraction of the nation's more than 4 million miles of roads. Many roadways are built with State, not federal, funds; and the States maintain those roads, as well.

State and local governments must also look after the physical safety of drivers on thousands of miles of roads and highways. Besides patrolling the roads, State and local governments set speed limits. The States license drivers to ensure their competence, and many States require periodic safety inspections of vehicles.

As indicated earlier, the many services the States and their local units provide are really far too numerous to be recounted here. That these services are not detailed here does not discount the importance of such functions as the setting aside of public lands for purposes such as conservation and recreation, the regulation of business practices, and the protection of consumers from a variety of dangers and inconveniences.

✔ **Checkpoint**
How do State and local governments ensure the safety of the people?

capacity
n. ability to hold

Essential Questions
Journal
To continue to build a response to the chapter Essential Question, go to your **Essential Questions Journal.**

SECTION **3** ASSESSMENT

1. **Guiding Question** Use your completed concept web to answer this question: What services do State and local governments provide?

Key Terms and Comprehension

2. What are the three largest spending categories in State and local budgets?

3. How is an **entitlement** program different from other spending programs?

Critical Thinking

4. **Drawing Inferences** Why do you think that many States asked the Federal Government to give them block grants to create their own welfare programs?

5. **Expressing Problems Clearly** What challenges do State and local governments face in providing for public welfare and safety? How are governments meeting these challenges?

Quick Write

Writing for Assessment: Write a Strong Opening Statement When writing for assessment, the opening statement should set forth the main idea of your response in an interesting and clear manner. Review your question and list of main points from Sections 1 and 2 and write an opening statement. Check it against your main idea and main points to be sure that all parts of your response are closely related.

ISSUES OF OUR TIME

State Taxation and Spending

▶▶ Track the Issue

The United States was founded, in part, on opposition to taxes. Nonetheless, governments have found many ways to raise money.

1646

The Massachusetts Bay Colony establishes the first property tax in the 13 colonies.

1765

Prompted by the Stamp Act, the colonists declare "taxation without representation" to be unfair.

1862

The Federal Government provides for a temporary income tax to meet the costs of the Civil War.

1911

Wisconsin establishes the first State income tax.

1964

New Hampshire institutes the first modern-day State lottery to pay for public programs.

1970s

Voters in several States rebel against rising property taxes with laws limiting tax increases.

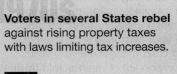

Governor Arnold Schwarzenegger (R., California). ▶

▶▶ Perspectives

Many Americans complain that the government takes too much money out of their pockets. However, limits on taxes have contributed to deficit spending or cuts in services in the States. What issues do State government officials and taxpaying citizens need to consider when trying to balance budgets?

"With California facing a possible $14 billion budget deficit, it is not surprising that legislators and the governor are considering tax increases. . . . The potential economic harm and unpopularity of tax increases should put spending increases on the back burner. . . . After all, it is spending increases, not tax breaks that got the State in a financial mess. State taxes take a larger share of personal income than ever before."

— Editorial, *Oakland Tribune,* January 2008

"[The governor's] budget all but ignores options for increasing revenues. . . . legislative leaders should adjourn and lock the doors for two weeks. That way, GOP lawmakers could go back to their districts and explain to voters why closing parks and plundering schools is preferable to closing tax loopholes. . . . Farsighted Republicans could agree to a one-year hike in taxes as part of a universal deal for long-term reform."

— Editorial, *Sacramento Bee,* January 2008

▶▶ Connect to Your World

1. **Understand (a)** Why do you think that taxes have increased in both number and rates since independence? **(b)** What is the central conflict in the relationship between taxation and government services?

2. **Compare and Contrast (a)** How does the editor of the *Oakland Tribune* suggest that California balance its budget? **(b)** How does the editor of the *Sacramento Bee* think that goal should be accomplished? **(c)** With which viewpoint do you agree? Why?

 GOVERNMENT ONLINE
In the News
To find out more about State revenues and spending, visit
PearsonSuccessNet.com

Financing State and Local Government

Guiding Question

How do State governments raise money to pay for services? Use a chart similar to the one below to record information about the sources of State revenue.

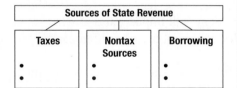

Sources of State Revenue		
Taxes	**Nontax Sources**	**Borrowing**
•	•	•
•	•	•

Political Dictionary

- sales tax
- regressive tax
- income tax
- progressive tax
- property tax
- assessment
- inheritance tax
- estate tax
- budget

Objectives

1. Describe the major federal and State limits on raising revenue.
2. List the four principles of sound taxation.
3. Identify major tax and nontax sources of State and local revenue.
4. Explain the State budget process.

Image Above: Sales taxes are a major source of revenue for State and local governments.

Altogether, despite the recent recession, the 50 States and their thousands of local governments take in and spend some $2 *trillion* per year. If you were to place 2 trillion dollar bills end to end, they would extend more than 185 million miles—farther than the distance from Earth to the planet Venus. Where do those governments get all that money, and what do they do with it?

Limits on Raising Revenue

The States now take in about $750 billion in taxes a year. And their local governments collect some 600 billion tax dollars every year. Those two basic levels of government also receive more than $1 trillion from several nontax sources, too—much of it from the Federal Government.

The power to tax is one of the major powers of the States in the federal system. In a strictly legal sense, then, their taxing power is limited only by the restrictions imposed by the Federal Constitution and those imposed by a State's own fundamental law.[7]

Federal Limitations The Federal Constitution does place some restrictions on the taxing abilities of State and local government. Although few in number, those limits do have a major impact.

The Constitution prohibits the States from taxing interstate and foreign trade. Remember, the Supreme Court's decision in *McCulloch* v. *Maryland,* in 1819, bars States from taxing the Federal Government or any of its agencies or functions.

The 14th Amendment's Due Process and Equal Protection clauses place important limits on the power to tax at the State and local levels. Essentially, the Due Process Clause requires that taxes be (1) imposed and administered *fairly,* (2) not so heavy as to actually confiscate property, and (3) imposed only for *public* purposes.

The Equal Protection Clause forbids the making of unreasonable classifications for the purpose of taxation. The clause thus forbids tax classifications

---

7 Remember, the power to tax is also limited by any number of practical considerations—including, especially, economic and political factors.

arbitrary
adj. unfairly determined by chance

contrived
adj. carefully planned, skillfully designed

exemption
n. freed, excused from a duty

based on race, religion, nationality, political party membership, or any other factors beyond what is reasonable.

Most tax laws do involve some form of classification, however. Thus, a cigarette tax is collected only from those who buy cigarettes, a classification most people agree is a reasonable one.

State Limitations Each State's constitution limits a State's taxing powers. State constitutions also limit the taxing powers of their local governments, often in great detail.

Most State constitutions create tax exemptions for religious and other nonprofit groups. State codes often set maximum rates for levies such as sales taxes or local property taxes. Some States prohibit certain taxes—for example, a general sales tax or a personal income tax.

Since local governments have no independent powers, the only taxes they can impose are those that the State allows them to levy. States have been restrictive in the matter. Even local units with home-rule charters are closely limited as to what and how they can tax.

Principles of Sound Taxation

Any tax, if taken by itself, can be shown to be unfair. If a government's total revenues were to come from one tax—say, a sales, an income, or a property tax—its tax system would be very unfair. Some people would bear a much greater burden than others, and some would bear little or none. Each tax should thus be defensible as part of a tax system.

In his classic 1776 work, *The Wealth of Nations,* Scottish economist Adam Smith laid out four principles of a sound tax system, which tax experts still cite today:

❝

PRIMARY SOURCE

1. The subjects of every state ought to contribute towards the support of the government as nearly as possible, in proportion to their respective abilities; that is, in proportion to the revenue which they respectively enjoy under the protection of the state.

2. The tax which each individual is bound to pay ought to be certain, and not arbitrary.

3. Every tax ought to be levied at the time, or in the manner, in which it is most likely to be convenient for the contributor to pay it.

4. Every tax ought to be so contrived as to both take out and to keep out of the pockets of the people as little as possible over and above what it brings into the public treasury. . . .

—*The Wealth of Nations*

Shaping a tax system that meets those standards of equality, certainty, convenience, and economy is just about impossible. Still, that goal should be pursued.

Sources of Revenue

Beyond the limits noted, a State can levy taxes as it chooses. The legislature decides what taxes the State will impose, and at what rates. It decides, too, what taxes localities can levy.[8]

The Sales Tax The sales tax is the most productive source of State-levied income today. It accounts for about a third of all tax monies the several States now collect.

A **sales tax** is a tax placed on the sale of various commodities; the purchaser pays it. It may be either *general* or *selective* in form. A general sales tax is one applied to the sale of most commodities. A selective sales tax is one placed on the sale of only certain commodities.

In 1932, Mississippi became the first State to levy a sales tax. Today, 45 States do so.[9] The rates range from 2.9 percent in Colorado to as much as 7.25 percent in California; most States now peg the rate at 5 or 6 percent. Some things are exempted from the tax almost everywhere—most commonly, food, medicine, and newspapers. A growing number of

---

8 Some State constitutions do grant certain taxing powers directly to some local governments, but this is not common practice.

9 Only Alaska, Delaware, Montana, New Hampshire, and Oregon do not levy general sales taxes, but each does impose various selective sales taxes.

cities, and some urban counties, also levy sales taxes today—a "piggy-back tax," added on to and collected with the State tax.

All 50 States impose a selective sales tax on gasoline, alcoholic beverages, cigarettes, and insurance policies. Many of them also place selective sales taxes on such things as hotel and motel accommodations, restaurant meals, and theater and other amusement admissions.

Sales taxes are widely used for two major reasons: They are easy to collect, and they are dependable revenue producers. Yet a sales tax is a **regressive tax**—that is, it is not levied according to a person's ability to pay. The tax falls most heavily on those least able to pay it.

States are prohibited from collecting the sales taxes on most Internet purchases. That is because products made in one State are sold online to customers across the country. As more and more people shop via the Internet, the States complain that the drain on their sales tax receipts could very well lead to a reduction of public services and/or an increase in their sales tax and other tax rates. Congress, acting under its commerce power, put a temporary <u>moratorium</u> on State taxation of e-commerce in 1998 and renewed it most recently in 2007.

The Income Tax The **income tax**, which is levied on the income of individuals and/or corporations, yields another one third of State tax revenues today. Wisconsin enacted the first State income tax in 1911. Today, 43 States levy an individual income tax; 46 have some form of corporate income tax.[10]

The individual income tax is usually a **progressive tax**—that is, the higher your income, the more tax you pay. Income tax rates vary among the States, from 1 or 2 percent on lower incomes in most States to 9

---

10 Nevada, Texas, Washington, and Wyoming levy neither type of income tax. Alaska, Florida, and South Dakota impose only the corporate tax.

✔ **Checkpoint**
What are the benefits and drawbacks of the sales tax?

moratorium
n. freeze, suspension

How **Government** Works

State and Local Revenues

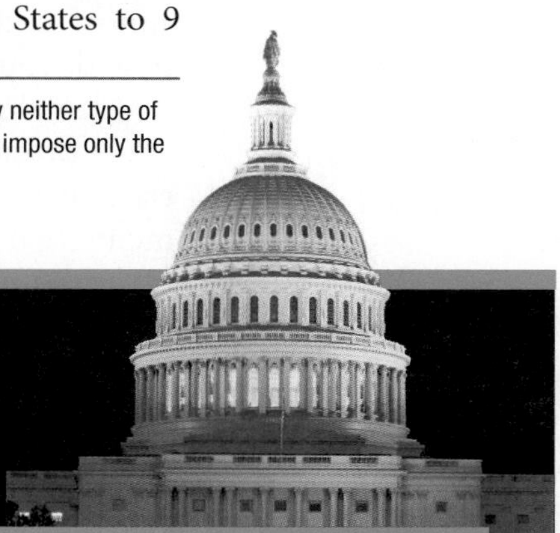

Most State and local governments rely on a balance of income tax, property tax, and sales tax to fund their expenditures. Other revenue sources include federal grants and income from government-owned electricity, universities, and hospitals. *Which sources of revenue draw most heavily from young people?*

10% PERSONAL INCOME TAX
is levied by 43 States. ▾

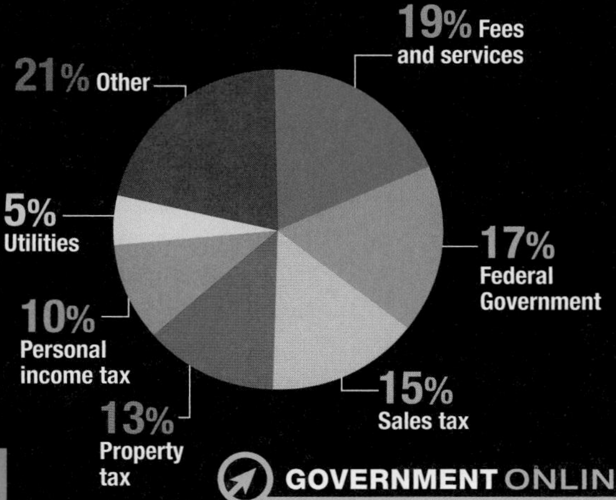

17% FEDERAL GOVERNMENT grants help pay for various programs administered by the States.

21% Other
5% Utilities
10% Personal income tax
13% Property tax
19% Fees and services
17% Federal Government
15% Sales tax

15% SALES TAX is the largest source of tax revenue for State and local governments.

SOURCE: U.S. Census

⊳ **GOVERNMENT** ONLINE
Audio Tour
Listen to a guided audio tour of this diagram at **PearsonSuccessNet.com**

beneficiary
n. one who benefits

graduated
adj. scaled

enterprise
n. initiative, drive, determination

percent or more on the highest incomes in a few States. Those who pay the tax receive various exemptions and deductions in calculating their taxable income.

Corporate income tax rates are usually a uniform (fixed) percentage of income. Only a few States set the rates on a graduated basis.

The progressive income tax is held by many to be the fairest—or the least unfair—form of taxation, because it can be geared to a person's ability to pay. If the rates are too high, however, the tax can discourage individual enterprise.

The Property Tax Property taxes have been a major source of governmental revenue since the early colonial period. Once the major source of State revenue, they are now levied almost exclusively at the local level. They provide roughly three fourths of all local governmental income today.

A **property tax** is a levy on (1) real property, such as land, buildings, and improvements that go with the property if sold; or (2) personal property, either tangible or intangible. Tangible personal property is movable wealth that is visible and the value of which can be easily assessed—for example, computers, cars, and books. Intangible personal property includes such things as stocks, bonds, mortgages, and bank accounts.

The process of determining the value of the property to be taxed is known as **assessment**. An elected county, township, or city assessor usually carries out the task.

Supporters of the property tax argue that, because government protects property and often enhances its value, property owners can logically be required to contribute to the support of government. They note that the rate at which the tax is levied can be readily adjusted to meet governmental needs.

Critics insist that the property tax is not progressive, not geared to one's ability to pay. They also argue that it is all but impossible to set the value of all property on a fair and equal basis. They also note that personal property is easily hidden from assessors.

Inheritance or Estate Taxes Every State has some form of inheritance or estate tax, sometimes called the "death tax." An inheritance tax is levied on the beneficiary's (heir's) share of an estate. An **estate tax** is one levied directly on the full estate itself.

Business Taxes A variety of business taxes, in addition to the corporate income tax, are important sources of revenue in most States. More than half the States impose severance taxes, levies on the removal of natural resources such as timber, oil, minerals, and fish from the land or water.

Every State has various license taxes that permit people to engage in certain businesses, occupations, or activities. For example, all States require that corporations be licensed to do business in the State. Certain kinds of businesses—chain stores, amusement parks, taverns, and transportation lines—must have an additional operating license. Most States also require the licensing of doctors, lawyers, hairdressers, plumbers, electricians, insurance agents, and a host of others.

Many States have levies known as documentary and stock transfer taxes. These are charges made on the recording, registering, and transfer (sale) of such documents as mortgages, deeds, and securities. Some States also impose capital stock taxes, which are levied on the total assessed value of the shares of stock issued by a business.

Other Taxes A variety of other taxes are imposed by the States and their local governments in order to raise revenues. As a leading example, payroll taxes produce huge sums; the monies generated by those taxes are held in trust funds to pay the benefits provided by unemployment assistance, accident insurance, and retirement programs. Most States levy amusement taxes for admission to theaters, sports events, circuses, and the like. Every State imposes license taxes for various nonbusiness purposes—notably, on motor vehicles and drivers, and for such things as hunting, fishing, and marriage.

Nontax Sources Taxes have never been very popular, and so State and local officials have long looked for nontax revenue sources. Today, the States and their many local governments take in more than a trillion dollars a year from these sources. Much

Property taxes may be charged on real estate, such as houses (left), and on personal property, which includes cars (right). **Why do you think real estate is easier for governments to value and tax than purchases or income?**

of that huge amount comes as grants from the Federal Government.

Business enterprises and user fees. State and local governments also make money from a variety of publicly operated business enterprises. Toll roads and bridges are especially popular in the East. Several States, notably Washington, are in the ferry business. North Dakota markets a baking flour, sold under the brand name "Dakota Maid," and is also in the commercial banking business. Eighteen States are in the liquor business, selling alcohol in State-operated stores.[11]

Many cities own and operate their water, electric power, and bus transportation systems. Some cities operate farmers' markets; rent space in their office buildings, warehouses, and housing projects; and operate dams and wharves. Receipts from such businesses support the local governments that own them. Other nontax sources include court fines, sales and lease of public lands, and interest from loans, investments, and late tax payments. Among the many public services for which those who use them must now pay a fee are hospitals, airports, parks, water, sewers, and garbage disposal.

Lotteries. For many years, nearly all forms of gambling were outlawed in every State except Nevada. Most States have relaxed their anti-gambling laws, hoping to attract dollars, jobs, and tourists. Today, only Hawaii and Utah do not permit any kind of gambling.

State-run lotteries net some $17 billion per year for 42 States, the District of Columbia, Puerto Rico, and the U.S. Virgin Islands.[12] Lotteries provide revenue without raising taxes. Supporters note that they are popular, voluntary, and offer an alternative to illegal gambling. Opponents say that lotteries prey on the poor and encourage compulsive gambling. Lottery proceeds are used for a number of purposes among the States. About half of States with lotteries earmark all or most of their revenue for education. Some channel the money directly to the State's general fund, while others dedicate most of it to economic development.

earmark
v. set aside for a specific purpose

Borrowing The States and many of their local governments regularly borrow money to pay for such large undertakings as the construction of schools, highways, hospitals, sports facilities, and college dormitories. Much of that borrowing is done by issuing bonds, much as the Federal Government does. Generally, State and local bonds are fairly easy to market because the interest paid on them is not subject to State or federal income taxes.

---

11 Those states are Alabama, Idaho, Iowa, Maine, Michigan, Mississippi, Montana, New Hampshire, North Carolina, Ohio, Oregon, Pennsylvania, Utah, Vermont, Virginia, Washington, West Virginia, and Wyoming. North Carolina's stores are operated by the counties; Wyoming's liquor monopoly operates only at the wholesale level.

12 Eight States do not operate lotteries: Alabama, Alaska, Arkansas, Hawaii, Mississippi, Nevada, Utah, and Wyoming.

✔ **Checkpoint**
How and why do State and local governments borrow money?

default
v. fail to pay

At various times in the past, many State and local governments <u>defaulted</u> on their debts. Thus, most State constitutions now place quite detailed limits on the power to borrow. Altogether, the 50 States' debts now total about $900 billion, and local governments owe more than a trillion dollars.

State Budgets

A public **budget** is much more than book-keeping entries and dollar signs. It is a financial plan, a plan for the control and use of public money, public personnel, and public property. It is also a political document, a highly significant statement of public policy. Here, in its budget, the State establishes its priorities and decides who gets what, and who doesn't.

For more than 150 years, State budgets were the product of haphazard and uncoordinated steps centered in the legislature. Various State agencies appeared before legislative committees, each seeking its own funding, often in fierce competition with one another. Their chances of success depended far less on need or merit than on whatever political muscle they could bring to bear. When the legislature adjourned, no one had any real idea of how much had been appropriated or for what. Inevitably, extravagance and waste, unresolved problems, debt, favoritism, and graft were all parts of the process.

State budgets are strikingly different things today. They remain highly charged political documents, but they are the end products of what is, by and large, an orderly and systematic process.

All but three States have now adopted the executive budget, which gives the governor two vital powers: (1) to prepare the State's budget, and, after the legislature has acted upon his or her recommendations, (2) to manage the spending of the monies set aside by the legislature.[13] The basic steps in the budget process are much the same at the State, local, and federal levels:

1. Each agency prepares estimates of its needs and proposed expenditures in the upcoming fiscal period.

2. Those estimates are reviewed by an executive budget agency.

3. Revised estimates, with supporting information, are brought together in a consolidated financial plan, the budget, which the governor presents to the legislature for its consideration.

4. The legislature reacts to the proposed budget, part by part, appropriates the funds it deems necessary, and enacts whatever revenue measures may be needed.

5. The governor supervises the execution of the budget—the actual spending of the funds provided by the legislature.

6. The execution of the budget is subject to an independent check—a postaudit.

---

[13] In Mississippi, South Carolina, and Texas, budget making is shared by the governor and the legislature.

SECTION **4** ASSESSMENT

Essential Questions
Journal
To continue to build a response to the chapter Essential Question, go to your **Essential Questions Journal.**

1. **Guiding Question** Use your completed chart to answer this question: How do State governments raise money to pay for services?

Key Terms and Comprehension

2. Explain why **income taxes** are generally described as progressive taxes.

3. What limits does the U.S. Constitution put on the States' ability to tax?

Critical Thinking

4. **Determining Relevance (a)** What are Adam Smith's four principles of sound taxation? **(b)** What do you think makes each principle important?

5. **Identifying Alternatives** What might be the advantages and disadvantages of raising revenue through **(a)** A State-run lottery? **(b)** A State-run business? **(c)** A State-wide property tax?

Quick Write

Writing for Assessment: Write a Summation Assessment essays often end with a summation. The summation should restate, briefly, your main points and echo the opening statement. Write a summation for the question you chose in Section 1. Check your summation against your main points to be sure that all are closely related.

Quick Study Guide

GOVERNMENT ONLINE
On the Go
To review anytime, anywhere, download these online resources at **PearsonSuccessNet.com**
Political Dictionary, Audio Review

CHAPTER 25

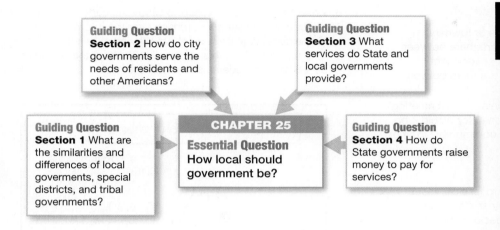

Guiding Question
Section 2 How do city governments serve the needs of residents and other Americans?

Guiding Question
Section 3 What services do State and local governments provide?

Guiding Question
Section 1 What are the similarities and differences of local goverments, special districts, and tribal governments?

CHAPTER 25
Essential Question
How local should government be?

Guiding Question
Section 4 How do State governments raise money to pay for services?

Political Dictionary

county p. 742
township p. 743
municipality p. 747
special district p. 748
incorporation p. 749
charter p. 750
mayor-council government p. 750
strong-mayor government p. 750
weak-mayor government p. 750
commission government p. 751
council-manager government p. 751
zoning p. 753
metropolitan area p. 755
Medicaid p. 757
welfare p. 757
entitlement p. 758
sales tax p. 762
regressive tax p. 763
income tax p. 763
progressive tax p. 763
property tax p. 764
assessment p. 764
inheritance tax p. 764
estate tax p. 764
budget p. 766

Local government responsibilities

- Provide essential services including education, security, road upkeep, and public records
- Conduct elections
- Administer justice
- Plan for future growth and development
- Collect taxes for local services

Revenues and Expenditures

Revenues	State and Local Government	Expenditures
Federal Government		Education
Fees for services		Public welfare
Sales tax		Public safety
Property tax		Healthcare
Income tax		Roads and transportation

Chapter Assessment

GOVERNMENT ONLINE
Self-Test
To test your understanding of key terms and main ideas, visit **PearsonSuccessNet.com**

Comprehension and Critical Thinking

Section 1

1. **(a)** How do counties differ from towns or townships? **(b)** What similarities and differences are there between the Federal Government and a tribal government? **(c)** What similarities and differences are there between tribal and State governments?

2. **(a)** What is the purpose of a New England town meeting? **(b)** What are its benefits and limitations? **(c)** Would it be a good form of government for your community? Why or why not?

Section 2

3. Think about large cities as opposed to less populous communities. **(a)** What types of services do city governments provide? **(b)** What types of special issues or problems do city leaders deal with?

4. Voters in a few cities have rejected zoning with noticeable results. **(a)** What do you think those results are? **(b)** How might a lack of zoning affect your quality of life?

Section 3

5. **(a)** What powers are delegated to the States that are denied to the Federal Government? **(b)** Does this division of powers make public services less efficient or more efficient, in your opinion?

6. **(a)** In what ways do States try to ensure the public safety of their citizens? **(b)** What challenges do States face in ensuring public safety?

Section 4

7. Some States are turning increasingly to nontax revenue sources. **(a)** Why do you think States prefer nontax revenues to taxes? **(b)** Some people are critical of using a lottery as a method for raising State revenue. Why do you think this is the case? Do you agree or disagree?

8. **Analyzing Political Cartoons** Study the cartoon below about a man making a purchase over the Internet with his personal digital assistant. **(a)** Why must he pay a sales tax? **(b)** What does this cartoon imply about the sales tax as a State, not federal, source of revenue?

CONCERNED CITIZENS WANT TO KNOW

IF I DRIVE OVER THE STATE LINE AND USE MY P.D.A. TO MAKE AN ON-LINE PURCHASE IN A THIRD STATE, DO I OWE SALES TAX IN MY HOME STATE?

STATE LINE

©05 AKRON BEACON JOURNAL

Writing About Government

9. Use your Quick Write exercises from the section assessments in this chapter to write a three-paragraph essay that answers your question about local government and finance. The question should be answered in at least three paragraphs—one for each of your main points—including a strong opening statement and a clear summation. Make sure that your essay is concise, correctly spelled, and demonstrates an understanding of correct grammar. See pp. S11–S12 of the Skills Handbook.

Apply What You've Learned

10. **Essential Question Activity** Research your local community or county government structure and budget. Answer the following questions:

    (a) What positions in local government are elected and what positions are appointed?

    (b) What are the most costly programs in the local government budget?

    (c) Which officials have the greatest authority over the budget?

    (d) What responsibilities does the State require of local government?

11. **Essential Question Assessment** Use the results of your research to prepare an election brochure that helps you answer the Essential Question: **How local should government be?** Create a brochure for a fictional candidate for local office explaining the responsibilities of the office and including specific promises to the voters, a description of the goals of local government, and how the candidate hopes to work with State government and other local officials.

Essential Questions Journal To respond to the chapter Essential Question, go to your **Essential Questions Journal.**

Document-Based Assessment

State Safety Laws and the Police Power

According to the Federal Constitution, the police power is reserved to the States. As these documents show, many question how far a State can go in legislating citizens' personal safety before it begins to intrude on personal privacy and choice.

Document 1

In 1987, Iowan John Hartog received a ticket for not wearing his seat belt. Hartog argued that Iowa's seat-belt law was unconstitutional because it violated rights to privacy and equal protection and went beyond the State's authorized police power. The following excerpt from the case transcript supports the court's finding that the seat-belt law was not unconstitutional.

"
   The government provides roads as a service to its citizens, and part of that service is assuring that these roads will be safe and efficient. The motorist is not being overly imposed upon when asked to comply with minimal standards of behavior designed to reduce the dangers of his driving to other drivers. It is also difficult to object to the State's attempt to stop an individual from making the rest of society pay for the consequences of his risk-taking. . . . our government provides services from the ambulance that delivers the injured motorist to the hospital to disability insurance. Having to buckle up may be inconvenient, but it is not an unreasonable price to pay for the use of public roads.

   —from *State of Iowa* v. *John Hartog,* 1989

Document 2

Use your knowledge of the police power and Documents 1 and 2 to answer Questions 1–3.

1. What is the main point of Document 1?
   A. Seat-belt laws are unconstitutional because they interfere with the right to privacy and to equal protection.
   B. Seat-belt laws are inconvenient and the State has no right to impose safety laws on individuals.
   C. Seat-belt laws are reasonable because the government bears costs incurred by injured people who were not wearing belts.
   D. Seat-belt laws are necessary to prevent accidents on public roads and to promote public safety.

2. What opinion about State regulations does Document 2 express?

3. **Pull It Together** Do you think that seat-belt laws and other public safety laws are a reasonable use of a State's police power? Do they intrude on individual rights? Why or why not?

> **GOVERNMENT ONLINE**
> **Documents**
> To find more primary sources on police power, visit **PearsonSuccessNet.com**

Perspectives

Essential Question

What is the right balance of local, State, and federal government?

The U.S. federal system divides power between two levels of government. Elected officials at each level have sought more power and authority for their governments—or to spread responsibilities to others.

" ON THE ROLE OF THE FEDERAL GOVERNMENT:

It is my intention to curb the size and influence of the Federal establishment and to demand recognition of the distinction between the powers granted to the Federal Government and those reserved to the States or to the people. All of us need to be reminded that the Federal Government did not create the States; the States created the Federal Government.

—Ronald Reagan, First Inaugural Speech, 1981

ON THE KEY ISSUES FACING THE STATES:

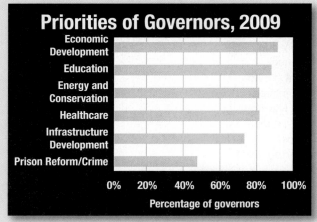

Priorities of Governors, 2009

Economic Development
Education
Energy and Conservation
Healthcare
Infrastructure Development
Prison Reform/Crime

0%   20%   40%   60%   80%   100%

Percentage of governors

Each year, the National Governors Association tracks the governors' State of the State addresses and identifies the subjects mentioned most often by the most governors.

" ON THE VALUE OF MAYORS:

As CEOs of the nation's cities, mayors know all too well the challenges American families face daily, so we are in the best position to offer solutions to local problems.

—Mayor Douglas Palmer, Trenton, New Jersey, 2007

Essential Question Warmup

Throughout this unit, you studied the roles, responsibilities, and powers of State and local government. Use what you have learned and the quotations, data, and opinions above to answer the following questions. Then go to your **Essential Questions Journal.**

1. Which issues are best handled at the local, State, and federal levels, respectively?

2. How do taxes, spending, and various programs link different levels of government?

3. Is any level of government more responsive and democratic than any other level?

4. What are the advantages and disadvantages of centralizing power?

| **Essential Questions** **Journal** | To continue to build a response to the chapter Essential Question, go to your **Essential Questions Journal.** |

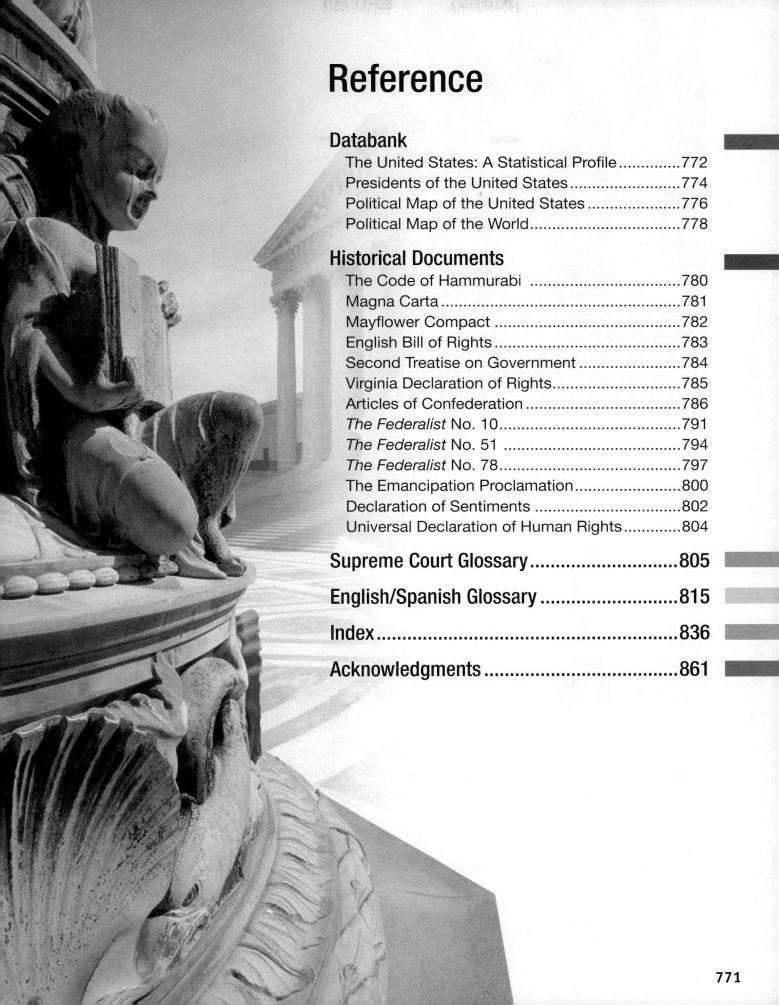

Reference

The United States: A Statistical Profile

State	Capital	Population (in thousands)					Land Area in Sq. Mi.	Population per Sq. Mi
		Year 2000	% Urban	African American	Hispanic Origin	% Foreign Born		
United States	Washington, D.C.	281,422	80.1	34,862	31,337	7.9	3,536,278	79.6
Alabama	Montgomery	4,447	70.1	1,139	45	1.1	50,750	87.6
Alaska	Juneau	627	41.5	24	25	4.5	570,374	1.1
Arizona	Phoenix	5,131	87.8	176	1,084	7.6	113,642	45.2
Arkansas	Little Rock	2,673	48.6	411	54	1.1	52,075	51.3
California	Sacramento	33,872	96.7	2,487	10,460	21.7	155,973	217.2
Colorado	Denver	4,301	84.0	176	604	4.3	103,729	41.5
Connecticut	Hartford	3,406	95.6	309	279	8.5	4,845	703.0
Delaware	Dover	784	81.6	149	28	3.3	1,955	401.0
Florida	Tallahassee	15,982	93.0	2,333	2,334	12.9	53,937	296.3
Georgia	Atlanta	8,186	68.9	2,236	240	2.7	57,919	141.3
Hawaii	Honolulu	1,212	73.1	34	95	14.7	6,423	188.7
Idaho	Boise	1,294	38.3	8	93	2.9	82,751	15.6
Illinois	Springfield	12,419	84.5	1,854	1,276	8.3	55,593	223.4
Indiana	Indianapolis	6,080	71.7	498	154	1.7	35,870	169.5
Iowa	Des Moines	2,926	44.6	58	62	1.6	55,875	52.4
Kansas	Topeka	2,688	56.4	157	148	2.5	81,823	32.9
Kentucky	Frankfort	4,042	48.3	288	35	0.9	39,732	101.7
Louisiana	Baton Rouge	4,469	75.2	1,415	119	2.1	43,566	102.6
Maine	Augusta	1,275	35.8	6	9	3.0	30,865	41.3
Maryland	Annapolis	5,296	92.7	1,454	199	6.6	9,775	541.8
Massachusetts	Boston	6,349	96.1	405	391	9.5	7,838	810.0
Michigan	Lansing	9,938	82.6	1,415	276	3.8	56,809	174.9
Minnesota	St. Paul	4,919	70.1	149	93	2.6	79,617	61.8
Mississippi	Jackson	2,845	35.9	1,010	24	0.8	46,914	60.6
Missouri	Jefferson City	5,595	68.0	617	91	1.6	68,898	81.2

State	Capital	Population (in thousands)					Land Area in Sq. Mi.	Population per Sq. Mi
		Year 2000	% Urban	African American	Hispanic Origin	% Foreign Born		
Montana	Helena	902	33.4	3	16	1.7	145,556	6.2
Nebraska	Lincoln	1,711	51.8	68	77	1.8	76,878	22.3
Nevada	Carson City	1,998	86.1	140	304	8.7	109,806	18.2
New Hampshire	Concord	1,236	60.2	9	20	3.7	8,969	137.8
New Jersey	Trenton	8,414	100.0	1,197	1,027	12.5	7,419	1,134.1
New Mexico	Santa Fe	1,819	57.0	46	708	5.3	121,364	15.0
New York	Albany	18,976	91.9	3,222	2,661	15.9	47,224	401.8
North Carolina	Raleigh	8,049	67.1	1,686	176	1.7	48,718	165.2
North Dakota	Bismarck	642	43.1	4	7	1.5	68,994	9.3
Ohio	Columbus	11,353	81.0	1,304	185	2.4	40,953	277.2
Oklahoma	Oklahoma City	3,451	60.5	262	137	2.1	68,679	50.2
Oregon	Salem	3,421	72.7	62	213	4.9	96,002	35.6
Pennsylvania	Harrisburg	12,281	84.5	1,170	326	3.1	44,820	274.0
Rhode Island	Providence	1,048	93.8	50	69	9.5	1,045	1,002.9
South Carolina	Columbia	4,012	70.0	1,157	54	1.4	30,111	133.2
South Dakota	Pierre	755	34.0	5	9	1.1	75,896	9.9
Tennessee	Nashville	5,689	67.8	913	67	1.2	41,219	138.0
Texas	Austin	20,852	84.5	2,470	6,045	9.0	261,914	79.6
Utah	Salt Lake City	2,233	76.7	19	151	3.4	82,168	27.2
Vermont	Montpelier	609	27.9	3	5	3.1	9,249	65.8
Virginia	Richmond	7,079	78.1	1,385	266	5.0	39,598	178.8
Washington	Olympia	5,894	82.9	204	377	6.6	66,581	88.5
West Virginia	Charleston	1,808	41.9	56	10	0.9	4,087	75.1
Wisconsin	Madison	5,364	67.8	293	140	2.5	54,314	98.8
Wyoming	Cheyenne	494	29.6	4	29	1.7	97,105	5.1
Washington, D.C.		572	100.0	319	38	9.7	61	9,377.0

George Washington   Zachary Taylor   Abraham Lincoln   Ulysses S. Grant   Chester A. Arthur

Presidents of the United States

Name	Party	State [a]	Entered Office	Age On Taking Office	Vice President(s)
George Washington (1732–1799)	Federalist	Virginia	1789	57	John Adams
John Adams (1735–1826)	Federalist	Massachusetts	1797	61	Thomas Jefferson
Thomas Jefferson (1743–1826)	Dem-Rep[b]	Virginia	1801	57	Aaron Burr/George Clinton
James Madison (1751–1836)	Dem-Rep	Virginia	1809	57	George Clinton/Elbridge Gerry
James Monroe (1758–1831)	Dem-Rep	Virginia	1817	58	Daniel D. Tompkins
John Q. Adams (1767–1848)	Dem-Rep	Massachusetts	1825	57	John C. Calhoun
Andrew Jackson (1767–1845)	Democrat	Tennessee (SC)	1829	61	John C. Calhoun/Martin Van Buren
Martin Van Buren (1782–1862)	Democrat	New York	1837	54	Richard M. Johnson
William H. Harrison (1773–1841)	Whig	Ohio (VA)	1841	68	John Tyler
John Tyler (1790–1862)	Democrat	Virginia	1841	51	none
James K. Polk (1795–1849)	Democrat	Tennessee (NC)	1845	49	George M. Dallas
Zachary Taylor (1784–1850)	Whig	Louisiana (VA)	1849	64	Millard Fillmore
Millard Fillmore (1800–1874)	Whig	New York	1850	50	none
Franklin Pierce (1804–1869)	Democrat	New Hampshire	1853	48	William R. King
James Buchanan (1791–1868)	Democrat	Pennsylvania	1857	65	John C. Breckinridge
Abraham Lincoln (1809–1865)	Republican	Illinois (KY)	1861	52	Hannibal Hamlin/Andrew Johnson[c]
Andrew Johnson (1808–1875)	Democrat	Tennessee (NC)	1865	56	none
Ulysses S. Grant (1822–1885)	Republican	Illinois (OH)	1869	46	Schuyler Colfax/Henry Wilson
Rutherford B. Hayes (1822–1893)	Republican	Ohio	1877	54	William A. Wheeler
James A. Garfield (1831–1881)	Republican	Ohio	1881	49	Chester A. Arthur
Chester A. Arthur (1829–1896)	Republican	New York (VT)	1881	51	none
Grover Cleveland (1837–1908)	Democrat	New York (NJ)	1885	47	Thomas A. Hendricks
Benjamin Harrison (1833–1901)	Republican	Indiana (OH)	1889	55	Levi P. Morton
Grover Cleveland (1837–1908)	Democrat	New York (NJ)	1893	55	Adlai E. Stevenson

William Howard Taft   Harry S Truman   Lyndon B. Johnson   Ronald Reagan   Barack Obama

Name	Party	State [a]	Entered Office	Age On Taking Office	Vice President(s)
William McKinley (1843–1901)	Republican	Ohio	1897	54	Garret A. Hobart/ Theodore Roosevelt
Theodore Roosevelt (1858–1919)	Republican	New York	1901	42	Charles W. Fairbanks
William H. Taft (1857–1930)	Republican	Ohio	1909	51	James S. Sherman
Woodrow Wilson (1856–1924)	Democrat	New Jersey (VA)	1913	56	Thomas R. Marshall
Warren G. Harding (1865–1923)	Republican	Ohio	1921	55	Calvin Coolidge
Calvin Coolidge (1872–1933)	Republican	Massachusetts (VT)	1923	51	Charles G. Dawes
Herbert Hoover (1874–1964)	Republican	California (IA)	1929	54	Charles Curtis
Franklin Roosevelt (1882–1945)	Democrat	New York	1933	51	John N. Garner/ Henry A. Wallace/Harry S Truman
Harry S Truman (1884–1972)	Democrat	Missouri	1945	60	Alben W. Barkley
Dwight D. Eisenhower (1890–1969)	Republican	New York (TX)	1953	62	Richard M. Nixon
John F. Kennedy (1917–1963)	Democrat	Massachusetts	1961	43	Lyndon B. Johnson
Lyndon B. Johnson (1908–1973)	Democrat	Texas	1963	55	Hubert H. Humphrey
Richard M. Nixon (1913–1994)	Republican	New York (CA)	1969	56	Spiro T. Agnew [d]/Gerald R. Ford [e]
Gerald R. Ford (1913–2006)	Republican	Michigan (NE)	1974	61	Nelson A. Rockefeller [f]
James E. Carter (1924–)	Democrat	Georgia	1977	52	Walter F. Mondale
Ronald W. Reagan (1911–2004)	Republican	California (IL)	1981	69	George H. W. Bush
George H.W. Bush (1924–)	Republican	Texas (MA)	1989	64	J. Danforth Quayle
William J. Clinton (1946–)	Democrat	Arkansas	1993	46	Albert Gore, Jr.
George W. Bush (1946–)	Republican	Texas	2001	54	Richard B. Cheney
Barack Obama (1961–)	Democrat	Illinois (HI)	2009	47	Joseph R. Biden

[a] State of residence when elected; if born in another State, that State in parentheses.
[b] Democratic-Republican
[c] Johnson, a War Democrat, was elected Vice-President on the coalition Union Party ticket.
[d] Resigned October 10, 1973.

[e] Nominated by Nixon, confirmed by Congress on December 6, 1973.
[f] Nominated by Ford, confirmed by Congress on December 19, 1974.

Political Map of the United States

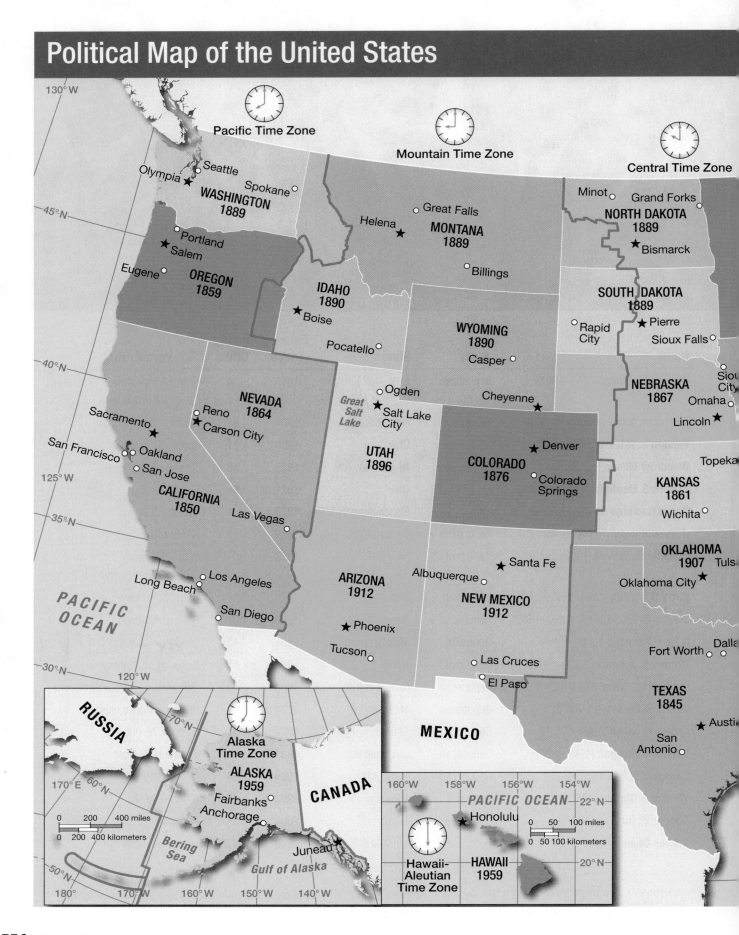

130° W

Pacific Time Zone

Mountain Time Zone

Central Time Zone

45° N

Olympia ★   Seattle ○   Spokane ○
WASHINGTON
1889

○ Great Falls
Helena ★   MONTANA
1889

Minot ○   Grand Forks ○
NORTH DAKOTA
1889
★ Bismarck

Portland ○
Salem ★
Eugene ○   OREGON
1859

IDAHO
1890
★ Boise

○ Billings

SOUTH DAKOTA
1889

40° N

Pocatello ○

WYOMING
1890
Casper ○

Rapid City ○   ★ Pierre
Sioux Falls ○

Sacramento ★

NEVADA
1864
Reno ○
★ Carson City

○ Ogden
Great Salt Lake   ★ Salt Lake City

Cheyenne ○
★

NEBRASKA
1867   Siou City ○
Omaha ○
Lincoln ★

San Francisco ○
Oakland ○
San Jose ○

UTAH
1896

COLORADO
1876
★ Denver
○ Colorado Springs

Topeka ○
KANSAS
1861

125° W

35° N

CALIFORNIA
1850   Las Vegas ○

Wichita ○

Long Beach ○   Los Angeles ○

ARIZONA
1912
★ Phoenix
Tucson ○

Albuquerque ○   ★ Santa Fe

NEW MEXICO
1912

OKLAHOMA
1907   Tuls
Oklahoma City ★

San Diego ○

PACIFIC OCEAN

Las Cruces ○
El Paso ○

Fort Worth ○   Dalla ○

30° N

120° W

MEXICO

TEXAS
1845
★ Austi
San Antonio ○

RUSSIA   70° N

Alaska Time Zone
ALASKA
1959
Fairbanks ○
Anchorage

CANADA

160° W 158° W 156° W 154° W
PACIFIC OCEAN   22° N
Honolulu ★   0 50 100 miles
0 50 100 kilometers

170° E   60° N

0 200 400 miles
0 200 400 kilometers

Bering Sea

50° N
180° 170° W 160° W 150° W 140° W

Juneau ★
Gulf of Alaska

Hawaii-Aleutian Time Zone

HAWAII
1959   20° N

DATABANK: Political Map of the United States

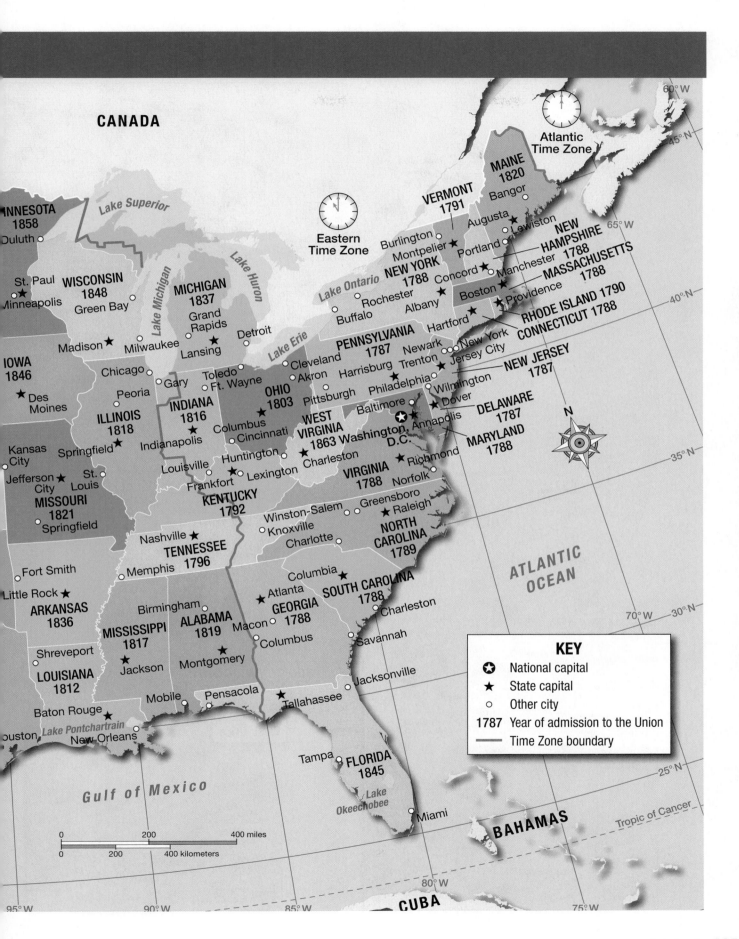

CANADA

MINNESOTA
1858
Duluth

Lake Superior

Lake Michigan

Lake Huron

MICHIGAN
1837

St. Paul
Minneapolis

WISCONSIN
1848

Green Bay

Madison
Milwaukee

Grand
Rapids

Detroit

Lansing

IOWA
1846

Chicago

Gary

Toledo

Ft. Wayne

Lake Erie

Eastern
Time Zone

Atlantic
Time Zone

MAINE
1820

Bangor

VERMONT
1791

Augusta

Lewiston

NEW
HAMPSHIRE
1788

65° W

Burlington

Montpelier

Portland

Concord

Manchester

MASSACHUSETTS
1788

NEW YORK
1788

Boston

Providence

RHODE ISLAND 1790

Des
Moines

Peoria

Rochester

Albany

Hartford

CONNECTICUT 1788

Buffalo

40° N

ILLINOIS
1818

INDIANA
1816

OHIO
1803

PENNSYLVANIA
1787

Newark

New York

NEW JERSEY
1787

Kansas
City

Springfield

Indianapolis

Columbus

Akron

Cleveland

Harrisburg

Trenton

Jersey City

Pittsburgh

Philadelphia

Wilmington

Cincinnati

WEST
VIRGINIA
1863

Baltimore

Dover

DELAWARE
1787

Jefferson
City

St.
Louis

Louisville

Huntington

Washington,
D.C.

Annapolis

MARYLAND
1788

N

MISSOURI
1821

Frankfort

Lexington

Charleston

Richmond

Springfield

KENTUCKY
1792

VIRGINIA
1788

Norfolk

35° N

Winston-Salem

Greensboro

Raleigh

Fort Smith

Knoxville

NORTH
CAROLINA
1789

Nashville

Charlotte

TENNESSEE
1796

Little Rock

Memphis

Columbia

ATLANTIC
OCEAN

ARKANSAS
1836

Birmingham

Atlanta

SOUTH CAROLINA
1788

70° W

30° N

MISSISSIPPI
1817

ALABAMA
1819

Macon

GEORGIA
1788

Charleston

Shreveport

Columbus

Savannah

Jackson

Montgomery

LOUISIANA
1812

Mobile

Pensacola

Jacksonville

Baton Rouge

Tallahassee

Houston

Lake Pontchartrain

New Orleans

Tampa

FLORIDA
1845

25° N

Gulf of Mexico

Lake
Okeechobee

Miami

BAHAMAS

Tropic of Cancer

KEY

⊛ National capital

★ State capital

○ Other city

1787 Year of admission to the Union

— Time Zone boundary

0   200   400 miles
0   200   400 kilometers

95° W   90° W   85° W   80° W   75° W

CUBA

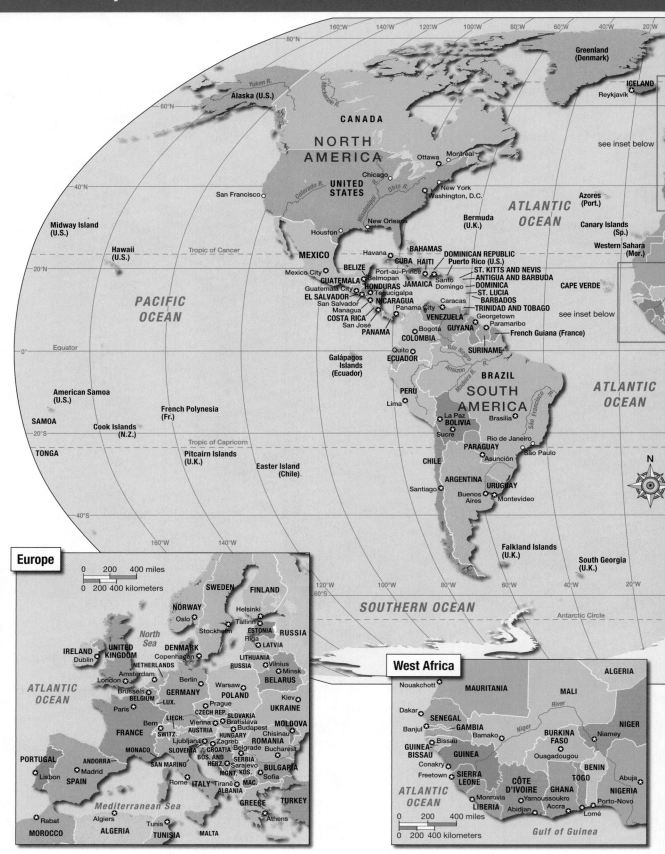

Europe

0   200   400 miles
0   200 400 kilometers

West Africa

0   200   400 miles
0   200 400 kilometers

KEY
- National capital
- Other city

Middle East

▶ The Code of Hammurabi

The Code of Hammurabi, believed to date before 1750 B.C., is a series of laws decreed by Hammurabi, the ruler of Babylon when that ancient city was at the peak of its power. Inscribed on stone columns over seven feet high, the Code consisted of 280 sections. Selected sections are excerpted below:

- If a man practice (robbery) and be captured, that man shall be put to death. . . .
- If a man has come forward in a lawsuit for the witnessing of false things, and has not proved the thing that he said, if that lawsuit is a capital case, that man shall be put to death. If he came forward for witnessing about corn or silver, he shall bear the penalty (which applies to) that case.
- If a man has concealed in his house a lost slave or slave-girl belonging to the Palace or to a subject, and has not brought him (or her) out at the proclamation of the Crier, the owner of the house shall be put to death.
- If a fire has broken out in a man's house, and a man who has gone to extinguish it has cast his eye on the property of the owner of the house and has taken the property of the owner of the house, that man shall be thrown into the fire.
- If a man is subject to a debt bearing interest, and Adad (the Weather-god) has saturated his field or a high flood has carried (its crop) away, or because of lack of water he has not produced corn in that field, in that year he shall not return any corn to (his) creditor. He shall . . . not pay interest for that year.
- If a man has donated field, orchard or house to his favourite heir and has written a sealed document for him (confirming this), after the father has gone to his doom, when the brothers share he (the favorite heir) shall take the gift that his father gave him, and apart from that they shall share equally in the property of the paternal estate.
- If an artisan has taken a child for bringing up, and has taught him his manual skill, (the child) shall not be (re)claimed. If he has not taught him his manual skill, that pupil may return to his father's house.
- If a man aid a male or female slave . . . to escape from the city gates, he shall be put to death. . . .

▲ Stone pillar with Hammurabi's Code

- If a man be in debt and sell his wife, son, or daughter, or bind them over to service, for three years they shall work in the house of the purchaser or master; in the fourth year they shall be given their freedom. . . .
- If a builder has made a house for a man but has not made his work strong, so that the house he made falls down and causes the death of the owner of the house, that builder shall be put to death. If it causes the death of the son of the owner of the house, they shall kill the son of the builder.
- If a man would put away [divorce] his wife who has not borne him children, he shall give her money to the amount of her marriage settlement and he shall make good to her the dowry which she brought from her father's house and then he may put her away.
- If a son has struck his father, they shall cut off his hand.
- If a man has destroyed the eye of a man of the "gentleman" class, they shall destroy his eye. If he has broken a gentleman's bone, they shall break his bone. If he has destroyed the eye of a commoner or broken a bone of a commoner, he shall pay one mina [about $300] of silver. If he has destroyed the eye of a gentleman's slave, he shall pay half the slave's price.
- If a gentleman's slave strikes the cheek of a man of the "gentleman" class, they shall cut off (the slave's) ear.
- If a gentleman strikes a gentleman in a free fight and inflicts an injury on him, that man shall swear "I did not strike him deliberately," and he shall pay the surgeon.

Analyzing Documents

Use the passage on this page to answer the following questions.
1. With what general topics is the Code concerned?
2. Why do you suppose the laws were written down and codified?

Magna Carta

Signed by England's King John in 1215, the Magna Carta (Great Charter) was the first document to limit the power of England's monarchs. The Magna Carta established the principle that rulers are subject to law—a major step toward constitutional government.

We . . . by this our present Charter have confirmed, for us and our heirs forever—

1. That the English Church shall be free and shall have her whole rights and her liberties inviolable. . . .

9. Neither we nor our bailiffs shall seize any land or rent for any debt while the chattels [possessions] of the debtor are sufficient for the payment of the debt. . . .

12. No scutage [tax] or aid [subsidy] shall be imposed in our kingdom, unless by the common counsel of our kingdom. . . .

14. And also to have the common council of the kingdom to assess and aid, . . . and for the assessing of scutages, we will cause to be summoned the archbishops, bishops, abbots, earls, and great barons, . . . And besides, we will cause to be summoned . . . all those who hold of us in chief, at a certain day . . . and to a certain place; and in all the letters of summons, we will express the cause of the summons; and the summons being thus made, the business shall proceed on the day appointed, according to the counsel of those who shall be present, although all who have been summoned have not come.

39. No free-man shall be seized, or imprisoned, or dispossessed, or outlawed, or in any way destroyed; nor will we condemn him, nor will we commit him to prison, excepting by the legal judgment of his peers, or by the laws of the land.

40. To none will we sell, to none will we deny, to none will we delay right or justice.

▲ King John signs the Magna Carta.

41. All merchants shall have safety and security in coming into England, and going out of England, and in staying and in traveling through England . . . to buy and sell, . . . excepting in the time of war, and if they be of a country at war against us. . . .

42. It shall be lawful to any person to go out of our kingdom . . . and to return safely and securely, by land or by water, saving his allegiance to us, unless it be in time of war, for some short space, for the common good of the kingdom. . . .

52. If any have been disseised [deprived] or dispossessed by us, without a legal verdict of their peers, of their lands, castles, liberties, or rights, we will immediately restore these things to them. . . .

63. Wherefore our will is . . . that the men in our kingdom have and hold the aforesaid liberties, rights, and concessions . . . fully and entirely, to them and their heirs, . . . in all things and places forever.

Analyzing Documents

Use the passage on this page to answer the following questions.

1. What basic American right has its origins in Article 39 of the Magna Carta?
2. Which article provides the basis for the Fifth Amendment to the Constitution, which states that no person can "be deprived of life, liberty, or property, without due process of law"?
3. What limits does Article 12 place on the king's power to tax?

▶ Mayflower Compact

The *Mayflower* landed in present-day Cape Cod in November, 1620. The document that became know as the Mayflower Compact contained the first written laws for the new land and established a government created by those who were to be governed. It was signed by 41 adult men.

In the name of God, Amen. We, whose names are underwritten, the Loyal Subjects of our dread Sovereign Lord, King James, by the Grace of God, of England, France and Ireland, King, Defender of the Faith, e&.

Having undertaken for the Glory of God, and Advancement of the Christian Faith, and the Honour of our King and Country, a voyage to plant the first colony in the northern parts of Virginia; do by these presents, solemnly and mutually in the Presence of God and one of another, covenant and combine ourselves together into a civil Body Politick, for our better Ordering and Preservation, and Furtherance of the Ends aforesaid; And by Virtue hereof to enact, constitute, and frame, such just and equal Laws, Ordinances, Acts, Constitutions and Offices, from time to time, as shall be thought most meet and convenient for the General good of the Colony; unto which we promise all due submission and obedience.

In Witness whereof we have hereunto subscribed our names at Cape Cod the eleventh of November, in the Reign of our Sovereign Lord, King James of England, France and Ireland, the eighteenth, and of Scotland the fifty-fourth. Anno Domini, 1620.

Analyzing Documents

Use the passage on this page to answer the following questions.
1. What goals are laid out in this document?
2. Why was this document necessary?
3. What might have happened if the Mayflower Compact had not be written?

▲ Selected signatures on the Mayflower Compact

Signing the Mayflower Compact aboard ship ▶

▶ English Bill of Rights

When the Catholic king, James II, was forced from the English throne in 1688, Parliament offered the crown to his Protestant daughter Mary and her husband, William of Orange. Parliament, however, insisted that William and Mary submit to a bill of rights. This document sums up the powers that Parliament had been seeking since the Petition of Right in 1628.

Whereas, the late King James II . . . did endeavor to subvert and exirpate [eliminate] the Protestant religion and the laws and liberties of this kingdom . . . and whereas the said late king James II having abdicated the government, and the throne being vacant. . . .

The said Lords [Parliament] . . . being now assembled in a full and free representative [body] of this nation . . . do in the first place . . . declare

- That the pretended [untruthfully claimed] power of suspending the laws or the execution of laws by regal authority without consent of Parliament is illegal;

- That the pretended power of dispensing with laws or the execution of laws by regal authority, as it hath been assumed and exercised of late, is illegal; . . .

- That levying money for or to the use of the Crown by pretence of prerogative, without grant of Parliament, for longer time, or in other manner than the same is or shall be granted, is illegal;

- That it is the right of the subjects to petition the king, and all commitments and prosecutions for such petitioning are illegal;

- That the raising or keeping a standing army within the kingdom in time of peace, unless it be with consent of Parliament, is against law;

- That the subjects which are Protestants may have arms for their defence suitable to their conditions and as allowed by law;

- That election of members of Parliament ought to be free;

- That the freedom of speech and debates or proceedings in Parliament ought not to be impeached or questioned in any court or place out of Parliament;

- That excessive bail ought not to be required, nor excessive fines imposed, nor cruel and unusual punishments inflicted;

- That jurors ought to be duly impaneled and returned, and jurors which pass upon men in trials for high treason ought to be freeholders [property owners with unconditional rights];

▲ Mary and William

- That all grants and promises of fines and forfeitures of particular persons before conviction are illegal and void;

- And that for redress of all grievances, and for the amending, strengthening and preserving of the laws, Parliaments ought to be held frequently.

Analyzing Documents

Use the passage on this page to answer the following questions.
1. Which rights and freedoms listed above do you think are most important? Explain your choices.
2. Review the American Declaration of Independence. What similarities do you see between the two documents?
3. What is the importance of this document for American government?

▶Second Treatise on Government

In 1690, English philosopher John Locke (1632–1704) produced two treatises (essays) on government. In his second treatise, he discussed the responsibilities of a government and claimed that the people have the right to overthrow an unjust government. Locke's ideas greatly influenced Thomas Jefferson and other supporters of the American Revolution. In this selection, Locke explains why people form governments.

To understand political power aright . . . we must consider what estate all men are naturally in, and that is, a state of perfect freedom to order their actions, and dispose of their possessions and persons as they think fit, within the bounds of the law of nature, without asking leave or depending upon the will of any other man. . . .

Men being . . . by nature, all free, equal and independent, no one can be put out of this estate and subjected to the political power of another without his own consent, which is done by agreeing with other men, to join and unite into a community for their comfortable, safe and peaceable living, one amongst another, in a secure enjoyment of their properties, and a greater security against any that are not of it. . . .

When any number of men have, by the consent of every individual, made a community, they have thereby made that community one body, with a power to act as one body, which is only by the will and determination of the majority. . . . . And thus every man, by consenting with others to make one body politic under one government, puts himself under an obligation to every one in that society to submit to the determination of the majority, and to be concluded by it. . . .

If man in the state of nature . . . be absolute lord of his own person and possessions, equal to the greatest and

▲ John Locke

subject to nobody, why will he part with his freedom, this empire, and subject himself to the dominion and control of any other power? . . . It is obvious to answer that though in the state of nature he hath such a right, yet the enjoyment of it is very uncertain and constantly exposed to the invasion of others; for all being kings as much as he, every man his equal, . . . the enjoyment of the property he has in this state is very unsafe, very insecure. This makes him willing to quit this condition which, however free, is full of fears and continual dangers; and it is not without reason that he seeks out and is willing to join in society with others . . . for the mutual preservation of their lives, liberties and estates, which I call by the general name—property.

The great and chief end, therefore, of men uniting into commonwealths, and putting themselves under government, is the preservation of their property. . . .

Analyzing Documents

Use the passage on this page to answer the following questions.

1. According to Locke, what freedoms did people have before the founding of governments?
2. What are the potential dangers of a person living in what Locke called "perfect freedom"?
3. According to Locke, how are governments formed?
4. What trade-off does Locke say occurs when people live under government?

▶Virginia Declaration of Rights

The Virginia Declaration of Rights was largely the work of George Mason (1725–1792), one of Virginia's wealthiest planters and a neighbor and friend of George Washington. The Declaration was adopted unanimously by the Virginia Convention of Delegates on June 12, 1776, and was later incorporated within the Virginia State Constitution. It influenced a number of later documents, including the Declaration of Independence and the Bill of Rights.

A declaration of rights made by the representatives of the good people of Virginia, assembled in full and free convention; which rights do pertain to them and their posterity, as the basis and foundation of government.

I That all men are by nature equally free and independent, and have certain inherent rights, of which, when they enter into a state of society, they cannot, by any compact, deprive or divest their posterity; namely, the enjoyment of life and liberty, with the means of acquiring and possessing property, and pursuing and obtaining happiness and safety.

II That all power is vested in, and consequently derived from, the people; that magistrates are their trustees and servants, and at all times amenable to them.

III That government is, or ought to be, instituted for the common benefit, protection, and security of the people, nation or community; of all the various modes and forms of government that is best, which is capable of producing the greatest degree of happiness and safety and is most effectually secured against the danger of maladministration; and that, whenever any government shall be found inadequate or contrary to these purposes, a majority of the community hath an indubitable, unalienable, and indefeasible right to reform, alter or abolish it, in such manner as shall be judged most conducive to the public weal.

IV That no man, or set of men, are entitled to exclusive or separate emoluments or privileges from the community, but in consideration of public services; which, not being descendible, neither ought the offices of magistrate, legislator, or judge be hereditary.

V That the legislative and executive powers of the state should be separate and distinct from the judicative; and, that the members of the two first may be restrained from oppression by feeling and participating the burthens of the people, they should, at fixed periods, be reduced to a private station, return into that body from which they were originally taken, and the vacancies be supplied by frequent, certain, and regular elections in which all, or any part of the former members, to be again eligible, or ineligible, as the laws shall direct.

VI That elections of members to serve as representatives of the people in assembly ought to be free; and that all men, having sufficient evidence of permanent common interest with, and attachment to, the community have the right of suffrage and cannot be taxed or deprived of their property for public uses without their own consent or that of their representatives so elected, nor bound by any law to which they have not, in like manner, assented, for the public good.

VII That all power of suspending laws, or the execution of laws, by any authority without consent of the representatives of the people is injurious to their rights and ought not to be exercised.

VIII That in all capital or criminal prosecutions a man hath a right to demand the cause and nature of his accusation to be confronted with the accusers and witnesses, to call for evidence in his favor, and to a speedy trial by an impartial jury of his vicinage, without whose unanimous consent he cannot be found guilty, nor can he be compelled to give evidence against himself; that no man be deprived of his liberty except by the law of the land or the judgement of his peers.

IX That excessive bail ought not to be required, nor excessive fines imposed; nor cruel and unusual punishments inflicted.

X That general warrants, whereby any officer or messenger may be commanded to search suspected places without evidence of a fact committed, or to seize any person or persons not named, or whose offense is not

George Mason

particularly described and supported by evidence, are grievous and oppressive and ought not to be granted.

XI That in controversies respecting property and in suits between man and man, the ancient trial by jury is preferable to any other and ought to be held sacred.

XII That the freedom of the press is one of the greatest bulwarks of liberty and can never be restrained but by despotic governments.

XIII That a well regulated militia, composed of the body of the people, trained to arms, is the proper, natural, and safe defense of a free state; that standing armies, in time of peace, should be avoided as dangerous to liberty; and that, in all cases, the military should be under strict subordination to, and be governed by, the civil power.

XIV That the people have a right to uniform government; and therefore, that no government separate from, or independent of, the government of Virginia, ought to be erected or established within the limits thereof.

XV That no free government, or the blessings of liberty, can be preserved to any people but by a firm adherence to justice, moderation, temperance, frugality, and virtue and by frequent recurrence to fundamental principles.

XVI That religion, or the duty which we owe to our Creator and the manner of discharging it, can be directed by reason and conviction, not by force or violence; and therefore, all men are equally entitled to the free exercise of religion, according to the dictates of conscience; and that it is the mutual duty of all to practice Christian forbearance, love, and charity towards each other.

Analyzing Documents

Use the passage on these pages to answer the following questions.
1. What similarities do you see in language and ideas between the Virginia Declaration of Rights and the Declaration of Independence? Between the Virginia Declaration of Rights and the Bill of Rights?
2. Choose one of the articles from the Virginia Declaration and explain the importance of the right that it describes using examples from your reading and general knowledge.

▶Articles of Confederation

The Articles of Confederation were approved on November 15, 1777, and were in effect from March 1, 1781, when they were finally ratified by all 13 States, until March 4, 1789. They established a weak central government, which led to conflicts among the States. Demand soon grew for a stronger central government, leading to the creation of the United States Constitution.

To all to whom these Presents shall come, we the undersigned Delegates of the States affixed to our Names send greeting. Whereas the Delegates of the United States of America in Congress assembled did on the fifteenth day of November in the Year of our Lord One Thousand Seven Hundred and Seventy seven, and in the Second Year of the Independence of America agree to certain articles of Confederation and perpetual Union between the States of New Hampshire, Massachusetts Bay, Rhode Island and Providence Plantations, Connecticut, New York, New Jersey, Pennsylvania, Delaware, Maryland, Virginia, North Carolina, South Carolina and Georgia in the Words following, viz. "Articles of Confederation and perpetual Union between the states of New Hampshire, Massachusetts Bay, Rhode Island and Providence Plantations, Connecticut, New York, New Jersey, Pennsylvania, Delaware, Maryland, Virginia, North Carolina, South Carolina and Georgia.

[ART. I.] The Stile of this confederacy shall be "The United States of America."

[ART. II.] Each state retains its sovereignty, freedom and independence, and every Power, Jurisdiction and right, which is not by this confederation expressly delegated to the United States, in Congress assembled.

[ART. III.] The said states hereby severally enter into a firm league of friendship with each other, for their common defence, the security of their Liberties, and their mutual and general welfare, binding themselves to assist each other, against all force offered to, or attacks made upon them, or any of them, on account of religion, sovereignty, trade, or any other pretence whatever.

[ART. IV.] The better to secure and perpetuate mutual friendship and intercourse among the people of the different states in this union, the free inhabitants of each of these states, paupers, vagabonds and fugitives from

Justice excepted, shall be entitled to all privileges and immunities of free citizens in the several states; and the people of each state shall have free ingress and regress to and from any other state, and shall enjoy therein all the privileges of trade and commerce, subject to the same duties, impositions and restrictions as the inhabitants thereof respectively, provided that such restriction shall not extend so far as to prevent the removal of property imported into any state, to any other state of which the Owner is an inhabitant; provided also that no imposition, duties or restriction shall be laid by any state, on the property of the united states, or either of them.

If any Person guilty of, or charged with treason, felony, or other high misdemeanor in any state, shall flee from Justice, and be found in any of the united states, he shall upon demand of the Governor or executive power, of the state from which he fled, be delivered up and removed to the state having jurisdiction of his offence.

Full faith and credit shall be given in each of these states to the records, acts and judicial proceedings of the courts and magistrates of every other state.

[ART. V.] For the more convenient management of the general interests of the united states, delegates shall be annually appointed in such manner as the legislature of each state shall direct, to meet in Congress on the first Monday in November, in every year, with a power reserved to each state, to recall its delegates, or any of them, at any time within the year, and to send others in their stead, for the remainder of the Year.

No state shall be represented in Congress by less than two, nor by more than seven Members; and no person shall be capable of being a delegate for more than three years in any term of six years; nor shall any person, being a delegate, be capable of holding any office under the united states, for which he, or another for his benefit receives any salary, fees or emolument of any kind.

Each state shall maintain its own delegates in a meeting of the states, and while they act as members of the committee of the states.

In determining questions in the united states, in Congress assembled, each state shall have one vote.

Freedom of speech and debate in Congress shall not be impeached or questioned in any Court, or place out of Congress, and the members of congress shall be protected in their persons from arrests and imprisonments, during the time of their going to and from, and attendance on congress, except for treason, felony, or breach of the peace.

[ART. VI.] No state without the Consent of the united states in congress assembled, shall send any embassy to, or receive any embassy from, or enter into any conference, agreement, or alliance or treaty with any King, prince or state; nor shall any person holding any office of profit or trust under the united states, or any of them, accept of any present, emolument, office or title of any kind whatever from any king, prince or foreign state; nor shall the united states in congress assembled, or any of them, grant any title of nobility.

No two or more states shall enter into any treaty, confederation or alliance whatever between them, without the consent of the united states in congress assembled, specifying accurately the purposes for which the same is to be entered into, and how long it shall continue.

No state shall lay any imposts or duties, which may interfere with any stipulations in treaties, entered into by the united states in congress assembled, with any king, prince or state, in pursuance of any treaties already proposed by congress, to the courts of France and Spain.

No vessels of war shall be kept up in time of peace by any state, except such number only, as shall be deemed necessary by the united states in congress assembled, for the defence of such state, or its trade; nor shall any body of forces be kept up by any state, in time of peace, except such number only, as in the judgment of the united states, in congress assembled, shall be deemed requisite to garrison the forts necessary for the defence of such state; but every state shall always keep up a well regulated and disciplined militia, sufficiently armed and accounted, and shall provide and constantly have ready for use, in public stores, a due number of field pieces and tents, and a proper quantity of arms, ammunition and camp equipage.

No state shall engage in any war without the consent of the united states in congress assembled, unless such state be actually invaded by enemies, or shall have received certain advice of a resolution being formed by some nation of Indians to invade such state and the danger is so imminent as not to admit of a delay, till the united states in congress assembled can be consulted: nor shall any state grant commissions to any ships or vessels of war, nor letters of marque or reprisal, except it be after a declaration of war by the united states in congress assembled, and then only against the kingdom or state and the subjects thereof, against which war has been so declared, and under such regulations as shall be established by the united states in congress assembled, unless such state be infested by pirates, in which case vessels of war may be fitted out for that occasion, and kept so long as the danger shall continue, or until the united states in congress assembled shall determine otherwise.

[ART. VII.] When land-forces are raised by any state for the common defence, all officers of or under the rank of colonel, shall be appointed by the legislature of each state respectively by whom such forces shall be raised, or in such manner as such state shall direct, and all vacancies shall be filled up by the state which first made the appointment.

[ART. VIII.] All charges of war, and all other expences that shall be incurred for the common defence or general welfare, and allowed by the united states in congress assembled, shall be defrayed out of a common treasury, which shall be supplied by the several states, in proportion to the value of all land within each state, granted to or surveyed for any Person, as such land and the buildings and improvements thereon shall be estimated according to such mode as the united states in congress assembled, shall from time to time direct and appoint. The taxes for paying that proportion shall be laid and levied by the authority and direction of the legislatures of the several states within the time agreed upon by the united states in congress assembled.

[ART. IX.] The united states in congress assembled, shall have the sole and exclusive right and power of determining on peace and war, except in the cases mentioned in the sixth article—of sending and receiving ambassadors—entering into treaties and alliances, provided that no treaty of commerce shall be made whereby the legislative power of the respective states shall be restrained from imposing such imposts and duties on foreigners, as their own people are subjected to, or from prohibiting the exportation or importation of any species of goods or commodities whatsoever—of establishing rules for deciding in all cases, what captures on land or water shall be legal, and in what manner prizes taken by land or naval forces in the service of the united states shall be divided or appropriated—of granting letters of marque and reprisal in times of peace—appointing courts for the trial of piracies and felonies committed on the high seas and establishing courts for receiving and determining finally appeals in all cases of captures, provided that no member of congress shall be appointed a judge of any of the said courts.

The united states in congress assembled shall also be the last resort on appeal in all disputes and differences now subsisting or that hereafter may arise between two or more states concerning boundary, jurisdiction or any other cause whatever; which authority shall always be exercised in the manner following. Whenever the legislative or executive authority or lawful agent [of any] state in controversy with another shall present a petition to congress stating the matter in question and praying for a hearing, notice thereof shall be given by order of congress to the legislative or executive authority of the other state in controversy, and a day assigned for the appearance of the parties by their lawful agents, who shall then be directed to appoint by joint consent, commissioners or judges to constitute a court for hearing and determining the matter in question; but if they cannot agree, congress shall name three persons out of each of the united states, and from the list of such persons each party shall alternately strike out one, the petitioners beginning, until the number shall be reduced to thirteen; and from that number not less than seven, nor more than nine names as congress shall direct, shall in the presence of congress be drawn out by lot, and the persons whose names shall be so drawn or any five of them, shall be commissioners or judges, to hear and finally determine the controversy, so always

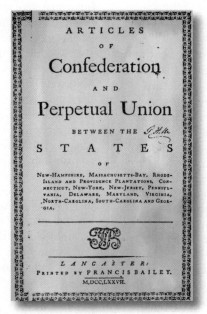

Cover of the Articles of Confederation

as a major part of the judges who shall hear the cause shall agree in the determination: and if either party shall neglect to attend at the day appointed, without shewing reasons, which congress shall judge sufficient, or being present shall refuse to strike, the congress shall proceed to nominate three persons out of each state, and the secretary of congress shall strike in behalf of such party absent or refusing; and the judgment and sentence of the court to be appointed, in the manner before prescribed, shall be final and conclusive; and if any of the parties shall refuse to submit to the authority of such court, or to appear to defend their claim or cause, the court shall nevertheless proceed to pronounce sentence, or judgment, which shall in like manner be final and decisive, the judgment or sentence and other proceedings being in either case transmitted to congress, and lodged among the acts of congress for the security of the parties concerned: provided that every commissioner, before he sits in judgment, shall take an oath to be administered by one of the judges of the supreme or superior court of the state, where the cause shall be tried, "well and truly to hear and determine the matter in question, according to the best of his judgment, without favour, affection or hope of reward;" provided also that no state shall be deprived of territory for the benefit of the united states.

All controversies concerning the private right of soil claimed under different grants of two or more states, whose jurisdictions as they may respect such lands, and the states which passed such grants are adjusted, the said grants or either of them being at the same time claimed to have originated antecedent to such settlement of jurisdiction, shall on the petition of either party to the congress of the united states, be finally determined as near as may be in the same manner as is before prescribed for deciding disputes respecting territorial jurisdiction between different states.

The united states in congress assembled shall also have the sole and exclusive right and power of regulating the alloy and value of coin struck by their own authority, or by that of the respective states—fixing the standard of weights and measures throughout the united states—regulating the trade and managing all affairs with the Indians, not members of any of the states, provided that the legislative right of any state within its own limits be not infringed or violated—establishing and regulating post-offices from one state to another, throughout all the united states, and exacting such postage on the papers passing thro' the same as may be requisite to defray the expences of the said office—appointing all officers of the land forces, in the service of the united states, excepting regimental officers—appointing all the officers of the naval forces, and commissioning all officers whatever in the service of the united states—making rules for the government and regulation of the said land and naval forces, and directing their operations.

The united states in congress assembled shall have authority to appoint a committee, to sit in the recess of congress, to be denominated "A Committee of the States," and to consist of one delegate from each state; and to appoint such other committees and civil officers as may be necessary for managing the general affairs of the united states under their direction—to appoint one of their number to preside, provided that no person be allowed to serve in the office of president more than one year in any term of three years; to ascertain the necessary sums of Money to be raised for the service of the united states, and to appropriate and apply the same for defraying the public expences—to borrow money, or emit bills on the credit of the united states, transmitting every half year to the respective states an account of the sums of money so borrowed or emitted—to build and equip a navy—to agree upon the number of land forces, and to make requisitions from each state for its quota, in proportion to the number of white inhabitants in such state; which requisition shall be binding, and thereupon the legislature of each state shall appoint the regimental officers, raise the men and clothe, arm and equip them in a soldier like manner, at the expence of the united states, and the officers and men so clothed, armed and equipped shall march to the place appointed, and within the time agreed on by the united states in congress assembled. But if the united states in congress assembled shall, on consideration of circumstances judge proper that any state should not raise men, or should raise a smaller number than its quota, and that any other state should raise a greater number of men than the quota thereof, such extra number shall be raised, officered, clothed, armed and equipped in the same manner as the quota of such state, unless the legislature of such state shall judge that such extra number cannot be safely spared out of the same, in which case they shall raise, officer, clothe, arm and equip as many of such extra number as they judge can be safely spared. And the officers and men so clothed, armed and equipped, shall march to the place appointed, and within the time agreed on by the united states in congress assembled.

The united states in congress assembled shall never engage in a war, nor grant letters of marque and reprisal in time of peace, nor enter into any treaties or alliances, nor coin money, nor regulate the value thereof, nor ascertain the sums and expences necessary for the defence and welfare of the united states, or any of them, nor emit bills, nor borrow money on the credit of the united states, nor appropriate money, nor agree upon the number of vessels of war, to be built or purchased, or the number of land or sea forces to be raised, nor appoint a commander in chief of the army or navy, unless nine states assent to the same: nor shall a question on any

other point, except for adjourning from day to day be determined, unless by the votes of a majority of the united states in congress assembled.

The congress of the united states shall have power to adjourn to any time within the year, and to any place within the united states, so that no period of adjournment be for a longer duration than the space of six Months, and shall publish the Journal of their proceedings monthly, except such parts thereof relating to treaties, alliances or military operations as in their judgment require secrecy; and the yeas and nays of the delegates of each state on any question shall be entered on the Journal, when it is desired by any delegate; and the delegates of a state, or any of them, at his or their request shall be furnished with a transcript of the said Journal, except such parts as are above excepted, to lay before the legislatures of the several states.

[ART. X.] The committee of the states, or any nine of them, shall be authorised to execute, in the recess of congress, such of the powers of congress as the united states in congress assembled, by the consent of nine states, shall from time to time think expedient to vest them with; provided that no power be delegated to the said committee, for the exercise of which, by the articles of confederation, the voice of nine states in the congress of the united states assembled is requisite.

[ART. XI.] Canada acceding to this confederation, and joining in the measures of the united states, shall be admitted into, and entitled to all the advantages of this union: but no other colony shall be admitted into the same, unless such admission be agreed to by nine states.

[ART. XII.] All bills of credit emitted, monies borrowed and debts contracted by, or under the authority of congress, before the assembling of the united states, in pursuance of the present confederation, shall be deemed and considered as a charge against the united states, for payment and satisfaction whereof the said united states, and the public faith are hereby solemnly pledged.

[ART. XIII.] Every state shall abide by the determinations of the united states in congress assembled, on all questions which by this confederation are submitted to them. And the Articles of this confederation shall be inviolably observed by every state, and the union shall be perpetual; nor shall any alteration at any time hereafter be made in any of them; unless such alteration be agreed to in a congress of the united states, and be afterwards confirmed by the legislatures of every state.

And whereas it hath pleased the Great Governor of the World to incline the hearts of the legislatures we respectively represent in congress, to approve of, and to authorize us to ratify the said articles of confederation and perpetual union. Know ye that we the undersigned delegates, by virtue of the power and authority to us given for that purpose, do by these presents, in the name and in behalf of our respective constituents, fully and entirely ratify and confirm each and every of the said articles of confederation and perpetual union, and all and singular the matters and things therein contained: And we do further solemnly plight and engage the faith of our respective constituents, that they shall abide by the determinations of the united states in congress assembled, on all questions, which by the said confederation are submitted to them. And that the articles thereof shall be inviolably observed by the states we respectively represent, and that the union shall be perpetual. In Witness whereof we have hereunto set our hands in Congress. Done at Philadelphia in the state of Pennsylvania the ninth Day of July in the Year of our Lord one Thousand seven Hundred and Seventy-eight, and in the third year of the independence of America.

JOSIAH BARTLETT
JOHN WENTWORTH JUNR
AUGUST 8TH 1778
On The Part & Behalf Of
The State Of New Hampshire

JOHN HANCOCK
SAMUEL ADAMS
ELBRIDGE GERRY
FRANCIS DANA
JAMES LOVELL
SAMUEL HOLTEN
On The Part And Behalf Of
The State Of Massachusetts Bay

WILLIAM ELLERY
HENRY MARCHANT
JOHN COLLINS
On The Part And Behalf
Of The State Of Rhode Island
And Providence Plantations

ROGER SHERMAN
SAMUEL HUNTINGTON
OLIVER WOLCOTT
TITUS HOSMER
ANDREW ADAMS
On The Part And Behalf Of
The State Of Connecticut

JAS DUANE
FRAS LEWIS
WM DUER.
GOUV MORRIS
On The Part And Behalf Of
The State Of New York

JNO WITHERSPOON
NATHL SCUDDER
On The Part And In Behalf Of
The State Of New Jersey.
Novr 26, 1778.—

ROBT MORRIS
DANIEL ROBERDEAU
JONA BAYARD SMITH.
WILLIAM CLINGAN
JOSEPH REED
22D JULY 1778
On The Part And Behalf Of
The State Of Pennsylvania

THO MCKEAN
FEBY 12 1779
JOHN DICKINSON
MAY 5TH 1779
NICHOLAS VAN DYKE,
On The Part & Behalf Of
The State Of Delaware

JOHN HANSON
MARCH 1 1781
DANIEL CARROLL DO
On The Part And Behalf
Of The State Of Maryland

RICHARD HENRY LEE
JOHN BANISTER
THOMAS ADAMS
JNO HARVIE
FRANCIS LIGHTFOOT LEE
On The Part And Behalf Of
The State Of Virginia

JOHN PENN
JULY 21ST 1778
CORNS HARNETT
JNO WILLIAMS
On The Part And Behalf
Of The State Of No Carolina

HENRY LAURENS
WILLIAM HENRY DRAYTON
JNO MATHEWS
RICHD HUTSON.
THOS HEYWARD JUNR
On The Part & Behalf Of
The State Of South Carolina

JNO WALTON
24TH JULY 1778
EDWD TELFAIR.
EDWD LANGWORTHY
On The Part And Behalf Of
The State Of Georgia

Analyzing Documents

Use the passage on these pages to answer the following questions.

1. What factors explain why the first government of the United States was a loose confederation of individual States?
2. List three reasons why the Articles of Confederation failed to establish a lasting government.
3. What do you think was the greatest flaw in the Articles? Why?

The Federalist No. 10

One of the 29 essays believed to have been written by James Madison, the tenth of *The Federalist* papers presents Madison's observations on dealing with the "mischiefs of faction" and the advantages of a republican (representative) form of government over that of a pure democracy. This essay was first published on November 23, 1787.

Among the numerous advantages promised by a well-constructed Union, none deserves to be more accurately developed than its tendency to break and control the violence of faction. The friend of popular governments never finds himself so much alarmed for their character and fate as when he contemplates their propensity to this dangerous vice. He will not fail, therefore, to set a due value on any plan which, without violating the principles to which he is attached, provides a proper cure for it. The instability, injustice, and confusion introduced into the public councils have, in truth, been the mortal diseases under which popular governments have everywhere perished; as they continue to be the favorite and fruitful topics from which the adversaries to liberty derive their most specious declamations.

The valuable improvements made by the American constitutions on the popular models, both ancient and modern, cannot certainly be too much admired; but it would be an unwarrantable partiality to contend that they have as effectually obviated the danger on this side, as was wished and expected. Complaints are everywhere heard from our most considerate and virtuous citizens, equally the friends of public and private faith, and of public and personal liberty, that our governments are too unstable, that the public good is disregarded in the conflicts of rival parties, and that measures are too often decided, not according to the rules of justice and the rights of the minor party, but by the superior force of an interested and overbearing majority. However anxiously we may wish that these complaints had no foundation, the evidence of known facts will not permit us to deny that they are in some degree true.

It will be found, indeed, on a candid review of our situation, that some of the distresses under which we labor have been erroneously charged on the operation of our governments; but it will be found, at the same time, that other causes will not alone account for many of our heaviest misfortunes; and, particularly, for that prevailing and increasing distrust of public engagements, and alarm for private rights, which are echoed from one end of the continent to the other. These must be chiefly, if not wholly, effects of the unsteadiness and injustice with which a factious spirit has tainted our public administrations.

By a faction, I understand a number of citizens, whether amounting to a majority or minority of the whole, who are united and actuated by some common impulse of passion, or of interest, adversed to the rights of other citizens, or to the permanent and aggregate interests of the community.

There are two methods of curing the mischiefs of faction: the one, by removing its causes; the other, by controlling its effects.

There are again two methods of removing the causes of faction: the one, by destroying the liberty which is essential to its existence; the other, by giving to every citizen the same opinions, the same passions, and the same interests.

It could never be more truly said than of the first remedy that it was worse than the disease. Liberty is to faction what air is to fire, an ailment without which it instantly expires. But it could not be less folly to abolish liberty, which is essential to political life, because it nourishes faction, than it would be to wish the annihilation of air,

Madison warned of "factions" leading to violence.

which is essential to animal life, because it imparts to fire its destructive agency.

The second expedient is as impracticable as the first would be unwise. As long as the reason of man continues fallible, and he is at liberty to exercise it, different opinions will be formed. As long as the connection subsists between his reason and his self-love, his opinions and his passions will have a reciprocal influence on each other; and the former will be objects to which the latter will attach themselves. The diversity in the faculties of men, from which the rights of property originate, is not less an insuperable obstacle to a uniformity of interests. The protection of these faculties is the first object of government. From the protection of different and unequal faculties of acquiring property, the possession of different degrees and kinds of property immediately results; and from the influence of these on the sentiments and views of the respective proprietors ensues a division of the society into different interests and parties.

The latent causes of faction are thus sown in the nature of man; and we see them everywhere brought into different degrees of activity, according to the different circumstances of civil society. A zeal for different opinions concerning religion, concerning government, and many other points, as well of speculation as of practice; an attachment of different leaders ambitiously contending for preeminence and power; or to persons of other descriptions whose fortunes have been interesting to the human passions, have, in turn, divided mankind into parties, inflamed them with mutual animosity, and rendered them much more disposed to vex and oppress each other than to cooperate for their common good. So strong is this propensity of mankind to fall into mutual animosities that, where no substantial occasion presents itself, the most frivolous and fanciful distinctions have been sufficient to kindle their unfriendly passions and excite their most violent conflicts. But the most common and durable source of factions has been the various and unequal distribution of property.

Those who hold and those who are without property have ever formed distinct interests in society. Those who are creditors and those who are debtors fall under a like discrimination. A landed interest, a manufacturing interest, a mercantile interest, a moneyed interest, with many lesser interests, grow up of necessity in civilized nations and divide them into different classes, actuated by different sentiments and views. The regulation of these various and interfering interests forms the principal task of modern legislation and involves the spirit of party and faction in the necessary and ordinary operations of the government.

No man is allowed to be a judge in his own cause, because his interest would certainly bias his judgment and, not improbably, corrupt his integrity. With equal, nay, with greater reason, a body of men are unfit to be both judges and parties at the same time; yet what are many of the most important acts of legislation but so many judicial determinations, not indeed concerning the rights of single persons, but concerning the rights of large bodies of citizens? And what are the different classes of legislators but advocates and parties to the causes which they determine? Is a law proposed concerning private debts? It is a question to which the creditors are parties on one side and the debtors on the other. Justice ought to hold the balance between them. Yet the parties are, and must be, themselves the judges; and the most numerous party or, in other words, the most powerful faction must be expected to prevail.

Shall domestic manufactures be encouraged, and in what degree, by restrictions on foreign manufactures? [These] are questions which would be differently decided by the landed and the manufacturing classes, and probably by neither with a sole regard to justice and the public good. The apportionment of taxes on the various descriptions of property is an act which seems to require the most exact impartiality; yet there is, perhaps, no legislative act in which greater opportunity and temptation are given to a predominant party to trample on the rules of justice. Every shilling with which they overburden the inferior number is a shilling saved to their own pockets.

It is in vain to say that enlightened statesmen will be able to adjust these clashing interests and render them all subservient to the public good. Enlightened statesmen will not always be at the helm. Nor, in many cases, can such an adjustment be made at all without taking into view indirect and remote considerations, which will rarely prevail over the immediate interest which one party may find in disregarding the rights of another or the good of the whole. The inference to which we are brought is that the causes of faction cannot be removed and that relief is only to be sought in the means of controlling its effects.

If a faction consists of less than a majority, relief is supplied by the republican principle, which enables the majority to defeat its sinister views by regular vote. It may clog the administration, it may convulse the society; but it will be unable to execute and mask its violence under the forms of the Constitution. When a majority is included in a faction, the form of popular government, on the other hand, enables it to sacrifice to its ruling passion or interest both the public good and the rights of other citizens. To secure the public good and private rights against the danger of such a faction, and at the same time to preserve the spirit and the form of popular government, is then the great object to which our inquiries are directed. Let me add that it is the great desideratum by which this form of government can be rescued from the opprobrium under which it has so long labored and be recommended to the esteem and adoption of mankind.

By what means is this object attainable? Evidently by one of two only. Either the existence of the same passion or interest in a majority at the same time must be prevented, or the majority, having such coexistent passion or interest, must be rendered, by their number and local situation, unable to concert and carry into effect schemes of oppression. If the impulse and the opportunity be suffered to coincide, we well know that neither moral nor religious motives can be relied on as an adequate control. They are not found to be such on the injustice and violence of individuals and lose their efficacy in proportion to the number combined together, that is, in proportion as their efficacy becomes needful.

From this view of the subject it may be concluded that a pure democracy, by which I mean a society consisting of a small number of citizens who assemble and administer the government in person, can admit of no cure for the mischiefs of faction. A common passion or interest will, in almost every case, be felt by a majority of the whole; a communication and concert result from the form of government itself; and there is nothing to check the inducements to sacrifice the weaker party or an obnoxious individual. Hence it is that such democracies have ever been spectacles of turbulence and contention; have ever been found incompatible with personal security or the rights of property; and have in general been as short in their lives as they have been violent in their deaths. Theoretic politicians, who have patronized this species of government, have erroneously supposed that by reducing mankind to a perfect equality in their political rights, they would, at the same time, be perfectly equalized and assimilated in their possessions, their opinions, and their passions.

A republic, by which I mean a government in which the scheme of representation takes place, opens a different prospect and promises the cure for which we are seeking. Let us examine the points in which it varies from pure democracy, and we shall comprehend both the nature of the cure and the efficacy which it must derive from the Union.

The two great points of difference between a democracy and a republic are: first, the delegation of the government, in the latter, to a small number of citizens elected by the rest; secondly, the greater number of citizens, and greater sphere of country, over which the latter may be extended.

The effect of the first difference is, on the one hand, to refine and enlarge the public views by passing them through the medium of a chosen body of citizens, whose wisdom may best discern the true interest of their country, and whose patriotism and love of justice will be least likely to sacrifice it to temporary or partial considerations. Under such a regulation, it may well happen that the public voice, pronounced by the representatives of the people, will be more consonant to the public good than if pronounced by the people themselves, convened for the purpose. On the other hand, the effect may be inverted. Men of factious tempers, of local prejudices, or of sinister designs may, by intrigue, by corruption, or by other means, first obtain the suffrages, and then betray the interests of the people. The question resulting is, whether small or extensive republics are more favorable to the election of proper guardians of the public weal; and it is clearly decided in favor of the latter by two obvious considerations:

In the first place, it is to be remarked that, however small the republic may be, the representatives must be raised to a certain number, in order to guard against the cabals of a few; and that, however large it may be, they must be limited to a certain number, in order to guard against the confusion of a multitude. Hence, the number of representatives in the two cases not being in proportion to that of the two constituents, and being proportionally greater in the small republic, it follows that, if the proportion of fit characters be not less in the large than in the small republic, the former will present a greater option, and consequently a greater probability of a fit choice.

In the next place, as each representative will be chosen by a greater number of citizens in the large than in the small republic, it will be more difficult for unworthy candidates to practice with success the vicious arts by which elections are too often carried; and the suffrages of the people being more free, will be more likely to center in men who possess the most attractive merit and the most diffusive and established character.

It must be confessed that in this, as in most other cases, there is a mean, on both sides of which inconveniences will be found to lie. By enlarging too much the number of electors, you render the representative too little acquainted with all their local circumstances and lesser interests; as by reducing it too much, you render him unduly attached to these and too little fit to comprehend and pursue great and national objects. The federal Constitution forms a happy combination in this respect: the great and aggregate interests being referred to the national, the local and particular to the state legislatures.

The other point of difference is the greater number of citizens and extent of territory which may be brought within the compass of republican than of democratic government; and it is this circumstance principally which renders factious combinations less to be dreaded in the former than in the latter. The smaller the society, the fewer probably will be the distinct parties and interests composing it; the fewer the distinct parties and interests, the more frequently will a majority be found of the same party; and the smaller the number of individuals composing a majority, and the smaller the compass within which they are placed, the more easily will they concert and execute their plans of oppression. Extend the sphere and you take in a greater variety of parties and interests; you make it less probable that a majority of the whole will have a common motive to invade the rights of other citizens; or if such a common motive exists, it will be more difficult for all who feel it to discover their own strength and to act in unison with each other. Besides other impediments, it may be remarked that, where there is a consciousness of unjust or dishonorable purposes, communication is always checked by distrust in proportion to the number whose concurrence is necessary.

Hence, it clearly appears that the same advantage which a republic has over a democracy, in controlling the effects of factions, is enjoyed by a large over a small republic—is enjoyed by the Union over the States composing it. Does the advantage consist in the substitution of representatives whose enlightened views and virtuous sentiments render them superior to local prejudices and to schemes of injustice? It will not be denied that the representation of the Union will be most likely to possess these requisite endowments. Does it consist in the greater security afforded by a greater variety of parties, against the event of any one party being able to outnumber and oppress the rest? In an equal degree does the increased variety of parties comprised within the Union increase this security? Does it, in fine, consist in the greater obstacles opposed to the concert and accomplishment of the secret wishes of an unjust and interested majority? Here, again, the extent of the Union gives it the most palpable advantage.

The influence of factious leaders may kindle a flame within their particular States but will be unable to spread a general conflagration through the other States. . . . A rage for paper money, for an abolition of debts, for an equal division of property, or for any other improper or wicked project will be less apt to pervade the whole body of the Union than a particular member of it; in the same

proportion as such a malady is more likely to taint a particular county or district than an entire State.

In the extent, and proper structure of the Union, therefore, we behold a republican remedy for the diseases most incident to republican government. And according to the degree of pleasure and pride we feel in being republicans, ought to be our zeal in cherishing the spirit and supporting the character of Federalists.

Analyzing Documents

Use the passage on these pages to answer the following questions.
1. What does Madison mean by "the mischief of faction"?
2. Why does Madison support a republican form of government over a pure democracy?
3. Do you agree with Madison's point of view? Explain your answer.

▶ *The Federalist* No. 51

In the passage below, first published on February 8, 1788, Madison discusses the need for a system of checks and balances to guard against "a gradual concentration of the same powers [of the new government] in the same department."

To what expedient, then, shall we finally resort, for maintaining in practice the necessary partition of power among the several departments as laid down in the Constitution? The only answer that can be given is that as all these exterior provisions are found to be inadequate the defect must be supplied, by so contriving the interior structure of the government as that its several constituent parts may, by their mutual relations, be the means of keeping each other in their proper places. Without presuming to undertake a full development of this important idea, I will hazard a few general observations which may perhaps place it in a clearer light, and enable us to form a more correct judgment of the principles and structure of the government planned by the convention.

In order to lay a due foundation for that separate and distinct exercise of the different powers of government, which to a certain extent is admitted on all hands to

be essential to the preservation of liberty, it is evident that each department should have a will of its own; and consequently should be so constituted that the members of each should have as little agency as possible in the appointment of the members of the others. Were this principle rigorously adhered to, it would require that all the appointments for the supreme executive, legislative, and judiciary magistracies should be drawn from the same fountain of authority, the people, through channels having no communication whatever with one another. Perhaps such a plan of constructing the several departments would be less difficult in practice than it may in contemplation appear. Some difficulties, however, and some additional expense would attend the execution of it. Some deviations, therefore, from the principle must be admitted. In the constitution of the judiciary department in particular, it might be inexpedient to insist rigorously on the principle; first, because peculiar qualifications being essential in the members, the primary consideration ought to be to select that mode of choice which best secures these qualifications; secondly, because the permanent tenure by which the appointments are held in that department must soon destroy all sense of dependence on the authority conferring them.

It is equally evident that the members of each department should be as little dependent as possible on those of the others for the emoluments annexed to their offices. Were the executive magistrate, or the judges, not independent of the legislature in this particular, their independence in every other would be merely nominal.

But the great security against a gradual concentration of the several powers in the same department consists in giving to those who administer each department the necessary constitutional means and personal motives to resist encroachments of the others. The provision for defense must in this, as in all other cases, be made commensurate to the danger of attack. Ambition must be made to counteract ambition. The interest of the man must be connected with the constitutional rights of the place. It may be a reflection on human nature that such devices should be necessary to control the abuses of government. But what is government itself but the greatest of all reflections on human nature? If men were angels, no government would be necessary. If angels were to govern men, neither external nor internal controls on government would be necessary. In framing a government which is to be administered by men

James Madison

over men, the great difficulty lies in this: You must first enable the government to control the governed; and in the next place, oblige it to control itself. A dependence on the people is, no doubt, the primary control on the government; but experience has taught mankind the necessity of auxiliary precautions.

This policy of supplying, by opposite and rival interests, the defect of better motives might be traced through the whole system of human affairs, private as well as public. We see it particularly displayed in all the subordinate distributions of power; where the constant aim is to divide and arrange the several offices in such a manner as that each may be a check on the other—that the private interest of every individual may be a sentinel over the public

rights. These inventions of prudence cannot be less requisite in the distribution of the supreme powers of the State.

But it is not possible to give to each department an equal power of self-defense. In republican government, the legislative authority necessarily predominates. The remedy for this inconveniency is to divide the legislature into different branches; and to render them, by different modes of election, and different principles of action, as little connected with each other as the nature of their common functions and their common dependence on the society will admit. It may even be necessary to guard against dangerous encroachments by still further precautions. As the weight of the legislative authority requires that it should be thus divided, the weakness of the executive may require, on the other hand, that it should be fortified. An absolute negative on the legislature appears, at first view, to be the natural defense with which the executive magistrate should be armed. But perhaps it would be neither altogether safe nor alone sufficient. On ordinary occasions it might not be exerted with the requisite firmness, and on extraordinary occasions it might be perfidiously abused. May not this defect of an absolute negative be supplied by some qualified connection between this weaker department and the weaker branch of the stronger department, by which the latter may be led to support the constitutional rights of the former, without being too much detached from the rights of its own department?

If the principles on which these observations are founded be just, as I persuade myself they are, and they be applied as a criterion to the several State constitutions, and to the federal Constitution, it will be found that if the latter does not perfectly correspond with them, the former are infinitely less able to bear such a test.

There are, moreover, two considerations particularly applicable to the federal system of America, which place that system in a very interesting point of view.

First. In a single republic, all the power surrendered by the people is submitted to the administration of a single government; and the usurpations are guarded against by a division of the government into distinct and separate departments. In the compound republic of America, the power surrendered by the people is first divided between two distinct governments, and then the portion allotted to each subdivided among distinct and separate departments. Hence a double security arises to the rights of the people. The different governments will control each other, at the same time that each will be controlled by itself.

Second. It is of great importance in a republic not only to guard the society against the oppression of its rulers, but to guard one part of the society against the injustice of the other part. Different interests necessarily exist in different classes of citizens. If a majority be united by a common interest, the rights of the minority will be insecure. There are but two methods of providing against this evil: The one by creating a will in the community independent of the majority—that is, of the society itself; the other, by comprehending in the society so many separate descriptions of citizens as will render an unjust combination of a majority of the whole very improbable, if not impracticable. The first method prevails in all governments possessing an hereditary or self appointed authority. This, at best, is but a precarious security; because a power independent of the society may as well espouse the unjust views of the major as the rightful interests of the minor party, and may possibly be turned against both parties. The second method will be exemplified in the federal republic of the United States. Whilst all authority in it will be derived from and dependent on the society, the society itself will be broken into so many parts, interests, and classes of citizens, that the rights of individuals, or of the minority, will be in little danger from interested combinations of the majority. In a free government the security for civil rights must be the same as that for religious rights. It consists in the one case in the multiplicity of interests, and in the other in the multiplicity of sects. The degree of security in both cases will depend on the number of interests and sects; and this may be presumed to depend on the extent of country and number of people comprehended under the same government. This view of the subject must particularly recommend a proper federal system to all the sincere and considerate friends of republican government, since it shows that in exact proportion as the territory of the Union may be formed into more circumscribed Confederacies, or States, oppressive combinations of a majority will be facilitated: the best security, under the republican forms, for the rights of every class of citizens, will be diminished; and consequently, the stability and independence of some member of the government, the only other security, must be proportionally increased. Justice is the end of government. It is the end of civil society. It ever has been and ever will be pursued until it be obtained, or until liberty be lost in the pursuit. In a society under the forms of which the stronger faction can readily unite and oppress the weaker, anarchy may as truly be said to reign as in a state of nature, where the weaker individual is not secured against the violence of the stronger: And as, in the latter state, even the stronger individuals are prompted by the uncertainty of their condition to submit to a government which may protect the weak as well as themselves. So, in the former state, will the more powerful factions or parties be gradually induced, by a like motive, to wish for a government which will protect all parties, the weaker as well as the more powerful. It can be little doubted that if the State of Rhode Island was separated from the Confederacy and left to itself, the insecurity of rights under the popular form of government within such narrow limits would be displayed by such reiterated oppressions of factious majorities that some power altogether independent of the people would soon be called for by the voice of the very factions whose misrule had proved the necessity of it. In the extended republic of the United States, and among the great variety of interests, parties, and sects which it embraces, a coalition of a majority of the whole society could seldom take place on any other principles than those of justice and the general good; whilst there being thus less danger to a minor from the will of the major party, there must be less pretext, also, to provide for the security of the former, by introducing into the government a will not dependent on the latter; or, in other words, a will independent of the society itself. It is no less certain that it is important, notwithstanding the contrary opinions which have been entertained, that the larger the society, provided it lie within a practicable sphere, the more duly capable it will be of self-government. And happily for the *republican* cause, the practicable sphere may be carried to a very great extent by a judicious modification and mixture of the *federal principle.*

Analyzing Documents

Use the passage on these pages to answer the following questions.
1. How will the new government guard against placing too much power in the hands of one individual or government body?
2. How will checks and balances be achieved in the new government?
3. What is the "double security" that Madison refers to in this passage?

▶ *The Federalist* No. 78

The Federalist papers were the brainchild of Alexander Hamilton, who conceived them and recruited James Madison and John Jay to the project. Hamilton is usually credited as the author of 51 of the 85 essays in the collection. Here, he discusses the national judiciary to be established by Article III in the proposed Constitution. He emphasizes the vital need for an independent judiciary and its role in the interpretation of laws and the determination of their constitutionality. First published April 11, 1788.

We proceed now to an examination of the judiciary department of the proposed government. In unfolding the defects of the existing Confederation, the utility and necessity of a federal judicature have been clearly pointed out. It is the less necessary to recapitulate the considerations there urged as the propriety of the institution in the abstract is not disputed; the only questions which have been raised being relative to the manner of constituting it, and to its extent. To these points, therefore, our observations shall be confined.

The manner of constituting it seems to embrace these several objects: 1st. The mode of appointing the judges. 2nd. The tenure by which they are to hold their places. 3rd. The partition of the judiciary authority between different courts and their relations to each other.

First. As to the mode of appointing the judges: this is the same with that of appointing the officers of the Union in general and has been so fully discussed in the two last numbers that nothing can be said here which would not be useless repetition.

Second. As to the tenure by which the judges are to hold their places: this chiefly concerns their duration in office, the provisions for their support, the precautions for their responsibility.

According to the plan of the convention, all judges who may be appointed by the United States are to hold their offices during good behavior; which is conformable to the most approved of the State constitutions, and among the rest, to that of this State. Its propriety having been drawn into question by the adversaries of that plan is no light symptom of the rage for objection which disorders their imaginations and judgments. The standard of good behavior for the continuance in office of the judicial magistracy is certainly one of the most valuable of the modern improvements in the practice of government. In a monarchy it is an excellent barrier to the despotism of the prince; in a republic it is a no less excellent barrier to the encroachments and oppressions of the representative body. And it is the best expedient which can be devised in any government to secure a steady, upright, and impartial administration of the laws.

Whoever attentively considers the different departments of power must perceive that, in a government in which they are separated from each other, the judiciary, from the nature of its functions, will always be the least dangerous to the political rights of the Constitution; because it will be least in a capacity to annoy or injure them. The executive not only dispenses the honors but holds the sword of the community. The legislature not only commands the purse but prescribes the rules by which the duties and rights of every citizen are to be regulated. The judiciary, on the contrary, has no influence over either the sword or the purse; no direction either of the strength or of the wealth of the society, and can take no active resolution whatever.

This simple view of the matter suggests several important consequences. It proves incontestably that the judiciary is beyond comparison the weakest of the three departments of power; that it can never attack with success either of the other two; and that all possible care is requisite to enable it to defend itself against their attacks. It equally proves that though individual oppression may now and then proceed from the courts of justice, the general liberty of the people can never be endangered from that quarter; I mean so long as the judiciary remains truly distinct from both the legislature and the executive. For I agree that "there is no liberty if the power of judging be not separated from the legislative and executive powers." And it proves, in the last place, that as liberty can have nothing to fear from the judiciary alone, but would have everything to fear from its union with either of the other departments; that as all the effects of such a union must ensue from a dependence of the former on the latter, notwithstanding a nominal and apparent separation; that as, from the natural feebleness of the judiciary, it is in continual jeopardy of being overpowered, awed, or influenced by its coordinate branches; and that as nothing can contribute so much to its firmness and independence as permanency in office, this quality may therefore be justly regarded as an indispensable ingredient in its constitution, and, in a great measure, as the citadel of the public justice and the public security.

The complete independence of the courts of justice is peculiarly essential in a limited Constitution. By a limited Constitution, I understand one which contains certain specified exceptions to the legislative authority; such, for instance, as that it shall pass no bills of attainder, no ex post facto laws, and the like. Limitations of this kind can be preserved in practice no other way than through the medium of courts of justice, whose duty it must be to declare all acts contrary to the manifest tenor of the Constitution void. Without this, all the reservations of particular rights or privileges would amount to nothing.

Some perplexity respecting the rights of the courts to pronounce legislative acts void, because contrary to the Constitution, has arisen from an imagination that the doctrine would imply a superiority of the judiciary to the legislative power. It is urged that the authority which can declare the acts of another void must necessarily be superior to the one whose acts may be declared void. As this doctrine is of great importance in all the American constitutions, a brief discussion of the grounds on which it rests cannot be unacceptable.

There is no position which depends on clearer principles than that every act of a delegated authority, contrary to the tenor of the commission under which it is exercised, is void. No legislative act, therefore, contrary to the Constitution, can be valid. To deny this would be to affirm that the deputy is greater than his principal; that the servant is above his master; that the representatives of the people are superior to the people themselves; that men acting by virtue of powers may do not only what their powers do not authorize, but what they forbid.

If it be said that the legislative body are themselves the constitutional judges of their own powers and that the construction they put upon them is conclusive upon the other departments, it may be answered that this cannot be the natural presumption where it is not to be collected from any particular provisions in the Constitution. It is not otherwise to be supposed that the Constitution could intend to enable the representatives of the people to substitute their will to that of their constituents. It is far more rational to suppose that the courts were designed to be an intermediate body between the people and the legislature in order, among other things, to keep the latter within the limits assigned to their authority. The interpretation of the laws is the proper and peculiar province of the courts. A constitution is, in fact, and must be regarded by the judges as, a fundamental law. It therefore belongs to them to ascertain its meaning as well

Alexander Hamilton

as the meaning of any particular act proceeding from the legislative body. If there should happen to be an irreconcilable variance between the two, that which has the superior obligation and validity ought, of course, to be preferred; or, in other words, the Constitution ought to be preferred to the statute, the intention of the people to the intention of their agents.

Nor does this conclusion by any means suppose a superiority of the judicial to the legislative power. It only supposes that the power of the people is superior to both, and that where the will of the legislature, declared in its statutes, stands in opposition to that of the people, declared in the Constitution, the judges ought to be governed by the latter rather than the former. They ought to regulate their decisions by the fundamental laws rather than by those which are not fundamental. This exercise of judicial discretion in determining between two contradictory laws is exemplified in a familiar instance. It not uncommonly happens that there are two statutes existing at one time, clashing in whole or in part with each other and neither of them containing any repealing clause or expression. In such a case, it is the province of the courts to liquidate and fix their meaning and operation. So far as they can, by any fair construction, be reconciled to each other, reason and law conspire to dictate that this should be done; where this is impracticable, it becomes a matter of necessity to give effect to one in exclusion of the other. The rule which has obtained in the courts for determining their relative validity is that the last in order of time shall be preferred to the first. But this is a mere rule of construction, not derived from any positive law but from the nature and reason of the thing. It is a rule not enjoined upon the courts by legislative provision but adopted by themselves, as consonant to truth and propriety, for the direction of their conduct as interpreters of the law. They thought it reasonable that between the interfering acts of an equal authority that which was the last indication of its will should have the preference.

But in regard to the interfering acts of a superior and subordinate authority of an original and derivative power, the nature and reason of the thing indicate the converse of that rule as proper to be followed. They teach us that the prior act of a superior ought to be preferred to the subsequent act of an inferior and subordinate authority; and that accordingly, whenever a particular statute contravenes the Constitution, it will be the duty of the judicial tribunals to adhere to the latter and disregard the former.

It can be of no weight to say that the courts, on the pretense of a repugnancy, may substitute their own pleasure to the constitutional intentions of the legislature. This might as well happen in the case of two contradictory statutes; or it might as well happen in every adjudication upon any single statute. The courts must declare the sense of the law; and if they should be disposed to exercise will instead of judgment, the consequence would equally be the substitution of their pleasure to that of the legislative body. The observation, if it prove anything, would prove that there ought to be no judges distinct from that body.

If, then, the courts of justice are to be considered as the bulwarks of a limited Constitution against legislative encroachments, this consideration will afford a strong argument for the permanent tenure of judicial offices, since nothing will contribute so much as this to that independent spirit in the judges which must be essential to the faithful performance of so arduous a duty.

This independence of the judges is equally requisite to guard the Constitution and the rights of individuals from the effects of those ill humors which the arts of designing men, or the influence of particular conjunctures, sometimes disseminate among the people themselves, and which, though they speedily give place to better information, and more deliberate reflection, have a tendency, in the meantime, to occasion dangerous innovations in the government, and serious oppressions of the minor party in the community. Though I trust the friends of the proposed Constitution will never concur with its enemies in questioning that fundamental principle of Republican government which admits the right of the people to alter or abolish the established Constitution whenever they find it inconsistent with their happiness; yet it is not to be inferred from this principle that the representatives of the people, whenever a momentary inclination happens to lay hold of a majority of their constituents incompatible with the provisions in the existing Constitution would, on that account, be justifiable in a violation of those provisions; or that the courts would be under a greater obligation to connive at infractions in this shape than when they had proceeded wholly from the cabals of the representative body. Until the people have, by some solemn and authoritative act, annulled or changed the established form, it is binding upon themselves collectively, as well as individually; and no presumption, or even knowledge of their sentiments, can warrant their representatives in a departure from it prior to such an act. But it is easy to see that it would require an uncommon portion of fortitude in the judges to do their duty as faithful guardians of the Constitution, where legislative invasions of it had been instigated by the major voice of the community.

But it is not with a view to infractions of the Constitution only that the independence of the judges may be an essential safeguard against the effects of occasional ill humors in the society. These sometimes extend no farther than to the injury of the private rights of particular classes of citizens, by unjust and partial laws. Here also the firmness of the judicial magistracy is of vast importance in mitigating the severity and confining the operation of such laws. It not only serves to moderate the immediate mischiefs of those which may have been passed but it operates as a check upon the legislative body in passing them; who, perceiving that obstacles to the success of iniquitous intention are to be expected from the scruples of the courts, are in a manner compelled, by the very motives of the injustice they mediate, to qualify their attempts. This is a circumstance calculated to have more influence upon the character of our governments than but few may be aware of. The benefits of the integrity and moderation of the judiciary have already been felt in more States than one; and though they may have displeased those whose sinister expectations they may have disappointed, they must have commanded the esteem and applause of all the virtuous and disinterested. Considerate men of every description ought to prize whatever will tend to beget or fortify that temper in the courts; as no man can be sure that he may not be tomorrow the victim of a spirit of injustice, by which he may be a gainer today. And every man must now feel that the inevitable tendency of such a spirit is to sap the foundations of public and private confidence and to introduce in its stead universal distrust and distress.

That inflexible and uniform adherence to the rights of the Constitution, and of individuals, which we perceive to be indispensable in the courts of justice, can certainly not be expected from judges who hold their offices by a temporary commission. Periodical appointments, however regulated, or by whomsoever made, would, in some way or other, be fatal to their necessary independence. If the power of making them was committed either to the executive or legislature there would be danger of an improper complaisance to the branch which possessed it; if to both, there would be an unwillingness to hazard the displeasure of either; if to the people, or to persons chosen by them for the special purpose, there would be too great a disposition to consult popularity to justify a reliance that nothing would be consulted but the Constitution and the laws.

There is yet a further and a weighty reason for the permanency of the judicial offices which is deducible from the nature of the qualifications they require. It has been frequently remarked with great propriety that a voluminous code of laws is one of the inconveniences necessarily connected with the advantages of a free government. To avoid an arbitrary discretion in the courts, it is indispensable that they should be bound down by strict rules and precedents which serve to define and point out their duty in every particular case that comes before them; and it will readily be conceived from the variety of controversies which grow out of the folly and wickedness of mankind that the records of those precedents must unavoidably swell to a very considerable bulk and must demand long and laborious study to acquire a competent knowledge of them. Hence it is that there can be but few men in the society who will have sufficient skill in the laws to qualify them for the stations of judges. And making the proper deductions for the ordinary depravity of human nature, the number must be still smaller of those who unite the requisite integrity with the requisite knowledge. These considerations apprise us that the government can have no great option between fit characters; and that a temporary duration in office which would naturally discourage such characters from quitting a lucrative line of practice to accept a seat on the bench would have a tendency to throw the administration of justice into hands less able and less well qualified to conduct it with utility and dignity. In the present circumstances of this country and in those in which it is likely to be for a long time to come, the disadvantages on this score would be greater than they may at first sight appear; but it must be confessed that they are far inferior to those which present themselves under the other aspects of the subject.

Upon the whole, there can be no room to doubt that the convention acted wisely in copying from the models of

those constitutions which have established *good behavior* as the tenure of their judicial offices, in point of duration; and that so far from being blamable on this account, their plan would have been inexcusably defective if it had wanted this important feature of good government. The experience of Great Britain affords an illustrious comment on the excellence of the institution.

Analyzing Documents

Use the passage on these pages to answer the following questions.
1. According to Hamilton, how long should judges stay in office?
2. What does Hamilton say is the role of judges?
3. What might Hamilton say about the judicial system as it exists today?

▶The Emancipation Proclamation

President Abraham Lincoln issued the Emancipation Proclamation on January 1, 1863, at the beginning of the third year of the bloody Civil War. The proclamation declared "that all persons held as slaves" within the rebellious states "are, and henceforward shall be free." Although the Emancipation Proclamation applied to a limited geographical area, it fundamentally changed the nature of the war to a conflict focused on freedom for all.

Whereas on the 22d day of September, A.D. 1862, a proclamation was issued by the President of the United States, containing, among other things, the following, to wit:

"That on the 1st day of January, A.D. 1863, all persons held as slaves within any State or designated part of a State the people whereof shall then be in rebellion against the United States shall be then, thenceforward, and forever free; and the Executive Government of the United States, including the military and naval authority thereof, will recognize and maintain the freedom of such persons and will do no act or acts to repress such persons, or any of them, in any efforts they may make for their actual freedom.

"That the executive will on the 1st day of January aforesaid, by proclamation, designate the States and parts of States, if any, in which the people thereof, respectively, shall then be in rebellion against the United States; and the fact that any State or the people thereof shall on that day be in good faith represented in the Congress of the United States by members chosen

thereto at elections wherein a majority of the qualified voters of such States shall have participated shall, in the absence of strong countervailing testimony, be deemed conclusive evidence that such State and the people thereof are not then in rebellion against the United States."

Now, therefore, I, Abraham Lincoln, President of the United States, by virtue of the power in me vested as Commander-in-Chief of the Army and Navy of the United States in time of actual armed rebellion against the authority and government of the United States, and as a fit and necessary war measure for suppressing said rebellion, do, on this 1st day of January, A.D. 1863, and in accordance with my purpose so to do, publicly proclaimed for the full period of one hundred days from the first day above mentioned, order and designate as the States and parts of States wherein the people thereof, respectively, are this day in rebellion against the United States the following, to wit:

Arkansas, Texas, Louisiana (except the parishes of St. Bernard, Plaquemines, Jefferson, St. John, St. Charles, St. James, Ascension, Assumption, Terrebonne, Lafourche, St. Mary, St. Martin, and Orleans, including the city of New Orleans), Mississippi, Alabama, Florida, Georgia, South Carolina, North Carolina, and Virginia (except the forty-eight counties designated as West Virginia, and also the counties of Berkeley, Accomac, Northhampton, Elizabeth City, York, Princess Anne, and Norfolk, including the cities of Norfolk and Portsmouth), and which excepted parts are for the present left precisely as if this proclamation were not issued.

And by virtue of the power and for the purpose aforesaid, I do order and declare that all persons held as slaves within said designated States and parts of States are, and henceforward shall be, free; and that the Executive Government of the United States, including the military and naval authorities thereof, will recognize and maintain the freedom of said persons.

And I hereby enjoin upon the people so declared to be free to abstain from all violence, unless in necessary self-defense; and I recommend to them that, in all cases when allowed, they labor faithfully for reasonable wages.

And I further declare and make known that such persons of suitable condition will be received into the armed service of the United States to garrison forts, positions, stations, and other places, and to man vessels of all sorts in said service.

And upon this act, sincerely believed to be an act of justice, warranted by the Constitution upon military necessity, I invoke the considerate judgment of mankind and the gracious favor of Almighty God.

Analyzing Documents

Use the passage on these pages to answer the following questions.
1. Recall the eight roles and the powers of the President. Which role and which power allow Lincoln to proclaim freedom for slaves?
2. In addition to proclaiming an end to slavery, what other action does the Proclamation declare? Why is this action significant?
3. Why was the Proclamation important even though no slaves were freed immediately?

Over the course of the Civil War, nearly 180,000 African Americans wore the Union uniform. ▶

▶Declaration of Sentiments

Elizabeth Cady Stanton and Lucretia Mott, two activists in the movement to abolish slavery, called together the first conference to address women's rights and issues in Seneca Falls, New York, in 1848. Using the Declaration of Independence as a model, the Declaration of Sentiments demanded that the rights of women be acknowledged and respected.

When, in the course of human events, it becomes necessary for one portion of the family of man to assume among the people of the earth a position different from that which they have hitherto occupied, but one to which the laws of nature and of nature's God entitle them, a decent respect to the opinions of mankind requires that they should declare the causes that impel them to such a course.

We hold these truths to be self-evident: that all men and women are created equal; that they are endowed by their Creator with certain inalienable rights; that among these are life, liberty, and the pursuit of happiness; that to secure these rights governments are instituted, deriving their just powers from the consent of the governed. Whenever any form of government becomes destructive of these ends, it is the right of those who suffer from it to refuse allegiance to it, and to insist upon the institution of a new government, laying its foundation on such principles, and organizing its powers in such form, as to them shall seem most likely to effect their safety and happiness. Prudence, indeed, will dictate that governments long established should not be changed for light and transient causes; and accordingly all experience hath shown that mankind are more disposed to suffer. while evils are sufferable, than to right themselves by abolishing the forms to which they are accustomed. But when a long train of abuses and usurpations, pursuing invariably the same object, evinces a design to reduce them under absolute despotism, it is their duty to throw off such government, and to provide new guards for their future security. Such has been the patient sufferance of the women under this government, and such is now the necessity which constrains them to demand the equal station to which they are entitled. The history of mankind is a history of repeated injuries and usurpations on the part of man toward woman, having in direct object the establishment of an absolute tyranny over her. To prove this, let facts be submitted to a candid world.

- He has never permitted her to exercise her inalienable right to the elective franchise.
- He has compelled her to submit to laws, in the formation of which she had no voice.
- He has withheld from her rights which are given to the most ignorant and degraded men—both natives and foreigners.
- Having deprived her of this first right of a citizen, the elective franchise, thereby leaving her without representation in the halls of legislation, he has oppressed her on all sides.
- He has made her, if married, in the eye of the law, civilly dead.
- He has taken from her all right in property, even to the wages she earns.
- He has made her, morally, an irresponsible being, as she can commit many crimes with impunity, provided they be done in the presence of her husband. In the covenant of marriage, she is compelled to promise obedience to her husband, he becoming, to all intents and purposes, her master—the law giving him power to deprive her of her liberty, and to administer chastisement.
- He has so framed the laws of divorce, as to what shall be the proper causes, and in case of separation, to whom the guardianship of the children shall be given, as to be wholly regardless of the happiness of women—the law, in all cases, going upon a false supposition of the supremacy of man, and giving all power into his hands.
- After depriving her of all rights as a married woman, if single, and the owner of property, he has taxed her to support a government which recognizes her only when her property can be made profitable to it.
- He has monopolized nearly all the profitable employments, and from those she is permitted to follow, she receives but a scanty remuneration.
- He closes against her all the avenues to wealth and distinction which he considers most honorable to himself. As a teacher of theology, medicine, or law, she is not known.
- He has denied her the facilities for obtaining a thorough education, all colleges being closed against her.
- He allows her in church, as well as state, but a subordinate position, claiming apostolic authority for her exclusion from the ministry, and, with some exceptions, from any public participation in the affairs of the church.

Lucretia Mott ▶

◀ Elizabeth Cady Stanton

- He has created a false public sentiment by giving to the world a different code of morals for men and women, by which moral delinquencies which exclude women from society, are not only tolerated, but deemed of little account in man.

- He has usurped the prerogative of Jehovah himself, claiming it as his right to assign for her a sphere of action, when that belongs to her conscience and to her God.

- He has endeavored, in every way that he could, to destroy her confidence in her own powers, to lessen her self-respect, and to make her willing to lead a dependent and abject life.

   Now, in view of this entire disfranchisement of one-half the people of this country, their social and religious degradation—in view of the unjust laws above mentioned, and because women do feel themselves aggrieved, oppressed, and fraudulently deprived of their most sacred rights, we insist that they have immediate admission to all the rights and privileges which belong to them as citizens of the United States.

Analyzing Documents

Use the passage on these pages to answer the following questions.

1. Why did Mott and Stanton base their Declaration on the Declaration of Independence? What additional goals does the Declaration of Sentiments include?

2. The Declaration of Sentiments attracted much controversy when it was first published. Why might this have been so?

3. Why is the Declaration of Sentiments an important document in the history of securing rights for all Americans?

▶Universal Declaration of Human Rights

The General Assembly of the United Nations adopted this declaration on December 10, 1948. The document sets forth the basic liberties and freedoms to which all people are entitled.

Article 1 All human beings are born free and equal in dignity and rights. They are endowed with reason and conscience and should act toward one another in a spirit of brotherhood.

Article 2 Everyone is entitled to all the rights and freedoms set forth in this Declaration, without distinction of any kind, such as race, colour, sex, language, religion, political or other opinion, national or social origin, property, birth or other status. . . .

Article 3 Everyone has the right to life, liberty and security of person.

Article 4 No one shall be held in slavery or servitude. . . .

Article 5 No one shall be subjected to torture or to cruel, inhuman or degrading treatment or punishment.

Article 9 No one shall be subjected to arbitrary arrest, detention or exile.

Article 13 Everyone has the right to freedom of movement. . . .

Article 18 Everyone has the right to freedom of thought, conscience and religion. . . .

Article 19 Everyone has the right to freedom of opinion and expression. . . .

Article 20 Everyone has the right to freedom of peaceful assembly and association. . . .

Article 23 Everyone has the right to work, to free choice of employment, to just and favourable conditions of work and to protection against unemployment. . . .

Article 25 Everyone has the right to a standard of living adequate for the health and well-being of himself and of his family, including food, clothing, housing and medical care and necessary social services, and the right to security in the event of unemployment, sickness, disability, widowhood, old age or other lack of livelihood in circumstances beyond his control.

Article 26 Everyone has the right to education. Education shall be free, at least in the elementary and fundamental stages. . . .

Analyzing Documents

Use the passage on this page to answer the following questions.
1. Which of the above rights are reflected in the Bill of Rights in the U.S. Constitution?
2. What additional rights are included in these excerpts? Why do you think these rights are not spelled out in the U.S. Constitution?
3. In what ways might the existence of this declaration benefit people living under an oppressive regime?

▲ A young girl carries water in Chennai, India

Supreme Court Glossary

Abrams v. United States (1919)

Decision: The Court ruled 7-2 that Congress could make it illegal to criticize the United States government and to encourage others not to obey the laws. When the defendants were convicted of distributing pamphlets that opposed certain U.S. military policies during World War I and urging people not to participate in the war effort, they were sentenced to 20 years imprisonment. The Court upheld their convictions. In his dissent, Justice Oliver Wendell Holmes argued that "the surreptitious publishing of a silly leaflet by an unknown man" did not create a clear and imminent danger to the United States and therefore should be protected by the First Amendment. The case was essentially overruled 50 years later in *Brandenburg* v. *Ohio*, which held that "mere advocacy" is constitutionally protected unless it is actually likely to produce imminent lawless action.

Agostini v. Felton (1997)

Decision: The Court decided that it was appropriate to reconsider *Aguilar* v. *Felton* as subsequent cases had undermined several of the assumptions, for example that public employees placed at parochial schools would "inevitably inculcate religion," upon which the decision was based. The Court then found that New York City's Title I Program did not violate any of the criteria used "to evaluate whether government aid has the effect of advancing religion: it does not result in governmental indoctrination; define its recipients by reference to religion; or create an excessive entanglement." As a result, the Court concluded that "a federally funded program providing supplemental, remedial instruction to disadvantaged children on a neutral basis is not invalid under the Establishment Clause when such instruction is given on the premises of sectarian schools by government employees pursuant to a program containing safeguards" against excessive entanglement between government and religion.

Alden v. Maine (1999)

Decision: In a 5-4 decision, the Court held that Congress does not have the power to force States to submit to being sued in their own courts without their consent. The structure of the Constitution and the Eleventh Amendment give the States "sovereign immunity" that allows the States to prevent people from suing them in their own courts, and Congress does not have the power to override this immunity.

American Insurance Association v. Garamendi (2003)

Decision: California's Holocaust Victim Insurance Relief Act interferes with the President's conduct of the nation's foreign policy and is therefore unconstitutional. Although the executive agreements do not specifically prohibit State action, they do pre-empt (override) the State's authority to act on the same subject matter, even in the absence of any direct conflict.

Baker v. Carr (1962)

Decision: Although in past decisions, the Court had called apportionment cases a "political thicket" and declined to intervene, in *Baker*, the Court held that it was within the scope of the judicial branch of government to rule on matters of legislative apportionment. The Court further ruled that Baker and other Tennessee citizens were entitled to a trial deciding whether their constitutionally guaranteed right to equal protection of the law (14th Amendment) had been denied. *Baker* opened the door to later cases on apportionment which led to the eventual reapportioning of nearly every State legislature according to population.

Board of Estimate of City of New York v. Morris (1989)

Decision: The reapportionment requirement of "one-person, one-vote" applies to the Board of Estimate. The Board has sufficient legislative functions that its composition must fairly represent city voters on an approximately equal basis. The fact that some members are elected city-wide is one factor to be considered in evaluating the fairness of the electoral structure, but it is not determinative. The City's expressed interests—that the Board be effective and that it accommodate natural and political boundaries as well as local interests—does not justify the size of the deviation from the "one-person, one-vote" ideal. The City could structure the Board in other ways that would further these interests while minimizing the discrimination in voting power.

Bob Jones University v. United States (1983)

(14th Amendment in conflict with 1st Amendment) Bob Jones University, a private school, denied admission to applicants in an interracial marriage or who "espouse" interracial marriage or dating. The Internal Revenue Service then denied tax exempt status to the school because of racial discrimination. The university appealed, claiming their policy was based on the Bible. The Court upheld the IRS ruling, stating that ". . . Government has a fundamental overriding interest in eradicating racial discrimination in education."

Brandenburg v. Ohio (1969)

Decision: The Court ruled unanimously that advocacy is protected under the First Amendment "except where such advocacy is directed to inciting or producing imminent lawless action and is likely to incite or produce such action." Therefore a Ku Klux Klan leader could not be convicted under an Ohio statute that prohibited advocating violence. The opinion effectively overruled prior Supreme Court cases such as *Whitney v. California* and *Abrams v. United States* that had allowed criminal convictions merely for urging violence or other unlawful acts.

Brown v. Board of Education of Topeka (1954)

(14th Amendment, Equal Protection Clause) Probably no twentieth century Supreme Court decision so deeply stirred and changed life in the United States as *Brown*. A 10-year-old Topeka girl, Linda Brown, was not permitted to attend her neighborhood school because she was an African American. The Court heard arguments about whether segregation itself was a violation of the Equal Protection Clause and found that it was, commenting that "in the field of public education the doctrine of 'separate but equal' has no place. . . . Segregation is a denial of the equal protection of the laws." The decision overturned *Plessy v. Ferguson*, 1896.

City of Boerne, Texas v. Flores (1997)

Decision: A 6-3 majority ruled that the Religious Freedom Restoration Act was unconstitutional. The majority concluded that the Act was not a legitimate attempt by Congress to implement the Free Exercise Clause of the First Amendment but was really an attempt to change constitutional law as previously determined by the Court. The Act therefore violated separation of powers.

The Civil Rights Cases (1883)

(14th Amendment, Equal Protection Clause) The Civil Rights Act of 1875 included punishments of businesses that practiced discrimination. The Court ruled on a number of cases involving the Acts in 1883, finding that the Constitution, "while prohibiting discrimination by governments, made no provisions . . . for acts of racial discrimination by private individuals." The decision limited the impact of the Equal Protection Clause, giving tacit approval for segregation in the private sector.

Cruzan v. Missouri (1990)

(14th Amendment, Due Process Clause) After Nancy Beth Cruzan was left in a "persistent vegetative state" by a car accident, Missouri officials refused to comply with her parents' request that the hospital terminate life-support. The Court upheld the State policy under which officials refused to withdraw treatment, rejecting the argument that the Due Process Clause of the 14th Amendment gave the parents the right to refuse treatment on their daughter's behalf. Although individuals have the right to refuse medical treatment, "incompetent" persons are not able to exercise this right; without "clear and convincing" evidence that Cruzan desired the withdrawal of treatment, the State could legally act to preserve her life.

Dennis v. United States (1951)

(1st Amendment, freedom of speech) The Smith Act of 1940 made it a crime for any person to work for the violent overthrow of the United States in peacetime or war. Eleven Communist party leaders, including Dennis, had been convicted of violating the Smith Act, and they appealed. The Court upheld the Act.

District of Columbia v. Heller (2008)

Decision: The Court ruled 5 to 4 that Washington, D.C.'s gun law was unconstitutional. The majority concluded that the Second Amendment "right of the people to keep and bear Arms" meant that individuals could have weapons for self-defense. An outright ban on gun ownership was therefore unconstitutional. In addition, since dismantled or disabled weapons would not be useful for self-defense, the part of the law requiring that all guns, including shotguns and rifles, be kept unloaded and either taken apart or disabled by a trigger lock was also unconstitutional. In dissent, Justice Breyer suggested a balancing test, under which gun control laws could be constitutional when they supported a compelling governmental interest in preventing crime.

Dred Scott v. Sandford (1857)

(5th Amendment, individual rights) This decision upheld property rights over human rights by saying that Dred Scott, a slave, could not become a free man just because he had traveled in "free soil" States with his master. A badly divided nation was further fragmented by the decision. "Free soil" federal laws and the Missouri Compromise line of 1820 were held unconstitutional because they deprived a slave owner of the right to his "property" without just compensation. This narrow reading of the Constitution, a landmark case of the Court, was most clearly stated by Chief Justice Roger B. Taney, a States' rights advocate.

Edwards v. South Carolina (1963)

(1st Amendment, freedom of speech and assembly) A group of mostly African American civil rights activists held a rally at the South Carolina State Capitol, protesting segregation. A hostile crowd gathered and the rally leaders were arrested and convicted for "breach of the peace." The Court overturned the convictions, saying, "The Fourteenth Amendment does not permit a State to make criminal the peaceful expression of unpopular views."

Engel v. Vitale (1962)

(1st Amendment, Establishment Clause) The State Board of Regents of New York required the recitation of a 22-word nonsectarian prayer at the beginning of each school day. A group of parents filed suit against the required prayer, claiming it violated their 1st Amendment rights. The Court found New York's action to be unconstitutional, observing, "There can be no doubt that. . . religious beliefs [are] embodied in the Regent's prayer."

Escobedo v. Illinois (1964)

(6th Amendment, right to counsel) In a case involving a murder confession by a person known to Chicago-area police who was not afforded counsel while under interrogation, the Court extended the "exclusionary rule" to illegal confessions in State court proceedings. Carefully defining an "Escobedo Rule," the Court said, "where. . . the investigation is no longer a general inquiry . . . but has begun to focus on a particular suspect . . . (and where) the suspect has been taken into custody . . . the suspect has requested . . . his lawyer, and the police have not . . . warned him of his right to remain silent, the accused has been denied . . . counsel in violation of the Sixth Amendment."

Ex parte Milligan (1866)

(Article II, executive powers) An Indiana man was arrested, treated as a prisoner of war, and imprisoned by a military court during the Civil War under presidential order. He claimed that his rights to a fair trial were interfered with and that military courts had no authority outside of "conquered territory." He was released because, "the Constitution . . . is a law for rulers and people, equally in war and peace, and covers . . . all . . . men, at all times, and under all circumstances." The Court held that presidential powers to suspend the writ of habeas corpus in time of war did not extend to creating another court system run by the military.

Flast v. Cohen (1968)

Decision: The Supreme Court concluded that the rule announced in *Frothingham* v. *Mellon* expressed a practical policy of judicial self-restraint rather than an absolute constitutional limitation on the power of federal courts to hear taxpayer suits. While mere status as a federal taxpayer ordinarily will not give sufficient "standing" to allow a person to challenge the constitutionality of a federal law, there may be times when taxpayers are appropriate plaintiffs. *Flast* v. *Cohen*, in which plaintiffs argued that the First Amendment specifically prohibited taxing them in order to support religious activities, was one in which their role as taxpayers was well suited to the challenge they sought to assert. The Court ruled that they had standing to sue, and allowed them to proceed with their case.

Furman v. Georgia (1972)

(8th Amendment, capital punishment) Three different death penalty cases, including *Furman*, raised the question of racial imbalances in the use of death sentences by State courts. Furman had been convicted and sentenced to death in Georgia. In deciding to overturn existing State death-penalty laws, the Court noted that there was an "apparent arbitrariness of the use of the sentence. . . ." Many States rewrote their death-penalty statutes and these were generally upheld in *Gregg* v. *Georgia*, 1976.

Gibbons v. Ogden (1824)

(Supremacy Clause) This decision involved a careful examination of the power of Congress to "regulate interstate commerce." Aaron Ogden's exclusive New York ferry license gave him the right to operate steamboats to and from New York. He said that Thomas Gibbons's federal "coasting license" did not include "landing rights" in New York City. The Court invalidated the New York licensing regulations, holding that federal regulations should take precedence under the Supremacy Clause. The decision strengthened the power of the United States to regulate any interstate business relationship. Federal regulation of the broadcasting industry, oil pipelines, and banking are all based on *Gibbons*.

Gideon v. Wainwright (1963)

(6th Amendment, right to counsel) In 1961 a Florida court found Clarence Earl Gideon guilty of breaking and entering and sentenced him to five years in prison. Gideon appealed his case to the Supreme Court on the basis that he had been unconstitutionally denied counsel during his trial due to Florida's policy of only providing appointed counsel in capital cases. The Court granted Gideon a new trial, and he was found not guilty with the help of a court-appointed attorney. The "Gideon Rule" upheld the 6th Amendment's guarantee of counsel of all poor persons facing a felony charge, a further incorporation of Bill of Rights guarantees into State constitutions.

Gitlow v. New York (1925)

(1st Amendment, freedom of speech) A New York socialist, Gitlow, was convicted under a State law on "criminal anarchy" for distributing copies of a "left-wing manifesto." For the first time, the Court considered whether the 1st Amendment applied to State laws. The case helped to establish what came to be known as the "incorporation" doctrine, under which, it was argued, the provisions of the 1st Amendment were "incorporated" by the 14th Amendment, thus applying to State as well as federal laws. Although New York law was not overruled in this case, the decision clearly indicated that the Supreme Court could make such a ruling. See also *Powell* v. *Alabama*, 1932.

Goss v. Lopez (1975)

(14th Amendment, Due Process Clause) Ten Ohio students were suspended from their schools without hearings. The students challenged the suspensions, claiming that the absence of a preliminary hearing violated their 14th Amendment right to due process. The Court agreed, holding that "having chosen to extend the right to an education. . . Ohio may not withdraw that right on grounds of misconduct, absent fundamentally fair procedures to determine whether the misconduct has occurred, and must recognize a student's legitimate entitlement to a public education as a property interest that is protected by the Due Process Clause."

Gregg v. Georgia (1976)

(8th Amendment, cruel and unusual punishment) A Georgia jury sentenced Troy Gregg to death after finding him guilty on two counts each of murder and armed robbery. Gregg appealed the sentence, claiming that it violated the "cruel and unusual punishment" clause of the 8th Amendment and citing *Furman* v. *Georgia*, 1972, in which the court held that Georgia's application of the death penalty was unfair and arbitrary. However, the Court upheld Gregg's sentence, stating for the first time that "punishment of death does not invariably violate the Constitution."

Griswold v. Connecticut (1965)

(14th Amendment, Due Process Clause) A Connecticut law forbade the use of "any drug, medicinal article, or instrument for the purpose of preventing conception." Griswold, director of Planned Parenthood in New Haven, was arrested for counseling married persons and, after conviction, appealed. The Court overturned the Connecticut law, saying that "various guarantees (of the Constitution) create zones of privacy. . ." and questioning, ". . .would we allow the police to search the sacred precincts of marital bedrooms. . . ?" The decision is significant for raising for more careful inspection the concept of "unenumerated rights" in the 9th Amendment, later central to *Roe* v. *Wade,* 1973.

Grutter v. Bollinger; Gratz v. Bollinger (2003)

Decision: (*Gratz*) The policy of the University of Michigan, giving undergraduate applicants twenty points just for being a member of a racial or ethnic group, violates the Equal Protection Clause of the 14th Amendment. The policy discriminates on the basis of race, but is not narrowly tailored to create a diverse student body. (*Grutter*) The policy of the University of Michigan's law school, considering an applicant's racial or ethnic background as just one factor in attempting to admit a diverse student body, is constitutional. Because the law school considers each applicant individually, and does not assign an inflexible value for race, the policy creates a diverse student body without discriminating on the basis of race.

Hazelwood School District v. Kuhlmeier (1988)

(1st Amendment, freedom of speech) In 1983, the principal of Hazelwood East High School in Missouri removed two articles from the upcoming issue of the student newspaper, deeming their content "inappropriate, personal, sensitive, and unsuitable for student readers." Several students sued, claiming that their right to freedom of expression had been violated. The Court upheld the principal's action: "a school need not tolerate student speech that is inconsistent with its basic educational mission, even though the government could not censor similar speech outside the school." School officials had full control over school-sponsored activities "so long as their actions are reasonably related to legitimate pedagogical concerns. . . ."

Heart of Atlanta Motel, Inc. v. United States (1964)

Decision: The Court ruled that Congress could outlaw racial segregation of private facilities that are engaged in interstate commerce. The Court's decision stated, "If it is interstate commerce that feels the pinch, it does not matter how 'local' the operation which applies the squeeze. . . . The power of Congress to promote interstate commerce also includes the power to regulate the local incidents thereof, including local activities. . . which have a substantial and harmful effect upon that commerce."

Hutchinson v. Proxmire (1979)

Decision: The Court held that the Speech or Debate Clause gives members of Congress immunity from suit for defamatory statements made within the legislative chambers, but the privilege does not extend to comments made in other locations, even if they merely repeat what was said in Congress. The newsletters and press release were not within the deliberative process nor were they essential to the deliberation of the Senate. They also were not part of the "informing function" of members of Congress, since they were not a part of legislative function or process. The comments were merely designed to convey information on the Senator's individual positions and beliefs. Finally, although Hutchinson had received extensive attention in the media as a result of his receipt of the Golden Fleece Award, he was not a public figure prior to that controversy and thus is entitled to the greater protection against defamation that is extended to non-public figures. The fact that the public may have an interest in governmental expenditures does not make Hutchinson himself a public figure.

Illinois v. Wardlow (2000)

Decision: The Supreme Court refused to say that flight from the police will always justify a stop or that it will never do so. Instead, the Court ruled that flight can be an important factor in determining whether police have "reasonable suspicion" to stop a suspect. The trial court will have to determine in each case whether the information available to the police officers, including the fact of a suspect's flight, was sufficient to support the stop.

In Re Gault (1966)

(14th Amendment, Due Process Clause) Prior to the *Gault* case, proceedings against juvenile offenders were generally handled as "family law," not "criminal law" and provided few due process guarantees. Gerald Gault was assigned to six years in a State juvenile detention facility for an alleged obscene phone call. He was not provided counsel and not permitted to confront or cross-examine the principal witness. The Court overturned the juvenile proceedings and required that States provide juveniles "some of the due process guarantees of adults," including a right to a phone call, to counsel, to cross-examine, to confront their accuser, and to be advised of their right to silence.

Johnson v. Santa Clara Transportation Agency (1987)

(Discrimination) Under their affirmative action plan, the Transportation Agency in Santa Clara, California, was authorized to "consider as one factor the sex of a qualified applicant" in an effort to combat the significant underrepresentation of women in certain job classifications. When the Agency promoted Diane Joyce, a qualified woman, over Paul Johnson, a qualified man, for the job of road dispatcher, Johnson sued, claiming that the Agency's consideration of the sex of the applicants violated Title VII of the Civil Rights Act of 1964. The Court upheld the Agency's promotion policy, arguing that the affirmative action plan created no "absolute bar" to the advancement of men but rather represented "a moderate, flexible, case-by-case approach to effecting a gradual improvement in the representation of minorities and women . . . in the Agency's work force, and [was] fully consistent with Title VII."

Korematsu v. United States (1944)

Decision: The Court upheld the military order in light of the circumstances presented by World War II. "Pressing public necessity may sometimes justify the existence of restrictions which curtail the civil rights of a single racial group." The Court noted, however, that racial antagonism itself could never form a legitimate basis for the restrictions.

Lemon v. Kurtzman (1971)

(1st Amendment, Establishment Clause) In overturning State laws regarding aid to church-supported schools in this and a similar Rhode Island case, the Court created the Lemon test limiting ". . . excessive government entanglement with religion." The Court noted that any State law about aid to religion must meet three criteria: (1) purpose of the aid must be clearly secular, (2) its primary effect must neither advance nor inhibit religion, and (3) it must avoid "excessive entanglement of government with religion."

Mapp v. Ohio (1962)

(4th and 14th Amendments, illegal evidence and Due Process Clause) Admitting evidence gained by illegal searches was permitted by some States before *Mapp*. Cleveland police raided Dollree Mapp's home without a warrant and found obscene materials. She appealed her conviction, saying that the 4th and 14th Amendments protected her against improper police behavior. The Court agreed, extending "exclusionary rule" protections to citizens in State courts, saying that the prohibition against unreasonable searches would be "meaningless" unless evidence gained in such searches was "excluded." *Mapp* developed the concept of "incorporation" begun in *Gitlow* v. *New York*, 1925.

Marbury v. Madison (1803)

(Article III, judicial powers) After defeat in the 1800 election, President Adams appointed many Federalists to the federal courts, but James Madison, the new secretary of state, refused to deliver the commissions. William Marbury, one of the appointees, asked the Supreme Court to enforce the delivery of his commission based on a provision of the Judiciary Act of 1789 that allowed the Court to hear such cases on original jurisdiction. The Court refused Marbury's request, finding that the relevant portion of the Judiciary Act was in conflict with the Constitution. This decision, written by Chief Justice Marshall, established the evaluation of federal laws' constitutionality, or "judicial review," as a power of the Supreme Court.

McCulloch v. Maryland (1819)

(Article I, Section 8, Necessary and Proper Clause) Called the "Bank of the United States" case. A Maryland law required federally chartered banks to use only a special paper to print paper money, which amounted to a tax. James McCulloch, the cashier of the Baltimore branch of the bank, refused to use the paper, claiming that States could not tax the Federal Government. The Court declared the Maryland law unconstitutional, commenting ". . . the power to tax implies the power to destroy."

Miranda v. Arizona (1966)

(5th, 6th, and 14th Amendments, rights of the accused) Arrested for kidnapping and sexual assault, Ernesto Miranda signed a confession including a statement that he had "full knowledge of [his] legal rights. . . ." After conviction, he appealed, claiming that without counsel and without warnings, the confession was illegally gained. The Court agreed with Miranda that "he must be warned prior to any questioning that he has the right to remain silent, that anything he says can be used against him in a court of law, that he has the right to. . . an attorney and that if he cannot afford an attorney one will be appointed for him. . . ." Although later modified by *Nix* v. *Williams,* 1984, and other cases, *Miranda* firmly upheld citizen rights to fair trials in State courts.

New Jersey v. T.L.O. (1985)

(4th and 14th Amendments) After T.L.O., a New Jersey high school student, denied an accusation that she had been smoking in the school lavatory, a vice-principal searched her purse and found cigarettes, marijuana, and evidence that T.L.O. had been involved in marijuana dealing at the school. T.L.O. was then sentenced to probation by a juvenile court, but appealed on the grounds that the evidence against her had been obtained by an "unreasonable" search. The Court rejected T.L.O.'s arguments, stating that the school had a "legitimate need to maintain an environment in which learning can take place," and that to do this "requires some easing of the restrictions to which searches by public authorities are ordinarily subject. . ." The Court thus created a "reasonable suspicion" rule for school searches, a change from the "probable cause" requirement in the wider society.

New York Times v. *Sullivan* (1964)

Decision: A unanimous Court announced that a public official could not win a suit for defamation (false statement) unless the statement was made with "actual malice," meaning either with the knowledge that it was false or with "reckless disregard" of the truth. The Court found a national commitment to "uninhibited, robust, and wide-open" debate on issues of public concern—even when this included "vehement, caustic, and sometimes unpleasantly sharp attacks on government and public officials." Without an "actual malice" standard, citizens might be unwilling to criticize elected officials for fear of being sued if something they said turned out to be inaccurate.

New York Times v. *United States* (1971)

(1st Amendment, freedom of the press) In 1971 The New York Times obtained copies of classified Defense Department documents, later known as the "Pentagon Papers," which revealed instances in which the Johnson Administration had deceived Congress and the American people regarding U.S. policies during the Vietnam War. A U.S. district court issued an injunction against the publication of the documents, claiming that it might endanger national security. On appeal, the Supreme Court cited the 1st Amendment guarantee of a free press and refused to uphold the injunction against publication, observing that it is the obligation of the government to prove that actual harm to the nation's security would be caused by the publication. The decision limited "prior restraint" of the press.

Nixon v. *Fitzgerald* (1982)

Decision: The Court ruled that a President or former President is entitled to absolute immunity from liability based on his official acts. The President must be able to act forcefully and independently, without fear of liability. Diverting the President's energies with concerns about private lawsuits could impair the effective functioning of government. The President's absolute immunity extends to all acts within the "outer perimeter" of his duties of office, since otherwise he would be required to litigate over the nature of the acts and the scope of his duties in each case. The remedy of impeachment, the vigilant scrutiny of the press, the Congress, and the public, and presidential desire to earn reelection and concern with historical legacy all protect against presidential wrongdoing.

Nixon v. *Shrink Missouri Government PAC* (2000)

Decision: In *Buckley* v. *Valeo*, 1976, the Supreme Court had upheld a $1000 limit on contributions by individuals to candidates for federal office. In *Nixon* v. *Shrink Missouri Government PAC*, the Court concluded that large contributions will sometimes create actual corruption, and that voters will be suspicious of the fairness of a political process that allows wealthy donors to contribute large amounts. The Court concluded that the Missouri contribution limits were appropriate to correct this problem and did not impair the ability of candidates to communicate their messages to the voters and to mount an effective campaign.

Olmstead v. *United States* (1928)

(4th Amendment, electronic surveillance) Olmstead was engaged in the illegal sale of alcohol. Much of the evidence against him was gained through a wiretap made without a warrant. Olmstead argued that he had "a reasonable expectation of privacy," and that the *Weeks* v. *United States* decision of 1914 should be applied to exclude the evidence gained by the wiretap. The Court disagreed, saying that Olmstead intended "to project his voice to those quite outside . . . and that . . . nothing tangible was taken." Reversed by subsequent decisions, this case contains the first usage of the concept of "reasonable expectation of privacy" that would mark later 4th Amendment decisions.

Oregon v. *Mitchell* (1970)

Decision: The Supreme Court was unable to issue a single opinion of the Court supported by a majority of the justices. However, in a series of separate opinions, differing majority groups agreed that (1) the 18-year-old minimum-age requirement of the Voting Rights Act Amendments is valid for national elections but not for State and local elections; (2) the literacy test provision is valid in order to remedy discrimination against minorities; and (3) the residency and absentee balloting provisions are a valid congressional regulation of presidential elections.

Plessy v. *Ferguson* (1896)

(14th Amendment, Equal Protection Clause) A Louisiana law required separate seating for white and African American citizens on public railroads, a form of segregation. Homer Plessy argued that his right to "equal protection of the laws" was violated. The Court held that segregation was permitted if facilities were equal. The Court interpreted the 14th Amendment as "not intended to give Negroes social equality but only political and civil equality. . . ." The Louisiana law was seen as a "reasonable exercise of (State) police power. . ." Segregated public facilities were permitted until *Plessy* was overturned by the *Brown* v. *Board of Education* case of 1954.

Powell v. *Alabama* (1932)

(6th Amendment, right to counsel) The case involved the "Scottsboro boys," seven African American men accused of sexual assault. This case was a landmark in the development of a "fundamentals of fairness" doctrine of the Court over the next 40 years. The Scottsboro boys were quickly prosecuted without the benefit of counsel and sentenced to death. The Court overturned the decision, stating that poor people facing the death penalty in State courts must be provided counsel, and commenting, ". . . there are certain principles of Justice which adhere to the very idea of free government, which no [State] may disregard." The case was another step toward incorporation of the Bill of Rights into State constitutions.

Printz v. *United States* (1997)

Decision: The Court ruled that the Brady Act's interim provision requiring certain State or local law enforcement agents to perform background checks on prospective handgun purchasers was unconstitutional. Although no provision of the Constitution deals explicitly with federal authority to compel State officials to execute federal law, a review of the Constitution's structure and of prior Supreme Court decisions leads to the conclusion that Congress does not have this power.

Reno v. *American Civil Liberties Union* (1997)

Decision: The Supreme Court unanimously ruled that the anti-obscenity provisions of the Communications Decency Act (CDA) abridged the freedom of speech protected under the First Amendment. Those parts of the CDA were intended to keep minors from "patently offensive" or "indecent" communications on the Internet. While the Court recognized the importance of Congress's goal of protecting children, it concluded that the terms "patently offensive" and "indecent" were too vague to be enforceable, especially since information on the Internet is easily transmitted to many different parts of the country where community standards of decency may vary. The decision suggested that the Court saw the Internet as more like books or newspapers, which have high First Amendment protection, rather than like radio and television, where content can be more closely regulated by the government.

Reno v. *Condon* (2000)

Decision: The Court upheld the federal law that forbids States from selling addresses, telephone numbers, and other information that drivers put on license applications. They agreed with the Federal Government that information, including motor vehicle license information, is an "article of commerce" in the interstate stream of business and therefore is subject to regulation by Congress. The Court emphasized that the statute did not impose on the States any obligation to pass particular laws or policies and thus did not interfere with the States' sovereign functions.

Republican Party of Minnesota v. *White* (2002)

Decision: The Supreme Court decided that the State prohibition on "announcing" a judicial candidate's views violates the 1st Amendment. It unduly restricts the candidates' rights of free speech without adequately furthering the expressed goal of improving judicial impartiality and the appearance of impartiality. The government may not restrict speech based on its content, as this rule does. In addition, the government may not restrict speech about candidates' qualifications for office, which the rule also does. In addition, the rule is not well designed to preserve impartiality,

since it has no effect on the candidate's beliefs. Finally, the lack of any longstanding tradition of such a rule shows there is no historical presumption of constitutionality.

Roe v. *Wade* (1973)

(9th Amendment, right to privacy) A Texas woman challenged a State law forbidding the artificial termination of a pregnancy, saying that she "had a fundamental right to privacy." The Court upheld a woman's right to choose in this case, noting that the State's "important and legitimate interest in protecting the potentiality of human life" became "compelling" at the end of the first trimester, and that before then, ". . . the attending physician, in consultation with his patient, is free to determine, without regulation by the State, that . . . the patient's pregnancy should be terminated." The decision struck down the State regulation of abortion in the first three months of pregnancy and was modified by *Planned Parenthood of Southeastern PA* v. *Casey,* 1992.

Rostker v. *Goldberg* (1981)

Decision: The Court ruled that women did not have to be included in the draft registration. The purpose of having draft registration was to prepare for the actual draft of combat troops if they should be needed. Since Congress and the President had both consistently decided not to use women in combat positions, it was not necessary for women to register either. The Court also noted that the role of women in the armed services had been debated extensively in the Congress, and concluded that the legislature had reached a thoughtful, reasoned conclusion on this issue.

Roth v. *United States* (1951)

(1st Amendment, freedom of the press) A New York man named Roth operated a business that used the mail to invite people to buy materials considered obscene by postal inspectors. The Court, in its first consideration of censorship of obscenity, created the "prevailing community standards" rule, which required a consideration of the work as a whole. In its decision, the Court defined as obscene that which offended "the average person, applying contemporary community standards." In a case decided the same day, the Court applied the same "test" to State obscenity laws.

Rush Prudential HMO, Inc. v. *Moran* (2002)

Decision: The Supreme Court decided that ERISA does not preempt the Illinois medical-review statute. The statute regulates insurance, which is one of the functions HMOs perform. Although HMOs provide healthcare as well as insurance, the statute does not require choosing a single or primary function of an HMO. Congress has long recognized that HMOs are risk-bearing organizations subject to state regulation. Finally, allowing States to regulate the insurance aspects of HMOs will not interfere with the desire of Congress for uniform national standards under ERISA.

Schenck v. United States (1919)

(1st Amendment, freedom of speech) Charles Schenck was an officer of an antiwar political group who was arrested for alleged violations of the Espionage Act of 1917, which made active opposition to the war a crime. He had urged thousands of young men called to service by the draft act to resist and to avoid induction. The Court limited free speech in time of war, stating that Schenck's words, under the circumstances, presented a "clear and present danger. . . ." Although later decisions modified the decision, the *Schenck* case created a precedent that 1st Amendment guarantees were not absolute.

School District of Abington Township, Pennsylvania v. Schempp (1963)

(1st Amendment, Establishment Clause) A Pennsylvania State law required reading from the Bible each day at school as an all-school activity. Some parents objected and sought legal remedy. When the case reached the Court, the Court agreed with the parents, saying that the Establishment Clause and Free Exercise Clause both forbade States from engaging in religious activity. The Court created a rule holding that if the purpose and effect of a law "is the advancement or inhibition of religion," it "exceeds the scope of legal power."

Shelley v. Kraemer (1948)

Decision: The Court ruled that "in granting judicial enforcement of the restrictive agreements . . . the States have denied petitioners the equal protection of the laws. . . ." No individual has the right under the Constitution to demand that a State take action that would result in the denial of equal protection to other individuals. The Court rejected the respondents' argument that, since State courts would also enforce restrictive covenants against white owners, enforcement of covenants against black owners did not constitute a denial of equal protection. "Equal protection of the laws is not achieved through indiscriminate imposition of inequalities."

Sheppard v. Maxwell (1966)

(14th Amendment, Due Process Clause) Dr. Samuel Sheppard was convicted of murdering his wife in a trial widely covered by national news media. Sheppard appealed his conviction, claiming that the pretrial publicity had made it impossible to get a fair trial. The Court rejected the arguments about "press freedom," overturned his conviction, and ordered a new trial. As a result of the *Sheppard* decision, some judges have issued "gag" orders limiting pretrial publicity.

Tahoe-Sierra Preservation Council v. Tahoe Regional Planning Agency (2002)

Decision: The 32-month moratorium imposed by the Tahoe Regional Planning Agency on development in the Lake Tahoe Basin between Nevada and California is not a taking of property for which compensation is required. It is impossible in the abstract to say how long a restriction would be permissible. Although 32 months is a long moratorium, it is not unreasonable in this case and does not restrict the property owners' economic use of their property sufficiently to amount to a taking for which compensation must be paid.

Tennessee Valley Authority v. Hill (1978)

(Article I, Section 8, Necessary and Proper Clause) In 1975 the secretary of the interior found that the Tennessee Valley Authority's work on the Tellico Dam would destroy the endangered snail darter's habitat in violation of the Endangered Species Act of 1975. When the TVA refused to stop work on the project, local residents sued and won an injunction against completion of the dam from the federal court of appeals. The TVA appealed, arguing that the project should be completed since it had already been underway when the Endangered Species Act had passed and, with full knowledge of the circumstances of the endangered fish, Congress had continued to appropriate money for the dam in every year since the Act's passage. However, the Supreme Court found the injunction against the TVA's completion of the dam to be proper, stating "examination of the language, history, and structure of the legislation . . . indicates beyond doubt that Congress intended endangered species to be afforded the highest of priorities."

Texas v. White (1869)

Decision: The Court held, in a 5–3 decision, that Texas had the right to bring suit as a "State" in the Supreme Court, even though it had claimed to secede from the United States in 1862. Writing after the end of the Civil War, with military rule imposed in Texas under the Reconstruction Acts of 1867, the majority concluded that the United States was "an indestructible Union, composed of indestructible States," so that Texas had never actually left the Union.

Tinker v. Des Moines School District (1969)

Decision: The Court upheld the students' First Amendment rights. Because students do not "shed their constitutional rights to freedom of speech or expression at the schoolhouse gate," schools must show a possibility of "substantial disruption" before free speech can be limited at school. Students may express personal opinions as long as they do not materially disrupt classwork, create substantial disorder, or interfere with the rights of others. In this case, the wearing of black armbands was a "silent, passive expression of opinion" without these side effects and thus constitutionally could not be prohibited by the school.

U.S. Term Limits, Inc. v. Thornton (1995)

Decision: The Arkansas amendment preventing any person who had already served three terms as U.S. representative or two terms as U.S. senator from being listed on the ballot violates Article I, Section 2, Clause 2 and Section 3, Clause 3 of the Federal Constitution. The Arkansas law in effect established term limits for members of Congress, but the Constitution is the sole source of qualifications for membership. Such limits can only be set by an amendment to the Federal Constitution.

United States v. American Library Association (2003)

Decision: Requiring public libraries to install filters to block obscene or pornographic Internet sites as a condition for obtaining federal funds for Internet access does not violate the 1st Amendment. Congress's substantial interest in protecting children from harmful materials justifies the minimal interference with free speech caused when library users are forced to request access to a specific site.

United States v. Amistad (1841)

In 1839 two Spaniards purchased a group of kidnapped Africans and put them aboard the schooner *Amistad* for a journey from Cuba to Principe. The Africans overpowered the ship's crew, killing two men, and ordered the Spaniards to steer towards Africa. The crew steered instead toward the United States coast, where the U.S. brig *Washington* seized the ship, freeing the Spaniards and imprisoning the Africans. A series of petitions to the courts ensued, in which the Spaniards claimed the Africans as their property, and the Americans who had seized the ship claimed a share of the cargo, including the Africans, as their lawful salvage. The Court, however, declared that the Africans were not property and issued a decree that the unlawfully kidnapped Africans "be and are hereby declared to be free."

United States v. Eichman (1990)

Decision: The Court agreed with the trial courts' rulings that the Flag Protection Act violated the 1st Amendment. Flag-burning constitutes expressive conduct, and thus is entitled to constitutional protection. The Act prevents protesters from using the flag to express their opposition to governmental policies and activities. Although the protesters' ideas may be offensive or disagreeable to many people, the government may not prohibit them from expressing those ideas.

United States v. General Dynamics Corp. (1974)

A deep-mining coal producer, General Dynamics Corp., acquired control of a strip-mining coal producer, United Electric Coal Companies. The Government filed suit against the company, claiming that the acquisition violated the Clayton Act by limiting competition in coal sales and production. The Court rejected the Government's argument, finding that, although the acquisition may have increased concentration of ownership, it did not threaten to substantially lessen competition and was therefore not in violation of the Clayton Act.

United States v. Leon (1984)

(4th Amendment, exclusionary rule) Police in Burbank, California, gathered evidence in a drug-trafficking investigation using a search warrant issued by a State court judge. Later a District Court found that the warrant had been improperly issued and granted a motion to suppress the evidence gathered under the warrant. The Government appealed the decision, claiming that the exclusionary rule should not apply in cases where law enforcement officers acted in good faith, believing the warrant to be valid. The Court agreed and established the "good-faith exception" to the exclusionary rule, finding that the rule should not be applied to bar evidence "obtained by officers acting in reasonable reliance on a search warrant issued by a detached and neutral magistrate but ultimately found to be invalid."

United States v. Lopez (1990)

(Article I, Section 8, Commerce Clause) Alfonzo Lopez, a Texas high school student, was convicted of carrying a weapon in a school zone under the Gun-Free School Zones Act of 1990. He appealed his conviction on the basis that the Act, which forbids "any individual knowingly to possess a firearm at a place that [he] knows . . . is a school zone," exceeded Congress's legislative power under the Commerce Clause. The Court agreed that the Act was unconstitutional, stating that to uphold the legislation would "bid fair to convert congressional Commerce Clause authority to a general police power of the sort held only by the States."

United States v. Nixon (1974)

(Separation of powers) During the investigation of the Watergate scandal, in which members of President Nixon's administration were accused of participating in various illegal activities, a special prosecutor subpoenaed tapes of conversations between Nixon and his advisors. Nixon refused to release the tapes but was overruled by the Court, which ordered him to surrender the tapes, rejecting his arguments that they were protected by "executive privilege." The President's "generalized interest in confidentiality" was subordinate to "the fundamental demands of due process of law in the fair administration of criminal justice."

Wallace v. Jaffree (1985)

(1st Amendment, Establishment Clause) An Alabama law authorized a one-minute period of silence in all public schools "for meditation or voluntary prayer." A group of parents, including Jaffree, challenged the constitutionality of the statute, claiming it violated the Establishment Clause of the 1st Amendment. The Court agreed with Jaffree and struck down the Alabama law, determining that "the State's endorsement . . . of prayer activities at the beginning of each schoolday is not consistent with the established principle that the government must pursue a course of complete neutrality toward religion."

Walz v. Tax Commission of the City of New York (1970)

(1st Amendment, Establishment Clause) State and local governments routinely exempt church property from taxes. Walz claimed that such exemptions were a "support of religion," a subsidy by government. The Court disagreed, noting that such exemptions were just an example of a "benevolent neutrality" between government and churches, not a support of religion. Governments must avoid taxing churches because taxation would give government a "control" over religion, prohibited by the "wall of separation of church and state" noted in *Everson v. Board of Education,* 1947.

Watchtower Bible & Tract Society v. Village of Stratton (2001)

Decision: The Court ruled the Village's ordinance requiring canvassers to get a permit to be unconstitutional. Although a municipality may have a legitimate interest in regulating door-to-door solicitation, there must be a balance between furthering that interest and restricting 1st Amendment rights. The ordinance restricts religious or political speech, and thus needs strong justification to be valid. Because the ordinance is not restricted to commercial activities, it is broader than necessary to protect fraud. Residents have other ways to protect their privacy—they can post "no solicitation" signs or refuse to talk with unwelcome visitors. Finally, the 1st Amendment protects the right to anonymous expressions of religious or political belief.

Watkins v. United States (1957)

Decision: The Court held that Watkins was not given a fair opportunity to determine whether he was within his rights in refusing to answer the Committee's questions. Congress has no authority to expose the private affairs of individuals unless justified by a specific function of Congress. Congress's investigative powers are broad but not unlimited, and must not infringe on 1st Amendment rights of speech, political belief, or association. When witnesses are forced by subpoena to testify, the subject of Congressional inquiry must be articulated in the Committee's charter or explained at the time of testimony if 1st Amendment rights are in jeopardy.

West Virginia Board of Education v. Barnette (1943)

(1st Amendment, freedom of religion) During World War II the West Virginia Board of Education required all students to take part in a daily flag-saluting ceremony or else face expulsion. Jehovah's Witnesses objected to the compulsory salute, which they felt would force them to break their religion's doctrine against the worship of any "graven image." The Court struck down the rule, agreeing that a compulsory flag salute violated the 1st Amendment's exercise of religion clause and stating that "No official, high or petty, can prescribe what shall be orthodox in politics, nationalism, religion, or other matters of opinion. . . ."

Board of Education of Westside Community Schools v. Mergens (1990)

(1st Amendment, Establishment Clause) A request by Bridget Mergens to form a student Christian religious group at school was denied by an Omaha high school principal. Mergens took legal action, claiming that a 1984 federal law required "equal access" for student religious groups. The Court ordered the school to permit the club, stating, "a high school does not have to permit any extracurricular activities, but when it does, the school is bound by the . . . [Equal Access] Act of 1984. Allowing students to meet on campus and discuss religion is constitutional because it does not amount to 'State sponsorship of a religion.'"

Wisconsin v. Yoder (1972)

(1st Amendment, Free Exercise Clause) Members of the Amish religious sect in Wisconsin objected to sending their children to public schools after the eighth grade, claiming that such exposure of the children to another culture would endanger the group's self-sufficient agrarian lifestyle essential to their religious faith. The Court agreed with the Amish, while noting that the Court must move carefully to weigh the State's "legitimate social concern when faced with religious claim for exemption from generally applicable educational requirements."

English and Spanish Glossary

A

absentee voting provisions made for those unable to get to their regular polling places on election day (p. 195)
voto en ausencia medidas para que voten, el día de las elecciones, aquellas personas que no puedan hacerlo en su lugar habitual de votación

acquit find not guilty of a charge (p. 319)
absolver determinar que alguien no es culpable de un delito

act of admission congressional act admitting a new State to the Union (p. 106)
decreto de admisión ley del Congreso mediante la cual se admite a un nuevo estado dentro de la Unión

adjourn suspend, as in a session of Congress (p. 271)
aplazamiento suspender, por ejemplo, una sesión del Congreso

administration the officials in the executive branch of a government and their policies and principles (p. 428)
administración funcionarios del poder ejecutivo de un gobierno, así como sus políticas y sus directores

affirmative action a policy that requires most employers take positive steps to remedy the effects of past discriminations (p. 627)
acción afirmativa política que exige que la mayoría de los empleadores lleven a cabo ciertas acciones para remediar los efectos de discriminaciónes pasadas

Albany Plan of Union plan proposed by Benjamin Franklin in 1754 that aimed to unite the 13 colonies for trade, military, and other purposes; the plan was turned down by the colonies and the Crown (p. 37)
Plan de Unión Albany proyecto propuesto por Benjamín Franklin en 1754 cuyo objetivo era unir a las 13 colonias en cuanto a asuntos comerciales, militares, así como para otros propósitos; las colonias y la Corona rechazaron el plan

alien a foreign-born resident, or noncitizen (pp. 156, 548, 634)
extranjero persona residente nacida en otro país o que no se ha nacionalizado

ambassador an official representative of the United States appointed by the President to represent the nation in matters of diplomacy (p. 485)
embajador funcionario oficial designado por el Presidente para representar a la nación en asuntos diplomáticos

amicus curiae brief legal Latin term meaning "friend of the court;" a document that consists of written arguments presented to a court in support of one side in a dispute (p. 257)
alegato amicus curiae término legal en latín que significa "amigo de la corte;" documento presentado ante la corte que expone argumentos escritos en defensa de una de las partes en una disputa

amendment a change in, or addition to, a constitution or law (p. 78)
enmienda cambio o adición a la Constitución o a una ley

amnesty a blanket pardon offered to a group of law violators (p. 420)
amnistía perdón general que se ofrece a un grupo de personas que han violado la ley

Anti-Federalists those persons who opposed the ratification of the Constitution in 1787–1788 (p. 59)
Anti-federalistas aquellas personas que se opusieron a la ratificación de la Constitución entre 1787 y 1788

appellate jurisdiction the authority of a court to review decisions of inferior (lower) courts; see original jurisdiction (pp. 523, 734)
jurisdicción de apelación autoridad de una corte para revisar decisiones de cortes inferiores; ver original jurisdiction/jurisdicción original

apportion distribute, as in seats in a legislative body (p. 273)
prorrateo distribuir, por ejemplo, los escaños de un cuerpo legislativo

appropriate assign to a particular use (p. 316)
asignar destinar a un uso particular

Articles of Confederation plan of government adopted by the Continental Congress after the American Revolution; established "a firm league of friendship" among the States, but allowed few important powers to the central government (p. 48)
Artículos de la Confederación plan de gobierno adoptado por el Congreso Continental, después de la Independencia de los Estados Unidos; se enunciaron como "un vínculo firme de amistad" entre los estados, pero le delegaron pocos poderes importantes al gobierno central

assemble to gather with one another in order to express views on public matters (p. 569)
congregar reunirse con otras personas para expresar puntos de vista sobre asuntos públicos

assessment the process of determining the value of property to be taxed (p. 764)
valuación proceso para determinar el valor de una propiedad que será gravada

assimilation the process by which people of one culture merge into, and become part of, another culture (p. 615)
asimilación proceso mediante el cual las personas de una cultura se integran en otra cultura y se convierten en parte de ella

at-large election election of an officeholder by the voters of an entire governmental unit (e.g., a State or country) rather than by the voters of a district or subdivision (p. 275)
elección general elección de un funcionario público por los votantes de una unidad gubernamental completa (por ejemplo, un estado o país), en vez de por los votantes de un distrito o subdivisión

Attorney General the head of the Department of Justice (p. 435)
Procurador General funcionario más alto del Departamento de Justicia

autocracy a form of government in which a single person holds unlimited political power (p. 14)
autocracia forma de gobierno en la que una sola persona tiene poder político ilimitado

B

bail a sum of money that the accused may be required to post (deposit with the court) as a guarantee that he or she will appear in court at the proper time (p. 602)
fianza suma de dinero que se exige que el acusado pague (en la corte) como garantía de que se presentará en dicha corte en la fecha señalada

balance the ticket when a presidential candidate chooses a running mate who can strengthen his chance of being elected by virtue of certain ideological, geographic, racial, ethnic, gender, or other characteristics (p. 372)

designar al compañero de fórmula acción que ejerce un candidato presidencial cuando elige al candidato a la vice-presidencia que refuerza sus oportunidades de ganar las elecciones, gracias a sus características ideológicas, geográficas, raciales, étnicas, de género, u otras virtudes

ballot the device voters use to register a choice in an election (p. 194)

papeleta electoral medio que los votantes utilizan para indicar su preferencia en una elección

ballot fatigue the phenomenon by which voters cast fewer votes for offices listed toward the bottom of the ballot (p. 171)

fatiga al votar fenómeno que se presenta cuando los votantes marcan menos casillas hacia el final de la papeleta electoral

bankruptcy the legal proceeding by which a bankrupt person's assets are distributed among those to whom he or she owes debts (p. 302)

bancarrota procedimiento legal mediante el cual los bienes de una persona se distribuyen entre las personas con las que tiene deudas

battleground States States in which the outcome of an election is too close to call and either candidate could win (p. 386)

estados reñidos estados donde los resultados de las elecciones indican que cualquier candidato podría ser el ganador

bench trial a trial in which the judge alone hears the case (pp. 597, 730)

juicio ante judicatura proceso en en el cual sólo el juez escucha el caso

bicameral an adjective describing a legislative body composed of two chambers (pp. 33, 268)

bicameral adjetivo que describe un cuerpo legislativo formado por dos cámaras

bill a proposed law presented to a legislative body for consideration (pp. 287, 343)

proyecto de ley ley propuesta que se presenta ante un cuerpo legislativo para su consideración

Bill of Attainder a legislative act that inflicts punishment without a court trial (p. 593)

Escrito de proscripción y confiscación acto legislativo que inflige un castigo sin que haya un juicio ante un jurado

Bill of Rights the first ten amendments to the Constitution (pp. 82, 547)

Declaración de derechos las primeras diez enmiendas a la Constitución

bipartisan supported by two parties (p. 127)

bipartidista apoyado por dos partidos

blanket primary a voting process in which voters receive a long ballot containing the names of all contenders, regardless of party, and can vote however they choose (p. 189)

elecciones primarias generales proceso de elección en el que los votantes reciben una papeleta electoral grande que contiene los nombres de todos los candidatos, independientemente del partido, y en el cual pueden elegir libremente

block grant one type of federal grants-in-aid for some particular but broadly defined area of public policy; see grants-in-aid (p. 109)

subsidio en conjunto tipo de subsidio público federal que se ofrece para un área particular pero definida en términos generales; ver grants-in-aid program/programa de subvención de fondos públicos

briefs detailed written statements filed with the Court before oral arguments are presented (p. 535)

alegato reseña detallada presentada ante la Corte antes de dar un argumento oral

budget a financial plan for the use of money, personnel, and property (p. 766)

presupuesto plan financiero para el uso del dinero, el personal y la propiedad

bureaucracy a large, complex administrative structure that handles the everyday business of an organization (p. 426)

burocracia estructura administrativa grande y compleja que gobierna los negocios cotidianos de una organización

bureaucrat a person who works for a bureaucratic organization; see bureaucracy (p. 426)

burócrata persona que trabaja en una organización burocrática; ver bureaucracy/burocracia

C

Cabinet presidential advisory body, traditionally made up of the heads of the executive departments and other officers (p. 87)

Gabinete cuerpo consultivo del Presidente que tradicionalmente está formado por los funcionarios más altos de los departamentos ejecutivos y otros agentes

capital all the human-made resources that are used to produce goods and services (p. 678)

capital todos los recursos creados por el hombre que se utilizan para producir bienes y servicios

capital punishment the death penalty (p. 604)

pena capital la pena de muerte

capitalism economic system in which individuals are free to own the means of production and maximize profits (p. 678)

capitalismo sistema económico en el que individuos tienen la libertad de poseer los medios de producción y de aumentar sus ganancias

categorical grant one type of federal grants-in-aid; made for some specific, closely defined, purpose; see grants-in-aid (p. 108)

subsidio categórico tipo de subsidio público federal; proporcionado para un propósito específico y rigurosamente definido; ver grants-in-aid program/programa de subvención de fondos públicos

caucus as a nominating device, a group of like-minded people who meet to select the candidates they will support in an upcoming election (pp. 185, 381)

junta de dirigentes en función de instrumento nominativo, grupo de personas que comparten la misma ideología y que se reúnen para seleccionar a los candidatos que apoyarán en una elección

censure issue a formal condemnation (p. 320)

amonestación pronunciamiento de una condena formal

certificate a method of putting a case before the Supreme Court; used when a lower court is not clear about the procedure or rule of law that should apply in a case and asks the Supreme Court to certify the answer to a specific question (p. 534)

certificación método de remitir un caso a la Corte Suprema; se utiliza cuando una corte inferior no está segura de qué procedimiento o regla deberá aplicar en un caso y consulta a la Corte Suprema para que certifique una respuesta a una pregunta específica

charter a city's basic law, its constitution; a written grant of authority from the king (pp. 33, 750)

carta constitucional ley básica de una ciudad, su constitución; concesión de autoridad escrita otorgada por el rey

checks and balances system of overlapping the powers of the legislative, executive, and judicial branches to permit each branch to check the actions of the others; *see* separation of powers (p. 72)

sistema de frenos y contrapesos sistema de equilibrio entre los poderes; mecanismo mediante el cual se traslapa la autoridad del poder legislativo, el poder ejecutivo y el poder judicial para permitir que cada poder verifique las acciones de los otros dos; *ver* separation of powers/separación de poderes

chief administrator term for the President as head of the administration of the Federal Government (p. 365)

administrador en jefe nombre que se le da al Presidente por ser el jefe de la administración del gobierno federal

chief citizen term for the President as the representative of the people, working for the public interest (p. 365)

primer ciudadano nombre que se le da al Presidente por ser representante del pueblo y trabajar por el interés público

chief diplomat term for the President as the main architect of foreign policy and spokesperson to other countries (p. 365)

diplomático titular nombre que se le da al Presidente por ser el arquitecto principal de la política exterior y un vocero ante otros países

chief executive term for the President as vested with the executive power of the United States (p. 364)

primer mandatario nombre que se le da al Presidente porque está investido con el poder ejecutivo de los Estados Unidos

chief legislator term for the President as architect of public policy and the one who sets the agenda for Congress (p. 365)

legislador en jefe nombre que se le da al Presidente por ser arquitecto de la política pública y por ser la persona que determina la agenda del Congreso

chief of party term for the President as the leader of his or her political party (p. 365)

jefe del partido nombre que se le da al Presidente por ser el líder de su partido político

chief of state term for the President as the ceremonial head of the United States, the symbol of all the people of the nation (p. 364)

jefe de estado nombre que se le da al Presidente por ser el funcionario ceremonial de los Estados Unidos, el símbolo de toda la gente de la nación

citizen a member of a state or nation who owes allegiance to it by birth or naturalization and is entitled to full civil rights (pp. 23, 632)

ciudadano miembro de un estado o nación por nacimiento o naturalización, que se beneficia de todos los derechos civiles y que le debe lealtad a ese estado o nación

civil case a case involving a noncriminal matter such as a contract dispute or a claim of patent infringement (p. 529)

caso civil caso relacionado con un asunto no criminal, como un litigio por contrato o una demanda por violación de patentes

civil disobedience a form of protest in which people deliberately but non-violently violate the law, as a means of expressing their opposition to some particular law or public policy (p. 569)

resistencia pasiva forma de protesta en la cual las personas violan la ley de una manera no violenta, como método para expresar su oposición a una ley o política pública

civil law the portion of the law relating to human conduct, to disputes between private parties, and to disputes between private parties and government not covered by criminal law (p. 728)

ley civil área de la ley que se relaciona con la conducta humana, con litigios entre entidades privadas, así como entre partes privadas y el gobierno, que no están cubiertos bajo la ley penal

civil liberties the guarantees of the safety of persons, opinions, and property from the arbitrary acts of government, including freedom of speech and freedom of religion (p. 547)

libertades civiles garantías que protegen la seguridad, las opiniones y la propiedad de las personas de actos arbitrarios del gobierno; entre ellas están la libertad de expresión y la libertad de religión

civil rights a term used for those positive acts of government that seek to make constitutional guarantees a reality for all people, e.g., prohibitions of discrimination (p. 547)

derechos civiles término que designa actos positivos del gobierno con el objetivo de hacer realidad las garantías constitucionales para todo el pueblo, por ejemplo la prohibición de la discriminación

civil service those civilian employees who perform the administrative work of government (p. 443)

servicio civil grupo de empleados civiles que desempeñan el trabajo administrativo del gobierno

civilian nonmilitary (p. 435)

civil que no es militar

civilian tribunal a court operating as part of the judicial branch, entirely separate from the military establishment (p. 539)

tribunal civil corte que actúa como parte del poder judicial y que está separado por completo de la institución militar

clemency mercy or leniency granted to an offender by a chief executive; *see* pardon and reprieve (pp. 419, 724)

clemencia misericordia o piedad que dispensa el Presidente a un delincuente; *ver* pardon/perdón y reprieve/suspensión

closed primary a party nominating election in which only declared party members can vote (p. 188)

elección primaria cerrada elecciones para una nominación de un partido en la que sólo los miembros declarados del partido pueden votar

cloture procedure that may be used to limit or end floor debate in a legislative body (p. 353)

limitación del debate procedimiento que puede utilizarse para restringir o terminar un debate verbal de un cuerpo legislativo

coalition a temporary alliance of several groups who come together to form a working majority and so to control a government (pp. 128, 667)

coalición alianza temporal de varios grupos que se juntan para alcanzar el poder mayoritario y controlar el gobierno

coattail effect the effect of a strong candidate running for an office at the top of a ballot helping to attract voters to other candidates on the party's ticket (p. 195)

efecto de refilón efecto que produce la presencia de un candidato fuerte en la parte superior de una papeleta electoral y que ayuda a atraer votantes hacia otros candidatos de su mismo partido

cold war a period of more than 40 years during which relations between the two superpowers were at least tense, and often hostile. A time of threats and military build up (p. 498)

guerra fría período de más de 40 años en el que las relaciones entre las dos superpotencias fueron por lo menos tensas, y a menudo hostiles; época de amenazas y de desarrollo armamentista

collective security the keeping of international peace and order (p. 498)

seguridad colectiva conservación de la paz y el orden internacionales

collectivization collective or state ownership of the means of production (p. 689)

colectivización hacer colectivos o propiedad del estado los medios de producción

colonialism the control of one nation over foreign lands (p. 651)

colonialismo control que tiene una nación sobre tierras extranjeras

command economy system in which government bureaucrats plan and direct most economic activity (p. 687)

economía dirigida sistema en el cual los burócratas del gobierno planean y dirigen la mayor parte de la actividad económica

commander in chief term for the President as commander of the nation's armed forces (p. 364)

comandante en jefe nombre que se le da al Presidente por ser el comandante de las Fuerzas Armadas de la nación

Commerce and Slave Trade Compromise an agreement during the Constitutional Convention protecting slave holders; denied Congress the power to tax the export of goods from any State, and, for 20 years, the power to act on the slave trade (p. 56)

Avenencia de comercio y trata de esclavos acuerdo durante la Convención Constitucional que protegió los intereses de los dueños de esclavos, al negarle al Congreso el poder de gravar la exportación de bienes desde cualquier estado y el poder de actuar, durante 20 años, en contra de la trata de esclavos

commerce power exclusive power of Congress to regulate interstate and foreign trade (p. 297)

poder mercantil poder exclusivo que tiene el Congreso para regular el comercio interestatal e internacional

commission government a government formed by commissioners, heads of different departments of city government, who are popularly elected to form the city council and thus center both legislative and executive powers in one body (p. 751)

junta municipal gobierno formado por comisionados, funcionarios altos de distintos departamentos del gobierno de la ciudad, que se eligen por voto popular para formar el Consejo de la ciudad y, por consiguiente, reúnen los poderes legislativos y ejecutivos en un solo cuerpo

committee chairman member who heads a standing committee in a legislative body (p. 336)

presidente de comisión miembro que encabeza una comisión permanente en un cuerpo legislativo

common law an unwritten law made by a judge that has developed over centuries from those generally accepted ideas of right and wrong that have gained judicial recognition (p. 727)

derecho consuetudinario ley que no ha sido sancionada por un juez y se ha desarrollado a lo largo de los siglos, con base en ideas generalmente aceptadas de lo bueno y lo malo que se han ganado un reconocimiento judicial

communism an ideology which calls for the collective, or state, ownership of land and other productive property (pp. 659, 686)

comunismo ideología que exige la propiedad colectiva, o estatal, de la tierra y de otros medios de producción

Communist Manifesto, The a political document written by Karl Marx and Friedrich Engels that urged workers to free themselves from "capitalist enslavement" (p. 685)

El manifiesto comunista documento político escrito por Karl Marx y Friedrich Engels en el cual se urge a los trabajadores a que se liberen de ser esclavizados por el capitalismo

commutation the power to reduce (commute) the length of a sentence or fine for a crime (pp. 420, 725)

conmutación poder de reducir (conmutar) la duración de una sentencia o el monto de la multa por haber cometido un crimen

compromise an adjustment of opposing principles or systems by modifying some aspect of each (p. 22)

transigencia acuerdo intermedio entre principios o sistemas opuestos, al que se llega mediante la modificación de algún aspecto de cada uno de ellos

concurrent jurisdiction power shared by federal and State courts to hear certain cases (p. 522)

jurisdicción coincidente poder compartido por cortes federales y estatales para atender ciertos casos

concurrent powers those powers that both the National Government and the States possess and exercise (p. 100)

poderes concurrentes aquellos poderes que el gobierno nacional y los estados poseen y ejercen

concurrent resolution a statement of position on an issue used by the House and Senate acting jointly; does not have the force of law and does not require the President's signature (p. 344)

resolución conjunta enunciado de una opinión sobre un asunto utilizado por la Cámara de Representantes y el Senado al actuar conjuntamente; no tiene el poder de la ley y no requiere la firma del Presidente

concurring opinion written explanation of the views of one or more judges who support a decision reached by a majority of the court, but wish to add or emphasize a point that was not made in the majority decision (p. 537)

opinion coincidente explicación escrita de los puntos de vista de uno o más jueces quienes apoyan una decisión alcanzada por una mayoría en la corte, pero desean añadir o recalcar un punto que no se remarcó en la decisión mayoritaria

confederation a joining of several groups for a common purpose (pp. 16, 37)

confederación unión de diversos grupos para un propósito común

conference committee temporary joint committee created to reconcile any differences between the two houses' versions of a bill (p. 342)

comité de consulta comité conjunto temporal formado para reconciliar cualquier diferencia entre las versiones de un proyecto de ley propuesto por las dos cámaras legislativas

Connecticut Compromise agreement during the Constitutional Convention that Congress should be composed of a Senate, in which States would be represented equally, and a House, in which representation would be based on a State's population (p. 56)

Acuerdo de Connecticut acuerdo alcanzado durante la Convención Constitucional que estableció que el Congreso debería estar integrado por un Senado donde cada estado estuviera representado de manera equitativa, y una Cámara de Representantes en la que la representación estuviera basada en la población de cada estado

consensus general agreement among various groups on fundamental matters; broad agreement on public questions (pp. 127, 314)

consenso acuerdo general entre diversos grupos sobre temas fundamentales; acuerdo general sobre asuntos públicos

constituency the people and interests that an elected official represents (p. 283)

circunscripción electoral las personas e intereses que un funcionario elegido representa

constituent power the non-legislative power of Constitution-making and the constitutional amendment process (p. 717)

poder constituyente poder no legislativo de la elaboración de la Constitución y del proceso de enmiendas constitucionales

constitution the body of fundamental laws setting out the principles, structures, and processes of a government (p. 5)

constitución cuerpo de leyes fundamentales que definen los principios, las estructuras y los procesos de gobierno

constitutionalism basic principle that government and those who govern must obey the law; the rule of law; *see* limited government (p. 70)

constitucionalismo principio básico que establece que el gobierno y los gobernantes deben obedecer la ley; el gobierno de la ley; *ver* limited government/gobierno limitado

containment a policy based in the belief that if communism could be kept within its existing boundaries, it would collapse under the weight of its internal weaknesses (p. 500)

contención Política basada en la creencia de que si se pudiera evitar la expansión del régimen comunista, éste colapsaría debido a la fragilidad de su estructura interna

content neutral the government may not regulate assemblies on the basis on what might be said (p. 570)

voto neutral el gobierno no regulará a las asambleas en lo concerniente a lo que se expresará en ellas

continuing resolution a measure that allows agencies to continue working based on the previous year's appropriations (p. 471)

resolución ininterrumpida medida que permite que las agencias continúen funcionando basándose en de las asignaciones del año anterior

continuous body governing unit (e.g. the United States Senate) whose seats are never all up for election at the same time (p. 283)

cuerpo legislativo ininterrumpido unidad gubernamental (por ejemplo, el Senado de los Estados Unidos) cuya totalidad de escaños nunca se elige al mismo tiempo

contract a legally binding agreement in which one party agrees to do something with or for another party (p.728)

contrato acuerdo legal mediante el cual una parte se compromete a actuar con o para otra parte

controllable spending an amount decided upon by Congress and the President to determine how much will be spent each year on many individual government expenditures, including environment protection programs, aid to education, and so on (p. 468)

gasto controlable cantidad de dinero determinada por el Congreso y el Presidente, que indica el monto anual de muchos gastos gubernamentales individuales, como programas para la protección del ambiente, ayuda a la educación, y otros

convene to begin a new session of Congress (p. 271)

convocar empezar una nueva sesión del Congreso

copyright the exclusive, legal right of a person to reproduce, publish, and sell his or her own literary, musical, or artistic creations (p. 307)

derechos de autor derechos legales y exclusivos de una persona para reproducir, publicar y vender su trabajo creativo literario, artístico o musical

council-manager government a modification of the mayor-council government, it consists of a strong council of members elected on a non-partisan ballot, a weak mayor, elected by the people, and a manager, named by the council; *see* mayor-council government; *see also* weak mayor government (p. 751)

gobierno de consejo-superintendente modificación del gobierno de consejo-alcalde, que consiste en un vigoroso consejo de miembros elegidos mediante un sufragio no partidista; un alcalde débil, elegido por el pueblo y un superintendente nombrado por el consejo; *ver* mayor-council government/gobierno de consejo-alcalde; *ver también* weak-mayor government/gobierno de alcalde débil

county a major unit of local government in most States (p. 742)

Condado unidad importante de gobierno local en gran parte de los estados

court-martial a court composed of military personnel, for the trial of those accused of violating military law (p. 538)

Corte marcial corte integrada por personal militar para juzgar a quienes han sido acusados de violar la ley militar

criminal case a case in which a defendant is tried for committing a crime as defined by the law (p. 529)

caso criminal caso en el que se juzga al acusado por cometer un crimen, tal y como éste se define de acuerdo a la ley

criminal law the portion of the law that defines public wrongs and provides for their punishment (p. 728)

derecho penal área de la ley que define los agravios públicos y que establece su castigo

custom duty a tax laid on goods brought into the United States from abroad, also known as tariffs, import duties, or imposts (p. 462)

derecho de aduana impuesto sobre los bienes traídos a los Estados Unidos desde el exterior, también se conoce como arancel, impuesto sobre importaciones o tasa sobre importaciones

D

de facto segregation segregation even if no law requires it, e.g., housing patterns (p. 621)

discriminación de facto o de hecho segregación, incluso sin que la ley lo exija, como en la asignación de viviendas

de jure segregation segregation by law, with legal sanction (p. 621)

discriminación de jure o de ley segregación con base en la ley, que implica una sanción legal

defendant in a civil suit, the person against whom a court action is brought by the plaintiff; in a criminal case, the person charged with the crime (p. 523)

acusado en un juicio civil, es la persona en contra de quien el demandante pide ejecutar una acción judicial; en un caso criminal, es la persona acusada de un crimen

deficit the yearly shortfall between revenue and spending (p. 463)

déficit diferencia anual entre los ingresos y los egresos

deficit financing practice of funding government by borrowing to make up the difference between government spending and revenue (p. 301)

financiamiento del déficit práctica que consiste en subvencionar al gobierno mediante préstamos, a fin de compensar la diferencia entre los gastos y los ingresos gubernamentales

deflation a general decrease in prices (p. 474)

deflación disminución general de los precios

delegated powers those powers, expressed, implied, or inherent, granted to the National Government by the Constitution (p. 96)

poderes delegados poderes explícitos, implícitos o inherentes que la Constitución transfiere al gobierno nacional

delegates representatives; members of Congress who cast votes based on the wishes of their constituents (pp. 37, 287)

delegados representantes; miembros del Congreso que votan según los deseos de sus constituyentes

demand-side economics the theory that the higher employment that results from government borrowing will produce higher tax revenues (p. 464)

economía de demanda teoría que establece que un alza de los empleos debido a préstamos del gobierno producirá un incremento en los ingresos tributarios

democracy a form of government in which the supreme authority rests with the people (p. 5)

democracia forma de gobierno en la cual la autoridad suprema reside en el pueblo

democratic consolidation the process of establishing the factors considered necessary for a democracy to succeed (p. 663)

consolidación democrática proceso mediante el cual se establecen los factores necesarios para el éxito de una democracia

democratization the change from dictatorship to democracy, marked by the holding of free and fair elections (p. 663)

democratización cambio de una dictadura a una democracia mediante elecciones libres y justas

denaturalization the process through which naturalized citizens may involuntarily lose their citizenship (p. 635)

desnaturalización proceso mediante el cual los ciudadanos naturalizados pueden perder su ciudadanía de manera involuntaria

deportation a legal process in which aliens are legally required to leave the United States (p. 637)

deportación proceso legal mediante el cual se exige a los extranjeros que abandonen los Estados Unidos

détente a relaxation of tensions (p. 501)

relajamiento disminución de las tensiones

deterrence the policy of making America and its allies so militarily strong that their very strength will discourage, or prevent, any attack (p. 498)

disuasión política que consiste en convertir a los Estados Unidos y sus aliados en una fuerza militar tan poderosa que su fortaleza desaliente, o prevenga, cualquier ataque

devolution the delegation of authority from the central government to regional governments (p. 670)

delegación transferencia de la autoridad del gobierno central a los gobiernos regionales

dictatorship a form of government in which the leader has absolute power and authority (p. 5)

dictadura forma de gobierno en la que el líder ejerce poder y autoridad absolutos

diplomatic immunity when an ambassador is not subject to the laws of the state to which they are accredited (p. 486)

inmunidad diplomática condición en la que un embajador no está sujeto a las leyes del estado anfitrión

direct popular election proposal to do away with the electoral college and allow the people to vote directly for President and Vice President (p. 392)

elección popular directa propuesta para abolir el colegio electoral y permitir que la gente elija de manera directa al Presidente y al Vicepresidente

direct primary an election held within a party to pick that party's candidates for the general election (p. 187)

elecciones primarias directas elecciones realizadas dentro de un partido para escoger a los candidatos del partido para las elecciones generales

discharge petition a procedure enabling members to force a bill that has been pigeonholed in committee onto the floor for consideration (p. 345)

petición de exoneración procedimiento que permite a los miembros reiniciar la discusión para considerar una propuesta de ley que se había suspendido en una comisión de debate

discount rate the rate of interest a bank must pay when it borrows money from a Federal Reserve Bank (p. 476)

tasa de descuento tasa de interés que debe pagar un banco que toma un préstamo del Banco de la Reserva Federal

discrimination bias, unfairness (p. 584)

discriminación prejuicio, injusticia

disenfranchised denied the right to vote (p.153)

privación del derecho al voto acción que consiste en negarle a alguien el derecho de votar

dissenting opinion written explanation of the views of one or more judges who disagree with (dissent from) a decision reached by a majority of the court; *see* majority opinion (p. 537)

opinión disidente explicación escrita de los puntos de vista de uno o más jueces que está(n) en desacuerdo con una decisión tomada por la mayoría de la corte; *ver* majority opinion/opinión mayoritaria

district plan proposal for choosing presidential electors by which two electors would be selected in each State according to the Statewide popular vote and the other electors would be selected separately in each of the State's congressional districts (p. 391)

plan de distrito propuesta para elegir a los electores presidenciales, mediante la cual se seleccionarían dos electores en cada estado, de acuerdo con el voto popular de todo ese estado, y los otros electores se elegirían de manera separada en cada uno de los distritos del Congreso de ese estado

divine right of laws the belief that God grants authority to a government (p. 650)

derecho divino creencia de que Dios le concede autoridad a un gobierno

division of powers basic principle of federalism; the constitutional provisions by which governmental powers are divided on a geographic basis (in the United States, between the National Government and the States) (pp. 16, 95)

división de poderes principio básico del federalismo; estipulaciones constitucionales que establecen que los poderes gubernamentales están separados según la ubicación geográfica (en los Estados Unidos, se dividen entre el gobierno nacional y los estados)

docket a court's list of cases to be heard (p. 530)

agenda lista de casos por atender en una corte

domestic affairs all matters not directly connected to the realm of foreign affairs (pp. 434, 482)

asuntos internos todas cuestiones no relacionadas con el campo de los asuntos exteriores

double jeopardy part of the 5th Amendment which says that no person can be put in jeopardy of life or limb twice. Once a person has been tried for a crime, he or she cannot be tried again for the same crime (p. 595)

doble juicio parte de la 5ª enmienda que establece que no se puede poner en riesgo la vida de una persona o su integridad física dos veces. Una vez que se ha juzgado por un crimen a una persona, no puede volvérsele a juzgar por el mismo delito

draft conscription, or compulsory military service (p. 445)

reclutamiento conscripción o servicio militar obligatorio

due process the government must act fairly and in accord with established rules in all that it does (pp. 31, 578)

proceso legal establecido el gobierno debe actuar con justicia y de acuerdo con las reglas establecidas en todo lo que hace

Due Process Clause part of the 14th Amendment which guarantees that no state deny basic rights to its people (p. 549)

Cláusula del proceso parte de la 14ª enmienda que garantiza que ningún estado negará los derechos básicos a su pueblo

E

economic protest parties parties rooted in poor economic times, lacking a clear ideological base, dissatisfied with current conditions and demanding better times (p. 138)

partidos de protesta económica partidos surgidos en tiempos de descontento económico, que carecen de una base ideológica bien definida, están insatisfechos por las condiciones presentes y exigen mejoras

electoral college group of persons chosen in each State and the District of Columbia every four years who make a formal selection of the President and Vice President (pp. 87, 375)

colegio electoral grupo de personas (electores presidenciales) elegidos cada cuatro años en todos los estados y en el Distrito de Columbia a fin de elegir formalmente al Presidente y Vicepresidente

electoral votes votes cast by electors in the electoral college (p. 375)

votos electorales votos emitidos por los electores en el Colegio electoral

electorate all of the people entitled to vote in a given election (pp. 132,152)

electorado todas las personas que tienen derecho a votar en una elección determinada

eminent domain power of a government to take private property for public use (p. 308)

dominio supremo poder de un gobierno de expropiar la propiedad privada para uso público

enabling act a congressional act directing the people of a United States territory to frame a proposed State constitution as a step towards admission to the Union (p. 106)

ley de habilitación ley del Congreso que orienta al pueblo de un territorio de los Estados Unidos para que redacte una propuesta de la constitución para el estado, como un paso hacia la admisión de dicho estado dentro de la Unión

encomienda a system instituted by the Spanish crown in which the monarch granted control of Indians to settlers for forced labor for mining and agriculture (p. 655)

encomienda sistema instituido por la corona española en el que el monarca les otorga a los colonos el control de los indígenas para ser forzados a trabajar en minas y en agricultura

English Bill of Rights document written by Parliament and agreed on by William and Mary of England in 1689, designed to prevent abuse of power by English monarchs; forms the basis for much in American government and politics today (p. 31)

Declaración inglesa de los derechos documento redactado por el Parlamento y aceptado por William y Mary de Inglaterra en 1689, elaborado para evitar el abuso de poder por parte de los monarcas ingleses; constituye la base de grande parte del gobierno y la política estadounidenses actuales

engross to print a bill in its final form (p. 349)

transcribir imprimir un proyecto de ley en su forma final

entitlement a benefit that federal law says must be paid to all those who meet the eligibility requirements, e.g., Medicare, food stamps, and veterans' pension (pp. 467, 758)

derecho beneficio que la ley federal establece que se debe pagar a todos los que cumplan los requisitos para ser elegibles, por ejemplo: el seguro médico, los bonos de comida y los pensión para los veteranos

entrepreneur an individual with the drive and ambition to combine land, labor, and capital resources to produce goods or offer services (p. 679)

empresario individuo con el impulso y la ambición de combinar los recursos de la tierra, la mano de obra y el capital para producir bienes u ofrecer servicios

espionage spying (p. 492)

espionaje acto de espiar

Establishment Clause separates church and state (p. 551)

Cláusula del establecimiento separa a la Iglesia del Estado

estate tax a levy imposed on the assets of one who dies (pp. 461, 764)

impuesto testamentario gravamen sobre los bienes de una persona que muere

ex post facto law a law applied to an act committed before its passage (p. 593)

ley ex post facto ley que se aplica a un acto cometido con anterioridad a la aprobación de la ley

excise tax a tax laid on the manufacture, sale, or consumption of goods and/or the performance of services (p. 461)

impuesto al consumo gravamen sobre la manufactura, venta o consumo de bienes y/o al suministro de servicios

exclusionary rule evidence gained as the result of an illegal act by police cannot be used against the person from whom it was seized (p. 588)

regla de exclusión evidencia obtenida como resultado de una acción ilegal de la policía y que no puede utilizarse contra la persona arrestada

exclusive powers those powers that can be exercised by the National Government alone (p. 99)

poderes exclusivos poderes que sólo el gobierno nacional puede ejercer

executive agreement a pact made by the President directly with the head of a foreign state; a binding international agreement with the force of law but which (unlike a treaty) does not require Senate consent (pp. 87, 413)

acuerdo ejecutivo pacto establecido de manera directa entre el Presidente y otro jefe un estado extranjero; pacto internacional obligatorio que tiene el poder de una ley pero que no requiere, a diferencia de un tratado, de la aprobación del Senado

Executive Article Article II of the Constitution. Establishes the presidency and gives the executive power of the Federal Government to the President (p. 400)

Artículo del ejecutivo el segundo artículo de la Constitución. Define la presidencia y le otorga el poder ejecutivo del gobierno federal al Presidente

executive departments often called the Cabinet departments, they are the traditional units of federal administration (p. 435)

oficinas del poder ejecutivo a menudo llamadas oficinas del gabinete; son las unidades tradicionales de la administración federal

Executive Office of the President an organization of several agencies staffed by the President's closest advisors (p. 431)

Oficina ejecutiva del Presidente organización compleja, que abarca diversas oficinas separadas, cuyo personal está integrado por los consejeros y asistentes más cercanos al Presidente

executive order directive, rule, or regulation issued by a chief executive or subordinates, based upon constitutional or statutory authority and having the force of law (p. 406)

orden ejecutiva directiva, regla o reglamento expedido por un primer mandatario o sus subordinados, con base en su autoridad estatutaria o constitucional, y que tiene el poder de una ley

executive power the power to execute, enforce, and administer law (p. 5)

poder ejecutivo poder para ejecutar, administrar y obligar al cumplimiento de la ley

executive privilege the President's power to refuse to disclose information (p. 409)

privilegio ejecutivo poder que tiene el Presidente para rehusarse a revelar información

expatriation the legal process by which a loss of citizenship occurs (p. 634)

expatriación proceso legal mediante el cual ocurre la pérdida de ciudadanía

expressed powers those delegated powers of the National Government that are spelled out, expressly, in the Constitution; also called the "enumerated powers" (pp. 96, 296)

poderes explícitos aquellos poderes delegados del gobierno nacional que se señalan explícitamente en la Constitución; también se conocen como los "poderes ennumerados"

extradition the legal process by which a fugitive from justice in one State is returned to that State (p. 113)

extradición proceso legal a través del cual un fugitivo de la justicia de un estado se retorna a ese estado

F

faction a conflicting group (p. 131)
facción un grupo disidente

factors of production basic resources which are used to make all goods and services (p. 678)

factores de producción recursos básicos que se utilizan para elaborar todos los bienes y servicios

failed states nations in which security is nonexistent, the economy has collapsed, healthcare and school systems are in shambles, and corruption flourishes (p. 665)

estados fallidos Países con un sistema de seguridad nulo, una economía muy deteriorada, sistemas de asistencia de salud y de educación en crisis y donde prospera la corrupción

fascism a system of government characterized by a centralized, authoritarian government with policies that glorify the state over the individual (p. 659)

fascismo Sistema político caracterizado por un gobierno centralizado y autoritario con políticas que destacan al estado por encima del individuo

federal budget a detailed financial document containing estimates of federal income and spending during the coming fiscal year (p. 433)

presupuesto federal documento financiero detallado que contiene las estimaciones de las recaudaciones y gastos que anticipan los ingresos y egresos federales durante el año fiscal venidero

Federal Government a form of government in which powers are divided between a central government and several local governments (p. 16)

Gobierno Federal forma de gobierno en la que los poderes están divididos entre un gobierno central y diversos gobiernos locales

federalism a system of government in which a written constitution divides power between a central, or national, government and several regional governments (pp. 75, 94)

federalismo sistema de gobierno en el que una constitución escrita divide los poderes del gobierno, entre un gobierno central (o nacional) y diversos gobiernos regionales

Federalists those persons who supported the ratification of the Constitution in 1787–1788 (p. 59)

Federalistas personas que apoyaron la ratificación de la Constitución entre 1787 y 1788

felony a serious crime which may be punished by a heavy fine and/or imprisonment or even death (p. 728)

felonía un crimen grave que puede castigarse con una gran multa, la prisión o incluso la muerte

feudalism a loosely organized system in which powerful lords divided their lands among other, lesser lords (p. 648)

feudalismo sistema relativamente organizado en el cual los grandes señores les concedían sus tierras a otros señores de menor autoridad

filibuster various tactics (usually long speeches) aimed at defeating a bill in a legislative body by preventing a final vote; associated with the U.S. Senate; *see* cloture (p. 352)

obstrucción tácticas diversas (por lo general, prolongar el debate verbal) con el objetivo de derrotar una propuesta de ley en un cuerpo legislativo, evitando que se tenga un voto final; a menudo se asocia con el Senado de los Estados Unidos; *ver* cloture/limitación del debate

fiscal policy the various means the government uses to raise and spend money (pp. 456, 474)

política económica métodos varios que usa el gobierno para obtener y gastar dinero

fiscal year the 12-month period used by a government and the business world for its record-keeping, budgeting, revenue-collecting, and other financial management purposes (p. 433)

año fiscal período de 12 meses utilizado por el gobierno y el mundo de los negocios para su contabilidad, presupuesto, recaudación de ingresos y otros propósitos financieros

five-year plan a plan which projects economic development over the next five years (p. 689)

plan quinquenal plan que hace proyecciones sobre el desarrollo económico durante los siguientes cinco años

floor consideration the process by which proposed laws are considered and acted upon by the full membership of the House or Senate (p. 287)

consideración de la sala proceso mediante el cual la Cámara de Representantes o el Senado consideran y reaccionan a las leyes propuestas

floor leaders members of the House and Senate picked by their parties to carry out party decisions and steer legislative action to meet party goals (p. 336)

líderes de fracciones partidistas miembros de la Cámara de Representantes y del Senado elegidos por sus partidos con el objeto de llevar a cabo las decisiones partidistas e impulsar la acción legislativa a fin de que se cumplan los propósitos partidistas

foreign affairs a nation's relationships with other countries (p. 482)
asuntos exteriores relaciones de una nación con otros países

foreign aid economic and military aid to other countries (p. 505)
ayuda extranjera auxilio militar y económico a otros países

foreign policy a group of policies made up of all the stands and actions that a nation takes in every aspect of its relationships with other countries; everything a nation's government says and does in world affairs (p. 483)
política exterior conjunto de políticas conformado por todas las posturas y acciones que una nación asume en cada uno de los aspectos de sus relaciones con otros países; todo lo que el gobierno de una nación expresa y hace respecto a los asuntos mundiales

formal amendment change or addition that becomes part of the written language of the Constitution itself through one of four methods set forth in the Constitution (p. 79)
enmienda formal cambio o adición que se convierte en parte del lenguaje escrito de la Constitución misma, mediante uno de los cuatro métodos enunciados de la Constitución

Framers group of delegates who drafted the United States Constitution at the Philadelphia Convention in 1787 (p. 52)
Redactores grupo de delegados que esbozaron la Constitución de los Estados Unidos en la Convención de Filadelfia en 1787

franchise the right to vote (p. 152)
sufragio derecho a votar

franking privilege benefit allowing members of Congress to mail letters and other materials postage-free (p. 289)
exención de franquicia beneficio otorgado a los miembros del Congreso que les permite enviar por correo cartas y otros materiales gratis

free enterprise system an economic system characterized by private or corporate ownership of capital goods; investments that are determined by private decision rather than by state control, and determined in a free market (pp. 23, 679)
sistema de libre empresa sistema económico caracterizado por la propiedad privada o corporativa de los bienes de capital; inversiones que están determinadas por una decisión privada, en vez del control estatal, y están sujetas a un mercado libre

Free Exercise Clause the second part of the constitutional guarantee of religious freedom, which guarantees to each person the right to believe whatever he or she chooses to believe in matters of religion (p. 551)
Cláusula de la libertad de cultos segunda parte de la garantía constitucional de libertad religiosa, que garantiza a todos el derecho de creer en lo que se escoja en cuestiones de religión

free market a market in which buyers and sellers are free to buy and sell as they wish (p. 679)
mercado libre mercado en el cual los compradores y vendedores tienen la libertad de comprar y vender como lo deseen

Full Faith and Credit Clause Constitution's requirement that each State accept the public acts, records, and judicial proceedings of every other State (p. 112)
Cláusula de fe y crédito cabal requisito constitucional (Artículo IV, Sección 1) según el cual cada estado acepta (da "fe y crédito cabal") los actos públicos, documentos y procedimientos judiciales de cualquier otro estado

fundamental law laws of basic and lasting importance which may not easily be changed (p. 710)
ley fundamental leyes de importancia primordial y duradera que no se cambiarán con facilidad

G

gender gap measurable differences between the partisan choices of men and women today (p. 174)
brecha de género diferencias medibles entre las elecciones partidistas actuales de los hombres y las mujeres

general election the regularly scheduled election at which voters make a final selection of officeholders (p. 185)
elecciones generales elecciones programadas regularmente en la que los votantes hacen una selección final de los funcionarios públicos

genocide the attempted extermination of a cultural, racial, or national group (p. 664)
genocidio intento de aniquilar a un grupo cultural, racial o nacional

gerrymandering the drawing of electoral district lines to the advantage of a party or group (pp. 165, 277)
demarcación arbitraria establecimiento de los límites de los distritos electorales de modo que den ventaja a un partido

gift tax a tax on a gift by a living person (p. 461)
impuesto a los regalos gravamen sobre los regalos que una persona viva otorga

globalization economic interdependence among nations of the world (p. 695)
globalización interdependencia económica entre naciones del mundo

government the institution through which a society makes and enforces its public policies (p. 4)
gobierno institución mediante la cual una sociedad lleva a cabo y hace cumplir sus políticas públicas

government corporation corporations within the executive branch subject to the President's direction and control, set up by Congress to carry out certain business-like activities (p. 448)
corporación gubernamental instituciones del poder ejecutivo que están sujetas a la dirección y el control del Presidente, formadas por el Congreso para que realicen determinadas actividades de tipo empresarial

grand jury the formal device by which a person can be accused of a serious crime (p. 594)
gran jurado dispositivo formal a través del cual puede acusarse a una persona de un crimen serio

grants-in-aid program grants of federal money or other resources to States, cities, counties, and other local units (p. 107)
programa de subvención de fondos públicos subvenciones de dinero o de otros recursos federales para los estados, sus ciudades, condados y otras unidades locales

grass-roots pressures pressures on public officials from members of an interest group or the people at large (p. 257)
presión popular presión que los miembros de un grupo de interés o la población en general ejercen sobre funcionarios públicos

Great Leap Forward the five-year plan for 1958 which was an attempt to quickly modernize China (p. 690)
Gran Salto Hacia Adelante plan quinquenal de 1958 que fue un intento de modernizar rápidamente a China

gross domestic product (GDP) the total amount of goods and services produced in a country each year (p. 473)

producto interno bruto (PIB) cantidad total de bienes y servicios producidos por un país cada año

guerilla warfare fighting carried out by small groups in hit-and-run raids (p. 657)

conflicto guerrillero armado lucha de golpe y fuga entre grupos pequeños

H

hard money campaign money that is subject to regulations by the FEC (p. 208)

fondos fiscalizados dinero de campaña que está sujeto a las regulaciones de la FEC

hardliners those who fight to maintain the status quo (p. 661)

radical los que luchan por mantener el status quo

heterogeneous of another or different race, family or kind; composed of a mix of elements (p. 612)

heterogéneo de diferente raza, familia o especie; compuesto por una mezcla de elementos

I

ideological parties parties based on a particular set of beliefs, a comprehensive view of social, economic, and political matters (p. 137)

partidos ideológicos partidos que se basan en un conjunto determinado de creencias, un punto de vista exhaustivo sobre asuntos sociales, económicos y políticos

immigrant those people legally admitted as permanent residents of a country (p. 612)

inmigrante persona que es admitida legalmente en calidad de residente permanente de un país

impeach to bring formal charges against a public official; the House of Representatives has the sole power to impeach civil officers of the United States (p. 319)

impugnar presentar cargos formales en contra de un funcionario público; la Cámara de Representantes tienen el exclusivo poder de impugnar a los funcionarios públicos de los Estados Unidos

imperial presidency term used to describe a President as an "emperor" who acts without consulting Congress or acts in secrecy to evade or deceive Congress; often used in reference to Richard Nixon's presidency (p. 403)

presidencia imperial término utilizado para describir a un Presidente como "emperador", quien actúa sin consultar al Congreso o de manera secreta para evadirlo o engañarlo

implied powers those delegated powers of the National Government that are suggested by the expressed powers set out in the Constitution; those "necessary and proper" to carry out the expressed powers; *see* delegated powers, expressed powers (pp. 96, 296)

poderes implícitos aquellos poderes delegados del gobierno nacional que se sugieren o están implícitos por los poderes explícitos; aquellos que son "necesarios y pertinentes" para realizar los poderes explícitos; *ver* delegated powers/poderes delegados, expressed powers/poderes explícitos

import quota a limit put on the amount of a commodity that can be imported into a country (p. 696)

cuota de importación límite sobre la cantidad de un producto que se puede importar a un país

income tax a tax levied on the income of individuals and/or corporations (p. 763)

impuesto sobre la renta gravamen sobre el ingreso de los individuos y/o corporaciones

incorporation the process by which a State establishes a city as a legal body (p. 749)

incorporación proceso mediante el cual un estado establece a una ciudad como un cuerpo legal

incumbent the current officeholder (pp. 131, 280)

titular funcionario público actual

independent agencies additional agencies created by Congress located outside the Cabinet departments (p. 441)

oficinas independientes agencias adicionales creadas por el Congreso y que se ubican fuera de los departamentos del Gabinete

independent executive agencies agencies headed by a single administrator with regional subunits, but lacking Cabinet status (p. 442)

oficinas ejecutivas independientes agencias dirigidas por un solo administrador que tiene subunidades operativas regionales pero que carecen del estatus del Gabinete

independent regulatory commissions independent agencies created by Congress, designed to regulate important aspects of the nation's economy, largely beyond the reach of presidential control (p. 445)

comisiones regulatorias independientes agencias independientes cuya función es regular aspectos importantes de la economía de la nación, en su mayoría fuera del control y dirección del Presidente

Independents a term used to describe people who have no party affiliation (p. 177)

Independientes término usado para describir a las personas que no están afiliadas a un partido

indictment a formal complaint before a grand jury which charges the accused with one or more crimes (p. 594)

denuncia queja formal que el fiscal expone ante un gran jurado, que incluye cargos al acusado por uno o más crímenes

inferior courts the lower federal courts, beneath the Supreme Court (p. 521)

cortes inferiores las cortes federales menores, que están por debajo de la Corte Suprema

inflation a general increase in prices throughout the economy (p. 474)

inflación incremento general de precios en la economía

information a formal charge filed by a prosecutor without the action of a grand jury (pp. 595, 729)

información acusación oficial presentada por un acusador sin acción de parte del jurado

inherent powers powers the Constitution is presumed to have delegated to the National Government because it is the government of a sovereign state within the world community (pp. 97, 296)

poderes inherentes aquellos poderes delegados del gobierno nacional que le pertenecen de manera inherente, debido a que es el gobierno de un estado soberano de la comunidad mundial

inheritance tax a tax levied on the beneficiary's share of an estate (p. 764)

impuesto sobre la herencia gravamen sobre lo que hereda un beneficiario

initiative a process in which a certain number of qualified voters sign petitions in favor of a proposed statute or constitutional amendment, which then goes directly to the ballot (p. 712)

iniciativa proceso en el que determinado número de votantes calificados firman peticiones a favor de una propuesta que se pasa después directamente a la papeleta electoral

injunction a court order that forces or limits the performance of some act by a private individual or by a public official (pp. 165, 562)

mandato orden judicial que fuerza o limita el desempeño de determinado acto, mediante la intervención de un particular o un funcionario público

integration the process of bringing a group into equal membership in society (p. 620)

integración proceso mediante el cual se ofrece a un grupo participación igualitaria dentro de la sociedad

interest a charge for borrowed money, generally a percentage of the amount borrowed (p. 462)

interés cargo que se hace por el dinero prestado, por lo general es un porcentaje de la cantidad prestada

interest group private organizations whose members share certain views and work to shape public policy (pp. 221, 242)

grupo de interés organizaciones privadas cuyos miembros comparten determinados puntos de vista y trabajan para dar forma a las políticas públicas

interstate compact formal agreement entered into with the consent of Congress, between or among States, or between a State and a foreign state (p. 111)

pacto interestatal acuerdo formal suscrito con el consentimiento del Congreso, entre dos estados o entre un estado y un estado extranjero, el cual está autorizado por la Constitución (Artículo I, Sección 10)

involuntary servitude forced labor (p. 583)

servidumbre involuntaria trabajo forzado

isolationism a purposeful refusal to become generally involved in the affairs of the rest of the world (p. 482)

aislacionismo rechazo voluntario a verse involucrado, de manera general, en los asuntos del resto del mundo

item veto a governor may veto one or more items in a bill without rejecting the entire measure (p. 724)

veto de artículo un gobernador puede vetar uno o más artículos de una propuesta de ley, sin rechazar toda la medida

J

Jim Crow law a law that separates people on the basis of race, aimed primarily at African Americans (p. 619)

Ley Jim Crow ley que separa a un grupo de personas del resto de la gente con base en la raza, dirigido principalmente a los afroamericanos

joint committee legislative committee composed of members of both houses (p. 341)

comité conjunto comité legislativo compuesto por miembros de ambas cámaras

joint resolution a proposal for action that has the force of law when passed; usually deals with special circumstances or temporary matters (p. 344)

resolución conjunta propuesta de acción que tiene el poder de una ley cuando se aprueba; a menudo tiene que ver con circunstancias especiales o asuntos temporales

judicial activism a judicial philosophy in which supporters believe that judges should interpret and apply provisions in the Constitution and in statute law in the light of ongoing changes in conditions and values (p. 524)

activismo judicial filosofía judicial que argumenta que los jueces deberían interpretar y aplicar las condiciones de la Constitución y del derecho escrito considerando los cambios progresivos de condiciones y valores

judicial power the power to interpret laws, to determine their meaning, and to settle disputes within the society (p. 5)

poder judicial poder para interpretar las leyes, determinar su significado y resolver las disputas que surgen dentro de la sociedad

judicial restraint a judicial philosophy in which supporters believe that judges should decide cases based on the original intent of the Framers or those who enacted the statute(s) involved in a case, or on precedent (p. 524)

restricción judicial filosofía judicial que argumenta que los jueces deberían tomar decisiones sobre sus casos basándose en la intención original de los creadores de la Declaración de Derechos o los que promulgan los estatutos del caso, o en el precedente

judicial review the power of a court to determine the constitutionality of a governmental action (p. 73)

revisión judicial poder de una corte para determinar la constitucionalidad de una acción gubernamental

jurisdiction the authority of a court to hear a case (p. 522)

jurisdicción autoridad de una corte para atender (juzgar y decidir) un caso

jury a body of persons selected according to law who hear evidence and decide questions of fact in a court case (p. 728)

jurado conjunto de personas seleccionadas de acuerdo con la ley para que escuchen la evidencia y decidan cuestiones de hecho en un caso de la corte

jus sanguinis the law of blood, which determines citizenship based on one's parents' citizenship (p. 633)

jus sanguinis ley de la sangre que define la ciudadanía con base en la ciudadanía de los padres

jus soli the law of soil, which determines citizenship based on where a person is born (p. 633)

jus soli ley del territorio que determina la ciudadanía con base en el lugar de nacimiento de la persona

justice of the peace a judge who stands on the lowest level of the State judicial system and presides over justice courts (p. 732)

Juez de paz juez que está en el nivel inferior del sistema judicial estatal y preside las cortes de justicia.

K

keynote address speech given at a party convention to set the tone for the convention and the campaign to come (p. 383)

discurso de apertura alocución dada en una convención de partido para establecer el tono de la convención y de la futura campaña

L

labor union an organization of workers who share the same type of job, or who work in the same industry, and press for government policies that will benefit their members (p. 248)

sindicato laboral organización de trabajadores que comparten el mismo tipo de trabajo, o que laboran en la misma industria y que busca impulsar políticas gubernamentales que beneficien a sus miembros

laissez-faire theory a theory which suggests that government should play a very limited role in society (p. 682)

teoría del dejar hacer teoría que sugiere que el gobierno debería desempeñar un papel limitado dentro de la sociedad

law of supply and demand a law which states that when supplies of goods and services become plentiful, prices tend to drop. When supplies become scarcer, prices tend to rise (p. 681)

ley de la oferta y la demanda ley que establece que cuando los suministros de bienes y servicios son abundantes, los precios tienden a bajar; cuando los suministros escasean, los precios tienden a subir

legal tender any kind of money that a creditor must, by law, accept in payment for debts (p. 303)

moneda de curso legal cualquier moneda que un acreedor debe aceptar, por ley, como pago de una deuda

legislative power the power to make a law and to frame public policies (p. 5)

poder legislativo poder para hacer una ley y redactar políticas públicas

legitimacy the belief of the people that a government has the right to make public policy (p. 650)

legitimidad crencia que un gobierno tiene el derecho de crear políticas públicas

libel false and malicious use of printed words (p. 559)

libelo utilización falsa y maliciosa de la palabra impresa

liberal constructionist one who argues a broad interpretation of the provisions of the Constitution, particularly those granting powers to the Federal Government (p. 314)

construccionista liberal aquel que argumenta una amplia interpretación de las estipulaciones de la Constitución, en particular las que otorgan poderes al gobierno federal

limited government basic principle of American government which states that government is restricted in what it may do, and each individual has rights that government cannot take away; *see* constitutionalism, popular sovereignty (pp. 31, 69, 709)

gobierno limitado principio básico del sistema estadounidense de gobierno que establece que el gobierno tiene restricciones en cuanto a lo que puede hacer, y en el cual cada individuo tiene ciertos derechos que el gobierno no puede enajenar; *ver* constitutionalism / constitucionalismo, popular sovereignty/soberanía popular

line agency an agency which performs the tasks for which the organization exists (p. 430)

agencia del ramo oficina que desempeña las tareas para las que la organización existe

line-item veto a President's cancellation of specific dollar amounts (line items) from a congressional spending bill; instituted by a 1996 congressional act, but struck down by a 1998 Supreme Court decision (p. 418)

veto de partida cancelación presidencial de ciertas cantidades de dólares (partidas) de una cuenta de gastos del Congreso; este veto se instituyó en 1996 mediante una ley del Congreso, pero la Suprema Corte lo derogó en 1998

literacy a person's ability to read or write (p. 161)

alfabetismo capacidad de una persona para leer o escribir

lobbying activities by which group pressures are brought to bear on legislators, the legislative process, and all aspects of the public-policy-making process (p. 254)

cabildeo actividades mediante las que un grupo aplica presión a los legisladores; al proceso legislativo, y a todos los aspectos del proceso de creación de políticas públicas

lobbyist a person who tries to persuade public officials to do those things that interest groups want them to do (p. 254)

cabildero persona que intenta persuadir a funcionarios a realizar cosas que ciertos grupos de interés quieren que se lleven a cabo

M

magistrate a justice who handles minor civil complaints and misdemeanor cases that arise in an urban setting (p. 733)

magistrado juez que atiende demandas civiles menores y casos de faltas leves que surgen en un contexto urbano

Magna Carta Great Charter forced upon King John of England by his barons in 1215; established that the power of the monarchy was not absolute and guaranteed trial by jury and due process of law to the nobility (p. 31)

Carta Magna constitución que los barones impusieron al rey John de Inglaterra en 1215; estableció el principio de que el poder del monarca no era absoluto y garantizó los derechos fundamentales, como el de un juicio con jurado y procesos establecidos legales para la nobleza

majority leader the floor leader of the party that holds the majority of seats in each house of Congress (p. 336)

líder mayoritario portavoz del partido político que posee la mayor cantidad de escaños en cada cámara del Congreso

majority opinion officially called the Opinion of the Court; announces the Court's decision in a case and sets out the reasoning upon which it is based (p. 537)

opinión mayoritaria llamada oficialmente Opinión de la Corte; anuncia la decisión de la Corte sobre el caso y describe el razonamiento sobre el que ésta se basa

majority rule in a democracy, the majority of the people will be right more often than they will be wrong, and will be right more often than will any one person or small group (p. 21)

gobierno por mayoría en una democracia, la mayoría de personas estarán en lo correcto con más frecuencia, y estarán en lo correcto con más frecuencia que una sola persona o un grupo pequeño

mandate the instructions or commands a constituency gives to its elected officials (p. 220)

mandato las intrucciones u órdenes que un grupo de votantes da a sus funcionarios electos

mass media those means of communication that reach large audiences, especially television, radio, printed publications, and the Internet (p. 217)

medios masivos de comunicación aquellos medios de comunicación que llegan a grandes audiencias, sobre todo la radio, televisión, publicaciones impresas e Internet

mayor-council government the oldest and most widely used type of city government—an elected mayor as the chief executive and an elected council as its legislative body (p. 750)

gobierno de consejo-alcalde el más antiguo y más utilizado tipo de gobierno municipal: un alcalde electo como Presidente y un consejo electo como su cuerpo legislativo

Medicaid a program administered by the State to provide medical insurance to low-income families (p. 757)

Medicaid programa administrado por el Senado para proporcionar seguro médico a las familias de bajos ingresos

medium a means of communication; something that transmits information (p. 228)

medio un medio de comunicación; algo que transmite información

mercantilism an economic and political theory emphasizing money as the chief source of wealth to increase the absolute power of the monarchy and the nation (p. 651)

mercantilismo teoría económica y política que destaca el dinero como la fuente primaria de riqueza para incrementar el poder absoluto de la monarquía y de la nación

metropolitan area a city and the area around it (p. 755)

area metropolitana la ciudad y el área que le circunda

minister cabinet members, most commonly of the House of Commons (p. 667)

ministro miembro del gabinete, y más frecuentemente de la Cámara de los Comunes

minority leader the floor leader of the party that holds the minority of seats in each house of Congress (p. 336)

líder minoritario portavoz del partido político que posee la menor cantidad de escaños en cada cámara del Congreso

Miranda Rule the constitutional rights which police must read to a suspect before questioning can occur (p. 599)

Ley Miranda derechos constitucionales que la policía debe especificar a un sospechoso antes de que se le pueda interrogar

misdemeanor a lesser offense, punishable by a small fine and/or a short jail term (p. 728)

falta leve delito menor que se castiga mediante una pequeña multa o un breve período de encarcelamiento

monetary policy a process through which the government can influence the nation's economy through changes in the money supply and the availability of credit (p. 475)

política monetaria proceso mediante el cual el gobierno toma decisiones que afectan a la economía del país mediante cambios en la oferta monetaria y la disponibilidad de crédito

monopoly a firm that is the only source of a product or service (p. 681)

monopolio empresa que es la única fuente de un producto o servicio

municipality an urban political unit within a township that usually exists as a separate government entity (p. 747)

municipalidad unidad política urbana dentro de un municipio que por lo general existe como una entidad gubernamental independiente

N

NAFTA (North American Free Trade Agreement) an agreement which removed trade restrictions among the United States, Canada, and Mexico, thus increasing cross-border trade (p. 697)

NAFTA (Tratado de Libre Comercio de América del Norte) acuerdo que elimina las restricciones comerciales entre los Estados Unidos, Canadá y México, con lo cual se incrementa el comercio transfronterizo

national convention meeting at which a party's delegates vote to pick their presidential and vice-presidential candidates (p. 381)

convención nacional Reunión en la que los delegados de un partido votan para elegir a sus candidatos a la presidencia y vicepresidencia

national popular vote plan proposal for electing the President whereby each State's election laws would provide for all of the State's electoral votes to be awarded to the winner of the national popular vote and enter into an interstate compact agreeing to elect the President by national popular vote (p. 393)

plan para el voto nacional popular propuesta para elegir al Presidente de la nación mediante la cual las leyes electorales de cada Estado decretan que los votos electorales sean otorgados al ganador del voto popular nacional y que de esta manera se llegue a un acuerdo interestatal donde se elija al presidente por voto popular

NATO (North American Treaty Organization) an alliance formed to protect the freedom and security of its members through political and military action (p. 506)

OTAN (Organización del Tratado del Atlántico Norte) alianza formada para proteger la libertad y seguridad de sus miembros a través de medidas políticas y militares

naturalization the legal process by which citizens of one country become citizens of another (pp. 309, 633)

naturalización proceso legal mediante el cual los ciudadanos de un país se convierten en ciudadanos de otro

Necessary and Proper Clause constitutional clause that gives Congress the power to make all laws "necessary and proper" for executing its powers; *see* implied powers (p. 312)

Cláusula de necesidad y conveniencia cláusula constitucional que otorga al Congreso el poder de expedir leyes "necesarias y pertinentes" para el ejercicio de sus poderes; *ver* implied powers/poderes implícitos

New Jersey Plan plan presented as an alternative to the Virginia Plan at the Constitutional Convention; called for a unicameral legislature in which each State would be equally represented (p. 55)

Plan Nueva Jersey plan presentado en la Convención Constitucional como una alternativa al Plan Virginia; proponía una legislatura unicameral en la que cada estado estuviera representado de forma equitativa

nomination the process of candidate selection in an electoral system (p. 184)

nominación proceso de selección de candidatos en una democracia

nonpartisan election election in which candidates are not identified by party labels (p. 190)

elección no partidista elección en la que los candidatos no están identificados por afiliaciones partidarias

O

off-year election congressional election that occurs between presidential election years (pp. 170, 275)

elección intermedia elección del Congreso que ocurre entre las elecciones presidenciales

oligarchy a form of government in which the power to rule is held by a small, usually self-appointed elite (p. 14)

oligarquía forma de gobierno en la que el poder de gobernar lo ejerce una elite pequeña y por lo general autonombrada

open market operations the processes by which the Federal Reserve buys or sells government securities from and to the nation's banks in order to alter the money supply (p. 476)

operaciones de mercado abierto proceso por el cual la Reserva Federal compra y vende valores del Estado a los bancos del país para controlar la cantidad de dinero en circulación

open primary a party-nominating election in which any qualified voter can take part (p. 188)

elección primaria abierta elección partidista de nominación en la que cualquier votante calificado puede tomar parte

opinion leader any person who, for any reason, has an unusually strong influence on the views of others (p. 218)

líder de opinión cualquier persona que por alguna razón tiene una poderosa influencia en los puntos de vista de otras

ordinance power power of the President to issue executive orders; originates from the Constitution and acts of Congress (p. 406)

poder de decreto poder del Presidente de emitir órdenes ejecutivas; se fundamenta en la Constitución y en los actos del Congreso

original jurisdiction the power of a court to hear a case first, before any other court (p. 523)

jurisdicción original poder de una corte de atender un caso antes que otra corte

oversight function review by legislative committees of the policies and programs of the executive branch (p. 288)

función de vigilancia revisión de las políticas y los programas de la rama ejecutiva por parte de los comités legislativos

P

pardon release from the punishment or legal consequences of a crime, by the President (in a federal case) or a governor (in a State case) (pp. 419, 724)

perdón exoneración que lleva a cabo el Presidente (en el caso federal) o el gobernador (en el caso estatal) del castigo o de las consecuencias legales de un crimen

parliamentary government a form of government in which the executive branch is made up of the prime minister, or premier, and that official's cabinet (p. 18)

gobierno parlamentario forma de gobierno en la que la rama ejecutiva está conformada por el primer ministro, o premier, y el gabinete oficial

parochial church-related, as in a parochial school (p. 552)

parroquial relacionado con la iglesia, como las escuelas parroquiales

parole the release of a prisoner short of the complete term of the original sentence (p. 725)

liberación bajo palabra libertad condicional de un prisionero poco antes de que termine el lapso de su sentencia original

partisan lawmaker who owes his/her first allegiance to his/her political party and votes according to the party line (p. 287)

partidista legislador que le debe fidelidad, en primer lugar, a su partido político, por lo que vota de acuerdo con la línea del partido

partisanship government action based on firm allegiance to a political party (p. 124)

partidarismo acción gubernamental basada en la vigorosa fidelidad a un partido político

party caucus a closed meeting of a party's House or Senate members; also called a party conference (p. 334)

junta de dirigentes de partido reunión cerrada de los miembros de la Cámara de Representantes o del Senado; también se conoce como Conferencia de partido

party identification loyalty of people to a political party (p. 177)

identificación con el partido lealtad de la gente hacia un partido político

passport a legal document issued by a state that identifies a person as a citizen of that state and permits travel to and from that state (p. 487)

pasaporte documento legal emitido por el estado que identifica a una persona como ciudadano de un país y le permite viajar al exterior y regresar

patent a license issued to an inventor granting the exclusive right to manufacture, use, or sell his or her invention for a limited period of time (p. 307)

patente licencia expedida a un inventor para garantizar el derecho exclusivo de manufactura, uso o venta de su invento, durante un tiempo limitado

patrician rich upper-class, landowning aristocrat of ancient Rome (p. 646)

patricio aristócrata propietario de tierras en la antigua Roma

patronage the practice of giving jobs to supporters and friends (p. 443)

patrocinio práctica de dar trabajo a los simpatizantes y amigos

payroll tax a tax imposed on nearly all employers and their employees, and on self-employed persons—the amounts owed by employees withheld from their paychecks (p. 460)

impuesto sobre la nómina gravamen tasado a casi todos los empleadores y sus empleados, así como a las personas autoempleadas; cantidad debida por los empleados que se les descuenta de su salario

peer group people with whom one regularly associates, including friends, classmates, neighbors, and co-workers (p. 218)

grupo de camaradas gente con la que uno se asocia regularmente y que incluye a socios, amigos, compañeros de clase, vecinos y compañeros de trabajo

perjury the act of lying under oath (p. 320)

perjurio mentir bajo juramento

persona non grata an unwelcome person; used to describe recalled diplomatic officials (p. 414)

persona non grata una persona que no es bienvenida; se utiliza para describir a los funcionarios diplomáticos destituidos

petition a citizen's right to bring his or her view to the attention of public officials by such means as written petitions, letters, lobbying, and marches (p.569)

petición derecho de un ciudadano a presentar su opinión ante funcionarios públicos, por medio de escritos, cartas, el cabildeo y marchas

Petition of Right document prepared by Parliament and signed by King Charles I of England in 1628; challenged the idea of the divine right of kings and declared that even the monarch was subject to the laws of the land (p. 31)

Solicitud de Derecho documento preparado por el Parlamento y firmado por el rey Charles I de Inglaterra en 1628; cuestionó la idea del derecho divino de los reyes y declaró que incluso el monarca está sujeto a las leyes de la tierra

picketing patrolling of a business site by workers who are on strike (p. 565)

vigilancia manifestación de los trabajadores en el sitio donde están en huelga

pigeonholed expression describing how most bills introduced in each session of Congress are buried, put away, or never acted upon (p. 345)

dar carpetazo expresión que describe cómo proyectos de ley que se presentan ante el Congreso se olvidan, se ponen a un lado o nunca se llevan a cabo

plaintiff in civil law, the party who brings a suit or some other legal action against another (the defendant) in court (p. 523)

demandante en el derecho civil, la parte que entabla un juicio u otra acción legal contra otra (el demandado) en una corte

platform a political party's formal statement of basic principles, stands on major issues, and objectives (p. 382)

plataforma un enunciado formal por parte de un partido político respecto a sus principios básicos, opiniones sobre cuestiones políticas importantes y objetivos

plebeians the common folk in the Roman Republic (p. 647)

plebeyos personas que pertenecían a la plebe en la República Romana

plurality in an election, the number of votes that the leading candidate obtains over the next highest candidate (p. 127)

mayoría en una elección, el número de votos que el candidato que va a la punta tiene de ventaja sobre su competidor más cercano

pocket veto type of veto a chief executive may use after a legislature has adjourned; when the chief executive does not sign or reject a bill within the time allowed to do so; *see* veto (pp. 356, 418)

veto indirecto tipo de veto que el Presidente puede utilizar después de que una legislatura se suspende; se aplica cuando un Presidente no firma formalmente o rechaza una propuesta de ley, dentro del tiempo comprendido para eso; *ver* veto

police power the authority of each State to act to protect and promote the public health, safety, morals, and general welfare of its people (pp. 580, 717)

facultad policial autoridad de cada estado para proteger y promover la salud pública, la seguridad, la moral y el bienestar general de su pueblo

political action committee the political extension of special-interest groups which have a major stake in public policy (p. 202)

comité de acción política extensión política de grupos de interés especial, los cuales tienen un gran interés en la política pública

political efficacy one's own influence or effectiveness on politics (p. 172)

eficacia política la influencia o eficacia individual en la política

political party a group of persons who seek to control government through the winning of elections and the holding of public office (p. 122)

partido político grupo de personas que buscan controlar el gobierno mediante el triunfo en las elecciones y ejerciendo puestos públicos

political socialization the process by which people gain their political attitudes and opinions (p. 173)

socialización política proceso mediante el que la gente obtiene sus actitudes y opiniones políticas

political spectrum the range of political views (p. 123)

espectro político gama de perspectivas políticas

politico lawmaker who attempts to balance the basic elements of the trustee, delegate, and partisan roles; *see* trustee, delegates, partisan (p. 287)

político legislador que intenta balancear sus responsabilidades como legislador independiente, partidario político y delegado; *ver* trustee/independiente, delegats/delegads, partisan/partidista

poll book list of all registered voters in each precinct (p. 159)

padrón electoral lista de todos los votantes registrados en cada distrito

poll tax a special tax, demanded by States, as a condition of voting (p. 154)

impuesto sobre el padrón electoral gravamen especial, exigido por los estados como una condición para votar

polling place the place where the voters who live in a certain precinct go to vote (p. 195)

casilla electoral lugar donde los votantes que viven en cierto distrito acuden a votar

popular sovereignty basic principle of the American system of government which asserts that the people are the source of any and all governmental power, and government can exist only with the consent of the governed (pp. 41, 69, 709)

soberanía popular principio básico del sistema estadounidense de gobierno que establece que el pueblo es la fuente de todos los poderes gubernamentales, y que el gobierno sólo puede existir con el consentimiento de los gobernados

precedent court decision that stands as an example to be followed in future, similar cases (pp. 524, 728)

precedente decisión judicial que se toma como un ejemplo a seguir en el futuro para casos similares

precinct the smallest unit of election administration; a voting district (pp. 146, 195)

circunseripción unidad mínima de la administración electoral; distrito de votación

preclearance mandated by the Voting Rights Act of 1965, the prior approval by the Justice Department of changes to or new election laws by certain States (p. 167)

preautorización ordenada por la Ley de Derechos de Votos de 1965, respecto a la aprobación anterior, por parte del Departamento de Justicia, de los cambios en las leyes electorales existentes o nuevas en ciertos estados

preliminary hearing the first step in a major criminal prosecution where the judge decides if the evidence is enough to hold the person for action by the grand jury or the prosecutor (p. 732)

audiencia preliminar el primer paso del procesamiento de un crimen mayor, en el que el juez decide si la evidencia basta para que la persona comparezca ante el gran jurado o ante el fiscal para ser sujeto de una acción

presentment a formal accusation brought by the grand jury on its own motion, rather than that of the prosecutor (p. 594)

declaración del Jurado una acusación formal hecha por el jurado de acusación en vez del acusador

President of the Senate the presiding officer of a senate; in Congress, the Vice President of the United States; in a State's legislature, either the lieutenant governor or a senator (p. 333)

Presidente del Senado funcionario que preside un Senado; en el Congreso es el Vicepresidente de los Estados Unidos; en la legislatura estatal, cualquier vicegobernador o un senador

President *pro tempore* the member of the United States Senate, or of the upper house of a State's legislature, chosen to preside in the absence of the president of the Senate (p. 334)

Presidente *pro tempore* miembro del Senado de Estados Unidos, o de la cámara superior de la legislatura estatal, elegido para ser Presidente, en caso de ausencia del Presidente del Senado

presidential elector a person elected by the voters to represent them in making a formal selection of the Vice President and President (p. 374)

elector presidencial persona elegida por los votantes para representarlos en la selección formal del Presidente y Vicepresidente

presidential government a form of government in which the executive and legislative branches of the government are separate, independent, and coequal (p. 17)

gobierno presidencial forma de gobierno en la que las ramas ejecutivas y legislativas del gobierno están separadas, son independientes y están en la misma jerarquía

presidential primary an election in which a party's voters (1) choose State party organization's delegates to their party's national convention, and/or (2) express a preference for their party's presidential nomination (p. 378)

elección presidencial primaria elección en la que los votantes de un partido: (1) eligen a varios o a todos los delegados de la organización partidista estatal para la convención nacional de su partido, y/o (2) expresan una preferencia por alguno de los distintos contendientes para la nominación presidencial de su partido

presidential succession scheme by which a presidential vacancy is filled (p. 370)
sucesión presidencial plan mediante el cual se resuelve la vacante presidencial

Presidential Succession Act of 1947 law specifying the order of presidential succession following the Vice President (p. 370)
Ley para la sucesión presidencial de 1947 ley que especifica el orden para la sucesión presidencial, después del Vicepresidente

preventive detention a law which allows federal judges to order that an accused felon be held, without bail, when there is good reason to believe that he or she will commit yet another serious crime before trial (p. 603)
arresto preventivo ley que permite a los jueces federales ordenar que un acusado de felonía sea arrestado, sin derecho a fianza, cuando existen buenas razones para creer que cometerá otro crimen grave antes del juicio

prior restraint the government cannot curb ideas before they are expressed (p. 562)
prohibición anticipada el gobierno no puede reprimir las ideas antes de que se expresen

privatization the process of returning national enterprises to private ownership (p. 690)
privatización regresar las empresas nacionales a la iniciativa privada

Privileges and Immunities Clause constitution's stipulation (Article IV, Section 2) that all citizens are entitled to certain "privileges and immunities," regardless of their State of residence; no State can draw unreasonable distinctions between its own residents and those persons who happen to live in other States (p. 114)
Cláusula de privilegios e inmunidades estipulación constitucional (Artículo IV, Sección 2), en que se conceden ciertos "privilegios e inmunidades" a los ciudadanos, sin importar su estado de residencia; ningún estado puede hacer distinciones no razonables entre sus propios residentes y aquellas personas que vivan en otros estados

probable cause reasonable grounds, a reasonable suspicion of crime (p. 586)
causa probable fundamentos razonables, sospecha razonable de un crimen

procedural due process the government must employ fair procedures and methods (p. 579)
procesos legales establecidos el gobierno debe emplear procedimientos y métodos justos

process of incorporation the process of incorporating, or including, most of the guarantees in the Bill of Rights into the 14th Amendment's Due Process Clause (p. 549)
proceso de incorporación proceso de integrar, o incluir, la mayor parte de las garantías de la Declaración de los derechos en la Cláusula de proceso legal establecido de la 14a enmienda

progressive tax a type of tax proportionate to income (pp. 459, 763)
impuesto progresivo tipo de impuesto que es proporcional con el ingreso

project grant one type of federal grants-in-aid; made for specific projects to States, localities, and private agencies who apply for them (p. 109)
subvención de proyecto tipo de subvención de fondos públicos; proporcionada para proyectos específicos de los estados, las localidades y las oficinas privadas que la solicitan

property tax a tax levied on real and personal property (p. 764)
impuesto a la propiedad gravamen sobre los bienes raíces y la propiedad personal

proportional plan proposal by which each presidential candidate would receive the same share of a State's electoral vote as he or she received in the State's popular vote (p. 392)
plan proporcional propuesta para seleccionar electores presidenciales, mediante la cual cada candidato recibiría la misma cantidad de votos electorales de un estado que recibió durante la votación popular del estado

proportional representation rule applied in Democratic primaries whereby any candidate who wins at least 15 percent of the votes gets the number of State Democratic convention delegates based on his or her share of that primary vote (p. 379)
regla de la representación proporcional procedimiento aplicado en las elecciones primarias del partido Demócrata, en el cual cualquier candidato que gane al menos el 15% de los votos emitidos en una elección primaria, obtiene el número de delegados a la convención estatal demócrata, que le corresponda a esa proporción de las primarias

proprietary organized by a proprietor (a person to whom the king had made a grant of land) (p. 33)
propiedad organizada por un dueño (persona a quien el rey le ha otorgado tierras)

prorogue adjourn, as in a legislative session (p. 271)
prórroga aplazamiento, por ejemplo, de una sesión legislativa

protectionism the practice of national governments trying to control imports to protect native industries from foreign competition (p. 696)
proteccionismo práctica en la que gobiernos nacionales tratan de controlar las importaciones para proteger a sus industrias de la competencia extranjera

public affairs those events and issues that concern the people at large; e.g., politics, public issues, and the making of public policies (pp. 215, 245)
asuntos públicos aquellos acontecimientos y asuntos que importan al público en general, por ejemplo: la política, los temas públicos y la determinación de las políticas públicas

public agenda the public issues on which the people's attention is focused (p. 234)
agenda pública asuntos públicos sobre los cuales está enfocada la atención de las personas

public debt all of the money borrowed by the government and not yet repaid, plus the accrued interest on that money; also called the national debt or federal debt (pp. 301, 466)
deuda pública todo el dinero que ha pedido prestado el gobierno a lo largo de los años y que todavía no paga, además del interés acumulado sobre ese capital; también se conoce como deuda nacional o deuda federal

public-interest group an interest group that seeks to institute certain public policies of benefit to all or most people in this country, whether or not they belong to or support that organization (p. 252)
grupo de interés público grupo de interés que busca instituir determinadas políticas públicas de beneficio para la mayoría de las personas de su país, sin importar si pertenecen o apoyan a la organización

public opinion the complex collection of the opinions of many different people; the sum of all their views (p. 215)
opinión pública colección compleja de opiniones de diversas personas; la suma de todos sus puntos de vista

public opinion poll device that attempts to collect information by asking people questions (p. 222)

    encuestas de opinión pública dispositivos que intentan recolectar información al hacerle preguntas a las personas

public policy all of the many goals that a government pursues in all of the many areas of human affairs in which it is involved (pp. 4, 242)

    políticas públicas todas las metas que un gobierno se fija, así como los distintos cursos de acción que toma en sus intentos por llevar a cabo esos objetivos

purge the process of reviewing lists of registered voters and removing the names of those no longer eligible to vote; a purification (p. 159)

    purga proceso de revisión de las listas de los votantes registrados y de la eliminación de los nombres que ya no son elegibles para votar; una depuración

Q

quorum least number of members who must be present for a legislative body to conduct business; majority (p. 348)

    quórum mínimo número de miembros que debe estar presente para que un cuerpo legislativo funcione; mayoría

quota a rule requiring certain numbers of jobs or promotions for members of certain groups (p. 628)

    cuota regla que requiere que determinado número de trabajos o ascensos se den a miembros de ciertos grupos

quota sample a sample deliberately constructed to reflect several of the major characteristics of a given population (p. 224)

    muestra de cuota muestra deliberadamente hecha para reflejar ciertas características importantes de una determinada población

R

random sample a certain number of randomly selected people who live in a certain number of randomly selected places (p. 224)

    muestra aleatoria determinado número de gente seleccionada al azar y que vive en ciertos lugares seleccionados de manera aleatoria

ratification formal approval, final consent to the effectiveness of a constitution, constitutional amendment, or treaty (pp. 48, 79)

    ratificación aprobación formal, consentimiento definitivo de la eficacia de una constitución, de una enmienda constitucional o de un tratado

rational basis test a test less intensive than the strict scrutiny test that the Supreme Court uses to decide equal protection cases; the test asks whether the classification in question bears a reasonable relationship to the achievement of some proper governmental purpose (p. 619)

    prueba de razonamiento básico examen menos intenso que el examen judicial riguroso que implementa la Corte Suprema para tomar decisiones en casos de protección equitativa; el examen pregunta si hay una relación razonable entre la clasificación en cuestión y el logro de algún propósito gubernamental

reapportion redistribute, as in seats in a legislative body (p. 274)

    reasignación redistribución, como los escaños en un cuerpo legislativo

recall a petition procedure by which voters may remove an elected official from office before the completion of his or her regular term (p. 721)

    retirada inesperada procedimiento de petición por el que los votantes puedan destituir a un funcionario oficial antes de terminar su mandato

recess a time when both houses of Congress temporarily suspend business (p. 271)

    receso período en que ambas cámaras del Congreso suspenden actividades temporalmente

recession an absence of economic growth (p. 474)

    recesión ausencia de crecimiento económico

recognition the exclusive power of a President to legally recognize (establish formal diplomatic relations with) foreign states (p. 414)

    reconocimiento el poder exclusivo de un Presidente para reconocer (establecer relaciones diplomáticas) a estados extranjeros

record a transcript of proceedings made in trial court (p. 531)

    registro trasunto de los procesos llevados a cabo en una corte tribunal

redress satisfaction of a claim payment (p. 540)

    resarcir satisfacer una queja, por lo general mediante un pago

referendum a process by which a legislative measure is referred to the State's voters for final approval or rejection (p. 719)

    referendo proceso mediante el cual una medida legislativa se consulta con los votantes de los estados para su aprobación o rechazo final

refugee one who leaves his or her homeland to seek protection from war, persecution, or some other danger (p. 615)

    refugiado persona que abandona su hogar para buscar protección contra la guerra, la persecución o algún otro peligro

regional security alliances treaties in which the U.S. and other countries involved have agreed to take collective action to meet aggression in a particular part of the world (p. 506)

    alianzas regionales de seguridad tratados mediante los cuales los Estados Unidos y otros países han acordado actuar colectivamente para enfrentar una agresión en una determinada parte del mundo

registration a procedure of voter identification intended to prevent fraudulent voting (p. 158)

    registro procedimiento de identificación del votante para evitar votaciones fraudulentas

regressive tax a tax levied at a flat rate, without regard to the level of a taxpayer's income or ability to pay (pp. 461, 763)

    impuesto regresivo gravamen con una tasa semejante, sin considerar el nivel de ingreso de los contribuyentes o su capacidad para pagarlo

representative government system of government in which public policies are made by officials selected by the voters and held accountable in periodic elections; *see* democracy (p. 31)

    gobierno representativo sistema de gobierno en el que las políticas públicas están elaboradas por funcionarios elegidos por los votantes y que rinden cuentas en elecciones periódicas; *ver* democracy/democracia

reprieve an official postponement of the execution of a sentence; *see* pardon (pp. 419, 725)

    suspensión un aplazamiento oficial de la ejecución de una sentencia; *ver* pardon/perdón

reservation public land set aside by a government for use by Native American tribes (p. 613)

    reservación terrenos públicos que un gobierno reserva para el uso de las tribus nativas estadounidenses

reserve requirement the amount of money the Federal Reserve determines banks must keep in reserve with one of the Federal Reserve Banks (p. 476)

reserva obligatoria cantidad de dinero que la Reserva Federal determina que los bancos deben mantener en reserva con uno de los Bancos de la Reserva Federal

reserved powers those powers that the Constitution does not grant to the National Government and does not deny to the States (p. 99)

poderes reservados aquellos poderes que la Constitución no otorga al gobierno nacional, pero que tampoco niega a los estados

resolution a measure relating to the business of either house or expressing an opinion; does not have the force of law and does not require the President's signature (p. 344)

resolución medida relativa al funcionamiento de cualquier Cámara, o una expresión de opinión sobre un asunto; no tiene la fuerza de una ley y no requiere la firma del Presidente

reverse discrimination discrimination against the majority group (p. 628)

discriminación inversa segregación en contra del grupo mayoritario

rider unpopular provision added to an important bill certain to pass so that it will "ride" through the legislative process (p. 344)

cláusula adicional provisión poco probable de ser aprobada por méritos propios, que se agrega a un proyecto de ley importante que se tiene la seguridad que será aprobado, así que dicha cláusula "cabalga" por todo ese proceso legislativo

right of association the right to associate with others to promote political, economic, and other social causes (p. 572)

derecho de asociación derecho de asociarse con otros para promover causas políticas, sociales, económicas y de otra índole

right of legation the right to send and receive diplomatic representatives (p. 485)

derecho de legación derecho a enviar y recibir representantes diplomáticos

rule of law concept that government and its officers are always subject to the law (p. 70)

gobierno de la ley el concepto en que el gobierno y sus oficiales estan sujetos a la ley

runoff primary a primary in which the top two vote-getters in the first direct primary face one another (p. 190)

elección primaria complementaria elección primaria en la que los dos candidatos con más votos en la elección primaria directa se enfrentan; el ganador de esa votación se convierte en el nominado

S

sales tax a tax placed on the sale of various commodities, paid by the purchaser (p. 762)

impuesto a las ventas gravamen sobre las ventas de distintos bienes, el cual paga el comprador

sample a representative slice of the public (p. 224)

muestra una porción representativa del público

search warrant a court order authorizing a search (p. 581)

orden de allanamiento autorización judicial para registrar algo

secretary an official in charge of a department of government (p. 435)

secretario funcionario a cargo de un departamento de gobierno

sectionalism a narrow-minded concern for, or devotion to, the interests of one section of a country (p. 133)

regionalismo preocupación estrecha, o devoción por los intereses de una región del país

Security Council a 15-member panel that bears the UN's major responsibility for keeping international peace (p. 509)

Consejo de Seguridad panel de 15 miembros de la ONU que tiene la máxima responsabilidad para la conservación de la paz internacional

sedition the crime of attempting to overthrow the government by force, or to disrupt its lawful activities by violent acts (p. 560)

sedición crimen de intentar derrocar al gobierno mediante la fuerza, o de interrumpir las actividades legales por medio de actos violentos

seditious speech the advocating, or urging, of an attempt to overthrow the government by force, or to disrupt its lawful activities with violence (p. 560)

discurso sedicioso la convocatoria o el apoyo a un intento de derrocar al gobierno mediante la fuerza, o a la interrupción de actividades legales por medio de la violencia

segregation the separation of one group from another (p. 619)

segregación separación de un grupo respecto a otro

select committee legislative committee created for a limited time and for some specific purpose; also known as a special committee (p. 340)

comité selecto comité legislativo creado por un tiempo limitado y para algún propósito específico; también se conoce como comité especial

senatorial courtesy custom that the Senate will not approve a presidential appointment opposed by a majority-party senator from the State in which the appointee would serve (p. 88)

cortesía senatorial costumbre de que el Senado no aprobará una nominación presidencial, si esa designación no es aprobada por el senador del partido mayoritario de ese estado, en donde la persona designada habría de servir

seniority rule unwritten rule in both houses of Congress reserving the top posts in each chamber, particularly committee chairmanships, for members with the longest records of service (p. 337)

regla de antigüedad regla no escrita de ambas Cámaras del Congreso, de acuerdo con la cual, los puestos más altos de cada una de ellas los ocuparán aquellos miembros que tengan un historial de servicio más antiguo; se aplica de forma más estricta a las presidencias de los comités

separate-but-equal doctrine a constitutional basis for laws that separate one group from another on the basis of race (Jim Crow Laws) (p. 619)

doctrina de iguales pero separados base constitucional para leyes que segregan a un grupo respecto a otro, con base en la raza (Leyes Jim Crow)

separation of powers basic principle of American system of government that the executive, legislative, and judicial powers are divided among three independent and coequal branches of government; *see* checks and balances (p. 70)

separación de poderes principio básico del sistema de gobierno estadounidense, según el cual los poderes ejecutivo, legislativo y judicial están divididos en tres ramas independientes e iguales; *ver* checks and balances/pesos y contrapesos

session period of time during which, each year, Congress assembles and conducts business (p. 270)

sesión período regular durante el cual se reúne el Congreso para atender a asuntos oficiales

shadow cabinet members of opposition parties who watch, or shadow, particular Cabinet members, and who would be ready to run the government (p. 668)

gabinete alterno miembros de los partidos de oposición que vigilan, o supervisan, a un miembro particular del gabinete, y que estarían listos para ejercer el gobierno

shield law a law which gives reporters some protection against having to disclose their sources or reveal other confidential information in legal proceedings (p. 563)

ley Escudo ley que ofrece a los periodistas cierta protección contra la revelación de sus fuentes o la publicación de otra información confidencial durante los procedimientos legales

single-issue parties parties that concentrate on only one public policy matter (p. 137)

partidos de un único asunto partidos que se concentran en un solo aspecto de la política pública

single-member district electoral district from which one person is chosen by the voters for each elected office (pp. 127, 275)

distrito de un solo miembro distrito electoral en donde los votantes eligen, en la papeleta electoral, una sola persona para cada cargo

slander false and malicious use of spoken words (p. 559)

calumnia utilización falsa y maliciosa del discurso hablado

socialism a philosophy based on the idea that the benefits of economic activity should be fairly distributed (p. 686)

socialismo filosofía basada en la idea de que los beneficios de la actividad económica deben distribuirse de manera equitativa a toda la sociedad

soft-liners those who want to reform governmental policies or procedures (p. 661)

blandos quienes quieren reformar las políticas o procesos gubernamentales

soft money money given to State and local party organizations for voting-related activities (p. 208)

fondos no fiscalizados fondos otorgados al estado y a organizaciones partidistas locales para actividades relacionadas con el voto, por ejemplo: registro de votantes, envío de propaganda por correo, anuncios

sound bite short, sharply focused report that can be aired in 30 or 45 seconds (p. 235)

informe sucinto informaciones breves y concisas que pueden despacharse en 30 ó 45 segundos

sovereign having supreme power within one's own territory; neither subordinate nor responsible to any other authority (pp. 7, 649)

soberano tener poder supremo y absoluto dentro de su propio territorio; no estar subordinado ni ser responsable ante ninguna otra autoridad

sovereignty utmost authority in decision making and in maintaining order of a state (p. 650)

soberanía autoridad suprema para tomar desiciones y mantener el orden en un estado

Speaker of the House the presiding officer of the House of Representatives, chosen by and from the majority party in the House (p. 332)

Vocero de la Cámara funcionario que preside la Cámara de Representantes y que es electo por el partido mayoritario en la Cámara, al cual pertenece

special district an independent unit created to perform one or more related governmental functions at the local level (p. 748)

distrito especial unidad independiente creada para llevar a cabo una o más funciones gubernamentales relacionadas a nivel local

special session an extraordinary session of a legislative body, called to deal with an emergency situation (p. 271)

sesión especial sesión extraordinaria de un cuerpo legislativo, convocada para tratar una situación de emergencia

splinter parties parties that have split away from one of the major parties (p. 138)

partidos de escisión partidos formados por la fractura de uno de los principales partidos; la mayor parte de los partidos pequeños importantes en el ámbito político estadounidense son partidos de escisión

split-ticket voting voting for candidates of different parties for different offices at the same election (p. 177)

voto diferenciado votar, en la misma elección, por candidatos de distintos partidos para puestos diferentes

spoils system the practice of giving offices and other favors of government to political supporters and friends (pp. 132, 443)

sistema de prebendas práctica de ofrecer cargos y otros favores gubernamentales a los simpatizantes y amigos políticos

staff agency an agency that supports the chief executive and other administrators by offering advice and other assistance in the management of the organization (p. 430)

oficina de apoyo tipo de agencia cuya función es dar respaldo al Presidente y a otros administradores, ofreciendo consejos y otro tipo de asistencia en la administración de la organización

standing committee permanent committee in a legislative body to which bills of a specified subject matter are referred; *see* select committee (p. 338)

comisión permanente comité permanente de un cuerpo legislativo al que se presentan las propuestas de ley sobre una materia específica; *ver* comité selecto

state a body of people living in a defined territory who have a government with the power to make and enforce law without the consent of any higher authority (p. 5)

estado conjunto de personas que viven en un territorio definido y que tienen un gobierno con el poder de legislar y de hacer cumplir la ley, sin tener el consentimiento de una autoridad superior

statutory law a law passed by the legislature (p. 713)

ley estatuida ley aprobada por los legisladores

straight-ticket voting the practice of voting for candidates of only one party in an election (p. 177)

voto duro práctica de votar en una elección por los candidatos de un solo partido

straw vote poll that seeks to read the public's mind by asking the same question of a large number of people (p. 222)

encuesta pre-electoral encuestas que pretenden conocer la opinión de la gente haciendo simplemente la misma pregunta a una gran cantidad de personas

strict constructionist one who argues a narrow interpretation of the Constitution's provisions, in particular those granting powers to the Federal Government (p. 313)

construccionista estricto persona que defiende una interpretación estrecha de las estipulaciones de la Constitución, en particular las referentes al otorgamiento de poderes al gobierno federal

strict scrutiny test a higher standard than the rational basis test a law must meet in equal protection cases (p. 619)

examen judicial riguroso estándar más alto que la prueba de fundamento razonable que una ley debe honrar en casos de protección equitativa

strong-mayor government a type of government in which the mayor heads the city's administration (p. 750)

gobierno de alcalde vigoroso tipo de gobierno en el que el alcalde encabeza la administración de la ciudad

subcommittee division of existing committee that is formed to address specific issues (p. 340)

subcomité división de un comité existente que se forma para atender asuntos específicos

subpoena an order for a person to appear and to produce documents or other requested materials (p. 322)

citación orden para que se presente una persona o para que se presenten documentos u otros materiales solicitados

subsidy a grant of money, usually from a government (p. 207)

subsidio una subvención de dinero, por lo general por un gobierno

substantive due process the government must create fair policies and laws (p. 578)

proceso legal duradero el gobierno debe crear políticas y leyes justas

successor a person who inherits a title or office (p. 319)

sucesor persona que hereda un título o un cargo

suffrage the right to vote (p. 152)

sufragio el derecho de votar

supply-side economics the assumption that tax cuts increase the supply of money in private hands and stimulate the economy (p. 464)

economía de oferta idea que supone que la reducción de impuestos aumenta el dinero de entidades privadas y estimula la economía

Supremacy Clause a provision of the U.S. Constitution that states that the Constitution, federal law, and treaties of the United States are the "supreme Law of the Land" (p. 101)

Cláusula de Supremacía Cláusula de la Constitución de los Estados Unidos que estipula que la Constitución, la ley federal y los tratados de los Estados Unidos son la "ley suprema del país"

surplus more income than spending (p. 463)

superávit cuando hay más ingresos que gastos

swing voters members of the electorate who have not made up their minds at the start of a campaign and are open to persuasion by either side (p. 386)

votantes indecisos miembros del electorado que no han tomado una decisión al comienzo de una campaña y están dispuestos a inclinarse hacia cualquiera de los candidatos

symbolic speech expression by conduct; communicating ideas through facial expressions, with body language, or by carrying a sign or wearing an armband (p. 565)

discurso simbólico expresión mediante la conducta; comunicación de ideas a través de expresiones faciales, lenguaje corporal o mediante el uso de un letrero o portando una banda en el brazo

T

tariff a tax on imported goods (p. 696)

arancel impuesto que se aplica a las importaciones

tax a charge levied by government on persons or property to meet public needs (p. 300)

impuesto cargo gravado por el gobierno a las personas o propiedades, con el objeto de satisfacer las necesidades públicas

term two-year period of time during which Congress meets (p. 270)

término lapso especificado durante el cual se desempeñará en el cargo un funcionario elegido

territory part of the United States that is not admitted as a State and has its own government (p. 308)

territorio no incorporado territorio de los Estados Unidos que no tiene calidad de estado y que tiene su propio gobierno

terrorism the use of violence to intimidate a government or society (p. 492)

terrorismo el uso de violencia para intimidar a un gobierno o sociedad

Three-Fifths Compromise an agreement at the Constitutional Convention to count a slave as three-fifths of a person when determining the population of a State (p. 56)

Avenencia de las tres quintas partes acuerdo logrado en la Convención Constitucional respecto a que un esclavo debería contarse como tres quintas partes de una persona, para propósitos de determinar la población de un estado

tort a wrongful act that involves injury to one's person, property, or reputation in a situation not covered by the terms of a contract (p. 728)

entuerto acto injusto que incluye daño a la propiedad de una persona, su reputación o a la persona en sí en una situación que no está cubierta por un contrato

township a subdivision of a county (p. 743)

municipio división de un condado

trade association interest group within the business community (p. 248)

asociación comercial grupos de interés dentro de la comunidad de los negocios

trade embargo a ban on trade with a particular country or particular countries (p. 697)

embargo comercial prohibición de comerciar con un país o varios países en particular

transient person living in a State for only a short time, without legal residence (p. 157)

transeúnte persona que vive en un estado sólo por un breve tiempo, sin residencia legal

treason betrayal of one's country; in the Constitution, by "levying war against the United States or offering comfort or aid to its enemies" (p. 606)

alta traición deslealtad hacia el país propio; en la Constitución, librar una guerra en contra de los Estados Unidos, proporcionar aliento u ofrecer ayuda a sus enemigos

treaty a formal agreement between two or more sovereign states (pp. 87, 412)

tratado acuerdo formal entre dos o más estados soberanos

trustee lawmaker who votes based on his or her conscience and judgment, not the views of his or her constituents (p. 287)

independiente legislador que vota en cada asunto de acuerdo con su conciencia y su juicio independiente, sin considerar las opiniones de sus electores o de otros grupos

U

unconstitutional contrary to constitutional provision and so illegal, null and void, of no force and effect (p. 73)

inconstitucional contrario a las estipulaciones constitucionales y, por lo tanto, ilegal, nulo e inválido, que no tiene fuerza ni efecto

uncontrollable spending spending that Congress and the President have no power to change directly (p. 468)

gasto incontrolable gastos que ni el Congreso ni el Presi-

gasto incontrolable gastos que ni el Congreso ni el Presidente tienen el poder de cambiar de manera directa, incluyendo los intereses de la deuda

unicameral an adjective describing a legislative body with one chamber; *see* bicameral (p. 34)

unicameral adjetivo que describe un cuerpo legislativo con una sola Cámara; *ver* bicameral

unitary government a centralized government in which all government powers belong to a single, central agency (p. 14)

gobierno unitario gobierno centralizado en el que los poderes ejercidos por el gobierno pertenecen a una única oficina central

United Nations a league of nations, with 192 members, that accepts the obligations of the United Nations Charter, a treaty drafted in 1945 (p. 508)

Naciones Unidas grupo de naciones compuesto por 192 miembros, que acepta las obligaciones de la Carta de las Naciones Unidas, tratado redactado en el año 1945

universe a term used in polling that refers to the whole population that the poll aims to measure (p. 224)

universo término que se usa en asuntos de elecciones que se refiere a la población entera que se intenta medir mediante una encuesta

V

veto chief executive's power to reject a bill passed by a legislature; literally (Latin) "I forbid"; *see* pocket veto (pp. 72, 356)

veto poder del Presidente para rechazar un proyecto de ley aprobado por una legislatura; literalmente (latín) "Prohíbo"; *ver* pocket veto/veto indirecto

Virginia Plan plan presented by delegates from Virginia at the Constitutional Convention; called for a three-branch government with a bicameral legislature in which each State's membership would be determined by its population or its financial support for the central government (p. 54)

Plan Virginia proyecto presentado por los delegados de Virginia en la Convención Constitucional; proponía un gobierno con tres poderes y una legislatura bicameral en la que la representación de cada estado estuviera determinada por su población o por su apoyo financiero al gobierno central

visa a permit to enter another country, obtained from the country one wishes to enter (p. 487)

visa permiso para entrar a otro país, otorgado por el país al cual se desea entrar

W

ward a unit into which cities are often divided for the election of city council members (p. 146)

barrio unidad en la que suelen dividirse las ciudades para la elección de los miembros del consejo municipal

warrant a court order authorizing, or making legal, some official action, such as a search or an arrest (p. 732)

mandamiento orden judicial que autoriza o hace legal alguna acción oficial, como la orden de allanamiento o la orden de arresto

weak-mayor government a type of government in which the mayor shares his or her executive duties with other elected officials (p. 750)

gobierno de alcalde débil tipo de gobierno en el que el alcalde comparte las obligaciones ejecutivas con otros funcionarios electos

weblogs (blogs) Web site postings usually devoted to a specific subject, often allowing visitors to post comments (p. 233)

blogs listados en un sitio web que por lo general se enfocan en un tema en específico y que muchas veces permite a los visitantes poner sus comentarios

welfare cash assistance to the poor (p. 757)

beneficencia ayuda en efectivo a los pobres

welfare state country that provides extensive social services at little or no cost to the users (p. 687)

estado benefactor países que ofrecen una amplia gama de servicios sociales a un bajo costo o de manera gratuita para los usuarios

whips assistants to the floor leaders in the House and Senate, responsible for monitoring and marshaling votes (p. 336)

whips auxiliares de los líderes de las fracciones partidistas en la Cámara de Representantes y el Senado que son responsables de vigilar y ordenar los votos

winner-take-all an almost obsolete system whereby a presidential aspirant who won the preference vote in a primary automatically won all the delegates chosen in the primary (p. 379)

el ganador se lleva todo sistema casi obsoleto en donde un aspirante presidencial que ganaba la preferencia del voto en las elecciones primarias, automáticamente obtenía el apoyo de todos los delegados elegidos en dichas elecciones

World Trade Organization (WTO) organization created in 1995 to increase trade (p. 697)

Organización Mundial del Comercio (OMC) organización creada en 1995 para aumentar el comercio

writ of assistance blanket search warrant with which British custom officials had invaded private homes to search for smuggled goods (p. 585)

auto de ayuda orden general de allanamiento con la que los funcionarios aduanales británicos invadían los hogares privados en busca de bienes de contrabando

writ of certiorari an order by a higher court directing a lower court to send up the record in a given case for review; from the Latin meaning "to be more certain" (p. 534)

auto de avocación *o certiorari* orden emitida por una corte superior dirigida a una corte inferior para que remita el expediente de un determinado caso para su revisión; el significado en latín de la expresión es "tener mayor certeza"

writ of habeas corpus a court order which prevents unjust arrests and imprisonments (p. 592)

auto de *habeas corpus* orden judicial que evita arrestos y encarcelamientos injustos

Z

zoning the practice of dividing a city into a number of districts and regulating the uses to which property in each of them may be put (p. 753)

zonificación práctica de dividir a una ciudad en determinado número de distritos y de regular los usos que se dará a la propiedad en cada uno de ellos

Index

Note: Entries with a page number followed by a (c) denote reference to a chart on that page; those followed by a (p) denote a photo; those followed by a (m) denote a map; those followed by a (g) denote a graph.

INDEX

elections in, 191*m*, 376*m*, 388*m*, 391*m*
gains statehood, 105*m*
governors of, 723*m*, 724
House of Representatives and, 273
immigrants in, 636*m*
local government in, 742
ratification of the Constitution and, 61, 61*c*, 61*p*
slavery and, 56*m*
state government in, 96, 719
statistical profile, 772*c*
voting rights in, 154*m*
delegated powers, 296–297
delegates, 287, 287*c*
demand-side economics, 464
democracy, 661
in Athens, 647
concepts of, 20–23
definition of, 5
difference between dictatorships and, 547
essentials of, 663, 663*c*
free enterprise system and, 23–24
government and, 13–14, 15*c*
indirect, 13–14
political parties and, 122–123, 124
roots of, 27
See also direct democracy
***Democracy in America* (De Tocqueville),** 244*q*, 245*q*, 551
democratic consolidation, 663, 663*c*
Democratic National Committee (DNC), 144–145
Democratic-Republican Party, 131, 186–187, 375–376, 376*c*, 376*m*
democratization, 661
definition of, 663
failures of, 664–665
of Haiti, 663–664
of Iraq, 664, 664*m*
of Soviet Union, 662–663, 662*p*
Democrat Party, 187
apportioned delegates, 378
civil rights and, 165
in Congress, 334*c*, 334–336, 335*m*
domination by, 129, 131–134
election of 2008, 206–208, 377*p*
fundraising by, 207–208
governors and, 723*m*
history of, 131
minor parties and, 138–140
organization of, 142–145, 142*p*, 143*p*
policy position of, 126, 128
political spectrum and, 126
primary elections, 378–381, 379*c*, 380*p*
symbols of, 133*p*
two-party system and, 124–128, 125*p*, 128*c*
voter behavior and, 174–178
See also elections; political parties
demonstrations, 258
denaturalization, 635
Deng Xiaoping, 690
***Dennis* v. *United States* (1951),** 561, 806
department, 428
deportation, 97, 637, 638
destroyers-for-bases deal, 413–414
détente, 501
deterrence, 498, 502, 515
De Tocqueville, Alexis, 244*q*, 245*q*, 247, 551
devolution, 670
Dewey, Thomas E., 134
Diaz, Porfirio, 657
***Dickerson* v. *United States* (2000),** 601
Dickinson, John, 39
dictatorships, 14, 15*c*, 129, 185, 547, 659–660, 659*p*, 661
digital age literacy, S24–S25
***Dillon* v. *Gloss* (1921),** 82
diplomatic immunity, 486–487, 486*p*
diplomatic powers, 97, 412–414, 412*p*, 413*p*, 421
diplomats, 407, 414, 486
direct democracy, 13–14, 739, 746–747
direct initiative, 719

direct legislation, 719
Director of National Intelligence (DNI), 492
direct popular election, 392–393
direct primary, 186*p*, 187–192, 191*m*
direct response electronic voting machines (DREs), 198
direct tax, 300–301, 458
disabled Americans, 299*p*, 315*p*, 629
discharge petition, 345–346
discount rate, 476
discretionary spending, 468
discrimination. *See* age discrimination; racial discrimination; religious discrimination; reverse discrimination; sex discrimination
disenfranchised citizens, 153, 153*p*, 164, 165
dissenting opinion, 537
district attorney, 744*c*
district courts, 521, 521*c*, 526, 528–530, 529*m*, 530*c*
districting, congressional, 528, 715–716
District of Columbia. *See* Washington, D.C.
***District of Columbia* v. *Heller* (2008),** 585, 806
district plan, 391–392
divided government, 359
divine right of kings, 650
divine right theory of the state, 8, 8*c*, 41
division of powers, 16, 16*c*, 17*c*, 17–18
divorce laws, 112
Dixiecrat Party, 138
DNI. *See* Director of National Intelligence
dockets, 530
documentary tax, 764
Document-Based Assessment
American electorate, 181
civil rights, 641, 641*p*
Congress, 359
congressional voting, 293
Constitution, U.S., 65
democracy, 27
direct democracy, 739
division of powers, 117
entitlement programs, 479
environmental protection, 453
fascism and communism, 675
federal judges, 543
foreign policy, 515
freedom of speech and assembly, 575
government and the economy, 703
impact of television, 239
lobbyists, 263
nominating process, 211
Patriot Act, 609
police power, 769
political parties, 149
presidential signing statements, 423
presidential term of office, 397
strict v. *liberal construction of the Constitution,* 327
Twenty-third Amendment, 91, 91*m*, 91*p*
Dole, Bob, 135, 385, 387
domestic policy, 434, 482
domestic violence, 104
Dominican Republic, 615
Dorr, Thomas W., 103
Dorr's Rebellion, 103
***Dothard* v. *Rawlinson* (1977),** 623
double jeopardy, 595–596
Douglas, William O., 163*q*
Douglass, Frederick, 244*p*
draft, military, 316, 445, 583, 813
Drake, Thelma, 343*p*
***Dred Scott* v. *Sandford* (1857),** 806
DREs. *See* direct response electronic voting machines
drivers' licenses, 716*p*
Drug Enforcement Agency, 492
drug testing programs, 588
drunk driving, 599
dual court system, 521
due process, 31, 32*c*, 80
definition of, 578–579
examples of, 579
privacy and, 581–582
Roe v. *Wade,* 581–582, 813

Due Process Clause, 549*c*, 549–550, 557–558, 569, 618, 761–762, 808, 809, 810, 811, 814
Dukakis, Michael, 135
Duncan, John J., Jr., 504*q*
***Duncan* v. *Kahanamoku* (1946),** 593
***Duncan* v. *Louisiana* (1968),** 597
Dunham, Frank, 519*p*
***Dunn* v. *Blumstein* (1972),** 157
Durbin, Dick, 333*p*
Durenberger, David, 284
Dwight D. Eisenhower System of Interstate and Defense Highways, 759
Dyer Act (1925), 520

E

Eckford, Elizabeth, 21*p*
e-commerce, 316, 763
Economic Advisors, Council of, 434
Economic and Social Council (UN), 509–511, 510*p*
economic protest parties, 138
economics and economic systems
capitalism, 678–684, 678*p*, 679*p*, 680*p*, 681*p*, 682*p*, 683*p*
command economy, 687
communism, 685–686, 688*c*, 689–691, 690*p*
demand-side, 464
Federal Reserve System, 693–694, 694*m*
fiscal policy, 474–475
global economy and, 693–700, 693*p*, 694*m*, 696*c*, 698*c*–699*c*, 700*c*
international organizations, 697–698
Labor Department and, 694–695
mercantilism and, 651
monetary policy, 475–476
Securities and Exchange Commission, 694
socialism, 685–688, 687*c*
supply-side, 464
trade policies, 696*c*, 696–697, 698*c*
economy
borrowing, 463–466
deflation, 474
domestic economy, 693–695
employment and, 473–474
foreign affairs and, 483
gross domestic product, 473–474
inflation, 474, 475
recession, 474
spending, 467–469, 468*c*
taxes and, 456–462
Edison, Thomas, 198
education
African Americans and, 21*p*, 257, 584
Brown v. *Board of Education,* 21*p*, 77, 257, 527, 620, 624–625, 624*p*, 625*p*, 628, 808
Congress and, 314–315, 314*p*, 315*p*
creation science, 554
freedom of speech and, 814
local government and, 756–757, 756*p*, 757*c*
Pierce v. *Society of Sisters* (1925), 552
public opinion and, 215–217, 217*p*
religion and, 552–555, 553*p*, 554*p*
school choice, 555
segregation in, 620–622, 621*p*
voter behavior and, 174
See also schools
Education, Department of, 437
Education Amendments (1972), 626, 627, 629
Edwards, John, 390, 692*q*
***Edwards* v. *Aguillard* (1987),** 554
***Edwards* v. *South Carolina* (1963),** 806
EEC. *See* European Economic Community
EEOC. *See* Equal Employment Opportunity Commission
Egypt, 5, 485, 502
Eighteenth Amendment, C21, 80, 82, 83
Eighth Amendment, C18, 82*c*, 549*c*, 602–603, 607, 809
Eisenhower, Dwight D., 134, 183*q*, 366, 367, 371, 397, 404, 416, 775*c*
election of, 384

INDEX

United States v. *Playboy Entertainment Group*, 564
United States v. *Salerno*, 603
Uttecht v. *Brown*, 605
Van Orden v. *Perry*, 556
Veazie Bank v. *Fenno*, 303
Vernonia School District v. *Acton*, 588
Virginia Bd. of Pharmacy v. *Virginia Citizens Consumer Council*, 567
Virginia v. *Black*, 566
Wallace v. *Jaffree*, 553
Washington v. *Texas*, 598
Watchtower Bible and Tract Society v. *Village of Stratton*, 558
Webster v. *Reproductive Health Services*, 581–582
Weeks v. *United States*, 588
Weems v. *United States*, 604
Welsh v. *United States*, 557
Wesberry v. *Sanders*, 278
Westside Community Schools v. *Mergens*, 553
West Virginia Board of Education v. *Barnette*, 547, 558
Whitney v. *California*, 575
Wilkerson v. *Utah*, 603
Williams v. *North Carolina*, 112
Wisconsin v. *Yoder*, 558
Wolman v. *Walter*, 554
Woodson v. *North Carolina*, 604
Wood v. *Broom*, 276
Wyoming v. *Houghton*, 587
Yates v. *United States*, 561
Youngstown Sheet & Tube Co. v. *Sawyer*, 402
Zelman v. *Simmons-Harris*, 555
Zobrest v. *Catalina Foothills School District*, 555
Zorach v. *Clauson*, 552
Supreme Court Glossary
Abrams v. *United States (1919)*, 805
Agostini v. *Felton (1997)*, 805
Alden v. *Maine (1999)*, 805
American Insurance Association v. *Garamendi (2003)*, 805
Baker v. *Carr (1962)*, 805
Board of Education of Westside Community Schools v. *Mergens (1990)*, 814
Board of Estimate of City of New York v. *Morris (1989)*, 805
Bob Jones University v. *United States (1983)*, 805
Bradenburg v. *Ohio (1969)*, 805
Brown v. *Board of Education (1954)*, 806
City of Boerne, Texas v. *Flores (1997)*, 806
Civil Rights Cases (1883), 806
Cruzan v. *Missouri (1990)*, 806
Dennis v. *United States (1951)*, 806
District of Columbia v. *Heller (2008)*, 806
Dred Scott v. *Sandford (1857)*, 806
Edwards v. *South Carolina (1963)*, 806
Engel v. *Vitale (1962)*, 806
Escobedo v. *Illinois (1964)*, 807
Ex parte Milligan (1866), 807
Flast v. *Cohen (1968)*, 807
Furman v. *Georgia (1972)*, 807
Gibbons v. *Ogden (1824)*, 807
Gideon v. *Wainwright (1963)*, 807
Gitlow v. *New York (1925)*, 807
Goss v. *Lopez (1975)*, 807
Gregg v. *Georgia (1976)*, 808
Griswold v. *Connecticut (1965)*, 808
Grutter v. *Bollinger (2003)*, 808
Hazelwood School District v. *Kuhlmeier (1988)*, 808
Heart of Atlanta Motel, Inc. v. *United States (1964)*, 808
Hutchinson v. *Proxmire (1979)*, 808
Illinois v. *Wardlow (2000)*, 808
In re Gault (1966), 808
Johnson v. *Santa Clara Transportation Agency (1987)*, 809
Korematsu v. *United States (1944)*, 809
Lemon v. *Kurtzman (1971)*, 809
Mapp v. *Ohio (1961)*, 809
Marbury v. *Madison (1803)*, 809
McCulloch v. *Maryland (1819)*, 809
Miranda v. *Arizona (1966)*, 809
New Jersey v. *T.L.O. (1985)*, 809
New York Times v. *Sullivan (1964)*, 810
New York Times v. *United States (1971)*, 810
Nixon v. *Fitzgerald (1982)*, 810

Nixon v. *Shrink Missouri Government PAC (2000)*, 810
Olmstead v. *United States (1928)*, 810
Oregon v. *Mitchell (1970)*, 810
Plessy v. *Ferguson (1896)*, 810
Powell v. *Alabama (1932)*, 810
Printz v. *United States (1997)*, 811
Reno v. *American Civil Liberties Union (1997)*, 811
Reno v. *Condon (2000)*, 811
Republican Party of Minnesota v. *White (2002)*, 811
Roe v. *Wade (1973)*, 811
Rostker v. *Goldberg (1981)*, 811
Roth v. *United States (1957)*, 811
Rush Prudential HMO, Inc. v. *Moran (2002)*, 811
Schenck v. *United States (1919)*, 812
School District of Abington Township, Pennsylvania v. *Schempp (1963)*, 812
Shelley v. *Kraemer (1948)*, 812
Sheppard v. *Maxwell (1966)*, 812
Tahoe-Sierra Preservation Council v. *Tahoe Regional Planning Agency (2002)*, 812
Tennessee Valley Authority v. *Hill (1978)*, 812
Texas v. *White (1869)*, 812
Tinker v. *Des Moines (1969)*, 812
U.S. Term Limits, Inc. v. *Thornton (1995)*, 812
United States v. *American Library Association (2003)*, 813
United States v. *Amistad (1841)*, 813
United States v. *Eichman (1990)*, 813
United States v. *General Dynamics Corp. (1974)*, 813
United States v. *Leon (1984)*, 813
United States v. *Lopez (1995)*, 813
United States v. *Nixon (1974)*, 813
Wallace v. *Jaffree (1985)*, 813
Walz v. *Tax Commission of the City of New York (1970)*, 814
Watchtower Bible and Tract Society v. *Village of Stratton (2002)*, 814
Watkins v. *United States (1957)*, 814
West Virginia Board of Education v. *Barnette (1943)*, 814
Wisconsin v. *Yoder (1972)*, 814
Supreme Law of the Land, 68
surplus, 463, 464*g*, 466
***Swann* v. *Charlotte-Mecklenburg Board of Education (1971)*,** 621
***Sweatt* v. *Painter (1950)*,** 620
swing voters, 386
Switzerland, 13, 16
symbolic speech, 565–567, 566*p*
symbols, 532, 709*p*

T

Taft, William Howard, 107, 133, 140, 403, 403*p*, 408, 440, 454*q*, 775*c*, 775*p*
Taft-Hartley Act (1947), 200
***Tahoe-Sierra Preservation Council* v. *Tahoe Regional Planning Agency (2002)*,** 812
Taiwan, 416
Taiwan Pact, 507
Taliban, 503, 507
talk radio, 231
Taney, Roger B., 592
TANF. *See* **Temporary Assistance to Needy Families**
Tariff Act (1789), 692
tariffs, 457, 696. *See also* taxes
taxation without representation, 37, 38
Tax Court, U.S., 521–522, 530*c*, 531, 540
taxes
Articles of Confederation and, 49–50
in capitalism, 687
Congress and, 299–301, 300*p*
Constitution and, 456–458
county government and, 745
cuts in, 474
definition of, 299
English colonies and, 37, 37*p*, 38–39
increases in, 474
on Internet purchases, 316, 763
limits on, 457–459
local government and, 761–764, 761*p*, 763*c*, 763*p*
progressive income, 140
regulation and, 457

in socialism, 687
state government and, 760, 760*p*, 761–764, 761*p*, 763*c*, 763*p*
See also capitation tax; direct tax; income tax; indirect tax; poll tax; tariffs; *individually named taxes*
tax return, 460
Taylor, Anna Diggs, 404
Taylor, Zachary, 132, 774*c*, 774*p*
***Taylor* v. *Louisiana (1975)*,** 597, 623
T-bills, 465
Tea Act (1773), 39
telecommunications, 231
telephone surveys, 225
television, 229, 229*c*, 230, 232*p*, 233, 233*p*, 236
freedom of speech and, 559*p*
interest groups and, 258
politics and, 235, 239
presidential elections and, 385
public opinion and, 218, 218*p*
regulation of, 563–565
Temporary Assistance to Needy Families (TANF), 758
Tennessee, 776*m*–777*m*
in Civil War, 284
congressional delegations from, 335*m*
congressional representation and, 274*m*
courts in, 529*m*
elections in, 191*m*, 376*m*, 388*m*, 391*m*
gains statehood, 105*m*, 106
governors of, 722, 723*m*
local government in, 743*p*, 745
statistical profile, 773*c*
Supreme Court cases in, 599
voting rights in, 154*m*, 157
Tennessee Valley Authority (TVA), 448, 449
***Tennessee Valley Authority* v. *Hill (1978)*,** 812
Tenth Amendment, C18, 82*c*, 95
Tenure of Office Act (1867), 321, 408
term limits, 366–368, 367*p*, 397, 543, 667, 815
Terrell, Mary Church, 244*p*
territorial courts, 522, 530*c*, 531, 540
territories, 308–309
acquisition of, 97
as characteristic of the state, 6–7, 8*c*, 8–9
The Terror, 655
terrorism, 275, 317, 402, 404, 490, 492, 493, 503, 548, 591, 665
courts and, 529
Foreign Intelligence Surveillance Court, 528–529
See also Patriot Act (2001)
***Terry* v. *Ohio (1968)*,** 587
testimonials, 260
Texas, 776*m*–777*m*
annexation of, 413
congressional apportionment and, 274*m*
congressional delegations from, 335*m*
congressional elections in, 278
courts in, 529*m*
elections in, 191*m*, 199, 388*m*, 391*m*
first amendment rights in, 553, 556, 566–567
gains statehood, 105*m*, 106
governors of, 723*m*, 725–726
local government in, 742, 743, 751
minority populations in, 612, 614, 636*m*, 637
presidential candidates from, 385
statistical profile, 773*c*
Supreme Court cases in, 566–567, 596, 598, 706*p*
voting rights in, 154*m*, 155, 162, 165, 166, 168
Texas Rangers, 758
***Texas* v. *Johnson (1989)*,** 566–567, 814
***Texas* v. *White (1869)*,** 812
Thatcher, Margaret, 481*p*, 667
think tanks, 251–252
Third Amendment, C17, 82*c*, 549*c*, 585
Thirteenth Amendment, C19, 56, 80, 83, 103, 547, 583–585, 607, 613, 632
Thomas, Clarence, 524, 531, 536*c*, 536*p*
Thomas, Norman, 140
***Thornburgh* v. *Abbott (1989)*,** 562
***Thornhill* v. *Alabama (1940)*,** 565–566

INDEX

Acknowledgments

The people who made up the **Magruder's American Government** team—representing design services, editorial, editorial services, education technology, fact-checking, library services, manufacturing and inventory planning, market research, marketing services, product management, production, planning and coordination, and technical operations—are listed below. Boldface type denotes the core team members.

Courtney Alexander, **Alyssa Boehm,** Kristen Braghi, **Peter Brooks,** Lynn Burke, Todd Christy, **Lori-Anne Cohen,** Brett Creane, Michael Di Maria, Laura Edgerton-Riser, Thomas Ferreira, Patricia Fromkin, Andrea Golden, Shelby Gragg, Thomas Guarino, Susan Hersch, Paul Hughes, Katharine Ingram, Stephanie Krol, Courtney Markham, **Dotti Marshall, Grace Massey,** Laurie McKenna, Angelina Mendez, Jennifer Paley, **Gabriela Perez Fiato,** Judi Pinkham, Charlene Rimsa, Amanda Seldera, Alexandra Sherman, **Mark Staloff,** Kara Stokes, Kristen VanEtten, Paula Wehde

Art Credits

Maps: XNR Productions, Inc.

Cover Image

Getty Images

Illustration

Kenneth Batelman, Kerry Cashman, Daniel Guidera, Gillian Kahn, Rich McMahon, Jen Paley, Cyndy Patrick, Ted Smykal, Robin Storesund

Picture Research

Kara Stokes

Photography

FRONT MATTER **Page i,** Getty Images; **v,** Catherine Karnow/Corbis; **vi,** REUTERS/Jason Reed; **vii,** DAVID NOBLE PHOTOGRAPHY / Alamy; **viii,** AP Photo/Doug Mills; **ix,** Catherine Karnow/Corbis; **x,** Zhukov Sergei/ITAR-TASS/Corbis; **xi,** AP Photo/Toby Talbot; **xiii,** Danny Kerr; **xiv T,** Getty Images; **xiv M and B,** istockphoto; **xvii,** Flip Schulke/Black Star; **xxii,** Bob Englehart, The Hartford Currant/politicalcartoons.com; **xxvi,** Swim Ink 2, LLC/Corbis; **C4,** Library of Congress, Washington D.C., USA,/The Bridgeman Art Library; **C6 L,** Bettmann/CORBIS; **C6 M,** British Museum / Art Resource, NY; **C6 R,** US Dept of Treasury; **C6 inset,** JUPITERIMAGES/ Comstock Images; **C9,** Scott J. Ferrell/Congressional Quarterly/Getty Images; **C10,** AP Photo/ Ron Edmonds; **C11,** Stockbyte/Getty Images; **C14,** The Granger Collection, New York; **C15,** The Granger Collection, New York; **C17,** Ron Chapple/Taxi/ Getty Images; **C18,** AP Photo/Ron Edmonds; **C20 L,** Drug Enforcement Administration; **C20 R,** David J. & Janice L. Frent Collection/Corbis; **C22,** Pearson Education/PH School Division; **S0,** Corbis; **S1,** JUPITERIMAGES/ BananaStock / Alamy; **S3,** Grapheast / Alamy; **S6,** Tetra Images / Alamy; **S13,** Blend Images/Getty Images; **S17,** PHOVOIR / FCM Graphic / Alamy; **S19,** Digital Vision / Alamy; **S20,** Juliet Brauner / Alamy; **S22,** Ed Fischer, Rochester (MN) Post Bulletin; **S24,** Red Chopsticks/Getty Images; **S25,** www.wikipedia.org; **S28 L,** Public Domain; **S28 R,** David J. & Janice L. Frent Collection/Corbis.

UNIT 1 **Page 1,** Catherine Karnow/CORBIS; **2-3,** Larry Chiger/ SuperStock; **4 TL,** Klaus Hackenberg/zefa/Corbis; **4 TR,** Romilly Lockyer/The Image Bank/Getty Images, Inc.; **5 T,** Mark Wilson/Getty Images; **5 M,** SANDY SCHAEFFER/MAI /Landov; **5 B,** Dennis Brack/Newscom; **7** REUTERS/Victor Fraile /Landov; **7 R,** Atlantide Phototravel/Corbis; **8 T,** Archive Photos/Getty Images; **8 TM,** Bridgeman Art Library; **8 BM,** Joseph Werner/Bridgeman Art Library/Getty Images; **8 B,** Library of Congress; **9,** By permission of Johnny Hart and Craetors Syndicate, Inc.; **10,** Mike Lutz/U.S. Coast Guard via Getty Images; **11,** Ed Fischer/CartoonStock; **12 both,** Tim Graham/Getty Images; **13 T,** AP Photo/Toby Talbot; **13 B,** AP Photo/Harry Cabluck; **15 L,** Christy Bowe/Corbis; **15 R,** Alain Evrard / Impact Photos / Imagestate; **18,** AP Photo/Benny Gool; **19,** AP Photo/Mike Stone; **20 both,** Richard B. Levine; **21 both,** Bettmann/Corbis, **26,** Baloo -Rex May/Cartoon Stock **27 L,** Bust of Aristotle **(384-322** BC) (marble) (b/w photo), Roman / Museo Nazionale Romano, Rome, Italy, Alinari / The Bridgeman Art Library International; **27 R,** Bust of Plato (c.**427-347** BC) (stone) (b/w photo), Greek / Vatican Museums and Galleries, Vatican City, Italy, Alinari / The Bridgeman Art Library International; **28-29,** The Battle of Lexington, 19th April **1775, 1910** (oil on canvas), Wollen, William Barnes (**1857-1936**) / National Army

Museum, London,   / The Bridgeman Art Library International; **30 L,** Copy of the Magna Carta (detail),   / Lincoln Cathedral, Lincolnshire, UK, / The Bridgeman Art Library International; **30 R,** The Granger Collection, New York; **31,** British Museum / Art Resource, NY; **32,** William Sumits//Time Life Pictures/Getty Images; **35 TL,** JEAN-PAUL PELISSIER/Reuters/Corbis; **35 TR,** AP Photo/Massimo Sambucetti; **35 B,** Peter Andrews/Reuters/ Corbis; **36 L,** The Drafting of the Declaration of Independence in **1776** (oil on canvas), Ferris, Jean Leon Jerome (**1863-1930**) / Private Collection, / The Bridgeman Art Library International; **36 R,** HIP / Art Resource, NY; **37 T,** American Antiquarian Society, Worcester, Massachusetts, USA, /The Bridgeman Art Library International; **37 B,** Library of Congress; **38 L,** Sloane MS **1622** Map of Virginia, showing in upper left hand a picture of Chief Powhatan by John Smith (**1580-1631**) **1624** (hand-coloured engraving), Bry, Theodore de (**1528-98**) (after) / British Library, London, UK, (c) British Library Board. All Rights Reserved / The Bridgeman Art Library; **38 ML,** The Granger Collection, New York; **38 MR,** The Granger Collection, New York; **38 M,** The Granger Collection, New York; **38-039 R,** The Art Archive; **39 L,** Photo Credit : HIP / Art Resource, NY; **39 M,** Bunker's Hill, **1775,** c.**1900** (w/c on paper), Simkin, Richard (**1840-1926**) / National Army Museum, London,   / The Bridgeman Art Library; **39 R,** The Granger Collection, New York; **41,** Bettmann/Corbis; **42 L,** English School/Bridgeman Art Library/ Getty Images; **42 R,** Bill Brooks / Alamy; **43,** Thomas Jefferson Writing the Declaration of Independence, from 'The Story of the Revolution' by Henry Cabot Lodge (**1850-1924**), published in Scribner's Magazine, March **1898** (oil on canvas), Pyle, Howard (**1853-1911**) / Delaware Art Museum, Wilmington, USA, Howard Pyle Collection / The Bridgeman Art Library; **45 L,** Bettmann/ Corbis; **45 R,** Eric Van Den Brulle/Riser/Getty Images; **47 L,** Todd Gipstein/ National Geographic/Getty Images; **47 R,** Bettmann/Corbis; **48 L,** Courtesy of the Federal Reserve Bank of San Francisco; **48 R,** The Granger Collection, New York; **49,** The Granger Collection, New York; **51,** R. Kord/Getty Images/ Retrofile; **52 both,** The Granger Collection, New York; **53 L,** Purestock/Getty Images; **53 ML,** Bettmann/Corbis; **53 TM,** The Granger Collection, New York; **53 BM,** VisionsofAmerica/Joe Sohm; **53 TR,** Burazin/Getty Images; **53 BR,** Photo by George Skadding/Time & Life Pictures/Getty Images; **55 TL,** John Locke (**1632-1704**) (plaster), English School, (19th century) / Yale Center for British Art, Paul Mellon Collection, USA, / The Bridgeman Art Library; **55 TR,** Bust of Charles de Secondat (**1689-1755**) Baron de Montesquieu, **1767** (marble), Lemoyne, Jean Baptiste II (**1704-78**) / Musee des Arts Decoratifs, Bordeaux, France, Lauros / Giraudon / The Bridgeman Art Library; **55 BL,** Bust of Jean Jacques Rousseau (**1712-78**) (terracotta), Houdon, Jean-Antoine (**1741-1828**) / Musee des Beaux-Arts, Orleans, France, Giraudon / The Bridgeman Art Library; **55 BR,** Library of Congress; **57,** The Granger Collection, New York; **58,** Independence National Historical Park Collection; **59 L,** Garry Black/Masterfile; **59 R,** Picture History; **60 L,** Stock Montage/ Stock Montage/Getty Images; **60 R,** The Granger Collection, New York; **61,** American Antiquarian Society; **64,** Library of Congress; **65,** Hulton Archive/ Getty Images; **66-67,** age fotostock / SuperStock; **68 both,** ROBERTO SCHMIDT/AFP/Getty Images; **69,** Visions of America, LLC / Alamy; **70-71 all,** Steve Artley;

76 BL, James Madison (oil on canvas), American School, (19th century) / Musee Franco-Americaine, Blerancourt, Chauny, France, Giraudon / The Bridgeman Art Library; **76 BM,** The Granger Collection, New York; **76 BR,** The Granger Collection, New York; **77 L,** public domain; **77 M,** Bettmann/ Corbis; **77 R,** New York Times Pictures; **78 L,** Library of Congress; **78 R,** Bettmann/Corbis; **80 L,** The Granger Collection, New York; **80 M,** Smithsonian Institution/Corbis; **80 R,** Bettmann/Corbis; **81 both,** Bettmann/ Corbis; **83,** ©Mark Parisi, reprint by permission; **84,** image100/Corbis; **85 both,** Tom Fox/Dallas Morning News/Corbis; **86,** AP Photo; **88,** AP Photo/ Gerald Herbert; **90,** Baloo -Rex May/Cartoon Stock; **91 T,** The New York Public Library / Art Resource, NY; **91 B,** The Granger Collection, New York; **92-93,** Emmanuel Dunand/AFP/Getty Images; **92-93,** UPI Photo/ Duncan McIntosh/Office of Governor Schwarzenegger; **94 both,** © Richard B. Levine; **95,** AP Photo/Chris Polk; **97 L,** Reuters/Carlos Barria; **97 R,** Bettmann/CORBIS; **98,** Image by © Michael Urban/POOL/epa/Corbis; **100 L,** David R. Frazier / Photo Researchers, Inc.; **100 R,** LUKE FRAZZA/AFP/ Getty Images; **101,** The Granger Collection, New York; **103 both,** AP Photo/ Nancy Bannick Collection, Hawaii State Archives; **106 L,** Tony Freeman / Photo Edit; **106 R,** Connie Ricca/Corbis; **108 L,** Bob Daemmrich / Photo Edit; **108 M,** Ric Dugan/Herald-Mail/AP Photo; **108 R,** Richard T. Nowitz/ Corbis; **110 TL,** Mark Constantini/San Francisco Chronicle/Corbis; **110 TR,** age fotostock / SuperStock; **110 B,** AP Photo/Energy Star, John Harrington; **111 both,** Corbis / SuperStock; **112,** Russ Lappa; **113,** Bettmann/Corbis; **116,** Mischa Richter/Condé Nast Publications/www.cartoonbank.com; **117 L,** Stock Montage / SuperStock; **117 R,** Getty Images; **118 L,** Free Agents Limited/Corbis; **118 R,** American Bar Association.

UNIT 2 **Page 119,** REUTERS/Jason Reed; **Page 119,** Ali Goldstein/NBC NewsWire **120-121,** AP Photo/Stephan Savoia; **122 both,** AP Photo/ Victoria Arocho; **123,** AP Photo/Jae C. Hong; **125 BL,** democrats.org; **125**

ACKNOWLEDGMENTS

TR, Carolyn Chappo; **125** Bkgrnd, Joshua Lott/Raleigh News & Observer/MCT; **125 BM,** facebook.com; **129,** J.B. Handelsman/The Cartoon Bank; **130 L,** Library of Congress; **130 M,** Bridgeman Art Library; **130 R,** Archivo Iconografico, S.A./Corbis; **131,** Library of Congress; **133 L,** The Granger Collection, New York; **133** inset L, Beathan/Corbis; **133 R,** The Granger Collection, New York; **133** inset R, Beathan/Corbis; **134 L,** The Granger Collection, New York; **134 ML,** Brooklyn Museum/Corbis; **134 M,** Portrait of Andrew Jackson, **1858** (oil on canvas), Sully, Thomas (**1783-1872**) / Private Collection, Photo (c) Christie's Images / The Bridgeman Art Library; **134 MR,** Bridgeman Art Library; **134-135,** Minnesota Historical Society/Corbis; **135 BL,** President Franklin D. Roosevelt (**1882-1945**) c.**1941** (photo), American Photographer, (**20**th century) / Private Collection, Peter Newark American Pictures / The Bridgeman Art Library; **135 M,** Bettmann/Corbis; **135 R,** Jean-Pierre Lescourret/Corbis; **135** inset R, Getty Images; **137 L,** Three Lions/Getty Images/Newscom; **137 R,** Bettmann/Corbis; **139 TL,** David J. & Janice L. Frent /Corbis; **139 BL,** Time Inc./Time Life Pictures/Getty Images; **139 TR,** David J. & Janice L. Frent Collection/Corbis; **140,** Underwood And Underwood/Underwood And Underwood/Time & Life Pictures/Getty Images; **141,** AP Photo/Kevork Djansezian; **142 both,** Chris Kleponis/Zuma/Corbis; **143,** Copley News Service; **144 M,** courtesy matt lundh at kcgop.org; **144 TR,** Image by (c) JASON REED/Reuters/Corbis; **144** BR, dnc.org; **144** Bkgrnd, MedioImages/Corbis; **146,** AP Photo/Kiichiro Sato; **148,** Mischa Richter/Cartoon Bank, Inc.; **149,** Harley Schwadron/CartoonStock; **150-151,** AP Photo/Springfield News-Leader, Christina Dicken; **152 both,** LOU DEMATTEIS/Reuters/Corbis; **153 L,** George Caleb Bingham/Bridgeman Art Library/Getty Images; **153 M,** The Granger Collection, New York; **153 R,** AP Photo;

155, Bettmann/Corbis; **156 both,** Barbara Davidson/Dallas Morning News/Corbis; **157 L,** AP Photo/Chuck Burton; **157 R,** AP Photo/Khampha Bouaphanh; **158,** Bettmann/CORBIS; **159** Bkgrnd, AP Photo/Ric Feld; **159 T,** AP Photo/ Robert E. Klein; **159 M,** AP Photo/Bill Waugh; **159 B,** Jonathan Nourok / Photo Edit; **160 TR,** AP Photo/Craig Fritz; **160 BL,** AP Photo/Ric Feld; **162,** Take Stock Images; **163,** Spencer Platt/Getty Images; **164 both,** Bettmann/Corbis; **166 L,** The Granger Collection, New York; **166 M,** Corbis; **166 R,** AP Pho[illegible] **167 L,** AP Photo; **167 R,** Jacques M. Chenet/Corbis; **168,** AP Photo/B[illegible] Tesfaye; **169,** Jim West / Alamy; **170 both,** Peter Turnley/Corbis; **172,** ©**2000** Mic Stevens from cartoonbank.com; **175 both,** Kara Stokes; **176,** Jeff Parker; **177,** EMMANUEL DUNAND/AFP/Getty Images; **180,** Marshall Ramsey/cnscartoons/Newscom; **181,** Library of Congress; **182-183,** Elaine Thompson/AP Images; **184 both,** AP Photo/Janet Hostetter; **185,** need credit and perm from paula; **186 T,** David R. Frazier Photolibrary, Inc. / Alamy; **186 M,** REUTERS/Eric Miller /Landov; **186 B,** AP Photo/Amy E. Powers; **188,** JIM WATSON/AFP/Getty Images; **189 TR,** AP Photo/Chris Carlson; **189 BL,** AP Photo/J. Scott Applewhite; **193 both,** AP Photo/Mark Humphrey; **194,** AP Photo/Elaine Thompson; **196,** Getty Images; **198,** AP Photo/Jamie-Andrea Yanak; **200 TL,** Getty Images; **200** TR AP Photo/David Crenshaw; **200 B,** AP Photo/Lawrence Jackson; **201 both,** AP Photo/Ben Margot; **203 L,** Getty Images/Richard Ellis; **203 M,** Jason Reed/Reuters/Corbis; **203 R,** Jason Reed/Reuters/Corbis; **204 both,** Joe Raedle/Getty Images; **206,** AP Photo/Josh Reynolds; **207,** Steve Artley; **210,** Steve Kelley/Cartoonist Group; **212-213,** Mario Tama/Getty Images; **214 both,** Alex Wong/Getty Images for Meet the Press; **217 TR,** Comstock Select/Corbis; **217 BL,** Image Source/Corbis; **218,** Dave Carpenter/Cartoon Stock; **219,** Minnesota Historical Society/Corbis; **220 both,** Billy E. Barnes / Photo Edit -- All rights reserved.; **221,** AP Photo/Shawn Patrick Ouellette; **222,** By permission of Gary Varvel and Creators Syndicate, Inc.; **227,** Tom Carter / Photo Edit -- All rights reserved.; **228 both,** Masterfile; **230,** The Granger Collection, New York; **232 L,** Bettmann/Corbis;

232 R, Yale Joel//Time Life Pictures/Getty Images; **233,** Matt Campbell/epa/Corbis; **234 L,** Harley Schwadron/Cartoon Stock; **234 R,** Leo Cullum/The Cartoon Bank; **238,** Adey Bryant/Cartoon Stock; **239,** Ray Jelliffe/Cartoon stock; **240-241,** Frances Roberts/Levine Roberts; **242 both,** Frances Roberts/Levine Roberts; **243,** Dave Coverly/The Cartoonist Group; **244 TL,** J. R. Eyerman//Time Life Pictures/Getty Images; **244** TML, Library of Congress; **244 BM**L, New York Public Library; **244 BL,** Minnesota Historical Society; **244 R,** The Granger Collection, New York; **246,** Norma Jean Garcasz/Courtesy Tuscon Citizen; **247 both,** AP Photo/Mark Humphrey; **249 T,** Bettmann/Corbis; **249 B,** PRNewsFoto/Panasonic Corporation of North America; **251 T,** Photo by Gary Dineen/NBAE via Getty Images; **251 B,** Scott Nelson/Getty Images; **253 TL,** Michael Geissinger / The Image Works; **253 BL,** Ian Wagreich Photography / www.iwphoto.com; **253 TR,** Catherine Karnow/Corbis; **254 both,** Scott J. Ferrell/Newscom; **255,** AP Photo/Charles Dharapak; **256** Bkgrnd, Justin Sullivan/Getty Images; **258 T,** Jupiter Images; **258 M,** www.avaaz.com; **258 BM,** Alan Schein Photography/Corbis; **258 B,** Polka Dot Images / SuperStock; **258** Bkgrnd, Momatiuk - Eastcott/Corbis; **258** TM, Getty Images; **259,** Lynne Fernandes / The Image Works; **260,** Mike Keefe/Courtesy Denver Post; **262,** The Cartoon Bank; **263,** Ann Telnaes/The Cartoonist Group; **264 L,** Free Agents Limited/Corbis; **264 R,** Charles Barsotti/The Cartoon Bank.

UNIT 3 Page 265, Ron Sachs/Consolidated News Photos; **266-267,** Shawn Thew/epa/Corbis; **268 both,** AP Photo/Susan Walsh; **269,** Brad Markel/Getty Images; **272,** Bonnie Kamin / Photo Edit; **273 both,** Stefan Zaklin/epa/Corbis; **278,** Bettmann/Corbis; **279 L,** courtesy Ileana Ros-Lehtinen; **279 R,** AP Photo/Times-News, Mike Dirks; **281 both,** UPI Photo/Kevin Dietsch; **282 L,** AP Photo/Jackie Johnston; **282** TM, JASON REED/Reuters /Landov; **282 BM,** Pearson Education/PH School Division; **283,** Matthew Cavanaugh/epa/Corbis; **284,** Bernard Schoenbaum/The Cartoon Bank, Inc.; **285 both,** AP Photo/J. Scott Applewhite; **287,** KEVIN LAMARQUE/Reuters / Landov; **288 R,** DON EMMERT/AFP/Getty Images; **289,** © **2006** RJ Matson/Cagle Cartooons. All rights reserved.; **292,** Library of Congress; **294-295,** Mark Wilson/Getty Images; **296 both,** AP Photo/Roberto Borea; **298 L,** Bill Frymire/Masterfile; **298 R,** Free Agents Limited/Corbis; **299 L,** David Pollack/Corbis; **299 MR,** Photofusion Picture Library / Alamy; **299 R,** Pearson Education/PH School Division; **300,** Robert Weber/Cartoonbank; **304 both,** Harris and Ewing/Corbis; **305,** Ames Madison (**1751-1836**) published by Nathaniel Currier (**1813-88**) (colour litho), Stuart, Gilbert (**1755-1828**) (after) / Private Collection, Peter Newark American Pictures / The Bridgeman Art Library; **306 L,** UpperCut Images/Getty Images; **306 R,** DK Stock/Getty Images;

307 L, Corbis Premium RF / Alamy; **307 M,** Getty Images; **307 R,** Getty Images; **308 TL,** David R. Frazier Photolibrary, Inc. / Alamy; **308 TR,** Don Smetzer / Alamy; **308 B,** Paul Springett / Alamy; **310 L,** Purestock/Getty Images; **310 BL,** Corbis Super RF / Alamy; **310 BM,** Alexander Hamilton, c.**1804** (oil on canvas), Trumbull, John (**1756-1843**) / (c) Collection of the New-York Historical Society, USA, / The Bridgeman Art Library; **310** BR, American Numismatic Association Money Museum; **311 L,** Portrait of Andrew Jackson, **1858** (oil on canvas), Sully, Thomas (**1783-1872**) / Private Collection, Photo (c) Christie's Images / The Bridgeman Art Library; **311 M,** American Numismatic Association Money Museum; **311 R,** Sandy Felsenthal/Corbis; **312 both,** AP Photo/Khampha Bouaphanh; **314,** A.Y. Owen/Time Life Pictures/Getty Images; **315 L,** AP Photo/Jason Hunt; **315 R,** Jeff Greenberg/Jupiter images; **316,** J.B. Handelsman/Cartoonbank; **317 TL,** AP Photo; **317 TR,** SHAMIL ZHUMATOV/Reuters/Corbis; **317 B,** Chris Hondros/Getty Images; **318 L,** AP Photo; **318 R,** AP Photo/Joe Marquette; **320,** AP Photo/File; **321 TL,** Najlah Feanny/Corbis; **321 ML,** Wally McNamee/Corbis; **321 BL,** Mark Wilson/Getty Images; **321 M,** AP Photo/Khue Bui; **321 TR,** Najlah Feanny/CORBIS SABA; **321 MR,** George Waldman/Getty Images; **322 L,** UPI Photo /Landov; **322 R,** Luke Frazza/AFP/Getty Images; **323 L,** Brandi Simons/Getty Images; **323 R,** Getty Images; **324,** Ed Stein, reprinted with permission of Rocky Mountain News; **327,** Bob Artley, Courtesy Washington (Minn) Daily Globe; **328-329,** Scott J. Ferrell/Congressional Quarterly/Getty Images; **330 L,** DOUG MILLS /The New York Times/Redux; **330** R Shawn Thew/epa/Corbis; **331,** Corbis; **333** all, United States Government (public domain); **336,** Harley Schwadron/Cartoonstock; **338 both,** Ken Cedeno/Corbis; **342,** AP Photo/Lauren Victoria Burke; **343 L,** Brooks Kraft/Corbis; **343 R,** Scott J. Ferrell/Congressional Quarterly; **344,** Mark Wilson/Getty Images; **347 L,** Getty Images; **347 R,** Chip Somodevilla/Getty Images; **348,** Jack Ziegler/The Cartoon Bank, Inc.; **350 TL,** Scott J. Ferrell/Congressional Quarterly/Getty Images; **350 TR,** William Thomas Cain/Getty Images; **350 BL,** United States Government (Publc Domain); **351 both,** Scott J. Ferrell/Congressional Quarterly/Newscom; **352,** Newscom; **354,** Mark Kauffman//Time Life Pictures/Getty Images; **355 T,** Scott J. Ferrell/Congressional Quarterly; **355 M,** United States House of Representatives; **355 B,** Scott J. Ferrell/Congressional Quarterly/Getty Images; **356,** AP Photo/Haraz N. Ghanbari; **358,** John Cole, The Scranton Times-Tribune/politicalcartoons.com; **359,** Bob Englehart/politicalcartoons.com; **360 L,** Free Agents Limited/Corbis; **360 R,** Nick Anderson/The Cartoonist Group.

UNIT 4 Page 361, AP Photo/Doug Mills; **362,** REUTERS/Jim Young; **364 both,** David Hume Kennerly/Getty Images; **365,** Reuters/Corbis; **367 L,** AP Photo; **367 TR,** Pearson Education/PH School Division; **367** BR, Pearson Education/PH School Division; **368,** Brooks Kraft/Corbis; **369,** Michael Newman / Photo Edit -- All rights reserved.; **370 both,** Bettmann/Corbis; **371,** National Archives/Handout/Getty Images; **372,** Peter Steiner/The Cartoon Bank; **373,** AP Photo/Terry Ashe; **374 L,** Bettmann/Corbis; **374 M,** ©Private Collection/ Peter Newark American Pictures/ The Bridgeman Art Library; **374 R,** ©Bristol City Museum and Art Gallery, UK/ The Bridgeman Art Library; **377 both,** Spencer Platt/Getty Images; **380,** Tribune Media Services, Inc. All Rights Reserved. Reprinted with permission.; **381,** AP Photo/Chris Carlson; **384 L,** AP Photo/Reed Saxon; **384 R,** Paul Drinkwater/NBC via Getty Images; **386 both,** Rock the Vote; **390 L,** REUTERS/Colin Braley/Corbis; **390 R,** Robert King/Newsmakers; **391,** DAEMMRICH BOB/CORBIS SYGMA; **393 L,** David Granlund, Metrowest Daily News; **393 TR,** JEFF HAYNES/AFP/Getty Images; **393** BR, AP Photo/Carolyn Kaster; **396,** ©**1986** The Philadelphia Inquirer. Reprinted with permission of Universal Press Syndicate.; **397,** Seeley G. Mudd Manuscript Library, Princeton University; **398-399,** Bettmann/Corbis; **400 L,** Paul Damien/NGS/Getty Images; **400 R,** Christie's Images/Corbis; **402 L,** Library of Congress; **402 R,** Chicago Historical Society; **403,** Harris & Ewing; Inc./Corbis; **404 TL,** Brooks Kraft/Corbis; **404 TR,** NSA via Getty Images; **404 B,** Brooks Kraft/Corbis; **405 both,** AP Photo/Ron Edmonds; **406,** Cynthia Johnson/Time Life Pictures/Getty Images; **408,** Dwayne Booth; **410 TL,** Purestock/Getty Images; **410 BL,** Joseph Sohm/Visions of America/Corbis; **410 BM,** AP Photo/stf; **410** BR, AP Photo/The Herald-Sun, Christine T. Nguyen; **411 L,** Owen Franken/Corbis; **411 M,** AP Photo/White House; **411 R,** Bettmann/Corbis; **412 L,** Dirck Halstead/ Getty Images; **412 R,** Bettmann/Corbis; **413,** LUKE FRAZZA/AFP/Getty Images; **414,** Bettmann/Corbis; **415,** Kevin

862 Acknowledgments

Lamarque/REUTERS/Corbis; **417** all, Alex Wong/Getty Images; **419,** Bettmann/CORBIS; **422,** Rex Rabin, Sacramento Bee; **424-425,** Melanie Steton Freeman/The Christian Science Monitor via Getty Images; **426 both,** UPI Photo/Roger L. Wollenberg; **427,** Clay Bennett/Christian Science Monitor; **429,** Jon Arnold Images Ltd / Alamy; **431 both,** Pete Souza/White House/Handout/Corbis; **432,** Brooks Kraft/Corbis; **433,** SAUL LOEB/AFP/Getty Images; **435 both,** AP Photo/Tim Larsen; **436 L,** Bettmann/Corbis; **436 M,** Frank Greenaway © Dorling Kindersley; **436 R,** H. Armstrong Roberts/Retrofile/Getty Images; **437 L,** Philip Nealey/Digital Vision/Getty Images; **437 R,** C. Sherburne/PhotoLink/Getty Images; **439 T,** Chuck Kennedy/White House/Sipa Press/0909141931/Newscom; **439 B,** Bettmann/Corbis; **440,** Bettmann/Corbis; **441 both,** AP Photo/Diane Bondareff, Pool; **443 L,** Helen Ashford/ Jupiter Images; **443 M,** Popperfoto/ Getty Images; **443 TR,** Heather Wright; **443** BR, AP Photo/Eugene Hoshiko; **444 L,** REUTERS/Jessie Cohen/Smithsonian's National Zoo /Landov; **444 M,** AP Photo/Rich Pedroncelli; **444 R,** REUTERS/Bob Care/Florida Keys News Bureau/HO /Landov; **447 T,** Comstock/Corbis; **447 B,** AP Photo/Keith Srakocic; **447 L,** Brooks Kraft/Sygma/Corbis; **447 R,** David Frazier / Photo Edit -- All rights reserved.; **448,** Bob/Thom Thaves/Cartoonist Group; **450 TL,** Walter Bibikow/Corbis; **450 TR,** Chris Howes/Wild Places Photography / Alamy; **450 B,** Cynthia Johnson/Time Life Pictures/Getty Images; **452,** Gary McCoy/Cagle Cartoons; **454-455,** GREG DERR photos/The Patriot Ledger; **456 both,** Monika Graff/Getty Images; **457,** Harley Schwadron/Cartoon Stock; **459** image **1,** Getty Images; **459** image **2,** Getty Images; **459** image **3,** Getty Images; **459** image **4,** Getty Images; **459** image **5,** Large blue and white Ming vase with the Hsuan Te mark, **1426-35** (porcelain), Chinese School, (**15**th century) / Private Collection, /The Bridgeman Art Library; **459** image **6,** Getty Images; **463 both,** Minnesota Historical Society/Corbis; **465,** Bryan Mitchell/Getty Images; **467 both,** Najlah Feanny/Corbis; **471,** Paul Morigi/WireImage; **472,** Getty Images; **473 both,** Scott J. Ferrell/Congressional Quarterly/Getty Images; **474 L,** Jeff Fusco/Getty Images; **474 R,** AP Photo/Manuel Balce Ceneta; **475,** David Horsey; **478,** Steve Kelley/Cartoonist Group; **480-481,** Bettmann/Corbis; **482 both,** Howard Sochurek//Time Life Pictures/Getty Images; **483,** Jim Borgman/Courtesy Cincinnati Enquirer; **484 TL,** Marwan Assaf/REUTERS/Corbis; **484 BL,** Voice of America; **484 TR,** Courtesy United States Government, State Department; **484** BR, Dimas Ardian/Getty Images; **485,** U.S. Department of State; **486 T,** MPI/Getty Images; **486 B,** Library of Congress; **487 L,** Sarah-Maria Vischer/The Image Works; **487 R,** Breck P. Kent; **488 both,** Shawn Thew/AFP/Getty Images; **491,** Brad Loper/Dallas Morning News/Corbis; **493 T,** Gerald French/Corbis; **493 BL,** Tom Pennington/Fort Worth Star-Telegram/MCT/Newscom; **493 BM,** Brooks Kraft/Corbis; **493** BR, NyxoLyno Cangemi/U.S. Coast Guard via Getty Images; **494,** Momatiuk - Eastcott/Corbis; **495 both,** Library of Congress; **496 L,** Bettmann/Corbis; **496 R,** The Art Archive / Culver Pictures; **497,** Library of Congress; **500,** Popperfoto/Getty Images; **501 T,** Bettmann/Corbis; **501 B,** AP Photo/Joe Marquette; **502,** Darren McCollester/Getty Images; **504 TL,** ACOB J. KIRK/US NAVY NEWS PHOTO/Newscom; **504 TR,** ROMEO RANOCO/Reuters /Landov; **504 B,** Sgt Andres Alcaraz/epa/Corbis; **505 both,** Bettmann/Corbis; **508,** REUTERS/Paco Sanseviero; **510 T,** im Zuckerman/Corbis; **510 BL,** Dung Vo Trung/Sygma/Corbis; **510 BM,** Tetra Images/Corbis; **510** BR, Dimas Ardian/Getty Images; **514,** Robert Mankoff/The Cartoon Bank; **516 L,** Free Agents Limited/Corbis; **516 R,** © John Deering.

UNIT 5 **Page 517,** Catherine Karnow/CORBIS; **518-519,** AP Photo/Evan Vucci; **520 L,** Gaetano/Corbis; **520 R,** SCOTT J. FERREL/Congressional Quarterly Inc./Newscom; **525,** Corbis; **527 TL,** Getty Images; **527 TR,** Richard Cummins / SuperStock; **527 B,** Image by © Ron Sachs/CNP/Corbis; **528 both,** Jerry Talfer/San Francisco Chronicle/Corbis; **532 L,** Digital Vision / Alamy; **532 R,** Stock Montage/Getty Images; **533,** The Granger Collection, New York; **536,** Dennis Brack/Newscom; **538 both,** AP Photo/U.S. Army, Pvc Ben Brody; **539,** © **2007** Paresh Nath /Cagle Cartoons. All rights reserved.; **542,** Bettmann/Corbis; **543,** picturehistory/Newscom; **544-545,** Levine Roberts Photography; **546 both,** AP Photo; **547,** Michael Newman / Photo Edit -- All rights reserved.; **551 both,** JUPITERIMAGES/Brand X / Alamy; **553,** AP Photo/Douglas C. Pizac; **554,** Peter Titmuss / Alamy; **556 L,** AP Photo/Steve Yeater; **556 R,** AP Photo/Mike Groll; **557,** AP Photo/The News-Tribune, Bob King; **559 both,** New York Times Pictures; **560,** Al Freni/Library Of Congress/Time Life Pictures/Getty Images; **562 both,** Minnesota Historical Society; **566,** Bettmann/Corbis; **568,** Tony Freeman / Photo Edit, Inc.; **569 both,** AP Photo/Nick Ut; **571 L,** Najlah Feanny/CORBIS SABA; **571 R,** AP Photo/Ric Francis; **574,** Steve Artley; **575,** Doug Marlette, Tallahassee Democrat/TMS Reprints; **576-577,** Steve Hamblin / Alamy; **578 L,** Photo Researchers, Inc.; **578 R,** Mark Harmel/Getty Images; **579 T,** Jon Shireman/Getty Images; **579 B,** Stockbyte/Getty Images; **580,** The New Yorker Collection **1970,** J.B. Handelsman from cartoonbank.com; **581,** Gunter Marx / Alamy; **583 both,** Masterfile; **584,** New York Public Library; **585,** Rolf Richardson / Alamy; **586,** Susan Van Etten / Photo Edit -- All rights reserved.; **588,** AP Photo; **589,** William Whitehurst/Corbis; **591 TL,** William Foley//Time Life Pictures/Getty Images; **591 TR,** Ralf-Finn Hestoft/Corbis; **591 B,** Reuters/Corbis; **592 both,** Douglas C. Pizac-Pool/Getty Images; **593 T,** American Stock/Getty Images; **593 B,** AP Photo; **597,** Flip Schulke/Black Star; **598 L,** JUPITERIMAGES/ Thinkstock / Alamy; **598 R,** David R. Frazier Photolibrary, Inc. / Alamy; **600 L,** Getty Images; **600 BL,** Bettmann/Corbis; **600** BR, John Loengard//Time Life Pictures/Getty Image; **601 BL,** Michael Newman / Photo Edit -- All rights reserved.; **601 BM,** Getty Images; **601** BR, AP Photo/Robert Houston; **602 both,** AP Photo/Nathan Martin; **603,** Dave Parker/Cartoon Stock; **608,** Mike Baldwin/Cartoonstock.com; **609,** Clay Bennett/© **2005** The Christian Science Monitor. All rights reserved.; **610-611,** Bruce Davidson/Magnum Photos; **612 both,** Chuck Savage/Corbis; **613,** Alison Wright/Corbis; **614,** Getty Images; **615,** Getty Images;

616, Clay Bennett, The Christian Science Monitor; **618 both,** AP Photo/Marcy Nighswander; **619,** Library of Congress; **621 L,** New York Times Co./Getty Images; **621 TR,** Center for American History, UT-Austin; **621** BR, Hulton Archive/Getty Images; **622,** Alex Wong/Getty Images; **624 L,** Bettmann/Corbis; **624 R,** Carl Iwasaki/Time Life Pictures/Getty Images; **625 L,** AP Photo; **625 M,** Bettmann/Corbis; **625 R,** Bettman/Corbis; **626 both,** AP Photo/File; **627,** Bettmann/Corbis; **628,** Robert W. Kelley/Time Life Pictures/Getty Images; **629,** Doug Pensinger/Getty Images; **631,** Newmann/zefa/Corbis; **632 both,** Carlos Barria/Reuters/Corbis; **634 L,** Bruce Forster/Getty Images; **634 R,** Jeff Greenberg / Alamy; **638,** Scott Stantis; **640,** Steve Artley; **641,** The Granger Collection, New York; **642 L,** Free Agents Limited/Corbis; **642 R,** Bob/Tom Thaves/ Cartoonist Group.

UNIT 6 Page 643, Zhukov Sergei/ITAR-TASS/Corbis; **644-645,** Lan Hongguang/Xinhua Press/Corbis; **646 both,** Jon Arnold Images Ltd / Alamy; **647,** Justin Kase zthreez / Alamy; **649,** Getty Images; **650,** MPI/Getty Images; **652,** Picture Partners / Alamy; **653 both,** The Granger Collection, New York; **654 L,** The Art Archive / Musée Carnavalet Paris / Gianni Dagli Orti; **654 R,** Ceiling of the Painted Hall, detail of King William III (**1650-1702**) and Queen Mary II (**1662-94**) Enthroned, **1707-14** (see **208087**), Thornhill, Sir James (**1675-1734**) / Royal Naval College, Greenwich, London, UK, Photo: James Brittain / The Bridgeman Art Library; **658,** public domain; **659 L,** Bettmann/Corbis; **659 TR,** Stapleton Collection/Corbis; **659** BR, Bettmann/Corbis; **661 both,** AP Photo/Lionel Cironneau; **662,** AP Photo/Dmitry Lovetsky; **666 both,** Erich Schlegel/Dallas Morning; **667,** RUSSELL BOYCE/Reuters/Corbis; **669,** Yerbury Photography / Alamy; **671,** AP Photo/Gregory Bull; **674,** Ed Fischer, Courtesy Omaha World-Herald; **675,** The Granger Collection, New York; **676-677,** AP Photo/M. Spencer Green, file; **678 both,** Don Mason/Corbis; **679 L,** Sean Masterson/epa/Corbis; **679 M,** Cultura/Corbis; **679 R,** Rick Friedman/Corbis; **680 L,** Tony Freeman / Photo Edit -- All rights reserved.; **680 M,** Getty Images; **680 R,** Robin Nelson / Photo Edit -- All rights reserved.; **681,** STEPHEN HILGER/Bloomberg News /Landov; **682,** AP Photo/George McLuskie/Fife College/PA; **683,** Shutterstock; **685 both,** Swim Ink **2,** LLC/Corbis; **687 T,** Bob Englehart, The Hartford Courant; **687 B,** ©Bill Proud/Cartoonstock; **688,** Gerd Schnuerer/Getty Images; **690,** Robert Van Der Hilst/Getty Images; **692 TL,** Masterfile; **692 TR,** Keith Dannemiller/Corbis; **692 B,** AP Photo/Joe Marquette; **693 both,** FRANK POLICH/Reuters /Landov; **696,** Bobby Bank/WireImage/Getty Images; **700,** Ed Kashi/Corbis; **702,** Chip Bok/Cartoonist Group; **703,** Bob Thaves/Cartoonist Group; **704,** Free Agents Limited/Corbis.

UNIT 7 Page 705, AP Photo/Toby Talbot; **706-707,** AP Photo/John David Mercer, Pool; **708 both,** Kara Stokes; **709 both,** public domain; **710 L,** AP Photo/Eckehard Schulz; **710 M,** AP Photo/Kevin P. Casey; **710 R,** VisionsofAmerica/Joe Sohm; **711 L,** Steven Puetzer/Getty Images; **711 M,** Jeff Greenberg / Photo Edit -- All rights reserved.; **711 R,** capt.digby / Alamy; **714 both,** AP Photo/Richmond Times-Dispatch, Bob Brown; **715 L,** AP Photo/Ric Feld; **715 R,** AP Photo/Doug Dreyer; **716 L,** Somos Images/Corbis; **716 R,** AP Photo/The Hawk Eye, John Lovretta; **720 both,** AP Photo/Judi Bottoni; **722,** © **2003** Monte Wolverton/Cagle Cartooons. All rights reserved.; **727 both,** Alan Klehr/Getty Images; **728 L,** Ruaridh Stewart/Ruaridh Stewart/ZUMA/Corbis; **728 R,** David Young-Wolff / Photo Edit -- All rights reserved.; **731,** Michael Kelley/Getty Images; **732 L,** AP Photo/Jim McKnight; **732 R,** AP Photo/Ric Feld; **733,** Pearson Education/PH School Division; **734,** Corbis; **735,** Leo Cullum/The Cartoon Bank, Inc.; **738,** J.B. Handelsman/The Cartoon Bank, Inc.; **740-741,** AP Photo/Matt Rourke; **742 both,** First Light/Corbis;

743, Jeff Greenberg / Photo Edit -- All Rights Reserved.; **744 T,** AP Photo/Charles Rex Arbogast; **744 B,** photocritic.org / Alamy; **747 both,** Google;

749 both, Andre Jenny / Alamy; **750,** Photo by Scott Olson/Getty Images; **754 L,** Michael Freeman/Corbis; **754 M,** Panoramic Images/Getty Images; **754 R,** VisionsofAmerica/Joe Sohm/Getty Images; **755,** Bruce Forster/Newscom; **756 both,** Thomas Barwick/Digital Vision/Getty Images; **757 TR,** Beth A. Keiser/Beth A. Keiser/Corbis; **757 BL,** Andersen Ross/Stockbyte/Getty Images; **757** BR, Ed Kashi/Corbis; **758,** AP Photo/Angela Rowlings; **760 TL,** WoodyStock / Alamy; **760 TR,** AP Photo/Paul Sakuma; **760 B,** AP Photo/Steve Yeater; **761 both,** AP Photo/The Tennessean, Sanford Myers; **763 TR,** Wes Thompson/Corbis; **763 BL,** Momentum Creative Group / Alamy; **763** BR, Ruaridh Stewart/ZUMA/Corbis; **765 L,** Steve Dunwell/The Image Bank/Getty Images; **765 R,** David Young-Wolff / Photo Edit -- All rights reserved.; **768,** Chip Bok/Cartoonist Group; **769,** Mike Marland, Concord Monitor; **770,** Free Agents Limited/Corbis.

END MATTER 772-773, Jose Luis Pelaez, Inc./Corbis; **774 L,** Christie's

ACKNOWLEDGMENTS

Images/Corbis; **774 ML,** Bettmann/Corbis; **774 M,** Corbis; **774 MR,** Corbis; **774 R,** Bettmann/Corbis; **775 L,** Bettmann/Corbis; **775 ML,** Bettmann/Corbis; **775 M,** Corbis; **775 MR,** Wally McNamee/Corbis; **775 R,** Courtesy barackobama.com;**780,** Time Life Pictures/Mansell/Time Life Pictures/Getty Images; **781,** King John signing the Magna Carta reluctantly (colour litho), Michael, A.C. (fl.1903-28) / Private Collection, The Stapleton Collection / The Bridgeman Art Library; **782 L,** Three Lions/Getty Images; **782 R,** The Granger Collection, New York; **783,** Ceiling of the Painted Hall, detail of King William III (1650-1702) and Queen Mary II (1662-94) Enthroned, 1707-14 (see 208087), Thornhill, Sir James (1675-1734) / Royal Naval College, Greenwich, London, UK, Photo: James Brittain / The Bridgeman Art Library; **784,** The Granger Collection, New York; **785,** The Granger Collection, New York; **788,** The Granger Collection, New York; **791,** The Granger Collection, New York; **794,** The Granger Collection, New York; **795,** James Madison (1751-1836) (colour litho), American School, (19th century) / Private Collection, Peter Newark American Pictures / The Bridgeman Art Library; **798,** Stock Montage/Stock Montage/Getty Images; **800,** Stock Montage/Stock Montage/Getty Images; **801,** MPI/Getty Images; **803 L,** National Portrait Gallery, Smithsonian Institution / Art Resource, NY; **803 R,** The Granger Collection, New York; **804,** Tai Power Seeff/The Image Bank/Getty Images; **809,** Tai Power Seeff/The Image Bank/Getty Images.

Text Acknowledgments

Grateful acknowledgment is made to the following for copyrighted material:

The Associated Press "Major Provisions of the Lobbying Bill" by The Associated Press from http://www.washingtonpost.com/wp-dyn/content/article/2006/03/29/AR2006032901950.html.

"School's Integration Legacy Looms Large" by Andrew DeMillo, The Associated Press from http://www.usatoday.com/news/nation/2007-09-22-littlerock_N.htm. Copyright © 2008 The Associated Press. Used by permission.

League of Women Voters "Ethics and Lobbying Reform" from http://www.lwv.org/AM/Template.cfm?Section=Lobby_Reform_and_Ethics. Copyright © 2008 The League of Women Voters of the United States. Used by permission.

The Honorable Lee H. Hamilton "Whose Team Should a Member of Congress Be On?" by Lee H. Hamilton from http://www.centeroncongress.org/radio_commentaries/whose_team.php. Copyright © Lee Hamilton. Used by permission.

The New York Times "Fewer Youths Jump Behind the Wheel at 16" by

Mary M. Chapman and Micheline Maynard from The New York Times, February 25th, 2008. Copyright © 2008 by The New York Times. All rights reserved. Used by permission and protected by the Copyright Laws of the United States. The printing, copying, redistributing, or retransmission of the Material without express written permission is prohibited.

The Oakland Tribune "Don't Balance California's State Budget by Raising Taxes" from The Oakland Tribune, January 2nd, 2008. Copyright © The Oakland Tribune/Zuma Press. Used by permission.

The Sacramento Bee "A new GI bill for a new generation of veterans" from The Sacramento Bee, May 26th, 2008. Copyright © The Sacramento Bee. Used by permission conveyed through Copyright Clearance Center.

"If you're into pain, you'll love this state budget" from The Sacramento Bee, January 11, 2008. Copyright © The Sacramento Bee.

The San Francisco Chronicle "Homeless project's army of citizens calls year success" by Kevin Fagan from The San Francisco Chronicle, October 19th, 2005. Copyright © The San Francisco Chronicle. Used by permission.

Writers House "I have a dream" by Dr. Martin Luther King Jr. Copyright © 1963 Dr. Martin Luther King Jr.; copyright © renewed 1991 Coretta Scott King. Used by arrangement with The Heirs to the Estate of Martin Luther King Jr., c/o Writers House as agent for the proprietor New York, NY.

Congressional Quarterly, Inc. "Clueless in Boise" by Alan Ehrenhalt from *www.governing.com*. Copyright © Congressional Quarterly Inc.

Note: Every effort has been made to locate the copyright owner of material reproduced on this component. Omissions brought to our attention will be corrected in subsequent editions.